Tourism Marketing and
Management Handbook

Tourism Marketing and Management Handbook

Editors

Stephen F. Witt
University College of Swansea

Luiz Moutinho
University of Glasgow

Prentice Hall

New York   London   Toronto   Sydney   Tokyo

First published 1989 by
Prentice Hall International (UK) Ltd,
66 Wood Lane End, Hemel Hempstead,
Hertfordshire, HP2 4RG
A division of
Simon & Schuster International Group

© 1989 Prentice Hall International (UK) Ltd

Printed and bound in Great Britain at
the University Press, Cambridge

British Library Cataloguing in Publication Data

Tourism marketing and management handbook.
  1. Tourist industries. Management 2. Tourism.
Marketing
I. Witt, Stephen F. II. Moutinho, Luiz
338.4′791′068

ISBN 0–13–925885–X

1 2 3 4 5 93 92 91 90 89

ISBN 0-13-925885-X

Contents

Foreword

Throughout the world more people than ever travel – for pleasure, on business, or for other reasons – in their own countries and abroad. Tourism generates large revenues for many firms and industries, as well as governments. It contributes significantly to economic growth, the balance of payments, employment and the regional balance of many countries. Tourism is also important socially, culturally, environmentally, and in other ways – for those who become tourists and for their hosts.

Writings to explain tourism and to formalize our knowledge and understanding of its many manifestations go back for only about half-a-century but have been increasing in volume and diversity in recent years. Academic institutions, tourist boards, professional associations and international organizations have led the way. Books and journals, articles and conference papers, bibliographies and libraries, testify to the growth of research and scholarship.

In this volume Stephen Witt and Luiz Moutinho have shown brave determination and a great deal of stamina to produce what amounts to an encyclopedia of tourism. They have brought together close on a hundred authors to contribute well over one hundred chapters dealing with most aspects of tourism. In addition to academics, a significant number of them are consultants and from public sector agencies. The authorship has a distinctly North Atlantic flavor but in their concerns the contributions range widely over developed and developing countries around the world.

What the reader wants to know about a topic is explained concisely with examples, and a particular effort is made to do so for the small business when appropriate. All but a few of the contributions include suggestions for further reading, which in some cases run to several dozen sources, with a total approaching two thousand references. This Handbook, therefore, also ranks among the major bibliographical sources on tourism. A few hundred information sources, databases, computer software programs and systems are included, and further enhance the value of the book.

Tourism Marketing and Management Handbook contains a wealth of information not found elsewhere. I welcome it as an author, consultant and educator, and commend it to all who need a comprehensive textbook and a reference book. It is essential for anyone with a professional interest in understanding tourism, whether as a practitioner, researcher, teacher or student.

PROFESSOR S. MEDLIK

Contributors

Louise Allard	Head, Tourism Division, OECD, Paris, France
John Allcock	Postgraduate School of Yugoslav Studies, University of Bradford, Bradford, UK
Brian H. Archer	Head, Department of Management Studies for Tourism and Hotel Industries, University of Surrey, Guildford, UK
J. Gerald Bailie	International Travel Section, Statistics Canada, Ottawa, Canada
Stephen Ball	Department of Catering Studies, Huddersfield Polytechnic, Huddersfield, UK
Charles D. Barnard	Assistant Director, Policy/Secretariat, British Tourist Authority, London, UK
Kevin B. Boberg	Department of Marketing, New Mexico State University, Las Cruces, USA
Jonathan A. Bodlender	Chairman, Horwath and Horwath (UK) Ltd, London, UK. Also Partner, Stoy Hayward
Ron Brathwaite	Centre for Hotel and Tourism Management, University of the West Indies, Nassau, Bahamas
P. Jane Broadbent	School of Management and Economic Studies, University of Sheffield, Sheffield, UK
J. M. Broadbent	Sheffield City Polytechnic, Sheffield, UK
Graham P. Brown	Department of Tourism, Dorset Institute, Poole, UK
Margaret Bruce	Department of Management Sciences, UMIST, Manchester, UK
Peter J. Buckley	Management Centre, University of Bradford, Bradford, UK
Neil R. Chisman	Department of Management Studies for Tourism and Hotel Industries, University of Surrey, Guildford, UK
Judy Cohen	Department of Marketing, Rider College, Lawrenceville, USA
Frederick M. Collison	School of Travel Industry Management, University of Hawaii, Honolulu, USA
Stavros T. Constantinou	Ohio State University, Mansfield, USA
Chris Cooper	Department of Management Studies for Tourism and Hotel Industries, University of Surrey, Guildford, UK
Jean-Claude Croizé	President, Ecole D'Architecture de Paris la Défense, Nanterre, France
Peter Cullen	School of Hospitality Management and Home Economics, Leeds Polytechnic, Leeds, UK
Steve Curry	Project Planning Centre for Developing Countries, University of Bradford, Bradford, UK
Bonnie Davis	Department of Human Environment and Design, Michigan State University, East Lansing, USA
Jamie Elwin	Department of Town Planning, Oxford Polytechnic, Oxford, UK
Stephen J. Essex	Department of Geographical Sciences, Plymouth Polytechnic, Plymouth, UK
John Fletcher	Department of Management Studies for Tourism and Hotel Industries, University of Surrey, Guildford, UK
Edward J. Friel	Chief Executive, Greater Glasgow Tourist Board, Glasgow, UK
Paul R. Gamble	Department of Management Studies for Tourism and Hotel Industries, University of Surrey, Guildford, UK
Frank Go	School of Hospitality and Tourism Management, Ryerson Polytechnical Institute, Toronto, Canada
Charles R. Goeldner	Editor, Journal of Travel Research, Business Research Division, University of Colorado, Boulder, USA
Anne Hampton	Department of Hotel and Catering Management, Oxford Polytechnic, Oxford, UK
Donald E. Hawkins	Travel and Tourism Programs, George Washington University, Washington DC, USA

John Heeley	Scottish Hotel School, University of Strathclyde, Glasgow, UK
John Holden	Department of Hotel, Catering and Institutional Management, Manchester Polytechnic, Manchester, UK
Terry Hudson	Department of Hospitality Management, Leeds Polytechnic, Leeds, UK
Howard L. Hughes	Department of Hotel, Catering and Institutional Management, Manchester Polytechnic, Manchester, UK
Jafar Jafari	Editor-in-Chief, Annals of Tourism Research, Habitational Resources, University of Wisconsin-Stout, Menomonie, USA
Keith Johnson	Department of Catering Studies, Huddersfield Polytechnic, Huddersfield, UK
Marion Joppe	Ontario Ministry of Tourism and Recreation, Toronto, Canada
L. Lynn Judd	School of Business and Public Administration, California State University, San Bernardino, USA
Howard Kahn	Department of Business Information Technology, Manchester Polytechnic, Manchester, UK
Claude Kaspar	President of AIEST, Institute of Tourism, University of St Gallen, St Gallen, Switzerland
Robert Lanquar	Consultant, Aix-en-Provence, France
Lena Larsson	University of Gothenburg, Gothenburg, Sweden
Patrick Lavery	Department of Tourism, Dorset Institute, Poole, UK
Rob Lawson	Department of Marketing, University of Otago, Dunedin, New Zealand
David Leslie	Department of Hotel and Catering Management, University of Ulster at Jordanstown, Newtownabbey, UK
Andrew Lockwood	Department of Management Studies for Tourism and Hotel Industries, University of Surrey, Guildford, UK
Robert D. Lockwood	Group Treasurer, Rowntree Mackintosh plc, York, UK. Formerly Head of Treasury Consulting, Coopers and Lybrand Associates Ltd, London, UK
Rosemary Lucas	Department of Hotel, Catering and Institutional Management, Manchester Polytechnic, Manchester, UK
Kelly J. MacKay	Consultant, Halifax, Canada
Margaret McKenna	Department of Hotel and Catering Management, University of Ulster at Jordanstown, Newtownabbey, UK
Matthew McQueen	Department of Economics, University of Reading, Reading, UK
Christine A. Martin	Management Centre, University of Bradford, Bradford, UK
Malcolm Martin	Department of Marketing and Tourism Management, Newcastle upon Tyne Polytechnic, Newcastle upon Tyne, UK
Josef A. Mazanec	Institute of Tourism, University of Economics, Vienna, Austria
Arthur Meidan	School of Management and Economic Studies, University of Sheffield, Sheffield, UK
Adolf Meinung	Director, Tourist Board of Rhineland-Pfalz, Koblenz, FRG
Victor Middleton	Department of Management Studies for Tourism and Hotel Industries, University of Surrey, Guildford, UK
George Moeller	USDA Forest Service, Washington DC, USA
Luiz Moutinho	Glasgow Business School, University of Glasgow, Glasgow, UK
Karl Heinz Müller	Director of Marketing, Austrian National Tourist Office, Vienna, Austria
Anna Murray	Department of Hotel and Catering Management, University of Ulster at Jordanstown, Newtownabbey, UK
Sam Okoroafo	Department of Marketing, University of Toledo, Toledo, USA
Ainsley M. O'Reilly	Centre for Hotel and Tourism Management, University of the West Indies, Nassau, Bahamas
Lynn Parkinson	Consultant, Henley-on-Thames, UK
Michael Pearlman	L & R Leisure Consultants, and Scottish Hotel School, University of Strathclyde, Glasgow, UK
Richard Prentice	Department of Geography, University College of Swansea, Swansea, UK
Dawn T. Pysarchik	Department of Human Environment and Design, Michigan State University, East Lansing, USA
Anthea Rogers	School of Business, Oxford Polytechnic, Oxford, UK
Jonathan N. Rounce	Associate Director, Coopers and Lybrand Associates Ltd, London, UK
Hanspeter Schmidhauser	Institute of Tourism, University of St Gallen, St Gallen, Switzerland
Markus Schwaninger	Institute of Tourism, University of St Gallen, St Gallen, Switzerland
Tony V. Seaton	Faculty of Business and Professional Studies, Newcastle upon Tyne Polytechnic, Newcastle upon Tyne, UK

John Seekings	Director, Tourism International, London, UK
Alberto Sessa	Director, Scuola Internazionale di Scienze Turistiche, Rome, Italy
Elwood L. Shafer	Pennsylvania State University, USA
Pauline J. Sheldon	School of Travel Industry Management, University of Hawaii, Honolulu, USA
Egon Smeral	Austrian Economics Research Institute, Vienna, Austria
Helena Snee	Cardiff Business School, UWIST, Cardiff, UK
Brenda Sternquist	Department of Human Environment and Design, Michigan State University, East Lansing, USA
Raymond E. Taylor	College of Business Administration, East Texas State University, Commerce, USA
Neda Telisman-Kosuta	Institute for Tourism, Zagreb, Yugoslavia
Anthony S. Travis	Consultant to Pieda on Tourism and Leisure, Reading and Edinburgh, UK. Also Emeritus Professor, Birmingham University, Birmingham, UK
Norbert Vanhove	Westvlaams Ekonomisch Studiebureau, Brugge, Belgium
A. H. Walle	School of Business and Administration, Alfred University, New York, USA
Stephen Wanhill	Department of Management Studies for Tourism and Hotel Industries, University of Surrey, Guildford, UK
Trevor J. Ward	Senior Consultant, Horwath and Horwath (UK) Ltd, London, UK
Sanda Weber	Institute for Tourism, Zagreb, Yugoslavia
Stephen Wheatcroft	Director, Aviation and Tourism International, London, UK
David R. Wheeler	School of Management, Suffolk University, Boston, USA
Philippe C. L. Wing	Department of Hotels and Tourism, University of Ulster, Londonderry, UK
Stephen F. Witt	Department of Management Science and Statistics, University College of Swansea, Swansea, UK
Ugur Yucelt	Division of Business Administration, Pennsylvania State University at Harrisburg, Middletown, USA
Ronald L. Zallocco	Department of Marketing, University of Toledo, Toledo, USA

Preface

The objective of this handbook is to provide a comprehensive business and academic reference source related to the most crucial issues in tourism marketing and management. Well over one hundred tourism topic entries are included, set in alphabetical order to provide quick and easy access to information. Our target users include managers in hospitality, travel, tourism, transportation, banking, market research, advertising and consultancy companies, local authorities and national tourist offices, as well as tourism educators, students and researchers.

This handbook only became a possibility as a result of the cooperation and efforts of the contributors. We wish to express our gratitude to these individuals, who include tourism academics and practitioners from many parts of the world, but concentrated mainly in Europe and North America. The broad coverage of topic areas is accompanied by a broad spectrum of countries of origin of contributors. We also wish to thank those individuals who provided support and suggestions throughout the process of design and preparation.

STEPHEN F. WITT
LUIZ MOUTINHO

Introduction

There can be no doubt as to the economic importance of tourism. World receipts from international tourism comprize 6 per cent of the value of international trade, placing international tourism second only to oil. It has been forecast that by the turn of the century international tourism will be the most important sector in world trade. When receipts from domestic tourism are also taken into account, world receipts from tourism exceed the GNP (gross national product) of any country in the world except Japan and the United States.* Tourism demand is expected to grow well into the foreseeable future, so the tourist industry is expected to become even more important in the years ahead.

Tourism has a marked impact on employment, the balance of payments and economic stability for many countries. It is labor intensive and hence a particularly good potential source of jobs, offering a relatively high proportion of job opportunities to the lower skilled occupations where unemployment tends to be concentrated. In addition, new jobs in tourism tend to be spread more widely geographically than other growth sectors in many economies.

It was in this context of the increasingly important role of tourism in the world economy that the editors perceived the need for this handbook. It was felt that a comprehensive collection of the main concepts and phenomena in tourism marketing and tourism management would prove to be a most useful reference work for the growing number of tourism practitioners and academics. We believe that the *Tourism Marketing and Management Handbook* makes a valuable contribution to the tourism literature because it provides a broad coverage of topics and effectively stimulates reader interest with its readable format and style and extensive use of interesting real-life examples. The breadth and depth of coverage in this text is intended to provide managers, teachers and researchers with a sound understanding of the tourism discipline. Tourism is a challenging and exciting field to study, and the format adopted for the handbook allows the reader to develop an appreciation of the types of problem that exist and to develop the skills of analysis and decision making necessary for success in the industry. Some of the topics emphasize and reinforce key tourism marketing and management concepts, whereas others challenge readers to analyze specific situations and develop creative solutions based on sound fundamental tourism knowledge.

Tourism marketing

The importance of sophisticated marketing is becoming widely recognized within the tourism industry. Tourists are far more complicated customers than in the past; thus, it is important for tourism-related businesses to know the specific characteristics of their clientele so that they might better serve their needs and reach them in the most effective ways. As the economic significance of tourism is more fully appreciated in the coming years, greater attention will be paid to marketing research in obtaining seasonal profiles of visitors and in determining how well promotions compete in the market.

Crisis marketing is now an essential ingredient for travel marketing professionals. Contingency planning, forecasting, and creative responses to rapidly changing world conditions are now essential elements of success in the tourism industry. The challenge for tourism managers is to realize that marketing activities do not just happen (they must be planned, implemented, controlled and evaluated) and that these are continuous processes not just undertaken on predetermined occasions.

Tourism marketing planning is the organized process of studying the market, identifying and measuring its trends, developing major marketing objectives and supporting marketing mix programs. All the elements of the marketing mix must complement each other and be presented in a balanced manner. The tourism marketer's goal in managing the promotion mix is to maximize successful communication to chosen target markets. Promotional consistency is essential. The component elements of tourism promotion are interdependent and must be combined into a mutually reinforcing whole. Proper management of the marketing mix is essential for the successful implementation of the tourism marketing approach. The marketing activity must be the major agent of change within the organization, and therefore continual evaluation and reappraisal of each marketing element is essential.

The development of an effective marketing strategy should be based on a consistent framework of policies, objectives and action programs that will enable the tourism organization to

---

* In the case of Japan, GNP is approximately equal to world tourism receipts, and for the United States GNP is approximately twice the value of world tourism receipts.

arrive at the best possible results by optimizing capabilities, resource, and market opportunities. A systematic and logical selection of target segments will require more efficient efforts in order to increase tourist product demand. It is not enough to generate tourist arrivals, or achieve a certain market share, but rather, it is necessary to produce profitable tourist product sales and profitable market penetration. Market penetration emphasizes more effective utilization of marketing tactics. A continual survey and review of new technology should be adopted in order to pursue new market opportunities arising from these.

Numerous tourism marketing concepts, techniques and application areas are introduced and explained. The topics cover the most important building blocks and managerial implications of marketing tourist products, services and destinations, ranging from marketing research approaches and the design of an effective tourism marketing mix, to the discussion and analysis of multiple marketing management issues.

Tourism management

Strategic planning and management in tourism take place within a highly dynamic environment and the tactical policies which contribute to the total planning strategy should be taken into consideration. The interweaving of short-term policies within the fabric of the total planning strategy calls for extreme skill, care, and sensitivity to the strengths and weaknesses of the tourism firm, the threats and opportunities present in the environment and a flow of recent, accurate and detailed information. Effective planning and control require a comprehensive understanding, both of the management processes and the management information required to support them. Precisely which strategy or combination of strategies will be adopted depends upon the specific circumstances of the tourism company, and its resources, as well as the corporate objectives.

Technology is one of the key driving forces influencing the competitive process in the tourism industry. Companies cannot strategically afford to neglect the opportunities and threats posed by new technologies: competitive strategies have to take account of technological changes and the market opportunities they may present in the shorter and in the longer term. The effective implementation of technological change will lead tourism organizations to business success and to the ability to gain and retain competitive advantages.

Concern is being expressed about the detrimental social and environmental impacts of tourism on host communities. Effective programs for the protection of wildlife and natural environments are becoming increasingly important, because public acceptance of what the tourism industry is doing and producing is vital for its survival. Furthermore, if a destination area wishes to retain tourism as a long-term economic activity, it must preserve and enhance those features that attract tourists. The absence of tourism planning in a destination can lead to irreversible social, cultural and environmental damage and to eventual loss of market share.

The tourism management areas and tools which are crucial for the implementation of an effective and proactive management approach are introduced and explained. The themes, which range from financial and personnel management to planning and forecasting, from training policies and technological trends to tourism legislation and resource allocation strategies, are designed to provide information for tourism managers in areas which should help them to improve their decision-making skills and minimize business risks.

Topic format

In order to provide the reader with the most relevant and concise information, the presentation format of the Handbook entries was designed, as far as possible, to contain the following sections:

Introduction: An overview of the topic, intended to describe the core content of the concept or issue under analysis.

Examples: An illustration of the ideas mentioned in the Introduction, presenting company case histories where appropriate.

Benefits: Highlighting the reasons why the concept/technique should be applied when its utilization is appropriate.

Implementation: Demonstrating how to apply the concept/technique.

Assessment: A critical evaluation of the concept/technique.

Conclusion: Emphasizing the key points previously developed for a clear understanding of the topic.

Focus on small business: A discussion of the specific case of the small business in tourism, making the material presented more meaningful and interesting to small business managers.

Software/databases: A section included only where very specific computer software or databases exist for the topic under consideration. More widely applicable software/databases are provided in the general section at the end of the Handbook.

Further reading: A list of bibliographical references (usually annotated) intended to supply the reader with the additional sources that will provide increased knowledge about the subject.

Clearly, given the very wide range of topics covered, complete uniformity of style was not possible. Furthermore, the imposition of very rigid style requirements on the large number of contributors was neither possible nor desirable; indeed, some topics lend themselves to a more practical treatment whilst others require a more academic approach.

Airline competition

Introduction

Airlines are the primary means of transport for longhaul and overseas travel. Most changes affecting the provision of airline services also impact on international tourism. On the supply side of the industry, technological and legal forces have reshaped the provision of services and, as a result, the profile of destinations served by air transport. The demand for travel also plays a role in shaping the types of air transport service provided.

The introduction of jet aircraft produced a boom in international travel as a result of the accompanying savings in both time and monetary expenditures. Thus, longhaul destinations such as Hawaii became more available to a wider spectrum of travelers. Continued innovations, such as the introduction of the Boeing 747-400 and -500 with attendant range and capacity improvements, promise continued expansion of the industry. Plans to develop a hypersonic aircraft, with speeds from mach 5, truly have the potential to revolutionize the international air travel industry.

Regulatory changes and changes in aircraft technology exhibit a mutual dependence, especially in international aviation. The 'open skies' policy of the United States, clearly enumerated in the International Air Transport Competition Act 1979, would largely be meaningless without current longhaul capabilities. With regulatory and technological freedom to reach new destinations, air carriers have reshaped route maps on the national, regional, and international levels.

Domestic and regional deregulation have produced their share of changes as well. The relatively unencumbered market policy of the United States has been copied to varying degrees elsewhere. Members of the European Community (EC) are currently moving to rewrite provisions of the Rome treaty with regard to airline service. Australia, New Zealand, and Canada have each enacted modified, although not total, deregulation programs.

In some respects, international regulatory changes have been affected by the changing composition of the world travel market. Many of the international airlines with the most dramatic growth come from developing areas of the world, notably the Pacific Basin. A number of the flag carriers of these nations have chosen to remain outside multilateral regulatory agreements, such as the rate-setting machinery of the International Air Transport Association (IATA). The freewheeling style of these carriers, in areas ranging from liberal fare policies to channels of distribution for selling the airline product, have a direct impact on tourism development and an indirect impact through the response that IATA carriers have made.

Air carrier managements have reshaped their competitive positions in response to evolving technological and regulatory standards which affect significantly the travel industry. Destination wholesale and retail operations must adjust their own positions to account for, if not coincide with, those taken by the airlines. All carrier decisions with respect to operations and marketing affect competition and, therefore, air travel.

Exogenous variables

To remain competitive, carriers must respond to numerous factors beyond their control or ultimately face the risk of bankruptcy. Examples can easily be found of airlines who chose not to respond to the new environment or who responded incorrectly. Pan American might be considered an example of the former, Braniff is an example of the latter. Gucci uniforms, Calder inspired liveries, rapid route expansion, and flying into Gatwick, at a time when all major connections were through Heathrow, proved to be interesting but noncompetitive operating policies.

Economic trends dating from the middle of the 1970s also caught the airlines in a predicament. Fuel prices and interest rates increased dramatically, boosting airline operating costs. Although these costs moderated somewhat by the mid-1980s, they then started to climb again. The consequences of these cost changes were felt foremost in the area of equipment selection and deployment. Airlines and aircraft manufacturers worked to improve fuel efficiency, in large part explaining the success of the Airbus consortium. A residual effect of the drive to reduce fuel consumption is that, as fuel prices moderated, the improved aircraft efficiency and technology gives airlines the ability to maintain acceptable profit margins while responding to more intense competition.

Financing the purchase of aircraft is directly affected by interest rates. The financial cost of even a slight increase in the interest rate on, for example, the recent Singapore Airlines order placed with Boeing for US $3 billion, would be staggering. Airlines forced to re-equip during the period of high rates found they had to reduce profit margins, as a result either of increased costs or of flying antiquated aircraft. Both factors contributed to the sea of red ink which plagued carriers worldwide at the start of the 1980s.

Even with interest rates moderating, some carriers may find it difficult to finance competitive operations. It is generally understood that equipment is a primary facet of airline competition, since new equipment is more competitive equipment. In addition, some carriers must finance fleet expansion to cover new operations, even if the current fleet is relatively new. United Airlines is faced with a multiple threat of rising interest rates and the need to purchase new aircraft for both its domestic operations and its relatively new international operations in the Pacific Basin. It is difficult to imagine how United can remain price competitive and maintain adequate profit margins, whether or not it does re-equip.

The economic recession of the early 1980s also adversely affected the industry. Declining discretionary incomes of consumers reduced the volume of longhaul pleasure travel. Business travel was also curtailed in response to the downturn in the business cycle and, at least in part, due to travel substitution techniques such as teleconferencing. The result was a decline in both the number of passengers and the actual service measured in passenger-kilometers for 1980 and 1981. Deregulation permitted airline management the latitude to respond competitively to declining traffic and profit margins. Many components of the air travel product taken for granted by travelers today were enacted by carriers in response to competitive pressures and financial hardship.

A more recent trend over which many airlines have little if any control is the privatization of heretofore nationalized carriers. Over the past few years, the airline industry has seen plans for the whole or partial privatization of British Airways, Japan Airlines, and Singapore Airlines, among others. Although it is too early yet to predict all of the outcomes of these moves, some are already evident. Foremost, the monopoly position of the flag carrier on international routes tends to be liquidated as a condition of privatization. For example, Japan Airlines has been joined by All Nippon Airways and Toa Domestic Airways on international operations based in Japan. The addition of new airlines and capacity on existing routes is intensifying competition, giving passengers and travel intermediaries a wider range of price and service offerings. While passengers may benefit from some reduced fares, the choice may reach bewildering proportions.

Privatization will also affect competition as the dictates of the private market replace government policy. Some of the former national carriers have been imbued with a new vigor as government bureaucracy is replaced by private management. These 'new' carriers are opening new routes, packaging their product in innovative ways, and generally becoming responsive to the traveler and the trade.

Accompanying privatization in reshaping airline structure and competition is the trend towards 'concentration' in the industry. Some airlines have been turned over to the private sector at least partially in response to the formation of mega-carriers, particularly those based in the United States. It has been suggested that some of these newly-private international airlines may themselves have to find merger partners if they are to survive. European-based carriers are most actively considering such actions at this time.

Concentration can have both beneficial and deleterious effects on competition. There can be economies of scale in the provision of airline services in areas such as aircraft purchases and management information systems. Therefore, continued concentration has the potential simultaneously to reduce travel prices and improve service levels. However, mergers may also be viewed as a threat to the long-term viability of a competitive market, since with size come problems with control of gate space, take-off and landing slots, distribution systems, and prices. Mergers may thus give a carrier the ability to control entry into the market, entry on individual routes, and the provision of service.

Endogenous variables

The increasingly competitive air travel environment has intensified the need for airlines to focus substantial effort on controllable variables, particularly those within marketing. Strategic management no longer means that success comes from understanding the political and regulatory environment. Airlines are giving more focus to what traditionally is referred to as the marketing mix.

Product

Deregulation has permitted carriers to differentiate an historically homogenous product. Inflight, transport, and ground services innovations have ranged from no frills carriers, pioneered by Sir Freddie Laker, to the luxury services of MGM Grand and the Concorde services of British Airways and Air France. Airlines are striving to identify profitable market niches, thus avoiding some competition and at the same time providing a better product in the segments served.

Inflight services now include elements such as airborne telephone and telex service, transmission of personal computer data, onboard personal computers, and inflight movies. Innovative food service, such as the use of fresh fruits and vegetables, has likewise become a major component of inflight services. These services have the multiple purposes of accommodating lifestyle changes of travelers while at the same time reducing the cost of customer services and generating additional revenues for the airline.

Competition and deregulation have also helped to reshape carrier route networks. Many airlines have implemented, or further refined, a 'hub-and-spoke' routing system. Airlines claim this is beneficial for passengers as it increases efficiency through control of feeder traffic at hub airports and better matches aircraft and flight segment requirements, although some travelers would not necessarily agree.

A hub-and-spoke system, combined with the current wave

of mergers, may effectively give the airline a near monopoly position at a hub airport. The airline is then in a position to control both prices and services, often at levels not comparable to those provided at competitive destinations. Passengers may also find that the number of direct services between a particular pair of points has been reduced, thereby increasing total travel time and equipment changes while decreasing schedule convenience.

Place

The burgeoning plethora of flight and service offerings has caused airline management to place increasing emphasis on the travel agency distribution system. While this generally has helped the traveler through increased access to the travel services offered by primary vendors, it has not come without cost to the airlines. In the United States, for example, travel agent commissions are increasing at a faster rate than passenger revenues, more than doubling as a proportion of total operating costs over the past decade.

The relationship between airlines and their sales agents has come under closer scrutiny. Faced with increasing government pressure to make the travel sales distribution system more competitive, IATA formed the International Airline Travel Agency Network. The practical outcome of these changes is that the airlines are forced to be more competitive in their dealings with product distributors. Increasing use of overrides and, allegedly, rebates and 'bucket shops', are now part of competition in the airline industry.

In order to control both product offerings and sales, airlines have developed computerized reservations systems, which very likely are one of the keys to future competitiveness. The introduction and use of these systems in foreign nations are at issue in, at least, the United States, Japan, and Germany, and also in the bilateral negotiations affecting these nations. Some have suggested that airlines use these systems to control competition through the dissemination of information, while others have suggested that they are an essential part of a highly successful competitive strategy.

Promotion

Promotional strategies have not only changed in response to competition but have also changed competition. One of the most successful programs ever developed in the industry is the frequent flier awards, in which the passenger receives bonuses such as upgrades and free tickets. Although initially offered by just a few airlines to develop customer loyalty, participation in a frequent flier program is a competitive necessity today.

Other programs have also been developed by airlines to create a greater demand for their services. Comprehensive travel and tour packages are a traditional element of airline competition. Deregulation, however, encouraged airlines to develop these packages more intensively and to go directly to the market rather than restricting themselves to selling packages through wholesalers.

The success of the above programs, and many others, seems to depend not only on innovation but also on the size of the airline offering them. In many ways this points to the continued oligopolization of the industry. Frequent flier programs of major airlines are more attractive to travelers since greater mileage can be earned on the carrier and more awards are available to those who qualify for benefits. Major airlines can also develop tour packages more successfully, particularly for prime destinations such as Hawaii, the Caribbean, and the Maldives (from the United States).

Pricing

Pricing is the most commented upon and analyzed aspect of airline competition. Its relative importance to the travel budget of the longhaul traveler warrants this interest. Approximately half of the total value of the Japanese outbound market is accounted for by air fares, which is a representative proportion for much overseas travel. Therefore, any changes in the price of airline service will have an immediate and relatively significant impact on the amount of world travel.

Most of the highly discounted fares are protected by relatively high, and rising, barriers or fences to their use. The most common and contentious barriers include advance booking requirements, minimum stay requirements, penalties for cancellations or changes in the itinerary, and capacity limitations. Discretionary travelers on longhaul, high density, tourism-dominated routes have benefited most from the new discount fares. Business travelers are effectively precluded from the discounts and, as a result, pay higher fares. For their part, airlines are managing profit margins through careful analysis and control of competition.

Conclusion

The degree and nature of airline competition has undergone vast changes in recent years. Carrier management has been freed from many of the regulatory and technological constraints which tempered competitive programs in the past. As competition emerges, travelers and other members of the travel industry will be faced with both opportunities and problems. The correct responses to these competitive challenges is not always easy to determine.

Focus on small business

The retail sectors of the travel industry, and to a lesser extent the wholesale operations, tend to be small and medium-size businesses. Recent trends, however, point to consolidation and increased size of individual businesses in the channel of distribution, at least partly in response to the increased competitiveness of the airline industry. Many retail travel agents find that they can remain profitable only if they increase the scope of their operations, thus enabling them to be in a position to take advantage of substantial cumulative discounts offered by the airlines. In the increasingly competitive business travel sector, large agencies dominate the market.

Other challenges to small agencies come from the increased automation now inherent in airline competition. Airlines are able to take their product directly to consumers through innovative new means such as public databases accessible through home computers, and even some specialty television programs. These changes, along with increasing activities by the airlines in direct marketing of tours, will require that many agencies redefine the mission of their business. A more active role in travel counseling and, perhaps, even taking title to some of the travel products they sell may be a way for small travel agents to proceed.

Software/databases

Smith, G. R. and Golden, P. A., *Airline: A Strategic Management Simulation* (Prentice Hall, 1987). This computer simulation allows for comprehensive decision-making in a competitive airline industry, taking into account many decision variables.

Further reading

Bailey, E. E., 'Airline deregulation in the United States: the benefits provided and the lessons learned', *International Journal of Transport Economics*, vol. 12, no. 2, (June 1985), pp. 119–44. This article, by one of the chief architects of deregulation in the United States, assesses the impact of deregulation on the airline industry.

Bailey, E. E., Graham, D. R. and Kaplan, D. P., *Deregulating the Airlines* (Massachusetts Institute of Technology, 1985). A rigorous microeconomic analysis of the competitive impacts of deregulation on airline competition.

Bitner, M. J. and Booms, B. H., 'Deregulation and the future of the US travel agent industry', *Journal of Travel Research*, vol. 20 (Fall 1981), pp. 2–6. Discussion of some early changes in the airline distribution system under deregulation.

Bitner, M. J. and Booms, B. H., 'Trends in travel and tourism marketing: the changing structure of distribution systems', *Journal of Travel Research*, vol. 20 (Spring 1982), pp. 39–44. Reviews how all members of the travel sales distribution system are coping with the changes brought about by deregulation.

Boberg, K. B. and Collison, F. M., 'Computer reservation systems and airline competition', *Tourism Management*, vol. 6, no. 3 (September 1985), pp. 174–83. This article discusses how CRS are reshaping airline competition and the controversy surrounding their use.

Brenner, M. A., Leet, J. O. and Schott, E., *Airline Deregulation* (Eno Foundation for Transportation, 1985). This text discusses the background of airline deregulation and the changes it has brought about in the marketplace.

Clark, T., 'Restrictions mar fares' appeal', *Travel Weekly* (2 February 1985) p. 4. Reviews deep discount fares in the industry, with particular attention given to consumer and trade reaction to the numerous barriers placed on budget fares.

Coker, B., 'In-flight services: an expanding world', *Airline Executive* (September 1984), pp. 22–4. Describes some of the new services airlines are adding to their in-flight services in an effort to attract and maintain customers.

Collison, F. M. and Boberg, K. B., 'Marketing of airline services in a deregulated environment', *Tourism Management*, vol. 8, no. 3, (September 1987), pp. 195–204. An analysis of how airlines are altering the marketing mix (the '4 Ps') to improve their competitive position.

Dempsey, S. P., 'Birth of monster airlines', *Traffic Management* (1 December 1986), p. 77. Discusses how the hub-and-spoke routing systems and the continuing merger trend in the industry are resulting in market dominance of some hubs by single carriers.

Durbin, F., 'ARC cancels record number of agencies for defaults', *Travel Weekly* (17 July 1986), p. 1. Author points to the toll that competition is having on retail travel agents, highlighting the impacts of low cost fares, the number of ticket rewrites, and increasing costs.

'ECAC approves liberalizing fare, capacity regulations', *Aviation Week and Space Technology* (12 January 1987), p. 36. A brief review of the memorandum of understanding drafted by the ECAC to affect deregulation in member nations.

Jenks, C., 'US airlines hub and spokes: developing hubs to dominate market share', *Travel and Tourism Analyst* (August 1986), pp. 29–42. An indepth discussion of the development of airline hub-and-spoke systems.

Ott, J., 'Carriers fine tuning discounts to control burgeoning demand', *Aviation Week and Space Technology* (25 February 1985) pp. 28–9. Views discount fares from a carrier management perspective, with special attention given to the concepts of yield management and inventory (seat) control.

US General Accounting Office, *Deregulation: Competition is Making Airlines More Efficient and Responsive to Consumers.* (GAO, Washington DC, 1985). A report to the US consumers on the impacts of increased competition on carriers and passengers.

KEVIN B. BOBERG and
FREDERICK M. COLLISON

Allocating tourism resources

Introduction

Tourism is a global industry. In the international league tables the aggregate value of international tourism expenditure stands second only to the expenditure on oil and oil-based products. Vast resources are committed annually to satisfying tourist demand and providing tourist products. The scale, complexity and significance of the tourist industry currently means that no individual nation can afford to ignore the resource use implications that are involved.

Resources can in general be defined as the inputs required by the transformation process that satisfies human needs or wants. Tourism resources are natural or manmade: they range from sun, sea and landscape through cultural and heritage assets to purpose-built amenity attractions. Invariably natural and manmade resources have to be combined to meet tourist needs and on balance the more sophisticated tourist products are capital intensive.

When mass tourism first started many optimistic observers believed that there were few natural resource limitations on development and that tourism resources were renewable: but successful tourism development can erode the very character-istics and features that provided the original attractiveness. The reality is, therefore, that all resources are finite and have alternative uses. Choices are an inevitable feature of resource use and an allocative process has to be determined to deal with the problems involved.

Examples

Natural landscapes of great beauty, e.g. remote Highland areas in Scotland, face different scenarios:

1. They may be left untouched as wilderness areas, their potential lying dormant with virtually no economic return, but a legacy for future generations.
2. Improvements in basic access could encourage hunting, shooting or fishing and some economic return.
3. Greatly improved infrastructure development in transport, hospitality and amenities could encourage mass-market tourism (e.g. skiing), and if successful high economic returns.

4. Options outside the tourism industry, e.g. afforestation and the long-term prospect of a fairly safe return.

This example is not exhaustive but a similar set of issues face virtually all tourist development, whether rural or urban. There is always an opportunity cost to be considered and there are economic, ecological and sociocultural repercussions to be appraised.

What criteria and procedures are to be used? Who is to be given the responsibility for the decision making:

1. Resource owners?
2. Local/destination communities?
3. Tourists?
4. Governments?

All of these issues have to be addressed if resources are to be transformed in an optimal fashion.

Implementation

In an ideal world the decision-making processes and procedures should be effective and efficient. To this end it is important to have a framework or mechanism that coordinates the process. At a national level there are two polarized alternatives – the market or the plan:

1. The market system where consumers and firms guided by self-interest and the profit motive interact through inter-pretation of price signals, insuring that an impersonal self-adjusting price mechanism meets consumer preferences constrained only by their ability to pay.
2. The planned system where an individual or group adopts an authoritarian role regarding the range of products and services to be produced, the production methods, quantities and to whom they should be distributed and at what price.

Both approaches have drawbacks and merits: real-world systems have features of both although the role of the government varies considerably.

Resource allocation involves various stages: *objectives* have to be clearly specified; *alternatives* have to be evaluated; *criteria* have to be established for option selection; *implementation* procedures need to be designed and *performance* appraisal has to be instigated. A free enterprise system abdicates these stages to the price mechanism. A planned economy has to carefully proceed through each stage if it is to be effective.

Analyzing tourism resource allocation over the last 30 years it is no surprise to find that features of both have been incorporated in the development, regulation and control of tourism but that the actual allocative process employed is closely linked to the type of economic and sociopolitical systems in operation. In the United States, for example, until very recently the government played a passive and low-key regulatory role; in Canada particularly at provincial levels a much more positive and facilitating role has been played; in Spain a very active and dominant role has been played by the State. This role has been replicated by more recent entrants to mass-tourist development, e.g. Yugoslavia and many Third World countries. The UK Government has displayed various attitudes towards tourism reflecting the perspectives of the political party in power. Currently it is acting as a facilitator for development, ostensibly by creating a free enterprise environment, but in reality, underwriting and subsidizing substantial development via its support network of tourist boards and development agencies.

The objectivies underlying government involvement are of crucial importance. If tourist development is seen primarily in economic terms then the price mechanism with its strictly commercial approach can be used as a vehicle. If however social, cultural or environmental considerations predominate then support or direct government involvement inevitably becomes necessary. Concepts and management tools necessary at a national level would include:

1. Planning – holistic and grass roots; carrying capacity (both physical and social); zoning; rationing; demarketing.
2. Impact analysis – opportunity costs; multiplier effects; input–output analysis; linkages; cost-benefit analysis.

Regional and local resource allocation

National perspectives and philosophical outlooks set the scene at regional and local levels. Although sociopolitical influences exert a considerable influence on the procedures adopted, generalization is dangerous. Sometimes it is difficult to explain the degree of variation found in apparently homogeneous sociopolitical frameworks. The contrasts highlighted by Heeley's (1986) research on Glasgow and Edinburgh is an interesting example. In Glasgow a leading role in tourist organization and policy has been taken by the District Council, resulting in new jobs, increased wealth, enhanced services and civic pride. In Edinburgh by contrast Heeley argues successive political administrations have failed to intervene authoritatively. It is interesting to speculate on the reasons for this variation in philosophy – could it be the role of tradition, the opportunity costs, or even the personality profiles of the decision makers? Similar examples could be found in most European countries.

Where planning is used it is important to understand that careful coordination is needed and that a top-down approach is rarely successful. Goodwill and cooperation of the host community is necessary for successful development and so grass roots planning or a community approach is preferable. The

same concepts and management tools need to be used as enumerated above.

Organizational resource allocation

Organizations transform inputs into outputs as a response to societal demands. There are two approaches to ensuring the efficiency of the transformation process: to maximize the output from a predetermined resource input, or to minimize the resource input for a predetermined output. Essentially this involves decisions regarding what services to offer, the production processes to be used, the location and the timescales involved.

Using the framework suggested earlier (objectives, alternatives, criteria, implementation, performance) the setting of operational objectives is particularly important and should be developed within the strategic dimensions of a corporate plan. The historical evolution of the organization, its ownership, size etc. will exert a significant influence on the setting of objectives and procedures used. In particular the criteria for evaluating performance will vary between private and publicly owned enterprise but the crucial question should always be whether the objectives have been met and how does the performance stand up to comparative evaluation.

Sometimes private sector commercial objectives may have to be controlled for the public interest. The objectives of publicly owned organizations in the United Kingdom are also being reappraised and debated. At Witney in rural Oxfordshire factions within the local council are in conflict regarding the overall objectives of Cogges Farm Museum: should it be preserved for its historic cultural and educational importance or developed as a self-financing commercially viable entertainment attraction? This illustrates at a local level how attitudes towards tourist development are all important in shaping the criteria and procedures to be used in allocating resources but similar difficulties arise at national and international levels because the role of tourism in society involves highly personal and subjective valuations.

Conclusion

The allocation of tourism resources has a significant impact in economic, social, cultural and political terms throughout the world. For some countries the economic benefits attainable in the short run may be particularly attractive but it is essential that they should be appraised against the long-term sociocultural and environmental implications. This means that the initial objective-setting stage is crucial in the process of resource allocation. The responsibility of the decision makers is onerous: the priorities that are established determine both the subsequent performance and societal effects. Inevitably implementation procedures will differ from country to country but in view of the vast global resources involved it is important that all approaches should be effective, efficient and socially responsible so that the assets and resources currently utilized will also be available for future generations to enjoy.

Further reading

Getz, D., 'Capacity to absorb tourism – concepts and implications for Strategic Planning', *Annals of Tourism Research*, vol. 10, no. 2 (1983). Presentation of a systems-type model to aid the general process of research and planning for tourism.

Gunn, C., *Tourism Planning* (Crane Russak, 1979). A general overview of planning for tourism.

Heeley, J., 'A tale of two cities and tourism', *Quarterly Economic Commentary*, vol. 11, no. 4 (1986).

McIntosh, R. W., *Tourism: Principles, Practices and Philosophies* (Grid, 1977). A general text with references to resource issues and problems.

Mill, R. and Morrison, A. M., *The Tourism System – an Introductory Text* (Prentice Hall, 1985). Chapters 9, 10, 11, 12 and 13 cover issues in tourism resource allocation, e.g. impacts, policy formulation, regulation planning and development.

Murphy, P., *Tourism: A community approach* (Methuen, 1986). Community planning for tourism development – an attempt to integrate ecological and social aspects into the more traditional economic-based development models.

Murphy, P., 'Perceptions and attitudes of decision-making groups in tourism centres', *Journal of Travel Research*, vol. 11, no. 3 (1983). Identifies, using discriminatory analysis, the differing attitudes of businessmen, administrators and residents when destinations are developed.

Trippier, D., 'Tourism in the 1990s – UK Government view', *Tourism Management*, vol. 8, no. 2 (June 1987). Review of role and objectives and responsibilities of government in UK tourism.

ANTHEA ROGERS

Appraising tourism potential

Introduction

The task of appraising a tourism project can cover a multitude of disciplines – economics, planning, environmental science, geography, historical research, architectural design, engineering, finance, management and marketing. These are all areas of specialist input which feed into project feasibility studies. The importance of these inputs varies from project to project and also according to the geographical coverage of the project – whether it is site-specific or an area strategy. Therefore a tourism planner requires a simple checklist of parameters which can be readily applied when assessing the tourism potential of a site or an area. The key parameters in this checklist are as follows:

1. Location and access: how well located is the site or area in relation to the market?
2. Concepts and themes: any tourism venture, development or marketing, requires a powerful concept to succeed. This necessitates the portrayal of strong identifiable themes and images to relevant market segments.
3. Products: themes must be translated into products which give added strength to the overall concept. Compatible products can be assembled to form a critical mass development which presents a clear and positive image to potential users.
4. Markets and economic benefit: is the market easily accessible? How can a site or area be developed and marketed to attract high value market segments which generate greater economic benefit?
5. Competition: a development scheme or strategy must take account of the location and image strength of the existing competition. Can a market gap be filled or is the scheme/strategy powerful enough to overcome the competition?
6. Commercial viability and funding: what is the scope for cross-funding tourism facilities from other more viable commercial elements of a scheme? Can grant aid be levered in to support the funding package?
7. Management and marketing: many tourism schemes stand or fall by the quality of operational management and the level of marketing activity. Successful tourism attractions require high standards of customer care to ensure the consumer feels he/she is receiving 'value for money'.

These parameters can be summarized in the form of a SWOT (strengths, weaknesses, opportunities, threats) analysis, examining the strengths, weaknesses, opportunities and threats for each component. A final assessment of the tourism potential of a site development or an area strategy will weigh up the costs and benefits of the project based on the summary appraisal of the key parameters. Tourism planners will accordingly be able to recommend whether the project should progress or whether an alternative strategy is more beneficial.

Site versus area

In developing a framework to assess tourism potential a clear distinction should be made between a site appraisal and an area appraisal. For the purposes of this exercise an area is deemed to be geographically represented by a county or region in the United Kingdom. The vast majority of professional consultancy studies in the tourism sector can be broken down between 1. site-specific feasibility study and 2. area tourism strategy. The costs and benefits of developing a particular site or pursuing a defined strategy will vary according to the target audience. For example the private sector project places greater emphasis on the financial rate of return on capital employed and profit generation whereas public sector projects are more likely to put job creation and economic benefit to the local community higher on the agenda.

A further distinction to be made is one of scale. One specific site, if developed for tourism, will only represent one component of a region's total tourism product. The latter is the sum of many individual site-related products. Whilst the whole will always be greater than its component parts, certain site products will contribute more to the area product than others. This can be measured in terms of visitor numbers or visitor spend. Thus Disneyland (California, USA) and Alton Towers (Staffordshire, UK) have a substantial impact on their regional tourism product in terms of visitor numbers and spend. Similarly, high quality flagship hotel developments such as the Mandarin (Singapore) or the Hilton (Budapest, Hungary) contribute significantly to national tourism spend. In addition they yield intangible benefits in terms of prestige and image.

The separation of site and area analysis is one which must be employed when establishing the importance of key parameters in appraising tourism potential. The relative importance of these factors differs between site appraisals and area appraisals and is a theme which recurs throughout this chapter.

Key parameters

The process of appraising tourism potential involves a thorough investigation of a number of key parameters. These are common to both site and area appraisals. For comparative purposes, however, it is difficult to assign values to these parameters. It is possible to consider them in relative terms when ranking projects but only for like projects. Thus Project A can only be assessed to be more beneficial than Project B if they are either both site appraisals or both area appraisals, not one of each type. Although the key parameters do not vary significantly between these two types of project, their relevance and importance does vary between project types. To illustrate this the key parameters are described below and applied to each project type.

Location and access

Many tourism projects can be dismissed on locational grounds alone at the site-specific level. For example a site development, whether it be an accommodation project or a day-visitor attraction, requires an attractive environment and location with good immediate access and signposting. Visitors will not walk half a mile to a site surrounded by dereliction and/or heavy industrial activity no matter how strong the product appeal is within the internal site boundary. A successful site development is one which has immediate car parking provision (80–90 per cent of visitors to day-visitor attractions arrive by car), is zoned within an attractive environment with good landscaping and is sited in close proximity to major road networks.

At the regional level an assessment of tourism potential would place greater emphasis on transport communications and general access to the area. The proximity of major international ports of entry (air and sea), the strength of linkages with the country's road and rail networks, and general infrastructure provision are the factors of most importance. Location also has to be assessed in relation to proximity to key feeder areas which already act as tourist magnets. Within the context of a SWOT analysis, for example, this can be interpreted as an opportunity or a threat – the opportunity to draw on a large immediately accessible market if the product is right, and the threat posed by brand loyalty to an existing location.

Concepts and themes

The notion of a concept in tourism terms is often a difficult one to explain to the layman, and is often confused with the product itself. For example, a meal in a restaurant is a product. If this is taken in a five star restaurant then the concept is one of a high quality culinary experience; if it is simply a meal in a fast food outlet the concept is entirely different – it is convenient cheap quick food. The quality of the environment and the food itself are of less importance in the fast food outlet. It is its convenience in terms of location and time availability which matter to the customer.

The above example demonstrates the importance of portraying a strong concept to potential markets. This is particularly so for site-specific tourist attractions whether they be theme parks with white knuckle rides (family fun and adventure), historic cathedrals (architectural and cultural heritage), or prestige conference and exhibition centres (quality business environment). Visitors to site attractions are becoming increasingly discerning and have high expectations of their visitor experiences. In the United Kingdom, for example, recent trends in museum development have placed much emphasis on providing the visitor with an interpretive experience. This is based on a strong portrayal of the themes and stories relating to social and industrial history, involves active participation by the visitor and often includes animated events.

In looking at the wider area, conceptual images play an important part in the success of tourism centres. The Lake District in the United Kingdom, for example, has a number of products which taken together portray strong marketable images, notably peace and quiet, grand countryside and romanticism. Clearly areas of strong historical and cultural appeal have natural advantages over areas of traditional industry in terms of their image in the marketplace. Tourism is increasingly seen in its wider context as a means of changing the conventional perception of an area and making it a more attractive place to live, work and invest in – the Wigan Pier development in the north-west of the United Kingdom is a pertinent example of the 'reversing the image' trend.

Products

A successful site attraction or tourist destination requires a critical mass of compatible products which have market relevance and appeal. In addition to the main theme of the attraction in its product format the overwhelming majority of day-visitor site attractions must provide standard add-on products such as a gift shop and catering outlet to improve viability. Product design implications are critical in this respect. Evidence suggests that locating the site exit through the gift shop for example significantly increases visitor spend. Similarly, visitor surveys at attractions indicate that approximately 60 per cent of spending by visitors on their day out is allocated to food and drink. This has clear financial and operational implications for many site attractions. However, very few site attractions, other than hotels and other accommodation-based products, are commercially viable in their own right and the critical mass concept is often extended to encompass neighboring sites. The aim is to create a more rounded development which improves both overall viability and the quality of the visitor experience. Increasingly many attractions are only one part of a wider retail and leisure complex which embraces core and speciality shopping and other commercial leisure operations (e.g. pub/restaurant, food court, cinemas).

Taking a wider perspective at the regional level, product development must relate available resources to target markets, concentrating where possible on those products which have unique appeal, can attract higher spending market segments and have greater employment generation potential. This necessitates financial resources being targeted on those product opportunities which can achieve the greatest impact. The product 'whole' for a region is greater than the sum of its constituent parts and targeted developments will help to raise the standards of support facilities. One single hotel, for example, can be viewed as an individual site product in its own right but in its wider context it supports a number of tourist-related activities in the area (attractions, shopping, business). By investing public funds in a new site attraction and its immediate environment the climate is created to encourage private sector investment in supporting facilities (accommodation) and encourage new higher quality development. An example of this would be public sector investment in a marina and its surrounding environment to create an attractive setting for private sector commercial leisure investment.

Markets and economic benefit

Taken together with location and access, market potential is fundamental to the success of many tourism projects. This applies to geographical accessibility as well as to the assessment of psychological factors which determine market penetration. The latter relates back to concepts and themes and translating these into products for which the market perceives a need.

A strict interpretation of the definition of a tourist as recommended by the World Tourism Organization would exclude day visitors since their trips do not exceed 24 hours and do not include an overnight stay. However many site attractions which have no accommodation element are ultimately dependent on the support of local day visitors to contribute to operational viability. Site surveys at visitor attractions indicate that on average upwards of 65 per cent of visitors are drawn from within the 1 hour drivetime catchment of the site. In market terms therefore it is essential that a site attraction has a location with a large immediate and accessible catchment population and that the product appeals to the dominant segments of that market (e.g. families with children, specific socioeconomic groups). Feasibility studies of site attractions examine the market characteristics of the one hour drivetime catchment population. This information can then be used to target the product more accurately. As the product is developed and marketed the scope for attracting higher spending market segments in the longer term increases.

A market assessment at the regional level will consider the existing product and the markets which are currently being attracted to the region. A ranking system could be applied to their current importance in terms of visitor numbers and visitor spend in the region. A thorough review of product opportunities would then be undertaken to establish which market segments have the greatest potential growth, again ranked according to visitor numbers and spend. A tourism development and marketing strategy will target resources at attracting those markets which generate the greatest economic benefit.

Tourism markets can be analyzed by market segment in

Table 1 Spending behavior of tourists.

Market		Ranking (average daily spend)
Business	– Overseas	1
	Domestic	2
Holiday	– Overseas	3
	Domestic	4
VFR*	– Overseas	5
	Domestic	6
Day trip		7

*Visiting friends and relatives

terms of the economic benefit generated by the spend of each segment using multiplier analysis to quantify the jobs benefit arising from this spend. This is a very complex technical calculation which has been subject to much discussion and disagreement amongst economists in its application to the tourism sector. It is not within the scope of this chapter to develop these arguments. In appraising projects it is sufficient for tourism planners to be aware of the relative and absolute value of the spending behavior of the defined market segments. Market segments can be broken down in a number of ways but at the regional level a recognized breakdown is shown in Table 1. These segments are ranked according to the relative value of their average daily spends. These vary from region to region and there may be some discrepancies. For example a study of the Cumbria region in the United Kingdom in 1986 indicated a higher ranking for the average daily spend of the VFR market than shown above. Taking a general view for the United Kingdom the average daily spend of the domestic holiday market is between five and eight times higher than the average spend of day trippers, whereas the overseas business market will spend, on average, two to three times more per day than the domestic holiday market.

With regard to the absolute value of visitor spend however the ranking of market segments may be quite different. The VFR market for example has a lower average daily spend but may stay twice as long in the region than the other tourist market segments. The day trip market is undoubtedly the largest volume market and it is often overlooked that day-visitor spend contributes significantly to the success of many site-based tourism attractions. A day trip is classified as a trip which starts and finishes on the same day, from the same base (home or holiday), is at least 3 hours in duration and does not have shopping or educational purposes as the main reason for the trip.

Clearly the relative importance of the average daily spend of each market segment indicates their ability to generate employment but it is the absolute spend of these segments which relates directly to jobs supported by tourist spend.

Competition

A feasibility study to determine tourist uses of a particular site must take into account competitive attractions within the 1 hour drivetime catchment. The strength of a new attraction will depend on the uniqueness of its product appeal, the portrayal of a strong marketable concept, the standards of management and customer care, pricing of the products and its ability to attract people from outside the 1 hour drivetime catchment. The scale of an attraction, its location in relation to major communications networks and the extent to which it is effectively marketed and promoted are other important factors. In effect a competition analysis will appraise all the key parameters described in this paper for the existing competition.

A regional view of competition is that there are many destinations and attractions competing for tourist spend, in neighboring regions, nationally and internationally. In fact a more comprehensive view is that tourism spend must compete for household income with other nontourist related products within the household budget. A region therefore needs to establish awareness of its products and attractions and a clearly identifiable image which expresses in simple terms what it has to offer to the visitor. The ability to keep ahead of the competition will depend upon the range and prices of products offered, the perceived image of a region, the uniqueness of its attractions, and the quality of the visitor experience. If these are of a high standard the tourist will perceive the region as providing him/her with 'added value' over other destinations.

Commercial viability and funding

A clear distinction should be drawn between private sector and public sector projects. Private sector projects are primarily site-based and the sponsors will be concerned with financial viability, cash flow and profitability. The wider intangible benefits of the project are unlikely to have a high priority in the project appraisal. However many private sector developers in the tourism and leisure sector recognize the value of a tourist attraction as a people draw. Within larger mixed use commercial schemes they may therefore wish to include an attraction as a 'loss leader' to improve the viability of other elements of the scheme. The provision of a leisure/tourist facility within such a scheme may also be the carrot which is required to persuade the local planning authority to accept the more profitable but politically sensitive scheme components (e.g. shopping).

Outside their statutory general cultural and leisure provision few local authorities will wish to invest heavily in tourist attractions because they often have large revenue deficit implications. They may be prepared however to fund environmental improvements, especially if grant aid is available, to create the climate for private sector investment in commercial schemes which incorporate a tourism element. A contribution towards the capital costs of the building structure is often 'thrown in' by the private sector as a negotiating stance for outline planning permission for a high value retail scheme. The more successful tourist regions take a pragmatic approach to this type of development recognizing the wider jobs benefit and, particularly in areas of industrial decline, the image-building potential of such a development.

For public sector funding agencies, such as the European Regional Development Fund (ERDF), it is necessary to set these schemes within the context of an overall tourism strategy. Initially tourism projects could only be supported through ERDF grants if an attraction or product demonstrated at least 50 per cent usage by staying visitors. This is rare for any attraction except for an accommodation-based development. The contribution day visitors make to tourism projects is now recognized by most funding agencies and the rules for grant support have been relaxed. Those regions which are able to utilize outside funding bodies to their maximum advantage are the ones located in areas of high priority for public sector grant support. Those which can also demonstrate the importance of a tourism-based project with regard to the economic benefit it generates in the region, are also strongly favored.

Management and marketing

For a site attraction, even if all the parameters thus far described are positive, success or failure is highly dependent on standards of site management and the level of customer care offered on site. This is extremely difficult to appraise in advance of any development scheme taking place and is often neglected by the management of many tourist attractions to their cost. It further emphasizes the need to offer the visitor an experience which is perceived as having added value. This is often expressed by the more general term 'value for money'. A further aspect of management and customer care is that it is an essential component of the marketing mix. If standards of customer care are high it is a very cost-effective method of marketing, encouraging both repeat business and word-of-mouth recommendation to friends and relatives. For many attractions it is the only effective marketing route available. The process of building up the image and awareness of the product through the media involves expensive advertising campaigns and requires vast marketing budgets far in excess of available resources.

A more strategic approach to management and marketing is necessary at the regional level. With the exception of large private sector leisure chains, notably in the hotel sector, there is little coordinated management of the marketing effort. Invariably the public sector has to take a leading organizational role in marketing and packaging products in the region. The ability to fulfil this role is often crucial in generating additional visitors and spend to the region. Potential operators in the tourist industry require saleable packages to offer to their customers. If the product can be packaged and made attractive to the travel trade, this will be a more cost-effective marketing strategy than expensive promotional campaigns directed at the general public.

SWOT analysis

In appraising tourism potential, particularly for site-specific projects, a SWOT analysis is a useful technique for summarizing the key issues. This is essentially a marketing concept but it can be usefully applied to project appraisal in the tourism sector. The analysis attempts to list the attributes of a site or area in terms of its: *S*trengths, *W*eaknesses, *O*pportunities and *T*hreats.

The SWOT analysis relates to all those key parameters which

form the basis of appraising tourism potential. Thus a simplified version of a representative SWOT analysis for a particular location for a local authority client could be:

Strengths
1. Building of historical interest.
2. Close proximity to the motorway network.
3. Large population catchment within the 1 hour drivetime zone.
4. Favorable grant regime.
5. Large area of land available for development.
6. Natural attraction of the waterside.

Weaknesses
1. Poor image of the location in the marketplace.
2. Present environment is one of industrial dereliction.
3. Immediate site access is constrained.
4. Poor quality of and lack of accommodation stock.
5. No overall development plan or concept for the site.
6. Limited marketing budgets and expertise in the tourism field.

Opportunities
1. Mixed use scheme with a visitor attraction focus.
2. Commercial leisure attractions (pub/restaurant) to maximize catering spend.
3. Marketing packages with complementary attractions in the region.
4. Accommodation upgrading scheme with tourist board grant support.
5. High profile events on site.
6. Moored vessels as a permanent feature.

Threats
1. Uncertain future of the direct main line rail link.
2. Complex land ownership threatens an integrated approach to development.
3. Competitive developments planned at other waterside locations within the region.
4. Poor standards of service and customer care at existing attractions.
5. Industrial uses on neighboring sites will hinder tourism development.
6. Existing clientele is low spending which has probable revenue deficit implications in the initial phase of operation.

This example is included for illustrative purposes only but the principle of the SWOT analysis provides a useful initial basis for appraising tourism potential.

Costs versus benefits

Whether a particular tourism project progresses or not will ultimately be dependent on the projected costs and benefits of the scheme. The definition of costs and benefits is interpreted differently by the private sector than by the public sector. Private sector developers and operators will in the main appraise a project purely in terms of financial viability and po-

tential development and operating profit. The wider benefits of the project will be of less importance, although the presentation of the job creation potential of the project may be instrumental in obtaining planning permission from the local authority. The public sector agencies' main criteria for assessing a project will be its potential impact in the regional economy and its importance in the context of a regional tourism strategy. Multiplier techniques can be applied to provide an indication of spending projections and jobs benefit.

Public sector projects will, in addition, consider a number of intangible costs and benefits of a particular scheme. It is difficult to assign monetary values to these intangible factors. Cost-benefit analysis has been applied to tourism projects but this technique is less than satisfactory. Tourism planners should be aware of the intangible costs and benefits of tourism development and take them into account in appraising projects. The most important costs are as follows:

1. Effect on the environment. Some geographical areas have such conservational value in terms of the flora and fauna of the landscape that a large influx of visitors will have a detrimental effect on the quality of that environment. The designation of national parks and conservation areas has attempted to tackle this intangible cost by not only restricting visitor access but also placing constraints on the built environment.
2. Cultural impacts. The spectrum of adverse cultural impacts can range from the resentment of highly visible affluent western lifestyles on the native population of developing countries, to the anger felt by local residents in a small town from a sudden influx of day visitors who spoil the normal peace and quiet of their day or who create traffic congestion problems for their town centre shopping trip.

The above factors relate to an area's capacity to absorb tourism. There are additional costs to consider:

1. Higher maintenance requirements of infrastructure. Due to intense usage, footpaths, roads, car parks and signposting need a heavier maintenance input.
2. Fluctuation in local employment patterns. This is due to the seasonal nature of tourist spending. Some towns/resorts may become ghost towns outside the tourist season.

The main benefits of tourism to a local area of an intangible nature are as follows:

1. Image building. If an area is seen as an attractive place to visit it will generate greater interest in the area generally by potential investors in commerce and industry.
2. Improvements to the quality of life. The very existence of tourists may help to improve the quality of life for local residents as higher standards of services and amenities are offered than would otherwise be provided.
3. Community pride. The self-esteem of the local community can be raised significantly if the area is regarded as an attractive place to visit. Community pride will be reflected in basic standards of cleanliness, litter control and floral decorations.
4. Educational value. Tourism by its very nature is educational

and broadens horizons. A new influx of culture, ideas, enterprise and intellect to an area can, if correctly harnessed, be used positively to benefit the future development of the area.

Conclusion

The recommendation to proceed with a particular tourism project or strategy or not will ultimately depend on the target audience. The assessment of the key parameters will be weighted according to that target audience. Developers and operators will wish to have evidence of viability and profitability; financiers will wish to be assured of market rationale; politicians will wish to see a social return as well as a commercial return from the project; funding agencies will wish to see a clear exposition of economic benefit. Many tourism studies have as their starting point that the client wishes to pursue development scheme A or strategy X. By undertaking a thorough assessment of the key parameters which determine tourism potential, a tourism specialist will not only be able to recommend whether scheme A or strategy X should be progressed but, where applicable, suggest alternatives, scheme B and strategy Y, which generate greater net benefit than the original proposals.

Further reading

Bryden, J., *Tourism and Development* (Cambridge University Press, 1973).

DRV Research, *Estimating the Level of Tourism-Related Employment* (English Tourist Board, 1986).

English Tourist Board, *Financing Tourist Projects* (ETB, 1983).

English Tourist Board, *Planning for Tourism in England* (ETB, 1983).

Gearing, C. E., Swart, W. W. and Var, T., *Planning for Tourism Development* (Praeger, 1976).

Gratton, C. and Taylor, P., 'Leisure economics: project appraisal', *Leisure Management*, vol. 6, no. 9 (September 1986).

Gunn, C. A., *Tourism Planning* (Crane Russak, 1979).

Jackson, G. and Taylor, P., 'Leisure consultancy', *Leisure Management*, vol. 7, nos. 5–8 (May–August 1987).

Kaiser, C. and Helber, L. E., *Tourism Planning and Development* (CBI Publishing Co., 1978).

Leiper, N., 'The framework of tourism', *Annals of Tourism Research*, vol. 6, no. 4 (1979), pp. 390–407.

Mill, R. C. and Morrison, A. M., *The Tourism System* (Prentice Hall, 1985).

Pearce, D. G., *Tourist Development* (Longman, 1981).

World Tourism Organization, *Evaluating Tourism Resources* (WTO, 1980).

World Tourism Organization, *Integrated Planning* (WTO, 1978).

MICHAEL PEARLMAN

Automation in the hospitality industry

Introduction

The term hospitality is more often perceived to be linked with personal services rather than automation. Automats, a group of vending machines which sell food, probably belong more to the retail industry than the hospitality industry. There are few indications that people are content to take important meals at work or socially in Automats. The closest equivalent to an Automat in the accommodation sector would be a down-market, budget hotel such as the Formula 1 concept being market tested by the French group Accor. Formula 1 involves self checkin and checkout using a credit card, modest guest rooms with a video player for in-room entertainment and little or no staff contact. Whilst there may be a market for an automated hotel, like an Automat it may not be perceived as part of the mainstream.

Automation of segments of the hospitality product can be considered in two parts, operating procedures and management systems. For basic operational tasks such as guest room servicing or even washing dishes, automating the entire function would stretch existing technology to its expensive limits. People are still cheaper than robots when it comes to changing beds and this fits in with a traditional perception of the hospitality industry as low-tech.

In common with some other service industries such as tour operation or banking, hospitality management systems are very closely intertwined with operating systems. This is distinctly different from manufacturing or most retailing industries where management information systems are designed to function in parallel with day to day operations. Thus the management information in a car factory is separate from process control devices on the production line. However, the clerical aspects of recording hotel reservations also generate the data for managing demand. Unfortunately operational demands have been allowed to overwhelm demands for management information so that decision support systems in the hospitality industry have been advanced very little by automation. The number of automated products now available for the industry is very extensive. Chervenak, Keene Associates, New York based hotel technology consultants, have estimated that there are over three thousand relevant technology products on the American market.

Examples

Accounting

The most widely automated function in the hospitality industry is accounting. Financial accounting systems in hospitality differ very little from those in any other and financial controllers have been using accounting machines for more than three decades. Payroll is the most common application followed by sales ledger, nominal ledger and, to a lesser extent, the purchase ledger.

Front office systems

The most effective way to automate a hotel would be to devise a completely integrated system. Clearly all the areas of a hotel operation are related to each other and such an approach would recognize these interrelationships. The one or two attempts to introduce completely integrated systems have been less than successful. Consequently, most hotels use partially integrated systems, often from several vendors.

Front office systems usually incorporate reservations, registration and billing because these three elements are linked by a high proportion of common data. In addition, such systems may incorporate a guest history system and integrate with at least the sales ledger functions of the accounting system. By and large, it is possible to classify front office systems by size of hotel and by expense. Large hotels of more than 300 rooms, especially in the first class and luxury markets, such as the London Hilton or the Concorde Hotel in Paris, use front office systems based on dual minicomputers. Costing in excess of $150,000 they are able to support a large number of terminals and provide direct links to systems such as telephone and energy control systems.

The most sophisticated front office systems now include self checkin and, more popular, self checkout. Self checkout may take place in the lobby where touch screens and laser disks support a very fast checkout for a guest with a credit card. However, it is also possible to install in-room checkout, sometimes via the hotel's video system. By punching a four-digit code on their telephone, guests can call up a folio display on their television screen. These systems have been very successful for large hotels with high checkout volumes. Typically they cost between $15,000 to $30,000 but rented with an in-room entertainment system they may be billed for as little as 80¢ per room per day.

Smaller hotels such as the Guildford Post House (Guildford, UK) are the main target area for microcomputer systems costing upwards of $10,000. Typically these employ one or two microcomputers and support a relatively small number of terminals. These microcomputers contain a hard disk with a capacity usually in excess of 30 megabytes. This allows them to support a wide range of features including guest history and accounting. For very small hotels, such as a 20 or 30 bedroom pension, it is possible to purchase very economical front office systems. The basic software may cost as little as $250 and will run on computers such as the Amstrad PCW which retails for under $500. Word processor and spreadsheet software is also cheaply available.

Food and beverage systems

In a hotel, food and beverage has a low significant contribution to profitability and this may partly explain the low levels of automation in the commercial sector of the industry. Most catering information systems are installed in the noncommercial sector such as Edinburgh's Astley Ainslie Hospital. Some large contract catering companies have developed their own systems like Caterfax used by Gardner Merchant Ltd.

A catering information system (CIS) provides real cost control on food, not possible on a manual basis due to the sheer volume of data. A CIS bases its reports on a file of recipes which can be re-priced for every ingredient cost change. The computer is used to calculate menu costings and summarize stores requisitions based on production forecasts. It may also be used for menu planning. In addition, stock control is possible for both main stores and kitchens. Reports are generated analyzing sales histories (the basis of future forecasts) and identifying production cost variances. Installation costs range from $7,500 to about $30,000 depending on features, particularly on the number of users.

Beverage control as such is generally a less complex problem. Since the unit of purchase and the unit of sale are more or less the same control can be exercized through standard inventory systems used in the retail sector. For specialist applications it is possible to install sensors linked in to optics and metered pumps, in turn connected to a microcomputer or to an electronic cash register.

Point of sale systems

The most common point of sale system is an electronic cash register (ECR), really a microcomputer programmed to perform certain functions. The market is very competitive with a large number of suppliers offering a wide range of machines and functions. The most interesting developments in ECRs include networking capabilities and display screens, which make them very sophisticated communication systems. However, even modest ECRs can cope nowadays with sales analysis, pre-pricing and change control. A little further up-market, features such as inventory control, memory protection, overprint facilities and touch sensitive keyboards become available. ECRs may also be linked directly to a computer system.

Waiter communication systems

Waiter communication systems usually comprise a number of units located on waiter work stations and in kitchens, linked together to provide messaging, billing and possibly inventory control. More sophisticated versions, such as the Remanco system, can make use of hand-held radio terminals for entering guest orders right by the table. A basic system is unlikely to cost less than $15,000.

Telephone systems

In 1987 there was only one hotel switchboard on the market with an inbuilt call-logger. However, call-logging systems are available from many vendors of microcomputer systems from about $7,500. It is useful to ensure that the company supplying software systems updates it regularly. Telephone systems may also be used as the basis of other functions such as room status, housekeeping, maid location or even security systems.

Voice messaging systems appeared on the market in 1986. These may be built into the PABX (private automatic branch exchange) or alternatively supported through the room entertainment system. Messages may be replayed either by recorded playback, television display or, in one case, printed on a compact printer installed in each guest room.

Security systems

The largest vendor of electronic locking systems is the Norwegian company Vingcard, which installed its 1,000th hotel system in late 1986. Controlled by a small computer in the front office, electronic locking systems can be operated by magnetic cards, magnetic keys or digital pads. Their value lies in providing a unique locking code for each guest arrival. Per door, they cost two to eight times as much as a mechanical locking system. Other back-of-house security systems may be based on motion detectors, infrared, closed circuit television or seismic sensors.

Energy control

Energy control, extensively employed in even the smallest hospitality businesses, uses both mechanical and electronic technology. Mechanical devices include waste water preventers, simple thermostats and timers. Electronically, load-cyclers, peak-power demand controllers, chiller optimization controls, automatic lighting, room-occupancy sensors and automatic shut-off systems are all common.

Guest room facilities

Vending systems linked directly to the front office are used in medium-size to large hotels. They are quite expensive to install and maintain and depend on well organized food and beverage servicing procedures to operate reliably. In-room entertainment may be controlled either through the telephone or the video system and is based on a billing system associated with certain channels on a television. The major growth area in the mid 1980s was cable and satellite channels. Indeed, Holiday Inns even has its own satellite network used for entertainment and teleconferencing. Automatic wake-up services allow the hotel to simultaneously call many rooms at an appointed time and to play a pre-recorded message. Finally, guest services may extend to fire and smoke alarms which operate through either the telephone or the television system.

Videotex and communications

Videotex describes television services controlled by a computer. The French system Minitel and the less successful British Prestel are telephone based systems charged on a per call method. Broadcast systems like Ceefax and Oracle are usually free. In-house videotex can be supported by a microcomputer and may even pay for itself through sales of advertizing space to local businesses.

The most important growth market in communications is facsimile transmission (fax). Anyone with a telephone, a modem and a personal computer can link to a fax transmission system. The additional cost of the necessary software can be as low as $500 but if a scanner is needed to encode pictures (or handwriting) then an extra $1500 to $3000 will be needed.

Microprocessor controlled catering equipment

Process control devices as part of catering equipment have been introduced extensively in the fast food industry and are now beginning to make their impact in other sectors. This equipment costs about five times as much as its conventional equivalent.

Benefits

Personnel displacement and tighter cost control are not the most productive ways of justifying increased automation. Some low-grade clerical jobs such as cashiers, income auditors and inventory controllers might be eliminated but studies have shown that savings will be in the order of 20 jobs per 1,000 employees. Most rewarding in terms of cost reductions are energy control systems; installations have been shown to have paybacks as short as 6 months.

Principal benefits should be expected, however, in improved marketing and better management information. Both of these strengthen the competitive position of a unit. Improved marketing generally takes the form of more effective selling and better provision of guest services. Front office systems in particular can enable a hotel to manage occupancy much more effectively. Thus the 800 bedroom Tara Hotel in London substantially increased both its occupancy and profit by using computers to manage the market segmentation of reservations. In a large city hotel with a short length of stay, effective demand management is virtually impossible manually.

Food quality can also be improved. The trend in catering is to recognize that most employees are not highly trained, well motivated chefs but semi-skilled or unskilled people who are taking a job for monetary reward. For consistency and quality control microprocessor regulated catering equipment allows service standards to be maintained without the need for heavy training costs and close, skilled supervision. Improved conformance to standard recipes resulting from the introduction of a CIS has led to reported improvements in food quality in many hospitals and the British army.

Other marketing benefits are related to better services. Improvements such as in-room entertainment or self checkout are obvious, others less so. Telephone control computers not only improve guest billing services and allow for more effective telephone management but in some markets, particularly North America, they play an important role in the cost-effective routing of guest calls. Electronic locking systems support better guest service for access control and provide an efficient basis for a personnel location system. In the long run, insurance costs are reduced and the possibility of having to re-install a complete new locking system does not arise. Fax has very significant advantages over telex not only in being faster and cheaper but in being able to transmit pictures as well as words.

Advances in management information are less apparent. Certainly there are some areas where real management is not possible without a computer, data volumes alone justify the power of a computer for food cost control. However, hospitality managers have been rather slow to take full advantage of modern business systems. The power and performance of small computers will not benefit hotels unless managers train themselves to use the technology directly. Productivity gains cannot be derived second-hand. The difficulties in this area are not confined entirely to computer literacy. Information literacy is also at stake and hospitality managers must be better trained to design and exploit information systems.

Implementation

The key factor for most guest services tends to be the cost of trunking for cables. Retrofit costs for cable connections can be very high and this affects systems from in-room vending through to electronic locking where control is maintained by a central computer. For this reason, systems which can share cabling are attractive, especially to older hotels. The most commonly used link is the coaxial cable installed for television services.

For administrative systems such as accounting, reservations and catering, key factors are changeover and training. Transferring manual records to a computer while continuing to process transactions requires special planning and careful testing. Careful attention must also be paid to organizational effects. Agreeing standard recipes with food production staff, setting them up on the computer and testing them for acceptability can take even a modest catering organization 6 months or more. Fortunately the industry has a good labor record in respect of new technology and studies show that the acceptability of computer-based systems by operators and supervisors has been high. Most resistance to new technology is experienced from middle and senior managers, concerned about job content and new demands for 'better' decision making.

Assessment

The extent to which automation in the hospitality industry can be evaluated depends on how well expected benefits are identified and understood. Some expected gains are hard to quantify, especially in the area of management productivity. Is the organization expecting more decisions or simply faster decisions? What distinguishes a good decision from a bad decision? There are few areas equivalent to energy management where the cost of utilities can be tracked precisely across the profit and loss account. No one can really say whether the new front office system has actually increased either occupancy or room rate. It is essential however, to establish the credibility of new systems. Evaluation must be related to carefully prepared feasibility studies which set out assumptions and objectives in precise, measurable terms. A formal review procedure must then be followed at fixed intervals to compare performance against benchmarks.

Conclusion

It must be acknowledged that the hospitality industry has been rather slow to recognize the management and the service potential in computer-based procedures. Luxury and first class hotels in most developed countries, and even developing countries, are using at least one computer system for room management. By contrast few large, commercial restaurants use any form of computerization. Even in the more progressive tions, market penetration in food control systems is probably still less than 5 per cent.

The range of automated hospitality systems is very extensive and it is clear that the potential for installations on both a national and international scale is very great. The rate of installations is expected to increase rapidly.

Focus on small business

Most hospitality businesses are small. Problems of definition make accurate data hard to obtain, but as an example, most sources are agreed that about 90 per cent of hotels have less than 25 rooms and employ less than 20 people. Data for catering services is even less complete but again it is evident that there are thousands of very small cafés and kiosks. Some applications like energy control produce affordable benefits at any scale of operation. However, there is clearly little need for a computerized front office system in a 25-bedroom hotel. Careful management and the effective application of technique is often more, not less, important to a small business. Large organizations have reserves to offset poor decision making or business recessions that will bankrupt a small company.

The answer lies in selecting inexpensive, domestic microcomputers and in purchasing one or more of the excellent, low-cost business applications software packages that are available for less than $100. More efficient business planning and costing by means of a spreadsheet or a database manager may well make the difference between survival and failure in the turbulent, highly seasonal environment of small hospitality businesses.

Software/databases

See table opposite.

Company	Nationality	City	Systems (Y=Yes; N=No)		
			Front office	Back office	Small hotel
A/S EDB	Norway	Oslo	Y	Y	N
Accomodata Systems	UK	Wokingham	Y	N	Y
Acom	Canada	Montreal	N	Y	N
Action Software	USA	San Diego	Y	Y	Y
Adapt Computer	USA	Wichita	Y	N	Y
Aldon Computer	USA	Bordentown	Y	Y	N
American Hotel Register	USA	Chicago	Y	N	Y
Applico	Finland	Abo	Y	Y	Y
Aptech	USA	Pittsburgh	Y	Y	Y
Archford Computers International	UK	London	Y	N	Y
Auditel	USA	Grand Prairie	Y	Y	Y
Avon Data Systems	UK	Bristol	Y	N	Y
BASIC	USA	Chicago	N	Y	Y
Balance Point Systems	USA	San Rafael	Y	N	Y
Barda	UK	Warrington	Y	N	Y
Cara Info. Systems	Eire	London	Y	Y	Y
Cashlink Software	UK	Caeathro	Y	Y	Y
Catchpenny in Progress	USA	Lexington	Y	N	Y
Champs Systems Ltd	UK	Frimley	Y	Y	N
Chart Software	UK	Taunton	Y	Y	Y
Check-Inns	USA	Halifax	Y	N	N
Checkout Services	UK	Houghton Regis	Y	Y	Y
Colos	USA	Independence	Y	Y	Y
Compass Computer	USA	Dallas	Y	N	Y
Compusolv	USA	Salt Lake City	Y	Y	Y
Computer Consultants Inc.	USA	Cleveland	Y	Y	Y
Computer Distribution Services	UK	Norwich	Y	N	Y
Computer Software Services	USA	Dallas	Y	Y	N
Computer Systems Consultancy	UK	Nottingham	Y	N	Y
Computerized Hotel Systems	USA	San Antonio	Y	Y	N
Computerized Lodging Systems	USA	Long Beach	Y	Y	Y
Computerline	USA	Tempe	Y	Y	Y
Conect	USA	Walnut Creek	Y	Y	Y
CPU	USA	Waitsfield	Y	Y	Y
Dapro Systems	Finland	Helsinki	Y	Y	N
Data-Bolagen	Sweden	Stockholm	Y	Y	N
Datapro	Norway	Alesund	Y	Y	N
Datastaben	Sweden	Backaryd	Y	Y	Y
Datatrac	USA	Atlanta	Y	Y	N
Dehan EDP	Canada	Dehan	Y	Y	Y
EECO	USA	Santa Ana	Y	Y	Y
Elite Software	USA	Saratoga	Y	N	Y
Elms	USA	Charlotte	Y	Y	Y
Eloquent Systems Corp.	USA	Manchester	Y	N	Y
Encore Lodging Systems	USA	Atlanta	Y	Y	Y
ERH Systems	Finland	Abo	Y	Y	N
Ericsson Information Systems	Sweden	Stockholm	Y	Y	N
Executive Systems Plus	USA	Irvine	Y	Y	Y
Fabco	USA	Fullerton	Y	Y	Y
Ffos	UK	Slough	Y	N	Y
G & M Mngt. Services	UK	Southampton	Y	N	Y
Hayes Associates	USA	Eliot	Y	Y	Y
Heineken	NL		Y	Y	N
HKC Data	Sweden	Stockholm	Y	N	N
Holiday Inns HMS	USA	Memphis	Y	N	N
Holtech Ltd	UK	London	N	Y	Y
Hospitality Info. Technology	USA	Dunwoody	Y	Y	Y
Host Software	UK	Bristol	Y	N	Y
Hotel Computers & Services	USA	Orlando	Y	Y	Y
Hotel Data Systems	USA	Norwalk	Y	Y	Y
Hotel Information Systems	USA	Pleasant Hill	Y	Y	Y
Hotel Master	UK	Alton	Y	Y	Y
Hotel Master Ltd	UK	Sunbury	Y	Y	Y
Hunting Computer Services	UK	Stockton	Y	N	Y
IBM	USA	Atlanta	Y	N	N

Company	Nationality	City	Systems (Y=Yes; N=No)		
			Front office	Back office	Small hotel
ICL Finland	Finland	Helsinki	Y	Y	N
Info. Resource Management	USA	St. Petersburg	Y	Y	N
Infodata Systems Ltd	UK	Newbury	Y	Y	Y
Innsight Hotel Services	UK	London	Y	Y	Y
Integrated Data Services	USA	Lancaster	Y	Y	Y
Integrated Hospitality Network	USA	New York	Y	N	Y
International Comp. Consultants	UK	Guernsey	Y	Y	Y
International Data Systems	USA	Phoenix	Y	Y	Y
International Guest Systems	UK	Isleworth	Y	Y	Y
IPCS	USA	Phoenix	Y	N	Y
ITD Wernor	Sweden	Stockholm	Y	Y	Y
Jonas & Ericson	Canada	Willowdale	Y	Y	Y
Knox Data Systems	USA	Saugus	Y	Y	Y
Lakeland Computer Systems	UK	Ambleside	N	Y	Y
Landsoft	UK	London	Y	Y	Y
Limes System	Denmark	Copenhagen	Y	Y	N
Lodgistix	USA	London	Y	Y	Y
Marlboro Computer	USA	Newark	Y	Y	Y
MDS Quantel	USA	Hayward	Y	Y	Y
Mer Com Computer Systems	UK	London	Y	N	Y
Micro-Connection	UK	London	Y	N	Y
Microciel	France	Grasse	Y	N	Y
Mirage Hotel Systems	USA	Beverly Hills	Y	N	Y
MIS Dynamic Solutions	USA	Lancaster	Y	Y	N
Modern Business Technology	UK	Haslemere	Y	N	Y
MODS Hoteldata	Sweden	Gothenburg	Y	Y	N
National Cash Register	USA	Dayton	Y	Y	Y
National Guest Systems	USA	Rockville	Y	Y	Y
Neptune	Germany	Stuttgart	Y	N	Y
New Generation Software	USA	Sacramento	N	Y	N
New Systems (ISI)	USA	Phoenix	Y	Y	Y
Nixdorf	Germany	Hounslow	Y	Y	Y
Nixdorf Finland	Finland	Helsinki	Y	Y	N
Norsk Data	Sweden	Stockholm	Y	Y	N
Northwest Info. Systems	USA	Kirkland	Y	Y	N
Omni Host	USA	Norcross	Y	Y	Y
Optim	UK	London	Y	Y	Y
PACS	USA	Honolulu	Y	Y	N
Palisades Comp. Corp.	USA	Pacific Palisades	N	Y	Y
PG-Yhtiot	Finland	Helsinki	Y	Y	N
Preferred Software	USA	Jackson	Y	N	Y
Prime	USA	Natick	Y	Y	N
Prolink Corp.	USA	Phoenix	Y	Y	N
Prologic (Accor)	France	Paris	Y	Y	N
Pulse	USA	St Augustine	Y	Y	Y
R. G. P. Micro Systems Ltd	UK	Plymouth	Y	N	Y
RCA Commercial Products	USA	Cherry Hill	Y	Y	Y
Resort Data Systems	USA	Camarillo	Y	Y	Y
Resort Mngt. Systems	USA	Denver	Y	Y	N
Resort Systems Intnl.	USA	Santa Barbara	Y	N	Y
Rural Computer Systems	UK	Bangor	N	Y	Y
Scandicom	Sweden	Stockholm	Y	Y	N
Scanvest Ring	Norway	Oslo	Y	Y	N
Scorpio Business Systems	UK	Isle of Man	Y	N	Y
Sense Computer Software	UK	Sanderstead	Y	Y	Y
Servitech	USA	Wayne	Y	Y	Y
Software Mine	USA	Rancho Bernardo	Y	Y	Y
Software Service	Sweden	Stockholm	Y	Y	N
Southcott Software Services	UK	Chorley	Y	N	Y
Southern Hotel Acctg. Sys.	USA	Orlando	N	Y	Y
Stendig Computer Systems	USA	Danville	Y	N	Y
Stored Info. Systems	USA	Hazlet	Y	Y	Y
Sunbelt Century	USA	Charlotte	Y	N	Y
Synerlogic	Canada	Vancouver	Y	Y	Y
Systell Software Assoc.	UK	Shanklin	Y	N	Y

Company	Nationality	City	Systems (Y=Yes; N=No)		
			Front office	Back office	Small hotel
Systemware	Sweden	Stockholm	Y	Y	N
Tammerdata	Finland	Tammerfors	Y	Y	N
Team Data	Sweden	Stockholm	Y	Y	N
Teleste	Finland	Helsinki	Y	Y	N
Welcome Hotel Software	UK	Spratton	Y	N	Y
Western Business Systems	UK	St Annes	Y	Y	Y
Winkelhorn & Co.	Denmark	Copenhagen	Y	Y	Y
Wisev Software Gmbh	Germany	Munich	Y	Y	N
Worldcom	USA	Mobile	Y	Y	Y
Xi-Data	UK	Leeds	Y	Y	Y
Ziegler & Co.	USA	Orangeburg	Y	Y	N

Further reading

CKC Report, The Hotel Technology Newsletter. Available monthly by private subscription from Chervenak, Keane & Co. of New York, USA. CKC are a leading international consultancy and possibly the only one which specializes in hotel technology.

Gamble, P. R., *Small Computers and Hospitality Management* (Hutchinson, 1984). The first part of this book deals with the nature of information technology, technical elements of computer systems, hospitality computer systems, systems analysis, applications software and future trends and issues. Part two is concerned with purchasing hardware and software development.

Godowski, S., *Microcomputers in the Hotel & Catering Industry* (Heinemann, 1987). An inexpensive, introductory text suitable for the beginner.

Hotel and Catering Technology. Available monthly by subscription from the publishers based in Norwich, England. Rather descriptive and uncritical but a useful source of ideas and contacts.

Kasavana, M., *Computer Systems for Foodservice Operations* (CBI Publishing Co., 1984). A book which concentrates mainly on point-of-sales systems for food and beverage but with a useful introduction to menu engineering.

Kasavana, M. and Cahill, J., *Managing Computer Systems in the Hospitality Industry* (CBI Publishing Co., 1987). A rewrite and development of Kasavana's earlier books combining front office with food and beverage. Given the lack of good books on hospitality computing, this text provides an overview.

Mitchell, I. D. and Phipps, D., *How to Buy Hotel Computer System* (*Caterer & Hotelkeeper*, 1986). A series of largely unsupported checklists asking questions which the purchaser is meant to answer for him/herself.

PAUL R. GAMBLE

Branding in tourism

Introduction

Branding is one of the long-term decisions involved in developing a tourism marketing strategy. It is an important part of product planning. A brand is a name, design or symbol (or combination of these) which is used to identify a service provided by an institution or organization. The branding process in tourism involves researching, developing and implementing the organization's brand decisions. Branding decisions involve the determination of a word or letter/number to identify the tourism service (brand name), a symbol, design or distractive coloring or lettering, and personified brand mark (trade character). When a brand name, brand mark or trade character is given legal protection, it is referred to as a trademark. Unless brand names, brand marks, and trade characters are registered as trademarks, competitors can use them. There are numerous examples of branding in the tourism and hospitality industry (e.g. hotel chains, rental car companies, cruise lines, tour companies and airlines).

The significance of branding in tourism can be explained by four factors.

1. Repeat business represents an important source of the tourism industry income, and repeat business depends on satisfied customers and a recognizable brand name. In other words, product acceptance is improved by popularizing brand names.
2. Considering the vast majority of new brands introduction (from cruise lines, to car rental companies, to tour package companies to hotels), the consumer can only be bemused and confused. For instance, between 1983 and 1985 the following brand names or concepts were introduced by the hotel industry alone: Renaissance, Emerald Hotels, Ritz Carltons, Royce Marriott's, Courtyards, Marquis, Holiday Inns, Embassy Suites, Brock Hotel's Residence Inns, Par Suites, Quality Inns, Trusthouse Forte's Exclusive, Excelsior, Viscounts, Wyndham's Wynfield Inns, Compri, Sofitel, Novotel, Ibis, Ciga. The rapid rate of new brand introduction complicates the tasks of travel agents and highlights the importance of obtaining customer brand recognition.
3. The choice of a brand has implications for the firm's marketing mix consisting of product strategies, promotional strategies, pricing strategies, and distribution strategies.
4. Customer loyalty in tourism is difficult to establish. A number of studies have shown that even when customers are reasonably satisfied with a travel experience, curiosity would attract them to try other alternatives. Vacationers and tourists continuously seek out new experiences, new locations, new airlines and new hotels. The more diverse the customers, tourism adventures, the richer their experience. For all these reasons, brand loyalty is difficult to obtain and hence branding is very important.

Examples

Branding in tourism is a decision that is integrated with other marketing mix decisions. The examples (from the lodging industry) discussed below show the firms progressively developing unique brand names to serve different markets.

Radisson has introduced five brand names. Radisson Hotel was established in 1962 and this brand name serves the upper middle class, provides full service and is located in commercial areas. It targets the broad business segment. Radisson Inn aims at businesses, small meetings and family. Its services include meeting rooms and it is located in second tier cities. Radisson Resorts was introduced in 1976 and targets the leisure market and association meetings. Services provided include recreational facilities and locations in scenic destinations. Radisson Plaza Hotel was introduced in 1978 and targets upscale business executives and the leisure markets. It provides full facilities and is located in city center and suburban sites. Radisson Suite Hotel was introduced in 1985 to service the extended-stay business market. Its services include complimentary breakfast and cocktails and it is typically located in office parks.

Quality Inn has also introduced five brand names. Quality Inn was first used in 1941, targeted to businesses, meetings groups and families. The services associated with this brand name were full amenities at reasonable prices. Next the company created Comfort Inns in 1981 to serve the business and family market on a limited budget. Services were limited; no food was served. In the same year it introduced Quality Royale to serve the upper end business and vacation traveler. A full service line was created. Comfort Inn Suites were conceptualized in 1984 to serve the business traveler exclusively. Hence it had only one room suites and provided limited service, although a health club and complimentary breakfast were available. In 1984, the Quality Inn Suite was introduced to serve the 'bread and butter' commercial traveler.

Holiday Corporation have successfully operated and used six brand names for lodging services. The original brand name was Holiday Inn Hotels created in 1952 to serve all markets – business and pleasure. Services were varied; locations in business centers, vacation destinations and travel routes were chosen. In 1975, Residence Inns came into being to serve extended-stay business clients. Services included all suites, one and two room accommodation in low-rise type structures. In 1983 H. I. Crowne Plaza was introduced to serve the market for businesses, meetings and conventions. Services were upscale, located in airports, business and convention centers. In the same year, Hampton Inns was created to serve both the pleasure and business market. Limited services were provided and they were usually located in high traffic areas. Also in 1983, two more brand names were established, Embassy Suites and Granada Royale. Embassy Suites targeted the upscale business traveler (weekdays) while Granada Royale targeted leisure guests (weekend). The services of both are similar.

Ramada operates under three brand names. Initially Ramada Inn, created in 1954, targeted the business traveler and families. In 1981 Ramada Hotels were created to serve the business travelers and associations. In the same year the Ramada Renaissance was established to serve the business traveler, individuals and groups and the upper end of the leisure market. Ramada's first inn near Phoenix, Arizona featured trademark columns, a design feature abandoned recently in favor of the Renaissance logo.

These examples show that branding is a major consideration in the hospitality industry. It is an integral part of a firm's marketing mix.

Benefits

The branding decision in tourism is very important for a variety of reasons.

1. Brand names enable customers to identify the product or service. A customer can then request the service by name; for example, a West German tourist may prefer the airline Lufthansa. Recognizability is important for patronage, implying that the name should be fairly simple and distinctive. From this premise, Western International Hotels changed its name to Westin Hotels in 1981.
2. Brand name assures the customer of a certain product quality. Related to the issue of quality is image: brand name suggests a product image. The Waldorf-Astoria in New York suggests high quality, while Comfort Inns suggest reasonable cost and economy. The Queen Elizabeth 2 (QE2) cruise liner suggests a more exclusive image than Carnival Cruise Lines.
3. The brand name does not just create an image for the product or service, it also suggests one for the firm. The producers of unbranded items cannot be identified, therefore customers do not have the opportunity to form an image of the firm.
4. Brand names enable customers to make fewer price comparisons. If a brand is unique, the customer will associate a set of marketing attributes to it. Thus it is easier for the customer to make decisions among brands that are closely related and not compare those that are not related. This is especially true when special characteristics are attributed to different brands. For the firm in the travel industry, the brand name enables it to advertise its sources and associate a brand and its characteristics in the minds of the customers. For instance, Carnival Cruise Lines associates the characteristic of 'fun ships' with its brand name, while Queen Elizabeth 2 associates 'unique experience' with its promotional theme, 'For once in your life, live'.
5. Simply having a brand name increases social visibility and product prestige. It shows the firm is willing to stand behind its service.
6. Consumers experience less risk when purchasing a brand that is familiar and toward which they have a favorable attitude.
7. Branding is a critical element of the firm's marketing plan since it helps segment markets. By using multiple brands, different market segments can be attracted. The Hilton Hotels group uses the Waldorf-Astoria brand name to attract the elite and politically influential, while the Hilton brand name is used to attract business executives and frequent lodgers.
8. A well-known brand name helps increase television channel cooperation. A strong brand increases control of the distribution channel, a particularly important factor in very competitive markets. The tourism and travel industry is a highly competitive industry, extremely dependent on travel agents and tour companies. In fact the agency market controls 70 per cent of all business ticketed on US airlines and 90 per cent on international carriers. In 1984, agents booked over $4.4 billion in hotel sales in the United States. A strong brand name is easily remembered by the customer and travel agent; travel agents are quick to recommend strong brand names to their clients.
9. A brand can be used to sell an entire line of products. The Holiday Corporation uses the brand names Holiday Inn Hotels, Residence Inn, H. I. Crowne Plaza, Hampton Inn, Embassy Suites Hotel and Granada Royale to market its line of lodging services.
10. Branding can be used to enter new markets and to serve new customer groups.

Implementation

Typically, implementation of branding decisions involves four steps: the choice of corporate sysbols, creation of a branding philosophy, selection of a brand name and deciding to seek legal protection.

Corporate symbols are a firm name, logo, and trade character. Although corporate symbols are designed or chosen to have elements of permanency, changes frequently have to be made. The firm operates in a dynamic environment, therefore no corporate symbol can serve all purposes and all times. Situations that call for a change, redesign and/or change of name are expansion of product lines to currently unrelated fields; going into new geographical markets; realization that the current name is indistinct, unwieldy or confusing; starting a completely new line. Recent brand name changes are Navistar from International Harvester, and Westin Hotels from Western International Hotels. Corporate symbols impact on a firm's marketing strategy and consequently should not be developed without considering elements of the marketing mix. Embassy Suites Hotel has successfully used Garfield the cat as its corporate symbol.

The brand philosophy is the basis for deciding whether to use manufacturer, dealer or generic brands or whether single or multiple brands should be used. The manufacturer's brand will appeal to a wide range of customers who need assurance of good product performance. On the other hand, there may be a need to create an image separate from the manufacturer's in order to offer distinctive marketing programs. The Radisson Corporation and Marriott use their corporate (manufacturer) name in all brand names, while Holiday Corporation does not. Dealer brands (private or distributor brands) contain the name of the intermediaries that account for a significant portion of product sales. Dealer brands tend to appeal to price conscious consumers that compare price and ingredients with manufacturer brands. The use of dealer brands is not widespread in the tourism industry, partly because intermediaries (travel agents, tour companies, telemarketing) individually deal in a tiny percentage of lodging sales or airline sales. A 1977 Federal study of perceived importance of information sources in destination choice listed 12 sources. Using a scale of 1 (not at all important) to 5 (extremely important), the highest mean score was only 3.62 (family) while the lowest was 1.51 (travel agents). Emphasizing the names of the product only (generic branding) is almost non-existent. Confidence and reliability are of significant concern to travelers. Even when price competition is a significant form of competition, the product is not emphasized exclusively. The defunct Peoples Airline used the strategy of no frills, low fares, but still emphasized its brand name.

A corporate philosophy also involves the choice of a family (blanket) brand or brand extension. A family name is when one name is used for several products. For instance, IBM uses the same family name to sell its product mixes (computers, typewriters etc.). The advantage is capitalization on a unique image and promotion of the same name continually (which reduces cost per exposure). The disadvantage lies in the inability to properly segment and target multiple markets. Brand extension, which is used in the lodging industry, involves attaching a name extension to what would be a family name. For instance, Marriott uses the extensions Hotels, Resorts, Courtyard, Marquis and Suites.

The third step in implementing brand decisions is to select a name. Alternatives include initials, invented names, numbers, mythological characters, personal names, geographical names, dictionary words, foreign words or a combination of words.

Lastly, the firm needs to legally protect the brand name to prevent others from using the name (licensed trademark) and to obtain royalty fees.

Assessment

A brand name, trade name, trade character or trademark can be used to achieve a multitude of objectives for the firm. The discussion here will be based on the more general objectives. Essentially the tourism marketer wants to move the firm's target market through different stages of service adoption: non-recognition, recognition, preference and insistence (brand loyalty). For a new brand, the consumer begins with nonrecognition of the name and the seller must then make the consumer aware of it. The first stage of evaluation, therefore, is determining the degree of recognition or awareness from an unaware state. Marketers use a number of measures of awareness depending on the media. For brand names that appear in magazines, awareness can be measured as either aided recall (using multiple choice questions) or unaided recall (using open-ended questions). Aided recall is a weaker measure than unaided recall since the respondent is given clues to help in recognition. A firm has the option of measuring consumer awareness itself or hiring a marketing research firm to do it.

The next measure of the effectiveness of branding decisions is the 'degree of preference' compared to 'dislike'. A good brand name should increase the chances of consumer preference. This measure however should be used with caution since a lot of other factors (marketing stimuli, buyer characteristics etc.) can also contribute to product preference or dislike. In other words 'brand-name hype' only cannot lead to sales unless backed by other substantive actions. While measuring sales is easy, the extent to which increased sales can be attributed to a good brand name is difficult.

The effectiveness of branding decisions can ultimately be measured on insistence on (or aversion to) the product. Repeat purchase or brand loyalty is the goal for the marketer. Brand loyalty however depends on satisfaction with product performance: repeat purchase or patronage can also be due to monopoly status which forces brand loyalty. In tourism this is prevalent.

Focus on small business

Small businesses are beginning to recognize the importance of branding. A good brand heralds good things, while a bad brand inhibits progress, so a small firm must strive to achieve brand recognition. A distinctive brand can make the task of marketing the product easier, possibly resulting in cost savings. For instance, a firm may not have to advertise a lot if it has a recognizable brand name. A recognizable brand name is useful in negotiating with intermediaries and commands a high position in the eyes of the consumer, allowing the firm's service to attract a high price.

Conclusion

Branding is a very important decision for firms in the tourism industry. The development of brand name over time can offer the firm a competitive edge, but the firm needs to plan and effectively execute branding decisions to ensure this benefit. Integration of the branding decisions into the marketing mix program can result in considerable synergistic effects. A brand cannot be treated as simply a name, rather it is an integral part of the firm's efforts to establish a unique image that is sellable to customers. Image building in service industries is significant because word of mouth advertizing is a major form of promotion. A firm operating in the tourism industry should pay special attention to its branding decisions. Brand loyalty and patronage may very well depend on a familiar brand name or symbol.

Software/databases

COMBI-NAME, Armstrong Marketing Services Inc., 34 N. Fifth St., Allentown, PA 18101, USA. Used to pick names for products and services; usable on IBM PC/XT/AT or compatibles.

NAMER, The Salinon Corp., Dept. M2, 7430 Greenville Avenue, Dallas, TX 75231, USA. Used to create new product, service or company names using 11 different name creation methods. More than 12 databases of pronounceable, categorized and indexed key words.

Further reading

Bahn, K. D., 'How and when do brand perceptions and preferences first form? A cognitive developmental investigation,' *Journal of Consumer Research*, vol. 13 (December 1986), pp. 382–93. Discusses children's brand discrimination and preference information.

Evans, J. R. and Berman, B., *Marketing* (Macmillan Publishing Company, 3rd edition, 1987). Discussion of branding decisions.

Gardiner, B. B. and Levy, S. J., 'The product and the brand', *Harvard Business Review*, vol. 33 (March–April 1955), pp. 33–9. Discusses how long-term brand success depends on marketers' abilities to select meaning names prior to market entry, operationalizing the meaning in the form of an image, and maintaining that image over time.

Giges, N. and Freeman L., 'Promos may not be hazardous', *Advertising Age*, vol. 58, no. 39 (16 February 1987). Discusses the results of studies that show that cutting advertizing expenditures to increase promotions does not result in declining brand loyalty.

Gunn, C. A., *Tourism Planning* (Crane Russak, 1979). Focuses on physical planning of tourism from a policy standpoint.

Hodgson, A. (ed.), *The Travel and Tourism Industry: Strategies for the Future* (Pergamon Press, 1987). A compilation of articles on the travel and tourism industry; Chapter 7, pp. 107–34, deals with marketing issues including branding.

Jarvis, L. P. and Mayo, E. J., 'Repeat guests: a loyal base or transient customers?', *Tourism Services Marketing: Advances in Theory and Practice*, Joseph, W. B., Moutinho, L. and Vernon, I. R. (eds), Academy of Marketing Science and Marketing Department of Cleveland State University Special Conference Series, vol. 2 (1986). Discusses a multi-dimensional framework for understanding lodging chain loyalty. Distinct loyalty 'types'.

Lappa, M., 'Market power of brand names', *Beverage World*, vol. 106, no. 110 (March 1987). Discusses the significant role played by brand names in marketing beverages.

Lee, D. R., 'How they started: the growth of four hotel giants', *The Cornell HRA Quarterly*, (May 1985), pp. 23–32. Discusses the start-up and growth strategies of four hotel chains – Hilton, Holiday Inn, Marriott and Ramada.

Mayo, E. J. and Jarvis, L., *The Psychology of Leisure Travel* (CBI Publishing Co., 1981). Discusses significant consumer behavior concepts relevant to the travel industry.

McIntosh, R. W., *Tourism Principles, Practices and Philosophies* (Grid, 1972). Discusses the significance, psychology, development and economics of the tourism industry; Chapter 11 focuses on aspects of tourism marketing including segmentation, integration and promotion of tourism.

Park, C. W., 'Strategic brand concept–image management', *Journal of Marketing*, vol. 50 (October 1986), pp. 135–45. Presents a framework, termed brand concept management (BCM), for selecting, implementing and controlling a brand image over time.

'Perspectives', *Marketing Communication*, vol. 11 (10 June 1986). A panel discussion of the role advertizing plays in the success of brands.

Wahab, S. L., Crampon, L. J. and Rothfield, L. M., *Tourism Marketing* (Tourism International Press, 1976). Part IV presents concepts on planning and strategy.

Withiam, G., 'Hotel companies aim for multiple markets', *The Cornell HRA Quarterly* (November 1985), pp. 39–51. Discusses the multiple brand strategies of firms in the hotel industry.

SAM OKOROAFO

Business travel

Introduction

People have traveled on business trips long before traveling for pleasure or vacations became a popular concept. Business travel is a vital sector of today's tourism industry, particularly in Europe and the United States. It can be divided into three distinct segments according to the purpose of travel: 1. regular travel. This chapter will deal with points 1 and 2, as incentive travel is essentially a hybrid of business and leisure travel.

Although business travel is discussed in terms of a single entity, it more correctly consists of a number of separate components such as accommodation, tickets or car rental. In addition to these are the all important service elements, which include the manner of dealing with the customer, the speed and efficiency of the service, and the ability to deal with problems successfully.

Business travel is not regarded by everyone as a legitimate part of the tourism industry on the grounds that people are not traveling for pleasure or leisure. However, there are many definitions of a tourist. A useful working definition adopted by the British Tourist Authority defines a tourist trip as 'a stay of one or more nights away from home for holidays, visits to friends or relatives, business, conferences or any other purpose except such things as boarding education or semi-permanent employment'. Whether or not a definition considers business travelers as being tourists depends on the perspective adopted. It is true to say that when a financial view is adopted, business travelers are most likely to be included as they provide a sizeable proportion of the total market. For example, business travel accounted for 24 per cent of tourist spending in the United Kingdom in 1985 and it is estimated that 50 per cent or more of all air travel is by business travelers. It should be remembered, however, that the business-pleasure mix varies according to destination. A recent study of first class hotels shows that 60 per cent of hotel guests are accounted for by business users and that the percentage is even higher in terms of value.

In deciding whether or not business travel should be considered a part of the tourist industry it should be remembered that it is often difficult to distinguish between business and pleasure travel. For, while a business person is attending a conference, exhibition or several professional meetings it is unlikely that the whole of the time away from home will be spent entirely on business duties. For example, attendance at a conference is likely to leave some free time for exploring the surrounding area or for a shopping expedition; evenings may well include an element of relaxation or use of leisure facilities at the hotel.

The business travel sector has grown rapidly over the last 20 years. For example, there was an 81 per cent increase in business visits by British people between 1973 and 1984. The industry continues to develop and is rapidly changing, especially through the increased sophistication and expectations of business travelers and through continued improvements in the technology available to meet the main requirements of business travelers. Such technology includes advancements in ticketing machine use, availability and reliability, computer-aided booking facilities, and improved use of videos. Forecasts for the development of the business travel market over the next decade predict relatively optimistic growth in the numbers of travelers.

Various travel agents, airlines, tour operators and hotel groups have recognized the value of the business travel market to their business and have designed their marketing and business policies and objectives with this in mind. The first to recognize the importance of the business travel sector were the airlines, who have operated special 'classes' of air travel targeted at the business traveler. The names of these 'business class' travel facilities are many, for example Executive Class, Business Club Class, and SuperClub, but they are all aiming to offer services close to those of 'first-class', a reflection of how they value their business clients.

Examples

Crest Hotels have realized the importance of one growing sector of the UK business travel market, namely business women. Crest have identified the special needs and requirements of this group and incorporated them into Lady Crest rooms which were introduced in 1983. The rooms have a more feminine character and include the provision of hairdryers and a range of special toiletries. Although targeted directly at female travelers, the concept has proved popular with males as well.

In the United States particularly, airlines have been operating Frequent Traveler clubs to attract and maintain loyal clients. Such clubs originally offered such rewards as a free ticket for two people to travel around the world or free holidays to exotic destinations. However, during the mid-1980s such prizes were becoming too expensive and many of the airlines, including Pan Am, TWA and Northwest have modified their schemes. Such schemes have also lost favor because the companies paying for the travel consider it more appropriate for them to receive some benefit rather than their employees. These modifications have led to restrictions on who can travel with the recipient and when the travel may be taken – usually during the quieter mid-week periods. Such rewards have been viewed differently in other countries. For example, consumer protection laws in Germany, Italy and Scandinavia make such awards to individuals illegal, and in the United Kingdom such benefits are viewed as income by the tax authorities and are therefore taxable.

Benefits

Business travel is a valued sector of the tourism industry because business travelers tend to spend more than the average holidaymaker. It is now generally accepted that business travelers spend approximately twice as much per trip as holidaymakers. In addition, business travelers make more trips per year than the average holiday tourist and are thus more likely to be considered frequent travelers. The average number of trips is considered to be approximately 12 per annum for a business traveler.

A major benefit to business travel suppliers is the lack of seasonality of the business travel market. Unlike most pleasure or vacation travel, business travel is not restricted to a particular time of year when a given destination is at its height of popularity. Of course, there may be periods of fluctuation in business travel numbers, but overall no seasonal trends are shown.

Implementation

Successful management of business travel involves gaining an understanding of the following special requirements or needs of business travelers:

1. Good, frequent and reliable transport.
2. Fast, simple and efficient booking services.
3. Last minute booking facilities.
4. Good quality accommodation.
5. Priority checkin and checkout facilities.
6. Efficient and polite staff.
7. Information readily available on the destination surroundings.

Product mix

This is an essential area for a successful involvement with business travel, requiring the following:

1. A full understanding of the business travel market.
2. The provision of the standards and quality of accommodation, facilities, and services to meet this requirement.
3. Facilities attractive to the business traveler.

It is recognized that the business travel product mix consists of both tangible and intangible elements. Tangible elements include the actual issue of, say, an airline ticket at a competitive price. This will be of low compensation if the staff issuing the ticket have been impolite or inefficient in dealing with the client, the latter elements being intangible.

The development and increasing expectation of sophistication within the business market has brought with it improvements to the level of services and facilities provided by the operators. For example, in hotels there has been a general movement to improve facilities in rooms (e.g. the provision of hairdryers, work areas and tea and coffee making facilities) and in the level of service provided. The rapid progress in high-technology which has increased, for example, the speed of checkin and the level of service this allows. Executive floors have been developed in large hotels specializing in the business travel sector; these often include areas for informal private meetings, secretarial and office support facilities, and executive lounges for relaxation.

Certain of these improvements are passed on to those traveling for pleasure, not only in hotels catering for both these market segments but also by enforcing general improvements throughout the industry. This is true, for example, of provision of facilities in rooms.

At the top end of the business travel market there has been a move away from the loyalty to large hotel chains toward smaller, more exclusive hotels where they are available. This has mainly arisen from the executive's desire for personalized service and more homely surroundings with a hint of luxury, which has not been provided by the hotel chains. However, it is not always possible for such facilities to be found in all destinations and their use may complicate booking arrangements for travel staff who may otherwise simply make the booking through the appointed hotel group.

Pricing

Pricing of the business travel product is complex and tends to be very competitive. There is no single pricing method used throughout the industry, although a common feature is the discounting of prices for group bookings or commitments to certain levels of booking. For example, most large hotel groups offer corporate rates to their regular user companies, many offering discounts of 15–20 percent for a firm commitment to book 100–500 room nights per annum.

Business travel has been viewed by some as a lucrative sector of the tourism industry because companies rather than individuals are paying. (It is often the larger businesses which are prepared to meet higher prices to provide their staff with a high quality of facilities and services, being more concerned with value for money than saving at the cost of reduced service.) Also, there is less likely to be a fluctuation in the numbers of business people traveling in times of economic recession, with many companies considering this the most appropriate period to retain contacts at a personal level. At times of recession, however, companies may be more likely to be cost-conscious regarding the additional expenses incurred by their staff, resulting in a reduction in their *ad hoc* spending.

Promotion mix

In promoting business travel an understanding of the market is essential. This is made more difficult by its complex nature, exacerbated by there being both companies and individual travelers to satisfy, and that the booking may be made by a third party, such as a secretary or company travel department, who has no other involvement with the travel arrangements. It is rare for the actual business traveler to be totally in control of his arrangements as they will almost always be influenced to some extent by the company travel policy.

These factors make promotional and marketing information difficult to target, as anything of this nature distributed at the point of client contact is unlikely to reach the purchasing decision maker and vice versa. Business travel promotion is necessarily aimed at different groups: the people traveling and the purchase decision makers. This is perhaps most clearly illustrated through the advertizing approach of the key business travel airlines. The 'personal' element of their service is targeted at the actual traveler through advertisements in business travel magazines and Sunday newspaper color supplements; whilst the communication of the pricing and business benefit approaches are directed through the company.

Distribution

A company marketing to the business traveler must determine the best means of selling its product and services to the determined target market. The distribution strategy adopted must be effective in reaching the market and be fully integrated with the other elements of the marketing mix. The main distribution tasks are to communicate information to the relevant people and to provide the necessary travel arrangements with easy purchase facilities. A key element is to identify the important people in the travel decision-making process. Once they have been identified and knowledge of their roles within the process developed the distribution strategy may be effectively directed to the correct people.

In the past, business travel users have achieved a sense of security in the proximity of the travel agent handling their travel needs. But recent developments in the computerization of travel services has led to a change in this distribution pattern, with a movement toward a centralized business travel operation within agencies. This change has also been facilitated by the majority of business travel arrangements being made by telephone, with visits to the agency being rare. Such a centralized operation allows the business travel agency to operate economies of scale in administration and organization.

The impact of technological change is likely to have major effects on the distribution processes in the future. New technology already allows faster information retrieval from vast databases of travel information and improved economical communications.

Assessment

Typical of any intangible product, the sale of business travel is made more difficult by the prospective customer being unable to inspect the product and service fully before purchase. The prospective client must therefore base his decision on promises and implications made by the seller and on past experience or the recommendations of a third party.

Familiarity with the differing business travel patterns of different industries and the differing sizes and types of organizations within those industries is an essential element in marketing business travel. Companies using business travel range from the small business to the large corporation, all having differing levels of travel activity and varying degrees of complexity in their requirements. Knowledge of the specific requirements of user-companies as well as of business travelers in general is essential. Therefore, good market research, marketing policy development and strategy play an essential role in business travel management.

Understanding the business travel market and the different purposes of travel is essential to the effective marketing and management of this sector of the tourism industry. Many different sectors of the industry have recognized this and have attempted to attract this lucrative area of the market. Traditionally, cities have been the major hosts for conference and exhibition travel which has led to the development of specialist centers providing the necessary facilities to hold large meetings and exhibitions. However, in recent years there has been a development of facilities in other areas so that leisure and recreation activities may be incorporated into the business routine where appropriate.

Certain sectors of the business travel market are likely to have specific requirements in addition to the general needs that may be applied to the business traveler. For example, recent surveys have shown that women business travelers require higher security levels within hotels and express a strong desire to be treated fairly and politely by staff. Many female executives spend their free time in hotel rooms rather than face discourteous or humiliating treatment by staff in the public areas of hotels. A US Travel Data Center report also suggests that women business travelers are more likely that their male counterparts to combine business and vacation travel – useful information for the marketing of hotel services.

It has been suggested that there is a need for companies using travel for business to have a written travel policy, enabling all levels of staff to be fully aware of company expectations and limitations. Larger corporations often employ fulltime travel planners to be responsible for all travel arrangements, giving them the advantage of staff that are familiar with booking arrangements and travel operator staff. Alternatively, some large travel agents, such as Thomas Cook, will take over the running of a company's travel organization providing the company remains responsible for its own travel policy decisions. It is customary for there to be no charge for this service as the travel agent takes all commission charges.

Conclusion

The business travel market has grown rapidly in the past decade and forecasts suggest that numbers of business travelers will continue to increase and that business travel will continue to play an important role in the development of the tourist industry. For the companies involved in the marketing or management of business travel it is important to be fully aware of the changing requirements, expectations and technologies within the complex market.

Business travel requires careful planning and management, including the accurate identification of the target market, organized study of the market to identify and quantify opportunities, and the development of the major marketing objectives.

Focus on small business

One major difference between the vacation and business sectors of travel agencies is that the bulk of the business travel market is with large travel contracts for multinational companies and therefore only the major travel agency chains are significant forces in the market place, whereas some independents survive in the holiday sector. However, there is still a niche for small businesses who specialize in specific areas of the business travel market. For example, specialist services are necessary for the incentive travel market and these are often serviced by small, personal companies. It is vital for a small business to identify clearly its objectives and target market within the business travel sector.

Small hotels which are able to provide high quality facilities and personal service may attract a specific type of business traveler. This may be particularly attractive to the traveler who has to return frequently to an area and prefers familiarity and a personal welcome. Equally, not all business travelers are on company expenses but may represent their own small business and be more cost conscious, preferring to stay in simple accommodation.

A small business must identify its niche in the market, establish the requirements of its market and attempt to satisfy these needs.

Further reading

American Express, *Travel and Entertainment Expenses in British Business* (1985). Reports on the travel expenditure patterns amongst UK companies.

Beaver, A., *Mind Your Own Travel Business: A Manual of Retail Travel Practice*, vol. 2 (Beaver Travel, 1980). Chapters 24 and 25 deal with business and group travel from a travel agent's viewpoint.

Cleverdon, R., *International Business Travel: A New Megamarket* (Economist Intelligence Unit Publications Ltd, 1985). This provides a comprehensive report covering most aspects of the business travel market.

Deller, A., 'New products for changing markets and the role of research and development', *The Battle for Market Share: Strategies in Research and Marketing*, TTRA 16th Annual Conference (Travel and Tourism Research Association, 1985). This deals with the approach of one airline to understand the special needs of the business travel market for air travel.

Foster, D., *Travel and Tourism Management* (Macmillan Education, 1985). This book briefly considers the type of accommodation requirements of business travelers and relates the business travel market within the tourism industry.

Gee, C. Y., Choy, D. J. L. and Makens, J. C., *The Travel Industry* (AVI Publishing Co., 1984). This covers the history of business travel and considers some of the distinctions and links between the business and pleasure traveler.

Henry, R., 'A case history: the woman business traveler and western international hotels', *Tourism: an Exploration* (J. van Harssel, National Publishers of the Black Hills, 1982). This article considers the specific travel needs of women business travelers and outlines one hotel group's response to their needs, including the implementation of a staff training program to improve staff awareness and handling of certain situations.

Hodgson, A. (ed.), *The Travel and Tourism Industry: Strategies for the Future* (Pergamon Press, 1987). Various topics of importance to the business travel sector are discussed. Chapter 7 on Marketing Business Travel Services is of particular interest.

Keynote Report, *Business Travel* (Keynote Publications, 2nd edition, 1987).

Lundberg, D. E., *The Tourist Business*, (CBI Publishing Company, 5th edition, 1985). Various topics relating to business travel are considered throughout the book. Chapter 5 covers examples of the importance of business travel to international airlines and hotels.

Lundberg, D. E., *International Travel and Tourism* (John Wiley, 1985). Chapter 1 considers business travel.

McIntosh, R. W. and Goeldner, C. R., *Tourism: Principles, Practices and Philosophies*, (John Wiley, 5th edition, 1986). Chapter 2 provides a useful introduction to the organization of the travel industry.

Mill, R. C. and Morrison, A. M., *The Tourism System: an Introductory Text* (Prentice Hall, 1985). Chapter 5 considers the characteristics of the business travel sector with particular discussion of the conference market in the United States.

US Travel Data Center, *1987 Outlook for Travel and Tourism: Proceedings of the 12th Annual Travel Outlook Forum* (US Travel Data Center, 1986). An interesting source of information and data. The sector on Business Travel Trends is particularly informative on the US market and characteristics of the US business traveler.

Welburn, H., 'Travel selling and distribution; new technology and trends in Europe', *Travel and Tourism Analyst* (The Economist Publications, July 1987). This is a detailed article on the impact of new technology and particularly considers its relevance to the business travel market.

ANNE HAMPTON

Capital budgeting

Introduction

Capital budgeting, the task of allocating funds to worthwhile and ultimately profitable projects, is one of the most fundamental management decisions. An ill-informed project because of its size and incidence can cause the downfall of the wider organization. Compare the failure of Laker Airways with the success of Virgin Atlantic.

Capital budgeting can be defined very simply as the task of allocating resources to the purchase of assets which will ultimately provide an organization with profitable projects, a simple definition but a most complex practical task. It involves four main activities, now considered in turn.

The search for potential activities

Tourism is a major growth sector in most economies today, and the search for activities might cover many areas.

1. The first time investment of the new entrant into the market.
2. Expansion of existing activities, either by expansion of an existing site, or by purchase of an additional site.
3. Replacement or redevelopment of existing facilities, e.g. addition to leisure facilities in a hotel.
4. Potential cost reduction schemes requiring new equipment, such as the introduction of computerized booking systems.
5. Expansion of operations using different management schemes such as franchising.

The ability to search the environment for potentially successful projects is an essential characteristic of an effective entrepreneur, and is one which cannot be totally prescribed. Any manager must be aware that this is not merely a decision which requires financial knowledge, but that marketing and technical skills are an essential input. It must be stressed that without a good environmental search opportunities will never be found.

The estimation of the incremental costs and income associated with the project

These must be realistic if a useful result is to be obtained from any evaluation technique employed. When evaluating capital schemes most, but not all, methods rely on cash flows, which are considered to be more objective than profit flows. The latter may be distorted by different methods which can be adopted under generally accepted accounting principles, e.g. in the calculation of items such as depreciation, or the subjective decisions taken in matching expenses and revenues.

It is important that all relevant cash flows are taken into consideration and great care must be taken in identifying these. A number of guidelines may be offered to aid this process.

1. Only incremental costs are relevant, that is to say the actual increase or decrease in total cash flows. The reapportionment of existing costs should not be undertaken.
2. Any past cost is a sunk cost and is not relevant to the future validity of the scheme.
3. Relevant costs may include the opportunity cost of not using resources in other ways, e.g. the loss in accommodation revenues if bedrooms are converted to conference rooms.
4. It may be thought necessary to provide a range of differing estimates of these cash flows based upon stated probabilities, in order to evaluate the project in more depth.

The use of one or more techniques to evaluate projects

Various evaluation techniques are available to enable a comparison between projects. Superior techniques will recognize both the risk inherent in the projects and the time value of money; that is, £1 received today is worth more than £1 received in the future. These methods will be examined in more detail in 'Examples'.

Post-audit of results

When the project is realized, then in the post-audit phase the actual results must be checked against the forecasts produced in order that any discrepancies which arise may be noted. This allows control of the existing situation as well as providing data to improve forecasting. It is at this stage that decisions about abandonment of unsuccessful projects will have to be taken.

A final point to stress, before moving on to examine evaluation techniques in more depth, is that the capital budgeting process is the primary method available for the implementation of the corporate strategy of a firm and as such is of prime importance in the management process.

Examples

Whatever method of evaluation chosen, the first stage of analysis must consider the target return to be used in appraising the scheme in question. Two different criteria must be considered in this context – the returns which will be generated by the project and the risk associated with the project. It is the interplay between the two which is a most important factor because the greater the risk the higher the expected return from the project. The target return is sometimes called the 'hurdle' rate.

Risk may be implicitly included by an entrepreneur in the decision-making process, but recent finance theory has sought to make this relationship explicit. The most sophisticated model provided to date, the Capital Asset Pricing Model (CAPM), deals with risk in a very specific fashion. This method recognizes that an investment will suffer two differing kinds of risk, systematic risk, which is related to the whole economic system, and unsystematic risk or unique risk, which relates solely to that project. Theory suggests that investors will only expect extra return from the systematic risk, as the unique risk can be diversified away. Thus the important risk is systematic risk, and an organization's sensitivity to that risk is measured by an indicator called its beta. The CAPM says that:

$$E(R) = R_f + (E(R_m) - R_f) \times \text{beta}$$

where $E(R)$ is the expected return on that investment; R_f is the risk-free rate of return; $E(R_m)$ is the expected market return; beta is the sensitivity of that investment to systematic risk.

The risk-free rate is considered to be equivalent to the return on investments in government stocks, and the excess of market return over the risk-free rate, $(R_m - R_f)$, has been observed over time to be 8–9 per cent. The beta of a project cannot be found directly but a surrogate may be obtained from databases such as Datastream, by taking the beta of an investment or company of a similar systematic risk class. Thus an expected return or hurdle rate may be calculated for any investment. At the least sophisticated level the hurdle rate may simply be the cost of bank or other borrowing. Once the hurdle rate is established then the evaluation may proceed using one or more of the following techniques, each simply trying to establish if the project gives superior returns to the hurdle rate.

Discounted cashflow techniques (DCF)

Net present value (NPV)

This technique rests upon the simple principle that, ignoring inflation, money received today is worth more than that received later. This is because of the lost opportunity to invest and the consequent loss of interest resulting from the later receipt of cash.

The NPV technique examines both relevant future cash outflows and inflows and converts them into present equivalent values, the NPV being the net effect of the two. There is sound academic proof that in a risk-free world any scheme which has a positive NPV should be adopted as it increases the wealth of the firm. For example:

Money received now (end of year 0)	£100
If invested @ 10%, at end of year 1, worth	£110
at end of year 2, worth	£121

Therefore, if the investment or borrowing rate is 10 per cent,

£121 received at the end of year 2 is the same as £100 now;
£110 received at the end of year 1 is the same as £100 now.

To convert cash flows at the end of year 2 into today's values, multiply by a factor of 100/121=0.826; to convert cash flows at the end of year 1 into today's values, multiply by a factor of 100/110=0.909; tables are available which show the discount factors for all interest rates for years 1–50.

Compare two projects using NPV techniques:

	A	B
Initial sum invested	£800	£800
Cash flow generated year 1	£100	£900
Cash flow generated year 2	£900	£100

If the expected return or hurdle rate is 10 per cent then NPVs for each project may be found by multiplying each cash flow by the appropriate factor;

		A		B
Outflow	(800) × 1	=(800)	(800) × 1	= (800)
Inflow year 1	100 × 0.909	= 91	900 × 0.909	= 818
Inflow year 2	900 × 0.826	= 743	100 × 0.826	= 83
Net present value				
		= +33		= +101

Therefore both projects will increase shareholder wealth, but project B is to be preferred as it has the greater NPV. This technique can be applied to any project or series of projects. The difficulty with the technique lies with the decision as to which discount rate to use, but this problem can be alleviated using the CAPM as described earlier.

Internal rate of return (IRR)

This is another discounted cashflow technique; whilst not theoretically superior to NPV it is sometimes preferred because it provides one return figure for a project, this is easily presented to managers and is seemingly understood by them. The IRR is the discount factor which, when applied to the estimated future cash flows, gives a zero NPV, i.e. where the discounted cash outflows and inflows are identical.

Whilst the method is easily presented it can give misleading results, particularly where the cashflows are such that there is a large cash outflow at the end of a project. Then the mathematics of the method will provide two discount rates which can confuse decision makers and lead to the wrong decision if the problem is not appreciated. Risk can be accounted for in the same manner as in NPV, by using the CAPM to calculate the hurdle rate which in this case will be the minimum IRR acceptable from the project.

Non-discounted cashflow techniques

Two methods which ignore the time-value of money are commonly used.

Accounting rate of return
This method compares the average annual profit generated by the project with the amount of money invested in the project, and is expressed as a percentage.

$$\frac{\text{Average annual profit generated by the project}}{\text{Amount of money invested in the project}} \times 100\%$$

It relates immediately to accounting measures of return on capital employed, and as such is easily understood. The basis of the method is that any acceptable project should return at least a given target. However as it is based on accounting profit, as discussed earlier, it is susceptible to the vagaries of profit measurement, and as such may not be totally consistent.

Pay-back period
This method considers cash flows like the DCF techniques and therefore avoids the problem of profit calculation. It simply examines the length of time which a project takes to return the investment in that project, and a firm may impose time limits for pay-back, any project not meeting this criterion being rejected. Thus this method is slightly different in that it deals with risk implicitly by assuming that the sooner a project pays back its original investment in terms of cashflows, the less the risk involved. It is easily understood and is a popular technique, but does ignore any cash flows which accumulate after the pay-back period and therefore tends to concentrate on risk at the expense of return. It may be especially relevant where sources of capital are restricted or where projects are subject to high risk, such as a development in a politically unstable environment.

Benefits

Whatever the method(s) of evaluation selected the benefits will be broadly similar. The importance of capital budgeting to a firm's ultimate survival cannot be overestimated as the ultimate survival of the firm may rest on its managers' ability to find projects which will increase the present value of the firm (and therefore the wealth of the shareholders). The larger the project the more important the assessment, because the risks of failure are more critical.

By adopting a comprehensive capital budgeting program a firm will set in action a cycle which will aid the following:

1. Attempts to insure that the only projects undertaken are those which will increase shareholder wealth.

2. Formalizing the manner in which new projects are conceived and developed, so that the financial implications of any project are considered formally and explicitly.
3. Fulfilling the corporate strategy of a firm; indeed, investment opportunities will flow from and be defined by that strategy.
4. Insuring that proper post-audit and monitoring is enacted to control current projects and provide better forecasts for any future projects under consideration.

Implementation

To implement a capital budgeting program, the following broad procedures can be usefully followed.

Search
There must first be a search procedure for investment opportunities. This may be activated by a 'trigger' either from within the company or externally. It is important at this stage to insure that schemes which accord with corporate strategy are sought, because capital budgeting is the main way of implementing this strategy. Innovation is to be emphasized – this is the point where entrepreneurial 'flair' can be exercized. The drop in beer sales in public houses has provided an internal trigger for the provision of different facilities in these outlets; opportunities created by UK Government policy to use agricultural land for recreational purposes is an example of an external trigger.

Screening
This is the first evaluation; it is not an 'in depth' and detailed examination but is an exercise designed to test the feasibility of using further resources to provide a future detailed study. Considerations must include the following:

1. Whether the project is technically possible.
2. Whether the expertise and financial resources are available.
3. What is the risk of the scheme?
4. How will this affect the risk structure of the firm as a whole?
5. An initial assessment of the return offered.

Definition
If a project passes the screening phase, it must be carefully defined in order that a detailed plan may be constructed and a rigorous evaluation conducted. Market research must be conducted to define the market and appropriate strategies. The sources of finance must be considered and verified, and wider economic factors considered. Finally, the expected cashflows will be constructed. If necessary the effects of a range of different circumstances should be quantified in order that a series of different outcomes may be considered.

Authorization and evaluation
When all information is gathered a final evaluation can take place. This will involve a critical appraisal of the detailed plans and the assumptions behind them, and a consideration of the

financial implications using one or more of the techniques described earlier. It must allow an appraisal of all alternatives. This evaluation will be carried out by senior management who have the final power to authorize a project. It is unusual for projects which reach this stage to be rejected as commitment to them has been accumulated throughout the process; lack of commitment leads to rejection at a much earlier stage.

Monitoring and post-audit

An important part of any budgeting cycle is the monitoring and post-audit phase. There is little use in controlling the planning phase if, once any subsequent decision is enacted, control is ignored. In this phase the actual expenditure and incomes must be compared with the estimated cashflows. Failure to meet targets should result in the preparation of supplementary plans and the initiation of corrective action. The post-audit will appraise whether a project has fulfilled the objectives which were set for it. In doing so existing decisions should be re-evaluated and updated in the light of post-audit findings. Future decisions should also benefit, as problems and mistakes may be pinpointed earlier in the capital budgeting cycle.

One major UK brewer uses sophisticated post-audit techniques in that actual performance of refurbished public houses is measured against the estimated IRR calculated during evaluation. If the target IRR is not achieved the project is deemed unsuccessful and a further refurbishment or a sale of the outlet may result.

Assessment

If capital budgeting is to be a useful exercise within an organization it must be seen as part of the wider organizational control procedures of the firm, rather than as an 'add-on' exercise. It must reflect the corporate strategy and culture, and provide incentives and opportunities for innovation and development, whilst still insuring that adequate control of the company's scarce resources is exercised.

There is a danger that the seemingly exact and technical methods of evaluation will lead to a misplaced belief that the results so obtained are accurate. This danger is to some extent reinforced by the large amount of literature which is geared towards the refinement of evaluation techniques alone. There is now an increasing body of opinion which is seeking to redress this preoccupation with technical measurement, aiming to establish capital budgeting as part of a wider management control and information system. Some studies have shown that sophisticated investment evaluation techniques (those using DCF techniques) will not in themselves lead to more corporate success.

The social system within the firm must be considered as it must be recognized that the objectives of managers may not always be those of the firm. Finally it should be noted that finance theory rests on the assumption that the main objective of the firm is the maximization of shareholder wealth, and this in itself may be problematic.

Conclusion

Capital budgeting should be based on a wide ranging management system which recognizes the need for and the methods of control. The importance of capital budgeting in relation to implementation of corporate strategy must not be underestimated. It must be recognized that sophisticated evaluation techniques, whilst being necessary, are not sufficient for implementation of a useful capital budgeting system, and that the search for investments and the post-audit are equally important stages in the cycle of control.

Focus on small business

There is no reason why the techniques which have been described earlier cannot be adopted and used by small business, but often those involved in this type of operation are so involved in day-to-day operations that the possibility of applying them is forgotten or not explored. If external funding is required for a project then the application of these techniques in addition to traditional cash flow and profit forecasts may aid the application considerably.

Because the business is smaller the techniques may in fact be easier to apply because the relevant cash flows and hurdle rates may be more easily recognized. The benefit achieved from such an exercise should always outweigh the cost of implementation and this may be a crucial limiting factor for a small business.

Software/databases

Datastream International Ltd, Monmouth House, 58–64 City Road, London EC1Y 2AL, UK, provide an on-line service with a wide range of financial and statistical information, including betas, on most companies.

Further reading

Bromwich, M., *The Economics of Capital Budgeting* (Penguin Books, 1976). A comprehensive coverage of the topic, which includes an explanation of the theoretical background to DCF techniques. Not an introductory text.

Cooper, D. J. 'Rationality and investment appraisal', *Accounting and Business Research* (Summer 1975), pp. 198–202. Examines capital budgeting in the context of the firm as a social system.

Copeland, T. E. and Weston, J. F., *Financial Theory and Corporate Policy* (Addison Wesley, 2nd edition, 1983). For those who require an in-depth explanation of the financial theory of capital budgeting. A comprehensive text with a mathematical bias.

Dobbins, R. and Witt, S. F., *Practical Financial Management* (Blackwell, 1988). Good coverage of capital budgeting.

Hakka, S. F., Gordon, L. A. and Pinches, G. E., 'Sophisticated capital budgeting selection techniques and firm performance', *The Accounting Review*, vol. LX, no. 4 (October 1985), pp. 651–69. Concludes that the adoption of sophisticated capital budgeting techniques will not, *per se*, result in superior firm performance.

Hayes, W. and Solomon, M., 'A misplaced emphasis in capital budgeting', *Quarterly Review of Economics and Business* (February 1962), pp. 39–46. Looks at the earlier stages of capital budgeting and emphasizes the importance of the search for alternatives and information on those alternatives as well as the correct processing of this information.

King, P., 'Strategic control of capital investment', *Journal of General Management*, vol. 2, no. 1 (Autumn 1974), pp. 17–28. Examines the process of decision making in capital investment decisions.

London Business School, *Risk Measurement Service* (quarterly). Provides summary information, including betas.

Lumby, S., *Investment Appraisal* (Van Nostrand Reinhold, 2nd edition, 1984). Another comprehensive review of the subject, presented in an easily readable fashion; covers the theoretical background to DCF techniques and the CAPM.

Pike, R. H., 'A review of recent trends in formal capital budgeting processes', *Accounting and Business Research* (Summer 1983), pp. 201–8. Surveys the use of capital budgeting techniques and the attitudes of firms to these techniques.

Pike, R. H. and Dobbins, R., *Investment Decisions and Financial Strategy* (Phillip Allan Publishers, 1986). A readable and comprehensive text, which also has the benefit of a series of four practical computer programs which can be used for capital budgeting problems. Covers all evaluation techniques and the theoretical background to them.

P. JANE BROADBENT and
J. M. BROADBENT

Career opportunities in tourism

Introduction

At some point in life, everyone must choose a career. Perhaps the best standards for that choice are to choose a field which is interesting, that has a healthy economic future, and where growth and advancement are possible. Fortunately, the tourism industry is such a field. Throughout North America and around the world, career opportunities abound for people of all ages, skill levels and backgrounds.

In *The Next 200 Years*, futurist Herman Kahn predicted that the tourism industry will be the world's largest industry by the year 2000. Somerset Waters, the author of *The Big Picture, The Travel Industry World Yearbook*, states that tourism is already the world's largest industry – that with spending an estimated $2 trillion in 1986 for domestic and international travel, Kahn's prediction is already true today. Waters reports that 12 per cent of the world's gross national product is now attributed to tourism, and that world spending for tourism has reached $5.5 billion per day.

However, whether tourism is the world's largest industry at this moment is hardly worth arguing. What is more important is to recognize its size and the direction it is going.

Outlook bright for future of world tourism

An analysis of travel and tourism worldwide shows the industry is strong and growing. The World Tourism Organization reports that tourist arrivals continue to set new records and that tourist expenditures continue to grow. In 1986 arrivals increased by 2.1 per cent and receipts by 5 per cent. Scheduled traffic on the world's airlines also continued to grow, setting new records. In 1986 air traffic increased 5 per cent over 1985 figures, a healthy increase considering the large base involved and several deterrents, such as terrorism and the Chernobyl nuclear reactor accident, which discouraged many people from travel.

All indications are that air travel will continue to contribute to tourism growth. Current world and domestic travel is expected to remain strong, and increases are expected with the growth in the Asia-Pacific area and new markets. For the world's jet airliner manufacturers, 1986 was a record year, orders for new jets totalled over $35 billion, a substantial increase over the $23 billion in 1985. This growth trend in air travel is predicted to continue through 1990, with average annual growth rates in air traffic of 6.1 per cent in Europe, 6.6 per cent in the United States, and 8.6 per cent in Asia and the Pacific region.

In spite of the rapidly growing numbers traveling by air, the automobile will continue to be the backbone of vacation travel far into the future. World passenger car ownership has been growing at an average annual increase of about 4.9 per cent, and most travel takes place in the family car.

These trends have important and interrelated implications. New highways are needed to connect suburbs with city centers; airport capacity must be expanded to handle rapidly increasing air traffic; open space must be preserved for recreation; new efforts must be made for improved land-use planning in many places. As all of these changes occur, efforts must also be made to preserve the historic sites, buildings and natural wonders that comprise the world's cultural heritage. All of these needs create jobs and indicate that the travel and tourism industry will create jobs at a more rapid rate than other sectors of the economy.

Growth in tourism is also related to increases in the world's standard of living. As discretionary income increases in the industrialized countries of the world, tourism continues to grow, making tourism one of the brightest spots in the world economy. In the majority of countries, tourism continues to be strong even in recessionary times; in the United States, the travel and tourism industry has added jobs even in recessionary years.

All of these facts demonstrate that when you consider a career in tourism, you are looking at a growth industry where the future outlook is bright, boundless and exciting.

A service industry

While growth and job creation appear to be safe forecasts for the travel and tourism industry, you must decide whether you wish to work in a service industry. A number of considerations may affect your decision. For example, service industries have a lower wage scale when compared to manufacturing industries, and they are affected by seasonal changes. Also, not everyone is suited to serve the public. You have to enjoy dealing with people, making sure all kinds of people in all kinds of moods are satisfied. In any job search, you must carefully analyze both the good and the bad aspects of a career in the industry to make sure it is right for you. The next section examines this aspect in some detail.

Is this the industry for you?

We have already discussed that tourism is a growth industry, one that has a remarkable record and one that is outpacing other segments of the economy. While there will be periodic dips, the future promises steady increases and job opportunities in the many sectors of the tourism industry will be good. Thus the future appears encouraging and inviting.

While all the statistics make an impressive case for the tourism industry some realities about the industry must be faced. As noted above, tourism is a seasonal business for most of the world, except for well established destination resorts and major urban centers. If you do not find a job in a major metropolitan area where meetings, conventions, vacations, attractions, entertainment and other activities take place the year around, you will have to be mobile. A worker at a winter ski resort frequently will have to look for summer employment at a different type of resort. One must be emotionally and practically prepared to move to where the jobs are.

Tourism is an industry of many small independent operators, particularly in the smaller communities. If you accept employment in a small community or a rural area, job advancement will be limited. While you will typically learn all facets of a business, you many feel you are stuck without opportunities for promotion and advancement unless you move to a larger community. On the other hand, you might enjoy the familiar routine and faces in a local property and being given more responsibility than in a larger property.

Salaries and wages vary a great deal. Pay scales in tourism are similar to those in other service industries and are low compared with manufacturing jobs. Entry level jobs are especially low paying; however, those working face to face with customers may improve earnings quite handsomely with gratuities. In the long run, as experience increases, skills improve and promotions to supervisor and manager come, the salary and wage rates become much more attractive and competitive.

Long hours and 'vacation' work periods are common in the tourism industry. Restaurants and hotels are typically open the year around, 7 days a week, and like the policeman, fireman and nurse, you will be working when others have time off.

Another consideration is that the tourism industry is a people industry. You have to like people or this is not the industry for you. Do you like people so well that you can have concern for customers' comforts and needs even if the customers are being rude and obnoxious? Courtesy comes easily when they are pleasant and gracious, but a great deal of self-discipline is needed to serve every type of customer. In the tourism industry, the customer is very likely to change his or her mind several times. This human condition requires patience and an unfailing 'hospitality personality'. Ask yourself, 'Can I handle it?'

Tourism jobs which frequently look glamorous and easy, are actually hard work. You must ask if you have the physical stamina required to carry out many of the jobs available in the

industry. Long hours on your feet, working in hot and humid environments, working in the cold, and handling the pressure of a crush of people are all difficult. Look at your physical attributes and determine whether you can perform. To make sure you would be able to handle a job, visit several operations. Watch the activities performed, talk to managers, supervisors and the employees – then make up your mind.

An advantage of a job in the industry is that once you have experience and have mastered the tasks to be performed, you can utilize these skills anywhere in the world! The tourism industry is international and a hotel manager, a chef, a meeting planner, a sales manager, a recreation director, a waitress or bartender can find a job almost anywhere as long as local legal requirements are met.

Advancement

One should always be concerned about job advancement. Experience is wonderful, but what will it lead to? When you go for a job interview, discuss with your prospective employer the likelihood of advancement, what the levels might be, and the responsibility and pay that go with those levels. If you are hired the employer will know your aspirations and hopefully you can work together to accomplish mutual goals. Advancement comes from hard work, initiative, emotional maturity, enthusiasm, a sense of responsibility and good quality of work. Another method of advancement is by education – taking a formal college or university program which will prepare you for management.

Examples

Tourism is such a broad field that describing all the jobs is not possible. For example, in the marketing area career opportunities exist in planning and analysis, new product and service development, research, advertising, public relations, sales and promotion. These opportunities are available in each of the tourism sectors, such as accommodations, food service, airlines, cruise lines, bus, rail, rental car, travel agents, tour operators, attractions, outdoor recreation, tourist offices and information centers, research, and journalism. Given the wide range of opportunities, you will want to focus on those sectors and jobs that fit your interest and ability level.

A way to get an idea of the kinds of jobs available in tourism is to read and review the books in the 'Information sources' section or review the chapters in an introductory tourism text. To provide a brief overview, the following paragraphs contain short descriptions of sectors and some of the job areas that are available.

Accommodation

This is one of the largest sectors and includes all types of overnight sleeping accommodation – hotels, motels, resorts, guest ranches, campgrounds and hostels. The multi-billion dollar lodging industry ranges from cozy country inns to bustling metropolitan hotels to seaside resorts providing comfortable rooms, delicious meals and excellent service. The American Hotel and Motel Association estimates that the hotel/motel industry employs approximately 1.4 million people and creates 100,000 new jobs every year.

The range of jobs in the lodging sector is very broad. The following list is representative: general manager, resident manager, convention/banquet manager, front office manager, comptroller, accountants, management trainees, director of sales, director of convention sales, director of personnel, director of research, mail clerks, room clerks, reservation clerks, front office manager, housekeepers, superintendent of service, bellhops, lobby porters, doormen, maids, chefs, cooks, kitchen helpers, storeroom employees, dishwashers, waiters, apprentice waiters, bartenders, heating and air conditioning personnel, maintenance workers, engineers, electricians, plumbers, carpenters, painters and laundry workers.

Resorts tend to have the same jobs as those mentioned for hotels and motels; the larger the resort the greater the job opportunities in all areas. In addition, resorts have a number of additional job opportunities in the areas of social events, entertainment, and recreation such as tennis and golf professionals.

Food service
This sector includes the many facilities offering food service to the traveling public. This is a giant sector: in the United States alone the food service industry employs over 8 million people and produces a sales volume of well over $100 billion. Travel food service consists of food operations in lodging establishments, roadside service to automobile travelers, and all food service on airplanes, trains, and ships.

Representative jobs are head waiters, captains, waiters, waitresses, bus persons, chefs, cooks, bartenders, restaurant managers, assistant managers, personnel directors, dieticians, menu planners, cashiers, food service supervisors, purchasing agents, butchers, beverage workers, hostesses, kitchen helpers, and dishwashers.

Travel agencies
The travel agent is an important cog in the distribution of travel. The agent acts on behalf of the client and makes arrangements with the airlines, hotels, tour operators and other suppliers of travel. The agent receives a commission from the suppliers for this effort. Travel agencies have enjoyed rapid growth in the United States, increasing in number from 6,700 in 1970 to over 30,000 today; agencies range in size from small single proprietorships to major chains with thousands of employees. Illustrative jobs in travel agencies include domestic travel counselors, international travel counselors, commercial account specialists, research directors, advertising managers, group sales consultants, accountants, file clerks, sales personnel, tour planners, tour guides, reservationists, groups coordinators, trainees, operations employees, administrative assistants, advertising specialists, and computer specialists.

Tour operators
The tour wholesaler or operator puts together tours and all their components to sell through travel agents and their own firm. Tour wholesaling is an important segment of the world-wide travel industry. Tour operators offer employment opportunities such as tour manager or escort, tour coordinator, tour planner, publicist, reservations specialist, accountant, sales representative, group tour specialist, incentive tour coordinator, costing specialist, hotel coordinator, office supervisor, and managerial positions.

Airlines
The airline business has been a glamour industry, attracting large numbers of people to its ranks. With deregulation, however, major changes have come to airlines with new entries, mergers and exits. Air travel is projected to continue growing at a 5 per cent annual rate because of demographics, personal income, a higher standard of living in industrialized nations and developing nations, and a desire to travel. This multibillion dollar sector offers numerous jobs at many levels. Illustrative jobs are reservation agents, flight attendants, pilots, flight engineers, aircraft mechanics, maintenance staff, baggage handlers, airline food service jobs, sales representatives, sales jobs, computer specialists, training staff, office jobs, clerical positions, ticket agents, ramp agents, marketing specialists, and research analysts.

Since airlines have to meet safety and other requirements, opportunities also exist with government agencies such as the US Federal Aviation Administration (FAA). The FAA hires air traffic controllers and various other specialists. Airports also use a wide range of personnel from parking attendants to accountants to managers. Other air-related jobs are available with associations such as the Air Transport Association and the International Air Transport Association.

Railroads
While rail passenger transportation is a minor force in the United States, it is a major mode of travel in many countries. The Orient Express is world famous. Railroads need managers, financial experts, marketing specialists, passenger service representatives, sales representatives, reservation clerks and other types of clerks, conductors, engineers, firemen, and station agents.

Cruise companies
The cruise industry presently is the fastest growing segment of the tourism industry. It is still considered to be in its infancy, with more growth in store as the cruise lines increase capacity and marketing efforts. Cruise lines have many of the same job categories as the hotel industry because of the similarity of operations; however, cruise lines have more opportunities in the social and recreation areas.

Road transportation
The largest number of travelers in the United States use the public road system and a variety of organizations exist to serve these travelers. Motorcoach, bus, taxi, and rental car companies are all potential employers. Tours and charters have proven to be a growing and profitable area for motorcoach operators. The growth of the rental car industry has been matching or exceeding the growth in air travel.

These companies require management personnel, ticket

agents, sales representatives, tour representatives, hostesses, information clerks, clerical positions, bus drivers, personnel people, reservation agents, rental sales agents, clerks of various kinds, service agents, mechanics, and district and regional managers.

Attractions

The attractions and theme park industry has been dominated by Disneyland and Disney World, but many other attractions are a part of this segment of tourism. Examples of other attractions in North America are Busch Gardens, the Six Flags parks, MCA's Universal Studios, the Harcourt Brace Jovanovich parks, Worlds of Fun, and Canada's Wonderland. As these examples indicate, attractions are big business. In the United States alone, they record over 220 million visits and over $4 billion annually in revenue.

The attractions sector has firms ranging from small to very large. These require the usual officers and managers, and have legal, accounting, marketing, administrative, and clerical needs. In addition, attractions need ticket agents, ticket takers, parking lot attendants, and hostesses.

Outdoor recreation and parks

Recreation is frequently a part of the tourism experience, and parks are frequently major tourist attractions. These areas offer numerous career opportunities with employment settings ranging from wilderness to rural to suburban and urban. Jobs can be found in municipal, county, special district, state and national agencies; public and private institutions; and commercial enterprises. Job examples include park superintendent, park rangers, park naturalist, outdoor recreation planners, landscape architects, foresters, grounds and facilities maintenance personnel, recreation directors, recreation consultants, mountain guide, ski instructor, ski patrolman, golf professional, tennis professional, and lifeguard.

Tourist offices and information centers

Almost every country, state, province, district, and destination area has a tourism office and/or information center. Political entities are recognizing how important tourism can be for its economic impact and its potential for economic development; consequently, they are allocating substantial funds for tourism development and promotion. Public sector tourism promotion is now an important professional career opportunity, whether it is in a national tourism organization, a foreign national tourist office, a state tourism office, or a city convention and visitors' bureau.

Numerous jobs are available in tourist offices and information centers. Chambers of commerce often function as information centers and hire employees to provide this information. Many states operate welcome centers. Job titles found in state tourism offices are director, assistant director, deputy director, travel representative, economic development specialist, assistant director for travel promotion, statistical analyst, public information officer, assistant director for public relations, marketing coordinator, communications specialist, travel editor, media liaison, media specialist, photographer, administrative assistant, information specialist, media coordinator, manager of travel literature, writer, chief of news and information, marketing coordinator, market analyst, research analyst, economist, reference coordinator, secretary, package tour coordinator, and information clerk.

Tourism education

The expectations of tourists have become more sophisticated as domestic and international travel has become available to a larger segment of society. These higher expectations have led to a need for increased professionalism to meet the tourists' requirements, and the desire of the tourist-serving organizations to deliver the product has caused rapid growth in education and training. In recent years many colleges and universities have added travel and tourism programs, vocational schools have launched travel programs, trade associations have introduced education and certification programs, and private firms have opened travel schools to make a profit. Illustrative job opportunities here are administrators, teachers, professors, department heads, and researchers.

Travel journalism

With the coming of the age of mass tourism have come many opportunities in travel journalism. Today's newspapers feature a travel section in the Sunday edition; others carry travel articles. Some consumer magazines are devoted entirely to travel and many others feature travel articles; in addition, there are inflight magazines, trade publications going to all sectors of the industry, guidebooks, consumer travel newsletters, radio, television, video, and books.

The huge publishing industry associated with tourism offers jobs such as travel editor, assistant travel editor, travel writer, photographer, researcher, advertising sales representative, broadcasters, and freelance writers.

Tourism research

Tourism research consists of collecting and analyzing data from both primary and secondary sources. The tourism researcher plans market studies, consumer surveys, and the implementation of research projects. Research jobs are available in tourism with airlines, cruise lines, management consulting firms, state travel offices, and lodging firms. The number of research firms specializing in travel has grown rapidly in recent years.

Other opportunities

While a fairly comprehensive list of sectors and career opportunities has been presented, still others exist. One example is meeting planning, which is a growing profession. Others include club management, corporate travel management, incentive travel, hotel representative companies, public relations, associations, advertising agencies, and computer services, all of which offer opportunities.

Conclusion

The information provided in this chapter should be an important starting point for you. However, it is really just the tip of the iceberg. It is up to you to explore the subject further and to gain additional information. You not only need to learn about careers in tourism and travel-related fields, but also about the task of marketing yourself – how to work up resumés and how to conduct yourself during interviews. *What Color is Your Parachute?* by Richard Bolles (Ten Speed Press, Berkeley, California) is particularly recommended.

Information sources

The purpose of this chapter has been to list some of the career opportunities available in the tourism field, to provide the reader with a guide, and to point out that the tourist industry is so large that it is worthy of much further study. Some of the best sources of information are industry associations. The names and addresses of some key associations for the tourist industry are listed below. (For calls to the United States from outside the country dial 0101 before the number given.)

Air Transport Association of America, 1709 New York Avenue NW, Washington DC 20006; (202) 626-4000.

American Bus Association, 1025 Connecticut Avenue NW, Washington DC 20036; (202) 293-5890.

American Hotel & Motel Association, 888 Seventh Avenue, New York NY 10019; (212) 265-4506.

American Society of Travel Agents, 1101 King Street, Alexandria VA 22314, or PO Box 23992, Washington DC 20026-3992; (703) 965-7520.

Caribbean Tourism Research & Development Centre, Mer Vue, Marine Gardens, Hastings, Christ Church, Barbados, West Indies; (809) 427-5242.

Cruise Lines International Association, 60 East 42nd Street, Suite 921, New York NY 10165; (212) 557-8448.

European Travel Commission, 630 Fifth Avenue, New York NY 10111; (212) 307-1200.

International Air Transport Association, PO Box 160, CH-1216 Cointrin, Geneva, Switzerland; (022) 98 33 66.

International Association of Convention and Visitors Bureaus, 702 Bloomington Road, PO Box 758, Champaign IL 61820; (217) 359-8881.

International Association of Amusement Parks and Attractions, 4230 King Street, Alexandria, VA 22302-9990; (703) 671-5800.

International Civil Aviation Organization, 1000 Sherbrook Street West, Montreal, Quebec, Canada H3A 2R2; (514) 285-8219.

National Restaurant Association, 311 First Street NW, Washington DC 20001; (202) 638-6100.

National Tour Association Inc., PO Box 3071, Lexington KY 40596; (606) 253-1036.

Organization of American States, Trade and Tourism Program, 1899 F Street NW, Washington DC 20006; (202) 458-3940.

Pacific Asia Travel Association, 228 Grant Avenue, San Francisco, CA 94108; (415) 986-4646.

Society of American Travel Writers, 1120 Connecticut Avenue NW, Room 940, Washington DC 20036; (202) 785-5567.

The Travel Industry Association of America, Two Lafayette Centre, 1133 21st Street NW, Washington DC 20036; (202) 293-1433.

Tourism Industry Association of Canada, 130 Albert Street, Ottawa, Ontario, Canada K1P 5G4; (613) 238-3883.

Travel and Tourism Research Association, Bureau of Economic and Business Research, University of Utah, PO Box 8066, Foothill Station, Salt Lake City UT 84108; (801) 581-3351.

United States Tour Operators Association, 211 East 51st Street, New York NY 10022; (212) 944-5727.

World Tourism Organization, Capitan Haya, 42, Madrid-20, Spain; (341) 279-2804.

Further reading

Some key references that deal with career opportunities are given below. It is important to gather information and absorb it before you go out to interview so you will be knowledgeable and make a good impression.

Alston, A. and Sharp, A., *Working in the Travel Business* (B. T. Batsford, 1979).

Career Guide to the Tourism & Hospitality/Recreation Industry (Tourism Canada, 1986).

Careers in Parks, Recreation and Leisure Services (National Recreation and Park Association, 3101 Park Center Drive, Alexandria, VA 22302, 1977).

English Tourist Board, *The Handbook of Tourism and Leisure* (Hobsons Publishing, 1988).

Hotel/Motel Careers (Educational Institute of the American Hotel and Motel Association, PO Box 1240, East Lansing, Michigan 48826, 1987).

Milne, R. S., *Opportunities in Travel Careers* (National Textbook Company, 1985).

Occupational Outlook Handbook (US Government Printing Office, 1986).

Rubin, K., *Flying High In Travel, A Complete Guide to Careers in the Travel Industry* (John Wiley, 1986).

Stevens, L., *Your Career in Travel, Tourism and Hospitality* (Delmar Publishers, 1988).

Witzky, H. K., *Your Career in Hotels and Motels* (Dodd Mead and Company, 1971).

CHARLES R. GOELDNER

Characteristics of tourism

Introduction

The heterogeneity of a productive tourism activity is a recent concept. Today, however, the tourism product comprises a number of activities and services related to lodging, food and beverages, transportation, the purchase of local products, and entertainment. The tourism product (consumption) is the result of a combination (aggregate) of productive activities and services.

It is necessary to recall that in this particular type of production it is not the goods that are shipped, but the tourist consumer who travels to the site of consumption. This characteristic helps us to understand the multiplicity of consumer activities that make the 'tourism product'. First there is a demand for transportation, then a demand for food, beverages, lodging, and so on. This multiplicity, this temporal progression, does not recognize the tourism product until the very act of consumption, thus the terms consumption and production are interchangeable, because it is impossible to identify the tourism product until the moment it is consumed.

If this is true from the macroeconomic viewpoint, it does not hold for the tourism microproduct, that is the product of hotel undertakings and industrial catering. Thus, there are two viewpoints – macroeconomic and microeconomic – which explain the theoretical and practical ambiguity which has always distinguished the economics of tourism.

340 million international tourist arrivals were recorded in 1986. In 1980, the arrivals were 280 million, while 10 years earlier, in 1970, there were 159 million. Thus arrivals around the world have more than doubled since 1970. From 1980 to 1986, arrivals increased from 280 million to 340 million, a net increase of approximately 20 per cent.

In 1986 $115 billion was the expenditure on international tourism, a 5.4 per cent increase over the previous year, while arrivals registered only a 2.1 per cent increase. The turnover registered in 1950 was $2 billion while in 1960 it was $7 billion, reaching $18 billion in 1970.

Under the term tourism, however, it is important to give due consideration also to the important role played by domestic tourism, particularly in the post-industrial societies. In some nations domestic tourism involves 70 per cent of the entire population.

We are discussing a phenomenon which gives rise to an annual flow of domestic and international tourists of over two billion, while the turnover for 1986 registered by the tourist industry was $2,000 billion (World Tourism Organization estimates).

Benefits

Tourists going to a tourist locality come from various regions or zones (see Fig. 1). The illustration is simplified with a single pole, but an urban region may have several urban poles or several tourist poles of an urban nature. Tourists make their way towards a typical tourist locality to meet their needs for biological, physical, or spiritual rebalancing. The diagram's single locality can represent different types of development. The tourist flows bring monetary flows and, through this spatial transfer of revenues, cause an accumulation of revenues in a locality otherwise devoid of economic growth. This accumulation brings about the transformation of revenues into consumption, saving, or investment, and subsequent revenues. This establishes, within the tourism pole, a process of growth beyond the original transformation from typically touristic primary revenue. A secondary 'induced' transformation establishes a whole series of new activities, businesses, and services.

The accelerated growth process within a region creates a certain national re-equilibrium, for it permits agricultural or poorer regions (such as mountain regions) to enter into a more advanced growth process of the urban type. Thus, there is a re-equilibrium between the richer regions and the less favored regions, stemming the flow of people from the agricultural regions to the city, ameliorating overcrowding in the great urban or industrial centers.

Hence the revenue coming from the tourist flows and the revenue flows going from the region to commerce or industry for the purchase of all those goods and services necessary for tourist consumption cannot be distinguished. This has always been a major problem in the study of the tourist region. From an economic perspective, tourism is a basic activity within a region whose production is destined to be exported outside of the region. Tourism's development arises from activities of the commercial and urban type but belongs to the tertiary or services sector.

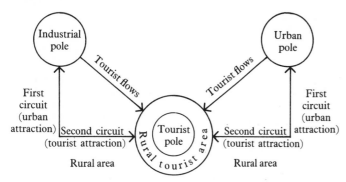

Figure 1 The process of tourism regional rebalancing.

Studies of the growth of regions, in attempting to measure the multiplier, have shown that following the initial growth, there is additional induced revenue which is more than proportional to the volume of revenue coming directly from the basic tourist activities themselves. The high supplementary fractions of revenues coming from this nontourist economic growth are spent, which creates a concentration of revenue in the locality.

Tourism stimulates investment, provides a means of earning foreign exchange and is a source of employment. Furthermore, tourism brings social change, and changes in attitudes, expectations and personal habits. It may radically alter the lifestyle of a remote area, introducing unexpected tensions and environmental erosion.

Implementation

Tourism appears atypical not only when one tries to study the phenomenon in its entirety, but also from just the economic perspective. In fact, when one was constrained to explain what constitutes tourist economic activity in the past few years, one has been forced to make a logical leap to create a pyramidal structure. This pyramid is divided into three levels: tourism infrastructure, tourism superstructure, and tourism industry in the strict sense (or the management phase). In other words, connecting the investment and management phases (normally economically distinct) is unavoidable in studying the economics of tourism.

The reason behind this is that economics has always considered tourism as a service activity. In other words, tourism in its production phase is a service: the typical case being that of the hotel. Service activities are, by definition, connected at the moment of investment to the marginal capital output ratio tied to the services themselves, which is the lowest ranked of all productive activities. Tourism services appear, on the contrary, to be connected to the highest marginal capital output ratio existing among the various productive activities, that of the building. Consequently, econotourism activity is a service activity with a high marginal capital output ratio. All the countries or regions which tried, in the post-war period, to develop tourism while considering it as a service activity have since changed their attitude.

Assessment

The tourism product is, therefore, a heterogeneous and highly composite product. All the activities indicated go into its production, but this sector also has its 'raw materials', without which no productive process could be set in motion. These raw materials are the natural and cultural assets. The introduction of natural assets and a country's cultural heritage into the national economic circuit is the fundamental justification for the establishment of a tourism industry, with its inherent financial burdens initially. Climate, deserts, beaches, mountains, museums, customs etc. become directly productive assets and participate in the general process of national economic expansion.

Natural and cultural assets can be compared to mineral or petroleum wealth. To introduce them into the economic circuit naturally involves meeting a series of transformation costs. As in the case of an oil field, a series of economic measures must be implemented to set this new process of production in motion and to make it beneficial to the country's economic development.

The major benefit from tourism activity is related, above all, to the assets utilized for this productive process and which are offered together with the other services and with the consumption of food products. Mineral wealth and oil fields are depleted as their exploitation continues. On the contrary, in tourism activity the services are always renewable, and the same is true of the food products. The natural and cultural assets can, however, deteriorate and the ecological cycle and cultural balance of a nation can be damaged, bringing an end to the flow of tourists. For this reason these assets must be used wisely and with moderation to permit their economic utilization for tourism activity without leading to definitive deterioration and, therefore, depletion. Such a policy should be contained in a series of measures designed to protect the environment.

Conclusion

The growth of tourism requires the adoption of a comprehensive development policy. This should anticipate and coordinate all forms of state intervention in the context of an accelerated growth of the sector and, even more important, in the context of the harmonious growth of the nation as a whole. This policy should have a dynamic nature, derived from the union and orientation of fragmentary measures toward a common end that has been clearly defined in advance.

A public tourism policy is the result of the twofold requirement to guarantee the tourist's satisfaction and to assure a harmonious and balanced tourism development in the framework of the national economy as a whole. In other words, the chief justification for public action is the necessity to develop tourism activity to satisfy the primary needs of a citizen's individual well-being. The satisfaction a tourist gains from his holiday is a basic element, whether one is referring to the national or international tourist.

The objective of this policy is valid above all for the countries that have yet to reach a high level of industrialization. In developing tourism, a new productive activity, these countries have a new instrument to achieve balanced and swift growth. It follows from this that the principal objective of a tourism policy is to bring about an increase in tourism activity.

Tourism policy will aim to achieve these objectives according to the institutional system of the individual country and in relation to each country's level of development. In every instance, however, it must aim to coordinate and harmonize the different forms of intervention in a single framework to reach well-defined objectives. Also government policy towards tourism can speed or retard its development.

Further reading

AIEST, *Problèmes Actuels de l'Economie des Entreprises Touristiques* (Gurten, 1968). This book defines the status and trends of tourist enterprises.

CESDIT, *Macro-economic Dimension of Tourism in the Post-industrial Economies.* (CESDIT, 1984). The book deals with the structure of economic activities in many European countries. The contributions of different authors are related to the net contribution of international tourism to the balance of payments; a theoretical model of foreign tourism flows; the role of tourism within the structure of the economy.

Erbes, R., *Le Tourisme International et l'Economie des Pays en Voie de Développement.* (OECD, 1973). Special attention should be given to chapters 2 and 3, concerning the cost-benefit analysis of tourism in the economy of developing countries.

Gray, H. P., *The Economics of International Tourism* (Pergamon, 1982). The intent of this special issue of *Annals of Tourism Research* (vol. 9, no. 1) is to focus on the economics of international tourism and its impacts on the exporting economies as well as the balance of payments of both generating and receiving countries.

Lundberg, D. E., *The Hotel and Restaurant Business* (CBI Publishing Co., 1979). This book is related to the field of restaurant and hotel management with an interdisciplinary approach. From this global approach are formulated analytical tools designed to make lodging and foods services satisfying for tourists.

Medlik, S., *Profile of the Hotel and Catering Industry* (Heinemann, 1978). The book is intended as a text for the students of the industry, and to be helpful to all those with an interest in the industry. The approach has been to provide a simple and reasonably comprehensive outline, rather than a detailed and exhaustive approach.

Medlik, S., *Tourism and Productivity: Report of a Study* (British Tourist Authority, 1986). The principal objectives of the study were to determine appropriate productivity measures and to examine trends in productivity in component tourism-related industries and in the tourism sector as a whole in recent years.

Peters, M., *International Tourism: The Economics and Development of the International Tourist Trade* (Hutchinson, 1969). The book sums up the economic importance which attaches to the present-day tourism phenomenon, looking at the benefits which derive from tourism.

Rogers, H. A., *Economics for the Hotel and Catering Industry: A Basic Course* (Barrie and Jenkins, 1977). The objective of the book is to consider and examine the potential contribution of the economist to management decision making in the hotel and catering industry. The catering industry is considered a significant user of the nation's resources, utilizing prime site locations, creating a large stock of fixed capital and employing labour.

Sessa, A., *Elements of Tourism Economics* (CATAL, 1983). This book contains three parts: the first part is on the tourism market, the second part is on tourism in the national economies and the third part is on tourism development policy.

Sessa, A., *Tourism and Third World: Theory of the Economic Tourism Development*, edited by S. Fossataro (Cagliari, 1972). A well balanced and comprehensive book on the theory of tourism economic development. The first part deals with tourism as a priority sector of economic development. Special attention should be given to Chapter 2, related to the added value of the nature and the culture in the economic circuit. The second part is related to the process of tourism economic development. Within this part Chapter 7 concerns the characteristics of tourism structure, Chapter 8 the theory of harmonious growth and Chapter 9 the mechanisms of tourism development. The third part is related to tourism policy; chapter 19 outlines state tourism policy and Chapter 20 tourism planning.

Sessa, A., *Tourism as a Factor of Progress in the Economy of Developing Countries* (Tipografia di Casamari, 1974). Special attention should be given to Chapter 1 which defines the relationship between public and private consumption and the value of nature and culture in the economic circuit.

Sessa, A. (ed.), *Megatrends in International Tourism* (Agnesotti, 1987). The book aims to establish the main trends of international tourism up to the year 2000. The picture that emerges has many lights and shades, with a tendency towards qualitative changes on the international market that need to be faced with a policy based on a wider knowledge and education.

Sessa, A. (ed.), *Systems Science for Tourism Development* (Agnesotti, 1985). The proceeding of an international seminar about a new global policy for tourism, which focussed on the application of systems science to tourism development.

Sessa, A. (ed.), *Tourism Development: Research, Theory, Education Policy* (Agnesotti, 1983). Research and theory, training, and policy.

Sessa, A. and Bernardi, R., *Hotel and Tourism Development* (Agnesotti, 1981). The book is concerned with the productivity of hotels and firm planning. Chapter 10 is related to the organization of labor in hotels.

Stavrakis, D., *Le Phénomène Touristique Internationale: Demande, Organisation, Problématique, Tendances Futures.* (Editions d'aujourd'hui, 1979). The first part is related to the analysis on basic elements and factors of international tourism demand. The second part concerns tourism services.

World Tourism Organization, *Appraisal and Social Value of Investments in Domestic Tourism* (WTO, 1983). Chapter 1 deals with the assessment and social value of investments in domestic tourism; chapter 2 is related to social optimization of domestic tourism investments; chapter 3 is concerned with the means for developing domestic tourism.

World Tourist Organization, *Tourism's Place in the Input–Output Tables of the National Economy* (WTO, 1985). The aim of this study is to furnish the basic concepts of input–output analysis applied to tourism. The study aims to show how this technique enables: the volume and the direction of flow of exchanges of goods and services between the tourism sector and other branches of the national economy to be evaluated; and the relationship existing between the tourism sector and the various branches of production to be charted.

ALBERTO SESSA

Commercial and consumer law in tourism

Introduction

'Consumer law' is a fairly recently-coined phrase. Odd fragments of law, drawn from many different sources, happen in combination (sometimes deliberately, but more often by historical accident) to apply to consumers, i.e. persons who purchase goods or services for their own, or for someone else's private use. This way of aggregating very different elements of law, thereby cutting across traditional patterns of legal concept, is dictated by non legal considerations. It is only within living memory that even the more firmly established 'commercial law' has come to be accepted by lawyers as valid and respectable. The law must, however, reflect the patterns of contemporary life, or fall in to discredit, and both 'consumer' and 'commercial' law are going to be increasingly important and influential categories of law for the foreseeable future.

Both areas of legal provision draw on statutory law (i.e. Acts of Parliament and statutory instruments, instances of which would be the Trade Descriptions Act 1968 and the Consumer Credit (Guarantees and Indemnities) Regulations 1983) and upon the common law (i.e. reported judicial decisions), as exemplified by the case of Pharmaceutical Society of Great Britain v. Boots (1953) 1QB401. Consumer law, in particular, involves criminal provision (where punishment of the wrong doer is the chief consideration) and civil provision (where compensation for the victim is of primary importance). Particularly where tourist consumerism is involved, the legal elements may be covered by municipal law, i.e. that of the state exclusively concerned with the issue, whether of this country (i.e. England, whose law includes that of the EC) or of another country – and that includes Scotland and Northern Ireland, for this purpose, but not Wales. Alternatively, it may have a Private International Law ('conflict of laws') dimension, i.e. it may draw on different systems, so that there is an initial problem of determining which of these is to apply to the situation.

It is impossible, in an article of this kind, to explore the substance of any of the vast areas of law which the topic covers in any depth. All that can be essayed is to sketch in the principal issues to which the law addresses itself in commercial and consumer contexts, as they affect tourism, and demonstrate the broad principles which it embodies and the methodology with which it seeks to deal with them.

General considerations

Consumer law provides protection for purchasers and users of goods, services and credit. Clearly, tourism activities are associated most obviously with services: and it is in respect of hotel, travel, leisure and recreational facilities that the law is concerned. Similarly, the commercial law of tourism is that which applies to a service, rather than to heavy industry and to business, whose concerns are rather more than office-orientated.

Specific provisions: contracts

A significant element of traditional civil law which affects both commercial and consumer matters is the law of contract, i.e. the law of enforceable agreements. Agreements among commercial undertakings and between such undertakings and members of the public will all be subject to the provisions of this area of law which, broadly speaking, was developed through successive judicial decisions. So far as contracts for the sale of goods are concerned, it is true that the law has been codified in statute since 1893, but it is only very recently that the contract for services has been incorporated into statute: Supply of Goods and Services Act 1983. Contract law sets out the criteria which make an agreement binding on the parties and those which may invalidate it. The law has to determine what constitutes the carrying out of agreements and in what circumstances failure, either wholly or in part, to comply with the agreed terms ought to be compensated. It also has to determine how to deal with situations in which an agreement becomes incapable of being implemented, without there having been fault on either part.

Commercial contracts in tourism would include the arrangements made between and among tour operators and travel agents, hoteliers and transport businesses. Consumer contracts would include those made between private individuals and any of the commercial enterprises mentioned above. All contracts emerge, by way of a firm offer and acceptance, from some degree of negotiation. Once offer and acceptance have been exchanged a binding commitment comes into existence. In tourism contexts, this will often consist in the making of a booking. Thus, purchasing a ticket to fly to Majorca; securing a berth on a ferry, or a room at a hotel would be contractual agreements, governed by established and fairly intricate principles, affecting the nature and timing of what is done. The making of the agreement in the presence of the other party, for example, may have different consequences for doing so by telephone, telex or letter.

Two aspects of contract law which have particular significance in respect of commercial and consumer law in tourism, are 1. the absence of real agreement, by reason of mistake or misrepresentation on the part of one or both of the parties during the process of negotiation, and 2. the introduction by one party, usually a large institution, of exclusion, exemption or limitation clauses aimed at opting out of, or reducing liability. As well as undermining the contract, misrepresentation, especially if fraudulent, may give rise to criminal proceedings in its own right, as well as possibly coinciding with the commission of offences under the terms of the Trade Descriptions Act. Exclusions are to be found in printed, often 'pro forma' or 'standard form' contracts. Such imposed terms are possible because the last vestiges of Victorian *laissez-faire* philosophy are called in aid to provide a philosophical justification for the theoretical freedom and equality of parties to agreement.

Other matters with which contract law deals are those of how agreements may validly be brought to an end, and how compensation is to be determined should one of the parties be found to be at fault. Assuming that the parties are found to have had the capacity to enter into a binding contract, and the contract itself is established as conforming with the general law of the land, the principal way in which an agreement will terminate, having been carried out in full, according to its terms, is by breach. Such a breach will be compensatable, but the same will probably not be the case where 'frustration' occurs, that is the happening of some event which makes performance impossible but over which neither party has any control. Although compensation is the basic purpose of awards of damages, the courts have come to make aggravated awards in situations where disappointment and distress have accompanied breach of contract in the provision of holidays: Jarvis v. Swan Tours (1973) 1AER71.

Torts

The other basic area of the civil law is the law of torts. This category includes such individual civil wrongs as trespass, nuisance, defamation and negligence: but it is with the latter (by far the most frequently litigated, rapidly growing and flexible and adaptable tort) that tourism is most directly concerned. In its present form, the law of negligence effectively dates from the seminal judgment of the House of Lords in 1932 (Donoghue v. Stevenson) in which the basic requirements of the tort were clearly stated for the first time. 'In order for a person claimed to have been negligent to be successfully sued, the party complaining (the plaintiff) will have to establish on the part of the person complained of (the defendant) the existence of a duty of care owed by the latter to the former, breach of that duty (i.e. failure to achieve the appropriate standard of care in discharging the duty) and consequential loss or damage.' Initially it was seen as being restricted to physical harm caused to persons in the physical ambit of the person claimed to be in default, the duty (and the kind of injury in respect of which it is

owed). Over the past half century of litigation, however, it has steadily expanded to encompass some forms of emotional damage, and some forms of economic loss, especially in the sphere of professional responsibilities and negligent misstatements.

Criminal law

Criminal law comprises long-standing common law offences, such as murder, rape, robbery and theft (although the latter, in some instances, is now incorporated into legislation, e.g. Theft Act 1968). It also comprises statutory offences, created by Parliament to meet changing social conditions, many of which apply to particular spheres of activity (e.g. the offences contained in the Food Acts 1986 and the Business Names Act 1985). Contravention of criminal provisions may be punished by the imprisonment of individuals in serious cases; in most situations, however (particularly in the case of companies which are regarded as entities separate from the human beings who set them up and operate them) there will be financial penalty in the form of a fine. Equally harmful in its consequences to the commercial undertaking is likely to be the adverse publicity which may accompany prosecution (whether successful or not).

Examples

Consumer tourism, seen through a lawyer's eyes, is concerned with holidays – the provision and use of transport, accommodation and leisure services and facilities. Commercial tourism, from the same viewpoint, concerns itself with the business transactions and activities undertaken, *inter se*, by tour operators, travel agents and the operators of hotels, restaurants, transport and leisure amenities. The crudity of this assessment is manifest, but, nonetheless, it provides a basis upon which to consider, in a little greater depth than heretofore, the effect of legal intervention in tourism activities.

Transport

Land (general)
A booking on a motor coach, or train will be a contract. The conditions which apply to the particular situation will be determined by the particular contract. Theoretically, at least, the terms will have been freely agreed between the parties in preliminary negotiation and the journey(s) will be undertaken on that understanding. Almost certainly the agreement will contain, often explicitly but sometimes implicit in the language of its terms, the relatively few legislative provisions which apply to the circumstances.

Road
The fundamental obligation of the coach operator will be to carry the contracting party to the ultimate destination via all agreed intermediate stops, and provide seating for the purpose, within the timescale specified. If he seeks to exclude or limit obligations to provide these basics, he may do so, as long as the terms are 'reasonable' and do not transgress the general

law of the states through which the vehicle is to travel. Similarly, he may introduce exemptions to cover his liability in respect of passengers' luggage; but he may not do so in regard to personal injury or death, for which (if caused by negligence or deliberate act) he will be liable at civil law, as well as possibly facing criminal prosecution. Dissatisfaction with any operation which is thought to be inadequate or actually dangerous can be referred to the Traffic Commissioners, as well as, or instead of, recourse to the courts. The Commissioners will not compensate the complainant, but in a serious case, established upon investigation, they will remove the licence to operate of the coach company.

Rail

Travelers by British Rail will be subject to the standard form 'Conditions of Carriage of Passengers and their Luggage'. (The same would essentially be true of carriage by most rail undertakings internationally, in that standard form provisions would apply.) It is a matter of some irritation to purchasers of rail tickets to discover that such a purchase, whether for first or second class travel, does not guarantee carriage in a seat. Even the special reservation of a place is subject to the condition of actual availability (to cover that situation of double-booking) and the only redress if a seat is not provided in such circumstances is the refunding of the reservation fee. Not only is there no guarantee that trains will depart and arrive on time, but the conditions make it clear that they need not necessarily run at all. The High Court has not been called on to pronounce directly on these provisions and, if challenged, they may well turn out to be unreasonable. Responsibility for loss of, or damage to luggage is fault-based and, therefore, negligence on the part of the carrier, except where property has been placed in the guard's van, will have to be established by a complaining passenger. Even before the Unfair Contract Terms Act 1977 was passed, with its general applicability, British Rail (and its predecessors) could not opt out of liability for death or injury to passengers, caused by negligence or deliberate act.

Sea

Contracts to carry passengers by sea are subject to the ordinary contract law, except with possible special provision as to liability exemption. The 1974 Athens Convention on the Carriage of Passengers and their Luggage by Sea, incorporated into English Law, provides that shipping companies must accept liability for negligence which caused injury or death.

Air

Since its inception in the 1920s, the international carriage of passengers by air has been fairly tightly regulated. The Warsaw Convention of 1929, re-enacted within successive UK statutes, controls the provisions which may be introduced into the relevant contracts for carriage by air. Compensation payable for death or injury is limited, as is that for loss or damage to property. Over-booking and delay will create liability on the part of the airline to its users, unless it can establish that the latter was 'reasonable' in the prevailing circumstances. The Air Transport Users Committee is able to provide advice on any of the above matters, but not compensation. In the case of charter

flights protection against being stranded abroad in the event of the failure by a company will be provided if the operator has an ATOL (Air Travel Operators Licence). Travel agents will need to be members of ABTA (Association of British Travel Agents) and appointed by IATA (International Air Transport Association).

Hotels

The Hotel Proprietors Act 1956 defines a hotel as an establishment held out by the owner as offering food, drink and accommodation to any bona fide traveler, without picking and choosing, at any time of day or night – provided that the person is in a fit state to be received and is able and willing to pay the bill. Establishments which have the physical appearance of hotels, and even provide the same characteristic services, but which seem to pick and choose their guests or limit the nature and duration of the services, are not 'hotels' at law. True hotels are obliged to look after the luggage of their guests (i.e. persons who have committed themselves to an overnight stay) and this is extended to involve providing safe-keeping facilities. In the absence of deliberate fault or negligence on the part of the hotel, compensation for loss or damage where items have not been so placed is restricted to £50 per item and £100 per person, if an appropriate notice is displayed in the reception area.

Package holidays

Space does not permit discussion of this topic which draws on the two broad areas of transport and accommodation, already dealt with. A specialist text which deals with the subject in great depth is Nelson-Jones and Stewart (1985). Two things are particularly worth noting, however. The need for commercial operators and consumers alike to cover liability and the absence of it respectively, draws in to sharp focus the need to seek protection through insurance, not only in respect of the hotel package but also of the component elements, already discussed. Secondly, the existence of the ABTA codes (alluded to earlier) provides for the solution of many problems without the need to go to court.

Benefits

Law is commonly supposed to be negative in character, whatever the context. This is because many laws, in the form of regulations, are prohibitions or restrictions of one kind or another. Even when seen to be imposing positive requirements, provisions are often the sort which prevent people from doing what they would otherwise wish to do for personal convenience, commercial advantage or the acquisition of power, control or financial profit. So far as tourism is concerned, consumer legislation is taken to exist simply to protect the interests of consumers, at the cost of any and every other consideration. All the benefits are seen as accruing to the consumer: all the burdens as being fixed on the trader or operator.

Law provides a framework within which ordered activities

may take place, determining what is mandatory, what permissible and what unfettered within a given context. Consequently, businessmen between themselves, and businessmen with their customers can regulate their affairs, reliantly and with coherence by reference to this framework. This can be called the 'referential' usage of law. Parties to a contract, for example, have the means of framing the arrangements they wish to make in their particular circumstances, within criteria of validity and effectiveness, tested over the years by the courts or established by statute.

The infrastructure of certainty can be infilled by terms as flexible or firm as the particular parties wish in order to secure the results they wish to achieve. This process is one of planning: by it, *inter alia*, the parties can arrive at a genuine pro-estimate of loss should their agreement fail, as well as providing for what it is to consist of, and how it is to be carried out. Thus, the law can be used as a constructive aid to effective commercial operation, and to compliance with consumer demand and consumer protection.

Besides offering referential guidelines, law provides a system for the adjudication of disputes. Where there has potentially been the commission of a criminal offence, the state will usually conduct the prosecution of the offender. This will occur, generally, where the referential opportunity has been ignored or miscalculated as, for example, in the compilation of a package tour brochure. In civil contexts, adjudication by the courts will be available for breaches of general obligations (torts) or specific agreements (contracts). Besides monetary compensation in the form of damages, the courts can offer (in appropriate cases) injunctions and specific performance of the obligation to the successful litigant.

Over the years, well-recognized arbitration procedures have been available for the settlement of some commercial contracts, without recourse to the courts. More recently, in the consumer sphere, apart from the provision of small courts, the operation of Codes of Practice such as the ABTA Codes frequently allows for the determination of consumer complaints against members of the relevant organization by independent arbitrators. These procedures can save time and money, but those having recourse to them should ascertain whether or not they are intended to augment, or to replace, their normal legal rights.

Implementation and assessment

Implementation and evaluation of policies to achieve compliance with the law must go 'hand in glove'. In simple terms, a tourism organization will implement the law by complying with the obligations which it imposes – carrying out effectively all duties and meeting all responsibilities, in respect of its commercial and consumer activities. This will involve the conscious adoption of measures to prevent contravention of the general law, civil and criminal, and the implementation of policies which are conducive to an awareness throughout the organization of specific commitments, consciously adopted or recognized by it. Thus, for example, contracts entered into will be clearly expressed, certain in content, free from misrepresenta-

tion and from mistake. They will be untainted by provisions repugnant to the general law, made with persons having the capacity to entertain and the intention to be bound by them, and soon.

The organization must, therefore, evaluate how it is established and monitor the legal dimensions of every operation in which it is involved, every activity it undertakes. First it must determine how professional advice, that of a lawyer or lawyers, is to be fed in to the organization – occasional access, retainer, on the payroll – so as to alert management to the often unperceived legal implication, rather than to perform a 'fire brigade' service when something has already gone seriously wrong. Second, and equally as important, all staff (at whatever level) need to be aware that virtually everything in which they engage is likely to have legal consequences.

If the organization does not see to its own means of meeting legal obligations it may be sure that national governmental, local governmental and consumer 'watchdog' organizations will do so – either as formally provided by statute or by inspection, testing and other inquisitional methods. In serious, criminal matters the police may become involved also.

Conclusion

There is no single, definitive body of law which applies to commercial and consumer tourism. The general law, both criminal and civil law, affects all aspects of tourism operation. No commercial enterprise providing services or amenities for tourists can afford to ignore these wider legal considerations, besides its being aware of what is involved when undertaking particular legal obligations.

The effectiveness of enterprise in coping with its legal problems will be determined by its use of appropriate devices for planning, monitoring and carrying out its activities. The impact of law on the organization is not the exclusive concern of its legal advisers but a crucial part of the necessary professional awareness of all staff.

Focus on small business

The problem which small businesses will have to confront is that of establishing and then keeping up to date with the law which controls the operation. It is unlikely that a lawyer will be employed fulltime and, therefore, the constant availability of legal advice and direction is likely to be limited, or altogether missing. In these circumstances, adequate and appropriate insurance for all the activities which involve legal risk (most activities) must, of necessity, be taken out. In any event, means will have to be found to enable the organization to imbibe, at the very least, the basic principles of the civil law most commonly to be found affecting the enterprise, and those criminal law provisions, failure to comply with which might lead to a heavy fine or imprisonment of the proprietors.

Software/databases

LEXIS, LAWTEL and *POLIS* provide libraries and files containing a wide range of United Kingdom Statutes, and decisions of United Kingdom, United States, Commonwealth and EC courts, contained in the appropriate reports. Statutes which searchers interested in the topics covered by this chapter would include are: Carriage by Air Act 1961; Civil Aviation Act 1971; Consumer Protection Acts 1961, 1971 and 1987; Hotel Proprietors Act 1956; Misrepresentation Act 1967; Supply of Goods and Services Act 1982; Theft Acts 1968, 1978; Trade Descriptions Act 1968; Transport Acts 1962, 1985; Unfair Contract Terms Act 1977; Unsolicited Goods and Services Act 1971.

Note also *Current Law Statutes* and *Current Law Yearbook* published by Sweet and Maxwell.

Further reading/information sources

ABTA codes (for Travel Agents and Tour Operators) are available from ABTA 55–57 Newman Street, London W18 4AH.

Baker, C. D., *Tort* (Sweet and Maxwell, 5th edition, 1987). Good, clear introductory text.

Barrett, F., *A Consumer's Guide to Air Travel* (Daily Telegraph/Woodhead-Faulkner, 2nd edition, 1984).

Beale, H. and Dugdale, T., 'Contracts between businessmen: planning and the use of contractual remedies', *British Journal of Law and Society*, vol. 2 (1975). Sets out the strategies to be adopted by businessmen in negotiating agreements.

Birds, J., *Modern Insurance Law* (Sweet and Maxwell, 1982). Very readable and comprehensive introduction.

Borrie, G., *The Development of Consumer Law and Policy: Bold Spirits and Timorous Souls*, Hamlyn Lecturer (Sweet and Maxwell, 1984). Fascinating description of law in the making.

Borrie, G. and Diamond, A. L., *The Consumer, Society and the Law* (Penguin, 2nd edition, 1981). Slightly out of date, but still *locus classicus* of consumer law.

Chandler, P. A., *The Hotel and Catering Manager's Guide to the Law* (Personal Data Service, 1981 and updating service). Wide-ranging compendium of information.

Clayton, P., *Consumer Law for Small Business* (Kogan Page, 1983). Good coverage of what the title claims, see especially, chapters 1, 2 and 7.

Consumers' Association, *A Handbook of Consumer Law – a Practical Guide to Consumers' Problems* (Consumers' Association and Hodder & Stoughton, 2nd edition, 1986).

Cranston, R., *Consumers and the Law* (Weidenfeld and Nicolson, 2nd edition, 1984). Interesting, general text.

Davies, F. R., *Contract* (Sweet and Maxwell, 5th edition, 1986). Well-written, beautifully clear introductory book.

Goode, R., *Commercial Law* (Penguin, 1981). Interesting treatment of a difficult subject.

Goudie, T. J., 'Spoilt holidays – where to sue', *New Law Journal*, vol. 135, no. 6217 (1985), p. 852.

Harries, J., *Your Business and the Law* (Longmans, 2nd edition, 1983). Practical, useful book.

Harvey, B., *Consumer Protection and Fair Trading* (Butterworth, 2nd edition, 1982). Slightly dated, advanced and scholarly work.

Hill, C., *Maritime Law* (Pitman, 1981). Read chapter 11, in particular.

Lowe, R., *Commercial Law* (Sweet and Maxwell, 6th edition, 1983). Standard text.

Lowe, R. and Woodroffe G., *Consumer Law and Practice* (Sweet and Maxwell, 2nd edition, 1985). Lucid text, supported by well-chosen cases. Wide-ranging collection of codes of practice included.

Marsh, S. B. and Soulsby, J., *Business Law* (McGraw-Hill, 3rd edition, 1985). Well written and concise. Good introductory text, helpfully laid out.

Miller, C. J. and Harvey, B. W., *Consumer and Trading Law Cases and Materials* (Butterworth, 1985). Excellent compendium of decided cases, regulations, statutes and consultative documents.

Nelson-Jones, J. and Stewart, P., *A Practical Guide to Package Holidays Law and Contracts* (Format, 1985). Is what it claims to be.

Savage, N. and Bradgate, R., *Business Law* (Butterworth, 1987). Interesting approach, new insights; assesses impact of governmental economic policy.

Schmitthoff, C.M. (ed.), *Journal of Business Law* (Sweet and Maxwell, bimonthly). Invaluable journal with a wide ranging coverage of topics.

Smith, G., Parry D. and Harvey B. (eds), *O'Keefe's The Law Relating to Trade Descriptions* (Butterworth, looseleaf, regularly up-dated). The practitioner's bible.

Stanesby, A., *Consumer Rights Handbook* (Pluto Press, 1986). See, particularly, Part II.

Tettenborn, A. M., 'Frustrated holidaymakers and frustrated contracts', *New Law Journal*, vol. 129, no. 5887 (1979), p. 12.

Tillotson, J., *Contract Law in Perspective* (Butterworth, 1981). Looks at contract law in its social, political and economic contexts.

Woodroffe, G., *Goods and Services – the New Law* (Sweet and Maxwell, 1982). Read, particularly, Chapters 6, 7 and 8.

Woodroffe, G. (ed.), *Consumer Law in the E.E.C.* (Sweet and Maxwell, 1981). Interesting collection of papers on the topic described in the title.

JOHN HOLDEN

Competitive analysis in tourism

Introduction

Every firm recognizes the need to analyze the markets in which it operates, to look at its strengths and weaknesses, for new opportunities and at the competition. Effective competitive analysis identifies the nature of the market, compares the selling points of competitors with the firm's, predicts the likely reaction of competitors, and determines the variables and the extent to which they can be used to increase the profitability of the firm. A conventional economic assessment of a firm's competitive position is based on the ability of the firm to vary price without being affected by the actions of rival firms. Markets are classified according to position of sellers and buyers. With respect to sellers, the following situations are identified:

1. Competitive or atomistic markets, characterized by many firms in the industry. Perfect competition occurs when any one firm by itself is unable to affect the price at which the good is sold. Price is determined entirely by general market demand and supply. This usually occurs when firms are selling the same or very similar products.

   Monopolistic competition occurs when firms sell similar but differentiated products. The degree of product differentiation may be so small that the firms have only relatively limited freedom of action, but price differentials can exist between the different firms' products.
2. Oligopoly, characterized by a few, usually large firms. Action by any one firm will have a significant impact on the other firms and so will bring a reaction from them. Depending on how each firm reads the market, this can lead to price stability, secret price cutting or open warfare. Situations can also arise where one firm will act as leader and others as followers.
3. Monopoly, where there is only one firm selling the product with no close substitutes. Traditional analysis shows that this can lead to high prices and reduced quantity of the product, and excessive amounts of profit being made by the firm.

This basic classification can be extended in various ways. For instance, in order to protect the large profits made, oligopolistic firms may form cartels which lay down by agreement prices and/or quality and/or quantity controls on the commodity. The cartel acts then as a virtual monopoly. Such a situation is often characterized by reductions in output and the existence of excess capacity. The cartel is often at risk from its own members. It normally benefits one member of the cartel to secretly undercut cartel prices or increase output as long as others do not perceive or react to this. Cartels in such situations may become unstable. Generally there is a presumption that these cartels or similar restrictive agreements work against the public interest.

Monopolistic situations can occur where one firm has a long established position in the market, having secured a large share of total sales. Smaller firms may accept the leadership of the large firm by not significantly undercutting price in the main market, or by concentrating on supplying more remote or more sparsely populated markets that the large firm does not consider worthwhile for development.

The small firms may also be a useful source of risk-taking in new ventures. Successful development will make these small firms of interest to large firms, either as rivals or as subjects of takeover bids. Similarly, in oligopolistic situations, price leadership may be established by one firm. The price leader will arise in two situations: either the firm is relied on as being more sensitive to changes in the market (in costs or demand) or the firm is capable of effectively waging a price war with sufficient spare capacity and financial resources against any non-compliant firm.

The profitability of monopolistic or oligopolistic arrangements will, sooner or later, attract new entrants to the market. The greater competition will erode both the generally high level of profits and certainty with which firms can make them. To maintain high levels of profit, existing firms may try to deter competitors, by limiting their prices or through creating or enhancing barriers to entry.

Barriers to entry can be either natural or artificial. A natural barrier occurs when the average cost of production falls as the rate of output is increased. Thus, larger firms have an advantage over smaller firms and new entrants have to establish their position in the market fairly quickly in order to survive. Similar unit cost reductions may accrue to firms as their total output over the previous years increases – this is known as 'the experience curve effect'. Other natural barriers may exist where, for instance, there are a limited number of good operating sites from which operators may serve customers.

An artificial barrier exists where, for instance, product differentiation puts a larger number of competing but similar products onto the market. This increases the risk in establishing any new product line and so the potential return relative to the costs of entry. These costs, incurred in the planning and installation of facilities, or in establishing networks or similar tourist flow channels, are sunk costs and may be substantial. Established firms do not have the same uncertainty in establishing a market, or expanding into new products. They may also benefit if production facilities are already geared to producing a basic product but where product differentiation is a fairly low-cost activity. This approach is often supported by high levels of advertizing. Natural barriers can also be artificially enhanced by similar activities. The analysis can be extended, where appropriate, to cover situations where control can be exercised over quantity and/or quality.

Competitive advantage also depends on the conditions in the markets from which the firm gets its resources. These markets can be classified as:

1. Competitive, where there are many buyers, with fixed prices to them.
2. Oligopsonistic, where there are few buyers, who generally can depress the price of the resource paid to the supplier.
3. Monopsonistic, where there is only one buyer, who would be able to depress the price of the resource even further.

The conventional classification of markets provides a useful backcloth for further analysis. However, effective analysis of the competitive position needs to be more firm-centered, with positive indications for behavior. The manager will supplement this by considering the strategic advantages available to the firm and potential rivalry in the market. The firm should look at the following factors:

1. Potential competition. Markets may not appear to be competitive, but latent competition may severely limit the ability of existing firms to keep prices and profits high.
2. Strategic groups. Some firms can operate on a national or international scale whilst other groups may only be able to operate on a regional basis. The national firms will maintain their position through large-scale promotional programs, small firms through price shading.
3. Strategic development. In a changing economic environment, a firm has always to look for new opportunities. Markets do not stand still, neither do competitors. Every new product development starts a process that tends to follow a general pattern.

For instance, a firm may succeed in establishing a new product such as a new type of hotel facility, holiday center or tour facility. Initially, high profits can be expected, but competitors will come in. They may be ignored temporarily as the original firm may be still dominant and the market growing, but the cumulative experience of the newcomers will enable them to cut costs, causing prices to decline. Increasing competition will eventually lead to a low-priced product in a saturated market. To ensure the long-term survival of the firm, management will need to establish dominance in a particular section of the market or generate an attractive variant of the product. The flush of enthusiasm for new or developing markets inevitably attracts excessive investment. In such cases, the firm must consider carefully demand in the longer term in deciding whether and when to follow or not, as price and profitability generally will fall.

Examples

There are several aspects to competition and the firm has to develop appropriate strategies for each. For instance, since the 1940s major airlines such as Pan-Am and TWA established or acquired hotels in major cities or tourist spots. The original purpose seems to have been chiefly to ensure accommodation for their passengers and to secure future development of their business, at a time when appropriate hotel accommodation seemed scarce. Developments since then have led to a variety of relationships, ranging from ownership to management contracts, depending on the strategic purpose. Inevitably, however, mistakes were made and some connections have been severed. One cause for failure seems to have been the attempt by some airlines to transfer their management style to an area unsuited to it.

The formulation of a competitive strategy is not enough: it has to be implemented. The organizational structure has to match the competitive strategy of the firm. If the firm is adopting a strategy of low-cost standardization, its target has been well defined from the center and there is little need for adjustment at the unit level. The organization will exhibit centralized control of standardized operations. Where, however, the firm is engaged in a policy of product differentiation to exploit new opportunities, a more decentralized system of decision making becomes appropriate, allowing the exercise of entrepreneurial discretion by unit managers. Such patterns have been found, for instance, among major hotel firms. In practice, it is a matter of determining where entrepreneurial flair is required and ensuring that the organizational structure encourages its development.

Benefits

A strategic development plan identifies sources of actual and potential competitive advantage, predicts their development over time, identifies the means of response and how and when adaptation will be implemented. The firm needs to understand its market in order to relate its objectives to it. For this, the firm has to be able to generate enough information about the market and its rivals and be able to feed the information into its decision making process.

The firm can then segment its market by analyzing the product characteristics, converting intangible features of the product where necessary into tangible characteristics. It can then identify those areas in which it is likely to be able to out-do its rivals and those areas in which it is relatively weak. Since the product contains a wide range of characteristics, the firm should devote few resources to the provision of the weaker characteristics and concentrate its resources on developing those characteristics where it has comparative advantage over its potential rivals. The firm has to concentrate on developing its own particular sector of the market. It must avoid the mistake of defining its market too widely, as this would spread its resources too thinly, raising cost through needless division of productive capacity and depressing profit margins by competing in areas where no real advantage exists. Continuing changes in the market mean that the firm still needs to review constantly its product lines and the emphasis on different characteristics.

Implementation

Competitive analysis must produce a plan that specifies objectives and identifies the instruments of action. No one planning model can cope with every type of situation in which the firm finds itself, but certain features are apparent.

Step 1
Identify the target market. The firm must not be deluded by apparent simplicity at first sight. Different conceptions of the product will produce different market considerations. Product characteristics must be identified so that a clearer perception of the market can develop. The product is specified, but not too rigidly at first, so that different perspectives on the market and their implications for product specification can be considered.

Each firm must create some form of goodwill between itself and customers: this creates stability in relationships and provides a basis from which the firm can work. This stability facilitates planning and leads to lower costs of supply. In establishing this goodwill, the firm has to succeed in differentiating its product in the mind of at least some consumers and create some identifying characteristic that other firms' products do not have and which has some special value to consumers. By branding the product or otherwise, the firm secures itself a form of localized monopoly: its product differs in some respect from competitors', but in such a way that the firm has a definite and sustainable advantage in production and supply.

Step 2
Determine the basic strategy in the market to build and retain competitive advantage. Is the firm pursuing some innovation to break into a new market, or is it looking to retain its position through price competition, based on cost reduction? Is it aiming to develop or consolidate its position across a wide market or some narrow segment of it? The choice of outlook must depend on the firm's previous development and current position.

Past decisions may limit the freedom of choice, locking a firm into a particular market strategy. For instance, a firm with a traditional luxury hotel in a particular area may face competition from more modern hotels catering for a changing market. The firm may not be able, initially, to make adequate defence by meeting the challenge head-on, since that could further damage their existing investment in that area. Instead it could treat the hotel as a mature and declining product and milk it until accelerated depreciation allows the investment to be scrapped and a more offensive strategy to develop.

An initiator strategy will generally emphasize product development. This will, according to circumstances, vary from changing the mix of characteristics of existing product to appeal to a particular segment of the market, to a change in the basic concept of the product in order to establish a more general and widespread market re-alignment.

A holding strategy by a well-established firm may employ price cutting based on the experience curve effect. This leads to declining unit costs as the total amount produced over the whole production life increases. Thus large firms should have a cost advantage over newer rivals and so may be able to employ price cutting to defend an existing product line. Smaller rivals must grow quickly to survive or must outflank the larger firms by producing a more attractive product for the consumer. Both initiator and holding strategies can vary in emphasis. For instance, the firm may mix price cutting with product differentiation.

Step 3
Determine probability of survival. This depends essentially on two things – the type of market demand and the likely costs of production. On the demand side, the firm needs to look at the nature of strategic groups in the market, to see where their dominance lies and to avoid a frontal assault on their entrenched positions. Both the product specification and the marketing strategy must avoid direct confrontation on a rival's own territory. Instead, the strategy must be to outflank the competitor's position by redefining the market. If necessary, the initial specification of the product is adjusted so that the firm can concentrate its strength where its opponents are weak in delivering the product to the market.

On the supply side, the firm needs to consider whether there are cost advantages to any particular size of firm. Cost conditions can be difficult to determine, but some indication can be gained through survivor analysis, which looks at the changing relative importance (measured by percentage of output or turnover) of different size categories of firms or, where appropriate, of establishments. This type of analysis could indicate where the small unit independent firm can best operate. For instance, if small firms account for a decreasing proportion of total turnover through time, then such firms may be suffering some cost disadvantage that prevents them from competing effectively. Even fairly crude data should be able to provide an indication as to whether this is the case or not. A more interesting analysis is to compare firms or establishments across space or market segment rather than time. For instance, large hotels seem to be predominant in large cities with high tourist and population densities. As the population and tourist density of the area becomes less dense, the average size of hotel declines. This trend seems to be continuing and indicates that small establishments face unfavorable conditions in large cities.

Step 4
Decide on the methods for achieving goals in step 2 (penetrating/consolidating the market). The firm must identify barriers to entry, new opportunities, new product requirements, and changing emphases in consumer requirements. From this it will determine the extent to which various methods can be used. For instance, a particular tourist activity may at the moment be

relatively novel, high cost, high priced and restricted to a small market. If capital investment is relatively small, the market relatively individualized and tastes are subject to frequent changes, an operator may attack the market by redefining the product and marketing accordingly. On the other hand, if the experience curve effect is considerable and capital investment is significant, an operator may try to capture a large slice of the market by large capital investment and low penetration pricing. Initial success can give such an operator considerable cost advantages in the future and push out rivals.

Step 5

Consider the scope for improving competitive advantage through forward, backward or horizontal integration. Integration can be partial, through tie-in or by agency arrangement, or complete by merger. Horizontal integration across different activities will be successful where similar skills or resources can be shared by all the sub-organizations. Forward integration secures a market for the product without the promotional effort required by rivals and may allow better planning by reducing uncertainty. Backward integration may allow the firm a more certain and cheaper source of inputs.

Assessment

Competitive analysis in tourism must recognize the difficulties in defining the markets to be served and in specifying appropriate products. Economic and social change lead to constant searching for new experiences by consumers. The novelty holiday of today becomes the standard of tomorrow and a declining product in the future. Defensive strategies based merely on cost and price-cutting without attention to specification run the risk of being outflanked in many situations where entry and exit are relatively easy. The firm operating along most stages of the tourist chain, from travel agent to hotelier, must regularly reassess its position to prosper. It must watch for signals of change. Where capital investment is high, the market must be precisely defined.

Conclusion

Competitive analysis is not a luxury, but essential for the continued well-being of the firm. No firm can take a buoyant market position for granted, and the threats from potential as well as existing rivals have to be understood before they can be adequately dealt with. A complacent firm may fail to appreciate that the changing socioeconomic structure of society may cause a decline in demand for its products. This may be disguised by the growth of sales of similar products that have been targeted effectively towards the lifestyle of groups that have been increasing their position in the market – upwardly mobile young or working women, for example. These groups are less inhibited by past habits and can respond quickly to fashion changes but will be unimpressed by product qualities that reflect an insensitive, production-oriented outlook on the part of the tourist operator.

The top management of the company may then blame wrongly lower level management for failure to grow and seek inappropriate remedies, such as cost reduction strategies, that will only worsen its longer-term position by continually reducing the necessary funding for its market repositioning.

Focus on small business

The small business can apply the lessons of competitive advantage to its own position. Large firms will either have a cost advantage in delivering standardized tourist products or control a significant section of the market. So the small firm should avoid challenging the large firms directly on their own ground by developing new markets or redefining markets where large firms have no particular advantage.

Thus, it can cultivate low-density tourist markets or those remote from a large firm's center of operations, where the inflexibility of the large organization prevents it from competing effectively. Similarly, it can take the initiative in developing new markets where capital investment requirements are not high. It can also develop specialist feeder services for the large firm where it can adapt better to local requirements.

Further reading

Bailey, E. C., *Competitive Leverage* (Conference Board, 1985). This short publication of ten articles shows that leading from strength and adjustment to changing market realities provide the ingredients for a firm's success.

Cowell, D. W., *The Marketing of Services* (Heinemann, 1985). This book has been published on behalf of the Institute of Marketing and the CAM foundation.

Faruqui, A., 'Marketing electricity – a military approach', *Long Range Planning*, vol. 20, no. 4 (1987), pp. 67–77. This article succinctly summarizes, with examples from several different markets, how ideas can be borrowed from military strategy to provide a guide for assessing market potential.

Henderson, B. D., *The Logic of Business Strategy* (Ballinger Publishing Co., 1984). This book provides a lively and provocative outline of strategy for improving the cutting edge of business in the market.

Lane, H. E., 'Marriages of necessity: airline–hotel liaisons', *Cornell HRA Quarterly*, vol. 27, no. 1 (1986); pp. 72–9. This article discusses the changing relationships between airlines and hotel firms.

Porter, M., *Competitive Advantage: Creating and Sustaining Superior Performance* (Free Press, 1985).

Porter, M., *Competitive Strategy: Techniques for Analyzing Industries and Competitors* (Free Press, 1985).

Schaffer, J. D., 'Structure and strategy: two sides of success', *Cornell HRA Quarterly*, vol. 26, no. 4 (1986); pp. 76–81. This article discusses alternative strategic approaches and the appropriate organizational structure for different types of firm.

PETER CULLEN

Components of tourism

Demand components

It is unusual in a professional handbook to have to start by defining the subject in question, in this case tourism. However, there are several aspects of tourism which necessitate a definition (or at least a description) before analyzing its components.

In the first place, the serious study of tourism is a remarkably recent phenomenon. The first recorded use of the phrase 'tourism management' occurred as recently as the early 1970s (in a document prepared by a group concerned with the planned development of tourism in London). The first international use of the phrase occurred in a textbook which was published in the mid-1970s and which for several years was the only textbook on the subject.

In the second place, because of widespread confusion (even within the travel industry) over the meaning of the word 'tourist' there is inevitable consequential confusion over the word 'tourism'. Although there is widespread agreement in official circles over the meaning of the word 'tourist', and the term has been clearly defined internationally for many years, the travel industry and the general public continue to understand a 'tourist' as being a person on holiday, or in some cases even more specifically as a person on a packaged holiday tour. To compound the confusion both the travel industry and the general public have increasingly in recent years used the term 'traveler' to describe a person on holiday who is *not* on a packaged tour.

A third reason for misunderstanding is that only a small minority of people working in the travel industry have an understanding of the wide range of activities and topics which are properly seen as being among components of tourism. It is common within the industry to restrict the scope of tourism to those providing primary facilities to travelers such as accommodation and transport. In fact, the providers of such services – essential as they are – constitute only a minority among the multitude of parties who collectively represent tourism.

The most convenient starting point in order to clarify the scope of tourism from the viewpoint of demand is not a definition but the diagram prepared by the World Tourism Organization (Fig. 1). This emerged after many years of debate which was unsuccessful in finding an acceptable definition for WTO members. The WTO description starts off with an assumption which must be emphasized: it relates to *international* travel. In fact it can be readily adapted to suit the needs of *domestic* travel, i.e. travel within a country by people normally resident in that country. The distinction is an important one for in most countries domestic tourism is more important in most respects than international tourism, even though many in the industry mistakenly continue to think of tourism only in international terms.

The WTO description is in the form of a 'classification of (international) travelers'. Anybody who moves across a border from one country to another is described simply as a 'traveler'. The part of this movement which concerns the tourism industry consists of those travelers known as 'visitors'. By definition, these are people considered to be making 'visits' to the foreign country concerned. Alongside this group are travelers who are not considered to be visitors for the simple reason that they are not traveling in order to 'visit' a foreign country but are traveling for some other reason. These are set out in the WTO classification; there are nine main categories of traveler involved, including such groups as members of armed forces on military operations, nomads and border workers. It must be stressed that many countries wrongly include among their visitors many travelers who are not visitors in this strict sense. In many cases this is a deliberate effort to inflate the apparent volume of incoming tourism, but in most countries it merely illustrates the primitive condition of tourism statistics for frontier arrivals. It is a striking fact that, almost without exception, countries with a military regime appear unable or unwilling to provide frontier statistics which comply with recognized international standards. Under the circumstances any use of these data for international tourism must be cautiously conducted.

According to the WTO classification, visitors are further subdivided into two basic groups: 'tourists' and 'excursionists', the distinction being on whether or not the visit includes one or more overnight stays in the destination country. For most island destinations such as the United Kingdom there will be little difference between the figures for visitors and tourists unless there is a substantial number of cruise visitors. However, for most countries with long land frontiers there will be a substantial flow of excursionists crossing the border to go shopping, to visit friends and relatives, to conduct business and to enjoy themselves. An extreme example of such a country is Monaco which annually welcomes some 3 million excursionists but only

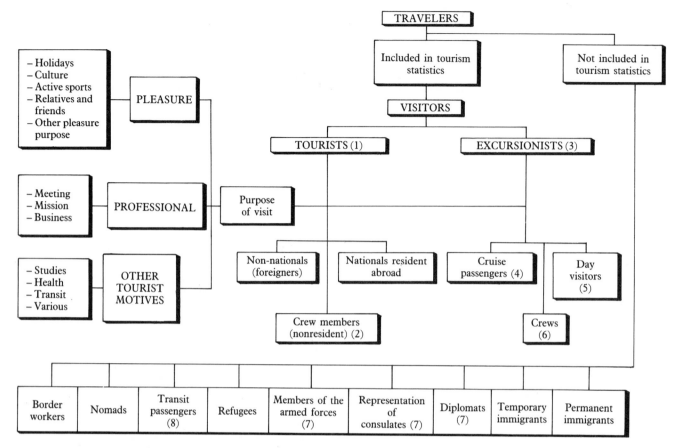

1. Visitors who spend at least one night in the country visited.
2. Foreign air or ship crews docked or in lay over and who use the accommodation establishments of the country visited.
3. Visitors who do not spend the night in the country visited although they may visit the country during one day or more and return to their ship or train to sleep.
4. Normally included in excursionists. Separate classification of these visitors is nevertheless recommended.
5. Visitors who come and leave the same day.
6. Crews who are not residents of the country visited and who stay in the country for the day.
7. When they travel from their country of origin to the duty station and vice-versa (including household servants and dependants accompanying or joining them.)
8. Who do not leave the transit area of the airport or the port. In certain countries, transit may involve a stay of one day or more. In this case, they should be included in the visitors statistics.

Figure 1 Classification of travelers (*Source*: World Tourism Organization).

one-quarter of a million tourists. Another extreme example is Macau. On the other hand, Italy and Austria are examples of countries with very large numbers of both tourists and excursionists.

A very important further division of tourists is between those who bear the passport of the country being visited and those who bear a foreign passport. Failure to appreciate the importance of this distinction is one of the most widespread forms of misunderstanding in the tourism industry, because many immigration authorities restrict their data on 'tourists' to those bearing foreign passports. As a result the true scale of tourism flow is often seriously understated. This problem is particularly difficult in those countries where substantial numbers of its citizens work abroad as 'expatriates'; this will often result in a

situation where the scale of their travel flow is larger than the flow of 'foreign' tourists. An example of this is provided by the very large flow of 'tourists' from Saudi Arabia to Britain where only one in three bear a non-British passport, the huge majority being British expatriate workers and their families, usually returning to Britain on leave.

Another important and often overlooked segment of the travel market consists of crew, particularly of airlines. It is not uncommon for aircrew to account for a significant share of the demand for good quality hotel accommodation. In recent years, for instance, it has been reckoned that aircrew accounted for a steady one-quarter of all bed-nights in so-called 'international' standard hotels in Cairo.

Although not recognized among travel statistics as a separate category, of at least equal significance to aircrew is the flow of people who are professionally employed in the travel industry and who are traveling in the course of their work. It has been estimated that around one in every ten people traveling internationally at any one moment are people in the travel business.

Despite the WTO's efforts to establish a generally accepted classification of travelers, many countries continue to cause confusion by failing to take account of the distinction between those visitors who utilize overnight accommodation ('tourists') and those who do not ('excursionists' or 'day visitors'). This distinction is of particular importance from the planning viewpoint because the economic benefit of short-stay visitors can often be eclipsed by the economic and social costs associated with their visits.

Because of its obvious use to the tourism industry, it has become increasingly common to classify the travel market into segments according to purpose of visit. The WTO classification divides travelers into two principal segments – pleasure and professional – plus a third rather amorphous segment which broadly includes all personal travel other than vacation or day-trip. Although these distinctions are valid, in practice the available information is often of doubtful use because of the tendency among many business travelers to prefer to describe the purpose of their visit as being 'holiday'. This is understandable given the more welcoming reception often given at frontiers to visiting 'holidaymakers'. This confusion is most marked in Third World countries, any of which impose annoying visa expenses and restrictions on visiting business people. As a result, it is common to much exaggerate the 'pleasure' share of the travel market to these countries.

Supply components

Whereas the World Tourism Organization has gradually evolved an acceptable classification of the components of tourism from the viewpoint of the market – the demand components – little matching work has been done to classify the components of tourism from the viewpoint of the product – the supply components. This is evident from the wholly inadequate so-called 'Classification of the tourist industries in the International Standard Industrial Classification (ISIC) of all economic activities' (Table 1).

The basic difficulty in classifying the supply components of tourism is that, by definition, they include the entire range of human activities. To be more precise, any and indeed every activity qualifies as tourism the moment it is combined with transport other than between the home and the normal workplace of the person concerned. To be even more precise, the scope of tourism in effect includes all activities undertaken except at home or at the normal workplace.

This virtually limitless description of tourism results first from the extension of tourism to include domestic travel as well as international travel, and then from its extension to include day trips. From a logical point of view, this twofold extension is wholly sensible. This explains why an ever increasing number of governments have, since the early 1970s, widened the scope of their tourism policies and official tourism machinery to include domestic tourism and day-trip tourism.

Another basic problem in classifying the supply components of tourism is that it is difficult in practice to distinguish between those elements of supply which are used by visitors, whether they are tourists or excursionists, and those which are used by (for lack of a better term) 'locals'. The nature of the tourism product is that most of its components are shared both by visitors and by locals. At the one extreme there are certain products such as overnight accommodation which are almost exclusively but not entirely used by visitors; at the other extreme there are certain products such as suburban transport services which are mainly used by locals. In reality it is quite surprising how few components of tourism are not used by locals as well as by visitors.

The one fundamental supply component which is common, by definition, to all tourism is transport. As it happens no generally accepted definition has yet evolved, either nationally or internationally, on the amount of transport which determines when a journey becomes a 'visit'. In some countries there is informal acceptance of a criterion based on journey distance, the most common basis being a one-way distance limit of either 100 km or 50 miles. Among some scholars there is a preference for a criterion based not on journey distance but on journey time; here the most commonly accepted limit is a one-way journey time of 1 hour. For working purposes, transport thus becomes regarded as tourism-related when the journey involves a one-way distance of over 100 km/50 miles or a one-way time of over 1 hour.

These limits effectively rule out virtually all nonpowered forms of transport. With the spread of car ownership and the improvement in road systems the private car has emerged as the dominant transport mode in tourism, nationally and internationally. Motoring statistics are notoriously inadequate but it is reckoned that some three-quarters of all tourism journeys – i.e. by people engaged on 'visits' – are by road. In the Third World most of this road travel is by bus and coach; in the developed world most is by private car.

Throughout the world intercity coach travel is expanding, partly as a result of improved roads and vehicles but partly too as a result of economic deregulation. Most of the economic restrictions on intercity coach travel were introduced by governments anxious to protect their national railways; it is therefore not surprising that the recent growth of coach travel has been at the expense of rail travel. Even in Western Europe, where the most energetic measures have been taken to improve the quality of rail service, the rail share of the travel market is tending to diminish.

Mainly as a result of the steady growth in motoring, ferry transport on short water crossings (usually on distances below 100 km) is also growing throughout the world. Cruising is also showing steady growth, although this is concentrated on inland waterways (of which the Rhine and the Nile are the two most important) and on relatively sheltered coastal waters (mostly in the Caribbean and the Eastern Mediterranean).

Although it still captures only a small share of total global tourism movement, air travel consistently shows the fastest growth – normally double the overall average growth rate for all

Table 1 Present classification of the tourist industries in the International Standard Industrial Classification of all economic activities (ISIC).

631   *Restaurants, cafés and other eating and drinking places*

Retail establishments selling prepared foods and drinks for immediate consumption, such as restaurants, cafés, lunch counters and refreshment stands. Catering is included in this group. Also included are dining-car services in railroad trains and other passenger transport facilities which are operated as an independent business; and canteens and eating facilities in plants and offices which can be separately reported. Restaurant facilities operated in connection with the provision of lodgings are classified in group 6320 (Hotels, rooming houses, camps and other lodging places).

632   *Hotels, rooming houses, camps and other lodging places*

The provision, on a fee basis, of lodging, camping space and camping facilities, whether open to the general public or restricted to members of a particular organization. Restaurant facilities operated in connection with the provision of lodgings are included in this group.

711   *Land transport*

　　7111   *Railway transport*

Companies furnishing transportation by interurban and suburban railroads; and services allied to railway transportation, such as sleeping-car services, railway express, and switching and other terminal services. Also included are dining-car services in railroad trains not operated as independent businesses; and the building, overhaul and repair of railway rolling stock and the construction and maintenance of railway right-of-way and buildings by railway transport companies which it is not possible to report separately. Excluded from this group are units operated by railroad companies which are primarily engaged in providing telegraph services (classified in group 7200); in operating hotels (classified in group 6320); and in providing water transport (classified in the appropriate group of 712).

　　7112   *Urban, suburban and interurban highway passenger transport*

Interurban and suburban bus and coach lines; and urban passenger transportation whether by electric railway, trolley coach, bus, tramways or subway. The operation of associated terminals, maintenance and service facilities is included. Urban transit systems may also include ferries and any other means of transport forming part of an integrated system of urban passenger transport.

　　7113   *Other passenger land transport*

Passenger transportation services, not elsewhere classified, such as sightseeing buses, limousines to airports or stations, school buses, taxicabs; and animal-drawn vehicles for the transport of passengers or freight. The rental of automobiles with drivers is also included. The provision of ambulance services is classified in group 9331 (Medical, dental and other health services).

　　7116   *Supporting services to land transport*

Services in support of land transport, such as the operation of toll roads, highway bridges, vehicular tunnels and parking lots and structures; the rental of railroad cars and of automobiles and trucks without drivers. Storage or warehousing of motor vehicles (dead storage) is classified in group 7192; and the rental of automobiles or trucks with drivers is classified in groups 7113 or 7114 respectively.

712   *Water transport*

　　7121   *Ocean and coastal water transport*

The operation of vessels for transport of freight and passengers overseas and coastwise.

　　7122   *Inland waterway transport*

The operation of vessels for the transport of freight and passengers by rivers, canals and other inland waterways. Included are ferries operated across rivers, domestic lakes and within harbors.

713   *Air transport*

　　7131   *Air transport carriers*

The transport by air of passengers and freight, whether by regular services or by private charter.

7191   *Services incidental to transport*

Services incidental to transport, such as forwarding; packing and crating; arrangement of transport (including travel agencies); inspection, sampling and weighing; ship and aircraft brokers. The operation of stock yards which provide pens, feed and selling areas for livestock temporarily held, either pending sale or in transit to or from the market, is also included.

94   *Recreational and cultural services*

Motion picture and other entertainment services:
　　Motion picture production
　　Motion picture distribution and projection
　　Radio and television broadcasting
　　Theatrical producers and entertainment services
　　Authors, music composers and other independent artists not elsewhere classified
　　Libraries, museums, botanical and zoological gardens, and other cultural services not elsewhere classified
　　Amusement and recreational services not elsewhere classified.

tourism – and has now captured virtually all tourism travel for journeys over 1,000 km and a major share of all travel over 500 km.

In addition to transport there is one other component which is fundamental to tourism: the attraction. Implicit in every tourism trip, in every visit away from home, is the process of being attracted towards something or somebody. Although the phrase 'tourist attraction' is often used to describe commercial establishments developed to attract tourists, it is a curious feature of tourism that most tourism journeys are undertaken to provide the visitor with an experience which is noncommercial. In many cases, perhaps most cases when business travel is included, the primary attraction of tourism is to meet somebody, usually a friend, a relative or a business contact. In many cases the primary attraction is a particular landscape, seascape or townscape, or even the opportunity to experience a different place and its people. Very often there are particular features of these places which are the specific attraction, often taking the form of local events which have developed without planning into tourist attractions.

The striking characteristics of these attractions, which together account for the vast bulk of all tourism flows, is that they are usually provided gratis. Visitors usually neither pay, nor expect to pay, for the experience which is the primary attraction. It is this peculiar, perhaps even unique, gratis element of the tourist product which causes the built-in problem of congestion or saturation. Because they are available gratis it is impossible, or at least very difficult, to control entry by pricing except where tight control can be exerted over numbers. This is possible in a small country like Bhutan where there is in effect only one gateway; in such a case control can be exerted by visa restrictions which inflict minimum daily expenditure levels on all visitors. But such a system could not work in neighboring India; it is therefore very difficult to control the number of visitors wishing to admire the Taj Mahal or to enjoy the beaches of Goa.

Alongside the primary tourism attractions there is a host of secondary attractions, at most of which the visitor expects to pay. Quite often these are provided at a nominal charge, well below what the visitor is in fact prepared to pay, normally because they are provided by a public authority which does not expect to finance its operations out of revenue from customers. Only in a relatively small number of cases is the tourist attraction a commercial enterprise, operated on commercial lines by a proprietor who has to make a profit in order to survive.

It is this intrinsic gratis or underpriced aspect of the main tourism product which has drawn governments into tourism. On the one hand, because it does not respond to the normal laws of supply and demand, governments find it necessary (in order to maximize the national benefit of tourism) both to promote the development of the tourism product and to control its use by visitors. On the other hand, because most of the product is generally not bought, the attractions lack funds for marketing and thus have to depend on governments to accept responsibility for marketing activities.

Although the two fundamental components of tourism supply are the attraction and the transport which allows access to the attraction, the scale and growth of tourism are dependent on the facilities which are available for visitors' convenience, comfort and pleasure. In a strict sense these are not really tourist attractions, but operators now realize that success results from making their facilities as attractive as possible. As a result, the dividing line between the attraction and the facility is becoming blurred. To many people, the primary attraction on a tourism trip will be to enjoy staying in one particular hotel, or even eating a meal in one particular restaurant. Of these facilities the most important as far as tourists are concerned is overnight accommodation. Although the hotel sector is most visible the dominant form of accommodation almost everywhere is the home of a friend or relative. Due to the lack of data it is difficult to be precise about other accommodation, now usually described as 'supplementary accommodation', but it is certainly the fastest growing sector of the accommodation industry and is likely soon to overtake the hotel sector in terms of visitor bednights if it has not already done so. The growth of timeshare is an important element here. Another is the development of the second home. Yet another, only in its infancy, is the development of farm tourism.

Alongside the provision of accommodation there has developed a wide range of other facilities for catering, entertainment and recreation which are used wholly or partly by visitors. A striking feature of the facilities component of the tourism industry, even among the hotel sector, is that supply is highly fragmented. Although chains are highly visible because of their intensive marketing, they account for only a small share of global hotel capacity, and only a microscopic share of all accommodation when private homes and supplementary accommodation is taken into account.

The intensely fragmented nature of this component is another reason why governments have been drawn into the tourism business, both to help in product development and in product marketing. As in all highly fragmented industries, without government interference there is too little research, too little training and too little attention to professional standards. In addition, as in the case of the actual attractions, it is difficult for small, fragmented enterprises to raise the funds needed to embark on effective marketing campaigns. This has meant that governments have felt obliged to accept responsibility for at least coordinating tourism marketing on a national level (normally through their national tourism offices).

Marketing sector

Because of another peculiar feature of tourism – the physical separation of supply and demand – another important component of the tourism industry is the marketing sector which serves to bridge the gap between the two. This basically falls into three parts. The largest is the retail sector, numbering at least 100,000 outlets worldwide, mostly in the form of small 'mom and pop' travel agencies operating on the local high street. In between these retailers and the suppliers (mostly of accommodation and transport) comes a smaller number (probably 10,000 at most) of rather larger companies which operate as wholesalers, many of whom produce their own range of branded travel packages. At the top end of this group are a small number of giants such as TUI in Germany and Thomson in the United Kingdom which each generate around a million clients a year. However, the bulk comprises small businesses run by somebody with great personal enthusiasm for his particular product and happy to generate a few hundred packages a year. Supporting these two groups, as well as the principals who provide transport and accommodation, is an assorted army of marketing specialists, each providing expertise in areas like reservations, information technology, public relations and advertising. Although at first sight this last component of the industry, the marketing sector, would seem capable of bridging the gap between supply and demand, it is a striking fact that most tourism transactions bypass the self-styled 'travel trade'. From many travel surveys it seems that the 'travel trade' accounts for only one in ten transactions at most, the bulk of travel business being transacted direct between client and supplier. This is comparable to a situation in which a prospective car owner has to buy several hundred components, each from its separate manufacturer, and assemble his car in the backyard. Here surely is opportunity for information technology.

JOHN SEEKINGS

Consumer behavior in tourism

Introduction

Marketing scholars and practitioners, in tourism like elsewhere, set out to investigate consumer needs and attitudes in order to develop influential measures. Consumer research has developed as a discipline giving recommendations on which explanatory variables should be monitored in order to understand consumer decision processes. Contemporary marketing science attempts to explain consumer behavior by employing models, i.e. systems of hypotheses relating one or more dependent variables (such as buying probability, trial or repeat purchase) to several independent variables (motives, product comprehension, attitude, behavioral intention etc.).

Market response may be modeled on an aggregate level. In tourism, such a *macromodel* is easily recognized since it uses, say, number of visitors or bed-nights recorded in a destination, tourist receipts or market share as endogenous (dependent) variables. Often, these response criteria are directly linked to input factors like travel cost or distance, disposable income, relative prices, tourist advertising etc. (*black box model*). The tourist researcher or manager interested in the interior structure of the consumer's/tourist's mind will turn to a *micromodel* (a *behavioral model* in the proper sense of the term). This is indeed the category to be discussed more extensively later on.

Beforehand, another method of consumer behavior model building should be introduced. Depending on the principles of the construction technique one has to differentiate between stochastic, econometric, structural, and simulation models.

Stochastic models are most popular in analyzing repeat purchase behavior and brand loyalty. In a very simple application to tourism one could try to predict the future travel market shares of competing destinations by the present values of market shares multiplied by a matrix of destination switching probabilities.

Econometric models work on the macro-level. In marketing research they usually appear as single equations or, less frequently, as simultaneous equation systems reproducing market response operationalized by an aggregate variable (sales, market share).

Structural models involve a lot of behavioral refinements. The bulk of consumer studies has concentrated on this area, postulating intervening variables inside the 'black box' of the consumer's mental system.

'What-if' analyses are supported by any model once it has been calibrated successfully. Sometimes, however, a *simulation model* is tailored specifically to serve this purpose. Obviously, it has to be programmed for straightforward computer processing. Judgemental data and managerial estimates partly replacing objective parameter validation are permissible.

Classifying the traveler's decision process from a micro-perspective requires a more discriminating approach. A novel tourist product and/or an inexperienced tourist are likely to entail a process called *extensive problem solving*. In order to arrive at a travel decision the tourist runs through a sequel of perceptual and learning steps. On becoming aware of the new travel options he actively searches for information, develops his choice criteria, sets up an overall attitude towards the range of alternatives, establishes a preference for a particular tour operator etc.

A decision process known as *limited problem solving* alleviates the traveler's endeavor in avoiding conflict and coming to a conclusion. A satisfactory amount of product knowledge and firmly established choice criteria help in shortening the information-seeking period and reducing the decision time.

In *routinized response behavior* consumer information processing drops to a minimum level. Preferences are stable and the main question is whether the favorite alternative is still available. Loyalty *vis-à-vis* a tour operator, an agency, a resort, or a hotel is quite common in travel behavior.

Conversely, *impulse buying*, the fourth type of consumer decision process is a rare phenomenon in travel and tourism. For most consumers holiday and travel decisions are highly important with a great deal of ego-involvement. Therefore, they may not be dealt with spontaneously in a rapid booking action.

From the managerial point of view, structural models implemented for explaining extensive or limited problem solving deserve indepth treatment and will be given priority in this chapter.

Examples

In 1981, the Tourist Board of the Province of Carinthia, Austria, commissioned a research project on the travel behavior of the residents of the eastern provinces. The primary objective was to derive the behavioral underpinnings of a subsequent marketing strategy suitable for increasing Carinthia's share in the Austrian domestic travel market.

In its strategic marketing, planning a tourist destination faces the problems of product positioning and market segmentation. Positioning means optimizing the product attributes and condensing appeals and arguments into an effective advertising message. Segmentation is equivalent to classifying travelers into homogeneous clusters and defining one's target groups for selective market operation.

The Carinthia Tourist Board considered three other Austrian Provinces (Salzburg, Styria, and the Tyrol) and the Italian Province of Southern Tyrol to be the major competitors. Thus, the study had to reveal strengths and weaknesses for five alternative destinations.

The structural model outlined in Fig. 1 was exployed as a frame of reference and a practical guideline for data collection. Intention to visit Carinthia in the next summer season is the dependent variable. Solid lines indicate direct influence of the predictors; dashed lines indicate indirect influence. Amongst these explanatory variables are the eminent theoretical constructs 'image', 'attitude', and 'perceived risk'. Their conceptualization will be elaborated in the Implementation section. For the time being, suffice to say that 'image' is made up of emotional feelings, 'attitude' comprises more rational knowledge-based evaluations, and 'perceived risk' covers undesirable consequences of a trip the traveler seeks to avoid.

Each construct was measured on a multidimensional scale. Tables 1 and 2 and Fig. 2 summarize the results. The reader may verify that strengths and weaknesses of a destination are easily recognized. If the tourism manager can be assured that the emotional, rational, and risk-bearing assessment criteria do have a significant impact on destination preferences and

Table 1 Relative frequencies of image items attributed to Carinthia (%).

Luxury	36	Adventure	26
Pleasure	51	Safety	33
Tradition	30	Culture	23
Naturalness	29	Cosiness	41
Health	45	Sex	31
Romance	25	Sun	74
Sympathy	40	Hospitality	49
Freedom	46	Cosmopolitan	45
Social life	48		

No. of cases is 900 (= 100 %)

Table 2 Relative frequencies of attitude criteria selected as subjectively important and attributed to Carinthia.

	Selected as important (%)	Attributed to Carinthia (%)
Not overcrowded	64	7
Festivals	14	5
Swimming, aquatic sports	62	67
Mountaineering	38	17
Nudist bathing	8	11
Walking tours	64	38
Folkloristic events	31	21
Modern camping sites	12	13
Animation programs	9	7
Unspoiled environment	80	44
Sightseeing	50	18
Shopping facilities (trips)	36	13
Special arrangements for children	16	9
Fitness training program	17	16
Dietary and medical treatment	11	11
Good eating and drinking	66	44
Disco-dancing	21	19
Gourmet restaurants	63	46
Sociable native people	52	31
Beautiful landscape	78	51
Comfortable hotels	42	34
Friendly waiting personnel	75	48

No. of cases is 994 (= 100 %) for first and 890 (= 100 %) for second column due to respondents refusing answer after giving importance judgments.

travel intentions, then a conversion into marketing strategy and action planning is straightforward. In particular, the Carinthia Tourist Board carried on with a campaign 'Holiday with Friends' exploiting evaluative criteria like the friendliness of the local population rather than adventure or good value for money.

Benefits

There are several reasons why consumer behavior evolved as one of the constituent subjects within marketing science and marketing management. It should have become apparent in the Examples section that consumer research provides a stockpile of hypotheses in a particular application study. When designing

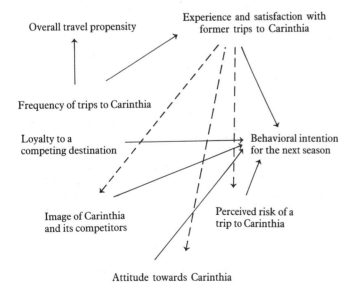

Figure 1 A structural model of travel behavior.

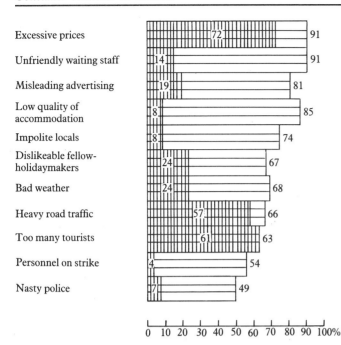

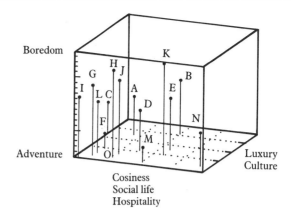

A: Salzburg – total sample
B: Salzburg – likers
C: Salzburg – dislikers

D: Carinthia – total sample
E: Carinthia – likers
F: Carinthia – dislikers

G: Southern Tyrol – total sample
H: Southern Tyrol – likers
I: Southern Tyrol – dislikers

J: Tyrol – total sample
K: Tyrol – likers
L: Tyrol – dislikers

M: Styria – total sample
N: Styria – likers
O: Styria – dislikers

Figure 3 Image space for five competing destinations.

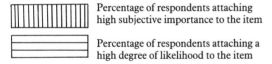

Percentage of respondents attaching high subjective importance to the item

Percentage of respondents attaching a high degree of likelihood to the item

Figure 2 Perceived risk towards Carinthia as a tourist destination.

a travel market, a guest or passenger survey, it is unnecessary or almost foolish to start from scratch each time and to neglect progress in behavioral model building.

It is also evident that influencing or even forecasting (combined with 'what-if' questions) travel behavior cannot succeed without, at least, some rudiments of an explanatory model. Behavioral research findings published in scientific journals, reports, and communications represent a collective learning process quite equivalent to an individual manager's collection of experience. (In fact, managerial expertise and learning by monitoring market response is systematically integrated into modern decision support systems.)

As consumer behavior deals with multiple causes and compound variables the measurement techniques are of special importance. Owing to a widespread reception of multivariate methods the marketing manager nowadays can rely on efficient data reduction and comfortable visualization of the research output. To continue with the Carinthia example, Fig. 3 depicts how the five competing destinations are located in a three-dimensional perceptual map. Separate measurements for the total sample, for Carinthia-likers and -dislikers increase the information yield. Long distances between the likers' and the dislikers' positions of a destination in the perceptual space signal a

highly distinctive image; short distances denote image erosion and lack of precision. Destinations far apart are unlikely to be substituted for each other while neighboring locations are under competitive threat.

Table 3 indicates another direction of how behavioral findings may be translated into strategic marketing. A concept known as *benefit segmentation* foresees that consumers be classified by their wants and desires sought in a tourist product. A cluster analysis applied to the Carinthia attitude data (i.e. to tourists' importance ratings for the benefits itemized) detects three 'natural' marketing segments of 1. Pretentious comfort seekers, 2. Juvenile water and sun lovers, and 3. Elderly walking tourists (age turned out to be a correlate of benefit bundles afterwards).

Implementation

Judging from consumer literature and research reports there is a limited number of variables particularly responsible for the explanatory power of behavioral models. A consumer's decision process reaches its crucial stage when the evaluation of alternatives takes place. Depending on the character of evaluative criteria employed the outcome may be portrayed by a theoretical construct such as 'image', 'attitude', 'perceived risk', and 'cognitive dissonance'. Only the fourth of these central constructs operates in the post-choice (post-purchase) situation whereas the remaining three are relevant to the cognitive mechanisms leading to a holiday/travel booking decision.

Table 3 Benefits sought by tourists as a basis for travel market segmentation.

Important benefits	Cluster 1 (%) $n_1=352$	Cluster 2 (%) $n_2=212$	Cluster 3 (%) $n_3=224$	Percentage of all travelers $(n=788)$
Not overcrowded	69.0	38.7	75.9	63.7
Festivals	19.9	7.1	9.8	13.6
Swimming, aquatic sports	74.7	78.3	25.4	62.2
Mountaineering	47.2	11.8	45.1	37.7
Nudist bathing	5.7	14.2	2.2	7.9
Walking tours	79.5	21.7	84.8	63.7
Folkloristic events	45.5	12.3	21.0	31.0
Modern camping sites	9.1	20.8	6.3	12.2
Animation programs	12.2	8.5	2.7	9.3
Unspoiled environments	91.8	49.1	86.6	80.3
Sightseeing	72.7	20.8	43.8	50.4
Shopping facilities (trips)	50.9	30.2	8.9	36.0
Special arrangements for children	23.3	8.5	6.7	16.2
Fitness training programs	18.5	15.6	5.4	16.5
Dietary and medical treatment	17.6	6.6	9.4	11.4
Good eating and drinking	83.5	57.7	38.4	66.1
Disco-dancing	19.0	33.5	2.2	20.8
Gourmet restaurants	92.9	42.5	30.8	62.7
Sociable native people	69.6	24.4	49.1	52.4
Beautiful landscape	92.3	45.3	84.4	77.6
Comfortable hotels	65.6	29.2	14.7	42.4
Friendly waiting personnel	94.9	54.2	64.7	75.0

Cluster 1: Pretentious comfort seekers
Cluster 2: Juvenile water and sun lovers
Cluster 3: Elderly walking tourists

Image

The image of a tourist product (a receiving country, a resort, a special type of trip, hotel services) consists of connotative and emotional criteria associated with the product. Images exist even in the absence of factual knowledge. Nevertheless, they simplify consumers' orientation *vis-à-vis* a puzzling world of consumables. Image measurement demands a multidimensional scaling instrument. Single word items, preferably nouns such as 'luxury', 'adventure', 'boredom' etc. are typical image attributes. A particularly equipped measurement technique uses a set of calibrated photos (nonverbal image measurement) instead of verbal material. Whatever the shortcomings in terms of objective assessment may be, as a stereotype the image governs (at least) the early stages of product evaluation and drags the consumer into a state of sympathy or aversion, high or low preference for a tourist product.

Attitude

Fortunately, consumer decision making is not entirely image-bound or governed by nonrational 'reasoning'. With an increase in product comprehension due to active search for information the consumer acquires choice criteria relating to the 'real' properties of tourist products. He generates an attitude while evaluating product alternatives by their goal-satisfying capabilities. Motives and some degree of emotional arousal are still implicit in attitude formation. However, whereas everybody is allowed to have an image, attitude measurement should be directed to respondents with personal experience or factual knowledge from reliable sources. In consumer research attitudinal measurement has matured into a behavioral subdiscipline.

Perceived risk

Human beings are not equally risk-prone. There are risk-averters, in tourism and elsewhere, who are inclined to approach a travel product by judging its undesirable or even dangerous implications. Bad weather, unfriendly locals, airport personnel on strike etc. are uncomfortable enough. Inedibility of local food, contagious diseases, political unrest etc. are worse. Consumer research invented the concept of perceived risk to capture the phenomenon of consumer risk reduction (minimizing disutility, economists might say). For a travel decision to have risky consequences two conditions must hold: the consequence is not negligible and avoiding it is of subjective importance, and there is some likelihood that the consequence can actually occur (i.e. the uncertainty component). Perceived risk motivates intensified information seeking and (if not properly reduced) erects a consumption barrier around the unacceptable alternatives. Of course, it is not equally operative in every consumer decision process. (But, perhaps, a tiny risk-averter hides in most of us.)

Cognitive dissonance

Imagine now a tourist who has booked an inclusive tour from an operator's catalog 4 months in advance. While waiting for his journey to start he gets exposed to competitors' advertising messages. Was it right or wrong to take just that decision? Then, immediately before departure that very travel agency where the consumer has booked announces a last minute £100 reduction. Post-choice conflict becomes rampant. In order to cover such post-decisional regret, consumer research adopted the concept of cognitive dissonance from behavioral science. In its worst appearance dissonance is conceived as consumer dissatisfaction due to a travel product that fails to come up to pre-purchase expectations. Obviously, dissonance prevents a tourist from becoming a loyal visitor to a resort or from patronizing a hotel or restaurant. Disturbances in the consumption pattern suspected of arousing dissonance have to be monitored carefully.

Other variables

There are motivational and cognitive states preceding, modifying, or succeeding the evaluative stage represented by the above-mentioned constructs. For example, *awareness*, *overt search*, or *product comprehension* may be considered prior to attitude formation. *Confidence* in one's own beliefs and values may moderate the effects of attitude on purchase intention. Many more demographic, socioeconomic, and psychological (personality traits, buying habits) variables beyond the scope of this chapter may also interfere.

Assessment

It is imperative for a practitioner in travel and tourism to understand correctly what he can expect from consumer research. Behavioral science is not an advanced discipline in a sense that it generates accurate forecasts deduced from a general theory. To give a trivial example, it is nonsense to state that a 5 per cent increase in the advertising budget of a tourist resort will always boost arrivals by 3.5 per cent. In brief, holiday and travel behavior necessitates parameter estimation in every single application; a particular model structure (i.e. the layout of relationships between variables) may, however, promise some degree of generalization.

Behavioral researchers often fail to pay proper attention to the conditions under which a proposed model is said to hold. Therefore, there are a few suggestions for the explanatory constructs outlined in the preceding section:

1. Tourist products exhibit a number of characteristics differentiating them from branded products/services for which the bulk of consumer studies has been conducted. Holiday planning usually arouses a considerable amount of ego-involvement comparable to purchasing consumer durables. The explanatory power of the product image, therefore, is confined to the early stages of a decision process and, on the whole, is lower than for convenience goods.

2. Tourist products are much more complex than managers themselves are willing to admit. Imagine, for example, a restaurant where numerous attributes – from the quality of menu items to sophistication of wine service, atmosphere, erroneously neglected details like closeness of tables and many more – accumulate into customer satisfaction. To allow for product complexity a multidimensional measurement technique is strongly advised for all 'central' constructs.

3. A travel product sometimes forces the tourist into an attraction-avoidance conflict (a desire for an exotic destination v. the inconvenience of a longhaul trip). Perceived risk in this case is recommended as a supplementary variable.

4. Tourist decisions may depend on compromise (one cannot maximize comfort and unspoiled nature simultaneously). An interview and analytical technique confronting respondents with a set of 'real-world' alternatives (conjoint measurement) should then be adopted.

5. The interval of time elapsing between the choice of a travel product (inclusive tour) and the beginning of consumption (departure) creates a favorable climate for dissonance arousal. Tour operators still do not take proper account of this phenomenon.

6. In travel or guest surveys the timing of field research is crucial and greatly influences the outcome. A holiday attribute like weather is of utmost importance to a tourist while

staying in his resort. Weeks later, after the past holiday has undergone a phase of glorification, weather drops in subjective importance and 'manmade' criteria such as friendliness of the local representatives dramatically gain salience. Unfortunately, there is no foolproof recipe for evading the pitfalls in diagnosing consumer behavior.

Conclusion

In a modern marketing textbook a chapter on consumer behavior is indispensable. Influencing the behavior of others is the kernel of marketing management. A solid background in consumer behavior makes the manager appreciate theory-guided market research rather than *ad hoc* data collection. A glimpse of model construction principles enables the decision maker to assess what the market research department or a commercial institute offers him.

Given the dominance of small, family-operated businesses in the tourist industry the commissioning of market studies by National Tourist Offices, Ministries, Tourist Boards, Trade Associations etc. becomes routine work in tourism policy and promotion. Thus, continuous checking of theoretical soundness and managerial relevance is not certain.

A check-list of control criteria should always touch upon the following questions:

1. Are the hypothesized relationships between dependent and explanatory variables made explicit?
2. What are the precautions to ascertain that the 'model algebra' (see Bettman *et al.*, 1975) of a behavioral study captures the tourist's cognitive algebra of travel product evaluation reasonably well?
3. Does the study utilize advanced measurement techniques (multidimensional instead of unidimensional methods) to provide the manager with concise but still informative research output?

Focus on small business

Management scientists should abandon the idea that everything in business needs a scientific treatment. In many instances common sense will do just as well. The owner of a 20-bed resort hotel knowing nothing about consumer research may be an excellent host just by keeping close personal contact with his most loyal guests and relying on word-of-mouth communication. The need for consumer behavior expertise arises as soon as customer relations become more anonymous, face-to-face contact is replaced by market research, and word-of-mouth communication is increasingly supported by advertising.

In principle, small business has one powerful remedy to offset economies of scale and other competitive advantages of large companies, i.e. cooperation and joint promotional programs. Combined efforts with respect to tourist behavior are customary both in *travel market surveys* (analyzing potential customers in their place of permanent residence) and in *guest surveys* covering a resort, a tourist region, or a receiving country.

In a multi-client travel market survey an individual hotel or travel agency can participate directly or through a trade association at low cost. Guest surveys have recently been extended to nationwide projects in Switzerland (since 1982), Austria (since 1984), and Yugoslavia (since 1987). The results are accessible by Federal and Provincial Governments, Communes, local tourist boards, and all sorts of nonprofit organizations and business units.

Further reading

So far, there is no textbook on tourist behavior which fully incorporates the recent developments in theory and measurement of buying behavior. Therefore, a few selective sources are recommended for consumer behavior in general:

Bagozzi, R. P., *Causal Models in Marketing* (John Wiley, 1980). The latest development in structural model building combining theory and measurement in an integrated latent-variable–multiple-indicator system.

Bettman, J. R., Capon, N. and Lutz, R. J., 'Cognitive algebra in multi-attribute attitude models', *Journal of Marketing Research*, vol. 12 (May 1975), pp. 151–64.

Green, P. E. and Tull, D. S., *Research for Marketing Decisions* (Prentice Hall, 4th edition, 1978). This is still the preferred option for readers interested in multivariate methods applied to consumer behavior measurement.

Howard, J. A. and Sheth, J. N., *The Theory of Buyer Behavior* (John Wiley, 1969). This famous book is still as fascinating as it was when it was published 20 years ago.

Howard, J. A., *Consumer Behavior: Application of Theory* (McGraw-Hill, 1977). Conveys a more concise treatment of fundamental concepts.

Kroeber-Riel, W., *Konsumentenverhalten* (Vahlen, 3rd edition, 1984). Beyond doubt, this would be the world's leading and most comprehensive textbook if it were written in English.

McFadden, D., 'The choice theory approach to market research', *Marketing Science*, vol. 5, no. 4 (Fall 1986), pp. 275–97. This author provides an up-to-date status report on consumer choice models recognizing how disciplines such as economics and econometrics, mathematical psychology, and marketing science encourage each other in exchanging results to their mutual benefit.

Mazanec, J. and Mikulicz, H., *Gästebefragung Österreich 1984–1986*, Vienna: The Austrian Society for Applied Research in Tourism. These reports demonstrate how to organize, draft and exploit a national guest survey.

Organization for Economic Cooperation and Development, *International Comparability of Tourism Statistics* (OECD, 1983). This document comments on global tourism statistics which are the base material for macro-modelling.

The progress of basic research is particularly documented in the *Journal of Consumer Research* and the *Journal of Marketing Research*, both published by the American Marketing Association.

Applications to travel and tourism

Darden, W. R. and Darden, D. D. 'A study of vacation life styles', *Marketing Travel and Tourism* (The Travel Research Association, 7th Annual Conference Proceedings, Salt Lake City, 1976), pp. 231–6. This article describes numerous attempts to construct a traveler typology suited for travel market segmentation.

Lewis, R. C., 'The basis of hotel selection', *The Cornell HRA Quarterly*, vol. 25, no. 2 (1984), pp. 54–69.

Lewis, R. C., 'Isolating differences in hotel attributes', *The Cornell HRA Quarterly*, vol. 25, no. 3 (1984), pp. 64–77.

Lewis, R. C., 'Predicting hotel choice: the factors underlying perception' *The Cornell HRA Quarterly*, vol. 25, no. 4 (1985), pp. 82–96. This series demonstrates convincingly how hotel and restaurant management can adopt behavioral hypotheses and advanced measurement techniques to streamline marketing action.

Mayo, E. J. and Jarvis, L. P., *The Psychology of Leisure Travel* (CBI Publishing Co., 1981). This is an easy-to-read introduction into the basics of travel behavior.

Mazanec, J., 'Practising the causal approach to consumer behavior model building: an example from tourism research', *Der Markt*, vol. 21, no. 4 (1982), pp. 127–33. This paper explains the latent-variable-multiple-indicator approach to travel behavior and outlines a sample study.

McIntosh, R. W. and Goeldner, C. R., *Tourism: Principles, Practices, Philosophies* (John Wiley, 5th edition, 1986). Chapters 4, 6, 11, 12, 13 of this widely used textbook are devoted to behavioral concepts.

Moutinho, L., 'Consumer behavior in tourism', *European Journal of Marketing*, vol. 21, no. 10 (1987).

Ritchie, J. R. B. and Goeldner, C. R., *Travel, Tourism, and Hospitality Research: A Handbook for Managers and Researchers* (John Wiley, 1987). Chapters 7, 8, 17, 35–39, and 42 deal with behavioral topics in a concise and introductory manner.

Holiday surveys

Medlik, S., *Holiday Surveys Examined* (London: Horwath & Horwath (UK) Ltd., 1983). The author briefly characterizes the methodology and contents of the major European Travel Market Surveys.

Studienkreis für Tourismus, *So Reisten die Europäer* (Starnberg: Studienkreis für Tourismus, 1982). The proceedings contain abstracts of European travel survey findings (papers translated into English).

JOSEF A. MAZANEC

Content analysis in tourism

Introduction

A fundamental aspect of international market analysis is obtaining viable global information for use in strategic analysis. Although the concept of marketing information systems was formulated to help managers incorporate internal and external factors into their planning, it did not offer any procedures to analyze themes, concepts, and values in various cultures. One such methodology that has yet to be used on a wide-ranging international basis is that of content analysis. Content analysis is a research technique for quantifying and comparing sociological, cultural, and political influences and trends, which has evolved since the 1920s, largely in social science applications. Today, aided by the use of optical scanners, which can read huge volumes of material inexpensively, and sophisticated, computer-aided coding and tabulation methods capable of reading languages such as Japanese, Chinese, Arabic, and many others, content analysis has great promise as a tool for international marketing analysis.

Marketing managers need an awareness of the world to be able to make global decisions. In international marketing, more than a general cultural and social 'awareness' is required to formulate effective international marketing strategy; managers require systematic global information-collecting techniques to support their analysis and decision making. There are many accepted marketing information systems and techniques which help managers incorporate internal and external factors into their planning. Content analysis provides reliable qualitative data on cross-cultural markets.

Content analysis uses an objective, systematic approach to measure the meaning of communicated material through the classification and evaluation of selected words, themes, concepts, and/or icons. It can be performed on books, motion pictures, radio and television programs. Most broadly, content analysis is any systematic attempt to codify the subject matter contained in a given set of communications. As we will see, this includes advertising and promotion, with the attendant implications and potential outcomes for marketing practitioners. It has been used extensively in analyzing US advertising content, particularly since 1975.

Examples

Early applications (1920s) of content analysis, involving nonobtrusive studies of cultures and societies, were first used by journalists searching for sociological interpretations. These investigations were centered at the Columbia University School of Journalism and studied American newspapers in order to discern trends and concepts. The technique is still used to monitor newspapers and, more recently, to perform more sophisticated analyses of content, with the aid of computers. A series of studies by De Weese (1976) described computer content analysis of *The New York Times* and *The Wall Street Journal*. DeWeese found combinations of categories and/or words in single sentences more useful indicators of meaning than mere frequency of occurrences of those words in an article or publication as a whole.

An article by Kale, McIntyre and Weir (1987) on marketing overseas tour packages to the youth segment is an example of content analysis in relation to tourism. The youth segment, consisting of 18- to 35-year-olds, is a potential market for tours and travel services. A content analysis was conducted to determine the elements stressed by tour operators and revealed that tours marketed to the youth segment used fewer verbal descriptions and more photographs in their literature than those marketed to the general public. The photographs tended to depict tour members engaged in a variety of activities.

Factor analysis, which assigns numerical values to various aspects of selected themes, and then positive and negative values, can be based on content analysis where both frequency and relationships can be determined within the verbal materials. Courtney and Lockeretz (1971) analyzed advertisements in *Life*, *Newsweek*, *The New Yorker*, and *US News & World Reports* during a 1-week period in April 1970. Codes were developed by number, sex, occupation, and activities of adults appearing in the advertisements, and by product type. Courtney and Lockeretz found few advertisements offensive to women, but most of the sampled advertisements emphasized the role of males in value systems (1.4 males to 1.0 females); and, 45 per cent of the men compared to only 9 per cent of the women were depicted in working roles. The content analysis revealed various sex differentiated stereotypes in the advertisements. Wagner and Banos (1973) conducted a content analysis study in 1973 and found twice as many magazine advertisements which portrayed women working and an emphasis on women with roles outside the home. Furthermore, Belkaoui and Belkaoui (1976) compared a content analysis of 1958 magazine advertisements, with advertisements in 1972 and 1973 and showed that the role of women as depicted in the advertisements was changing.

Namenwirth and Bibee (1975) reported a study of US and UK newspaper editorials using factor analysis to derive the relevant themes for the content analysis. Factor analysis produces a numerical value for each factor or theme. To determine whether the themes identified are real rather than statistical artifacts, Weber (1983) suggests that three steps should be taken:

1. Examine editorials with the highest positive and negative scores.
2. Examine how the words in the texts are classified.
3. Compare the texts with other texts containing the same theme.

Themes at the positive and negative poles are typically opposing resolutions of this controversy.

Implementation and assessment

Early content analysis methods were relatively simple. The researcher used various means to determine what words or themes were important in a given type of material by looking in the indices of textbooks on the subject; asking scholars in the field; or holding group interviews with appropriate experts. Later refinements were added in better methods of definitions of unit analysis; and, applying distinctions such as latent v. manifest content, measurement of meanings, and conceptual understanding.

Units of analysis were further specified to include: words, characters (persons or institutions cited), themes (concepts), and topics (whole units of communication – an article, news item etc.). North *et al.* (1963) led early development of these refinements and of methods of measuring the intensity and frequency of variables.

According to Berelson (1952), 'The theme is among the most useful units of content analysis, particularly for the study of the effect of communications upon public opinion, because it takes the form in which issues and attitudes are usually discussed. But it is at the same time among the most difficult units of analysis.... One elaborate, complex method of attacking this problem is to break the theme down into its components, to analyze them, and then to reconstruct the theme by mechanical process.' Defining categories permits a classification of data on the basis of selected concepts and measures of the intensity and frequency of occurrence can be represented by the categories. North *et al.* (1963) developed coder skills in reducing paragraphs and sentences into 'atomic themes', or perceptions of what constituted an unbreakable unit.

In 1957, Osgood *et al.* made a contribution to the refinement

of meaning in the content of verbal materials as a methodology with their definition of semantic differentiation *The Measurement of Meaning*. They described 'the successive allocation of a concept to a point in the multidimensional semantic space by selection from among a set of given scaled semantic alternatives. Difference in the meaning between two concepts is then merely a function of the differences in their respective allocations within the same space, i.e. it is a function of the multidimensional distance between the two points'. Selection and the precise definition of the units to be analyzed is the most complex part of content analysis. Once those have been established, researchers can use the more mechanical means to count the frequency of occurrence.

Innovations in automated content analysis

Although content analysis was used in an objective and systematic manner starting in the 1920s and 1930s, it was performed largely by hand until the 1960s when computers began to play an important role. Stone and his associates (1969) explained that the introduction of optical scanners solved a key problem in content analysis by greatly reducing the cost of reading large volumes of material.

'Today, researchers can employ an optical scanner that reads almost any typed or printed page and then transfers the text to an electronic storage medium such as tape or disk. This device, the Kurzweil Data Entry Machine (KDEM) is very accurate and fast' (Weber, 1985). Such devices have encouraged development of much more complex content analysis techniques than were feasible previously. One electronic database known as VU/TEXT now allows access to the full text of major newspapers from coast to coast in the United States, as well as a number of national magazines.

Computers further improved the processes of content analyses by counting and cross-tabulation of data quickly and economically, and often according to more sophisticated schemes than had previously been feasible. 'One of the most important advantages of computer-aided content analysis over hand-coded and interpretive content analysis is that the rules for coding text are made explicit. The public nature of the coding rules yields tools for inquiry that, when applied to a variety of texts, generate formally comparable results' (Stone *et al.*, 1969).

The use of computers forces the researcher to state explicit categories and rules for identification of the characteristics under study. It disciplines researchers by making them focus on objective content as a function of both inference and measurement, without becoming preoccupied or biased in either direction.

Paradoxically, one drawback of computer-aided content analysis lies in the very strength of computers, being able to handle a huge volume of data compared to manual methods. To obtain meaningful analysis of optically-scanned and computer-tabulated material requires sophisticated methods of data reduction, to consolidate masses of detail to enable computer processes to yield richness without diffusion or loss of content.

There are dozens of firms providing thousands of computer accessed, online information databases. The growth in the electronic information industry grew out of the need to control the massive documentation inherent in medical research and the space program. The Lockheed Corporation worked for NASA and then turned its expertise in storing and searching enormous files to commercial ends with its subsidiary, Dialog Information Services. There are also electronic databases available, one of the first dealt with Japanese markets. The Japanese Economic Daily has the latest trend-shaping business news, and it is transmitted by satellite to the United States each day. 'In just 90 seconds you can download more than 50 headlines that will tell you whether business ventures or political events that occurred 15 hours ago in Japan will affect your corporate activities today' (Stein, 1987). Japan Computer Technology and Applications Abstracts is another electronic data source which tracks over 700 Japanese technical journals with 7,000 abstracts a year. Although the Japanese language prevents many business executives from learning about Japanese inventions, there are now technological advances that document Japanese patent applications (in English). These are available electronically through JAPIO database, the Japanese Patent Information Organization.

A global information network is growing which will lead to improved strategic analysis and planning.

International marketing applications

Content analysis can be used productively in international marketing to monitor the social, economic, cultural and technological environment in which the marketing organization is operating or wishes to operate. It can be a valuable predictor of the characteristics and behavior of target markets. Content analysis can be used to find international/cultural differences in communication content; to gain an understanding of psychological states of mind (including attitudinal, personality, and behavioral variables) of individual, group, and cultural units. Abell (1978) described a 'strategic window' through which the corporation could see the right mix of cultural, economic, and business conditions for success in the international environment.

Global technology monitoring is based on the premise that innovations are visible in the verbal materials of society before their commercialization and acceptance. Monitoring developments around the world can reveal marketing opportunities. Companies lack sophisticated intelligence networks or the research methodology to use electronic searches effectively. By developing an integrated information system, a multinational firm can gather information globally to support potential marketing strategies. Marketing executives who rely on their reading and their judgment for international intelligence gathering are usually interested in news, or information from subordinates, and various external sources, none of which are known to be dependable, coordinated, or systematic.

A comparison of advertising content in India and the United States was done by Singh and Huang (1962), selecting a representative magazine from each country. Through content analysis it was found that larger advertisements were used in the United States than in India; there was a tendency toward multicolor advertisements in the United States; Indian adver-

tisers always used black and white illustrations; US advertisements have more food, prestige, social approval, sex appeal, luxury and reliance appeals than Indian advertisers. Singh and Huang (1962) determined a trend toward more isolation in US advertisements than in India: 'Indian advertising is similar to American advertising around 1900–1920. The changes in US advertising resulted from the growth of the "affluent economy" and the application of scientific methods to the study of advertising.'

Suzuki (1979; 1980) documented the changing pattern of advertising strategy by Japanese business firms in the United States. He analyzed every page of *Business Week* and *Newsweek* from 1965 to 1977 on which Japanese business firms appeared. Suzuki discovered that the Japanese must adapt to the US way of marketing to be competitive in the US market. The results of the study indicated that Japanese advertising strategy in the United States passed through the following stages: nationalism, product attributes, challenge, and world market orientation.

Madden, Caballero, and Matsukubo (1986) analyzed the information content of US and Japanese magazine advertising. Japanese advertising was found to be more informative than US magazine advertising. The authors advised American advertisers to '...employ an agency with expertise distinctly relating to magazine advertising. Rather than going in with a monolithic view of Japanese advertising, foreign firms should recognize each medium's unique role in the total media mix.'

Researchers at the Free University of Amsterdam (led by Irmtraud Gallhofer) are using human coders to measure decision making based on ministerial debates. Using computers, Boden (1977) analyzed wire service reports concerning terrorist incidents. Cultural systems have been studied using computers to count words and categories of political documents (Namenwirth, 1973; Weber, 1981.) Content analysis has been used successfully to evaluate political conflicts in various international contexts. Content analysis seems to be quite useful in research on international values. Lasswell and Leites (1949) used content analysis during the 1930s to develop a set of structures of political symbols and themes (freedom, democracy, fascism, and communism); characteristic cultural responses (violence, negotiation, and the manipulation of cultural symbols); and cultural-political values pertaining to acquisition (indulgence, deprivation). Since content analysis can be used unobtrusively to assess political and cultural forces, it is ideal for measuring, at a distance, prevalent beliefs, values, ideologies, and other indicators of culture. Various indicators can be used to assess how the society is organized, and how its institutions function. Also, comparative studies using content analysis can be used to view differences and similarities among various groups at particular times, or over centuries.

Conclusion

The development of valid cultural indicators is lagging behind computer applications in content analysis. It is difficult to measure the amount of influence there is in communication content. Although the making of inferences from a symbolic medium is the essence of content analysis, inferences are at best very inexact science.

The purpose of marketing, especially advertising, is somewhat like propaganda – it is to persuade. In order to persuade, the elements which influence must be known. Content analysis has been used to determine the influence of political concepts, and this objective technique is equally well-suited for advertisers who wish better to understand themes which influence international target audiences, as well as international advertisers who need better to understand the themes prevailing in the cultures in which they intend to advertise/market.

Today, moving into a new market with inadequate understanding of the prevailing social, cultural, political and economic norms is almost a formula for disaster. The availability of content analysis as a reliable and economically feasible indicator of the local climate is an auspicious development for international marketers and one which should not be overlooked as they assemble a sophisticated kit of international marketing analysis and planning tools.

Software/databases

Several software programs have been developed to assist in data reduction and analysis, including TEXTPACK (distributed in Mannheim, Federal Republic of Germany). TEXTPACK is available in English or German and runs on micros (Apples, IBM-PCs), minis (Prime Computers), and larger mainframes with FORTRAN 77 compilers. TEXTPACK will perform frequency counts of words, key-word-in-context (KWIC) lists, key-word-out-of-context (KWOC) lists, comparisons of vocabularies, cross-references, procedures for iterative dictionary construction, retrievals of text units, reduction of text, and interfaces for statistical packages.

While it is beyond the scope of this chapter to evaluate computer packages for content analysis, there are many systems available. One product which bears mention because it is a practical application of computer-assisted content widely used commercially in libraries and businesses is InfoTrac. The system consists of a central unit consisting of one controller, one multihost, one videodisk player and interface cards and cables attached to PCs. References to nearly a half-million articles drawn from business, technical and general interest publications are integrated into a single comprehensive database. Several years of retrospective material are included with indexing to the latest issues of the covered publications added monthly. *The New York Times* and *Wall Street Journal* are included for the tracking of current events.

A proliferation of new computer software packages dealing with foreign languages, computer translation, optical scanning of languages using non-Roman alphabets or characters, and the like are being marketed at the time of writing. The Apple computer Macintosh, for instance, can accommodate Chinese (FeiMa, Kaihin Brushwriter), Japanese (EgWord, KanjiTalk), Korean (MacHangul), Hebrew (Mac-InHebrew, Achbar), and Arabic (Lukos, 1987; 'Arabic Mac' 1987). [The Arabic Macintosh software provides right-to-left word processing, conforms completely to the idiosyncrasies of the written Arabic language, and controls for ligatures, numeric formats, and accommodates Urdu, Farsi, and Malay languages.] These software programs contain dictionaries and translation guidelines. Further development of optical scanners, word processing, and computer translation will facilitate rapid advances in multi-lingual applications of international content

analysis, some of which will be of direct benefit in international marketing applications.

Further reading

Abell, D. F., 'Strategic windows', *Journal of Marketing* (July 1978), pp. 21–6.

Alsop, R., 'US concerns seek inspiration for products overseas', *The Wall Street Journal* (3 January 1985), p. 13.

'Arabic Mac', *Macworld*, vol. 4, no. 6 (June 1987), p. 109.

Belk, R. W. and Pollay, R. W., 'Images of ourselves: the good life in twentieth-century advertising', *Journal of Consumer Research*, vol. 11, no. 4 (March 1985), pp. 887–97.

Belkaoui, A. and Belkaoui, J. M., 'A comparative analysis of the roles portrayed by women in print advertisements: 1958, 1970, 1972', *Journal of Marketing Research*, vol. 13 (May 1976), pp. 168–72.

Berelson, B., *Content Analysis in Communication Research* (Free Press, 1952).

Boden, M., *Artificial Intelligence and Natural Man* (Basic Books, 1977).

Bonoma, T. V. and Rosenberg, H., 'Theory-based content analysis: a social influence perspective for evaluating group process', *Social Science Research*, vol. 7 (September 1978), pp. 213–56.

Bright, J. R., 'Evaluating signals of technological change', *Harvard Business Review*, vol. 48 (1970), pp. 64–72.

Burton, D. M., 'Automated concordances and word-indexes: machine decisions and editorial revisions', *Computers and the Humanities*, vol. 16 (1982), pp. 195–218.

Courtney, A. E. and Lockeretz, S. W., 'A woman's place: an analysis of the roles portrayed by women in magazine advertisements', *Journal of Marketing Research*, vol. 8 (February 1971), pp. 92–5.

DeWeese, L. C., 'Computer content analysis of printed media: a feasibility study', *Public Opinion Quarterly*, vol. 40 (1976), pp. 92–100.

DeWeese, L. C., 'Computer content analysis of "Day-old" newspapers: a feasibility study', *Public Opinion Quarterly*, vol. 41 (1977), pp. 91–4.

Festinger, L., *A Theory of Cognitive Dissonance* (Stanford University Press, 1957).

Fuchs, P. E., 'Macintosh invades Japan', *BCS* [Boston Computer Society] -*Mac* (August 1985), pp. 9–10.

Healey, J. S. and Kassarjian, H. H., 'Advertising substantiation and advertising response: a content analysis of magazine advertisements', *Journal of Marketing*, vol. 47 (Winter 1983), pp. 107–17.

Holsti, O. R., *Content Analysis for the Social Sciences and Humanities* (Addison-Wesley, 1969).

Kale, S. H., McIntyre, R. P. and Weir, K. M., 'Marketing Overseas Tour Packages to the Youth Segment: An Empirical Analysis', *Journal of Travel Research*, vol. 25, no. 4 (Spring 1987), pp. 20–4.

Kassarjian, H. H., 'Content analysis in consumer research', *Journal of Consumer Research*, vol. 4 (June 1977), pp. 8–18.

Klingemann, H. D., 'Cultural indicators based on content analysis', *Quality and Quantity*, vol. 16 (1982), pp. 1–18.

Krippendorff, K., *Content Analysis: An Introduction to its Methodology* (Sage Publishing, 1980).

Lasswell, H. D. and Leites, N., *Language of Politics: Studies in Quantitative Semantics* (Steward Publishing, 1949).

Lukos, G., 'More multilingual computing', *BCS – Mac* (May 1987), pp. 19–23.

Madden, C. S., Caballero, M. J. and Matsukubo, S., 'Analysis of information content in US and Japanese magazine advertising', *Journal of Advertising*, vol. 15, no. 3 (1986), pp. 38–45.

Namenwirth, J. Z., 'The wheels of time and the interdependence of value change', *Journal of Interdisciplinary History*, vol. 3 (1973), pp. 649–83.

Namenwirth, J. Z., 'Why cultural indicators?' *Cultural Indicators: An International Symposiom*, G. Melischek (ed.) (Austrian Academy of Science, 1984).

Namenwirth, J. Z. and Bibee, R., 'Speech codes in the press', *Journal of Communication*, vol. 25 (1975), pp. 50–63.

North, R. C., Holsti, O. R., Zaninovich, M. G. and Zinnes, D. A., *Content Analysis: A Handbook with Applications for the Study of International Crisis* (Northwestern University Press, 1963).

Oakman, R. L., *Computer Methods of Literary Research Columbia* (University of South Carolina Press, 1980).

Oakman, R. L., Stone, P. J. and Kelly, E. F., 'Computer aided content analysis', *Handbook of Social Science Research Methods*, R. B. Smith and P. K. Manning, eds (Irvington Publishing, 1980).

Osgood, C. E., Suci, G. J. and Tannenbaum, P. H., *The Measurement of Meaning* (University of Illinois Press, 1957).

Popko, E. S., *Key-Word-in-Context Bibliographic Indexing: Release 4.0 Users Manual.* (Harvard University, Laboratory for Computer Graphics and Spatial Analysis, 1980).

Sebald, H., 'Studying national character through comparative content analysis', *Social Forces*, vol. 40 (May 1962), pp. 318–22.

Simmons, E. S., 'JAPIO – Japanese Patent Applications Online', *Online*, vol. 10, no. 4 (July 1986), pp. 51–8.

Singh, P. N. and Huang, S. C., 'Some socio-cultural and psychological dominants of advertising in India: A comparative study', *Journal of Social Psychology*, vol. 57 (Spring 1962), pp. 113–21.

Snider, J. G. and Osgood, C. E. (eds), *Semantic Differential Technique: A Sourcebook* (Aldine Publishing, 1969).

Stein, P., 'The latest import', *Dowline* (May/June 1987), pp. 10–11.

Stone, P. J., Dunphy, D. C., Smith, M. S. *et al*, *The General Inquirer: A Computer Approach to Content Analysis* (MIT Press, 1969).

Suzuki, N., 'Changing patterns of advertising strategy by Japanese business firms in the US market: content analysis' (Paper presented to the annual conference of the Academy of International Business, Las Vegas, Nevada, June 17–20, 1979).

Suzuki, N., 'The changing pattern of advertising strategy by Japanese business firms in the US market: Content analysis', *Journal of International Business Studies*, vol. 11 (Winter 1980), pp. 63–72.

Tomita, H., 'The latest import', *Dowline*, (May/June 1987), pp. 10–11.

Wagner, L. C. and Banos, J. B., 'A woman's role: a follow-up analysis of the roles portrayed by women in magazine advertisements', *Journal of Marketing Research*, vol. 10 (May 1973), pp. 213–14.

Weber, R. P., 'Society and economy in the western world system', *Social Forces*, vol. 59 (1981), pp. 1130–48.

Weber, R. P., 'Measurement models for content analysis', *Quality and Quantity*, vol. 17 (April 1983), pp. 127–49.

Weber, R. P., 'Content analytic cultural indicators', *Cultural Indicators: An International Symposium*, G. Melischek (ed.), (Austrian Academy of Science, 1984).

Weber, R. P., *Basic Content Analysis* (Sage Publications, Series: Quantitative Applications in the Social Sciences, Series No. 49, 1985).

DAVID R. WHEELER

Convention market

Introduction

Business travel is estimated to be worth in excess of £1 billion annually to the UK alone and is considered a major growth opportunity for world tourism. The expansion of international organizations, associations and multinational corporations, has created a demand for increased communication and interrelation at all levels.

There are as many organizations and associations as there are reasons for meeting and topics to discuss, but broadly speaking there are five categories which can be identified.

1. International organizations (government)
2. International organizations (nongovernment)
3. Multinational corporations
4. National, provincial and local associations and institutions.
5. National and local businesses/corporations.

Commercial traffic has been excluded on the grounds that it is nondiscretionary travel and, as such, would respond less to promotional stimulus than the other market sectors.

The Union of International Associations (UIA) estimates there were 4,864 meetings held by international governmental and nongovernmental organizations during 1983, a growth rate of 5.6 per cent since 1950. However, the last 3 years have produced some of the fastest growth – an average of 8.5 per cent per year.

However the 'International' segment represents the tip of the iceberg of the meetings industry, accounting for less than 5 per cent of the total with national, regional, and local associations and corporations accounting for the lion's share of the meetings market.

In addition, current estimates place visitor spending by convention delegates at 3 times that of the 'leisure' visitor, making this an extremely attractive sector in cost-benefit terms to destinations equipped to service the needs of the conference delegate.

The criteria considered desirable for a successful conference destination are as follows:

1. An attractive destination
2. A variety of meeting facilities
3. A range of good accommodation
4. Good access by air, road and rail, etc.
5. Civic commitment to hosting delegates
6. A coordinated approach to destination marketing and visitor servicing

The growth of purpose-built convention centers not only in the United Kingdom and Europe but particularly in Asia, ensures the international convention organizer continues to enjoy a 'buyers' market' with a wide range of destinations to choose from. In turn, competing destinations are now spending vast sums of money on upgrading existing facilities or investing in new infrastructure to allow them to increase their market share.

There is a growing awareness of the need for a coordinated approach on the part of a destination wishing to make an impact on the conventions or meetings market, and a number of cities (London; Birmingham; Glasgow) have established Convention and Visitor Bureaux along the lines of the US model.

Examples

The International Association of Convention and Visitor Bureaux (IACVB) comprises more than 280 members worldwide. A Bureau is a non profit-making organization which represents a city or urban area in a 'corporate destination' approach to marketing and visitor servicing, irrespective of purpose of visit.

In UK cities many tourist attractions, amenities and convention facilities are in the care of the public sector, whereas the servicing of the visitor is largely in the hands of the private sector. Any organization purporting to represent the total destination must therefore forge a partnership between the public and private sectors.

The Bureau is the single entity which brings together all the component parts – local government, accommodation suppliers, transportation companies, venues, restaurants, attractions, entertainment, the arts, retailers, travel suppliers – in a 'one-stop' shopping approach to tourism.

There is an increasing commitment to tourism as a tool of economic development. Business tourism is considered particularly important in the revitalization of inner cities, being a major revenue earner and an increasingly important source of employment.

Visitor and Convention Bureau professionals offer the association and corporate meeting planner a wide variety of advisory and administrative services which are not available elsewhere. Since the Bureau marshals the informational resources of the entire area it is in an ideal position to advise the planner on site selection, scheduling, transportation, accommodation, entertainment, social program, pre- and post-convention tours etc., and act as honest broker between the suppliers and conference organizers.

A recent UK example of a coordinated approach to destination marketing and visitor servicing is the Greater Glasgow Tourist Board and Convention Bureau. Established in 1983, its current budget of £1.2 million consists of contributions from six local authorities (Glasgow, Renfrew, Strathkelvin, Monklands and Inverclyde District Councils and Strathclyde Regional Council), membership fees from the private sector, and income from various services offered by the organization throughout its network of tourist information centers. The Board's affairs are governed by an Executive Committee comprising equal representation from the public and private sectors.

Glasgow is Scotland's largest city and has suffered a negative image in the past, largely associated with the decline of the traditional industries of heavy engineering and shipbuilding which led to increased levels of unemployment, poor housing and high emigration, leading to population decline.

During the 3-year period ending in December 1987, the city enjoyed a massive investment program in excess of £2 billion, the result of a genuine partnership between the public and private sectors in the provision of new infrastructure geared to the service industries. A number of these, the £20.6 million Burrell Collection and the £36 million Scottish Exhibition and Conference Centre built on reclaimed dockland on the River Clyde, allied to new hotel developments, suggested that tourism could play a major role in the economic regeneration of the city.

An extensive study of Glasgow's tourism potential was completed in 1983 by Pannell Kerr Forster at the request of the Scottish Development Agency. The study identified the city as a commercial destination and as a result of past emigration, there was a high concentration of VFR (visits to friends and relatives) traffic. The city did not perform well in the leisure/holiday or conference sectors. Occupancy levels in the serviced accommodation sector dropped significantly during June, July and August. In addition, 90 per cent of Scottish tourism was UK based and centered on family motoring holidays. In 1983 Glasgow's product profile did not meet the requirements of Scotland's 'traditional tourist'.

On the plus side, the city had the finest examples of Victorian architecture anywhere in Europe, extensive parkland, a wealth of artistic riches in museums, art galleries, performing arts organizations (72 in all) and theaters. It had an excellent stock of hotel accommodation, a recently opened purpose-built Conference and Exhibition Centre and an International Airport 10 minutes from the city center which was handling close to 3 million passengers a year.

The impact of the Burrell Collection on Glasgow as a tourist destination was to prove of critical importance in two respects.

First, it enabled the city's stock of cultural assets to be offered realistically on the market place as a major tourist attraction. Second, it provided major impetus to the highly successful 'Glasgow's Miles Better' public relations campaign which was a powerful antidote to the 'industrial slum' image which had acted as a strong deterrent to potential visitors in the past.

The Greater Glasgow Tourist Board and Convention Bureau identified its priority objectives as follows:

1. Increasing the number of leisure tourism visitors from May to September to correct the low occupancy of the serviced accommodation sector during that period.
2. To increase the number of conventions and meetings held in the city to ensure maximum utilization of meetings' facilities, leading to a year-round tourism development strategy.

In the short term it was believed that the overseas markets provided a better opportunity for Glasgow to be positioned as an essential part of a Scottish tour within the holiday sector. This required thorough analysis of the British Tourist Authority's overseas market profiles to determine where Glasgow's strengths and weakneses lay. Once the priority target markets were identified, a program of press facility visits and travel trade familiarization programs was introduced to create high awareness of the attractions of the destination within the minds of those capable of producing volume traffic.

In addition, acting as the corporate destination marketing organization, the Greater Glasgow Tourist Board set about commercially organizing the component parts of the tourist product for presentation in the selected target markets. Advertising was concentrated on the travel trade, as consumer advertising in the overseas market place was not considered cost effective at that stage of the destination's development. Within the United Kingdom the concentration was on the short-break market segment geared to events.

The Glasgow product profile as examined in 1984, was ideally suited to business travel. However, the conference product had not been commercially organized on a corporate basis in the past. Various component parts tended to operate independently, presenting a fragmented or confused message in the market place. An analysis of the conference market sector profiles (international associations, national associations, corporate sales meetings, national and regional product launch, business information) demonstrated that Glasgow matched the requirements of any meeting from 10 to 10,000.

A case was then presented to Strathclyde Regional Council, Glasgow District Council and the industry at large, to provide additional funding for a corporate business travel strategy. This was agreed and the Greater Glasgow Convention Bureau was formed in January 1987 as the Business Travel division of the Greater Glasgow Tourist Board.

Benefits

In 1982 Glasgow had 700,000 visitors, in 1986 2.6 million, and in 1988 an estimated 4 million visitors will attend the Glasgow Garden Festival.

The Convention Bureau serviced over 850 conference enquiries during the first 4 months of its existence. Because of its role as the corporate destination marketing organization, the Greater Glasgow Tourist Board and Convention Bureau was able to bring together all the interested parties in the formulation of Glasgow's bid to secure the designation of European City of Culture 1990. The benefits to the public sector are increased employment and regeneration of the inner city. The private sector enjoys increased profitability.

Implementation

Product evaluation

Identify strengths and weaknesses in current product mix.

1. Image or attractions
2. Facilities, accommodation supply etc.
3. Access

Monitor utilization of infrastructure

1. Determine volume and value estimates of existing business.
2. Establish the profile of existing visitors.
3. Set up a regular review of occupancy levels of serviced accommodation sector.
4. Monitor visitor numbers at all tourist attractions etc.
5. Monitor all passenger surveys.
6. Monitor the conversion rate of all conference enquiries.

Market surveys

1. Maintain data on all relevant markets.
2. Update the market sector profile on an annual basis.
3. Interface with all conference industry organizations for research purposes:
   (a) International Association of Visitor & Convention Bureaux;
   (b) International Congress & Convention Association;
   (c) British Association of Conference Towns;
   (d) European Federation of Conference Towns;
   (e) Association of Conference Executives.

Identify objectives

Set specific and measureable targets.

Develop marketing plan

1. Advertising campaign.
2. Sales promotion campaign.
3. Production of collateral materials:
   (a) brochure;
   (b) mailing leaflets;
   (c) shell folders;
   (d) video;
   (e) exhibition display materials;
   (f) brochure wallets;
   (g) bid documents;
   (h) enquiry service.
4. Determine distribution channels and measure results.

Assessment

The basic philosophy attending business travel evaluation on the part of most destination marketing organizations is that every enquiry should be converted into business at some point. Conferences are rarely one-off affairs and for the most part are held annually, with the major international conventions being held every 2 or 3 years; so that the destination failing to secure the conference in 1990 should continue to pursue it annually until the conversion is made. At its most simplistic, failure to convert will be due to one of two reasons: 1. The product mix was wrong or 2. The promotion mix was wrong.

Conclusions

Convention destination marketing to be truly effective requires first and foremost a commitment on the part of all those who make up the collective will of the city. There has to be a commitment from the public sector which creates the environment for the private sector to flourish. Those who, to date, have affected genuine partnerships based on common interests such as the regeneration of an urban area, are reaping significant rewards.

Tourism, be it of the leisure or business variety depends on cooperation not conflict but above all must be managed professionally if a destination is to succeed into the 1990s and beyond.

Further reading/information sources

Cleverdon, R., *International Business Travel: a New Megamarket* (Economist Intelligence Unit Publications Ltd, 1985).

English Tourist Board, *Providing for the Future* (ETB, 1984). The UK conference market.

Greater Glasgow Tourist Board & Convention Bureau, *Annual Report and Accounts 1986/87* (1987).

Heeley, J., 'A tale of two cities and tourism', *Fraser of Allander Economic Quarterly*, vol. 11, no. 4 (May 1986). Economic perspective.

International Association of Convention & Visitor Bureaux: General Information, PO Box 758, Campaign, Ill. 61820, USA.

EDWARD J. FRIEL

Cooperative marketing

Introduction

The understanding of cooperative marketing starts with comprehension of the players in a marketing system. Marketing is the process of seeking out the needs of a group of people (customers or target market) and satisfying those needs. The players involved are firms (manufacturers, wholesalers, retailers) and the customers. Cooperative marketing therefore is an agreed arrangement between any of these distinct groups designed to help facilitate performance of the marketing function. In cooperative arrangements, channel members share the costs of some aspect of the marketing task. It therefore could be horizontal (i.e. two or more independent channel members at the same stage of distribution) or vertical (i.e. two or more independent channel members at different stages of the distribution process).

Cooperative marketing typically involves activities such as developing products that satisfy customer needs, communicating the availability of the product and its attributes to a target audience, establishing a value (price) for the product and finally providing the product at a place and time desirable to the customer. Cooperative marketing arrangements are most common with firms that belong to the same marketing system. For instance, cooperative marketing efforts are commonplace between manufacturers and either wholesalers, agents or retailers; cooperative marketing arrangements with competitors are not typical.

Cooperative marketing is, in a sense, a broad term reflecting cooperation in advertising, sales promotion, product development, distribution, and price arrangements. Cooperative advertising is probably the most popular arrangement. It involves the joint presentation of ideas and products belonging to two or more firms. Typically competitive products (i.e. two competing brands from different firms) are not used. Cooperative sales promotion arrangements cover the typical sales promotion tools such as coupons, trading stamps, point-of-purchase displays, special events, gifts, demonstrations, rebates, samples, and contests or sweepstakes.

Cooperative distribution is where two or more channel members share the costs of delivering the goods to the customer at the right place and time. The functions typically agreed upon are inventory costs, transportation and storage, for instance, when a manufacturer decides to team up with a retailer and share costs of transportation of a product. Cooperative pricing arrangements exist between channel members to effectively execute price strategies.

Examples

In the early 1980s, faced with a declining share of the West German travel market, the former United States Travel Service (USTS) embarked on a program to increase tourism called 'Tour Development Program'. This was a cooperative effort between USTS, tour operators and US travel suppliers. The USTS personnel abroad identified the most productive tour operators in their respective markets and helped them plan and assemble US tour packages. US travel suppliers were solicited and given slides and photographs for use, in part, for promotional materials and to produce tour catalogs for distribution to retail travel agents and the general public. Also, travel agencies designated at least one travel counselor to serve as a 'visit USA travel planning specialist'. The specialists were instructed through a series of structured workshops including a short 'field inspection' trip to observe US travel facilities first hand. The result of this effort has been that the United States is now a featured destination in tour catalogs and brochures distributed in major markets.

Days Inns based at Atlanta, Georgia, the fastest growing lodging chain in the nation, hopes to boost its occupancy rate significantly with its new consumer promotion. The promotion was aimed at some 40 million potential guests who also shop at K-Mart stores. It was the first joint retail/travel consumer promotion of its kind in the lodging industry. According to the program, Days Inns will award guests $2.50 worth of K-Mart gift certificates for night lodging at any of the chains 350-plus locations nationwide. To participate, a guest simply picks up a redemption envelope at the service desk of any of the more than 2,000 K-Mart stores in the United States, then mails the original or a copy of his hotel bill to the address listed on the material and receives a K-Mart certificate, redeemable for merchandise at any store.

Thrifty Car Rental and Continental Airlines also have participated in a program giving travelers an opportunity to earn a significant amount in gift certificates during their business and leisure trips. Thrifty and Continental will award 5 per cent of the price of any car rental or airline ticket that is purchased and reserved through International Tours.

California State University, San Bernardino, in a joint effort with the San Bernardino County Tourism Development Council and some local newspapers, has been involved in projects designed to maintain a database on tourism and tourists in the country.

Benefits

The benefits of cooperative marketing depend on the nature and objectives of the arrangement. For instance, joint sales promotions provide sales personnel increased leverage and also help participating companies obtain additional shelf exposure. There are, however, some generic benefits which any cooperative arrangement provides.

1. All cooperative arrangements help improve cost efficiency. By sharing the costs of a full page advertisement, for instance, the costs are halved while the firm's products are shown. This is especially useful for products whose pictorial representation is not a selling point such as the products offered by the hospitality industry. Producers that are cooperative with local retailers can also benefit from favorable media rate structures available to local retailers.
2. Cooperative marketing makes it possible for two firms to combine resources (personnel, capital) to tackle huge projects. Joint marketing research projects can make use of the firms' combined resources. Related to this point is that the firms' weaknesses can be made up if such weaknesses constitute the other party's strength. By sharing each others' strengths, both firms minimize their weaknesses.
3. Cooperative marketing is particularly beneficial for new product introduction. A new product can be tied into an already established brand. A newly formed travel agency can enter a joint sales promotion effort with an established car rental company like Hertz. Customers implicitly accept the new travel agency and associate it with Hertz.
4. Cooperative marketing gives customers the feeling that firms endorse each others' products. A joint advertisement between IBM and Allegis Airlines required Allegis booking desks to make use of IBM computers.
5. Joint marketing programs give a firm access to established distribution channels.

The decline in the value of the dollar in 1985–1986 prompted the United States Travel and Tourism Administration (USTTA) to undertake initiatives to re-establish US competitiveness in the international travel market. The USTTA launched a major cooperative advertising program to enlist more of the one million US travel related businesses, states and cities in an endeavor to market the United States abroad. The cooperative approach offered a number of benefits to participating firms, states, and cities:

1. A 20 to 40 per cent saving on space costs.
2. A 24 to 36 page magazine or newspaper supplement providing more visibility than a one page advertisement.
3. The use of USTTA language professionals for space negotiations and media selection.

Implementation

Horizontal and vertical cooperative arrangements in advertising, sales promotion, distribution and pricing are common. This is partly due to today's competitive marketplace and rising marketing costs. Cooperative marketing, while providing cost savings, poses some problems for participants, resulting from the mountain of paperwork associated with such arrangements and meeting Federal Trade Commission (FTC) guidelines.

To improve the effectiveness of cooperative marketing programs, a New York City based firm, Crimur's Coop Marketing has suggested 10 steps to follow.

1. Cooperative arrangements should be kept simple. Channel members typically do not have the time or patience to deal with complicated programs. Arrangements that involve few parties and programs are recommended.
2. The arrangement should not be complex. The simpler, the better. Asking travel agencies to comply with complex regulations is a mistake.
3. All arrangements must conform to legal provisions. Fines and legal fees for violations can be expensive. Agreements between a country's tourism agencies and travel agencies in the United States must conform to regulations.
4. It is important to work within the framework of the participating firms' operations. Don't force a hotel chain to advertise on television, if the chain prefers newspaper advertising. If the tourism agency desires, it should select those firms that use television advertisement and deal with them.
5. All claims promised must be paid promptly. Many of the cooperative arrangements involve sales promotion techniques with car rental companies, restaurants and the hospitality industry. These have contact with the tourists and typically most cooperation plans are set up so that the retailer who places the advertisement pays for them, and files a claim for reimbursement. Don't hassle the retailer about reimbursements.
6. Image-building programs seem to be the objective of tourism agencies. This directly conflicts with many of the objectives of the hospitality industry. Restaurants and car rental firms are also interested in sales. Don't encourage long-range, image-building programs.
7. Do not delegate a lot of the tasks. Provide the necessary tools. All parties must know what to expect.
8. Information necessary for proper implementation of the program should be provided to the other party. For example, information such as when advertisements will run in the car rental company's area, and what it will feature should be known to the car rental company.
9. The concerned parties must know when and how they will

be reimbursed. The steps involved in filing claims should be simple and completely understood by all parties.

10. The cooperative arrangement should be part of the company's overall marketing strategy. There is no point in entering into cooperative sales promotion arrangements if the objective of the tourism firm is to enhance its image. It is better off using advertising.

Firms engaging in cooperative marketing efforts should try to match various forms of complementary linkages such as seasonality, distribution channels or use time. Thus firms offering services and products that are frequently used at the same time of day (use time) or that use the same retail outlets (distribution) should engage in cooperative marketing.

Assessment

The goals of cooperative marketing are numerous, therefore its evaluation will be based on the extent to which these objectives are achieved. Discussion of evaluation criteria will be organized around the marketing activities. Cooperative agreements in the communications (promotional) area can be judged on: 1. increased awareness of the firm's products, 2. a change in attitude, and 3. the extent to which sales are stimulated.

The hierarchy of effects – model-awareness, knowledge, liking, preference, conviction, purchase – can be used to evaluate the effectiveness of joint promotional efforts. Cooperative agreements can be evaluated on the increased customer service level achieved. Customers desire to have the right product at the right time (product availability).

Other customer service measures that can be used are:

1. Time involved in taking and delivering orders (order cycle time).
2. Ability to expedite back order.
3. Substitute orders (distribution system flexibility).
4. Ability to provide information on inventory or order status (distribution system information).
5. Ability to reduce packing and shipping errors (distribution system malfunction).
6. The ability to provide repair services (post sale product support).

Agreements made in the area of new product introduction can be evaluated on achieved customer brand loyalty and new product acceptance.

Conclusion

Cooperative marketing arrangements will continue to increase. There is a tremendous pressure on firms to control costs and be competitive. As we move into the global marketing era, new firms and products will heighten competition. Marketing costs (advertising, sales promotion) are also increasing.

Focus on small business

Cooperative marketing is probably more beneficial to small firms than large firms. By combining resources, small firms can achieve greater economies of scale and reduce per unit costs than if they acted alone. By joining together, small firms can increase their negotiatory leverages with marketing intermediaries and institutions such as banks, wholesalers, and retailers. Small firms stand to benefit because they can serve customers better. Servicing the customers satisfactorily leads to increased sales and customer loyalty. In the tourism industry cooperative arrangements are almost inevitable. The diversity of firms, products and services in the hospitality industry increase the opportunities for cooperative agreements.

Further reading

Allvine, F., *Marketing Principles and Practices* (Harcourt Brace Jovanovich, 1987). A section deals with coordination between wholesalers, retailers and manufacturers.

'Avoid coop ad headaches', *Sales and Marketing Digest*, vol. 3, no. 3 (March 1985), p. 11. Illustrates the benefits of cooperative advertising.

'Cooperation helps cut advertising costs', *Sales and Marketing Digest*, vol. 3, no. 12 (December 1985), p. 1. Suggests ways to improve the effectiveness of cooperative programs.

Everett, M., 'A force in the field', *Sales and Marketing Management*, vol. 124, no. 7 (13 May 1985), pp. 81–8. Shows examples of cooperative advertising in action, involving vertical and horizontal arrangements.

Everett, M., 'Just the weapon for a tough fight', *Sales and Marketing Management*, vol. 128, no. 7, (17 May 1982), pp. 62–82. Shows examples of cooperative advertising in action, involving vertical and horizontal arrangements.

'General foods and national park service team up for promotional campaign', *Sales and Marketing Digest*, vol. 4, no. 7 (July 1986), p. 1. Illustrates a cause-directed marketing program that relates sales of a breakfast cereal product to better awareness and understanding of a diverse park system.

'How Polaroid and TWA created a monster', *Business Week* (21 January 1985), p. 39. Discusses the success of the cooperative arrangement between Polaroid and TWA.

'Joint sales promotions provide numerous beneficial growth opportunities', *Sales and Marketing Digest*, vol. 4, no. 7 (July 1986), p. 1. Lists the advantages offered to marketers who use cooperative sales promotions.

Rothstein, L., 'Building dealer relations with coop', *Sales and Marketing Management*, vol. 136, no. 2 (3 February 1986), p. 59. The author states the case for using cooperative agreements as a means for strengthening dealer relations.

Rozen, M., 'What's new in joint promotions', *New York Times* (10 March 1985), p. 64. Discusses examples of innovations in joint promotions.

Schewe, C. D., *Marketing Principles and Strategies* (Random House, 1987). A section discusses cooperatives in marketing.

Seely, R., 'USTTA's cooperative marketing program stimulates new business', *Business America*, vol. 10, no. 4 (16 February 1987), p. 1. Describes the US Travel and Tourism Administration's cooperative efforts to stimulate US tourism business.

Tuttle, D., 'The "visit USA" program after 25 years: changing markets, growing competition, and new challenges abroad', *Business America*, vol. 9, no. 4 (17 February 1986), p. 3. Illustrates a cooperative marketing effort designed to increase tourism in the United States.

Varadarajan, P. R., 'Joint sales promotion: an energizing marketing tool', *Business Horizon*, vol. 28, no. 5 (September–October 1985), pp. 43–9. Discusses the rise in cooperative arrangements, their advantages and problems.

Varadarajan, P. R., 'Horizontal cooperative sales promotion: a framework for classification and additional perspectives', *Journal of Marketing*, vol. 50, no. 3 (1986), pp. 61–73. Identifies several potential opportunities for growth through joint sales promotion. Also, presents a framework for classification of horizontal cooperative sales promotion.

Young, R. F. and Greyser, S. A., *Managing Cooperative Advertising: A Strategic Approach* (Lexington Books, 1983). The author examines five firms in the appliance and fashion/soft goods fields and discusses the problems and objectives of cooperative advertising and other marketing issues such as brand/store identities.

SAM OKOROAFO

Cost–benefit analysis

Introduction

Cost–benefit analysis is a technique for assessing the viability of new investments or expenditure programs. It has developed as a decision-making tool in commercial organizations, but is used particularly in the public sector in developing countries.

Application of the technique involves tabulating the estimated costs of an investment or project for each year of the project life. Costs will include initial and replacement investments, working capital and all operating cost items. Similarly, the estimated benefits arising from these expenditures are written out for each year of the project life. A comparison is then made of the costs and benefits in each year. Typically, these net benefits will be negative whilst investment is taking place, turning positive shortly after operation commences.

The viability of an investment is assessed by evaluating the net benefits over the full project life. This involves adding up values appearing in different years. In cost–benefit analysis it is generally recognized that net benefits occurring in earlier periods are more valuable than net benefits in later periods (and net costs in earlier years more punitive than net costs later). Net benefits in the future are discounted at a specified annual compound rate of discount to convert future values into an equivalent present value. The question then is whether the present value of net benefits in total is positive, in which case discounted benefits exceed discounted costs and the investment is worthwhile, or whether discounted costs exceed discounted benefits and the investment should not be undertaken. This decision criterion can be expressed as follows:

$$\text{Is } \sum_{t=0}^{n} \frac{(B_t - C_t)}{(1 + d)^t} \geq 0 ?$$

where B_t and C_t are the annual benefits and costs respectively, d is the discount rate and n is the number of periods over which the investment is being assessed.

The costs and benefits in the above expression can be evaluated using different sets of prices. Both private investors and governments are interested in returns in real terms, that is, returns on an investment after adjusting the calculations to remove the effects of price increases. For this reason, costs and benefits over the life of the investment are generally evaluated at a set of constant prices; the prices at the time the investment is being evaluated can be used for every year. Additional forms of analysis at actual prices should also be used to ensure the project will remain liquid in financial terms.

Cost–benefit analysis can be used by different agencies to evaluate investments: by the owner of a new project, by lenders, by the management agents, and by government. Each application will take account of the costs and benefits from a different point of view. An adjustment to organizational or financial arrangements may be necessary if different points of view give different conclusions. A successful project must be acceptable to all interests.

Examples

A new restaurant may be constructed to complement other resort investments. In order to estimate the investment, the size of building required is assessed against the likely restaurant demand. The costs of the building, kitchen equipment, furnishings, operating assets, food and drink purchases, transport, overheads and labor are forecast for each year of investment and operation, bearing in mind the way in which business is likely to build up. The benefits in the form of revenue will be related to the number of tables and covers, the expected turn-round of customers at different times of the day and week, and their anticipated expenditure. Both the benefits and costs are related to the anticipated demand; the length of time over which they are estimated will depend upon the period for which the investment will be suitable to serve that market without any major alterations or refurbishments.

A commercial assessment of the restaurant investment will include costs of taxes and loans to the owners. The rate at which net benefits each year should be discounted is normally the interest rate at which investment funds are available, adjusted for risk; that is, the investment should at least earn a rate of return equal to the real costs of borrowing, and preferably more. If the value of discounted net benefits is positive, the restaurant investment can be undertaken. If it is negative, further consideration will have to be given as to how the food and drink needs of tourists could be met in a way that would be profitable to the owners.

Hotel investments are the major component of most tourism development. Assessing the viability of a hotel investment must begin from an assessment of the tourist market. This will indicate the type of services a hotel needs to provide, and the standard of construction, as well as size. Against these basic parameters, an estimate of investment and operating costs can be made; a distinction should be drawn between fixed, semi-variable (utilities, promotion, linen, cutlery, maintenance materials) and variable operating costs (commissions, food and drink, cleaning materials).

The forecast benefits will depend upon the seasonality of demand. For business tourism, seasonality may be small and room occupancy consistent; for several types of holiday tourism seasonality will be considerable and average annual occupancies below full capacity use. The size of investment must be fixed somewhere between the demand for accommodation at peak times of year and a size giving an annual occupancy of at least 50 per cent. Benefits in the form of revenue will come from the price for basic services (accommodation and inclusive meals) plus discretionary expenditure on food, drink and other purchases by tourists in hotels. In many locations, such discretionary expenditure will be by tourists who are not hotel guests, especially food and drink purchases.

The period over which to evaluate the benefits is a matter of judgment. The longest possible life will correspond to the life of the major fixed assets, the buildings. However, it is more appropriate to restrict the life to a particular tourist market; few hotels can go more than 15 years at more without considerable re-investment and a possible change in clientele. If a market life approach is adopted, the cost-benefit analysis should include as a benefit in the final year the remaining value of the fixed assets. They can be substantial.

The assessment of a hotel investment can tell the investor whether it is likely to be worthwhile. If it is not, then alternative forms of investment should be sought for the investment funds available, including other types of tourism investment or tourism investments elsewhere.

Benefits

There are several advantages of applying the technique of cost–benefit analysis.

1. It enforces a strict consideration of all the costs and benefits from an investment and their timing. In order to build up the project statement, the relationship between type of market, standard of construction and service and price must be considered.
2. It provides a clear decision-making criterion. Projects that do not match this criterion can be stopped or redesigned.
3. It allows the consideration of alternatives: by drawing up different project statements, the advantages of different technologies and locations can be compared; by considering the effects of additions to project costs and benefits, a decision can be taken on whether to extend services or not.
4. By an adjustment of values in the cost and benefit flows, an assessment of the sensitivity of the results to possible changes in prices or quantities can be made. This information can be assessed in relation to the risks of such changes.

In these several ways, the application of cost–benefit analysis on a systematic basis can lead to informed decisions and a better use of investment resources.

Implementation

Most commercial decisions in tourism involve some form of cost–benefit analysis. Forecasts are made of annual expected net profits from an investment, taking all material, service and financial costs into account. Applying a discount rate to the flow of net profits is a means of bringing to bear on the investment the alternative return that could be earned on all expenditures elsewhere at a comparable level of risk. By dividing the net profits between owners and lenders, an assessment is possible of whether the rate of return is adequate to each. A viable project can generally be redesigned to ensure an adequate return to all participants.

Economic analysis

Cost–benefit analysis can be taken further than straightforward commercial decisions; the technique is most appropriate in evaluating decisions from a wider perspective. For example, a new hotel may have negative repercussions on demand for existing hotel beds; the new hotel managers or owners should include in their analysis the additional promotion costs of attracting custom away from existing hotels. However, lenders (who may already be committed to existing hotels) and sectoral or national planning agencies must consider the incremental value of the new hotel. The incremental costs will be the full project costs of the new hotel, less the variable and semivariable costs saved at existing hotels as customers switch; the incremental benefits will be the new hotel revenues less the revenues lost at existing hotels. This incremental statement of costs and benefits will show how a new investment will contribute commercially to the sector as a whole and not just the owners. New investments will be preferable if they can tap a new tourist market, involving little lost custom in existing hotels, or if they can produce the same type of tourism as existing hotels but at considerably lower cost. Incremental cost–benefit analysis in this form thus provides an essential assessment of innovation in the sector.

This wider perspective can also include the costs of infrastructure associated with a new development. Where services like water and sewerage, electricity and telephones are charged for, the additional costs of connections to new tourism investments are generally included in the charges. Where tourism requires a major new infrastructure investment in these fields, or where services are not charged for (or only partially) like roads, then explicit account must be taken of the extra expenditures involved even though project owners do not meet the cost. Extra infrastructure costs necessary to yield the commercial benefits must be added on to the costs of new investments, both investment and maintenance costs.

In making these additions, a judgment has to be made about how much of shared facilities to allocate to specific investments. Infrastructure investments may be shared with nontourism uses; an allocation to tourism must be made only if tourism has prompted the investment (allowing some of the costs to be apportioned to other uses) or if tourism has prompted a higher quality provision (in which case the costs of the additional quality are relevant). Making these allocations on a project-by-project basis can be difficult; in principle it should be done, although infrastructure costs are frequently included in sector level rather than project level assessments.

Some types of indirect expenditure can be evaluated in their own right. For example, a government promotion and advertising campaign can be closely costed. The benefits of such a campaign are the net expenditures of additional tourists that would not have arrived without the campaign. The net expenditures of these additional tourists may or may not be the same as existing tourists; some idea of the numbers of additional tourists may be estimated after the event, but will be difficult to estimate before the event. There is considerable uncertainty about the returns to this type of expenditure; however, the application of cost–benefit analysis requires an enumeration of all the costs and benefits even where they cannot be fully measured.

Accounting or shadow prices

A more far-reaching adjustment to the way in which cost–benefit analysis in tourism is carried out relates to the prices at which resources are evaluated. The analysis can be used to assess the value of investments not from a commercial point of view but considering its contribution to the national economy. The purpose is to assess the net resources produced in the economy regardless of who owns the project and how it is financed. This form of analysis excludes tax and financing items from costs. On the other hand, incremental effects are included in costs and benefits: extra infrastructure costs; and effects on the benefits and costs of other investments.

A major issue in cost–benefit analysis, particularly in developing countries, is whether the prices which operators can charge for outputs or have to pay for inputs represent the value of those outputs and inputs to the national economy. Prices may depart sharply from opportunity costs where supply is monopolized or as a result of government decisions on taxes, subsidies, exchange and trade controls. Methods of revaluing all costs and benefits of an investment have been advocated in order that the net value of resources from a national point of view can be better assessed.

Operational methods of 'shadow pricing' are based on the use of international prices for valuing outputs and inputs; for a particular country these are the border prices of resources as they enter or leave. Traded goods, like kitchen equipment, furnishings, imported foods and fuel, can be valued directly at their border prices. Nontraded goods, like electricity, telephones, construction and local transport, cannot be directly valued at border prices; their price can be broken down progressively into their cost components which will include mostly traded goods. Labor can be valued at its full cost (for expatriate labor) or at its opportunity cost for domestic labor – what will be the value of production lost elsewhere in the economy as new tourism jobs are taken up?

In revaluing resources in this way, an assessment is in effect being made of an investment's contribution to an economy's capacity to command resources, either by producing them or by trade. Investments should proceed if the net resources produced are more valuable than the level of traded goods given up to make the investment. In such an application, the government will estimate an appropriate discount rate representing an alternative economic rate of return that could be achieved in other investments valued in this same way.

Applications of cost–benefit analysis from a wider, national point of view are generally favorable to tourism investments, especially those oriented to international tourism where the benefits (revenues) are measured directly at border prices. In most developing countries, the resource costs of inputs are lower than their financial costs; when these resource costs are used the rate of return improves. Where the national returns are greater than the private returns, there may be a case for providing financial assistance to new investments (or relaxing financial demands) in order that the national benefits can be achieved.

This process of subsidy must be justified, however, through an analysis that considers incremental benefits only (and therefore, for example, such subsidies should not be available in large measure to all hotel investments regardless of the interaction of demand). All incremental costs, including extra infrastructure costs, should also be taken into account. This wider national viewpoint may also demonstrate a less favorable result than commercial analysis. This can occur where, for example, land costs are high because tourism takes land away from other productive uses, or where the opportunity cost of labor is high, with an induced migration of labor to tourism resulting in lost agricultural output. These types of effect are likely to be larger in smaller economies where tourism represents one of very few options; for each investment, a careful assessment of such effects must be made.

Savings and income distribution

Methods of economic analysis have been extended to consider the effects of projects on the level of savings and consumption and on income distribution. These are additional objectives that may be relevant from a national but not a commercial point of view. The net benefits from a project valued at shadow prices can be broken down by recipient; the net benefits going to owners, foreigners, lenders, workers and government can be calculated. The propensity to consume (or save) of these different groups can be estimated and the project's contribution to future savings assessed. The government may wish to attach a weight to incomes that will be saved to represent its commitment to the objective of economic growth.

The same statement of net benefits, broken down between savings and consumption, can be used to incorporate the government's income distribution objectives. Favorable weights can be placed on consumption that will go to those with lower present levels of consumption (unskilled workers) with little weight on that by owners. Consumption and saving by government are treated as equally valuable, that is, subject to direct government decision, unlike the consumption of other groups that has to be indirectly valued. To some extent, application of consumption distribution weights giving priority to consumption by those at low levels will negate the application of savings weights, giving priority to those with higher incomes and savings.

The costs of earning foreign exchange

Tourism investments are frequently oriented to earning extra foreign currency. Although the methods of economic analysis provide an assessment of an investment's contribution to the national economy as a whole, it does not do so in a manner which directly highlights effects on net foreign currency earnings. An alternative indicator of economic viability, the 'domestic resource cost', measures the amount of domestic resources in the form of inputs that an investment uses to produce a net unit of foreign currency. An investment should not use up domestic resources having a greater equivalent value than the net foreign exchange generated, and preferably should use up much less. This can be expressed as:

Domestic Resource Cost < 1.0

Unit of net foreign currency generated

Where an investment is viable at shadow prices, then the domestic resource cost criterion, using present values discounted over the life of the investment, will also indicate viability from the foreign exchange point of view.

Such calculations can also include foreign exchange flows associated with financing. This includes equity and loan inflows as well as the outflow of interest, loan payments and profits. Including such flows is justified where the funding is project-specific; that is, the inflow of foreign funds to the economy would not occur outside the particular investment being analyzed. The inclusion of such flows can alter domestic resource costs considerably by changing the net foreign exchange earnings. The values of projects with an average rate of profit are likely to be improved by foreign inflows covering some of the investment costs; for projects with a very high rate of profit, the outflow of profit is likely to outweigh the advantages of the initial investment inflows, reducing the overall return to the economy.

Assessment and conclusion

Cost-benefit analysis of a tourism investment can play an important role in the decision-making process. The anticipated costs and benefits of a new investment need to be related to a market analysis of the types of service and facilities tourists will demand and for how long. Particularly with the inclusion of infrastructure expenditures, the analysis needs to concentrate on the incremental effects of new projects on costs and benefits, and not just on the commercial effects for the operator.

Not all costs and benefits can be valued for quantitative analysis. For example, the effects of a concentration of tourists on beach pollution, or the demonstration effects of the lifestyles of high-income tourists on lower-income residents, are frequently referred to but cannot properly be quantified. However, cost-benefit analysis will encourage the consideration of all beneficial and deleterious effects even when the predominant purpose is to provide an investment decision based on numerical values.

Cost–benefit analysis provides a systematic approach to investment decision making which allows a proposed investment to be compared with other alternatives. It is particularly useful when applied from a national perspective; cost–benefit analysis can help investors decide whether an investment is worthwhile; it can also help to identify projects that the government should be supporting or those that the government should seek to modify.

Software/databases

A microcomputer program developed by the United Nations Industrial Development Organization can be used for directly productive projects in tourism. However, the program assumes a standard project life and has limitations on the number and type of costs and benefits that can be included. It does connect up different forms of financial analysis and allows an assessment from the national point of view. A spreadsheet package for the financial and economic analysis of projects has also been developed and used within the World Bank (IBRD).

The project statements necessary for carrying out cost–benefit analysis can be built up on commercial spreadsheet packages such as Multiplan or Lotus. This allows the project statement to represent the features of the particular investment under consideration. An advantage of such applications is that they allow an easy treatment of the sensitivity of the results to different assumptions and values, and can easily be extended to include cost–benefit analysis from different points of view.

Further reading

Adhikari, R., 'Efficiency and social analysis of projects in the Nepalese economy', *Industry and Development*, no. 17 (1986), pp. 91–109. This article applies a full set of shadow prices to investments in Nepal, including a large international city hotel. It distinguishes between the results at efficiency prices, allowing for the opportunity cost of resources, and at social prices including the distributional effects of incomes.

Anderson, R. W., 'Estimating the recreation benefit from large inland reservoirs', *Recreational Economics and Analysis*, G. A. C. Searle, ed. (Longman, 1975), pp. 75–88. This paper illustrates a method of identifying and estimating the present value of recreational benefits within a multi-purpose water project.

Archer, B., 'The economic costs and benefits of tourism', *Tourism. A Tool for Regional Development*, B. Duffield, ed., (Leisure Studies Association Conference, Edinburgh, 1977). This article argues the need for an assessment of costs and benefits from the viewpoint of a region, comparing tourism development with alternative forms of regional resource use.

Bryden, J. M., *Tourism and Development: A Case Study of the Commonwealth Caribbean* (Cambridge University Press, 1973). Chapter 10 contains an economic evaluation using shadow prices of a holiday hotel and the associated extra government promotional expenditures.

Chapter 11 calculates an economic rate of return for two proposed programs of development of hotels, infrastructure and promotion.

Curry, S., 'Hotel investment in Tanzania: an evaluation', *Project Appraisal*, vol. 2, no. 4 (1987), pp. 221–30. This article presents the results of an application of shadow prices to different types of hotel, comparing the commercial and national returns.

Etzel, M. J. and Swensen, P. R., 'Taking the mystery out of travel investment decisions', *Journal of Travel Research*, vol. XX, no. 2 (Fall 1981), pp. 24–8. This brief article outlines the elements of discounted cash flows for the financial analysis of new investments in tourism.

Forbes, A. M., 'The Trinidad Hilton: a cost–benefit study of a luxury hotel', *Using Shadow Prices*, I. M. D. Little and M. F. G. Scott, eds (Heinemann Educational, 1976). This case study applies the Little– Mirrlees method of shadow prices to investigate the national economic returns from an international city hotel.

IBRD, *Terms of Lending. Hotel Projects, Draft Report* (Tourism Projects Department, 1973). This working paper establishes financial models of different types of hotel investment to investigate the effects of variations in loan terms and interest payments.

Latimer, H., 'Consumer and producer surpluses in tourism', *Tourism Management*, vol. 2, no. 3 (September 1981), pp. 147–61. This article discusses the costs and benefits of tourism from the point of view of residents, distinguishing between monetary estimates of costs and what residents would be willing to give up to restrict changes brought by tourism.

Latimer, H., 'Project evaluation. The need for a rigorous approach', *Tourism Management*, vol. 1, no. 1 (March 1980), pp. 30–41. This article reviews the basic concepts behind the application of project evaluation methods to tourism projects, including broader forms of economic analysis.

Latimer, H., 'Some considerations in project analysis of tourism', *Journal of the Mugla School of Business Administration*, Special Issue (October 1978), pp. 185–94. This paper outlines some basic issues in cost-benefit analysis and tourism and argues for the inclusion of all indirect and induced effects in such an analysis, net of opportunity costs.

Ministry of Overseas Development, *A Guide to the Economic Appraisal of Projects in Developing Countries* (Revised edition, HMSO, 1977). In this guide to economic analysis, Appendix D.25 (pp. 154–58) provides a checklist of questions involved in building up and justifying a tourism sector project.

National Council of Applied Economic Research, *Cost Benefit Study of Tourism* (National Council of Applied Economic Research, 1975). This study includes in chapter 3 a cost–benefit analysis of a new beach resort assessing the conomic viability of the development.

Powers, T. A., 'Economic appraisal of international projects', *Journal of Travel Research*, vol. XV, no. 2 (Fall 1976), pp. 10–13. This brief paper outlines the elements of the cost–benefit decision criterion including the way in which costs and benefits are identified in international tourism projects.

Powers, T. A., 'Using accounting prices to evaluate international tourism projects in developing countries', *Tourism Planning and Development Issues*, D. E. Hawkins, E. C. Shafer and J. M. Rovelstad, eds, (George Washington University, 1980), pp. 411–42. This chapter outlines an economic appraisal method including growth and income distribution adjustments, applies it to a simplified resort complex investment, and discusses the special features of economic appraisal of tourism projects.

Powers, T. A. and Powers, P. A., 'A dynamic programming model for optimizing economic returns to tourist resort projects in developing countries', *Journal of Travel Research*, vol. XV, no. 2 (Fall 1977), pp. 16–21. This paper uses cost-benefit calculations in the determination of an optimum construction schedule for different types of hotel in an illustrative tourist resort development.

Shvedow, L. U., 'Evaluating the effectiveness of capital investment in the tourist industry', *Problems of Economics*, vol. 18, no. 12 (1976), pp. 45–54. This article proposes a method for including broad indicators of effect in choice between tourism alternatives, as well as returns on investment.

Vanhove, N., 'Cost benefit analysis. Theory and techniques applied to tourism', *Managerial Aspects of Tourism*, S. Wahab, ed. (International Seminar Proceedings, Alexandria, Egypt, September 1975). This paper outlines decision-making criteria from the commercial point of view, and then illustrates how these need to be extended in a full cost-benefit analysis within a macroeconomic framework.

Vickerman, R. W., *The Economics of Leisure and Recreation* (Macmillan, 1975). Chapter 3 outlines the main principles in the application of cost – benefit analysis to leisure projects.

Vincze, I., 'Foreign currency income and profitability of Hungarian tourism', *Acta Oeconomica*, vol. 29, nos 3–4 (1982), pp. 361–70. This article calculates the domestic resource cost of foreign exchange earned by selling food and other products to foreigners through tourism and compares the results with direct exports of similar products.

World Bank, *Appraisal of the Bali Tourism Project* (Tourism Projects Department, 1973). This study illustrates the application of cost-benefit analysis to a large tourism complex, allowing for the opportunity cost of drawing labor away from other sectors.

STEVE CURRY

Decision design for tourism chief executive officers

Introduction

This process can be used to rank a wide range of budget items in tourism planning and development activities when the anticipated combined social, economic, managerial, environmental, and political benefits of those items cannot be adequately described in economic terms; and, budgetary constraints do not permit funding all items under consideration. The process accounts for subjective judgment and contains a formal, rigorous decision strategy that takes the place of intuition when qualitative and quantitative tourism values need to be evaluated.

What was the last major tourism management or planning decision you made where some of the benefits and costs of one or more of the items you were evaluating were either not readily quantifiable or easily accessible – and how did you make it? There is a good chance you collected a mountain of data, read it, studied it, paged through it, contemplated it, and then made your decision. But do you really know why you made the decision you did? Could you describe each of the specific factors you weighed in the decision making process, and how much weight each of those factors carried? Very likely, the answer is 'no'. If so, don't feel badly. It just proves that you are not unlike most of the rest of us. So say the experts (Peters and Austin, 1985; McCormack, 1984; Naisbitt and Aburdene, 1985).

The literature is filled with examples of how tourism managers and planners, and many other types of executives, when faced with a difficult, complex decision, traditionally gather information or appoint a committee to do it, or both (Austin, 1966; Kahn *et al.*, 1964; Richards and Greenlaw, 1972). As a result, decision makers may be overwhelmed with difficult-to-evaluate data, or become mired in trade-off considerations as proponents push favorite ideas, programs, or options. When a decision is finally reached, it may be difficult to trace the process and discover why one item was chosen instead of another. There is no 'audit trail'.

The process described in this article was developed and used originally by chief executive officers (CEOs) to set priorities on a large number of research items involved in the National Resource Planning Act (USDA Forest Service, 1983). The design's premise: human judgment is indispensable to solve complex priority-setting problems. The solution: use the perceived values and beliefs of CEOs responsible for making the final decisions thus insuring coherent decisions consistent with stated values. Since its conception, the design has been applied by a wide range of managers, negotiators, policy makers and analysts in a variety of decision-making situations related to tourism in government and industry (National Agricultural Research and Extension Users Advisory Board, 1983 and 1984).

Example and implementation

The process is best described by sitting in on a typical meeting of a CEO and her/his staff where it is being used. The purpose of the meeting could be to set priorities on a list of different public involvement options, tourism development opportunities, environmental impact alternatives, tourism development possibilities, or a complex combination of items in all of the above. The process applies equally well to all of these and any other type of priority-setting situation where classic economic cost–benefit analysis cannot be used to evaluate the combined social, economic, managerial, environmental, and political effects of some, or all, of the items to be evaluated. Typical items to be evaluated, and quotations from participants in previous proprietary studies, are included in this hypothetical example to describe the process as realistically as possible.

Selecting the items to be evaluated

When the participants were invited to attend the meeting, the only information they were asked to bring was that inside their heads. Once inside the conference room, they are literally sealed off until they make their decisions. Let us assume in this hypothetical example that the group has a specific number of dollars to invest over a certain period of years in the following ten items:

1. Purchase more water-related sports equipment.
2. Improve hiking trails to scenic vistas.
3. Restore historic landmarks on the property.
4. Promote public relations efforts with local populations.
5. Enlarge bar facilities.
6. Acquire more land for future development.
7. Increase marketing/advertising efforts.

8. Send key personnel to graduate school management courses.
9. Invest in ski area development at another location.
10. Make major renovations in beach houses.

Cost constraints

The group cannot afford to invest in all ten items. Some items can be evaluated in terms of economic cost-benefit analysis; some cannot. Which ones should the group go for? In this hypothetical example, the names of these items are not as important as the fact that they are very different in terms of the kinds of perceived benefits they eventually will provide or evoke in the minds of the meeting participants.

Facilitators are essential

Although their postures are relaxed, all eyes of the participants are riveted near one end of the conference table where a wall board is gradually being filled, by one of the group's facilitators, with definitions of the various terms that need to be positioned in order of priority. Two group facilitators, with backgrounds in decision analysis, play distinct roles in shepherding the participants through the tangle of possibilities, values, and risks the group is considering. Facilitator number one stands at the front, eliciting information, asking questions, responding to comments and objections from the table. Facilitator number two darts back and forth, taking copious notes and filling in on the board when needed. The facilitators are helping structure the definition of the items to be evaluated, along with each individual's description of perceived qualitative and quantitative benefits of the items.

The facilitators are essential to the success of the meeting. They are individuals who are able to: think quickly and clearly on their feet in the midst of intense, people-oriented situations; exhibit strong leadership skills; remain results-oriented; portray unusual self-confidence; and remain objective, dispassionate

non-members of the decision making group throughout the entire process. In effect, the facilitators act as praetorian guards, managing the entire process and making sure all players know what is required of them.

Detailed description of items and benefits

Early in the discussion, one or more members of the group will point out: 'This whole process depends entirely on how clearly we initially define the items to be evaluated and their respective benefits.' A facilitator replies, 'Exactly; that's why the group should be in agreement on this information before we take the next step.'

'How specific should we be in trying to describe the perceived benefits of each item?', another member of the group asks. A facilitator responds, 'Each of you has imperfect knowledge about the overall benefits of each item. Some benefits are difficult (and in some cases impossible) to define in a totally objective way. Try to describe the benefits of each item as best you can in terms of how you perceive the *combined* social, economic, managerial, environmental, and political benefits.'

At the close of the first day's session, the facilitators leave the room with a briefcase full of notes to be edited and consolidated that evening for the next step the following day. Incidentally, this process may not require several days – it has been applied in situations that only require a few hours.

Comparing items two at a time

The next morning, participants receive the edited material and a survey form (Table 1) for comparing the items – two at a time – in terms of their overall benefits. Now the facilitators begin to play a different role as they move about the room, coaching and assisting individuals as they complete the survey form.

Periodically, the facilitators will explain that this method for estimating any one item's value under these circumstances has been developed in a wide range of disciplines – including

Table 1 Survey forms and hypothetical entries of how one panelist compared all two-way sets of ten items.

Ten items	1. Water sports equipment purchases	2. Hiking trail improvement	3. Historic landmarks restoration	4. Public relations promotion	5. Bar facilities enlargement	6. Land acquisition	7. Marketing effort increases	8. Management training efforts	9. Ski area investment	10. Beach houses renovations
1. Water sports equipment purchases	X	1	1	1	0	1	1	0	1	0
2. Hiking trail improvement		X	1	1	0	1	1	0	0	0
3. Historic landmarks restoration			X	1	0	0	1	0	0	0
4. Public relations promotion				X	0	0	0	0	0	0
5. Bar facilities enlargement					X	1	1	1	1	1
6. Land acquisition						X	1	0	0	0
7. Marketing effort increases							X	0	0	0
8. Management training efforts								X	1	0
9. Ski area investment									X	0
10. Beach houses renovations										X

'1' indicates the benefits of the column item was judged more favorable than the benefits of the row item. '0' means just the opposite.

economics, political science, psychology, and sociology. Despite differences in approach, these methods tend to blend. Paired comparisons – comparing all items two at a time – may be used, for example, to derive an attitude scale for a psychologist (Edwards, 1957; Thurston, 1927; Torgerson, 1958), or a utility scale for an economist (Sinden and Worrell, 1979). In fact, the various disciplines often use different terms for the same things. Economists make the most use of these methods as value indicates for setting priorities in marketing strategy decisions.

Computing benefit scores for each item

When all participants complete Table 1, which usually requires about 30 minutes for a ten-item exercise, they take a coffee break and the facilitators compute the benefit score for each item. Essentially, the proportion of times all respondents select each item over every other item provides the basic data for computing benefit scores (Table 2).

It is likely at this point that one or more economists in the group will remark, 'I believe calling the results of panel judgments "benefits" is a misnomer. Benefits have a definite economic meaning – contribution to social welfare. In economics, quantified benefit estimation is imperfect, but the goal is to estimate total benefits generated; generally based on willingness to pay.' A facilitator replies, 'For many of the items being compared here, it may be impossible to describe the related benefits in pure economic terms. Remember, we have asked each of you to make judgment calls based on your perception of the *total* social, economic, managerial, environmental, and political benefits associated with each item. The challenge of comparing items two at a time is characterized by multiple criteria, both objective and subjective; an imperfect state of knowledge; and, a plethora of relevant information that requires evaluation and rational choice under complexity, uncertainty, and risk. Thus, we are using the word "benefits" in this exercise in a much broader context than that ordinarily used in economics.'

Cost estimates

Next, the group estimates the annual cost of each item. Cost estimates are made *after* the benefit scores are computed because costs are independent of benefits, and therefore should not influence perceptions of the related benefits. It is important that the group estimate the cost of each item before the facilitators report the benefit scores to the group. Costs are discounted to present worth – the money needed today in order to fund the item in total; the rate of interest is selected by the group. The total cost of all items in the hypothetical example is approximately $23 million – $8 million more than the group can afford to spend with a $15 million budget.

Developing criteria for decisions

Using a *benefit-only criterion*, facilitators now list the 10 items on the wall board in order of their priority according to the initial

Table 2 Hypothetical example of how benefit scores were calculated for ten items.

Ten items	1. Water sports equipment purchases	2. Hiking trail improvement	3. Historic landmarks restoration	4. Public relations promotion	5. Bar facilities enlargement	6. Land acquisition	7. Marketing effort increases	8. Management training efforts	9. Ski area investment	10. Beach houses renovations	
	Proportion of times column effort was judged more favorable than row effort										
1. Water sports equipment purchases	0.00	0.70[1]	0.15	0.10	0.15	0.15	0.60	0.00	0.60	0.10	
2. Hiking trail improvement	0.30[2]	0.00	0.00	0.00	0.15	0.30	0.45	0.25	0.45	0.25	
3. Historic landmarks restoration	0.85	1.00	0.00	0.30	0.60	0.70	0.60	0.25	0.60	0.30	
4. Public relations promotion	0.90	1.00	0.70	0.00	0.85	0.70	0.75	0.55	0.75	0.85	
5. Bar facilities enlargement	0.85	0.85	0.40	0.15	0.00	0.55	0.60	0.40	0.75	0.60	
6. Land acquisition	0.85	0.70	0.30	0.30	0.45	0.00	0.75	0.30	0.60	0.55	
7. Marketing effort increases	0.40	0.55	0.40	0.25	0.40	0.25	0.00	0.25	0.55	0.25	
8. Management training efforts	1.00	0.75	0.75	0.45	0.60	0.70	0.75	0.00	0.75	0.70	
9. Ski area investment	0.40	0.55	0.40	0.25	0.25	0.40	0.45	0.25	0.00	0.25	
10. Beach houses renovations	0.90	0.75	0.70	0.15	0.40	0.45	0.75	0.30	0.75	0.00	
Totals	6.45	6.85	3.80	1.95	3.85	4.20	5.70	2.55	5.80	3.85	**45.00**
Benefit scores	143[3]	152	84	43	86	93	127	57	129	86	**1000**

[1] Let's assume ten panelists were used in this survey. We add the individual raw scores from the survey forms (for example, $1 + 1 + 0 + 1 + 1 + 0 + 1 + 1 + 1 + 0 = 7$) and divide by the number of panelists ($7/10 = 0.70$).

[2] The value in a cell to the left of the diagonal dashed line is: 1.00 minus the corresponding paired comparison value to the right of the diagonal. For example, the 0.30 in the first column, row two, is the result of $1.00 - 0.70$; the 0.70 being located in the second column, row one.

[3] $6.45/45.0 \times 1000 = 143$. Multiplying by 1000 is a convenience to avoid the use of decimal points in the benefit scores.

benefit scores obtained from Table 2. Item 2 is first, 1 second, 9 third etc. In a second, third, and fourth column, respectively, facilitators also record each of the items' benefit scores; the discounted costs; and, the cost–benefit criterion values – the benefit score divided by its discounted cost (Table 3). Pointing to the board (Table 3) a facilitator explains, 'Notice that if we have listed these items in column one in order of priority according to a *cost–benefit criterion*, rather than the way we have listed them here, item 4 would be first, 8 second, 7 third etc.'

Inevitably at this stage a participant will ask, 'If we only want to use the cost–benefit criterion for setting priorities, why even bother to record the benefit-only criterion data?' 'Because we need to be aware of the magnitude of the difference if we reverted to a benefit-only criterion for making decisions in a situation that involves qualitative as well as quantitative estimates of the benefits for the items involved', the facilitator answers.

The group takes a coffee break and the facilitators use the data in Table 3 to cumulatively plot the costs and benefits of the ten items in their order of priority: first, according to a benefit-only criterion; next, by the cost–benefit criterion (Fig. 1).

The resulting diagram provides a design for decisions the group can use to examine the priorities of the ten items under any budget constraint. As Fig. 1 shows, the order of priority of the items along the cost–benefit criterion curve (the decision curve) always provides the most benefits for a given budget. For example, since the group's total budget is $15 million, a program (on the cost–benefit curve) that contains items 4, 8, 7, 2, 5, 1, 6, and 3 with a total benefit score of 800 is preferable to a $15 million budget (on the benefit-only curve) with items 2, 1, 9, 7, and 5 with a total benefit score of only 660.

Fine tuning the priorities

Also at this point, one or more members of the group will comment, 'Now that I understand how this whole process works, I am not quite satisfied with the benefit scores we've assigned to each item. Can we go back and adjust them?' 'Of course', a facilitator replies, 'But we may not have to go back

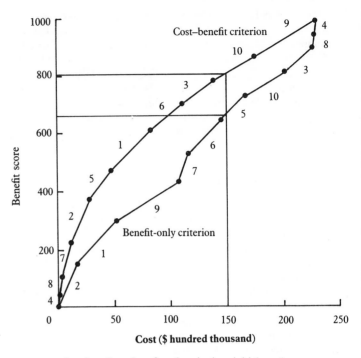

Figure 1 Cost-benefit v. benefit-only criterion: initial results.

and compare the items two at a time again if we only want to make *minor* adjustments.'

Pointing to the display board, the facilitator explains, 'If we only wish to make minor corrections the only constraint is that, regardless of the number of adjustments we make in benefit scores, the sum of the benefit scores for all items must still only equal 1000 – as we originally agreed (Table 3). For example, if participants want to increase the benefit score of one item, they must reduce the value of another, or others, an equal amount. Up to this point, the system was designed to facilitate consensus as quickly as possible; now we can "fine tune" your perceptions of the benefit scores.'

During this period of adjusting benefit scores, facilitators

Table 3 Initial and final results, after fine-tuning the benefit scores, of the ten items.

Ten items	Initial results			Final results	
	Initial benefit score	Discounted cost ($ hundred thousand)	Initial cost–benefit criterion value	Final benefit score	Final cost–benefit criterion value
1. Hiking trail improvement	152	16	9.50	216	13.50
2. Water sports equipment purchase	143	36	3.97	123	3.41
3. Ski area investment	129	56	2.30	164	2.93
4. Marketing effort increases	127	9	14.11	110	12.22
5. Land acquisition	93	30	3.10	80	2.67
6. Bar facility enlargement	86	20	4.30	74	3.70
7. Beach houses renovations	86	35	2.46	74	2.11
8. Historic landmarks restoration	84	26	3.23	72	2.77
9. Management training efforts	57	2	28.50	49	24.50
10. Public relations promotion	43	1	43.00	38	38.00
Totals	1000	231		1000	

record participants' comments that describe the additional benefits associated with those items that are assigned higher benefit scores.

The final decision

On the basis of participant suggestions, facilitators make final adjustments in benefit scores on the display board, recalculate final cost–benefit criterion values (Table 3), and plot the end results (Fig. 2). Now, for a $15 million dollar budget, for example, the most efficient budget program should contain 4, 8, 2, 7, 5, 1, and 9 for a total benefit score of 800; rather than 2, 9, 1, 7, and 6 for a total score of 693.

Conclusion

This decision design for CEOs and their staff facilitates consensus and serves the decision-making process primarily by enabling attention to be directed at different items in a complex priority-setting problem without losing sight of the interdependencies. Individual CEOs, managers and planners may use the process without the aid of group consensus to discipline their own reasoning and to enhance communication among individuals at various levels in their organization. The process has been used effectively in tourism planning to communicate the basis for recommendations, to identify sources of disagreement, and to focus expertise on appropriate parts of decisions needing more attention. Because the process specifically focuses on policy or CEO decision options, results can be incorporated directly by lower management levels into planning and operating proced-

ures. It is important to note that the process is not intended to stand on its own merits without, whenever possible, the benefits of additional information from other studies to improve the final priority-setting process within the constraints of a fixed budget.

This decision design recognizes that human judgment is indispensable to serious CEO decision making. With this realistic acceptance of human limitations, the potential for more balanced decision making emerges. The process takes exception to Shakespeare's optimistic assessment: 'What a piece of work is man. How noble in reason, how infinite in faculties...' Rather, the underlying pragmatic premise of the design is more closely related to the skepticism of Francis Bacon, who said, 'We do ill to exalt the powers of the human mind, when we should seek out its proper helps.' In the words of one of today's modern managers, 'The qualities that make a good manager...come down to decisiveness. You can use the fanciest computers in the world and you can gather all the charts and numbers, but in the end you have to bring all your own information together, set up a timetable, and *act*' (Iacocca, 1984). The decision design described above is intended to assist CEOs in taking that action.

Further reading

Austin, C. F., *Management's Self-inflicted Wounds* (Holt, Rinehart and Winston, 1966). Seventy-six types of managers are examined, with practical business solutions to illustrate each one.

Edwards, A. L., *Techniques of Attitude Scale Construction* (Appleton-Century-Crofts, 1957). This book describes the various methods that have been used in the construction of attitude scales.

Iacocca, L., *Iacocca, an Autobiography* (Bantam Books, 1984). This book is a compelling and thought-provoking assessment of US business, illustrated with examples from Iacocca's career at Ford and Chrysler.

Kahn, R., Wolf, D. M., Quinn, R. P. *et al.*, *Organizational Stress: Studies in Role Conflict and Ambiguity* (John Wiley and Sons, 1964). Using the framework of role theory, this book examines the pressures that occur in various echelons of modern, large organizations.

McCormack, M. H., *What They don't Teach You at Harvard Business School* (Bantam Books, 1984). The author shares the business skills, techniques, and wisdom gleaned from his own experience and that of top executives with whom he has worked in a powerful, on-target, straight-talking book.

Naisbitt, J. and Aburdene. P., *Re-inventing the Corporation* (Warner Books, 1985). This book asks the questions and provides the answers and guidelines to transform organizations for the new information society and provide an environment where both people and profits can flourish.

National Agricultural Research and Extension Users Advisory Board, *Appraisal of the Proposed Budget for Food and Agricultural Sciences* (USDA, 1983). This report is an evaluation of the research programs and priorities for the United States Department of Agriculture.

National Agricultural Research and Extension Users Advisory Board, *New Directions for Science, Education, and Agriculture: Executive Summary* (AGR 101, USDA, 1984). This report is a summary of the research priorities of the United States Department of Agriculture.

Peters, T. and Austin, N., *A Passion for Excellence* (Random House, 1985). This book highlights the methods and accomplishments of those who have always had strong leadership qualities and stressed

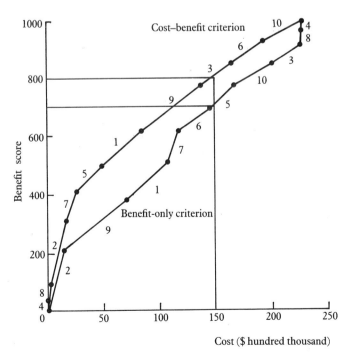

Figure 2 Cost-benefit v. benefit-only criterion: final comparisons.

superior service and constant innovation.

Richards, M. D. and Greenlaw, P. S., *Management Decisions and Behavior* (Richard D. Irving, 1972). This book outlines the inter-relation of the components in difficult decisions in management issues.

Sinden, J. A. and Worrell, A. C., *Unpriced Values – Decisions without Market Prices* (John Wiley, 1979). This book presents a compre-hensive and systematic compilation of information concerning the problem of placing comparative values on benefits and costs that have no market value.

Thurston, L. L., 'A law of comparative judgment', *Psychological Review*, vol. 34 (1927), pp. 278–86. This article evaluates the strengths and weaknesses in procedures designed to set priorities through comparative judgment techniques.

Torgerson, W. S., *Theory and Methods of Scaling* (John Wiley, 1958). This book describes the wide range of techniques used to provide quantitative values for qualitative attributes.

USDA Forest Service, *Draft Environmental Impact Statement: 1985–2030*. (Resources Planning Act Program Staff Report, USDA, 1983). This report evaluates the social, economic and environmental impacts of various forest management alternatives in which all the variables being considered cannot be described quantitatively.

ELWOOD L. SHAFER

Delphi method applied to tourism

Introduction

Environmental trends may have a significant impact on the tourism industry in general or on selected parts of the tourism industry. Forecasting environmental trends can be especially important to those communities and regions whose economy is dependent on tourism rather than manufacturing industries. In fact, the ability to forecast environmental trends in the tourism industry is extremely important for most organizations who are involved in tourism as well as those considering entering the business. The purpose of this chapter is to present a method for environmental forecasting: the Delphi method.

The Delphi method

Figure 1 presents the basic steps in the Delphi method, adapted from a model by Tersine and Riggs. The Delphi method, a group decision process, was developed by the RAND Corporation for technological forecasting. It includes the following elements:

1. A series of questionnaires are completed by a panel of experts.
2. The responses of the panel members to the questionnaires are anonymous.
3. The responses are statistically categorized by the median score which represents the midpoint of the responses.

The primary usage of the Delphi method has been long-term technological and environmental forecasting. It has also been successfully applied to marketing research and sales forecasting. The basic logic of the Delphi method is:

1. The range of responses by panel experts will decrease and converge toward the midrange of the distribution.
2. The median, or total group response, will move toward the 'true' or 'correct' answer with each succeeding round of questionnaires.

The Delphi method was developed to make use of the advantages of group decision making without the disadvantages. The major disadvantages of group decision making include the domination of the group by one or two individuals, the tendency of developing a 'bandwagon effect', and the reluctance of group members to change their positions. The advantages of the Delphi method include the following. First, a panel of experts are brought together to provide an expertise that they commonly share to solve a problem. Second, the panel through a consensus process will converge toward the best response. This consensus process does not mean 100 per cent agreement by everybody in the panel. It means a majority response as represented by the median. Third, because the panel members' responses are anonymous, this will allow individuals to respond freely and to change their minds without ego involvement. Therefore, one or two persons will not be able to control the panel and stifle the creativity of other persons on the panel. Thus, any 'halo effect' or 'bandwagon effect' will be greatly reduced.

Example

Mr John Smith (a pseudonym), president and founder of Southern Queen Incorporated (a pseudonym), had just finished reading an article in a travel magazine. The article, about the boon to the travel industry because of lower gasoline prices, perplexed Smith. Tourism analysts predicted that this trend would drastically increase the number of people traveling, and to greater distances. At first Smith was happy with the thought of the prospect of people further away visiting his area. The Southern Queen Incorporated operated three paddle wheel steamships on excursions from New Orleans to St Louis. Therefore, if more people come to the St Louis and New Orleans areas it should mean more business. After thinking about it, however, his excitement died down. The thought came to him that even though more people further away will be coming to his area, the people in the nearby areas may go elsewhere too. Therefore, the increase in one area might be offset by a decrease in the other area. Another concern Smith had was the long-term trend of gasoline prices. The prices are down now but how long will it last?

While Smith thought about the article, another article that he had recently read came to mind, about proposed legislation by the federal government in restricting navigational activities on the US inland waterways. Smith was obviously concerned about this development.

Both of these environmental trends weighed heavily on Smith's mind because they were likely to have serious impacts

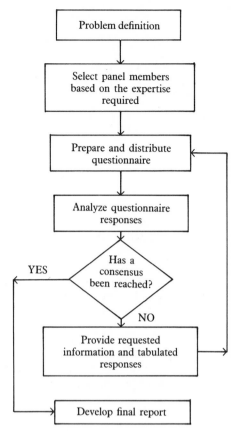

Figure 1 The Delphi method.

on Smith's business. He was particularly sensitive to these issues because he was considering expanding his operations at great expense. What really bothered Smith was the thought of other environmental trends of which he was not aware.

Implementation

Figure 2 presents a model that demonstrates the use of the Delphi method in the process of environmental forecasting. The example of Southern Queen will be used to discuss the model's application to tourism and to discuss some of the Delphi method's finer points.

Without question, the most important step in the Delphi method is the selection of panel members. The panel should include individuals who have expertise in the subject under consideration and who are willing to participate. This expertise may be defined either through formal education (e.g. PhD) and/or informal education (e.g. experience). The nature of the subject is important in deciding on the makeup of the panel. If the subject area is abstract in nature and cuts across a number of operational areas, the panel should include a broad representation of individuals. If the subject area is technical in nature and focuses on one operational area, the panel should include mostly technical members. If the makeup of the panel members

is basically homogeneous (e.g. mostly technical members), a panel size range of 10 to 15 individuals would be appropriate. However, if the panel members are basically heterogeneous (e.g. broad representation), the panel size would need to be increased to 20 or 30 individuals for appropriate results.

In the Southern Queen situations Smith would want to select a narrow representation of individuals focusing on tourism particularly in regard to the type of business in which Smith is involved. Smith would select 10 to 15 individuals; the most likely candidates would include but not be limited to, the following: other knowledgeable administrators or staff persons at Southern Queen, other channel members who are willing to participate, individuals from noncompeting organizations who have mutual concerns and interests, and industry experts who are willing to participate (for a fee). Since Smith would be supervising the process, he would not be included in the panel. If he wanted to be included in the panel, he would need to select someone to oversee the project.

Once the panel members are selected, the next step as presented in Fig. 2 is to identify the major environmental trend categories to consider. This will require input from the panel members. For the sake of argument, let us say the panel members suggested the following: foreign competition, demographic changes, technological changes, social/cultural changes, energy resources, and governmental regulations. Two of these areas were specifically thought of by Smith. The others were not.

The purpose of the first series of questionnaires as depicted in Fig. 2 is to develop a priority listing of the environmental trends that the company should be most concerned about. Along with this a more specific definition of these trends should be developed. In preparing the initial questionnaire Smith would want to use primarily an open-ended questionnaire. This is important in the initial questionnaire to allow panel members to freely express their opinions. The succeeding questionnaires can be more specific and more structured. With the initial questionnaire, Smith would ask the panel members to specifically define the major environmental trends they see developing, to list these trends according to the importance of their effects, and to assign a probability to their occurrence.

Along with the initial questionnaire (this could be done earlier) Smith would provide each panel member with a packet of information regarding the topic areas. This packet would most likely include internal data as well as external data. It is important that panel members have a common body of information to make their assessments. As additional information becomes available it too would be provided to the panel members.

After distributing and collecting the questionnaire, Smith would tabulate and analyze the responses. He would note the median response (representing the midpoint of the responses) and any responses that fall outside of the interquartile range of responses. The interquartile range represents the response between the 25 per cent and the 75 per cent response levels. The median response would be at the center of the interquartile range. Any panel member whose response falls outside of the interquartile range (e.g. 15 per cent level) is asked to justify his or her position. Of course this is done anonymously through written correspondence. The person's justification is then given

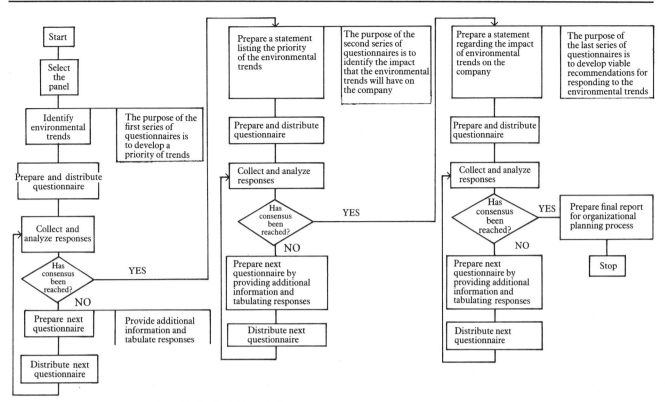

Figure 2 Environmental forecasting with the Delphi method.

to the other panel members with the next questionnaire. After studying the justification, the other panel members might change their positions. Since the responses are anonymous this can be done easily without the fear of losing face.

In analyzing and tabulating the responses, Smith would determine whether a consensus has been reached. If not, he would prepare the next questionnaire based on the tabulated results of the previous questionnaire. Normally, a consensus will be reached in three to five iterations. Each succeeding questionnaire becomes more specific and more structured than the last.

After reaching a consensus on the first series of questionnaires, Smith will be able to develop a list of specifically defined environmental trends ranked according to their priority of importance to the company. This list will also include the probability of each trend occurring. For example purposes, let us say that ten specific environmental trends were ranked by the panel and assigned probabilities. Of these, a demographic trend was ranked as number one. It was specifically stated as follows:

Within the next 10 years there will be a 50 per cent increase of people 55 years or older who will be visiting the area from St Louis to New Orleans as tourists.

The probability assigned by the panel members to the likelihood of this trend occurring was 80 per cent. By ranking this trend as number one the panel is saying that this is more important than either the decrease of gasoline prices or the federal

restrictions of navigational activities. This was a trend that Smith had not thought of.

The purpose of the second series of questionnaires is to identify the degree of influence that the list of trends will have on Southern Queen's future success. Smith will again take the panel through other iterations of questionnaires until a consensus is reached on the degree of these influences. Continuing with the above demographic trend the following statement might represent the panel's feelings in regard to the influence that this trend will have on Southern Queen.

Since the Southern Queen's marketing program is primarily directed at individuals under the age of 35, there is an 80 per cent probability that Southern Queen will lose 20 per cent of its market share to other competitors unless preventive actions are taken.

After the panel has reached a consensus on the influences of the environmental trends, Smith would develop a list of statements reflecting the influence(s) that each trend will have on Southern Queen, similar to the one above.

The purpose of the last series of questionnaires is to develop viable alternatives to each of the trends. These recommendations will give Smith a solid base for developing appropriate strategies to respond to the environmental trends. The panel will again be taken through a series of questionnaires until a consensus is reached on the viable alternatives. The purpose is not making strategy decisions. That will be left to Smith. The panel is simply providing suggested recommendations.

In regard to the demographic trend of an increase in older tourists, the following recommendations might be examples of what the panel would suggest for Southern Queen.

1. Rather than adding additional ships, Southern Queen needs to remodel its existing ships to appeal to older persons as well as younger persons.
2. Southern Queen needs to develop advertising programs that are directed at the person aged 55 or over.
3. To complement the above advertising effort, a sales promotion program will need to be developed to appeal to the person aged 55 or over.

Once the panel has reached a consensus on recommendations, the environmental forecasting process would be completed. Smith would then have a solid foundation to make strategic decisions, taking into consideration long-term environmental trends affecting his industry and his tourism business.

Assessment

The effects of environmental trends can be enormous on an organization or for an industry. These effects may be either positive or negative. The Delphi method is particularly suited for environmental forecasting, but there are some weaknesses that need to be noted. First, the successful outcome of the Delphi method depends on the selection of an appropriate panel of experts – not an easy task to perform. Second, to complete the necessary rounds of questionnaires, it may take several weeks. The time required to complete the process can be decreased through refinements in the method, in making use of data processing procedures, and in selecting suitable panel members who are really willing to participate.

The above weaknesses can be significant, but the advantages outweigh them. First, the Delphi method allows a group of experts to bring to bear their expertise in dealing with a problem. Because their input is anonymous they can respond more freely and creatively to the subject. Ego involvement is greatly reduced. Second, because some of the panel members may be directly affected by the outcomes, they will tend to have a higher level of support for the decisions that are made. Third, the Delphi method reduces the effects of a self-fulfilling prophecy regarding the decision made by one or two decision makers. This tendency is reduced by allowing more individuals to participate in the process in a nonthreatening manner.

Conclusion

Tourism organizations need to forecast environmental trends significant to their specific areas of business. The Delphi method can provide a valuable tool to accomplish this task.

Further reading

Basu, S. and Schroeder R. G., 'Incorporating judgements in sales forecasts: application of the Delphi method at American Hoist and Derrick', *Interfaces*, vol. 7, no. 3 (1977), pp. 18–27. This article presents the use of the Delphi method in sales forecasting.

Dalkey, N. C., *The Delphi Method: An Experimental Study of Group Opinion* (RAND Corporation, 1969, RM-5888-PR). This publication represents the original development of the Delphi method by the Rand Corporation.

Jolson, M. A. and Rossow, G. L., 'The Delphi process in marketing decision making', *Journal of Marketing Research*, vol. 8 (November 1971), pp. 443–48. This article presents the basic logic of the Delphi method.

Taylor, R. E., 'Using the Delphi method to define marketing problems', *Business*, vol. 34, no. 4 (1984), pp. 16–22. This article presents the use of the Delphi method in marketing research.

Tersine, R. J. and Riggs W. E., 'The Delphi technique: A long-range planning tool'. *Business Horizons*, vol. 19, no. 2 (1976), pp. 51–6. This article presents a model of the Delphi method process.

RAYMOND E. TAYLOR and
L. LYNN JUDD

Determinants of the attractiveness of a tourism region

Introduction

There are different determinants of the attractiveness of tourism regions, which apply equally to whole countries and continents. Their relationships and interactions are determined by their own intrinsic nature and the qualities associated with them and/or attributed to them. Accordingly we can identify three different groups of determinants:

1. Primary factors of an unchangeable kind (static factors).
2. Secondary factors of a partially variable kind (dynamic factors).
3. Tertiary factors of an unstable kind (current decision factors).

Before these factors are defined and explained it is necessary to specify the area of interest precisely. Here we shall deal with the attractiveness of tourism regions only from the point of view of flexible *demand*, not from the perspective of supply. Thus one is looking for a marketing approach which will avoid fixing the determinants in a too rigid theoretical manner. Marketing is a management philosophy which, in the light of tourist demand, makes it possible through research, forecasting and selection to place tourism products on the market which are most in line with the organization's purpose for the greatest benefit. Accordingly, this chapter will give more space to dynamic factors and unstable factors, changes to which can be especially critical with regard to demand. Destinations compete, even in a growing market, for tourists since their products are often close substitutes.

Primary factors of an unchangeable kind (static factors)

Any geographical, cultural or political area which possesses tourism attractiveness has, as a rule, one or more dominant primary factors.

1. The landscape:
   (a) natural landscape;
   (b) cultivated landscape.
   The landscape, its natural form, its comparability to and also its contrast with the usual life situation of the consumer, is (from the demand point of view) one of the most import-

ant elements in attractiveness leading to involvement in tourism.
2. Forms of landscape:
   (a) plain;
   (b) hills;
   (c) mountains;
   (d) coast and sea;
   (e) rivers and lakes.
   Regardless of the kind of tourism demand, whether it is the main or the second holiday, a summer or winter holiday, a short break or just a weekend break, the form of the landscape is always a significant factor in the primary decision in favor of this landscape.
3. The climate and its curative qualities:
   (a) climatic zones;
   (b) natural cures (air, altitude, mineral waters etc.).
   Frequently it is not direct knowledge but merely vague notions about a landscape which influence or even decide demand. This concept of halo effect plays an important role in shaping tourist demand. The climate is part and parcel of the landscape. Every landscape has a typical climate and generally possesses certain natural curative factors which can be crucial where demand is related to health.
4. Means of travel:
   (a) to the region;
   (b) in the region.
   As with the general public infrastructure, means of travel are basic factors in attractiveness. A tourism region can only be developed if the infrastructure exists and functions.
5. Culture:
   (a) history;
   (b) monuments, objects;
   (c) local crafts, folklore, local customs.
   Cultural determinants are of growing importance in global demand for tourism. Areas with an important history, e.g. anywhere in Europe or in Asia, generate significant demand simply because of their historical and cultural credentials, whether displayed in natural settings or in museums.

The broad category of social/cultural resources for tourism is perhaps the most difficult factor to evaluate, as so many subjective considerations emerge. The peculiar mix of social, cultural and political factors experienced by each country may serve both to attract and deter tourists.

Secondary factors of a partially variable kind (dynamic factors)

These secondary factors are only partly variable because their presence can generally be regarded today as a fixed supply factor as far as demand for tourism is concerned. They are only variable to the extent of their proportions, quality and time availability.

Where the market in tourism is ruled by free competition the secondary factors have a considerable effect in determining demand. The general factors of supply, administration and trends itemized below can have a major impact on demand, developing it or undermining it. Whereas, to a certain extent, the primary factors represent standard values in tourism, the most important criteria are to be found in the secondary factors. It is they which can directly bring about the demand decision because they can be in part changed, albeit only in detail.

1. Tourism supply:
   (a) accommodation;
   (b) catering;
   (c) personal attention and service;
   (d) entertainment and sport.

   Tourism supply in the narrower sense of accommodation, catering, personal attention and service, entertainment and sport, are provided today in absolutely comparable quality in competitive markets, e.g. on the Mediterranean coasts and in the winter sports centres of the Alps. The result is that supply in terms of quantity and quality can no longer operate as a variable decision factor. This can only happen now in association with other, partly personal, preferences or in connection with tertiary factors which are yet to be dealt with. Modern tourism has led in certain mass markets to a uniformity of supply and demand, which hardly reveal different personal decision factors. Tourism destinations and organizations must find sustainable differential advantages which then translate into clear tourist preference patterns, with the resulting attainment of high demand growth rates and tourist product effectiveness.

2. Administrative and political setting:
   (a) free access to the market (without visas, foreign currency restrictions, permits etc.);
   (b) restricted access to the market;
   (c) conditions associated with the political system (planned economy, market economy, developing country etc.).

   There remains a considerable demand which is completely freely decided upon, and for which the determinants set out above are a natural variable. In general this applies to high quality tourism supply of accommodation, catering, service and entertainment. It also applies to the removal of administrative and political obstacles.

3. Trends in tourism:
   (a) growth market;
   (b) currently established market ('cash cow');
   (c) declining market ('dog');
   (d) competitive situation of similar markets.

   It is remarkable that, with growing economic importance, access problems to hitherto difficult markets such as Albania

are removed and, in their place, attributes of quality and levels of provision assume importance. International tourism is on its way to becoming the first branch of industry to achieve complete market penetration worldwide. The decisive economic factor in winning the central market position is not the available supply, but demand which can be continuously activated.

Logically, then, 'tourism marketing' can be designated as a further determining factor in demand attractiveness. A satisfied tourist results from many independent businesses each providing a satisfying part of the total vacation. The marketing efforts of each of the parts are then affected by the efforts of the others providing a part of the total tourist product.

Tourism planning is an essential activity for every destination area, especially in today's fast-changing business environment.

Tertiary factors of an unstable kind (current decision factors)

These tertiary factors are not subsidiary determinants, but of equal importance to the primary and secondary factors, ensuring the attractiveness of tourism regions. These factors are unstable with regard to demand. They both depend on the market and influence it.

1. Marketing of the region:
   (a) total marketing concept;
   (b) partial marketing concepts (marketing mix efforts).

   The attractiveness of tourism regions can be small, despite the existence of other favorable determinants, if the regions do not succeed in constructing a total marketing strategy for all direct and indirect suppliers of services. A total marketing strategy is based on an effective allocation of resources and the implementation of action plans to achieve well-defined goals and objectives, as well as measurable results. A region focused on long-term demand will produce a segmented regional marketing concept which takes account of the individual needs of all subregions, of private and public providers of services and of the possible utilization of the environment and the cultural assets. In such a concept the optimum supply conditions can also be ascertained by cost–benefit analysis. Cost–benefit analysis is a technique used to determine which economic sector will produce the most benefit in terms of foreign exchange, employment, taxes or income generated relative to the cost of development. The marketing plans of tourism regions are economic factors which generate demand or change it and are, thus, always based on changeable factors and flexible policies.

2. Price situation:
   (a) prices in the target region;
   (b) prices in the country of origin.

   Prices are a direct instrument of marketing and, especially in international competition, doubly effective via foreign exchange fluctuations, disparities in purchasing power, differences in the costs of labor and goods, taxes, fees etc.

In terms of their stimulation of demand, prices promote competition particularly when they are relatively favorable in the target region as compared to other competing regions, including the country of origin. Recent scholarly research into tourism in West Germany often gives price only a subsidiary role after tourism product performance, comfort, availability, service and weather. This is explained by the growing requirement of the consumer for comfort and safety – which cost more. In other closely related product markets, however, price is likely to continue to be an essential factor in attractiveness.

3. Organization:
   (a) administration;
   (b) economic organization.

The organization of tourism can be advanced as a final tertiary factor. In general, the organizational form which is involved commercially is to be preferred to one that only has an administrative role. Its flexible and needs-oriented activity makes it possible for it to react more quickly to changes in the market. Yet in many tourism regions in the East and the West there are tourist enterprises of a public nature; the development of tourism is regarded as a general public area of activity. This does not need to be a disadvantage for the attractiveness of tourism regions if the organization is promoted according to a true marketing orientation.

Conclusion

There are interrelationships among all factors of a primary, secondary and tertiary kind. These interrelationships are greater where variability is greater, i.e. in the secondary and tertiary factors.

The determinants of the attractiveness of tourism regions include today a large number of variables whose importance can only be fully appreciated in competitive conditions. Many alternative ways of raising or reducing the attractiveness are possible, depending on the degree of adoption of the marketing concept.

ADOLF MEINUNG

Development and investment policy in tourism

The volume of international travel and its importance in world trade flows, together with increasing demands from the domestic population for leisure and recreation, make tourism an investment opportunity that few countries can afford to ignore. For many governments, the roots of their tourism policy lie in balance of payments considerations. The prize is the foreign tourist, who on average stays longer and spends several times more than his domestic counterpart, and is seen as a ready source of foreign exchange. Most developing countries are pressured into earning foreign exchange in order to service their debts. Faced with limitations in their traditional exports, the attractiveness of tourism as a fast earner of foreign exchange is obvious.

Any decision as to the appropriate investment policy depends on the interested parties and the prevailing economic philosophy. On the one hand there is the private sector which may have many reasons for investing in tourism, but in general must be concerned with the viability of the investment in terms of generating adequate returns on capital employed or returns to owners' equity. On the other hand, the degree of involvement of the government sector in tourism will depend upon how society decides on the dividing line between public and private provision. Those who argue for the market mechanism as the sole arbiter in the allocation of resources for tourism are ignoring the lessons of history and are grossly over-simplifying the nature of the product. In the United Kingdom, for example, the growth of the seaside resorts during the nineteenth century was as a result of a partnership between the public and private sectors. The local authorities invested in the promenades, piers, gardens and so on, while the private sector developed the revenue-earning activities which enhanced the income of the area and in turn increased property tax receipts for the authorities.

Tourism is a multifaceted product: it includes accommodation, transport, restaurants, shopping facilities, attractions, entertainment, public infrastructure support and the general way of life of the host community. Embodied in the tourist product are goods and services which are unlikely to be provided in sufficient quantity by the market mechanism. These are known as public goods: items which everyone can enjoy in common and are equally available to all. Their principal feature is that they are non-excludable. If the good or service is to be provided at all, it may be consumed by everybody without exception, and usually without charge at the point of use. The single-minded pursuit of profit may be self-defeating, as several Mediterranean resorts have found to their cost. The outcome may not be the integrated tourism development which distils the essence of the country in its design, but a rather crowded, over-built and placeless environment with polluted beaches. What is clear is that the complex structure of the product lends itself to the fact that in any tourism development program there is often a marked difference between private and social benefits and costs.

The precise nature of a country's stance on tourism investment is determined by the kind of development the government is looking for and what role it envisages for the private entrepreneur. Eastern European countries lay considerable importance on social tourism; Yugoslavia, for example, allows for all of the population to benefit from subsidized holidays through workers' organizations and central government provision. African countries have recognized the importance of tourism for conservation. By giving wildlife an economic value, funds are generated to support game reserves, preserve endangered species and help eradicate poaching. Many Caribbean countries have strong views about the wisdom of developing casinos for tourists – because of the possibility of criminal involvement and also on moral grounds.

Benefits

Generally speaking, economics forms the basis of nearly all tourism development plans. Within the economic framework there are three themes which are continually given prominence:

1. Foreign exchange: tourism is a 'cash' business and so is an activity which is a fast earner of foreign exchange.
2. Employment creation: the variety of tourist spending is seen to have important 'spillover' effects which, through job creation, spread the benefits of tourism growth as widely as possible.
3. Regional development: tourism has been made to work in

areas where there are few opportunities for alternative forms of employment.

Implementation

To achieve these benefits governments have to put forward an investment policy which is conducive to developers and investors. In situations where there is a clear commercial profit potential the government may only be required to demonstrate a commitment to tourism by:

1. Marketing and promoting the region, particularly abroad.
2. Giving advice and information to prospective developers.
3. Simplifying planning procedures.
4. Initiating liberal transport policies, especially air access.
5. Easing frontier formalities.
6. Giving guarantees on investment security, e.g. repatriation of capital and earnings.

Where the social rate of return to tourism projects is greater than the assigned public sector discount rate, but private profit rates are inadequate, governments will need to give financial incentives to investors to encourage the desired pattern of tourism development. The extreme case is where governments themselves set up a Tourist Development Corporation and invest directly in revenue-earning activities such as hotels which are traditionally regarded as the preserve of the private sector. Examples around the world include New Zealand, Malaysia, India, Egypt and many African countries.

Financial incentives

International competition to obtain foreign investment is such that countries can become trapped in a bidding process to secure clients. As a consequence the variety of financial incentives multiplies together with an escalation in the rates of benefit, without any true consideration of the cost to the economy and the need for them in relation to the quality of the natural resource elements of the tourist product on offer. The result of this 'bidding-up' of incentives may be that too much money is given away when all that is required is an answer to the question: 'Will this project not go ahead if £x financial support or the equivalent benefits in kind are not forthcoming?' The implication of this question is an ideal situation where all incentives are discretionary and therefore offered selectively. The legislation would be fairly general, empowering the ministry responsible for tourism to offer loans, grants, tax exemptions and equity investment as it sees fit. The granting of incentives to prospective developers would be in accordance with ministerial guidelines. The latter should be regularly reviewed in response to the level of tourism activity. Such guidelines might include the following:

1. Location of the project.
2. Bias towards projects which lengthen the tourist season, e.g. all-weather pools.
3. Preference for projects which enhance the overall tourist

package offered by an area rather than competing with existing operations.
4. Reserving some kinds of projects for local investors.
5. Favoring specific projects, e.g. holiday villages, farm tourism, theme parks, craft centers, leisure complexes and health spas.
6. Appropriate ceilings on the level of financial benefits available.

To have only discretionary incentives, however, is a counsel of perfection. Competition for tourism investment frequently requires countries to legislate for automatic financial help in order to attract investors in the first instance. This financial help falls into two categories:

1. Reduction of capital costs: these include capital grants or loans at preferential rates, interest rate relief, a moratorium on capital repayments for a certain number of years, provision of infrastructure, provision of land on concessional terms, tariff exemption on construction materials and equity participation.
2. Reduction of operating costs: to improve operating viability governments may grant tax 'holidays' (5 to 10 years), give a labor or training subsidy, offer tariff exemption on materials and supplies, provide special depreciation allowances and ensure that there is double taxation or unilateral relief.

Some countries may legislate for all the incentives outlined above; others for a subset of them. The appropriateness of the various financial incentives available depends on understanding the nature of the business risk and the likely returns of the tourist industry, as well as the ability of the country to afford them. Thus developing countries may find themselves in no position to offer grants or cheap loans.

It is well known that part of the business risk in tourism projects lies in the fact that services are non-storable (a hotel bed unsold is lost forever) and in demand being generally seasonal. This implies that peak demand determines capacity so that the industry is always facing excess capacity at other times. Not always apparent is the dominant cost structure in the industry. Typically, tourist projects have a high operating leverage, i.e. a high level of fixed costs arising out of the initial capital investment and low operating costs. This makes pricing difficult, because operating costs are no longer a reliable guide to what to charge, and also results in businesses which are very sensitive to variations in demand.

A 1 per cent variation in load factors on aircraft may be critical to the profitability of tour operators; thus when things do go wrong the losses are often spectacular. Further, although tourism (perhaps more than any other industry) deals with the development of real estate, the non-transferability of assets such as hotels hinders their worth as a property investment. The upshot of this is that the preferred form of financial incentives are those which reduce capital costs. The most common are grants and loans: grants have an immediate impact on the investment funding and are relatively simple to administer. Loans require a more elaborate administrative structure and need to be long term, for in tourism a healthy trading profit does not necessarily mean an ability to service the debt structure of the enterprise.

Conclusion

A country's investment policy with regard to tourism depends on the development objectives of the government. The authorities should decide upon the structure of the industry they would like to see and set policy instruments accordingly. The focus of investment incentives should be on the capital structure of projects and on encouraging a secure economic and political climate for developers. Incentives to reduce operating costs may be considered secondary in importance.

Focus on small business

For many countries, much of their investment legislation is aimed at attracting international investors, although it may be equally applicable to the domestic market. Small, local businesses may be offered preferential rates of benefit, particularly as they form the dominant economic unit in the industry.

Raising commercial finance for small businesses is always difficult because their asset backing is limited and they often lack managerial expertise. On the other hand, owner-managers frequently see the enterprise as a way of life and are prepared to sacrifice returns to equity to ensure that the operation does not founder. The tourist authorities can play a key role: they may act as a catalyst by 'pump-priming' the project through cash grants, by expressing confidence in the project and in so doing stimulating the flow of commercial funds, and by giving or obtaining expert advice and training. On the basis that the authorities are acting as lenders of the last resort so as to maximize the leverage on public funds, i.e. the ratio of private to public capital, grants are preferable to loans since by this stage the debt burden on the small business is already likely to be severe.

By definition, individual disbursements to small operators will not be large. It is important, therefore, that any grant as a percentage of the capital cost should not fall to a point where it is not worthwhile putting in an application form. The threshold is considered to be around 20 per cent. Further, because the sums involved are relatively small, it is possible to streamline aid procedures and the documentation.

Further reading

Bodlender, J. A., *Guidelines on Tourism Investment* (World Tourism Organization, 1980). This publication covers the criteria that governments should use to evaluate tourism investment proposals and some of the actions they should take to improve the climate for tourism investment.

Bodlender, J. A. and Davies, E. J., *A Profile of Government Financial and Grant Aid to Tourism* (World Tourism Organization, 1984). Grants and loans are covered in some detail together with guidelines on how to use investment incentives and the rationale for them.

Bodlender, J. A., 'The financing of tourism projects', *Tourism Management*, vol. 3, no. 4 (December 1982), pp. 277–84. Expands on earlier work and covers some of the same ground as Jenkins (1982).

Bodlender, J. A. and Ward, T. J., *An Examination of Tourism Incentives* (Horwath & Horwath, 1987). An extensive document, the first part of which covers the motives for tourism development, the use of state aid and a profile of the various investment incentives. The second part is a directory of aid available in selected countries.

Jenkins, C. L., 'The use of investment incentives for tourism projects in developing countries', *Tourism Management*, vol. 3, no. 2 (June 1982), pp. 91–7. Introduces a classification of incentives and argues for selectivity.

Skinner, J., 'How to attract developers', *Tourism–Managing for Results* (Peat Marwick, 1984). Papers given at a seminar for ministers of tourism and directors of national tourist organizations, November 1984. A hotelier's view of providing incentives to encourage developers.

Wanhill, S. R. C., 'Which investment incentives for tourism?', *Tourism Management*, vol. 7, no. 1 (March 1986), pp. 2–7. Examines investment incentives within a probabalistic model of the cost structure of tourist enterprises.

STEPHEN WANHILL

Direct sell

Introduction

The concept of direct selling has been the subject of attention in many industries in recent years. Direct selling is the process of offering a product (or service) for sale directly to the consumer, bypassing the need for intermediaries, such as agents or distributors. Direct selling in tourism has been an especially controversial topic.

Direct selling in tourism concerns the sale of either individual components of tourist products or of packaged holidays by their providers directly to customers. For example, an airline may sell seats in response to a customer's telephone call, a hotel may sell accommodation directly to business customers or an inclusive tour (IT) operator may sell a ski holiday through a brochure and inbound telephone operation. In the United Kingdom the main focus of attention on direct selling has been on IT operators offering package holidays directly to the market. Accordingly this chapter will focus on this aspect of direct sell, but its messages can be applied equally to all sectors of the tourism industry.

Direct selling of IT holidays involves the tour operator distributing brochures directly to existing or potential customers, who, in turn, make reservations directly with the tour operator. This approach bypasses travel agents as a means of distributing brochures or assisting with reservations and invoicing. The two alternative approaches are illustrated in Fig. 1. Typically, UK buyers have made hotel, train, holiday camp and coach tour arrangements directly with the respective suppliers, i.e. using a direct selling approach. Package tours bought in the United Kingdom have, however, been booked predominantly through travel agents.

In many types of business operation, a company may choose to sell to some customers directly, and may use intermediaries to reach others. In tourism, a company will generally be viewed as either a direct selling operation or a business which uses travel agencies. The distinction refers to whether the tour operator offers trade terms to travel agents, rather than indicating the source of all bookings. Indeed a compay which sells through agents will normally also receive bookings directly. Further, direct sell operators may sell to group organizers, who receive payment or incentives to sell to others. These could be classified as intermediaries in the distribution channel.

The distinction between direct selling and selling through travel agencies has become increasingly unclear in recent years, with some tour operators having interests in travel agencies, e.g. Thomsons interest in Lunn Poly, or companies operating as both travel agents and tour operators, e.g. Thomas Cook. Vertical integration in these distribution channels could change the meaning of direct sell in tourism in the near future.

Direct selling of mass market IT holidays in the United Kingdom developed when the Danish operator, Tjaereborg, entered the market in 1978. Other companies followed, including direct sell companies which were owned by existing travel principals, who were users of traditional travel trade channels. At this time, direct sell operators were accounting for large shares of the package holiday market in West Germany and Scandinavia. It was expected that the market share of direct sell operators in the United Kingdom would follow this trend and expand rapidly. However, it is clear with hindsight that these predictions were over-optimistic. Some operators have now withdrawn from the market; others have switched to using traditional trade channels.

Portland Holidays, who are part of the Thomson group, are the market leaders in the direct sell holiday sector, followed by Martin Rooks and Tjaereborg. It is difficult to establish the precise market share of the direct sell operators in the total markets, although 10 per cent is a good estimate. Direct selling operations appear strongest in specialist sectors (or 'niche' markets), based either on the product features (such as ski holidays) or market features (such as the over-sixties market). There are also many small operators selling under 10,000 places per annum who use direct sell.

Direct selling is often used synonymously with direct marketing, because to be effective in the longer term companies need to develop a comprehensive customer database and use this effectively. One reason for the development of direct sell in some areas of tourism has been the adoption of new technology which makes management of a customer database easier to control, and also enables the tour operator to reply speedily to customer enquiries.

Examples

Saga Holidays is a UK-based tour operator which caters for the over-sixties market. It originally sold direct because it was

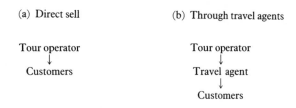

(a) Direct sell   (b) Through travel agents

Tour operator   Tour operator
↓   ↓
Customers   Travel agent
↓
Customers

Figure 1 Alternative distribution channels for package holidays.

unable to achieve adequate distribution through travel agents. As Saga's business expanded, travel agents were able to book Saga Holidays for their clients and sales through travel agents accounted for 20 per cent of sales by the mid-1980s. In late 1987, Saga decided to withdraw from selling through the retail travel trade, feeling that retail travel agents could no longer provide the level of service needed for the range of products which they offered. Bookings are now only to be made directly via a booking form or telephone. Saga have a mailing list of 2 million customers which is used as the basis for their direct selling operations.

A major user of direct sell has been in the group travel area, including schools' and educational groups. Schools Abroad is a UK-based direct sell operator, which started by offering school trips during the 1970s. Its major products were ski holidays, but in recent years, it has added a wide variety of educational and activity programs to its range. In addition to extending the range of packages the company has expanded its customer base. It is no longer exclusively a schools operator. It sells to clubs, businesses and other groups of travelers, and even to individuals or families. Schools Abroad with its related operations (such as Skiscope) is the largest specialist ski operator in Europe, selling more ski holidays than Thomsons and Inghams combined.

Martin Rooks are a long established tour operator in the direct sell market. Initially set up in the 1950s as a direct sell operator, they were acquired by British Airways in the 1970s to act as their direct selling operation. British Airways had hoped that Martin Rooks would become a major direct sell operator, by combining the value for money product with the name and strength of British Airways. Martin Rooks was sold to the SunMed Group in 1987.

Benefits

There are many reported benefits of direct selling to the operator. However, it is clear that for companies operating in the United Kingdom, potential benefits have not always been realized.

The fundamental benefit of direct sell is that it cuts out the use of a middleman between the operator and the customer. This means that the operator can retain control over his entire marketing process, ensuring that the customer relationship is managed at the chosen level. He can communicate directly with his customers, record information on them which can be used to target his marketing effort more effectively, and ensure that

advice, reservations, ticket distribution and all other communications conform to his desired minimum standard of operation. This reduces the fear that a consumer using an agency may fail to book a holiday because of lack of effort, indifference or delays by travel agency staff. Indeed, until recently, travel agents have played a passive role in all aspects of the holiday buying process, relying on operators to stimulate demand.

The operator can also retain control over the characteristics of the holiday package. Recently, travel agents (mainly the national chains) have offered promotional incentives to encourage holidaymakers to book, such as reduction in deposits, reduction in price, inclusion of insurance etc. The direct sell operator may wish to utilize these incentives, but by retaining control over the distribution system, he can identify when and if they are appropriate and select benefits for all customers, or for specific types of customers to meet set targets.

Arguably, the most significant difference between direct selling and selling through agents is that the direct sell operator does not have to pay commission to an agent or middleman. This has the effect of reducing the cost of the holiday package or alternatively increasing the operator's profit margin. There is some dispute regarding the amount of work which the agent exerts to attract business, but there is little doubt that agencies provide a local and convenient outlet for customers. Indeed a major factor underlying the development of the travel agencies was the major tour operator's need to have an extensive national distribution system. Some direct sell operators have found it necessary to open regional offices or establish regional sales networks to achieve such coverage.

Dealing directly with customers can mean that the operator's cashflow can be improved. The terms of package holiday bookings usually request full payment for the holiday 6–8 weeks before departure. Travel agents will normally retain this money for a while, enabling them to earn interest on it. When this money is paid to the operator directly, the company has its benefit earlier than if dealing through agents.

The elimination of travel agents' commission is not the only area of potential cost reduction. Further cost reductions are possible because the operator no longer has to spend money on maintaining relationships with travel agencies and providing point of sale promotional material. Brochure wastage should be lower, and the conversion rate to sales higher, because the brochure should be distributed to interested customers. However, it has been difficult for UK direct sell operators to achieve the level of success in brochure-to-sales conversions of some of the major tour operators dealing in traditional channels.

A major benefit of direct selling has been the ability to segment the market effectively. By retaining detailed customer records, it is possible to identify key segments and determinants of demand within segments. This enables products, prices and promotional activity to be tailored around the needs of specific customers. Examples of this could include identifying those people who book at short notice and mailing them with details of last-minute breaks, or identifying those people who like to visit new destinations in the product range or those who are loyal to specific hotels, resorts or countries and preparing a specific mailing highlighting relevant points to them. Management of this customer database can thus be used to increase repeat buying. Costs of promotional effort can also be reduced, and through this, marketing efficiency is improved.

The costs of advertising for direct sell operators are not necessarily higher than for companies using travel agencies. This is because, even when selling through travel agencies, the responsibility for generating brand awareness and preference still lies with the operators. Traditionally the agent's role has been to provide information on a wide range of options and not offer one particular supplier's products, although the developments in vertical integration may alter this. Accordingly the burden of responsibility for advertising falls on the operator, irrespective of whether he is using a direct sell approach or not. The information which the direct sell operator has on his market may enable him to make more informed decisions about placing advertising.

The overall success of a direct selling operation depends on the extent to which the tour operator can improve marketing efficiency by improving customer contact and service quality and achieving lower promotional costs per unit of sale than would be achieved if selling through agencies. For example, if they determine that they are likely to get one booking for every six brochures distributed through travel agents, then they would aim for a better conversion rate through direct selling.

Implementation

In the UK any company which wishes to offer flight-based IT holidays, including direct selling operators, must be ATOL (Air Tour Operator's License) registered with the CAA (Civil Aviation Authority). All operators must pay into the Air Travel Reserve Fund. Once registered they can offer their tours to the market through their chosen channel.

Start-up costs in direct sell operations may be low, if the operator develops to meet the needs of specific, clearly identified groups of travelers. However, where it is necessary to generate market awareness (through advertising or personal selling) and to develop or buy a mailing list, start-up costs can be high.

The critical factors in implementing a direct sell policy in tourism are the management of a customer database (which is often called a mailing list, but which should include more than customers' names and addresses), achieving the target level of customer service or response and monitoring the effectiveness of aspects of the direct selling process.

Managing the customer database

The overall process of ensuring that the customer database is effective and comprehensive is clearly critical to the long-term success of a direct selling operation. There are three distinct phases in managing this resource effectively.

Database development

A database can be drawn up from a variety of different sources. The most obvious starting point for a company which is currently operating is from existing records of past customers.

Other sources are open to new and existing companies alike – people who respond to advertising or editorials, those approached at exhibitions, etc. Other sources for the direct sell databases are names from competition entries, or bought–in mailing lists which meet specified criteria. Additionally, names should be added to the database when brochure requests are received by mail or phone.

Housekeeping

Once a database has been developed it is important to keep it current and correct. Housekeeping is the term used to describe tasks which are part of the process of ensuring that the database is accurate and up-to-date. The most basic housekeeping task is de-duplicating – checking to ensure that each person is only entered once on each list in the database. This task may prove difficult in practice, because while it is simple to determine whether two people of the same name are on the list, there may be several variations in any one entry. Variations may exist for a variety of reasons, for example, spelling mistakes, use of initials rather than full names, or house names rather than numbers. These errors can be reduced by making updating a highly disciplined exercise, or alternatively by using sophisticated computer software to check the list.

Database use

The efficiency of direct selling operations relies on using the database effectively and creatively. By accessing information on the database, a direct sell operator can follow-up brochure dispatch (or any other activity) with telephone calls or letters, distribute newsletters, identify those customers who should be sent details of special offers etc. The database can help beyond the promotional area. Its details on customer buying patterns can lead to identification of profitable market segments. It can also be used to form the sampling framework for surveys on customer satisfaction with the sales process or with the end product. Some direct sell operators are not using their database effectively, using it only as a mailing list to distribute brochures.

Levels of customer service or response

When developing a direct sell operation, it is important to set levels of customer service in all aspects of operation. People wishing to book a holiday may visit a travel agent and collect brochures on the same day. If they respond to an advertisement, then they should be able to expect a brochure in a (specified) set period of time. Operators who fail to distribute brochures promptly will not manage to impress customers with their reliability and attention, and will be unlikely to convince a prospect that a direct sell operator offers the same level of attention as a travel agent. The same standards should also apply for confirmation of bookings, ticket dispatch and other correspondence. Equally, information on availability and resorts, hotels, departure times etc. should be given quickly to prospects (preferably over the phone in response to their query). This can counteract the view that a local travel agency can service the customer's needs more efficiently or promptly and also add to his buying experience.

Monitoring the effectiveness of the selling operation

It is important that standards are set for each aspect of the selling operation For example, target response rates should be set for advertising, conversion rates (from brochure receipt to reservations) should be established, and acceptable quantity and quality of leads must be determined to justify participation in shows and exhibitions. All these tasks can be difficult to establish in the first instance, but are necessary for the operator to identify when support is needed in a particular area of activity, on a particular product and/or market. It also helps the operator to establish their role as a proactive one, rather than passively waiting to see whether the distributed brochures will result in conversions to sales.

Two particularly critical areas are the sales team performance and the brochure. Many direct sell operators have networks of representatives or telesales-type activities. Where these exist, call rates and conversion rates should be established and monitored on a daily, weekly and monthly basis to identify the performance of each member of the team, the customer base they are working with and perhaps the sales pitch or script they are using. The brochure is particularly important for direct sell operators because the customer will make their initial judgment of the company on it. Accordingly, brochures need to be particularly clear and easy to use, and give adequate information on the company and its reliability and quality. All forms and price lists should be clear and easy to follow. Ideally, these aspects should be tested prior to the launch of a new brochure, and they should also be monitored continuously.

Assessment

It is difficult to determine precisely *why* direct selling operations have a relatively small share of the total UK package tour market. A recent survey by the Henley Centre for Forecasting on home shopping reported that 31 per cent of respondents reported that they would shop for a foreign holiday from home, a higher level than for any other category of product. This indicates that customers are not against the principle of direct selling in tourism, although this does not convert into actual sales of directly booked IT holidays. Clearly, direct sell operators have problems competing against existing branded tour operators and national travel agency chains.

An operator may ask the following questions, for example, on the brochure dispatch and reservations area. What is the minimum period from dispatch of a brochure to obtaining a sale from it? What is the average period of time from brochure dispatch to a booking? What percentage of bookings will come within, say, 1 month of brochure dispatch? What percentage will come within 3 months? How many people (or what percentage) book within 6/3/1 month(s) of the departure date?

Other questions concern the holidaymaking behavior of clients. What percentage of the customer base take more than one holiday per year? What is their average length of stay? What is the average party size? What percentage of customers fly from their nearest airport? What percentage of customers

live in any specific region? These questions can be linked to external data, such as commercial psychodemographic analyses, in addition to internally generated data.

Alternatively, operators can undertake evaluation which is based on monitoring their product offering. This type of evaluation can also be undertaken by tour operators using travel agencies. Which are the most popular departure times? Which are the most popular departure airports? Does this vary through the year? Which are the most popular forms of accommodation? Which are the most popular resorts?

It is clear that it is important to evaluate the effectiveness of promotion. Questions here can include identification of the advertisements/editorials which generate the greatest or quickest response. It is also useful to identify those which show the highest conversion rates to sales, or the greatest average value of holidays.

Conclusion

Despite the benefits detailed in this chapter, the profitability of the direct sell operators in the UK mass market has been variable. While specialist operators have achieved a degree of success, the established channels (from tour operator to travel agency to final consumer) have proved difficult to change for the mass market. The failure of direct sell operators to achieve a substantial share of the package holiday market has resulted in a trend from direct selling. Recent press reports detail operators who have specialized in direct sell focusing on development of their travel agency relations. For example, Club Med is aiming to increase sales through use of travel agents, reversing its current ratio of 70 per cent direct sales and 30 per cent of retail sales. Recently, sales through travel agents have accounted for over 90 per cent of increased bookings, while direct selling operations have only increased sales by 2–3 per cent.

The process of vertical integration in the travel trade is likely to have further effects on direct selling of package tours. The relationship between Thomsons Holidays and Lunn Poly is causing some disquiet, because of the strong brand preference for Thomsons which existing customers have. Some trade members have expressed fears that Thomsons may sell their holidays exclusively through Lunn Poly in the future. Currently, approximately 25 per cent of Lunn Poly's sales are for Thomsons holidays, a fact which explains that concern.

Direct selling operators may develop a substantial customer database which will enable them to focus their marketing activities more precisely. The adage of database marketing being data-based marketing is an appropriate one to those involved in direct selling. This can enable more efficient and effective marketing operations to be developed.

While this chapter has focused on direct sell in package tours, direct sell is applied in other areas of travel and tourism. While travel agents account for a large percentage of airline ticket sales in Europe, the mechanisms of direct selling of airline seats which have been used in the United States following deregulation have now appeared in the United Kingdom. This may result in an increase in direct sales of airline seats.

Automatic ticket sales machines using credit cards, and self-ticketing schemes where companies (or individuals) can buy quantities of tickets and write out the details having phoned to check availability, also offer potential for expansion of direct sales for carriers. In addition, online information systems, where individuals can call up information on seat availability and tariffs at home, may also affect the acceptance of direct selling.

Focus on small business

The direct selling operation can be an effective form of distribution for a small business. A major objective will be to ensure an adequate level of awareness exists in their market. This can be achieved through the development of a suitable customer database or sufficient promotional effort. While advertising can be an effective medium of communication with the market, for some small businesses, such as hotels, personal selling may be more efficient.

A benefit of the direct sell approach for small businesses is the ability to monitor and control all aspects of the selling process and simultaneously to establish and maintain contact with customers. This enables the business to obtain constant feedback on their marketing efforts and also to monitor changes in the market-place. This information, gathered as part of the normal business routine can help small businesses compete against the resources of larger companies.

Further reading

Beaver, A., *Mind Your Own Travel Business* (Beaver Travel, 1980). This comprehensive two volume publication is a manual for travel agency personnel and so gives an alternative perspective on direct sell operations.

Bishop, J., *Travel Marketing* (Bailey Bros and Swinfen, 1981). Various chapters in this well known and practical text refer to the establishment of package tours and the alternative distribution options. Chapter 15 is especially useful for a novice operator.

Cowell, D., *The Marketing of Services* (Heinemann, 1984). This com-prehensive text on the marketing of services discusses alternative channel decisions of service suppliers in Chapter 10, including a brief review of the advantages of direct selling.

Fitch, A., 'Tour operators in the U.K.', *Travel and Tourism Analyst* (March 1987), pp. 29–43. A comprehensive review of the practice of tour operators in the UK, which examines the various influences on the inclusive tour sector, including the nature of the travel agency – tour operator relationship.

Henley Centre for Forecasting, *Planning for Social Change* (Henley Centre for Forecasting, 1987). Amongst other topics, this explores the concept of home shopping of various products, including holidays.

Hymas, R., 'Marketing business travel services', *The Travel and Tourism Industry*, A. Hodgson (ed.), (Pergamon, 1987), pp. 107–34. While focusing on business travel, this article questions commission levels to agents, and reviews possible strategies for direct selling airlines and for travel agents to maintain customer contact and service levels.

Mayhew, L., 'The travel agent – rise or fall', *The Travel and Tourism Industry*, A. Hodgson (ed.), (Pergamon, 1987), pp. 49–73. A review of the role of the travel agent which identifies many of the issues in the debate on their role in the tourism distribution process, as well as many operation issues facing travel agents.

Middleton, V. T. C., 'A marketing argument for direct sell in the holiday market', *International Tourism Quarterly*, no. 2 (1980), pp. 44–55. This article reviews the basic principles which underly direct selling in tourism, and also details the state of direct sell operations at the time.

Mill, R. C. and Morrison, A. M., *The Tourism System: An Introductory Text* (Prentice Hall, 1985). Chapter 16 of this text examines the nature of tourism distribution channels and influences on distribution policy.

Stern, L. and El-Ansary, A. I., *Marketing Channels* (Prentice Hall, 3rd edition, 1987). A classic textbook on channel management, this recently revised edition includes a chapter on marketing channels for service business.

Wardell, D., 'Airline reservation systems in the USA', *Travel and Tourism Analyst* (January 1987), pp. 45–56. In addition to covering the range of airline reservation systems in the USA, this article identifies the trend to direct sales and reviews the future of agency carrier relations in the USA.

Welburn, H., 'Travel selling and distribution', *Travel and Tourism Analyst* (July 1987), pp. 3–15. This article makes predictions on the use of technology in selling of tourism products in the short, medium and long term.

LYNN PARKINSON

Economic models
of tourism

Introduction

This chapter attempts to give an overview of the use of economic theory in analyzing tourism. Hypothetically, modeling in tourism could have originated with the development of private consumption theory in economics. In this respect, tourism can be considered as just a specialized form of consumption theory.

A warning should be given at the outset however – tourism is a complex subject: it is not sufficient to study tourism alone without also considering the influence of such relevant issues as sociodemographic and sociopsychological factors, the impact of personal values and lifestyles, the continuing development of technology and transportation, urbanization, the growth in leisure time, and so on. These additional issues are covered in other sections of the Handbook.

The consumer theory approach

In the framework of microeconomic consumption theory, tourism demand can be·explained by the utility maximization of an individual or household under budget constraint, given complete information.

In neoclassical theory, the consumer distributes his known budget across the goods and services available at given prices in order to receive a maximum utility from the total amount of consumed goods and services. In order for this process to take place, the consumer must have complete information concerning all possible combinations of goods and services as well as the ability to evaluate and rank them. The utility function provides complete information about what utility can be gained from the various goods and services. The individual demand for tourism originates from a budget allocation process which maximizes utility. The demand for each good or each specific tourism service is a function of all prices and the consumer budget; leisure time is assumed to be constant and given.

Through time, complete demand systems were developed. One of the most well-known demand systems, called the 'linear-expenditure-system', was developed by R. Stone (1954). One direct application of demand systems was demonstrated through the work of O'Hagan and Harrison (1984) and Smeral (1988).

Within the framework of the neoclassical allocation model, one can integrate tourism demand in the following manner:

$$D_{ij} = \mathbf{f}(p_{ij} \ldots p_{nj}, Y_j)$$
.
.
$$D_{nj} = \mathbf{f}(p_{ij} \ldots p_{nj}, Y_j)$$

$D_{ij} \ldots D_{(n-2)j}$ = demand for nontourism consumer goods in country j

$D_{(n-1)j}$ = domestic consumption of tourism services by country j

D_{nj} = tourism consumption abroad by country j

$p_{ij} \ldots p_{(n-2)j}$ = prices of nontourism consumer goods in country j (expressed as units of a homogeneous currency)

$p_{(n-1)j}$ = prices of domestic tourism goods and services in units of a homogeneous international currency in country j

p_{nj} = prices of foreign tourism goods and services in units of a homogeneous currency for country j with

$$p_{nj} = \sum_{k=1}^{l} g_k p_{(n-1)k}, \text{ where } g_k = \frac{D_{njk}}{D_{nj}},$$

$$\text{and } \sum_{k=1}^{l} g_k = 1, j \neq k$$

Y_j = disposable income in units of a homogeneous international currency in country j

$$\sum_{i=1}^{n} p_{ij} D_{ij} = Y_j$$

n = number of consumer goods, $i = 1 \ldots n$

m = number of countries of origin, $j = 1 \ldots m$

l = number of destination countries, $k = 1 \ldots l$

With a model thus developed, the demand for each consumer good, including that for tourism goods and services, is a function of prices and of disposable income. Savings can be thought of as a future consumption good and thus also find a place within the model.

In the above model, if one makes the assumption of a two-stage decision process separable for each country, one can find an equation for the tourism demand of origin country j for the destination country k. In the first step, the volume of demand for domestic and foreign tourism goods and services from the consumers in the origin countries is determined. In the second step, the country of destination is determined according to prices of tourism goods in all possible destinations and the foreign travel budget restriction.

$$D_{njk} = \mathbf{f}\left(p_{(n-1)k} \cdots p_{(n-1)l}, \sum_{k=1}^{l} D_{njk}\right)$$

$$k = 1 \ldots l, \ k \neq j$$

Total foreign tourism demand of all countries of origin j for a destination country k can be expressed as:

$$D_{nk} = \mathbf{f}\left(p_{(n-1)k} \cdots p_{(n-1)l}, \sum_{j=1}^{m} D_{nj}\right), \ k = 1 \ldots l$$

$$D_{nk} = \sum_{j=1}^{m} D_{nkj}$$

$$\sum_{k=1}^{l} D_{nk} = \sum_{j=1}^{m} D_{nj} = \sum_{j=1}^{m} \sum_{k=1}^{l} D_{njk}$$

$$\sum_{k=1}^{l} D_{njk} = D_{nj}$$

The following functions represent the market shares in international travel:

$$D_{njk}/D_{nj} = S_{njk} = \mathbf{f}(p_{(n-1)k} \cdots p_{(n-1)l}); \ k \neq j$$

$$D_{nk} \bigg/ \sum_{j=1}^{m} D_{nj} = S_{nk} = \mathbf{f}(p_{(n-1)k} \cdots p_{(n-1)l}); \ k = 1 \ldots l$$

A simple empirical application of this developed equation system based on an approximation of neoclassical theory can be found in the appendix on page 116.

The explanation of tourism in the framework of microeconomic consumption theory progressed further through the contribution of K. J. Lancaster (1966). Contrary to the tenets of neoclassical theory, Lancaster's theory classifies goods and services *not* as the direct utility objects, but rather according to their characteristics. Consumption is assumed to be an activity. The inputs of this activity are goods or services, alone or in combination. The output is a bundle of characteristics. This input–output relationship is called the 'consumption technology'. The ranking of preferences is assumed to be an evaluation of characteristics; the goods or services themselves are only indirectly ranked through their characteristics. The consumer decision is based on the maximization of a utility function according to the characteristics of the goods and services as arguments, with a given consumption technology and a linear budget constraint.

In general, the utility maximization problem can be formulated as a nonlinear programming problem in the following manner: let $\mathbf{z}$ be a vector whose characteristics are the quantities of various attributes; let $\mathbf{x}$ be a vector the elements of which are quantities of various commodities; let $\mathbf{p}$ be a vector of cor-

responding prices, and $\mathbf{y}$ the level of income (U = utility). Thus, the consumer desires to maximize:

$$U = U(\mathbf{z})$$
$$\mathbf{z} = \mathbf{f}(\mathbf{x})$$
$$\mathbf{p}'\mathbf{x} \leq \mathbf{y}$$
$$\mathbf{x}, \mathbf{z} \geq 0$$

The function $\mathbf{f}(\mathbf{x})$ describes the 'production' of attributes by commodities. A simplification is provided by replacing it by the linear approximation $\mathbf{Bx}$, where $\mathbf{B}$ is a matrix with as many rows as there are attributes and as many columns as there are commodities. The matrix $\mathbf{B}$ is then the consumption technology.

The special application of this theory to tourism is based on the assumption that, under certain conditions, it is possible to separate a set of activities and characteristics. Therefore vacation trips are for the most part independent of the nontouristic consumption of the traveler. In this manner, the whole spectrum must not be taken into consideration as it would be in the neoclassical theory. One consequence of the independence assumption is that changes in the prices of nontouristic goods or services cause no reaction in the travel behavior. Lancaster's approach is useful for introducing new goods or services without the necessity of a reformulation of the utility function as would be the case with the neoclassical theory.

For practical application of Lancaster's theory, it is useful to become familiar with the ideas of Young (1969). Young shows that, when an individual maximizes a utility function according to commodity characteristics that are subject to budget and commodity constraints, then the resulting demand function contains commodity attributes as explanatory variables.

Many other models used to explain tourism demand are developed based on the central ideas of microeconomic theory, but not all explanations of special variants can be included in this survey (see references). The gravity and trip generation models are another special group of models which attempt to explain tourism demand. Their main assumption is that the number of visits to a certain destination or city is a function of the population size of both the area of origin as well as the area of destination and the distance between them.

In the framework of macroeconomic consumption theory, a general relationship between income and consumption (with tourism demand as a special group in consumption) is assumed. Here we find a difference between short-term development and long-term growth.

Ideally, one assumes that, in the long run, total consumption will depend on the development of income, specifically the development of that part of income upon which the individual can rely. However, in the short run, total consumption will depend also upon the economic expectations of the individual. Because of travel and tourism's positions in the needs hierarchy, it can be considered a superior form of consumption (travel as a luxury good). The income elasticity of demand for travel and tourism will therefore be higher than that of total demand of households and is in general greater than 1. This property of travel is the main reason for its strong dependence on developments in the 'consumption climate' and on economic expectations. In periods of economic instability, such as when unemployment threatens, households tend to save more (preventive motive) and to reduce their consumption of high quality goods such as travel and durable consumption goods. It is much easier for the household to go without a holiday than to deprive itself of basic goods such as food, heating, lighting, and clothing. However, an increase in saving at the cost of vacations causes only in the most extreme case a cancellation of the planned vacation. Normally, a reduction of vacation length, distance or lower daily expenditures will be the result.

The possibility also exists that a household in a situation of short-term income losses will not reduce its usual travel standard but rather finance travel from its savings. However, in the long term, an adaption in the level of tourism expenditures to the new income level will be necessary.

The implicit assumed rank-order of needs or the changes in the needs hierarchy are based on the idea that, in the process of economic development, special demand waves exist. After the satisfaction of a certain group of needs, the expenditures in the next level or group of needs grows above average. Upon the approximation of a certain satisfaction level, expenditures in the next level begin to rise rapidly. The best known relationship between the income level and a certain need group in the hierarchy was discovered by E. Engel in the year 1857. He established 'Engel's Laws', which claim that the income elasticity of food is less than 1. Following this, the relationship between other commodity groups and income became the focus of many research programs.

The results of research demonstrate the existence of a hierarchy, which starts with food, shelter and clothing, goes through the durable consumption goods to services, including travel. The described demand waves or the structural change in the growth process have the following impact on tourism demand: as with private consumption, it can be assumed in the growth process that the demand for tourism goods with a higher quality (such as entertainment, meals in restaurants, shopping, cultural attractions etc.) receive a greater weight. In contrast, the expenditure shares of tourism goods of a lower quality (such as low priced accommodation, food and transportation) become less important. These changes in the consumption structure can occur due to structural changes in the specific vacation styles or because of the traveler's selection of other vacation styles.

Specific vacation styles go through a special product life cycle. According to this concept, a single destination area can support several different vacation styles. The older, supply-oriented approach argues that a destination can have only one life cycle. The application of the product-cycle theory for travel is none other than a mix of explanation factors originating from demand, production and trade theory. The cycle by itself offers no explanation; it is just a statistical documentation.

The foreign trade theory approach

The traditional view of foreign trade theory, such as the factor proportion theory of Heckscher (1949) and Ohlin (1933) (the 'H-O-model') or Ricardo's (1817) theory of 'comparative costs', ignores demand, an important factor in international travel.

The H-O-model can be used reservedly, however, to explain intersectoral exchange of industrial goods and tourism services. For production to take place, certain necessary factors must be available in each country, but the amount of factor per country can vary. The provision of tourism services is relatively labor intensive, while the production of industrial goods is relatively capital intensive; the factors are measured as flows. In the industrialized countries, the capital intensity is higher than in the developing countries. The result is that the industrialized nations attempt to specialize in the production of capital goods while the developing countries focus on the production of services, such as tourism; both types do their trade in their own specific manner.

The classical 'Ricardo model', although not a thorough explanation for international trade either, is (like the H-O-model), a supply-side oriented model similarly useful for explaining the international exchange between developing or socialistic countries and industrial countries. The exchange is mostly complementary (raw material or island-beaches against industrial goods). For example, countries which have just raw materials or just unspoiled landscapes with certain climate conditions must become specialized in this direction in order to have goods to exchange for industrial goods or technologically advanced products not produced in that country ('availability hypothesis'). Developed countries which have good natural resources like climate, island beaches and mountains, or culture or special technical knowledge, do not become specialized to the same degree.

Contrary to most orthodox trade theories, which assume a given demand and focus more attention on the supply side, neoclassical theory attempts to create a synthesis between supply and demand. The 'neoclassical synthesis' has a high degree of abstraction and a very low empirical content; however, the neoclassical model has the important didactic function of focusing on the demand side.

For the new differentiated forms of tourism the 'new view' of trade theory approach is more appropriate and explanatory. This 'new view' focuses on the international exchange of differentiated products and services between countries with similar stages of development and similar preferences (an *intra*sectoral view as opposed to the *inter*sectoral view of the classical theories).

These kinds of international exchanges are dominated by the preferences of the people; they are a trade of differentiated goods and services or an exchange of equal goods of different types. These goods and services are produced in the supplier countries with a different input mix and are in competition with similar, but not identical, products in imperfect markets; on the supply side economies of scale are generated. Each good or service has its own demand curve with a negative slope. An increase in relative price induces an imperfect substitution. In this case, international exchange is created so that the consumers purchase goods or travel to a given destination which is perceived as having real or subjective qualitative advantages or prestige.

One consequence is that goods are purchased in the foreign

destination even when the price is higher than at home. It is possible that an equal assortment of tourism services are bought in the home country by foreign visitors as are purchased by citizens from the home country abroad. Some examples of this are the exchange between cities in the framework of urban tourism (Paris v. London or Rome v. Vienna) or in other forms of tourism such as ski vacations (Vermont v. Tyrol). This exchange, mostly free from the influence of prices, will grow in the future with the growth of wealth.

In the framework of monetary trade theory, tourism is a flow of aggregated exports and imports of services. Given this perspective, the basic points of importance are:

1. The effect of an autonomous increase in tourism demand on the economy or the size of the tourism export multiplier.
2. The effect of increases in income on foreign travel by residents or the size of the propensity to import.
3. The elasticity of travel demand in relation to changes in prices and exchange rates.

Tourism and the theory of services

One of the best known explanations of long-term development of services is the three-sector hypothesis. The main content of this approach with respect to tourism can be summarized as follows: with growing per capita income, the demand for goods changes from primary production to secondary production, and then to goods from tertiary production, or the service sector. The fast growth of the service sector has two main components:

1. The change in the needs structure of private households to bank and insurance services, travel, education etc.
2. The growth in the intermediary demand from producers who need always more tertiary goods, such as business trips and consulting, for the production of secondary goods.

As a result of this growth, tourism – and in the future, its specialized forms such as city tourism – will gain advantages from the structural change.

In general, technical progress has a lesser impact at the tertiary level than in the primary or secondary level. This is mostly the case for all sectors which, like the tourism sector, are dominated by personal services because of the few possibilities for mechanization and rationalization. Certain areas in the tourism industry could receive advantages from technical and organizational innovations, such as traveling with large tour buses, large hotels located at the city limits, jumbo jets, airlines with their own hotel chains, and so on.

The special conditions for service production can be summarized as follows: tourism is dominated by the special services of the hotel and restaurant industries. The special conditions for production in these industries are generated through the nonstorable and nontransportable character of their services. Contrary to industrial production, production and demand in the hotel and restaurant industries are identical. Changes in demand cannot be equalized by stock changes; rather, cycles

in the capacity utilization are the result. In short, supply in the tourism industry is simply a supply of capacity, with the number of services produced a function of demand.

Assessment and conclusion

In summary, many parts and aspects of economic theory may be applied in the development of models for tourism. The challenge for the future remains the unresolved question of how to go beyond the purely economic factors in model development. Other aspects which might be included in the modeling process are the aforementioned issues of the impact of values and lifestyles, developments in the technological environment, urbanization, sociodemographic factors, and the like. In other words, new directions in the development of modeling in tourism should reflect not only changes in purely economic variables but also possible changes in other influencing factors as well.

Appendix

In order to estimate the foreign tourism demand in nine European countries, an econometric model has been developed and is presented below. The demand for, or real revenue from, international tourism in each of the destination countries is given as functions of dollar prices (and therefore implicitly exchange rates) in all competing countries, and income, or travel budgets.

The source of the data on the revenues of international tourism are the balance of payments statistics of the International Monetary Fund (IMF); the calculation of the different price indices is based on the 'Verbrauchergeldparitäten' from the Statistisches Bundesamt in Wiesbaden (FRG) and on information from the national statistics of the specific countries involved. The information about the dollar exchange rates is from the OECD (Organization for Economic Cooperation and Development).

$$x_k = a_k + b_k X + c_k (p_k/P) + u_k$$
$$.$$
$$x_l = a_l + b_l X + c_l (p_l/P) + u_l$$

$l (= 9) =$ number of countries of destination k, $k = 1 \ldots l$

$x_k =$ real revenue from international tourism of country k expressed in US\$

$$X = \sum_{k=1}^{l} x_k$$

$p_k =$ prices of tourism goods in country k in US\$, $1979 = 100$

$P =$ average prices of tourism goods in all n countries of destination in US\$

$$P = \sum_{k=1}^{l} g_k p_k, \ g_k = \frac{x_k}{X}, \ \sum_{k=1}^{l} g_k = 1$$

u_k = residual

a_k, b_k, c_k = constant parameters

In the model presented above, real revenue from international tourism has been expressed as a function of relative prices and real foreign travel budgets. In order to carry out an econometric estimation based on a small sample, the OLS (ordinary least squares) method was used. In the model, linear equations were taken.

One could argue that a 2SLS (two-stage least squares)-estimation procedure should be applied. However, for the sake of practicality and also because the data sample is too small in this example for a 2SLS-estimation, this method was not used; the 2SLS-model needs a large amount of data to become at least 'asymptotically consistent'.

The results of the estimation are presented in Table 1. In general, a sufficient statistical explanation could be found for the development of revenues from international tourism, except for Switzerland and Yugoslavia. All coefficients have the sign expected from theory.

In order to obtain estimates for the future development of foreign tourism demand in each of the chosen countries, a number of simulations was conducted using the model. Using different scenarios with differing growth rates in Western Europe, reactions in foreign tourism demand could be calculated.

For comparing results, different growth rates of 2 and 3 per cent were taken for the analysis. The volume of the total real travel budget spent in the nine destination countries by travelers from the origin countries was determined using regressions (Table 2) which correlate the development of total real revenues from international tourism in the nine countries with the real gross national product (GNP) of OECD Europe (X). The values thus calculated were used recursively to find x_k. In solving the equations, constant relative prices were assumed in order to monitor accurately the growth effects.

The results obtained by increasing growth rates by 1 per cent have been computed in Table 2. The increase in growth rates has the largest effect for Italy, the United Kingdom, France and Spain. An increase in the growth of demand leads to larger market shares for all these countries. The other countries show no gain from increases in the growth rate and suffer losses in their market shares. These are minimal for Greece and West Germany, and rather large for Austria.

Table 1 General form of the estimation function $x_k = a_k + b_k X + c_k(p_k/P)$. Time period: 1973–1984.

Country	a_k	b_k	c_k	R^2
Austria	7686.321	0.055	−47.134	0.845
France	2189.426	0.218	−48.225	0.969
West Germany	4927.132	0.098	−35.386	0.955
Greece	3933.683	0.023	−34.870	0.706
Italy	103.597	0.277	−47.145	0.939
Spain	14519.273	0.208	−177.042	0.782
United Kingdom	4699.462	0.175	−65.998	0.684

Table 2 The effect of an increase in growth rates on the increase in real revenues from international tourism.

	Growth rate[1] (change in %)		Effect on real revenues in percentage points[2]
	2%	3%	
Austria	1.4	2.1	0.7
France	3.8	5.7	1.9
West Germany	2.2	3.2	1.0
Greece	2.1	3.1	1.0
Italy	4.9	7.2	2.3
Spain	3.6	5.3	1.7
Switzerland	/	/	/
United Kingdom	4.4	6.6	2.2
Yugoslavia	/	/	/

[1] Real GNP of OECD Europe (GNP_{Eur}). The development of foreign tourism demand in the chosen destination countries (X) was calculated on the basis of the estimation function given below and used under the assumption of constant relative prices:
X = −22203.446 + 32.837 GNP_{Eur}; R^2 = 0.902
[2] Additional growth in the first year.

Further reading

The following references provide the basis for an understanding of how microeconomic theory can be applied to tourism:

Henderson, J. M. and Quandt, R.E., *Microeconomic Theory: A Mathematical Approach* (McGraw-Hill, 1958).

Lancaster, K. J., *Consumer Demand: A New Approach* (Columbia University Press, 1970).

Lancaster, K. J., 'A new approach to consumer theory', *Journal of Political Economy* (1966), pp. 132–57.

Quandt, R. E. (ed.), *The Demand for Travel: Theory and Measurement* (Lexington, 1970).

Smeral, E., 'Ein Entscheidungsmodell für Konsumieren und Sparen', *Empirica*, vol. 2 (1978), pp. 243–77.

Smeral, E., 'Ein Exportallokationsmodell für die westlichen Industrieländer', *Weltwirtschaftliches Archiv*, vol. 3 (1979), pp. 450–66.

Smeral, E., Alternative Modelle und Hypothesen der Konsum- und Sparentscheidung', *Empirica*, vol. 1 (1980), pp. 89–120.

Stone, R., 'Linear expenditure system and demand analysis', *The Economic Journal*, vol. 64 (1954), pp. 511–27.

Young, K. H. 'An abstract mode approach to the demand for travel', *Transportation Research*, vol. 3 (1969), pp. 443–61.

The following references present a comprehensive overview of consumer theory and are useful for understanding its relationship to tourism.

Ando, A. and Modigliani, F., 'The life cycle hypothesis of saving: aggregate implications and test', *American Economic Review*, vol. 53 (March 1963), pp. 55–85.

Duesenberry, J. S., *Income, Saving and the Theory of Consumer Behavior* (Harvard University Press, 1949).

Friedman, M., *A Theory of Consumption Function* (National Bureau of Economic Research, 1957).

Katona, G., *The Powerful Consumer* (McGraw-Hill, 1960).

Keynes, J. M., *General Theory of Employment, Interest and Money* (Macmillan, 1936).

Philips, L., *Applied Consumption Analysis* (North Holland, 1974).

Streißler, E. and Streißler, M., *Konsum and Nachfrage* (Kiepenheuer, 1966).

Streißler, M., *Theorie des Haushalts* (Fischer, 1974).

Excellent examples of the product life cycle theory and its implications for tourism are:

Haywood, K. M., 'Can the tourist-area life cycle be made operational', *Tourism Management*, vol. 7, no. 3 (1986), pp. 154–67.

Palme, G., *Tourismus in der Steiermark: Ein Produktzykluskonzept*, Österreichisches Institut für Wirtschaftsforschung (WIFO, 1986).

The following references give an excellent overview of the possibilities for integrating travel and tourism in foreign trade theory:

Breuss, F., *Österreichische Außenwirtschaft, 1945–1982* (Signum, 1983).

Chacholiades, M., *International Monetary Theory and Policy* (McGraw-Hill, 1978).

Chipman, J. S., 'A survey of the theory of international trade'; Part 1, 'The classical theory', *Econometrica*, vol. 33, no. 3 (July, 1965), pp. 477–519; Part 2, 'The neoclassical theory', *Econometrica*, vol. 33, no. 4 (October 1965), pp. 684–760; Part 3, 'The modern theory', *Econometrica*, vol. 34, no. 1 (January, 1966), pp. 18–76.

Gray, H. P., *International Travel – International Trade* (Heath and Co., 1970).

Heckscher, E. F., 'The effect of foreign trade on the distribution of income' (englische Fassung von: 'Utrikshandelns verkan pa inkomstfördelningen', *Ekonomisk Tidskrift*, vol. 21, del. 2 (1919), pp. 1–32), *Readings in the Theory of International Trade*, H. S. Ellis and L. A. Metzler, eds (Macmillan, 1949), pp. 272–300.

Jarchow, H. J., and Rühmann, P., *Monetäre Außenwirtschaft: I. Monetäre Außenwirtschaftstheorie* (Gustaf Fischer, 1982).

Kravis, I. B., 'Availability and other influences on the commodity composition of trade', *Journal of Political Economy*, vol. 64 (April, 1956), pp. 143–55.

Leontief, W. W., 'The use of indifference curves in the analysis of foreign trade', *The Quarterly Journal of Economics*, vol. 47 (May 1933), pp. 493–503.

Lerner, A. P., 'The diagrammatical representation of cost conditions in international trade', *Economica* (August 1932), pp. 346–56.

Lerner, A. P., 'The diagrammatical representation of demand conditions in international trade', *Economica* (August 1932), pp. 319–34.

Marshall, A., *The Pure Theory of Foreign Trade* (Macmillan, 1930).

Ohlin, B., *Interregional and International Trade* (Macmillan, 1933).

Ricardo, D., *On the Principles of Political Economy and Taxation* (Macmillan, 1817).

Tourism's relationship to services in economics can be studied in the following sources:

Bhagwati, J., 'Why are services cheaper in the poor countries', *Economic Journal* (June, 1984), pp. 279–86.

Clark, C., *The Conditions of Economic Progress* (Macmillan, 1960).

Kravis, I. B., Heston, A. and Summers, R., 'The share of services in economic growth', *Trade in Services: Economic Determinants and Development – Related Issues*, F. G. Adams, B. G. Hickman, A. Sapir and E. Lutz, eds (World Bank, Staff Working Paper, no. 480, August 1981).

The following sources contain some interesting economic applications of the theory of tourism demand.

Martin, C. A. and Witt, S. F., 'Substitute prices in models of tourism demand', *Annals of Tourism Research*, vol. 15, no. 2 (1988), pp. 255–68.

Menges, G., 'Die touristische Konsumfunktion der Schweiz 1929–1956', *Schweizerische Zeitschrift für Volkswirtschaft und Statistik*, vol. 94 (1958), pp. 329–31.

Morey, R. E., 'The choice of ski areas: estimation of a generalized CES preference ordering with characteristics', *Review of Economics and Statistics*, vol. 4 (1984), pp. 584–90.

O'Hagan, J. W. and Harrison, M., G., 'Market shares of US tourist expenditure in Europe: an econometric analysis', *Applied Economics*, vol. 16 (1984), pp. 919–31.

Smeral, E., 'Tourism demand, economic theory and econometrics: an integrated approach', *Journal of Travel Research*, vol. 26, no. 4 (1988), pp. 38–43.

Witt, S. F., 'An abstract mode-abstract (destination) node model of foreign holiday demand', *Applied Economics*, vol. 12, no. 2 (1980), pp. 163–80.

Witt, S. F., 'A binary choice model of foreign holiday demand', *Journal of Economic Studies*, vol. 10, no. 1 (1983), pp. 46–59.

Witt, S. F. and Martin, C. A., 'Forecasting future trends in European tourist demand', *Tourist Review*, no. 4 (1985), pp. 12–20.

Witt, S. F. and Martin, C. A., 'International tourism demand models – inclusion of marketing variables', *Tourism Management*, vol. 8, no. 1, (March 1987), pp. 33–40.

The following texts provide empirical explanations and analyses of tourism in the framework of economic theory:

Smeral, E., Kramer, H. and Walterskirchen, E., *Situation des österreichischen Fremdenverkehrs und Perspektiven bis zum Jahr 2000* (Österreichisches Institut für Wirtschaftsforschung, 1984).

Smeral, E., 'Längerfristige Entwicklung und struktureller Wandel im internationalen und Österreichischen Tourismus' (Österreichische Strukturberichterstattung 1984; vol. II, 1985, pp. 197–264).

Smeral, E., 'Ökonomische Erklärungsfaktoren der langfristigen Entwicklung der touristischen Nachfrage', *Zeitschrift für den Fremdenverkehr*, vol. 4 (1985), pp. 20–6.

Smeral, E., 'Makroökonomische Aspekte des Reiseverkehrs', *Wirtschaftspolitische Blätter*, vol. 5 (1985), pp. 407–19.

Smeral, E., *Reiseverkehr und Gesamtwirtschaft* (Österreichisches Institut für Wirtschaftsforschung (WIFO), 1986).

Schulmeister, S., 'Internationale Rezession und Reiseverkehr', *Monatsberichte des Österreichischen Instituts für Wirtschaftsforschung*, vol. 4 (1975), pp. 160–73.

Schulmeister, S., *Internationaler Reiseverkehr und Wirtschaftswachstum* (Österreichisches Institut für Wirtschaftsforschung, 1975).

Schulmeister, S., *Modellprognosen für den Reiseverkehr* (Österreichisches Institut für Wirtschaftsforschung/Fischer, 1978a).

Schulmeister, S., 'Reiseverkehr und Wirtschaftswissenschaft', *Festschrift zur Vollendung des 70. Lebensjahres von Prof. Dkfm. Dr. Paul Bernecker*, W. A. Ender, ed. (Österreichisches Institut für Wirtschaftsforschung (WIFO), 1978b), pp. 215–51.

EGON SMERAL

Education and training in tourism

Introduction

Service industries in general and the tourist industry in particular make a significant contribution to the economy of many countries. In the European Community (EC) over 20 million people are currently employed either directly or indirectly in the tourist industry and it directly accounts for 4 per cent of the Community's GNP (gross national product). The subject of education and training for careers in tourism has been poorly quantified to date, however, and little or no research has been done in this field of study. Yet any policies to promote the growth of the tourist industry must depend on adequate numbers of trained people being available at all levels within the industry. If the tourist industry is to be encouraged as a major growth area within the Community and in those Third World countries associated with the Community, it is essential that there are sufficient numbers of qualified people for preparing and implementing tourism development plans, managing regional and national tourist organizations and staffing the many firms which make up the tourist industry.

Examples and assessment

This chapter is a summary of information originally contained in a much longer report (Lavery, 1984), concentrating on the main findings of that report and the central issues of education and training. The study was carried out on behalf of the EC although any views and opinions expressed here are solely those of the author. The aims of the study were to examine the existing provision for education and training in the EC, to determine shortfalls in this provision and to propose changes needed to overcome existing gaps in provision.

'Education and training' is taken to mean education and vocational training courses, covering the whole field of further and higher education from technical colleges through to universities which are aimed at raising the level of skills and knowledge needed to work in the tourist industry. The study focused on sectors of the tourist industry other than hotels because it was felt that the hotel and catering sector was well developed. Training in the tourist services sector is at a much earlier stage of development and has quite different manpower and training requirements.

Methodology

The first phase of the study consisted of preparing an inventory of existing education and training courses in Europe, drawing upon data from the following sources:

1. World Tourism Organization, *Annual Reports* (WTO, annually).
2. *Annual Yearbooks* of the Tourism Society (Tourism Society, 1983).
3. European Parliament draft working documents concerned with youth, culture, information and sport (European Parliament, 1983).
4. Commission of the European Community, *Directives on Education and Training* (European Commission, 1982).
5. Journal articles (Airey, 1979).
6. Economist Intelligence Unit, *Special Reports* (EIU, 1976).
7. Reviews of education and training for careers in tourism published in 1972 and 1975 (IUOTO, 1972; Lawson, 1975).
8. A questionnaire survey of the National Tourist Organizations of each Member State, designed to identify all the schools of tourism responsible for education and training.

This first phase produced a database to be used in the main study together with a clearer definition of education and training for tourism. The literature review suggested that the Tourism Society definition of courses offering at least 20 hours per week of tourism topics should be considered as primary tourism courses. On this basis visits were made to all the main schools of tourism teaching in the Member States. Using a structured questionnaire, face-to-face interviews were held with senior members of staff and a wide range of information was obtained on teaching programs, curriculum content, course objectives, demand for places, links with industry, careers of graduates and related issues. One final aim was to forecast, with the consensus of this expert opinion, the likely developments in the main schools of tourism up to 1990.

Existing provision for education and training

A threefold classification was made, based on the existing nature and the level of tourism education courses in the Member States of the EC.

1. University courses containing tourism studies.

2. Business studies courses containing some tourism study.
3. Technical courses focused on a narrow definition of tourism.

Each is discussed in more detail below:

University courses

Three types of course existed (in 1983): those where tourism formed an option in an undergraduate degree programme; postgraduate degrees in tourism offered either as taught Master's courses or by research: and short diploma courses. The Swiss have the longest established degree courses. The University of Berne started a Tourism Research Institute in 1941 and in 1943 the St Gallen School of Economics first offered a tourism option. In 1961 the University of Paris began a fulltime 2-year course leading to an Advanced Diploma in Tourism Studies. In 1972 the Universities of Strathclyde and Surrey in the United Kingdom offered Master's degrees in tourism. The UK Universities of Bradford, Birmingham and Swansea (Wales) also offer courses of study with a tourism specialism. Elsewhere in Europe the University of Aix-en-Provence (France) in 1968 began a course in tourism studies which leads to a doctorate in either Economic or Legal aspects of Tourism and in 1976 the International School of Touristic Studies was established in Rome, offering postgraduate courses in Tourism mainly for students from developing countries. There are no fulltime university courses in tourism studies in Norway, Denmark, Belgium, Holland, West Germany, Ireland or Luxembourg. The relatively recent origin of the few existing university courses highlights the limited recognition of tourism as a subject worthy of serious academic study, and it generally has been the newer, more technically oriented universities that have pioneered tourism studies at first degree level.

As the body of knowledge about tourism has grown and become more sophisticated it has had two effects. First, it has begun to obtain a recognized place in more university courses (for example in geography degrees) albeit in a limited way; secondly, there is now a common curriculum emerging in relation to the topics covered. These generally include the following:

1. The signficance and characteristics of tourism.
2. The social and economic impact of tourism.
3. International tourism trends.
4. Planning and development of tourism.
5. The impact of tourism development on the Third World.

Unlike the continental universities where languages form an integral part of the undergraduate courses, in the United Kingdom languages are offered as options only. A further contrast between UK and continental university practice is that the UK first degree courses place more emphasis on periods of industrial placement within the course. There is a general tendency, however, particularly in Europe to place most emphasis on the theoretical aspects of tourism. This is in part a reflection of the background of the staff teaching on the tourism courses. At Surrey and Strathclyde the majority of the staff have experience of working in the tourist industry whereas staff in the continental universities generally lack such experience. This tends to perpetuate a theoretical, as opposed to an applied approach, towards the teaching of the subject.

The majority of tourism education within the EC is concentrated outside the universities, either in Polytechnics, Institutes of Higher Education, or their equivalent. Here, tourism is usually taught as an adjunct of business studies, with emphasis on vocational courses designed to provide a foundation of knowledge and experience of business principles and practice related to the tourist industry.

Business studies courses including tourism studies

Such courses are in the minority in Europe, but have grown in popularity in the United Kingdom since the late 1970s. In Europe the main centres are the Netherlands Institute of Travel and Tourism Studies, Breda, the Fachhochschule (Technical Universities) at Heilbronn, Munich, Wurms and Kempen in West Germany. In Italy and Greece there are no high level state schools of tourism. In the United Kingdom in 1983 there were five institutions offering business studies (tourism) courses; by 1987 there were 17 institutions offering HND courses. In the United Kingdom these are validated by the Business and Technician Education Council and therefore a common format generally exists, with a number of core subjects studied together with several travel and tourism options.

The Netherlands Institute for Travel and Tourism was established in 1964 and offers a 3-year course which the Institute regards as being equivalent to university standard. In West Germany the tourism courses are taught over 4 years, with two semesters per year. The emphasis during the first 2 years is on the broad spectrum of business studies and in the third and sixth semesters there are two 20-week periods of practical training. The first placement can be in business generally, but the second must be in the tourist industry.

Because of the strong vocational emphasis in these tourism courses and the national regulations of these tourism schools, there is a strong and sustained demand for places with a ratio of applicants to places of 10 to 1. Many of the staff teaching on these courses have experience of working in the tourist industry and they have generally retained and developed industrial contacts so their links with industry are very evident. It was generally felt that the graduates of these institutes were better equipped than their university counterparts for careers in the tourist industry, given their awareness of the theoretical underpinning of tourism as a phenomenon and their business training in operations management, law, personnel management, marketing and financial management.

Technical courses

The students on these courses tend to be quite young (16 to 18 years old) and there are considerable variations in the entry requirements between one Member State and another. Most of these courses run for one year and the overall emphasis is less on the academic aspects of tourism and rather more on the development of a rather narrow range of technical and practical skills. In the United Kingdom there has been a very rapid growth in such courses, mainly in the further education sector. At the time of the survey in 1983 there were 170 travel and tourism courses at the BTEC (Business and Technician Education Council) National level or below. By 1987 there were 351 nonadvanced tourism courses – a doubling of provision in just 4 years.

In the United Kingdom three types of qualification were available, the Certificate of Travel Agency Competence (COTAC), the Business and Technician Ordinary National or General Diploma and the Institute of Travel and Tourism Examinations. Throughout each course the emphasis is on practical training and the main topics are ticketing and air, rail, coach or hotel reservations, finance/travelers' cheques, sales techniques and customer relations. Most of these colleges also seek the approval of the education and training board of the Association of British Travel Agents (ABTA) and the successful students generally find jobs with retail travel agents.

In France there are two nationally recognized vocational qualifications in tourism, the Brevet de Technicien du Tourisme (16+) and the Brevet de Technicien Supérieur du Tourisme (18+) which is taught at four state schools located at Paris, Strasbourg, Nice and Bordeaux. The lower level course concentrates on travel and passenger transport, tourist information and customer care. The higher level courses include techniques of production and selling (aimed at travel agents and transport companies); administration and management; and reception for guides, couriers and interpreters.

Ireland has eight technical colleges based in Dublin and the main provincial cities, each offering vocational courses for the tourist industry which are approved centrally by the Council for Education Recruitment and Training (CERT) for the Hotel, Catering and Tourism Industries, in cooperation with the Ministry of Education. They offer a 1-year fulltime course with a strong emphasis on skills training (ticketing, reservations, hospitality) linked to a work experience program.

In Belgium and Italy there is a similar pattern of technical schools with a 16+ intake teaching a common curriculum approved by the Ministry of Education. Belgium has four such institutions. Italy has 12. In Belgium the main tourism related topics include guiding techniques, ticketing, typing and office organization. In Italy, as in France, there are two levels of technical training. There are the *Institute Professionali* (vocational institutes) who take students aged 14 to 17 and offer a 3-year tourism course leading to an Institute diploma. Secondly, there are the *Institute Tenenici per Il Turismo* that provide a 5-year course leading to a state diploma. This is for students aged 14 to 19. Numbers on these courses are large and the technical content is at a low level, with an emphasis on basic office skills, history of art and three foreign languages.

In Greece there are five basic schools for tourism vocational training as well as a School for Guides in Athens administered by the National Tourist Organization. The technical schools offer 1- to 3-year courses in a range of skills, with a greater emphasis on business administration and principles of management in the 3-year course.

The clearest distinction lies between the vocational training courses offered in the United Kingdom and those offered elsewhere in the EC. In Ireland, Belgium, France, Italy and Greece the courses are all controlled by the Ministry of Education and the state has established a countrywide spread of institutions to provide vocational training. Moreover, in these countries the state has recognized that tourism training should come within the province of the educational establishments. In the United Kingdom there is no clear, recognized system of vocational training and several bodies have independently of one another attempted to establish training programs and levels of competence. At the national level there are four different and overlapping sets of qualifications – the Certificate of Travel Agency Competence, the Business Education Council qualifications, those of the Institute of Travel and Tourism, and the Air Transport and Travel Industry Training Board. In addition, the Manpower Services Commission sponsors a Youth Training Scheme in tourism and individual colleges offer their own diploma courses in tourism.

In the Member States with standardized, state-supported training programs the industry has a clear understanding of the level of vocational training and the standards achieved regardless of where this training was received. In the United Kingdom the value of the award often relates to the reputation of a particular institute rather than a general recognition of the course completed.

Conclusion

The general conclusions have been grouped under three main headings: staff teaching on tourism courses; courses available and qualifications obtained; policies on education and training.

Staff teaching on tourism courses
There is a general shortage of experienced and trained teachers of tourism and this has prevented tourism teaching being more effectively developed in the further and higher education sector. Too few teaching staff have experience of working in the tourist industry and this is reflected in the way in which tourism is taught. In nearly all cases the courses that exist have been developed as a result of academic enterprise rather than industrial demand. This has resulted in an *ad hoc* approach to course development and in part explains the variety of courses available.

Qualifications and courses
Since tourism is a relatively new subject of study, no common curriculum has emerged, and there are a variety of training courses and policies on education and training for careers in tourism. Within the EC there are disparities between similar level courses in terms of their entrance requirements, course content and duration. The mechanisms for changing course content are often slow and time-consuming so that institutions are unable to keep up with new developments and ideas. At the technical education level there is a marked contrast between the content and emphasis of courses in the United Kingdom and those offered in the rest of the EC. In the United Kingdom the emphasis is on a much narrower range of skills aimed at the

travel agency/tour operation firms – language skills tend to be neglected.

Education and training policy

There has been a general absence of research into the demand for tourism diplomats or graduates at either national or international level. There was a limited awareness of the importance of tourism education on the part of politicians. (Since the study in 1983 the UK Government has given this matter increased attention.) Only a limited number of colleges keep records of the career history of former students, and thus lack any objective standard by which to measure the usefulness and relevance of their courses. There is a general absence of a clear career development path for new entrants to the industry. Few schools of tourism have established a regular dialog with the industry, so that they can communicate their perception of what is required and obtain from industrialists a view of the industry's needs. There is a lack of post experience courses to provide education and training for people already working in the tourist industry.

Career prospects

Although many tourism courses have been successfully developed over the past 10 years, a large proportion of the industry has reservations about employing graduates. However, if this attitude persists, the industry risks losing this source of managerial talent to more far-sighted industries. This is exacerbated by the relatively low levels of pay and sometimes poor working conditions which usually result in students graduating and finding that the positions offered do not live up to expectations.

On a more positive note, the future prospects are probably brighter as several initiatives have been introduced since this study was completed in 1984. The UK Government has given much greater priority to tourism matters: it has established an Education and Training Unit in the English Tourist Board, the Department of Education and Science and Manpower Services Commission has sponsored over 40 local collaborative projects between colleges and the tourist industry as part of the PICKUP program (Professional and Commercial Updating), and the MSC in conjunction with the national training board of the Association of British Travel Agents have established a Youth Training Scheme focused on travel and tourism.

Within the EC there is a need to adopt similar measures and to seek greater reciprocity of tourism education and training between Member States and to widen the scope for post entry education and training. Finally, there needs to be further research into the exact requirements of the tourist industry and the motivations and aspirations of new entrants to the industry.

There is also an urgent need to relate the annual output of students seeking careers in the tourist industry with the manpower requirements of the industry. Unless this is done there is a danger of over-provision for this sector of the economy.

References

Airey, D., 'Tourism education in the United Kingdom', *Tourist Review*, no. 2 (1979), pp. 13–15. This outlines the levels of education provision in the United Kingdom in the late 1970s.

AIEST Working Commission on Education, 'Key components for education in tourism', *Tourist Review*, no. 2 (1980), p. 19. This paper sets out the main components of the body of knowledge of tourism as perceived by the experts who are members of AIEST.

Economist Intelligence Unit, *Tourism Education in Europe*, special issue no. 20 (EIU, 1976). This is a comprehensive analysis of the main levels of tourism education in Europe in 1975.

European Community, *A Community Policy on Tourism*, Supplement 4/82 (European Commission, 1982). This booklet provides a full account of the EC policies on tourism and related matters.

European Parliament, *Draft Working Document on Tourism in the European Community* (Committee on Youth, Culture, Education, Information and Sport, 1983).

International Union of Official Travel Organizations, *Compilation and Preliminary Analysis of Information on Educational and Vocational Training Programmes* (IUOTO, 1972). This is now somewhat dated but does provide an early review of levels of provision in the 1970s.

Lavery, P., *Education and Training for Careers in Tourism in the European Community* (Commission of the European Community, 1984). This report provides a comprehensive review of all education and training courses within the ten Member States of the EC in 1984. It deals with all courses from 16+ to postgraduate level.

Lawson, M., *Teaching Tourism: Education and Training in Tourism in Western Europe* (Tourism International Press, 1975). This is a largely descriptive work which nevertheless raised a number of important questions relating to education and training. However, they are not developed as major elements of the study.

Tourism Society Yearbook 1983/4 (Britmark). This provides a comprehensive summary of all tourism courses available in the United Kingdom in 1983.

Note Since this study was undertaken three first degree courses in Tourism Studies have been approved at the Dorset Institute of Higher Education, Newcastle Polytechnic and South Glamorgan Institute of Higher Education. The comments on this paper are based on a study carried out in 1983/84, but where new developments have taken place since then, these are referred to.

PATRICK LAVERY

Effects of new technology on job motivation and job design of travel agent employees

Introduction

The travel industry is essentially an information-based industry. It supplies a complete range and mixture of travel, accommodation and tour offerings as packaged or specialist holidays, or for business travelers. Consequently, travel offerings have to be packaged in ways that are attractive to customers and an effective information and communications infrastructure has to be in place to achieve the movement of people and goods from their points of departure to their arrival destinations across the globe. The communications system between principals and retail outlets, the agents, has undergone significant technical changes since the late 1970s, particularly with the development and installation of videotex systems to facilitate booking and confirmation procedures. Information technology has become such an integral part of the communications process that it is practically impossible to survive and attain a sustained competitive advantage as principal, carrier or agent without investing in automation.

Even though the travel industry has undergone major technical and structural changes, there is little understanding about the effects of these on skill levels, and on the quality and nature of employment of travel agent employees. What are the training needs of travel agency staff? How is their job design and job motivation linked? What implications does information technology have for customer service? This chapter describes some of the effects of new technology on job motivation and job design, as revealed in a survey undertaken in 1986 of over 180 travel agencies in the north-west of the United Kingdom (Kahn, 1987). The research investigated factors affecting staff attitudes to work and motivation, such as payment structure and overall satisfaction with the work following the introduction of new technology. The findings of the study, as discussed here, have implications for training, job design and other concerns which influence the effective management of technical change. Some effects on customer service are also drawn out.

Effects of technical change

There is ample evidence that the introduction of new technology influences not only the number of jobs and levels of employment, but also the quality of work for those remaining in employment.

However, there are conflicting views as to whether greater automation downgrades or upgrades the skills of the employee and how technical change influences job motivation and job satisfaction. The pessimists argue that the outcome of the uncritical implementation of information technology reduces the skill content of jobs and ultimately negatively affects job satisfaction and attitudes towards job motivation and enables greater control to be exerted over the workforce (Sherman, 1985; Mumford and Weir, 1979).

In contrast, the optimists suggest that new technology improves the quality of work by, for example, enabling job rotation, enhancing the variety of tasks performed and improving the overall quality of the working environment (Giuliano, 1982).

There have been few, if any, empirical studies of travel agency employees to examine their attitudes to job motivation and job satisfaction following technical change, even though technology has fundamentally and rapidly altered the nature of their work. In the mid-1970s, the average agency used the telex, telephone and mail for bookings, checking availability and confirming reservations. Ten years later, highly sophisticated automated reservation and booking procedures are the norm (Bruce, 1983; 1987). Indeed, the expansion of computer systems in travel agencies has meant that there may be much less need in future for agency employees to maintain large amounts of product knowledge and retain a wide range of job skills. For instance, some computer systems can automatically match customer needs to specific destinations via a database. At the same time, then, as computer systems are increasingly being installed in travel agencies, the amount of the travel agent's job that can be done by the computer is also expanding. From the basic ability to answer enquiries from customers regarding holiday availability, the more sophisticated computer systems have now taken over a wide range of the tasks historically carried out by the travel agent, for instance automatically issuing and printing tickets and receipts.

Technical change not only affects the nature of the work of travel agency clerks but alters their attitudes to and relations with customers. One assumption prevalent in the industry is that technical change necessarily improves the quality of customer service, for example by providing access to many databases and so opening up available options. But if staff become demoralized by the effects of technical change, then this may not be the case. The aim of the above-mentioned survey of travel agency employees (Kahn, 1987) has been to investigate some of the effects of information technology on their attitudes to work and to assess how effective new technology has been in terms of job design.

Factors affecting attitudes to job motivation

Factors influencing attitudes to job motivation and satisfaction can be classified into two types: those intrinsic to the job itself like achievement and job content, and those extrinsic to the job like payment schemes.

A more sophisticated approach, taking account of the multi-faceted nature of job motivation, has been developed by J.R. Hackman and G.R. Oldham, two American academics. They have produced a model of those job characteristics which together impact on motivation and satisfaction (Hackman and Oldham, 1980). They indicate that there are five 'core' job characteristics which make work interesting to people and which take account of both the individual and the organizational structure, and they regard 'job satisfaction' as being 'an overall measure of the degree to which the employee is satisfied and happy with the job'. These five core dimensions which determine job motivation are defined as follows:

1. Skill variety – the degree to which a job requires a variety of different activities in carrying out the work and involves the use of a number of different skills and talents by the employee.
2. Task identity – the degree to which the job requires completion of a 'whole' and identifiable piece of work; that is, doing a job from beginning to end with a visible outcome.
3. Task significance – the degree to which the job has a substantial impact on the lives or work of other people, whether in the immediate organization or in the external environment.
4. Autonomy – the degree to which the job provides substantial freedom, independence and discretion to the employee in scheduling the work and in determining the procedures to be used in carrying it out.
5. Feedback from the job itself – the degree to which carrying out the work activities required by the job results in the employee obtaining direct and clear information about the effectiveness of his or her performance.

By increasing the presence of these five core job characteristics within a job, Hackman and Oldham claim that it is possible for managers to increase the challenge and richness of a job, and thus improve productivity, since a job which is seen by the employee as highly motivating will result in high quality work performance, high satisfaction with the work and low staff absenteeism and turnover. The questionnaire associated with the model, the Job Diagnostic Survey, produces other employee attitudes, but the five noted above, and a sixth which is mathematically derived from them – the motivating potential score of a job (that is, the overall motivation of a job) – are seen as the most important measures for determining the personal and work outcomes of a particular type of job.

Hackman and Oldham have applied their model in various industries; for example, clerical employees in a bank (Oldham *et al.*, 1976). Others have used it with white-collar professional employees and blue-collar employees with low levels of formal education (Wall *et al.*, 1978). One of the main criticisms of the model has been its failure to take into account the power/control perspective which influences employees' attitudes to their work. It is clear, however, that Hackman and Oldham's model does obtain a broad, general picture of the perceptions of employees in an organization, so the model was used as the basis for our survey of the travel agency employees.

Example

For the purposes of this survey of north-west UK travel agencies, the Job Diagnostic Survey was modified to focus particularly on those factors which might potentially influence the attitudes of agency employees to job motivation. The first part of the questionnaire consisted of 53 questions aimed at determining various job attitudes of agency employees – their attitudes to pay, how motivated by their job they felt etc. The second part of the questionnaire consisted of 20 questions seeking demographic information from the employee, such as age, sex, job status etc.

A number of questions were specifically related to the job attitudes of computer users in travel agencies. For instance, employees were questioned about what percentage of their time they spent using a computer (usually a visual display unit) in their job; the sophistication of the computer system used (i.e. whether it could automatically print tickets, whether it supported a form of electronic mail etc); how much training had been given in how to use the computer system, and whether this was perceived as being adequate; and so on.

The two parts of the questionnaire were to be correlated with each other, so that is would be possible to show what aspects of a computer-based job in a travel agency results in higher (or lower) staff motivation and job satisfaction. After piloting, and subsequent minor amendment, multiple copies of the 73-question paper were sent, with reply-paid envelopes, to 189 travel agencies in the Greater Manchester area (as listed in the *Travel Directory*, July 1985 edition, covering almost all listed agencies in the Manchester city region and various suburbs). The database was formed from the 185 usable questionnaires which were returned. Some of the main findings of the survey are presented below.

There is an optimum amount of time that employees can spend using the agency's computer system

While it was found that those employees who use computer-based systems consider their jobs as more motivating than those who do not (i.e. those using the traditional methods noted earlier), employee performance is related to the amount of time spent using the system. Either too little time or too much time spent daily working with a visual display unit (VDU) results in a significant reduction in those characteristics which are seen as making a job sufficiently motivating, and thus performance is affected negatively. The explanation may be as follows: staff who make little use of the computer system are unwilling to invest time to learn how the system functions, whereas, too much time spent using a VDU may result in 'computing stress' (Kahn and Cooper, 1986). The optimum time lies somewhere between 25 and 75 per cent of the day. Below and above these respective figures, travel agency terminal users see their job value as being reduced, particularly in the areas of skill variety and autonomy. Therefore, managers should provide alternative forms of work for employees, and not require them to sit all day, and every day in front of visual display units answering telephone enquiries. This was a more typical problem in the larger, national or multiple-office organizations. Some form of *job rotation* was desired by most employees participating in the survey and this reinforces the points made above.

Many employees do not seek computer systems that can provide more functions

The study showed that the more of the travel agent's work which could be carried out by the computer, the less motivating the employee found the job, so that a system which could, for instance, cope with customer holiday enquiries and accept confirmations, was seen as more motivating them a system which could, in addition, automatically produce tickets and receipts for the customer. This was true with all five of the core job dimensions described earlier, particularly so of skill variety, autonomy and feedback from the job itself. Thus, in the typical travel agency, employees seem not to want the most sophisticated computer system, which perhaps makes them feel as merely an extension of the machine and 'button-pushers'. Even the diversion of completing paperwork in the form of issuing tickets, receipts, itineraries and so on, gives the employee a chance to feel some autonomy, to feel as though they had accomplished something for themselves. Surprisingly, those travel agencies whose computer systems offered a form of electronic mail produced higher motivation in computer users – it is suggested that this facility is not seen by all employees as an integral part of the travel agent's job, and is used for more personal, frivolous reasons!

The importance of training

Almost 18 per cent of travel agents who use computer systems as part of their job reported that they see their training to use the system as inadequate, and this had a significant negative effect upon their overall satisfaction with the job. The methods by which training was obtained, however (on-the-job; using computer training packages; via in-house courses; or by external courses) made little difference. More important in terms of motivation was the amount of time allotted to computer training – an initial scheme of 3–5 days seems sufficient; below this is seen as inadequate, more than this may result in 'over-training'. Overall, the quality and quantity of computer training are more important than the method of training and these factors directly influence job motivation.

Older employees can cope with computer systems

Results from the study indicate quite clearly that the age of the computer user is not significantly related to the core job characteristics, and thus to the performance, etc. of the employee. Employers and employees alike should reconsider the traditional attitude which suggests that mature employees find it difficult to adapt to major changes in job activities, and to computer systems in particular. Given the appropriate environment, older employees are fully able to make the transition from traditional paper-based to computer-based travel agency systems. Consequently, employers can make financial savings by retraining existing staff rather than by recruiting and training new, younger, employees.

Additional support for this argument has been obtained by a further set of results produced by the study. Employees who had experience of working in a travel agency without using computer systems were more motivated and satisfied by their present, computer-based job, and since these will tend to be older employees, it is clear that it is quite possible to make the transition given the appropriate training, as suggested above.

Methods of pay are important

Employees using computers in travel agencies were asked the basis on which they were paid. The group which recorded its payment system as 'salary and concessions' recorded the lowest mean scores for overall job satisfaction, skill variety, task identity and task significance, and tied for second lowest of the groups for 'autonomy'. Thus, this group's motivating potential was the lowest by far of the six payment methods examined. The highest scores were generally recorded by those employees working with an incentive scheme as part of their payment system – the lowest by any employee whose conditions included concessions or educational travel. In summary, employees using computer terminals in travel agents report higher job motivation where an incentive scheme is in operation.

Assessment

The technology considered in this survey may have been intended to improve the communications between principals and carriers on the one hand, and agencies on the other, and ultimately to provide a better quality of service to the customer. This can be achieved, for example, by speeding up the process of booking, confirmation and ticketing; searching many databases quickly to check availability and open up options for the customer; and so on. However, the impression gained from this study of north-west UK travel agents is that the technology has mainly been implemented in ways which enable a greater volume of transactions to be made in order to enhance the profit margins of travel trade wholesalers and retailers. This has been attained by introducing new technology in the retail outlets without involving the travel agencies' employees in the design and implementation process; the technology has been imposed upon them in a way which requires them to be flexible and adapt their working practices to the machine. Consequently, strategies for improving the quality of their working practices are now being developed, such as playing with electronic mail and introducing job rotation. The effect of technical change on customer service has not typically been thought out by those responsible for implementing new technology, other than to assume that the service must be improved. In particular, employee training courses focus on the interaction between operator and machine and not the wider aspects of how such an interaction affects their ability to sell travel offerings to a customer. Nor do such courses consider how agents can market themselves in the local marketplace.

Conclusion

The overall results of this detailed study of terminal users in travel agents suggest that to increase the personal satisfaction and work outcomes of the job with the introduction of new technology, operators need the chance to undertake a variety of tasks. Some of these should be unconnected with the use of computers, and should provide at least the possibility of moving around the workplace and meeting and talking to colleagues or customers. The least attractive scenario exists where an employee is required to repeat continually the same tasks, sitting in front of a dedicated terminal. In this situation, customer relations are relatively poor. Getting the design of the job right is important, as are the appropriate methods of remuneration and training and recognizing the effects of the technology on customer service which can also include aspects of customer relations and marketing. In sum, an approach to the management of technical change which is human-centered and market-oriented is likely to be more effective in the long run.

Software/databases

TALISMAN; Travel Agency Computer System from Data Management Group, London, UK; (01) 888 6779.
TRAVELPACK; Management and Accounting System for Travel Agents from Independent Computer Co. Ltd, Altrincham, UK; (061) 941 6065.

Further reading

Bruce, M., 'Information technology: changes in the travel trade', *Tourism Management* (December 1983), pp. 290–95.

Bruce, M., 'New technology and the future of tourism', *Tourism Management* (June 1987), pp. 115–20.

Giuliano, V., 'The mechanization of office work', *Scientific American*, vol. 3, no. 247 (September 1982), pp. 148–65.

Hackman, J. R. and Oldham, G. R., *Work Design* (Addison-Wesley, 1980).

Kahn, H. 'New technology and job satisfaction – A case study of travel agents', *Human Computer Interaction, Interact '87*, H. J. Bullinger and B. Shackel, eds (Elsevier Science Publishers, 1987).

Kahn, H. and Cooper, C. L., 'Computing stress', *Current Psychological Research and Reviews*, vol. 2, no. 5 (1986), pp. 148–62.

Mumford, E. and Weir, M., *Computer Systems in Work Design: The Ethics Method* (Associated Business Press, 1979).

Oldham, G. R., Hackman, J. R. and Pearce, J. L. 'Conditions under which employees respond positively to enriched work', *Journal of Applied Psychology*, vol. 4, no. 61 (1976), pp. 395–403.

Sherman, B., *The New Revolution: The Impact of Computers on Society* (John Wiley, 1985).

Wall, T. D., Clegg, C. W. and Jackson, P. R. 'An evaluation of the job characteristics model', *Journal of Occupational Psychology*, vol. 51 (1978), pp. 183–96.

MARGARET BRUCE and
HOWARD KAHN

Entertainment

Introduction

The ability of any location to attract tourists depends on a multitude of factors, each of which is related in a complex manner to the others. One factor in that multitude is entertainment. The word 'entertainment', both in its everyday usage and dictionary definition has overtones of undemanding amusement or diversion. It has often been distinguished from 'the arts' which, in some sense, are considered to be more demanding, more civilizing and valuable. This distinction is arbitrary and unhelpful and for this chapter 'entertainment' will include live performances of both the 'high arts' and the 'popular arts'.

The features which attract tourists to a place may be manmade (museums, historic buildings, sporting events, entertainment), natural (sea, mountains, beaches) or cultural (aspects of a way of life). Other factors are secondary and may be enabling or encouraging. They will include accommodation, catering, entertainment and internal transport. The two categories are obviously not mutually exclusive. The actual significance of entertainment in any tourist's choice of destination will vary according to the characteristics of the tourist, of his/her decision unit and the motivations he/she has for being a tourist.

To some tourists, entertainment may be a major pull in its own right, equal to or more powerful than other possible attracting features. Entertainment can also be an incidental or secondary activity for tourists pulled by other factors. Finally, there will be those tourists for whom entertainment plays no part in the choice of destination. Such tourists may, nevertheless, attend entertainment events at the destination.

It would appear that a substantial minority of both overseas and domestic tourists do see some live entertainment whilst on holiday. There is little evidence, however, to demonstrate clearly that entertainment did bring to a destination people who otherwise might not have come.

For certain 'lively' resorts entertainment is a primary attraction, although probably in combination with other factors. Even where a tourist does not attend any holiday entertainment it is possible that the presence of the entertainment could have had a significant role to play in choice of resort. Entertainment is one of the necessary ingredients that contribute to the identity of place as a holiday destination.

The importance of live entertainment may be greater in inland urban areas. Most of the attractions of such areas will be manmade and entertainment can be a major or sole reason for visits. It may, in practice, be difficult to disentangle the relative pull of attractions. For many domestic visitors, London may be a desirable destination because of the variety and combination of attractions; the absence of any one (such as shops and museums) may reduce the pull of another (such as entertainment). There are also instances where tourists visit a destination solely because of the entertainment. Most noticeably this is where there is some major entertainment event such as an arts festival.

Examples

Attractions with tourist potential use entertainment to encourage tourists; for example, English Heritage has concerts and mock battles at the castles and other historic buildings and monuments under its care. Trusthouse Forte has, for over 21 years, offered 'Music at Leisure', weekends of classical concerts at a small number of its hotels. Concerts are usually held in the hotels and accommodation is available at an all-inclusive price. More often, hotels or hotel groups offer packages of accommodation (and perhaps travel) and tickets for a show/concert at a venue other than the hotel (e.g. Stardust Showtime Break and Thistle Hotels' London Reveller). Many of these packages are based in London.

At many seaside resorts in the United Kingdom, theaters and entertainment centers are owned by local authorities. At many of these theaters the traditional summer show has declined or disappeared because of a combination of reduced numbers of holidaymakers and increased costs. In many cases, seasons of two- or three-night stands with weekly changes have been introduced. Ticket prices are usually quite low but seat capacity sold over the season averages only just over a third. These theaters are usually a net cost to the local authority.

The English Tourist Board launched, in 1985, a major three-year promotion 'England Entertains', with the objective of encouraging live entertainment, especially as a platform for tourism development. It has not concerned itself solely with summer shows but has sought to encourage the widest variety of entertainment in the widest variety of venues. Some hotels sell themselves through entertainment, some actually providing the entertainment themselves.

There are a number of tour operators with a particular interest in entertainment packages. The Theatre and Concert Rail Club, in exchange for a subscription, allows members a reduced package price covering theater tickets, rail travel and hotel accommodation. An offshoot of the Club is 'That's Entertainment' which offers low rail-fare packages to entertainment venues throughout the country (including the BBC Proms and Edinburgh Festival). Leeds City Council has itself developed and marketed a number of 'Entertainment Breaks' centered on the city.

Artistic organizations have themselves encouraged these developments. The Welsh National Opera and Royal Shakespeare Company have both successfully stimulated and marketed packages based on their own products. Many of the arts festivals in the United Kingdom have encouraged the provision of packages through cooperative ventures with local hotels, e.g. 'Aldeburgh at Ease' at the Aldeburgh Festival and 'Opera Stopovers' at the Buxton Festival. A number of specialist tour operators (such as JMB Travel) also offer packages to these and other festivals. Most festivals sell event tickets through agencies, thus encouraging a tourist audience: Edinburgh and Aldeburgh use a ticket agency with principal sales offices in London and New York.

Benefits

Holidays may be considered as being out of the ordinary sphere of life; they are often undertaken partly to compensate for the deficiencies of ordinary life. It may be that the arousal through entertainment is as much, or as easily, satisfied in hotels and pubs and by television and video, as by productions in resort theaters. Whatever the form, it would appear that entertainment is perceived by holidaymakers to be a desirable constituent of most holidays. This is regardless of how much use, if any, is actually made of it.

It may be that certain theaters and entertainment events only continue to exist because of the tourist. Whatever benefits the community as a whole may derive from a thriving entertainment industry may, in part, be attributable to tourism.

During the 1980s, overseas visitors have been estimated at between one-quarter and one-third of London West End theater audiences; the proportion is, of course, considerably greater during the summer. Local populations at seaside resorts are able, during the summer, to consume the entertainment products that are offered primarily to the tourist. In some places, the tourist season may be the only occasion when there is entertainment of any significance. The tourist, whether domestic or foreign, may present a sizeable and profitable opportunity to ensure the survival of much of the live entertainment industry. In addition, package tourists may be encouraged to use theaters at times when they would otherwise be relatively empty.

Entertainment, especially in the form of 'the high arts', may succeed in giving a destination and the community a sense of pride and a prestigious image. This in turn may stimulate tourists to pursue other attractions at the destination at the same and at other times of the year, as a sideline from the entertainment events or as a result of receiving a favorable image of the destination because of its arts provision. There may also be an influx of industry or of residents because of an area's attractiveness in terms of entertainment provision.

If some of these entertainments are perceived to be 'elitist' and many of the audience are non-local, they may be seen to have little local relevance or even as divisive. Some concern has been expressed too about the possibility of over-commercialization of the arts and the trivializing of the product.

Nonetheless, the expenditure of 'entertainment-tourists' has been estimated as being greater per day than that of other tourists. Unlike business or conference tourists, such a tourist is likely to have free time during the day to devote to other tourist activity and expenditure.

Tourism which is specifically entertainment-based is currently only a minor segment of the total tourism market, though it is possibly a growing segment. Its particular significance is likely to be the second holiday and/or short-break market.

Implementation

The English Tourist Board (1984) urged that local authorities still have a part to play in the provision of entertainment, even though demand had fallen. They were advised to refurbish theaters, raise the standard of theater management and update booking systems. Computerized booking systems are being linked directly with travel agents and other tourist-related outlets. Theaters should be more welcoming as day-long activity centers. Main shows produced would need to satisfy an audience used to TV. Persuading stars to appear in long summer seasons is difficult and local authorities may have to accept short seasons. Combined resistance to the demands from performers for high fees and guarantees should improve the 'economics' of summer shows, especially if the councils themselves are persuaded to regard entertainment more sympathetically as an investment in tourism.

Local authorities were also recommended to encourage local talent contests, buskers and traveling theater groups, street entertainment and the inclusion of entertainment in package holidays. Packages are more likely to feature in domestic visits to London. Many already include entertainment or an option to purchase theater tickets. Packages of travel, accommodation and theater tickets can be particularly successful if combined with talks, lectures and backstage tours. The costs of brochures can be shared between tour operators and entertainment organizations. Packages usually mean that theater tickets have to be allocated to tour operators; theater management may be reluctant to do this without financial guarantees and tour operators may only be willing to take tickets on a sale-or-return basis.

For non-package tourists there are a number of developments that might encourage ticket sales. The introduction of 24-hour phone centralized booking services (accepting credit card bookings) makes ticket purchase easier. Central booking agencies or 'ticket shops' are also beneficial. Of particular significance in adding to 'tourist' ticket sales in London has been the Leicester Square Half-Price Ticket Booth, selling unsold tickets from West End theaters.

Some means of increasing the awareness of the range and quality of entertainment outside London is also desirable. Familiarization tours for travel writers and travel agents should focus more on entertainment. Regional arts associations and entertainment organizations could themselves continue to initiate and encourage such awareness and cooperation with the travel trade.

The tourist potential of many entertainment events (especially in the 'high arts') is underestimated and often considered undesirable. More positive steps to foster the tourism connection should be encouraged. Some organizations have been sufficiently aware of tourism to reschedule their events in such a way as to encourage overnight stays, especially at weekends. Local authorities, regional arts associations and tourist boards should develop and distribute annual events publications or calendars specifically aimed at the tourism market. (There are very real difficulties, however, in many entertainment organizations, in being able to supply details of their programs very far in advance.) A form of national clearing-house might be established to put arts organizations and tour operators in contact with each other.

The establishment of new entertainment events and venues may be desirable. Tourist boards can assist through development or promotion grants. The 'attractiveness' of entertainment events may need to be complemented by a 'bundle' of other attractions. Consequently, joint funding of any promotion would be appropriate as would be the development of packages to include some of these other attractions (such as golf or admission to historic houses). It is important that a range of facilities should be available at a destination; the development of some major events has been hindered by a lack of convenient local transport (including taxis) or suitable local restaurant facilities.

It may be that a number of entertainment organizations could undertake joint promotion to develop a tourist 'circuit' of entertainment events; such a scheme could include concessions for tickets purchased for more than one event.

Conclusion

Little is known about the role of live entertainment in stimulating tourists, although there is a widespread belief that it has considerable significance. That significance is very varied, but as most holiday trips are to do with refreshment, relaxation and regeneration, it is likely that entertainment has a part to play. The continuation of live entertainment in many seaside resorts is one of several factors that are important for their prosperity. For business and conference tourists and those visiting friends and relatives, the pull of entertainment may be less but it may, nonetheless, be an important activity during the visit.

For some holidaymakers, choice of destination may be influenced by the provision of entertainment, either to see specific event or performer, or because of a more generalized awareness of availability. The potential of some entertainment as a tourist attraction in its own right is perhaps not fully appreciated by the entertainment or tourist industries.

Most holidaymakers may be little influenced by entertainment in their choice of destination and some may even prefer to avoid destinations with an abundance of entertainment.

Focus on small business

There are opportunities for most small businesses in tourism to be involved in the provision of entertainment. Hotels and guest houses may themselves hire entertainers; such entertainment need not be lavish or costly since entertainment is a product that can be based on a one-person input. Groups of independent hotels may jointly hire entertainers for performances in one or several of the hotels and use such entertainment in their promotional literature. There are a number of hotels already offering entertainment as a focal point of visits and they could cooperate to promote 'entertainment-hotels' nationally. Hotels in an area can jointly sponsor events such as carnivals, festivals, mock battles etc. As a tourist draw, the impact of many small entertainment enterprises can be considerable when concentrated, for instance, in a festival. Individual tourist firms can sponsor individual events or performers.

There is a number of package-tour operators specializing in this particular field. It is a limited market in terms of the total number of tourists and as such it is well suited to the small operator. In addition to packaging entertainment in the United Kingdom, UK tour operators can offer a large number of events abroad. There are some large firms in this market already but their involvement is usually subsidiary to their main tour market. It generally remains the domain of the small specialist operator.

Most theaters give discounts for group bookings at levels which are relatively low: from 10 or 12 tickets. Thus, packaged parties need not be large. A large outlay on an expensive brochure is not always necessary in these minority markets. Precise targeting is required, however, and is usually achieved by advertisements in newspapers and special-interest journals and magazines.

Further reading/information sources

American Council for the Arts, *The Arts and Tourism: A Profitable Partnership* (ACA, 1981). A collection of conference papers. They cover a wide range of topics relating to the actual and potential arts-tourism connection.

Barbour, S. (ed.), *Arts Festivals in Britain and Ireland, 1987–1988* (Rhinegold, 1986). A reference book of over 400 festivals with dates, aims, contacts, etc.

Bibliography of Resources at the Department of Arts Policy and Management (City University, 1987). Listing of the material in the resources unit of this department. A very comprehensive collection of published and unpublished works on all aspects of the 'popular' and 'high' arts.

British Tourist Authority, *A Survey of Overseas Visitors to London, Summer 1983* (BTA, 1983). Section 12 is concerned with evening activities that overseas visitors took part in.

British Tourist Authority, *The Arts as an Attraction for Overseas Visitors to Britain* (BTA, 1983). This report draws together data from several BTA surveys on the role of the arts (including theater) in Britain as an attraction for overseas visitors.

British Tourist Authority/English Tourist Board, *BTA Overseas Visitor Survey 1984* (BTA/ETB, 1985). Section 2 considers the effect that the absence of various attractions (including theater) would have had on the decision to visit.

British Tourist Authority/English Tourist Board, *Overseas Visitor Survey 1985* (BTA/ETB, 1986). Sections 5 and 6 of this report deal specifically with entertainment; section 8 deals with activities of overseas visitors.

Cultural Assistance Center and the Port Authority of New York and New Jersey, *The Arts as an Industry: Their Economic Importance to the New York–New Jersey Metropolitan Region* (Cultural Assistance Center, 1983). The report considers the contribution to the area of several art forms including Broadway theater and the contribution from the tourist.

English Tourist Board, *Scarborough District Tourism Study* (ETB, 1981).

English Tourist Board, *Torbay Tourism Study* (ETB, 1982). These are two of several similar reports that look at factors influencing choice of resort, resort image and activities of holidaymakers.

English Tourist Board, *Provincial Theatre and Tourism in England: An Analysis of Trends between 1975 and 1981–82* (ETB, 1982). This report considers theater developments, theater closures and openings and endeavors to relate them to tourism.

English Tourist Board, *A Guide to Some Lively Entertainers* (ETB, 1984). Part of the 'England Entertains' campaign; it includes over 300 performers and contacts.

English Tourist Board, *England Entertains: A Selection of Live Entertainment Holidays and Breaks* (ETB, 1985). Details of hotels and tour operators etc. which have put together special live entertainment packages.

English Tourist Board's Resorts Entertainments Working Party, *Curtain Up on the Resorts* (ETB, 1984). The report of an inquiry into live entertainment in English seaside resorts. It contains the results of surveys and makes many recommendations for tackling problems identified.

Hughes, H. L., 'Tourism and the live performance of opera and classical music', *Journal of Arts Policy and Management*, vol. 2, no. 3 (1986), pp. 12–16. This reviews the current evidence relating to the significance of the tourist in arts audiences and the significance of certain arts as tourist attractions. It also considers some of the confusion surrounding the term 'cultural tourism'.

Hughes, H. L., 'Culture as a tourist resource – a theoretical consideration', *Tourism Management*, vol. 8, no. 3 (1987), pp. 205–16. This explores the potential of a particular form of cultural product as a tourist attraction and develops a framework for further analysis.

Mellor, G., *Pom-Poms and Ruffles: The Story of Northern Seaside Entertainment* (Dalesman, 1966). This book deals in a readable, anecdotal way with pre-war seaside summer shows in the United Kingdom.

Society of West-End Theatres, *Britain at its Best: Overseas Tourism and the West-End Theatre* (SWET, 1982). Draws on BTA surveys as well as its own and attempts to assess the importance of tourism to the West-End theater.

Tighe, A., 'Cultural tourism in the USA', *Tourism Management*, vol. 6, no. 4 (1985), pp. 234–51. This considers the developing relationship between the arts and tourism in the USA and makes recommendations for the way forward.

Tighe, A., 'The arts/tourism partnership', *Journal of Travel Research*, vol. XXIV, no. 3 (1985), pp. 2–5. Summarizes a report on areas of practical cooperation between the arts and tourism in the United States.

Travel and Tourism Research Association, *Innovation and Creativity in Travel Research and Marketing – Keys to Survival and Opportunity*, 12th Annual Conference Proceedings (TTRA, University of Utah, 1981). Contains two papers describing the experiences of Seattle and Miami in developing tourism through the arts.

Vaughan, D. R., *The Economic Impact of the Edinburgh Festival 1976* (Scottish Tourist Board, 1977). A report on a pioneering British project to assess the tourist and other effects of a major artistic event.

Vaughan, D. R. and Wilkes, K., *An Economic Impact Study of Tourist and Associated Arts Developments in Merseyside: The Tourism Study* (Merseyside Arts, 1986). This report is one part of a two-part study covering both tourism and the arts. This study specifically considers the importance of the arts and heritage in the decision to visit Merseyside, UK.

Young, K., *Music's Great Days in the Spas and Watering-Places* (Macmillan, 1968). This book looks at the place of music in the resorts 1880–1950. It pays particular attention to resort orchestras and bands.

HOWARD L. HUGHES

Environmental analysis in tourism

Introduction

The year 1987 was designated the *European Year of the Environment* to enhance environmental awareness and education. Environmental analysis is an awareness of the environment, and has an immediate objective in tourism development; namely, the conservation of the very environment the tourist seeks to enjoy. Because much recreational activity involves trips into and through the countryside, 'landscape design' is becoming increasingly important, and as the *Cynefin Strategy* for Wales has outlined, 'If we are to become more aware visually, this should start from primary schools upwards' (Cynefin, 1984, p. 3). The Welsh concept of Cynefin is an appropriate shorthand for environmental analysis, for it refers to those parts of the environment to which we belong. It is the home, the refuge, the starting point from which our thoughts and actions emerge, and the places to which we return for strength and renewal. It embodies that with which we are familiar, and conveys the twin concepts of men and women in their environment and the environment within human control.

As a strategy Cynefin is both an attempt to appreciate the present and to structure a sustainable future. For tourism development this means 'environmentally sensitive' developments, ranging from signposting to buildings, and from the recognition of the interests of both residents and heritage conservation locally, to the recognition of these interests at a regional or national scale in the planning of developments. At an international level this is the *World Conservation Strategy*, that is, the acceptance of the need for both sustainable growth and of the retention of genetic diversity to enable long-term adaptation to changing environmental circumstances. This is not to say that tourism development is the only conflict in our environment, nor to imply that all agree on the desirability or objectives of conservation. Instead, the purpose of environmental analyses in tourism is to place environmental issues to the forefront of an agenda for development. Questions of morality and of public policy immediately arise in the degrees of compulsion and education necessary or desirable in affecting environmental conservation.

Examples

Analyses of the impact of tourists on the environment – physical, social and economic – abound, as do management solutions. At the most stringent, in some countries, but notably not in the United Kingdom, comprehensive environmental impact studies are required to support developments (e.g. O'Riordan and Hey, 1976). Studies in response to the erosion caused by tourists include those of country parks (e.g. Daniels, 1985a, b, c, d), footpaths (e.g. Aitken, 1984), beaches (e.g. Countryside Commission for Scotland, 1980) and lakeside shores (e.g. Countryside Commission for Scotland and Nature Conservancy Council, 1979; Tivy, 1980). Further problems studied include those of litter (e.g. Countryside Commission, 1971; Jones and Crofts, 1980), caravans (e.g. Angus District, 1981) and access (e.g. Miles, 1972; Countryside Commission for Scotland and Fife Regional Council, 1981). These topics are only illustrative of the range of literature which is available. Major sponsors of studies have included, for example, the Countryside Commission and the Countryside Commission for Scotland. At a broader level, the Welsh Cynefin Strategy is a further example of a conservationist response, but one prompted by other factors as well as tourism developments. Whereas at site level physical conservation tends to be expressed in terms of surface and visitor management, at broader levels the response is both educational and frequently political.

Benefits

The most important benefit of environmental analysis is the conservation and compatible improvement of the resource which the tourist seeks and the residents enjoy. This is effected either through the design of new developments or through the repair of the damage caused by tourists, often unintentionally, at existing attractions. These benefits are most readily noticeable in attempts to avoid or to repair the physical damage caused by tourists and other visitors. In large numbers tourists can damage soils, vegetation and animal life, and can disrupt other industries, most notably agriculture. In their development, recreational activities can affect the local removal and relocation of soils. The activities of tourists may variously cause soil creep, slides and scree movement, the break-up or compaction of soils, changes in run-off and drainage, and the erosion or enrichment of soils (e.g. Speight, 1973). Clearly, these effects are varied and depend both on the soil type and on other natural and semi-natural factors, such as vegetation, as well as on the type of tourist activity. Vegetation can likewise be damaged mechanically. For example, sand dune and machair systems along our coasts frequently suffer trampling. Wildlife may be disturbed by tourists, particularly ground nesting birds in open or accessible cliff-nesting habitats. Agriculture can suffer and direct effects include damage to walls and fences, the worrying of livestock, straying and trespass. Such effects can lead to reduced stocking rates or losses of livestock, and need to be expressed quantitatively as costs to the farmer (e.g. Gibbs, 1976).

Clearly, the benefits to be gained from environmental analyses are the avoidance or repair of such effects. However, it should be emphasized that the assessment of the physical effects of tourism on the environment is fraught with difficulties. For example, the destruction of dune systems can arise from overstocking or from rabbits, as well as from the impacts of tourists' feet. Pye-Smith and Blackie (1980) have identified the following difficulties:

1. Pressures from tourists are nearly always superimposed on effects caused by other land uses.
2. It is unlikely that accurate ecological carrying capacities can be determined for vegetation types.
3. There is a need to distinguish between aesthetic and ecological degradation. Assessments of aesthetics, however, are likely to be more controversial still, as people disagree on the attributes of design. However, the retention of the vernacular styles of architecture in the National Parks of England and Wales and in building conservation areas, using design briefs, shows what may be achieved with will (e.g. Knowles, 1976; Reynolds, 1976).

Implementation

Measures to assist conservation include: private maintenance; planning controls; other administrative action; legal and financial arrangements short of ownership; public ownership; preservation; and recording of the site. Standards of conservation may be thought of as fivefold (An Foras Forbartha, 1969), namely:

1. Photographic and documentary records.
2. Basic protection of the items of heritage.
3. Protection of their setting.
4. Provision of access.
5. Restoration, if necessary, and active use.

A critical concept in seeking to predict environmental impact is *capacity*, the amount of use a site can sustain before it begins to deteriorate (e.g. Gilg, 1978). Four broad types of capacity may be delimited:

1. Economic capacity, defining the intensities of use at which maximum economic benefit will be gained.
2. Physical capacity, the absolute capacity of car parks or ski lifts, for example.
3. Ecological capacity, which has already been discussed.
4. Perceptual capacity, which is dependent upon the expectations of visitors.

An example of the varied nature of the latter is the comparison of tourists' tolerance of crowds and queues on skiing slopes, but dislike of similar crowds generally in upland areas. The critical difference, of course, is that skiers are not generally seeking 'wilderness', unlike ramblers. It is important to recognize that not only are some environments more fragile than others, but the applicability of capacities may be difficult to determine.

Implementation of environmental analysis must begin with an awareness of heritage types and objectives, and with an inventory of the range of heritage items. Heritage types include both the scientific and the historical and artistic. Scientific heritage types include terrestrial, freshwater and marine habitats, and sites of geological or topographical interest. For example, planning for heritage conservation in Ireland has recognized areas of outstanding landscapes; archaeological sites and monuments; buildings of architectural or historic interest; areas of scientific interest; and wildlife (e.g. An Foras Forbartha, 1969 and 1985). Formally, the United Nations identifies ten categories of area for the management of wildlife resources (IUCNNR, 1985); these range from the scientific reserve, through national parks and protected landscapes and seascapes, to biosphere reserves and world heritage sites. In the United Kingdom the following twelve designations apply for promoting the management of land for landscape, amenity and nature conservation (Nature Conservancy Coucil, 1986):

1. Areas of Special Protection (Bird Sanctuaries).
2. International Sites (Biosphere Reserves and Ramsar Sites).
3. Local Nature Reserves.
4. Marine Nature Reserves.
5. National Nature Reserves.
6. Non-statutory or private reserves.
7. Sites of Special Scientific Interest.
8. Areas of Outstanding Natural Beauty.
9. Areas of Archaeological Interest.
10. Country Parks.
11. Environmentally Sensitive Areas.
12. Heritage Coasts.
13. International Sites (Special Protected Areas and World Heritage Sites).
14. National Forest Parks.
15. National Parks.
16. National Scenic Areas.
17. National Trust land.
18. Areas with planning conditions which give them high conservation status.
19. Voluntary marine reserves.

These sites range both in number and in extent. For example, up to May 1986 no Marine Nature Reserve had been declared; yet there are in excess of 200 country parks and a like number of National Nature Reserves. Individually, the ten National Parks of England and Wales are the most extensive, covering 9 per cent of these countries. The range of legislative requirements associated with these designations is beyond the scope of this chapter. Despite the impression given by the length of the above list, many, and probably most, tourism developments in Britain are on land not designated in these ways, and in these cases local authority planning statements, approved plans and associated development control are the major administrative controls on developments which change the use of land.

At best, local conservation in the countryside may be integrated into an overall plan, as for example, in the Heritage Zone concept, in which different types of conservation are integrated. An example is at Clonmacnoise, in Ireland, integrating landscape, ecological, historical and archaeological heritage (Jeffrey, 1983). A further example is the integrated approach to environmental education adopted by certain of the National Parks, for example, by the Northumberland National Park, where a range of subjects is presented as different facets of the heritage, natural and manmade, of the area. Country parks are further attempts to combine physical management with management by education. The legal definition of a country park conveys their purpose: 'a park or pleasure ground in the countryside which by reason of its position in relation to major concentrations of population affords convenient opportunities to the public for enjoyment of the countryside or open-air recreation' (Countryside Commission for Scotland, 1986a). Simply, a country park is a place, usually quite close to an urban area, where the countryside can be enjoyed and outdoor activities pursued. The location of the 33 country parks in Scotland illustrates this locational requirement, for they are to be found in a broad band across the central lowlands and along the coastal parts of Tayside and Grampian. Further criteria of country park designation illustrate management criteria and include the sites' capacities 'of being developed to withstand intensive recreational use without detriment to their attractiveness, judged in terms of their ability to provide open air recreation in a countryside setting' and individually to 'be run to a single co-ordinated plan' (Countryside Commission for Scotland, 1986a). Country parks vary in type: for example, in Scotland they range from Culzean, with its castle, to Strathclyde Park, the latter with international water sports activities. In the jargon of recreation, these are planned 'honeypot' sites; that is, sites attracting large concentrations of tourists and other visitors.

Local conservation in the countryside may also be affected by management agreements with land owners. For example, the Countryside Commission for Scotland enters into agreements 'with persons having an interest in land, to preserve or enhance the beauty of the countryside or to promote the enjoyment of the countryside by the public' (Countryside Commission for Scotland, 1986b). Such agreements may include granting permission to the public to enter onto private land, the operation of a ranger service or the making of by-laws. Rangers are a managerial response to environmental impact, and their major task is educational, namely 'to advise and assist the public as to any matter relating to the use' (Countryside Commission for Scotland, 1986c) of the designated land or waterway. Management agreements also have a parallel in urban areas in the *Little Houses* projects of the National Trust for Scotland. These projects involve the conservation of the vernacular domestic architecture of Scotland, and began at Culross in Fife, with Dunkeld in Perthshire a second project. Since its introduction in 1960, the Trust's *Little Houses Improvement Scheme* has extended widely the geographical spread of these projects which not only conserve buildings, but also townscapes. The Trust generally sells the buildings to prospective occupiers who then restore them. An owner enters into a conservation agreement with the Trust not to alter the design or use the building without the Trust's consent (National Trust for Scotland, undated).

The importance of the countryside as a backcloth to recreation is recognized in attempts to educate farmers in landscape conservation and environmental interpretation – the explanation of the environment to others. The importance, and potential importance, of tourism to many rural areas is aptly summarized by 'conservation as a cash crop' (Shoard, 1980). In Mid-Wales the *Festival of the Countryside* has been promoted jointly by Mid-Wales Development, the Countryside Commission and Cynefin. In 1986 this Festival incorporated over 500 'events', such as farm open days, nature walks and day courses. In terms of countryside management, in Scotland, for example, the following seven stage planning and action guide has been produced to encourage conservation by farmers and other rural landowners:

1. Assess the landscape and wildlife interest of the farm.
2. Review past and likely future changes.
3. Determine the aims and objectives of a conservation plan.
4. Prepare a conservation plan.
5. Manage existing features of landscape and wildlife interest.
6. Create new features.
7. Consider conservation in day-to-day management (Cobham Resource Consultants, 1986).

The general applicability, beyond farmers alone, of these stages in conservation makes them a model structure for the managers of space-extensive tourism developments to consider. The basis of the guide's recommendation is ultimately the basis of all environmental awareness, namely '. . . countryside conservation can bring increased personal satisfaction' (Cobham Resource Consultants, 1986). This is the main benefit of environmental awareness, and may compensate for any immediate financial costs resulting from management practices more in keeping with carrying capacities and public aesthetics.

Assessment

Studies of the effectiveness of conservation schemes are twofold: those reviewing the management of sites, and those considering wider issues of policy, such as the roles of the

National Parks or of the Countryside Commission, or of the effectiveness of specific legislation. For example, Shoard (1980) has described these major bodies as 'toothless watchdogs' and Lowe *et al.* (1986) have criticized the application of the Wildlife and Countryside Act of 1981. Shoard has argued for firmer planning for tourism and recreation through the creation of Regional Countryside Planning Authorities, and the creation of six further national parks in England and Wales. Likewise, MacEwen and MacEwen (1982) have asked whether the national parks are about 'conservation or cosmetics?'. Scotland, despite its scenic heritage, has no national parks, but instead has national scenic areas and regional parks. Shoard (1987) has similarly questioned the effectiveness of this system.

More generally, environmental awareness requires the acceptance of environmental ethics. Williams *et al.* (1982) set out such a system of ethics for the Cynefin Strategy, arguing that such a system should 1. be comprehensive across diverse disciplines; 2. be practical; 3. be forward looking; 4. be relevant; 5. give proper care for what is irreplaceable of the past; and 6. recognize the interdependence of all parts of our world. Ultimately, environmental conservation is a moral stance, as is environmental analysis directed to conservation.

Conclusion

The main objective of environmental analysis is the same as that set for the European Year of the Environment of 1987; namely, to raise awareness of the importance of environmental conservation so that better progress can be made in conserving and improving the environment. Conservation is ultimately a moral, and thus in practice a political stance, based both on education and awareness, and on an acceptance of the need both for sustainable utilization of our resources and of genetic diversity. Not to consider the environmental consequences of tourism developments is at its worst to destroy the very resource which many tourists and others seek to enjoy. Conservation is a classic example of the aggregation of individual investment decisions not necessarily leading to maximum social benefit. Management issues range from the practical to the organizational and legislative. However, not only does the success of designations such as the European Year of the Environment ultimately depend on participation, so does any scheme of environmental analysis with a serious conservation objective.

Focus on small business

The practical response of the small business person is twofold. Firstly, to recognize the collective desirability of both planning requirements and the particular requirements in any specially designated areas. Secondly, and more fundamentally, to accept the need to consider the environmental impacts both of individual actions and the collective actions of developers. Unlike many of the concepts outlined in this book, environmental

concerns have an immediate moral dimension. The small business person should seek to develop environmentally sensitive tourism, and, if possible through the tourism product offered, to educate others in an appreciation of our environmental heritage.

Further reading

Aitken, R., *Scottish Mountain Footpaths: A Reconnaissance Review of Their Condition* (Countryside Commission for Scotland, 1984). A review of the form and function of footpaths, changes and options and opportunities for future action.

An Foras Forbartha, *Planning for Amenity and Tourism*. Specimen Development Plan Manual 2–3 (An Foras Forbartha, 1966). A classic tourism planning study for an area of high scenic value, produced as part of a United Nations funded project, and illustrated from the Model Amenity-Tourism Study of County Donegal. The manual sets out to demonstrate a means of measuring capacity, posing development options, and assessing budgets to show not only the financial impacts of the options considered, but also the impacts of these options on the heritage of Donegal. Despite its age, this study is strongly recommended as a starting point for applied environmental analysis.

An Foras Forbartha, *The Protection of the National Heritage* (An Foras Forbartha, 1969). A review of the types and importance of heritage, of conservation standards and of the role of agencies.

An Foras Forbartha, *The State of the Environment* (An Foras Forbartha, 1985). This review of Irish environmental change includes sections on amenity and recreation and on the Irish National Heritage, including the 'National Heritage as an Economic Resource'.

Angus District Planning Department, *Angus District Caravan Site Location Policy* (Angus District Council, 1981). This is a good example of a district council policy review on the environmental impact of caravans: trends, benefits, provision, resource potentials, landscape character, accessibility, site development considerations and criteria to be met.

Biswas, A. K. and Geping, Q. (eds), *Environmental Impact Assessment for Developing Countries* (Tycooly International, 1987). A text outlining and illustrating the requirements of environmental impact assessments, principally: impact identification; impact prediction and measurement; impact interpretation and evaluation; and impact monitoring.

Bowyer, J., *Vernacular Building Conservation* (Architectural Press, 1980). A handbook on building conservation, restoration and replacement.

Clark, B. D., Chapman, K., Bisset, R. and Wathern, P., *Environmental Impact Assessment in the U.S.A.: A Critical Review. Research Report no. 26* (Department of the Environment, 1978). A review of US federal, state and local environmental impact statements, and of the methods for their preparation.

Cobham Resource Consultants, *Countryside Conservation: A Guide for Farmers* (Countryside Commission for Scotland, 1986). This booklet sets out a planning and action guide in seven stages for countryside conservation.

Countryside Commission, *Litter in the Countryside. CCP 43* (1971). A review of the types of litter problem, methods of clearing litter, education and publicity and a digest of legislation.

Countryside Commission for Scotland, *Highland Beach Management Project 1977–79: Final Report* (Countryside Commission for Scotland, 1980). Review of coastline management, including approaches to development, the management of trampling, and re-seeding and planting.

Countryside Commission for Scotland, *Scotland's Countryside: Who's Who* (Countryside Commission for Scotland, 4th edition, 1985). This is a gazetteer of the organizations with an interest in or responsibility for the Scottish environment. Earlier editions had the title, *Who Does What For Scotland's Countryside.*

Countryside Commission for Scotland, *A Policy for Country Parks in Scotland* (Countryside Commission for Scotland, 1986a). Sets out the Commission's policies for country parks: their definition, functions, and registration.

Countryside Commission for Scotland, *Management Agreements* (Countryside Commission for Scotland, 1986b). Sets out the Commission's policies for management agreements.

Countryside Commission for Scotland, *Grants for Countryside Ranger Services* (Countryside Commission for Scotland, 1986c). Sets out the Commission's policies regarding ranger services.

Countryside Commission for Scotland and Fife Regional Council, *Wee Mary the Country Bus: An Experiment in Transport to the Countryside for Recreation: The Lomond Hills Project* (Countryside Commission for Scotland, 1981). Review of this accessibility experiment including surveys of residents and passengers. Followed in 1982 by a second report.

Countryside Commission for Scotland and The Nature Conservancy Council, *Shore Erosion around Loch Lomond* (Countryside Commission for Scotland, 1979). Proceedings of a conference on the impact of visitors on the Loch's shoreline.

Cynefin, *One Year on* (Cynefin, 1984). This report reviews the Cynefin Strategy, setting out its objectives and achievements.

Daniels, J. L., *Cannock Chase Country Plan Project. Technical Reports nos. 1, 2, 3 and 4. CCP 182, 183, 184 and 185* (Countryside Commission, 1985a, b, c, d). This series reviews eroded hillslope repair, heathland management trials, visitor redistribution and vegetation restoration at informal car parks.

Edington, J. M. and Edington, M. A., *Ecology and Environmental Planning* (Chapman and Hall, 1977). A review of the impacts of man-made environment on ecology, including the tourism impacts of a National Park in Wales as a case study.

Environmental Pollution This technical journal publishes papers on a full range of impacts, including recreational.

Gibbs, R. S., *The Impact of Recreation on Upland Access Land.* Agricultural Adjustment Unit Research Monograph no. 7 (University of Newcastle Upon Tyne, 1976). This monograph reviews the costs of public access to Uplands, with particular attention to impacts on farming and grouse shooting.

Gilg, A. W., *Countryside Planning: The First Three Decades 1945–1976* (David and Charles, 1978). A review of countryside planning, including recreational planning and the conservation and planning of landscape.

Green, B., *Countryside Conservation* (George Allen and Unwin, 1981). A book setting out conservation concepts and organizations, ecosystem management, and countryside planning.

International Union for Conservation of Nature and Natural Resources, *United Nations List of National Parks And Protected Areas* (IUCNNR, 1985). United Nations categories of conservation management; areas of special international significance; growth of the world coverage of protected areas; and lists of national parks and protected areas.

Jeffrey, D. W., *Creation and Management of a Heritage Zone at Clonmacnoise, Co. Offaly, Ireland.* Second Interim Report (Environmental Sciences Unit, University of Dublin, Trinity College, 1983). Review of the content and boundaries of the proposal.

Jones, H. E. and Crofts, R. S., *Litter: A Review of the Problem and Approaches Towards its Reduction* (Central Research Unit, Scottish Development Department, Scottish Office, 1980). A review of the nature of the problem and approaches towards litter control and reduction.

Knowles, P., *Peak National Park Building Design Guide* (Peak Park Joint Planning Board, 1976). A design guide to altering buildings of traditional architecture in the Peak, and the conservation of this heritage.

Lowe, P., Cox, G., MacEwen, M. *et al.*, *Countryside Conflicts: The Politics of Farming, Forestry and Conservation* (Gower, 1986). A review of changing land use conflicts, and, in particular, a review of the Wildlife and Countryside Act of 1981.

MacEwen, A. and MacEwen, M., *National Parks: Conservation or Cosmetics?* (George Allen and Unwin, 1982). A review of the operation of the National Parks, their administration, policies and land use issues.

Mathieson, A. and Wall, G., *Tourism: Economic, Physical and Social Impacts* (Longman, 1982). A review of the range of tourist impacts. A good text for those wanting a comprehensive and international introduction to environmental analysis in tourism, and in particular for those unable to gain access to a major tourism research library. Reprinted for the third time in 1986.

Miles, J. C., *The Goyt Valley Traffic Experiment, 1970–1971* (Countryside Commission, 1972). An assessment of this experiment and its effects on environmental management.

National Geographic This journal of the Washington-based National Geographic Society often includes introductory papers on a range of tourism impacts worldwide.

National Trust for Scotland, *Little Houses* (National Trust for Scotland, undated). An introduction to the objectives of Trust with regard to vernacular architecture, and to the evolution and management of the program.

Nature Conservancy Council, *Nature Conservation Guidelines For Onshore Oil And Gas Development* (Nature Conservancy Council, 1986). This includes a comprehensive list of the statutory framework for UK nature conservation.

Northumberland County Council National Park and Countryside Committee publishes a series of field guides which integrate a range of disciplines in environmental interpretation, primarily for schools' use. These are available from the County Council at Hexham, and include: *A Field Guide to the Hadrian's Wall Area* (1982); *Look around Hadrian's Wall* (1982); *A Field Guide to Plessey Woods Country Park* (1983); and *A Field Guide to the Cheviot Hills* (1985). These guides are an excellent example of literature designed to promote environmental understanding.

O'Riordan, T. and Hey, R. (eds), *Environmental Impact Assessment* (Saxon House, 1976). This text reviews the methdologies of environmental impact assessment.

Pennyfather, K., *Interpretive Media and Facilities.* Part 2 of *Guide to Countryside Interpretation* (HMSO, 1975). This is a gazetteer of interpretative media with site examples in Britain. It forms a comprehensive guide to this form of environmentally sensitive development.

Pye-Smith, C. and Blackie, J., 'The impact of tourism on nature conservation', *Tourism and the Environment* M. Romeril and D. Hughes-Evans, (eds) (London Institution of Environmental Sciences, 1980), pp. 45–55. This paper reviews the mechanical damage to vegetation; pollution; fire; disturbance; management strategies.

Recher, H. F., Lunney, D. and Dunn, I., *A Natural Legacy: Ecology in Australia* (Pergamon, 2nd edition, 1986). This introductory text includes reviews of planning and conservation of the natural resource in Australia, and includes a discussion of National Parks as an agency of conservation.

Reynolds, J. (ed.), *Conservation Planning in Town and Country* (Liverpool University Press, 1976). Papers illustrating conservation, produced for European Architectural Heritage Year of 1975.

Rogers, A., Blunden, J. and Curry, N., *The Countryside Handbook* (Croom Helm, 1985). A gazetteer of legislation, official bodies, private groups and reports pertaining to the countryside. Produced by the Open University in association with the Countryside Commission.

de Santo, R. S., *Concepts of Applied Ecology* (Springer Verlag, 1978). This text reviews ecological impacts and outlines the requirements of environmental impact statements (EISs). Included are guidelines for the preparation of the ecological documentation for statements and an extensive glossary of ecological terms.

Shoard, M., *The Theft of the Countryside* (Maurice Temple Smith, 1980). A text reviewing, in part, the effectiveness of the National Parks.

Shoard, M., 'No space for parks', *Geographical Magazine*, vol. 59 (1987), pp. 291–5. This paper reviews the evolution of park policies in Scotland, and the effectiveness of the policies adopted.

Speight, M. C. D., *Outdoor Recreation and its Ecological Effects: A Bibliography and Review*. Discussion Papers in Conservation, no. 4 (University College, 1973). This paper reviews some ecological effects of recreational activities, and the use of information on ecological change caused by these activities.

Tivy, J., *The Concept and Determination of Carrying Capacity of Recreational Land in the U.S.A.* (Countryside Commission for Scotland, 1972). This text reviews definitions of carrying capacity, factors affecting capacities and recreational space standards.

Tivy, J., *The Effects of Recreation on Fresh Water Lochs and Reservoirs in Scotland* (Countryside Comission for Scotland, 1980). A review of the characteristics of Scottish freshwater lochs and reservoirs, the impacts of recreation, and types and levels of management.

Wall, G. and Wright, C., *The Environmental Impact of Outdoor Recreation*, Department of Geography Publication Series no. 11, (University of Waterloo, Ontario, 1977). A monograph reviewing environmental impacts, not all of which are necessarily caused by tourists.

Williams, G. O., ap Nefydd Roberts, E. and Morgan, B. C., 'Ethical considerations', *Cynefin, Conference Papers* (Cynefin, 1982), pp. 3–9. This paper sets out an ethical system for conservation.

de Zouche Hall, R., *A Bibliography on Vernacular Architecture* (David and Charles, 1972). An extensive bibliography of work published on vernacular buildings up to the end of the 1960s.

RICHARD PRENTICE

Ethnic identity and tourism marketing

Introduction

The tourism industry often postures itself as the merchant of adventure, unique experiences, and even the unimagined. In this spirit, agency offices are habitually bedazzled with posters of strange lands and folk attired in ethnic garb. In reality, of course, pleasure trips are often less exotic; many clients simply seek to visit relatives or return 'home'. Serving the homeward bound, however, is apt to be unprofitable; the agency might sell an airline ticket and nothing else. Everytime an 'Uncle Charlie' picks your client up at the airport and loans out the guest room, you lose. You lose commissions on hotel accommodations, rent-a-cars, and excursion packages. In short, what Uncle Charlie provides, you can't sell.

Not all people visiting their heritage, however, are marginal clients; on the contrary, some present profitable opportunities. Ethnic groups who wish to return to their ancestral home are such a target market.

This chapter deals with members of ethnic groups who live far from their ancestral home and who are permanently located in 'alien' lands as citizens or permanent residents. Many such people wish to embark on a rather lavish excursion to their place of origin and, perhaps, do so on a regular basis. To facilitate dealing with such individuals, we will provide some concrete hints on how to find such people, how to assess the opportunities they provide, and how to best provide tourism services to this target market. We will also remind the tourism professional that such people are apt to make more than one such pilgrimage and, therefore, deserve special attention as potential repeat customers.

Not only that, travel agencies which cater to specific ethnic groups may be able to use their expertise to spawn successful sidelines, such as selling specialty goods made in a specific country to members of ethnic communities. Due to our research experience, we will concentrate upon ethnic communities living in North America, although the strategies discussed can be applied elsewhere.

Examples

The cultural diversity of North America provides an example of how ethnicity can provide a window of opportunity to the tourism profession. One of the truisms of North American history is that the various ethnic groups which settled in the United States have slowly, but inevitably, been alloyed into a new, distinctively 'American' culture. In 1909, for example, Israel Zangwill observed, 'There she lies, the great melting pot – listen! Can't you hear the roaring and bubbling? Ah, what a stirring and seething – Celt and Latin, Slav and Teuton, Greek and Syrian, Black and Yellow – Jew and Gentile' (pp. 198–9). Since that time, the 'melting pot' theory has dominated interpretations of American society.

Recently, however, this paradigm of cultural intermingling has come under attack. Ethnic identity, once believed to be a mere vestigal remain destined for oblivion, has staged a vital resurgence. Today, social theorists acknowledge that ethnic identity in the United States is enjoying a robust, though unexpected, revival despite great distances in time and space between ethnic subcultures and their old world progenitors. Perhaps a definitive statement of this perspective is Phillip Roth's novel *Goodbye Columbus* (1959) which portrayed the dilemma faced by members of the New York Jewish community poised between almost total assimilation and the maintenance of Jewish identity. Although Judaism, of course, is a religion not merely an ethnic group, Roth portrays the costs of assimilation and suggests ethnic identity will continue to survive in many situations.

Scholars such as Milton Gordon (1964) draw a distinction between 'cultural assimilation' in which the ethnic group learns the appropriate means of behavior in the new culture and 'structural assimilation' in which a person can enter into primary relationships such as marriage without regard to ethnicity. In general, ethnics of European origin can, at will, blend into the mainstream of American life. Increasingly, however, they choose to assert and celebrate their ethnic identity. Of course, such groups have evolved in the United States and are profoundly different from their old world cousins. Still, they celebrate their ancestral heritage and make consumer decisions based on this identity.

European-derived ethnics are now 'mainstream' North American residents and citizens who have typically been economically successful and have the discretionary income which makes 'investing' in one's heritage a financial possibility. These developments offer opportunities to entrepreneurs who wish to satisfy the needs and demands which stem from ethnic identity. Travel to an ancestral home is one such need or demand.

Benefits

What is most striking about this survival of ethnicity in the new world is that, even in the United States where cultural assimilation has led to a degree of cultural homogeneity and where travel to an ancestral place of origin is rather difficult, a potentially significant market for such tourism services exists. In many other markets (such as Europe), circumstances may be even more lucrative: often assimilation is not taking place rapidly and members of ethnic communities often have less difficulty in returning to their place of origin.

In general, when people make such a pilgrimage to their ancestral home, luxury and lavishness are the norm. Such people have often been separated from their friends and loved ones for decades. Understandably, during such a triumphant return, people want to indulge themselves and give their relatives a taste of the success they have found in their new home. As a result, these clients can be lucrative and a relatively 'easy sell'.

Some travel agencies, furthermore, have found that selling standardized Christmas gifts (such as fine foods) which are sent to loved ones in the old world can be a lucrative sideline. This would be especially true if a travel agency had many ethnic clients and/or access to mailing lists of specific ethnic groups.

By profiling the travel agencies' geographical marketing range and concentrating upon ethnic targets, tourism professionals can not only sell foreign travel services, they will have a good chance of attracting repeat business and customer loyalty since ethnics who return home tend to do so periodically. In addition, an agency might be able to innovate sidelines which serve ethnic communities. For these reasons, catering to the needs of ethnic groups can have significant long-term implications and emerge as a particularly attractive strategy.

Implementation

Many ethnic groups live far from their 'roots' and they constitute a lucrative target market. A major problem exists, however: can the tourism professional effectively implement a plan to serve and satisfy this target market?

Here we will give some practical hints on how to tap such a market by analyzing one group: Greek Americans living in the State of Ohio, USA. We will examine their propensity to travel to Greece, their motivation for doing so, and identify surrogate measures which can be used to predict the likelihood of a pilgrimage to their place of origin. Significantly, such a purchase is beset with risks to the consumer; not only is foreign travel expensive, travel to an ancestral homeland involves significant social and psychological risks and payoffs – dangers and opportunities not felt by the typical tourist. Although we realize that Greek Americans are unique, we believe the kinds of questions we ask and the types of strategies we recommend can be used by other tourism professionals wishing to market their services to other ethnic groups.

Our research involves Greek Americans living in north-eastern Ohio and members of six parishes of the Greek Orthodox Church in the area. The literature dealing with Greek ethnicity in America supports such a choice for there is a strong interrelation between community (*koinotis*) and parish (*paroikia*), at least with reference to the Greek cohorts. In addition, membership of the Greek Orthodox Church provides a good basis for a sample, since 80 per cent of all Greek Americans belong to the church (Moskos, 1980, p. 67; Constantinou and Harvey, 1985, pp. 237–8).

Data collection was based on a survey conducted between December 1980 and April 1981. Five hundred questionnaires were randomly distributed and 448 (89.6 per cent) were usable. The questionnaires were available in Greek and English. The specific mutually exclusive criteria for inclusion in the sample were the following:

1. Immigrants from the nation of Greece as it expanded territorially in modern years.
2. Immigrants from the Hellenic Diaspora, that is, Greek ethnics who live outside the boundaries of Greece.
3. Descendents of 1 and 2.

Respondents had to be at least 20 years of age and permanent residents or citizens of the United States (Constantinou, 1982, pp. 114–15).

The following variables were examined with respect to times of visitation to the homeland: sex, marital status, age, education, income, employment status, occupation, place of birth (Greece v. United States), location of residence, participation in folk societies, participation in nationwide ethnic associations, church membership, attendance at church services, vacationing patterns, correspondence with the homeland, knowledge of the Greek language, subscription to Greek and/or American newspapers and/or magazines, retirement intentions, listening to Greek radio stations, and generation status (Constantinou, 1982, pp. 120–30).

Ultimately, the goal was to ascertain what variables were truly linked with a propensity to travel to Greece and which were false indicators. Variables indicating a propensity to visit Greece include the following (Thanopoulos and Walle, 1988):

1. Being born in Greece or first generation Americans.
2. Speaking Greek fluently.
3. Corresponding with Greece on a regular basis.
4. Subscribing to Greek magazines and newspapers.
5. Participating in folk societies which relate to a *specific* region of Greece.
6. Having lower levels of education.
7. Listening to Greek radio stations.

According to these findings, each of the above is a legitimate measure of the propensity to travel to Greece and, as such, may be used by tourism professionals in their marketing research and in their strategic planning.

Just as it was possible to isolate a host of true indicators, various 'red herrings' were also found which could easily throw tourism professionals 'off the right track' (Thanopoulos and Constantinou, 1985). In specific, inappropriate indicators of

Greek Americans' preference to visit Greece include the following:

1. Participation in nationwide associations formally linking Greek Americans to Greece (like American Hellenic Educational Progressive Association 'AHEPA').
2. Membership of the Greek Orthodox Church.
3. Subscription to English newspapers and/or magazines relating issues from Greece.
4. Age, sex, income, or other socioeconomic variables (except education).

These variables were not found to be correlated with a high rate of visitation to Greece, even though some are clearly linked to the Greek American subculture. By alerting the tourist industry to such potential pitfalls, perhaps nonproductive promotions can be eliminated and marketing efforts can be made more effective.

One question remains. How can such knowledge be evaluated and forged into a viable marketing strategy aimed at members of their ethnic group which are most receptive to the possibility of foreign travel?

Assessment

Having established that a host of important measures indicates a propensity of an ethnic group to travel to their ancestral homeland, it is important to be able to evaluate which indicators are useful to the tourism professional. Corresponding on a regular basis with relatives, friends, and loved ones in Greece, for example, is significant but hard to measure in a cost-effective manner. Although good parameters, gathering this information can be difficult.

Indicators which are easy, quick and cheap to analyze are logical choices when planning marketing research and promotional campaigns. They include: participation in folk societies, subscribing to ethnic newspapers and listening to ethnic radio stations or programs. Folk societies are usually high profile organizations and can be identified with little difficulty. Ethnic newspapers sell advertising space which is cheap and reaches likely prospects. Many ethnic newspapers, furthermore, have a nationwide circulation which expands the range of a relatively cheap advertisement. Ethnic newspapers may also sell their mailing lists for a direct mail campaign planned by a travel agency. Ethnic radio provides another means of advertising which reaches the target market. If ethnic programming is on noncommercial radio, sponsorships and a resultant air-time acknowledgement might still be possible.

The beauty of such promotional strategies is their simplicity, their cheapness, and the ability to reach a high number of bona fide prospects. Such proposals, of course, only scratch the surface; many other cheap and efficient promotional strategies can be employed. They all have one thing in common, however, concentrating upon those measures which lead to cheap, but efficient, communication with a desirable target market.

Conclusion

As we have argued, ethnic communities are not homogeneous entities. As a result, marketing efforts can be made more efficient by locating market segments which are particularly likely to travel to an ancestral homeland; by doing so, tourism professionals can employ more efficient marketing strategies.

Through an indepth study of a sample of Greek Americans living in Ohio, we were able to identify traits linked to such foreign travel among this group. Such measures both indicate the likelihood of travel and provide means of cheaply and efficiently communicating with lucrative target markets. We also found that the propensity to travel to Greece atrophied as actual contact with the old world decreased.

Although some ethnic groups may behave somewhat differently to the Greek Americans discussed in this chapter, we have established a framework with which to conceptualize and accomplish the marketing of tourism to a specific ethnic group. We recommend the following means of identifying market segments and communicating with them:

1. Assume that the ethnic group is made up of a number of heterogeneous groups.
2. Do not assume that being a visible or active member of an ethnic community inevitably indicates a propensity to travel to the place of origin.
3. When gathering data and locating variables which indicates a propensity to travel concentrate upon characteristics which can be relatively easily isolated and/or which enhance the ability of the marketer to communicate with the target group in a cheap and efficient manner.

In the final analysis, in various regions of the United States as well as other parts of the world, ethnicity is vital and subcultures can be profitably served. It has been claimed, for example, that between 1 and 4 million Greek Americans live in the United States and approximately 30 per cent of the sample survey appear to be likely prospects for travel to Greece. Greek Americans, we add, are a relatively small ethnic group; many other groups offer even larger opportunities.

Further reading

Cohen, J. and Cohen, P., *Applied Multiple Regression/Correlation Analysis for Behavioral Sciences* (Lawrence Erlbaum Associates, 2nd edition, 1983). Standard statistical text used in the analysis part of this work.

Constantinou, S. T., *A Geographic-Systems Approach to Ethnicity: The Greek Americans in Northeastern Ohio* (PhD dissertation, Kent State University, 1982). Data derived from this source were used as pointers to marketing applications.

Constantinou, S. T. and Harvey, M. E., 'Basic dimensional structure and intergenerational differences in Greek American ethnicity', *Sociology and Social Research*, vol. 69 (January 1985), pp. 234–54.

Constantinou, S. T., Thanopoulos, J. and Walle, A. H., 'Ethnicity and its relevance to marketing: the case of tourism', *Journal of Travel*

Research (Winter 1988), pp. 11–14.

Gordon, M., *Assimilation in American Life: The Role of Race, Religion and National Origins* (Oxford University Press, 1964).

Green, P. E. and Tull, D. S., *Research for Marketing Decisions* (Prentice Hall, 4th edition, 1978). Standard marketing research text used in the analysis part of this work.

Moskos, C., *Greek Americans: Struggle and Success* (Prentice Hall, 1980). Indepth analysis of the Greek–American cohort and their motivation toward progress and ethnic identity.

Roth, P., *Goodbye Columbus and Five Short Stories* (Houghton Mifflin, 1959). Fiction by a noted New York Jewish author which dramatizes the plight of those who must choose between ethnic identity and cultural assimilation.

Thanopoulos, J. and Constantinou, S. T., 'Tourism and ethnic groups: behavioral patterns and marketing implications', *Developments in Marketing Sciences*, N. K. Malhotra, ed. (Academy of Marketing Science, 1985). Abstract of a paper that attempted to capitalize on cultural variables as determinants of market behavior.

Zangwill, I., *The Melting Pot: A Drama in Four Acts* (Macmillan, 1909). Play written by American immigrant of Jewish descent about assimilation in America. Compare with Jacob Riis' *The Making of an American* (1901).

A. H. WALLE and
STAVROS T. CONSTANTINOU

European destination marketing

Introduction

This chapter considers the issues and challenges involved in marketing Europe as a tourist destination particularly for long-haul tourists. Three interrelated topics need to be examined. These are the type of tourist market that Europe caters for; the effect that European Community (EC) policies have on tourism in Europe, and the evidence from market research on the types of tourist who perceive Europe as a holiday destination. The chapter concludes with an outline marketing strategy for Europe.

Tourism marketing is different to the marketing of almost any other product. In the first place the tourist product is not a single product, but rather an amalgam of products. The EC consists of twelve countries from Greece to Denmark, with a great variety of attractions, scenic and cultural, both between and within member states. Secondly, the tourist product has to be consumed on the spot and to do this it is necessary to transport the market (i.e. the tourist) to the product, which is the opposite of any normal economic transaction. Seasonality is a key factor in marketing tourism, because unless an airline seat, or hotel room or package holiday is sold by a particular date it is lost. It cannot be reduced in price and sold at a later date. It is also a highly discretionary product and is competing with many other choices facing the potential tourist. For example a family in the United States may choose to buy a new boat or a time-share apartment or a Caribbean cruise rather than a trip to Europe. Very often the tourist is not buying a specific product or service but rather an experience, a dream.

The European tourism product

This consists of the mountains and beaches, lakeside resorts, ski slopes, historic towns and rural villages and sheer diversity of natural attractions. It also includes the vast cultural heritage of Europe with museums such as the Vatican Museum in Rome, the British Museum in London, art galleries including the Prado, the Uffizzi, the Louvre and the Rijksmuseum. It includes archaeological features such as the wealth of Greek and Roman remains around the Mediterranean and the prehistoric sites such as Stonehenge. It includes cultural events, the arts from La Scala to Covent Garden and historic traditions. In fact Europe contains a greater diversity of attractions both natural and man-made, cultural and historical, than any other tourist destination in the world. However, at present Europe is not marketed as a single tourist destination. Each individual European country markets itself and no account is taken of marketing Europe as a package for the longhaul tourist.

Existing patterns of European tourism

A study of existing tourism statistics helps to explain the emphasis on marketing tourism at national rather than Community level. By the mid-1980s Europe alone took up 70 per cent of international tourist arrivals. The Americas absorbed 20 per cent and other regions of the world accounted for the remaining 10 per cent (World Tourism Organization, 1986). Between 1967 and 1987 Europe almost doubled its number of international tourist arrivals (Casini et al., 1984). The greatest individual increases during this period were Greece (500 per cent) and the United Kingdom (168 per cent). Belgium, Luxembourg and Denmark had the lowest rates of growth of international tourism. However, 80 per cent of 'international' tourism in Europe is intraEuropean, so it is tourist movements within the EC and adjacent countries that are of greatest significance. The remaining 20 per cent of tourist movements are longhaul traffic from North America, Japan and Asia. In the last 15 years the volume of travel for tourism in Europe has trebled whilst international tourist arrivals have doubled (Casini et al., 1984).

Within Europe the main tourist destination countries are Italy and Spain, where intraregional arrivals accounted for 91 and 95 per cent of international arrivals respectively in 1983 (World Tourism Organization, 1986). In 1984 Europe received over $57,000 million from international tourist spending (World Tourism Organization, 1986). Seven countries account for 75 per cent of Europe's tourist receipts. They are Austria, the Federal Republic of Germany, France, Spain, Italy, the United Kingdom and Switzerland. The two leading destinations are France and Italy, with Spain and Greece increasing in importance during the 1970s.

The main tourist-generating countries are West Germany,

France, the United Kingdom and the Netherlands, with Denmark and Ireland also having more outgoing than incoming tourists. This pattern has remained the same for the past decade.

Despite the importance of Europe as an international tourist destination, and the contribution that tourism makes to Europe's economy, there are still several problems related to its future development in Europe. As a tourist destination there is a marked degree of seasonality in the demand for tourism which still tends to be concentrated in July and August. This seasonality does not lead to an efficient tourist industry and results in an overloading in the tourist infrastructure, which is geared up to peak season demands and is consequently underused during much of the rest of the year. Hotel occupancy figures, airline seats sold and other capacity indicators all show a downturn in the autumn – spring period with less effective use of capital investment. More effective destination marketing, including promotion of off-season travel and special air/hotel discounts and a new approach to off-season pricing could increase the demand for off-peak holidays. Where the climate is an important factor, incentive tours, cultural programs and sporting events could be part of the package.

Tourism promotion and development by the public sector in Europe

All the countries of Europe promote tourism through their national tourist organizations, although the scale and extent of this support varies from country to country. Tourism is particularly important to the economies of Austria, France, Greece, Italy, the United Kingdom, Spain and Switzerland. Its social role is particularly recognized in Belgium, France, West Germany, the Netherlands and Switzerland. In France and the United Kingdom tourism is given high priority by the central government in terms of promotion and development. Because of the impact that tourism can have on the balance of payments, in recent years the national tourist organizations have played a greater role in promoting domestic tourism.

The Commission of the EC prepared a community policy on tourism in July 1982, and this has greatly strengthened tourism in Europe for a number of reasons. It has encouraged the integration of tourism in Europe by measures designed to provide freedom of movement and the protection of tourists. Before the Treaty of Rome was passed establishing the EC, the many national frontiers represented a very real barrier to the movement of travelers from one country to another. Since 1958 frontier formalities have been steadily relaxed and liberalized. Customs duties between the member states have gone, as has much of the paperwork and the long queues at customs posts. There are no major problems concerning the personal effects that tourists bring with them and most formalities have been relaxed concerning cars, caravans and boats. All EC nationals are entitled to the medical services of the host country if they are so entitled under their domestic health insurance. The Commission is also seeking to harmonize car insurance and

tourist assistance. All of these measures put tourism within the Community at a greater advantage over other regions in the world.

There is a highly efficient and well trained labor force working in the tourist industry and the Commission has established a common market in tourist services by providing the right of nationals of one member state to set up and manage firms in other member states. Moreover, the European Social Fund provides, on a co-financing basis, aid to tourism and those employed in the tourist industry to improve job prospects or to develop vocational training.

Seasonality is a worldwide problem with most tourist activity concentrated into a summer or winter season. This is exacerbated by the tendency to concentrate school and industrial holidays into a short period of the year so that the tourist infrastructure is overloaded during the summer and underused for the rest of the year. The Commission has jointly financed two studies to look at various approaches to staggering school and industrial holidays so as to spread the tourist season over a longer period of the year.

The Community also has the full use of the extensive rail and road network throughout Europe by providing common rules for the international carriage of passengers by coach and allowing coach and bus services from an individual member state to operate throughout Europe. The Commission has promoted high speed international rail passenger services and is seeking ways to improve air services and lower air fares. The European Regional Development Fund and the European Investment Bank have provided funding for over 2,000 km of motorways in Europe. Two of the priority projects examined by the Commission are a permanent link between France and the United Kingdom and a motorway linking Germany with Greece via Austria and Yugoslavia.

The Community is also anxious to develop the poorer regions of Europe and sees tourism as an important means of developing regional economies. The European Regional Development Fund has financed over 350 tourist projects between 1975 and 1981 with a total investment of over £80 million.

A further reason for the importance of Europe as a tourist destination is that over half of the population takes a period of paid holidays and leisure every year. In Sweden 83 per cent, and in Norway 74 per cent of the population take at least one holiday away from home. In some European countries such as the United Kingdom, West Germany and Switzerland the main holiday market has leveled off, and the growth has been in second or third holidays with short breaks being more common.

Figure 1 shows the overall growth in the European travel market between 1968 and 1983, and Fig. 2 shows the main tourist-generating countries.

Market analysis of overseas tourists visiting Europe

A limited number of surveys have been carried out in the main countries providing the bulk of longhaul tourists to Europe. However, it is worth looking at the United States and Canadian

Number of holiday trips taken (millions)
(including children)

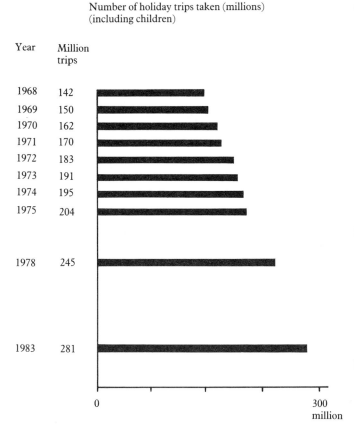

Year	Million trips
1968	142
1969	150
1970	162
1971	170
1972	183
1973	191
1974	195
1975	204
1978	245
1983	281

Figure 1 Evolution of market size over time (*source:* TPRA estimates).

a) main generators of European holiday trips (*Source:* TPRA estimates)

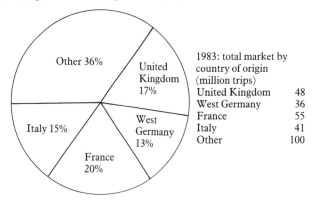

1983: total market by country of origin (million trips)

United Kingdom	48
West Germany	36
France	55
Italy	41
Other	100

b) European foreign travel

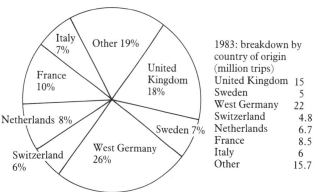

1983: breakdown by country of origin (million trips)

United Kingdom	15
Sweden	5
West Germany	22
Switzerland	4.8
Netherlands	6.7
France	8.5
Italy	6
Other	15.7

Figure 2 Market dimensions.

market in order to develop a marketing strategy for Europe. As Fig. 3 shows, the five biggest dollar earners since 1960 have been Switzerland, West Germany, United Kingdom, France and Italy. The United Kingdom is the major destination, attracting more American tourists than the rest of Europe in 1984 (Fig. 4). Their reasons for visiting the United Kingdom are summed up below.

1. History and culture.
2. A shared heritage and language.
3. Quaintness and charm.
4. Ease and convenience of public transport system.
5. Safeness.

Americans who visit the United Kingdom (and Europe) tend to be more affluent, better educated, more likely to be in professional/technical occupation and older than Americans in general. Almost 60 per cent are 45 or older. Very often they are first time visitors, and they spend more per day than visitors from other EC countries.

A survey of the Canadian vacation market (Commission of the European Communities, 1982) found that 6 million Canadians formed the potential market for tourists to Europe*. When asked about their actual choice of holiday destination in the past 5 years, the results were as follows:

1. The largest group chose Canada (over 60 per cent) closely followed by the United States; Europe was the next most popular destination (over 5 per cent) well ahead of the Caribbean, Mexico and Hawaii.
2. Of those who chose Europe, over one-third visited the Continent only, while just under one third visited the United Kingdom only and just under one third visited both the United Kingdom and the Continent (Commission of the European Communities, 1982, p. 19).

Where does Europe fit in people's future vacation plans? Continental Europe came easily in front (over half the sample) followed by the United Kingdom/Ireland (over a third). About a third identified the United States, Caribbean, Mexico and Hawaii as potential destinations. They were also asked about their perception of the type of vacation that Europe would be good for (European Travel Commission, 1978, Table 5, p. 18). Europe is perceived as offering a wide range of vacation opportunities for Canadian tourists. However, they were also asked

---

* The sample consisted of adults aged 18 or over living in households with an annual income of $10,000 and more, who live in metropolitan areas and who either have taken a major vacation in the past 5 years or expect to do so in the next 5 years.

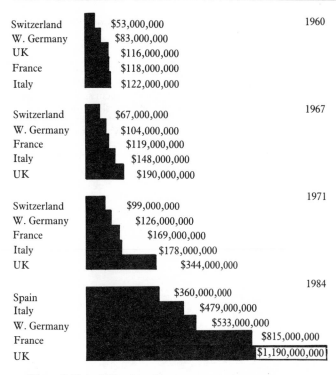

		1960
Switzerland	$53,000,000	
W. Germany	$83,000,000	
UK	$116,000,000	
France	$118,000,000	
Italy	$122,000,000	

		1967
Switzerland	$67,000,000	
W. Germany	$104,000,000	
France	$119,000,000	
Italy	$148,000,000	
UK	$190,000,000	

		1971
Switzerland	$99,000,000	
W. Germany	$126,000,000	
France	$169,000,000	
Italy	$178,000,000	
UK	$344,000,000	

		1984
Spain	$360,000,000	
Italy	$479,000,000	
W. Germany	$533,000,000	
France	$815,000,000	
UK	$1,190,000,000	

Figure 3 United Kingdom: biggest earner in Europe from US travel.

about factors that might deter them from visiting Europe, and there were several negative factors, listed below:

1. It is expensive to get there.
2. It is not always safe there.
3. Canadians are usually thought to be American.
4. It is crowded with tourists from other countries.
5. Not enough people speak English.
6. Hotels are not very clean.
7. They tend to distrust North Americans.
8. It is difficult to get help if you are in trouble.
9. Service is not good.
10. It is hard to get the kind of food you want.

In order to obtain a more detailed picture of their concerns the sample were shown a list of things tourists might encounter on vacation anywhere. The issues of major concern were the following:

1. High prices.
2. Delays at airports/rail stations.
3. Bad public washrooms.
4. Bad weather.
5. Strikes.
6. Water not safe.
7. Lack of hygiene.
8. Being cheated.
9. Bad political situation.

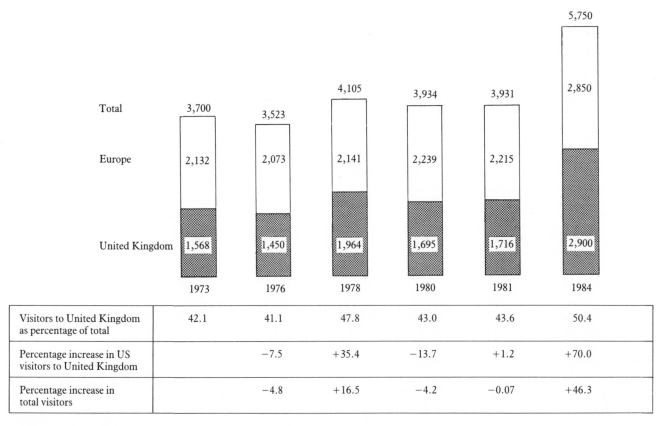

	1973	1976	1978	1980	1981	1984
Total	3,700	3,523	4,105	3,934	3,931	5,750
Europe	2,132	2,073	2,141	2,239	2,215	2,850
United Kingdom	1,568	1,450	1,964	1,695	1,716	2,900
Visitors to United Kingdom as percentage of total	42.1	41.1	47.8	43.0	43.6	50.4
Percentage increase in US visitors to United Kingdom		−7.5	+35.4	−13.7	+1.2	+70.0
Percentage increase in total visitors		−4.8	+16.5	−4.2	−0.07	+46.3

Figure 4 US visitors to the United Kingdom and Europe 1973–84.

In part some of these negative factors stem from a lack of knowledge about Europe and an absence of detailed information about the region in general and individual countries in particular. About half of the North Americans hoping to vacation in Europe will first make a visit to one or more of the national tourist offices over there. The welcome to Europe starts in the national tourist office and the staff there must be competent and knowledgeable with a good supply of brochures and information.

The lesson from the North American market research is that more could be done to promote Europe as a tourist destination by stressing the integrated nature of the tourist infrastructure and by taking advantage of the EC policies designed to encourage the freedom of movement and protection of tourists throughout the EC. In tourist regions within individual countries small tourist businesses in the same sectors, for example hotels or attractions, are encouraged to group together to form marketing consortia. The same approach could be adopted for countries in Europe marketing the whole region as a tourist destination. Considerable economies of scale could be achieved in terms of marketing and promotional budgets in the longhaul markets.

A marketing strategy for Europe

In preparing a marketing strategy it is worthwhile 'regionalizing' Europe to put together different types of holiday destination based on social, cultural and other characteristics. For example Austria, West Germany and Switzerland have a similar culture and language and are linked by a modern rail and motorway network. Similarly the three Scandinavian countries Denmark, Norway and Sweden have a distinctive culture and close associations. In fact the tourist boards of these Nordic countries jointly promote inter-Scandinavian travel, although this may be done through the rest of Europe rather than in the longhaul markets. Similarly, France, Italy, West Germany and Switzerland can promote the Alpine region, although this is unlikely to attract North American visitors for the winter sports as they have comparable facilities. The three Benelux countries (Belgium, the Netherlands and Luxembourg) could also engage in joint promotions stressing their close proximity and varied cultural heritage. However the predominant trend is for individual countries to market their country as a single tourist destination, when it is clear that the majority of longhaul tourists wish to maximize their visit because of the time and cost of traveling to Europe, and wish to visit as many countries as possible during their visit. Although this chapter has concentrated on the North American market which is a high spending one with still further potential for tourism traffic, events in 1986 showed the wisdom of adopting a marketing strategy that seeks to diversify into as many longhaul markets as possible.

One immediate repercussion of the Libyan bombing raid in April 1986 was a dramatic decline in the number of Americans traveling to Europe because they feared terrorist reprisals. In May 1986 there were 40 per cent fewer American visitors to the United Kingdom, than in the same period in 1985. In Greece and France there were 60 per cent fewer US tourists and 50 per cent fewer in Italy.

Australia, South-East Asia and Japan are growing in importance as generators of tourism to Europe and have considerable scope for expansion despite the great distances involved. Europe accounts for about 12 per cent of the Japanese overseas visitors (over 350,000 tourists) and they are among the highest spending tourists in Europe. Despite the distance and the high air fare, Europe has steadily increased in importance as a destination for Japanese tourists since 1964. It is also the destination where they stay longest. Since the 1970s the European Travel Commission (who have representatives of all the European national tourist organizations [NTOs]) have been very successful in promoting Europe as a whole, and supplementing the individual efforts of each national tourist office. Their main efforts are targeted at travel agents, who handle 92 per cent of the overseas market in Japan. A small group of companies associated with major finance houses, are often wholesalers and retailers selling package tours to Europe. The future for this market is likely to be less emphasis on a packaged tour (particularly for the 20 per cent of the Japanese who are on repeat visits) and more emphasis on special interest travel opportunities. What we are selling to Japan is a small size Continent with 23 different countries, cultures and an endless variety of both historical and natural environments. It is a destination that can be visited several times without repeating previous experiences.

Assessment

What are the implications of these trends and these market surveys for the European tourism and hospitality industry? The strength of the European tourist product is the sheer variety and diversity of opportunities in a relatively compact area, the ease of travel within the Continent and the wide range of accommodation. The weaknesses are the high cost of travel for the longhaul tourist, the failure to market Europe as a single tourist 'package' and the emphasis on national promotion rather than Community promotion, the limited number of inclusive tour charters from North America or Asia, and the varied exchange rates between the US or Canadian dollar and major European currencies. The opportunities to market Europe are considerable especially in Japan, the Far East and Middle East. The threats to Europe are competition from destinations in the Pacific, Caribbean or South-East Asia where travel costs are lower, accommodation may be cheaper and the overall package can be sold at a more competitive price. As almost all longhaul tourists to Europe travel by air it is important for tourist organizations and tourist companies in Europe to take steps towards the following:

1. Closer cooperation between national tourist offices and airlines.
2. Selling more inclusive tour packages. These could take the form of cooperative ventures by NTOs or by hotel consortia arranging 'tie-in' deals with the major airlines.

3. Targeting market segments such as the conference market, special interest holidays/the cultural tourism market.
4. Spreading the demand in time by hoteliers encouraging long-haul tourists to come in the shoulder months with special price packages and seasonal discounts.
5. Funding, by the public sector NTOs and the European Commission, hotel development schemes and tourism-related developments that will attract longhaul tourists.
6. Selling more surface travel in Europe. This is efficient, inexpensive, quick and often overlooked.
7. To put more emphasis on marketing good quality second class accommodation. The use of budget hotels and second class hotels can have a marked impact on the cost of a visit to Europe, and this is a key factor in the highly competitive international market.
8. Taking advantage of the important market for cruise travel in North America and the Far East. Although only 4 per cent of the population of the United States has taken a cruise, the majority of that 4 per cent is repeat business. Companies could promote fly-cruise deals with cruises originating in Europe.

Conclusion

The 1987 figures for the US bookings have shown a substantial improvement over 1986. In June, tour operators were reporting increases in business of 30 to 100 per cent and the revival is so strong that the challenge is to find last minute space for the unexpected volume. More than 80 per cent of US travel agents experienced increases in bookings for Europe. The highest increases in bookings were for the United Kingdom and France. Other countries sharing a marked increase in US bookings over 1986 figures were West Germany, Austria, Switzerland and the Netherlands. However, there is considerable scope for improving the marketing of Europe. In a recent poll of US travel agents (*Travel Weekly*, 1987) less than 30 per cent felt that European countries were promoting tourism adequately, less than 20 per cent felt that hotels were promoting Europe as a destination and less than 25 per cent felt that cruise lines were marketing Europe effectively. Airlines did rather better, and 85 per cent of those polled gave them credit for promoting Europe as a tourist destination.

What is needed is better coordination of activity between the airlines, the hotel companies and the national tourist organizations to provide more competitive packages for potential tourists to Europe. Although Europe is a major destination, much of the tourism activity is concentrated in the summer months. The load factor for the tourism infrastructure, transport and accommodation is about 60 per cent year round, so there is considerable spare capacity and resources that could be used. Special price packages for the early summer/early autumn periods and more innovative marketing could help to spread the tourist season.

The prospects are good, but complacency must be avoided at all costs. There are many other tourist destinations competing in a highly discretionary market place. The European Commission is in a strong position to assist in developing tourism by taking further steps to ease the free movement of tourists throughout Europe, by encouraging the education and training for careers in tourism, by providing grants, loans on favorable terms, loan guarantees and interest subsidies to encourage the development of new hotels and resort areas, or the refurbishment of existing ones. The European Regional Development Fund is particularly important in this respect.

There needs to be greater recognition at policy level by individual countries and by the private sector of the tourism and hospitality industry of the advantages of the cooperative marketing of Europe in the international marketplace. The national tourist organizations have an important role to play here because the tourism industry is mainly made up of small firms which often do not have access to international market research or lack the knowledge of where to go for specialized advice.

Further reading

'Agents show big revival for Europe', *Travel Weekly*, vol. 46, no. 55 (25 June, 1987).
British Tourist Authority, *Guide to the US Market* (BTA, May 1985).
Buhler, J. *et al.*, 'The Japanese travel market', *Europe's New Tourism: A Look at the Prospects in the 1980s* (European Travel Commission, 1978).
Casini, S., Varalado, S., Masetti, P. *et al.*, *The Tourism Sector in the Community: A Study of Concentration and Competitiveness* (EC, 1984). This report by a group of Italian economists was commissioned by the EC and provides an overview of trends in the early 1980s.
Commission of the European Communities, *A Community Policy on Tourism*, Supplement 4/82 (EC, 1982).
European Community. There are numerous additional reports and papers from the EC, notably Council regulations (EC) no. 724/75, establishing a European Regional Development Fund, and nos. 2615/80 and 2619/80, which are referred to in the guidelines on EC policy on tourism.
European Travel Commission, *Europe's New Tourism: A Look at the Prospects in the 1980s* (European Travel Commission, 1978), pp. 18–20.
Medlik, S., *Trends in Tourism: World Experience and Englands' Prospects* (English Tourist Board, 1982).
World Tourism Organization, *Economic Review of World Tourism* (WTO, 1986).

PATRICK LAVERY

Family life cycle

Introduction

In the areas of consumer behavior research and marketing management one of the most important concepts that has been developed is that of the family life cycle. The life cycle is one of the social stratification techniques commonly used by consumer researchers and marketing analysts for analyzing data and has particularly important potential applications in the area of segmentation strategy. It will be seen from this chapter that the idea of the family life cycle is a useful complement to the other criteria usually referred to for segmentation purposes such as age, occupation, income, lifestyle, and benefit segmentation (Meidan 1984).

The concept originated in the sociology literature at the turn of the century and has been used in consumer analyses since the 1950s to examine both general patterns of consumption and demand for specific products. Amongst these evaluations there have been several which have investigated leisure and tourism (Landon and Locander, 1978; Hisrich and Peters, 1974; Rapoport and Rapoport, 1975; Reynolds and Wells, 1977). The general conclusion from these studies is that, in this area of consumer behavior, the family life cycle is one of the most significant techniques that can be used for analyzing purchasing.

Even today perhaps the most widely used scheme is that devised by Wells and Gubar (1966) which divided the history of a family into nine possible phases. Table 1 gives a summary of the most important features of their review of buyer behavior over the life cycle and despite the fact that this work is 20 years old the general consumption characteristics associated with the life cycle still remain valid. The table also shows how the family life cycle is a multidimensional construct which takes into account age, the presence of children and income. It is implicit in concept that absolute levels of income will rise over the life cycle until retirement. However the differences between the stages are especially important in describing that amount of income which is likely to be uncommitted after meeting the basic needs of the family and is therefore available for expenditure on more discretionary items. Typically much expenditure on leisure and tourism is of this nature and this is probably the key reason why the family life cycle is such a potentially important concept for tourism management. The review highlights how the bachelor, newly married, full nest 3 and empty nest 1 stages of the life cycle are the particularly important periods for heavy expenditure on leisure and tourism.

Examples

Some of the most obvious examples of the actual use of the family life cycle in tourism management are to be found in the strategies employed by tour operators dealing in the package holiday business. A short examination of a number of brochures from UK firms reveals many illustrations of how the market may be segmented to concentrate on the needs of customers in particular stages of the life cycle.

Club 18–30, run by International Leisure Group, is specifically targeted towards the bachelor/young singles phase of the life cycle. The kind of holiday characteristics emphasized by the operators are facilities such as bars, discos, nightlife and sports; all aimed at securing the 'time of their life' for the customer who will 'meet new friends' and make the most of their 'youthful freedom'. In contrast, under the Intasun name, the Group offer their Golden Days package designed for the over-50s. Superficially this may seem like segmentation simply on the basis of age. However the emphasis on freedom and new friends places the Club 18–30 package directly towards Young Singles rather than equivalent aged married couples while Golden Days are really looking towards the childless stages associated with the empty nest periods and are not designed for older married people who still have dependent children. Comparisons with other Intasun holidays show how the company carefully adjust the holiday attributes for Golden Days to meet the particular needs of the more elderly group; for example by including full- or half-board instead of bed and breakfast or self catering, and providing singles clubs at chosen resorts for the solitary survivor categories of the life cycle. Further comparisons across a range of roughly equivalent holidays from a number of companies also show how the person booking through Golden Days might expect to pay a slight premium at most times of the year compared to the alternative holiday not specifically targeted to that group. This reflects a policy consistent with the presentation from Wells and Gubar given above. The general principles of the pricing structure are also adjusted to take into account the fact that more elderly people without the ties of children are less constrained on the season of their holiday. This means that their price response is more elastic over the year and that operators cannot charge such a great differential between peak and other seasons as compared to families who have more constraints on the timing of their holiday.

Table 1 Consumption characteristics over life cycle.

Stage	Characteristics	Consumer behavior
Bachelor	Young, single people not living at home	Few financial burdens; recreation orientated; buy basic equipment, cars, vacations
Newly married	Young, no children	Financially better off than will be later; buy cars, durables, vacations
Full nest 1	Youngest child under 6	Low liquid assets; buying conditioned by young children
Full nest 2	Youngest child 6 or over	Financial position better; buy bicycles, educational items
Full nest 3	Older married with dependent children	Financial position still improving; buy durables, leisure items
Empty nest 1	Older married, no children at home, still working.	Optimum financial position; buy luxuries, vacations
Empty nest 2	Older married, no children at home, retired	Income falls; health/medical products important
Solitary survivor in labor force		Income good; similar to empty nest 1 but often gives up home commitments
Solitary survivor retired		As for other retired but special needs for affection and security

The two examples given above both refer to stages of the family life cycle which Wells and Gubar highlighted as being important for expenditure on leisure and vacations. However people in other stages of the life cycle still have holiday needs and there are many companies who target their products to those groups. Family First from Lancaster holidays (also part of International Leisure Group), Falcon Family holidays or Skytours provide examples of products which are specifically geared towards the full nest 1 and full nest 2 categories. In the literature produced by Skytours they are keen to emphasize 'kids' of all ages and highlight the provision of cots, highchairs, and family games as well as the usual sun, beaches and swimming pools, A key feature of Skytours marketing is the price strategy. Almost every page of their main summer brochure for 1987 contains a claim about reductions and low prices. The full nest phases of the life cycle which probably form the largest part of Skytours' target market are also the stages of the family life cycle where family finances are typically at their most stretched and price becomes a very dominant consideration in the holiday decision process. The product characteristics and the price strategy knit together to form a unified whole carefully

constructed to meet the needs of potential tourists in those stages of the life cycle.

In all the instances mentioned above the different market segments are targeted with separate brochures which keep the products very discrete. In the case of Club 18–30 the Group have built up a separate brand image which is not linked into its other brands at all. Other operators do not take their strategies to such definitive lengths. For example, Sunmed offer three different products aimed at different stages of the life cycle within their one Greek brochure. 'Young and Lively' is positioned to appeal to young singles and newly marrieds, 'Family Holidays' seem particularly targeted towards the earlier full nest stages where families may need child-minders and possibly want quiet evenings to avoid too much disturbance to young children. 'Carefree' holidays are devised for the older tourist, probably without the ties of dependent children, who seeks a more mature and seemingly slightly more exclusive holiday.

Benefits

All the examples quoted in the section above showed not only how tour operators have carefully adjusted their products to meet the specific needs of their customers but also how those needs are often well described by the stage of the family life cycle.

A clearer idea of the possible benefits offered by the family life cycle as a basis for segmentation can be gained by taking a brief look at the work of Rowntree (1903), who is credited with the original idea. Figure 1 shows how he related income and needs in the family to produce a life cycle reflecting alternative periods of 'want' and 'plenty'.

Thus in Rowntree's definition a life cycle starts at 0 and includes childhood and is defined around a series of critical points such as marriage, birth of children and retirement. At each of these critical points the needs and income relationships of the family will change with consequent effects on the buying behavior of the family. One difference between Rowntree's original life cycle and those found in the marketing literature (e.g. Wells and Gubar, 1966) is that the latter typically commence when the subject leaves home and do not include

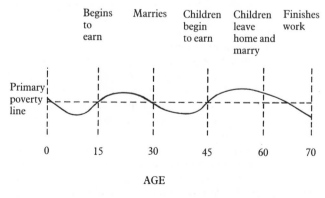

Figure 1 Life cycle of Rowntree's laborer, 1901.

childhood itself. In most instances the marketer is trying to deal with distinct family units and requires an analytical tool which can be used for the classification of markets in cross-sectional studies. In these cases a scheme is obviously required which does not result in overlap between family groups.

As well as being related to the needs and therefore purchases of the family, the family life cycle is also related to actual decision-making processes within the family. Research on this aspect has not covered all the possible relationships which are of interest to marketing managers, although sufficient work has been done to show, in general terms, how the amount of joint decision making between husband and wife goes down over the life cycle, and also how children become more important with age in contributing to the actual decision, instead of merely influencing it by their presence. In consequence the use of the family life cycle to define target markets not only tells the firm something about the needs and possible income constraints of the family but it also may allow the firm to adjust the presentation of its information in ways which suit the likely decision-making processes within the family.

The final substantial benefit that management can derive from using the concept as a basis for segmentation derives from its definitiveness as a concept. The three criteria always held up as being appropriate when assessing the viability of potential market segments are substantiability, accessibility, and profitability. Although the proportion of the population covered by each of the stages of the family life cycle is obviously very different it is always likely that they will be large enough to represent a substantial enough segment.

Accessibility to segments defined on the basis of the life cycle will vary with the overall media habits of the population, but even simple age correlations with media consumption will provide the marketer with access to most of the target segment without excessive wastage. Ultimately, the provision of separate brochures for each segment, as illustrated in some of the examples above, gives absolutely direct access.

Substantiability and easy access are likely to be key factors in profitability but that characteristic must remain for the company to evaluate in the light of the competitive market situation. The definition of consumer needs may not always be so accurate with the family life cycle as it is with direct benefit segmentation, or with lifestyle segmentation (Meidan, 1984) but the classification will nearly always have the key features of substantiability and accessibility which are not always so assured with the other methods.

Implementation

Throughout this chapter it has been emphasized that the concept is one which is primarily related to needs. All marketing people should be careful to distinguish between the more basic needs that people have and the wants that they may seek to meet those needs. The failure to remember this distinction has sometimes resulted in unwarranted criticism of the life cycle as a concept to explain consumer behavior (Wagner and Hanna, 1983). However it does mean that it is perhaps best imple-

mented at what might be termed the strategic level of market segmentation policy where the marketer is looking to define broad bands of the population and their needs. Those population bands will cover people from all social classes and a range of different lifestyles and it may be that a combination of a few descriptor variables is required to produce very exact classifications of potential customers and their requirements. Work on such combinations in the tourist industry which involve the family life cycle are not generally available but a good illustration of how they can be used is given by Ellis (1975) for the US telephone market.

The second important feature about implementing the life cycle is to remember that it is a static concept which periodically requires updating to meet changes in demographic patterns (Murphy and Staples, 1979; Lawson, 1987). Thus, in the context of the United Kingdom and the United States, two important modifications have been suggested for Wells and Gubar's scheme: firstly to make provision for divorced people and one-parent families and secondly to include a phase to cover the time when children are dispersing from the family. Both these aspects could be important in tourism marketing since divorced people and one parent families may provide specialist market segment opportunities and the dispersal phase of a family is typically one where the amount of income available for more discretionary purchases such as tourism is relatively high.

The need to adjust the family life cycle to demographic patterns also suggests that it must be adapted for the requirements of different cultures. The form of life cycle discussed in this chapter has been one devised for nuclear families in western style societies. If the marketing manager was considering a culture where extended families were the norm, then the solitary survivor phase would not be so important and may not warrant status as a separate phase. The view of the concept and its implementation would have to be adjusted accordingly.

Assessment

As with everything else in business, the evaluation of the family life cycle as a management tool ultimately comes back to the long-term contribution that the strategy makes to the 'bottom line'. However the more direct questions that need to be asked to gain an assessment of its potential usefulness relate to how well it describes the target market and differentiates between the requirements of potential sets of customers. This can only be achieved by detailed consumer research. In the final analysis it need not be the only, or even main, base for market segmentation which a company may choose to employ. Among the examples given earlier in this paper it is noticeable that both of the International Leisure Group subsidiaries – Intasun and Lancaster – choose different criteria for some of their products. Thus it seems fairly typical for companies to sell Greek holidays separately on the basis of lifesyle (often a 'simple style, real Greek flavor theme'), rather than employing the family life cycle categorizations which they use more generally across other parts of the Mediterranean.

Conclusion

The family life cycle gives an indication of the requirements of a family at each of its various stages of development and shows how these are likely to be related to the income of the family. Literature related to leisure and tourism has consistently shown how the life cycle reflects important variations in the behavior of consumers and therefore its potential as a criterion for segmenting markets should be emphasized. The examples show how it has gained widespread acceptance in the UK package holiday business but its potential applications reach into every area of the tourism industry across every culture.

Focus on small business

It is worthwhile reiterating the basic logic of market segmentation which argues that no company can provide all things to all customers and therefore specialization must take place within markets. This is even more important in the case of a small business which must seek to identify, and occupy, profitable niches in the market. In most instances it will be likely that the broad categorizations of the life cycle are too general for a small business to consider without further refinement. Even so the concept may act as a basic element of a strategy and when combined with other variables may result in the definition of small market niches.

Further reading

Ellis, R. B., 'Composite population descriptors: socio-economic/life cycle grid', *Advances in Consumer Research*, vol. 2, M. J. Schlinger, ed. (Association for Consumer Research, 1975), pp. 481–93. Ellis shows how one can combine social class and the family life cycle together in a matrix to provide a more detailed classification of consumers.

Hisrich, R. D. and Peters, N. P., 'Selecting the superior segmentation correlate', *Journal of Marketing*, vol. 38 (1974), pp. 60–3. This article relates leisure activities to age, social class and the family life cycle and concludes that the latter is the best correlated variable.

Landon, E. L. and Locander, W. B., 'Family life cycle and leisure behaviour research', *Advances in Consumer Research*, vol. 6, W. K. Wilkie, ed. (Association for Consumer Research, 1978), pp. 133–8.

Landon and Locander used the family life cycle to analyze recreation behavior in the United States and found it significant in explaining the frequency and kind of recreation chosen as well as perceptions about facilities and therefore satisfaction with the products.

Lawson, R. W., *The Family Life Cycle: A Demographic Analysis* (School of Management and Economics, University of Sheffield, 1987). This article provides a comprehensive review of all the consumer and management literature on the life cycle and analyzes the structure of different life cycle schemes in relation to UK demographic patterns.

Meidan, A., 'The marketing of tourism', *The Service Industries Journal*, vol. 4, no. 3 (November 1984), pp. 166–86. Presents a sound overview of tourism marketing and has a useful section reviewing other market segmentation techniques as they are applied in the tourist industry.

Murphy, P. E. and Staples, W. A., 'A modernised family life cycle', *Journal of Consumer Research*, vol. 6 (1979). Reviews the development of the concept and updates the structure in line with changes in American demography.

Rapoport, R. and Rapoport, R. M., *Leisure and the Family Life Cycle*, (Routledge Kegan and Paul, 1975). This book does not provide any empirical analysis but instead offers an in-depth study with a number of families in the UK into leisure behavior over the life cycle.

Reynolds, F. D. and Wells, W. D., *Consumer Behavior* (McGraw-Hill, 1977), pp. 49–190. Chapters 3–7 of this book analyze the needs and interests of the American public by the stages of the family life cycle.

Rowntree, B. S., *Poverty: A Study of Town Life* (Macmillan, 1903). Rowntree is credited with the original idea of the family life cycle and the simple schematic approach from Rowntree's original work helps a great deal in understanding the workings of the concept. A short and more easily available review of Rowntree's work is to be found in M. Wynn, *Family Policy* (Penguin, 1972), Chapter 6.

Wagner, J. and Hanna, S., 'The effectiveness of family life cycle variables in consumer expenditure research', *Journal of Consumer Research*, vol. 10 (1983). This paper analyzes clothing consumption in relation to the life cycle and is included in this reference list because it provides a critical appraisal of the concept. When reading this article the reader should bear in mind the nature of the concept in reflecting needs not wants, the fact that clothing is often a fairly basic commodity, and whether expenditure or product choice is the most appropriate dependent variable for the analysis.

Wells, W. D. and Gubar, G., 'Life cycle concept in marketing research', *Journal of Marketing Research*, vol. 3 (November 1966), pp. 355–63. This is perhaps the seminal paper on the subject of the life cycle and buyer behavior. Twenty years on it still provides a generally accurate description of the concept and its implications for marketing.

ROB LAWSON

Financial analysis in tourism

Introduction

Expense accounting and operating ratios are friendly barometers of how a tourist business is doing. Rather than wait for the financial walls of a business to come crashing in it is better to find a hole and repair it. The analysis of a business's operating ratios is not a hard and fast science, but rather a diagnostic tool. To be meaningful, the ratios need to be compared with others in a trade similar to the business being analyzed. Several primary sources are available that summarize ratios in retailing: *Expenses in Retail Businesses* published by National Cash Register Corporation and *Barometer of Small Business* published by the Accounting Corporation of America. In addition, Dun and Bradstreet and Morris Associates publish standard operating ratios for retailing, wholesaling, and manufacturing.

It is important to realize that operating ratios are interrelated. If a tourist business spends too much for the advertising ratio this may be offset by a lower than average rent ratio. By identifying business ratios that are significantly different from the standards and understanding why the ratios are different, the business person develops a greater understanding of the financial performance of the business.

Table 1 contains a typical profit and loss (P & L) statement for a fictitious company – Fun and Sun. It is the information from this document that provides the basis for the computation and analysis of operating ratios. Gross sales includes the total amount of sales for a particular company. The operating ratios are computed not on gross sales but rather on net sales. Net sales is gross sales minus any merchandise returns or allowances. For instance, a retail store may have gross sales of $1,000 for a day, but one customer may return an item worth $100, and another customer may bring back a product that will have to be repaired which will cost $25. In total then the store had net sales of $875 (gross sales − $100 return − $25 repair).

Implementation and assessment

Operating ratio analysis

Gross-margin ratio
The gross-margin ratio is a direct reflection of the cost of merchandise required to obtain sales. Since merchandise in a retail store does not conveniently disappear at the end of a fiscal period it is important to determine what proportion of the inventory supported sales during the period. To determine the cost of goods sold first add the value of the goods obtained from the preceding period (the prior accounting period) to the cost of the goods received for sale during the current period. Then subtract the value of the goods remaining on hand (the closing inventory). An example of this will clarify these terms. You are interested in computing the cost of goods sold for your sporting goods business for 1986. When you begin the year on 1 January 1986 you have an inventory value of $35,000. During the year you order merchandise that is worth $74,000. At the end of the year you are left with an inventory of $40,000 which you will carry over to next year. Therefore your cost of goods sold for 1986 would be the value of goods obtained from the previous year ($35,000) plus the cost of the goods received for sale during the current period ($74,000) minus the value of the goods remaining on hand at the closing inventory ($40,000). Therefore cost of goods sold for this company is $69,000.

The gross-margin ratio is net sales minus the cost of the inventory used to produce those sales, divided by net sales. The formula looks like this:

$$\text{Gross margin} = \frac{\text{Net sales} - \text{Cost of goods sold}}{\text{Net sales}} \times 100$$

Now plug in the figures for the Fun and Sun Company:

$$\text{Gross margin} = \frac{130,000 - 70,000}{130,000} \times 100 = 46\%$$

A high gross margin ratio may indicate that inventory was purchased at low prices, that the inventory has been sold at very high prices, or a combination of both of these explanations. In other words a high gross margin is very good. A low gross margin may indicate that the inventory was sold at a low mark-up or high merchandise costs occurred because of poor buying and related write-offs. A low gross margin could be part of a business strategy. If goods are sold at a low mark-up and a large volume of the goods are sold, a very healthy profit margin could result. In general, a low gross margin must be accompanied by a low total operating expense ratio and large sales volume to be profitable. Discount stores are good examples of where this retail policy has been highly successful.

Table 1 Fun and Sun: statement of profit and loss.

Net sales		$130,000
Cost of goods sold:		
Inventory on hand, beginning of year	$22,000	
Merchandise purchases	66,000	
Goods available for sale	88,000	
Inventory on hand, end of year	18,000	
		70,000
Gross margin		60,000
Expenses		
Salaries	15,000	
Utilities	1,000	
Depreciation	2,000	
Rent	6,000	
Insurance	1,000	
Office and supplies	500	
Advertising	1,000	
Taxes and Licenses	1,000	
Shrinkage (shoplifting)	1,000	
Miscellaneous	200	
		28,700
Net income		$ 31,300

Total operating-expense ratio

Operating expenses include all the costs of running the business, such as payroll, rent, insurance, advertising and office supplies. The total operating expense ratio is a percentage cost of the total operating expenses in relation to net sales. The formula is:

$$\text{Total operating expense ratio} = \frac{\text{Operating expenses}}{\text{Net sales}} \times 100$$

The figures for Fun and Sun would be:

$$\text{Total operating expense ratio} = \frac{28,700}{130,000} \times 100 = 22\%$$

A store with an operating expense ratio that is higher than the ratio for similar stores is likely to be unprofitable. Usually higher than average figures for this ratio indicate that there is poor control of expenses and therefore low efficiency. A higher than average operating expense ratio combined with a higher than average gross-margin ratio and a satisfactory profit figure does not carry a negative connotation. Instead it is probably a reflection of the image of the store. For instance, if a store offers high mark-up merchandise and provides a great deal of service this store could have a higher than average operating expense ratio yet have favorable profits.

Net profit ratio

The net profit ratio is the percentage return on sales after all expenses have been subtracted. Most of the time we just call it the percent profit. The formula for the net profit ratio is:

$$\text{Net profit ratio} = \frac{\text{Net income}}{\text{Net sales}}$$

The figures for Fun and Sun would be:

$$\text{Net profit ratio} = \frac{31,300}{130,000} \times 100 = 24\%$$

Needless to say, the higher the net profit ratio, the better.

Employees' wage ratio

The employees' wage ratio tells the manager what percentage of sales is spent on employee compensation. The formula is:

$$\frac{\text{Employees'}}{\text{wage ratio}} = \frac{\text{Salaries}}{\text{Net sales}} \times 100$$

The figures for Fun and Sun would be:

$$\frac{\text{Employees'}}{\text{wage ratio}} = \frac{15,000}{130,000} \times 100 = 11.5\%$$

A high employees' wage ratio is generally an unfavorable sign. It signals that the company is either employing too many people for the sales volume or that excessive wages are being paid to the employees in relation to the sales they generate. In the tourism industry, because sales are seasonal and often erratic, the employee wage ratio is an important barometer to monitor. Like the total operating expense ratio, however, the employees' wage ratio may be higher than the average because of a planned policy. The retailer may be obtaining sales by providing additional sales service rather than spending more on rent, fixtures or advertising. A low employees' wage ratio is generally evidence of efficient management, particularly if it is accompanied by a low total operating expense ratio and a satisfactory profit figure.

Rent/occupancy expense ratio

This ratio is an indication of the importance of location to the tourist business. There is an accepted generalization that the higher the ratio for rent, the lower should be the ratio for advertising and vice versa. In other words, a location with much traffic (customers passing by) is a form of advertisement. One estimate is that the ratio for rent plus the ratio for advertising should equal 10 per cent. The formula for rent expense is:

$$\text{Rent expense ratio} = \frac{\text{Rent}}{\text{Net Sales}} \times 100$$

The figures for Fun and Sun are:

$$\text{Rent expense ratio} = \frac{6,000}{130,000} \times 100 = 4.6\%$$

A higher than average rent expense ratio may mean that the store is larger than necessary to handle the present sales volume or it may mean that the owners have obtained a high demand location, which allows them to spend less on advertising their business. A lower than average rent expense ratio may mean that the retailer has been able to find an excellent rental value, or it may mean that the building is too small for the volume of business.

Advertising expense ratio

Advertising, or sales promotion, includes all of the nonpersonal sales efforts expended by the tourist business to generate sales. These nonpersonal methods include television, newspaper, outdoor billboards and direct mailing. The formula for the advertising expense ratio is:

$$\text{Advertising expense ratio} = \frac{\text{Advertising expense}}{\text{Net sales}} \times 100$$

The figures for Fun and Sun are:

$$\text{Advertising expense} = \frac{1,000}{130,000} \times 100 = 0.8\%$$

A higher than average advertising expense ratio is not necessarily positive. In order for advertising to sustain itself in the long run it must result in added dollar gross margin which is more than sufficient to cover the added dollar advertising. A lower than average advertising expense ratio, when combined with low net profits, usually indicates that one of the causes of poor profits is insufficient advertising. In the tourism industry because there is little repeat customer patronage it is even more important to have a reasonable amount allocated to promotion.

Inventory turnover rate

Inventory turnover is the number of times a retailer sells the average stock of merchandise. To determine average stock, the merchandise for the beginning of a particular period is added to the value of the merchandise available at the end of the period and then the sum is divided by 2. The formula for inventory turnover rate is:

$$\frac{\text{Inventory}}{\text{turnover rate}} = \frac{\text{Cost of goods sold}}{\text{Average inventory at cost}}$$

$$\frac{\text{Average}}{\text{inventory}} = \frac{\text{Beginning inventory} + \text{ending inventory}}{2}$$

The figures for Fun and Sun are:

$$\text{Average Inventory} = \frac{22,000 + 18,000}{2} = \$20,000$$

$$\text{Inventory turnover rate} = \frac{70,000}{20,000} = 3.5 \text{ times}$$

A very low inventory turnover may mean that the average inventory is too large for the store. In this case the merchandise becomes stale before it is sold in addition to tying up working capital for long periods of time. Neither an excessively high nor an excessively low inventory turnover is desirable. Businesses with a very high inventory turnover ratio usually have an inventory which is too small; therefore, they deplete this inventory and customers are lost when they are out of stock. Because the tourist business does not depend on repeat customers for financial solvency, being out of stock is not as detrimental to the business as it would be to business catering to long-term clientele. In general, tourist businesses can benefit from carrying a too small rather than a too large inventory.

Break-even analysis

Break-even analysis is used to determine at what sales volume the firm begins to make a profit. It is useful to any business to know at what point sales exceed costs. In order to calculate the break-even point for a business it is necessary to identify the

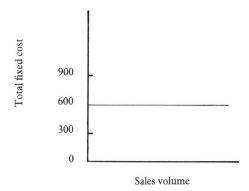

Figure 1 Fixed cost line.

costs that are constant regardless of sales volume (fixed costs) and to identify the costs that vary according to the level of sales volume (variable costs).

Fixed costs

A fixed cost does not vary with sales volume. So regardless of whether the business is open or closed, these costs will still occur. Costs that are included in this category are rent, mortgage payments, leased equipment payments, property taxes and interest on debts. In addition, if there are employees that work on a basis other than hourly, their salaries, at least in the short run would be considered fixed. Graphically represented, the line for fixed costs is a horizontal line, originating at the dollar amount of the fixed cost. For example if a business had daily fixed costs of \$600; the fixed cost line would originate at \$600 (Fig. 1).

Fixed costs can be altered. Reducing the level of fixed costs contributes to the flexibility of the business. For instance a business might decide that the \$400 per month rental charge for their building is much too steep, and they could search and find a building for \$250. This move might reduce their total fixed costs but could decrease their overall sales volume, thereby reducing profits. The purpose of breakeven analysis is to estimate how changes in the expense structure will affect sales and thereby profitability.

Variable costs

Variable costs change in proportion to the sales volume of the business. As sales increase variable costs also increase because they are tied to sales volume. Some examples of variable costs are hourly wages and costs of goods sold (the cost of merchandise sold in the business). A variable cost line is illustrated in Fig. 2. The origin of the line is at the zero sales because by definition, if operations ceased, variable costs would not exist. The variable cost line ranges from zero to infinity.

Consider a small business which is run principally by the owner. If the owner wanted to close the business during the winter because there is little demand for his product, he could tell the hourly employees not to return until spring. Since he would not be selling any merchandise, he would not be spending money on the cost of goods sold. This represents a variable cost. However, even if he closed his operation during

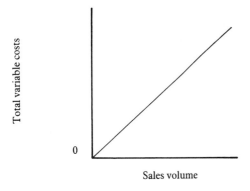

Figure 2 Variable cost line.

the winter months he would still be expected to pay the rent or mortgage payment for the building and he would still be obligated to pay the property tax. These costs are fixed costs.

Calculating the break-even point
The following equation is used to compute the break-even point, which means that profit is equal to zero.

$$P = S - (FC + pS)$$

where:

P	= Profit
S	= Sales
FC	= Fixed costs
p	= Variable cost for dollar of sales, expressed as a ratio

Using the following steps and the figures from Table 2 compute the break-even point for the Fun and Sun Company.

1. First compute the variable cost per dollar of sales, the formula is Variable cost divided by Total sales income.

$$\text{Variable cost per dollar of sales} = \frac{\text{Variable cost}}{\text{Total sales income}}$$

$$\text{Variable cost per dollar of sales} = \frac{\$40,000}{\$100,000} = 0.40$$

2. Compute the break-even point (where profit is equal to 0).

$$P = S - FC - 0.4S$$
$$0 = S - 30,000 - 0.4S$$
$$30,000 = 0.6S$$
$$S = \$50,000$$

The break-even point is $50,000.

Table 2 Break-even point for the Fun and Sun Company.

Total sales income for the period		$100,000
Total cost at that sales volume:		
Fixed cost	$30,000	
Variable cost	40,000	70,000
Profit		$30,000

The break-even point is graphically represented in Fig. 3, the marginal increase in profit above the zero profit level and the marginal decrease in profit below the zero profit level are represented.

3. Experiment, compute the same company's expected profit if sales volume increased to $200,000.

$$P = S - FC - 0.4S$$
$$= 200,000 - 30,000 - 0.4(200,000)$$
$$= 200,000 - 110,000$$
$$= \$90,000$$

Above the break-even point, increasingly greater profits are earned when sales volume increases but below the break-even point, increasingly greater losses occur as sales volume decreases.

Total costs include both fixed and variable costs incurred at different sales volumes. Total revenue is the sales generated. The difference between the total cost line and the total revenue line indicates the profit or loss at any level of sales. The higher the break-even point, the smaller are the chances of a business operating at a profit over the long run.

When sales exceed the break-even volume and all fixed costs are covered, sales revenue minus variable costs equals profit. Therefore a relatively small increase in sales volume above the break-even point may produce a sharp increase in profits.

Software/databases

Gifford, J., *Strategic Retail Management: A Computer Simulation for Lotus 1, 2, 3* (South-Western Publishing Co., 1988). A computer simulation of accounting financial management, productivity analysis and merchandise planning for retailers.

National Retail Merchants Association, *Financial and Operating Results of Department and Specialty Stores in 1985* (National Retail Merchants Association, 1986). Database of retail financial operating ratios classified by retail sales volume, Useful for evaluation of a company's financial performance against industry ratios.

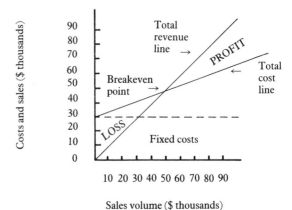

Figure 3 Break-even point for Fun and Sun Company.

Further reading

Baumback, C. and Lawyer, K., *How to Organize and Operate a Small Business* (Prentice Hall, 1988). A comprehensive and thorough guide for small business profitability analysis. Mini cases are provided in the text and a workbook companion is available for more complex analysis.

Broom, H. N., Longenecker, J. and Moore, C., *Small-Business Management* (South-Western Publishing Co., 1983). This book contains a particularly good section on using the computer for financial control in a small business.

Davis, B., Pysarchik, D., Sternquist, B. *et al.*, 'A profile of tourism-dependent and non-tourism-dependent retailers', *Research Report No. 484*, Michigan State University Agricultural Experiment Station (August 1987). Business demographics comparing the two types of businesses.

Dobbins, R. and Witt, S. F., *Practical Financial Management* (Blackwell, 1988).

Helfert, E., *Techniques of Financial Analysis* (Irwin Publishing, 1972). Helfert gives a concise treatment of the basic fundamentals of finance. Here is a good quick reference manual.

Patrone, F. L. and DuBois, D., 'Financial ratio analysis', *Journal of Small Business Management*, vol. 19 (1981), pp. 35–40. Creative discussions of which financial ratios are of significance to smaller companies.

Stegall, D. P., Steinmetz, L. L. and Kline, J. B., *Managing the Small Business* (Irwin Publishing, 1976). This book uses some good conceptual models to show how financial ratios are related to the earning power of the firm.

Sternquist, B. J., 'Tourism and the 1980 economy: the case of traverse city retailers', *Research Report No. 475*, Michigan State University Agricultural Experiment Station (May 1986). A report analyzing factors which contributed to business success during the US energy crisis.

Wemple, W. B., 'Where are your receivables right now?', *INC.*, vol. 3, no. 4 (April 1981), pp. 86–88. The life-cycle of receivables is examined using actual experiences of several businesses. Some suggestions for improving cashflow are included.

BRENDA STERNQUIST,
BONNIE DAVIS and
DAWN PYSARCHIK

Financial planning and control in tourism

Introduction

The businesses and nonprofit organizations which constitute the tourism industry are very disparate in nature. The factors which are crucial to a hotel – such as occupancy rate or speed of checking out – may be irrelevant to an airline, a tour operator, a restaurant, a National Tourist Organization or an attraction operator. Financial matters are important to all organizations, however, because profit is usually the aim and even where it is not, cost is always a major constraint.

Because finance is important, managers need to ensure that their organization's activities are financially feasible. This is the role of *planning*. They also have to ensure that the plans, once set, are carried out, or at least modified to meet changing circumstances. This is the role of *control*. Financial plans and controls do not stand alone. It is not possible to have one financial plan and a different physical (or activity) plan; the financial plan is the result of the physical plan. Financial results arise because of physical activities. Because money offers a convenient unit of measurement for all aspects of an organization, there is a tendency for all planning and control to be swept up, in the final analysis, into financial planning and control. This point of view – popular among accountants – is valid provided the financial results are clearly seen to derive from the physical ones. Neither is more important. Finance is simply the end result.

Although all organizations are different, the elements of planning and control functions are common. Different businesses may give different emphases to the constituent parts (for example a small one-product business may not require a complex strategic planning process) but all are, or should be, present. These required managerial processes, comprising the cycle of strategic control, are illustrated in Fig. 1.

The *strategic planning* process makes the broad resource allocation decisions, identifying the activities that will be undertaken over a lengthy time scale (5 years being common). It is supported by other processes of external monitoring, objective setting and decision support. *Operational planning and budgeting* is familiar to most managers. It addresses the more detailed and more pragmatic planning of day-to-day operations. The timescale is shorter (one year is almost universal) and the end result is the budget which sets out the financial implications of the physical plan. *Operations* is what the organization does, what is

to be planned and controlled. *Recording results* is self explanatory but it should be noted that while this activity includes accounting, the recording of nonfinancial results is equally important. *Performance monitoring and control* is a major managerial process requiring a lot of time and considerable expense. Control implies the need to take corrective action in order to achieve required results. This requires reports, or management information, to be available so that performance is monitored and problems identified. Again decision support is required to determine appropriate actions to correct deviations from plans.

Objectives and activities

Any organization aims to ensure that its activities (what it does) meet its objectives (what it wants to achieve). Although this is self evident it is not necessarily simple, because it must do this at all levels of detail and for all future time periods. It must have managerial processes to address issues as far apart as 'should we move into the accommodation sector over the next five years?' and 'the computer has gone down'. Planning and control processes set out a pragmatic framework in which all such issues are dealt with by the appropriate manager at the appropriate time.

Objectives and activities are two important concepts that provide the building blocks of this framework. There is a confusing mass of terminology surrounding the two concepts. The concept *objectives* includes such phrases as goals, mission, aims, performance indicators, critical result areas. *Activities* includes such things as strategic business unit, business, responsibilities, duties, functions. A key feature of both concepts is that they are hierarchical in nature and the hierarchy is linked to that of organization structure. Starting at the top of an organization, corporate objectives (such as growth in earnings per share) and activities (such as businesses or subsidiary companies) are the domain of the Chief Executive. Responsibility for both is delegated down the organization chain in finer and finer detail until jobs may be described as very specific activities, such as waiting at table, with very specific performance indicators, such as covers per day and average bill.

The converse view of these hierarchies is that of aggregation and summary of responsibilities – up the hierarchy. More

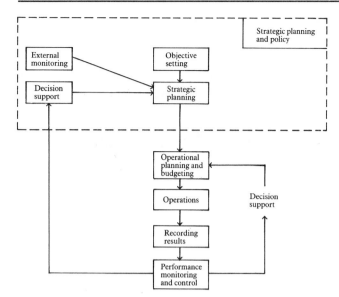

Figure 1 The cycle of strategic control.

senior positions have broader responsibilities, require more summarized information (because of the wider coverage) and deal more with long-term decisions. Senior posts tend to have more to do with planning and less to do with control than junior posts.

The definition and clarification of objectives is crucial in setting this framework – objectives being a precursor to decisions on activities, organization structure and control mechanisms. Although companies might spend a great deal of effort drafting their objectives, it is often found that clarity is lacking. While avoiding a full discussion of this subject two very useful tips can be given to assist:

1. Quantify to clarify – for example '15 per cent growth in earnings per share' is a much sharper, more useful objective than 'maximize profits'.
2. Distinguish *purpose* from *ethos* – Argenti (1981) makes this distinction. An organization has only one objective of purpose – its *raison d'être*. It may have several objectives of ethos relating to how it intends to operate.

Strategic planning

The purpose of strategic planning is to establish (usually in document form) the organization's conscious and evaluated resource allocation decisions. This determines the activities that will be undertaken but is arrived at after systematic consideration of alternatives, evaluations of potential results, priority setting and sensible phasing. The process is described in Fig. 2. It is not completely objective but when made as systematic as possible it uses (as inputs) the following:

1. Corporate objectives.
2. Information from external monitoring.

3. Internal historic information.
4. Forecasting and decision support tools.

The key starting points are thorough *internal* and *external analyses* to ensure a comprehensive understanding of the business, its history, its products, its strengths and weaknesses, its people, the markets it operates in, the economic, political and sociological factors that affect it and much more. There are techniques, such as SWOT (strengths, weaknesses, opportunities, threats) analysis, that can help with this and many authors provide checklists of the kind of issues that should be explored.

One of the results of these analyses is the compilation of a document describing the *existing situation and forecast* – sometimes referred to as a 'momentum forecast' or 'F_o forecast' (Argenti, 1981). This describes the key features of the internal position of the business and the (very important) key assumptions about the external factors that are expected to influence the business. These findings are combined into a prognosis of what is likely to happen over the period of the plan. In financial terms they are analyzed into a financial forecast – in the normal format of financial statements – showing the results that the business is expected to achieve from its existing activities *if the business makes no changes to its present plans*. This can be compared with objectives and gives the starting point for creating ideas for the changes that will be required in order to close the gap between forecast results and those required by objectives.

Idea generation is a creative process. It goes on all the time and is merely given a focus when a strategic plan is being prepared. Internal and external analyses, in particular, are prolific generators of ideas. Again there are techniques to assist the process – brain storming and lateral thinking being examples. Ideas tend to concentrate upon the organization's activities – developing new products, dropping old ones or modifying them to meet external trends and changes. A great deal of marketing activity, such as the four 'P' decisions (product, price, promotion, place), features here. However, ideas are not limited to this area and other strategic thrusts (on information systems, people or other areas) may be appropriate.

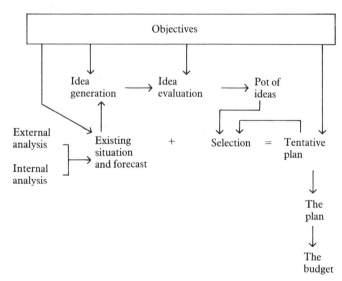

Figure 2 Strategic planning.

Idea evaluation is the logical next step. Idea generation produces an unmanageable array of different possibilities. These have to be evaluated to determine which are feasible and which are likely to be the best performers. Any dynamic organization will generate far more ideas than it can actually carry out. Constraints, usually of cash, will limit the number of things that *can* be done. Evaluation provides the basic details of performance which will allow later prioritization decisions – fixing what *will* be done. Investment appraisal techniques in general, and discounted cash flow analysis in particular, are very common approaches to evaluation.

The result of evaluation is a *'pot' of ideas*, all of which are feasible, from which selections may be made in order to formulate the plan. Formulation of the plan is an iterative process. A selection of the best ideas is made and their total financial effect evaluated by 'adding' them to the existing forecast to produce forecast financial statements for the organization. This provides a tentative plan which can be judged for forecast performance against objectives, for feasibility against the organizations constraints (usually cash or debt) and for risk. Several or many permutations of ideas will be tried until one is reached which is satisfactory. This then becomes the adopted strategic plan and its basis, the analysis that led to it and its key features are written as explanatory text which can be disseminated within the organization and often outside it (for example to bankers).

Operational planning and budgeting

A strategic plan is necessarily set out at a high level of aggregation and summary. There is an additional need for a very detailed plan which coordinates planned activities throughout the organization, almost universally for one year ahead. This is the operational plan and the financial expression of its forecast results is the budget.

One function of this document lies in its nature as a plan. It specifies the activities that will be carried out and does so in a hierarchical manner so that managers at all levels can understand their role in meeting corporate goals. It coordinates decisions in this area, often having the important function of specifically omitting 'pet' activities that it is decided will not be undertaken, and addresses the issues of prioritization that are involved. In its planning function it provides a link with the strategic plan, essentially specifying in detail how the first year of the plan will be achieved. Therefore the activities that it addresses are both the normal, continuing activities of the organization and the very important projects which are required in order to bring about the change dictated as required by the strategic plan. Too often companies treat the strategic plan merely as an extension of the budget instead of the budget as a derivative from the plan. If a new head office is needed in 4 years time, the embryonic project of building design must be a budgeted activity now.

The budget does not only express what the organization will do, it also specifies what it expects to achieve. The forecast results (not only financial) act as vital comparators for the subsequent exercise of budgetary control over the execution of the plan. The format of the budget for this purpose is the normal one for financial statements, but supported by a hierarchical mountain of analyses of these statements into the results required of individual managers.

The process of budgeting is fairly familiar to most managers. Although it varies from one organization to another the following key features are common:

1. Continuing activities are normally addressed first in the form of schedules of sales and direct cost forecasts.
2. Each manager makes a first 'bid' for the overhead costs he wishes to incur.
3. Costs of the projects required by the strategic plan are forecast.
4. Draft financial statements are produced and when (usually) they are unsatisfactory iterations are made to amend them.

Budgeting is an iterative process. Until fairly recently the sheer volume of the computations required in each iteration was a constraint. With the advent of cheaper information technology support it is now possible to iterate much more (one aspect of asking 'what if' questions) in order to produce more coherent and reliable budgets.

One technique worthy of brief mention here is that of priority (or zero) based budgeting (PBB or ZBB). This addresses the problem of overhead cost insensitivity to activity levels. There is commonly a ratchet effect, in that once an overhead resource is hired or acquired, it takes a significant managerial effort to get rid of it or amend its use. The cost of people is a particular case in point. PBB addresses this problem, requiring managers to justify their overheads in terms of the benefit they produce, but it is an expensive exercise and is not normally carried out as an annual routine.

Performance monitoring and control

Performance monitoring and control (PM&C) is perhaps the most familiar of the management processes. Within the overall scheme of strategic control its very blinkered aim is to ensure that the organization meets its budget (and therefore its strategic plan and therefore its objectives). It does have a very important, but small, function also in ensuring routinely that the strategic plan (upon which the budget is based) remains valid. PM&C is such a major process that the terminology surrounding it often appears to hijack terms equally applicable to the other processes. Routine reports are the basis of PM&C so terms such as monthly report, MI, and information systems are all relevant. Indeed the key feature of PM&C is the MI required to support it. The key component of PM&C is budgetary control.

The PM&C process can be illustrated as in Fig. 3. As any engineer will recognize, this is a simple feedback loop to achieve control over an output. Indeed PM&C is no more complex in concept than that; the complexities lie within the management information that forms the feedback. The process itself involves management control meetings (the board meeting normally being the most significant) considering routinely reported results. Problems are identified, corrective action

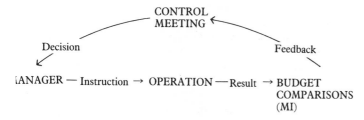

Figure 3 Performance monitoring and control.

determined and instructions issued. The essence is *action* – to correct operations where they deviate from budget, or (more dynamically) where it is foreseen that they will. The conduct of such a meeting can be characterized by three questions that the participants might ask:

1. Is our strategic plan still valid?
2. Are any managers underperforming?
3. Will we meet budget?

The first question is usually quickly dealt with since the strategic plan should not normally become invalid within a year. It is answered by considering whether any of the assumptions made on key external factors are now thought to be significantly wrong. If they *are* wrong this question can prompt major managerial action. However, usually they are right and the function of this question is to receive the 'yes' answer (once per month) which gives comfort to managers that there are no major perturbations outside normal day-to-day operations.

The second question is the one that gives the whole process its discipline. Because managers know that they are accountable for their results they will be motivated both to achieve good results and to provide constructive explanations and suggestions when results are not as forecast. That is the theory. Unfortunately, in practice, far too often, control meetings degenerate into heated discussions as to who is to blame. It is the function of good, accurate management information to avoid this kind of unhelpful discussion.

The last question is the one that is most constructive. The whole process aims at ensuring that the budget is achieved. If the latest view is that it will not be achieved, minds are focused onto the actions that can be taken to correct performance.

The effectiveness of the whole process is keenly dependent on the quality of the management information that supports it. Companies with poor information are severely handicapped in competition with those with effective systems. The required qualities of management information can be encapsulated into the following seven principles:

1. Timely – produced frequently enough and soon enough after the event to enable managers to take effective action.
2. Relevant – to the manager receiving it. Compliance with this principle is often poor since it relates to the fundamental design of management information and systems. It is considered further below.
3. Accurate – but only accurate enough. There is often a conflict between accuracy and timeliness and in many cases it is appropriate to present an early approximate report.

4. Credible – although credibility encompasses accuracy it also addresses the need to ensure the coherence of the overall information system. Managers should get the same messages from reports from different sources, whether these be financial or operational information systems.
5. Forward looking and action oriented – *all* accounts are history. Latest forecasts are often more useful, although necessarily inaccurate.
6. Easily digestible – neatness and consistency of presentation, commonality of format, structured commentaries to accompany figures, highlighting, exception reporting, graphical presentations, and avoidance of excessive detail are all examples of areas in which management information can be made more effective.
7. Worthwhile – there is always a cost associated with the production of management information. Its benefit, although almost impossible to quantify, should clearly exceed the cost.

The question of relevance is crucial to the whole design of management information and the systems to produce it. This can be addressed systematically, and the management consultancies make a lot of money doing this for their clients, but it is usually a major exercise which can be discussed only briefly here. Each manager can be given key result areas (KRAs) to describe the major achievements he has to make. These will derive from a systematic analysis of corporate objectives down the organization hierarchy. KRAs will be textual descriptions such as 'meet production schedules' or 'maintain employee morale'. Each KRA may be given one or several performance indicators (PIs) to provide a quantified guide to performance. Some PIs may be straightforward measures (such as sales value), although in many cases performance may not be directly quantifiable and a less direct indicator is used instead (such as employee turnover or absentee rate for morale). Each PI then has a target value set for it as part of the budgeting process.

The required management information for any manager is then a set of reports setting out his own PIs, and those of his immediate subordinates, against budget. If a firm base of this sort is built, it provides almost all of the information that is then required to meet the preferences of individual managers. Its hierarchical nature also provides a continuous path for investigation of problems down the organization hierarchy.

Although many individual points can be of interest within the subject of PM&C the following represent a few commonly encountered mistakes or misconceptions:

1. PM&C is not only budgetary control: marketing information and operational (or production) control, in particular, are also extremely important.
2. Comparisons with last year are misleading. For example, it may be that the budget requires sales to double from last year. Ten per cent growth is then a severe underachievement which comparison with last year would obscure (often, of course, deliberately).
3. Historical figures are not as useful as reforecasts. Reforecasts address directly the question 'will we meet budget?' but they are by necessity inaccurate and therefore cannot address the sensitive issue of the performance of individual managers.

4. The management information requirements of projects are quite different from those relating to continuing activities. Projects require emphasis on the completion of work and on (reforecast) costs to or at completion. The phasing of costs normally implicit in budgetary control is less important.

Conclusion

Effective planning and control require a comprehensive understanding both of the management processes and the management information required to support them. The processes are necessary to all businesses. It is common to find strategic planning absent from small businesses, but this is a sad omission. Even a quick strategic review can provoke a different view and consequently a more effective strategy. Budgeting and PM&C are indispensible to all businesses – they are just more complex in large organizations.

Consideration of the quality of management information yields two independent approaches to improvement:

1. Design of the management information itself.
2. Design of the systems to deliver it.

In small businesses sophisticated information technology systems are often unavailable. This does not preclude activity on basic management information design and addressing the question of relevance (to managers and therefore indirectly to corporate objectives) often yields substantial benefits from minor, totally comprehensible, improvements. Even where sophisticated information technology is available good management information design must precede it.

Advances in information technology have made sophisticated management information provision affordable by a much expanded range of businesses. Routine budgetary, operational and marketing control systems are very often available in software packages. Planning tools such as spreadsheets and modeling software are available for many complex iterative computational requirements. Database approaches allow the development of very sophisticated decision support systems.

Planning and control are fundamental managerial activities. If they are poor, performance will almost certainly be poor. Attention to the processes, and to the information that supports them, is essential for effective management.

Software/databases

There has been a recent trend for software to be made available from specialist suppliers in packaged form. Custom designed programs still have their place but they are usually most significant in the larger companies. Even here the use of packages can make the acquisition of software cheaper and more effective in functionality. The packages available vary enormously in complexity and in price. Many very useful products sell for less than £100 while others may have a price guide of £50,000. Usually price and complexity go hand in hand, but not

always, and the evaluation of software is not yet a highly developed science.

In a large organization using mainframe computers, accounting and other facets of control (such as for logistics) are likely to be handled by routine, albeit sophisticated systems. These systems can establish a large corporate database which allows more advanced applications for modeling and planning. The phrases 'decision support systems' and 'information center' have connotations of the individual manager using his personal computer to access the database and use modeling tools to assist in his decision making. Software selection is complex and is likely to be made by specialists, either as employees or consultants.

For the smaller company microcomputers (or minis) are likely to be more appropriate – either a single machine or several linked in some form of network. The accounting system is likely to be central to most control. Adjuncts to it may provide other features of control as well as planning facilities. There is a vast array of micro-based accounting packages which may be basic or may include advanced features such as multi-user, multi-company, multi-currency, stock control, bill of materials and many more. The Committee of Accounting Software Houses (73/74 High Holborn, London WCIV 6LE) was formed recently as a trade association of the more reputable suppliers of such products in order to provide some protection to users. The National Computing Centre, Manchester, runs an independent evaluation scheme for such software and potential purchasers can buy reports from them on the products that have been tested.

For planning purposes the ubiquitous spead sheet allows many applications such as budgeting, modeling and 'what-if' questioning to be developed. Lotus 1-2-3 is by far the most widely used but other packages increasingly offer similar or better facilities and prices. Database packages are available on micros to allow *ad hoc* analyses in decision support. There are also specialized planning systems which allow the building of sophisticated models.

Further reading

Argenti, J., *Systematic Corporate Planning* (Nelson, 1981). A comprehensive guide to the process of strategic planning.

Arnold, J. and Hope, T., *Accounting for Management Decisions* (Prentice Hall, 1983). Gives a wide ranging view of how information may be presented and used for various types of decision.

Claret, J., 'Sign of the times points outward in financial world', *Accountancy Age* (10 September 1987). This article elaborates on the need to incorporate external monitoring into management information systems, particularly for planning.

Coltman, M. M., *Hospitality Management Accounting* (CBI, 1982). A good introductory guide to management accounting within the hospitality industries.

Cowe, R., 'Making models keeps B-Cal on course', *Accountancy Age* (October 1985). This article outlines the practical experience of British Caledonian with the use of models for forecasting, reporting and decision support.

Cowe, R., 'Zeroing in on the basics of budgeting', *Financial Decisions*

(November 1986). This article outlines and advocates the use of PBB.

Drucker, P. F., *Managing for Results* (Pan, 1967). Now a classic exposition of strategic control processes.

Drury, C., *Management and Cost Accounting* (Van Nostrand Reinhold, 1985). A comprehensive guide to many issues within the accounting aspects of planning and control.

Goch, D., Shailer, P. and Bishop, D., 'Forecasting and budgeting', *Certified Accountant* (December 1985). Three connected articles dealing with the practical implications of budgeting.

Grudy, T., 'Big can be beautiful with strategic culture', *Accountancy Age* (2 October 1986). This article advocates consideration of corporate culture to remove bureaucracy from strategic planning.

Kotas, R., *Management Accountancy for Hotels and Restaurants* (Surrey University Press, 1977). An industry-specific guide to the subject.

Nixon, B., 'Defining "true and fair" boundaries is a matter of opinion', *Accountancy Age* (10 September 1987). This articles illustrates the conceptual difficulties of accuracy and relevance of information even at the level of statutory financial statements.

Rutherford, B. A., Palmer, D. R. and McSweeney, B., 'Value for money', *Certified Accountant* (September 1985). These separate articles deal with the difficulties of performance evaluation and the quantification of PIs.

Samuels, J. M. and Wilkes, F. M., *Management of Company Finance* (Nelson, 1980). Planning and control of the balance sheet is often underrated. This book gives a comprehensive guide to the various ways of financing companies and the planning and control of these financing arrangements.

Sizer, J., *An Insight into Management Accounting* (Pelican, 1985). A concise and practical description of the planning and control processes in practice.

Westwick, C., 'Relevance of ratios', *Certified Accountant* (March 1987). This article, while directed at local authorities, is interesting in that it addresses the difficulties of devising PIs where these are not directly quantifiable.

NEIL R. CHISMAN

Forecasting international tourism demand: the econometric approach

Introduction

International tourism is a major world industry and has grown rapidly; the current level of international tourist arrivals is approximately four times that of the early 1960s. However, many tourism-related companies have experienced considerable turbulence in the economic environment since the oil crisis of 1973, and face great uncertainty about what the future might bring. Within the context of such a changing and competitive business environment it is necessary for companies to plan. Reliable forecasts of international tourism demand are essential for efficient planning by airlines, railways, ferry operators, coach operators, tour operators, travel agents, hoteliers, food and catering establishments, providers of entertainment facilities, manufacturers producing goods primarily for sale to tourists, and other industries connected with the international tourism market. A realistic appraisal of likely future demand is also of great interest of national tourist offices.

The usual approach to forecasting the sales of a product by an individual firm is to consider a two-stage forecasting model. The first stage is a forecast of the total market demand for the product, that is a market size forecast. The second stage is a market share forecast – what share of the total market for the product the individual firm is likely to obtain. The company sales forecast is then given by

Company sales = Market size × Market share
forecast   forecast   forecast

This chapter concentrates on market size forecasting in international tourism. Demand is expressed either in the form of the number of tourist visits from an origin country to a foreign destination country, or in terms of tourist expenditures by visitors from the origin country in the destination country.

The econometric approach to forecasting involves the use of regression analysis to estimate the quantitative relationship between the variable to be forecast and those variables which appear likely to influence the forecast variable. The estimation is carried out using historic data, and future values of the forecast variable are obtained by using forecasts of the influencing variables in conjunction with the estimated relationship.

Examples

The first stage in the construction of a market size forecasting model is to examine those variables which are likely to influence the demand for international tourism. The market demand function is given by:

$$Y = \mathbf{f}(X_1, X_2, \ldots X_k) \tag{1}$$

where:

Y is the demand for international tourism to a given destination from a particular origin,
$X_1, \ldots, X_k$ are the influencing variables, and
$\mathbf{f}$ denotes some function.

Examples of the variables which may be included in the demand function are now considered.

Forecast variable
Tourism demand is measured in terms of tourist visits or tourist expenditures/receipts. As the level of foreign tourism from a given origin is expected to depend on the origin population, the forecast variable is usually expressed in per capita form.

Income
It is usual in demand analysis to include income as an explanatory variable. Income usually enters model (1) as origin country real income per capita. If holiday visits or visits to friends and relatives are under consideration then the appropriate form of the variable is personal disposable income, but if attention is focused on business visits a more general income variable (such as national income) may be used.

Own price
Price is usually included in demand functions. For international tourism there are two elements of price – those costs incurred in reaching the destination and those costs to be met whilst at the destination. Transport cost can be measured using representative air fares between the origin and destination for air travel, and representative ferry fares and/or petrol costs for

surface travel. Transport cost should enter model (1) in real terms in origin country currency.

It may be possible to measure the cost of tourism in the destination by a specific tourists' cost of living variable if appropriate data are available. Otherwise the consumer price index in a country is likely to be a reasonable proxy for the cost of tourism variable. Tourists' cost of living should be specified in real terms in origin currency for model estimation purposes. It is sometimes suggested that exchange rate should also appear as an explanatory variable influencing international tourism demand. Although exchange rates are already incorporated to some extent in the other price variables, in practice people may be more aware of exchange rates than relative costs of living for tourists in the origin and destination countries, and thus pay considerable attention to this price indicator.

Substitute prices

Economic theory suggests that the prices of substitutes may be important determinants of demand. Potential tourists compare the price of a foreign holiday with the price of a domestic holiday in reaching their holiday decision. However, they also compare the costs of holidaying in a particular foreign destination with the costs involved in visiting other foreign countries. Thus substitute travel costs and substitute tourists' living costs may be important determinants of the demand for international tourism to a given destination from a particular origin. Substitute prices can be accommodated in model (1) through the inclusion of: 1. a weighted average substitute transport cost variable, and 2. a weighted average substitute tourists' cost of living variable. The weights should reflect the relative attractiveness of the various destinations to residents of the origin under consideration, and are often based on previous market shares.

Dummy variables

Dummy variables can be included in econometric models explaining international tourism demand to allow for the impact of 'one-off' events. For example, the 1973 and 1979 oil crises are likely to have temporarily reduced international tourism demand on account of the resultant uncertainties in the world economic situation. Tourism flows to Greece were lower than expected in 1974 because of the heightened threat of war between Greece and Turkey as a result of the Turkish invasion of Cyprus. When governments impose foreign currency restrictions on their residents, this is likely to reduce outward tourism, as was the case, for example, in the United Kingdom during the period late 1966 to late 1969.

Trend

A trend term may be included in international tourism demand models if it is thought relevant. This represents a steady change in the popularity of a destination country over the period considered as a result of changing tastes.

Promotional activity

National tourist offices often spend considerable sums in foreign countries on promoting the particular country as a tourist des-

tination. Hence, promotional expenditure is expected to play a role in determining the level of international tourism demand and thus should feature as an explanatory variable in the demand function (1). The appropriate form of the variable is promotional expenditure by the destination in the origin, expressed in origin country currency and real terms.

A major problem regarding the inclusion of promotional variables as determinants of tourism demand relates to difficulties in obtaining the relevant data. A further problem concerns the form of the relationship; the impact of advertising on tourism demand may be distributed over time, so that advertising in a given period is likely to influence not only demand in that period but also in subsequent periods, although the effect will diminish with the passage of time.

Lagged dependent variable

A lagged dependent variable is sometimes included in tourism demand functions to allow for habit persistence and supply rigidities. Once people have been on holiday to a particular country and liked it, they tend to return to that destination. Furthermore, knowledge about the destination spreads as people talk about their holidays and show photographs, thereby reducing risk for potential visitors to that country. Supply constraints may take the form of shortages of hotel accommodation and passenger transportation capacity, and these often cannot be increased rapidly. If a partial adjustment process is postulated to allow for rigidities in supply, this results in the presence of a lagged dependent variable in model (1).

Benefits

Considerable benefits derive from an accurate forecasting system. If forecasts of international tourism demand are too high, then firms in tourism-related industries will suffer; for example, there may be empty seats on aeroplanes and coaches, empty rooms in hotels, unoccupied apartments, unused hire cars, and so on. It is likely that in general capital investment will be excessive, the labor force will be too big and excess stocks will be held of goods normally sold directly to or used by tourists. If, on the other hand, forecasts of international tourism demand are too low, then firms will lose opportunities; for example, there may be insufficient hotel accommodation or too few flights to cater for all those wishing to visit a certain area at a given time. Even if supply can be expanded to a limited extent at short notice, this is likely to impose additional costs on firms as, say, less efficient aircraft are used, and excessive overtime is worked.

Forecasting future events precisely is impossible because of the uncertainty which inevitably attaches to the future. A forecasting system therefore cannot be expected to eliminate future uncertainty, only reduce it.

Forecasting techniques may be divided into causal and noncausal methods. Noncausal techniques assume that a variable may be forecast without reference to the factors which determine the level of the variable, and include time series models in which past history on the forecast variable is extrapolated. By contrast, econometric models specifically relate the forecast variable to a set of determining forces.

A major advantage with econometric forecasting is that it explicitly takes into account the impact on the variable to be forecast of changes in the causal variables, whereas forecasting by extrapolation presupposes that the factors which were the main cause of growth in the past will continue to be the main cause in the future, so any alteration in the trend is likely to generate poor forecasts. Furthermore, econometric models may be used for active ('what if') forecasting, that is to assess the consequences of possible changes in the causal factors. An additional advantage with econometric forecasting is that it provides several statistical measures of the accuracy and significance of the forecasting equations. However econometric models may be inappropriate in certain cases on account of lack of data or incomplete knowledge regarding the causal structure, and are generally more expensive than noncausal models. Econometric forecasting also requires considerable user understanding in order to develop the correct relationships. Although more sophisticated forecasting methods provide no *guarantee* of greater forecasting accuracy, econometric forecasting models provide considerable benefits over extrapolative methods.

Implementation

The process of forecasting tourism demand by regression may be summarized as follows:

1. Select those variables which are expected to influence the forecast variable (the demand determinants) and specify the relationship in mathematical form.
2. Assemble data relevant to the model.
3. Use the data to estimate the quantitative effects of the influencing variables on the forecast variable in the past.
4. Carry out tests on the estimated model to see if it is sufficiently realistic.
5. If the tests show that the model is satisfactory then it can be used for forecasting.

The mathematical form most commonly specified for international tourism demand models is log-linear. In such cases the estimated coefficients (which show the effects of the explanatory variables on the forecast variable in the past) may be interpreted directly as elasticities.

Assessment

It is necessary to evaluate the parameter estimates obtained in a regression model in terms of both sign and magnitude in order to determine whether these estimates are theoretically meaningful. Economic theory imposes restrictions on the signs and values of the parameters in demand functions, and the estimates need to be examined to see whether they satisfy these constraints. For example, foreign holidays are 'superior' goods and thus a positive income elasticity is expected. In fact, most

foreign holidays are regarded as 'luxuries' and in such cases the magnitude of the income elasticity is expected to exceed unity. Similarly, the own-price elasticity of demand should be negative and cross-price elasticities for substitutes positive. Changes in consumer tastes may move towards or away from a particular holiday and therefore the trend variable could have a positive or negative coefficient. The promotional expenditure and lagged dependent variable coefficients are both expected to be positive. If an estimated parameter has an 'incorrect' sign or does not satisfy the restrictions on magnitude it should be rejected, as it is theoretically implausible. In general, an unexpected parameter sign or size is the result of deficiencies in the model.

The empirical results may also be evaluated in terms of statistical measures of accuracy and significance of the forecasting equations. For example, the 't' test can be employed to examine the hypothesis that a particular explanatory variable coefficient is significantly different from zero, or whether the estimated value may simply have been generated by chance. If the hypothesis that a coefficient is equal to zero is true, then the corresponding explanatory variable does not influence the dependent variable and should be excluded from the tourism demand function. However, when a parameter is not statistically significant (at, say, the 5 per cent level), this does not prove that there is no relationship between the explanatory and dependent variables; the insignificance of the parameter may be a result of statistical problems. Prior belief plays a vital role in the decision regarding which explanatory variables should be retained in the equation in view of the statistical evidence. If there are strong theoretical grounds for expecting a particular explanatory variable to influence the dependent variable and a 'correct' coefficient sign is estimated but the parameter is insignificant, the explanatory variable should not be eliminated from the equation as weak support has been obtained for the hypothesis. If the 'correct' sign is estimated for a coefficient and it is statistically significant, this provides strong support for the hypothesis that the variable has an impact on the dependent variable.

Conclusion

Forecasts of international tourism demand are crucial for planning by those industries connected with the international tourism market, and the more reliable the forecasts, the more efficient the planning. A major advantage with econometric forecasting is that it explicitly allows for the impact on the forecast variable of changes in the determining forces. The process involves estimating the quantitative relationship between the forecast variable and explanatory variables, and then inserting forecasts of the influencing variables into the estimated relationship.

Focus on small business

Sophisticated forecasting and formal corporate planning were until recently only carried out by medium size and large companies. With the introduction of widespread availability of computing facilities, more and more small companies are making use of advanced forecasting techniques. The advent of the microcomputer and appropriate software for regression analysis have considerably lowered the real costs of econometric forecasting.

More reliable forecasts would clearly be advantageous to small businesses. However, the potential benefits to be derived from more accurate forecasts than those available under the current system must be compared with the extra costs which would be involved in changing to econometric forecasting methods. For very small tourism businesses the potential benefits may well not outweigh the likely costs.

Software/databases

Many computer packages are available for generating econometric forecasts, and in particular a considerable amount of software has now become available for use on microcomputers. As well as specific econometric packages such as RATS (Regression Analysis of Time Series), Shazam and TSP (Time Series Processor), there are many general statistical packages (such as SPSS-X) and forecasting programs (such as ORION) which include regression analysis.

Further reading

Johnston, J., *Econometric Methods* (McGraw-Hill, 1984). A thorough and comprehensive discussion of econometric methodology.

Kliman, M. L., 'A quantitative analysis of Canadian overseas tourism', *Transportation Research*, vol. 15A, no. 6 (1981), pp. 487–97. Construction and estimation of econometric models to explain inward and outward Canadian overseas tourism using pooled cross-section and time series data.

Koutsoyiannis, A., *Theory of Econometrics* (Macmillan, 1981). A thorough and comprehensive discussion of econometric methodology.

Little, J. S., 'International travel in the US balance of payments', *New England Economic Review* (May/June 1980), pp. 42–55. Econometric models are presented which explain tourism expenditure by USA residents traveling abroad to various countries and also by UK residents in the United States.

Loeb, P., 'International travel to the United States: An econometric evaluation', *Annals of Tourism Research*, vol. 9, no. 1 (1982), pp. 7–20. Builds and estimates econometric models to explain foreign tourist expenditure in the United States from various origins.

Makridakis, S., Wheelwright, S. C. and McGee, V. E., *Forecasting: Methods and Applications* (John Wiley, 1983). Discusses the practical use of econometrics for business forecasting. See particularly Chapters 5, 6 and 7.

Martin, C. A. and Witt, S. F., 'Tourism demand forecasting models: Choice of appropriate variable to represent tourists' cost of living', *Tourism Management*, vol. 8, no. 3 (September 1987), pp. 233–46. An empirical comparison of the use of a specific tourists' cost of living variable with a general consumer price index in the context of tourism demand forecasting models.

Martin, C. A. and Witt, S. F., 'Substitute prices in models of tourism demand', *Annals of Tourism Research*, vol. 15, no. 2 (1988), pp. 255–68. An empirical analysis of the impact of prices of competing holidays on international tourism demand.

Martin, C. A. and Witt, S. F., 'Forecasting tourism demand: a com-

parison of the accuracy of several quantitative methods', *International Journal of Forecasting*, vol. 5, no. 1 (1989). A statistical comparison of the accuracy of econometric forecasts with those obtained using exponential smoothing, trend curve analysis etc., using out of sample data.

O'Hagan, J. W. and Harrison, M. J., 'Market shares of US tourist expenditure in Europe: an econometric analysis', *Applied Economics*, vol. 16 (1984), pp. 919–31. Analysis of factors influencing share of US tourism expenditure achieved by various European countries.

Papadopoulos, S. I. and Witt, S. F., 'A marketing analysis of foreign tourism in Greece', *Proceedings of Second World Marketing Congress*, S. Shaw, L. Sparks and E. Kaynak, eds (University of Stirling, August 1985), pp. 682–93. Econometric models are developed to explain Greek inward tourism. Promotional expenditure by the Greek NTO features as an explanatory variable.

Paraskevopoulos, G., *An Econometric Analysis of International Tourism*, Center of Planning and Economic Research Lecture Series 31, Athens (1977). Econometric models are presented which explain outward tourism flows from five European origins, using cross-section and time series data.

Quayson, J. and Var, T., 'A tourism demand function for the Okanagan, BC', *Tourism Management*, vol. 3, no. 2 (1982), pp. 108–15. Econometric model explaining tourism expenditure by residents of five North American regions in British Columbia.

Saunders, J. A., Sharp, J. A. and Witt, S. F., *Practical Business Forecasting* (Gower, 1987). Provides a discussion of econometric forecasting within a practical business context. See particularly Chapters 5 and 6.

Stewart, M. B. and Wallis, K. F., *Introductory Econometrics* (Basil Blackwell, 1981). A thorough introduction to the methodology of econometrics.

Stronge, G. B. and Redman, M., 'US tourism in Mexico – an empirical analysis', *Annals of Tourism Research*, vol. 9, no. 1 (1982), pp. 21–35. Econometric models explaining US tourist expenditure in Mexico as a whole, in the border area and in the interior.

Witt, S. F., 'An abstract mode–abstract (destination) node model of foreign holiday demand', *Applied Economics*, vol. 12, no. 2 (June 1980), pp. 163–80. Construction and estimation of econometric model to explain UK outward holiday visits by destination, transport mode and independent/inclusive tour using pooled cross-section and time series data.

Witt, S. F., 'An econometric comparison of UK and German foreign holiday behaviour', *Managerial and Decision Economics*, vol. 1, no. 3 (September 1980), pp. 123–31. Extension of above model to accommodate two origins.

Witt, S. F., 'Special industrial sectors-service: tourism', *Handbook of International Trade*, P. J. Buckley and M. Z. Brooke, eds, Issue 2 (Kluwer Publishing, 1982), pp. 6.3-01–6.3-18. Revised 1983 (Issue 4), 1985 (Issue 10) and 1987 (Issue 16). Examines the growth and structure of UK outward tourism split by holidays, visits to friends and relatives, business visits and miscellaneous visits, and discusses a framework for econometric forecasting.

Witt, S. F., 'A binary choice model of foreign holiday demand', *Journal of Economic Studies*, vol. 10, no. 1 (April 1983), pp. 46–59. Uses probit analysis to construct and estimate a model explaining the sea and sand/lakes and mountains holiday choice split for UK outward tourism.

Witt, S. F. and Martin, C. A., 'Forecasting future trends in European tourist demand', *Tourist Review*, vol. 40, no. 4 (October/December 1985), pp. 12–20. Describes the construction and estimation of econometric models for forecasting outward tourism flows from West Germany and the United Kingdom.

Witt, S. F. and Martin, C. A., 'Deriving a relative price index for inclusion in international tourism demand estimation models: comment', *Journal of Travel Research*, vol. XXV, no. 3 (Winter 1987), pp. 38–40. Discusses the problems associated with incorporating substitute prices as determinants of demand.

Witt, S. F. and Martin, C. A., 'Econometric models for forecasting international tourism demand', *Journal of Travel Research*, vol. XXV, no. 3 (Winter 1987), pp. 23–30. Describes the use, construction and estimation of econometric models for forecasting international tourism flows.

Witt, S. F. and Martin, C. A., 'International tourism demand models – inclusion of marketing variables', *Tourism Management*, vol. 8, no. 1 (March 1987), pp. 33–40. Discusses the problems associated with

incorporating marketing variables as explanatory variables in econometric models explaining international tourism flows.

Witt, S. F. and Rice, R. A. C., 'An empirical comparison of alternative forecasting methods as applied to the UK foreign holiday market', *Business Forecasting for Financial Management*, J. R. Sparkes and S. F. Witt, eds (Barmarick, 1981), pp. 16–20. Compares the accuracy of econometric and trend forecasting methods using out of sample forecasts.

Wonnacott, R. J. and Wonnacott, T. H., *Econometrics* (John Wiley, 1979). A thorough and comprehensive discussion of econometric methodology.

STEPHEN F. WITT

Forecasting international tourism demand: univariate time series methods (noncausal quantitative techniques)

Introduction

International tourism is a major industry in which international tourism receipts account for 5–6 per cent of world exports. Over the last 25 years the industry has grown at a rapid but uneven rate, and hence an accurate forecasting system is necessary for tourism-related firms to be able to take appropriate decisions regarding the future. The perishable nature of the tourism product increases the importance of the role of forecasts in planning.

Forecasting techniques may be split into causal and noncausal methods. The latter assume that a variable may be forecast without reference to the factors which determine the level of the variable, and include time series models in which past history on the forecast variable is simply extrapolated. By contrast, econometric models specifically relate the forecast variable to its determinants (see the chapter by the author on *Forecasting International Tourism Demand: The Econometric Approach* p. 163).

Univariate time series methods determine future values for a single variable through a process of identifying a relationship for past values of the variable. Thus a great problem with forecasting by extrapolation is that it presupposes that the factors which were the main cause of growth in the past will continue to be the main cause in the future, which may not be the case. It is rarely possible to justify time series models on the basis of theory. The reasons for their use are essentially pragmatic; they often generate acceptable forecasts at low cost.

Although time series extrapolation models are 'naive' in the sense that the impacts of the forces which determine the behavior of the time series are not taken into account, they often predict relatively well. Indeed Barnard (1971) found in his study that when forecasting overseas visits to the United Kingdom, non-causal models provided more accurate forecasts than econometric models. More recently, Martin and Witt (1988) found that when comparing the forecasting accuracy of econometric models with several time series extrapolation models over many data sets, the econometric models performed relatively poorly, even though the form of the causal model was

quite sophisticated compared with many earlier econometric models of international tourism demand.

In this chapter several noncausal quantitative methods commonly used in business forecasting are considered. These univariate time series methods are discussed in the next section.

Examples and benefits

Moving average (arithmetic)

In a survey of tourism practitioners and academics, Martin (1987) and Martin and Witt (1988) found that the most widely used univariate time series forecasting techniques were moving average and exponential smoothing. The arithmetic moving average forecast is very easy and cheap to compute, the data for previous periods are added together and divided by the number of observations to give an average figure, and then as a new data point becomes available this is included in the set, the oldest observation is removed, and a new average is calculated. For seasonal data with seasonality of s periods, a moving average s periods long is free of seasonal effects. The moving average forecast for periods $t + 1$, $t + 2$, etc. is given by:

$$F_{t+2} = F_{t+1} = [x_t + x_{t-1} + \ldots + x_{t-s+1}]/s \qquad (1)$$

where:

x_t is the value of a time series in period t
F_{t+j} is the moving average forecast of x_{t+j} (i.e. the forecast for j periods ahead)
s is the length of the seasonal cycle.

The moving average model (1) attempts to estimate the nonseasonal portion of a time series. It is not applicable to series containing steps or trends (as is often the case with tourism data), as these would cause the moving average to lag behind the movement of the data. Thus, for example, if tourism demand were increasing the method would underforecast. If a trend were present in our time series, we could difference the data to remove the trend and subsequently apply the moving average technique.

Exponential smoothing (exponentially weighted moving average)

Exponential smoothing models provide a relatively simple set of forecasting methods that tend to perform well in practice. As they are cheap to compute, smoothing models are well suited to high volume applications. Provided that the previous period's parameters are given as a starting point, smoothing models can be cheaply re-estimated each period, and this procedure tends to give better forecasts. The simplest smoothing method is single exponential smoothing; more complicated methods include adaptive smoothing, Brown's double exponential smoothing and Holt-Winters' double exponential smoothing.

Single exponential smoothing

The single exponential smoothing model in effect attempts to reduce forecast error by correcting last period's forecast by a proportion of last period's error:

$$F_{t+1} = F_t + k\,(x_t - F_t) \tag{2}$$

where:

x_t is the value of a time series in period t
F_{t+1} is the single exponential smoothing forecast of x_{t+1} (i.e. the forecast for one period ahead)
k is a constant, such that $0 < k < 1$.

Equation (2) states that the forecast for period $t + 1$ is given by the forecast for period t plus a proportion (k) of the forecast error for period t. This equation may be rewritten to give:

$$F_{t+1} = kx_t + (1 - k)F_t \tag{3}$$

To fit the model the forecaster needs to do two things: estimate a forecast F_1 for the first value of the time series x_1; and choose the 'best' value of k. A simple way to do this is as follows:

1. Take $F_1 = x_1$.
2. Try generating forecasts using equation (2) for the whole time series using a number of values of k, e.g. 0.05, 0.15....0.95 and choose the value of k that gives the lowest forecast error. Commonly applied measures of forecast error are mean absolute error and mean square error.

Single exponential smoothing methods are only applicable to stationary series, i.e. to data without steps, trend or seasonality components and with constant variance. If a trend were present in our time series it would be necessary to difference the data so that we could subsequently apply the single exponential smoothing technique. If seasonality were present in our time series (as is almost certainly the case if monthly or quarterly tourism data are under consideration), it would be necessary to seasonally difference the data prior to forecasting using single exponential smoothing. Finally, a data series exhibiting changing variability may be rendered stationary in the variance by applying the logarithmic transformation.

Adaptive smoothing

A modification of the single exponential smoothing model is adaptive smoothing. Here, instead of using a constant value for k, the value of this parameter changes in accordance with the

forecast error. When the forecast error is large, the value of k in equation (3) is set close to 1 so that the forecast adjusts rapidly towards the previous actual value. When the forecast error is small, the value of k is set close to 0 so that the forecast remains almost unchanged. k is set equal to the absolute value of the ratio of the smoothed forecast error to the smoothed absolute forecast error. If the forecasts show consistent under- (or over-) forecasting the ratio will be near 1, but where there is no consistent bias the smoothed error and hence the ratio will be near 0. Thus the following equations apply:

$$F_{t+1} = k_{t+1}\,x_t + (1 - k_{t+1})\,F_t \tag{4}$$

$$k_{t+1} = \left| \frac{SE_t}{SAE_t} \right| \tag{5}$$

where:

x_t is the value of a time series in period t
F_{t+1} is the adaptive smoothing forecast of x_{t+1}
k_t is the smoothing constant in period t
SE_t is the smoothed forecast error in period t
SAE_t is the smoothed absolute forecast error in period t.

Adaptive smoothing models, in common with single exponential smoothing models, are only applicable to data series that are stationary in the variance and that do not exhibit trend or seasonality. However, whereas single exponential smoothing models are also only applicable to data without steps, adaptive smoothing models can accommodate sudden upward or downward steps in a series.

Double exponential smoothing – Brown's model

Whereas single exponential smoothing and adaptive smoothing are not suitable for time series containing a trend, this is not the case with double exponential smoothing models. Brown's (1963) double exponential smoothing method produces forecasts containing both a constant level term and a linear trend term. In general, the forecasts produced by Brown's double exponential smoothing method tend to be better than applying single exponential smoothing to a series that has been transformed to render it stationary in the mean.

Double exponential smoothing – Holt–Winters' model

Brown's double exponential smoothing method is not suitable for use with seasonal data, but the Holt (1957)–Winters' (1960) double exponential smoothing method is specifically designed to be used with time series exhibiting seasonality. The Holt–Winters' method produces forecasts containing a constant level term, a linear trend term and seasonal factors.

Trend curve analysis

Trend curve analysis is widely used in business forecasting situations. In general regression analysis is used to find a curve of best fit through time series data, which is then projected forward into the future. Trend analysis is relatively quick and easy to use, and using transformations can be employed to produce forecasts from data showing a range of patterns, for example, straight line progressions, exponential growth or patterns that display a gradual approach to a saturation level. A variety of trend expressions is shown below, where Y is the forecast variable, T is time, $e = 2.718$ and a, b, c are coefficients to be estimated using regression analysis:

Linear	$Y = a + bT$	(6)
Constrained hyperbola	$Y = T/(a + bT)$	(7)
Exponential	$Y = ae^{bT}$	(8)
Log-log	$Y = aT^b$	(9)
Semi-log	$Y = a + b \log T$	(10)
Modified exponential	$Y = ae^{b/T}$	(11)
Hyperbola	$Y = a + b/T$	(12)
Modified hyperbola	$Y = 1/(a + bT)$	(13)
Quadratic	$Y = a + bT + cT^2$	(14)
Log quadratic	$Y = e^{(a+bT+cT^2)}$	(15)

Examples of some of the possible shapes are given in Fig. 1.

Trend analysis gives equal weights to all data. This can be problematical if there is a sudden change at the end of a series. Regression analysis will try to fit a curve to all the data so a

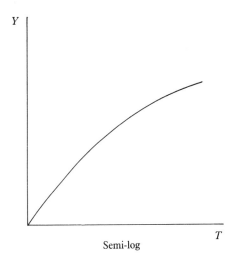

Semi-log

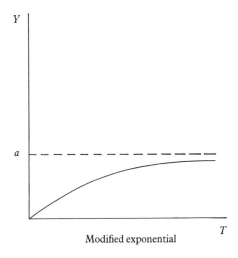

Modified exponential

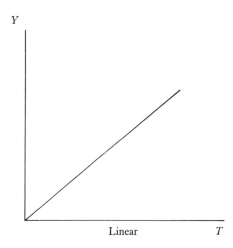

Linear

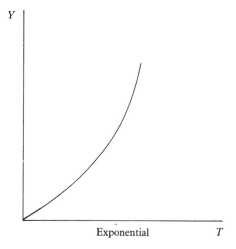

Exponential

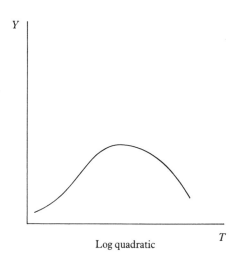

Log quadratic

Figure 1 Examples of trend curve shapes.

forecast may pay little attention to new and important variations. There are no rules to suggest how many data points should be used so trial and error must predominate.

Trend analysis is limited by its reliance on the extrapolation of historic patterns to produce forecasts. Curve fitting methods should not be used blindly. Forecasters should choose the shape of the curve to be projected before using analytical methods to find the best fit. Trend analysis is therefore best viewed as a three-part process. The first part is the selection of the general shape or expression to represent the trend to be forecast. The second part of the process uses regression analysis to fit the chosen expression to a historic pattern. R-squared, or other validation statistics, can be used to check the quality of the fit but the most important test is a visual comparison of the time series and the forecast. The final stage of trend analysis produces a forecast by extrapolating the trend equation. It is dangerous to collapse parts one and two of trend analysis. Forecasting programs can often automatically fit a set of curves to a data series, but it should be noted that several curves may yield a reasonable fit but do not produce the same shape or forecasts.

Autoregressive models

In many time series, there is a strong relationship between this period's value and next period's. More generally, the last few periods' values may serve as a very good basis on which to forecast next period's value. Autoregressive models attempt to exploit this fact. One of their useful properties is that they can follow nonlinear trends. Regression methods are used to estimate the autoregressive model.

The autoregressive model takes the form:

$$F_1 = a_0 + a_1 x_{t-1} + a_2 x_{t-2} \ldots + a_n x_{t-n} \qquad (16)$$

where: x_t is the value of a time series in period t
F_t is the autoregressive forecast of x_t
and the a_is are coefficients to be estimated using regression analysis.

Where the time series is seasonal the past values x_{t-1}, x_{t-2}, etc. should comprise a complete past year of data. An alternative approach, that is almost always better, is to seasonally difference the data first. It will be assumed here that seasonality has been removed in this way. Where the data are nonseasonal, no more than four or five immediate past values should be used. Furthermore, the regression package should be allowed to select only the minimum set of independent variables necessary by means of stepwise regression, i.e. the addition of independent variables one at a time by the regression package until no further variables would be statistically significant. Autoregressive models are very flexible and tend to work well in practice.

Decomposition methods

Decomposition methods, although not now in common use in business forecasting, have been applied in the tourism forecasting area, and are often associated with the work of BarOn (1975). Now the observed values of a time series are usually the

result of several influences, and here we are concerned with isolating and measuring those parts of the time series that are attributable to each of the components. Customarily time series variations are considered to be the result of three or four basic influences: secular trend, seasonal variations, irregular or random changes, and possibly cyclical fluctuations.

Classical decomposition

The starting point of the classical decomposition approach is that the observation of the time series at period t, x_t, can be represented as:

$$x_t = T_t \times S_t \times I_t \qquad (17)$$

where:

T represents the trend value
S represents the seasonal component
I represents the irregular (unpredictable) component
t represents the time period.

Sometimes an additional longer term cycle component is added to the classical decomposition model but often this factor is ignored and hence it has been omitted from the model presented here. This can be justified if the cyclical component is so small as to be of little or no consequence, or if there are insufficient data to detect it (which is likely to be the case with tourism series). Sometimes, however, it is ignored because it is the most difficult component to identify. The difficulty of forecasting cyclical patterns in economic and business activity arises because, among other things, the causes of cyclical movements are generally not well understood; and the duration and amplitude of cycles vary from one oscillation to another. This makes projections of future occurrence especially hazardous.

In broad terms the classical decomposition method works as follows. Seasonality is removed from the data by taking a moving average with a period of one year. A linear trend is then fitted to the deseasonalized data using regression of the deseasonalized data against time. This provides a value T_t for the trend at each time period. The seasonal component is estimated by dividing the time series value x_t by the computed trend value to give a seasonal index for that period. The seasonal component S_t is derived by averaging the values for corresponding periods in the year, e.g. with monthly data the seasonal term for January is derived by averaging all the seasonal indexes corresponding to January. Finally the irregular term I_t is computed using equation (17) and the values of T_t and S_t previously derived. Classical decomposition is best suited where trend or seasonality, and preferably both, are marked.

Census XII

An alternative (though considerably more complex) approach to decomposition is provided by the Census XII model originally devised for the US Bureau of Census. This also extends the basic decomposition model of equation 17 by allowing the trend term T_t to be nonlinear. The XII model involves considerably more computation than the classical decomposition model because of the relative increase in sophistication. It is mainly used by practitioners on account of the excellence of its seasonal decomposition.

Box–Jenkins univariate method

The Box–Jenkins (1970) univariate forecasting method is a highly sophisticated technique and is rather more difficult than the other techniques considered in this chapter for the non-specialist to apply successfully. Nevertheless it has been used in various studies that have appeared in the tourism forecasting literature (see, for example, Wandner and Van Erden (1980)). The model incorporates autoregressive and moving average terms, and the method involves identifying the most suitable form of model for analyzing the data. The Box–Jenkins model-building approach can provide relatively accurate forecasts, but it involves complex mathematical and statistical algorithms, together with subjective judgments on the part of the modeler. Experience is an essential prerequisite for improving the final models in the analysis of a time series and thus for successful application of the technique.

Conclusion

Forecasts of international tourism demand are essential for planning by tourism-related industries, and univariate time series methods are often cheaper than causal models, and may also be used where causal models are inappropriate because of lack of data or incomplete knowledge regarding the causal structure. Furthermore, trend extrapolation models often give better predictions than econometric models in the short run. Generating forecasts using univariate time series methods such as moving average, exponential smoothing, trend curve analysis and autoregressive models is quite straightforward if there is access to one of the many suitable forecasting computer packages that are available.

Care should be taken to select a noncausal quantitative technique which is appropriate for the particular time series, for example several of the exponential smoothing techniques are not appropriate for tourism data exhibiting seasonal patterns, whereas decomposition methods specifically examine the seasonal characteristics of a data series. Furthermore, it should be noted that the nature of the assumptions underlying univariate time series forecasting methods means that in general they are only suitable for fairly short-term forecasting. In an industry as highly volatile as international tourism, and one that is influenced by so many factors, trend extrapolation is a technique that should be used with extreme care.

Focus on small business

Forecasting future levels of activity is just as important for small businesses as larger ones, and with the introduction of widespread availability of computing facilities, it is now possible for small firms to use not just the simplest of noncausal quantitative techniques at relatively low cost and with relative ease.

More accurate forecasts would clearly be of benefit to small businesses in the tourism industry, but the benefits to be derived from more accurate forecasts need to be weighed against the extra costs. For the highly sophisticated forecasting techniques such as Box–Jenkins, the potential benefits may well not outweigh the likely costs for rather small businesses.

Software/databases

ORION is a general forecasting package developed by Comshare Inc., 3001 S. State St., Ann Arbor, MI 48108, USA. It contains moving average, exponential smoothing, trend curve analysis, autoregressive, decomposition and Box–Jenkins forecasting methods.

Forecast Plus is a similar type of forecasting package available from Walonick Associates, 6500 Nicollet Ave. S., Minneapolis, MN 55423, USA. It is designed specifically for use with microcomputers.

Statgraphics is another similar forecasting package and is available from the Statistical Graphics Corporation, 2 Wall St., Princeton, NJ 08540, USA. It is available for use with microcomputers.

Further reading

Archer, B. H., 'Forecasting demand: quantitative and intuitive techniques', *International Journal of Tourism Management*, vol. 1 (March 1980), pp. 5–12. Discusses the use of time series models (among others) in tourism forecasting.

Archer, B. H., 'Demand forecasting and estimation', *Travel, Tourism and Hospitality Research*, J. R. B. Ritchie and C. R. Goeldner, eds (John Wiley, 1987), pp. 77–85. A comprehensive review of tourism demand forecasting methods including time series models.

Barnard, C. D., 'BTA's method of forecasting', *European Travel Commission, Papers Presented at a Seminar on Forecasting Tourist Movement* (British Tourist Authority, January 1971).

BarOn, R. R., *Seasonality in Tourism* (Economist Intelligence Unit, 1975). Uses decomposition analysis to forecast tourism demand.

Box, G. E. P. and Jenkins, G. M., *Time Series Analysis: Forecasting and Control* (Holden-Day, 1970). The Box–Jenkins forecasting technique is presented in detail.

Brown, R. G., *Smoothing, Forecasting and Prediction* (Prentice-Hall, 1963). See Chapter 9 for Brown's double exponential smoothing model.

Calantone, R. J., Di Benedetto, C. A. and Bojanic, D., 'A comprehensive review of the tourism forecasting literature', *Journal of Travel Research*, vol. XXVI, no. 2 (Fall 1987), pp. 28–39. Discusses the use of time series models (among others) in forecasting.

Duke, K. E., 'Survey of travel forecasting techniques', *Looking Ahead: Proceedings of 8th Annual Travel Research Seminar, Christchurch, N. Z.* (PATA, 1981), pp. 32–64. Discusses the use of time series models (among others) in forecasting.

Holt, C. C., *Forecasting Seasonal and Trends by Exponentially Weighted Moving Averages* (Carnegie Institute of Technology Research Paper, Pittsburgh, 1957).

Martin, C. A., *International Tourism Demand Forecasting* (PhD Thesis, University of Bradford, 1987). Includes the results of a survey of tourism practitioners and academics regarding forecasting techniques.

Martin, C. A. and Witt, S. F., Forecasting performance', *Tourism Management*, vol. 9, no. 4 (December 1988), pp. 326–9. Survey results including usage of various time series methods.

Martin, C. A. and Witt, S. F., 'Forecasting tourism demand: a comparison of the accuracy of several quantitative methods', *International Journal of Forecasting*, vol. 5, no. 1 (1989). A statistical comparison of the accuracy of forecasts obtained using exponential smoothing, trend curve analysis, autoregressive models etc., using out of sample data.

Saunders, J. A., Sharp, J. A. and Witt, S. F., *Practical Business Forecasting* (Gower, 1987). Provides a discussion of moving average, exponential smoothing, autoregressive and decomposition methods in Chapter 3, and trend curve analysis in Chapter 9.

Sheldon, P. J. and Var, T., 'Tourism forecasting: a review of empirical research', *Journal of Forecasting*, vol. 4, no. 2 (1985), pp. 183–95. Discusses the use of time series models (among others) in forecasting.

Trigg, D. W. and Leach, A. G., 'Exponential smoothing with an adaptive response rate', *Operational Research Quarterly*, vol. 18 (1967), pp. 53–9. An adaptive smoothing model is presented.

Uysal, M. and Crompton, J. L., 'An overview of approaches used to forecast tourism demand', *Journal of Travel Research*, vol. XXIII, no. 4 (Spring 1985), pp. 7–15. Discusses the use of time series models (among others) in forecasting.

Wandner, S. A. and Van Erden, J. D., 'Estimating the demand for international tourism using time series analysis', *Tourism Planning and Development Issues*, D. E. Hawkins, E. L. Shafer and J. M. Rovelstad, eds (George Washington University, Washington DC, 1980), pp. 381–92. Incorporates an application of the Box–Jenkins univariate technique.

Winters, P. R., 'Forecasting sales by exponentially weighted moving averages', *Management Science*, vol. 6 (1960), pp. 324–42.

STEPHEN F. WITT

Foreign exchange management

Introduction

The profitability of any organization that buys goods or services in one currency and sells them in another is directly affected by changes in exchange rates. As a large part of the travel and tourist industry is concerned with persuading and assisting people to cross national boundaries and thus to buy goods and services priced in a foreign currency, the identification and management of exchange rate exposures is vital to the profitable operation of a travel and tourist business.

Three examples of the sort of risks that can arise are given below:

1. A package holiday operator selling Spanish holidays to British tourists. This company will receive most of its revenue in sterling but will have a large part of its costs in Spanish pesetas. In order to price its holidays it will have to estimate the sterling–peseta exchange rate. If subsequently the peseta is weaker than expected the company will make larger profits. But if it is stronger, the profits will diminish and losses could be incurred.
2. An airliner operating solely within the United Kingdom. At first sight, this company may not appear to have a foreign exchange exposure as its income and expenditure are both in sterling. In fact, large parts of its operating costs are priced in dollars: both aviation gas and the airplane itself for instance. A rise in the value of the dollar will increase the operating costs but revenue will remain unchanged.
3. A UK hotel company which borrows sterling to purchase an hotel in Paris. The hotel will earn revenue in francs and incur its costs in francs so that a problem does not seem to arise. But the profits made in francs have to pay an interest cost in sterling and hopefully leave some extra available to pay a dividend. A fall in the value of the franc will reduce the sterling value of the net profit. The value of the dividend will be reduced and ultimately the profits could be insufficient to pay the interest costs.

In each case the risk arises because of uncertainty about the future exchange rate between two currencies. It is important, therefore, to explore whether it is possible to predict future exchange rates. Two principal schools of prediction exist: the fundamentalists and the chartists.

Fundamentalists believe that in the long run changes in exchange rates will reflect comparative economic performance (economic fundamentals) and that monitoring economic fundamentals, therefore, allows prediction of long-term exchange rates. This may be so, but it is of limited practical use to companies. Such fundamental analysis suggested that the dollar was undervalued by around 30 per cent at the end of 1987 and so should strengthen. But if it is undervalued now why should it not be undervalued next year and the year after. It could be 5 years before the correction takes place. Knowing that the dollar will strengthen in the long run does not help tourist companies stay in business in the short run.

Chartists believe that short-term exchange rate movements are driven by psychological factors and that by graphing or charting exchange rates and recognizing patterns, it is possible to predict short-term movements. Again this may be so but it requires fulltime resources devoted to it that a bank may be able to afford but few nonfinancial services companies can justify. And the short term really is short term, measured in hours and perhaps days.

Neither the fundamentalists nor the chartists can claim to be accurate predictors over the period from 2 weeks to 2 years that is of prime concern to most travel and tour operators and so for all practical purposes it is not possible to predict future exchange rate movements.

If a company cannot predict future changes in exchange rates, then it must consider whether any increased costs arising from changes in exchange rates can be passed on to the final consumer. If an increase in costs can be passed on to the final consumer with no adverse impact on the business, then the company is unaffected by the change in exchange rates and no exposure exists. The exposure only arises when changes in rates have an impact on the company and its business. If a company sells a unique product to people who are not price sensitive, then the increase in cost can be passed on. For example, the seller of holidays to the South Pole, the North Pole or, in future, to the moon, may not feel that he has an exposure: his customers will pay an increased cost if exchange rates push up prices. But the seller of tours to Egypt has an exposure if his potential customers will switch to Greece or India if those destinations look better value for money. And if the price of holidays in Spain increases, tourists will change to France, Italy, Greece, and North Africa.

Although it is not possible to predict accurately the future exchange rate, most companies are not able to ignore such changes. It is important, therefore, to identify and control these exposures, which are generally classified under three headings:

1. Transaction exposure: this term describes the uncertainty that exists when a company has an amount to pay in foreign currency or is due to receive some foreign currency at a future date. Having contracted to pay or receive such amounts there exists uncertainty about what its cost or value will be in the domestic currency of the company concerned.
2. Translation exposure: translation exposure arises because a company is required to present a balance sheet to its shareholders at least once a year. To prepare the balance sheet, all assets valued in a foreign currency are translated into domestic currency at the rate of exchange ruling on the date at which the balance sheet is prepared. If a British hotel company bought a French hotel company it would acquire a hotel priced in francs. Each year, when the balance sheet was prepared, the value of the hotel would be translated into sterling at the exchange rate ruling at the date of the balance sheet, thus giving rise to a gain or loss in value when measured in sterling terms. Some people argue that such changes in value are artificial as the company still owns the same bricks and mortar and fixtures and fittings. But there has been a real change. The bricks and mortar, fixtures and fitting will still earn a stream of profits in francs but these will be worth more or less to the British company. The gain or loss in sterling value of the hotel reflects a gain or loss in the sterling value of the future stream of profits. Shareholders who see a loss in the value of their assets are not always quick to ignore the loss as unimportant.
3. Economic exposure: this is probably the most complex of the exposures to identify but, in many ways, the most important. A few examples may help to explain it. Firstly, a seller of Spanish package holidays expects to sell them next year and the year after. If the peseta strengthens, the price of Spanish holidays will rise and he will sell fewer holidays. He has, therefore, an economic exposure to the value of the peseta. Secondly, the seller of Spanish holidays will be affected by a change in the sterling French franc exchange rate. If the French franc weakens, holidays in France become cheaper, more British tourists will go to France and fewer to Spain. So the seller of Spanish holidays has an exposure to the French franc exchange rate. Indeed, the hotel operator in Torquay or Bournemouth selling accommodation to British tourists has a similar economic exposure to the value of both the peseta and the franc as cheaper foreign holidays will reduce his volume.

Benefits

Several benefits flow to companies from identifying, quantifying and then controlling their foreign exchange exposures. The most obvious of these benefits is the avoidance of sudden and very large losses although this will often involve giving up the potential of equally sudden and large windfall profits. The

real benefit, therefore, is the introduction of certainty in the short term as a basis for forecasting profits and planning future business activity. Such benefits are especially important if a sudden large profit from exchange movements leads to praise and a small bonus payment whereas a sudden large loss leads to redundancy.

Another key benefit that follows from controlling exposures properly is that the impact of a change in exchange rates is delayed, thus allowing a business time to react to the change and to readjust its activities to reflect the new circumstances. Indeed, a first step in controlling exposures is for management to determine the time they need to react to changes in exchange rates. If a tourist company is committed to buying accommodation in dollars and selling it at a fixed sterling price to holidaymakers for the next 6 months, then the exposure management must delay the impact of changes in the value of the dollar for 6 months. This buys management the time it needs to react to the change in rates.

A less obvious benefit that derives from exposure management is a better understanding of the business itself and the influences on its profitability. In short, every senior member of a company should know how a 10 or 20 per cent change in any exchange rate would affect the business. A general increase in such awareness of itself makes companies better able to cope with such changes.

Finally, a full understanding of the exposures allows companies to eliminate some of the risks by diversification or by matching one risk with an equal and opposite risk so that the business overall is unaffected by a particular change in rates.

Implementation

Transaction exposure

Identification of transaction exposure can start with the identification, recording and reporting of all invoices received or issued in a foreign currency. However, an exposure does not arise when an invoice is received or despatched but when the commitment to buy or sell in a foreign currency is taken and so it is more appropriate to identify purchase orders placed in foreign currency and commitments to sell goods or services for a fixed price in a foreign currency. A commitment to sell could arise, for instance, if a company issues a fixed price list in a foreign currency. Having identified the risk the company can now start to control it.

The first course of action available is to avoid the exposure. Some companies simply refuse to buy or sell in any currency other than their own. This is generally not recommended as it can drive away customers and most suppliers will charge a premium for the work involved in them covering the risk of selling in your currency.

If the exposure cannot be avoided it can be controlled. A number of techniques exist:

1. Identify an opposite exposure which can be netted against the original exposure. A future commitment to buy one item and sell another in the same currency at the same time

effectively covers the exposure. The gain in price in one will be offset by an exactly similar gain in revenue on the other.

2. Pass it on to another party. Most travel companies in the early 1970s included an exchange rate surcharge whereby if rates went against them they would charge their end consumer a supplement (few, interestingly, offered to share the benefit of falls in cost from a change in currency with their end consumers).

3. Take out forward cover in the foreign currency markets whereby you set the exchange rate today that will be applied to a future transaction. This is only really possible where there is a degree of certainty about the time and value of the currency flows. Taking a forward contract to sell dollars for sterling reduces risk if there is a certain receipt of a known amount of dollars in the future. However, if that receipt fails to materialize, then having a forward contract in place creates an exposure that otherwise would not exist.

4. Take an option whereby, in exchange for a premium you are guaranteed an exchange rate but do not have to take the contract up. If the exchange rate ruling on the date the currency is received is better, the option is ignored and the better market rate is taken. And, if the receipt of foreign currency fails to materialize, the option does not create an exposure because you are not committed to it. Options therefore are like an insurance contract but, of course, do involve the payment of a premium.

Translation exposure

Identification of translation exposure starts with the identification of all assets and liabilities in each currency. Whenever an excess of assets or liabilities in a foreign currency exists, an exposure also exists. For example, in the early 1960s, several major UK companies were very pleased with Swiss Franc borrowing at 3 or 4 per cent per annum. But unless the borrowing was related to investment in Swiss Franc assets, a rapid rise in the value of the Swiss Franc left such companies with borrowings that were very expensive to repay.

The usual method of controlling translation exposures is to use currency borrowings to finance currency assets. In this way an increase or decrease in the asset value is offset by a corresponding increase or decrease in the value of borrowings. It should usually be the case, also, that the stream of earnings generated by the currency assets can be used to repay the interest on the currency borrowings. Translation exposure can also be covered by forward contracts and options in the short term but this is generally regarded as an expensive and inappropriate method of obtaining cover.

Economic exposure

Not surprisingly this is the hardest exposure to identify and quantify and generally involves management in asking what impact a 10 per cent rise or fall in any currency would have on their businesses. In the case of a seller of foreign holidays it is possible to cover all of next year's holidays with forward contracts or options although if the relevant currency gets weaker, rivals who have not covered will be able to offer cheaper holidays. The risk can be lessened by selling holidays to a number of different foreign destinations so that only a part of the business will be affected if a particular currency strengthens. Indeed if holidays are also sold to a wider variety of destinations, then customers who turn away from countries with increased prices can be sold holidays to the relatively cheaper resorts so that the company does not suffer overall.

Such a strategy still leaves the company exposed to a weakening of sterling against all other currencies. In that case UK travelers would tend to stay at home and more overseas travelers come to the United Kingdom because it would now be cheaper for them. A full risk diversification strategy, therefore, could involve ownership of UK resorts to catch the stay-at-home holidaymaker or the sale of UK holidays to overseas travelers. The activity providing the diversification does not, of course, have to be tourist or travel related. The sale of American holidays to UK people and UK china and cut glass to Americans provides a perfectly good hedge against economic exposure.

The above approach to economic exposure is appropriate in respect of exposure to major western countries where convertibility and exchange control are not a problem. A different approach is required in respect of exposures to Third World currencies, as additional risks arise from lack of convertibility and inability to create equal and opposite currency cash flows. In such cases, a more normal approach would be to seek a very quick payback on any investment so that the period of exposure is as short as possible. Once any investment has been recovered the risk can be lived with on the grounds that if the investor lost everything he would still have shown a profit overall.

Assessment

Travel and tourism companies must ensure that steps are taken to identify and control foreign exchange exposures. The following are among the questions which must be addressed:

1. Is responsibility for management of foreign exchange exposure vested in the correct level of management? As a rough guide, its control should probably be the responsibility of the Chief Executive in smaller organizations and of the Finance Director in medium-sized organizations. Larger travel and tourist companies should have a specialist treasury department headed by a functional specialist reporting directly to the Finance Director and with easy access to and the full confidence of the Board of Directors.

2. What frequency and format of reporting should be implemented? This obviously depends on the size and complexity of the business so that in the smaller company where the Chief Executive may be expected to have an intimate knowledge of the day to day activities a formal reporting system may not be required. Where responsibility lies with the Finance Director or Group Treasury a formal reporting of transaction exposure and actions taken should take place at least monthly. A weekly report may be necessary where the impact of foreign exchange movements is large. A less

frequent but equally formal review of translation exposure should take place either quarterly, half yearly or annually.

3. Who is responsible for setting the strategy for handling exposures? Whilst the execution of transactions is best delegated to a specific individual, the decision taking rarely is. Regular meetings of a small group of senior executives should take place to review reported exposures and formulate or reappraise the strategy for dealing with them. A monthly meeting may be appropriate comprising the Chief Executive, senior financial executive, group treasurer if one exists, and the senior sales and marketing executives. Provision must also exist, however, for changes of strategy to be agreed at short notice between such meetings in response to unforeseen changes in the market place.

4. Does the person with responsibility for foreign exchange exposure have sufficient time free from routine work to assess the economic exposure of the group and how it changes over time? Economic exposure is not capable of precise definition and reporting and requires free thinking time to assess its impact.

5. Are all senior executives aware of the impact of movements in exchange rate on the business? Each executive should be conscious of how a 10 or 20 per cent change in the value of any currency would impact on the business.

6. Does the company have predetermined reactions for dealing with significant shifts? You can bank on rates between independent currencies moving by approximately 20 per cent each year and movements of 40 per cent are not uncommon. The businesses that survive and indeed prosper from such movements are those that have prepared for them.

Conclusion

Foreign exchange risk management is the process of identifying, reporting and controlling the impact of changes in foreign exchange rates on the business. The impact on a tourist and travel company is likely to be major affecting the short-term profitability and long-term viability of the business. The process starts by identifying or appointing an individual with responsibility for it. The designated person is then responsible for identifying exposures, recommending action and executing it. Responsibility for decision taking, however, should rest with a group of senior executives who understand the overall business. In addition to the formal allocation of responsibilities, each senior executive must be aware of the potential impact of currency movements on their areas of responsibility.

Focus on small business

As has already been indicated, the risks from foreign currency movements apply equally to large and small businesses. Consequently the same principles of identification, reporting and control apply although the systems and routines may be less formal.

Clearly the smaller business cannot afford the specialist resource and so the Chief Executive and Finance Director must develop the skill themselves. Discussion with fellow tourism operators or other local businessmen through social contact and local business associations will probably play a key role in this process. Specific advice, often free, can also be obtained from the local bank manager, auditors and accountants.

Software/databases

Reuters Monitor. Real time data on foreign exchange rates. Also includes real time data on interest rates in different currencies, news service, and other items.
Telerate. Similar service and coverage to Reuters.

Further reading

Antl, B., ed., *Currency Risk* (Euromoney Publications, 1980). Good general introduction.

Austin, M. and Reynier P., eds, *International Treasury Management Handbook* (Euromoney Publications, 1986). A good general introduction to theory and practice. Chapters 10 to 13 deal specifically with foreign exchange management.

Donaldson, J. A., *Corporate Currency Risk* (Financial Times Business Information, 1980). General introduction to exposures and their management by the former Group Treasurer of ICI.

Donaldson, J. A., *Corporate Currency Risk – A Reappraisal* (Financial Times Business Information, 1987). An update of his 1980 book.

Ensor, R. and Antl, B., eds, *The Management of Foreign Exchange Risk* (Euromoney Publications, 1982). Good general handbook.

Financial Times (every Tuesday). FT guide to world currencies.

Heywood, J., *Foreign Exchange and the Corporate Treasurer* (A. & C. Black, 1979). General textbook covering most aspects.

Hodson, D., ed., *Corporate Finance and Treasury Management* (Gee & Co., 1984). A loose-leaf manual dealing with all aspects of treasury management. Section C1 by Stephen Crompton, the Group Treasurer of Unigate, covers currency exposure management.

Lassen, R., *Currency Management* (Woodhead-Faulkner, 1982). General textbook with practical advice, written by someone who learnt much of his treasury at Thomas Cook.

Spencer, P., ed., *The Treasurer* (Association of Corporate Treasurers). A monthly magazine issued by the ACT covering all aspects of corporate treasury including foreign exchange, funding, cash management and bank relationships. Articles and special features on foreign currency management appear two or three times a year.

Tygier, C., *Basic Handbook of Foreign Exchange Risk* (Euromoney Publications, 1983). Good first introduction.

Zenoff, D. B., ed., *Corporate Finance in Multinational Companies* (Euromoney Publications, 1986). A series of case studies on the approach to treasury management in 25 or so multinational corporations. Most include sections on foreign exchange. Most suitable for larger organizations with well-established treasury operations.

ROBERT D. LOCKWOOD

Franchising

Introduction

Franchising in the United Kingdom accounts for approximately 2 per cent of retail sales, whilst in the United States it accounts for about ten times that figure. Sales by such companies in the United Kingdom reached the £2.2 billion per annum rate in 1986 representing an increase of 26 per cent. This sector of the economy has a clear prospect of achieving sales of £6.1 billion per annum by 1991 at today's prices. Direct employment in companies is reported at 150,000. The number of separate businesses created by companies is over 19,800.

The major factors influencing the growth of franchising are as follows:

1. The franchising concept works. The advantages to be gained for both the franchiser and franchisee can reduce the risk in starting your own business.
2. In many areas the product/service being presented to the consumer could be improved upon, therefore creating a 'new markets for old'. A way to enter this 'new market' quickly, with least capital outlay and therefore risk, is franchising.
3. The present economic climate lends itself to the strategy to franchise, e.g. the high unemployment rate; increase in the service sector; high redundancy payments.
4. Influence of certain parties including the FA (Franchising Association) and the Americans.
5. Finance facilities being offered specifically for franchising operations by (*inter alia*) the big banks.
6. Increased technology has enabled goods/services to be offered quicker and cheaper without a great deal of skill on the part of the dispenser.
7. The outlawing of pyramid selling by virtue of the Fair Trading Act 1973.
8. Increasingly sophisticated marketing techniques.
9. Franchising can be an ideal business strategy for growth for the small business (franchiser) and a vehicle for starting one's own business (franchisee).

Franchising arrangements can take many forms and cover a multitude of business categories. There are two main types of franchise to consider of relevance to tourism at present. *The business format franchise* is likely to be operated from a shop or restaurant. Here the franchisee will sell to the public any one of a wide variety of products/services which has been bought from the franchiser and for which demand has been created through marketing, advertising and promotion by the franchiser. Examples are fast food restaurants, health food shops and exchange travel shops. The hours will be long and staff will be needed. Eventual expansion to ownership of more than one outlet is not unusual. *The investment franchise* is usually entered into by a company rather than an individual as the sheer size and scale of some franchises can be very large indeed. Typical examples are hotel chains, car rental services and soft drink manufacturers.

Although all the above forms of franchising continue to flourish, business format franchising is more prevalent and that which is referred to in most definitions, because it meets the commercial needs of the present time. The main features are as follows:

1. It is a licence for a specific period of time to trade in a defined geographic area under the franchiser's name and to use an associated trade mark or logo.
2. What is franchised is an activity, usually some sort of product/service which has already been tried and tested to produce a formula of operating that has been found to work elsewhere.
3. The franchiser provides the entire business concept of that formula or blueprint, for the conduct of operations. This must be followed by the franchisee. In fast food, for example, the ingredients of any secret recipes for the type of food being offered are strictly laid down as are the specifications for the surroundings in which it is served. The blueprint is generally set out in an operating manual which is given to the franchisee when negotiations are completed.
4. The franchiser educates the franchisee in how to conduct the business in accordance with the blueprint.
5. The franchiser also provides back up services in order to ensure that the franchise operates successfully. This should certainly cover advertising and promotion of the franchise's name in general and may also cover promotion of the particular franchise in its locality. It can cover many other aspects: ongoing business advice including help in raising finance, market research into the viability of a particular location for trading purposes, assistance with negotiating leases and obtaining planning permission, site development,

the provision of building plans and specifications, a standard accounting system, virtually anything connected with setting up a new business.

6. In exchange for the business blueprint and the services the franchiser provides, the franchisee is expected to make an initial investment and to pay a weekly or monthly royalty to the franchiser, normally based on turnover. There may also be an obligation on the franchisee to buy some or all of the goods and equipment from the franchiser, or sources nominated by the franchiser.

7. The business belongs to the franchisee and he is free to dispose of it. The franchise agreement will, however, contain clauses regulating such a sale. Franchising can then be defined as a contractual bond of interest in which the franchiser, which has developed a pattern or formula for the manufacture and/or sale of goods/services, extends to others (the franchisee) the right to carry on the business, subject to a number of restrictions, controls and consideration.

Examples

The first SPUD U LIKE outlet opened in Edinburgh in 1974. The chain now enjoys some 50 outlets across the country. A SPUD U LIKE outlet is one that offers both eat-in and take-away facilities based around the concept of a baked potato filled with a choice of over 20 fillings. The food concept has been thoroughly researched and developed. SPUD U LIKE conduct initial feasibility studies regarding site location and assist in securing such location. Franchisees benefit from the advantages of bulk purchasing. Marketing personnel assist and advise and promotional campaigns are planned to provide maximum consumer impact at national and local levels. SPUD U LIKE is primarily targeted at the young adult with spill-over into the family sector. Initial and regular training programs are provided in: food preparation techniques, equipment maintenance, hygiene, selling techniques, and inventory and cost controls. In addition, a franchise department is available to assist in any matter.

Capital costs for an average outlet are £57,500 (including VAT) which includes a £5,000 signing-on fee. Average projected profits vary between 15 and 24 per cent return on sales (before tax depreciation and any loan interest). Projected sales figures range between £2,000–£3,000 per week. A franchise fee of 5 per cent of turnover plus advertising fees of 3 per cent of turnover are payable.

Advantages and disadvantages of taking up a franchise

The advantages and disadvantages of taking up a franchise depend, to some extent, on the type of franchise and therefore the content of the agreement. However, the factors identified are largely common because they relate to the nature of the kind of activity which franchising involves.

The franchiser

Advantages

1. Franchising enables the franchiser to increase the number of distribution outlets for his organization's product or service for minimal capital investment. It is the franchisee who provides the capital with his investment stake in the business.

2. Since the franchisee owns his own business, he is assumed to be highly motivated to maximize profits.

3. The franchisee is more likely to be responsive to local market needs and conditions and be readily accepted by the community as being a local business.

4. The franchiser has limited wages, rent and administrative overheads, because the very nature of the operation requires franchisees to be self-employed, although there are heavy start up costs and continuation costs in maintaining advice, training and general administrative back-up.

5. As well as the franchiser achieving a wider distribution network for his product or service, the nature of most franchise contracts ensures that franchisees are, in some measure, tied to him. They are often obliged to purchase their equipment from or through the franchiser plus the necessary ingredients that actually go to make up the final product.

Disadvantages

1. It has been claimed that company-owned units tend to be more profitable to the parent company than franchised outlets.

2. It may be difficult for the franchiser to exercise tight control over the franchisee, simply because he is not an employee of the franchiser and cannot be closely supervised. The poor reputation of one outlet in terms of product quality or service can be damaging to the general trade name and reputation of the franchiser and, in turn, the whole franchise organization.

3. A franchiser cannot always be certain that any franchisee is declaring his true level of business activity. Many franchisers employ a central accounting system, though no system can be expected to be totally successful in this respect.

4. A franchisee may lose some of his initial motivation once a desired lifestyle has been achieved, yet the operation may have much potential to be exploited.

5. The management of a franchising company could be limited in its flexibility. Ordinary companies can move in any direction to exploit market potential when a modified selling strategy is required. However, to bring about such a change can be a lengthy and cumbersome operation when dealing with individually-owned franchised outlets. Any changes need to be carefully handled to avoid conflicts stemming from perceived threats to the franchisee's independence.

6. The franchiser may have difficulty in recruiting suitable franchisees.

7. The franchiser may feel that by all the work and effort he is putting in to train the franchisee, he is, in fact, preparing a competitor.

The franchisee

Advantages

1. *Operational*: Upon joining a franchise system, the franchisee has access to a proven format, which should reduce the risk of business failure. The modification to a devised and operational 'blueprint' should have been made by the franchiser, thus eradicating inherent problems. Franchisers offer assistance during setting up and continuous support in all aspects of the business.
2. *Marketing*: The franchisee should be in receipt of a marketing concept which has already been tested.
3. *Purchasing*: The negotiating capacity and size of the franchiser enables the franchisee to receive economies of scale handed down to him from bulk purchasing and discount prices and benefits are gained through transferring some of the responsibility to the franchiser, since less time and cost is expended on purchasing activities.
4. *Financial*: Although commencing a franchise may not be cheaper than starting on your own, it is considered that the percentage of expensive errors made by individuals starting on their own is substantially reduced by adoption of tested format.

Disadvantages

1. There is virtually no scope for franchisees to be involved in matters of product, service or design. A franchisee cannot therefore impose his own personality on his business.
2. The royalty paid by the franchisee, which is usually based on a percentage of turnover, can be the subject of dispute, particularly once the franchisee is conversant with the operation of the business. The franchisee may feel he no longer requires the advice of the franchiser, or that the franchiser is not pulling his weight.
3. Should the trade name of the franchise company become tarnished, perhaps through mismanagement by the franchiser, or the shortcomings of other franchisees, then there is a possibility that the franchisee may suffer simply because he is seen by the public as a representative of the franchise organization in question.
4. The services provided by the franchiser may constitute a heavy expense to the franchisee. The franchisee may be obliged to purchase equipment and ingredients from the franchiser which he could have bought more cheaply from other sources.
5. There is the possibility that the franchise agreement may not fulfil the franchisee's initial expectations, both in terms of anticipated sales and the franchiser fulfilling his obligations. It is also possible through franchiser mismanagement that the company could go bankrupt.

Assessment

In franchising, there are two main participants, the franchiser and the franchisee. Therefore, to ensure the success of the partnership, both parties are dependent upon each other. It is essential, therefore, that before either party enters into an agreement, thorough research is undertaken by the franchisee into the franchiser and vice versa. The potential franchisee should research the franchiser, his organization and business strategy. Particular attention should be paid to the business history, costs of entering the franchise, methods of business operation, contractual obligations and continual services/advice being offered.

Conclusion

Franchising is becoming an increasingly popular method of developing a business. The success rate of franchises is quoted as high as 98 per cent, whilst the failure rate of conventional methods of starting in business is quoted as high as 90 per cent. Like many good ideas there are dangers as well as benefits and any person contemplating this method of business is strongly recommended to study the wider implications fully before implementation. While franchising can eliminate the many specialized areas of knowledge required for a franchisee, it is not an easy way to riches. Franchising can offer a compromise between self employment and working for someone else. There are always unscrupulous operators who tend to emerge whenever there are inexperienced people around with money to invest in business ventures.

Focus on small business

Most franchises would be classified as a small business and in times of recession, indeed in present times, they become increasingly important as a source of employment. Hope for the future economic recovery therefore lies in the development of small firms. This makes it all the more worrying that, despite great personal and financial commitment by their owners, so many go under within the first two years. Often the reason is that what sounds like a good idea in theory has not worked out in the market place. A very much better success rate is claimed for business format franchising.

The small business (and therefore franchising) has an important role to play in the nation's problems.

The following are the main reasons chronicled for failure of small business:

1. Lack of expertise.
2. Lack of product and marketing strategy.
3. Over-optimism about the market size.
4. Underestimating the start up time.
5. Lack of working capital.
6. The start up costs are too high.
7. The consequences of early growth and therefore over-trading.
8. Mistaking profit for cash and forgetting VAT and National Insurance payments that need to be made in arrears.
9. The wrong location.

10. Poor selection and management of people.
11. Lack of management accounts.

As can be viewed from the advantages of franchising, failure may in some cases be avoided with the aid of a franchise.

Franchisees should be provided with expertise, product and marketing strategy and assistance with regard to siting. Theoretically, the market size should have been defined, enabling a reasonably accurate cashflow, but there is no guarantee that the franchiser's projections will be precise. Therefore, while franchising can eliminate some of these problems, it is not the only solution. The self employed need to be disciplined not to take short cuts as they rarely pay off. Before going into business a potential entrepreneur should seek professional advice including the small firms service. They can give advice and help in producing a business plan that is realistic and viable.

Further reading/information sources

Barron, C., *Small Business Guide*, 2nd Edition (BBC Publications, 1984). A very comprehensive guide to sources of information for small and new businesses.

The British Association, Franchise Chambers, 75a Bell Street, Henley on Thames, Oxfordshire RG9 2BD, UK; Tel: (0491) 578049. The Association was formed in 1977 to establish a clear definition of ethical franchising standards, and to help members of the public, press, potential investors and government bodies to differentiate between sound business opportunities and suspect business offers. It currently has some 76 full members. Although being a member of the BFA does not guarantee the likely success of a franchise, it does show acceptance of a code of practice. The Association will provide a checklist of questions to ask a franchiser and will answer questions on non BFA members if it has the information.

Clegg, G. and Barron, C., *How to Start and Run your own Business* (Macmillan, 1984).

Directory of Franchising (Franchise Publications, every 18 months). This publication has over 400 entries with a series of articles by well known specialists. Suitable for both prospective and existing franchisees/franchisers.

European Franchise Federation; President: Mr Duncan Whitfield, Home Tune Ltd, Home Tune House, Guildford Road, Effingham, Nr Leatherhead, Surrey KT24 5QS, UK.

Financial Times Survey; 'Franchising' (7 October 1985).

Franchise Opportunity Handbook; US Government Printing Office, Administrative Division (SAA), Washington DC 20402, USA. The handbook provides an interesting insight into the official American views on franchising and also gives an idea of the scope of the franchising phenomenon.

Franchise Rights: A Self Defence Manual for the Franchisee; Alex Hammond, Hammond and Morton, 1185 Avenue of the Americas,

New York, NY 10036, USA. The manual contains perceptive insight into franchiser/franchisee relationship.

Franchise World Magazine (Franchise Publications, published quarterly). Of general interest to franchisees and franchisers. Each issue has a franchise directory describing the franchise organizations and cost of entry.

Franchisers Association of Australia; Executive Officer: Mr B Bell, Suite 7, Ground Floor, Corporation Centre, 123 Clarence Street Sydney, New South Wales, Australia 2000.

Grant, C., *Business Format Franchising* (The Economist Intelligence Unit, Report No 15, February 1985). The main emphasis of this report is on the substance and nature of Business Format Franchising in the United Kingdom. Drawing on a major survey commissioned by the BFA, the EIU presents a detailed examination of the sector and considers the impact of franchising on the UK economy, forecasting very rapid growth over the next 5 years.

Housden, J., *Franchising and Other Business Relationships in Hotel and Catering Services* (Heinemann, 1984). With fast food being a large sector of franchising it is interesting to study the concept within the framework of the Hotel and Catering Industry, which this book does. The text also examines the advantages and disadvantages of franchising from the standpoint of the national economy and the consumer.

The International Franchise Association; 1025 Connecticut Av NW, Suite 1005, Washington DC 20036, USA. Founded in 1960, this nonprofit organization represents franchising companies in the USA and around the world. It could be particularly useful in providing information on the growing number of 'new' franchises arriving in the United Kingdom with claims of US parentage.

Izraeli, D., *Franchising and the Total Distribution System* (Longman, 1972). Sets franchising in its context in the economic environment.

Mendelsohn, M., *The Guide to Franchising* (Pergamon Press, 4th edition, 1985). The standard work on franchising, covering the basic principles including the advantages and disadvantages and the franchise contract.

Mendelsohn, M. and Nicholson, A., *The Law and Practice of Franchising* (Franchise Publications, 1982). The book has three parts: an overview of franchising, precedents of franchising agreements and clauses with commentary and the law applicable to franchising.

National Franchise Association Coalition; PO Box 366, Fox Lake, Illinois 60020, USA. The coalition was formed in 1975 by franchisees in order to provide a center for the views of franchisees as distinct from franchisers. No such organization exists in the United Kingdom.

Pollock, A., 'Franchising – the business of working in chains', *Accountancy Age* (24 October 1985).

Popular Food Service Magazine (December 1984; January 1985; May 1985; June 1985; November 1985).

Solzen, G. and Barron, C., *Taking up a Franchise* (The Daily Telegraph Guide, 1986). Tells prospective franchisees what exactly franchising is, how it operates, who the main franchisers are and the possible pitfalls. A very comprehensive publication.

TERRY HUDSON

Government controls on and support for tourism

Introduction

Through its very nature, tourism touches on all economic sectors. Its growth is closely linked to that of a group of countries, an individual country or a region...But the growth of what might loosely be called the 'tourism industry' poses problems for the receiving as well as the generating country or region. Thus the involvement of governments with tourism has become a fact, but, in many instances, tourism growth has overtaken policy, which, in the best of cases, deals with the problem of tourism in a piecemeal fashion.

The role that governments should play in the process of developing tourism industries has given rise to much controversy. In fact, the degree of government involvement is the result of a country's history, socioeconomic conditions or development, the political philosophy of the ruling party and the extent to which tourism supply is already developed.

The nature of government involvement can be passive or active, and the actions employed can aim for the control, the support, the financial (and sometimes managerial) assistance, or the orientation and planification of the tourism market. Furthermore, the actions can have an effect on the tourism supply and its distribution channels (product and producer-oriented), or the demand (consumer-oriented).

Product and producer-oriented government actions

Government involvement can aim at the object of tourism, that is to say all aspects that directly or indirectly make up the tourism industry. This not only concerns the capacity, quality and price of supply, but also the natural, human and manmade resources of a country.

Tourism resources

The authorities can, through legislative means, safeguard those natural and human resources that are part of the tourism attractions of a country or a region (laws for the protection of monuments and historical sites, national parks, beaches, indigenous populations etc.), or control land speculation by instituting preemptive rights or special taxes. But the administration can also become directly involved through the purchase of sites and monuments with public funds, the granting of financial aid for their restoration and improvement or the creation of museums and art galleries. Indirectly, the authorities can encourage private actions of improvement, maintenance and conservation of the national heritage through subsidies, loans, tax exemptions or promotional efforts, such as special features on the work undertaken to restore a castle, for example. However, all of the measures will remain limited, unless the country has elaborated a coherent policy which includes all aspects of tourism development, and presented clearly stated objectives. The program relating to tourism resources must include all means of action at the government's disposal, covering their safeguarding, their financing, their improvement and their commercialization.

Infrastructure

The general infrastructure almost always comes under the responsibility of the public authorities for the necessary investments as well as their maintenance and management. Nonetheless, under certain circumstances, a private investor may assume the cost of an infrastructure usually considered to be of public interest (for example, the access road to a ski resort). Although too vast a subject to be dealt with here, it is important to remember that the general infrastructure plays a determining role in the development of the tourism potential of any country.

Contrary to the general infrastructure, the tourism infrastructure depends as much on the regional and local authorities as on the private sector investors, even though the authorities usually play a determining role through the control of the norms applied, the investment incentives available, or even the direct or indirect management of these infrastructures. Where investment incentives are available, these usually aim at reducing the required capital outlay. Although direct capital grants are fairly rare in the developed countries, except for such major projects as ski-lifts or yacht harbors, the practice of loan guarantees (the underwriting of loans granted by commercial banks, by government or some specified institution), preferential loans (loans at preferential rates) by government and interest relief subsidies (government pays the difference between a fixed rate of interest and that charged by a commercial bank) are fairly widespread.

Tourism and leisure facilities and amenities

Although traditionally the responsibility of the private sector, government involvement in most countries is concentrated on the investment and management aspects of the facilities and amenities directly related to the tourism industry. Control can be exerted on the private firms, through legislative or statutory means, for various reasons, such as the protection of the consumer or assuring the financial soundness of the market. Controls on investment can include restrictions as to the localization, the capacity or even the construction of the tourism facilities, the price of transaction to minimize land speculation, the safety and hygiene standards applied etc. Price control measures, whether through government approval of prices charged or the payment of subsidies (for example, to make certain sports more readily accessible), and the official classification of accommodations and camp sites etc., are ways for the government to exercise a direct influence on the running of tourism facilities.

Most countries use some form of investment incentives as part of a national or regional tourism development strategy. These fall into two basic categories according to their area of impact:

1. Reduction of required investment outlay (direct capital grants, loans at preferential rates, loan guarantees, interest rate subsidies, duty-free import of construction materials, sale or lease of land at below market value etc.).
2. Reduction of operating costs (accelerated depreciation allowances, loans and subsidies for the modernization or extension of the accommodation sector, tax 'holidays', duty remit on equipment, exemption from indirect taxes, training grants etc.).

The guarantee of repatriation of capital and profits can also be an important incentive for foreign investors. The selective use of these incentives allows the government to control the development of the tourism supply: it can favor luxury or, on the contrary, modest accommodations, big cities or rural areas, big or small establishments etc.

The public authorities can also decide to intervene directly by managing parts of the tourism and leisure facilities and amenities themselves. Many governments own, in fact, the major transportation firms (air and rail), hotel chains (often through the national airline or railway), leisure facilities etc. Furthermore, the government may also assume a large part (if not all) of the training costs associated with qualified personnel. At the same time, the administration can institute a certain number of restrictions concerning the employment of nationals and foreigners; the working conditions (numbers of hours worked, time off, salary and social benefits etc.) and the qualifications of the personnel.

Distribution channels

All the intermediaries, such as tour operators, travel and rental agencies, guide services etc., are closely controlled by the authorities, usually through a licensing process and the professional status of the individual branches. The major concern here is the protection of the consumer, since the 'product' bought cannot be viewed or tested before its 'consumption', usually many miles away from where it was bought. Many governments own, directly or indirectly, tour operators and/or travel agencies, or subsidize those who provide services considered to be of public utility (to the young, the elderly, the handicapped . . .).

Every country also possesses an official agency charged with the promotion of the country as a tourist destination, whether for foreigners or for the nationals. Often part of central government or subsidized by it, the agency can also be an autonomous legal entity which is co-financed by private industry. Although the bulk of the budget is usually spent on marketing efforts, many of these national tourist agencies also engage in research or provide technical assistance for tourism projects.

Consumer-oriented government actions

Government involvement can also aim at the subject of tourism, that is to say the tourist, whether real or potential. The main concern is to increase the number of users of the tourism facilities, or at least avoid their underutilization. By making it possible for ever increasing numbers of people to take a holiday, the government not only fulfils a social objective, but also assures that the occupancy rate, and thus the profitability, of the various tourism industry branches is favorably influenced.

Tourism promotion

Unless a person feels the need (physical or psychological) to take a holiday, he will not become a tourist. All promotional actions, whether direct publicity or through the development of the mass culture, determine, maintain or increase that need. It is thus not surprising to note the important sums of public funds spent on the promotion of tourism, whether on the foreign or the national market, and whose only objective is to increase the number of tourists. But the imitation factor also plays a large role: the fact that everyone else seems to go on holidays creates the need to do likewise. The state, the largest single employer, can thus set an example by facilitating the vacation-taking of its employees.

Working conditions

The potential tourist must have enough time to go on holidays. The general legislation on the length of the annual holiday (extremely varied from one country to another), the regulations concerning the possibility of splitting up this holiday period into several shorter vacations, as well as those relating to flexible working hours, 3- and 4-day weekends, and even school holidays will have a very definite influence on tourism demand.

Economic policy measures and social tourism

Unless the discretionary income is sufficient, the potential tourism demand will remain latent, even if the person feels the need to go on holidays and possesses the necessary time to do so. Through economic policy, the government has a direct influence on tourism demand, whether through its legislation relating to salaries (especially minimum wage), social contributions which reduce the salary more or less severely, price of services rendered especially in the major tourist-receiving regions, or loans for such purchases as camping equipment, caravans, boats, secondary homes or vacation apartments.

Even if judiciously employed, all these measures are not enough for low-income groups and the 'disadvantaged' (elderly, disabled, socially disadvantaged). These must receive financial assistance if they are to benefit from an occasional break. In the long run, no government can afford to ignore these economically weak classes as they contribute heavily to a lasting social equilibrium. The financial assistance can take the form of direct subsidies or reductions, especially for the use of transportation, or indirect means such as grants to holiday villages, youth hostels, etc. Either way, the primary objective is to adjust their purchasing power to the prices of the tourism services.

Tourism flow

The government can also elaborate a series of regulations in order to control the flow of tourism demand. For instance, camping can be restricted to certain approved sites, bathing and nautical sports limited to certain areas for safety or ecological reasons, access by car prohibited in certain parks or city centers etc. When it comes to international tourism, the measures can be even more prohibitive, as explained below.

Quantitative and qualitative barriers to international tourism

Tourism and international travel, as entered in balances of payments, have, for more than a decade, accounted for a quarter of world trade in services. While there is little doubt that some countries enjoy natural advantages (such as climate or geography) with regard to tourism, other factors can influence the volume and direction of international tourist trade, such as poor transportation and communications, political stability, standards of services, exchange rates and favorable prices, inferior health and sanitary conditions, inadequate accommodation and leisure facilities etc.

Concerns of a general economic, financial and social nature have led many governments to take more or less unintentional protectionist measures to promote service exports while reducing imports and/or to give domestic export firms more favorable treatment than foreign enterprises. These impediments fall into two categories: those affecting the traveler and those affecting the enterprises which produce, market and sell the services related to tourism. A number of international organizations are currently studying the liberalization of trade in services, and the specific problem of facilitating international tourism, the most important of which are the World Tourism Organization (WTO), the Organization for Economic Coopera-

tion and Development (OECD) and the General Agreement on Tariffs and Trade (GATT).

Government-imposed impediments on travelers

Obstacles affecting the individual intending to travel can be imposed either by the home country or by the host country. In both cases, they relate essentially to exchange control, administrative documents and formalities as well as customs regulations. When the country of residence restricts the departure of travelers, this, in a way, represents restrictions on imports. More than 100 countries impose restrictions limiting the amount of currency their citizens may purchase for travel abroad. Whatever form the restrictions take, travel allowances limit expenditures on goods and services outside the home country, and in extreme cases impede outbound travel altogether. The conditions or procedures for delivering travel documents can also be a deterrent in some cases, while other measures, such as tax deductions, can act as an incentive for travelers to use the service of domestic enterprises in preference to others for their journey abroad. High duties, small duty-free allowances, time consuming procedures and inspections also serve to discourage international tourist spending.

Measures applied by the country of destination constitute obstacles, the effect of which, whether intentional or not, has been compared to self-imposed restriction of tourism exports. Many countries use, for instance, a system of entry visas for health, safety and immigration reasons. While sometimes justified politically, they become an impediment when applied arbitrarily, or are too time-consuming or expensive. Restrictions concerning, or unfavorable terms of, exchange of currency and special taxes applied to foreign visitors may be a way of increasing the amount of foreign currency collected per visitor, but also discourages a global increase in their numbers. On the other hand, the establishment of an official, preferential exchange rate for visiting foreign tourists can be compared with the practice of 'dumping'. As far as restrictions on the acquisition of property by non-nationals are concerned, these are often part of a policy of national sovereignty, especially in the lesser developed countries.

Government-imposed restrictions on enterprises in the tourism sector

Normally included under this heading are travel agents and tour operators, professions or occupations related to tourism (guides, interpreters etc.), the hotel and catering trade, tourist transport, and the offer of tourist attractions such as casinos and leisure parks. Each of these branches may, of course, serve both international and domestic tourism. Among the numerous government-imposed impediments, the more common of these are: payment and exchange restrictions (foreign remittances), rules governing the right to establish a business, local equity requirements for foreign nationals involved in these activities, and access to an appropriate local commercial presence.

The motivation behind regulations governing the tourism sector or professions are the protection of the consumer, concerns about competition and cultural differences that might lead to clashes. In state trading countries, market access by foreign companies is regulated by agreements with the authorities. Companies from foreign countries have been allowed to set up hotels in the form of joint or other types of venture, but they are often permitted to deal with foreign customers only. As far as the lesser developed countries are concerned, many claim their social and economic situation as a justification for the application of practices that might be considered protectionist, such as requirements as to a local controlling interest, conditions as to the nationality of the owner or manager, rules as to the recruitment and training of nationals (including appointment to managerial posts), unfavorable rules of taxation, restrictions on imports of goods, preferential treatment given to domestic firms with regard to advertising in the public media etc.

Within the European Community and the member countries of the OECD, considerable efforts have been undertaken to liberalize trade in services, but the restrictions applicable to airlines remain particularly severe. Thus even within these countries, foreign airlines do not usually have access to domestic air transport. The national airline is further given various advantages over foreign competitors: restrictions on advertising by foreign companies, instructions to local travel agents to direct business rather towards the domestic carrier, obligations for national civil servants and equivalent personnel to use the national airlines, difficulty for foreign airlines to access reservation systems controlled by the national carrier, nonconfirmation by the national carrier of reservations on the domestic part of a flight unless it has undertaken the international part, discriminatory treatment given to foreign airlines in airports (allocation of less attractive locations, discriminatory landing taxes), impossibility for non-national airlines to establish their own ground handling facilities, etc. Most countries are particularly sensitive when it comes to deregulating airlines, and most of the international organizations will not therefore deal with the problem. Bilateral negotiations derived from international conventions continue to regulate the field of air transport. The interests involved (national carriers are often state-owned monopolies) do not permit us to be very optimistic, even within the European Community, that substantial progress can be expected before 1992 at the earliest.

Assessment

In the western world (mainly member-countries of the OECD), the revival of the economic activity which began in 1981/82 was associated with rising unemployment. This situation has led many governments to review their manpower policy to facilitate the redistribution of the labor force from declining to expanding sectors. In the United Kingdom, responsibility within government for tourism matters was even transferred from the Department of Trade and Industry to the Department of Employment in 1985, and funding to the British Tourist Authority and the English Tourist Board increased considerably. These funds are to be concentrated on improving employment opportunities, especially in regions of high unemployment.

The impressive variety of businesses that make up the tourism industry has also led a good number of countries to make efforts to harmonize better government and private operations. Through contractual arrangement or development plans between the state and local or regional public authorities, central governments hope to progressively decentralize development decisions while keeping a control on the overall economic policy. Furthermore, cost-sharing between government authorities, especially the national tourist board, and private enterprises is becoming a widespread practice: in an increasingly competitive climate, official tourism organizations have accentuated the commercialization of their countries as a destination, efforts sometimes accompanied by (considerable) budget increases, in cooperation with interested parties in the tourist industry and often with their financial support.

But the increasingly liberal climate which reigns in many industrialized nations has led not only to the decentralization of decisions and cost-sharing, but also to the privatization of certain national transport networks, or at least a much more competitive attitude towards their exploitation. Since the deregulation of the US airlines, several other countries have also started loosening the state control on their national airline(s), the most tightly controlled means of transportation and where the advocates of liberalism have faced the most opposition.

Conclusion

After having addressed the list of government-initiated actions that control or support tourism, it becomes clear that other policies (political, economic, monetary, financial, social, etc.) often conflict with, and override, tourism policy. In short, tourism is still regarded as an adjunct in spite of its importance, and is affected by restrictions which are imposed upon it for the benefit of other spheres of government activities.

The highly interdisciplinary nature of the tourism sector and the nonrecognition of its importance to economic and social policies, has led governments to deal with tourism in an *ad hoc*, haphazard manner. Although governments usually increase their interventions when their country is heavily dependent on this industry, this does not mean that the coordination and harmonization between the variety of measures taken is any better. This leads to much wastage, especially of public funds. Investment incentives, for instance, should only be used as a selective, tactical application of the general development strategies, which presumes the existence of a development plan which seeks to match development priorities and available resources in a realistic framework. But their effective use also supposes a monitoring process of incentive-aided companies on which a regular review of the legislation is based. Unfortunately, in most countries there is no indication of the real size of investment incentives nor of their true effectiveness in job creation, for example.

Whether the government opts merely for the creation of an ambience conducive to the growth of a successful tourism industry, or decides to becomes more actively involved, perhaps even assuming an entrepreneurial role, intervention by the government should not be a manifestation of political rhetoric, but rather an organized, sustained, and flexible approach to tourism planning with the aim of optimizing the social and economic returns from tourism.

Focus on small business

Businesses involved in the tourism industry are faced with two major problems: identification and size. Aside from such traditional branches such as transport, accommodation, restaurants, tour operators and travel agencies, many companies are not associated (or do not associate themselves) with the tourism industry. The result are government measures that can be disastrous for the entire sector, as was, for instance, the weekend closure of gas stations in the United States during the last oil shock. This nonidentification with the tourism industry and the small size of the vast majority of businesses, makes the creation of lobbies difficult. Furthermore, the interests of the various sectors that make up the tourism industry are divergent and sometimes even conflicting, so that no association could ever unite all of them and act as its spokesman or put real pressure on government.

The result is that government – aside from just plain ignoring the industry when defining a policy – often only takes into account the large, structured businesses. Thus, for example, many development plans contained (and some still do so) clauses effectively limiting incentives to larger hotel units and upper level accommodation (often controlled by international hotel chains). In more recent years, unemployment and regional disparities (but not the industry!) have led governments to concentrate their action more on small budget accommodation amongst which are found rural and farm tourism, bed and breakfast, chalets or cottages etc.

Further reading

Ascher, B., 'Obstacles to international travel and tourism', *Journal of Travel Research*, vol. XXII, no. 3 (Winter 1984), pp. 2–17. Following the work undertaken by the OECD and WTO, this article identifies and examines restrictions on the international tourist trade and suggests possible approaches for the future. Particular attention is given to government actions and regulations, classifying them in a very logical and comprehensive manner.

Bodlender, J. A. and Davies, E. J. G., *A Profile of Government Financial and Grant Aid to Tourism* (World Tourism Organization/Horwath & Horwath International, 1984). Prepared for the Working Party on Investment in Tourism of the WTO, the paper sets out the principal methods by which governments can provide financial aid for tourism projects. Essentially concerned with the relationship between governments and private sector investment, some of the relationships examined have implications within planned economies and through social tourism. Case studies in selected countries have been employed to illustrate the current or past use of the various forms of aid.

Bodlender, J. A., 'The financing of tourism projects', *Tourism Management* (December 1982), pp. 277–84. The author considers the financing of tourism projects under its macro and micro aspects, covering the role of the public and private sectors and the bodies and organizations in each, as well as the difficulties in obtaining finance

for developing countries and the direction and type of grant aid.

Colley, G., *Possibilités et limites de l'Action économique et financière des Pouvoirs publics en matière de tourisme* (Editions Gurten, 1967). A theoretical approach to interventionism by governments, he lists the direct and indirect actions available to the authorities in order to influence the tourism market. Although somewhat dated, the clear approach is still a very worthwhile base for reflection.

Hughes, H. L., 'Government support for tourism in the UK – a different perspective', *Tourism Management*, vol. 5, no. 1 (March 1984), pp. 13–19. The nature of government support for industry in the United Kingdom is examined and the circumstances where a free enterprise economy could be reconciled with increased government support for tourism are argued. The article opposes the traditional arguments for further support, particularly employment-generating and balance of payments effects.

Jenkins, C. L. and Henry, B. M., 'Government involvement in tourism in developing countries', *Annals of Tourism Research*, vol. 9 (1982), pp. 499–521. The article examines the case for involvement of governments in the tourism sector in developing countries and makes definitional distinctions between passive and active involvement, which can be applied to government intervention in the developed countries as well. Five areas of concern for government involvement are discussed, and conclusions relate to the need for government-private sector cooperation for development purposes.

Organization for Economic Cooperation and Development, *Report of the Tourism Committee on Obstacles to International Tourism in the OECD Area* (OECD, 1984). As part of the general subject of trade-in-services within the OECD, the Tourism Committee has undertaken to seek to identify and analyze the existing obstacles to the liberalization of international tourism. The paper considers impediments which discriminate either between nationals and non-national persons or companies, or against persons or companies of a particular nationality or nationalities.

Organization for Economic Cooperation and Development, *Tourism Policy and International Tourism in OECD Member Countries* (OECD, yearly). This publication contains a section on government policy and action, listing the actions and measures taken within a given year concerning the development of supply, marketing, protection of the tourist as a consumer, staggering of holidays, international cooperation and frontier formalities and currency restrictions.

Richter, L. K., 'Tourism politics and political science – a case of not so benign neglect', *Annals of Tourism Research*, vol. 10 (1983), pp. 313–35. The paper argues that in the absence of political science interest, important dimensions of the political costs and advantages of tourism have been neglected. As a consequence, the developmental potential of tourism has frequently collided unnecessarily with the public interest and even the long-term interest of the tourism industry.

Wanhill, S. R. C., 'Which investment incentives for tourism?', *Tourism Management*, vol. 7, no. 1 (March 1986), pp. 2–7. The article argues the case that high operating leverage is the principal source of financial risk, that grants to reduce initial capital costs are more effective in reducing this risk, and that apart from guaranteed investment security most tourism incentives are unnecessary. It also gives a complete list of investment incentives.

World Tourism Organization. Work undertaken by, and reports submitted to, the Facilitation Committee. An ongoing process within the WTO, facilitation has been the subject of numerous studies and reports on current measures and practices likely to constitute an obstacle to the development of the travel and tourism sector as well as the problems of protectionism and measures to reduce, if not eliminate, obstacles to international trade in tourism services.

MARION JOPPE

Hotel marketing

Introduction

The practice of marketing is increasingly being heralded as the savior of all business activities, especially in the current dynamic and turbulent environment. It is particularly relevant in the hotel industry, but it is important at the outset to recognize that whilst effective and efficient marketing has a vital role to play it must not be to the exclusion of sound financial and human resource management. To many marketing managers in hotels the marketing concept consists of advertising, selling and other promotional activities. They are just the tip of the iceberg, however; there are a large number of varied and sophisticated techniques which can be put into practice in any size of hotel whatever the level of expenditure allocated to the marketing function.

It is obvious that hotels offer a heterogeneous product; they vary in location, scale, size, range, quality and style of food, accommodation and facilities offered, resources available, and organizational structure. In this chapter basic concepts and theories of marketing are discussed, the principles of which can be applied in organizations whatever their situation.

Examples

It has already been noted that the structure of the hotel industry varies along a continuum from large corporate international chains (for example Trusthouse Forte plc, Stakis plc, Grand Metropolitan plc and Ladbroke Groups plc) to consortiums (such as Best Western) and small family owned and managed establishments that exist in every locality. In the larger, company-owned hotels where marketing departments have been established it is the role of the marketing manager to participate in the strategic management process. The marketing manager's brief then is to interpret the corporate objectives, and formulate, implement and evaluate marketing plans. The organization for marketing within these large hotels is very different from smaller establishments as the personnel are free to concentrate and specialize in their task. In smaller organizations the day-to-day operations tend to take precedence over extensive marketing tasks. In this classification of hotels it is quite probable that general management staff are responsible for all the marketing activities as well as the everyday running of the hotel. Even within this context, however, marketing can be undertaken with positive results.

In the hotel industry market segmentation is widely practised. Crest Hotels, for example, developed new products for one of their major market segments – women executives – which they identified some time ago as a market opportunity. In addition, the Senior Citizens market and retired people have been identified by Crest, Thistle and Stakis hotels as a lucrative sector deserving a separate market package. Promotional activities can range from the 'happy hour' in the bar of the local hotel to media advertising on television, and in national and regional newspapers and magazines.

Benefits

The hotel customer is fickle, not particularly loyal to one organization and is currently being subjected to changes in the social and technological environment. Most people are receiving a higher standard of education and have experienced a wider range of services and standards through business life or leisure activities. In addition there are more competitors in the catering and leisure industries attempting to persuade customers to use their goods/services. Consequently hotel managers have to work harder in order to market their products if they want to achieve their business objectives – normally to survive and be profitable.

For hotels to be market oriented it is essential that customers' needs are ascertained by the use of systematic market research in conjunction with market segmentation. The move towards customer orientation leads to higher standards throughout the industry, thus improving its general perception. Staff may also be motivated by the adoption of the marketing concept as most employees wish to be associated with successful business ventures and of course the benefits to the organization are obvious.

Implementation

The concepts and principles of marketing are implemented by practitioners through the framework of the marketing mix which consist of the 'four Ps' – Product, Promotion, Price and Place.

Product

The three main aspects of the product which must be taken into account are as follows:

1. The product in the hotel industry is different to that in manufacturing industries and may in some ways cause the marketing effort to be more difficult. These differences are generally recognized as being the qualities of heterogeneity, intangibility, inseparability and perishability.
2. The elements of the product offered to each market segment also differ and marketing personnel must take this into account when planning marketing activities. For example, the product package on offer to the businessman differs from that offered to the tour operator. The marketing manager must take this into account when planning marketing activities.
3. The concept of the product life cycle, which recognizes that all products have a limited life during which they retain profitability, and hence the need for new product development, are of particular relevance in the industry. An example of this process is the decline of hotels at railway stations and the emergence of large modern hotel complexes located near major airports.

Promotion

Promotion is the generic term used to explain the communication activities in marketing. The promotion mix or techniques consist of the following:

1. Advertising through the media – television, newspapers, magazines, radio, cinema and hoardings.
2. Personal selling – where one person tries to persuade another to buy, face to face or by telephone. This is the most frequently used technique as all staff can be trained to sell.
3. Sales promotions which are short-term incentives to buy – for example a free bottle of wine with each meal booking.
4. Public relations – the aim of which is to establish good relationships with influential groups in the market place who may be potential buyers.
5. Direct mail which includes sending postal communications to potential purchasers.
6. Merchandizing which usually takes the form of displays or exhibitions either at trade fairs or in hotels; for example, the wedding package exhibition.
7. Publicity – free advertising through sports events/personalities; for example, the reporting in a local newspaper of a celebrity visiting the hotel.
8. Sponsorship where the hotel contributes financially to (for example) a charity or sports event.

The choice of technique depends on the target audience to be reached, the resources available and the past success rate of a particular acitivity.

Pricing

Pricing is one of the most important variables in the marketing mix for hoteliers, although it does not always receive the attention it deserves. Customers perceive a strong relationship between price and quality of the product; some are not particularly price conscious and many are prepared to pay for the exclusiveness of, for example, a highly priced meal in a restaurant which is known as being 'up-market'.

Within the hotel industry there is normally a high proportion of fixed costs which do not vary whatever the level of business. Pricing strategy is therefore an important factor in the marketing mix. Two main approaches tend to be used: cost orientation and market orientation. Even within a particular hotel, different pricing strategies are used for different elements of the product.

The pricing tactics employed in hotels include the following:

1. Cost-plus pricing. One of the most popular methods is where the price charged is calculated to allow for the total costs of the product item plus a percentage mark up. The problem which the marketer encounters is centered around which costs to use – variable, total or marginal.
2. Break-even pricing. Here the establishment's objective is to arrive at a price which will allow it to 'break-even', recovering its total costs and neither making a loss nor a profit. This is then used as a base to ascertain how prices can be increased in order to ensure profitability.
3. Contribution pricing. This method ensures that the price charged covers the variable costs and makes a contribution to the fixed costs.
4. Market pricing. Here the price charged is determined by what the market will bear. This method takes into consideration the price adopted by competitors in the industry, cost structure and the objectives of the company.
5. Differential pricing. This is where different prices are charged for the same product item which is sold to differing market segments – senior citizens, package holiday and the business market, for example.

Place

The location of a hotel is a prime factor in determining market success but once decided it cannot readily be changed. For this reason it is essential that the optimal site is chosen to facilitate customer convenience.

Assessment

The marketing activity must be the major agent of change within the organization, therefore continual evaluation and reappraisal of each element of marketing is essential. The aims and objectives must be reassessed immediately they are determined as well as at frequent intervals along the time span of the plan. Product policies and the products available should be examined to ensure continuing customer satisfaction.

Market segmentation strategies also must be continuously

evaluated to ensure that the most lucrative segments are currently being reached. Changes in consumer demand patterns for the product should be monitored and conclusions ascertained regarding the implications for the future.

The location of each element of the product mix should be assessed to maximize customer demand and satisfaction within each market segment. An example of this would be the positioning of food and beverage outlets, bars, and bedrooms in response to customer perception and its effect on consumer buying behavior. Close monitoring of price changes is also essential to determine overall profitability.

Promotional policies and their implementation are the core marketing activity in most hotels. The promotional techniques must be evaluated for profitability – in particular, those activities such as advertising which are costly. An analysis of each promotional tactic within the mix must be undertaken for homogeneity and appropriateness for the target market within the total promotion package. Management must assess how far each promotional tactic contributed to the overall promotional objectives and assess the costs and benefits of each. The timing of special promotions should be continuously reappraised and recognition given to better positioning in order to achieve more satisfactory results.

The need for market research, the type undertaken, the relevance of the information supplied by the research project, the cost of the project and the implementation of the recommendations must be evaluated. The formation and implementation of continual market research systems and the value of such lines of communication is an important factor for evaluation.

Conclusion

Marketing is essential in every industry in the developed countries of the world. In addition, the concepts of marketing are currently being given recognition in many of the underdeveloped and controlled economies. In instances where the customer has a choice of many products to buy and where his information has reached a high level of sophistication, the level of marketing practised by the firm can determine the success or failure of the business.

The concept of being customer orientated should permeate the heart of the business, color each activity and be one of the main controlling factors in decision making.

The challenge for management is to realize that marketing does not just happen, it must be planned, implemented, controlled and evaluated. Furthermore, these are continuous processes not just undertaken on predetermined occasions. Marketing is essential if a hotel is to maximize its opportunities and minimize the threats and risks to survival.

Focus on small business

The concept of marketing is relevant to all organizations, regardless of their size or organizational structure. The catering

industry which has an abundance of small, privately-owned hotels is no exception to this. The principle of a hotel providing the right product in the right place at the right price and with appropriate promotional activities can just as easily be applied to a 15-bedroom hotel as to a 500-bedroom unit within an international company.

There are aspects of marketing which may be practised more effectively in a small unit, for example the individual needs of guests may be more easily served. There is closer and more frequent contact between the manager responsible for marketing and staff in smaller establishments, therefore the ideology and practices of marketing may be easily communicated. The marketing mix elements are relevant to small units. Market segments can be identified and product packages developed. In addition staff are able to acquire a wide understanding of their customer behavior.

Nevertheless, there are several problems in implementing marketing within small businesses. The major one is the lack of any one person with extensive specialist knowledge necessary to develop and implement marketing plans. There are generally less financial resources available to implement marketing plans in small units. One way of overcoming this problem is to organize promotion and research on a cooperative basis with other hotels in similar situations. Market research may, of necessity, have to be undertaken at a less sophisticated level, however this does not mean that the results are less effective.

Severe changes in the market place may have a devastating effect on a small business whose resources are more limited than a multinational organization so it could be argued that marketing is even more important in the small unit which could more easily adapt to the changing environment.

Further reading

Buttle, F., *Hotel and Food Service Marketing* (Holt, Rinehart and Winston, 1986). An excellent text on the marketing process related to the hotel and catering industry.

Caterer and Hotel Keeper (Reed Business Publishing, weekly). Examines issues related to hotel management and marketing. Directed towards the practitioner.

Cornell Quarterly, *Hotel and Restaurant Administration* (Cornell University NY). This journal examines many marketing issues relevant to practitioners in the hotel industry but in addition contains other articles on management.

Crouch, S., *Marketing Research for Managers* (Heinemann, 1986). A book which assists the manager to use marketing information rather than how to undertake it.

Hotel Catering and Institutional Management Association. Reference Book 1987/88. This contains useful information including directories of hotel operators, consortia, catering operators, organizations in the United Kingdom, as well as manufacturers of catering equipment. Available from 191 Trinity Road, London SW17, UK.

Hotel Companies in the UK (Kleinwort Grievson Securities, Spring 1987). A report on the UK hotel market which examines the recent performances of major UK companies.

International Journal of Hospitality Management, vol. 5, no. 4 (Pergamon Press, 1986). This particular volume of the journal is devoted entirely to the marketing of hospitality, but the journal in general contains articles related specifically to management in the hotel and catering industry.

Greene, M., *Marketing Hotels and Restaurants into the 1990s* (Heinemann, 1987). An essential book for every marketing manager as it contains practical information with respect to increasing sales.

Kotler, P., *Principles of Marketing* (Prentice Hall, 1986). A comprehensive text which sets out marketing principles, concepts and practices clearly. Suitable for applications.

Merricks, P. and Jones, P., *The Management of Catering Operations* (Holt, Rinehart and Winston, 1986). Examines how different types of catering operations can be successful. Case study examples are included.

Miller, S., *Menu Pricing and Strategy* (CBI Publishing Co., 1980). This book provides practitioners with a direct, basic body of information in relation to the development of menu strategies and methods of menu pricing.

McDonald, M. W. B., *Marketing Plans and How to Use Them* (Heinemann, 1984). This book sets out the main aspects involved in formulating plans for marketing activities.

Summer, J. R., *Improve your Marketing Techniques* (Northwood Books, 1982). This book is a guide for hotel managers and caterers and sets out the steps involved in the marketing process in a clear straightforward framework.

MARGARET MCKENNA and
ANNA MURRAY

Hotel marketing audit

Introduction

Most businessmen are familiar with the annual accountancy audit, but the term 'marketing audit' is less widely understood. The marketing audit, like its accountancy counterpart, aims to subject the operations of the firm to particular review. The focus of the marketing audit, as its name suggests, is an organization's marketing effort. The marketing audit reviews the organization, objectives and operations of marketing to ensure that they are best suited to the emerging threats and opportunities in the business environment. Accordingly, the focus of a marketing audit is not to comply with legal requirements, but rather it is an activity aimed at improving a company's marketing performance.

A widely used definition of the marketing audit identifies its key elements. It states that 'the marketing audit is a comprehensive, systematic, independent and periodic examination of a company's (or business unit's) marketing environment, objectives, strategies and activities with a view of determining problem areas and opportunities and recommending a plan of action to improve the company's marketing performance' (Kotler *et al.*, 1977, p. 27).

The characteristics of the marketing audit can be explained by expanding on the four criteria identified in this definition. The first of these, that a marketing audit should be *comprehensive*, means that the marketing audit should cover all aspects of the organization, planning and implementation of marketing activities. Failure to examine all aspects of the organization's marketing effort may mean that a problem, or the cause of a problem, may not be correctly identified. Accordingly, the company's plans, which result from this audit, may not be the most appropriate for the company's situation.

In order to be completely comprehensive, a marketing audit should cover a predetermined range of topics, and thus it should be *systematic* in approach. Some organizations, such as consultancies, have identified the range of topics which any consultant should assess in undertaking a marketing audit and have compiled these into a checklist. This not only ensures that the scope of the audit is sufficiently comprehensive but also that the basis for comparison of activities over time will exist. Unlike an accountancy audit, the scope of the marketing audit will vary slightly between companies, although there are many common issues.

Kotler believes that the marketing audit should be *independent*. While the accountancy audit should be an independent appraisal of a company's financial activities, there is no requirement that a marketing audit must be undertaken by an independent consultant. However, the objectivity of an independent auditor may be central to identifying the company's situation. Those involved in an organization's activities on a daily basis, or over a period of time, may not be able to take the objective stance which is required of an marketing auditor. Audits may be undertaken by company personnel, however. For example, a large group of companies may invite a member of staff of another division to undertake the review.

Finally, Kotler states that the marketing audit should be *periodic*. While the accountancy audit is conducted at regular intervals, the marketing audit is less likely to be undertaken on a similar basis. Many companies will only undertake or commission a marketing audit when the business appears to be underperforming; often it is undertaken after consultants have been invited to help identify the root of a company's problems. Other organizations may believe their business to be sound, and feel that a marketing audit is not needed. Neither of these extreme perspectives are ideal. The marketing audit should be undertaken on a periodic basis, with the frequency reflecting the nature of planning activities in the organization. For example, a small independent hotel may need to review its operations quarterly; a hotel group's marketing division may need this review only once or twice yearly. The level of frequency should be reassessed in periods of rapid change in the marketing environment, such as when changes in exchange rate affect the level of tourist flows or when new competitors or products are entering the market.

Examples

A national company operates pubs and restaurants, most of which have basic residential accommodation. Despite the growth in the market for budget accommodation, accommodation occupancy levels were low. There was no obvious reason why they should be unable to profit from these rooms. A limited budget was allocated for promotion of these rooms. A marketing audit identified that the accommodation was of an acceptable standard, but even regular customers were unaware of its availability, standard and prices. The marketing audit proposed that this issue was addressed immediately as the market was developing rapidly. It was important that the company became established as a budget accommodation provider while there was still potential for growth in this sector. The low budget allocated to this sector for this financial year was fixed and could not be changed easily. The audit proposed that all planned national advertising for both restaurants or pubs should mention the availability of budget accommodation, and special promotional literature was prepared for display in all outlets. This low-cost solution enabled the company to increase market awareness levels within current budget levels and also directed management to assess the level of promotional support for this product in future years.

A privately owned hotel, which had recently been bought from its original owners in a rather poor state, faced a problem with future bookings. Despite a key location, close to a major tourist center in the United Kingdom the hotel had to offer discount rates to attract custom in the peak tourist season, even after refurbishing all rooms. A marketing audit revealed that most visitors who stayed for more than one night in this town came on coach tours. The existing size of the hotel was too small to accommodate coach parties. A building program was brought forward, and negotiations with coach tour operators resulted in confirmed bookings following the extension's completion. Selective mailshots to past customers, informing them of the new management and refurbishment also increased the level of independent bookings. This example shows the importance of examining external data as well as internal operations.

Benefits

The definition of the marketing audit given above explains that the purpose of the marketing audit is to examine both the marketing operation and the marketing environment to make recommendations of approaches which will improve the organization's marketing direction and operations. This reveals the three main areas in which a marketing audit may benefit a company.

First, it identifies the role of the marketing audit in investigating the range and context of a company's marketing operations to determine the key areas which affect its performance. The marketing audit reviews all relevant issues, first independently and then it also examines their interdependence. While narrow functional reviews (such as an appraisal of sales force operations) can examine precise topics in depth, they may reveal symptoms of a problem rather than an underlying cause. Further, a marketing audit enables marketing activities which are not consistent with company objectives to be identified. It can also establish those areas which receive too much or too little attention, in terms of the time spent on their management, the budgets allocated and/or the profits which are earned. The

balance of a company's product mix is also assessed, in terms of consistency, market growth and profitability ensuring that neither natural obsolescence nor market change could leave the company's offering and activities exposed.

The systematic and comprehensive nature of the activities involved in the marketing audit enables the trappings and substance of marketing activity to be determined. Marketing personnel's attitudes on particular brands, promotional approaches and future performance of different products or divisions should be examined. The auditor's objectivity and independence enables an objective assessment of the current and future allocation of time and resources in these areas.

Secondly, the marketing audit reviews the company's complete operations in terms of the changing market conditions. Trends in the market, whether social or cultural, political or legal, technological or competitive, will be assessed to identify growth sectors and emerging segments. These can then be matched against the company's current and future offerings. This consideration of market trends can enable companies to prepare for developments and take remedial action where necessary, such as investing in research or product modification. Through early identification of trends which may threaten business, the company has sufficient time to develop considered plans.

Finally, the recommendations which result from a marketing audit will benefit a company by advising on actions which will improve the performance of its marketing efforts. This area is known as marketing productivity. In addition, it will guide the company's marketing plans, based on its comprehensive assessment. The recommendations which result from a marketing audit will thus provide a solid foundation on which the company can build.

Any size and type of organization can benefit from a marketing audit. A small business can benefit from objective assessment, resulting in a better return on its marketing budget. A chain of hotels may wish to conduct a marketing audit to investigate the marketing activities of one hotel, one division (e.g. the European or UK division) or the entire operations of the chain worldwide. In addition to helping identify the critical aspects of its marketing organization, objectives and operation, undertaking an audit can focus the marketing division on the need for continuous gathering of market and competitive data. The need to amend its plans in light of the resultant information will also become clear.

The marketing audit is useful to young companies which are developing, by focusing their efforts and directing their growth; long-established companies, which often have set patterns of activity, will also benefit from an objective review which identifies where their resources can be most effectively used. Successful companies can benefit from an independent review of this type; often their popularity can mask inefficiencies. Unsuccessful companies will look to an audit to remedy their problems. However, while the audit may identify problem areas and suggest solutions, a company must undertake recommendations effectively for the process to be of value. Unfortunately, implementation of plans can be the major weakness in many companies.

Implementation

There are three basic stages in a marketing audit – agreement of purpose and scope, collection of data, and analysis and presentation of findings.

Agreement of purpose and scope

It is important to clarify the purpose, scope and methods to be used in any research activity. A marketing audit is no different. Generally, the audit will begin with clarification of its aims. Some marketing audits may be focused towards solving specific marketing problems despite their broad remit. However, it is important to recognize that the auditor should be allowed some flexibility in this matter, as other areas with more fundamental and pressing problems may become clear once the data collection has started. Once the aims have been clarified, the auditor and the company must agree on a suitable level of depth, and an appropriate timescale for reporting. The auditor must determine the available sources of information and key personnel to be interviewed. It is useful to ensure that these staff have been briefed about the role of the marketing audit. Some people feel that it is a personal review and withhold information which shows poor performance of their products, personnel or promotional efforts. It is useful to identify some customers or distributors whose opinions of the company can be compared with the perceptions of company employees. This contrast can often reveal key areas for further research. Finally, it is important to agree a suitable format for the final report. While some companies prefer a detailed written document, others require a draft document followed by a review session.

Collection of data

The collection of data for a marketing audit can be a time consuming process. Often the data which is required by the auditor will not have been collected by the company being audited, or is not available in the form required. Where possible, outline details of the data required should be left with the company once the scope of the audit has been agreed. This enables the auditor to spend his time on interviewing key personnel and customers, rather than wasting time while staff look for records. All interviews need scheduling in advance. Interviews should be semi-structured to ensure that the main topics are considered, but allowing the chance to develop other relevant issues in depth. It can be useful to issue a list of topics to interviewees before the meeting, as this can focus their attention on its purpose. Typically, one component of the data collection stage is the analysis of competitive companies and products. This can be more difficult in the hotel sector, because of the element of personal service. However, this is an important part of a hotel marketing audit. Much can be learnt by staying as a hotel guest or eating in hotel restaurants. This should be undertaken before staff are notified of the role of the auditor in the sponsoring hotel to ensure that the auditor is not treated favorably.

Analysis and presentation of findings

While the data collection stage will normally be the most time-consuming stage of the marketing audit, the analysis of the data requires most insight. The auditor must assess the quality and completeness of the data collected, and examine the present and past practices and position of the company in view of changing market conditions. It is normally the case that the strategic options open to a company are limited after this analysis. It is the auditor's task to examine those options which remain, and select the approach which builds on the company's strengths and protects its weaknesses, considering the opportunities and threats in the marketing environment.

The recommendations which result from a marketing audit can cover many different areas, including marketing objectives, organization of the marketing department and/or sales department, marketing planning and control, new product development, pricing strategy, distribution policy and/or implementation of the marketing plan. The content will depend on the auditor's analysis of the critical issues from the data collected. A marketing audit may identify areas which merit further investigation. Although the audit is meant to be comprehensive, it cannot cover every area of operation in depth.

When the report is presented in the chosen form, it is useful to have a seminar focused on how the findings of the audit should be implemented. This can help clarify the problems and justification behind specific courses of action. Further, it ensures that there is a common understanding of the existing problems and can help build the teamwork and commitment necessary to ensure that the recommendations are implemented effectively.

It was stated earlier that the marketing audit should be undertaken by an independent auditor where possible. The reality is that it is often difficult to find or use an auditor. Various alternatives have been suggested to overcome this problem, including asking people in related activities in the business to audit each other, or developing a 'task force' from the company which will undertake the audit. Some large organizations can develop an auditing office, which will undertake marketing audits for all hotels and divisions. In this latter instance, an external auditor may also be appointed to the audit team on occasions.

Assessment

It is difficult to establish the success of the marketing audit. It should identify the major problems in a company's marketing effort and suggest priorities for action to remedy them. However, attempts to determine whether the audit has identified the underlying problems is a complex activity. Even if the symptoms still exist after remedial action, it may demonstrate poor implementation rather than a poor audit.

Checklists of key questions asked at each stage of the audit process should ensure that the audit will gather information of sufficient quality and covering the defined areas. Few check-lists focus on the specific situation facing either independent hotels or hotel groups. While some questions in traditional checklists could be rephrased to accommodate the require-ments of hotels or hotel groups, others need to be added. Areas which should be included are:

1. Levels of occupancy (in different types of accommodation, at different times of the week and year, at different rates, and by method of sale).
2. The nature of direct and indirect competition.
3. Turnover rates in the restaurants and bars.
4. Location and property assessment.
5. Questions relating to the service element of the product, specifically, identifying staff skills, labor intensive tasks, and management of the quality of the service activities.

It is particularly difficult to evaluate the data analysis stage, yet this is critical to the success of an audit. Accordingly, anyone who manages or commissions a marketing audit must ask key questions at other stages of the audit process to ensure that it will run smoothly and efficiently and be built on solid foundations.

The following questions should be asked when commission-ing a marketing audit:

1. What is the scope of the audit?
2. How much should the audit cost/what can we spend on the audit?
3. Who should undertake the audit, and why?
4. Have the audit team (or the auditor) got sufficient exper-ience to undertake the data collection?
5. Have they got the skills to evaluate the data?
6. What will the audit results be used for?
7. How long will each stage take?
8. When will the results be ready?
9. What form will the results take?
10. When do we need the results?

Once these issues have been resolved, the focus should then be on ensuring that the data collection stage is undertaken in an efficient and comprehensive manner. Have staff been informed about the nature and purpose of the audit? Has the data collection plan been established? Have interviews been set, both internally and externally? Has existing desk research been made available? Are past sales or occupancy figures com-plete and available? Has access to these studies/figures been arranged?

When the report has been presented it will normally raise many specific questions. Before these are addressed, the fol-lowing general questions should be answered:

1. Is the report in the form required?
2. Does it cover the scope detailed at the outset?
3. Does it explain any assumptions which were made?
4. Are there any omissions?
5. Are the recommendations included?
6. Is the logic underlying the recommendations clear?
7. Are there any obvious examples of data which appear to have been misunderstood or misinterpreted?

Once these have been answered, findings and recommen-dations should be considered in depth too. The assumptions and data which underlie these should be examined to ensure that the auditor's analysis is based on accurate and complete data.

Conclusion

The marketing audit is a valuable tool for assessing the mar-keting performance of any business, and identifying areas for remedial action. Marketing audits should cover all aspects of the marketing operation, and not be limited to appraisals of specific functional areas. The success of a marketing audit depends on the ability of the auditor to gather data on the marketing systems and operations from a variety of internal and external sources of information and analyze this to identify the problems and opportunities which exist. Recommendations for future action will be based on these findings. Key factors in the success of the marketing audit are the completeness of data, and the quality of its analysis and of the resultant recommen-dations. Checklists of key areas can be useful in ensuring that all areas are covered, albeit at a general level. Where possible, marketing audits should be undertaken by someone from out-side the existing marketing operation to ensure that the work is undertaken objectively. Further, marketing audits should be undertaken on a regular basis (although not necessarily at fixed intervals) to ensure that any problems are recognized early enough to enable corrective action to be effective. Recommen-dations from a marketing audit can be used as the basis of policy development and marketing planning.

Focus on small business

A major problem facing small hotel businesses which wish to undertake a marketing audit is how to obtain the required level of objectivity in assessment. Generally, it is difficult for per-sonnel in small companies to be objective about their operation, as they are invariably involved in all aspects of the business, either directly or indirectly. Major consultancy groups are a costly alternative. However, by using key clients, staff at all levels, and assessors from independent agencies (such as sup-port agencies), these businesses can produce a valid review. The integration and assimilation of different perspectives may be a time-consuming task, but the results can be revealing.

Checklists have already been mentioned as being useful in ensuring that some coverage is given to the key areas of the business operation. A regular review using these checklists can provide valuable information on marketing performance, even if the audit is undertaken internally. Over time, this can build a useful database of the marketing performance of the small business which can be used to model outcomes of alternative actions.

Further reading

Grashof, J. F., 'Conducting and using a marketing audit', *Readings in Basic Marketing*, E. J. McCarthy, J. F. Grashof and A. A. Brogowicz, eds (Irwin, 1975), pp. 318–29. A well written review article on the marketing audit, including listings of key areas to cover.

Hooley, G. and Cowell, D., 'The status of marketing in the UK service industries', *The Service Industries Journal*, vol. 5, no. 3 (November 1985), pp. 261–72. Among the many issues investigated in this interesting study was the use of marketing audits by service companies. The level of acceptance (below 17 per cent) indicates that use of this approach is not widespread in the UK services.

Kotler, P., *Marketing Management: Analysis, Planning and Control* (Prentice Hall, 2nd edition, 1972). The section on pp. 773–9, reviews the background behind the marketing audit in an old version of one of the best-selling marketing textbooks.

Kotler, P., Gregor, W. and Rodgers W., 'The marketing audit comes of age', *Sloan Management Review* (Winter 1977), pp. 25–43. A comprehensive article on the marketing audit, which includes a marketing audit checklist as an appendix.

McDonald, M. H. B., 'Planning the marketing function', *The Marketing Book* (Heinemann, 1987), pp. 70–93. This chapter reviews the entire marketing planning process and, in doing so, considers the role of the marketing audit in the marketing planning cycle.

McDonald, M. H. B., *Marketing Plans: How to Prepare Them; How to Use Them* (Heinemann, 1984). A detailed review of the marketing planning process which gives more detail on each of the areas identified in the above chapter.

Morse, S., *Management Skills in Marketing* (McGraw-Hill, 1982). This book aims to develop the reader's skills in the marketing area, and in doing so, includes several checklists which could be used when undertaking a marketing audit.

Peters, C. H., 'Pre-opening marketing analysis for hotels', *Cornell HRA Quarterly* (May 1978), pp. 15–22. This article identifies key information (partly in a checklist form), which should be assessed prior to development of a new hotel business.

Porter, M. E., *Competitive Strategy* (Free Press, 1980). A popular book which focuses on techniques of competitive analysis, one element of the marketing audit.

Tybout, A. M. and Hauser, J. R., 'A marketing audit using a conceptual model of consumer behaviour: application and evaluation', *Journal of Marketing*, vol. 45 (Summer 1981), pp. 82–101. This article details the approach taken in undertaking a marketing audit for a service sector company, and focuses on the use of a theory of consumer behavior to assess the market position of a company. Although it is rather technical in places, it provides a good description of issues raised when undertaking a marketing audit.

Willborn, W., 'Quality assurance audits and hotel management', *The Service Industries Journal*, vol. 6, no. 3 (November 1986). This article explains what is meant by a quality assurance audit for hotels and the steps involved in undertaking a hotel quality assurance audit. As such, it provides interesting reading on an important area which is considered (in less depth) in the marketing audit.

Wilson, A., *The Assessment of Industrial Markets* (Associate Business Programmes, 1973). Although this is an industrial marketing research book, its checklist in Appendix A is considered useful, clear and easy to follow by many in different industries.

Yesawich, P. C., 'Post-opening analysis for hotels', *Cornell HRA Quarterly* (November 1987), pp. 70–81. A review and checklist of the key issues to be investigated by a hotel when trying to improve its marketing performance, with some general information on strategic options which can be considered following the review.

LYNN PARKINSON

Hotel marketing budgeting

Introduction

The marketing budgeting process is crucial for the total profitability of the hotel and the resource allocation for the marketing mix programs. It is a planning and control tool.

The objective of the planning process is the identification of opportunities and the allocation of resources towards strategies. A well-conceived strategy includes four basic components: scope, resource deployment, competitive advantages, and synergy. The scope component of a strategy specifies the present and planned interactions between the hotel and its environment, in order to achieve a strategic fit. The strategy should include an outline of the hotel's projected resource deployment – how it will distribute its resources across various areas. Resources should be allocated towards successful hotel services or units and away from less successful ones. The strategy should specify the competitive advantages that result from the hotel's scope and pattern of resource deployment. Strategy should also take into account the synergy expected to result from decisions about scope, resource deployment and competitive advantages. This allocation must take place in such a way that the overall performance of the multi-business hotel can be optimized. Each strategy can serve as a framework for developing specific action plans and for specifying associated programs, expenditures and risks.

Budgeting involves expressing a set of planned activities for the coming time period in dollar or other quantitative terms. Budgets are the foundation of most control systems. Because of their quantitative nature, they provide yardsticks for measuring performance and facilitate comparisons from one time period to another. In particular, budgets serve four primary purposes. They help managers coordinate resources and projects. They help define the standards needed in all control systems. They provide clear and unambiguous guidelines about the organization's resources and expectations, and they facilitate performance evaluations of managers and units.

One important factor governing the financial success of a hotel group is how control of its individual hotels is exercised. Activities such as payroll, accounts payable, and capital spending above certain levels, should be centralized.

Examples

ARGE (asset revenue generating efficiency)

Ideally, capacity-constrained service firms would like to be operating at a high capacity (which may or may not be 100 per cent of available capacity) at all times outside scheduled 'downtime' periods. Many capacity-constrained service organizations use percentage of capacity sold as a measure of operational efficiency. For instance, hotels talk of their 'occupancy rate'. However, by itself, this percentage figure tells us little of the relative profitability of the business attracted, since high utilization rates may be obtained at the expense of heavy discounting. What is needed, then, is a measure of the extent to which the hotel's assets are achieving their full revenue-generating potential. This must take into account the relationship between the average price actually obtained per unit of service and the maximum price that might potentially have been charged – what might be termed the unit price efficiency rate. Should a hotel accept an advance booking from a tour group of 200 room-nights at $30 each when these same room-nights might possibly be sold later at short notice to business travelers at the full room rate of $50?

Based upon past experience and an understanding of current market conditions, prices can be set by reflecting the demand curves of different market segments. At the same time, 'selective sell' targets can be assigned to advertising and sales personnel, reflecting how management expects to allocate available capacity among different market segments at a specific point in time. By multiplying the capacity utilization rate by the unit price efficiency rate, one can derive an index of asset revenue generating efficiency (ARGE).

Consider, for example, a 200-room hotel where all rooms carry a maximum posted price of $50. If only 60 per cent of rooms are occupied one night, with 60 rooms being sold at $50 and another 60 at $30, then the average unit price efficiency rate is 80 per cent and the ARGE is $(0.6 \times 0.8) = 48$ per cent. Another way to arrive at the ARGE is to divide total revenues received ($4,800) by the theoretical maximum revenues that could have been obtained by selling all rooms at the highest price ($10,000).

The value of the ARGE approach to performance measurement is that it forces explicit recognition of the opportunity cost of accepting business from one segment when another might subsequently yield a higher rate. The decision to accept or reject business should represent a realistic estimate of the probabilities of obtaining the higher rated business, together with a recognition of any incremental costs involved. Incremental revenues should always be greater than incremental costs, unless the hotel service is to be marketed as a 'loss leader' or the action program is part of a pre-specified marketing strategy.

CRM (critical ratio method)

The critical ratio method is based on the expected contribution of an incremental available room. A room will generate a positive contribution if it is occupied. The expected contribution of an incremental available room can be seen as:

$$C = r - (s + c)$$

where:

C = the expected contribution of an incremental available room
r = the occupancy-variable revenues
s = the occupancy-variable (servicing) costs
c = the capacity-variable (carrying) costs.

Then the hotel manager can further calculate the expected contribution of the nth room of a contemplated capacity of n rooms as follows:

$$EC_n = P_n (r - s - c) - (1 - P_n) C$$

where:

EC_n = the expected contribution of the nth room of a contemplated capacity of n rooms
P_n = the probability that at least n rooms will be demanded on a given night
r = the occupancy-variable revenues in dollars per occupied room-night
s = the occupancy-variable costs in dollars per occupied room night
c = the capacity-variable costs in dollars per available room
C = the expected contribution of an incremental available room.

The optimal probability that at least n rooms will be demanded on a given night can also be found as follows:

$$P_n^\star = \frac{c}{r - s}$$

$$1 - P_n^\star = \frac{r - s - c}{r - s}$$

where:

$\star$ = at optimality

As an example, suppose that a hotel's occupancy-variable revenues per occupied room-night are $100 and that its occupancy-variable costs per occupied room-night are $40. If the hotel's capacity-variable costs per available room-night are $20, one can find that the most profitable capacity for which the hotel is expected to be fully occupied is only $1/3$ of the nights in the given year.

The second equation gives the demand level equivalent to the probability that capacity will exceed demand and so the nth room will not be occupied.

e.g.

$$1 - P_n^\star = \frac{(\$100 - \$40 - \$20)}{(\$100 - \$40)} = \frac{\$40}{\$60}$$
$$= 2/3 = 0.67 \text{ (the same as } 1 - 0.33)$$

ERC (efficiency–risk coefficient)

The strategic problem is not merely one of how much to invest in the marketing mix as a whole, nor in each element of the marketing mix, but how much to spend in relation to the hotel's total resource budget. Clearly, the higher the proportion spent, the greater the risk (unless a higher degree of certainty is available concerning the outcome). Supposing the hotel has a total advertising budget that may be spent in different media, with different coverage and response rates and... assuming the risk to be uniform, a comparative efficiency-risk coefficient (ERC) can be established to compare the effectiveness and risk of each medium. This would be calculated by multiplying the *IPC* factor (income generated as a percentage of cost) by the total budget (B) available and dividing by the campaign cost (C):

$$\text{ERC} = \frac{IPC \times B}{C}$$

This will give an order of preference in which to allocate the hotel marketing resources to the media available, in order to combine the highest return for the outlay with the least risk in regard to the total resources available. Of course, the income generated is not the same as profit generated. For instance, the profit on the $800,000 of income generated by a TV campaign will probably not be sufficient to cover the $200,000 cost of the campaign. Hence, it will be useful, not merely to establish an order of preference in the relative expenditure on the different media, but also to find a cut-off point below which the expected return for expenditure in the next medium proposed is quite simply unprofitable.

Benefits

The importance of the hotel marketing budgeting process should be seen within the development of hotel marketing plans, in particular, regarding its role as a planning tool, its interrelationship with forecasting procedures, its linkage with the definition of hotel marketing objectives and alternative marketing strategies, its crucial role in terms of the allocation of financial resources to marketing mix programs, and in terms of a monitoring device within a marketing control system.

There is a very close relationship between budgeting as a planning technique and budgeting as a control technique. Since we prepare budgets prior to operations, budgeting is part of planning. With the passage of time and as the hotel engages in its activities, the actual results are compared with the budgeted (planned) results. This analysis may lead to corrective actions and this is the essence of control.

In every business undertaking, budgeting constitutes the core of the business-running exercise. It is the concept of planning put in concrete financial terms after other phases of planning have been gone into. It is thinking ahead to justify that activities thus budgeted should lead to achieved planned results through a well-thought-through surplus of revenue over expenditures. In addition to being a planning tool, a marketing budget is a means of communicating the decision-making process, a tool of control, and link between cost and the scope of marketing activities to be undertaken.

The hotel should seek to create a differential advantage (DA), the set of unique features in a hotel's marketing program that attract customers and cause them to patronize the hotel and not its competitors. Without a DA, a hotel adopts a 'me-too' philosophy and offers the customer no reason to select its offerings over a competitor's. A DA can be achieved through a distinctive image, new products/services or features, quality of services, low rates, and other hotel characteristics. The hotel marketing mix requires a number of decisions and the budgeting of marketing activities does not mean a guesswork allocation of sums between various marketing activities. Budgeting involves forecasting, selection of priority customer-generating markets, and the planned manipulation of all the variables that determine the hotel's performance in an effort to arrive at some preferred market position in the future.

In order for the marketing budget to be a useful and effective tool for planning, organization, implementation and control of the hotel marketing plan, it has to be comprehensive, detailed, realistic, and flexible. By comprehensive, it is meant that the budget should contain all planned marketing expenditures from the planned cost of all communication activities to the cost of research.

A marketing budget should include all the details pertaining to the expenditures of the marketing plan expected to be implemented. Thus, the budget document should itemize all marketing mix activities in a systematic manner. The budget should be realistic. It should strike a good balance between ambition in marketing activities and financial resources available. The cost of each item of the marketing activities should be estimated at the time the expenditure is going to be incurred. The budget should not contain doubtful cost information or assumptions about cost which are not tenable as this might destroy the whole hotel marketing plan. Marketing budgets should be as flexible as possible in order to specify the budgeted level of costs without need for revision when the situation changes during the period of the budget. It achieves this by distinguishing between those costs which vary with changes in the level of activity and those that do not. In other words, a flexible marketing budget is usually based on complete knowledge of cost-behavior patterns.

The programming, allocating and budgeting tasks focus on short-term programs and the allocation of scarce resources. Each program tends to focus on one element of the marketing mix. For several hotel services or on several elements of the mix for one product, the resources being allocated vary from production capacity to promotional funds.

Marketing mix impact on profit/sales and resource allocation

The hotel marketing-mix strategy should be set in relation to corporate and marketing goals. We can then derive profit and sales equations by incorporating the different marketing mix elements. Every marketing mix strategy will lead to a certain level of profit. The profit can be estimated through a profit equation:

$$Z = [(P - k) - c]Q - F - M$$

where:

Z = total profits
P = hotel list price/room rate
k = allowance per unit (trade allowances, commissions, discounts)
c = service production variable cost (such as labor costs)
Q = numbers of units sold
F = fixed costs (such as salaries, electricity)
M = discretionary marketing costs.

The expression $[(P - k) - c]$ is the gross contribution margin per unit – the amount the hotel realizes on the average unit (room/service/meal) after deducting allowances and the variable costs of producing the average unit. The expression $[(P - k) - c]Q$ is the gross contribution margin – the net revenue available to cover fixed costs, profits, and discretionary marketing expenditures.

In order to use the profit equation for planning purposes, the hotel manager needs to model the determinants of sales volume (Q). The relationship of sales volume to its determinants is specified in a sales equation (also called a sales-response function);

$$Q = f(X_1, X_2, \ldots X_n, Y_1, Y_2, \ldots, Y_M)$$

where:

$(X_1, X_2, \ldots, X_n)$ = sales variables under the control of the hotel
$(Y_1, Y_2, \ldots, Y_M)$ = sales variables not under the control of the hotel.

Y variables include such things as the cost of living index, the size and the amount of discretionary income of the served market, and so on. As these variables change, so does the hotel market's buying rate. The hotel manager has no influence over the Y variables but needs to estimate them for use in forecasting. When the hotel manager has estimated the Y variables and their effect on sales volume, this can be conveyed by:

$$Q = f(X_1, X_2, \ldots, X_n/Y_1, Y_2, \ldots, Y_M)$$

or:

$$Q = f_{(Y_m)}^{(X_n)}$$

which says that hotel sales volume is a function of the X variables, for given levels of the Y variables. The X variables are the variables that the manager can use to influence the sales level. The X variables include the hotel list price (P), allowances and discounts (k), variable cost (c) (to the extent that high variable costs reflect improved product/service quality and customer service), and marketing expenditures (m). Thus sales, as a function of the hotel manager's controllable variables, is described by:

$$Q = f(P, k, c, m)$$

One additional refinement can be made. The marketing budget, m, can be spent in several ways, such as advertising (A), sales promotion (S), sales force and distribution (D), and marketing research (R). The sales equation is now:

$$Q = f(P, k, c, A, S, D, R)$$

where the elements in the parentheses represent the hotel marketing mix.

After having defined corporate goals, marketing goals, marketing strategies and the level of manipulation of the marketing mix variables, one can start defining the appropriations and the allocation of the financial resources of the hotel.

Implementation

The task of constructing a hotel marketing budget in order to attain a given level of sales and profits is a crucial step in the hotel planning process. A common approach is to link marketing budget-setting to the target profit planning of the hotel.

The hotel manager first estimates the area's total market for hotel lodging for the coming year. An estimate can be formed by applying the recent growth rate of the market to this current year's market size. This forecasts the market size for next year. One then includes the estimated annual average occupancy rate for the industry in the region and forecasts the total real market. The manager then forecasts the hotel sales volume based on the assumption that the hotel's past market share will continue. Next the hotel manager sets an average room rate for next year based mainly on expected increases in labor, material, and maintenance costs. Then one can calculate the sales revenue. The manager then estimates next year's variable costs per room and by doing that he can calculate the contribution margin to cover fixed costs, profits and marketing costs. The hotel manager now brings in the target profit goal. Now the manager subtracts the target profit from what remains of the contribution margin to learn how much is available for marketing. In the final step, he splits the marketing budget into its mix elements, such as advertising, sales promotion, and marketing research. The split is done according to the hotel marketing plan objectives.

Although this method produces a workable marketing plan and budget, several improvements are possible:

1. The hotel manager estimates market size and share by extrapolating past trends. He should consider changes in the marketing environment that would lead to a different demand forecast.
2. He may continue to use his past marketing strategy. But one of the reasons for the planning process is to consider alternative marketing strategies and their potential impact on hotel sales and profits. The hotel manager should not estimate the hotel's market share until after he develops his marketing strategy. He may have set next year's room rate largely to cover expected cost increases, but setting the price mainly on cost is not a market-oriented pricing method.
3. He may have developed the marketing mix on 'more-of-the-same' thinking rather than on figuring out each marketing mix element's potential contribution to the marketing objectives at this stage of the hotel's product life cycle. Taking these limitations into consideration, a revised target profit plan could be devised. The hotel manager should take into account the 'objective-task' nature of budgeting rather than budgeting based on 'what is left over' (after profit) or considering the budget as being just a function of sales.

No magic formula exists for setting the advertising budget. How much to spend is always a perplexing question. Commonly used methods include a percentage of last year's sales, a percentage of potential sales, or the hotel industry percentage (competitive-parity or going-rate method). These methods are all flawed because advertising should create sales and cause things to happen, not react to what has happened in the past or in other hotels. Consequently, the best method of setting advertising budgets is to determine the objectives to be performed and allocate the proper amount to reach these objectives. This budgeting system (the objective – task method) involves decision making related to four essential stages: market, message, medium, and measurement. The specific amount to budget for advertising and sales promotion will depend on each situation.

The implementation of computer systems tailored to the needs of an organization may contribute to the setting up of a fully-integrated budgeting system for hotel management. The most important part of the system will be its forecasting ability, since oversupply or shortages of supplies are a major problem in the lodging industry. This will permit the hotel manager to take a systematic approach to his marketing management goals. It also can help him to spot trends in costs that otherwise will go unnoticed. The computer system will allocate costs and expenses by marketing entity and/or activity, providing running financial statements, and comparing actual performance to projections.

Assessment

Since the planning budgeting process is seen as an important control device in marketing planning, it should also be used to monitor the hotel's action programs. Adequate follow-up must be instituted to properly monitor progress on the hotel marketing plan's action programs. A simple worksheet can help the hotel manager in allocating the marketing budget by marketing tool/type of expenditure and by market segment. The worksheet will be of particular value if it is modified and applied at the individual property level. Also, the updating and scheduling of periodic research inputs will help provide the hotel manager with an ongoing flow of relevant applicable data.

The principle of allocating funds to target markets (TMs) to equalize the marginal response is used in the planning technique called zero-based budgeting (ZBB). The primary advantage of ZBB is that it helps maintain vitality by constantly assessing and questioning existing programs. It also facilitates the development of new programs. The hotel manager can formulate a marketing plan for each TM and estimate sales, for example, for three levels of marketing expenditure, such as 30 per cent below the normal level, the normal level and 30 per cent above the normal level. An example is shown in Table 1, outlining what a hotel manager would do with each budget level and the estimate of sales volume (the sales-response function). Then management reviews this response function against those of other hotel products/services with different TMs and gives serious consideration to shifting funds from TMs with low marginal responses to TMs with higher marginal sales responses.

The application of a broad budgeting concept will help the hotel manager prioritize where he or she wants to spend his or her limited resources. The ZBB concept states: 'no expenditure is justified just because it was spent last year'. Every expense is re-analyzed and justified each year on the basis that this expenditure will yield more favorable results than spending

the same amount in another way. Hence, one needs some caution when applying this concept. For example, a hotel that relies on a reservation system, should see this feature as a 'core' or vital element which at the minimum must be maintained at a certain level. One approach is to subdivide the budget into the 'vital core' and an 'all other category', and only apply the ZBB concept to the 'all other category'.

Conclusion

Dynamic hotel marketing management calls for great flexibility in meeting emerging and new challenges. The budgeting process is a major, essential input to all hotel marketing decisions. Marketing budgeting is a highly interactive process with direct implications to the definition of marketing goals and objectives, choice of alternative marketing strategies, forecasting procedures, tactical decisions and their consequent allocation of financial and other (such as labor and materials) resources, and on the models of control to be used in the hotel marketing plan.

From a practical standpoint, the hotel marketing budgeting process involves four distinctive stages:

1. Target profit planning.
2. Implementation of the right combination of the marketing mix elements.
3. Application of suitable and effective budgeting techniques.
4. Monitoring of action programs.

Budgeting facilitates effective control. The hotel manager can better monitor marketing operations and pinpoint problem areas. Budgeting facilitates coordination and communication between hotel departments. In a sense, hotel unit budgets are like pieces of a puzzle that fit together to yield an overall strategic and tactical framework.

Table 1 Illustration of zero-based budgeting.

Budget (M) ($)	Summary of the marketing plan	Sales forecast (Q) (service units)
1,400,000	Maintain sales and market share in the short term by concentrating sales effort on business travelers, advertising only in magazines, newspapers and direct mail; sponsoring two promotions a year, and carrying on only limited marketing research.	60,000
2,000,000	Implement a coordinated effort to expand market share by contacting 80 per cent of all tour operators and travel agents, adding magazine advertising, adding point-of-purchase displays, and sponsoring three promotions during the year.	70,000
2,600,000	Seek to expand market size and share by adding two new hotel products, enlarging the sales staff, increasing marketing research, and expanding the advertising budget.	90,000

Focus on small business

Capital budgeting concepts can assist small business within the hospitality industry in deciding which marketing alternative strategies and mix tools to choose. These techniques are particularly relevant for decisions involving marketing research, segmentation, targeting, hotel product policy, new product development, pricing, advertising, sales promotion, channels of distribution and after-sales service.

Complex and sophisticated computer hardware is not a necessary condition for the small business which wants to apply capital budgeting to its marketing operations. Many capital budgeting problems can be quickly solved with the use of pen and paper. Despite modest investments and resources available, marketing tools can be applied when properly adjusted to their situational context in order to improve hotel performance. Marketing on a small budget can be effective, efficient and profitable. Market opportunities should be defined, assessed and based on a solid budgeting process and pursued. Segmentation and concentration strategies are crucial for small hotel businesses. Low budget promotional campaigns can be designed and implemented. An overall marketing plan, sustained by a well thought out marketing budget, can be devised incorporating marketing strategies and action plans that will help the hotel to attain realistic goals and objectives in the future competitive environment. Marketing control mechanisms such as cost analysis, sales analysis, profitability analysis and customer/guest segment analysis should be used.

Software/databases

HOTCAP (hotel capacity) MODEL, developed by Joseph M. Waddell, Stanford Research Institute, California, USA. This is a computer model capable of handling any capacity decision problem for the hospitality/lodging industry. It accepts the revenue and cost factors for a particular hotel, a summary of demand history, and the rates and types of expected market growth as input, and computes the expected demand distributions for as many years as desired.

Further reading

Anthony, R. N. and Dearden, J., *Management Control Systems* (Irwin, 4th edition, 1980).

Buttle, F., *Hotel and Food Services Marketing: A Managerial Approach* (Holt, Rinehart and Winston, 1986). Chapters 7, 17 and 19, in particular.

Dean, J., 'Does advertising belong in the capital budget?', *Journal of Marketing* (October 1966). The article asserts that advertising belongs in the firm's capital budget since advertising's effects occur over the years and advertising outlays are substantial.

Greene, M., *Marketing Hotels into the 90s: A Systematic Approach to Increasing Sales* (Heinemann, 1983). Important chapters are: 3, 5, 7, 10, 15, 16, and 20.

Griffin, R. W., *Management* (Houghton Mifflin Company, 1984).

Hedley, B. A., 'A fundamental approach to strategy development', *Long Range Planning*, vol. 9, no. 6 (December 1976), pp. 2–11.

Hise, R. T. and Strawser, R. H., 'Applications of capital budgeting techniques to marketing operations', *MSU Business Topics* (Summer 1970), pp. 70–5. Discusses a survey of the extent to which 190 Fortune 500 companies apply capital budgeting techniques to channels of distribution, sales management, advertising marketing research, and new product development.

Kotler, P., *Marketing Management – Analysis, Planning, and Control* (Prentice Hall, 5th edition, 1984). Chapter 9 deals with the marketing planning process and budgeting.

Lorsch, J. W., Banghman, J. P., Reece, J. *et al*, *Understanding Management* (Harper and Row, 1978), pp. 187–8.

Lovelock, C. M., 'Strategies for managing demand in capacity-constrained service organizations', *Marketing in the Service Industries*, G. Foxall, ed. (Frank Cass and Co., 1985). This article explains the usefulness of the ARGE approach and ERC technique.

Norkett, P., 'Financial success: elusive goal for the hotel trade', *Accountancy* (UK), vol. 96, no. 1097 (January 1985), pp. 69–74.

Nykeil, R. A., *Marketing in the Hospitality Industry* (CBI Publishing Co., 1983). Chapter 14 contains practical examples of hotel marketing budgeting (worksheets, ZBB etc.)

Waddell, J. M., 'Hotel capacity: how many rooms to build?' *Cornell H. R. A. Quarterly* (August 1977), pp. 35–47. This article explains the rationale and methodology of the HOTCAP Model and CRM technique.

Wahab, S. L., Crampon, L. J., and Rothfield, L. M., *Tourism Marketing* (Tourism International Press, 1976). Parts III (marketing mix) and IV (planning and strategy) in particular.

LUIZ MOUTINHO

Hotel marketing strategies

Introduction

The simple fact that different people demand different products has given rise to a large variety of hotels: motels, inns, business and conference centers etc. In order to classify hotels then, different criteria must be used: location, size, type of rooms, positions, services, facilities, licences, as well as purpose of visit.

Until the twentieth century, hotels mainly followed collective transportation systems – the railway hotels and inns serving the transit passengers, for example. The growing use of automobiles led to a new demand for hotels along the highways. We can see a similar trend with the development of air transportation: the building of hotels close to airports. Other factors do of course influence the location of hotels; economic activities or appealing environments can also attract holiday travelers.

Each segment of the consumer population creates a distinct pattern of demand for accommodation and often for a special type of hotel. It is thus important, for successful marketing, to understand who your guests are: their background, purpose of traveling, as well as their behavior in consuming, buying and decision making. The guest market at present consists of the following:

1. Travelers on business: people who travel for their work, take part in conferences, congresses etc. They do not pay themselves.
2. Travelers on recreation: people who travel for pleasure or for family reasons. They pay for themselves.

The purposes of traveling on business include the following:

1. Trade fairs or exhibitions.
2. Congresses, e.g. at UN or at governmental levels.
3. Conferences.
4. Negotiations, meetings.
5. Sales, with few people involved.
6. Purchase journeys, with few people involved.
7. Service, maintenance, control etc.
8. Incentive travel programs (participants, often salesmen, may be offered a journey as a reward for selling, as encouragement or to be introduced to a new product (Larsson, 1986).

It is very difficult to show exact figures for each of these markets because a traveler can have more than one purpose for a visit. A trade fair is often held in connection with a congress or conference. Sometimes it can be difficult to distinguish between the travelers on business and the travelers on recreation – accompanying family members enjoy a holiday during a congress or a holiday follows a conference.

When discussing the travelers on recreation one must bear in mind the distinction between group and individual travelers. Many package deals include special group activities. The hotel might be part of an arrangement with a boat and/or bus company and an entertainment producer, where journey, food, lodging and entertainment are combined in a complete holiday program.

Examples

What then is the ideal business mix? It deals with the definition of the segments as well as with how to direct the sales efforts to these segments at various times of the year. A hotel in Fredrikshamn, Denmark offers an incredible indoor pool area to the Swedish market. In this case the pool is aimed at both conference and family segments. The Sunwing chain, owned by a charter-tour organizer in Sweden, has the family segment as its target market – it arranges activities suited to all family members from early morning to late evening every day. Another example is a Swedish ski resort hotel which, in selling to different segments, talks about the metaproduct: the snow guarantee, the ski lift, the nearness to activities, pleasant restaurants in the surroundings, a picturesque village etc.

What the above examples have in common with many hotels is that they sell through activities within or outside of the hotel area – only basic attention is paid to the rooms. The guests expect an acceptable standard but are more interested in the different activities. These activities can also be offered in combination with other types of service geared to making traveling easier. SAS (Scandinavian Airline System)-owned hotels, for example, advertise their airline check-in service, available at the hotel. Time and ease factors seem to be of overwhelming importance even for travelers other than the business segment.

Benefits

A marketing strategy in the tourism industry must take into account the interaction between the tourist products' suppliers, the environmental factors (including competition), and the customers/target markets (Meidan, 1986). The formulation of marketing strategies basically includes four consecutive stages:

1. Segmenting the market: geographic, demographic, psychographic and behavioral aspects.
2. Defining environmental constraints: technical, demographic, economic, political, social, religious and cultural.
3. Goal formulation (after identification of the target market segments and the environmental constraints), specifying the objectives of the marketing strategy.
4. Allocation of marketing resources to reach the target market – the marketing mix.

Many hospitality firms use the same methods to market services as other firms do to market goods, even though services and goods are different in many ways. Services are intangible – they cannot be stored, transported or resold as goods can be. Further, the product cannot easily be standardized since each service experience will be unique, depending as it does on the individual customer's expectations and interactions with the service organization (Bitner and Booms, 1981). The simultaneity of production and consumption makes location important and limits the consumer's choice of alternatives. Explicitly, a service is an activity, an action or a process. A service is consumed as long as this activity continues. When the activity discontinues, the service ceases to exist.

The customer chooses, uses and experiences the product and evaluates it on a level of satisfaction or dissatisfaction. 'Consumer satisfaction can be viewed as a function of customer expectations and perceived performances. The larger the shortfall between expectations and performance, the greater the customer dissatisfaction' (Booms and Nyquist, 1981). In traditional marketing it is common to use the marketing-mix theory. This theory must be modified for hotel marketers. The marketing mix is a combination of product, price, place and promotion – often summarized by McCarthy's label, the 4 Ps. These 4 Ps will differentiate the product of the company from that of the competitors and will help the company to reach its strategic goals.

Bitner and Booms (1981) suggest that each of these marketing-mix elements must be modified to provide maximum usefulness to the service marketer and that the marketing mix should expand to include three new Ps: *Participants* (the firm's personnel and customers); *Physical evidence* (the environment in which the service is assembled and where the firm and customer interact); *Process of service assembly* (the actual procedures, mechanism, and flow of activities by which the service is delivered).

Renaghan (1983) develops another marketing mix for the hospitality industry, arguing that one problem with using the traditional 4 P framework is that the traits that distinguish services from products have not been accounted for. The mix Renaghan suggests contains three major submixes: the *product-service mix* (a combination of products and services); the *presentation mix* (all elements used by the firm to increase the tangibility of the product-service mix in the perception of the target market at the right place and time), the *communication mix* (all communications between the firm and the target market that increase the tangibility of the product-service mix, that establish or monitor consumer expectations, or that persuade consumers to purchase). Crissy *et al.* (1975) lists the *customer-service mix*, the *service mix*, and the *promotion mix*. Mindak and Fine (1981) suggest instead another P, *Public relations*. Gummesson (1985) divides marketing of services into *mass marketing*, *interactive marketing* and *internal marketing*.

In this chapter we try to explain the marketing program using product, price, location, promotion, and discuss interactive marketing and internal marketing as applied to the hotel business.

Implementation

Product

With such a diverse market to cater for, it is natural that the hotel has become a complicated product, a conglomeration of a great many parts. The hotel offers accommodation with varying standards and varying service levels. A growing category of products is offered in close cooperation with travel agencies and tour operators: conferences, courses, group journeys, low-budget weekends and package offers of various kinds.

Several hotel marketers have mentioned, as the most important qualities, location, service and personnel, and the image of the hotel itself. As the production and consumption of services occur simultaneously interactions between buyer and seller and between customers should be included in product-planning decisions (see **interactive marketing**). When marketing intangible products, as service-oriented firms do, one expects prospective customers to buy promises, i.e. it is necessary to provide metaphorical reassurances of quality and to 'mechanize' the service-delivery process (Levitt, 1983). The hotel's evaluation of its qualities should be compared with the values and needs of the guests. It is important to know what each guest is in reality looking for. When planning and marketing one section of the hotel, it is necessary to look at the total product. The core product is the accommodation; the restaurant, bar, and pool are examples of additional services. It is not enough to have a very good standard for some of these services, or products and not for others. All sections of the hotel have to match and function with each other.

Price

Hotels need to develop a special price policy. A guest's price sensitivity can be part of the motive for his visit. However, the majority of hotel guests do not pay for their stay themselves and it is difficult to estimate just how sensitive such visitors are to prices. The travelers on recreation usually pay themselves and are consequently more clearly price conscious in one way or another.

If a visitor unfamiliar with the hotels of the area is looking for a first-class hotel, the reputation and price of the hotel can be determining factors. If a potential visitor chooses a hotel belonging to a chain of hotels, certain expectations may be involved (Sheraton for example is known around the world for its high standard). When setting prices at first-class hotels, psychological factors must always be considered. If the price is low, the visitor might assume that the hotel has a low standard and choose another hotel. For the customer, price can be an indicator of what the hotel has to offer. The more unusual and special a service is, the greater the price-setting freedom will be (Anttila, 1985).

The price is, however, not just a technical problem; it has to be seen as part of marketing. There are many pricing methods, such as cost pricing, competitive pay pricing, fixed prices, contract prices, and customer oriented prices. Hotels have a lot to gain by focusing on customer-oriented pricing because of the early detection of differences in the way buyers value the same product benefits. Many hotels could not survive if they treated all guests alike. In other words, this method focuses more on value than cost, and on what the guests are willing to pay. For example guests do pay different rates for a room depending on when they are staying at the hotel and special weekend offers are common means for hotels to fill up empty rooms (Ryan, 1986; McDaniel and Jarboe, 1986).

A steady demand is, for obvious reasons, not possible. It can be a matter of fluctuation between weekdays and weekends or between summer and winter seasons. Some hotels, e.g. in a ski resort, are open only during a short season. The problem with periods with varying demands is that free capacity one day cannot be saved to sell the next. Price can therefore be an instrument with which to develop a more even demand.

Location

The location is part of the hotel product inasmuch as the service is consumed and produced at the same time, i.e. it must be provided where the demand exists. Location is thus of key importance for the business and in part responsible for success. 'Consumers are willing to travel a distance to locate the right offering if the cost of making the wrong decision is high enough. If the decision is less important, however, consumers will pick the most conveniently located offering' (Renaghan, 1983, p. 36).

Location describes both the place where the hotel is actually located and the accessibility measured in time and convenience, i.e. how easy it is to move between the hotel and desired activities – by car, bus, train, or a combination of vehicles. In some cases the hotel has its own transport for the guests' convenience. If the hotel is catering for guests coming in their own cars, enough safe parking space should also be a part of the total product. If many guests come by air, it is important that they can quickly and comfortably travel from the airport to the hotel. Different guests prefer different modes – the most common are taxi, limousine or bus.

If the guest is visiting a company outside the city center he/she could prefer either a hotel near the company or accommodation closer to entertainment and shopping. Hotel profiles can be determined by the location: motels are usually situated outside cities, whereas the large international hotels, e.g. Hilton and Sheraton, are often located in the metropolitan center close to a wide spectrum of activities.

Promotion

Potential customers must be informed, and reminded, of the existence of the hotel. To be convinced of the advantage of choosing a certain hotel the potential visitor needs complete and correct information concerning everything that the hotel can offer. This can be achieved with traditional methods of promotion. Promotion can be divided into advertising, sales promotion, public relations and personal selling, which all together make up the promotion mix. When creating a promotion mix, the company has to be aware of the total product. Which instrument the company uses varies from company to company depending on which profile it is trying to build up and maintain.

Promotion of a hotel can be divided into the instrumental (advertising and sales promotion) and personal (public relations and personal selling). The purpose of this distinction is to make it clear that personnel are part of the interactive marketing and the service quality. When we talk about public relations (PR), everyone in the company has to be involved; the personal contacts made by the employees play a great role in the PR. Personal selling is not solely a task for the marketers in the hotel; it includes all the employees with customer contacts.

Public relations and personal selling can be referred to as interactive marketing. Satisfied guests telling friends and relatives about their experiences are of course the best marketers. Internal marketing is important to create and maintain an appropriate atmosphere at the hotel. Interactions contribute to the service quality. Advertising and sales promotion will help the company to inform potential customers about the hotel and possibly persuade them to stay there, but ultimate success is dependent on the quality created through positive internal and interactive marketing.

Interactive marketing

Interactive marketing relates to buyer-seller relations, i.e. different kinds of contacts between the guest and the company. This mode of marketing can be applied to a guest's stay at a hotel. With production and consumption happening at the same time, buyer-seller interactions begin as soon as the guest is in actual contact with the hotel. The four main types of interaction occur between the guest and the hotel personnel, the milieu at the hotel, the environment outside the hotel and the other guests.

On arrival the guest meets the receptionist and, successively, the cleaners, bartenders, waitresses and so on. These are marketers inasmuch as they shape the offering to the needs of individual customers. This of course requires that they understand the marketing concept and its focus on identifying and satisfying customers' needs.

The milieu can be a feature of the room, equipment in the conference room or other facilities in the hotel. The physical environment can be used as an effective marketing tool for a hotel because of the intangible characteristics of the product. (For goods' manufacturers the environment has much less impact on the customer since many are unaware of where the product is produced.) Guests are influenced by tangible cues, e.g. architecture, lighting, furnishings, color. 'These elements communicate information to the customer about how the firm sees itself and about how it wishes its customers to behave' (Booms and Bitner, 1983, p. 223). The outside environment can include transport facilities, the weather, unexpected high prices in the city, pollution, pleasant parks and opportunities for entertainment.

Interaction between guests is also important. The physical environment with big lounges, nice reception areas etc. may be designed to influence guests to interact with each other. At the same time the hotel has to be aware of potential problems when mixing different segments staying at the hotel, for example congress delegates mixing with teenagers. A football team and a wedding party can create an uncomfortable atmosphere in both groups.

> Although the firm's personnel and the human interaction between the customer and others in the environment are of key importance in the service experience, the marketer rarely has any control over these elements. This is another frustration expressed by service marketers today. They can plan, price, and promote the service forever, but all is lost if the firm's contact personnel do not recognize the importance of their roles and interact with customers in a way that reflects a marketing or customer-oriented philosophy. (Booms and Bitner, 1981, p. 48)

Interaction consists of human communication – a process by which the actors create and exchange messages. The process has certain characteristics: it is complex, transactional, continuous and dynamic, situational and expressed in verbal and/or nonverbal codes (Booms and Nyquist, 1981). It is necessary to understand the human communication process to be able to manage the interaction between the guests and the hotel.

All four interaction modes being discussed here should be involved in the marketing process but the fourth, the outside milieu, is obviously most difficult to influence. Even so, it is important to be aware of this element when planning the marketing program.

Internal marketing

The concept of internal marketing refers to the application of externally proven marketing know-how to the 'internal market', i.e. a firm's personnel (Gummesson, 1985, p. 98). Successful interactive marketing through intensive involvement of the personnel is often the result of good internal marketing. Some aims for internal marketing can therefore be to recruit and retain capable employees and to motivate these to do a good job. This requires that the managers are positive and understand the importance of both internal and interactive marketing, which is essentially a question of communication. 'The hospitality manager's responsibility then, consists initially of conceptualizing hospitality enterprise communications in total.

His/her role remains that of fostering open channels of communication – internally and externally, maintaining a healthy communication climate and integrating the operations and customer-contact functions' (Reid and Reid, 1986, pp. 198–99).

An internal milieu has to be created, e.g. through a satisfying motivational and educational policy and through functional planning and control. Generally, a number of the employees in a hotel are employed only part-time, are poorly educated and not paid very well. The turnover is also comparatively high. The hotel branch in general is personnel intensive, often on a seasonal employment basis. If, as determined earlier, the personnel is to be counted upon as a key element of the product, i.e. actively involved in the production process, then the above factors can obviously make control of the quality of the service difficult. One goal of the company is therefore to create loyalty, understanding, motivation and hospitable attitudes among the personnel. In particular, those personnel with extensive customer contacts are very important marketing instruments for the company. This implies that these employees have to be offered training which focuses their roles as interacting marketers.

Assessment

Marketing strategy is, in short, the selection of a target market or target markets and the development of a marketing mix for each target market selected. An understanding of the market and the needs of the potential guest are of prime importance. Factors such as size, trends and conditions in the market have to be identified and profiles of resulting segments have to be developed. To avoid wasting resources, it is important for a marketing manager to recognize the segments of this market so that products can be developed that suit each target market, and so that promotional resources can be allocated to each specific market.

Typical questions which a marketing manager at a hotel will ask are:

1. Has the hotel sufficient knowledge of the market to be able to divide it into well defined segments?
2. Can the hotel reach the segments effectively?
3. According to which criteria have the competing hotels segmented the market?
4. Where does the hotel stand *vis-à-vis* the competition?
5. Which types of guests is the hotel concentrating on?

Another step must be to define environmental constraints. Relevant questions for this could concern the trends in the following environments:

1. Economic (e.g. devaluations, instability in exchange rates).
2. Political (e.g. airport tax, hotel tax).
3. Social (e.g. travel behavior).
4. Demographic (e.g. more elderly people, and women on business).
5. Technological (e.g. more computerized systems).

This is of special interest and importance in the light of tourism's constant vulnerability.

The next step is to formulate objectives and compose a marketing mix. Questions to be asked are: Are objectives devised to meet changing environmental conditions? The hotel product is far more extensive than just the difference in rooms and with this in mind: Is this an appropriate mix to meet the needs of the different target markets? How is the service rendered? Is the design chosen for the distribution system for the market and the promotion program the most effective? Do the pricing strategies meet the needs of the various segments? Hotel marketing is a planning process which implies a systematic approach to serving guests, i.e. a planned application of marketing resources to achieve marketing objectives.

Conclusion

Hotel marketing strategies include reformulation of the marketing strategy several times during the product's life, in response to changing conditions in the market. Marketing strategy depends on each hotel's size and position; large hotels can naturally use strategies not affordable by small hotels. Being large, however, is not the same as choosing the winning strategies. Marketing planning is a long-term activity; strategies should be maintained but different tactics could be changed. The hotel management determines the marketing strategies, but the selected strategy will affect all areas of the hotel. It must be accepted by all employees even in the long run, because the face-to-face service encounter is important to foster loyal guests. Buyer-seller interactions cannot be neglected; with production and consumption occuring at the same time, the customer experiences the production process on the basis of his/her participation.

Focus on small business

Marketing cannot be ignored by even the smallest hotel. It is essential that a small tourist business uses a sound marketing program to be effective (Harris, 1986). The budget for marketing in the small business is often tight, but the management is responsible for success through good planning and a well defined strategy. The quality of communication both internally and externally is of great importance. It is therefore especially necessary for the small hotel to pay attention to its personnel.

The traditional marketing instruments can suffice as a complement to the level of service a well motivated and stimulated personnel can achieve. Satisfied guests answer for a vital part of the marketing process. A good profile, motivated personnel and good relations with the external environment can create a satisfying milieu. This in turn will give the hotel goodwill, a better atmosphere, more inspired personnel, as well as create customer loyalty and, hopefully, attract new guests.

Strategic planning for long-term success must include recognition of the importance of customer loyalty. It is usually easier and less costly to retain an existing guest than it is to attract a new one. Open and responsive communication between the management and the employees is a crucial element if the hotel is to be customer oriented. Only when employees understand the vital role they and their service play, and rely on the rationale of the management's decisions, can they feel committed to the job at hand and to work for future development.

Further reading

Anttila, M., 'Pricing in service marketing', *Service Marketing – Nordic School Perspectives*, C. Grönroos and E. Gummesson, eds (Proceedings, University of Stockholm, 1985), pp. 120–30. This article emphasizes the classification of services and service-pricing policies.

Booms, B. and Bitner, M., 'Marketing strategies and organization structures for service firms', *Marketing of Services*, J. Donnelly and W. George, eds (Proceedings, American Marketing Association, 1981), pp. 47–51. The environment emphasized here includes atmosphere, architecture and physical setting.

Booms, B. and Bitner, M., *Marketing Services by Managing the Environment* (The Educational Institute of the American Hotel & Motel Association, 1983), pp. 222–6. This article emphasizes the differences between services and goods and the problems faced by service marketers as a result of these differences.

Booms, B. and Nyquist J., 'Analyzing the customer/firm communication component of the services marketing mix', *Marketing of Services*, J. Donnelly and W. George, eds (Proceedings, American Marketing Association, 1981), pp. 172–7. This article analyzes the marketing implications of customer/firm communication in services delivery.

Cowell, D., *The Marketing of Services* (Heinemann, 1984). A comprehensive book which gives the reader a good understanding of service marketing. Of special interest for this topic is Chapter 4, about marketing strategy and the marketing mix in service marketing.

Crissy, W. J. E., Boewadt, R. J. and Laudadio, D., *Marketing of Hospitality Services: Food, Travel, Lodging* (Educational Institute of the American Hotel and Motel Association, 1975), pp. 59–89. The authors present a marketing mix consisting of the customer service mix, the service mix and the promotional mix.

Gummesson, E., 'Applying service concepts in the industrial sector – towards a new concept of marketing', *Nordic School Perspectives*, C. Grönroos and E. Gummesson, eds (Proceedings, University of Stockholm, 1985), pp. 95–109. The article focuses on a new concept of marketing in which new theories of services and industrial marketing merge with the traditional marketing-mix theory.

Harris, R. L., 'A six step marketing approach for the small business', *Tourism Services Marketing: Advances in Theory and Practice*, B. Joseph, L. Moutinho and I. Vernon, eds, Special Conference Series, vol. II (Academy of Marketing Science and the Marketing Dept of Cleveland State University, 1986), pp. 270–82. A case which explains how to use a comprehensive and systematic marketing plan for the small business.

Jarvis, L. P. and Mayo, E. J., 'Repeat guests: a loyal base or transient customers', *Tourism Services Marketing: Advances in Theory and Practice*, B. Joseph, L. Moutinho and I. Vernon, eds, Special Conference Series, vol. II (Academy of Marketing Science and the Marketing Dept of Cleveland State University, 1986), pp. 119–28. The multidimensional framework presented for the understanding of lodging-chain loyalty considers patronage behavior and attitudes.

Kotler, P. and Bloom, P. N., *Marketing Professional Services* (Prentice Hall, 1984). This book presents organizing and planning for marketing, researching and targeting the market, and managing the marketing program for the professional services.

Larsson, L., 'Marknadsföring av hotell', *Nordiskt forskarsymposium om*

Turism (Göteborgs Universitet, 1986), pp. 176–8. The focus of the article, written in Swedish, is on definitions and marketing strategies for the hotel industry.

Lehtinen, V. and Lehtinen, J. R., 'Service quality: a study of quality dimensions', *Proceedings from Second World Marketing Congress* S. Shaw, L. Sparks, and E. Kaynak, eds (University of Stirling, 1985), pp. 296–308. The concept of this study is a customer-oriented interactive approach where service quality is produced in interaction between a customer and interactive elements in the service organization. An empirical case from a restaurant.

Levitt, T., 'Marketing intangible products and product intangibles', *Strategic Marketing Planning in the Hospitality Industry*, R. L. Blomström, ed. (The Educational Institute of the American Hotel & Motel Association, 1983), pp. 27–33. This article analyzes the characteristics of intangibility of services and the need for their tangibility.

Lovelock, C. M., *Services Marketing* (Prentice-Hall, 1984). Special attention should be paid to Parts IV (Managing the Customer Mix) and VII (Planning, Organizing, and Implementing the Marketing Effort).

Mayo, E. J. and Jarvis, L. P., *The Psychology of Leisure Travel* (CBI Publishing Co., 1981). This book gives an understanding of consumer behavior related to travel.

McCarthy, E. J., *Basic Marketing: A Managerial Approach* (Irwin, 4th edition, 1971). The '4 Ps': Product, Place, Promotion and Price, are introduced.

McDaniel, C. D. and Jarboe, G. R., 'A study of attitudes and print media preferences of weekend guests staying at hotels/motels in centerport', *Tourism Services Marketing: Advances in Theory and Practice*, B. Joseph, L. Moutinho and I. Vernon, eds, Special Conference Series, vol. II (Academy of Marketing Science and the Marketing Dept of Cleveland State University, 1986), pp. 249–59. Presents insights into weekend visitors' motivations and activities and recommendations on how to use this information for promotion campaigns.

Meidan, A., 'Marketing strategies for tourism', *Tourism Services Marketing: Advances in Theory and Practice*, B. Joseph, L. Moutinho and I. Vernon, eds, Special Conference Series, vol. II (Academy of Marketing Science and the Marketing Dept of Cleveland State University, 1986), pp. 294–310. This article deals with the major marketing strategies in tourism and the way they are actually implemented.

Mindak, W. and Fine, S., 'A fifth P: public relations', *Marketing of Services*, J. Donnelly and W. George, eds (Proceedings, American Marketing Association, 1981), pp. 71–3. The authors suggest a synthesis of public relations with marketing, arguing that each discipline can derive benefits from the other.

Renaghan, L., 'A new marketing mix for the hospitality industry', *Strategic Marketing Planning in the Hospitality Industry*, R. L. Blomstrom, ed. (The Educational Institute of the American Hotel & Motel Association, 1983), pp. 34–7. This article deals with a new marketing mix, one that reflects the difference between products and services.

Reid, L. and Reid, S., 'Communicating hospitality services: from the inside out', *Tourism Services Marketing: Advances in Theory and Practice*, B. Joseph, L. Moutinho and I. Vernon, eds, Special Conference Series, vol. II (Academy of Marketing Science and the Marketing Dept of Cleveland State University, 1986), pp. 190–200. With focus on the employees in hospitality firms this article shows the link between internal communications, managing employees and marketing tourism-hospitality services.

Ryan, C., 'The short break holiday market for hotels in the UK', *Tourism Services Marketing: Advances in Theory and Practice*, B. Joseph, L. Moutinho and I. Vernon, eds, Special Conference Series, vol. II (Academy of Marketing Science and the Marketing Dept of Cleveland State University, 1986), pp. 217–25. This paper discusses the 'weekend break' and the marketing reasons and problems that gave rise to this activity.

LENA LARSSON

Hotel tariffs – price taker or price maker?

Introduction

The price, as the saying goes, is the amount that people are prepared to pay. True enough, and for the auctioneer it is a principle on which his business is founded. But such a principle, when applied to a hotel bedroom, must be supported by hard information. The auctioneer is able to find out what people are prepared to pay at the time the sale is made – in most circumstances the hotel keeper must determine this many months in advance. He must stick his neck out and make a statement: 'this is the price of my product; if you're not prepared to pay that price, we must regretfully decline your custom'. So how does the hotelier arrive at the tariff for his bedroom?

For most hoteliers and hotel companies, price setting is an annual or biannual event; indeed, in some countries hotels are obliged by law to submit their proposed tariff structures to the appropriate authority for approval, as much as 6 months in advance. In the vast majority of cases, the task of price setting is a question of 'how much more', i.e. the appropriate increase on the existing tariff. This will represent the maximum price payable by any guest, because once the 'how much more' has been established, the hotelier will enter into a process of deciding 'how much less', i.e. the reduction in tariff which he is prepared to allow to different guests, or groups of guests. Where this latter is a formal process – the setting of a group tariff, for example – then this is normally part of the formal tariff setting prior to the beginning of the period, and often in fact becomes itself a 'how much more' decision (more than last year's group tariff).

Examples

The 'how much less' decision is most often an informed, *ad hoc* procedure, and can even become akin to the auctioneer's situation, especially where the price charged is settled at the time of sale – where rooms remain unsold at 10.30 at night, and the customer knows what he's about, the hotelier must have a fixed idea already of how little he is prepared to accept, especially where the customer knows the extent of the need of a hotel to sell that room.

The price quoted or charged for a hotel room is a statement from the hotelier which conveys information to the consumer. On an occasion several years ago when a 5 star hotel in London announced its intention to be the most expensive hotel in town, it received much criticism from other hoteliers and from the trade press.

But the statement wasn't made for their benefit, it was made for the information of the clients, both present and future, of that hotel. It was a statement which conveyed the information that that hotel believed itself to be the best and that it believed in its product to such an extent that it was prepared to charge a premium for the use of that product. And it was a statement that said 'if you are willing to pay the price to stay in this hotel, then you yourselves are making a statement that you have not only wealth, but also the necessary level of discernment to choose a quality product upon which to spend that wealth'. The decision of that hotel's management to be the most expensive hotel in London was very much one of 'how much more', not only how much more than last year, but more importantly how much more than the competitors' do we believe our product is worth and people will pay?

Implementation and assessment

At the risk of doing an injustice to those operators who are more sophisticated in their approach, the 'how much more' decision in tariff setting is invariably intuitive, and based on an assumption as to how much the market will bear. Even where a hotel has been refurbished and upgraded, the new tariff will be based upon the old one. But how is that differential assessed, and how does a new hotel, which does not have the benefit of historical tariffs on which an increase can be applied, determine its tariff? In manufacturing, and indeed in the hotel industry in terms of its food and beverage sales, price can be based partially or wholly on direct input (the principle of cost-plus pricing) in order to achieve a preordained gross margin. However, in terms of room sales there is no direct input, it is basically a sale of space and time, and therefore it is difficult to apply this method of pricing.

Rule of thumb method

The ultimate objective of any hotelier is the optimization of the return on his investment, and therefore the price of a room must play a part in achieving this objective. The price must be set at such a level as to produce long-term sales volumes, which in turn produce long-term profits. As a starting point, there are two mathematical formulae which can assist in tariff setting. There is the 'rule-of-thumb' formula, often scorned by hoteliers, which says that for every 1000 units of cost per bedroom unit, the hotel must derive one unit of *achieved average room sales*, at an annual occupancy of 60 per cent or higher. Thus a hotel which cost an average of £60,000 per room to construct (excluding the cost of the land) should achieve an average room rate of £60 (excluding VAT), which could, after adding back discounts and VAT (and often also breakfast), result in a published tariff in excess of £80.

Apart from the initial market feasibility study for the project, which would presumably have contributed to the decision to build for £60,000 per room, such a calculation has no regard at all to the original hypothesis of the price being what people will pay. It could result in a price being set, mathematically, which will deter people from staying, whilst a price some 10 per cent lower would have brought them flocking in. Or it may result in a tariff which produces a reasonable return on the investment, but one which is lower than could in fact be achieved. It is clear that a £50 room rate at 80 per cent occupancy, for example, is preferable in most cases to a £60 room rate at 60 per cent occupancy. The objective in both good and poor years will be to maximize the contribution made to overheads and debt service, and it is not certain that the 'rule-of-thumb' method will achieve this aim.

The Hubbart formula

The second formula for calculating room tariffs is the Hubbart formula, and is somewhat more sophisticated than the 'rule-of-thumb' method. The formula works by taking a required level of return on the investment, and by working *backwards* through the profit and loss account, using assumptions regarding expenses, departmental profits from all profit centers other than rooms, and with the underlying assumption of the number of rooms occupied during the period, calculating the amount of rooms revenue, and then the average room rate necessary to achieve this return. As with the 'rule-of-thumb' method, it is then possible to derive the tariff which will achieve the required average room rate.

While the Hubbart formula has its attractions, it has one evident flaw which makes it useful only as a starting point. In a competitive environment, where demand is price elastic (i.e. demand varies as price changes) it is highly unsatisfactory to make assumptions on sales volumes without taking into consideration the price, yet the Hubbart formula uses a forecast of

sales volume to *determine* price! This fault is enough for many practising hoteliers to dismiss this formula entirely, and not without reason.

A refinement on Hubbart is 'return-on-investment' pricing which follows a similar process but which, having established the required level of total revenue to generate the required level of return on investment, then provides the facility to assess and alter the various mixes of departmental revenues.

Pricing strategy

Of paramount importance in the tariff setting process must be market conditions, historic, current and predicted. To make the correct statement to this market, the hotelier must fully understand and believe in his product. Although there is no workable formula into which one can slot the size of the room, the quality of the curtains, the size of the soap or the fluffiness of the towels, all have an impact on the price which customers will be prepared to pay. Having identified exactly what the product is, the hotelier must decide upon his philosophy, or his pricing strategy.

What statement does he wish to make? Does he wish his product to be seen as the most expensive in the market place, and therefore the best available? Does he wish his product to be compared on equal terms with all other hotels, to some extent removing the element of price from the consumer's decision-making process? Or does he wish to attract a high volume of customers by offering a lower price than that charged by other hotels? In all stages of this process, he may be guided by the results of the 'rule-of-thumb' method or the Hubbart formula, together with a break-even chart, which will tell him at what stage it becomes unprofitable to open the doors of the hotel.

While deciding which price strategy to adopt, the hotelier will be conscious also of the market stance he wishes to adopt – who does he want his clientele to be (from those available, or from those new markets which can be created)? The hotelier must know his intended markets intimately and must be fully aware of their product needs and their perceptions of price, because the tariff that is decided upon, which is printed on the sheets and which is announced to the buying public, is as much a part of the hotel as the restaurant, or the four poster beds, or the front door itself. Everybody at some time or other has said 'I'm not buying that, it's not worth the money' or 'it's too cheap, there must be something wrong with it'. Equally the hotel tariff, a statement of fact, is an invitation to buy.

Further reading

Buttle, F., *Hotel and Food Service Marketing* (Holt, 1986). A comprehensive introduction to marketing and the hospitality industry, designed for students. The principles and mechanics of pricing are included as part of the marketing mix, with ways of calculating price.

Greene, M., *Marketing Hotels into the 90s* (Heinemann, 1983). A well respected text on the changing requirements of hotel guests and how hoteliers can plan to meet these in the future, including price setting.

Rogers, H. A., 'Pricing in hotels', *Managerial Economics for Hotel Operations*, R. Kotas, ed. (Surrey University Press, 1980). An academic paper which investigates the theory and practice of pricing.

Acknowledgement: This article first appeared in the 1987/88 HCIMA Reference Book, and is reproduced with the kind permission of Sterling Publications Limited.

TREVOR WARD

Impact of tourism

Introduction

Tourism has many dimensions and therefore impinges upon a society in a number of different ways. The most persuasive arguments in favor of the development of the tourist industry in a country or region relate to its positive impact on the economy. However, if viewed from an environmental or sociocultural standpoint, the negative impacts of this industry come to the fore. The development of tourism, therefore, must be planned with the aim of maximizing its benefits and minimizing its costs.

The size of the economic impact of tourism, be it positive or negative, is determined by a number of factors, the most critical being the level of economic development of the host country, the degree of diversification of economic activity and to what extent the economy is dependent upon imports of goods, services and capital. It will also be determined by the volume and nature of tourism, the crucial economic variables here being the size and pattern of tourist expenditure. It is important to note that the development of a tourism industry may have a significant effect upon the allocation of resources and that the degree of distortion will be greater the less developed the host economy.

The physical environment is a vital ingredient in the tourism product since it is a powerful attraction to tourists. The relationship between tourism and the environment tends to be symbiotic in the sense that conservation of natural areas, wildlife and scenery and preservation of sites and monuments of archaeological and historical interest are often a response to tourism demand, but have the effect of stimulating and maintaining a flow of visitors to the region. However, although tourism may act as a stimulus to conservation, it may generate a substantial negative impact upon the environment of the host country or region. Among the costs of tourism in this context are damage to wildlife and vegetation, pollution of lakes, rivers and coastlines, air pollution and the destruction of both natural and manmade features. There may also be a radical impact upon the manmade environment as infrastructure, such as motorways and tourist resorts, are developed.

Tourism has marked social and cultural impacts upon both hosts and visitors, with the effects upon the host traditionally being regarded as detrimental whereas the effects upon visitors are generally seen to be beneficial. Among the negative social impacts are the demonstration effect of affluence in poor regions, the overcrowding of resources used by the indigenous population, such as roads, communications and leisure facilities, an increase in undesirable activities such as crime, prostitution and drug-pedalling and the erosion of the local language and culture. It has been claimed that the interest expressed by tourists in the native arts, crafts and ceremonies stimulates and perpetuates the traditional culture, but in many cases it has the effect of diluting it. Artifacts produced, or even ceremonies, music and dance performed for tourists tend not to be authentic. The main sociocultural benefit of tourism is held to be a wider understanding of people of different nationalities and cultures, but studies of mass tourism indicate that there is likely to be very little contact between visitors and hosts.

The economic impact of tourism

Tourism has an impact on the economy through several different avenues. Tourist expenditure raises national income in the host country both directly, through the initial increase in output and incomes, and indirectly through the tourism multiplier. Since tourism expenditure is spread over a variety of economic sectors, including travel and transport, hotels and other accommodation, restaurants and bars and retail distribution, it has a broad initial impact even before the multiplier effect comes into play. In addition to this contribution to the economic growth of a country or region, the labor-intensive nature of tourism and tourism-related industries results in a significant impact upon employment in these sectors. Furthermore, as in the case of output and incomes, activity in these sectors stimulates employment in other sectors of the economy through the employment multiplier.

Increased economic activity as a result of tourist expenditure is not confined to the private sector of the economy, but also has an impact upon the public sector. A proportion of tourism demand will be for publicly provided goods and services, such as public transport, communications and public utilities. In terms of tourist attractions, such services as leisure and sports amenities, museums and art galleries and monuments of historical interest are often provided or run by the national or local government. Since there is a component of taxation in many of the goods and services demanded by tourists, whether provided by the public or private sectors of the economy, tourism also has an impact upon government revenue. In some cases the tax is explicitly levied on the tourist, as with airport departure tax, but much of the extra revenue raised will be from taxes on expenditure, such as sales tax or VAT, and on imports, where import duties are levied. The additional indirect and induced activity generated by tourism will have a multiple effect upon government revenue, through the government revenue multiplier, as receipts from both direct and indirect taxes increase.

All of the above arguments apply both to domestic and to international tourism, but one of the major economic advantages of tourism, as far as most countries are concerned, is its contribution to the balance of payments. International tourism is an invisible export from the host nation and as such represents, potentially at least, an important source of foreign exchange and especially of hard currency. However, the balance of payments effects which stem from tourism are complex and much wider than the (easily measureable) initial inflow of foreign exchange. The critical factor, which will determine whether or not tourism has a beneficial effect on the balance of payments, is the size of the import content of goods and services provided to tourists. There will be not only a direct effect upon imports as, for example, tourists purchase imported products in the shops, but also indirect and induced effects. The indirect effect is the imports required by suppliers of goods and services to tourists and the induced effect is the demand for imports which results from the extra income which is generated in the economy. In addition, if a high proportion of the labor force in the tourism industry is foreign, there may be substantial outflows in terms of remittances to families abroad. In countries where the tourist industry has a predominantly overseas ownership, as is the case for many less developed countries, there will also be a continual outflow of profits and dividends. On the other hand, a thriving tourist industry is likely to stimulate substantial inflows of capital investment.

Tourism has the effect of stimulating capital investment through two routes, the first being direct investment in the tourist industry and the second being investment in the infrastructure required to supply the tourism product. Private investment in tourism is often carried out by overseas companies and, in particular, by multinational corporations. Thus, there may be costs as well as benefits for the host, the main costs being the subsequent outflow of funds, lack of control over the development of the industry, the employment of expatriate labor in all key positions and a dependency on one or two countries, or even one or two companies. Investment in infrastructure is likely to benefit the indigenous population, but, particularly for less developed countries, there will be competing uses for the resources. The resource costs of the development of tourism, then, must be weighed against its potential economic benefits.

Examples

The share of tourism in gross national product (GNP) is calculated by estimating expenditure levels for domestic and inter-

Table 1 Contribution of international tourism to GNP, 1975 (*Source*: WTO, 1978).

Country	GNP (%)
Australia	0.3
Austria	7.4
Canada	1.0
Ireland	2.8
Japan	5.1
Spain	3.4
Switzerland	3.0
United Kingdom	1.0
USA	0.3
West Germany	0.7

national tourism and subtracting from this figure the purchases of goods and services by the tourism industry. It is, therefore, the direct contribution which is being measured. Table 1 shows the contribution of international tourism to GNP for various developed countries. It can be seen that the contribution in the European countries is substantial, but the addition of domestic tourism to the figures makes a considerable difference. For example, for Canada, the contribution rises from 1 to 5 per cent of GNP.

The power of tourism to generate increases in incomes in the host region or country is described by the income multiplier. A selection of income multipliers for countries, regions and towns and cities is shown in Table 2. It can be seen that, with the exception of Gibraltar which is smaller than even the small regions, the income multipliers for countries and large regions are far larger than those for small regions or towns and cities. This direct relationship between the size of an economy and its value is a function of its degree of openness to trade. The smaller the region, the higher leakages, in the form of imported goods and services, will be.

Table 2 Selected tourist income multipliers.

Countries	Income multiplier
Turkey	1.98
United Kingdom	1.73
Jamaica	1.27
Gibraltar	0.57
Regions	
Northern Ireland	1.10
Missouri State	0.88
Grand County, Colorado	0.60
Door County, Wisconsin	0.55
Sullivan County, Pennsylvania	0.44
Small regions	
South-west England	0.33
Tayside	0.32
Exmoor National Park	0.24
South East Dorset	0.23
Towns and cities	
Carlisle, Cumbria	0.40
St Andrews, Fife	0.34
Keswick, Cumbria	0.26
Bournemouth, Dorset	0.18

In terms of its balance of payments impact, tourism may benefit a country, by earning a surplus, or have a detrimental effect where there is a net outflow of tourism expenditure. In Spain, tourism receipts reduce the trade deficit substantially, whereas in Canada the trade deficit is worsened as a result of a high deficit on the travel account. International tourism has been one of the United Kingdom's major invisible exports in recent years alongside other service industries such as banking and insurance.

Assessment

The majority of studies which focus on the impact of tourism have been devoted to its economic impact with the emphasis on its benefits rather than its costs. Some research has simply estimated the direct effects of tourism activity in the economy by calculating its contribution to GNP or exports. More sophisticated analyses tend to rely upon output, income and employment multipliers which include the indirect and induced effects of tourism as well as its direct impact. The two main techniques are to construct *ad hoc* multipliers for the tourist industry or to use the multipliers which are generated by an input-output model for the region or country. Both of these techniques are outlined elsewhere in this Handbook (see pp. 223 and 529).

Studies of the impact of tourism upon the environment have been more limited and tend to be restricted to one specific component, such as water or air. These *ex post* studies also suffer the drawback that the impact of tourism cannot be readily separated from the effects of other economic activities. Analysis of the sociocultural impacts of tourism has generated a number of studies in recent years but researchers in this area encounter problems in measurement and in isolating the behavior associated with tourism from other behavioral changes. Efforts have been made to devise a framework within which to systematically analyze the interaction between tourists and hosts, such as the index of tourist irritation devised by Doxey (1976) or the matrix of behavioral responses suggested by Butler (1974; 1975).

Conclusion

Tourism has a wide variety of impacts on the economy, physical environment, social behavior and culture of a nation or region. The main benefits of this industry are related to its contribution to economic activity and are often the reason why tourism is developed. Although not all of the effects upon the physical environment and sociocultural impacts are negative, tourism may bring with it substantial costs. It is important to note, however, that other industries also cause pollution, sociocultural change and a change in the allocation of resources.

Studies of the impact of tourism have become more diverse and sophisticated in recent years, but the majority of the research focuses upon a narrow range of effects. It is apparent, however, that tourism should be planned in each destination with a view to minimizing the costs and maximizing the benefits. This type of planning requires not only a broader approach, but also improvements in data collection and forecasting techniques.

Further reading

Airey, D., 'Tourism and the balance of payments', *Tourism International Research – Europe* (3rd Quarter, 1978). This article examines the contribution of tourism activity to the balance of payments. Airey examines the primary, secondary and tertiary effects of tourism activity.

Archer, B. H., *Tourism Multipliers: The State of the Art*, Bangor Occasional Papers, no. 11 (University of Wales Press, 1977). A thorough examination of the concept of the various types of tourism multipliers, together with an analysis of their applications and usefulness.

Butler, R. W., 'Social implications of tourist development', *Annals of Tourism Research*, vol. 2 (1974), pp. 100–11.

Butler, R. W., 'Tourism as an agent of social change', *Tourism as a Factor in National and Regional Development*, F. Helleiner, ed., Occasional Paper no. 4 (Dept. of Geography, Trent University, Peterborough, Ontario, 1975), pp. 85–90.

Doxey, G. V., 'When enough's enough: the natives are restless in Old Niagra', *Heritage Canada*, vol. 2 (1976), pp. 26–7. The Butler and Doxey article includes the development of frameworks to enable the examination of the interaction of host and guest communities.

Henderson, D. M. and Cousins, R. L., *The Economic Impact of Tourism: a Case Study in Greater Tayside* (Tourism and Recreation Unit, University of Edinburgh, 1975). A very comprehensive study of the economic impact of tourism at the local, regional and national levels.

Mathieson, A. and Wall, G., *Tourism: Economic, Physical and Social Impacts* (Longman, 1982). An excellent summary and review of the research on the impact of tourism.

Plog, S. C., 'Why destination areas rise and fall in popularity', *Domestic and International Tourism*, E. M. Kelly, ed. (Institute of Certified Travel Agents, Wellesley, MA, 1977). Plog develops a scenario to demonstrate the factors which cause resort destinations to rise in popularity and then to lose favor. This scenario brings with it clear implications for the long-run impact of tourism on an economy.

Richards, G., *Tourism and the Economy: An Examination of Methods for Evaluating the Contribution and Effects of Tourism in the Economy* (PhD thesis, University of Surrey, 1972). Richards uses the technique of input-output analysis in order to determine the economic impact of tourism on the United Kingdom and Ireland.

Rothman, R. A., 'Residents and transients: community reaction to seasonal visitors', *Journal of Travel Research*, vol. 3 (1978), pp. 8–13. This study analyses the increased crime rates, both actual and perceived during the peak tourism periods.

Turner, L. and Ash, J., *The Golden Hordes: International Tourism and the Leisure Periphery* (Constable, 1975). The authors examine how culture, history and archaeology is condensed down into a few recognizable features and sold as a package to tourists.

JOHN FLETCHER and
HELENA SNEE

Impact of world events
on tourism

Introduction

In 1979, the famed futurist Herman Kahn predicted that tourism will be the world's largest industry by the year 2000. Eight years later, Waters (1987) stated that tourism is now the world's largest industry comprising about 12 per cent of the world's gross national product (GNP). Spending for the world's domestic and international tourism is larger than the GNP of any country in the world except Japan and the United States. Waters also reported that worldwide spending for trips 25 miles or more from home reached almost 2 trillion in 1986 – $5.5 billion per day. Tourism generated 64.3 million jobs directly or indirectly in 1984.

The volume of global trips resulted in 3.7 billion arrivals at domestic and international destinations in 1984, an increase of 2.5 per cent over 1983. Domestic tourism, representing more than 90 per cent of travel worldwide, rose 2.4 per cent. By region, domestic travel rose in Europe, South and East Asia, and the Pacific. Domestic travel declined in the Americas and remained the same in Africa and the Middle East.

Strengthening economic recovery worldwide, according to Waters (1987) pushed travel volumes and expenditures to new heights:

1. The airline industry had solid gains in both business travel and passengers carried. Gains from 1985–87 were in the range of 5 per cent worldwide, 10 per cent in the United States. Load factors declined by a point worldwide. The weak dollar and terrorist threats caused a decline of 52 per cent traffic over the North Atlantic routes, but traffic recovered in 1987. Over the next several years, traffic across Pacific routes is expected to show average annual increases of 9–10 per cent. Boeing forecasts that air traffic will grow until 1990 at an average annual rate of 6.1 per cent in Europe, 6.6 per cent in the United States and 8.6 per cent in the Asia and Pacific areas.
2. Worldwide international travel reached 340 million trips in 1986, a 58 per cent increase since 1975.
3. Worldwide passenger car registrations totalled 364.8 million in 1984. Some 36 per cent were in the United States, which has the lowest ratio of population/car – 1.8 persons per car,

compared with the highest in China – 10,221 persons per car. Most tourism spending in the industrialized world takes place as part of a private automobile trip. Auto registrations have been closely correlated with tourism growth.

At its 1985 general assembly is Sofia, Bulgaria, the World Tourism Organization (1985) released a report on the accommodation sector worldwide. In 1983, the world total of rooms was estimated at 9.64 million, which is 430,000 rooms more, or a 4.7 per cent increase, than for the previous year. These rooms represented an estimated 18.86 million beds, nearly 790,000 more beds, or a 4.3 per cent increase, as compared to 1982. Of the total capacity, 80 per cent is concentrated in Europe and North America. The highest rate in 1982 and 1983 included the following: the Middle East where foreign markets comprised over 60 per cent of hotel occupancy; North America where 75 per cent was attributable to the domestic market. By purpose of trip, business travelers continued to be the most important segment (43 per cent), followed by tourists (26 per cent), and conference participants (13 per cent). The latest statistics show an increase to an estimated 10.6 million hotel rooms in 1986, reporting occupancy in the range of 61 to 68 per cent.

Significantly according to the World Tourism Organization, domestic tourists favor accommodations other than traditional hotels. Such lodging alternatives often express the local architecture and reflect the traditions and way of life of resident populations – for example, the 'Chisakime' in Malawi, the 'Mishuku' in Japan, 'Yokoan' in Korea, and 'Funduk' in Yemen. Other types of accommodation operations included camping and caravaning, bungalows, flats, two- and three-star hotels, villas, guest houses, vacation homes shared with family and friends, park lodges, youth hostels, condominiums, health spas, bed and breakfast inns, apartments, boarding houses, holiday villages, trekking huts, fishing camps, and bare boat chartering. Increasingly, self-catering options are being demanded.

Innovative financing approaches involving individual investors or owners are achieving success worldwide, e.g. timeshare ownership, condo hotels, fractional ownership of vacation properties. The Marriott Corporation is now operating timeshare resorts at Hilton Head and on its 11,503 room Orlando World Center.

Examples

Transportation issues

Efforts worldwide to build national and international systems of highways will continue the automobile's dominance as the major mode of transportation.

Although fuel prices are expected to rise, disruptions as during previous energy crises are unlikely to occur. Engineering improvements in automobiles by the year 2000 are expected to result in using 31 per cent less gasoline. Newly built airplanes (e.g. the Boeing 757) are also more energy efficient.

Deregulation of the transportation industry is being judged a qualified success in terms of lower prices, expanded service, and higher load factors in the United States:

1. Airline fares, on average, are between 20 to 30 per cent lower than in 1980; about 90 per cent of fares are discounted compared with 57 per cent in 1980.
2. Passenger load efficiency increased 10 per cent after deregulation.
3. Smaller cities and towns have experienced a 20 to 30 per cent increase in service.
4. The number of airlines increased from 43 in 1978 to over 180 today.
5. The number of passengers doubled from 200 million in 1978 to 400 million in 1986.

Deregulation has resulted in the widespread adoption of hub-and-spoke cities. Problems such as safety, aircraft congestion, overbookings, lost baggage, labor strife existed before deregulation and continue to present problems.

Airline mergers are taking place in record numbers, creating a new breed of carrier – the megacarrier. The six largest airlines in the United States will soon control 75 to 80 per cent of air travel if all of the proposed mergers are completed.

Airline deregulation, or the preferred European term 'liberalization', is happening now in Europe. The European Community Commission's Office for Competition Policy recently sent letters to 10 carriers from 9 of the 12 EC countries citing anticompetition policies. Promotional fares, proposed last summer to bolster the weak market by American carriers which the French rejected, are an example of the problems that can occur.

Motorcoach tour operators have experienced revitalization. The cruise ship industry continues to grow. In Europe, passenger train systems continue to provide efficient and cost-effective service.

Travel agencies, under deregulation, are now undergoing diversification and consolidation. Corporate travel departments are growing; new relationships are being developed by corporate buyers, travel agency intermediaries, and travel suppliers.

Attractions development

It is encouraging to note that after the difficulties experienced by the World's Fair in Knoxville and New Orleans, EXPO in Vancouver passed an attendance goal of 21 million.

Rand McNally is now publishing a 'vacations rated' guide, which ranked Seattle as the United States' number 1 vacation destination. The National Conference of Mayors has developed a new computer database for US city attractions which is linked to the SABRE, APOLLO, and COMPUSERVE systems. Information on attractions and activities is becoming increasingly critical to destination promotion efforts designed to attract the pleasure, conference and business market segments.

Los Angeles was able to diffuse fears of terrorism affecting the successful 1984 Olympics, but the riots and civil disturbance which surrounded the Asian Games in South Korea cast doubts on the 1988 Olympics. The promise of the European Disney World development has been dampened by terrorist incidents recently targeted on France.

The new National Riverpark and Waterfront Association will hold its first conference in San Antonio, calling attention to the enormous success of water-based developments in Boston, Baltimore, New Orleans, San Juan, New York, Louisville, and others.

Attractions, like EPCOT are integrating entertainment with education. Popular natural resource-based attractions are being protected from overuse and saturation with effective substitution strategies like the National Park Service's 'Lesser Known National Park's' information program which has been so successful.

Nonprofit-making and publically operated attractions (natural, historical, cultural, arts etc.) are increasingly using marketing approaches adopted from the private sector. New destinations will be developed. Completely new frontiers and adventure opportunities will open to tourists – including underwater, underground, polar and space settings.

Technology

New technology continues to change the operation of the tourism industry. Environmental impact studies of proposed tourism developments are now required by destination governmental and regulatory bodies. The social and cultural impact of tourism development is equated with the economic/business aspects.

Compunications (a term describing an integration of telecommunications and computing) and fiberoptic cable technology will result in postal pricing – in other words, every telephone call will be a local call.

Thus, more individuals will choose to work at home. These telecommuters will have the ability to work anywhere they please – on vacation, at conferences, wherever they are. Individuals in more traditional work settings will be freed from the constraints of the office. Voice messaging systems will provide access to business communications to and from any remote location in the world to your home, hotel or any designated point.

If more work is done at home, tourism, as an escape from the home's familiar settings and chores, will be essential to maintain balance, and to provide social interaction and personal communication with others.

Other factors

1. External forces continue to create industry problems. Terrorism can be expected to escalate and continue to disrupt

world travel. New destinations in safer and more secure areas are being discovered or developed.

2. Crisis marketing is now an essential ingredient for travel marketing professionals. Contingency planning, forecasting, and creative responses to rapidly changing world conditions are now essential ingredients of success in the tourism industry.

3. The propensity to travel has been correlated with employment in the service industry and disposable income. However, service industry employment is difficult to measure and classify; for example, in the United States the Standard Industrial Code (SIC) is hopelessly outdated. Also, the underground economy (estimated to be 15 to 20 per cent of disposable income in the United States) is a significant factor as well.

4. Leisure time and its distribution will become more important in the marketing process. The trend toward short but more frequent vacations will continue. Marketing messages will increasingly focus upon decisions about how to spend discretionary time – i.e. in terms of quantity available and quality of experience desired – and not simply how to spend discretionary income.

5. Travel market segmentation will increasingly use psychographic approaches emphasizing lifestyle, attitudes/interest, and benefit/experience data and inferences.

6. The major competition in the travel industry may be home-based luxury living and community recreation opportunities which continue to expand and offer substitutes for travel.

7. Responsible traveling will become the norm worldwide. Tourists will increasingly seek opportunities to meet, talk and establish meaningful contacts with people in the indigenous cultures they visit. Customs, etiquette, language forms, gift giving, jargon and baffling idioms will no longer be mysteries to hosts and guests; and once known they will facilitate communication immensely.

Assessment and conclusion

It is unfortunate that some of the facts above are dated due to the lag in reporting statistics. Although useful, such facts need to be supplemented by future estimates of world conditions and events significant to travel professionals.

Tourism is directly dependent upon economic conditions conducive to GNP growth and disposable income increases, which signal higher propensities to purchase travel and recreation products. Approximately 25 per cent of the world's countries have reached developed or newly industrialized status, yet they represent 85 to 90 per cent of the world's economy and travel market. Forecasters have estimated that 50 to 60 per cent of the world's countries will reach industrialized status by the year 2000, which could more than double the world's travel market.

World events could inhibit growth, however. In addition to more obvious economic uncertainties, the tourism industry has experienced positive and negative impacts caused by technological factors, consumerism, energy shortages/gluts, interest rate variations, inflation/recession/deflation cycles, terrorism and political instability, and (most recently) the liability insurance crisis. Too often, major tourism-related events and their impacts were not forecast or given appropriate weighting in business decision making.

Recent industry conferences have warned tourism to be prepared to cope with rapidly changing world conditions. Herman Kahn, in 1979, stated that, 'We must not expect the expected'. Kahn cited the expected continuation of escalating energy costs as an example of the 'expected' event following the conditioned response of industrialized countries to two energy crises. Kahn forecasted 'unexpected' world events which eventually resulted in the present oil glut/deflation economic situation.

Toffler calls our attention to 'The Third Wave', i.e. information society with market demassification. Naisbitt cites 'Megatrends' – new values, rapid institutional change, and product differentiation responsive to the communications revolution and in *Reinventing the Corporation*, he forecasts severe labor shortages, company ownership by employees, and flexible work schedules and benefits.

Have tourism leaders taken the time to reflect on world events related to the tourism industry? Table 1 gives a listing of major events which have potential impact on tourism worldwide. Each event listed has been rated by industry Delphi panels or futurists as having a 50/50 chance of occurrence or reoccurrence over the next 10 years.

Table 1 World event statements by environmental category (50/50 likelihood of occurrence over the next ten years).

Physical and built environment

1. Effective programs in most countries establish economic incentives to private industry for the protection of wildlife, scenic beauty, and natural environments.
2. Regional areas of the world establish and enforce programs to monitor and reduce pollution (e.g. air, water, noise etc.)
3. Reliable short-term weather predictions of one week or less are the norm.
4. Limited access to natural resources is achieved by rationing, drawing lots, or residential qualifications.
5. Completely new frontiers and adventure opportunities are open to tourism (sea and underwater, underground, polar, desert and space environments).
6. Visitors are responsible for preserving ecological habitats of the host country.
7. Artificial environments are commonly used as substitutes for outdoor recreation areas and facilities to provide tourism opportunities.
8. Regional areas of the world establish and enforce programs to monitor and reduce pollution (e.g. air, water, noise, etc.) and to control development.
9. Urban and regional population centers are overcrowded throughout 75 per cent of the world.
10. Agriculture and light manufacturing are integrated with tourism in developing countries.

Economic environment

1. An international currency is used for monetary exchange among nations of the world.
2. The number of developed and newly industrialized countries

Table 1 Continued

Economic environment (continued)
    increases to 50 per cent of the world's countries.
3. Rocketing insurance liability rates result in business closings and unaffordable pricing situations.
4. Labor shortages and value shifts require major organizational changes by employers, e.g. flexible work schedules, personal growth opportunities, and ownership options.
5. A major oil crisis causes major supply disruptions and gasoline price increases of 300 per cent.
6. Real estate value boom pushes purchase prices up and encourages investment in rental properties.
7. The dollar continues to decline dramatically against major foreign hard currencies.
8. The prime interest rate increases to 20 per cent and more.
9. Vertical and horizontal consolidation/integration of travel and tourism industry components and suppliers increase dramatically.
10. Worldwide spending for international travel doubles by the year 2000 as compared with 1986 expenditures in real terms (i.e. without inflation).
11. Major 'flag' franchisers, management contractors, and developer/operator companies will penetrate both traditional (hotel, motel, resort, inn etc.) and non-traditional forms of accommodation (camping, timeshare, cruise ship, etc.).
12. A network of international travel routes for most of today's national air carriers is established.
13. Worldwide stock market crashes reoccur, and reduce travel spending and inhibit industrial expansion.

Political environment
1. Restrictions on foreign ownership of land and transnational companies inhibit economic expansion.
2. The escalation of terrorism throughout the world significantly reduces international travel.
3. Border formalities (e.g., requirements, visa, customs) of most countries are increased.
4. Mandatory retirement age in OECD countries is increased to 75.
5. The public and private sectors work together through education and cultural projects to reduce hostility toward tourists.
6. Energy saving 55 mile speed limit raised to 70 plus miles per hour in most developed countries including the United States.
7. Global efforts to coordinate tourism-related environmental protection, consumer protection, multinational cooperation, regulation, and facilitation intensify and produce a widely accepted Tourist Bill of Rights, Code of Ethics, and widespread international cooperation.
8. Deregulation of commercial transportation carriers becomes the norm in developed countries with market economies.
9. Unfair competition becomes a major political action issue of the private sector designed to limit commercial involvement of nonprofit-making and public agencies.
10. Liberalization of international airline agreements makes travel movements between East and West almost as easy as within the

West.
11. Tourists involved in human rights and political action contribute measurably to world peace.

Personal and social environment
1. The two-income family is predominant in developed countries.
2. Most people travel on other continents as commonly as in their own country today.
3. Half the urban working population throughout the world work primarily for life fulfilment rather than economic necessity.
4. The 30-hour work week and annual month-long paid vacations characterize the normal work patterns in developed countries.
5. Biochemical developments and wellness programs retard ageing and extend the average human lifespan to 90 years.
6. Two separate holiday periods (summer and winter) and frequent shorter trips are dominant in developed countries.
7. Industrialized countries experience increasing resistance to travel due to cultural insularity, home/leisure substitutes for travel, saturation of tourist destinations, etc.
8. Increasing weekend travel to long-haul destinations, 500–1,000 miles and more.
9. Nontraditional work lifestyles like telecommuting – i.e. work at home with advanced communications/computers capabilities – and other home-based compulsive time uses (chores, shopping, etc.) increase demand for travel.
10. AIDS becomes major risk factor inhibiting travel to some countries.

Technological environment
1. Fully automated data retrieval systems are developed on a global basis to provide travel information on a real-time basis.
2. Automation replaces most labor-intensive administrative and industrial jobs in urban areas of developed countries.
3. Major technological advances lower international travel costs to affordable prices on a middle-class budget.
4. Computer-based voice messaging systems (i.e. a voice mail box) are commonly provided as a basic hotel service.
5. Inexpensive longhaul (over 100 miles or 167 km) mass transport by water is feasible.
6. 50 per cent of the world's cash transactions occur through computerized credit, audit, buying and billing systems.
7. Air taxis to destination locations within 200 miles are integrated with major metropolitan airports in developed countries.
8. An international reservation system and data bank with video real-time communications are established for tourist information and attractions.
9. *Compunications* (integration of telecommunications and computing), and fiberoptic cable technology, will result in 'postal pricing' – i.e. every telephone call will be a local call.
10. Super conductor technology produces magnetic trains and energy transmissions resulting in cost-effective access to remote destinations.

The Delphi Method is a way of determining the consensus of informed professionals in a given field. For example, a Delphi poll correctly predicted the year of the first human heart transplant. Delphi surveys conducted by the author predicted the oil shortage (1971) and terrorism effects on tourism (1979), but missed the interest rate increase surge and the insurance liability crisis. Despite the efforts of many to predict world events, the rapidly accelerating rate of change requires us to both think about the future and do something about it in order to benefit the tourism business and its consumers.

In order to improve the accuracy of forecasts, larger Delphi panels will be used in future studies; also, more emphasis will be placed on divergent and visionary thinking.

Futher reading

Waters, S., ed., *The Big Picture* (Child and Waters, 1987).
World Tourism Organization, *Report on the Development of the Accommodation Sector* (WTO, 1985).

DONALD E. HAWKINS

Input–output analysis

Introduction

Input–output analysis is a general equilibrium approach to examining the structure of an economy, its dependencies and the economic impact of exogenous changes in final demand. For any change in exogenous final demand, for example, tourist expenditure, there will be three levels of economic impact:

1. The direct effect. This is the most obvious effect and is concerned with the level of output, income, employment, government revenue and imports associated directly with tourist expenditure. This effect is also known as the first round effect and is confined to those sectors directly involved with the provision of tourist goods and services.
2. The indirect effect. This second round effect occurs because those establishments directly related to tourism activity will purchase goods and services from other establishments within the economy as part of their production inputs. Similarly, the suppliers to those industries supplying the tourist-related industries will also purchase factor inputs from other establishments within the economy. In this way the monies received from tourists will circulate throughout the economy.
3. The induced effect. As the monies created by tourist expenditure circulate throughout the economy, there will be both a direct and indirect addition to income levels in the economy. Part of this income will, perhaps, be saved, but a large portion of it will be respent as household expenditure, causing the monies generated by tourism activity to circulate throughout the economy again.

Input–output analysis can be used to determine all three effects of such a change in final demand. The modeling procedure is a compromise between the general theory of economics and its practical application. Nevertheless, this method of analysis is widely used in Eastern, Western, developed and developing economies alike. It is the most comprehensive method available for studying the economic impact of tourism. Its major drawbacks are related to the data requirements, which make model construction an expensive task in terms of both resources and time.

Input–output analysis involves the construction of a set of accounts, similar to national income accounts, except for the fact that the emphasis is on the final demand section of the economy and the extent of sectoral interdependence within the economy. This set of accounts, generally referred to as an input–output (or transactions) table, records the flows of transactions which take place between industrial sectors and between industrial sectors and final demand. The flows show the origin of factor inputs and the destination of sales, output, hence the name given to this type of analysis. Once the input–output table has been constructed it can be transformed into an operational model by the incorporation of some simplifying assumptions together with a process of algebraic manipulation.

Throughout the analysis, attention is focused upon the concept of economic interdependence between economic agents, be they business (public or private) or consumers of final goods and services. In view of the fact that the framework of the analysis is created by the transactionary flows which take place between the various sectors of the economy over a specified period of time (normally a year), the major task of the input–output analyst is to identify and quantify these backward and forward linkages. The concept of economic interdependence between the various sectors of the economy was first noted during the mid-eighteenth century, but it was almost 200 years later before this concept was developed into an operational model.

Once the input–output modeling is complete, it is possible for the analyst to determine the direct, indirect and induced effect of any change in final demand on the levels of output, income, employment, government revenue and inflow of foreign exchange. This knowledge is invaluable to policy makers who wish to assess the importance of, say, tourism activity, relative to other domestic industries. Furthermore, the input–output model will enable the analyst to determine where supply constraints will occur, given a projected increase in final demand. Thus, remedial action can be implemented before such supply constraints become a reality.

Examples

As well as being comprehensive in nature, input–output analysis is one of the most flexible tools available for studying interdependencies and impacts. It is this flexibility that has led to the model's use in studies concerned with assessing the economic impact of tourism at both local and national levels, educational studies, airline systems, national and regional economic studies. The level and technique of disaggregating the economy into industrial sectors is, in general, constrained by the assumption that all establishments included within a single sector must have similar production functions i.e. they all use similar factors of production in the same proportion in order to produce their output. Subject to this constraint, the economy can be aggregated in such a way as the emphasize the area(s) under analysis (e.g. the tourism related sectors). The general guidelines which should be adopted when deciding upon the structure of the model are as follows:

1. The different sectors should fully reflect the area of study and the purpose of the analysis.
2. The model should be easy to understand and use.
3. The above two guidelines may need to be compromised by the availability of data – input–output models generally require a great deal of primary data, thus the level of disaggregation should bear in mind the possibility of collecting such finely detailed data.
4. Irrelevant information should, as far as possible, be suppressed.
5. Provision should be made for future changes to the economic structure; this is particularly true in the case of developing countries where significant, rapid changes to economic structure are quite common.

The Spanish input–output table of the Spanish tourism economy is an excellent example of the detail that can be achieved using this type of economic analysis. Hotels and hostel accommodation is broken down into three sectors, eating and drinking establishments are subdivided into five different sectors, transport and related services are covered by twelve different sectors and other tourist-related services and their interindustrial dependencies are so finely detailed that they reflect such things as bullfighting, theater, and museums and libraries as separate sectors.

The Jamaican tourism input–output model distinguishes between 27 different categories of visitor arrivals, according to the purpose of the visit (business, vacation, conference, honeymoon etc.), the time of year that visitors arrived (winter/summer) and whether it was a first-time visit or repeat visit to Jamaica. This type of analysis can be invaluable when deciding upon the marketing strategy to be adopted. If it is found, for instance, that first-time vacation visitors who arrive in the summer generate the greatest economic impact then this may well be the major target area for future marketing, or it may be found that conference trade, which tends to be more lucrative on a per capita per day basis, is a particularly attractive segment of the market to aim for.

In the Bahamas, a tourism orientated input–output model was constructed which demonstrated the local 'value-added' generated by each major tourism-related sector. The local value-added is an important indicator because it may generally be assumed that a sector with a relatively high level of local value-added is also likely to be a sector which makes a significant contribution to the level of household incomes per dollar of turnover.

Regional models have been constructed to determine the economic impact of different categories of visitors to specific geographical areas of an economy, such as the study of the economic impact of tourism on Anglesey which distinguished between hotel guests, bed and breakfast guests, campers, caravanners and day visitors. The data requirements for regional models tend to be more demanding than for national economies simply because there are fewer sources of secondary data, e.g. goods and services imported from outside the region and the difficulties associated with apportioning tax revenues to specific areas when people may live in one locality, work in another and yet make their expenditure in, perhaps, a third area.

Implementation

1. Disaggregate the economy into distinct sectors which reflect the purpose of the study. Basic guidelines for such disaggregation can be found in the International Standard of Industrial Classification (SIC), and emphasis for particular industries, such as tourism, can then be achieved by using greater detail for that industry.
2. The data is set out in matrix form; the horizontal rows depicting the sales made by each sector to other sectors and final users; the vertical columns depicting the purchases of each sector from other sectors and primary inputs (i.e. wages, salaries, profits). Table 1 shows a hypothetical transactions table to demonstrate the form that such a table will take. It shows that the tourist industry sells (row 1) £80 of goods/services to tourist establishments within the economy, £140 to the distributive trade sector, £40 to the building and construction industry and £140 to 'final users', yielding a total sales, or gross output of £400.

   Reading down column 1 shows that the tourist industry purchases £80 worth of goods/services from establishments within that industry, £40 from the building and construction sector and £80 worth of goods/services from the distributive trade sector. Furthermore, it purchases £40 of imports, £120 is spent on wages and salaries and £40 is kept as profit, making total purchases £400. Providing all elements of sales are included in the row and all elements of purchases (inputs) are included in the column, then the row total and the column total will always be equal.

   The transactions table is a very useful framework for analyzing the linkages within an economy. For instance, it can be seen from Table 1, that some sectors have a greater direct impact on household incomes than other industries, whilst other industries contribute more to the nation's import bill than others. However, input–output analysis offers much more than this.
3. The most successful and acceptable method of converting the accounting matrix shown in Table 1 into an operational model is the Leontief (1954) inverse. To do this, it is necessary to reduce the specific transactions table (Table 1) to a more general technical coefficients table (Table 2). Take the first three colums and divide the value in each cell by the corresponding column total; in this way the table reflects the

Table 1 A hypothetical transactions table.

Sales to / Purchases from	Intermediate demand			Final demand	Gross output
	Tourist industry	Distributive trade	Building and construction		
Production					
Tourist industry	80	140	40	140	400
Distributive trade	80	40	400	280	800
Building and construction	40	40	40	280	400
Primary inputs					
Imports	40	80	120	160	400
Labor	120	80	120	–	320
Profits	40	20	80	–	140
Gross inputs	400	400	800	860	2,460

level in inputs required from each other sector in order to produce one unit of output.

Table 2 shows that, for the tourism industry to produce one unit of output, it must purchase £0.20 of inputs from other tourism establishments, £0.10 from the distributive trade industry, £0.20 from the building and construction industry and £0.50 from the primary input sectors (imports £0.10, labor £0.30 and profits £0.10). It also shows that the tourism industry uses relatively more labor input per unit of output than the other industries, relatively less imports, and so on.

4. Using the first three rows of Table 2:

$$\begin{matrix} 0.20 & 0.35 & 0.05 \\ 0.10 & 0.10 & 0.05 \\ 0.20 & 0.10 & 0.50 \end{matrix} \quad \text{Let this} = A$$

The final demand for these sectors may be shown as:

$$\begin{matrix} 140 \\ 280 \\ 280 \end{matrix} \quad \text{Let this} = Y$$

The gross output of these sectors is:

$$\begin{matrix} 400 \\ 400 \\ 800 \end{matrix} \quad \text{Let this} = X$$

The economy may now be represented by the following:

Table 2 A hypothetical technical coefficients table.

	Tourist industry	Distributive trade	Building and construction
Production			
Tourist industry	0.20	0.35	0.05
Distributive trade	0.10	0.10	0.05
Building and construction	0.20	0.10	0.50
Primary inputs			
Imports	0.10	0.20	0.15
Labor	0.30	0.20	0.15
Profits	0.10	0.05	0.10
Total	1.00	1.00	1.00

$$X = AX + Y \tag{1}$$

which is,

$$\begin{matrix} 400 \\ 400 \\ 800 \end{matrix} = \begin{matrix} 0.20 & 0.35 & 0.05 \\ 0.10 & 0.10 & 0.05 \\ 0.20 & 0.10 & 0.50 \end{matrix} \begin{matrix} 400 \\ 400 \\ 800 \end{matrix} + \begin{matrix} 140 \\ 280 \\ 280 \end{matrix}$$

Bringing AX over to the left-hand side gives

$$X - AX = Y \tag{2}$$

Which can be written as

$$(I - A)X = Y \tag{3}$$

where I is the identity matrix (a matrix with zeros in every cell except the diagonal which has 1s). However, this presentation still shows Y as the dependent variable. In order to express the model with output (X) as the dependent variable, it is necessary to transfer (I − A) to the right-hand side

$$X = (I - A)^{-1} Y \tag{4}$$

Now let Δ represent a change in a variable and the equation can demonstrate the full effect (direct plus indirect) of a change in final demand (Y) on output (X)

$$\Delta X = (I - A)^{-1} \Delta Y \tag{5}$$

Equation (5) reads as follows: the change in final output (ΔX) will be equal to the Leontief inverse matrix $(I - A)^{-1}$ multiplied by the change in final demand (ΔY).

This provides the policy maker with a basic input–output model which depicts the partial multiplier values associated with each industrial sector and the complete multiplier values associated with each category of final demand. The example shown above will give the direct plus indirect effect of any change in final demand. In order to determine the induced effect the household sector must be brought into the inverted matrix (the column representing household expenditure and the row representing household income).

Further reading

Archer, B. H., 'Input–output analysis: its strengths, limitations and weaknesses', Paper presented at the Annual Conference of the Travel

Research Association held in Scottsdale, Arizona (June 1977). A concise and useful summary of input–output analysis, its advantages and disadvantages.

Carter, A. P. and Brody, A. (eds), *Input–Output Techniques, Vol. 1, Contributions to Input–Output Analysis* (North-Holland, 1970). A thorough guide to the technique of input–output analysis together with some useful applications.

Diamond, J., 'Tourism and development policy: a quantitative appraisal', *Bulletin of Economic Research*, vol. 28 (1976), pp. 36–50. The paper was one of the earlier papers to use input-output analysis as a means of assessing the performance of tourism.

Dorfman, R., 'The nature and significance of input–output', *Regional Economics and Statistics*, vol. 36 (1954).

Fletcher, J. E. and Snee, H. R., 'The service industries and input–output analysis', *Service Industries Review*, vol. 2, no. 1 (1985). This article examines the assumptions of input–output analysis and then compares them with the reality of service industries.

Fletcher, J. E., Snee, H. R. and Macleod, B., *An Input–Output Study of Gibraltar* (The Institute of Economic Research, UCNW, Bangor, March 1981). A detailed analysis of the economy of Gibraltar using the technique of input–output analysis.

Leontief, W. W., *The Structure of the American Economy 1919–1939* (Oxford University Press, 1954). The original input–ouput model of the United States.

O'Connor, R. and Henry, E. W., *Input–Output Analysis and its Applications* (Griffin's Statistical Monographs and Courses, no. 36, 1975). A comprehensive manual for the construction and applicability of input–output analysis, together with examples using a model of Ireland.

Sadler, P. G., Archer, B. H. and Owen, C., *Regional Income Multipliers: The Anglesey Study*, Bangor Occasional Paper (University of Wales Press, 1973). This study looks at different categories of tourists coming into a region and estimates their economic impact.

JOHN FLETCHER and
HELENA SNEE

International regulation of tourism

Introduction

Tourism has become an object of national policies because it procures an increase in the national product, diversifies its currency resources, and causes an outward flow of currency in the tourists' countries of origin. Legislative and statutory texts have been elaborated, controlling regulations have been decreed and special public services created. All these measures have contributed to the fact that international tourism is no longer regarded as a transnational relationship, managed, administrated and carried out by private persons and enterprises. Tourism has taken on the dimension of an intergovernmental relationship and has led to the conclusion of many bilateral and multilateral treaties. Although the law on international tourism should really be an independent chapter of international law, the questions raised by this activity are usually treated in a dispersed manner under the more classical headings of international law: the legal status of the tourist, the international regulations on transport, foreign investment, currency transfers, the environment, sport and culture, or even the status of holy places such as the Vatican City.

Contemporary international law can be divided into two types: the international law of coexistence, which attempts to assure the peaceful coexistence between sovereign states (in particular East–West relations), and of cooperation, which lays out and organizes the cooperation between states (in particular North–South relations).

Tourism and the international law of coexistence

The international law of coexistence tends to affirm the sovereignty of states and to define its limits in order to safeguard' international peace. Although tourism is not dealt with directly under this type of law, it comprises two series of specific rules: the first one tends to emphasize the right to tourism, the second one tends to regulate tourism exchanges.

Tourism appears as a private activity, whether individual or collective, and therefore favorable to maintaining peaceful coexistence. As such, tourism is indirectly, as well as explicitly, recognized by international law. The 13th article of the Universal Declaration of Human Rights confirms the right of each

person to leave and to return to his country freely, which constitutes an implicit recognition of the right to tourism. In addition, the final act of the Helsinki Conference on Security and Cooperation in Europe incorporates this right explicitly by affirming that the participating governments consider tourism to contribute to a better understanding of the life, the culture and the history of other countries, to increase the mutual comprehension between the peoples, to improve contact and to widen the use of leisure time, and that they have every intention of facilitating tourist trips in their respective countries.

As far as the regulation of tourism exchanges is concerned, they are usually covered by more general rules adapted to the problems raised by the increasing tourist flows. The regulations tend to lay out the rights of tourists while protecting the interests and rights of the governments concerned. Two examples are particularly pertinent: the adaptation of the international transport law and that of the legal provisions concerning foreigners.

The international regulations that govern the different means of transport (by air, sea, rail or road) are too numerous to list here, but some of the more significant multilateral treaties are: for air transport, the Warsaw Convention (12 October 1929) modified by The Hague Convention (28 September 1955) regulates the issue of tickets, the responsibility of the carrier and the transport of luggage. The many resolutions adopted by the International Civil Aviation Organization (ICAO) and the International Air Transport Association (IATA) regulate the flying over national territories (at the origin of many bilateral treaties on income sharing), the common exploitation of certain air routes and international air tariffs (with the delicate problem of charters). Sea transport is regulated, amongst many others, by the Brussel Convention (29 April 1961) stipulating the obligations of the carrier and the conditions of his responsibility, while transport by rail in Europe is governed by the Berne Convention (25 February 1961, modified 26 February 1966), in particular. But it is road transport that has probably the most numerous treaties, since each type (private car, tour bus, road haulage etc.) has its own, regulating such things as insurance, acceptance of driving licences in foreign countries, and the right to haul (freight, caravans, boats, . . .), for instance.

The adaptation of the legal provisions concerning foreigners is becoming an increasingly important problem since tourists are often considered by treaties to be privileged temporary residents, but the line between a 'tourist' and an illegal immigrant (or terrorist and other 'undesirables') is very fine. Still, through the influence of certain international organizations, the trend towards a suppression of entry visas, the acceptance of national identity cards instead of passports, and collective passports for members of a group, is becoming very strong. Customs formalities have also been eased considerably and currency transfers are now quite liberal within the OECD (Organization of Economic Cooperation and Development) countries.

Tourism and the international law of cooperation

While elaborating national tourism policies in order to develop or orient the tourism flows and activities, governments also felt the need to endow themselves with the appropriate legal means to facilitate cooperation among each other on an international level. But tourism development can be a double-edged sword, whether for the industrialized or developing countries: it can be an important factor of growth just as much as means to intensify the existing dependence of the developing countries (or regions) on the industrialized ones.

Recognized as a lever in the economic development of the poorer countries, often particularly attractive to tourists because of their climate, culture and environment, many bilateral agreements on cooperation refer to tourism directly and provide for technical assistance in this field. Thus, the developed country will send consultants and technical experts to the lesser developed one, while the latter will send students or trainees who receive an education in the tourism field (often in hotel schools) in the partner country. Agreements that deal specifically with tourism can also contain clauses assuring that trips for tourism purposes will be encouraged, that the necessary visas will be granted, and that the promotion of tourism as a whole will be furthered. Since development will not take place without investment, the agreements sometimes stipulate that foreign investors enjoy certain privileges such as customs and fiscal exonerations or facilities, the possibility to transfer benefits etc.

Certain international organizations have contributed much to cooperation in the field of tourism. The World Tourism Organization (WTO) actively promotes cooperation and attempts to change the balance of power currently existing between the North and the South. The United Nations and its various Commissions and Councils as well as the World Bank were quite active for a while and at the origin of several major studies relating to tourism. The World Bank has also helped to finance several large projects in the lesser developed countries: Kenya, Tunisia, Turkey, Mexico etc. But the most decisive work has doubtlessly been undertaken by the OECD and the European Community, both of which are dealt with in more detail under the heading 'Examples'.

International law also tries to regulate tourism in order to minimize its negative impact, especially the aspects of neo-colonialism or neoimperialism for which tourism development is so often decried in the Third World. In fact, the wealthy countries, from which tourists originate, not only control and orient the demand almost at will, they also control the means of transportation and quite often the investments realized in the receiving countries from where they repatriate benefits. Numerous countries have therefore 'closed their frontiers' to these practices, demanding a share in airline revenue, the reinvestment of profits in their own country, the training of personnel to replace foreign staff etc. A vast diplomatic offensive is trying to establish a new economic order in the world based on the acceptance of a code of conduct of the activity of transnational companies, the reform of the international monetary system, a new regulation on invisible exchanges and an increase in international development loans. All these measures concern the field of tourism directly and indirectly and as such can modify the relationships that currently dominate.

Examples

Ever since its establishment in 1948, the Organization of Economic Cooperation and Development (OECD), then OEEC, has regarded the progressive liberalization of trade in goods and services as one of its prime objectives, and through various codes and instruments at its disposal, has maintained pressure on governments to remove unjustified impediments to international trade in services and to improve international cooperation in the service sector. In 1985, the Council adopted a Decision-Recommendation on International Tourism Policy as part of its intersectoral work program on the liberalization of trade in services. This Decision-Recommendation consists of three main elements. Firstly, the Act sets out the objectives which it aims to attain and the procedures to be followed to reach these objectives: avoid all measures that distort competition, that discourage the movements of travelers, goods, services and capital, encourage the equitable treatment of national and foreign companies, and reduce administrative requirements. Secondly, it lists in detail the obligations which member countries have accepted in a number of specific tourism sectors, concerning such matters as the duty and tax-free import of personal effects, duty-free allowances, circulation of private cars and caravans, temporary importation, tourist publicity and promotion by official tourist organizations, etc. Thirdly, it sets out a number of guidelines covering facilitation matters in order to encourage governments to make the movement of travelers easier.

In 1992, the objective set by the second article of the Treaty of Rome is to be attained: a genuine interior market of persons, goods and services within the European Community (EC) is to be set up and all obstacles resulting from the diversity of national regulations are to be eliminated. The challenge of 1992 as it concerns tourism, is the harmonization of the rules regulating the different means of transportation, the hotel and travel industries, the different levels of value added tax, the carrying out of activities such as tour guiding or busing of groups. The elimination of frontiers between the various member countries also poses the problem of internal security and immigration. This is a monumental task in light of the existing disparity and the many protectionist measures that still dominate a good number of national regulations.

Assessment

Just as the study of international tourism is interdisciplinary, so the international regulation of tourism draws on all aspects of international law. However, with the steady increase in developed countries of the amount of leisure provided to the working population and the number of people who are retired, the importance of the use of leisure and its economic implications have become progressively more apparent. The actions by the OECD and the EC will have a definite impact on tourism and the coming years should see a steady removal of excessive government restrictions leading to a progressive blurring of frontiers. In many areas international law will dominate national regulations; with the completion of an 'economic space' in Europe, the national laws will, furthermore, resemble each other in the way they approach various issues and the contents of the regulations themselves.

Conclusion

While the adoption of the International Tourism Policy Decision-Recommendation constitutes a significant advance in the concept that tourism is a service industry in its own right, the great frontierless market to be established in Europe could serve as a testing ground for the innovations that will have to be made in the area of tourism legislation. The technical standards that will have to be adopted could be spread to the rest of the world, while many highly protected activities, such as air transport for instance, will have to adapt to much fiercer competition. This weeding out of weak and unadapted companies and practices should be very beneficial in a climate of increasing liberalization in all parts of the world and in all fields. It will also force governments to consider tourism on a par with the 'main' concerns of the national economy, and perhaps give rise to a treaty on the specific legal aspects of tourism.

Further reading

Ascher, B., 'Obstacles to international travel and tourism', *Journal of Travel Research*, vol. XXII, no. 3 (Winter 1984), pp. 2–17. Following the work undertaken by the OECD and WTO, this article identifies and examines restrictions on the international tourist trade and suggests possible approaches for the future.

Commission of European Communities, *A Community Policy on Tourism Initial Guidelines*, Bulletin of European Communities, supplement (April 1982). The communication by the Commission illustrates the large number of Community policies which, directly or indirectly, have a bearing on tourism and which must therefore be given a 'tourist dimension'. Topics cover freedom of movement and protection of tourists, working conditions for those engaged in tourism, transport, regional development, and safeguarding the European heritage.

Hollier, R., 'Le défi de 1992', *ESpacES*, no. 88 (1987), pp. 5–7. The author addresses an inventory of the problems which the travel and tourism industry must face in order to prepare for 1992. The harmonization of value-added taxes and the loss of revenue it represents for certain governments is treated in particular detail.

Organization for Economic Cooperation and Development, *Report of the Tourism Committee on Obstacles to International Tourism in the OECD Area* (OECD, 1984). As part of the general subject of trade-in-services within the OECD, the Tourism Committee has undertaken to seek to identify and analyze the existing obstacles to the liberalization of international tourism. The paper considers impediments which discriminate either between nationals and non-national persons or companies, or against persons or companies of a particular nationality or nationalities.

Organization for Economic Cooperation and Development, *Decision-Recommendation of the Council on International Tourism Policy* (November 1985). This instrument is intended to bring together, in a single document, the main strands where progress needs to be made to remove impediments to international tourism and distortions of competition within the sector.

Organization of American States, *Hemispheric Policy on Tourism Development and Strategy for Implementation*, Occasional Papers (OAS, 1979). A very short paper outlining the main tourism objectives.

Rapp, L., 'L'harmonisation de la réglementation du tourisme', *ESpacES*, no. 88 (1987), pp. 8–12. The author analyzes three problems posed by the freedom of movement for merchandise, persons, services and capital: the harmonization of national legislations, the application of the rules set out by the Treaty of Rome, and the adoption of common technical standards.

Ronkainen, I. A., 'The conference on security and cooperation in Europe, its impact on tourism', *Annals of Tourism Research*, vol. 10, no. 3 (1983), pp. 415–26. A very good study of the inner working of international conferences and the impact they may have on individual countries' policies.

Wackerman, G., 'Acte unique et transports touristiques', *ESpacES*, no. 88 (1987), pp. 15–18. Until now, only the airlines have generally been considered as posing a particular problem under a frontierless market, but the author points out that all means of transportation will have to adapt. He also insists on the limits of a too liberal policy, as far as transportation is concerned, and favors certains 'soft' interventionist measures.

World Tourism Organization, *World Conference on Tourism* (Manila, 27 September – 10 October 1981). The main objective of this conference was to define a new international economic order, in line with the general discussions on North–South cooperation. Particularly interesting are volumes 10 on contraints, 11 on the new objectives and 16 on the objectives concerning the freedom to travel.

World Tourism Organization. Work undertaken by, and reports submitted to, the Facilitation Committee. An ongoing process with the WTO, facilitation has been the subject of numerous studies and reports on current measures and practices likely to constitute an obstacle to the development of the travel and tourism sector as well as the problems of protectionism and measures to reduce, if not eliminate, obstacles to international trade in tourism services.

MARION JOPPE

International travel patterns

Introduction

Preliminary estimates from the World Tourism Organization (WTO) show that approximately 325 million international overnight trips were taken globally for holiday, leisure, business and other reasons in 1985. Receipts from international travel, excluding international transportation expenditures, are estimated at US$105 billion, representing approximately 5 per cent of the overall value of world trade. While international travel continues to expand, with total global volumes up 4 per cent in 1985 over 1984, the growth has been declining over the last 25 years. During the 1960s, international travel increased by 9 per cent, in the 1970s by 6 per cent, while the average for the eighties has been only 3 per cent. In absolute numbers, global arrivals grew by 55.3 million between the years 1970–1975, 64.9 million between 1975 and 1980 and only 45.0 million between 1980 and 1985.

A regional disaggregation of global international travel patterns shows a clear geographical concentration in Europe and North America which together represent about 80 per cent of the worldwide movements between nations. East Asia and the Pacific account for 9 per cent while the Caribbean and Latin America receive 6 per cent of total arrivals. Africa and the Middle East (at 2 per cent each) and South Asia at 1 per cent complete the geographical distribution. While Europe and North America continue to be the main tourist receiving (and generating) areas, their dominance has been declining over the last two decades. In recent years, developing and newly developed countries, particularly in East Asia and the Pacific and Africa, have recorded the strongest growth in international travel.

International travel is basically intraregional tourism. It is estimated that about 80 per cent of total international tourism originates in countries of the same region. Intraregional tourism as a percentage of total arrivals varies among the regions of the world; from approximately 80 per cent in Europe and North America to only 38 per cent in South Asia and 25 per cent in Africa. The ease of movement among the countries of Europe and North America and the existence of substantial tourism infrastructure and facilities, particularly in the southern regions of these two continents, have promoted intraregional tourism in these two areas of the world. Within intraregional tourism, the largest number of arrivals are between neighbouring countries, with the volumes decreasing as the distance between the countries of origin and destination increases.

With the dominance of Europe and North America in terms of international tourism generation, the trip characteristics of international travel reflect the travel patterns of inhabitants of these two continents. For example, the arrival figures confirm a typically seasonal pattern reflecting the traditional holidays of the residents of the northern hemisphere – the greatest number of arrivals are in the summer months with a secondary (and growing) peak to southern destinations around the Christmas and Easter holidays. Regionally, there are differences to this pattern; for example in South Asia, the highest number of arrivals occur in the months of October to March, coinciding with the optimum weather conditions.

In terms of purpose of visit, 70 per cent of international tourist arrivals are due to the main motive of holiday and leisure, 14 per cent due to business and the remaining 16 per cent to other reasons such as religious, health, family and sports. The Americas show the highest relative share for holiday purposes, as a result of the importance of this motive to tourism in the Caribbean and the United States. Countries with a large immigrant population exhibit a larger share of 'visiting friends or relatives' travel.

Transport by land accounts for 70 per cent of total international travel, followed by air and by sea transport. Travel by private car in Europe and North America accounts for 75 per cent of total arrivals – a share that has remained remarkably stable over the period 1973–1984, despite the quadrupling of oil prices. Air transport is the most important mode of international travel (80 per cent) in the countries of South Asia followed by East Asia and the Pacific where it accounts for 70 per cent of arrivals. Conversely, in Europe, air transport represents less than 15 per cent of international arrivals. Naturally, air and sea transport play a dominant role in those regions of the world with an insular geography. Rail transport is important for a limited number of countries – most are in Europe where continental rail transport counts for more than 10 per cent of international arrivals.

The spending associated with international tourists is documented as part of services in the current account of a nation's balance of payments. The travel account is comprised of receipts, the spending of visitors in a country, payments, the spending of residents abroad and, in some countries, international fare payments. Since international tourism receipts and payments are essentially separate activities, there are those that question the importance or relevance given to the balance between them. While it may be recognized that the travel balance is of little significance as an indicator of a nation's success in the international tourism marketplace, it does measure the net result of the primary effects of incoming and outgoing tourism on a nation's balance of payments and the economy as a whole.

An examination of the travel balance of 84 countries by the WTO identified common characteristics among the countries recording a surplus or deficit. Countries which recorded a positive travel account balance were: European countries of the Mediterranean basin; some developed countries which had a large tourism sector; developing countries with a developed tourism sector; Caribbean countries; and, some developing countries with a relatively small tourism sector. The countries with a travel account deficit included: the countries identified as the greatest international tourism generators (among which were those with the highest deficits); oil-generating countries; and, developing countries whose total amount of international tourism receipts and payments was low.

It is generally recognized that there is a duality of motivations responsible for international travel demand. One set of essentially socioeconomic factors (personal disposable income, unemployment rates, labor force and family composition) explain the propensity for the overall level of international travel demand in a nation. Another set of factors – such as the spatial distance between countries, the presence or absence of international connectivity (historical, military, business, cultural, migratory or political), climate, exchange rates and transport linkages– explain the distribution of tourists between particular countries. Generally, the total number of tourists going abroad from a country annually varies much less than the proportional distribution by country of destination. In addition, the factors responsible for the overall level of tourist demand are both less numerous and more easily definable in statistical terms than those effecting the destination patterns.

Although the total and spatial distributions of international travel volumes are related to the aforementioned motivations, unforeseen short-term events can play a significant role in disrupting these flows from time to time. International terrorism, natural disasters, labor strikes (particularly in the accommodation or transportation sectors), environmental pollution, currency revaluations or restrictions and changes in passport or visa requirements can all adversely impact the number of tourists planning to visit a particular destination. These incidents, which may or may not have occurred with a view of disrupting tourism, can quickly negate the best conceived tourism marketing plans and strategies. While some locations suffer a decrease in the number of visitors, other sites may experience an increase in visitation as tourists alter their travel plans to 'safer' destinations at home or abroad. As a result, the total volume of travel may remain relatively unchanged while individual destinations experience an increase or decrease in visitation.

Examples

In 1985, Canada recorded 26.2 million resident and nonresident tourist trips, of which 85 per cent were with the United States. Of the 22.3 million overnight trips between the two nations, 10.7 million were by Canadian residents and 11.6 million by residents of the United States. The remaining 3.9 million were between Canada and all other countries of the world with 2.3 million person-trips originating from Canada and 1.6 million trips to Canada. These figures clearly demonstrate the importance of intraregional or transborder tourism within Canadian international travel patterns.

Between 1972 and 1985, total international travel volumes in and out of Canada increased by 11 per cent, however, intraregional travel between the United States and Canada grew by only 2 per cent. Within the intraregional volumes, the proportion originating from the United States and Canada is now nearly equal (52 and 48 per cent respectively) compared to the 60 and 40 per cent recorded in 1972.

During the same period, intercontinental travel more than doubled to 3.9 million trips and represents 15 per cent of the total, up from 8 per cent in 1972. Travel between Canada and nonEuropean countries increased at a faster rate than travel to and from European countries. In 1985, nonEuropean countries accounted for 46 and 42 per cent of all intercontinental destinations and origins; in 1972 their share had been 39 and 29 per cent respectively. Asia in particular recorded the largest gain in its market share, increasing as an origin to 23 per cent in 1985 from 12 per cent in 1972 and as a destination to 5 per cent from less than 2 per cent.

The seasonal pattern of Canadian international travel movements is related to the origin of the traveler. Travelers to this country tend to visit during the third quarter of the year – nearly half of the American visits and 44 per cent of the visits by residents of all other countries occurred in the summer quarter. Travel by Canadian residents to both the United States and other countries is more evenly distributed throughout the year. Only 37 per cent of the transborder travel from Canada took place in the third quarter with the other quarters recording approximately 20 per cent each. Canadian travel to other countries recorded two distinct peaks of approximately 30 per cent to southern destinations in the first quarter and to intercontinental (mainly European) destinations in the third.

The automobile dominated the travel patterns between Canada and the United States, with plane travel accounting for the second largest percentage. Plane travel represented 17 per cent of American entries into Canada and 27 per cent for Canadian travelers – the higher Canadian proportion is a result of the longer distances involved to particular destinations popular in the first quarter of the year. While most intercontinental travel between Canada and all other countries was by air, there was a sizeable proportion of visitors from these other countries who entered Canada by land (car, bus and train) while visiting the United States.

In terms of purpose-of-trip statistics, nearly two-thirds of all Americans came to Canada for pleasure, recreation or holiday reasons, with the remainder visiting a friend or relative (VFR) or on business, in equal proportions. Pleasure, recreation or holiday accounted for just over half of the Canadian travel to the United States, while another quarter planned to visit a friend or relative and 13 per cent were on business. VFR travel was much more important among the intercontinental travel patterns. Over two-fifths of the visitors from other countries and over half of all Canadians quoted this purpose – a much higher percentage than was recorded at the global level by the WTO.

In 1985, Canada's travel account recorded (Cdn) $5.0 billion in receipts and $7.1 billion in payments, resulting in a deficit of $2.1 billion. Canada has habitually recorded a travel account deficit even though the numbers of international travelers both in and out of the country are relatively equal. The critical factor, in terms of the travel deficit, is the length of stay of visitors and residents. On average international visitors stay less time in this country than Canadian travelers do on visits to foreign nations. Residents of the United States and all other countries stayed 4.7 and 14.4 nights respectively in this country in 1985. On the other hand, Canadians spent on average 7.6 nights in the United States and 21.3 nights on visits to all other countries. The longer length of stay translates into increased average spending per trip for Canadians.

Preliminary statistics for 1986 show that Canadian international travel patterns were significantly different from those recorded during the last two decades. Short-term events such as Expo 86 in Vancouver, a decline in the Canadian dollar against most European currencies, increased terrorism, natural disasters and environmental pollution elsewhere in the world combined to make Canada an attractive destination. As a result, international tourists to Canada increased to 15.6 million in 1986, up 19 per cent from 1985 and the highest level ever. Canadian residents returning from an international trip numbered 13.1 million, virtually unchanged from 1985. The deficit on Canada's travel account fell from (Cdn) $2.1 billion to $1.2 billion in 1986, the lowest level for the deficit since 1981. Whether these increased levels of international tourism into Canada will continue or were just the result of the unusual conditions of 1986 remains to be seen.

Implementation (of international tourism marketing)

There are three principal economic reasons why approximately 175 national governments of the world finance international tourism promotion. First, the governments themselves are recipients of substantial revenues through direct and indirect taxation. Second, the governments have an interest in a healthy international balance of payments to which tourism contributes substantially. Third, tourism is a generator of employment opportunities of major proportions, particularly for low-skill work at entry level.

Governments also become involved in tourism promotion because much of the industry is made up of numerous small to medium-size enterprises who do not have the know-how nor financial resources to promote their services in many widely dispersed markets upon which they depend. Tourism promotion is a logical extension of their responsibility for the planning and managing of facilities and installations. Important elements of the infrastructure, such as airports, airlines, roads and parks, are wholly or in part owned by public authorities. As a result, governments have a stake in tourism development and promotion.

Important objectives of a national tourism marketing plan are to increase the number of foreign visitors, their length of stay and ultimately the amount of foreign exchange received by the host country. Governments cannot 'order' the future development of tourism as there are too many external factors that influence the future scale and pattern of demand. Even if these could be forecasted accurately, many independent authorities and commercial organizations make decisions which determine whether the supply of facilities is properly matched to demand.

National tourism marketing plans are in practice generally composed of two interrelated elements – research and promotion. The foundation of any marketing plan is based on solid, detailed research of a country's tourism supply – the infrastructure (food services, accommodation and transportation), attractions (manmade and natural) and other related facilities. The accurate measurement of who a nation's tourists are, their profiles, trip characteristics and expectations, are prerequisites to any successful marketing plan. In addition, a knowledge of those consumers who are not tourists and an analysis of the competition elsewhere will aid the host country in assessing its own strengths and weaknesses in the international marketplace. A structured approach to analyzing the potential and relative importance of travel markets will help in assessing the relative marketing viability of each country.

From a pragmatic point of view, the essence of any marketing plan is the promotion of accurate images of the country which both attract and inform the consumer and potential traveler. The development and promotion of accurate images is usually led by the national tourism organization but it must be supported by all the components of the industry if a clear picture is to emerge. Governments, through their national tourism offices, generally assume prime responsibility for generic promotion to expand the size of the overall market. The government's efforts enhance the impact of the promotion undertaken by the private sector on an individual service or product basis.

A successful tourism marketing plan requires coordination and integration among the different levels of government and the private sector. While governments may help international tourism by providing a fertile environment for development, it is the private sector which is the driving force of the industry. The industry is comprised of a large number of organizations, both big and small, providing a multitude of goods and services. The nature of the industry almost dictates that governments lead the cooperative efforts among the numerous competitive but complementary service components.

Since the overall growth in international tourism has declined during the 1980s, marketing has become that much more important. Countries are no longer able to rely on the overall growth of international tourism to maintain their respective market shares. With more and more countries regarding international tourism as an important economic tool, the marketplace is becoming increasingly competitive as more countries become involved.

Assessment (of international tourism marketing)

An integral part of any marketing strategy consists of methods to measure the effectiveness of the promotional programs. Unless some program evaluation is made, no measure of effectiveness can be accomplished. Ineffective programs must be eliminated and productive ones strengthened and enlarged. This is only possible when a systematic evaluation is conducted to see what kinds of promotional schemes have the best pay-off. Pre-tests and post-tests should be conducted in order to measure the impact of the promotional campaigns and the evolution of the images.

Since international travel plans are made months in advance, any promotional strategy must be given time to influence the marketplace. Generally, a program should be continued for 2–3 years to give the travel publicity investment time to earn travel income dividends. In addition, it must be recognized that a country's marketing strategies are not being received by the consumers in isolation. Therefore, external factors must be recognized in the evaluation of the success or failure of a particular marketing strategy.

Focus on small business

Small businesses, like national tourism offices, must begin by researching their present customers and comparing their analysis to those of their competition and to the regional level. This exercise will help to determine the strengths and weaknesses of the current market and identify areas of potential growth, subject to the appropriate marketing strategies. In addition, operators must work together at the local and regional level to ensure a maximum return for every dollar spent, without duplication of effort.

There are many ways small businesses can be involved in international tourism marketing. Businesses can increase their level of exposure by listing in government sponsored industry or regional guide books. By pooling financial resources in a consortium, individual enterprises may be able to afford to advertise in expensive overseas markets. All businesses can obtain and benefit from the research completed by national tourism offices as a base for their own marketing strategies. Finally, small businesses can influence all levels of governments by being active in their respective industry or trade associations.

Further reading

Armstrong, C. W. G., 'International tourism: coming and going – the methodological problems of forecasting' *Futures*, vol. 4, no. 2 (June

1972). An early attempt to model statistically international tourist flows. However, limitations with the data prohibited any departure from the relatively straightforward classical econometric type.

British Tourist Authority, *Strategy for Growth, 1984–1988* (BTA, 1984). The document provides guidelines for a marketing plan for the United Kingdom.

Buckley, P. J. and Papadopoulos, S. I., 'Marketing Greek tourism – the planning process', *Tourism Management*, vol. 7, no. 2 (June, 1986). An examination of the tourism-marketing process including a tourist profile and a marketing audit of Greece.

Harris, G. and Katz, K. M., *Promoting International Tourism* (The American Group, 1986). The book is designed to help a country (state, region) attract foreign tourists. Chapters such as Defining the Product, Inventorying the Resources, Analyzing the Marketplace and Developing Promotional Material give a step by step, itemized/listing approach to the subject matters under discussion.

Schmoll, G. A., *Tourism Promotion* (Tourism International Press, 1977). Chapter 2 deals with the role of national tourism organizations in terms of marketing – why they are involved, their research requirements and promotion effectiveness measurements and criteria.

Tourism Canada, *1986 Marketing Plan* (TC, 1986). A strategic international tourism marketing plan for Canada within the United States and all other countries.

Travel Association of America, *Competitiveness in the International Tourism Market* (TAA, 1984). An international tourism marketing plan for the United States.

Wahab, S., *Tourism Management* (Tourism International Press, 1975). Chapter 9 deals with tourism marketing while chapter 11 documents the role and structure of national tourism organizations. Four case histories (France, Italy, the United Kingdom and Switzerland) are included.

Wahab, S., Crampon, L. J. and Rothfield, L. M., *Tourism Marketing* (Tourism International Press, 1976). Chapter 11 deals with the marketing activities of national tourist organizations.

Williams, A.V. and Zelinsky, W., 'On some patterns in international tourist flows', *Economic Geography*, no. 46 (October 1970). A pioneering work that attempted to explain the pattern of flows among a selected group of countries which dominate the international tourist flows.

Wood, M., *Tourist Marketing for Small Business* (English Tourist Board, 1980). Short guide on how a small business can maximize its marketing potential through improved marketing techniques and existing industry and government organizations.

Wynegar, D., 'Estimating the potential of international markets', *Travel, Tourism and Hospitality Research*, J. R. B. Ritchie and C. R. Goeldner, eds (John Wiley, 1987). A model is developed which utilizes a weighted indexing system for evaluating the cumulative significance of pertinent variables for the countries under study and provides decision makers with an indication of the relative marketing viability of each country.

J. GERALD BAILIE

Managing tourist information

Introduction

Hospitality is one of the three major industries of tourism which accounts for a major proportion of the direct spending by tourists in the destination area. The location of the hospitality outlets must, of necessity, be where demand is clearly evident, as is the case in popular tourist destinations, and areas of high business activity. Locating suitable outlets in such areas is relatively easy, as is probably the general case with the experienced traveler. Yet is this true in all instances? Apparently not – as suggested by the wide range of information services and publications available to the tourist to facilitate finding suitable outlets.

While appropriate hospitality outlets are essential to tourists they are in many instances the last aspect of any trip to be considered. Take, for example, someone who is considering a holiday. Having decided on a destination, or the type of holiday, he/she will then visit a travel agent who will most likely offer a range of options, or packages, each invariably including accommodation. Ultimately the deciding factor as to where the client goes and where he/she stays will depend on the cost. Therefore it appears that the hospitality aspect of tourism is of lesser importance than either the destination or the cost. Undoubtedly this is not true in practice; the fact is that the presence of suitable hospitality outlets is often taken for granted. When booking package tours, for example, the need for locating hospitality outlets, at least for accommodation, is negated. However, what is the situation in those instances when a package tour is not suitable? For business trips, contacts in the destination area will be able to arrange any necessary accommodation. A knowledge of the ways in which hospitality outlets may be located therefore appears superfluous. This is not necessarily so, particularly as no account has been taken of the usefulness of being able to locate outlets that are especially appropriate to the needs of the potential customer. Such a task will invariably be facilitated if the potential customer is either at home or at his place of business where information may be more readily accessed.

In general tourists do not wish to spend their day concerned about where they are to stay the night, nor to have doubts about the quality and standards of the selected accommodation. What happens in cases where either the information is not forthcoming or a tourist is already in the destination area, for example in the case of the 'wanderlust' type of tourist, or visitors travelling without having made prior arrangements for catering and accommodation? In such instances difficulties may be encountered in locating hospitality outlets, particularly those that meet the tourists' expectations regarding price, quality, standards, and, increasingly important, whether they accept the appropriate credit card.

How then does a visitor, potential or otherwise, locate hospitality outlets and ideally gather sufficient information as to the suitability of any one outlet to meet his needs? There are a number of ways through which this may be achieved: travel agents; national and international organizations; consortia; government agencies and tourist boards; guide books. In the latter case the fact that there are a great many 'guides' indicates that there is a demand for aids to locating hospitality outlets and to gathering some information about them.

Managing tourist information may, therefore, be seen as the accessing of appropriate information to meet the needs of the traveler.

Examples

A tourist, either before departure or during his stay in any destination, can easily identify whether or not a particular hotel chain has a unit located in the area where he is visiting. The likelihood of at least one of the international or national hotel chains having a unit in the destination area is very high when one considers that some three-quarters of the hotels in the world are probably controlled, either by direct ownership, management contract or franchise by organizations based in the United States, France or the United Kingdom, e.g. Holiday Inn, Sheraton, Club Mediterranee, Novotel, Trusthouse Forte, Ladbrokes. This proportion is likely to increase with the growth of tourism and the consequent rise in the number of hotels. The number of hotel rooms worldwide has been consistently growing since the late 1940s with a marked increase in the growth rate since the 1960s boom in tourism. This has been a key factor in the development of the hotel chains arguably due to the realization of the 'eco-bubble' concept and the orientation of their marketing policies accordingly. By adopting a consistent company style regarding presentation, standards and service the large companies aim to provide a guarantee to their customers, thereby alleviating concern. Today most hotel chains have a central reservations system to facilitate reservations at any one of their units. The telephone number of the reservations office is invariably noted on their hotel brochures, and should this not be to hand then it should be obtainable either from one of the hotels, or a travel agent.

In the context of international tourism, travel agents are probably the most useful and reliable source of information regarding the identification and location of accommodation, ideally furnishing information relating to the categories of accommodation available (i.e. hotel, guest house, bed and breakfast etc.), the classification of that accommodation, and some guidance as to the charges. Further they may be able to advise about the destination area's culture, an important aspect to take into account when considering the hospitality industry in any particular area. The destination having been decided, the travel agents will normally be able to supply the necessary details about the location and access of accommodation, but probably not about other hospitality outlets. They may also be able to arrange reservations, although this will often be only for outlets in the hotel sector. In many cases they will have contracts with various groups such as international hotel companies, and are more likely to recommend these if a commission is applicable. The development of marketing consortia has helped to further the range of information the agents have at their disposal. Also broadening the information available in the hands of travel agents, and generally assisting reservations with hotels not part of large national or international chains is 'Roomwatch', a hotel room reservation guide on British Telecom's 'Prestel' service, which has been designed primarily for travel agents. Agents may use the associated 'Roomservice' system which facilitates direct reservations.

Some consideration may also be given to other types of hospitality outlets that are also part of national or international companies. It is suggested that many people are wary of entering unknown catering operations, especially if the type, or style, of operation is not clear from the outside. In realizing this we again find companies whose primary aim is to market a particular product and/or image, for example Macdonalds, Kentucky Fried Chicken, Thank God It's Friday's (TGIF's), Wimpy, and Little Chef. Franchising is usually the key to expansion in these cases. The tourist rapidly becomes familiar with the various companies and can usually be assured of his expectations being met and thus relieve any anxieties regarding finding an acceptable catering outlet. Problems arise when such an operation is not available or alternatively when an outlet of this type does not meet the requirements of the tourist.

Possibly one of the hardest instances for locating hospitality outlets is in those areas which might be described as being undeveloped for tourism. In such cases one method would be to contact the appropriate government agency with responsibility for the promotion of tourism or, where applicable, the appropriate tourist board. In the case of the United Kingdom this is relatively straightforward as there is an umbrella organization, i.e. The British Tourist Authority, and a National Tourist Board for England, Scotland, Wales, and Northern Ireland. It is interesting to note that probably the first organization to be

formed to promote international tourism was the 'Come to Britain Campaign' in the 1920s. An association was formed by some of the leading London hoteliers with the primary objective of encouraging Americans to visit London and stay in their hotels. Locating the hospitality outlets in that instance was clearly not a problem!

Today most countries have some form of organization to oversee and promote tourism, e.g. the US Travel and Tourism Administration, Tourism Canada, and the Department of Tourism in Japan. Such organizations are invariably oriented to encouraging international tourists and will often devolve the main promotional efforts to other government related organizations. In some cases international groups have been formed to facilitate tourism promotion for the whole area, e.g. Pacific Area Travel Association or the European Travel Commission. In well developed areas there will often be found local tourist boards and tourist associations, all of which can supply information about hospitality outlets. Promotional material published by these various organizations will often be available through travel agencies, and in some cases they will have their own offices in those countries which generate a substantial volume of visitor traffic. The increasing presence of such organizations leads to the suggestion that locating hospitality outlets will be greatly facilitated. In all likelihood this will be the case, although the related problems will not necessarily be resolved.

Guide books are perhaps the most useful aids available for finding information about hospitality outlets, particularly for those tourists who are touring unfamiliar areas. The best known guide books are probably seen as a source of reference solely for accommodation yet many of them will include references to other sectors of the hospitality industry. There is also an increasing number of guide books that specialize in specific types of hospitality outlets. It is as a reference to the non-accommodation sector that guide books are particularly helpful in aiding the tourist to locate, for example, catering outlets to meet their own particular requirements. In such cases reference to appropriate guides will go some way towards removing the 'chance' element.

There are basically two types of guide book, those that are predominantly collections of advertisements placed by the outlets, or those that are independent and provide in addition to the more general information, some analysis of the services available. The first category is by far the most numerous and includes, for example, *Signpost*, and many of the publications produced by tourist boards, e.g. *Let's Go* by the English Tourist Board, and *The Best Getaway* by the Scottish Tourist Board. At an international level American Express and Diners Club both produce a guide to all those hospitality outlets that enter into a trade agreement with their companies. Another example is the *A–Z Worldwide Hotel Guide* which is very commercially oriented and claims to include all known hotels. (Further examples are noted at the end of the chapter.) The second category of guide books, i.e. the independent guides, may be split into those that only provide limited data and those which include some critical analysis of the outlets mentioned. The latter type are arguably the most useful. Examples of the first type are the Automobile Association's Hotels and Restaurants in Britain, and the RAC Guide and Handbook (further examples are provided at the end). Two organizations particularly renowned for guides which include some critical analysis are, at an international level, 'Michelin', and mainly at the national level in the case of the United Kingdom, the Consumers' Association. Michelin guides provide comprehensive and detailed information on each hotel mentioned. The Consumers' Association produces a range of guides, for example, the *Good Hotel Guide: Britain and Western Europe*, which is particularly useful, providing information on outlets in less well known areas. The Consumers' Association also serves to illustrate the increasing range of guides available in that they also produce the *Budget Good Food Guide*, the *Good Pub Guide*, and the *Good Wine Bar Guide*.

Assessment and conclusion

Centralized reservation systems save time, effort and costs through quick and accurate reservations. There are disadvantages, however, in that the customer may not be able to gain full details about the accommodation; nor is he guaranteed that the central office will be able to provide information regarding actually locating the unit once he is in the area, or of traveling times and distances between the hotel and, for example, airports or rail stations. With regard to the information available from travel agents customers should be cognisant of the fact that such agencies charge commission on their sales and thus it is probable that the hotels represented are generally higher priced. Small hotels that might be more the type the customer is seeking are less likely to be located through agencies.

While there appears to be a plethora of information available through either travel agents or by contacting the large hotel companies, tourists may find little particularly useful information when visiting rural and less developed areas. In such instances tourist organizations are probably the most useful of the examples discussed. Information centers would appear to be particularly helpful as a source of information and advice, although the visitor could encounter problems in that the information available may be very basic and a poor guide as to the suitability of any of the accommodation referenced. A further factor to take into consideration is that the visitor may arrive in the locality at a time when these centers are closed, perhaps due to the hour or because it is off-season. The unprepared tourist is then left with few options.

The final example we looked at was that of guide books and their particular advantages are to be found when one is seeking to gain some detail about the type of the establishment, and further in locating hospitality outlets in unfamiliar areas. However there are drawbacks to guide books, not least because there are so many on the market. The majority are mainly a collection of advertisements for the various outlets included, providing little information beyond basic data such as category, classification, and an indication of cost. The principle that tourists generally like to have some degree of confidence in the outlets they are about to use is an aspect which many guides fail to deal with, a criticism also applicable to information often provided by tourist information centers. Classification schemes, to some extent, do alleviate concern but care should be exercised in placing too much emphasis on such schemes as the bias to different aspects may vary, with the main attention being given to the basic facilitites, indicating little about the overall quality and standards of service.

The more information there is available, the more discerning the tourist can be, and thus more indepth information is required. This, however, still may not resolve problems that could arise in locating suitable hospitality outlets in the less popular and less populated areas.

Focus on small business

Increasingly, centralized reservation systems are being set up for small businesses, e.g. small hotel groups and individual hotels who are not in a position to have their own exclusive system. They may be included in the Roomwatch and Roomservice systems used by travel agents. They may also use a hotel representative agency, e.g. Utell International, and R.M. Brooker. However this is unlikely as the commissions charged by such agencies may make them a nonviable opportunity. Perhaps the most useful method for informing a wider audience is through a consortium, e.g. Consort Hotels, a grouping of independent hotels with connections throughout the world. (Further examples are listed at the end of the chapter.) The advantages of such schemes are clear: for example, enabling any one hotel to reach a wider audience and in reducing costs. A consortium may also decide to promote a particular style of hotel, for instance the Prestige Group of Hotels which aims to promote hotels with a high reputation. The growth in the number of consortia is a boon for locating hospitality establishments that are 'off the beaten track', or in those cases when the tourist wishes to find a more individual style of hotel.

At the more regional and particularly at local levels information about small businesses is probably to be gained to the greatest extent through tourist information centers. These centers will either be run by the regional or area tourist board, or by the local authority. Normally the center will be able to provide information about all types of hospitality outlets and, further, they may operate a system providing information about the availability of accommodation. These centers can certainly help to avoid the possible 'chance' element that is present if, when touring for example, one accepts the first hospitality outlet that appears which offers the required services.

Consortia

Best Western, Vine House, 143 London Road, Kingston on Thames, Surrey KT2 6NA, UK.
Consort Hotels, Ryedale Building, Piccadilly, York YO1 1PN, UK.
Golden Tulip Hotels, c/o Times Life Buildings, New Bond Street, London W1Y 0AD, UK.
Transchannel Consort, 24 Rue De St Quentin, 75010 Paris, France.
Hotel and Travel Service, Friedrichstrasse 32, 6000 Frankfurt-am-Main, FRG.

Intelco, Sagasta 22-5-15, 28004 Madrid, Spain.

International Leading Association, 26/6 Schuttersvest, B-2800 Mechelen, Belgium.

Leading Hotels of the World, 15 New Bridge Street, London EC4V 6AU, UK.

Pan Travel, 5 Via Lambertenghi, PO Box 3208, 6900 Lugano, Switzerland.

Relais et Chateaux, Hotel du Crillon, 10 Place de la Concorde, 15008 Paris, France.

Selective Hotel Reservations, 19 West 34th Street, Suite 700, New York NY 10001, USA.

Guide books

Ashley Courtenay's Hotel Guide, *Let's Halt Awhile*, published by Macdonald. Correspondence to Ashley Courtney Ltd, 16 Little London, Chichester, West Sussex PO19 1PA, UK.

Britain: Hotels and Restaurants, published by the British Tourist Authority.

British Hotels and Restaurants, published by the British Hotels, Restaurants and Caterers Association.

BTA Commended Guide, published by the British Tourist Authority. Note: A highly recommended guide for locating attractive country hotels.

Classic Country Pubs: a CAMRA guide published by Guild, London, UK.

Egon Ronay's *Guinness Pub Guide* published by Egon Ronay Organization Ltd, Greencoat House, Francis Street, London, UK.

Good Value Guide in Britain, published by Routiers (Britain and Commonwealth) Ltd, 354 Fulham Road, London SW10 9UH, UK.

International Hotel Guide, published by the International Hotel Association, 80 Rue de la Roquette, 75011 Paris, France.

The Small Hotel Guide, edited by C. Gill and published by Macmillan.

The Financial Times World Hotel Directory, published by Longman. A very extensive reference guide containing a great deal of useful, and highly relevant information.

DAVID LESLIE

Market analysis

Introduction

Analysis is part of a process that organizations engage in to detect opportunities and threats in the market. Based on the analysis of a market companies may decide to respond or not to respond.

Market or demand analysis consists of four steps:

1. Identifying a market. One fundamental concept underlying demand analysis is that a market for a product or service is actually a composite of smaller markets, each with identifiable characteristics. The travel market can be considered as a large market composed of smaller submarkets or segments. The purpose of the trip different customers intend to take could be used to identify at least three submarkets or segments: commercial, pleasure, and convention/meeting. This process of breaking the heterogeneous market into homogeneous parts is usually called market segmentation. The basic premise is that consumers in one segment are different from the consumers in another segment, and so each group represents a separate entity.

   Market segmentation is based on the reality that markets are too complex and diverse to consider all consumers within the market as homogeneous. If a new product or service is to appeal to 'frequent travelers', for example, then that segment or part of the total commercial travel market between 25–44 age group, is the market of interest. In order to save time and money, only the identified segment's size and characteristics should be studied, rather than those of other segments which are not included.

2. Identifying market factors. Market factors are those realities that 'drive demand' for a product. For example, an important factor for foodservice is population increase/decrease each year. Since a market consists of people with needs, wants, money, and motivation to buy, population and additional demographic factors such as 'mobility', sex, income, are commonly used as market factors.

   It is usually possible to be specific in identifying market factors for a given organization, product, or service. The interest in identifying market factors is threefold:
   (a) to identify the factors that influence the demand for the product/service;
   (b) to determine the relationship between the factors and the product or service;

(c) and to forecast those market factors for future years. Since many of the same market factors are used by different forecasters, much of the forecasts may have already been completed and simply need to be located.

3. Estimating market potential. Once the characteristics of demand factors in the market, in conjunction with its various segments have been analyzed, the next step is to estimate the size of the market. The term market potential is used to refer to expected sales of a product or service for an entire market. Put in a different way, if everybody who could buy would buy, how many units or dollars worth of sales would occur? The answer to that question is the market potential which exists for a product/service.

   Market potential is a quantitative measure of a market's capacity to consume a product in a given time period. This measure is a prerequisite to assessing profitability.

4. Estimating the revenues anticipated from a given venture. Although estimating potential revenues is extremely difficult, it should be done to prepare, for example, the pro forma income statement.

Examples

The Marriott Corporation utilized market analysis successfully in the product development process of its newly created Courtyard concept. The Washington DC-based company realized through its analysis that the US lodging market had become saturated and extremely competitive, especially in urban markets. Management understood that in order to expand successfully in suburban and secondary sites, the corporation had to come up with an appropriate lodging 'formula'. Segmentation studies combined with market analysis, in particular focus group interviews, revealed two potential target markets: 'security seekers' and 'functional roomers'. Rather than confirming Marriott management beliefs, the research results were a complete surprise.

The threat of terrorism, the dollar's depreciation, and concerns about radiation from Chernobyl have been blamed for cutting American tourism to Europe in 1986. Take for example, Lucerne, the Swiss city that draws a great number of American tourists. The director of Lucerne's tourism office estimated losses at $60 million. This turned out to be no exaggeration. Lucerne dropped from 271,000 American visitors in 1985 to 116,000 American visitors in 1986. This represents a 26 per cent drop in tourism to the lakeside city where Americans normally constitute half of the visitors.

Benefits

Perhaps the most important research task in the hotel industry is to analyze the area's sources of demand for transient accommodation. In this analysis, one must typically: 1. quantify total demand by source and type, 2. establish the subject hotel's share of total demand by type, and 3. make judgements about trends or shifts in area demand that may affect occupancy in both the short and long term.

The major advantage of market analysis is that it can provide hoteliers with an insight of the limits within which their hotels must compete. Specifically, lodging market analysis gives operators an opportunity to assess the present demand for lodging and other revenue generators, and forces them to identify the existing supply of competitive properties and their probable growth. The demand for transient accommodation is typically measured in room nights. It is essential to quantify demand in terms of room nights, identify the generators responsible for demand, and specify demand by segment.

Within the context of total travel volume, many factors influence lodging demand. The consumer's lodging choice is affected by the means and cost of transportation available, the difficulties of travel, the availability of alternative forms of entertainment or communication, and a host of other variables ranging from the weather to a personal decision to stay home this year. Once the consumer decides to travel, where to go, how to get there, how long to stay, and what type of accommodation to take, there is still the final choice of a specific hotel.

The largest segment, the pleasure travel market, comprises persons taking both the typical one- or two-week vacations and those on shorter weekend trips. About 80 per cent of all US residents travel for pleasure each year, taking an average of two vacation trips. The predominant form of transportation is the family car; air travel ranks a distant second. Roughly 60 per cent of all pleasure trips are weekend trips, but the substantial number of longer trips brings the average length of a pleasure trip from six to seven nights.

Pleasure travelers are more prone than other travelers to share rooms or avoid hotels altogether. About 20 per cent of nights spent away from home are spent with friends or relatives and 15 per cent use camping facilities. Hence, while they account for almost 80 per cent of all travelers and 65 per cent of nights spent away from home, pleasure travelers account for only about 40 per cent of the lodging room nights sold each year in the United States.

The pleasure market is the most price-sensitive of all the travel industry's market segments and easily affected by economic conditions. Furthermore, the travel industry faces great competition from other industries, especially the entertainment industry, for both the consumer's leisure time and discretionary income. In addition, factors such as fuel shortages, transportation worker's strikes and poor weather may have dire effects on the discretionary travel decision.

Business travel embraces trips to attend corporate gatherings to make commercial sales visits, and so on. Business travelers are important to the lodging industry, because they are more likely to stay in a hotel room than other travelers and less likely to share the room. The business market accounts for 45 per cent of the room nights sold each year in the United States, making it the single most important of the lodging market segments.

Although the largest portion of US business-oriented lodging demand stems from travelers who are visiting clients (26 per cent), the travelers associated with meetings and conventions (3 per cent of total demand) are more important than their numbers indicate, since meetings and conventions result in considerable sums spent on banquet and meeting rooms' facilities, guest rooms, and food service, and in some cases such traffic can be scheduled to occupy a hotel during shoulder-season periods.

Personal travel includes jobseeking trips, funeral attendance, and other nonbusiness travel. It may be a minor part, but is a stable portion of the total travel market, accounting for perhaps 8 per cent of US lodging demand. Personal travel is often necessary and usually at the individual's expense. Despite its stability, therefore, personal travel is marked by price-sensitivity. People will travel on personal business even in difficult times, but they will probably seek economical transportation and lodging. Incentive travel is used as a motivational device whereby a company rewards salespeople, dealers, distributors, and employees who meet or exceed sales objectives.

Implementation

The overall objective of market analysis is to establish the relative market position of a given organization *vis-à-vis* the competition in a particular industry. Competition may be defined as those organizations which produce goods or services of a like function and nature seeking to serve the same market(s) as the subject firm.

In order to conduct an effective analysis one has to evaluate one's product, market, and competition on a number of variables. The following relates to the lodging industry, but may be applied to other tourism facilities.

Product

1. Location (city center, suburban, airport, highway).
2. Classification (commercial, conference, resort).
3. Operating status (independent, chain, franchise).
4. Guest composition (commercial, tourist, group, independent).
5. Facilities (guest rooms, meeting rooms, restaurants).
6. Rates (single, double, suites, by season [dates]).
7. Reservation system and representation ('800' number).

Market

1. Hotel was developed for what primary markets (e.g. business and conference)?
2. Present major market as percentage of total room sales:
   (a) transient;
   (b) corporate group meetings;
   (c) convention;
   (d) family travel.
3. Present minimarkets:
   (a) medical;
   (b) sports;
   (c) military.
4. Available but undeveloped markets:
   (a) educational;
   (b) senior citizens.
5. Market demographics of subject hotel:
   (a) sex;
   (b) age;
   (c) marital status;
   (d) income;
   (e) education;
   (f) occupation;
   (g) residence.

Competition

Identifying the competition is an important task. The same items presented under 'Product' and 'Market' should be used to analyze principal competitors. Information should be verified in every detail, for example by visiting, inspecting, checking, and if possible measuring competitive facilities. Comparing results of the research conducted should provide an operator insight into his organization's strengths *vis-à-vis* the competition.

In order to formulate an effective marketing plan, the hotel operator should develop a profile of guests to identify market segments, travel patterns, and responses to products and services offered. The questions that should be posed by a hotel operator include:

1. Who visits the hotel (general profile)?
2. Where do present guests come from?
3. What are the business reasons, attractions or other interests that bring travelers to our hotel?
4. What type of accommodation do guests request most often (single/double/conference rooms)?
5. What is the average length of stay?
6. How much do guests spend during their stay and in what departments (lounge/coffee shop/restaurant)?

Assessment

As the tourism industry has entered the mature phase of its life cycle, its business environment has become more competitive, complex, and characterized by change. More often than ever before, managers have to come up with quick solutions despite the constraints and conflicts the market imposes on them.

Effective decision making and market analysis are based on accurate information systems and databases. Observation indicates that in the tourism industry, information systems often lag behind new developments and techniques. In an uncertain business environment, most travel industry companies appear to lack the appropriate management information systems to produce the reports that are desired by management.

In terms of lodging market analysis, the data required to support enhanced marketing efforts can be broken down in two main areas: information about current and past guests, and information about target groups of possible future guests. This information comes from a combination of internal and external sources. The internal sources derive primarily from 'front-of-the-house' databases. The external sources of data range from automated reservation systems to independent market surveys. Currently, it appears, that management information systems are inadequate to produce the information desired by management, especially in the marketing area. In marketing lodging facilities, it is important to understand that all analysis is based on information. The more accurate, reliable, and concise the information is, the more effectively management will be able to analyze and market their properties to travelers the world over.

Conclusion

Market analysis is an important component in the marketing process, which includes measuring market size, identifying trends, and forecasting revenues from a particular venture. Typically, analysis would be used to detect market opportunities and threats. Decisions by management are usually based on market analysis.

In marketing travel-related products, abroad or domestically, it is essential to realize that decision makers have a common need – INFORMATION which is concise, up-to-date, reliable, and accurate – in order to analyze the marketplace effectively.

Focus on small business

The marketing function in smaller operations in the tourist industry is often overlooked, because owners/managers are concerned with other functions, especially operations. However, in an increasingly competitive business environment, small business in particular should analyze its market situation *vis-à-vis* the chain operations and other 'independents'. Experience shows that when marketing is applied by small business operators, modifications are typically made in the manner in which the establishment operates. In addition, the financial results often improve as a result. Small business operators should analyze from time to time several factors, which directly and indirectly influence business results: consumer perceptions, industry trends, competition, and government.

Numerous factors contribute to the failure of many small

businesses, including inconsistent service, poor marketing execution, and lack of analysis. Successful companies are usually engaged in planning and analysis, never losing sight of their objective. Small business operators must watch not to become overly concerned with day-to-day concerns, so that they fail to see the overall picture. Small business operators must be aware of trends, so that when the competitive environment changes, they are prepared for it.

Further reading

Cooke, B., 'Analyzing markets for services' *Handbook of Modern Marketing*, V. P. Buell, ed. (McGraw-Hill, 1970).

Daltas, A. J., 'Protecting service markets with consumer feedback', *Cornell HRA Quarterly*, vol. 18 (May 1971), pp. 73–7.

Frechtling, D. C., 'Five issues in tourism marketing in the 1990s', *Tourism Management*, vol. 8, no. 2 (June 1987), pp. 177–8.

Jarvis, L. P. and Mayo, E. J., 'Winning the market-share game', *Cornell HRA Quarterly*, vol. 27 (November 1986), pp. 73–9.

Morrision, A. M., 'Selling the USA, tourism promotion by the States', *Travel & Tourism Analyst* (The Economist Publications Ltd., April 1987), pp. 3–18.

Reid, R. D., '*Foodservice and Restaurant Marketing*' (CBI Publishing Co., 1983).

Yesawich, P. C., 'Hospitality marketing for the '90's: effective marketing research', *Cornell Quarterly*, vol. 28 (May 1987), pp. 49–57.

FRANK GO

Market penetration

Introduction

In marketing, market penetration has two meanings. First, it is used as a measure of the effectiveness of a marketing program. In this context, the penetration rate is the ratio of users generated to total target market potential. The penetration rate for a specific company in the tourism industry is the proportion of all potential tourists in a specific target market that the company has been able to capture. For example, if an airline defines one of its target markets as families interested in comfort and luxury, it would determine its penetration rate for this target market by comparing sales of its first-class tickets to families relative to estimates of potential industry sales of first-class tickets to all families.

The second meaning of market penetration is in the context of a marketing strategy. As a strategy for growth, market penetration describes efforts to expand sales and/or market share among current products/services in existing target markets. A market penetration strategy is one of four generally recognized growth strategies. The others are: market development (growth through targeting new markets or segments of the tourist market), product development (modifying existing products or developing new products for existing customers), and diversification (targeting new markets with modified or new products).

Greater market penetration can be achieved by increasing usage or loyalty among existing users, by attracting competitors' users, or by convincing nonusers in the targeted market segment(s) to try the product/service.

In the early stages of a product or service life, market penetration can be achieved by preemptive techniques such as penetration pricing. In later stages, greater penetration is usually achieved through intensifying or more effectively utilizing elements of the marketing mix – product, price, promotion, and distribution. Market penetration is a low cost – low risk strategy compared to the other growth strategies. However, it can be a difficult means of achieving modest gains in the marketplace, particularly in mature segments of the tourist market.

Examples

The US Travel and Tourism Administration (USTTA) conducts continual seminars throughout the country designed to help organizations successfully penetrate foreign markets at reasonable costs. Seminar topics include marketing research, promotional activities, formulation of plans for overseas marketing efforts, and methods for implementing programs. These efforts have helped to reverse the decline of foreign visitors to the US that occurred during the first half of the 1980s.

St Louis, Chicago, and Indianapolis were successful in increasing their share of the regional tourist market by combining forces to run a cooperative advertising program promoting their Midwest cities. One objective of the promotions was to increase weekend trips to the cities. Extensive advertising inserts were developed for newspapers in each city. The marketing package also included special weekend prices and promotions such as discount meals, complimentary gifts, and free local attraction tickets. One result of the program was a 200 per cent increase in inquiries and an increase in billings for St Louis between 1985 and 1986.

One of the clearest examples of linking a specific marketing tactic – pricing – with increased market penetration objectives can be found in the airline industry. Since deregulation in the United States, airlines have discovered the power of the pricing variable to affect market share rates between specific pairs of cities. The result has been tremendous pricing variability designed to achieve specific objectives relative to different segments of the travel market.

Benefits

In order to implement a market penetration strategy, careful analysis of the consumers' decision process regarding selecting among alternatives is necessary. This analysis must be done for specific market segments. One benefit of the analysis is greater understanding of what product/service attributes are important to each segment. A better understanding of how to approach the consumer should also emerge.

Many of the benefits of market penetration relate to the concepts of organization size and market domination. Some of the advantages of a large share of a market are: it acts as a buffer during downturns in the economy, when tourists might rely on larger, better known, more reliable airlines, hotels etc.; it portrays a positive image to tourists which helps build long-term loyalty; and it provides a base of power from which to deal with suppliers, travel agents, tourist groups etc.

Size is dependent upon market served. Even a small firm can use market penetration to help build a share in fewer, more narrowly defined markets. This concentration on increasing share in one or a few markets provides a firm specializing in tourist products/services with the same advantages that accrue to larger firms targeting more market segments.

A final benefit is in program evaluation. Market penetration requires precise delineation of markets and objectives. Monitoring of results allows for a determination of whether penetration tactics are successful.

Implementation

Market penetration emphasizes more effective and efficient utilization of marketing tactics. Increased penetration can be achieved by: increasing the level or intensity of marketing efforts (e.g. increase the advertising or promotions budget), improving the utilization of tactics (e.g. maintaining the existing advertising budget but increasing efficiency by better placement of advertisements in tourist-related media), or some combination of both.

Strategies for achieving market penetration fall into two categories – those designed to increase usage or loyalty among existing customers and those designed to attract competitors' customers or nonusers. Increasing usage among current customers can be achieved by increasing the frequency of use (e.g. frequent flyer programs), increasing the amount used (e.g. extending the average stay of a hotel guest), developing new attractions or services for current users (e.g. adding children's programs to a resort package), or some combination of the above. Techniques to support these strategies include, but are not limited to: pricing to encourage off-peak usage; bundling services to achieve greater overall facility utilization; adding attractions or services; and modifying promotional efforts to encourage expanded utilization of facilities, longer stays etc.

Attempts to attract competitors' customers generally are more risky than attempts to increase usage of existing customers. They are likely to result in competitive retaliation. Short-term gains can be achieved through promotions, discounts, and aggressive advertising programs. Longer-term gains at the expense of competitors have to be based on something more substantial – a lasting competitive advantage that cannot be easily duplicated.

A penetration strategy can be solidified by discouraging competitors from entering the market. One technique to achieve this, common in the airline industry, is penetration pricing, which is setting a relatively low price level. The low price tends to yield lower gross margins, but builds share quickly and gives the firm a cost advantage built on volume and capacity utilization. The combination of low margins and an aggressive market leader developing experience and volume advantages creates a market less attractive to potential entrants. Other preemptive strategies include offering customers such a complete tourist attraction that there is no unique opportunity for competitors to exploit, offering quality services, and utilizing intensive advertising. In general, anything that helps build a positive distinctive image is useful to building and defending market share.

Market penetration is usually more difficult to achieve when a tourist industry has reached maturity. Competitors are entrenched and will fight to maintain market shares. Brand loyalty patterns are established. The market is not expanding rapidly. While share gains are possible under these conditions, the efficiency of such achievements must be closely monitored.

Assessment

The value of market penetration as a strategy rests on the proposition that increased market share and increased profitability are positively related. There is empirical evidence to support this relationship. Others, however, have suggested that the relationship between market share and profitability is not that clear – they are both achieved simultaneously because of a third factor, superior overall management of the firm.

Much of the success of a market penetration strategy is dependent on the ability to create a differential advantage. The organization must be able to develop a distinctiveness that translates into increased usage from existing customers, competitors' customers, or nonusers in the target market.

Under what conditions is a strategy of market penetration appropriate?

1. When a positive image, which usually accompanies increased market share, is a significant factor in achieving long-term market success.
2. In the early stages of a tourist industry's life, when the market is volatile and share gains require less investment.
3. When the firm has significant marketing management skills relative to those of competitors.
4. When there is a unique competitive advantage (such as superior physical facilities at a ski resort or when an airline has greater maintenance facilities) upon which to build.
5. When the competitive situation is appropriate; it is harder to succeed with market penetration when competitors vigorously defend their market position.

Longer-term consequences of employing a market penetration strategy also need to be considered. What are the risks involved if the program is unsuccessful? Would the resources allocated to a program of market penetration be more effectively used in product/service development or in going after new segments of the market? Are there any possible regulatory consequences in increasing market share? Will increases in market share have any lasting impact on profitability and market position?

Finally, specific measures must be developed to determine the results achieved from a program of market penetration. Specific measures are:

1. The percentage increase in sales achieved by an organization in a specific target market relative to the percentage increase in that target market's growth. This will determine whether sales or revenue increases are coming from an expanding market or from more effective performance.
2. Revenues generated from the organization's target market relative to the total potential revenues from that target market. Changes in this ratio over time, market share gains or

losses, are the 'bottom-line' determinant of success or failure of a market penetration program.

3. Brand loyalty rates. This is an indirect measure of market penetration that, if increasing, should lead to share improvements in the long term.

4. Product/service usage rates relative to capacity. This helps determine whether specific objectives established for the penetration program are being achieved.

Conclusion

Market penetration is an important strategic alternative for firms in the tourism industry. It is the fastest way to achieve gains in facility utilization. Also, it can be employed by all tourist-related organizations regardless of size. Implementation of a program to achieve greater market penetration 'forces' the organization to establish specific objectives, clearly define target markets, carefully evaluate the relative effectiveness of possible marketing tactics, and systematically measure marketplace results.

There are two primary risks in pursuing market penetration. The first is the opportunity cost of not pursuing other strategies that may yield greater returns in the long term. The second involves possible inefficiencies. Share gains may be achieved at a cost that outweighs benefits. For example, increasing advertising intensity may yield increased market share that is not economically justified given the added advertising costs.

Focus on small business

For the small organization in the tourism industry, market penetration is probably the most important strategy available. Alternatives such as market and/or product/service development require capital and resources the small business may not have access to. Successful market penetration, on the other hand, relies on more effective and efficient utilization of whatever resources are available.

There are many ways for a small organization to succeed with market penetration. They include: more customization of products and services to meet the needs of the target market, more direct promotional efforts, concentrating on serving the needs of a few key customers more thoroughly, and providing a more intimate and personal relationship with customers. Overall, the most critical element is to have a clearly defined business with a distinctive image serving the needs of a specific market. Do not try to be all things to all possible consumers.

Further reading

Aaker, D. A., *Strategic Market Management* (John Wiley, 1984), pp. 232–6. A good discussion of techniques for achieving market penetration.

Ansoff, H. I., 'Strategies for diversification', *Harvard Business Review* (September/October 1957), pp. 113–24. Discusses a framework of alternative strategies for achieving intensive growth. Market penetration is discussed.

Beik, L. and Buxby, S. L., 'Profitability analysis by market segment', *Journal of Marketing* (July 1973), pp. 48–53. Describes methods for allocating marketing costs to specific market segments. Has implications for measuring the efficiency of market penetration programs.

Buzzell, R. D. and Wiersema, F. D., 'Successful share building strategies', *Harvard Business Review* (January/February 1981), pp. 135–44. Discusses factors leading to success in gainng market share.

Day, G. S., 'A strategic perspective on product planning', *Journal of Contemporary Business* (Spring 1975), pp. 1–34. Strategies for growth, including market penetration, are presented. Summarizes the advantages and disadvantages of pursuing a strategy of building market share.

Fogg, C. D., 'Planning gains in market share', *Journal of Marketing* (July 1974), pp. 30–38. Identifies and explains techniques for increasing market share and the internal processes to develop and implement strategies for market share gains.

Hodgson, A., 'The concept of strategy within the travel industry', *The Travel and Tourism Industry, Strategies for the Future*, A. Hodgson, ed. (Pergamon Press, 1987). A summary chapter outlining some of the major issues in strategy formulation and presenting a model of the intraorganizational planning process.

Jarvis, L. P. and Mayo, E. J. 'Repeat guests: a loyal base or transient customers?', *Tourism Services Marketing: Advances in Theory and Practice*, W. B. Joseph, L. Moutinho and I. R. Vernon, eds (Academy of Marketing Science and Dept. Marketing Cleveland State University, 1986), pp. 119–28. Discuss the strategies for defending market share positions in the lodging industry. Also identifies strategies for achieving and maintaining user loyalty.

Lovelock, C. H., *Services Marketing* (Prentice Hall, 1984). Many of the chapters, written by separate authors, provide insight useful in formulating strategies in service industries. Also, cases in the ski resort, airline and hotel industries are provided.

McDaniel, C. D. and Jarboe, G. R., 'A study of attitudes and print media preferences of weekend guests staying at hotels/motels in Centerport', *Tourism Services Marketing: Advances in Theory and Practice*, W. B. Joseph, L. Moutinho and I. R. Vernon, eds (Academy of Marketing Science and Dept. Marketing Cleveland State University, 1986), pp. 249–59. Describes the research conducted to determine consumer attitudes and behavior relative to weekend use of motels and hotels in a specific city. Also describes methods used to evaluate a promotional program with specific objectives.

McIntosh, R. W., *Tourism, Principles, Practices, Philosphies* (Grid, 1972). Chapters 10 and 11 describe techniques for measuring and increasing tourism demand through marketing.

Meidan, A., 'Marketing strategies for tourism,' *Tourism Services Marketing: Advances in Theory and Practice*, W. B. Joseph, L. Moutinho and I. R. Vernon, eds (Academy of Marketing Science and Dept. Marketing Cleveland State University, 1986), pp. 294–309. Relates market penetration to the tourism industry. Comparisons are made with other strategies such as market and product development.

US Travel and Tourism Administration, *Developing a US Regional Approach for Promoting Travel From Foreign Markets* (USTTA, 1985). Provides information on how to organize for and promote in order to achieve increases in tourism from overseas markets.

Weber, J. A., 'Market structure profile analysis and strategic growth opportunities', *California Management Review* (Fall, 1977), pp. 34–46. Methods for analyzing strategies, including the concept of Market Structure Profile Gaps, are discussed. Many of the Profile Gaps relate to the effectiveness of market penetration efforts.

RONALD L. ZALLOCCO

Market targeting

Tourist market targeting is the process of aiming a company's, or public authority's, marketing efforts to identified groups of potential tourists who are accessible to the company or authority in terms both of promotional media and of product design. Market targeting should be an integral part of producing the marketing part of a company's business plan, namely the identification of what sales and marketing position the company currently holds, what it believes it can achieve, the steps to be taken to achieve its aims, and where the company considers it will be placed in the future market. The company's effectiveness depends in this area on both its ability to define markets and on its skill in producing products or services which the identified groups of tourists see as providing sufficient added benefit to buy. In this sense target marketing applies both to situations which are market-led (those situations where a product is designed for a predefined market) and to those which are product-led (situations in which an existing product is found a new market). It should be emphasized that target marketing is not equated with promotion, but rather that successful promotions of products or services are dependent on the adequate definition of markets, their targeting and associated product design.

Critical to target marketing is the identification of groups of potential customers, or market segments, from among the heterogeneous population of tourists, who have varying tastes, expectations and abilities to pay. Successful market segmentation depends on identifying groups of consumers who are accessible by media and whose tastes, expectations and abilities to pay can be met by product designers. To be of use, therefore, market segmentation must select like consumers by attributes which can relate directly both to media and products. Tourist market segmentation commonly takes several forms, which in practice are intermixed. These segmentations include geographical location, demographic or social attributes, psychological attributes, past purchasing or trip making decisions, benefits gained, affinity through ancestral links (for North Americans, in particular, making European holidays), media exposure, usage rates and price sensitivity. Once identified, the market segments need to be assessed for their size in terms of population, their value, their level of demand for different products, the levels of likely growth or decline in size and demand,

and the degree of present and likely future competition in meeting these demands. It should be recognized in such assessments that products frequently have 'life cycles' in terms of their rate of demand, and that consequently market segments may change in importance during this cycle.

Examples

Market targeting has been used, for example, by the Wales Tourist Board in the promotion of Wales as a holiday destination, and in the promotion of the Swansea marina, the focal point of the dockland redevelopment as the Maritime Area in central Swansea. In 1984 the Wales Tourist Board began an extended program of market research to help pinpoint more clearly the needs of existing and potential visitors, so as to enable the production of a marketing plan. One of the new targeted campaigns which resulted was designed to encourage people living in Wales to 'See Wales First', namely, to choose Wales as a holiday destination in preference to elsewhere in the United Kingdom (mainly England) or continental Europe. The campaign was launched in November 1984 and consisted of a promotional bilingual brochure, together with a series of 30-second commercials on the two Wales-based commercial television stations, HTV and S4C. For the general United Kingdom market in 1985 the Wales Tourist Board supplemented general promotional campaigns aimed at projecting a positive and attractive image of Wales, with targeted marketing campaigns aimed both at geographical market sectors offering potential for growth and at special interest markets. The United Kingdom marketing in part involved a market-led response, the development of a wider range of easily bookable package holidays in conjunction with tour operators and carriers, and the encouragement of the retail travel trade to offer and promote them. Overseas marketing was, in contrast, concentrated on those sectors for which the product was already developed or available in Wales, and as such was product-led. The Board's overseas marketing aims were targeted to six market segments, namely:

1. The independent leisure traveler attracted by 'go as you please' as opposed to package holidays.
2. Special interest groups with interest in such things as history, archaeology, music, and culture.

3. Senior citizens attracted by the general ambience of peacefulness and the quiet pace of holidaying in Wales.
4. The youth market with interest in such things as hiking, climbing, riding, sailing and windsurfing.
5. The ethnic market involving Welsh communities overseas, especially in North America; but not forgetting relations of ethnic groups who have settled in Wales.
6. Business travel which included conference, exhibition and incentive travel, together with the business traveler who may be induced when visiting Wales to extend his visit by taking a holiday.

Targeting promotional efforts to these overseas segments was supplemented by the promotion of Wales in London to 'footloose' overseas visitors. In contrast, the target marketing of the Swansea marina in 1985 utilized small area census data from 1981 to identify areas in the West Midlands of England of similar socioeconomic profile to existing marina users, in order to minimize local advertising costs in reaching potential marina users.

The two examples outlined above are only illustrative of many applications of target marketing, of varying sophistication. The owner of an attraction for day trip family visitors who, on the basis of a survey, finds that most of his visitors come from within 40 miles, and on this basis advertises on Fridays in the local newspapers circulating in this area, is in a basic sense target marketing. Clearly, further refinements in the targeting may be added, such as targeting to certain social classes, but three basic ideas of targeting are to be found in this strategy: market research (the visitor survey), geographical segmentation (the spatial range of the product offered) and accessibility to the potential customers (the selection of an appropriate medium in which to advertise). The critical point is that this is a reasoned and researched strategy based on an understanding of the market for the attraction.

Benefits

The major benefit of target marketing is that by tightly relating the product to the market, both development and advertising costs may be reduced, or the productivity of advertising expenditures, increased. But effective targeting may do more than minimize advertising expenditure, it may expand demand for the product, or counter a previous decline. The process of target marketing, principally in the identification of accessible market segments, may in itself generate product development, and the production of new tourist products or services. Critical to success is both the correct identification of market segments and the accurate prediction of market size and competition. The sale of unbooked Mediterranean package holidays in the United Kingdom at much less than the cost of their provision in the summer of 1987 is a reminder of the consequences, in this case, of incorrectly predicting the size of the popular 'Sun, Sea, Sand and Sex' segment of the UK holiday market.

Implementation

Implementation of target marketing follows five stages:

1. The identification of accessible market segments.
2. The evaluation of these segments in terms of size, likely growth and competitive provision.
3. The tailoring of a product to an appropriate market segment.
4. The selection of appropriate media.
5. The design of advertising material to reach this selected market segment.

Market targeting itself involves the first of these two stages, whereas the further three stages operationalize the targeting. Essential to market targeting is market research, or the formal investigation of a market. Market research is designed to answer such questions as: who buys?, why do they buy?, and how are their needs satisfied? Research of this kind yields both the data needed to define, rather than to guess at, segments and to evaluate them. For targeting, market research takes two forms, either the use of existing sources and surveys, or the production of new data by specific surveys. It is pointless to spend money and other effort in undertaking, or paying an agency to undertake, a survey if the information needed is already known, or if information on a similar product or service can be sensibly applied to the task. Various official and institutional bodies in the United Kingdom undertake research which the small business person can gain access to. These bodies include the British Tourist Authority (Hammersmith), the national Tourist Boards, (based in Hammersmith, Edinburgh, Cardiff, Belfast, Dublin and Douglas), the National Trust (London), the National Trust for Scotland (Edinburgh), the Countryside Commission (Cheltenham and Newtown) and the Countryside Commission for Scotland (Perth). The Office of Population Censuses and Surveys (London) publishes not only Census material but much other survey material, particularly on social trends, and population estimates and projections. The National Tourist Boards and the Countryside Commissions have libraries which are open to genuine researchers. Organizations, such as the Leisure Studies Association (Birmingham) and the Society for the Interpretation of Britain's Heritage (Church Stretton), may be able to put the businessman in contact with appropriate researchers. A major problem for the small businessman is simply finding out what previous market research or statistics may apply, especially as much market research or statistics may apply, especially as much market research is unpublished and available in research libraries only. SEREN, a group of leisure industry researchers at the University College of Swansea, in association with the South Wales Tourism Research Group, offer an annotated leisure and tourism bibliography, focusing on Tourist Board and Countryside Commission material.

If no applicable market research exists for the required targeting analysis a specific survey may need to be undertaken. There are many market research agencies and universities or other higher education bodies willing to undertake this kind of research. Alternatively the businessman can undertake the survey himself. The latter is obviously easier if existing visitors can be appropriately surveyed; some organizations offer packages in which the agency designs the survey, prints the survey schedules or questionnaires, and analyzes the data. The businessman is responsible for either providing interviewers or distributing questionnaires. Analysis can vary widely in sophistication, and price, from the distribution of visitor attributes to lifestyle segmentation, occupational segmentation, psychographics, principal components analysis, multidimensional scaling, association analysis and discriminant analysis. In commissioning market research the businessman should specify the segmentation that is usable to him, in terms both of media and product.

One official segmentation is fundamental to much research: namely, the equation of tourists with travelers as visitors staying overnight away from home, and not with people away from home for leisure reasons. This is the World Tourism Organization's segmentation of the visitor travel market into tourists and excursionists. A literal definition of a tourist is a person who makes a tour, or performs a journey in a circuit. This clearly includes day tourists, or more commonly, day trippers. But day trippers are explicitly termed excursionists by the World Tourism Organization, and not tourists. Similarly, this official definition includes business and conference travelers as tourists, irrespective of any explicitly leisure purpose to their trip. At an international scale these definitions may be sensible, but at a national scale this segmentation is questionable as a universal segmentation. Implicitly, this definition equates the tourism industry with the accommodation industry and with international trip-making. The owner of an attraction should not only consider whether this official segmentation applies to his product, but also whether other attributes are likely to be more important in differentiating visitors into groups.

It is useful to consider some common attributes of tourist market segments, attributes which depending on the sophistication of the subsequent analysis may separately or interrelatedly define market segments. Basic social attributes can be used both to produce a general differentiation of a population and to describe visitors to an area or attraction. The SAGACITY groupings of the adult population are an example of a general social differentiation, which classifies the population on the attributes of life-cycle stages, income levels and occupational types. Surveys of visitors to areas or at attractions are common in the tourism industry; less common because of their cost are surveys of households to ascertain their patterns of visits. Visitor surveys usually generate basic descriptive data. Examples include the International Passenger Survey and the National Survey of Tourism in Scotland. A variant of surveying visitors or households is to survey households who have expressed an interest in visiting an area, say by applying for a brochure.

Spatial targeting takes two forms, either the identification of the catchment area of a district or attraction, or the identification of sub-areas by social criteria within the catchment area. There is a clear spatial market declining over distance for holidays in the United Kingdom by UK residents; however, at a more refined scale the spatial range of tourist products can vary substantially, as it may for superficially similar products. Spatial targeting may be associated with areal subdivision using the Small Area Statistics of the 1981 Census. The extent of analysis achievable may be very localized, as there are approximately 130,000 enumeration districts, the basic areal unit of the Census. These districts have been grouped, for example, into 36 neighborhood types under the ACORN classification (*A Classification Of Residential Neighbourhoods*) which is linked to the postcode system to facilitate postal identification.

The activities engaged in while on holiday may be used to segment tourists and to indicate the comparative size of the segments. Expectations can be used in a similar manner. Affinity to the destination may be an important attribute of segmentation, particularly for repeat visiting and the possibly different destinations within an area of repeat visitors, compared to first time visitors. Lifestyle analyses are attempts to derive groupings across a range of activities, expectations and values. These have varying relevance for target marketing, dependent on the applicability of the attributes included. A recent example of lifestyle analysis may be found in the Countryside Commission's *Recreation 2000 Trends Project*. A more general classification is the MONITOR system of Value Groups, which is an indirect method of classification deriving from attempts to understand social change. These groups were defined by Taylor Nelson Associates Ltd on the basis of extensive social surveying. Seven groups were defined, namely:

1. Self explorers: creative individuals seeking intellectual and emotional satisfaction.
2. Social resisters: critics of the way the United Kingdom has developed.
3. Experimentalists: fashion followers looking for novelty, fun and excitement.
4. Achievers/conspicuous consumers: status conscious, acquisitive and emulative.
5. Belongers: home centered, future oriented, self sacrificing, achievement directed group.
6. Survivors: conventional, conservative, chauvinistic.
7. Aimless: demoralized, goalless, apathetic.

The question of discovering the causes of consumer behavior leads to the concept of *benefit segmentation*. Benefit segmentation is based on the realization that consumers gain different benefits from the same product. Consumers are essentially grouped by the benefits they gain from a product or service. In this way benefit segmentation produces reasons why certain products are favored, rather than merely describing the members of a particular segment. Benefit segmentation is a current growth area of marketing, but clearly requires comparatively expensive and product-tailored research.

The accessibility via media of market segments is an essential criterion once a potential segmentation has been defined. Studies of media exposure include both those of the general population, occupational groups and of participants in specific activities. Of the national Tourist Boards, the Scottish Tourist Board, in particular, has undertaken surveys to measure media exposure and recall of its advertising. Examples of media surveys are included in the references appending this chapter. Direct mailing using a commercial mailing list is a further alternative, although Scottish Tourist Board research has indicated mailing lists to be less effective than their general advertising. Mailing lists of previous applicants may in themselves be considered an unsophisticated form of targeting.

Assessment

Target marketing depends for its effectiveness not only on the appropriateness and accessibility via media of the groups or segments defined, but also on the product and advertising design. As such there is ready scope for disagreements over its effectiveness or ineffectiveness. Target marketing by the Wales Tourist Board has been criticized by a House of Commons Select Committee for substantially diverting funds away from general advertising and, thus, implicitly for its comparative ineffectiveness in this case. The Select Committee did not elaborate on this issue further, although it systematically questioned the Tourist Board on this matter. Central to such evaluations is the concept of the 'conversion rate' to a destination, the extent to which a promotion converts potential tourists to holidaying in the destination rather than going elsewhere. As the decision process cannot be observed, the true extent to which a promotion, compared to other influences, effects a conversion is always unknown, and such analyses rely, for example, on brochure recipients' views on their changed likelihood to choose a destination, or on where they actually holidayed. Such studies are most useful if different media are being compared. To properly measure the effectiveness of target marketing a comparison with general advertising is necessary; otherwise the apparent performance of targeting may in reality be the result of the weather or even different dates of brochure distribution! Ultimately, target marketing can only be justified on its cost-effectiveness, and if the market is so disaggregated or inaccessible general advertising may be equally as cost-effective. However, this is unlikely.

Conclusions

Target marketing depends for its success only in part on the appropriateness of the market segments defined and used as targets. Critical also are both the accessibility of the segments via media and the appropriateness of the products offered. Segmentation of a market may take many forms of varying sophistication, but the central idea is always the same: to group prospective tourists meaningfully with a view to securing their holiday or trip destination. Ultimately, benefit segmentation is to be preferred.

Focus on small business

The small tourist business, whether an accommodation enterprise or attraction, is frequently reliant on other public and private bodies to distribute its advertising, via an area brochure, accommodation list, information office or Tourist In-formation Centre. Attractions often also advertise locally in the press and at camp sites and the like. With the possible exception of the latter, these are nonspecific, but comparatively cheap, means of advertising. Individually the small business is unlikely to be able to afford to target its promotion. However, local authorities and tourist associations do not need to be so nonspecific in their marketing and promotion. Small businesses should press these bodies to justify or redirect their efforts. Owners of attractions can readily survey their customers and both seek to place their advertising and develop their products accordingly.

Software/databases

ESRC Date Archive. This is located at the University of Essex, Colchester (0206 873333), and has recently acquired data sets from the Scottish Tourist Board. The Archive also contains data sets on time budgets, social and economic indicators, social groups, professional groups and attitudinal studies.

University of Manchester Regional Computer Centre have both the Small Area Statistics of the 1981 British Census on file, and SASPAC, a program to analyze this data.

Further reading/information sources

Central Statistical Office, *Social Trends* (HMSO, yearly). Summarizes other UK statistical sources, with chapters on basic demographic, income and social data, including leisure and participation.

Crouch, S., *Marketing Research for Managers* (Pan Books, 1985). This book includes a review both of the SAGACITY adult groupings and of the ACORN classification.

Edwards, J. A., *The Identification and Location of Potential Users of the Swansea Yacht Haven in the West Midlands* (1985). Report to the Economic and Social Research Council (contract no. F 09 25 0058), and available from the ESRC library or from the Department of Geography, University College of Swansea. This report includes a target marketing exercise, identifying census wards with disproportionate numbers of persons with comparable characteristics in the West Midlands to those already using the Swansea marina.

Evans, J. R. and Berman, B., *Marketing* (Collier Macmillan, 3rd edition, 1987). This text contains both a review of the bases of segmentation and of the techniques of defining marketing strategies based upon segmentations. Included are descriptions of the VALS program for blending demographics and lifestyle analyses, and of the selection of segments.

Frain, J., *Principles and Practice of Marketing* (Pitman, 1986). This text contains a review both of the common types of segmentation and of the place of targeting in marketing. In particular, the MONITOR Value Groups, ACORN system and SAGACITY groupings are described.

General Register Office for Scotland (Ladywell House, Edinburgh, EH12 7TF). The 1991 Census for Scotland is likely to be aggregated from spatial areas based upon post codes. These areas should be smaller in spatial extent than the enumeration districts currently used as the basis of small area census statistics, and will relate to commercial data sources based upon post codes. Circular SC91/M2 outlines the policy options. Refinements of this kind should enable more accurate spatial targeting than is available from the 1981 Census.

Harris Research Centre, *Effectiveness of ATB Promotions Report* (1984). Report to the Scottish Tourist Board, and available for inspection in the Board's library. This report includes an estimation of 'conversion' rates by media, and data on holiday takers who had received the area Tourist Boards' brochures.

House of Commons Committee on Welsh Affairs, *Tourism in Wales*, vols I and II (HMSO, 1987), 256-I; 256-II. This is an extensive review of both tourism in Wales, including the characteristics of visitors to Wales, and of the Wales Tourist Board, including the Board's target marketing and promotions.

Leisure Consultants, *Recreation 2000 Trends Project*. Report to the Countryside Commission, and available for inspection at the Commission's library in Cheltenham. This report presents projections for recreational participation, including an analysis based on lifestyle groups.

Media Research Bureau, *Local Government Publications Survey* (Media Research Bureau, 1987). This report assesses the media exposure to selected occupational publications of local government administrators.

NOP Market Research Ltd., *STB Marketing Follow Up Study* (1985). Report to the Scottish Tourist Board, and available in the STB library. This marketing follow up study includes an evaluation of 'conversion' rates.

Office of Population Censuses and Surveys (Saint Catherine's House, 10 Kingsway, London WC2B 6JP). As well as the Census, this agency produces both a *Monitor* series and *Population Trends*, and is the central British source for population estimates, movements and trends.

Prentice, R. C., *Rural Residents' Leisure Use of Manx National Glens* (Saint John's, Isle of Man, Isle of Man Forestry, Mines and Lands Board, 1986). This report demonstrates the varying spatial market segmentations for similar products, the Manx glens.

Rhind, D. (ed.), *A Census User's Handbook* (Methuen, 1983). This book examines the uses to which the Small Area Statistics of the British Census may be put, including the classification and grouping of areas.

Scottish Tourist Board, *Research and Planning Information Handbook*. This handbook summarizes all the STB's past and current research, and is updated annually by the Board.

SEREN (Social-Economic Research and Environment), in association with the South Wales Tourism Research Group, have an annotated bibliography of leisure and tourism research, including that to be found in the national Tourist Boards' and Countryside Commissions' libraries, available to the small business. Contact Dr R. C. Prentice, University College of Swansea (0792 205678).

Survey Research Associates, *National Survey of Tourism in Scotland, 1985* (1986). Report to the Scottish Tourist Board, and available for inspection in the Board's library. This report includes basic social data on the characteristics of tourists to Scotland, and the media exposure of groups.

Wertheim, E., *Survey of British Golfers* (1979). Report to the Scottish Tourist Board, and available for inspection in the Board's library. This report includes an analysis of the media exposure of different groups of golfers, as a basis for promotional targeting.

RICHARD PRENTICE

Marketing feasibility study

Introduction

The hotel or tourism marketing feasibility study, as its name would suggest, forms part of the wider project feasibility study. Indeed, it can be considered as the frame or base on which other aspects of the project feasibility study – the master plan and financial and social cost–benefit analyses – depend. For example, a study or analysis of the market for any project will determine whether the project merits further analysis.

Thus, as shown in Table 1, the general format of a feasibility study should begin with a market study after the preliminary concept of the project has been stated.

Many projects have failed or have proven costly due to no market studies being done at the feasibility stage or at the wrong time during this stage. For example, if the market study is done after great amounts of money have been spent on project design by the developer, this can result in wasted finances, as a different size and design of the project may be determined from the market study. Therefore, it is advisable for the developer and project analyst to follow the planning profile in Table 1, which could save the developer considerable sums of money in the long run.

The market study can be defined, therefore, as a very important or major part of any feasibility study, which basically attempts to determine the level of demand for the proposed project by analyzing trends and showing how these trends might enhance the feasibility of the project, or prove it not worthwhile. The study should analyze the two major components, demand and supply, from a macroeconomic point of view, that is, looking at the market in the broad sense and anticipating what changes may occur in the long run, which may or may not affect the viability of the project.

Implementation

The aim of international/regional demand analyses is to show tourism growth trends in international and regional tourism and to consider the country and the project in relation to these world/regional trends. Here would be indicated factors such as major flows, reasons for these flows, means of transport, types of accommodations, facilities favored and the like. This section should be brief. Sources from which data for this purpose can be drawn are the publications by the World Tourism Organization (WTO) and Organization for Economic Cooperation and Development (OECD).

In analyzing the demand for a tourism project, say, in a resort area, the general characteristics of the market should first of all be determined. This is done by the project analyst giving a brief general description of the proposed location of the project, its population, business activities and other ancillary characteristics, e.g. tourist attractions (natural or manmade), access to the site (airport, roads), which may relate directly or indirectly to the project. However, the basic demand, which may influence these other demands, is the demand for the project itself, namely whether there will be a sufficient number of visitors to the tourism project to make it viable.

Demand analyses should also incorporate the following for a meaningful assessment of the market:

1. A review of international and regional tourism demand over the past 3–5 years.
2. A look at economic, social, political, demographic and behavioral trends in the main tourist market(s) to the country.
3. An analysis of trends in the domestic market.
4. Demand at the project level.

Existing demand to the country is extremely important as it indicates potential demand for the project. These trends can be analyzed from an economic point of view, by showing, for example, whether more discretionary income is being earned by potential visitors; from a social point of view, whether more people in the marketplace are taking time for outside leisure/recreation or staying at home; from the political point of view, whether the governments of the main tourism-generating countries enjoy a friendly relationship with the country in which the project is being conceptualized or whether overseas travel from these generating countries is becoming tighter; from the demographic point of view, what types of people are traveling to the country in question, their age groups, income levels, family sizes etc.; from the behavioral point of view as to what types of vacations are being taken by travelers to the destination, their motive for visits, activities that visitors would prefer in the country of the project, means of arrival, length of stay and what type of accommodation is favored. These types of data are important in order that not only the propensity to

Table 1 Planning profile for feasibility study of tourism projects.

Step 1. Preliminary concept including financing possibilities
Step 2. Market study
Step 3. Revised concept including project design
Step 4. Revised costings of project including financing arrangements
Step 5. Financial and social cost–benefit analyses
Step 6. Sensitivity analyses

travel will be determined, but also to show the types of people who are traveling, their characteristics, and how these factors may affect the project.

The reasons and motivations for travel are many and varied, but they can be grouped into certain significant categories: pleasure (sports, attractions, vacation) – the sun, sand, sea or the snow/skiing combinations; business; visits to friends and relatives (VFRs), ethnic travel, travel for religious, study or health reasons. All of these travel motivations should be analyzed separately from the economic and noneconomic points of view, as each category will have different demand behavior as far as economic, social and psycholiogical patterns are concerned. For example, VFRs returning home may not take up accommodation in the hotel sector, but will most likely stay with friends and relatives as the acronym suggests. Also business travelers may have shorter stays than pleasure tourists, and travelers to a destination for religious or study reasons may not stay in expensive resort hotels, but may seek the unbeaten track. Information relative to these demand characteristics can be gleaned from data usually compiled by Tourist Boards and Ministries in their exit studies.

Trends in the domestic market should also be analyzed, e.g. with regard to the local people using attractions, convention halls, resorts and other local facilities constructed for tourist use. Some projects may depend on foreign trade while others may have a dependence on both the foreign and local markets.

Comparisons should also be made of present demands for similar projects at the regional and local levels. Analyses should be made of these especially if there is a link between facilities in different territories, e.g. the building of cruise ship facilities in one territory will probably depend on the successful interdependence with cruise ship facilities that may exist in a nearby destination. As far as hotel projects are concerned, a supply–demand analysis should consist of an inventory of all accommodations including any new hotel construction within the area where the new hotel project is to be built, subgrouped to indicate those that are 'most competitive', 'fairly competitive', 'somewhat competitive', and identification of the principal competitive hotels as to their location, size, room rate, occupancy, facilities and services offered and composition of trade, and an analysis of principal sources of demand with their forecasted or anticipated growth rate. The idea is to obtain the total number of rooms needed in future years by multiplying the current demand level by the anticipated growth in demand which is the composite rate of growth of the various sources of demand or market segments (see Fig. 1).

Demand at the project level should be considered the most important for the investment question, and should be as accurate as possible. It would of course be much easier to gather more correct data for a project which is being considered in an

already developed resort destination than in a pristine, undeveloped area of a country. Information for the former situation can be gathered from any number of sources, e.g. public statistics from Government ministries, occupancy levels and room rates from existing hotels, and entrance prices for public parks. For a development in a more virgin area, attitudinal surveys of tourists and information from more knowledgeable sources will be needed. The demand analysis at the project level should cover the same areas as for the demand at the country level, but it should be carried out in much more detail.

Market projection techniques

Demand projection, or demand forecasting as it is usually referred to, differs according to the type of project. Normally it will consist of the numbers of tourists that are expected to visit the site (if it is a tourist attraction); or be accommodated (if it is a hotel or an airport); their length of stay; the prices that they will be willing to pay, and how these expenses are distributed. The aim of demand forecasting in project evaluation is to predict the most probable level of demand that is likely to occur in the light of known circumstances. Therefore, demand forecasting should be based on some knowledge of the market and the demand analysis, that has been described in the preceding paragraphs, can serve as a basis for future demand. Forecasts can be done intuitively (by guesswork), or scientifically, using complex techniques. The accuracy of the forecasts will definitely affect the accuracy of the market analysis.

The choice of the technique used for demand forecasting depends on: the accuracy of the data that are available, time constraints, the size of the budget etc. These analyses can be done either quantitatively or qualitatively; the simplest and most used quantitative method is trend analysis, which consists of extrapolation from the past into the future. However, past growth rates merely tell what has happened in the past, and trends based on extrapolation are therefore no more than a gesture of faith in the accuracy of the past growth trends, rather than being firmly based on an understanding of what the future will bring. Thus, the accuracy of the forecast, in this case, will depend on the accuracy of past data. Trend analysis can be done by simply extrapolating past annual rates of change into the future or in more sophisticated ways by applying moving averages, where relevant, to each of the data series, or by exponential smoothing or by adopting regression analysis using the least squares method. In addition to its dependence on the accuracy of past data, data extrapolated beyond one-third of the base data can be considered suspect in some cases. Quantitative forecasting techniques are discussed in the chapters on 'Forecasting international tourism demand: the econometric approach' and 'Forecasting international tourism demand: noncausal quantitative methods'.

In order that a more accurate forecast may be achieved, these quantitative techniques could be used in conjunction with the market analysis, where the socioeconomic characteristics of the market are taken into consideration, and each characteristic forecasted individually to estimate market growth within that sector.

Qualitative methods are used in demand forecasting when

Step 1: Data section

Statistics on major competitors over the past 12 months (1987)

Hotel	Number of rooms	Average occupancy (%)	Nightly occupancy (no. of rooms)
1	400	72	288
2	350	80	280
3	180	76	137
4	290	82	238
5	450	70	315
6	350	75	263
	2020	75	1520

Step 2: Demand statistics

Source	Percentage of total	Actual (1981)	Actual (1987)	Compound growth rate (%)	Composite growth rate (%)
Business travelers	20	400,000	550,000	4.65	0.93
Convention delegates	20	400,000	578,000	5.40	1.08
Vacationers	60	1,200,000	1,600,000	4.20	2.52
					4.53

Step 3: Supply statistics

Rooms available (1981)	Rooms available (1987)	Compound growth rate (%)
1650	2020	3

Step 4: Answer section 1

Assume normal break-even occupancy of 75%
Assume normal room supply growth rate of 3.0%

Year	Demand	Current supply	Required supply	New rooms required
1987	1520	2020	2027	7
1988	1589	2081	2119	38
1989	1661	2143	2215	71
1990	1736	2207	2315	107
1991	1815	2274	2420	146
1992	1897	2342	2529	187
1993	1983	2412	2644	232
1994	2073	2484	2763	279
1995	2166	2559	2888	330
1996	2264	2636	3019	384
1997	2367	2715	3156	441

Answer section 2

Assume new break-even occupancy of 78%
Assume new room supply growth rate of 3.5%

Year	Demand	Current supply	Required supply	New rooms required
1987	1520	2020	1949	−71
1988	1589	2091	2037	−54
1989	1661	2164	2129	−35
1990	1736	2240	2226	−14
1991	1815	2318	2327	9
1992	1897	2399	2432	33
1993	1983	2483	2542	59
1994	2073	2570	2657	87
1995	2166	2660	2777	117
1996	2264	2753	2903	150
1997	2367	2849	3035	185

Figure 1 Supply/demand analysis.

data are insufficient or unreliable or there is not enough time to conduct a quantitative analysis. Qualitative forecasts are quite suitable for long-term forecasting when large and unprecedented changes in trends in the marketplace may be expected. However, in project analysis where there are time constraints and where time means money, and the delay of a project may result in severe losses, qualitative techniques, like the Delphi technique, may not be considered.

Comparison of business and leisure travel

In many small territories, where the urban and resort areas are very closely positioned, the business and leisure markets can be quite difficult to differentiate. This distinction is made more difficult by tourists traveling for both business and pleasure. There are, however, some very major differences between business and leisure travel. The main characteristics of business travel are that it is linked to the economic activity in the destination country while the leisure or resort market is linked to the economic activity in the country of origin and is dependent on a level of per capita income that will create sufficient disposable income to permit comfortable travel and accommodation. Other differences in characteristics of these two types of travel is that business travel usually occurs in the low season, while leisure travel occurs mainly during the high season, and business travel is price insensitive while leisure travel is price sensitive. Single occupancy is more common among business travelers as compared with double occupancy for leisure tourists. Finally location is also important here, where business hotels are usually located in city centers, e.g. London, Paris and other major business-oriented cities, or on the outskirts of cities, e.g. the motel market in the United States. However, in many continental or island resort cities, e.g. Orlando (US), Miami (US), San Juan (Puerto Rico), Nassau (Bahamas), there is in many cases travel both for business and leisure, and the urban and resort areas are physically close to each other, or are one and the same.

Definition of this market and physical possibility is important in doing a feasibility study, as this can help to determine the masterplan of the hotel: should the rooms be standardized as twin rooms, or should a portion of the hotel be reserved for the construction of single rooms only, as in urban areas. Because of economies of scale in building construction, it is more feasible to have standardized double rooms in resort areas, especially if the forecasted single room occupancy capacity is less than 20 per cent.

Examples

A marketing feasibility comparison

In the mid-1970s a project feasibility study was carried out for a small, 10-room, family-owned hotel in Canouan, one of the unspoilt islands in the territory of St Vincent and the Grenadines in the Caribbean. There was difficulty in identifying a market for this hotel because of a lack of attitudinal surveys

of tourists and information from knowledgeable sources about this area which was undeveloped, touristically and otherwise. In addition, communications to Canouan were very difficult, there being only one out-of-date dirt airstrip on the island. The main source of visitors that was identified at that time to Canouan was the yachting market, and although there were three safe anchorages on the island, with the primary one being only a few yards from the project site, this market was proven to be inadequate. Today, a decade later, Canouan is being marketed as an exotic destination, and there is now more hope for the hotel, if properly advertised.

On the other hand, in the feasibility study done in 1980 of a 230-room resort hotel in Nassau, Bahamas, a prime tourist destination, there was no difficulty in identifying a market. In the year ending 1979, the arithmetic average of hotel room occupancy percentages was 81 per cent, an increase over the previous 12 months of nearly 10 per cent. Among the main reasons for the improvement in arrivals and occupancies at that time were the well organized and aggressive promotional campaign of the Ministry of Tourism, increased accessibility by air and a good image in the travel market due to an improved tourism product. With a good tourism product, beefed up by extensive marketing not only from the Government but from numerous international hotel groups, and a lack of hotel rooms at the time, the marketing feasibility proved very positive.

These two examples show some of the factors that can affect or enhance the development of hotel facilities in the West Indies. These factors may apply to situations in other developing and maybe some developed countries. They are location, accessibility, size of property, a well-established product versus a product which was hardly known, and professionalism or the lack of it in the developer. Let us examine them Canouan, situated in the Grenadines in the Eastern Caribbean was barely accessible to the North American market, from where the great majority of tourists to the Caribbean originate. In order to reach the facility, a North American tourist, say, from Miami would have had to fly to the main hub in the Eastern Caribbean, Barbados, a four to five-hour journey, dependent on the stops along the way, then take a shuttle service for another half-hour to St Vincent, the main island in the archipelago of St Vincent and the Grenadines, and then another light plane to Canouan (another half-hour). If everything was on schedule travel would take 5 to 6 hours (not including waiting time in the airports). Canouan at that time (any maybe now) was not an established tourist market. Nassau, on the other hand has had a very well established tourism product. The tourism product is well known and Nassau is only 35 minutes away from its nearest US hub, Miami. The questions of size of property and professionalism of the small hotelier versus the large one is also evident and well documented (see 'Focus on small business' (pp 257–8), and the 'Project feasibility' chapter later in this handbook (p. 329)).

Computer applications in marketing feasibility – supply/demand analysis

Figure 1 illustrates the calculations of a hotel developer who wishes to build a 200-room hotel in a resort area. As mentioned above, an inventory of all accommodation in the area has to be taken. In this example, let us assume that there are six hotels in the 'most competitive' hotel grouping. First of all, the average occupancy of these six hotels was calculated. This was done by dividing the total nightly demand by the total rooms and multiplying the result by 100:

$$\frac{1520}{2020} \times 100 = 75\%$$

Next, the composite growth rate of demand from the various market segments was calculated. The source of visitors in this example has been broken down into three segments, and then multiplied by the anticipated compound growth rates which have been estimated from historical growth rate figures. The composite growth rate was calculated at 4.53%.

Step 3 considers the supply statistics of the rooms available in 1981 as compared with those available in 1987. Over this 7-year span, there is a compound growth rate of 3%.

In Step 4, the future demand was calculated year by year, using the composite growth of 4.53%. Next the future supply of rooms required was calculated. With a current average occupancy rate of 75%, assuming a normal break-even occupancy of 75, then the required supply will be the present demand divided by the occupancy percentage, the result of which is shown in the required supply column for each of the eleven years.

This shows, in Answer section 1, that new rooms are required from 1987 with a break-even occupancy percentage of 75 per cent and a normal room supply growth rate of 3 per cent. However, the market will not be able to support the developer's 200-room hotel until 1993, all things being equal, as we can see that 232 rooms can be supported in that year and more from that year onwards. We can also see that at the end of 5 years 146 rooms can be supported, assuming a break-even occupancy of 75 per cent and a normal room supply growth rate of 3 per cent. However, to reduce risk, we might assume that a higher break-even occupancy, say of 78 per cent may be a more feasible figure and the room supply growth rate may grow say, by 0.5 per cent as refurbished rooms and small guest houses come on stream. The result would be that a smaller number of new rooms would be required as shown in Answer section 2 and the market in this case could theoretically not support the 200 rooms. Therefore from these two illustrations, it is clear that the two most important variables, which can substantially change the new demand for rooms are the break-even occupancy and the room supply growth rate percentages. In doing a supply/demand analysis like this some other factors may have to be considered. For example, if there are rooms that are coming off the market, then the room supply growth rate has to be adjusted downwards to reflect this, just as it was adjusted upwards in this example to reflect a small percentage of rooms coming on stream.

Conclusion

The marketing feasibility study seeks to determine the level of demand for the proposed project by analyzing trends in the marketplace, examining the general characteristics of the market and producing a market analysis, which considers both demand and supply. The study is a prime requirement for any hotel/tourism project, as it helps in justifying the conceptual plan of the project. The marketing feasibility study also helps in reducing investment uncertainty and improving investment decisions, and is usually material that is requested by lending institutions in the feasibility process.

Focus on small business

Small hotels in the Caribbean and other developing regions of the world are more and more being faced with a dilemma in marketing and management. On the one hand, the small entrepreneurs in many of these countries are being encouraged to build, develop or improve their hotels, while, on the other hand, the large multinational and local entrepreneurs are being allowed to indulge in the closed-market concept of the all-inclusive package tour, which lends itself to the vertical and horizontal integration of the various segments of the tourist industry. The package tour is being forced upon the travel trade, and this results in the requirement of *en masse* travel facilities and larger capacity hotels and leisure complexes. Some smaller hotels have been involved in this trade, but they usually form part of a grouping of hotels. By and large, however, the travel trade and airlines have recognized the economies of scale in the travel business, and larger aircraft and hotels have been the result.

This leaves the small hotel operator in a predicament, and over the years, he has had to depend on the larger operator for overflow business to make ends meet. Indeed, in many feasibility or investment studies done by the small hotel developer, a marketing analysis is often not evident. For example, in the feasibility study for the construction of a 20-unit apartment hotel in a developing country in the Caribbean, done by the developer for consideration by a lending agency, the market survey read thus: 'A detailed market survey has not been undertaken but preliminary enquiries from the Tourist Board Sector indicate an increase in the demand for apartment hotels. The recent introduction of major airline charter flights to the island has resulted in a very good season last year. Indeed all available hotel beds were full during the months of March to April last year'.

The developer had not segmented the market into those wanting apartment-type accommodation and those opting for hotel accommodation. Apartment hotels have cooking facilities within the apartments, but may have very limited dining and entertainment facilities generally. Some of the questions that should have been asked are:

1. Was a survey done to distinguish between those potential tourists using apartment facilities as opposed to hotel facilities?
2. What types of markets would have preferred apartment facilities to hotel facilities – tourists from the United States, Canada, Europe, other Caribbean islands?

3. Where did tourists to the island generally come from at that time?
4. Would the price per apartment to the tourist have been more or less than the price per hotel room?
5. Would there have been goods and services, e.g. supermarkets, close to the proposed project?

The developer was obviously considering the 'very good season last year' and the fact that 'all available beds were full during the months of March and April last year' as prime points for consideration. But this was not enough. Undoubtedly, a more indepth consideration of the market should have been done so that the lending agency might have considered the financing proposal put up by the developer.

Marketing feasibility or prefeasibility studies done for the small hotel operator have to be on a par with those done for the large multinational hotel corporation. Local hotel developers may not have the expertise nor the funds to have these studies done. Development Banks and Finance Corporations can and do offer technical assistance in this area. However, as mentioned in the chapter *Project Feasibility*, 'small entrepreneurs must come together as small hotel bodies to try to solve their problems'; in particular, together they can gain expertise in the various areas of management, including project analysis and development.

Further reading

Archer, B. H., 'Forecasting demand: quantitative and intuitive techniques', *International Journal of Tourism Management* (March 1980), pp. 5–12. This article explains the various methods of demand-forecasting used for the prediction of tourist demand.

Beals, P. and Troy, D. A., 'Hotel feasibility analysis, part I', *Cornell HRA Quarterly*, vol. 23, no. 1 (May 1982), pp. 10–17. In this first of two parts the authors offer a critique of methods currently used in evaluating lodging-industry investments. The critique looks at the four types of economic studies most commonly encountered in the evaluation of hotel investments – market, marketability, feasibility and appraisal.

Beals, P. and Troy, D. A., 'Hotel feasibility analysis, part II', *Cornell HRA Quarterly*, vol. 23, no. 3 (November 1982), pp. 58–64. In this second part the authors offer specific suggestions for more useful feasibility reports, especially in the area of market analysis.

Caribbean Tourism Research and Development Centre (CTRC), *Caribbean Tourism Statistical Report* (CTRC, Mer Vue, Barbados 1982).

This manual gives the format of tourism statistical reports on countries of the Caribbean as compiled by the CTRC.

Coffman, D. C., *Marketing for a Full House* (Cornell University, 6th edition, 1979). This text gives a thorough analysis of marketing in the hospitality industry. Chapter 9 entitled 'Planning the New Property' explains in great detail each step of the feasibility study of a new hotel property.

Coltman, M. M., *Financial Management for the Hospitality Industry* (CBI Publishing Co./Van Nostrand Reinhold, 1979). This is a very concisely-written and factual text on financial management for the hotel and restaurant industries. Chapter 10 deals with feasibility studies, and gives a very good account of supply and demand analysis for a new hotel project.

Doswell, R. and Gamble, P. R., *Marketing and Planning Hotel and Tourism Projects* (Barrie and Jenkins, 1979). This text, as its title suggests, describes in detail *inter alia* the steps, format and data that are required for the marketing feasibility study of hotel and tourism projects.

Gee, C. Y., *Resort Development and Management for Operators, Developers and Investors* (Educational Institute of the American Hotel and Motel Association, 1981). This text covers the broad spectrum of resort management. The resort development cycle including the market feasibility study is covered in Chapter 4 entitled 'The Process of Planning and Development'.

Keiser, J. R., *Principles and Practice of Management in the Hospitality Industry* (CBI Publishing Co., 1979). This text encompasses the hospitality 'environment', and discusses all relevant subjects in hospitality management. Chapter 13 explains the concept of the feasibility study, with more emphasis placed on the restaurant business.

Kendell, P. J., 'Recent experiences in project appraisal', unpublished paper presented at University of Surrey International Conference on 'Trends in Tourism Planning and Development' (1982). In this paper the author discusses recent experiences in project appraisal and gives a synopsis of how an appraisal should be done.

Lundberg, D. E., *The Hotel and Restaurant Business* (CBI Publishing Co., 3rd edition, 1979). This is a very comprehensive text which looks at all aspects of the hotel and restaurant business starting with its history. Site selection, market and economic feasibility studies are explained in Chapter 3 entitled 'Hotel/Motel Finances and Building'.

Organization of American States, *Methods for Tourism Project Pre-investment studies*, Research and Bibliography Series No. 4 (OAS, 1978). This manual serves as a reference to methods and orderly procedures in preparing preinvestment studies of tourism projects and gives a practical analysis of the techniques. The manual is designed for tourism authorities in the member states of the OAS.

AINSLEY M. O'REILLY

Marketing of tourism

Introduction

Tourism marketing can be defined as the management process through which tourist organizations identify their selected tourists, actual and potential, and communicate with them to ascertain and influence their needs, desires, and motivations on local, regional, national and international levels, in order to formulate and adapt their tourist products accordingly in view of achieving optimal tourist satisfaction and maximizing organizational goals.

Tourism marketing involves discovering what tourists want (market research), developing suitable tourist services (product planning), telling them what is available (advertising and promotion), and giving instructions where they can buy the services (channels of distribution – tour operators and travel agents) so they will receive value (pricing), and the tourist organization will make a profit and attain its goals (marketability).

The structure of the tourism industry is highly fragmented in terms of size, styles, location, and ownership pattern; however, it has four major common characteristics:

1. Inflexibility of supply: for example, the hotel bedroom cannot be adjusted to fluctuations in demand and cannot be stored for periods of peak demand.
2. Tourism services are perishable: that is, any unoccupied bed in a hotel or seat in a plane represents a loss which affects industry's profitability and ability to compete.
3. Fixed location and, therefore, the importance of communication methods such as advertising and/or sales promotion in order to bring the customer to the tourist destinations where the service can be consumed.
4. Relatively large financial investments are required for every modern tourist establishment, and therefore, both the level of risk and the return on investment are of critical importance to tourism management.

Tourism marketing management is the setting of marketing goals (considering the resources of the tourism company and the market opportunities) and the planning and execution of marketing activities required to meet the goals. When carried out effectively, tourism marketing management results in creating and satisfying customers in a manner acceptable to society and leads to profitable growth for the organization.

Examples

The French-owned hotel group NOVOTEL is investing £60 million to build 24 new hotels in the United Kingdom, aimed at mid-market customers. The expansion, during the next 4 years, will take the number in its total chain to 30. It is aiming squarely at a three-star slot, weighted heavily towards business travelers, and has targeted Trust House Forte's Post House and Bass-owned Crest as major competitors in its positioning strategy. NOVOTEL is stepping up its marketing thrust and is backing it with a public relations push.

Coach operator National Express plans a joint venture with the British Tourist Authority to grab a share of the fast growing short break sector, which is even now worth £1 billion. The move is National Express's biggest diversification since the deregulation of the bus system. The company has been testing the appeal of the concept, called tourist trail, in Australia and North America. There will be three pop-on/pop-off services, two running from London to Edinburgh via the East and West coasts, and one from London to Lincoln. The packages, including stays at hotels or guest houses, run from 3 days to a 28-day version costing £1700. The launch is likely to coincide with British Rail's updating of its Anglo-Scottish sleeper services, where many of the overnight sleepers will be routed down the West coast in an attempt to provide passengers with more comfortable services.

Benefits

Tourism organizations that practice the marketing concept study the consumer to determine consumer needs and wants and then organize and integrate all activities within the company towards helping the consumer fulfil these needs and wants while simultaneously achieving organizational goals. There are three pillars to the marketing concept:

1. consumer orientation,
2. integrated or total company effort, and
3. achievement of organization goals.

The development of a tourist market depends on the analysis

of actual and potential tourists' needs and wants and on market segmentation in order to pursue profitable opportunities. The overall size of the market for tourism in a given market area – country, region, city, or for a tourist organization – is determined by: purchasing power, and especially discretionary income; demographic structure and trends; social and cultural factors; travel motivations and attitudes; the range of available travel opportunities; the existence (or absence) of travel restrictions; intensity and quality of travel marketing efforts and distribution system; and the economic situation and expectations about its future development.

The consumer's perspective centers around the needs a tourist product or service satisfies or fulfils. But the tourist buying-decision is unique in several ways:

1. There is no tangible rate of return on the investment.
2. The expenditure is often considerable in terms of the after-tax income earned during the year.
3. The purchase is not spontaneous.
4. The expenditure is prepared and planned through savings made over a considerable time.

Tourists seek a variety of satisfactions, each in its own way contributing to the richness of the travel experience.

Tourists do not represent a homogeneous group of people striving to travel and pushed by identical motivations. There is a complex of various, and sometimes conflicting desires, needs, tastes, likes and dislikes. An important part of the consideration of tourism psychology and motivation is the fact that a person usually travels for more than one reason. Basic travel motivators can be divided into four categories: physical, cultural, interpersonal, and status and prestige. The individual has also needs for both stability (psychological security) and change (novelty), of familiarity versus novelty, relaxation versus activity, and order versus disorder, in his travel experiences and behavior.

Marketing research should help pinpoint target markets, help determine the proper tourist marketing mix, and help make most effective use of marketing efforts and expenditures. The concept of market segmentation arises from the recognition that consumers are different. Market segmentation is a strategy of allocation of marketing resources given a heterogeneous tourist population. Tourist markets can be segmented or subdivided in many different ways. Geographic segmentation, demographics, psychographics, benefit segmentation, usage rate, and price sensitivity are some of the most commonly used segmentation techniques in the tourism industry. When travel consumers are grouped according to their psychological make-up (psychographics), emphasis is placed on values, attitudes, feelings, and desires. The various elements in the marketing mix and plans are designed in order to exploit the different elasticities of demand for travel and tourism of the various segments.

The concept of market segmentation is the basic point of origin for all tourism marketing strategies. Tourism segments should be identified by population size and proportions in various geographically defined market areas. The segments should then be ranked according to their economic value (substantiality), by the level of demand for various tourist product opportunities, by the variance in responsiveness among market segments to available opportunities, by the accessibility of market segments in terms of communication strategies, by growth potential, and by the degree of competitive vulnerability. Market segmentation contributes to the synchronization of the marketing mix with the tourist/customer, to the delineation of different demand curves, to a focused form of promotion and to greater tourist product loyalty because of the tailoring of the product to fit the market. Linked with market segmentation and market targeting is the concept of market positioning, which is the act of formulating a competitive positioning for the tourist product and a detailed marketing mix.

Once the target markets have been determined, the marketing mix must be defined. The elements of the marketing mix include pricing, branding, channels of distribution, personal selling, advertising, promotion, packaging, product service, personal contact, displays, and the merchandising strategy. In formulating a marketing mix, one must make sure that the elements are not considered in a vacuum but are, instead, considered as they are affected by changes in tourist attitudes and habits, changes in competition, changes in the economic outlook, and changes in government activity. When adjusted to external forces, the marketing mix consists of all those strategies that attract the target markets. Ideally, target markets must be of a sufficient size to promise a profit, have the potential for future growth, not be the target of excessive competition, and exemplify some more or less unsatisfied tourist needs that can be met by the tourist operation.

Implementation

Product mix

The optimal tourist product mix is the one that best allows an organization to reach its goals. Each item in a tourist product mix makes some contribution towards a company's goals. For example, Holiday Inn's product mix also includes institutional furniture manufactured by a company division and other products, in addition to its lodging line. In turn, the tourism organization's goals serve as yardsticks by which management can measure performance and the need for some type of action. Tourism management makes product decisions to close gaps between goals and achievements.

Pricing

Pricing in tourism is a complex matter, particularly where the individual suppliers, airlines, hotel groups and so on determine their prices independently of one another. Pricing goals pursued by the tour operator or tourist establishment can include pricing to realize a target market share, pricing to meet or prevent competition or pricing subordinated to tourist product differentiation. There is no universally accepted pricing method in tourist establishments. Indeed, the approach to pricing varies quite considerably, depending on the sector of the industry. Whatever the different approaches to pricing in the tourism business they are all variants of two well-established pricing methods: costs-plus pricing and rate of return pricing.

Promotion mix

Advertising should influence the tourist's assessment of the tourist product's performance on a given attribute, or on the combination of product attributes regarded as 'ideal'. The messages must create or reinforce existing positive attitudes or images and correct negative attributes or image elements. Tourist promotion should also be aimed at key influentials in the buying process, such as travel agents. Various possible advertising objectives can be sorted into whether their aim is to inform, persuade or remind.

In terms of media planning the tourist company should deal with a basic question: which medium delivers the most key prospects at the lowest cost within a supportive editorial environment? The relative cost-effectiveness of the different communication channels is also an important factor to be evaluated. Advertising and sales promotion activities in tourism are even more effective when supplemented by publicity and personal selling.

Distribution

The most crucial question for tourism distribution analysis is what channels are the most productive and whether a new channel strategy is needed. A distribution strategy involves determining the best way in which the industry will try to sell its products to designated end markets. The leading factors for a tourism distribution policy to be effective are the market coverage, the costs of distribution involved, and the effectiveness in generating sales in terms of motivation and image of the channels. The tourism industry relies on tour operators, travel agents and airlines for most point-of-sale contacts. The distribution strategy must be supported by information services, publicity material, training seminars, joint special promotions, and trade advertising.

The allocation of available marketing funds among the various components of the tourism marketing mix (advertising, publicity, sales force, travel agents' commissions, discount coupons, pre-opening campaigns, new product development, research etc.) should be determined. For tomorrow's tourism marketing strategies, the name of the game will, above all, be how to achieve a sustainable competitive advantage.

Assessment

Tourism management must determine what can be done to improve marketing performance, effectiveness and efficiency. Various aspects related to the planning, organization, and control process and to the tourist product's marketing mix must be examined. Typical questions which management will ask are as follows:

1. Are objectives devised to meet changing environmental conditions?
2. What is the company/organization's competitive situation?
3. What are the trends in competition?
4. Did the organization study tourist needs, attitudes, and behavior?
5. Are the marketing efforts organized in a systematic way?
6. Does the organization engage in comprehensive sales forecasting?
7. Does the organization have clearly stated contingency plans?
8. Does the organization control activities through marketing cost analysis, sales analysis etc.?
9. Does the organization utilize marketing research for planning as well as problem solving?
10. Does it utilize a systematic tourist product planning process?
11. Does it have suitable procedures for developing new tourist products?
12. Does it motivate tour operators, travel agents, and other channel members?
13. Does the tourist organization have an overall promotional plan?
14. Is there an established creative strategy, indicating the desired appeal to be used for each target market?
15. Are there clear objectives for advertising, sales promotion, and publicity?
16. Does it seek out favorable publicity?
17. Does the organization have a pricing strategy that satisfies channel members?
18. Does it estimate tourist demand and cost factors before setting prices?
19. Does the tourist organization set prices that are consistent with image?

By using a tourist marketing audit, which is a systematic, critical, and unbiased review or appraisal of the organization's marketing objectives, strategy, implementation, and organization, the tourist company will be able to maximize its long-term and tactical goals and objectives.

Conclusion

Marketing is a management philosophy which, in light of tourist demand, makes it possible through research, forecasting and selection to place tourism products on the market most in line with the organization's purpose for the greatest benefit. Tourism marketing planning is the organized process of studying the market, identifying and measuring its trends, and developing major marketing objectives and supporting programs. The process includes developing targets (timing, costs, results expected) and monitoring the actual achievements against these targets. A basic starting point for tourism marketing effort is a marketing plan. The marketing plan should include careful selection of market segments. A systematic and logical selection of target segments will require more efficient efforts and/or reduce marketing costs while increasing tourist product demand. It is not enough to generate tourist arrivals or achieve a certain market share, but rather, it is necessary to produce profitable tourist product sales and profitable market penetration.

Focus on small business

No business in the tourism industry can afford to ignore marketing. Anyone operating a small tourist business needs to apply the marketing concept and its techniques. Unfortunately, many small independent hotels, travel agencies, and other business owners are so busy with the day-to-day operations that they overlook the marketing activities of their tourist products and, therefore, they are unable to expand business and achieve higher levels of profitability. Despite their modest investments and resources, marketing tools can be applied when properly adjusted to the small business context, and improve company performance.

Few small businesses in the industry recognize how important they are to the expanding business of tourism. Marketing on a small budget can be effective and profitable. Market opportunities should be defined and pursued; marketing research can be undertaken; a simple marketing information system can be implemented; segmentation and concentration strategies are crucial for small tourist businesses; product mix and product planning decisions should be made; new tourist products can be developed; low-budget promotional campaigns can be defined and implemented; relations with travel agents can be developed and enhanced; and after sales service policy can be pursued; an overall marketing plan can be devised as well as marketing strategies designed to attain realistic goals and objectives; and marketing control mechanisms such as cost analysis, sales analysis, profitability analysis, and tourist/customer segment analysis should be implemented.

Software/databases

Airways – A Marketing Simulation, by Jamie Fisk and Raymond Fisk, John Wiley Inc., 605 Third Avenue, New York, NY 10158, USA. This simulation game enables users to act as key marketing decision makers in a highly competitive and rapidly changing service industry – the airlines.

Further reading

Bryant, B. E. and Morrison, A. J., 'Travel market segmentation and the implementation of market strategies', *Journal of Travel Research*, vol. XVIII, no. 3 (Winter 1980), pp. 2–6. The article indicates how the segmentation approach should be used to implement marketing strategies.

Cowell, D., *The Marketing of Services* (Heinemann, 1984). A very well-balanced and comprehensive book on services marketing. Chapters 3–10 and 14–17 give an excellent overview of marketing activities as applied to service industries. These chapters deal with topics such as organization, marketing strategy, marketing mix, market analysis and marketing research, service product planning and development, pricing of services, promotion, place decisions, international marketing of services, competition policy, productivity, and the future for services.

Crask, M. R., 'Segmenting the vacationer market: identifying the vacation preferences, demographics, and magazine readership of each group', *Journal of Travel Research*, vol. XX, no. 2 (Fall 1981), pp. 29–33. This article deals with the application of segmentation techniques as related to media planning.

Etzel, M. J. and Woodside, A. G., 'Segmentary vacation markets', *Journal of Travel Research* (Spring 1982) pp. 20. Presents perspectives about segmentation issues as related to the vacation market.

Fridgen, J. D., 'Environmental psychology and tourism', *Annals of Tourism Research*, vol. 11 (1984), pp. 19–39. The article emphasizes the analysis of some travel behavioral concepts such as tourist travel planning, imagery, proxemics and social interaction, environmental perception, on-site behavior, return travel and vicarious exploration.

Greene, M., *Marketing Hotels into the 90s: A Systematic Approach to Increasing Sales* (Heinemann, 1983). Chapters 3, 5, 7, 10, 15, 16 and 20 emphasize concepts such as redefining markets, successful marketing, market segmentation, sales action plans, advertising, publicity, and face-to-face selling.

Gross, C., W. and Peterson, R. T., *Marketing – Concepts and Decision Making* (West Publishing Company, 1987). This book contains several areas that have expanded in significance to today's marketers and deserve indepth treatment.

Hawkins, D. E., Shafer, E. L. and Rovelstad, J. M., *Tourism Marketing and Management Issues* (George Washington University Press, 1980). Presents a thorough review of tourism marketing management topics.

Keiser, J. R., *Principles and Practice of Management in the Hospitality Industry* (CBI Publishing Co., 1979). Chapter 10 presents several marketing and sales management concepts related to the hospitality industry.

Levitt, T., 'Marketing intangible products and product tangibles', *Cornell HRA Quarterly* (August 1981). Explores the characteristics of intangibility of services and the need for their tangibility.

Lovelock, C. M., *Services Marketing* (Prentice Hall, 1984). Special attention should be given to PART IV (Managing the Customer Mix) and PART VII (Planning, Organizing, and Implementing the Marketing Effort).

Lunberg, D. E., *The Tourist Business* (CBI Publishing Co., 4th edition, 1980). Special attention should be given to Chapters 6 and 12, which deal with tourist motivations and travel market research.

Lusch, R. and Lusch, V. N., *Principles of Marketing* (Kent Publishing Company, 1987). This book is designed and written for those who want a basic solid understanding of the critical concepts and phenomena in marketing. It is written in a modular format.

Mayo, E. J. and Jarvis, L. P., *The Psychology of Leisure Travel* (CBI Publishing Co., 1981). This book presents some of the most important consumer behavior concepts as related to travel.

McIntosh, R. W. and Goeldner, C. R., *Tourism: Principles, Practices, Philosophies* (Grid, 4th edition, 1984). Special attention should be given to Chapters 5, 8, 9, and 10. These chapters deal with topics such as tourism psychology and motivation, the consumer market, tourism marketing, and tourism research.

Meidan, A., 'The marketing of tourism', *Marketing in the Service Industries*, G. Foxall, ed. (Frank Cass, 1985). This is a very well-balanced and comprehensive chapter dealing with such topics as an overview of the tourism industry, market segmentation, factors affecting the tourism market, the tourism marketing mix, and tourism marketing strategies.

Meidan, A. and Lee, B., 'Marketing strategies for hotels', *International Journal of Hospitality Management*, vol. 1, no. 3 (1982). This article presents a framework for marketing strategy formulation, development stages, and the most effective marketing strategies for the hotel industry.

Mill, R. C. and Morrison, A. M., *The Tourism System: An Introductory*

Text (Prentice Hall, 1985). This is an excellent and comprehensive book on tourism marketing. Sixteen chapters full of interesting content and useful examples.

Nykiel, R. A., *Marketing in the Hospitality Industry* (CBI Publishing Co., 1983). Special attention should be called to Chapters 2–6, 8, 10, 13 and 14. These chapters deal with segmentation, positioning, channels of distribution, marketing strategy, advertising, promotions, pricing and the total marketing plan.

Reibstein, D. J., Lovelock, C. H. and Dobson, R. De P., 'The direction of causality between perceptions, affect, and behaviour: an application to travel behaviour, *Journal of Consumer Research*, vol. 6 (March 1980), pp. 370–4. This article presents important concepts related to attitude development in travel behavior.

Reilly, R. T., *Travel and Tourism Marketing Techniques – A Handbook of Travel Agency Advertising and Promotion* (Merton House, Travel and Tourism Publishers, 1980). The book covers all aspects of travel agency advertising and promotion techniques. The manual contains virtually everything necessary to plan, develop, and implement a total travel marketing campaign.

Renaghan, L. M., 'A new marketing mix for the hospitality industry', *Cornell HRA Quarterly* (August 1981). Explores new combinations of the marketing mix elements as applied to the hospitality industry.

Varadarajam, P. R., 'Product diversity and firm performance: an empirical investigation', *Journal of Marketing*, vol. 50, no. 3 (July 1986), pp. 43–57. An excellent article on product policy decisions.

Wahab, S. L., Crampon, L. J. and Rothfield, L. M., *Tourism Marketing* (Tourism International Press, 1976). Part I deals with the marketing approach in tourism; Part II contents are related to tourism marketing information; Part III discusses tourism marketing mix; Part IV presents concepts on planning and strategy; Part V deals with marketing in national tourist organizations (NTOs), and Part VI gives an overview of travel industry marketing.

LUIZ MOUTINHO

Marketing plan

Introduction

The marketing plan is a formal document designed to act as a guide in marketing decision making. Historically, marketing plans were very tactical in nature and concentrated on developing detailed methods for implementing marketing strategies. More recently, marketing plans have been used more in strategic marketing management. Within this latter context, the marketing plan takes on a broader role in helping to specify longer-term, more fundamental directions for the business. In this chapter, the more strategic perspective will be adopted.

The marketing plan itself is a document that specifies an integrated program for achieving business objectives within a prescribed time span. While emphasizing marketing objectives and programs, issues in other functional areas within the business that are affected by marketing must be included.

Formulation of a marketing plan is the last step in the strategic marketing planning process. In a sense, it documents the issues considered and analysis undertaken in the determination of business strategies. Company direction and strategies and tactics for getting there are specified. Equally important, the plan acts as a guide for daily decision making. A manager should constantly ask whether specific decisions are being made in a manner consistent with the strategies and tactics included.

Examples

Each year American Airlines develops a System Marketing Plan that summarizes the marketing program for the upcoming year. Some of the plan's key components include: planning assumptions (in areas such as economic growth) and how they will affect travel and tourism markets; forecasts of market potential and revenues by market segment; marketing objectives and strategies to be employed; and action programs (quality and reliability programs, ticketing programs, reservation programs, service levels, special vacation packages etc.)

In the late 1970s and early 1980s, the Dunfey Hotels Corporation instituted a planning approach to marketing manage-

ment. The objective was to develop a standardized approach to management across a rather diverse group of 22 hotels. As a part of that process, managers of each hotel prepare an annual plan and a series of three 4-month plans. Major provisions of each plan include: assessing the supply (number of competitors and their strategies) and demand (market potential by segments such as conventioneers, tourists and business travelers) relationship; determining what market position the hotel should occupy; a gap analysis (the difference between the desired market position and the one currently occupied); and a strategic analysis (moves needed to bridge the position gap).

Recently, United Airlines, Hertz, Westin and other companies have merged into the Allegis Corporation. The marketing plan for Allegis emphasizes the synergism of the individual companies around the concept of travel. Also included are strategies for achieving increased loyalty and delivering quality, value and service to customers.

Benefits

A sound marketing plan provides many benefits, including:

1. Pinpointing organizational strengths and weaknesses.
2. Identifying threats and opportunities in the marketplace.
3. Helping establish an overall, long-term direction for the business.
4. Clarifying the business definition and mission of the organization.
5. Delineating competitive and marketplace position.
6. Pinpointing environmental changes and directions that impact on the business.
7. Coordinating all marketing tools.
8. Quantifying objectives in measurable terms.
9. Specifying strategies for achieving objectives.
10. Establishing dates, deadlines, and responsibilities.
11. Identifying resource acquisition and utilization strategies.
12. Allowing for evaluation of marketing program effectiveness.
13. Providing a working document that can be used as a guide for a manager's continuous decision making.

Implementation

A marketing plan should be developed for each Strategic Business Unit (SBU) in the organization. A SBU is a unit that has: a distinctive mission, a source of marketplace revenue (an external client base), a unique competitive situation, an identifiable resource base, and some strategic independence relative to other SBUs in the organization.

The exact format for the marketing plan varies by organization. This is due partially to the fact that each organization faces different environmental and internal circumstances. It is also the result of different management styles and individual preferences of managers. Each tourist organization should strive to develop plans in a format that best suits its circumstances and style.

Although formats vary, there are certain elements that all marketing plans should include. Table 1 is an ordered summary of what should be included. When formulating the plan, a 3–5 year time frame is used when forecasting changes in markets, competition etc. The plan itself usually covers 1 year with this longer-term dimension used for an analytic base. The plan format shown in Table 1 assumes an ongoing business, but could be modified for use by a new one.

Assessment

A good marketing plan should accomplish six things:

1. It should contain management's thoughts on the SBU's future direction or course. In so doing, a sense of direction is communicated to all parts of the business.
2. It should specify results to be achieved.
3. Strategies to be employed and resources to be acquired and allocated to implement the strategies specified should be laid out. The rationale for strategy selection should also be present.
4. It should provide enough tactical detail to become a working document helpful to daily decision making.
5. A system of program evaluation should emerge.
6. The marketing plan should be a tool managers look forward to generating and using; not something they view as an unnecessary exercise.

The following questions will help determine whether marketing plans are being effectively utilized:

1. Has the process of creating marketing plans helped the business clarify its role within the tourism industry and set a direction for it to take?

Table 1 Sample format for a marketing plan.

Topic	Issues included
Situation analysis Internal	Self-assessment of where the business has come from and where it is going. Current business definition, mission and resources are identified. Emphasizes marketing, operational and financial performance. Marketing strategies currently used are identified. Summarized by a prioritized statement of internal strengths and weaknesses.
External	Analysis of market size and trends overall and by segment, competitive evaluation, consumer decision-making processes by segment, regulatory–political–social environment, industry trends, and general economic conditions affecting tourism. Emphasize both existing and projected future environments. Summarized by a prioritized statement of external threats and opportunities.
Business definition	Statement establishing the general boundaries or parameters of business operation. Includes consumers or segments of market to be served, and generic statement of products/services to be offered. If a business definition already exists, it should be evaluated in the light of factors emerging from the situation analysis.
Mission statement	A general statement of directions the business wants to take (e.g. expand market share, improve service, improve ROI (return on investment). Missions should be realistic and built upon the business's resources and distinctive competencies. Long-term v. short-term trade-offs must be considered.
Objectives	Concise, specific, measureable performance criteria, attainment of which will achieve the business mission. Objectives are usually established for market performance (growth rate, market share etc.), financial performance (profit, ROI etc.) and other key performance areas (e.g. consumer awareness, image)
Marketing strategies	Statements of how the objectives will be met. Should address the following: market segments to be targeted, positioning relative to competition, facility/service requirements, and timing. Rationale for the strategies should be presented. It might be useful also to present other strategies considered and the rationale for their rejection.
Maketing tactics (action programs)	Specific tactics to be used to implement strategies. Should be as detailed as possible, but realistic. Should include specifics in functional areas including pricing, promotions, facility/service offering, and distribution (e.g. use of travel agents). If multiple segments are targeted, tactics in the functional areas must be developed for each segment.
Resource statement	Forecast sales and profit. Establish a budget. Also, identify capital, manpower, physical facility, and other resource additions and/or changes necessary to implement strategies and tactics. Specify responsibilities of other departments in organization necessary to implement the plan.
Evaluation and control	Identify how objectives are to be measured to determine whether they are being achieved, who is responsible, and when evaluation is to occur. Be exact. Identify contingencies if events differ from those built into the plan (e.g. economic conditions are better or worse than assumed) or if results vary significantly from objectives.

2. Has a better understanding of the marketplace emerged and have critical success factors been identified?

3. Are competitive, target market and position issues clearer?

4. Has the plan helped identify clear objectives?

5. Has the plan helped determine more precisely resource needs and allocation?

6. Have marketing managers responsible for implementing programs gained experience and value by being actively involved in the creation of the marketing plans?

7. Has the plan helped specify more precisely criteria to be used in performance evaluation?

8. Have strategic alternatives for approaching the tourist market been identified and analyzed?

9. Has a more thorough, integrated marketing program emerged?

10. Have managers actually been using the marketing plans as a guide to short-term decision making?

Conclusion

Marketing plans help set a long-term direction for a business. Plans can also be used as a guide for more tactical decisions. Much of the value from a marketing plan comes from its formulation. In the volatile tourism industry – where competition, markets and economic/political/social conditions are in flux – the planning system forces continuous monitoring and analysis of these factors by managers at all levels.

Effective use of marketing plans results in a coordinated approach to the marketplace. Business units gain a greater appreciation of their role and how they fit into the overall organization.

Focus on small business

It is important for a small business to formulate a marketing plan. Small tourist businesses usually concentrate on a particular market segment and have a narrow product/service line. Concentrating creates risks from competitive duplication and shifts in market demand. It is important, therefore, for the small tourist business to constantly monitor the environment for threatening changes and new opportunities. A second major value to the small business comes from developing strategies to differentiate from larger firms and develop a distinctiveness. Finally, there is a tendency for small firms to add services and broaden target markets in order to grow. The market planning process forces a systematic evaluation of strategies so that haphazard changes do not occur.

Developing a marketing plan for a small tourist business is not an impossible task. Data on markets, competitors etc. is available from government agencies and trade associations. Also, many of the complexities of formulating marketing plans in a diversified tourist firm do not exist. Finally, there are many executive development programs put on by governments, universities and private companies that provide training on how to develop marketing plans.

Further reading

Abell, D. F. and Hammond, J. S., *Strategic Market Planning* (Prentice Hall, 1979). Excellent presentation of the concept of strategic market planning, planning tools, and the planning process. Chapter 10 focuses on the process of preparing a strategic market plan.

Cravens, D. W., *Strategic Marketing* (Irwin, 2nd edition, 1987). Chapter 17 discusses preparation of an annual marketing plan and methods for implementation of the plan.

Day, G. S., *Strategic Market Planning: The Pursuit of Competitive Advantage* (West Publishing Co., 1984). Chapter 3 describes the strategic market planning process and outlines the key features of a marketing plan.

Dircks, W., *Types of Statistics Needed Most From Tourism Research* (US Travel Service, 1971). Provides information on the determination of market segments and market potential by segment for numerous countries. Useful in marketing plan development.

Gunn, C. A., *Tourism Planning* (Crane Russak, 1979). The best single source dealing with planning in the tourism industry. Entire book devoted to formulating plans and strategies for a tourist firm. Chapter 12 discusses the written plan. Focuses on marketing and other topics such as land development.

Hopkins, D. S., *The Marketing Plan* (Conference Board, Report No. 801, 1981). Discusses utilization of marketing plans by businesses. Describes steps in preparation of plans and provides numerous examples of those developed by companies.

Kopp. R. J., 'Dunfey hotels corporation', *Services Marketing*, C. H. Lovelock, ed. (Prentice Hall, 1984), pp. 463–75. A case discussion of the philosophy behind and use of marketing plans by a mid-sized hotel chain.

Luck, D. L. and Ferrell, O. C., *Marketing Strategy and Plans* (Prentice Hall, 1979). The marketing plan is the topic of Chapter 15. Emphasis is placed on techniques for measuring the outcome of a plan's implementation.

Lundberg, D. E., *The Tourist Business* (Cahners Books, 2nd edition, 1974). The chapter entitled, 'Tourism destination development' discusses the role of marketing planning in development of master plans for tourist destination. Also discussed is the value of an interdisciplinary approach to planning.

McIntosh, R. W., *Tourism: Principles, Practices, Philosophies* (Grid, 1972). Chapters 10 and 11 discuss marketing research and data input necessary to formulate marketing plans.

Marcus, B. H. and Tauber, E. M., *Marketing Analysis and Decision Making* (Little, Brown and Co., 1982). Detailed summaries of actual marketing plans are presented in Chapter 13. One of the plans is for a major airline.

RONALD L. ZALLOCCO

Marketing of tourism in small island states

Introduction

The development of tourism in small island economies is constricted by their small economic and geographical size and often their remoteness. Any island state with a population of less than 5 million people can be classified as small. Small island economies are confronted with a host of problems such as high population density, limited resources, low agricultural productivity, unequal land distribution, high unemployment and underemployment, small domestic markets and high production costs, low economic growth, and foreign debt. As a major earner of foreign exchange and an important creator of employment, tourism is expected to alleviate some of these problems, to reduce their substantial dependence on a small range of export commodities, and to broaden the islands' narrow economic base.

In many island states, tourism has become the dominant economic sector while, in others, it has not been possible to develop tourism on a commercial scale because either the facilities needed are not available yet, or their problem of remoteness and accessibility has not been resolved. Unlike the islands' traditional agricultural exports which are threatened by lower demand, declining prices and protectionist measures, tourism has relatively few restrictions as tourists are allowed to move from the developed to developing nations. Such freedom of movement becomes inconsequential unless the tourist product is properly promoted and marketed.

So, the marketing of tourism in small island states is a challenging exercise in view of their small promotional budgets which are insufficient to make any impact in the highly competitive tourism market. The policy makers and the National Tourist Offices (NTOs) must formulate the appropriate marketing policies and strategies which will be conducive to tourism growth. There must also be close collaboration with all those involved with the tourist industry so that the marketing efforts of the private and public sectors can be coordinated.

Examples

Most of the small island states which had recently acquired their political independence had a weak tourist industry during the colonial rule. Their former rulers failed to encourage the development of tourism as their economic structure was oriented towards the supply of raw materials to the metropoles. After independence, their narrow and weak economic foundation was so severely exposed that diversification of the economy was regarded as the only solution to economic viability. Their small size compounded by the availability of limited resources circumscribes the scope for diversification. But, the presence of natural and environmental resources may facilitate the development and marketing of tourism in the small island economies.

Two small island nations, Mauritius and the Seychelles, in the Indian Ocean typify the successful development of tourism. Equipped with an initially small tourist base, they have been able to develop and expand tourism to such an extent that it has been transformed into an important economic sector. The development of tourism in these two islands is essentially due to their skill in exploiting their remoteness and isolation to their own advantage through their easy accessibility by sea and air. Both countries have seemingly adopted the same marketing strategies in their effort to direct more tourists to their destinations.

Their marketing policies are based on creating a 'mix' market for their tourist industry for two main reasons. First, they want to attract a diversified market. Secondly, both islands are in a position to provide different types of accommodation. In their main longhaul markets (e.g. Western European countries) and in their principal mediumhaul market (South Africa), the aim of their promotional and marketing strategies is to emphasize their exclusivity. Unlike most of the Caribbean island states where charters are allowed to operate, Mauritius and the Seychelles do not countenance their operation from Western Europe and South Africa because of the necessity not to damage their high quality image in their principal tourist generating markets. Above all, the success of their marketing campaign hinges on their continued ability to attract the high-spending tourists from these markets. In their shorthaul market (Reunion Island), they have promoted their product as cheap and affordable.

Demand for selective tourism poses major problems to most small island economies. The Seychelles and Mauritius will prefer to concentrate their marketing campaign in South Africa and Western Europe because tourists from the latter have a higher propensity to spend in relation to those from their shorthaul market. This implies that the supply of superstructure, more particularly accommodation and entertainment, should be of international standard. Access to this market demands expensive facilities which the local entrepreneurs are unable to develop and finance. If the development of up-market tourism results in the tourist industry being dominated by foreign companies, then a cautious approach must be adopted towards the development and marketing of this type of tourism.

No island state should depend entirely on one type of tourism, especially where local participation might be excluded on the ground of cost. Even though there is a definite tendency to favor selective tourism because of its income and price inelasticities, policy makers must rationally formulate policies which will have more positive effects on the economy. A marketing strategy favoring a 'market-mix' approach is important for tourism development because the hotel establishments catering for the up-market tourists are under the virtual monopolistic control of foreign enterprises. Relying entirely upon this type of tourism is inappropriate for small island economies as there is a danger that this will result in increased dependency.

On the other hand, the market for low- and middle-income tourism is normally dominated by local entrepreneurs who operate and manage the small to medium-sized hotels. Such hotels do not require the high level of service provided by the luxurious hotels. One major advantage is that these establishments will make more use of local food and products. Although the marketing of this type of tourism is more beneficial to the local economies, their governments have failed to encourage the establishment of the small to medium-sized hotels because there is a feeling that this type of tourism does not have the same effect as selective tourism.

Benefits

The marketing of tourism in small island economies must emphasize the quality of the product in relation to the other competing ones because of the multitude of destinations selling an undifferentiated product. Small island economies must concentrate their marketing efforts on creating positive aspects of the products in the mind of the potential tourists. The high quality usually associated with island tourism must be preserved and enhanced since it represents an important asset in the marketing process. But, the benefits of tourism marketing vary for each island as these will depend on their level of tourism development. Islands with an advanced stage of tourism development will not adopt the same marketing strategies as those whose tourist industry has just been established; the former can attempt to diversify their markets by marketing and promoting their product in other potential tourist generating countries while the latter must start their marketing campaign by initially concentrating in a few markets.

An island state where tourism development is still at an embryonic stage cannot be expected to tap all the potential markets because of the limited amount of financial resources available for the promotion and marketing of tourism. Its mar-

keting efforts must be concentrated on a relatively up-market clientele which can be expected to bring in the maximum net economic and employment benefits per bed space because this segment of the market has a high level of disposable income. In marketing their product, on the other hand, the more established destinations are concerned to attract more tourists because their aim is to improve the utilization of existing facilities.

The need to preserve a good image is acknowledged to be beneficial in the marketing process. Since tourists do not have prior knowledge of the product they are buying, they take into consideration the image projected by NTOs, tour operators and media. Because of the intense competition in the international market place, image becomes a critical factor in directing tourist flows. The relatively high cost of a holiday to these small islands states excludes a large section of the potential tourists and as such, in marketing their tourist product, their images must be projected with care in a few specialized publications with a view to reaching the targeted segment.

Since most of the small islands offer an undifferentiated product, there is a strong case for countries in the same region to enter into a 'cooperation' marketing agreement. This will not only allow them to complement each other but also, perhaps, to explore the possibility of breaking into other potential markets. Small island states will not, however, be able to benefit from the development and marketing of tourism unless a climate of political stability prevails. In order to gain the maximum benefits from tourism, their marketing strategy must not be directed exclusively to the up-market tourists, because of the volatility of the tourist industry and because demand for tourism is dominated by foreign enterprises, over which the tourist receiving island states do not have any control. It will be more appropriate and beneficial to small island economies if a 'mix' marketing strategy is implemented since they will not depend entirely upon a single type of clientele.

Implementation

The implementation of policies to market and promote tourism is influenced by a number of factors which will determine its success. Location, for instance, plays a decisive role in the type of tourism development that can be initiated. Some islands are more favorably situated than others. Those which are not far from the large tourist markets (e.g. The Bahamas and Bermuda close to the United States and Canada) have a great advantage in transport costs while those remote from their main markets (e.g. Samoa and Vanuatu distant from New Zealand and Australia) are in a disadvantageous position because they are scattered out of the way of the principal shipping and airline routes.

Some of these remote islands are also a long distance from each other. This implies that the organization of multidestination holidays, which can increase the tourist flow to the region, can only be organized with difficulty unless regular transport links can be established. But, with the possible exception of the Caribbean islands which are located near their very important North American markets, other island states do not share the same advantage. On the other hand, because of their location, islands in the South Pacific have identified the cost of transport as representing a natural barrier to the movement of tourists. Since the high cost of a holiday to these destinations makes it unfeasible to compete against cheaper island tourism, in marketing their tourist product, they must emphasize their isolation and their resulting uniqueness because relatively easy accessibility to most countries of the world has made isolation a scarce commodity.

It is indispensable for all small island economies to differentiate their tourist product in terms of price, quality and scarcity since these destinations are to some extent in competition with one another. 'New' island tourist destinations, unlike islands at an advanced stage of tourism development are products which need far more intensive and specialized marketing support to win acceptance, market share and sustained demand.

As demand for international tourism is concentrated geographically, in theory it looks facile to tap all these potential markets. In practice, it is difficult to achieve this goal because of two inhibiting factors. First insufficient promotional and marketing expenditures are available to penetrate all the markets. It will be more beneficial to market the product in a few selected markets. Secondly, there is intense competition to attract tourists in the highly competitive marketplace because most island destinations seem to offer the same 'exotic tropical destination'.

Although a degree of competition between the islands is inevitable, destinations within the same region must cooperate on joint marketing campaigns, especially when the trend towards 'island hopping' circuits involving two or more island states is gaining in popularity. In this case, the differentiation of their products must avoid emphasizing them as being competitive destinations but rather as complementary to each other. In the long term, most small island economies must regard multi-destination holidays as necessary to their tourism development because their small size will only permit limited tourist capacity. Once saturation level has been reached these countries will have to encourage the marketing of this type of tourism in order to increase average spending per visitor-day.

Assessment

Those involved in the marketing of tourism will be judged by their ability to attract more tourists. The principal factor determining the type of tourists likely to visit any destination is pricing. The high price of a holiday to small island states is based on their distance, and the high quality of the product. Since their main objective is to appeal to the up-market tourists, then the standard of facilities must be equally high. In principle, there should not be any objection regarding the high price of island tourism but tourists, like any consumers, are primarily concerned with value for money. Criticisms have been leveled against some tourist receiving countries for their failure to match the expectations of their visitors.

A drop in demand caused by recession or any other economic problems in the 'trigger' markets must not be reacted to by

excessive price reduction because that will only attract a different type of clientele. Once an island destination has become known as a mass tourism package destination, it will be difficult to recover its exclusive image because, for small islands, the country is the destination. Small islands can also lose control over the type of tourism they want to market unless the proper management of their fragile ecosystem and cultural assets is undertaken with a view to preserving the high quality and exclusivity of the product.

There might be a conflict of interests between the tour operators and the local tourist authorities. On the one hand, the former are more influenced by profit-maximization through high volume, high-turnover, and lower-cost product if there is a drop in demand, while on the other hand, the latter, because of the islands' limited tourist capacity, wish to maximize the benefits derived from tourism by attracting the high-income clientele. So, the tourist-receiving countries must offer a high quality product in order to satisfy their visitors and the tour operators because of the high level of substitutability that exists among the tourist destinations.

The distribution system of the international tourist industry is such that the ability of the small island destinations to influence demand through their own marketing and promotional campaigns is severely restricted because of the high costs involved. The distribution channel is dominated by transnational corporations with extensive interests in hotel operations, airlines, tour operation and retailing. Tour operators and travel agents are so powerful that they can make or break a destination because, since tourists may not have a clear notion of their holiday destinations, they act as go-between between the tourist-receiving nations and the potential tourists.

Conclusion

The marketing of tourism represents a critical challenge to both the private and public sector involved in the development of tourism in the small island states. The latter must formulate a coherent marketing strategy that will spell out the policies required to sell their tourist product more effectively. Unlike any other products, the tourist product is lost if tourists are not attracted to buy it. Because of the high costs needed in the marketing of tourism in the principal tourist generating countries, the NTO must forge close links with all those involved in the development and promotion of tourism so that the benefits of tourism can be maximized. The marketing of island tourism must, above all, emphasize the need to maintain a high quality product and an exclusive image.

Further reading

Archer, B. H. and Wanhill, S., *The Economic Impact of Tourism in Mauritius* (University of Surrey, 1981). A report prepared for the World Bank.

Beekhis, J. V., 'Tourism in the Caribbean', *Ambio*, vol. 10, no. 6 (1981), pp. 325–33. This article examines the role played by tourism in the development of small island economies.

Bertram, G., 'Sustainable development in Pacific micro-economies', *World Development*, vol. 14, no. 7 (1986), pp. 809–22. This article examines the viability and continued dependency of small islands upon the metropolitan powers.

Britton, R., 'The image of the Third World in tourism marketing', *Annals of Tourism Research*, vol. 6, no. 3 (1979), pp. 318–29. Explores the importance of image in the marketing of tourism in the developing nations.

Bryden, J. M., *Tourism and Development: A Case Study of the Commonwealth Caribbean* (Cambridge University Press, 1973). This book deals with the merits and demerits of tourism development in small island economies.

Burkart, A. J., 'Small island phenomena', *Tourism Management*, vol. 6, no. 1 (1985), pp. 2–3. This short introduction states the main reasons why tourism should be developed in small island states.

Burkart, A. J. and Medlik, S., *The Management of Tourism* (Heinemann, 1975). Attention should be given to Chapters 12–14 which deal with the importance of tourism marketing and tourism promotion.

Butler, A., *An Introduction to Mini-economies* (Gruner, 1985). This book outlines the main constraints which affect small economies.

Cheung Young, P., 'Tourism in the development of small states: Jamaica's experience', Conference on small economies (1981). This article looks at the main factors affecting tourism growth.

Cohen, R., *African Islands and Enclaves* (Sage, 1983). This book discusses the emerging strategic importance of these countries and their limited scope for economic development.

Commonwealth Secretariat, *Vulnerability: Small States in the Society* (Commonwealth Secretariat, 1985). This book describes the needs for small developing nations to become less dependent upon the developed countries.

Demas, W. G., *The Economies of Developments in Small Islands with Special Reference to the Caribbean* (Montreal University Press, 1965). This book analyzes the main economic weaknesses of small island states.

Dilley, R. S., 'Tourist brochures and tourist images', *Canadian Geographer*, vol. 30, no. 1 (1986), pp. 59–65. Presents the view that the image of a destination plays an important role in its tourism marketing.

Dommen, E. C. and Hein, P., *States, Microstates and Islands* (Croom Helm, 1985). This book analyzes the main problems confronted by small economies and Chapters 4 and 7 are concerned with the use of tourism as a tool for economic development.

Economic Commission for Africa, *Study on Tourism in the Indian Ocean* (ECA, 1981). This study explains why small island states must formulate marketing strategies and policies to develop tourism.

Faber, M., 'Island microstates: problems of viability', *The Round Table*, no. 4 (1984), pp. 372–6. This article stresses the reasons why this type of country has failed to achieve it development.

Harden, S., *Small is Dangerous – Microstates in a Macroworld* (Frances Pinter, 1985). This book analyzes the disadvantages that economic smallness might cause to small nations.

International Bank for Reconstruction & Development, *A Study of the Contribution of Tourism to the Antiguan Economy* (1975). This study formulates the appropriate marketing strategy needed to initiate tourism development in a small island economy.

Jalan, B., *Problems and Policies in Small Economies* (Croom Helm, 1982). This book looks at the limited economic options available for the development of small economies and tourism is regarded as one of the possibilities.

Latimer, H., 'Developing-island economies – tourism and agriculture', *Tourism Management*, vol. 6, no. 1 (1985). This article discusses one

of the conflicts that tourism gives rise to in economies where there is a scarcity of land.

Legarda, B., 'Small island economies', *Finance and Development*, vol. 21 (1984), pp. 42–3. This article analyzes the industrial policies that can be implemented in the small island states.

Livingstone, I., 'International transport costs and industrial development in the least developed African countries', *Industry and Development*, no. 19 (1986), pp. 1–54. This article asserts that the failure to establish a sound internal and external transport network has inhibited the development of Third World nations.

MacNaught, T. J., 'Mass tourism and the dilemma of modernization in Pacific island communities', *Annals of Tourism Research*, vol. 9, no. 3 (1982), pp. 359–81. This article emphasizes the problems caused by tourism development in small island communities.

McEachern, J. and Towley, E. L., *Ecological Guidelines for Island Development* (International Union for Conservation of Nature and Natural Resources, 1974). This study argues the case for the protection of the fragile environment in the development of island tourism.

Naya, S., 'Asian and Pacific developing countries: development issues and challenge,' *Asian Development Bank*, vol. 1, no. 1 (1983), pp. 1–40. Examines the different economic structures of these nations and the development problems faced by the islands in the Pacific Ocean.

Oglethorpe, M., 'Tourism in a small island economy: the case of Malta', *Tourism Management*, vol. 6, no. 1 (1985), pp. 23–31. This article emphasizes the successful growth of tourism in Malta.

Organization for Economic Cooperation and Development, *The Impact of Tourism on the Environment* (OECD, 1980). This study takes the view that if tourism development is properly managed, the damages to the environment can be minimized.

Ostheimer, J. M., *The Politics of Western Indian Ocean Islands* (Praeger, 1975). This book examines the political, economic and social conditions prevailing in those nations.

Pearce, D. G., *Tourism in the South Pacific* (UNESCO, 1980). This collection of articles looks at the diverse aspects of tourism development, including tourism demand, tourism promotion and tourism marketing.

Pepplenbosch, P. G. W. and Templeman, G. T., 'Le tourisme international et les pays en voie de développement', *Les Cahiers d'Outre Mer*, vol. 27 (1974), pp. 77–87. The article details the benefits and disbenefits of tourism development in the Third World nations.

Rajotte, F. and Crocombe, R., *Pacific Tourism as Islanders see it* (University of the South Pacific, Fiji, 1980). This book outlines the dangers of tourism development as perceived by the small tourist-receiving island states.

Rawat, R., 'Product marketing' Tourism and Air Transport Conference, Manila, 1985. This paper articulates the policies that need to be adopted in tourism marketing.

Shand, R. T. (ed.), *The Island States of the Pacific and Indian Oceans: Anatomy of Development* (The Australian National University, 1980). This book presents the issues that are likely to affect the development of small island economies and tourism is one of them.

Selwyn, P. (ed.), *Development policy in small countries* (Croom Helm, 1975). This book formulates policies which might result in reducing dependency upon the developed nations.

Tata, R. J., 'Poor and small too: Caribbean mini-states', *Focus*, vol. 29, no. 2 (1978), pp. 1–12. This article analyzes the main economic characteristics of underdevelopment in small island economies.

Treaster, J. B., 'Finding the right Caribbean island', *International Herald Tribune* (20 November 1987), pp. 7–9. This article looks at the different stages of tourism development in the Caribbean region.

Tsusaka, A., 'South Pacific developing countries: development issues and challenge', *Asian Development Review*, vol. 2, no. 1, pp. 65–81. Explores the main geographical and economic constraints facing small island economies.

United Nations Committee on Trade and Development, *Developing Island Economies* (United Nations, 1974). This study emphasizes the importance of economic diversification and the need to develop tourism as a means to that end.

United Nations Development Advisory Team, *South Pacific: Guidelines for the Development of Tourism* (United Nations, 1979). The last section of this report examines marketing strategies for small island economies.

Virahsawmy, R., *The Characteristics of Island Economies*, Seminar Papers (University of Mauritius, 1975). Presents the view that these economies must be restructured so that they may overcome their development problems.

Williamson, P. F., 'Tourism in small island nations: a fragile dependence', *Leisure Studies*, vol. 6, no. 2 (1987), pp. 117–46. Discusses the danger for small island economies to depend exclusively upon tourism for their development.

Wing, P. C. L., *Tourism in Mauritius* (MSc Dissertation, University of Strathclyde, 1981). Discusses the importance of formulating and implementing the right policies for the development of tourism.

Wing, P. C. L., *Tourism and Small Island Economies: A Comparative Study of Seychelles and Mauritius* (Forthcoming Ph.D Thesis, University of Strathclyde). This study looks at the relevance of tourism as a tool for development in the small island economies.

World Development, Special issues on Islands, vol. 8, no. 12 (1980). This collection of articles discusses the development policies that are needed to make them more viable.

PHILIPPE C. L. WING

Methods of measuring market volume and market shares in European tourism

Introduction

The development of the tourism market is marked by increasingly tough competition. New developing destinations enrich the wide range of tourist offers. The fast growth of aircraft for mass transportation and a wider travel experience make holiday destinations more easily interchangeable. In order to use marketing to meet this tough competition an increasing demand for market knowledge has developed. For national tourist offices, international hotel chains or tour operators the travel volume of tourism-generating nations and the respective market share is a fundamental aspect for the planning of market activities.

The Austrian National Tourist Office has developed a 'marketing information system' (MIS), which is based on electronic data processing. It contains three major elements:

1. Database.
2. Forecasting elements.
3. Budget allocation model.

The forecasting elements and the budget allocation model depend to a large extent on the data of the market volume and market share in the database. Measurements for market volume and market share in the MIS include the following:

1. National bednights matrix.
2. Cities bednights matrix.
3. Travel surveys and microcensus.
4. International tourist receipts and expenditures.

Continuous travel surveys like the travel survey of the British Tourist Authority or the Studienkreis für Tourismus, Starnberg in West Germany exist only for few countries. Travel surveys are in many cases only concerned with the major trip of the year and don't look into the segment of shorter trips. Last but not least, most of the travel surveys are not comparable. Owing to this lack of comparable data in travel surveys the Austrian National Tourist Office has developed a national bednights matrix. The idea is rather simple: by adding the bednights of a generating country such as West Germany, to the major receiving countries, the market volume of the German travel market and the market share of each receiving country can be estimated. This method allows an estimation for countries, which do not have travel surveys and makes the market volume of the generating countries comparable.

In the MIS so far nine European receiving countries were used for estimating the market volume of 19 generating countries.

Receiving countries

Austria	West Germany
Switzerland	France
United Kingdom	Greece
Italy	Yugoslavia
Spain	

Generating countries

Austria	Australia + New Zealand
Belgium + Luxembourg	Canada
France	Denmark
West Germany	Greece
Netherlands	Italy
Sweden	Japan
Switzerland	Yugoslavia
United Kingdom	Norway
United States	Finland
	Spain

As the bednight statistics of the nine receiving countries were not fully comparable and in some cases not even complete, the missing data had to be estimated by different means like arrival data, corresponding travel surveys and statistics on receipts and expenditure.

The market volumes and market shares of the bednights matrix are estimates and include errors as all estimates do. Nevertheless, so far the system of the bednights matrix seems to be the best way to estimate comparable market volumes of the 19 major generating countries and the market shares of receiving countries. As the data for the bednights matrix have existed continuously since 1959, the long-term development of tourism flows in Europe can be measured. Comparison with the existing travel survey shows that the bednights matrix is a useful instrument for measurements.

Example: the West German travel market

Development of the market volume

The West German travel market is, compared to other travel markets, well documented. The Studienkreis für Tourismus in Starnberg has carried out, since 1970, a German travel survey, which allows a continuous picture of the market development.

Figure 1 shows the MIS-bednights of Germans in West Germany and in the eight major receiving countries. More than 90 per cent of all German bednights occur in these nine countries. The German travel survey shows a very similar development from measurement of the number of trips.

The Austrian market share of the West German travel market

Travel surveys show in most cases only the market share in the 'major trips' segment. These are trips which last at least four

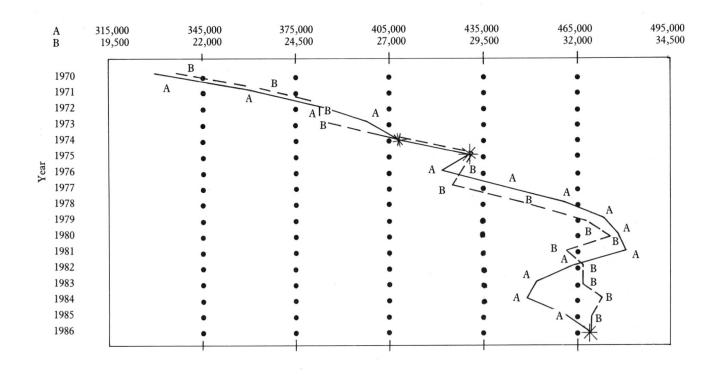

Year	A	B
1970	328.173	21.100
1971	358.234	23.300
1972	378.066	25.100
1973	397.858	25.100
1974	405.938	27.000
1975	429.343	29.200
1976	421.102	28.800
1977	440.116	28.600
1978	460.662	30.600
1979	472.925	32.100
1980	279.466	32.800
1981	480.970	31.600
1982	462.619	32.100
1983	450.775	32.000
1984	449.653	32.600
1985	459.016	32.300
1986	470.953	32.400

Figure 1 The West German travel market (thousands) A = number of bednights of West Germans in their own country and in eight foreign countries (MIS); B = number of trips (*Source:* Travel survey, *Studienkreis für Tourismus*).

nights. The tourism traffic of short trips, especially in border countries, is in most cases neglected.

Figure 2 shows the comparison between the Austrian market share in the bednights matrix and the results of the German travel survey. It shows clearly that Austria loses stronger market shares with trips longer than four nights (German travel survey) than in the overall volume of all kinds of trips (short trips and trips longer than four nights) measured by the bednights matrix.

Figure 3 is a comparison between the Austrian market share in the bednights matrix and the Austrian market share of the spending of Germans on tourism abroad.

Conclusion

The bednights matrix in the MIS of the Austrian National Tourist Office allows the estimation of the following:

1. A comparison of market volumes generated by major tourism countries.
2. The development of market volumes.
3. The market share of major receiving countries.
4. The development of market shares.

The bednights matrix cannot be regarded as a substitute travel

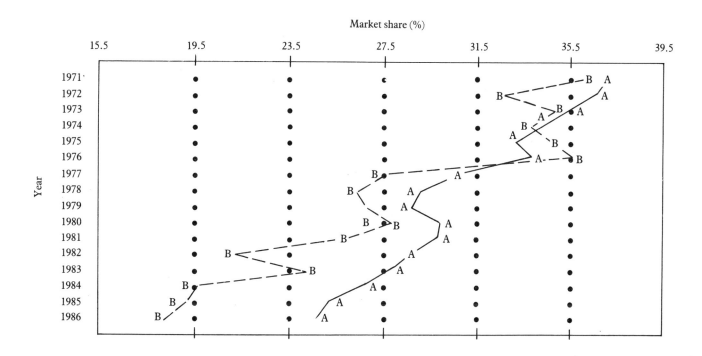

Year	A	B
1971	37.036	36.131
1972	36.697	32.420
1973	35.170	34.943
1974	33.903	33.630
1975	33.363	34.396
1976	33.668	35.874
1977	30.407	27.332
1978	28.836	26.132
1979	28.573	26.349
1980	29.573	27.719
1981	29.558	25.620
1982	28.434	20.930
1983	27.859	24.217
1984	26.630	19.246
1985	25.053	18.824
1986	24.638	18.271

Figure 2 The Austrain market share of the West German travel market. A = Austria's market share in the total of West German bednights in eight countries (MIS); B = Austria's market share in the number of travelers to eight countries (*Source:* Travel survey, *Studienkreis für Tourismus*).

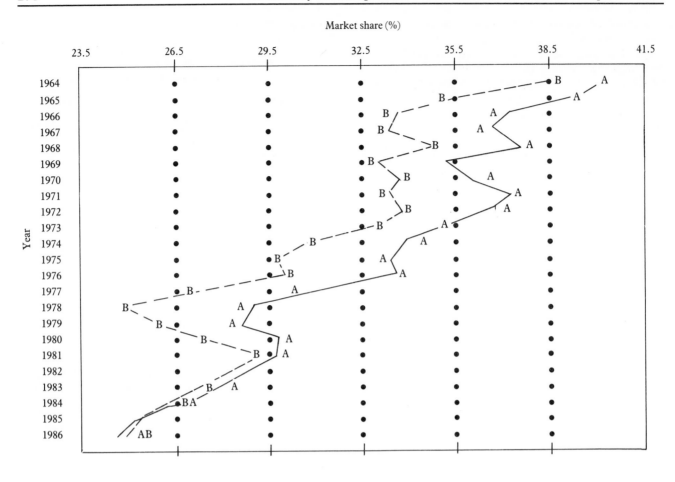

Year	A	B
1964	40.026	38.350
1965	39.263	35.400
1966	37.189	33.630
1967	36.667	33.230
1968	37.424	34.610
1969	35.059	32.860
1970	36.057	33.430
1971	37.036	33.360
1972	36.697	33.560
1973	35.170	32.900
1974	33.903	31.000
1975	33.363	29.550
1976	33.668	29.820
1977	30.407	26.950
1978	28.836	24.940
1979	28.573	25.810
1980	29.573	27.310
1981	29.558	29.050
1982	28.434	28.730
1983	27.859	27.550
1984	26.630	26.490
1985	25.053	25.290
1986	24.638	24.940

Figure 3 Comparison between the Austrian market share in the bednight matrix (MIS) and that in the spending of West Germans abroad. A = Austria's market share in the total of West German bednights in eight countries (MIS); B = Austria's market share in the tourism spending of West Germans abroad (*Source:* WIFO, Austrian Institute for Economic Research).

survey; travel surveys give a much better survey of the travel behavior of a country.

The same methodology as described earlier was applied to 30 European cities. This allows the estimation of the demand for tourism to these cities from each generating market, and the market shares of each city.

The bednights matrix is the foundation of our macroeconomic forecasting models and the budget allocation model to optimize the marketing budget allocation of the Austrian National Tourist Office.

Further reading/databases

British Tourist Authority, *British Travel Survey* (BTA, 1985).

Central bureau voor de statistik, *Vakantie – Onderzoek* (Central bureau voor de statistik, 1975–1985).

Fuhri, R., *Die Auskunfts- und Reportfunktion des MIS* (Austrian National Tourist Office, June 1984).

Gabinete de Investigacion Turistica, *Las Vacacienes de los Espanoles* (Gabinete de Investigacion Turistica, 1981–1984).

Hruschka/Rosenmayr, *Musteranalysen Touristischer Marktdiagnosen und Prognosen* (Austrian National Tourist Office, December 1983).

Insee, *Les Vacances des Françaises* (Insee, 1974–1986).

Institut für Fremdenverkehr, *Österreichische Reisemarktanalyse 1981/82* (Institut für Fremdenverkehr, 1981/82).

Institut für Fremdenverkehr und Verkehrswirtschaft, *Reisemarkt Schweiz* (Institut für Fremdenverkehr und Verkehrswirtschaft, 1970–1986).

Istituto Centrale di Statistica, *Indagine sulle Vacanze Degli Italiani* (Istituto Centrale di Statistica, 1968–1986).

Mazanec, J., *Budopt-Ein Dialogmodell zur EDV-unterstützenden Budgetplanung* (Austrian National Tourist Office, November 1983).

Müller, K. H., *Das Marktvolumen der Europäischen Herkunftsländer* (Austrian National Tourist Office, 1983).

Müller, K. H., *Entwicklungstendenzen der Deutschen Sommerurlaubsreise nach Österreich* (Austrian National Tourist Office, 1985).

Müller, K. H., *Meßinstrumente für Marktvolumen und Marktanteile im Europäischen Fremdenverkehr* (Austrian National Tourist Office, 1984).

Müller, K. H., *MIS* (Marketing Information System), (Austrian National Tourist Office, 1985).

Organization of Economic Cooperation and Development, *Tourism Policy and International Tourism* (OECD, 1974–1986).

Österreichisches Statistisches Zentralamt, *Reisegewohnheiten der Österreicher Mikrozensus* (Österreichisches Statistisches Zentralamt, 1970–1986).

Steiner, M., *Die EDV-Technische Umsetzung der MIS-Anfragen* (Austrian National Tourist Office, June 1984).

Studienkreis für Tourismus, *Deutsche Reiseanalyse* (Studienkreis für Tourismus, 1970–1986).

Westvlaams Ekonomisch Studienbureau, *Les Belges en Vacances* (Westvlaams Ekonomisch Studienbureau, 1979–1985).

World Tourism Organization, *World Travel and Tourism Statistics* (WTO, 1974–1986).

KARL HEINZ MÜLLER

Multi-nation tourism promotion

Introduction

Tourism, one of the fastest growing industries, is expected to become the world's largest in the twenty-first century. Since 1960, this industry has experienced an average growth of over 10 per cent and it is estimated that by the year 2000, there will be over two billion tourists traveling. In spite of this phenomenal growth, the developing countries' share of the international tourist market has remained small as the expansion of tourism has taken place predominantly within the developed world. So, the developing nations want to capture a bigger share of this growing market.

The main factor affecting tourist flow to a particular destination is promotion. Most countries, developed and developing alike, have acknowledged the crucial importance played by tourism promotion since financial resources, though in short supply in the latter, are allocated to this end. Any tourist development strategy without the inclusion of promotion is likely to result in failure because the tourist product cannot be sold unless it is properly promoted and marketed. Developed countries, however, are better able to promote their products in the main tourist-generating markets than the developing countries, because of less financial constraints.

Multi-nation tourism promotion will facilitate cooperation between two or more countries in a region so that they can promote their tourist products, their image and their regional attractions. This type of promotion is particularly attractive to the developing nations because of their inability to launch individual promotional campaigns in the main trigger markets. Some of the governments of the developing world may be misguided into believing that the presence of environmental and cultural attractions is a sufficient prerequisite for tourism growth, but the flow of international tourists to their destination will depend on creating an awareness of the product.

If countries within a region find it uneconomic to promote their product individually multi-nation tourism promotion might be the answer. Since tourism is becoming increasingly important to the economies of the Third World nations, it is imperative that this scheme works so that their financial problem can be overcome.

Examples

Various examples exist to prove that multi-nation tourism promotion can be effective, provided there is good understanding and close cooperation among the participating nations. The European Travel Commission (ETC) whose membership is composed of the National Tourist Organizations (NTOs) embodies the success of a regional approach to tourism promotion. Although all its members are financially able to undertake their own individual promotional campaigns, the ETC tries to supplement their promotions by undertaking marketing research in their leading tourist-generating countries, namely the United States, Canada and Japan. Because of the absence of political interference, the ETC is able to function efficiently and effectively in the promotion of European tourism.

The sustained success of the ETC as a vehicle for multi-nation tourism promotion has led many multilateral organizations such as the United Nations Development Programme (UNDP), World Tourism Organization (WTO) and European Community (EC) to encourage the establishment of a similar model for the developing countries. Tourism is still not well-established in developing countries, however, and since the scarcity of financial resources prevents many of them from promoting tourism effectively, the creation of a regional tourism organization will give them the opportunity to combine their knowledge and their resources in promoting their product in a larger number of countries. Although multi-nation tourism promotion implies promoting one's competitors as well as oneself, the benefits will accrue to all the countries in the region, as tourism grows.

Third World nations are equally aware of the merits of multi-nation tourism promotion. Regional tourism organizations such as the Pacific Asia Travel Association (PATA) and the Caribbean Tourism Association (CTA) have been primarily occupied with promoting tourism within their member countries. Since its formation in 1951, the CTA has been actively engaged in developing a regional image for its tourist product with a view to benefiting the entire region. Since most of its members are underdeveloped, they find it difficult to find the resources required to initiate and promote tourism. Initially, the CTA was concerned with the marketing of tourism in the United States and Canada, but the islands in the Caribbean region have become overdependent on these two markets. As a result, the CTA is formulating policies to diversify so that other potential markets such as the Western European countries can be tapped.

Joint tourism promotion involving two or more countries is gaining in popularity among the developing countries. In South Asia where Sri Lanka had emerged as the gateway for multi-destination tourism, there was a high level of cooperation to encourage and promote the organization of regional circuits. Sri Lanka, the leading-tourist receiving country in the region was promoted in conjunction with Nepal, Maldives and India and the foreign tour operators were offering tours involving these countries. Close cooperation combined with joint promotional campaigns had benefited all the participating nations and had also facilitated the movement of tourists from one country to another. Attractive packages for multidestination holidays, for example Sri Lankan culture integrated with Nepalese mountains and beaches in the Maldives, were available. The popularity of this type of tourism, benefiting all three countries, was evident from increased demand.

Benefits

The rationale for multi-nation tourism promotion hinges primarily on economic factors. Tourism promotion is such a costly exercise that it is not feasible for an individual poor, developing country to break into all the leading tourist-generating markets. The developing nations have a small proportion of the global tourist market and this proportion cannot justify the huge promotional expenditures needed to capture a larger share of the market. Even in countries where tourism plays a dominant economic role, it will be difficult to promote in all the main trigger nations.

By pooling their individually meagre but collectively substantial resources, the developing countries can have a greater impact in promoting their destinations and their region. After all, multi-nation tourism promotion is oriented towards influencing and guiding the potential tourist towards taking a holiday within a particular region since there are so many competing regions. Two key factors must be given due regard in the multi-nation promotion process. First, the poor qualitative image of the developing countries must be corrected as they are too often misrepresented in the developed world and secondly, more information must be made accessible to tour operators since they are generally under-informed about the tourism products available.

Since the majority of the Third World tourist destinations are considered as being longhaul, the cost of a holiday is relatively high. The potential tourist will find it more attractive if a multi-destination package results from their high expenditure and long travel time. Thus, tour operators can satisfy their customers and maximize profits by organizing packages for multidestination holidays. The trend towards this type of tourism offers

countries within a region the possibility of promoting a regional image. Countries within the region at a more advanced stage of tourist development might, however, oppose this concept because they would prefer the tourists to stay in their own country so that they can derive maximum benefit.

Mutual benefits have been gained by Nepal, the Maldives and Sri Lanka through their joint tourism promotion since their tourist products – mountain, beach and culture, respectively – exhibit complementary characteristics for an attractive package tour. Their different levels of tourism development have, furthermore, meant that Nepal and the Maldives were not opposed to the dominant role played by Sri Lanka, which has a more established tourist industry. Although the benefits are distributed disproportionately, as tourists stay longer in Sri Lanka, the less dominant partners are able to develop their tourist industries at a more controlled pace. In the Maldives, the development of an international airport where wide-bodied aircraft can land has permitted it to become independent now.

Implementation

Although the case for multi-nation tourism promotion is overwhelming, conflicting economic and political ideologies have often militated against its successful operation. If the developing nations want to increase their small share of the international tourism market, less nationalistic attitudes must be adopted to ensure that their regional tourism organizations and their joint tourism promotions can work for their own benefit. Even the contrasting level of tourism development among countries in a particular region must not act as a deterrent against such ventures because countries with an early stage of tourism development are unlikely to attract more tourists than countries with an advanced stage of tourism development.

Without the development of an internal and external transport system, the development and promotion of tourism becomes insignificant. The movement of tourists to developing countries is affected specially by the high air fare charged by airlines, because of their location and poor demand. Since tourism is still in its infancy in many of these nations, airlines must be persuaded to offer cheaper air fares to boost tourism growth. The low level of tourism development among the developing nations necessitates the organization of regional tourism circuits, especially if their capacity is limited. Moreover, the absence of a regional transport network connecting neighboring nations might make the movement of tourists more difficult.

Political difficulties remain the main reasons why policies favoring multi-nation tourism promotion cannot be implemented with success. In East Africa, the development of East African Airways (EAA), a regional airline under the joint ownership of Tanzania, Kenya and Uganda was regarded as a success. The impact of EAA was obvious as this had permitted the growth of tourism in the region, had facilitated the promotion of multidestination holidays, and had reduced their dependency upon the metropolitan airlines. As a result of political instability in the region, the regional airline collapsed, leading to the creation of individual national airlines. During the period of political instability, the growth of regional tourist circuits suffered. However, the current trend towards multi-nation holidays has forced Tanzania and Kenya to cooperate in the promotion of a regional tourism product.

Because of the continuing internal political problems, the image of Sri Lanka as an exotic tourism destination has been tarnished to such an extent that all its hotels have an occupancy rate of less than 30 per cent. Consequently, its joint tourism promotion with the Maldives has been terminated; Sri Lanka is currently a liability to its neighbors since it is considered an insecure and unsafe destination. Neighboring countries which once associated their tourist product with Sri Lanka want to preserve their image – once a good image is damaged it costs a lot in financial resources and human effort to restore confidence in the destination. Even Air Lanka, which was a major regional carrier and a leading promoter for multidestination holidays, has a drastically reduced operation because of falling demand for its seats.

Assessment

In the absence of multi-nation tourism promotion, countries within a region must promote their tourist product individually but such cooperative schemes can only be justified if all partners make net gains in terms of tourism flow and if these gains are perceived to be distributed relatively equally among the participating nations. Failure to do so may lead to the collapse of multi-nation tourism promotion. The only way to attract more visitors to a regional tourism circuit is to offer good tourism products. Satisfaction with this type of vacation can be translated into 'repeat' business, which remains a powerful weapon in the promotion of tourism.

This type of tourism must work for the benefits of the developing nations within a region. Each country must attempt to complement each other as opposed to being fierce competitors. Tours lasting 3 weeks, for example, would provide sufficient benefits to be shared among several tourist-receiving countries. The obvious merits of multi-nation tourism promotion may convince doubtful countries of the necessity not to wreck this concept. If more tourists can be attracted towards a particular region, then the sphere of cooperation should not be limited to tourism. Governments of developing countries must encourage the establishment of such schemes because not only are costs of promotion minimized, the region will also gain maximum exposure.

Multi-nation tourism promotion will fail, however, if the Third World nations continue to manifest political divergence and a high level of political instability. What will happen if a country is faced with political turmoil? Are the neighboring countries likely to be affected? International tourists are highly sensitive to political instability in any country and they often classify all developing countries in the same category when there are distinct differences between them. When there is internal strife in a particular country, multi-nation tourism promotion will fail to offer the security needed to attract more tourists, with disastrous results for the entire region.

Conclusion

The effectiveness of multi-nation tourism promotion will depend upon the willingness of the participating countries to cooperate. Since the developed nations do not encounter the same financial restraints, they are able to promote and market their tourist product individually while at the same time, relying on regional promotional campaigns to boost their regional image. In the case of the developing nations, there is an urgent need for strong cooperation with a view to creating a strong regional image, free from political troubles. Furthermore, the huge cost involved in the penetration of the international tourist markets means that developing countries must pool their limited resources to give their promotional campaigns greater impact.

Focus on developing nations

New tourist destinations need to adopt tough measures to improve their share of the global tourist markets. A few developing nations have carefully concentrated their promotional efforts in a handful of developed nations in order to have a greater impact. The danger in market concentration lies in the high level of market dependence. If market diversification is to take place, then the limited financial resources will be thinly used in as many markets as possible. Despite their unwillingness to support the concept of multi-nation tourism promotion, developing nations must be aware of their limitations in promoting their product individually. If two or more countries can unify their promotional efforts, more tourists can be attracted.

In the end, most developing countries, irrespective of the amount of resources available, prefer to promote their tourist product individually even though it means spending large amounts to create the right image. Most of them dislike the concept of multi-nation tourism promotion as this will result in the organization of regional circuits. Even the more developed tourist destinations have challenged the merits of multidestination holidays because, like the developing nations, they want potential tourists to spend their entire vacation in their own countries so that they can obtain the maximum benefits possible. The current trend towards multidestination holidays, however, exposes the need for cooperation and for promotion of a regional image.

Further reading

Ascher, F., *Transnational Corporations and Cultural Identites* (UNESCO, 1985). This study examines the role of foreign private enterprises in the development and promotion of tourism.

Balassa, B., *The Theory of Economic Integration* (George Allen & Unwin, 1961). This book analyzes the various schemes available for economic cooperation and integration.

Brandt Commission, *Common Crisis. North–South: Cooperation for World Recovery* (Pan Books, 1980). This book argues the case for better cooperation among the developing nations.

Dupon, J. F., *Contraintes Insulaires et Fait Colonial aux Mascareignes et aux Seychelles*, PhD Thesis (Aix-Marseille University, 1977). This thesis looks at the failure of a particular regional tourism organization in the Indian Ocean.

Economic Commission for Africa, *The Impact of Tourism in the Indian Ocean Islands* (ECA, 1981). This study recommends joint tourism promotion and closer cooperation as a basis for tourism development.

Economist Intelligence Unit, *The Impact of Tourism on the Developing Countries*, Report no. 60 (EIU, 1979). Section four of this report is concerned with the concept of tourism cooperation.

Ffrench-Davis, R., 'The Andean Pact: a model of economic integration for developing countries', *World Development*, vol. 5, nos 1 and 2 (1977), pp. 137–53. This article emphasizes the merits for cooperation and for a high degree of economic independence among the developing nations.

Franco, M., 'A suggested methodology for the evaluation of projects for regional cooperation', *Industry and Development*, no. 1, pp. 38–85. This article describes the need for developing countries to identify projects which can be developed on a regional basis.

Friedland, E. A., 'The Southern African development coordination conference and the West: cooperation or conflict', *Journal of Modern African Studies*, vol. 23, no. 2 (1985), pp. 287–314. The article exposes the advantages for neighboring nations to cooperate so that they can become economically viable.

Haq, M., 'Beyond the slogan of South–South cooperation', *World Development*, vol. 8, no. 10 (1980), pp. 743–52. This article advocates stronger collaboration and less division among the poor nations to combat their poverty.

Hiller, H. L., 'Escapism, penetration and response: industrial tourism and the Caribbean', *Caribbean Studies*, vol. 16, no. 2 (1980), pp. 92–116. The article articulates the necessity not to overlook the dangers of uncontrolled tourism development.

Kuyvenhoven, A. and Mennes, L. B., 'Projects for regional cooperation: identification, selection, evaluation and location', *Industry and Development*, no. 1 (1979), pp. 3–37. This article presents the case for economic cooperation to achieve economies of scale.

Nugent, J., 'The potential for South–South trade in capital goods industries', *Industry and Development*, no. 14 (1985), pp. 99–141. This article emphasizes the absence of strong trading links among the Third World nations.

Nyamora, P., 'Seychelles tourism leaps ahead', *African Business* (March 1980), pp. 63–5. This article argues that tourism will develop more efficiently and effectively in collaborating with other neighboring nations for joint tourism promotion.

Palling, B., 'Sri Lanka needs peace to bring tourists back', *The Independent* (27 August 1987). This article discusses the impact of political instability on tourism development.

Papson, S., 'Tourism: world's biggest industry in the twenty-first century', *Futurist* (August 1979), pp. 249–59. This article examines the importance of marketing in the continuing growth of tourism.

Pearce, D. G., *Tourism in the South Pacific* (UNESCO, 1980). This collection of articles discusses the different issues affecting tourism development, including tourism cooperation.

Ravenhill, J., 'Regional integration and development in Africa: lessons from the East African community, *Commonwealth and Comparative Politics*, no. 3 (1979). This article investigates the reasons why regional integration schemes often fail.

Robson, P., 'Regional economic co-operation among developing countries: some further considerations', *World Development*, vol. 6, no. 6 (1978), pp. 771–8. The article regards cooperation as an economic necessity for development.

Sathiendra, K. and Tisdell, C. A., 'Tourism and the development of the Maldives', *Massey Journal of Asian and Pacific Business*, vol. 1, no. 1 (1985), pp. 27–34. This article shows the development of tourism in a small island state, and how it affects its marketing strategy.

Seekings, J., 'Regional tourism organisations', *Travel and Tourism Analyst* (September 1987), pp. 47–57. This article identifies the main regional tourism organizations engaged in the promotion of regional tourism.

United Nations Development Advisory Team, *South Pacific: Guidelines for the Development of Tourism* (UN, 1979). One of the recommendations of this study is concerned with the development of tourism on a regional basis.

Vaitsos, C. J., 'Crisis in regional economic cooperation (integration) among developing countries: a survey', *World Development*, vol. 6, no. 6 (1978), pp. 719–69. This article discusses the failure of regional cooperative schemes.

Wing, P. C. L., *Tourism in Mauritius*, MSc Dissertation (University of Strathclyde, 1981). This study examines the importance of political stability and regional cooperation in the development of tourism.

PHILIPPE C. L. WING

Multinationals in tourism

Introduction

The conventional paradigm of a multinational company is of a giant industrial enterprise, very often vertically integrated, responsible for large flows of foreign direct investment and owning major sections of industrial activity in a number of countries. In fact there are many forms of multinational enterprises which do not fit this picture and international tourism provides a good example of this. It is most useful to envisage the multinational enterprise (MNE) as a multiplant firm whose operations transcend national boundaries. An MNE may, therefore, simply be defined as an enterprise owning outputs of goods and services originating in more than one country. Note that the MNE does not need to own foreign productive assets, as all resources can be hired.

In principle, the tour operators, hotels and carriers (airlines, road and rail transport) in the tourist-receiving countries could, together, market tourism products and not require the services of MNEs. In practice, this is not possible because, unlike other exports, tourism is consumed in the exporting country. It is therefore an 'experience good' whose value to the consumer cannot be established by inspection, rather than a 'search good' whose attributes can be examined and compared to the requirements of the consumer. It is this factor which gives a fundamental competitive advantage to the MNE. Tourism is a highly differentiated product and in the context of international tourism, includes both vacation and business travel (see *Marketing of Tourism* on page 259). Entrepreneurs in the tourism-generating country will have proprietary knowledge of the requirements and various segments of the market. Consumers, especially first-time tourists to a destination, will face considerable uncertainty regarding the quality of the tourism product but will have much greater knowledge of the reliability of the MNE's operation in the home market and this essentially acts as a substitute for knowledge of the quality of the tourism product. Alternative guarantors of quality may be provided by government agencies in the host country or private sector guide books and advisory services. However, to be effective, such 'honest brokers' must be regarded by consumers as wholly independent of producers and sellers and concerned solely with the interests of the tourist. At the same time they must also be highly knowledgeable about a product whose quality from a producer can vary considerably over a relatively short period of time. In practice few organizations outside the MNEs will have this reputation in the eyes of the consumer.

The MNE may acquire knowledge of product quality either through inspection or direct control of the production process and the degree and form of market integration varies considerably in international tourism. The greater the degree of vertical integration the greater the control over the volume and quality of production. However, this benefit must be weighed against inflexibility in responding to variations in demand. This risk is particularly important in international tourism where there are substantial seasonal and annual fluctuations in the volume and direction of flows of tourists.

Examples

The greatest degree of vertical integration of MNEs in international tourism is to be found among mass market 'sunlust' tour operators such as Neckerman und Reisen in West Germany, Thomson Travel in the United Kingdom, and Tjaereborg and Vingessor in the Scandinavian countries. Tour operators are not simply wholesalers of tourist activities but rather supply a package service which comprises the separate elements of a business trip or vacation. In the context of the mass market tour operators, intense competition ensures that profit margins on tourists are a small proportion of the total price of the holiday and depend on maintaining high passenger load factors on 'back-to-back' charter operators between the home and host countries. These firms are, therefore, characterized either by the ownership of a charter airline (for example Britannia Airways by Thomson) or a close working relationship with a charter airline (for example Condor in West Germany, Scanair and Transair in Scandinavia) which guarantees adequate and flexible airline seat capacity. The largest Scandinavian and West German tour operators also dominate the retailing operations of their segment of the market either through shops or by mail order, although this is not true of the United Kingdom. Equity and management participation in hotel operations by tour operators is much more limited and is confined either to areas where the tour operator has a long-term assurance of utilizing capacity, such as Spain, or where there has been (at least in the past) an inadequate supply of appropriate accommodation, such as North Africa.

Some of the major scheduled airlines also have significant charter and tour operating subsidiaries, notably British Airways, which owns British Airtours and Enterprise Holidays. The involvement of scheduled airlines with hotels has, however, always been very limited and the sale of Hilton International by Trans World Airlines and Inter-Continental Hotels by Pan Am has confirmed this pattern of minimum involvement.

The international operations of the large hotel chains such as Inter-Continental, Hilton International, Sheraton, Trust House Forte, Ramada, Hyatt International, and Grand Metropolitan Hotels are primarily oriented towards business travel, both in developed and developing countries. They retain their high market share by providing not only an ambience and high standard of basic services of room, food and drink but also a wide variety of services both on and off the premises.

Benefits

Knowledge of *what* to produce, gained as a result of operating in the same market as that of the tourists, can be expected to be only part of the source of the competitive advantage of MNEs. They can also be expected to have a competitive advantage over enterprises in the tourist receiving country on *how* to produce the service, particularly where international tourism is not well developed. This particularly applies to the international hotel sector where the dominance of the US-, and to a lesser extent, UK-based chains cannot simplybe explained in terms of the international flows of tourists. For example, hotels from West Germany are considerably underrepresented in terms of flows of tourists or importance in international trade. This suggests that the size and structure of the hotel industry of the home country of the MNE is an important factor in generating management expertise, in the acquisition and analysis of knowledge of markets, and in developing a pool of trained labor. The West German domestic hotel industry is not characterized by chains of hotels and therefore management lacks the necessary experience of such multi-plant operations necessary for the establishment of international hotel chains.

Having built up a set of logistic skills and proprietory knowledge in the home market the hotel chain can then make these available to a new hotel at a much smaller transaction cost than new entrants into the hotel business. This would explain the observation that there is a greater similarity between international hotels in different countries under the same ownership than there is between hotels in the same country under different ownership, supplying similar groups of customers.

Second, as the international hotel chain grows so further competitive advantages will accrue partly as a consequence of increased size and partly from operating in a number of different countries. Larger size enables economies of scale associated, for example, with spreading fixed costs over a greater number of hotel guests, obtaining finance and purchasing inputs on the most favorable terms, and enabling greater functional specialization of staff. The international dimension enables the MNE to enhance these factors by drawing on the availability of resources at a world and not simply a national level. Operating in different countries with different social and economic environments also forces the MNE to adjust and refine its operations and management techniques and this in turn increases the efficiency of its worldwide operations. The combined effect of size and multinationality enables the MNE to have an expertise in the overall planning and design of hotel complexes and methods of operation, control and maintenance of international business class hotels which the individual hotel in the host country will have great difficulty in matching.

Underlying all of these factors is the key element of training. As research and development are often essential elements in the maintenance of the competitive advantage of MNEs in manufacturing industries, so investment in training may be regarded as essential to maintaining that of MNEs in tourism. This is partly a matter of overcoming buyer uncertainty referred to in the first section, so that confidence in the safety and reliability of the airline, the integrity of the tour operator and the quality of the hotel chain become a substitute for inspection of the service by the consumer. It is also a key aspect of product differentiation, with marketing seeking to portray a distinctive 'brand image'. For example, in the case of scheduled airlines where airfares are negotiated through IATA conferences and approved by the governments concerned, emphasis is placed on the quality of 'inflight' services provided to the business traveler. A good example of the success of such a campaign is Singapore International Airlines, where despite having to compete with 28 other airlines servicing Singapore, among them many of the market's largest and most prestigous carriers, just under half the foreign visitors to Singapore are carried by the airline.

International hotel chains similarly invest substantial amounts in maintaining training facilities at each hotel, in regional centers and at the 'flagship' hotel. In addition, there is a constant process of preparing training literature, visual aids and manuals, organizing seminars and disseminating information on new designs and decor management procedures, techniques, equipment etc. Internalizing training is also complementary to promoting personnel largely from within the organization since it enables the MNE to accurately monitor and assess employees' abilities and prospects while maintaining a ready pool of skilled and mobile labor for expansion. Promoting from within the organization, allied with other incentive schemes, are also techniques used by MNEs to retain key staff within the organization and reduce the spread of unpatentable knowledge to competitors.

Implementation

Industrial organization theory differentiates between the ownership and control over resources and this is a particularly important distinction in the context of international tourism.

The best example of this distinction is in international hotel chains where the predominant form of involvement of the MNE (especially in developing countries) is either through a franchise (for example Holiday Inns) or, more usually, a management contract. The MNE may have a loan or equity participation in the hotel but this is very often a minority holding. Investment in hotels is therefore largely portfolio investment, rather than direct investment as is generally the case of MNEs in manufacturing. The ownership of hotels is best analyzed separately as investment in assets which will produce a return through income and capital appreciation, dependent on these assets being profitably utilized without the necessity for direct intervention by the owner.

MNE involvement in foreign hotels through the nonequity route has the characteristics usually associated with direct investment in the sense of providing *de facto* control. A very great deal of influence is exerted on the day-to-day operation and on the long-term production and marketing strategy of the hotels through the management contract. The period of the management contract is normally between 10 and 20 years with the right to renew the agreements for a further period on the same terms and conditions, except if the option to renew is deleted. A typical clause in a management contract allows the MNE to:

Supervise, direct and control the management and operation of the hotel and render, supervise and control the performance of all services and do or cause to be done all things reasonably necessary for the efficient and proper operation of the hotel.

Control over the day-to-day organization and operation of each hotel is often detailed and complete. It includes the setting of all room and other prices for the hotel, the negotiation and execution of contracts for the operation of the hotel and the provision of technical consultants and other specialized experts for nonroutine services. The structure of the remuneration of the management usually combines a basic fee, irrespective of profitability of the hotel, with an incentive fee plus charges for various services (e.g. technical consultants, reservations systems, sales promotion, administrative expenses etc.).

Apart from financial questions, other decision-taking procedures are written into the contract. In most cases, the MNE will reserve the right to make such alterations, additions or improvements in or to the hotel as are customarily made in the operation of modern international hotels. Major alterations usually require the consent of the owners of the hotel but there is usually a clause in the agreement that this should not be 'unreasonably' withheld.

Most agreements also have escape clauses for the MNE. For example, agreements may be terminated if the MNE is prevented from, or materially restricted in, obtaining foreign currency or in remitting foreign and/or local currency out of the country in which the hotel is located. It may also be ended by circumstances constituting *force majeure* which has a substantial adverse effect upon the operation of the hotel. Terms of compensation are also laid down in the event of compulsory purchase.

The balance between ownership and control will vary between different MNEs in different locations. Some groups may consider that they have the required in-house expertise to manage property investment (for example, Trust House Forte) others may consider that their expertise lies exclusively in managing hotel operations and leave the ownership to local or international investors (for example, Hilton International).

Control of hotel operations either *de jure* or *de facto* is essential to guarantee that the quality of the hotel service is consistently maintained in all the MNE's hotels throughout the world so that the tourist and especially the business tourist, is saved the transaction costs of having to identify a suitable hotel in each country visited and instead relies on the brand name guaranteeing the service required. Equally, poor service in one hotel will reduce the tourist's confidence not only in that hotel but towards all other hotels in the group. Strict accountability of each hotel is therefore fundamental to the success of the group as a whole.

A further reason for the use of management contracts may lie in the 'approprobility problem', that is, the inability of innovators to obtain for themselves the social value of an idea. In the case of goods and technology this can often be efficiently handled by markets if the legal system clearly establishes property rights. In the case of hotels, enforceable property rights will largely be limited to the brand name(s) and trademark of the hotel chain. The design concepts and operations of the hotel can be freely copied by competitors, provided they also obtain the proprietory knowledge and expertise held by key staff. Long-term management contracts and attempts to 'lock-in' staff into the organization, combined with raising barriers to entry by increasing the size and complexity of the technology of the individual hotel, may also be interpreted at least in part, as methods by which MNEs may limit the diffusion of knowledge to actual or potential competitors.

Computerized reservation systems are another powerful means by which MNEs may gain a strong competitive advantage by providing a superior standard of service to customers as well as raising the entry price into the industry. Airlines, for example, provide online booking facilities to travel agents to ensure that their airlines appear first in the listings and, therefore, increase passenger load factors. Links between airlines and hotels (for example, British Airways Associated Hotels) relieve the business traveler of the transaction costs of obtaining information about each separately. Tour operators similarly use computer reservations systems to efficiently market group inclusive tours, provide constantly updated information on demand for aircraft and hotels at specific times and places and if necessary discount prices to match more precisely demand with committed capacity.

Assessment

Unlike manufactured goods, the value of a hotel or holiday to clients cannot be separated from the location but this does not mean that the locational advantages of a country are irrelevant to an MNE in deciding whether or not to be involved with the tourism sector of a country.

Managerial or organizational constraints may well limit the number of new hotels or inclusive tours which can be effectively handled and involvements in alternative locations may be mutually exclusive. The MNE must also protect its quality standards and, therefore, has to be assured that adequate resources are available to ensure that this objective is met. The factors determining the involvement of an international hotel chain or tour operator will be broadly similar to those facing foreign firms in other sectors of economic activity, for example the size and rate of growth of demand; the policy of the host government towards foreign enterprise; the general political, social and economic stability of the country. Specific factors will concern the general infrastructure for tourism and the availability and quality of hotel inputs.

Decisions will then have to be made as to *where* to locate in the host country, what *size* and *features* the hotel should have, and what *form* the participation should take. For example, MNEs very rarely have anything other than a small financial stake (if that) in hotels located in developing countries because they perceive the risks of such investment to be unacceptable relative to the return they can obtain through contractual forms of involvement. Also, as mentioned earlier, the decision on whether or not to invest in a foreign hotel is more in the nature of a portfolio investment decision and as such will depend, among other factors, on the attractiveness of investments in countries with weaker currencies than that of the home country of the MNE.

Conclusion

The competitive advantages of MNEs in international tourism derive from the nature of tourism as an 'experience good' often consumed in an unfamiliar environment, where the trademark of the MNE guarantees a standard of service with certain characteristics demanded by the tourist (principally business tourist). International hotel chains may also operate on a superior production function to local hotels, partly because, being multinational, there is a wider learning process derived from operating in different economic environments and a wider sourcing of inputs, improving both quality and competitiveness. Fundamentally, there are significant economies of size and logistical skills which enable the knowledge and expertise developed by the organization as a whole to have many of the characteristics of a public good within the organization, that is, the human and physical resources and coordinating ability of the MNE may be supplied to a newly associated hotel at a much lower marginal cost than that of a new entrant into the market.

An important element in maintaining confidence in the trademark of the MNE, and thereby consolidating and improving market share, is investment in training, which can be likened to the importance of research and development to MNEs in certain areas of manufacturing.

Focus on small business

Large size is clearly a major factor underlying the competitive advantage of airlines, the mass market tour operators and international hotel chains. Opportunities exist, however, in other areas of international tourism where the 'entry price' is much lower. This particularly applies to 'wanderlust' tourism and certain types of special interest tourism where the specialized knowledge of the tour operator can be marketed either in conjunction with an MNE, for example, by organizing local tours in the host country, or independently using local knowledge to obtain suitable accommodation and arranging part-charter seating on scheduled flights of established airlines.

The competitive advantage of international hotel chains appears, at least in part, to derive from the unfamiliarity of clients with the destination. This suggests that when business travelers return to a destination they may be more willing to use locally owned and managed hotels provided a similar standard of service is available. Size is of course one important factor in this respect but some medium sized hotels in the Caribbean, for example, have overcome this problem by grouping around central tourism facilities. This, of course, may not be possible in a city location. Furthermore, smaller hotels will also have to obtain staff with the relevant training and skills.

Further reading

American Hotel and Motel Association, *Annual Directory of Hotel and Motel Systems* (American Hotel Association Directory Corporation, New York). Lists, for every hotel chain in the world, the name, location and size (in terms of numbers of rooms) of each hotel associated with the chain.

Casson, M. C., 'Transaction costs and the theory of the multinational enterprise', *New Theories of the Multinational Enterprise*, A. M. Rugman, ed. (Croom Helm, 1982), Chapter 2. This article develops the theory of internalization in the context of non R and D intensive industries (such as international hotels).

Dunning, J. H., *International Production and the Multinational Enterprise* (George Allen & Unwin, 1981). Part I outlines the eclectic theory of the MNE which emphasizes the need to explain MNE activities in terms of the ownership, locational and internalization advantages.

Dunning, J. H. and McQueen, M., 'The eclectic theory of the multinational enterprise and the international hotel industry', *New Theories of the Multinational Enterprise*, A. M. Rugman, ed. (Croom Helm, 1982), Chapter 5. As the title implies, this article applies Dunning's theory to the hotel industry.

Dunning, J. H. and McQueen, M., 'The eclectic theory of international production: a case study of the international hotel industry', *Managerial and Decision Economics*, vol. 2, no. 4 (1981). This article is different from above in that it presents the results of a survey carried out by the authors in 1980 on the size, distribution, and forms of involvement of MNEs in the hotel industry.

McQueen, M., 'Appropriate policies towards multinational hotel corporations in developing countries', *World Development*, vol. 11, no. 2 (1983). This article concentrates on the forms of involvement and impact of MNEs on host developing countries and suggests conclusions for policy formulation.

United Nations, *Transnational Corporations in International Tourism* (UN, 1982). ST/CTC/18. Study prepared by Dunning and McQueen for the UN Center on Transnational Corporations, presenting original data on international hotels, tour operators and airlines.

MATTHEW MCQUEEN

New product development in tourism

Introduction

New product development in tourism refers to the activities undertaken by tourism organizations in the course of bringing new services to the marketplace. New product development is a sequential process which begins with the step of idea generation and ends with the commercialization of the tourist service. In the context of the entire organization, new product development is often an ongoing process, and there may be several potential services at various stages of development at any one time.

New products are those whose degree of change for customers is sufficient to require the design or redesign of marketing strategies. Replacing old tourist products with new products is essential to the growth and vitality of tourist organizations. One of the major challenges in marketing planning is to develop ideas for new products and to launch them successfully: customers want new products, and competitors will do their best to supply them. The new product planning gap can be filled in two ways: acquisition or new product development. The acquisition route can take three forms: corporate-acquisition, patent-acquisition or licence-acquisition. The new product route can take two basic forms: internal new product development or contract new product development. This chapter will focus on the new product development process in tourism as a growth strategy, because of the heavy role that marketing plays in finding, developing and launching successful new products.

Examples

London City Airport is Europe's first stolport – an airport specially designed to handle short take-off and landing (STOL) aircraft. London City's marketing concept is simple. The £30 million airport aims to tap the buoyant City of London business travel market by offering a fast, hassle-free route to Europe that will get executives to Paris in less than the time it takes to get to Heathrow. It should appeal greatly to the time-pressed business traveler and if it prospers, the airport will radically alter the capital's business travel patterns.

The job of designing the vacations to suit the various segments of the market was done by Air Canada's product development group, having ascertained which lifestyle groups and which vacation types went together. What went towards the make-up of each holiday type (e.g. accommodation, destination, activities) was used to design new holidays around specific Air Canada destinations. The desire among extravagant consumers for a holiday in the sun with the luxuries of high class hotels and good service became one of Air Canada's 'Sun Living' vacations. It included a 1 or 2-week stay in Montego Bay, Ocho Rios, and Kingston, accommodation in first class hotels, entertainment, sightseeing, beach parties etc. The desire of the cautious home bodies to be led around and made to feel secure as opposed to being on a wild solo fling, was recognized and turned into a guided coach tour of England. In total, 20 vacation concepts were designed, based on consumer profile and need information.

Benefits

New products are the lifeblood of a business. The primary benefits of a successful, continuous new tourist product development program include increased sales and profits, reduction of the financial risk of failure inherent in introducing a new product or service, and enhancement of the organization's overall market position. Also, a successful new tourist product development program facilitates diversification and may provide a competitive advantage. New tourist products may stimulate sales of complementary products offered by the tourism organization.

Under modern conditions of competition, tourism companies that do not develop new products risk much. Such companies will find their products falling victim to changing consumer needs and tastes, new technologies, shortened product life cycles, and increased domestic and foreign competition.

New product development is an essential activity for companies seeking growth. By adopting the new product strategy, tourism companies are better able to sustain competitive pressures on their existing products and make headway. New products are essential to the long-term health of a tourism company: they are needed to provide growth and to offset the inevitable leveling or decline of sales from present products.

Implementation

In general, tourism companies that have established formal development procedures have been more successful than firms that introduce new products or services haphazardly. Although the scope of these activities varies among tourism companies, most major corporations have systematic programs for the development of new tourist products or services. Product development activities often consume a considerable amount of time.

Sound new product development occurs in a series of stages. First, the company should formulate a new tourist product strategy. The strategy should include: the type of new products/services desired – true product innovations; repositioning improved products; products new to the company but not to the market ('me-too' tourist products); modifications of existing products. Resources need to be allocated to new product development as part of this strategy. The company's overall business objectives, goals, and strategies should always guide the design of new product strategy.

Once the strategy is in place, the development process starts with the idea generation stage. All possible sources, both internal and external, should be considered in the search for new product ideas in tourism. Many firms use creativity techniques (i.e. brainstorming, morphological analysis, discovery matrices, checklists, wordlists etc.) to help the generation and evaluation. Only the best and most suitable ideas are allowed to pass through this phase. Ideas are then translated into specific image and benefit concepts. Concept testing is done with potential customers through the utilization of 'storyboards' and written concept statements. Then the company evaluates the proposed tourist product's 'fit' with existing product lines and 'service production' feasibility.

Business analysis is the next phase. Here, initial sales and repeat purchase rates are forecast, costs and profits are projected, and preliminary product/service specifications are developed. This is followed by product/service development. When it is applicable, tourist product/service prototypes can be developed, refined, and tested by potential users and customers, or even in the lab. The tourist product may then move into test market. This stage carries high costs, somewhat long time periods, and its application is not always recommended in the tourism industry.

At this time, alternative marketing mix combinations (i.e. price levels, promotional messages and media, alternative distribution channels, and different tourist product configurations) are evaluated. Customer repurchase rates and tourism trade acceptance can also be measured. Finally, potential tourist products that have not been rejected, which may occur at any stage in the new product development process, are commercialized. The new tourist product commercialization may occur across the whole market at the same time, or more typically, in a phased rollout fashion.

The new product development process is shown in Fig. 1. While the new product development phases are sequential, the stages often overlap timewise, and proper scheduling of activities is an important factor for an efficient development

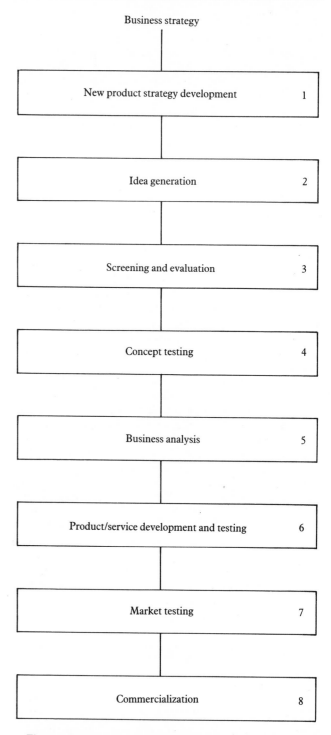

Figure 1 New product development process.

process. Several organizational alternatives exist for coordinating the new product development process. Some tourism firms use new product committees, or venture teams, while other organizations have created new product departments, or have new product managers or product managers among their staff.

Proper timing in new product development is a critical factor – moving too quickly on a late entry into the market can be disastrous. All possible competitor reactions to proposed new products should be anticipated and evaluated. Profit and cost projections should be updated on a continual basis, since they often change significantly over the course of a new product development project. The time between the generation of new product ideas and their introduction into the marketplace often spans several years. This means that changes in markets, competitive strategies, supply conditions, and economic trends can substantially alter a tourist product's attractiveness by the time it reaches the market.

Developing an explicit new product strategy is an essential step to be undertaken. New product strategy provides corporate strategic guidelines for the new tourist product development process through assessing internal experience and abilities as well as external opportunities. Environmental forecasting methods can be used to identify new tourist product ideas. A changing environment often means changing markets and these, in turn, lead to new product opportunities.

Central to the screening process is setting criteria that represent the standards that management believes must be surpassed by a new tourist product opportunity. Management must also evaluate new product ideas in terms of whether the company has the ability and the resources needed to take advantage of the opportunities they afford. Assessing the profitability of a new product helps management decide whether to introduce the new tourist product, continue the development and evaluation process, or drop the idea.

Once an idea has passed the screening stage, work on the design and testing of supporting strategies and tactics can begin, concurrently with product development. Planning supporting strategies at this stage can significantly reduce the total lead-time between idea screening and product introduction.

Information from concept and product-use tests does not directly measure what happens after a new tourist product is offered for sale, nor does it give the market's reaction to an entire marketing strategy. Test marketing is intended to duplicate a real market suitation for the new products, but on a smaller scale and at less cost. Competitors may also try to disrupt a test market, which can cause inaccuracies in test data.

Commercialization is the actual introduction of the tourist product into the marketplace, with all of the related decisions and resource commitments. A crash introduction is the full-scale commercializaton of a new tourist product as quickly as possible. For a rollout introduction, target markets are divided geographically and initially the new tourist product is introduced in only one or a few areas. If the new product is successful in these areas, the process continues until all geographic target markets are being served. All rollouts offer the advantage of giving management time to monitor and adjust the new product strategy before all resources are committed. Introductions of new tourist products that occur before their time often fail. At the other extreme, delays or overly slow rollouts can help competitors gain a substantial advantage. There is often a window of opportunity that gradually closes due to changing preferences, competitive entries and a changing environment.

Assessment

Companies and organizations in the tourism industry can use many different criteria for determining the effectiveness of a new product/service development program. Some of the more widely used measures include the contribution to total revenue, the profits generated by new tourist products compared to the costs of the development programs, success/failure rates for new products, and return-on-investment rates. The integration of new products into the company's organizational structure, product mix and product lines, as well as into the marketing function is an essential requirement for success.

New products in tourism fail for a variety of reasons, two of which are related to a lack of effective customer demand and intense competitive pressure. Internal reasons for failure include inadequate market assessment and analysis, poor planning and execution processes, lack of suitable resources, poor organizational structure, the development of imitative products and services with no clear differential advantages or benefits to customers, and lack of, or poor, product positioning. Effective control mechanisms should be used in order to minimize the risk of new product failure. New product development control ranges from the efficient scheduling of activities to the willingness to drop a new product idea when a 'red flag' goes up, despite the amount of investment already 'sunk' into the project.

Generally speaking, the more novelty and change a product presents to customers, the more risk-laden the tourist product. Most customers tend to resist change. Tourist products in which significant new benefits are not perceived will join the huge and ever-growing product failure junkyard. Managerial problems also account for new tourism product failures. These problems include inadequate budgeting to cover introduction costs, incomplete controls over performance, poor timing of introductions, and failure to establish a competitive market position. Management must carefully coordinate the entire process with the intended strategy to ensure a high probability of success.

Conclusion

New product development is not easy, and almost all companies have experienced costly failures. Tourism companies that do well at managing new products direct their development activities in support of specific new product strategies, so that new tourist products are ready for introduction when they are needed, to maintain a consistent profitable growth record.

Top management can affect the implementation of new product strategy in the following ways:

1. By establishing policies and broad strategic directions for the kinds of new products the company should seek.
2. By providing the kind of leadership that will create the environmental climate needed to stimulate innovative drive in the tourism organization.
3. By instituting review and monitoring procedures so that the

manager is involved at the right decision points and can know whether or not work schedules are being met in ways that are consistent with the broad policy direction.

Focus on small business

Unfortunately, only very few small businesses in the tourism industry are seriously engaged in new product development activities. The majority of small business owners or managers often fail to realize how important new products and services are to the continued growth and survival of their sector. Despite their limited financial and human resources, small businesses should become more oriented towards innovation and the launch of new tourist products and services.

The new product development process can easily be adapted for use by the smaller firm. While it may not always be feasible to develop totally new products and services, the small company can usually consider modifications of its existing products. Another option, offering additional services, should not be ignored, since it may stimulate growth.

Software/databases

Expert Choice, Decison Support Software Inc., 1300 Vincent Place, McLean, VA 2210, USA. Uses qualitative data and subjective judgments for strategic planning and product selection decisions.

Mind Sight, Execucon Systems Corp., 3410 Far West Boulevard, Austin, TX 78731, USA. Helps in forecasting, planning, and evaluating risks of new products.

New Product Scheduling, Superior Software Systems, 3115 White House Road, Suite 145, Greenville, SC 29611, USA. Helps in tracking components of new products from concept to commercialization.

Further reading

Buell, V. P., *Marketing Management – A Strategic Planning Approach* (McGraw-Hill, 1985). This is a very comprehensive book on marketing management. Special attention should be given to Chapter 17 which deals with new product planning and development issues.

Cooper, R. G., 'The performance impact of product innovation strategies', *European Journal of Marketing*, no. 5 (1984), pp. 5–54. Introduces the results of an extensive study of new product strategies. Describes common strategies leading to superior performance.

Cravens, D. W., Hills, G. E. and Woodruff, R. B., *Marketing Management* (Irwin, 1987). This book contains a very elaborate chapter on new product development (Chapter 12).

Crawford, C. M., *New Products Management* (Irwin, 1983). Provides a comprehensive discussion of the process of new product development.

Feldman, L. P. and Page, A. L., 'Principles versus practice in new product planning', *Journal of Product Innovation Management* (January 1984), p. 44. An excellent overview of pragmatic issues related to the topic.

Hawkins, D. E., Shafer, E. L. and Rovelstad, J. M., *Tourism Marketing and Management Issues* (George Washington University Press, 1980). Offers a thorough review of tourism marketing management topics.

Kotler, P., *Marketing Management – Analysis, Planning, and Control* (Prentice Hall, 5th edition, 1984). This classic book contains an excellent chapter on the new product development process (Chapter 10).

Mattson, B. E., 'Spotting a market gap for a new product', *Long Range Planning* (February, 1985), pp. 87–93. Discusses the relationship between the new product development process and market opportunity analysis. Addresses the 'strategic entry window' concept and describes an analytical technique to facilitate its application.

Mill, R. C. and Morrison, A. M., *The Tourism System: An Introductory Text* (Prentice Hall, 1985). This book introduces excellent coverage of tourism-related topics. Chapter 4 includes good reading on the design of products for the leisure travel market from market definition to product information.

Rothberg, R. R. (ed.), *Corporate Strategy and Product Innovation* (The Free Press, 1981). This book includes many of the classic leading articles covering a wide range of product development topics.

Takeuchi, H. and Ikujiro N., 'The new new product development game', *Harvard Business Review* (January/February 1986), pp. 137–46. Describes a holistic approach to new product development where the stages in the process occur near-simultaneously, thereby facilitating greater speed and flexibility.

LUIZ MOUTINHO

Personnel management

Introduction

The tourist industry is a large employer. In 1984, the British Tourist Authority estimated that 1.5 million people were to be found in tourist-related employment in the UK. In 1986, explicit government recognition that tourism would continue to be a significant generator of new jobs was given in 'Action for Jobs in Tourism' and has been continually re-emphasized by subsequent ministerial statements.

Many sectors of the tourist industry are labor intensive; personnel management deals with what the organization needs to do with one of its key resources – people. The efficient and effective utilization of its human resources is a major contributory factor towards the achievement of organizational objectives. To this end staff need to be obtained, developed and motivated, and their skills and capacities utilized to best effect. The success of an organization's personnel policies and the subsequent achievement of organizational objectives will also be dependent upon the existence of an appropriate organization structure and culture. Such a 'framework' should be designed to promote cooperation and commitment and at the same time provide recognition for any social or legal responsibilities incumbent upon the organization.

Personnel management centers on three major groupings of activities:

1. Employee resourcing, concerned with all aspects of the employment of people exemplified by the following inter-related activities: organizational design and development; job design and work structuring; manpower planning; recruitment and selection; performance appraisal; remuneration and conditions of employment; health, safety and welfare, termination of employment and equal opportunities.
2. Employee development, concerned with training and management development.
3. Employee relations, concerned with dealing with employees individually and collectively (when the workforce is unionized the term industrial relations is generally used) through procedures designed to regulate grievance and disciplinary matters, negotiations, communications, consultation and participation.

All of the above mentioned activities take place in the tourist industry, their extent depending upon a variety of different factors such as organizational objectives, size, structure and type of business.

Personnel management is not the preserve of specialists but its elements form an important part of every manager's job, e.g. interviewing or carrying out training. Only the larger organizations, employing around 200 staff or more can justify (on grounds of cost) the existence of a personnel manager/ officer whose role may vary from one of high level strategist to, perhaps most typically, that of 'technical adviser' to the busy manager who remains the implementer of the personnel management function.

Examples

In the 1980s, Manchester International Airport has enjoyed considerable growth in terms of sales revenue, passenger numbers and staff employed on a single site. Past and planned continued expansion have led to the need for a review of objectives and policy in the area of employee or industrial relations. A long-term strategy involving a fairly radical solution has been developed to change the current industrial relations climate and existing attitudes at the airport, within a highly unionized environment. The 'new deal' includes replacing fragmented wage bargaining with a single local agreement; introducing performance-related pay; improving communication and consultative arrangements; harmonizing conditions of employment and inexhaustible procedure agreements. The objectives of these changes include greater management control, fostering more identity and higher morale among heterogeneous work groups, and creating equity through harmonization of conditions of employment and the standardization of pay settlement dates. The importance of effective personnel management has been recognized in the elevation of the most senior personnel specialist to board level.

The brewers, Greenall Whitley, established their hotels division in 1979 and have since followed a policy of growth and development, largely effected through takeovers, and now own 35 hotels operating as De Vere and GW Hotels. Commitment to people is clearly expressed at board level, 'the people who work in our hotels are the company's most valuable resource', and there is strong emphasis on employee development. Overall personnel objectives, policies and procedures are coordinated and controlled through a head office personnel manager, e.g. a company training plan and many general conditions of employment, but much local personnel management practice is left to each hotel general manager's discretion, including local wage rates, to reflect the individual circumstances of each establishment.

Benefits

An effective and efficient workforce is an important element of a profitable tourist organization to enable it to challenge, adapt and survive in increasingly competitive circumstances. To illustrate the benefits of successful personnel management practice, examples which relate to specific activity areas are given below.

An organization will expect to see some or all of the following benefits from adopting a systematic approach to training: decreased learning time on the job; greater motivation and commitment; improved performance; faster progress; increased loyalty to the organization; fewer bad habits transmitted from one generation to another; reduced rates of absenteeism, labor turnover, accidents and wastage of materials; fewer irate customers; higher standards of service; reduced time in dealing with queries and fewer mistakes. This list is by no means exhaustive but indicates the sort of results that organizations should expect from commitment to training.

In the area of employee/industrial relations, the benefits of formal written procedures, e.g. grievances, disputes and discipline, will avoid misunderstanding and ensure consistency in operation. The benefits of comprehensive disciplinary rules and procedures will ensure the promotion of fairness and order in the treatment of individuals; assist the organization to operate effectively through the setting of standards of behavior and conduct and by ensuring that those standards are adhered to.

The benefits of enlightened welfare practice can be justified both economically and socially. Undue anxiety can result in reduced effectiveness; welfare services such as employee counselling or assistance with health or sickness problems, can help minimize such decreases. People do not leave their personal problems at home; organizations do have a social responsibility towards their workforce in matters of equity, consideration, the quality of working life and working conditions.

Finally, the benefits of good personnel administration will ensure compliance with the many legal requirements that now underpin the personnel management function in the United Kingdom. This could avoid potentially costly industrial tribunal or court proceedings, e.g. equal opportunity, the transfer of undertakings, redundancy, dismissal and health and safety. Sound personnel administration will also ensure that organizations satisfy government regulations and thereby receive their due financial entitlements, e.g. statutory sick and maternity pay, and allowances and grants relating to government employment and training schemes, including the Youth Training Scheme.

Implementation

A prerequisite to successful personnel management in any organization, is commitment from top management which permeates throughout the management structure. Successful personnel management stems from stated organizational objectives about its employees. Personnel policies are derived from these objectives; strategies and systematic procedures are devised to secure policy implementation.

A vital factor in successful personnel policy implementation is accurate information. Personnel records and statistics provide the facts necessary for rational, informed decision making. Personnel record systems may be very simple in the small travel agency but the introduction of computers has provided opportunities for even the small business to hold basic personnel data and process employees' pay. MANIS, British Rail's manpower information system, has the capability to interrelate some 110 separate sets of records in respect of all or any of British Rail's 170,000 staff. Apart from the obvious benefits of greater control and efficiency from the provision of rapidly available high quality and up-to-date information, the system is considered to have enhanced the personnel department's credibility with other managers and its involvement in mainstream organizational policy matters.

The manpower plan – the keystone of the personnel management process – cannot be realistic or effective unless formulated with the corporate and other functional plans; hence the importance of top level personnel management commitment. The manpower plan helps determine not only future staffing requirements quantitatively, but is also concerned with qualitative issues such as the correct utilization of staff, controlling labor costs and increasing productivity. Thus the manpower plan forms the basis for future programs in recruitment, training, redundancy, productivity and retention.

But in service industries, customer satisfaction is the key to success and as such is overwhelmingly influenced by front line staff courtesy. British Airways and Thistle Hotels are examples of organizations who have developed service enhancement programs to this end. Training through behavioral modeling, transactional analysis, staff involvement, competitions and incentives, has been carried out. But to make such a training program work, a radical rethink and re-examination of recruitment criteria, induction, promotion criteria and work organization has been necessary. In other words, to be successful, training aimed at improving customer satisfaction is much more than 'just a training course' and involves conversion in an almost evangelical sense.

In many organizations sound personnel policies exist yet at the implementation stage, personnel matters are pushed to the bottom of the busy manager's in-tray. This may be because the manager, who is simply faced with too many and often conflicting demands, perceives that top management is more concerned about financial operational performance. Conforming with management in these areas becomes the prime consideration; the figures must look right. Personnel issues are often less tangible to the manager who finds it easier to comprehend the need to set about selling more package holidays to boost profits than it is to improve staff morale and attitudes. But if business performance is being hampered by a rapid turnover of disgruntled staff, with the subsequent loss of expertise and skill, improved profitability will not be solved just through a simple marketing exercise.

Organizations must also give some thought to the feasibility and practicability of implementing personnel policies and procedures. If a performance appraisal system is hide-bound by too many forms and instructions, it will be derided as more 'irrelevant personnel matter' by managers and is thus doomed to fail, technically sound though it may be. Tourist organizations must relate personnel policies and activities to their needs. Managers must consider what is feasible and viable to meet their organization's needs and not implement new techniques which are either inappropriate or unworkable in their particular environment.

Assessment

Apart from the particular problems of achieving a balance between efficiency and effectiveness, measuring successful personnel management is especially difficult. One problem stems from the inherent difficulties that exist in measuring accurately many personnel management activities which are frequently impossible to define precisely, or demonstrate little cause and effect. Personnel management at the strategic level and in areas of key policy formulation is perhaps the most difficult to evaluate, e.g. organizational development, manpower planning, management development, motivation and good employee/industrial relations. It is much easier to assess the effectiveness and efficiency of administrative personnel management tasks on a more localized level, e.g. a recruitment exercise, by looking at factors such as the speed of filling vacancies; advertising costs; recruitment costs per head and voluntary terminations made within 3 months of employment.

Whilst the fact that the recruitment service is working satisfactorily or that the company is kept from defending unfair dismissal claims at industrial tribunals, may on the face of it suggest success, it is often difficult to measure the extent to which this is contributing to profitability. It can be argued that the importance of good personnel management is to provide a basis on which profit can be built and by helping prevent situations where productivity can be diminished.

Quantifiable measures such as labor costs as a percentage of sales revenue do provide valuable business management control information, particularly in labor-intensive organizations, but must relate to those organizations' standards. For example, a five-star hotel will expect to carry higher labor costs:sales revenue than a family run boarding house. British Airways' evaluation of success in its 'Putting People First' campaign is to be measured in the longer term through commercial success, improved return on investment, increased market share and successful defence against new market intruders. On a more interim level, staff response and changed behavior and 'has the customer noticed?' are considered to be positive indicators of achievement.

Conclusion

Personnel management is concerned with the efficient and effective use of an organization's workforce, not for altruistic reasons but because it makes sound business sense. People are a costly resource and need to be moulded into a beneficial asset. To achieve this, organizations must be committed to sound personnel management practice from the highest level downwards; set clear objectives; formulate personnel policies and procedures that reflect their needs and priorities; and ensure that these policies and procedures are implemented, monitored, evaluated and updated to remain relevant in a rapidly changing economic and social climate.

Focus on small business

Even in the smallest firm, a personnel management need exists. Staff have to be recruited, trained, paid or dismissed, and legal constraints cover areas such as sex and race discrimination. Managers must use clear and analytical thinking in staff matters. In recruitment this would include defining the job, the standards that are expected, and the skills and qualities required of the job holder. For effective selection, interview skills training would be a valuable asset. Job Centers offer excellent personnel experience and expertise to assist managers to fill vacancies.

The main problem for the smaller firm, in personnel management terms, is reached typically when the firm has expanded to the point where the manager can no longer deal with matters such as employee grievances on a relatively informal or personal basis. Sheer numbers employed begin to demonstrate the need for simple yet more systematized and formal personnel procedures. In such a case, the manager (in the United Kingdom) could seek advice on what to do from the Advisory, Conciliation and Arbitration Service (ACAS) which provides assistance on all personnel and industrial relations matters to firms regardless of their size, but may be particularly beneficial to small firms because it does not charge for its services. Advice may be given verbally; alternatively an ACAS officer might spend a few days undertaking a mini-consultancy exercise at the firm.

The small businessman cannot afford to pay scant attention to the effective and efficient use of his staff. The typical cost of a travel agent's staff salaries may be as high as 60 per cent of total costs. If in doubt, managers can seek specialist help from a variety of sources including government-funded or voluntary organizations (which are generally free), or from fee-charging consultants.

Further reading/information sources

Albrecht, K. and Zemke, R., *Service America! Business in the New Economy* (Dow Jones-Irwin, 1985). Valuable analysis of the importance of improving people performance in service industries.

Armstrong, M., *A Handbook of Personnel Management Practice* (Kogan Page, 2nd edition, 1983). Presents an integrated picture of personnel management as a key function in any organization. Very comprehensive; well referenced.

Boella, M. J., *Human Resource Management in the Hotel and Catering Industry* (Hutchinson, 1987). Updates previous 'nuts and bolts' personnel management text.

Bramham, J. and Cox, D., *Personnel Administration Made Simple* (IPM, 1984). Practical guidance on record keeping and administration; over 100 examples of forms and records.

Brewster, C. and Connock, S., *Industrial Relations: Cost-Effective Strategies* (Hutchinson, 1985). Practical guidance on key employee/industrial relations issues of the 1980s and 1990s, including flexibility of task; initiatives in working time; alternative forms of contract.

Computerfile, Personnel Management (Institute of Personnel Management). Contains a monthly review of computing in personnel and references to firms offering software packages (see also Evans, 1986).

Cuming, M., *The Theory and Practice of Personnel Management* (Heinemann, 5th edition, 1985). Comprehensive general text.

Evans, A., *Computerising Personnel Systems: A Basic Guide* (IPM, 1986). Includes a directory of leading suppliers of complete systems, software packages and bureau services.

Fitz-Enz, J., *How to Measure Human Resources Management* (McGraw-Hill, 1984). Emphasis on the measurement of quantitative results and the contribution of personnel management to productivity.

Hackett, P., *Success in Management: Personnel* (Murray, 1985). General text designed for self-study courses.

Hotel and Catering Training Board, *Employee Relations* (HCTB, 6th edition, 1986). Invaluable handbook, particularly on employment law and organizations that offer assistance.

Humphrey, P., *How to be Your Own Personnel Manager* (IPM, 1987). Practical reference book for the small business or where no personnel expertise is readily available.

The Compleat Anbar (Anbar Publications Ltd). This annual publication is a compilation of five abstracting journals published eight times a year which form the ANBAR service. One of these is *Personnel and Training Abstracts* which contains brief summaries of newly published papers.

Thomas, M., 'Coming to terms with the customer', *Personnel Management* (February 1987). Indicates the training and communication initiatives used by British Airways to establish quality and service objectives.

Thomason, G. F., *A Textbook of Personnel Management* (IPM, 4th edition, 1981). 'Heavyweight' general text with a very broad bibliography.

Torrington, D., *Face to Face in Management* (Prentice Hall, 1982). Practical guidance for managers on interactive encounters at work including training for skill, the selection interview, counseling, discipline and negotiation.

Torrington, D. and Hall, L., *Personnel Management: A New Approach* (Prentice Hall, 1987). Very comprehensive and up-to-date general text on the personnel management process, aimed at the student and incorporating extensive empirical research. Well referenced.

Tyson, S. and Fell, A., *Evaluating the Personnel Function* (Hutchinson, 1986). Explores the issues of effectiveness and eficiency and the type of specialist personnel function that organizations might best select.

ROSEMARY LUCAS

Present and future demand for transport

The present pattern of world travel

To make predictions about the future demands for transport for tourism throughout the world we must first establish a base line of current operations. This is no easy task because the pattern of transport activities varies enormously from country to country and from region to region. Some fairly sweeping generalizations therefore have to be made to present a global picture which is sufficiently summarized to be comprehensible.

Something of the scale and nature of international transport operations can be portrayed by an analysis of the pattern of international travel disclosed by the statistics published by the World Tourism Organization (WTO). The 1985 WTO figures for world tourist arrivals are presented in Table 1 to show the broad division of tourist travel into seven major geographical regions. The table shows the numbers of tourist arrivals in each region and the percentage share which these represent of total world travel.

Europe has by far the largest international travel market with over two-thirds of world arrivals. This predominance is, however, a reflection of the large volumes of travel within Europe between neighboring countries. This is similar, in many ways, to domestic travel in other countries like the United States. An attempt has therefore been made in Table 1 to differentiate between the intraregional travel within the largest geographical regions, which tends to involve shorthaul means of transport, and the interregional travel which is normally of a longhaul nature.

It must be noted that Europe is not unique in having a substantial part of its international travel originating within its own region. Intraregional travel is 82 per cent in Europe but it is also 61 per cent in the East Asia and Pacific region, 72 per cent in North America and 80 per cent in Latin America and the Caribbean. The percentage for East Asia and the Pacific would almost certainly be higher if the large, but unrecorded, flow of excursionists between Hong Kong and China were included. In the world total of tourist arrivals intraregional travel is estimated to be about 78 per cent and, correspondingly, the longhaul interregional traffic is approximately 22 per cent.

World air traffic

The foregoing analysis of regional travel gives one immediate indication of the present demand for transport because longhaul, interregional travel is almost entirely an air transport market. Travel by sea has virtually disappeared on long distance routes leaving the airlines with a monopoly of this market. The major flows of longhaul interregional air traffic are illustrated in Fig. 1 in which the relative sizes of the flows are measured by passenger kilometers (km). The North Atlantic route is by far the largest air traffic artery. It is twice as large as the traffic flow between Europe and the East Asia and Pacific region, and 4.5 times as large as the traffic flow between North America and the East Asia and Pacific region. The longhaul air traffic flows illustrated in Fig. 1 represent approximately 80 per cent of total international passenger km and, since international traffic is 48 per cent of all world air traffic, these major flows are 38 per cent of total world air traffic including domestic.

The overall pattern of world air traffic is summarized in Table 2 to show the main components which can then be compared with the world pattern of travel by all means of transport. Further consideration will be given later to the large domestic segment of the air traffic market but it must be noted that domestic operations in the United States are 30 per cent of all world air traffic.

One further feature of world air traffic must also be noted. In most parts of the world air traffic is predominantly carried on scheduled airline services. Europe is the one marked exception and in 1985 well over 60 per cent of European air traffic was carried on inclusive tour (IT) charter services which are classified as nonscheduled. These European IT charter services are over 70 per cent of total world nonscheduled air traffic. The future importance of this aspect of the European transport system will be discussed later.

Transport for tourism in Europe

From the statistics of the world travel pattern and the major flows of air traffic it can be deduced that air transport in Europe

Table 1 The pattern of world tourist travel, 1985 (*Source:* WTO, 1986).

Geographical region	Tourist arrivals from abroad (millions)	Proportion of world arrivals (%)	Proportion from within region (%)
Europe	224.5	67.4	82
East Asia and Pacific	37.0	11.1	61
North America	32.5	9.8	72
Latin America and Caribbean	20.3	6.1	80
Africa	9.1	2.7	–
Middle East	7.1	2.1	–
South Asia	2.5	0.8	–
WORLD TOTAL	333.0	100.0	–

Table 2 The pattern of world air traffic, 1985.

	Proportion of international (%)	Proportion of world (%)
Longhaul traffic between major geographical regions	80	38
Intraregional traffic within geographical regions	20	10
Domestic traffic within countries of each geographical region	–	52★
TOTAL	100	100

★ Of which domestic traffic in the United States is 30 per cent and in the USSR is 15 per cent.

carries a much smaller share of intraregional travel than of interregional travel, where it predominates. This overall impression is supported by more detailed statistics of visitor arrivals by different modes of transport. Table 3 sets out the transport used in 1985 by visitors from abroad for 13 European countries (WTO, 1986).

Although there are very large variations in the transport used by visitors to these European countries, most of the differences can be explained by geographical circumstances. Two factors are of most importance. The first relates to the large volumes of

travel between contiguous countries, like West Germany and Austria, which almost entirely moves by private car. The second factor is the existence of a water barrier, like the English Channel, which gives a great advantage to air travel in saving journey times. These factors explain why air travel is such an important mode for the United Kingdom and why road transport (primarily by private car) predominates for most other European countries.

Some further information about transport used in Europe was given in a report 'Europeans and their Holidays' (EC, 1986). This report was commissioned by the EC Directorate for Transport (Tourism) and was based on a survey carried out in each of the 12 EC countries. The survey covered all holidays,

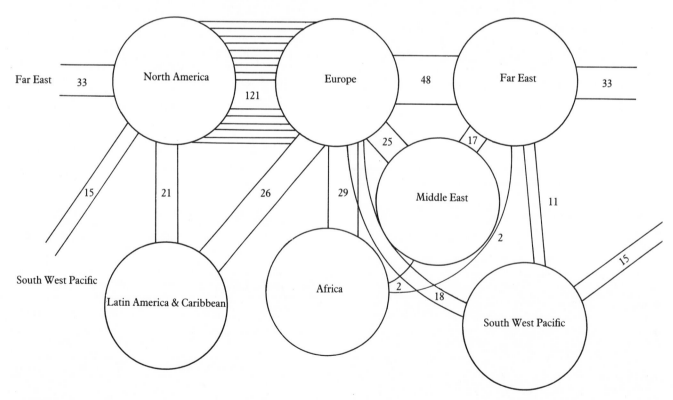

Figure 1 Major longhaul international air passenger traffic flows, 1986 (billions of passenger kilometers) (*Source: World Air Transport Statistics*, IATA, 1986).

Table 3 Mode of transport used by visitors to each European country (*Source*: WTO, 1986).

	Air (%)	Sea (%)	Road (%)	Rail (%)
Austria	0.8	–	93.4	5.8
Czechoslovakia	2.2	–	71.7	25.8
West Germany	5.9	3.4	84.4	6.3
Greece	68.9	9.7	12.4	2.3
Hungary	3.5	0.4	75.7	20.3
Italy	9.0	2.1	79.3	9.6
Romania	7.8	3.2	54.1	34.9
Spain	29.3	3.3	61.5	5.9
Turkey	33.2	19.9	44.8	2.1
United Kingdom	64.9	35.1	–	–
Yugoslavia	5.6	2.7	97.1	4.7
Bulgaria	13.0	0.4	78.5	8.2
Portugal	15.4	1.8	81.8	1.0

not just those taken abroad, and therefore includes domestic travel as well as international.

Table 4 presents one aspect of the data derived from this extensive survey and shows the method of transport used by holidaymakers from each country. This data differs from that presented in Table 3, not only because it covers domestic as well as international travel, but also because it relates to the travel generated by each country and not to the traffic coming into the country. The variations shown between the twelve countries are again of considerable interest but most important are the Europe-wide indications of the relative importance of each transport mode. Travel by private car shows up as by far the most important transport mode with 68 per cent of total traffic. To this must be added a further 10 per cent of travel by coach (and 1 per cent for bicycle or motorbike) to bring the road transport total to 79 per cent. Travel by rail and air are almost equal in their shares of the total with rail at 14 per cent and air at 13 per cent. Travel by boat is only 5 per cent for the whole of Europe.

A further feature of the travel pattern is the relationship

Table 4 Method of transport used for European holidays (*Source:* EC, 1986).

	Car (%)	Train (%)	Plane (%)	Boat (%)	Bike (%)	Coach (%)
Belgium	77	6	10	1	2	7
Denmark	59	14	18	11	3	4
West Germany	61	16	17	3	1	7
Greece	78	4	13	25	1	–
Spain	70	16	5	2	–	12
France	81	15	6	2	2	7
Ireland	51	11	31	18	1	6
Italy	73	15	5	5	2	11
Luxembourg	62	10	19	4	–	15
Netherlands	70	8	14	5	6	14
Portugal	76	17	3	3	1	16
United Kingdom	59	11	24	8	–	14
AVERAGE	68	14	13	5	1	10

between journey length and the mode of transport used. Road transport is most convenient for short journeys, rail has advantages for rather longer distances, and the time savings of air travel become more pronounced as the journey length increases. A generalized picture of the relationship between journey length and transport mode is presented in Fig. 2. This is based on survey work undertaken by Professor Bo Bjorkman (1983). It shows that travel by private car predominates on short distances but declines from over 80 per cent of the total at 150 km to less than 10 per cent at 700 km. Rail travel peaks at just over 50 per cent of the total at 350 km and air travel, which is less than 5 per cent at 200 km, rises to 75 per cent at 700 km.

Consideration will be given later to the most likely changes in the pattern of European transport and travel as a result of future economic and technological developments.

Transport in the United States

The US market for transport and travel is of special interest in establishing the base line for future projections. First because it is a very large part of the world's travel market and second because some of the developments in the US transport industry may presage changes to be expected in other parts of the world as income levels increase.

International travel from the United States is important in the world picture: the top six generating countries in 1985 were the United States ($17.0 billion), West Germany ($14.6 billion), the United Kingdom ($6.3 billion), Japan ($4.8 billion), France ($4.6 billion) and Canada ($4.1 billion). Some of this US foreign travel is by private car to Canada and Mexico and some by shipping cruises (a business which has boomed in recent years). No breakdown is available of the sizes of these two transport modes in international travel but it is evident that air travel now wins an overwhelming share of US foreign travel.

Despite the importance of US foreign travel in the world

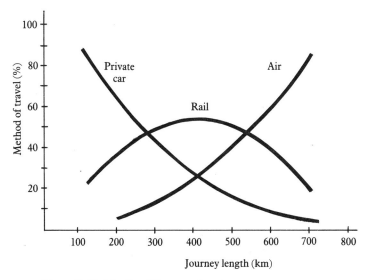

Figure 2 Modal split of European travel.

Table 5 US domestic intercity traffic distribution of passenger miles (*Source:* TPA, 1985).

	1960 (%)	1970 (%)	1980 (%)	1984 (%)
Private car	90.4	86.7	83.4	83.0
Air	4.4	10.1	14.1	14.8
Bus	2.4	2.1	1.7	1.5
Rail	2.8	0.9	0.7	0.7

market, international travel is an insignificant part of total US transport. An annual report of the US Department of Transportation (1986) presents a fascinating breakdown of all travel measured by passenger miles by each mode of transport. This shows that the passenger miles of international travel are only 2 per cent of the national total. This figure is, of course, a reflection of the huge volume of domestic travel by private car. But the relationship between international and domestic air travel also reflects the much greater importance of domestic travel. International air passenger miles are only 21 per cent of total air passenger miles. And in the vacation market it has been estimated that only one in ten holidays is taken abroad.

The domestic travel and transport market is clearly a very interesting field for more detailed analysis. The use of the private car for local trips and travel on urban transport systems have been eliminated in the definition of 'intercity travel' which includes only those journeys of more than 100 miles. Table 5 sets out the mode of transport used in this intercity travel market and shows how the pattern of transport has changed over the past 25 years. Travel by private car still predominates but its share of the total has fallen from 90 per cent in 1960 to 83 per cent in 1984. This drop reflects the increase in the airline share of the total from 4 per cent in 1960 to 15 per cent in 1984. Over the same period the share of bus transport and rail have fallen, with rail having an insignificant 0.7 per cent of total passenger miles in 1984. More recent statistics (as yet unpublished) will undoubtedly show a further increase in the air share and a further drop in the bus share.

Domestic journeys of over 100 miles have also been analyzed by purpose of travel and the shares of each of four major categories are set out in Table 6. In the overall intercity travel picture business travel is only 22 per cent of the total. The percentage is significantly higher for air travel, although even here the business share has dropped from 55 per cent in 1978

Table 6 Reason for travel by US residents – trips of more than 100 miles from home, 1984 (*Source:* USDT, 1986).

Purpose of trip	Numbers (millions)	%
VFR*	180.3	34
Other pleasure	170.4	32
Business or convention	114.5	22
Other	63.0	12
TOTAL	528.2	100

* Visits to friends and relatives

to 44 per cent in 1986, reflecting the competitive appeal of discounted air fares to leisure and personal travelers.

The most interesting questions for other regions of the world which arise from the trends in the US domestic travel market concern the future of rail traffic and long-distance coach services. Will these suffer the same decline in Europe and elsewhere as they have in the United States? Before trying to answer this question we must look at the most likely developments in longhaul air transport.

Future developments in intercontinental air transport

A marked feature of the pattern of international tourism which has been observed over the past three decades is the trends for holidaymakers to go further afield in search of new travel experiences. This trend shows up very clearly in international air transport statistics which disclose that the average passenger journey length increased from 2,500 km in 1975 to 3,143 km in 1985, an increase of 26 per cent. An International Civil Aviation Organization (ICAO) forecast predicts an average passenger journey of 3,690 km in 1995, a further increase of 17 per cent from 1985.

Such forecasts, together with those of continuing longhaul air traffic growth of about 7–8 per cent a year, rest heavily upon the assumption that air fares will continue to fall in real terms. The presumption of most aviation forecasters is that developments in aeronautical technology and improvements in airline efficiency and labor productivity will more than offset any likely rise in the price of aviation fuel in the next decade.

Far from having reached a technological plateau, as is sometimes suggested, there are many improvements in technology already in the pipeline which will significantly improve aircraft efficiency in the decade or more ahead. In particular, significant improvements in fuel efficiency and other aspects of operating costs can be expected from the following:

1. Aerodynamic improvements in wing design and the greater use of active controls.
2. The increased use of composite materials which will reduce structural weights and correspondingly increase payload.
3. Continuing improvements in engine efficiency and a resulting reduction in specific fuel consumption.
4. Improvements in flight systems which will not only make aircraft easier and safer to fly but which will also save fuel by the more precise operation of flights.

Two important features of intercontinental airline operations in the 1990s will be the use of even larger aircraft and the introduction of even more very long nonstop flights. A stretched version of the Boeing 747 with about 650 seats will almost certainly be in service in the 1990s and this will offer a substantial reduction in seat-mile costs for heavy density traffic routes. Moreover, there will be very few major traffic routes which are not served by nonstop flights like those which have recently been introduced from Europe to Hong Kong and Tokyo.

A major uncertainty is whether there will be a supersonic

replacement for Concorde in the 1990s. It is now technically possible to produce a new supersonic aircraft with operating costs lower than those of Concorde. But whether such a project will attract the very large development funds required for production must be a matter for doubt. In any event, the share of intercontinental air traffic likely to be carried on supersonic services in the next decade seems certain to be very small.

Future transport developments in Europe and the United States

It has been noted earlier that the use of the private car has declined as a percentage of intercity travel in the United States. Will this also happen in Europe in the next decade? The most likely prediction is that it will not and there are several reasons to support this conclusion. The first factor is that, unlike the United States, the European trunk road system is still in a developmental stage and considerable improvements are to be expected in the next decade which will make long road journeys easier and quicker. The second factor is that the developments to be expected in motor car technology will make motoring more comfortable and, through improvements in fuel efficiency, will make car journeys cheaper.

This second factor may be questioned in the face of US evidence which shows that the share of private car travel in the total has fallen in a period in which the fuel efficiency of cars has considerably improved. From 1974 to 1984 the average miles per gallon of private cars in the United States increased from 14 to 17, an average annual increase of 1.8 per cent. The fuel efficiency of new cars increased even more over the same period from 13 to 26 miles per gallon. It is possible that much of this improvement was related to the use of smaller cars which are less comfortable for long journeys. Whatever the reason, the share of private cars in intercity traffic has steadily fallen.

Despite the contrary evidence from US experience it is predicted that the share of private car traffic in European travel will not fall in the decade ahead. It is more likely that in some markets the share will slightly increase. A good example is travel to and from the United Kingdom where travel by private car may be increased because of the greater convenience of the Channel Tunnel compared with sea ferry services.

In other respects the development of transport in Europe in the decade ahead is likely to be similar to US experience in the past decade. Air transport is likely to increase its share of the market though not, perhaps, so dramatically as the change seen in the United States. The most likely forecast is that, whilst the total European travel market will increase at approximately 5 per cent a year, the air travel market will increase at 7 per cent a year. Hence, in a market in which air travel is currently 30 per cent of the total, it can be expected to increase to 35 per cent in 10 years time.

The market shares of both rail and coach services in Europe are expected to decline in the next decade. The forecast decline in the rail share is in spite of planned improvements in the speed and comfort of long distance trains. US experience suggests that rail travel has increasing difficulty in finding a slot in the market for its particular combination of speed and fare level. Fares are much higher than coach travel by road and speeds, except on relatively short distances, are outclassed by air travel. Rail travel is therefore in a competitive squeeze from which it has not been able to escape. As noted earlier the rail share of US domestic intercity travel has fallen to less than one per cent of the total, and this despite a very large investment through Amtrak in the improvement of rail services. A decline in the rail share of travel in Europe also seems likely in the next decade.

It is possible, if one looks further ahead into the twenty-first century, that this decline might be reversed by the exploitation of new developments in railway technology. One of the most exciting technological possibilities in the years ahead is the harnessing of the advantages of superconductivity to produce trains which use magnetic levitation and linear induction motors. These developments are theoretically capable of revolutionizing the railway system and could greatly increase the speed competition of trains on routes up to 700 km. But an enormous investment will be required before this competitive advantage can be realized and it is likely to be well into the next century, if ever, before this comes about.

Travel by long distance coach is an interesting part of the European transport system. The importance of this sort of travel appears to vary inversely with the economic climate. In the years of economic recession from 1980 to 1983 there was an increase in the coach travel market and there was some evidence that this was explained by a 'trading down' in the holiday travel market. In the United States in the past few years long distance bus travel has been badly hit by the competition of low air fares. Low cost airlines, like People Express (before its failure) and Continental (after its restructuring), were able to draw a great deal of their expanding traffic by diversion from the bus travel market. The more competitive air transport system which is emerging in Europe as a result of the reduction of regulatory controls within the EC may well produce a similar situation with lower cost airlines drawing traffic from coach services. The most likely prediction is, therefore, that coach traffic, like rail traffic, will experience a decline in its market share in the next decade.

Conclusion

In summary, therefore, the main changes in the transport markets in the United States and Europe in the next decade are likely to be a continued growth in the air share in both regions but with this increase coming in the United States from a continuing fall in private car travel whereas in Europe it will come from a fall in the rail and coach travel shares of the market.

Further reading

Bjorkman, B., 'The role of air transport in the inter-regional passenger transport system', Paper presented at ECNT Conference, Paris (1983).

Commission of the European Communities, *Europeans and their Holidays* (EC, 1986).

International Air Travel Association, *World Air Transport Statistics* (IATA, 1985).

Transport Policy Associates, *Transportation in America* (TPA, 1985).

US Department of Transportation, *National Transportation Statistics* (USDT, 1986).

World Tourism Organization, *Yearbook of Tourism Statistics* (WTO, 1986).

STEPHEN WHEATCROFT

Pricing in tourism

Introduction

Tourism pricing is a very complex decision, made even more so by the variability of the product, the high degree of competition in certain tourism markets, and difficulties in accurately forecasting the level of demand. The latter may vary not only due to the special characteristics of this industry, but also due to factors such as weather, terrorism, strikes, etc. As a result, there is no one universally accepted pricing method, and the approach can vary considerably from one tourism organization to another.

A number of basic characteristics of the tourist industry affect pricing, for example:

1. *Perishability*. As the touristic product cannot be stored for future use, this means that an unsold service/product is revenue lost, which cannot be recouped later. This will influence the profitability of the tourism organization/establishment, especially when the high fixed costs incurred by the industry are considered.
2. *Intensive capital investment*. In most investments in touristic facilities, up to 90 per cent of the capital is invested in fixed assets. Consequently, the level of fixed costs is very high in relation to other industries. This affects pricing decisions as explained below.
3. *The costs of intensive staff employed.* The quality of the product of the tourism industry depends, to a large extent, on the number and quality of the staff employed, and the special and professional skills they need to deal with guest/ staff relationships. Another problem here is that most of the tourism establishments and facilities are very dependent on occupancy levels at off-peak times, in order to justify the retention of staff at these periods.
4. *Customer characteristics*. Different touristic destinations will appeal differently to various income groups and social classes, who will have different patterns of spending, of length of stay, and different price sensitivities.

Examples

Pricing in tourism can be employed to communicate with the consumers (Virgin Atlantic flights to the United States), at-

tracting new customers into the market (Laker Airways), or enticing them from competitors. In areas where customers find it difficult to assess quality in advance of purchase, price can act as an indication of quality. As a result of this, some hoteliers, for example, have expressed the view that pricing can also be used as a device to control the marketing thrust of a hotel. For instance, if a hotel wants to get out of a particular market and concentrate on another type of business it can adjust its rates accordingly.

In setting menu prices certain pricing methods have a specific role to play. The cost-plus approach is employed in setting menu prices, by setting the food cost at a chosen percentage of the selling price. A 'menu-pricing multiple' may then be defined by taking the reciprocal of this fraction, i.e. if the food cost is to form 25 per cent of the selling price, the multiplier is $1/0.25 = 4$. Menu items are hence costed by food content and the multiplier used to yield an approximate selling price.

Another possibility is price discrimination by time. This practice has gained momentum following the Grand Metropolitan Hotels 'Stardust' holidays initiative in 1964. Now nearly all the major hotel groups, airlines, travel organizations etc., offer various sorts of 'bargain' holidays, at discounts up to 70 per cent of the normal price. Weekend packages are the most popular, but with the trend for increased holiday entitlements, mini-holidays in spring and autumn are growing in popularity and a trend is developing for second and third holidays.

Benefits

Tourism pricing affects future demand, so the impact of price must be considered carefully: should one use a low price initially to encourage long-run demands, and as a weapon aimed at capturing market share from existing competitors and discouraging potential ones from entering? Alternatively, if the market situation is monopolistic (this sometimes does happen, due to location, for example), should the price be high, aiming at gaining short-term profits and risking attracting potential competitors?

Basically, there are three factors that influence pricing decisions:

1. *Cost structure*. In the long term, the price of a touristic

product or service must be higher than the full costs incurred by the tourism organization.
2. *Competition prices*. These should be taken into account in formulating price strategies.
3. *The price the customers/guests are 'willing to pay'*, i.e. their relative elasticities of demand for the particular tour, holiday, touristic experience etc.

Prior to deciding the pricing objectives, the tourist organization must identify and quantify the potential demand for the particular tourist establishment. In order to achieve this, a market feasibility study must be conducted which should examine a number of factors such as: the nature and extent of existing facilities in a particular location, socioeconomic structure of potential visitors, potential business from industries and other sources, infrastructure, the form of existing and proposed transport networks etc. Market research must also be conducted to identify who are, or will be, the customers on whom its strategies will eventually be targeted, and what needs they have in terms of standard of services, facilities, atmosphere, location etc.

The main pricing objectives in the tourism industry are:

1. *Profit maximization*. This is the most commonly cited pricing objective, because it (a) acts as a measurement of management efficiency; (b) provides cashflows; and (c) in the hotel industry, it can be used to compensate for lower income in the off-peak season.
2. *Maximization of return on investment*. This is very important in the tourism industry, which normally has a very high level of fixed costs.
3. *Survival*. This objective is applicable where low levels of demand are experienced due to seasonality, intense or superior competition, economic recession etc. Examples include cheap holiday packages for off-season periods, and cost cutting exercises such as the ones undertaken by, say, Spanish hotels following a period of very high labor inflation which resulted in a trend towards self-service buffets, instead of the usual sit-down meals.
4. *Volume of sales*.
   (a) Maximizing occupancy. This is closely connected with profitability – unsold beds mean lost profits;
   (b) Stable occupancy. Again this is aimed at achieving high sales which are connected with profitability, but in this case increased occupancy may have to be achieved at the expense of profitability. It is usually achieved through low rates and special discounts for long stays; certain hotels offer particularly low rates to guests staying long periods during the winter season; airport hotels operate special (lower) prices at weekend when occupancy tends to fall sharply.

Implementation

In the tourism industry fixed costs are notoriously high, therefore by this commonly quoted analysis, the scope for strategic pricing is high. It should therefore be expected that the pricing systems used in practice are found to be market oriented. Traditionally this has not been the case, as more formal cost-oriented pricing structures have been used, such as those outlined below.

Cost-plus

This method calculates the price on the basis of variable costs to which is added a certain percentage which is regarded as covering other fixed costs and providing a satisfactory profit margin. Typically an operator will set this percentage on known industry practice or by analysis and projections of the market conditions. This method is easy to use and apply, but it has a number of drawbacks, especially so for the accommodation sector of the tourism industry.

The cost-plus method does not take into account demand for the product/service. This method of pricing is appropriate for cost-oriented industries, but not so for market oriented ones. There is little justification in using it for hotel rooms, for example, since a room selling for, say, $16 may have a direct cost of less than $6.

Rate of return

Those concerned with financial analysis will argue that the true function of a tourist enterprise, be it an airline or a restaurant, is to provide a satisfactory return on the capital invested. Therefore, whereas the cost-plus method concentrates on the costs associated with running the business, the rate of return method concentrates on the profits generated in relation to the capital invested. The criticism of rate of return pricing is that it is a rather mechanistic, rigid and unduly profit-oriented approach. It ignores more factors influencing pricing policy, e.g. the importance of sales volume. Its approach to pricing problems is therefore too simple to be realistic. Its greatest failure is that it loses sight of the customer and market demand generally. Thus in a market-oriented business it cannot be wholly acceptable.

Backward pricing

This method of pricing adopts the procedure of going from price (normally that of a competitor) to cost. It starts with a predetermined market price and a given specified profit, and it then attempts to achieve the latter by adjusting variable service and qualitative aspects to reduce costs.

As such it must be used with care, as a thorough analysis of attitudes, psychology and requirements of the tourist customer must be made before price selection, whilst making allowance for existing or potential competition and for the psychological effects of pricing in implying quality levels.

Marginal pricing

The marginal cost approach to pricing decisions recognizes that decision-making is essentially a process of choosing between competing alternatives, each with its own combination of income and costs. By estimating the demand curve for a particular product, it is possible to see what would happen to total profits if the selling prices are raised or lowered.

Such an approach could be useful in a highly competitive

industry with corresponding elastic demand and a high ratio of fixed to variable costs. In such an industry it is possible to set a range of prices all of which are economically possible, i.e. each price generates enough revenue to cover total costs and provide some profit. The crucial question to be answered here is what price would maximize total contribution to fixed costs and profits. This is a useful technique for industries with high fixed costs, like tourism.

Marginal pricing permits a more aggressive pricing policy, by segmenting the market and using product differentiation to gain advantage of the different layers of consumer demand, and for selecting the most profitable pricing when capacity is limited, as for example, in the peak season.

Flexible pricing
This method takes into consideration the market demand and enables discrimination according to time, place, version or volume. Although clearly the most profitable way to price is according to what the market will bear, it is not always easy to discover the correct level, and in the process some costly mistakes may be made. 'Charging what the market will bear' comes down to segmenting the market and producing different prices for the different segments based on willingness and ability to pay. In other words, this is price discrimination. Several types of discrimination are possible in the hotel industry.

1. *Discrimination by time.* This is applicable where there are peaks and troughs of demand, e.g. hotels and airlines charge more at peak holiday times and may be prepared at off-peak to accept low prices that merely make a contribution to the necessary costs of keeping a hotel ready for business. This is a way of maintaining necessary services and retaining reliable and quality staff. Additionally, it can be argued that significant amounts of business can be generated in other departments, e.g. from sales of food or beverages, resulting from accommodation bookings, and thus it might even be feasible to accept accommodation tariffs below variable costs.
2. *Discrimination by place.* An example of this could be hotel rooms wth a balcony overlooking the sea, commanding higher prices than the ones overlooking the service yard or in close proximity to the hotel's disco.
3. *Discrimination by product/service version.* Hotel rooms with bath can be charged at a higher rate than those without.
4. *Discrimination by volume.* Here we are concerned with volume and quantity discounts where end-users are concerned, e.g. in the case of tour operators care must be taken that the actual bookings reach their promised level, otherwise concessions are not related to the size of the booking.

Market penetration
This involves setting a price below that of the market or competition to capture custom in the hope that prices may be raised at a later date while retaining a high proportion of the custom that has been built up. This approach offers economies of scale both in production and in marketing.

Skimming
In tourism this may be applied to a very differentiated product, such as a new transportation method, or a new destination, where premium prices may be charged. Indeed, this pricing policy could be adopted only in circumstances where a strong (or inelastic) demand exists for the touristic products offered. Ownership of a certain unique location often offers an opportunity to charge particularly high prices.

Assessment

An assessment of the various alternative pricing methods and techniques available in tourism is presented in Table 1.

Conclusions

Pricing is one of the most important elements in the tourism marketing mix. Tourism customers rate the product at a price and without price there is no indication of value. Pricing decisions are therefore essential for the profitability of the tourist establishment, as it has a tremendous impact on demand and sales volume. Pricing is also often considered an indication of quality.

Setting the price is a critical decision for any tourism establishment. It is easy to discover when a product is underpriced. The psychology of price is important in determining a person's price/value relationship. Attitudes to price also relate very closely to the amount of risk the buyer feels is involved in the purchasing decision. For all these reasons, cost-based methods of setting tourism prices can be dangerous – their real value is in determining lower limits of price.

Although the pricing element is the most important one of the marketing mix in terms of profitability, pricing cannot be seen in isolation from the other elements. Pricing must be viewed as an integral part of the market process and the inter-relationship with the other elements in the mix, must be taken into consideration.

Focus on small business

Some of the pricing methods presented above are particularly suitable to small touristic enterprises and operators; examples are the cost-plus method, marginal pricing technique and market penetration pricing. However, even small tourism businesses, in developing a pricing policy, must carry out the following before arriving at a decision.

1. Undertake a market feasibility study and market research to determine:
   (a) the customers and the nature of demand;
   (b) the quality/quantity of the product/service required and its costing elements;

Table 1 The main tourism pricing methods.

Pricing method(s)	Content	Advantages	Limitations
Cost-plus	Calculates the price by totaling the variable costs incurred and adding a certain percentage for profit and fixed costs.	Easy to use and apply.	Not very appropriate for the hotel industry because of the high fixed costs; costs dependent on occupancy levels, but these depend on prices (i.e. are affected by the level of costs allocated); not suitable for use by market-oriented establishments.
Rate of return	Calculates the profits generated in relation to the capital invested (e.g. Hubbart formula)	Suitable in particular for calculating rooms rates; problematic when there are several interrelated service facilities.	Estimates are based on forecasted business/guests numbers; provides only an *approximate* figure for the mark-up required; ignores partially the importance of sales volume, the market and the customer.
Backward pricing	Adjusts the levels of service and product components (costs) to a certain predetermined market price.	Takes into consideration competitors' prices, as well as customers' attitudes, wants and needs via market research studies.	Requires substantial research in order not to 'dilute' the tourism product quality and consequently lose custom, create dissonance etc.
Marginal pricing (or *contribution analysis*)	The price should 'cover' the additional variable (or direct) costs *and* contribute towards the fixed costs.	Suitable particularly to hotels or similar establishments, with high fixed costs, high competition, and elastic demand. This method permits a more aggressive pricing policy including adjustments/ flexibility to low/high demand and seasonality.	Rather difficult to apply in the catering industry, e.g. restaurants, because of difficulty in identifying clearly direct costs, on each/different menu products (as these are interchangeable). Marginal pricing requires constant calculations as variable costs change over time.
Flexible pricing	Takes into consideration market demand and suggests changes in prices (i.e. price discrimination) according to time, place, product version or volume of sales.	Relies heavily on segmentation and market demand analysis. Handles changes in customers' demand. Very much a market-oriented method.	Requires constant attention, and control of marketing factors in the market place.
Trial and error pricing	Raising or lowering the price on a random basis, while continuously monitoring customers' reactions and adapting the price accordingly in order to maximize departmental contribution.	Takes account of the competition; attempts to optimize profits in the short-term.	Customers' reactions do not occur in a sufficiently short period of time to facilitate adequate changes in prices. In practice, it is difficult to assess customers' attitudes to prices as their perceptions change over time.
Market penetration pricing	Setting prices at a level lower than the market in order to capture market share.	Offers economies of scale both in production and in marketing.	The tourism organization should or could expect 'retaliation' from competitors; if the market penetration is not successful, low levels of profitability will be achieved.
Skimming pricing	Setting a particularly high price to indicate a highly differential product.	Suitable when there is a strong inelastic demand for, say, a certain tourism facility, with limited (or weak) competitors.	It is very difficult to operate this price policy for a long period of time, as alternatives are developed by competitors.

(c) the nature of the competition;
(d) the price that the customers are 'willing to pay' for the product in question.
2. Set clear pricing objectives (e.g. attain a certain level of return/ profitability, sales volume/occupancy level(s), survival etc.).
3. The price strategies selected depend highly on the customers serviced, the small tourist organization strengths and weaknesses, the opportunities and threats in the market place, the competition, and certain tourism noncontrollable marketing variables, e.g. weather, government intervention and regulation of tourism activities, economic circumstances (e.g. inflation, unemployment) etc.

Further reading

Greenberg, C., 'Focus on room rates and lodging demand', *Cornell HRA Quarterly* (November 1985).

Kotas, R., *Management Accounting for Hotels and Restaurants* (Surrey University Press, 1983), Appendix 1.

Meidan, A. and Lee, B., 'Marketing strategies for hotels', *International Journal of Hospitality Management,* vol. 1, no. 3 (1982), pp. 169–77.

Miller, J., *Menu Pricing and Strategy* (CBI Publishing Co., 1980).

Pavesic, D., 'Prime numbers: finding your menu's strengths', *Cornell HRA Quarterly* (November 1985).

Quest, M., 'Room rates: options open to maximise profits', *Caterer and Hotelkeeper* (UK) (20 October 1983), pp. 57–8.

Renaghan, L. M., 'A new marketing mix for the hospitality industry', *Cornell HRA Quarterly* (February 1986), pp. 76–81.

Rogers, H. A., 'The psychological aspects of pricing', *HCIMA Journal* (UK) (January 1977), pp. 15–16.

Ryan, C. A., *A Study into Pricing Policies and Impact of Bargain Break Holidays in the Hotel Industry,* M. Phil. (Trent Polytechnic, Nottingham, 1981).

ARTHUR MEIDAN

Priority base budgeting

Introduction

Each winter the major tour operators of Western Europe nervously prepare to launch their summer sun holiday brochures for the coming season. They hold back brochure publication as long as possible, not wanting to be the first to publish for fear of the competitive advantage that such a move could give the other operators. And so begins a vigorous and much publicized ritual battle for competitive advantage. Every conceivable ploy is tried as all the major operators seek to sustain and hopefully gain all-important market share. The tour operating business is very much one of high volumes and low margins and so growth in market share is extremely important.

Behind the scenes the launch of the forthcoming season's programs will have been preceded by months of intensive planning as the tour operators struggle with price:volume projections, foreign exchange exposure risks, air-seat allocations, hotel contracts, new resorts, brochure production and numerous other pieces of the inclusive airtour holiday jigsaw puzzle.

Tour operators are not alone in the search for higher volumes and better margins, however. The tourism industry generally, whilst being a major growth sector, is highly competitive. There is only so much disposable time and income that can be spent on tourism and leisure, but each day brings more competition – new attractions, more hotels, larger airlines and so on. It is an increasingly competitive marketplace. The budgetary process is therefore more important than ever before in the corporate search for growth and prosperity. And as competition continues to grow there has never been a greater need to plan these operations more rigorously and to ensure that resources are used more cost-effectively.

Decisions on the use of resources have to be made or confirmed at the time of preparing the annual budget, but traditional budgeting systems do not usually meet the more demanding requirements of the present economic climate. With the traditional approach to budgeting, attention tends to be focused on proposed changes from the previous year's level of spending. Little if any information is provided about the activities to be carried out, performance levels to be achieved, optional levels of service which might be considered, or the savings and consequences arising from them. As a result the budget review process is often unsatisfactory and may lead as a matter of expediency to arbitrary decision making. This incremental approach to budgeting is typified by adjusting last year's actual spending levels by an estimated inflation factor together with a possible increment for new activities (Fig. 1).

Priority Base Budgeting (PBB) is a process which is designed to help management overcome the limitations of traditional budgeting. Quite simply the PBB process is a structured approach to planning and budgeting overhead and service activities. It is not an investigation by external consultants, but a process carried out by managers who are themselves directly responsible for the areas under review. PBB has been used successfully in a large number of service organizations, albeit to-date principally in the manufacturing, industrial and retailing sectors, for the following:

1. Better allocation of resources to achieve the organizations' business aims.
2. To improve productivity, reduce costs and gain greater value for money.
3. To build commitment within management teams to the changes required and the performance targets and resource levels to be met.

Examples

PBB has been designed to overcome the most common limitations of traditional budgeting systems. It enables senior management to review more thoroughly the underlying activities and thereby establish tighter control on the use of resources in indirect and service functions which, in the tourism industry generally, can represent a significant level of costs.

Under PBB, the managers involved are required to make a radical reassessment of their activities and to document proposals for review by senior management. In doing so, each manager has to: establish the purposes of his activities and evaluate alternative means of achieving them; define the absolute minimum level (and the lowest cost) at which service could be provided, to satisfy essential requirements only; identify successive incremental levels of service and their costs and benefits, to satisfy the more discretionary requirements of the function.

In developing these proposals, the managers are required to discuss them with their senior managers and with representative

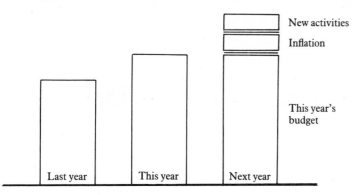

Figure 1 Traditional budgeting.

users of the service(s) provided to ensure realism and consistency. The managers then present them to a review panel, where the proposals are challenged to ensure that they are sound and cost-effective, and the requests for resources are ranked in order of priority for funding. The resulting priority listing provides the basis for top management to decide which plans to approve and to determine a budget and action plan within the constraints of expected revenue. This process is summarized in Fig. 2.

An important feature of the process is that it is led by senior management and allows a high degree of involvement of managers at all levels in the organization. It thereby enables the ideas, creative energy and commitment of the budget center managers to be harnessed, whilst senior management gain greater insight into all activities, assign priorities and are assured that current and emerging needs are given their due weight.

In the first year of the process PBB requires a significant commitment of management time and effort to produce results. Much of this time will, however, be spent necessarily in addressing management issues highlighted through the process. This time is amply rewarded, however, by the continuing benefits obtained through the PBB process.

Benefits

In many organizations, very substantial cost savings and other measurable benefits have been obtained with PBB. These bene-

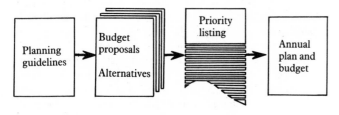

Figure 2 Priority base budgeting.

fits have been particularly great in organizations where top management have used the process to achieve objectives of strategic importance to the business and where they have been strongly committed to improving performance.

In addition to the measurable benefits, most organizations have found that the benefits arising from the participation of managers in the process are, in the longer term, at least as important. These include management training and development, improvements in communications and the development of more commercial attitudes and readier acceptance of the need for change.

Implementation

Setting the framework

The first step is for senior management to decide the budget areas or subjects to be covered. In many cases, budget areas will coincide with established cost centers. In other areas, management may wish to focus attention on particular areas of cost in order to address issues which are better tackled directly, as they cannot be addressed adequately when the costs are included within departmental budgets.

Challenging established activities

The second step involves budget line managers who are required to make a radical reassessment of their activities and propose outline budget proposals for review by senior managers. Top management has to give clear policy guidelines and provide direction which should govern the budgeting process and determine boundaries. The particular relevance of this is that it allows senior management to bring in incidental areas of planning which may be overlooked and while these do not necessarily create major problems in aggregate, they can be significant, e.g. company cars, security services etc.

This is the crucial phase in which the status quo should be challenged and alternative (more cost-effective) methods considered. The budget proposals should also identify different levels of service, starting with the absolute mandatory or minimum level, and identify the costs and benefits of each level, so that the implications are apparent to senior managers, but accurate costings are not necessary at this stage.

Senior management review

This is the stage at which each manager has to justify his budget to senior managers who are at liberty to question its validity. Therefore they will be challenged to ensure that the analysis has been sufficiently radical and that the proposals are realistic and cost-effective.

The strength of this step is that it has to involve both user-managers and senior managers from different functions, for example, operational managers and service/administrative managers, who can be involved in challenging aspects in order to achieve the necessary degree of objectivity.

Preparing detailed budgets

So far, the basis on which budgets should be prepared has been agreed. Now it remains to prepare the budget proposals in more detail. In particular, the proposals should specify the cost of each level of service. Budget managers now proceed to prepare their detailed budget proposals. Each proposal will comprise an absolute minimum level (and lowest cost) and usually up to four incremental levels. The budget proposals should describe for each level: the annual cost of the level proposed; the resources (staff) required and how they are to be used; the benefits to the business of the service provided.

This is the information senior management needs to be able to justify whether the activity should be provided and at what level. For instance, in a recent PBB assignment a particularly controversial area was the head office staff canteen where it was recognized that, at the absolute minimum level, it could involve sandwiches and drinks served by dispenser, and at another, waitress service. Quite clearly these two alternative levels of service involved very different levels of cost.

Rank proposals in order of priority

This is the point at which top management considers the proposals emerging from the PBB process. The budget manager presents his proposals to a senior management review panel which will include some senior managers from different functions, for example, operations and service/administrative managers.

A simple technique is used to ascertain the relative priority of each service level by using a rating scale to rank the proposals is descending order of importance as seen by the reviewing panel. The priority listing includes the cost of the ranked levels. This is used in the next stage to identify the service levels to be funded.

In addition to the priority listing, it is usual for the review and ranking process to highlight opportunities for profit or operational improvements which may require further study or effort before the benefits can be realized. The review panel is ideally placed to initiate and prioritize further work. The review and ranking process also provides substantial benefits in improving senior management understanding of operations within the business and helps to develop communications across functional boundaries (for example between operations and support functions) and to clarify corporate goals and strategies.

Budget and implementation

In the final stage of the process, top management should use the priority listing to decide which budget levels to approve in order to meet financial and other objectives. This allows top management to draw a cut-off line at the point in the list where funds are no longer available to support activities below the line. Once the funding decisions have been confirmed, however, senior management should ensure that the decisions are communicated to line managers and that an implementation plan is developed so that the benefits that have been identified are realized.

Conclusion

What can be learnt from all this? That management does have a choice in the approach it adopts to controlling overhead costs. Recent experience in a variety of sectors has shown that the new approach – PBB – does yield major benefits and has much to offer the burgeoning tourism industry. It demands a more critical assessment of costs than in the normal budgeting process. It stimulates management to be much more objective and cost conscious in establishing their budgets and in the words of the managing director of a recent PBB client, 'it made my managers appreciate more clearly their role in relation to the total company operation'.

Priority base budgeting is a practical management process which, in our experience, is particularly suitable for planning and controlling indirect costs in most industrial and commercial organizations. In addition to the facility which PBB provides for achieving reasoned and balanced reductions in indirect costs which are required to meet a profit or revenue plan, PBB can also provide a number of important additional benefits:

1. Closer top-management understanding of the operations and priorities of indirect services and functions.
2. Improved management communications.
3. Better commitment of managers to achieve planned objectives and costs.
4. Closer integration of annual budgets with longer-range plans.
5. Improved allocation of scarce resources, e.g. between functions of different importance to the future of the organization.

In times of financial constraint PBB is a valuable alternative to the more arbitrary allocation of resources which management is often forced to take as a matter of expediency. PBB can be helpful also in developing implementable operating plans within the constraints imposed by an arbitrarily reduced financial budget, and it can be equally helpful in planning the reallocation of resources when an organization moves into an expansionary phase.

One of the major advantages of the priority base approach over contemporary methods of overhead cost improvement is that PBB ties planned cost improvements into the annual budgeting and monitoring system. This enforces a discipline both in terms of ensuring that the process is completed to a deadline, and also in providing a control through the management reporting system to ensure that planned improvements are in fact achieved.

Experience suggests that the benefits of PBB outweigh the costs and that the tourism industry should look at PBB as a useful and proven management tool.

JONATHAN N. ROUNCE

Production/operations management in tourism

Introduction

The tourism industry, with its many and varied component parts which include airlines, hotels, travel agents, tour operators etc., is generally accepted to be a part of the service sector rather than the manufacturing sector. This is not an issue which is disputed. What is sometimes a matter for disagreement is the definition of a service industry; Lockyer (1986) argues that the usage of the term can often be misleading. If one were asked to define 'a service industry' various issues such as 'intangibility of the product', or 'perishability of the product', or 'involvement of the customer in the transformation process' might be raised. Lockyer points out that none of these criteria are peculiar to the service industry. With the purchase of a watch a customer is not only buying a tangible product, i.e. an artefact which allows the user to tell the time, he/she may also be concerned with the appearance of the watch – what image does it create – one of glamor, manliness, etc? These are not attributes which can be readily measured, they are as intangible as the 'welcome' which a customer receives on entering a hotel.

There exists a continuum of products with a low intangibility element at one end and a high intangibility element at the other, as illustrated in Fig. 1. Generally speaking, the production or manufacturing sector will have products which lie towards the lower end of the intangibility spectrum whilst the service sector 'products' will lie towards the higher end. A similar illustration may be used for perishability or customer/organization interaction. The important point is that in all cases a *transformation* is taking place '. . . inputs (which may be physical, nonphysical or both) pass through a set of facilities to create outputs (which again can be physical, nonphysical or both)' (Lockyer, 1986, p. 5).

Industries, such as tourism, which are classified as being in the 'service sector' all have transformation processes that are similar in many cases to those found in the 'manufacturing sector'. So of what relevance is this to production/operations management in tourism? The answer is quite simple – many managers in the so called 'service' industries perhaps do not appreciate that many techniques which have proved highly successful in manufacturing are also applicable in their sphere of operations.

The remainder of this chapter will be devoted to illustrating just how some of the production management techniques may be of use in the tourism industry. It is intended to provide an overview, rather than a detailed treatment, and the reader is referred to some of the excellent texts and articles which have been written on the subject of operations management.

The 5 Ps

There are a range of tasks and problems which face a production manager which are usefully categorized into one of five areas: product, plant, process, programs and people – known as the 5 Ps of Production. This classification provides a framework for dealing with the tasks and analyzing the problems. This framework can also be used by any operations manager in the tourism industry.

The product

Before looking at specific tasks which relate to the product and at the techniques which may be used to solve problems, it is important to understand what is meant by 'product' in the service context. For a vacation the 'product' which is purchased comprises many parts: the journey to the airport, the flight, the hotel accommodation, meals, entertainment, sightseeing and so on. It is important that the suppliers of each component part of the 'product' realize just what it is that they are providing. Take, for example, a theater; what is the product? All too often theater management consider only the play, ballet or opera as the product. But this is a very myopic picture. A night out at the ballet is much more than the excellence of the performance. Other things which will affect the audience are for example:

1. Comfortable seating.
2. View of the stage.
3. Heating – whether it is too warm or cold.
4. Air conditioning.
5. Attentive and helpful staff.
6. Bar facilities – are these adequate to meet demand during an interval? Do the bar staff seem to spend all their time chatting to each other?
7. Decor – are the surroundings shabby?
8. Toilet facilities – is the queue so long that people are late back after the interval?

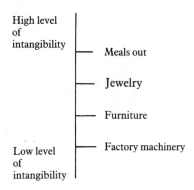

High level
of
intangibility

— Meals out

— Jewelry

— Furniture

Low level
of
intangibility

— Factory machinery

Figure 1 Continuum of products.

9. First-aid facilities – are they provided? Are they adequate?
10. Booking facilities – how difficult is it to acquire tickets?

Theater goers expect to enjoy the whole of the time that they spend within the portals of the theater. Intangible aspects such as atmosphere are clearly difficult to measure and as such are often ignored. Attention focuses on the more tangible aspects of the product. However if one realizes that what are often thought of as support functions are actually part and parcel of the product, success is far more likely to result.

One example of management not fully realizing the importance of such issues is in evidence at a large theater in the north of England, which has recently undergone major renovations with improved facilities for both performers and audience. However at least two of the issues listed above appear to have been forgotten. During the interval the audience face a dilemma: to rush to the bar in the hope of getting a drink or to rush to the toilet to make sure they get back for the start of Act 2!

Quality

Quality may be defined as meeting the customer's requirements. Thus one may have a high quality camping site or a low quality so-called luxurious hotel. A level of decor which is perfectly acceptable in a two-star hotel may be totally unacceptable in a five-star hotel. Here one is involved with the expectations of the customer, which is exactly the same as the situation facing a car manufacturer making a Mini or a Jaguar, for example. A strategic decision has to be made regarding the market segment which is being targeted. This decision should not be made by the marketing department alone – the operations department need to be consulted about the feasibility of providing the product. This strategic decision must cover policy regarding quality, i.e. a conscious decision must be made about the level at which a product is being offered. The quality should then be *designed* into the product, and clear specifications put into writing. The other facet of quality is *conformance* to design – does the product actually meet the specifications when produced or delivered? This will depend on how well the transformation process has been designed, and whether the methods laid down have been adhered to. Techniques concerned with

ensuring quality of conformance will be dealt with later under 'Process'.

Value

The value of a product is reflected in the price of that product. However, the price or exchange value may be seen to be comprised of two parts, use value and esteem value, thus:

Exchange value = Use value + Esteem value

where 'use value' is the price the purchaser will offer in order to ensure that the purpose (or function) of the product is achieved and the 'esteem value' is the price which is offered for the product beyond the use value. In the tourism sector many products have a very large esteem value element, for example, at a high class expensive restaurant the actual worth of the meal will be far exceeded by the price.

Value analysis is just one of the techniques which may help when designing the product. This technique entails following a routine which involves identification of the function of the product, making an examination of ways of achieving this function and analyzing the costs associated with the various options.

Variety

Excessive variety of tourism products or parts brings with it increasing problems and costs. For example the more destinations and hotels offered by a tour operator, the more complex become the scheduling problems. In a restaurant the greater the choice on a menu, the more storage space required, the higher the committed capital etc. This problem often causes conflict between marketing and operations, with the former wishing to increase product range whilst operations need to maximize the efficiency of production of the services on offer. A technique which is very easy to use but which leads to logical choices with respect to which products or services to maintain, is Pareto Analysis, sometimes known as ABC analysis. In many cases 20–30 per cent of products may be seen to earn 80 per cent of the total contribution. Thus the vital few products may be identified. This technique may be used in many other situations, for example in the analysis of complaints or identification of the most persistent debtors.

The process

Quality management

The process of making or providing the 'product' is an area where many production management techniques may be applied. Statistical Process Control (SPC) comprises a range of techniques which have been introduced into the manufacturing environment to ensure that products are made 'right first time'. This leads to reduced rework costs, guarantee claims, loss of goodwill etc. Prevention rather than detection and cure is the underlying strategy. This approach is equally applicable in the tourism sector and is probably of even greater importance.

When the author decided to take a short break in the Lake District last autumn, recommendations were sought from a few colleagues before choosing a hotel. The stay in the hotel was very disappointing with many trivial, and one or two more serious shortcomings. These were brought to the attention of the deputy manager who was most apologetic and indeed agreed to a slight reduction in the price of the stay. The manager (who had been absent that weekend) subsequently wrote, again apologizing and repeatedly expressing the hope that they would be granted 'another chance' to demonstrate how things usually operated. A letter of explanation is not the answer, however apologetic. By that stage of the proceedings the custom had already been lost and a poor image indelibly created. Reassurance that a repeat performance would be totally satisfactory had little chance of proving successful in counteracting the reality of the experience. As this particular hotel is part of a large chain, the effect of this bad experience is likely to extend to other hotels in the chain. Also some of the previously consulted colleagues, enquiring about the break, may be deterred from visiting the hotel. In such a case it is difficult to assess the cost of loss of goodwill, but there is clearly a great deal to lose.

The only way to control quality and ensure that the products are made 'right first time' is to follow the total quality management philosophy. Quality should be everyone's business and there must be a total commitment from the top of any organization downwards. Quality manuals should exist in which standards, together with the ways of meeting these goals, are defined. To be able to do this the whole transformation process must be studied and the right methods, materials and equipment identified. Staff will have to be trained to perform the process correctly. Quality can *only* be controlled at the point of operation – it must be where the meal is cooked, the bedroom cleaned, at the information desk etc.

Cause and effect analysis and control charts are techniques which may be used. For example, if a client arrived at a hotel reception to find that there were no rooms available despite having made a reservation, the cause of the problem must be identified to prevent similar problems in the future. Tour operators or travel agents may use cusum (cumulative sum) charts to facilitate early detection of changes in trends.

Work study

One of the essential factors for ensuring that the required standards are consistently met is that the method of work is correct. Method study and work measurement are two aspects of work study which may be of use in the service sector. The mnemonic SREDIM which stands for *S*elect, *R*ecord, *E*xamine, *D*evelop, *I*nstall and *M*aintain provides a systematic framework for analyzing tasks. Each step is important and techniques are available to facilitate the implementation of each step. For example flow diagrams and process flow charts may be used in the Record step; a questioning technique may be used in the Examine and Develop steps. Method study is a useful technique in all sectors at all levels and has wide application in tourism operations. Whatever the job, there will always be a better way of doing it. This is particularly important in the tourism sector where the manner in which a job is done often directly affects the tourist. For example, Levitt (1972) explains that the way an airline hostess performs her job is part of the product and goes on to show how 'the product' was improved using just such an analytical approach.

There may be instances where a work measurement technique such as Activity Sampling may be of use to help identify new areas needing attention. A hotel manager may feel that a bar is overstaffed because every time he passes the bar the barmen seem to be standing around doing nothing. He may suspect that exactly the opposite is true in the restaurant or elsewhere. It is possible to analyze the situation quantitatively by taking a number of observations at random times and calculating, with a given level of accuracy, the proportion of time the barmen were unoccupied. The result may of course show that the barmen were busy 95 per cent of the time and that a false impression had been created because the manager always happened to pass the bar just after it had opened.

Materials

Part of any process will involve the purchasing of materials. This may take the form of brochures/paperwork in the case of the travel agent or tour operator, food/drink in hotels, or restaurants, or airlines etc. Material Requirements Planning (MRP) and Just-in-Time (JIT) techniques are applicable in all sectors of the tourism industry.

Plant (equipment)

All sectors of the tourism industry will have equipment of some kind. It may be computers and office equipment or kitchen/restaurant facilities, or bedroom furniture, linen, coffee-making facilities, etc. in hotels. Decor too is part of the 'equipment' in many cases.

Techniques used in planning layout, ergonomics and maintenance will lead to greater efficiencies, less waste and smoother operations. These aspects may be of particular importance when trying to create intangible characteristics such as atmosphere. Maintenance should also be planned. For example showers that do not work properly will cause severe annoyance to the hotel guest and counteract much good work put in elsewhere in the establishment to create atmosphere, provide good food and service etc.

Programs

One of the attributes of the service industry is that of 'perishability' of the goods. An unfilled seat on a plane, train or coach, a fillet steak, a sunny day cannot be 'stored'. The opportunity of making a product for stock and supplying from stock is therefore often precluded. Nevertheless, scheduling problems do exist and just as jobs must be allocated to machines, hotel guests must be allocated to rooms; meals must be ready at a certain time; planes, coaches and trains must run to timetables. Some of these tasks may be dealt with by using similar scheduling techniques to those used in manufacturing. The answer to some of the problems, however, may be to try to manipulate demand. The marketing function may be able to redistribute demand to smooth out peaks and troughs.

People

People are clearly involved in all aspects of production/operations management and the problems of training and motivation apply to all sectors of industry. Some of the experience gained from the use of quality improvement teams and the evolution of quality circles in manufacturing may be of interest to the operations manager in the tourist organization in the development and motivation of his/her staff.

In general in the manufacturing sector, the customer is not directly involved in the transformation process and the organization/customer interface takes place with the marketing department and not with the production department. In many areas of the tourism industry, however, the customer is involved in the transformation process and the operative comes in direct contact with the client. Hence the development of special staff training programs is essential and much can be learned by observing the effects of, for example, British Airways' Customer Care campaign on improving service and lifting both staff and customer perceptions of the service being offered.

Conclusion

Clearly, there are differences between managing service operations and manufacturing operations, and there will be situations where the experience of the production manager is not directly transferable to the operations manager. Overall there is a great deal of overlap and the tourism based operations manager should learn from the production manager where possible.

In both situations the task facing the operations manager or production manager will be multifaceted and the bulk of the enterprises' employees will be under their control. The consequences of this are as follows:

1. The large numbers of people together with the volume of tasks will generate many problems.
2. There will be enormous pressure to solve the problems *rapidly* because of the magnitude of the resources involved and the sheer number of tasks.

Lockyer and Oakland (1987, p. 11) incorporate the ideas of Simon (who suggests that problems range from those that are programmable for which a definable route to a solution can be set down to those nonprogrammable problems which depend for solution upon personal knowledge, skills, intuition and flair), when they point out that:

Broadly, the non-programmable problems are the most difficult to resolve, so that the more problems which can be made programmable the more time can be devoted to non-programmable resolution. One task of the operations manager, therefore, is to cast as many problems into a programmable form.

It is exactly in this area of programmable problems that the production manager has the experience to pass onto the operations manager.

Further reading

Berry, L. L., Zeithaml, V. A. and Parasuraman, A., 'Quality counts in services too', *Business Horizons*, vol. 28, no. 3 (May/June 1985), pp. 44–52. Discusses ways of improving quality in the service context.

Chase, R. B. and Aquilano, N. J., *Production and Operations Management* (Irwin, 4th edition, 1985). This textbook comprehensively covers production/operations management techniques for use in both the manufacturing and service sectors.

Killeya, J. C. and Armistead, C. G., 'The transfer of concepts and techniques between manufacturing and service systems', *International Journal of Operations and Production Management*, vol. 3, no. 3 (1983), pp. 22–28. This paper contains a framework for thinking about organizations and a suggestion for research to facilitate the transfer of expertise across the production/operations interfaces.

Leslie, D., 'The control function and the hospitality industry', *The Service Industries Journal*, vol. 7, no. 2 (April 1987), pp. 207–15. Outlines how controls have developed and examines the role of the control function.

Levitt, T., 'Production-line approach to service', *Harvard Business Review*, vol. 50 (September/October 1972), pp. 41–52. Illustrates how the manufacturing approach can be taken in the service industries.

Lockyer, K. G., *Production Management* (Pitman, 4th edition, 1983). This textbook covers the whole of the production management function but is not oriented towards the service sector.

Lockyer, K. G., 'Service – a polemic and a proposal', *International Journal of Operations and Production Management*, vol. 6, no. 3 (1986), pp. 5–9. Discusses the definitions of a service industry.

Lockyer, K. G. and Oakland J. S., 'An operations manager's audit', *The Service Industries Journal*, vol. 7, no. 1 (January 1987), pp. 5–13. Sets out a conceptual framework for analyzing and auditing transformation management situations, specifically in service-providing organizations.

Van der Hoeven, W. H. M. and Thurik, A. R., 'Labour productivity in the hotel business', *The Service Industries Journal*, vol. 4, no. 2 (July 1984), pp. 161–73. Studies differences in labor productivity in the hotel business using cross-section data of one West German and two Dutch samples.

Willborn, W., 'Quality assurance audits and hotel management', *The Service Industries Journal*, vol. 6, no. 3 (November 1986), pp. 293–308. Outlines audits of quality assurance systems as an important management aid in hotel operations.

Acknowledgement: The author wishes to thank John S. Oakland for helpful comments on an earlier draft of this chapter.

CHRISTINE A. MARTIN

Productivity measurement in hotels

Introduction

Productivity management programs aim to ensure that business organizations use their resources in ways which are both efficient and effective. The importance of such schemes has been recently highlighted by the realization that modest increases in productivity are quickly outstripped by inflation. Therefore, for short-term survival and longer-term growth and prosperity, productivity advances need to be more substantial. The key pressures for productivity improvement are as great, if not greater, in hotels as elsewhere. They include the following items:

1. The problem of utilizing expensive labor: labor costs have increased more sharply than the general rate of inflation. The inherent unpredictability of the pattern of business in hotels generates severe difficulties for the control of staff time and the consequent maximization of labor efficiency.
2. The difficulty of passing on cost increases to customers: the more competitive market associated with the industry's increasing maturity has heightened many operators' reluctance to charge higher prices.
3. The need to increase service levels without a corresponding increase in costs: rising customer expectations produce demands for upgraded services, but at affordable prices.
4. The need to withstand both national and international competition and to hold off predatory hotels or hotel groups: tourism is now conducted on an international scale and hotels must be competitive in this market. Takeover bids are a common feature of an industry approaching maturity.
5. The continued employee demands for better working conditions and improved wages: rising expectations are not limited to customers.
6. The requirement in many hotels to replace unproductive and obsolete equipment and facilities: the refurbishment costs of some of the 'grand' hotels are on a par with the building costs of more modern units.
7. The necessity to provide increased profits to the owners of hotels: rising expectations are not limited to customers and workers!

The improvement and management of productivity in any context is dependent upon measurement which in turn requires a clear understanding of the productivity concept. Productivity has many contemporary connotations depending upon the discipline and reference point of the definer. However, it is generally regarded as the relationship between output(s) obtained from a system and one or more of the input(s) employed in yielding these outputs. Thus:

$$\text{Productivity} = \frac{\text{Output(s) obtained}}{\text{Input(s) employed}}$$

For hotels, the concept can basically be expressed in either a partial or total form. Partial productivity is the ratio of output(s) to one class of resource input. For example, labor productivity is represented as the ratio of output(s) to labor input. In total form the numerator is total output(s) and the denominator is the sum of all the contributing and associated resource inputs. The traditional quantitative dimension to outputs should be supported by a qualitative dimension within the hotel output(s). This is because quality is a key factor in the customer's evaluation of hotel outputs. Thus, whilst it might be possible to fill more bedrooms (outputs) or produce and serve more meals (outputs) to more customers the desirability and satisfaction of these bedrooms, meals and service outputs might fall. In other words, a 'trade off' between the quantity and quality of hotel outputs may result in an adverse effect on productivity in hotels. Hotel productivity can therefore be expressed as:

$$\frac{\substack{\text{Partial} \\ \text{hotel} \\ \text{productivity}}}{} = \frac{\mathbf{f}\ (\text{quality of outputs, quantity of outputs})}{\text{Single class of resource input, e.g. labor}}$$

$$\substack{\text{Total} \\ \text{hotel} \\ \text{productivity}} = \frac{\text{Total } \mathbf{f}\ (\text{quality of outputs,}\ \text{quantity of outputs})}{\substack{\text{Labor} + \text{Energy} + \text{Raw Materials} \\ +\ \text{Capital} + \text{Other resource inputs}}}$$

Productivity measurement basically consists of three separate elements: the measurement of hotel outputs for a given period of time, the measurement of the hotel inputs responsible for these outputs and the expression of the related outputs and inputs in the form of a ratio. Once a ratio has been calculated its meaning and significance for the management of productivity within a hotel can be evaluated via comparisons against predetermined yardsticks.

Examples

Commonwealth Hotels International Co. is a multiple, and one of the largest, franchisees of Holiday Inns Inc. It operates throughout Canada, the Caribbean and the United Kingdom. In the United Kingdom its hotels are positioned at a four-star market level and are located in urban areas offering a branded package of broadly similar products, facilities and services. The 1980s has been a period of growth for the company with the number of hotels it operates having increased.

Work performance within a labor productivity context has been regarded by the company as a contributory factor to its competitiveness and growth. The company has considered both market (output) and workforce (input) factors simultaneously in its quest to measure and manage levels of labor productivity in the food and beverage departments of its hotels. In these departments customer use was most variable and the potential for performance improvement greatest.

The uniform operational and financial information produced monthly by each hotel provided the data to compile both revenue (output) and cover (output) to labor input measurements. These measurements were utilized to provide a picture of workforce productivity for each hotel, each food and beverage department and each monthly period. The identification of exceptionally good and bad productivity periods and food and beverage departments was facilitated by comparative analyses. For example, a comparison of room service activity revealed that one hotel was able to achieve productivity levels eightfold greater than that of another. An examination of the characteristics of provision and consumption in these two hotels allowed the company to determine whether these performances were actually as good and as bad, for each hotel respectively, as they seemed on first inspection. The recognition of the causes underlying good or bad productivity levels was then used to improve future productivity within the company's hotels.

Benefits

The basic purposes of measuring productivity in hotels are to determine appropriate and realistic target productivity levels, to take stock of productivity levels for a given time period, to ascertain how satisfactory these levels are and to direct the hotel towards the future improvement of productivity in conjunction with the quest for other organizational performance objectives.

The potential benefits of productivity measurement to hotels can be grouped under the following three headings:

Strategic

The first category of benefits is associated with helping hotels acquire greater flexibility in response to external conditions. This category includes the comparison of the productivity of hotels or hotel groups with that of their competitors. Along with other information, these assessments can aid decision making and the formulation of strategies for survival, profit-

ability and growth. Such assessments are not an easy task since the late entry of hotels into the arena of productivity has meant that few comparative hotel derived yardsticks, other than those based upon accounting information, are available for public use. Productivity measurements are useful for hotels in decision making with regard to unit development, geographical expansion, refurbishment, business contraction, market exit etc.

Operational

Productivity measurement offers numerous advantages related to the internal operation and conduct of hotels. Hotels can assess the efficiency with which they have consumed resources in the course of yielding outputs, at a constant quality level. The extent to which this performance has improved or regressed can be judged through comparisons with earlier operating periods. The efficiency with which labor is used is particularly significant in the management of hotels as labor is present in most output generating endeavors, and invariably accounts for the greatest proportion of total hotel costs. Employees are crucial to the success of hotels where direct contact is made with customers and where automation is limited. These areas can be significant labor productivity focal points.

The ultimate goal of productivity measurement is to improve productivity by increasing output without a corresponding increase in input. The determination of the extent of variance between the actual and planned productivity levels can aid hotels in their selection of one or more of the available improvement techniques or methods. These can be grouped as follows:

1. Technology-based, such as energy conservation or computer-aided design.
2. Employee-based, for example, incentive schemes or job enrichment.
3. Materials-based, such as the use of convenience foods or the use of standardized equipment, furnishings and fittings.
4. Task-based, for instance ergonomics or job evaluation.
5. Customer-based, such as business trough discounting or the subtle replacement of employee effort by customer effort in carveries or to make tea/coffee in bedrooms.
6. Organization-based, including the adjustment of size and structure within hotels and the improvement of communications.
7. Product/service-based, for instance monitoring standards or auditing outputs.
8. Combinations of the above.

The choice of enhancement technique is very much dependent on the particular hotel. The success, or otherwise, of employing these techniques in hotels can also be appraised, other factors considered, through productivity measurement.

Productivity measurement has the potential to act as a vehicle to improve the conduct of operations within hotels and provide direction for employees. The internal climate and operating performance could benefit from encouraging employees to participate in a productivity program and from involving them in the analysis, interpretation and discussion of the measurements.

Such cooperation could be reinforced by, linking productivity to pay through incentive schemes and commission systems based upon the achievement of specific sales levels per sales person or group. Productivity measurement could improve conduct by enabling more rational collective bargaining between hotel management and employee groups. The negotiations over the introduction of a cook chill system for banqueting and conference catering can be made easier by relating bonuses to increased productivity (compared to a conventional catering system) and by smoothing out temporal productivity fluctuations as a consequence of separating production from service.

Planning

The third group of benefits relates to program or resource planning. Productivity measurement can facilitate the setting of targets and timetables for future activities. Targeting hotel and departmental managers against both their own historical performance and that of any counterparts, if in a hotel group, is seen as a simple way of highlighting the significance of productivity and its subsequent improvement.

The objectives and direction of a hotel or hotel group can be prioritized as a consequence of productivity measurement and particular programs developed according to their contribution to objectives. Hotels, seeking cost savings as a means of improving profits, have planned and pursued industrial engineering programs to enhance productivity. A Holiday Inn in the United States, for example, has formulated new procedures, redesigned and rearranged equipment, set new standards, developed job descriptions and improved training as part of such a program for food and beverage, laundry, housekeeping, maintenance and front office departments.

Productivity measurement can enable a comparison of the potential benefits accruing from the use of different types of inputs or from the use of different forms of the same input type. An example of the first option is where hotels are considering whether to substitute machines for employee time through the replacement of manual front office systems by computerized systems. The decision over whether to purchase a flight dishwasher or a 'roll in-roll off' dishwasher for a hotel wash up is an example of the second.

Manpower planning and, in particular the determination of staffing complements and the scheduling of staff within hotels, can also be facilitated as a result of productivity measurement and forecasting future business load and patterns of business.

Implementation

The measurement of hotel outputs

Hotels supply customers with a diverse range of products, facilities, services and forms of hospitality. At the hotel level outputs such as turnover, value-added, housecount and number of meals and drinks served are quantifiable. They also incorporate a quality dimension and reflect the receipt by customers of the complete, or a major part of, the hotel package. The beauty of such outputs is that associated data is readily available in hotels as it is collected for other purposes.

Within the hotel an array of outputs is identifiable and can be utilized for more specific productivity measurement. For instance, outputs of interest to the sales department might be the number of bedrooms, conferences or functions booked and taken up; to the switchboard, the number of calls dealt with satisfactorily; to the housekeeping department, the number of bedrooms cleaned to standard; to maintenance, the number of effective repairs of a certain type. All hotel outputs can be conceived as secondary or primary outputs. Secondary outputs are those which result from the transformation of inputs, but are not sold or delivered to the customer. The production of food in the kitchen or the preparation of a bedroom prior to occupancy are examples, whereas primary outputs are those which have a 'sales' element such as net profit, covers sold and room occupancy. The choice of output and, indeed, productivity ratio is dependent upon the use to which it is to be put.

There are approaches to overcome the pitfalls associated with quality changes to outputs. These include adjusting quantity to the number of usable, saleable or acceptable outputs such as refining the number of customers served to the number of satisfied customers served. The need for any adjustments due to quality changes could be minimized through the use of quality control techniques such as hotel standards packages, service audits and direct customer feedback mechanisms including guest questionnaires. These techniques are being increasingly used in hotels with one key intention which is to maintain quality at a constant level.

The measurement of hotel inputs

Inputs are simply the resources needed to operate hotels and can be categorized into such broad types as labor, capital, raw materials, energy and customers. While the measurement and accumulation of total factors, particularly if the resources are based on financial costings, is feasible at the hotel level it is more difficult for individual departments and activities. However, single inputs can be more readily quantified for specific productivity monitoring. Measurement of labor input related to the numbers of employees, the hours which they work, payroll costs etc. can be used to monitor labor productivity, while energy conservation and utilization can be measured using kilowatt hours and energy cost inputs.

Hotel productivity ratios

A catalog of ratios can be compiled by fitting outputs to associated inputs. Each ratio relates to different aspects of operating performance and to different organizational activities. The use of primary or secondary outputs would result in the formation of primary or secondary productivity ratios. The choice of measure depends greatly on the purposes for which it is intended and a combination of different measures might be most appropriate. Dysfunctional consequences however might arise if too narrow a definition of productivity is taken leading to employees focusing on certain operational aspects at the expense of others. Those concerned with energy management will be attracted to those ratios which relate energy inputs to outputs. Those concerned with measuring financial performance will be most interested in accounting ratios. In fact, productivity ratios can be identified for any feature of hotel operation once the inputs and outputs have been recognized.

Conclusion

Productivity is a key performance area in hotels. Hotel productivity can be broadly defined as the utilization of labor, customers, capital and natural resources in creating hotel outputs. The qualitative dimension of outputs is vital in any consideration of productivity in hotels, for if hotels increase quantity of output at the expense of lower quality, they gain little if any overall productivity.

The measurement of hotel productivity is fundamental to its improvement as it allows management to know how well they are doing, to know which areas are problematical and should be further investigated, and to decide the course of action most suited to solve the problems. The potential benefits to hotels of measuring productivity can be categorized as strategic, operational or planning benefits. Productivity measurement comprises the selection of both output and input variables in hotels and the development of a ratio which expresses a measurement of outputs to a measurement of associated inputs. Productivity ratios should be developed for the specific purpose to which they will be applied in hotels.

Focus on small business

In many countries most hotels, defined by any of a variety of size criteria, are small. In the United Kingdom, for instance, small hotels currently comprise the majority of all hotels both on the basis of numbers employed and in terms of the numbers of bedrooms. The need for productivity maintenance and improvement through productivity measurement is no less important and beneficial in small hotels than in larger hotels. Indeed, evidence for the UK hotel market suggests that larger hotels invariably perform better in terms of room occupancy than smaller hotels, that the numbers of small hotels have decreased in recent years concurrent to an increase in the numbers of larger establishments and that larger companies who tend to own a higher proportion of the larger hotels, have become more competitive.

The principles of productivity measurement are common to all hotels, but the actual practices should be shaped according to the size, complexity and business type of hotel. A small owner-managed hotel would not require the same range and degree of productivity measurement information as a large multi-departmentalized hotel belonging to a hotel group. Moreover, the involvement of the owner/manager of a small hotel with everyday activities is likely to reduce the need for the broad measurement of secondary productivity levels as the owner/manager would have a 'feel' of the rate at which inputs are converted into many secondary outputs, and would presumably be taking any necessary corrective action. Conversely,

it is less likely that the owner/manager will have his 'finger on the pulse' of primary productivity levels if only because of the time involved in related measurement and analysis. In this case, the expertise of external specialists may be required to design and operate measurement systems and interpret the results.

Productivity data can be obtained from the basic records and accounts if they are maintained in an appropriate form. These records should aid productivity measurement in small hotels as they are simpler than in larger hotels due to fewer purchases, reduced customer transactions, fewer departments, less staff, etc. Furthermore, if the small hotel does not belong to a group it will not have to collect and provide data to satisfy the needs of the corporate offices. The limited departmentalization of small hotels facilitates interhotel productivity comparisons more so than between large hotels, and this enables operating weaknesses to be more readily identified.

Further reading/information sources

Adam, E., Jr., Hershauer, J. and Ruch, W., *Productivity and Quality – Measurement as a Basis for Improvement* (Prentice Hall, 1981). This book is directed at service functions within all types of organization and refers to hotels. Chapters 1, 2 and 7 provide an overview of quality measures for productivity. Chapter 3 develops productivity measurement systems, and Chapters 5 and 6 discuss conceptual models of productivity.

Anon, 'Industrial engineering comes to Holiday Inns', *Hotel and Motel Management* (January 1978), pp. 27–9. This article explains, with reference to Holiday Inns Inc., how productivity can be increased in hotels through industrial engineering.

Bailey, D. and Hubert, T. (eds), *Productivity Measurement: An International Review of Concepts, Techniques, Programmes and Current Issues* (Gower, 1980). A number of excellent conference papers are contained in this book, ranging over the whole field of productivity and performance measurement examining both policies and methods and describing how productivity measurement techniques have been successfully applied to a wide variety of organizations in different cultures. The introduction and Chapters 1, 5, 6, 7, 10, 12 and 17 are particularly recommended.

Ball, S. D., Johnson, K. and Slattery, P., 'Labour productivity in hotels: an empirical analysis', *The International Journal of Hospitality Management*, vol. 5, no. 3 (1986), pp. 141–7. This paper introduces approaches to the measurement of hotel productivity and, within the context of one hotel company's quest to manage productivity, concentrates upon productivity measurement and evaluation.

Blois, K., 'Productivity and effectiveness in service firms', *The Service Industries Journal*, vol. 4, no. 3 (November 1984), pp. 49–60. This paper describes some of the pressures for change which are forcing service industries to re-examine their methods of 'producing' services and outlines possible responses. The difficulties of measuring productivity in service firms are discussed. Types of information needed by service firms for their response to the pressures for change are suggested.

Carnes, R. B. and Brand, H., 'Productivity and new technology in eating and drinking places', *Monthly Labour Review* (September 1977), pp. 9–15. An exposition of productivity levels in eating and drinking establishments, labor-saving developments in the preparation of meals and the growth of firms is provided within this article relating to the US Food Service industry.

Cowell, D., *The Marketing of Services* (Heinemann, 1984). Chapter 16 deals with productivity of service organizations and includes sections upon the meaning of productivity, a comparison of services and manufacturing productivity and methods of improving productivity. Hotel examples are present.

Filley, R. D., 'IEs make good use of people-orientated skills in helping their organisations provide service productivity', *Industrial Engineer* (January 1983), pp. 36–47. This article describes how six progressive US service organizations, including the Burger King restaurant company, have used industrial engineering to improve productivity.

Fletcher, J. and Snee, H., 'The need for output measurements in the service industries: a comment', *The Service Industries Journal*, vol. 5, no. 1 (March 1985), pp. 73–8. This article discusses both definition and measurement problems with illustrations from various service activities.

Freshwater, J. F. and Bragg, E. R., 'Improving food service productivity', *Cornell HRA Quarterly*, vol. 15, no. 4 (February 1975), pp. 12–18. This article describes methods of measuring productivity and summarizes four labor productivity research studies conducted in commercial food service establishments in the United States.

Fuchs, V. R. and Wilburn, J. A., *Productivity Differences within the Service Sector* (National Bureau of Economic Research, 1967). This book examines productivity variations and the factors affecting productivity among service industries, including hotels.

Harper, J., *Measuring Business Performance: a Manager's Guide* (Gower, 1984). This book explains how managers should measure the performance of basic economic units. Reference is made to productivity measurement and hotel performance.

Hotel Companies in the UK (Kleinwort Grieveson Securities, Investment Research, Spring 1987). Produced in connection with the Hotel and Catering Research Centre at Huddersfield Polytechnic, this publication contains a performance index for 12 major hotel companies. The performance of these, and a number of other related companies, is also analyzed in some depth.

Hughes, H. L., *Economics for Hotel and Catering Students* (Hutchinson, 1986). This book covers the main concepts of economics applied to hotel and catering activities within the wider economic context. Chapters 1 and 3 should be given special attention as they deal with such topics as the service economy and influences (including productivity) upon it, and the market structure of the hotel and catering industry with particular reference to small firms and establishments.

Inman, R. P. (ed.), *Managing the Service Economy: Prospects and Problems* (Cambridge University Press, 1985). Chapters 4, 11 and 12 concentrate upon the measurement of output and productivity in the service sector and productivity policy and future research for the service sector.

Kazarian, E., *Work Analysis and Design for Hotels, Restaurants and Institutions* (AVI Publishing Co., 1979). Chapter 1 is an introduction to the use of work analysis and design in the hotel/restaurant industry and includes an analysis of productivity in the United States. The bulk of the book is devoted to the principles, knowledge and techniques required to analyze and design work systems in hotels, restaurants, and institutions to make them efficient and productive.

Keiser, J., *The Practice and Principles of Hospitality Management* (CBI Publishing Co., 1979), pp. 174–99. Keiser discusses various aspects of hospitality productivity, including the concept of productivity, the problems caused by low productivity, the factors influencing productivity and productivity–pay schemes.

Lane, H. E., 'The Scanlon Plan: a key to productivity and payroll costs', *Cornell HRA Quarterly*, vol. 17, no. 1 (May 1976), pp. 76–80. This article introduces the productivity problem in hotels and suggests how it can be improved through an incentive scheme, such as the Scanlon Plan.

Lovelock, C. H. and Young, R. F., 'Look to consumers to increase productivity', *Harvard Business Review*, vol. 57 (May/June 1979), pp. 168–78. Five service examples are described where productivity improvement has been less successful than it might have been due to a failure to consider the consumers' needs. Then three marketing strategies are discussed which take into account the needs of consumers. Reference is made to hotels and restaurants.

McIntosh, R., *Employee Management Standards* (AVI Publishing Co., 1984). Chapter 4 is concerned with increasing productivity in food service and concentrates in particular upon staff planning and scheduling.

Medlik, S., *The Business of Hotels* (Heinemann, 1980). Chapter 9 is concerned with productivity in hotels and focuses specifically on measures and standards of productivity. Chapter 13 considers small hotels, their management and future.

Pavesic, D. V., 'The myth of labor-cost percentages', *Cornell HRA Quarterly*, vol. 24, no. 3 (November, 1983). This article discusses the failings of the traditional labor cost percentage and explains the use and value of productivity measures in the management of food service operations.

Pedderson, R. B., Avery, A. C., Richard, R. D. *et al.*, *Increasing Productivity in Food Service* (Cahners, 1973). This book considers productivity theory and various techniques that will increase productivity. Topics covered in detail include: motivation, equipment arrangement, task planning, the stored labor concept, convenience foods, disposables, automation, the role of management and work simplification.

Pine, R., *Management of Technological Change in the Catering Industry* (Gower, 1987). This book provides an appreciation of technology and the management of technology in hotel and catering businesses. Chapter 8 is concerned with manpower productivity and technology.

Pine, R. and Ball, S., 'Productivity and technology in the UK catering industry', *Food Science and Technology Today*, vol. 1, no. 3 (September, 1987), pp. 174–6. This article highlights the employee reaction to productivity improvements in catering and the eventual effect on customers.

Pizam, A., Lewis, R. C. and Manning, P. (eds), *The Practice of Hospitality Management* (AVI Publishing Co., 1982), Chapters 15 and 16. These chapters concern themselves, respectively, with improving productivity in the operations function, and productivity measurement and improvement in the hospitality industry.

Rives, J. M., West, J. M. and Krenk, C. G., 'Productivity and pay: a survey of workers' perceptions', *International Journal of Manpower*, vol. 2, no. 4 (1981), pp. 26–31. This excellent article examines workers' perceptions of productivity and the productivity–pay link, including those in service organizations.

Slattery, P. and Roper, A., *UK Hotel Groups Directory* (Cassell). This is an annual publication containing up to date information on the hotel groups, companies and consortia operating in the United Kingdom.

Whiteman, J., *The Services Sector – a Poor Relation?: A Review of its Role, Performance and Prospects in the UK* (National Economic Development Council, London, 1981), pp. 9–12. A description of the productivity record of the UK service sector is contained in these pages.

Worldwide Hotel Industry (Horwath and Horwath International). An annual publication which presents information about hotel operations in five major regions of the world. For each region a variety of performance measures and productivity indices is tabulated.

Wyckoff, D. D. and Sasser, W. E., *The US Lodging Industry* (Lexington Books, 1981), pp. lx–lxiv. These pages deal with labor force and productivity aspects in the lodging industry.

KEITH JOHNSON and
STEPHEN BALL

Profile of investment incentives

Introduction

Investment incentives, when applied to tourism development, can be said to have three main purposes. Firstly, there is the acceleration of the realization of developments, so that government may enjoy the resultant benefits – economic, environmental, social and political – sooner. Whilst incentives may not necessarily be required to bring about the eventual realization of a project, they will indirectly assist in the decision-making process if another destination initially has higher development priority for the private sector, or they may assist in completing the financing of a project, or merely demonstrate a commitment on the part of government to the future of the tourism sector in that region.

Secondly, investment incentives are used to remove or overcome the obstacles which prevent a private sector developer satisfying the profit motive, and thus assist in the generation of profits at a level sufficient to meet corporate objectives.

Thirdly, investment incentives can be used to discriminate positively in favor of certain types of development, or certain locations, so making projects of other types, or in other locations which are not favored, less attractive to the private sector. Measures such as these are used extensively to rejuvenate depressed areas, or to achieve a balanced supply of tourist facilities. In favouring specific locations, government will give regard to any existing infrastructure, and to the expense of installing infrastructural facilities where none exist – generally a prerequisite for obtaining private sector investment. Although not specific to tourism, the United Kingdom's system of Urban Development Grants is a good example of an incentive used to discriminate in favor of specific areas, in this case certain inner urban areas in need of regeneration, or where future urban decay is foreseen.

For the purposes of this paper, investment incentives are categorized into four separate headings – financial, quasi-financial, fiscal and others. Whilst their application and effect will differ according to the category, the end objective of each is to encourage development which would not otherwise have taken place.

Examples

Government financial incentives

Grant aid

Government financial aid to tourism projects can either be in the form of a grant (in cash or in kind) or a loan. Grant aid is considered to be the best method of 'seeding' tourism projects, as it has an immediate effect upon the realization of a project. Many tourism projects, particularly hotels and leisure centers, require a large 'up-front' investment in fixed assets before operation can commence, and servicing this investment can have a serious effect upon cashflow in the early years of a project.

A grant can be either discretionary, i.e. subject to the satisfaction of certain conditions relating to location, type or other factors and requiring approval from the funding authority, or nondiscretionary, where conditions will also normally have to be met, but approval is not necessary. Nondiscretionary grants can be extremely effective in achieving objectives in a short timeframe. A grant to a tourism project may be a cash payment which does not require a return, injection of an equity stake requiring profit share, or payment in kind, e.g. rent-free land, which would otherwise have had to have been purchased, and therefore would have required capital outlay.

Loan aid

Instead of, or in addition to grant aid, but with the similar objective of reducing the requirement for a developer to raise finance from other sources, government can provide loan financing. The effect of a government loan upon a tourism project is entirely conditional upon the terms of the loan. A loan on the same terms as those offered by commercial sources does not affect the profitability of the operation of a project, but it may remove an obstacle to development, i.e. the developer's difficulty in raising finance from the private sector. However, in these circumstances, and in fact in all circumstances where governments give loan aid, the reason for that obstacle being present in the first place must be recognized and evaluated against the motives for promoting tourism growth. If the obstacle is a perceived 'country risk', then government aid in this form should satisfy whatever motives are present, including any purely political motive, by demonstrating the government's own confidence and commitment to the tourism sector.

If the obstacle preventing a developer from raising finance is doubt regarding the financial viability of the project itself, then government must consider whether it is prepared to jeopardize the economic motive – as default on the loan may occur – in order to satisfy another motive. For example, the construction of a hotel project may be particularly costly in a specific location and, although market demand might be able to support the project's operation, the return on investment is low. However, government may wish to promote the project to create employment, or to increase the opportunities for social tourism, to accrue the social benefits rather than the economic ones. By funding in this manner, government is tacitly accepting that default on the loan is possible, in order that its own social motive and the private sector's profit motive can be satisfied.

Because of the risks involved in commercial loan funding, government loan finance is most commonly given to tourism projects at preferential rates. This can be in a number of forms – interest relief schemes giving a lower interest rate, longer-term, longer payment moratorium, reduced repayment in 'balloon' funding – all of which would be more favorable to the project than the terms available from private sector sources.

Implications of financial incentives

The provision by government of grant or preferential loan finance to tourism projects is evidence of a commitment to tourism growth, and of a recognition of the opportunity cost involved. A system of financial incentives which operates within the framework of a tourism policy will recognize and evaluate the opportunity cost of grant and loan financing. The tourism policy will be formulated and will operate within the context of a broader economic plan (whether local, regional or national) and therefore financial assistance given to tourism projects may have direct links to other sectors of the economy.

Administration of financial aid

The most easily administered form of financial aid for tourism projects is a nondiscretionary grant. The awarding authority need only set the conditions for the grant, and ensure that the grant is used, and continues to be used, for the designated purposes. Discretionary awards require the interim process of deciding whether or not to award a grant, according to the applicable criteria, and therefore the exercise of opinions and public accountability, and also public pressures. Conversely loan finance requires continued administration throughout the term of the loan.

For the private sector developer, grants are also the easiest to administer, although the effect on cashflow of a grant or loan may both be favorable. Although a grant is normally more attractive, both in cashflow terms and as no conditions apply which have not been satisfied at the outset, government loan finance in a project can provide ready access to additional capital funds should the project require assistance, and if government wishes to preserve its original investment.

The choice for government as to whether to give grant aid or

loan finance to a specific project, or to tourism development in general, will be a political decision, influenced by many factors. Both require the availability of funds 'up-front', but whilst a grant to a project has a permanent opportunity cost, loan finance delays that opportunity until repayment is made★. Loans are politically more widely acceptable, as the perceived direct cost to public funds will only be the 'preferential' element of the loan, as opposed to the whole amount of a grant, while the economic and social benefits will be very similar, for example employment opportunities, tax revenues and provision of leisure facilities.

The financial benefits of loans are also readily quantifiable, for example the number of jobs created, or the amount of tax revenue received: they are politically presentable and acceptable, and easily understood. Grants in kind – the provision of land, the development of essential infrastructure – carry the least risk of all forms of financial aid. State-owned land which is developed has a greater value than undeveloped land, and the provision of infrastructure is the creation of social capital which contributes to the wealth of the country, and aids further development.

Quasi-financial incentives

Financial incentives in the form of grants and loans are the best method of promoting and directing tourism development, by removing obstacles to project profitability. Paradoxically, those economies with immature tourism sectors which could most benefit from overall growth are often those with insufficient access to funds, and are therefore unable to offer assistance in a planned, comprehensive manner.

Such countries are often perceived by private sector funding sources as risk areas for investment, and therefore, regardless of project profitability, private sector developers can experience difficulties in project financing. In these circumstances governments can provide loan guarantees to commercial funding sources, thus demonstrating their commitment to and confidence in the tourism sector, at no initial cost and, in most cases, no cost at all to public funds.

Alternatively a government may choose to make a financial commitment by offering a loan subsidy, which finances the differential between the (commercial) rate of interest charged by the lending institution, and a lower rate decided by the government (which may be fixed, or may be related to the flexible commercial rate).

When there is an element of foreign currency loan funding in a project, governments can offer a quasi-financial incentive in the form of an exchange rate guarantee. The exchange rate for loan interest and capital payments is fixed, and the government undertakes to relieve any adverse effects from exchange rate fluctuations. This form of incentive therefore alleviates one form of risk associated with tourism development in areas

---

★ In the case of the United Kingdom, special circumstances prevail in that loan repayments are taken into the Treasury and not into the Agency giving the loan. As the Agencies cannot recycle funds received in loan repayments, they have tended to favor grants, not loans.

where exchange rate fluctuations can seriously affect profitability.

Fiscal incentives

Fiscal incentives can have the dual role of removing obstacles to project profitability, where this would otherwise be marginal, and of accelerating the development process by making the investment climate more attractive than that in other destinations. Fiscal incentives can apply both to the development stage of a project and to the actual operation of the facility. They can be specific to the tourism sector or, more usually, are part of an overall economic policy aimed at encouraging capital investment, and particularly at attracting foreign investment. In general, fiscal incentives preserve or increase profits during operation, although some are intended to reduce the initial construction cost through duty exemption etc.

A particular feature of most fiscal incentives, of both political and economic significance, is that the benefit to the developer often will not accrue until the project is profitable, and therefore (paradoxically) is no longer in need of assistance. A careful assessment of projects will identify those developments of marginal profitability for which a fiscal incentive will actually realize a surplus. Fiscal incentives can include the following:

1. Income tax reduction.
2. Net operating loss carryover.
3. Tax credit on interest on foreign loans.
4. Real estate tax exemption.
5. Preferential energy tariffs.
6. Reduced importation duties on equipment.
7. Tax credits on domestic capital equipment.
8. Tax exemption on re-invested profits.
9. Capital expenditure allowances.

Because they generally have no significant effect upon the cashflow in the early years of a tourism project (unless they can be used against profits generated by other activities), fiscal incentives are most commonly used in conjunction with financial incentives. The cost related to the provision of fiscal incentives is readily assessed, as they are specific, e.g. 50 per cent profits tax reduction is easily measured. However the benefits accruing to government (as opposed to the private sector, whose benefits is equal to the cost to the government) are less readily measured. Where a grant or loan is offered, it is often the case that the project would not have been realized without it, and indeed this may be a condition for obtaining the award. It is therefore appropriate for all the benefits accruing from the project to be directly related to the cost of the incentive. Such ease of measurement is not possible with fiscal incentives, and their cost must often be written off against more general benefits, such as reduced unemployment or increased per capita income, rather than against specific benefits.

Other incentives

It is appropriate in a chapter of this kind to touch briefly upon certain other factors which, although not strictly investment incentives as they do not affect the cost, nor directly the profitability of a project, are relevant to a discussion of investment incentives and tourism development as they form part of the investment climate. Experience shows that in some cases one or more of these factors have restricted tourism growth, or have even brought about a decline in the sector. A formal tourism policy would consider and evaluate these factors as they impact on the investment decision.

1. Training. Are there sufficient trained personnel available to staff a new tourism enterprise? Does the government provide training facilities and courses to increase the qualified workforce? Or are these additional costs to be borne by the project?
2. Marketing. Governments who wish to and who have the resources are always best able to promote a new destination. Is the tourism promotion effective?
3. Repatriation of earnings. Are there restrictions on the international transfer of operating profits, capital gains and expatriate staff salaries?
4. Access to materials. If the materials required for the construction and operation of a tourism project are not available locally, is it possible to import them?
5. Work permits. Where there is a shortage of professional and technical skills locally, is it possible to employ and to retain foreign staff?
6. General attitude to tourism. Despite the existence of a range of tourism investment incentives, do other factors indicate a more negative attitude, for example excessive visa regulations, prohibitive transport costs and inconvenient timetabling?

Of most importance is the economic and political stability of a destination. Although certain incentives can be offered to alleviate the effects of instability, or perceived instability, project profitability, although commercially attractive, may be insufficient to compensate for the risks involved in development.

Assessment

In addition to that review of an individual project which takes place prior to and as part of the decision whether to give that project specific tourism investment incentives and additional also to the review of an individual project which takes place during its operational life (to ensure that the incentive is applied for the purpose intended), there is the essential review of the entire spectrum of tourism incentives available, on a regular basis. This review will be seeking answers in a number of different areas, but in particular the following:

1. Are the tourism incentives contributing to and furthering the tourism policy within which they are intended to operate?
2. Are the tourism incentives furthering and contributing to the profit motive of the private sector, and to what degree?
3. What are the cost–benefit implications of the policy to give tourism incentives?

4. How does the range of tourism incentives offered compare with those in other regions or countries?
5. What is the monetary amount of tourism incentives committed in the future, but not yet taken up (for budgetary purposes)?

Answers to questions such as these should enable government to refine both its range of tourism incentives and its tourism policy, to meet the changing needs of itself, its people, the private sector and, of course, of tourists themselves. While the review should take place on a regular basis – probably not less than every 2 years – it is important that stability is maintained, as a continuously changing tourism policy and range of tourism incentives (or changes in their detail or conditions) can be as (if not more) damaging than no policy at all. Where policies and incentives do change, private sector investors should receive forward assurance that incentives already granted to a specific project will not be reduced in quality or quantity as a result of a review.

Conclusion

It is possible that all countries of the world, from the most undeveloped to the most developed, have on their statute books measures which are, or which can be construed as being, tourism investment incentives. The use to which these are put depends upon the existence and application of a tourism policy, upon the maturity of a country's tourism sector and other, less tangible factors, including political will.

It is certain that, as global tourism continues to grow at a rate matched by few other economic activities, tourism investment incentives will continue to be an integral part of that growth – initiating, promoting and directing. The effectiveness of incentives in performing these roles will depend upon the manner in which they are applied, either piecemeal or selectively, and the manner in which they are administered. An investment incentive which is difficult to obtain due to the workings of bureaucracy (and all too often a succession of government departments must be satisfied) can become a dis-

incentive through the effects of inflation and missed market opportunities. And a range of investment incentives which are 'available', but not attainable, can be worse than no investment incentives at all. Private sector developers, both domestic and international, can normally satisfy their profit motive elsewhere, and will do so, in the face of claims of a political will to develop tourism, which is not supported by political action.

Further reading

Bodlender, J. A., *Guidelines on Tourism Investment* (World Tourism Organization, 1980). This publication covers the criteria that governments should use to evaluate tourism investment proposals and some of the actions they should take to improve the climate for tourism investment.

Bodlender, J. A. and Davies, E. J., *A Profile of Government Financial and Grant Aid to Tourism* (World Tourism Organization, 1984). Grants and loans are covered in some detail, together with guidelines on how to use investment incentives and the rationale for them.

Bodlender, J. A. and Ward, T. J., *An Examination of Tourism Incentives* (World Tourism Organization, 1987). An extensive document in which the first part covers the motives for tourism development, the use of state aid and a profile of the various investment incentives. The second part is a directory of aid available in selected countries.

Holloway, J. C., *The Business of Tourism* (M & E Becbooks, 1983). This textbook for OND, HND and other students of tourism aims to provide a basic understanding of the nature, structure and organization of the tourist industry. Of particular relevance is Chapter 12, 'Public Sector Tourism'.

Pearce, D., *Tourist Development* (Longman, 1981). One of Longman's Topics in Applied Geography series, this textbook provides a systematic overview of tourist development. Of particular relevance is Chapter 2, 'Structures and Processes of Tourist Development', which provides a general basis for analyzing tourist development.

Wanhill, S. R. C., 'Which investment incentives for tourism?', *Tourism Management*, vol. 7, no. 1 (March 1986), pp. 2–7. Examines investment incentives within a probabilistic model of the cost structure of tourist enterprises.

JONATHAN A. BODLENDER and
TREVOR J. WARD

Project feasibility

Introduction

Tourism is arguably the biggest business in the world today, and is widely considered as one of the fastest growing. With the 'shrinking of the world', because of the advent and improvements in jet travel making previously-considered faraway places within easy reach of travelers the world over, the supply of tourist facilities to meet the ever-growing demand is of prime concern for governments and private investors. This is especially true for countries that depend on tourism to a large extent for foreign exchange and employment benefits. This chapter will mainly view the topic as it applies to the developing country, where this situation most commonly applies.

In defining project feasibility, we have first to consider what is meant by a project. A project can be defined as a scheme or activity or parts of a scheme or activity, in which resources are invested in expectation of returns, and which lends itself to reasonable analysis and evaluation as an independent unit. Being an independent unit, it can therefore be considered a specific scheme or activity, with specific starting and ending points, intended to achieve a specific result or objective.

The starting point of a project is usually considered at the time when investment funds are poured into the project for the cost of land development, construction, furniture, fittings and equipment (F, F and E) and other capital expenditures. Before the project is given the 'go-ahead', however, it has to be proven feasible. What, then, is meant by being feasible? This suggests that the project is capable of being done, that it is practicable, and that it has met the objectives as set out by the developers, who may be private or entrepreneurs who only consider the financial viability of the project or governments who should look at the economic and social benefits of the project to the society.

For a project to be proven feasible, two studies should be carried out, firstly a preinvestment study to see whether the project meets the minimum requirements within the economy, whether or not it is technically feasible, or whether or not it can be considered of priority to the tourism sector. The preinvestment study will indicate whether or not to consider the second study, which is called the final full feasibility study. Even if the 'go-ahead' is not given after the preinvestment stage is done, it may highlight certain parts of the project that may be studied in greater detail for future development.

The full, extensive feasibility analysis or appraisal is a more detailed analysis which considers and analyzes all of the pertinent aspects of the project: technical aspects, capital costs, the market for and marketability of the project, its financial gains to the developers/owners (usually the private entrepreneurs) and the socioeconomic gains to the society. The cost of the preinvestment and feasibility studies, dependent on the size of the project, may be built into the overall cost of the project, thus making those stages a part of the project also. The end of the project is usually when the loan payments are fully repaid. (This should not include the rescheduling of loans, however.) The result or objective of the project may depend on whether it is a private, public, or private and public venture. As mentioned above, private entrepreneurs may only be interested in the financial gains accruing from the project; the government that represents the public may be more interested in the social and economic benefits to the society, i.e. the value added to the economy in the form of more foreign exchange generated by the project itself, and the added employment that the project will need.

Thus a Tourism Project Feasibility study can be defined as the analysis or appraisal of a tourism scheme, or part of a scheme, by means of application of technical, marketing, financial and economic evaluation techniques, which may show if the scheme or project can be proven acceptable or practicable to be carried out, within certain financial and socioeconomic boundaries. Some synonyms that can be used for the term Project Feasibility are Project Analysis, Project Appraisal, Project Evaluation, Investment Analysis and Investment Appraisal.

A project can involve parts of a scheme or subprojects. Each subproject can be considered as a project or scheme in itself, as it will have a specific starting point, ending point and objective. But, because these various subprojects may be interlinked, one activity being dependent on another, it may be better to consider the sum of the parts as the whole project. A hypothetical example of a tourism development project consisting of various interdependent subprojects, is the development by a government of an undeveloped region of a country, where infrastructure, e.g. roads, electricity, water, telephones, an airport, is considered together with the development of superstructural elements of the project, e.g. hotels, condominiums, villas, timesharing facilities and a convention center. Each element of both the infrastructural and superstructural developments can be considered a separate project, but it is obvious that the superstructural elements will have to depend on the completion of the infrastructural elements. Hotels and condominiums, for example, cannot be built without power, water, sewerage and roads being introduced first onto the site.

The objectives of the tourism project should be compatible with those of the tourism sector and national plans and there should be integration between all levels of the planning process. Therefore, the role of the project developer, who will be in charge of the overall planning process, is crucial in the implementation of planning proposals in relation to other levels of planning. It should also be remembered not to confuse the objectives of a project with its definition. For example, to state in a tourism project that 'In building this hotel the objective is to accommodate 600 more tourists in the tourism sector...' is incorrect: this is not an objective but a description. Objectives of a tourism project should state the increased income or increase in value-added to the society because of the project, or the enhancement of a site, which can be considered a qualitative instead of a quantitative judgment, or linkages that the project will create with the rest of the society. Objectives or the purpose of a project are being demanded more and more by lending agencies today, and as mentioned above, they should be compatible with national development and sectoral plans of the country in question.

Types of tourism projects and problems faced by developers

There are mainly three types of tourism project – resorts, hotels and ancillary facilities. Resort development involves the development of public or private land. The projects may include infrastructure, e.g. roads, power, water, sewerage, airports; common facilities such as sports and recreational areas (tennis, golf, marinas), bars, nightclubs, restaurants, convention centers; and accommodation facilities such as hotels, condominiums, apartels, villas, holiday villages and timesharing facilities. A development project should make a positive contribution to the development goals of the economy by contributing more resources to the economy than it would expend in operating to fulfil its purpose. In other words, the value of the outputs from this development project in the form of value-added to the economy must exceed the value of inputs it draws from the rest of the economy, e.g. labor and capital.

The financial aspects of resort development, however, are a large initial investment, high debt, high risk of cost overruns and cashflow problems. The success of a tourism venture such as this will depend on the rate of the sale or lease of land facilities, resulting in the profitability of hotels and other superstructure. The same financial problems are indicative of luxury (first class) hotel projects where the investment cost had escalated from about US$50,000 per room in 1975 to over US$100,000 per room 10 years later, thus usually providing a high debt burden on the developer. Other very important questions that have to be asked are the marketability of the destination and hence the project itself. What types of arrangements are there already existing in the marketplace, e.g. with tour operators or wholesalers? Will the developers of the project have to seek new markets? As far as management is concerned, is it better for a government-owned hotel to be leased by a multinational firm? Or rather to have a management contract with them? What do these types of arrangements or contracts bring to the host country? Finally, problems that may affect the small hotel development as opposed to the large one also have to be taken into account, e.g. management, marketing and promotional problems that do exist with the small, local entrepreneur.

As far as ancillary facilities are concerned, tourism also involves links with other sectors of the economy, e.g. agricultural (the production of meat, fish and vegetables); industrial (production of handicrafts, furniture); transport (transport of tourists by ground transportation at the destination – tour buses, taxis); restaurants and bars outside the project development, which tourists from the development may patronize. These links, provided by the project development, can also result in benefits to the suppliers of the goods and services mentioned above, so that a large proportion of the economy becomes dependent on the development.

Assessment

After having defined the objectives of the project at hand, related them to the tourism sectoral and national plans of the country, and defined the project, the next phases in the project feasibility study or appraisal are more analytical in content. These are the market analysis, the project technical description, the financial analysis and the social cost–benefit analysis. In addition, sensitivity analyses can be done in the latter two phases, to prove the project's feasibility or infeasibility when certain unforeseen circumstances arise during the life of the project.

The market analysis looks at tourism supply of like and other facilities and the tourist demand to the country and maybe to the region (if the country is large enough) in which the project will be situated. The markets for the particular project are also identified. In other words, a Marketing Feasibility Study will be done. This is looked at in detail in another chapter in this handbook (p. 253). The project technical description should include all the project's superstructural and infrastructural elements, and these should be costed out. Alternatives should be discussed and the rationale given for the one chosen. The role of each component in the overall design should be described. Quantities and types of materials, equipment and the skilled and unskilled labor content should also be discussed, and a Project Construction Schedule should be drawn up, either by using the simple bar chart or the more refined project network schemes such as the Project Evaluation and Review Technique (PERT) or the Critical Path Method (CPM). This section of the Project Analysis is very technical in content, and architects, engineers, and quantity surveyors should be involved in the preparation of it.

Approximate costs should be determined for each element of the project and subprojects. This can be done on a cost per square foot (or square meter) basis or on a per-room cost basis. Costs for similar construction can be used as a guideline, but one has to be careful here, as costs of hotel construction, for example, have escalated considerably over the past 10 to 15 years. These costs of the tourism project and subprojects will make up the investment costs of the project. As they may be extended over a few years for the construction, furnishing and equipping of the project, cost contingencies, usually 10 per cent of total costs, should be built into the overall costs of the project. This could prevent cost overruns, due, for example, to the project construction time not keeping pace with the schedule in the project analysis. These cost overruns could be caused by work stoppages, imported materials not reaching the project site on time or other unforeseen problems.

The financial appraisal of the tourism project is analyzed in a similar way to any other development project. A development project has a certain lifespan, usually a long one. The procedure for this analysis is to list the revenues and expenditures (including both capital and operational), discount the cashflow values for each year and then use certain evaluation techniques to determine the project's feasibility. The two evaluation techniques commonly used are the Net Present Value (NPV) and the Internal Rate of Return (IRR) methods. These are discounting methods, which endeavor to allow for the timing of cashflows and which calculate the present value of future cashflows. Discounting may appear to be a complex technique, but it is simply the opposite of compounding, or compound interest, as explained mathematically below.

In compounding, we find the future value (F) by multiplying the present value (P) by 1 + the rate of interest (r) as many times as the number of years (n) involved. This is expressed by the following formula:

$$F = P (1 + r)^n$$

Hence to calculate P, we must multiply F by the reciprocal of $(1 + r)^n$

$$\therefore \quad P = F \times \frac{1}{(1 + r)^n}$$

Compounding and discounting tables, found in many financial management texts, simplify the process of compounding and discounting by providing a single multiplication factor corresponding to the various values of r and n. As we are only interested in discounted methods to arrive at the NPV and IRR of cashflows in a project, the present value, therefore, is multiplied by the discount factor $1/(1 + r)^n$. Discount factors are therefore always less than 1. There are certain advantages and disadvantages in using the NPV and IRR concepts. Suffice to say that the NPV gives an absolute measure of profit in monetary terms and is particularly useful for choosing between mutually exclusive projects, while the IRR gives a measure of profitability in percentage terms which is easy to interpret. As with any other development project, in order that the project may be proven financially acceptable, the NPV must be greater than zero and the IRR greater than the cost of capital. The financial analysis shows the estimated profitability of the project to the developer, whether private, public, or private and public. Financing agencies whether private or public, e.g. development banks, generally insist on the financial analysis being done in detail even if a social cost–benefit analysis or economic evaluation is necessary. The financial analysis will also include a financing plan for the capital investment required, pro forma income statements and a projected cashflow.

The financial analysis also forms the basis for the social cost–benefit analysis or economic evaluation (analysis), where benefits accruing from the project to the island or region of the country as a whole are considered. In developing countries especially where there are limited capital resources, the choice of putting these resources to their best use, i.e. directing them into projects that will yield the greatest social and economic benefits to the country, has to be taken into consideration. Using these scarce resources in one economic sector reduces the resources available to other economic sectors. Therefore, a choice of employing the best use of these resources is necessary. Policy makers should be concerned to know which among alternative projects, whether in the same or different sectors yields the highest social and economic return. Cost–benefit analysis can help policymakers to distinguish between projects competing for these scarce resources.

The basic concept in cost–benefit analysis in pricing the outputs and inputs of the project is that of 'opportunity cost', the value the good or service would have if utilized in the best alternative use. For example, the construction of a new tourism project means that labor, capital, land and management are withdrawn from an alternative use in order that a certain satisfaction of needs may be realized through the project. Thus it is seen as a reallocation of factors of production. The benefits of the project are the satisfaction of needs by the project. The costs are the satisfaction of needs forgone by the withdrawal of factors of production from alternative allocation within the society. If the benefits outweigh the costs, by the process of rate of return computation, as used in the financial analysis, then the project is acceptable.

The socioeconomic impact of the project is assessed by adopting the use of certain measures where the value placed on the costs and benefits of the project as shown in the financial analysis are 'shadowpriced' to reflect their value to the national economy. Costs are measured in terms of their 'opportunity costs', while regarding benefits, the additional benefits accruing to the economy because of the project are measured together with those of the project. In addition to commensurables, which are benefits and costs that can be quantitatively measured in economic terms, there are also incommensurables and intangibles, which are benefits and costs that cannot be so measured or may go beyond economic values. These values must also be emphasized in the project, as they may involve certain qualitative judgments, which may prove important to the project and to the wider society. The economic benefits of tourism-related projects can be identified as follows:

1. Tourist expenditures within and outside hotels which constitute food, accommodation, local transportation, souvenirs, entertainment and other benefits.
2. International transportation benefits, especially where a national carrier is concerned. These are external benefits, as

they accrue because of the project, but do not form part of the direct benefits of the project.

3. Other external benefits such as the creation of agricultural and/or industrial links (and environmental conservation), because of a hotel project, and consumer surplus.

Costs usually involve the investment and operating costs of accommodation facilities, other facilities, e.g. restaurants, convention facilities and the costs of infrastructural components.

In considering the wider benefits of tourism to any economy, it should be apparent that not all tourist expenditure can be counted as a benefit since resources will be used up in providing tourist facilities. The correct value of such expenditure is the difference between revenue and costs at 'shadow' prices, expressed in the form of an accounting ratio. In order to do this however, tourism expenditure has to be divided into its economic categories and accounting ratios determined for each sector. For purposes of analysis, tourism expenditure is usually divided into two main categories, namely: 1. accommodation, food and beverage; 2. shopping and other. There are other economic components that may have to be included in these two categories. For example, if a country (like some of the Caribbean and other regional island destinations) is heavily involved in casino gambling, which may be concessions operating in major hotels or casino companies that own hotel development, this major economic sector has to be included in (1) above. Also, because of the nature of resort tourism in these developing island regions, marine sports activities that constitute a substantial part of the resort attraction would also have to be included in category 1.

From the above analysis, it might be thought that projects should be both financially and economically feasible for them to be accepted, but a project can be financially infeasible, but socially and economically acceptable, or vice versa (if the government is not involved). Even though these analytical methods may help in identifying which project or group of projects will increase social income more quickly, pure economic benefits may not be the only yardstick that may be considered in the acceptability of a project. A hotel and a convention facility may have similar economic benefits, but the hotel project may be chosen over the convention facility because of its greater employment generation. Thus, political and social decisions may determine whether one project may be chosen over another.

Examples

In a project feasibility study done on the 'Redevelopment of the Nassau International Airport', involving US$25 million (1983/84 figures), the financial analysis suggested that with the project, airport revenues would barely cover operating and capital costs. In fact the NPV at an IRR of 2.74 per cent, which was far below the opportunity cost of capital figure of 11 per cent, was only $2.7 m. This position would have worsened considerably if the residual value attributable to depreciating assets was omitted. The social cost–benefit analysis showed, however, that to

the economy of the capital, Nassau (which is the hub of air travel in the country) and the Bahamas in general, the redevelopment of the airport would have very positive implications. This was shown from a qualitative point of view, where not developing the airport at the given time (1983/84 onwards) would have had serious negative consequences for the tourist industry, which is the mainstay of economic life in the territory; increasing tourist arrivals would depend to a great extent on adequate airport facilities, which had almost reached their full capacity. From a quantitative point of view, there were also positive benefits, in that tourist expenditure played a very important role, representing 93 per cent of the total benefits of the project which received a NPV of approximately $717 million at the cut-off rate of 11 per cent.

This example shows the socioeconomic importance of an infrastructural project, in this case an airport, to the continuing development of the tourism industry in a tourism-dependent country. Other tourism project examples, especially of the infrastructural type in the Caribbean and elsewhere, also show much lower financial rates of return when compared with economic rates of return. Hotel investments usually have higher financial IRRs and NPVs, when compared with infrastructural projects, as their revenue base is much more lucrative. However, hotel projects can be considered of the high risk variety, and moratoriums are usually set for the first few years of the project, dependent on the project life.

Conclusion

Project feasibility studies and cost–benefit analyses should be considered as methods for reducing investment uncertainty and improving investment decisions by the investor, the state, the development aid agency and other participants in the development process. Any national investment, however, is to be considered by the policy maker. Feasibility studies can only provide a guideline which may help the policy maker in considering all alternatives objectively, so that serious errors resulting from bad judgement may be avoided.

Focus on small business

Development Banks and Development Finance Corporations have been set up in the Caribbean and other developing countries to finance projects in the main economic sectors: agriculture, industry and tourism. In the Caribbean, the Caribbean Development Bank (CDB) has given special (but not exclusive) attention to the development needs of owner-managed guest accommodation of under 40 rooms in scale. In other words, the Bank has seen the necessity of involving the local entrepreneur, who in most cases is the retired professional, who knows little or nothing of the hotel business, in owning and managing his property. This thinking has been echoed by Development Finance Corporations and territorial Development Banks, to which money has been loaned by the CDB for small projects, including hotel and tourism projects in these territories. The CDB views the growth of a balanced and financially healthy regional tourism industry as one major potential contributor to increased employment and incomes among the population which it serves, and has identified the small or medium-sized local entrepreneur as the main vehicle in pursuing this ideal. This is also true in the Indian Ocean islands such as the Seychelles where tourism started on a 'cottage industry' basis in the 1970s before the arrival of foreign entrepreneurs, who built larger hotels. The average number of rooms among the 46 hotels and guesthouses (relais des iles) is 30 (1986 figures) with the largest having 184 rooms and only five hotels with over 100 rooms. In some of the smaller and less developed countries of the Caribbean (e.g. St Vincent and the Grenadines, Granada, St Kitts, Dominica and Montserrat) the averages are even smaller.

The majority of problems seem to lie in the fact that, with few exceptions, there is a lack of management skills among the small hoteliers. This has caused, in some instances, the rejection of prefeasibility or preinvestment studies by development and other banks in the Caribbean region, although development banks can and do offer technical assistance. Local small hotel owners and developers cannot, in most cases, employ trained managers or lease out their properties. Among the small hoteliers, however, there are also foreign entrepreneurs who can do this, and who, nevertheless, may possess management and marketing skills. Developing territories are also in most cases short of capital and entrepreneurship, yet are burdened by investment restrictions, which affect the small entrepreneur as far as equity participation is concerned.

Small entrepreneurs must come together as small hotel bodies to try to solve their problems. This has been evident in some territories. However, even in cases like this, the parochial image sometimes still persists. But as a body, much can be done like collective, low-budget promotional and marketing campaigns and training programs. In the 1970s the Caribbean Hotel Association (CHA) set up the Small Hotel Advisory Council (SHAC) which produced very effective training programs for both employers and employees. Universities and hotel schools can also be involved (and in some cases have been) in ventures like this, by giving short programs to owner-operators of hotels and by training supervisors within the small organization to train their employees. The potential small developer can also be involved in these training programs in courses dealing with administration, financial and property management, marketing, feasibility studies and the management of service. Governments should review policies on investment restrictions, seeing that many potential small developers may have equity in the form of land and buildings but not in cash. In many cases, cash has had to be raised from other sources or the project has been abandoned.

Further reading

Barham, C. H., 'The Caribbean development bank: functions and view of tourism development in the Caribbean', *Caribbean Tourism Policies and Impacts*, compiled by J. S. Holder (Caribbean Tourism Research and Development Centre (CTRC), 1979), pp. 135–52. This paper sets out the CDBs views for tourism development in the Caribbean, discusses certain major problems inherent in the Caribbean tourism industry and outlines a plan of action.

Bhatt, V. V., 'On a development bank's selection criteria for industrial projects', *Aspects of Development Banking Policy*, Seminar Paper No. 12 (Economic Development Institute, World Bank, 1975), pp. 1–38. This article deals with the bases on which development banks select industrial projects, explains the objectives of a development bank, the choice criteria based on international prices, other feasible and choice criteria and looks at the process of economic analysis.

Davis D. H. and Simmon, H. A., 'World bank experience with tourism projects' (University of Surrey International Conference 1982 on *Trends in Tourism Planning and Development*, 1–3 September 1982). This paper deals with the authors' views on the complex problems encountered in the execution of World Bank supported projects in tourism.

Irvin, B. *Modern Cost–Benefit Method* (Macmillan, 1978). A very concisely written book on the appraisal of projects. Chapters 1, 2 and 3 deal with principles of project appraisal and selection, principles of financial accounting, project appraisal and forecasting, risk and uncertainty and probability theory.

Kendell, P. J., 'Recent experiences in project appraisal' (University of Surrey International Conference 1982 on *Trends in Tourism Planning and Development*, 1–3 September, 1982). In this paper the author discusses recent experiences in project appraisal and gives a synopsis of how an appraisal should be done.

Kotas, R., *Management Accounting for Hotels and Restaurants* (Surrey University Press, 1977). An applied text on the above subject. Chapter 16 deals with the 'Assessment of Capital Projects' where concepts and examples of financial project feasibility are discussed.

Little, I. M. D. and Mirrlees, H. A., *Project Appraisal and Planning for Developing Countries* (Heinemann, 1974). This book deals with the entire concept of project analysis, the economics of social cost–benefit analysis, project analysis and planning, the estimation of accounting prices, among other topics.

Lumby, S., *Investment Appraisal and Related Decisions* (Van Nostrand Reinhold (UK), 1983). This text presents a thorough and vigorous analysis of the concepts and principles of long-term financial decision making.

Organization of American States, *Methods for Tourism Project Preinvestment Studies*, Research and Bibliography Series No. 4 (General Secretariat, OAS, 1978). This manual serves as a reference to methods and orderly procedures in preparing preinvestment studies of tourism projects and gives a practical analysis of tourism preinvestment techniques. The manual is designed for tourism authorities in the member states of the OAS.

O'Reilly, A. M., *Airport Capacity: A Case Study for the Redevelopment of the Nassau International Airport, Bahamas* MSc. dissertation (Department of Hotel, Catering and Tourism Management, University of Surrey, 1983/84). The thesis examines airport capacity at the Nassau International Airport, and analyzes present capacity, determines future capacity, looks at the airport's performance and analyzes the financial and cost–benefit implications of the proposed development.

O'Reilly, A. M., 'Sketches of development of leisure and recreation facilities in the Commonwealth Caribbean', *The Tourist Review*, no. 4 (1981), pp. 17–23. This article presents the possibilities of the development of leisure and recreation facilities in the Commonwealth Caribbean and the author examines four such projects that were done by the Caribbean Development Bank between 1976 and 1977. The author suggests that planned facilities should be used by a larger percentage of the population of the host country with more interaction between the tourist and the local.

Price, G. J., *Economic Analysis of Agricultural Projects* (World Bank/ Johns Hopkins University Press, 1972). This text gives a simple outlook on cost–benefit analysis, with reference to agricultural projects. A basic book for cost–benefits analysis.

Squire, L. and van der Tak, H., *Economic Analysis of Projects* (World Bank/Johns Hopkins University Press, 4th edition, 1981). This book sets forth the general approach to the economic analysis of development projects recommended for use within the World Bank and other agencies that are engaged in project appraisal. The methodology used deviates in some respects from traditional analytical practice, e.g. from Gittinger, Little and Mirrlees, OAS methodologies of analysis.

Todaro, M. P., *Economic Development in the Third World* (Longman, 1981), pp. 451–55. In this chapter on 'Development Planning: Theory and Practice', the author looks, *inter alia*, at the concept of project appraisal and social cost–benefit analysis.

Vanhove, N., 'Interrelation between benefits and costs of tourist resources – an economic approach' (Publications AIEST [International Association of Scientific Experts in Tourism], 1982), pp. 29–43. This paper, presented as a basic paper for the 32nd AIEST Congress held in Yugoslavia in 1982 looks at the economic impact of tourism. Of special importance to the subject 'Project Feasibility' is the section on 'How to Interpret Cost–Benefit Analysis' – p. 36 onwards.

Winpenny, H. T., 'Some issues in the identification and appraisal of tourism projects in developing countries' (University of Surrey International Conference, 1982 on *Trends in Tourism Planning and Development*, 1–3 September 1982). This paper is general in nature.

AINSLEY M. O'REILLY and
RON BRATHWAITE

Promotional strategies in tourism

Introduction

Promotion is the name given to the mix of communication activities designed by tourist organizations to influence those target audiences upon whom their sales depend in both the short and long term. These audiences include not only past and potential customers, but also opinion formers such as journalists and travel writers, retail influences such as travel agents and brokers, as well as diverse other groups that may variably include: local government departments, tourist boards, business societies, schools etc.

Benefits

The purpose of promotional strategy is to allow tourism organizations to decide priorities and goals before allocating money and resources to detailed implementation of promotional campaigns in the form of advertising, publicity etc. Specifically, it is beneficial to view promotional strategy from two complementary perspectives:

Promotion as a macro-process

At the macro-level promotion can be seen as a method of demand management: 'The ultimate goal of all promotion is to obtain a level of demand which is favorable to the promoter – to increase, decrease, or maintain demand, and/or to influence the elasticity of demand by using channels of communication which allow access to a defined target audience' (Buttle, 1986, p. 301).

In macro-terms, promotional strategy in tourism involves determining exactly how communication activity is to be designed to influence demand for holidays, travel etc. There are eight possible demand states which tourism promotion may be designed to address (Kotler, 1973):

1. No demand: there is no demand for a particular tourism offering (e.g. package tours to industrial locations). Promotion is helpless in this situation unless the project is improved or repackaged to include additional benefits and features.

2. Latent demand: there is a need for a product but no product to fulfil it (e.g. the need for a museum of photography and television before one was pioneered in Bradford). Promotion can be highly effective once a suitable product has been designed.

3. Faltering demand: a once-successful tourism offering is in decline (e.g traditional seaside holidays in the United Kingdom). Remedial promotion can often be used to arrest or improve faltering demand, e.g. the relaunch by the Torbay Tourist Board of Torquay as the 'English Riviera' in 1982/83 (IPA, 1982).

4. Full demand: supply and demand are about equal and match production capacity (e.g. full bookings at certain hotels during high season). Promotion in this situation should be maintained at its existing level or, if there is none, not used at all. There is no point in stimulating an increased demand which cannot be met.

5. Irregular demand: demand is cyclic or seasonal and does not meet the total potential supply (e.g. fall-offs in holiday letting and timesharing during the winter). Promotion can be extremely successful in generating off-peak demand, especially when tied to price deals and special offers.

6. Overfull demand: demand continuously exceeds supply. In tourism this may result in environmental deterioration and consumer frustration (e.g. jams on certain motor routes and crowding and pollution in prime tourist locations such as Florence or Paris during the summer). Promotion may be used to shift demand either in time or place (e.g. advertisements for out-of-season holidays in Spain; the French Tourist Board's provision of Bison Fute maps to travelers driving off car ferries, routing them from major to minor roads). Overfull demand in one kind of tourist offering may be a promotional stimulus to competitors to provide more acceptable substitutes (e.g. the promotion of the Algarve in Portugal during the 1970s and 1980s as a new alternative to overcrowded French and Spanish 'sunshine' beaches).

7. Unwholesome demand: demand for a tourist product may be thought to be socially or physically damaging, and thus susceptible to intervention by public regulatory measures or exploitation by commerce. This is so far rare, although it is possible to discern the start of a medical lobby publicizing the dangers of skin cancer from sun exposure, which could affect the huge 'sun, sea and sand' market. In 1987 there was

also a fashion campaign, among some cosmetic firms, aimed at marginalizing sun tans and promoting white skin as fashionable.

8. Negative demand: segments of the population dislike the product, even though it may have social or physical advantages (e.g. some groups dislike adventure holidays requiring large physical inputs; others avoid 'high' cultural tourism such as museum visiting). Promotion is unlikely to reverse strong negative demand; but it should be precisely channelled in such a way as to avoid the wastage of reaching hostile or apathetic segments.

Promotion as a micro-process

At the micro-level promotional strategy can be seen as an attempt to forge relationships with individuals (customers and potential customers) and elicit their loyal patronage. Coffman and Recknagel (1979, p. 165) writing on hotel/motel management, identify promotion with several practical tasks:

1. Getting a prospect to try us.
2. Giving him/her the absolute in service so that:
   (a) He/she spends a maximum amount with us for all our varied services;
   (b) He/she comes back.
3. Making him/her into a sales agent for us by:
   (a) Telling friends and associates;
   (b) Getting from him/her direct prospect leads from which we can promote additional patronage.

Example

The Alternative Travel Group of Oxford, an English firm specializing in culturally-oriented/trekking holidays for ABC1 markets, use a diversity of promotional activities which include: press advertising in the quality press; well produced brochures with distinct arty/historical connotations for direct mail shots; and public relations wine and cheese parties at historic/prestige venues in UK cities. In direct mail shots, the firm invites respondents to suggest new holiday ideas and also to provide the name and address of a friend likely to be interested in their holidays. Former customers are annually canvassed and the emphasis of the firm's promotional strategy is on forming a highly personalized feeling of 'elite' community among past and potential customers.

Implementation

Promotion, which is also called the Marketing Communications Mix (see Rothschild, 1987, for a comprehensive text which uses this designation), commonly includes four major components: advertising, publicity and public relations (including sponsorship), sales promotion, and personal selling. Some writers (e.g.

Foster, 1985) add 'merchandizing and packaging' to this list. These options will be individually defined and examined in a subsequent chapter ('Tourism promotion mix' p. 545).

Fundamental features of tourism promotion

There are six major underlying features of promotion in tourism which need to be considered before strategy can be decided upon and implemented.

Identity building

Promotion should be seen as an *identity building* activity for the firm. All the elements of the promotional mix should pull in the same direction. Promotional consistency is essential. Activities as diverse as brochures, media advertising, the behavior of employees (particularly sales staff), in-store merchandising, special offers and so on all go to create an image of the organization (place, transport line, travel agent etc) in addition to relaying discrete units of information.

Promotion should be seen as both a short-term activity (spanning a particular day, week, season or year), but also as a middle- and long-term investment aimed at building up a consistent and credible corporate identity. Such identities act as valuable warranties of good service. Once this cumulative, long-term effect is understood it means that there are good reasons for coordinating all promotional planning under one executive or within one department to achieve consistency and integration: 'The component elements of promotion. . .are interdependent and must be combined into a mutually reinforcing whole. This can only be the case if the various promotional activities are governed by goals and objectives common to all of them' (Schmoll, 1977). A good method of achieving this integration of effort is to appoint a Marketing Communications Manager to oversee promotional strategy (Ziegenhagen, 1984).

Intangibility of product

Recognition must be made of the fact the promotion *is* the product as far as the tourist-prospect is concerned. The customer buys a trip or a holiday purely on the basis of symbolic expectations established promotionally through words, pictures, sounds, images etc. The prospect cannot see the actual product the way he/she could examine the goods in other markets. You can't test drive a holiday, or try on a new airline schedule. This means that the role of promotion is critical. Promotion must generate desire and acceptance in the absence of more tangible kinds of evidence. Promotion thus has a greater role in establishing the nature of the product in tourism than in many other markets.

Perceived risk

Promotional strategy should be seen as the cumulative reduction of the risks the customer perceives to exist in travel/tourism decisions. Some of these decisions include (Foster, 1985): where to go, where to stay, how to travel, how much to spend, where to book, and the type of travel (as a group or individually). All these decisions are fraught with perceived risk because of the following factors:

1. They involve committing large sums of money to something which cannot be seen.
2. They involve large emotional investments. Whole families look forward to and backward from holiday activity, so each year the fear of failure is high.
3. The opportunity cost is irreversible. If a holiday backfires, that's it for another year. Most people do not have the additional vacation time or money to make good the holiday that went wrong.
4. They often involve encounters with the unknown (in terms of destination, accommodation, transportation etc), and the unknown always involves risk.

People attempt to reduce risk in many different ways, most importantly by seeking out information (from commercial sources, the media, friends etc.) The purpose of promotional strategy is to identify and anticipate, through research preferably, what the major perceived risks in the holiday decision process are, and then devise a promotional plan that reduces or eliminates them, at the points at which they occur in the overall decision sequence. For example, Thomas Cook's '10 Point Guarantee' promotional package, presented in travel agencies, literature and media advertising in the early 1980s was devised to address the major forms of perceived risk identified as central to customer tourist decisions, by offering a covering guarantee about each one.

Tourism decision making

Promotional strategy, then, can only be realistically conceived if the planner has a detailed knowledge of the way in which tourism decisions are made. Numerous general models of buyer behavior exist, but there is no substitute for focused, specific data on the particular tourism market within which a given firm or tourism offering is located. This requires the firm to know how long tourism decisions take; what sequence of steps is involved; who is involved at different stages; when and how final commitment comes and so on. Once the nature of the tourism decision is understood, promotional strategy can be geared to affect some or all of the key points in the process.

In understanding the tourism decision process a useful analytical tool is the concept of the Decision Making Unit (DMU). This postulates that consumer decisions can be understood by differentiating several functional influences that may operate to affect the ultimate sale:

1. Buyers (the person who pays the money).
2. Users (the people who actually take the holiday). For example, children or elderly relatives may be a significant factor in holiday choice, though they rarely pay for them.
3. Personal referentials (social contacts whose opinions may be sought such as friends, business peers, society members etc.).
4. Media referentials (travel writers, editors and broadcasters). Research at Newcastle Polytechnic (Seaton, 1989), showed that negative comment in the Travel Page of an ABC1 newspaper could dramatically depress an airline's bookings, while positive coverage could result in hotels completely selling out room space.

5. Deciders (the person or persons whose opinions precipitate the final decision). For example, in tourism offerings in the Middle East, clerics and educators can play the crucial decider's role in leading parties of 20 or more people (church groups, classes etc.) to such destinations as Jerusalem and the Holy Land. Teachers may do the same for school parties to other European destinations. Promotional strategy must recognize these influences.
6. Trade influence. Not merely in the sense of keeping travel outlets well stocked with brochures and mailshots, but also in providing other forms of contact and communication about planning, particularly when new tourist offerings are involved.

As an example, Townsend Thoresen introduced a new ferry service in the mid-1960s and launched it with consumer advertising but little travel trade promotion. As a result, it failed for the first year, until a public relations trade campaign was devised, which involved sailing one of the new ferries around Britain and holding parties for regional travel agents at important provincial ports.

Cultural expectations

Tourism promotion operates within a cultural field which it also affects. Anyone involved in devising strategy should be aware that travel and holiday decisions are strongly affected by cultural expectations (De Souza, 1985; Mill and Morrison, 1985). Consider the following examples:

1. Iceland has a strong cultural connection with Viking culture but very little topographical evidence of it still exists. Official Icelandic Guides are therefore briefed in Viking history so that, in conducted tours of the island, they can verbally bring to life the culture at particular historic locations, where it would otherwise be hard to 'see'.
2. The Italian Tourist Board has the opposite problem. Italy is primarily seen as a network of 'cultural' sites (buildings, monuments, galleries etc.), rather than as a 'sun, sea and sand' destination. In 1987 promotional strategy was aimed to extend the country's image by emphasizing Italy's coastal resorts and seaside attractions, to reduce dependence on 'cultural' locations (Tommasi, 1987).

Attitudes and behavior

All promotion is aimed at influencing the attitudes and behavior of audiences, but there are three different directions in which it may do so. Strategists should clearly determine which or what combination of the following is desirable in their policies:

1. Confirmation and reinforcement. Much promotion is not aimed at getting people to do or think anything different, but to remain the same. In many consumer goods fields the main communication task is to 'hang onto what you've got', and there are reasons to think that tourism markets consist of significant numbers of people with previous experience of a product. People tend to repeat their holiday behavior (see, for example, Schmidhauser, 1984). Thus the confirmation/reinforcement role of promotion must always be considered,

even when the aim is also to win new customers. In 1982 the agency Pictorial Publicity and the Torbay Tourist Board discovered that two-thirds of all visitors to the Torquay seaside area had been before. This was a key factor in shaping the kind of promotional plan they developed (IPA, 1982).

2. Creation of new patterns of attitude or behavior. Some tourism organizations need to educate potential customers to consider completely new travel options. In 1986 the Seychelles Tourist Board conducted a highly visible campaign to put this remote island on the tourist map for the first time.

3. Changing of attitudes and behavior. This is the most difficult of all forms of behavioral influence because people resist change. One striking example of its successful accomplishment was the reversal of Puerto Rico's adverse image among American businessmen in the early 1960s due to promotion devised by David Ogilvy (Ogilvy, 1983).

Checklist of decision areas

Having considered some of the major general factors behind the implementation of promotional strategy, it is possible to finish with a final checklist of decison areas that must be agreed as a basis for promotional planning.

1. Audience decisions. *Who* needs to be reached? Who are customers/potential customers? What influences make up the buying unit? What is the market for a tourist offering like in terms of the quantitative and qualitative characteristics of its constituents (number of people; age; class; lifestyle; education; family status etc)? What are the trade influences who might need reaching? What priorities should be allocated to the various audiences who must be reached?

2. Message decisions. *What* needs to be said? What benefits should be promoted? What information is necessary to push prospects through the various phases of the decision process? How do information requirements vary among the different audiences targeted? *From whom* should information be seen to come? (The firm? The travel agent? A travel writer or broadcaster? A former customer? A personal contact? etc.)

3. Timing decisions. *When* should promotion be phased to the chosen audiences? Once audiences and messages have been decided timings must be assessed and integrated. *How often?* In addition, considerations of frequency and continuity of promotional effort must be assessed. One useful question to consider is how close to the moment of decision the promotional options need to be implemented. One pattern is to use media advertising to stimulate early interest, direct mail as follow-up to consolidate it, and personal or telephone selling after that to convert interested prospects into customers.

4. Media and channel decisions. *Where* should promotion appear and *how* should it be channelled? (Media adverts? Publicity in the news media? Through face-to-face contact with customers? etc.) Different media and channels can be used for different purposes. For example, the Shetland

Isles in the United Kingdom are promoted through media advertising and direct mail shots to gain initial awareness and interest, but videos offering 20 minute guides to the Islands are located on the ships taking already committed tourists from Scotland to the Shetlands.

Finally, all these strategic decisions should be put down in writing for agreement within the firm and as a guide to any outside agencies or consultancies involved (e.g. advertising agencies, design groups etc.) If written objectives are not established, they are likely to be fudged or misinterpreted later.

Assessment

All strategic objectives should be conceived within the parameters of a known budget and an agreed program for measuring results (see Beaver, 1980, for an excellent practical discussion of these). Promotional strategy must involve two-way communication. In order to say the right thing promotionally, it is necessary to know what needs saying and then to measure to what extent it has been said with effect. Promotional strategy involves providing feedback mechanisms, so that the firm can anticipate consumer information needs and provide for them, and then check that they have been met. 'Ask, Listen and Observe' should be the promotional planner's watchwords. Thomas Cook spent considerable time and money on questionnaire-based research to determine what the consumer felt to be the main problems and risks in booking holidays, before developing the 'Ten Point Guarantee' mentioned above (Burfoot, 1987). They were also to monitor its effects using sales data and other means.

Conclusion

Promotional strategy is the art of defining the audiences the firm needs to reach; the messages needed to influence them; and the channels that will deliver those messages to the designated audiences. When these have been agreed it requires monitoring mechanisms to provide feedback on achievements and feedforward for future strategic modifications, where necessary.

Focus on small business

Strategic decision making and the assessment of alternative promotional strategies is as important to the small business as the global company. A tourist enterprise as small as a bed-and-breakfast guest house needs to assess who its likely target audiences are (customers? a tourist board? local travel journalists? etc.) and establish promotional avenues for targeting and communicating with them. The procedures enumerated in this chapter are of universal relevance in approaching these key decisions.

Further reading

Beaver, A., *Mind Your Own Travel Business* (Beaver Travel, 1980). A massive (2 vols-over 1,000 page) handbook on travel agency practice, which is excellent for its personal style and practical recommendations and examples. Chapters 5–7 are good on marketing and promotion, with a particular emphasis on budgeting and cost-effectiveness.

Burfoot, T., 'Quality control in Thomas Cook', *Are They being Served: Quality Consciousness in British Industry*, B. Moores, ed. (Philip Allan, 1987), pp. 166–78. This article provides an interesting insight into the questionnaire design used in Cook's surveys. The book includes other interesting articles on consumer perceptions of airline services (pp. 60–87) and package holidays (pp. 201–13).

Buttle, F., *Hotel and Food Service Marketing* (Holt, Rinehart & Winston, 1986). Particularly good on behavioral aspects of hotel marketing and a whole section on promotion (pp. 299–406).

Coffman, C. D. and Recknagel, H. J., *Marketing for a Full House* (Cornell University, School of Hotel Administration, 1979). Focused on hotel/motel management in America, this is a lively and well illustrated book with a particularly good section on promotion (pp. 163–327).

De Souza, M., 'Contribution of qualitative research techniques to the definition of product and communication strategies', *Behavioral Travel Modelling*, D. A. Hensher and P. R. Stopher, eds (Croom Helm, 1985), pp. 209–14. Based on indepth interviews with visitors to France, this paper provides a thoughtful consideration of cultural factors in travel choices.

Foster, D., *Travel and Tourism Management* (Macmillan, 1985). Contains a good section on 'The communications mix' (pp. 250–83) which provides a clear analysis of the nature of tourist buying decisions, and the influences on them.

Institute of Practitioners, *Advertising: Advertising Works*, P. Broadbent, ed. (Holt, Rinehart & Winston, 1982). This case history compendium of successful advertising campaigns includes data on the Torbay relaunch of the 'English Riviera'.

Kotler, P., 'The major tasks of marketing management', *Journal of Marketing*, vol. 37 (October 1973), pp. 42–9. A classic article by marketing's major guru on the eight kinds of demand which marketing and promotion may be used to affect.

Mill, R. C. and Morrison, A. M., *The Tourism System* (Prentice Hall, 1985). Based on US examples but with a short section on promotion (Chapter 15) and an interesting chapter (3) on some of the social and cultural factors involved in tourism choices.

Ogilvy, D., *Confessions of an Advertising Man* (Cape, 1964).

Ogilvy, D., *Ogilvy on Advertising* (Pan Books, 1983). Both these are highly entertaining memoirs by advertising's most hyped celebrity, and include comments on tourism promotion. There is a whole chapter in *Ogilvy on Advertising* – 'How to advertise foreign travel' (pp. 127–36) – on tourism.

Ornstein, E. and Nunn, C. A., *The Marketing of Leisure* (Associated Business Press, 1980). A useful overview of the 'Leisure Boom' and its commercial implications. Specially relevant are: Chapter 3, 'Holidays' (pp. 115–33); Chapter 9, 'Channels of Communication' (pp. 176–96) and Chapter 10 'Promotion-Including Advertising' (pp. 197–224). Each of these chapters ends with a practical checklist of questions relevant to executive decisions in the area of promotional strategy.

Rothschild, M. L., *Marketing Communications–From Fundamentals to Strategies* (D.C. Heath and Co., 1987). A lively, comprehensive and well-referenced textbook covering the main aspects of both planning and implementation of promotion.

Schmidhauser, H. P., 'Travel experience segmentation as a predictor of holiday behaviour', *Behavioural Travel Modelling*, D. A. Hensher and P. R. Stopher, eds (Croom Helm, 1984), pp. 149–65. This article uses statistical techniques to show that over a 10-year period Swiss holiday venues and forms stayed much the same, and that past holiday behavior thus affords a more discriminating basis for segmentation than sociodemographic criteria.

Schmoll, G. A., *Tourism Promotion* (Tourism International Press, 1977). Still the only book devoted entirely to tourism promotion and essential for its relentlessly systematic approach, though light on examples and color. Chapters 4–6 are essential reading for all promotional strategists.

Seaton A. V., *Freebies, Puffs, Belles Lettres and Vade Mecums: the Occupational Ideologies and Practices of Travel Page Editors* (Newcastle Polytechnic, 1989). This examines the relationship between travel and the media, based on interviews with travel editors of national newspapers, and content analysis of travel pages. It provides data on the influence of the travel press and the policies which shape its content.

Tommasi, E., 'Changing role of a national tourist office,' *Tourism Management*, vol. 8, no. 2 (June 1987), p. 89. This is a useful short summary of the evolving role of a tourist office in promoting Italy.

Ziegenhagen, M. E., 'Why you need a marketing communications manager', *Business Marketing* (September 1984), pp. 107–16. Although primarily addressed to executives in business marketing, this short article gives a succinct argument for appointing a manager to oversee the whole promotional/communications mix.

TONY V. SEATON

Psychographic segmentation

Introduction

The concept of market segmentation is based on the fact that buyers are basically heterogeneous in their demands, or in other words, each has unique needs and wants. Market segmentation is the identification and aggregation of individual consumers coming from a heterogeneous population into groups or segments where the members of the group or segment are relatively alike, yet different from other groups. Marketing functions such as pricing, distribution and product planning are determined and the resources are allocated according to different market segments.

Tourists as buyers of tourist products differ in one or more respects. They may differ in their wants, needs, motives, attitudes or lifestyle. Any one of these variables can be used for segmenting a market. The best known ways of segmenting the tourist market include geographic, demographic and benefit segmentation, as well as segmentation based on the characteristics or behavior of the buyer (volume of use) and psychographic segmentation.

Geographic segmentation is very often used by the statistics offices in many tourist countries and it identifies the tourist by country (region) of origin. Demographics describe personal characteristics of travelers. Age, sex, family size and life cycle, education, occupation and income are demographic variables which have been found to be associated with travel behavior. Segments based on usage levels differentiate heavy buyers from low volume users. Market segmentation based on benefits assumes that consumers buy a product for the potential benefit experienced from using it. Its focus is on product attributes which consumers perceive to have goal-satisfying capabilities and this method employs some psychographic variables.

Psychographics, also referred to as data on lifestyles and on activities, interests and opinion (AIOs), attempt to provide a detailed understanding of consumers in terms of their way of living. They take into account how people spend their time (daily activities, hobbies, entertainment), what they place importance on (interests, community involvement) and their opinions and attitudes towards various types of vacations.

In the travel literature a number of other ways of market segmentation have been reported and discussed, i.e. distance traveled, means of travel, vacation attributes and the number of previous visits. However, these methods are often associated with some other ways of segmenting, either demographic or psychographic.

Demographic and socioeconomic characteristics portray the basic differences which are the determinants of a traveler's behavior. But they merely describe and do not provide an understanding of why buyer segments respond to a product the way they do. There is increasing evidence that these variables are insufficient means of effectively delineating the market segments. Psychographics allow a substantially deeper grasp of the psychological side of the tourist. Therefore, psychographic segmentation as an analytic tool has been shown beneficial in describing and understanding the tourist. Such understanding has had substantial rewards in developing effective and efficient communication programs.

Examples*

Cunard Lines, as a shipping company, operate a variety of vessels all over the world. In recent years their strategy has been to try to attract the middle and the upper middle class, the wealthy and the super rich consumers. They have different products with which they try to cover different needs of such different markets. Aiming to increase their market share within the above mentioned segments Cunard did some surveys on the modern lifestyle trends such as the health movement and how it affects daily lives. Based on the results, they introduced a health program, including diets on the menus, which was so successful that the company is now putting health facilities in all their ships. Another item resulting from the research of lifestyle trends was the need for computer knowledge or literacy expressed by people in their forties, fifties and sixties who did not grow up with computers. Cunard proceeded to install a learning center on one of its big ships. It was also a great success. In this way Cunard was able to advertise products which differentiated the company and which are usually not expected on cruiseliners but for which, as their psychographic research showed, there was an obvious need.

* The examples explained here were presented at the Fifteenth TTRA Annual Conference, held in 1984 in Philadelphia, Pennsylvania, and are printed in the anthology *Travel Research: The Catalyst for Worldwide Tourism Marketing*.

The other example concerns Amtrak – the rail passenger service in the United States. The result of their study, which employed national surveys, led them to develop an entirely new advertising and sales promotion strategy designed to establish in the travelers' minds that Amtrak is a truly viable transportation system for all types of trips. Their new marketing programs and promotion efforts were redesigned to increase 'top-of-mind' awareness of the passenger train as well as awareness of the quality of services that the passenger train provides. A test and evaluation of these concepts and findings enabled Amtrak to determine their primary target markets. They were able, therefore, to define more clearly the demographics and psychographics of their prime prospects and core travelers. This new emphasis and focus for Amtrak was incorporated into an umbrella 'All Aboard Amtrak' marketing campaign with a message that on Amtrak it is easy to go where you want to go in a pleasurable, comfortable fashion.

Benefits

The tourism market has become increasingly competitive in recent years, making it necessary to sharpen the research tools which would generate more accurate data for strategic tourism development and planning. Recognizing the needs and the motives of the various market segments provides the marketer with a very powerful and practical tool for achieving need/motive satisfaction. While demographic variables are still important, there is growing recognition that demographic variables alone do not in many cases provide an adequate degree of differentiation between segments resulting in a need for additional information about consumer groups.

The concept and application of psychographics has been widely accepted in the field of marketing. Knowledge about relevant segments of travelers, their desires, motives, attitudes and lifestyles allows travel marketers to become more focused and effective in their efforts. Psychographics can help in answering some marketing queries such as how to make/design the tourist product (what services and products to offer), whom to sell it to (personality characteristics) and how to sell it (distribution and communication channels). A lot of activities and services that make up the tourism product could position the product on the market, at the same time also adapting the development of the destinations.

Psychographics provide a unique way of viewing the tourist/consumer. It starts with people and reveals how they feel about a variety of subjects. Insight into a vacationer's personality, attitudes and motivations is gained by asking questions about many aspects of life. Psychographics enables inferences to be drawn from general questions on social status, profession or a tourist's income bracket and possible travel expenditure levels. It must be remembered that respondents are more often than not unwilling to provide accurate answers to questions pertaining to their income. Therefore, an indirect method of obtaining such data can be extremely valuable.

Psychographic research provides detailed profiles that allow a marketer virtually to visualize the people he is trying to reach.

It seeks to determine why people travel (and why they do not), how they think, what their values and attitudes are, what types of destinations they want to visit and what they want to do while staying in a destination. When implemented in the segmentation process it can lead to more effective advertising strategies aimed at each market segment. Marketing management attempting to segment travel markets and to develop promotional programs needs to rely on information about the lifestyles of potentional travelers as well as on demographic characteristics. But, information about a traveler's personality may be more important in predicing foreign and domestic travel behavior.

Successful advertising depends upon effectively discerning the audience that the marketer can reach. One of the vital links of message development is to understand why consumers want the benefit they desire. This suggests the copy appeal should reflect the consumer's desires, expectations, preferences and perceptions about a travel destination. Certain special attributes of a place may be more appealing to a specific target audience. Also, proper selection of media units and optimal scheduling of advertising time can be essential to the success of an advertising campaign. In this, psychographic variables can be an invaluable aid to media research since people with different lifestyles have different media habits. So, psychographics provides valuable information for media selection and scheduling, and for creative thinking in developing advertising copy or theme. In that way, promotional messages and travel incentives as well as communication channels can be better tailored to the receptive market segments.

Implementation

Psychographic segmentation is a research tool which provides new insights into consumer behavior permitting a better understanding of the market conditions and an improvement of the marketing strategies. Research based on psychographics may offer particularly useful findings for persons who will implement the results – developers and planners, marketing executives, advertising directors and creative types at advertising agencies. Proper use of this approach in segmenting a consumer market rests on dividing the total market into finely tuned market segments. The objective is to create profiles which carve out characteristics of each segment and at the same time substantially differentiate the segments from one another. Psychographic segmentation can be a useful tool in planning and developing product strategies, such as package tours or theme parks, as well as in creating promotion strategies. For example, it would appear that knowing whether a traveler prefers historic sites, nightlife, gambling or indoor/outdoor sports activities can be useful for creating a package, or knowing that psychographic characteristics such as impulsiveness in the decision-making process, escaping form every day life, enjoying wildlife or physical activities are more correlated with visiting National Parks as vacation destinations. It is important to answer which psychographic characteristics directly influence product attributes the traveler is evaluating when making a purchase decision. Thus, psychographics allow the creation of a tourism product which is more compatible with the motivation, the attitudes and the opinions of the travelers.

Segmentation of potential tourist markets has a number of benefits for government tourism organizations. Since the size of their advertising budgets is limited, the development of different compaigns, aimed at different market segments may not be possible. In such a case, information about psychographic patterns shared by large proportions of the total market are most helpful in developing an advertising campaign that would cover a large number of potential consumers and be more effective.

It should be remembered, however, that psychographic segmentation is an analytic tool which helps in the decision-making process and that implementation leads to real or actual product/service. And implementation depends on the degree of skill and creativity of the researcher and the marketer.

Assessment

Does psychographic data add anything beyond demographic analysis that is real, meaningful and relevant? Is lifestyle information superior to demographics? Psychographic information is more difficult to obtain than demographics and it is also more expensive, both in development and survey costs. Furthermore, since using psychographics in market segmentation usually involves a great number of variables, computer facilities and sophisticated statistical techniques have to be available.

Collection of demographic data has been, by far, the most frequently used technique for identifying the tourist markets. Demographics are more readily available than information on why a person chooses a particular trip or a vacation destination. Furthermore, demographics are much easier to analyze and understand and practitioners involved in marketing travel may not be aware of other techniques for identifying their consumers. But psychographics provide designers of the tourism product with some additional information over and beyond the demographic profile. This does not imply that lifestyle analysis should replace demographics. Psychographics cannot do the job alone. Although this is a very useful means in developing copy and message strategy, without additional guidelines in selecting the media, psychographics cannot help deliver the proper message, in a proper manner, to the proper target. It is highly probable that a combination of psychographic and demographic data would offer still greater insights into traveler preferences.

A combination of consumer lifestyle and demographic data can be used to predict travel behavior with substantial accuracy. Psychographics attempt to identify the characteristics of travel segments and discover the actual motives for travel preferences and behavior. Many practitioners believe that personality measures are more descriptive and thus more useful than standard demographic measures. An individual's way of life is not fixed and immutable. As a person goes through the life cycle, values, preferences, needs, wants, attitudes and beliefs may change significantly. So, continued monitoring and examination of the psychographic data in the tourism market (research) is needed to help keep the data up-to-date and, thus, to satisfy the needs of the consumers.

Conclusion

Psychographic segmentation is an approach to tourism market segmentation based on personality characteristics of consumers. In contrast to other ways of segmenting the market, psychographics examine the actual motives for travel behavior and offer answers about why people travel, allowing the tourism managers to focus their efforts.

Segments based on psychographic variables provide travel marketers with valuable information for planning, designing, positioning and distributing tourism products, for promoting and advertising them, as well as for creating copy appeals and selecting the proper media. It also enables the identification of certain segments of tourists as well as helping in better defining the majority of potential consumers and in that way achieves better effectiveness of marketing and promotional budgets. In a competitive environment it is a useful stategic marketing tool.

Focus on small business

Owing to a high degree of competition in the marketplace, all types of enterprises, regardless of their size or field of specialization, are today forced to implement a marketing concept and the marketing techniques. This simply means they have to adapt to the demands of the market. In a narrower sense, such an approach presupposes the use of market segmentation. In tourism, small organizations, such as hotels or travel agencies, very often neglect such a market approach.

In many industries, segmentation is a commonly recognized principle of differentiated marketing and strategic market planning. Tourism management, especially on the local level of resorts still lacks a proper understanding of how to evade competitive pressure by using the strategic tools of segmenting and positioning. Psychographic profiles may provide policymakers in small business with more insights than specific attitudes alone. Moreover, defining market segments through psychographics is an especially helpful tool for those with limited promotion and advertising budgets. Psychographics allow one to define the different segments and approach only those of interest, or they make it possible to creat messages which appeal to individuals with certain psychographic characteristics within a large heterogeneous population. Small enterprises can really afford to address only a 'known buyer' or a well defined buyer, and this is where psychographic segmentation can be of significant assistance.

Software/databases

American Marketing Association, Chicago, USA, offers their members computer search services on DIALOG. The relevant Bibliographies for psychographic segmentation are Bibliography series No. 23 – *Personality Research in Marketing*, edited by D. Twelt (1977) and Bibliography No. 28 – *Market Segmentation*, edited by R. Michman, F. Gable and W. Groff (1977).

Further reading

Abbey, J. R., 'Does life-style profiling work?', *Journal of Travel Research*, vol. XVIII, no. 1 (Summer 1979), pp. 8–14. The research discussed in this article deals with the relevance of lifestyle and demographic information in the design of package travel tours.

Darden, W. R. and Pereault, W. D., 'A multivariate analysis of media exposure and vacation behavior with life style covariates', *Journal of Consumer Research*, vol. 2 (September 1975), pp. 93–103. The article describes a study investigating consumer media exposures, vacation behaviors and lifestyles and how these are interrelated.

Hawes, D. K., 'Psychographics are meaningful...not merely interesting', *Journal of Travel Research*, vol. XV, no. 4 (Spring 1977), pp. 1–7. The article presents the psychographic variables used in segmenting the travel market.

Kotler, P., *Principles of Marketing* (Prentice Hall, 3rd edition, 1986). Special attention should be given to Part IV, Chapter 10, which deals with market segmentation, targeting and positioning of the product.

Mayo, E., 'Tourism and the national parks: a psychographic and attitudinal study', *Journal of Travel Research*, vol. XIV, no. 1 (Summer 1975), pp. 14–18. The article points out the psychographic characteristics of tourists who visit National Parks in the United States.

McIntosh, R. W. and Goeldner, C. R., *Tourism: Principles, Practices, Philosophies* (John Wiley, 5th edition, 1986). Special attention should be given to Chapter 12 which deals with tourism marketing and market segmentation.

McQueen, J. and Miller, K. E., 'Target market selection of tourists: a comparison of approaches', *Journal of Travel Research*, vol. XXIV, no. 1 (Summer 1985), pp. 2–6. The study described in this article evaluates a number of alternative ways to segment tourist markets using the criteria of profitability, variability and accessibility of the segments.

Pitts, R. E. and Woodside, A. G., 'Personal values and travel decisions', *Journal of Travel Research*, vol. XXV, no. 1 (Summer 1986), pp. 20–5. This article discusses the relationship between personal values and travel or leisure decisions and the application of the 'value profile' to the development of a marketing strategy.

Ritchie, J. R. B. and Goeldner, C. R., *Travel, Tourism and Hospitality Research* (John Wiley, 1987). Special attention should be given to Chapter 17, 'Understanding Psychographics in Tourism Research', where a comprehensive overview of psychographic research used for travel and tourism purposes is given.

Schewe, C. D. and Calantone, R. J., 'Psychographic segmentation of tourists', *Journal of Travel Research*, vol. XVI, no. 3 (Winter 1978), pp. 14–20. The article explains how psychographics and demographics can be used for segmenting the market and planning advertising strategies for different target markets.

Shih, D., 'VALS as a tool of tourism market research: the Pennsylvania experience', *Journal of Travel Research*, vol. XXIV, no. 4 (Spring 1986), pp. 2–11. This article focuses on the concept of value and lifestyles (VALS) which provides new insights into consumer behavior related to tourism development.

Soloman, P. J. and George, W. R., 'The bicentennial traveler: a lifestyle analysis of the historian segment', *Journal of Travel Research*, vol. XV, no. 3 (Winter 1977), pp. 14–17. The study described in this article uses lifestyle analysis to examine travelers who are particularly interested in history.

Taylor, G. D., 'Multi-dimensional segmentation of the Canadian pleasure travel market', *Tourism Management*, vol. 7, no. 3 (September 1986), pp. 146–53. The article explains segmentation based on three broad criteria – travel philosophies, benefits and activities/interests, related to the types of pleasure trips chosen by individuals.

Travel and Tourism Research Association, *Travel Research: The Catalyst for Worldwide Tourism Marketing*, fifteenth annual conference, Philadelphia, Pennsylvania, 24–27 June 1984 (Bureau of Economic and Business Research, Graduate School of Business, University of Utah, 1984). The conference papers under the headings 'An overview from industry leaders' and 'Travel research: the catalyst in action – major case histories', give examples of market research and implementation of results in the tourism industry.

Travel and Tourism Research Association, *The Battle for Market Share: Strategies in Research and Marketing*, sixteenth annual conference, Palm Springs, California, 9–12 June 1985 (Bureau of Economic and Business Research, Graduate School of Business, University of Utah, 1985). The conference papers that are relevant for this topic are presented under the headings: 'New products of changing markets', 'Role of research and marketing and strategic planning: the maturing of the tourism industry'.

Wellls, W. D. 'Psychographics: a critical review', *Journal of Marketing Research*, vol. XII (May 1975), pp. 196–213. The article gives a comprehensive review of psychographic studies in areas other than tourism.

Woodside, A. G. and Pitts, R. E., 'Effects of consumer life styles, demographics and travel activities on foreign and domestic travel behavior', *Journal of Travel Research*, vol. XIV, no. 3 (Winter 1976), pp. 13–15. The article highlights the importance of life-style information in predicting foreign and domestic travel behavior.

SANDA WEBER

Quality control: the key to excellence in tourism

Introduction

In industrialized countries, the implementation of quality control started only about 40 years ago. The concept of quality control first appeared in the United States under the name of Statistical Quality Control (SQC), and extended, after World War II, all over the developed world. In Japan, in particular, between 1948 and 1960, an experiment was carried out which led to training on issues of quality control. This concept continues to evolve with CWQC (Company-wide Quality Control) and TQC (Total Quality Control). Quality must be the responsibility of all and its concern becomes a state of mind, a behavior, even before the development of its methods, its tools and its standards.

In industry development of quality control was helped by the appropriate management and production techniques and a strong intention to master the future markets. On the other hand, the concept of quality control as applied to tourist products and services is relatively new. One of the first documented articles which emphasized the importance of quality control in the field of tourism was published in the mid-1970s (Lanquar, 1975). This does not mean that quality is a recent preoccupation of professionals and officials of tourism. Good work and fair prices were the untold elements in quality control before its concept was introduced in the tourism industry.

Security and protection of the consumer

Concern to assure the security and the protection of consumers led countries, starting at the end of the nineteenth century, to lay down the laws and rules to be applied to lodging and catering activities (security against hotel fire, control of food products' quality). In the 1930s many people began to go on vacation through travel agencies; competence, respectability and solvency were essential on the part of the agents, and soon legislation became necessary. The granting of licences to the different participants in the tourist business–guides, interpreters, travel agents, hotelkeepers – was designed to protect the customer. Now such regulations have become commonplace. It

is no longer just a question of assuring the security and the protection of the consumer. Factors such as new means of information, increases in the number of destinations and of tourist products, reservation facilities and the average level of education have led to fundamental modifications in the behavior of the consumer. Tourist satisfaction has become the keystone of the whole of the tourism marketing area.

A response to crisis

After 30 years of fast growth (1946–1975), our societies have been confronted with difficulties and challenges. The numerous causes of these difficulties have been analyzed: shortages of raw materials, energy scarcity, monetary disorders and economic resurgence of some developing countries which have, in the last few years, taken off economically. Quality control fits into this context because the modern firm finds itself confronted with phenomena which can be summarized as follows:

1. Productivity slowing down.
2. Social climate deterioration.
3. International competition becoming tougher.
4. Changing lifestyles and deterioration of the firm's traditional values such as authority, success, career development etc.

In this context, the question arose: Why are some Asian airline companies so successful with business people, customers known to be the hardest to please? Their success does not have any secrets. It is not a question of seating arrangements, since the planes of these companies carry as many passengers as the other companies, nor the quality of the food served on board, which is similar to others. The 'plus' is somewhere else – in the service. During the entire flight, the staff remain efficient and vigilant. Requests are quickly satisfied, whether it is a question of defective earphones, of bringing an extra blanket or of exchanging a drink for another. All these small attentions given with a smile quickly convince the passenger that he is really welcome on board and that everything possible will be done to make his flight a pleasant one.

Another strong point is reliability. Planes arrive and leave on time, a quality particularly appreciated by business travelers. They are on time because the companies' managers have chosen to run a policy of systematic preventive maintenance. Mechanics change the engine before breakdown occurs, because unforeseen breakdowns lead to delays, customer annoyance and loss of money by the airline. Other airline companies have understood the importance of being very attentive to all their customers' actions, starting with information research on their buying decision, and finishing at the airport exit, when the passenger takes a means of transportation to go to his lodging place.

Likewise, hotel managers have systematically looked into the problem of quality. The International Hotel Association held a workshop on the necessity to reach quality and control the costs by appropriate training. The American Hotel Managers have also carried out a program called 'Guarantee Program of Quality' which identifies the cost of errors. Its principle could be used as information by all those who care about the problem of quality; more precisely, it involves organizing all operations for the consumer's benefit by allowing staff to take immediate decisions when faced with the problems to be solved.

Tourist satisfaction

Tourist satisfaction leads to the satisfaction of tourist staff (WTO, 1985): 'The satisfaction of the tourists has direct effects on the satisfaction of the hotel staff... A well-done job lets the employee have feelings of competency, confidence in himself, sense of success, pride for his work, and also a feeling of being important. Thus in tourism distribution, one realizes that an unsatisfied customer is a lost customer and the common saying "one lost, ten found" is a lie for many firms. Losing a customer is often felt as a hard blow for a firm (especially when the staff gets much involved in his work, putting not only energy but even feelings into the organization of a tour or a tourist project ...) and one must analyse the reasons for this dissatisfaction' (WTO, 1985, sections 31 and 34).

The problem of quality is therefore one of the most delicate problems with which the trade is confronted for the following reasons:

1. It is difficult to know whether the customer is satisfied. Current marketing techniques provide knowledge about the customer, his needs and expectations (Crosby, 1980; Joseph, 1983), but professionals remain relatively helpless in perceiving what it is that the customer wants or does not want and what he is ready to accept.
2. On the whole, the customer always wants more and his perception of quality is different from that which the professional can offer him. Only experience, listening and attention at every instant may let one have a more or less true idea.

The increase in the number of tourist services puts the customer in a strong position: he/she is able to choose, as he/she creates the supply and forces the professionals to adapt themselves to what he/she is looking for. Customers are, nowadays,

well-informed. They intend to optimize satisfaction considering the time and money they put in to the product. This optimization can only be perceived in terms of quality. Customers will go to the service supplier which seems to offer the best quality; if, for various reasons, quality is not what it ought to be, they will turn away from this supplier.

Customer and supplier do not perceive quality in the same way. The customer does not talk in terms of products, but in terms of vacation, travels, living experiences. The tourism professional must sell him this abstraction, his expected dream. As the customer's perceptions are distorted by the environment, and as tourism is an impalpable, intangible service, one cannot rely on the price to evaluate its quality. There is, finally, another aspect which may modify the customer's perception: the tendency to compare the service which is given to him with what he could have accomplished by himself. It must be underlined that in all the cases where the customer can substitute himself for the professionals, he becomes very difficult to please, especially when he is looking for the cheapest service for a specific destination.

For these reasons, the image given by the firm to sharpen the customer's perception must stick to reality: an advertisement cannot sell a dream at any price for fear of deceiving the customer. Displeasure will not often result in a complaint. Very few customers complain, perhaps for one of the following reasons. (1) Because they fear that in attesting their dissatisfaction, they will implicate somebody, a travel agent employee, a guide, a receptionist who, deep down, are not responsible for the poor quality of the service. (2) Because they have the feeling that their complaints will serve no purpose. (3) Because they do not have the material means to make their complaints quickly.

The practice of quality: the search for excellence

Quality is determining and researching an optimum excellence. Fundamental changes are in progress in many countries. Conflicts resulting from it show that it is not easy to enter an era where one must produce the best quality at the best price. *Some professionnals of quality say that it is better to point at perfection and not reach it than to point at imperfection and reach it.*

This level of excellence must be determined according to the expectations of the consumer, but not to any customer. The supplier should, as a priority, target the customer who is most loyal or who brings in the majority of his business.

The control of quality, in practice, answers the following three questions:

1. What is control?
2. Who controls?
3. How is control achieved?

Two essential variables enable the determination of the optimum level of excellence (Peters and Austin, 1985):

1. The price (the customer anticipates a quality of service for a given price).
2. The customer's needs.

One must therefore manage the expectations of the customer according to the communication that has been established with him. It is necessary to avoid the mistake of associating luxury with quality. A fast-food restaurant may offer hot and cold sandwiches of quality, while a luxury restaurant can offer services of very poor quality.

Quality itself focuses on two aspects:

1. The quality of the product or service.
2. The customer's personality: one may sell safety, atmosphere and surroundings, availability and choice. In this case, everything will depend on each individual's expectations. It is necessary to be constantly aware of one's customers, before, during and after service has been given. This means that one should get information from market studies on the expectations of the customers and that the staff will have to pay attention to the expressed wishes of the users. This requires evaluation of the users' satisfaction through different means such as questionnaires.

Content and economic characteristics of quality

Quality control implies a relative abundance of the supply in relation to the demand for goods and services. This state of competitive pressure may lead the tourist operator to make an effort to rationalize and control before and after. Among other things, quality control leads to a better allocation of the different scarce resources in the firm, to use, at their best, men and stocks; but too often, in more numerous sectors, the tendency is to replace men by machines.

The economic content of quality covers the targets to be reached, and the possible means and the adjustments of optimization needed for these controls. In so far as one can break down an activity into measurable objectives, one is often brought back to the four following dimensions: quantity, quality, delay and profitability.

Generally, in the secondary industry of production of goods, quality is measured according to the amount of wastage or failures. The cost of these wastages forms a first economic evaluation, but poor quality may have diffuse results which are hard to evaluate. Dissatisfaction of customers – harmful to future sales – and disturbance in the running of a department are examples of hidden costs.

Concerning the delay criterion, advance or lateness on the operation calendar characterizes the nonrespect of a set timetable. It results in an excess or a lack of products or services. 'Over-stocking' is another problem. In hotels and other lodgings, this is expressed by 'over-booking'. Unfortunately, too often, in peak periods, some professionals overbook up to 20 per cent of their occupancy without having contingency plans to allow them, for instance, to send the surplus customers to neighboring professionals.

Costs of quality

Quality leads to costs and expenses which must be compared to the advantages one gains from it: on the whole, quality induces three types of expenses:

1. A preventative cost. All the expense involved in preventing a mistake from happening – in succeeding first time. This can include material or training charges.
2. An insurance cost. Costs of covering any breakdowns and accidents in the service or duty.
3. A failure cost. Covering the loss of earnings due to the dissatisfaction of the customer.

So, it is necessary to establish a quality budget. Every time one dollar is spent preventatively, it may lead to a hundred in turnover: customers will come back or advertise by word of mouth. As to the costs of insurance, they will cover many risks related to the survival of the firm. Today most of the travel agencies systematically include insurance in their packages, offering substantial guarantees for a modest price. The insurances cover the entire trip, starting from departure. The travel assistance in general covers unanticipated homecoming, a round-trip ticket to be used by a family member when the insured is hospitalized for 7 or more days abroad, payment abroad of medical care, medicines, surgery and hospitalization, and even legal assistance.

Psychosociological characteristics of quality

The researching of quality has a psychosociological content. In order to comply with quality, one must try to achieve *zero-defect*, that is to do well the first time. This research is a state of mind that amounts to being proud and demanding of the service one provides. This state of mind is a fundamental condition of self-quality control. Only those who are interested in modifications, in progress and who do it in an economic perspective can put it into practice.

Researching a level of excellence thus corresponds to a profile of people: one must know how to recruit, how to train and motivate one's colleagues. Recruited people must be sensitive to work well done, which often leads to the congratulations of the customers and which can help to enhance staff enthusiasm. It is essential that an employee knows that he has the support of his organization and that he will not be contradicted when taking an initiative. This makes a staff member aware of his responsibilities, and is fundamental in case of complaint by a customer: the employee will be able in a confident atmosphere to take the responsibility to compensate the customer and to increase satisfaction all round.

Another psychological characteristic of quality is to know how to correct one's own errors. Generally mistakes are concentrated on a small number of causes that must be identified in order to remove them. An error hunt should not be a manhunt: blaming someone for these faults will not help at all in the long run if the problem is deeper rooted.

Quality control and service quality standards

The establishment of service standards is a powerful means to guarantee *a priori* a level of excellence. For instance, an important travel agency can commit itself to its customers with a professional code and rules of ethics written in the service contract: *X travel* fulfils its obligations to business people and firm customers as follows:

- in respecting the instructions given by the firm to reduce or eventually to reimburse any travel expenses,
- in looking for the most interesting fare from a financial point of view or looking for the best quality–price ratio,
- in accepting the entire discretion of the firm for trips – for the destinations, the frequencies and the volume – during the contractual agreement with the firm and after its end...

As to service quality standards, according to the given example, they affect what could be guaranteed by the same travel agency for its business customers:

1. *Reception*: opening hours, punctuality, telephone standards, information service, VIP procedure (after having specified who is VIP).
2. *Taking orders*: registering orders, controlling items, frontier formalities (passports, visas, ...), service linking (controlling the whole service).
3. *Reservations*: choice of the right fare price, seat allocation, systematic research of solutions in case of difficulties.
4. *Document presentation*: informing about delays, issuing tickets, rental car exchange vouchers, hotel exchange vouchers, billing.
5. *Document delivery*: presentation, frequency (for firms which make their staff travel, it is in fact important to know when in the week the travel agent or tour operator will deliver the tickets and documents), to whom should one deliver (decision as to the person or the service to whom the travel documents will be delivered).
6. *After-sales service*: reimbursements, visiting regular customers, visiting new customers, evaluation of the customer's satisfaction.

On this last point, it is a matter of knowing if the quality perceived by the customer is equivalent to the conceived quality. The travel agent or the organizer does not have at his/her disposal an option other than to ask his customers directly. How to question them? A simple way is to start on the basis of the complaint rate while remaining aware that this rate is not truly representative of the real dissatisfaction percentage. One must also take into account the reimbursement procedures and the complaints letters as well as the loyalty rate.

The International Hotel Association (IHA) published in 1984 a list of services and attractions likely to be offered by hotels and which include the following elements:

1. Staff in uniform.
2. Business services (i.e. secretarial office, translations, copying machine etc.).
3. Sports installation.
4. Rooms.
5. Private bathroom (with hairdryer and suitable light for make-up).
6. Bathroom products and installations.
7. Buying services (newspapers, souvenirs and various items).
8. Room service and others.

Quality standard is therefore a reference value for the economic action of the tourism firm. Such quality standard belongs to the system of rules and values that the firm or organization asks for – knowing how to behave and how to find its bearings when it must choose between several paths. The more the firm has contacts with other economic partners (customers, suppliers etc...) the more the firm understands the importance of good behavior from the economic viewpoint as well as the socially responsible one. Its standard system is widely determined by the interpretation it gives itself of the situation.

How can norms be specified and developed to standards which will serve as a scale in the search for the optimal level of excellence? It is extremely difficult to establish this type of standard for all the tourist products. One can, for instance, fall into a kind of professional self-discipline which won't let the phone ring more than three or four times, or will not allow more than a 6-day delay for the delivery of an airplane ticket. One must then give oneself the means to reach the standards of excellence. In order to do it, one must anticipate all that can fail at each sequence the customer goes through. This is why it is important to determine some basic principles for the preparation of such standards.

Quality measures

Finally, these standards can facilitate the elaboration of ratios to measure some characteristics of quality. This simple concept has been used for a long time by management supervisors and by those who are in charge of quality control. Quality processes are continuous, starting with the product or service and leading to after-sales service, which means that they apply to the following from the perspective of the optimal quality/price ratio:

1. Product or service conception.
2. Creation of the manufacturing process.
3. Manufacturing itself.
4. Marketing.

In this framework, the tourist organization must implement quality control report recommendations via quality managers, after having worked out a quality policy. This latter must be developed with its staff and the control of quality must allow, on the one hand, correction of malfunctioning and, on the other hand, systematic searching for improvements, for competitive reasons and economic and social good health. Quality policy is then everybody's business and must be directed towards at least four aims:

1. To improve the product/service quality.
2. To improve the quality of the working conditions.

3. To improve productivity.
4. To improve organizational and working methods.

Conclusion

The 'quality state of mind' should permeate all levels of the firm and all its functions. Management should implement quality training for all the staff, including the executives and the board, with a training program incorporating a capacity for expression and determination of some quality problems at the level of employees, because the quality processes represent responsible behavior.

Quality then becomes a regulating mechanism through which the elements of quality are maintained at an optimal value from the point of view of the tourist firm and the tourist. In this policy, one must particularly emphasize the importance of training. Because quality control is a new approach of management, it needs tremendous efforts of training at all levels. There must be first a complete involvement of all in the firm. It is under this condition that the leaders will have the necessary enthusiasm and the power to lead their colleagues. Then quality control asks for a deep knowledge of marketing. It is a subject which must be properly taught. Finally, quality control asks for sustained training in the field of communication and in the leadership of teams.

Further reading

Crosby, P. B., *Quality is Free: The Art of Making Quality Certain* (McGraw Hill, 1980).

Joseph, W., *Professional Service Management* (McGraw Hill, 1983).

Lanquar, R., *Répertoire des Voyages* (Les Editions Touristiques, September 1975).

Peters, T. and Austin, N. K., *A Passion for Excellence* (Random House, 1985).

World Tourism Organization, *Identification and Evaluation of Controlled Elements of Tourist Services Controlling the Tourist Satisfaction and State Measures Intended to Guarantee the Level of Quality of Tourist Products* (WTO, 1985).

ROBERT LANQUAR

Quality management in hotels

Introduction

The management of quality is a key issue in the management of any hotel property. It has been described as one of three key areas underpinning corporate success in the hospitality field (Haywood, 1983). The profitability of the operation is seen as being supported by the quality of hospitality services, management and the market. Hotel companies are increasingly aware of the importance of quality and clearly use it in their advertising and promotion to customers and in the standards of performance set for their employees. There is still, however, some confusion about what quality means. Dictionary definitions talk about quality as 'the degree or standard of excellence of something' and no self-respecting hotelier would think of his product as being substandard. This view is particularly prevalent where hoteliers adopt a product orientation. If the room itself is seen as the product, then the problems of quality management are the technical problems of ensuring high and consistent standards.

The increasing realization of the need for a marketing orientation in hotel management has changed the quality emphasis to one of 'fitness for purpose'. A more appropriate definition, therefore, is that of the British Standards Institute, which stresses the product or service's ability to satisfy the customers' needs. This shifts the evaluation of quality away from the provider, the hotelier, onto the consumer. The hotelier should not be concerned with providing the 'best' but the best for his particular customers. The management of quality is not, therefore, just a technical problem but a behavioral one too. The hotelier must consider the customer's attitudes, preferences and perceptions to be able to provide 'quality'.

There are many different approaches to quality but it is now becoming accepted that to be effective quality must be integrated into all activities of the organization. It cannot simply be added in at the end of the production cycle. Total quality management combines all the elements needed to 'imply that quality is a discipline to be implemented throughout an organization, and it suggests the complete dedication essential to making a quality programme work' (Hart and Casserley, 1984).

A model of the quality management system is given in Fig. 1. This model shows quality as the result of the matching of the customer's expectations and the actual performance delivered by the hotel. Customer expectations are obtained through the marketing research function and customer feedback at unit level. This information is interpreted by management to determine the type and style of product that they should produce, or changes they should make to an established product, given their own particular financial and operational constraints. This original product design must then be translated into performance standards for the physical and technical operation of the hotel property. It is then the responsibility of operational management to ensure that these standards are maintained to safeguard the availability of the expected product to the customer. Marketing plays a role not only in generating market research data but also in communicating with the customer to influence his or her expectations of that product.

Examples

Holiday Inns is the largest hotel chain in the world with approaching 2,000 hotels in more than 52 countries. The chain started from one property opened in Memphis (US) in 1952 with a particular market in mind – the family traveling by road. For this reason, all Holiday Inns rooms were given two double beds, to accommodate the whole family; they all had swimming pools, to provide a leisure facility for the family; and all had convenient roadside locations. This basic policy still exists but has been amended to cope with modern customer needs and a move to a more business-oriented market. One of the strengths of the chain has been the consistency of the product. This has been reinforced by the franchise operation of the company which has maintained strict control over buildings, facilities, equipment and operating standards. In fact one criticism leveled at Holiday Inns is that their properties are so similar that it is difficult to know where in the world you are when you wake up in the morning.

Since 1984, however, the renamed Holiday Corporation has been operating a market diversification strategy, which has aimed to develop products targeted more closely to the various types of clientele involved. Holiday Inns remain a three- to four-star hotel chain as before; Crowne Plaza are upmarket luxury hotels responding to the requirements of business clien-

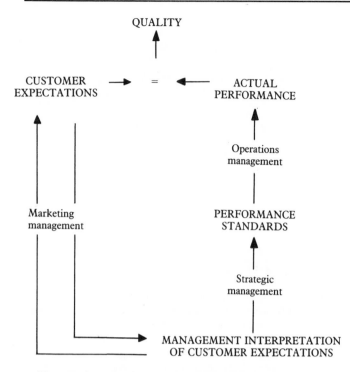

Figure 1 A model of the quality management system.

tele; Hampton Inns are a low budget chain for the traveler; Embassy Suites are all suite hotels designed for longer business stays; and Harrahs are hotels/casinos.

Holiday Inns in Europe have recently introduced a room guarantee to support their international reputation for room standards. This guarantees that the room will be clean; that the heating, ventilation, telephone, television, shower, in fact everything in the room, will work properly. If there is something wrong with the room, notification of the problem will bring prompt action to correct the situation or to move the guest to an alternative room. This example not only demonstrates the importance of quality in ensuring the satisfaction of the guest during their stay but also its role in the marketing of the property.

Benefits

The hotel market is highly competitive, and like any industry which markets a product in a highly competitive market, competing for the consumer's disposable income, it has to be aware of the quality issues. This is especially important to the hotel situation where there is little obvious competition on price, and competition therefore centers on issues of facilities, image, service and the quality of that provision. Hotels have been quick to use quality as a marketing strategy and have themselves fueled higher expectations of the hotel product.

There has also been a recent growth in 'consumerism' generally which has resulted in customers expecting to receive pro-

ducts and services of a higher minimum acceptable level. UK customers have also traveled more widely than ever before, due to package holidays and cheaper transportation, returning with new ideas and new standards regarding hotel provision.

The hotel market is characterized by high levels of repeat business through regular clientele at either the individual or institutional level. This reliance on repeat business and the effects of word of mouth recommendation make quality and the resulting guest satisfaction of paramount importance in maintaining high occupancy levels.

The benefits above have concentrated on the importance of quality to the customer but there is also a role to play in 'internal marketing' to the employees. Many establishments have found that improving the quality image of a hotel has resulted in increased staff commitment and improved levels of performance. It must be recognized that any marketing effort aimed at customers will also influence employee perceptions. Hotels in general, however, have been slow to respond to changes in customer expectations for a number of reasons. Firstly, modification of the hotel product requires a substantial capital investment; secondly, the time involved in renovating a property is lengthy and must be scheduled around periods of slack demand; thirdly, the hoteliers' ability to respond to change is restricted by the physical structure of the hotel itself; and finally, the large amount of mediated demand, that coming through third parties such as travel agents, tour operators or corporate offices, has restricted the direct influence of the customer who, on average, does not stay in the hotel very frequently anyway. There is obviously then much scope for hotels who do respond to the call for quality to make substantial improvements in their market share.

Implementation

The first stage in quality management is to determine the product characteristics that will satisfy the target market. In the hotel industry there has been a tendency to concentrate on those aspects of the operation for which consumer preferences are easy to measure. This has led to an emphasis on the tangible physical aspects of the provision. Even the latest Crown Criteria devised by the English Tourist Board are based on physical criteria. For example, the one crown criteria require a single bed to be of a minimum size of 6ft 3 inches by 3ft but do not make any comment that it should be comfortable. The bathroom requirement is one for every 10 resident guests but little mention is made about its cleanliness or the availability of hot water. There is evidence, however, that customers do not evaluate the quality of their stay in a hotel on this basis. They are more likely to consider such factors as the availability of a service; the smoothness or speed of the response to a request; ease of use; comfortable, pleasant and relaxing surroundings; spaciousness; value for money; the provision of reasonable facilities and adequate choice (Nightingale, 1985).

In fact the hotel product is made up of a combination of tangible and intangible elements relating both to the physical characteristics of the provision and the interpersonal contact

Characteristics of
the experience

	TANGIBLE	INTANGIBLE
PHYSICAL Nature of the contact	The product Facilitating goods Information processes	Atmosphere Esthetics Feelings Comfort
INTERPERSONAL	Actions Process Speed Script Corrective action	Warmth Friendliness Care Service

Figure 2 The quality matrix for hotel provision (adapted from Lockwood and Jones, 1988).

that occurs during the stay. These elements have been combined to form the quality matrix shown in Fig. 2. In designing the hotel product all aspects of this matrix must be considered. It would appear from the matrix that each quadrant is equal in importance but this is not the case. The relative importance of each quadrant is difficult to measure but evidence suggests (Parasuraman *et al.*, 1985; Nightingale, 1985) that the material/ tangible component is more significant than the material/intangible component. From the hotel operator's point of view it is of course also a lot easier to control. On the other hand the interpersonal/intangible component is more significant than the interpersonal/tangible and this is very difficult for the hotel operator to influence.

Market segmentation has major implications for quality management. Each market segment has discrete quality requirements which must be communicated both to the customer and the staff. One advantage of segmentation is that such accommodation can be sold at a premium, for example Holiday Inns' Club Europe rooms or Crest's Lady Crest rooms. At the same time the product should be more closely matched to the specific customer's requirements. However, very few hotels do not have a mix of clientele through weekly and seasonal demand patterns. A hotel designed and aimed at the business customer from Monday to Friday cannot be easily transformed into a weekend retreat for tourists or leisure travelers. The transformation involves not simply a change in the physical attributes of the property but also a change in the attitude and approach of staff to different types of customers.

When the hotel has determined its customers' requirements and has assessed the viability of providing the level of service requested in financial and operational terms, it can then translate these into product specifications. These specifications will include the layout, decor and design of rooms, the furniture and equipment to be provided, the ancillary items such as toiletries, stationery and linen and in a broader context the scale and nature of other hotel services and facilities. These might include the provision of room service, the leisure and recreation facilities, business and office services and so on. In addition, operating procedures must also be devised to determine the way

in which the services are to be provided. This will involve the production of detailed standards of performance manuals, the training of staff and the development of operational systems.

Once the product standards and operating procedures have been determined the manager's job is to ensure the conformance to these standards. There are two basic strategies that can be adopted to ensure conformance – the 'control' strategy and the 'assurance' strategy. The quality control strategy concentrates on the physical/tangible aspects of the provision and therefore is more concerned with what goes on in the back of house. The quality assurance approach is more suited to the interpersonal aspects that take place in the front of house.

The control approach to checking on conformance can monitor both the actual outcomes and the process or working practices employed. Checking on the outputs attempts to measure objectively how actual output has matched up to the predetermined standards. For example the floor housekeepers in a hotel will be responsible for checking every room that a chambermaid cleans before it is 'given back' to reception as ready for sale. At the same time as checking on the output, the housekeeper will be checking on the process. This will involve not only monitoring the technical performance of how the bed is made or how the bath is cleaned but also the behavioral aspects such as smoking on duty or playing the radio in the bedrooms while cleaning. The final stage of the control approach is to 'correct nonstandard output'. This means that if the housekeeper finds a room that is not up to standard, then it will be put right before being occupied by a guest. Any deviations from standard should be investigated so that action can be taken to ensure that the problem does not recur. These failures may be due to poor staff selection, inadequate training, malfunctioning equipment or nonadherence to operating procedures. If there is a persistent failure to meet standards it may be necessary to revise the standard of performance expected in the light of experience.

Whereas the control approach is primarily concerned with the checking and correction of faults, the assurance approach tries to make sure that the faults do not arise in the first place. This is particularly important when there is face to face contact with guests. Any breakdown in a personal interaction is very difficult to put right once it has gone wrong and has a very strong influence on guest satisfaction. Quality assurance is more a matter of management philosophy and style than of systems and procedures. In practice it involves bringing quality to the forefront of management thinking and using the term throughout the operation and through the selection, recruitment, induction, training and treatment of staff. This emphasis then becomes central to the shared value system of the operation where management praise high quality performance; promotion or bonuses are seen to relate to the quality of work done; the physical resources such as tools and equipment and the general working environment in front and back of house are themselves of high quality. It is impossible for the manager to engender a desire for quality if the staff changing rooms are filthy, uniforms are unfashionable and ill-fitting and management do not seem to care about their own timekeeping, appearance and standards. This approach involves not just role modeling from management but the active involvement of employees in the quality process.

One technique for creating an appropriate climate for quality is the quality circle. This is a group of between four and ten volunteers working in the same area who meet on a regular basis for about one hour with their supervisor to identify, analyze and solve their own work-related problems. The reported benefits of quality circles are many. They change attitudes within the organization; staff are better motivated; supervisors gain confidence; problem solving is improved; communications at all levels are improved and there is an emphasis on solving problems, not blaming them on someone else.

Assessment

The final stage in the quality management process is to evaluate the success of the operation in matching the customers's expectations. There are two main approaches to this problem. The first is to monitor in some way the satisfaction level of guests who have used the hotel. The second approach is to use an objective assessment of the unit's performance by an external expert through observation and participation – a quality audit.

Guest satisfaction can be monitored in three main ways: unsolicited compliments or complaints, customer comment cards and customer surveys. Reliance on compliments and complaints is potentially dangerous as it only takes into account those guests that were sufficiently motivated to take action and ignores those that were only moderately satisfied or dissatisfied or who simply did not want to make a fuss. Comment cards have also come in for criticism (Lewis and Pizam, 1982) as being meaningless, unreliable, product dominated and statistically insupportable. A carefully planned customer survey, on the other hand, can provide detailed information about the overall level of guest satisfaction and identify areas where improvements in service may be made. This survey should be approached in the same rigorous way as any marketing research project.

The quality audit process should provide an objective judgment of the hotel's performance. Quality audits can be conducted by consultants external to the operation or by specialist staff within the organization. Once the objectives of the study are established, the auditor must try to adopt the customer's frame of reference and make an assessment for a particular market segment. Information for the audit will be obtained both through the observation of guests experiencing the service and direct participation as a guest. In most cases, to avoid bias, staff will be unaware of the auditor's identity. On completion of the participation period a detailed report of the study will be written and an analysis of the findings made. This report will attempt to identify the key issues affecting the quality performance of the hotel. The report can then form the basis for corrective action.

Conclusion

Quality management is fundamental to the successful operation of hotels. The quality management process can be seen as

determining the customer's requirements for the hotel product, designing a hotel which satisfies these needs, operating the hotel to adhere to established standards of performance and monitoring the resulting level of customer satisfaction. Quality in these terms is very closely related to the marketing of the hotel. The marketing policy of the organization will determine the market segments to be attracted and the market positioning to be adopted. The marketing of the product to the customers will create or modify the customers' expectations from the hotel which must be reflected in the hotel's actual provision to be seen as giving quality.

Focus on small business

All the issues discussed above are applicable to the small business. Small hotels are often seen as operating at higher standards than those of the groups. The Lygon Arms at Broadway, UK, now part of the Savoy group, has always had a reputation for quality, as has the Swan at Lavenham or the Waterside Inn at Bray. The average hotel in the United Kingdom has approximately 25 rooms and is just as likely to offer a quality product as a hotel with 500 or 600 rooms. In fact the small business is in some ways in a better position to give a quality product than the large chains. The manager of a small hotel has more direct contact with the customers and more direct control and influence on the employees and their standards of performance. In addition the small hotel is able to attract a very specific market segment and cater very closely to its needs.

Further reading

British Standards Institute, *British Standard 4778* (BSI, 1979). Good source of definitions of quality related terms, includes a model of the factors influencing service quality.

Czepiel, J. A., Solomon, M. R. and Surprenant, C. F., *The Service Encounter* (Lexington Books, 1985). A fascinating collection of readings on the service encounter. Chapters 1 and 2 make specific reference to quality but almost all have relevance.

English Tourist Board, *Standards for Serviced Accommodation* (ETB, 1986). Full details of the ETB Crown Classification scheme.

Hart, C. W. L. and Casserley, G. D., 'Quality: a brand new time tested strategy', *Cornell HRA Quarterly* (November 1984), pp. 52–63. Uses the case of Ringer Hut, a US restaurant chain, to examine approaches to quality management programs.

Haywood, K. M., 'Assessing the quality of hospitality services', *International Journal of Hospitality Management*, vol. 2, no. 4 (1983), pp. 165–77. A good review of quality management in the hospitality industry; proposes a method for conducting quality audits.

Jones, P., 'The restaurant – a place for quality control and product maintenance', *International Journal of Hospitality Management*, vol. 2, no. 2 (1983), pp. 93–100. Applies a number of quality control techniques to restaurant operations, including Hazard Analysis Critical Control Point.

King, C. A., 'Service oriented quality control', *Cornell HRA Quarterly* (November 1984), pp. 92–8. Converts the manufacturing approach to quality control to the hospitality industry.

Lewis, R. C., 'The measurement of gaps in the quality of hotel services', *International Journal of Hospitality Management*, vol. 6, no. 2 (1987), pp. 83–8. A mathematical approach to identifying gaps in hotel service, based on the Parasuraman model.

Lewis, R. C. and Pizam, A. 'The measurement of guest satisfaction', *The Practice of Hospitality Management*, A. Pizam *et al.*, eds (AVI Publishing Co., 1982), pp. 189–201. Criticizes guest comment cards and suggests a statistically valid approach to customer surveys.

Lockwood, A. J. and Jones, P. L. M., *The Management of Hotel Operations* (Cassell, 1988). Proposes a conceptual model of hotel management with quality as a central issue. Chapter 9 gives an indepth review of the problems and approaches.

Martin, W. B., 'Measuring and improving your service quality', *Cornell HRA Quarterly* (May 1986), pp. 80–7. Suggests ways of improving the procedural and convivial dimensions of service.

Merricks, A. P. M. and Jones, P. L. M., *The Management of Catering Operations* (Holt, Rinehart and Winston, 1986). Chapters 5 and 6 are concerned with product and service quality respectively.

Nightingale, M., *Determination and Control of Quality in Hospitality Services*, MPhil. Thesis (University of Surrey, 1983). An authoritative review of the literature on quality; provides interesting insights into customer perceptions of hotels.

Nightingale, M., 'The hospitality industry: defining quality for a quality assurance programme – a study of perceptions', *Service Industries Journal*, vol. 5, no. 1 (1985), pp. 9–22. Provides a conceptual framework for looking at quality in the hospitality industry based on his MPhil thesis.

Nightingale, M., *Managing Standards of Service* (HCTB, 1987). An open learning text giving a detailed method of analysis of standards of service in an organization.

Parasuraman, A., Zeithaml, V. A. and Berry, L. L., 'A conceptual model of service quality and its implications for future research', *Journal of Marketing*, vol. 49 (Fall 1985), pp. 41–50. Describes a model of quality as a series of gaps between expectations and outputs and identifies a series of determinants of service quality.

Robson, M., *Quality Circles – A Practical Guide* (Gower, 1983). As the title suggests a practical approach to using quality circles primarily in a manufacturing context.

Sasser, W. E., Olsen, R. P. and Wychoff, D. D., *Management of Service Operations* (Allyn and Bacon, 1978). One of the few texts on service operations with many case histories of relevance to quality.

Voss, C., Armistead, C., Johnston, B. *et al.*, *Operations Management in Service Industries and the Public Sector* (John Wiley, 1985). Chapter 6 takes a primarily operations perspective on quality management.

Willborn, W., 'Quality assurance audits and hotel management', *Service Industries Journal*, vol. 6, no. 3 (1986), pp. 293–308. A detailed review of approaches to and principles of quality audits.

Wyckoff, D. D., 'New tools for achieving service quality', *Cornell HRA Quarterly* (November 1984), pp. 78–91. Adopts a quality assurance perspective on service operations.

ANDREW LOCKWOOD

Rate of return analysis

Introduction

The two methods of evaluating the desirability of capital projects considered conceptually most sound are the net present value (NPV) and internal rate of return (IRR). The average rate of return (ARR) and the payback-period methods are two other techniques used. These two methods are simple to interpret and calculate, but, apart from other deficiencies, they both fail to address the time value of the relevant cashflows, a major factor to consider when long-term investments are being evaluated.

Most of the capital budgeting problems and concepts used in textbooks address situations in which the initial capital investment is provided, 100 per cent, through equity financing. As a result, discounted cashflow models rarely incorporate debt financial and the related debt servicing factor. When preparing financial feasibility studies for tourist-related facilities, and the financing package comprises debt and equity, difficulties are thus often encountered in distinguishing the project's net cash benefits and/or losses from the net cashflows associated with the project.

The conceptual framework for computing the IRR is as follows:

At time period zero there is an initial investment in the form of one or more cash outflows. Over the life of the project, there is a series of cash inflows and outflows which are netted out to produce net cash inflows or outflows. The IRR analysis is conceptualized as finding an interest rate at which these net flows can be discounted so that the sum of their present values equates with the initial investment made in time period zero. This rate, the IRR, will produce a net present value of zero. Salvage values, including working capital, are treated as cash inflows at the end of the project's life. Another way of looking at these salvage values is to consider their present values as discounts on the initial investment received at the end of the project's life.

This conceptual framework works well when the initial investment is financed totally with equity. However, when debt is introduced into the financing package, issues arise that present conceptual difficulties in the computation of IRR. The major conceptual problem is to determine the cashflows that must be discounted. The following more appropriately defines the problem:

When debt is introduced into the financing package, the question of debt servicing emerges. There are two elements in the amounts expended to service the debt: principal repayments and interest charges. Should both these elements or some part of them be included to compute the net cashflow to be discounted to determine the IRR, seeing that they can be associated directly with a particular project? Or should they be excluded totally from the analysis? What conceptual framework must this decision be within?

Most textbooks recommend four basic steps for the analysis of capital expenditures using internal rate of return:

1. Determine the initial net cash investment required.
2. Determine the net annual after-tax cash benefits.
3. Calculate the rate of return of the after-tax cash benefits on the initial net investment.
4. Compare the rate of return with the after-tax cost of capital.

The shortcoming of this approach is that no distinction is made between project-related *net cash flows* and *net cash benefits*. Obviously, since most texts that address the subject of capital budgeting, explicitly or implicitly, assume one hundred per cent equity financing, the issue seldom arises. Whenever it arises, as it often does in the preparation of financial feasibility studies for tourist-related projects, discounted cashflow techniques are rarely requested.

In this chapter we argue that there is a subtle but critical distinction between net cashflows and net cash benefits as these relate to any particular project. Unless this distinction is formally noted and treated appropriately in discounted cashflow models, students and practitioners will find it confusing to calculate the IRR of proposed capital projects. First, we make the distinction between net cashflows and net cash benefits. Next a concise and general formula is presented that can be used for all discounted cashflow models, regardless of the financing selected. Finally, the use of this formula is illustrated in assisting users to avoid the conceptual pitfalls in selecting the correct cashflows to be used in computing IRR.

Reformulation of formulae

The general formula used to calculate the after-tax net cash flows is:

> Revenues – Operating expenses – Fixed charges (which include depreciation and interest on initial debt financing) – Income taxes + Depreciation – Principal repayments

In this formula, depreciation is added once and deducted once. It is deducted before income taxes are calculated so that it could reduce taxable income and, consequently, income taxes. This process indicates that depreciation does not matter in the analysis, except for the tax-savings it produces. In government-sponsored projects and in projects where the government extends tax holidays to private developers, depreciation is excluded totally from the analysis. Both interest on debt and the repayment of principal are deducted to arrive at the net cashflow generated during any particular period.

An alternate expression of the after-tax cashflow formula is:

> Revenues – Operating expenses – Fixed charges (which exclude depreciation but includes interest on initial debt financing) – Income Taxes + Tax-savings from depreciation – Principal repayments

In the second formula depreciation is excluded totally from the calculation of net cashflows. It does not belong in the analysis for two reasons:

1. It does not involve a cash outflow.
2. To deduct depreciation and the initial investment would be to count the same item twice.

Only the tax-savings from depreciation matter, and these can be calculated simply by multiplying the depreciation by the marginal tax rate.

In both formulae shown above, principal repayment and its related interest are deducted from revenues to obtain after-tax net cashflows. Interest is deducted before income taxes are calculated because it is tax-deductible and principal repayment after income taxes because it is non tax-deductible.

Principal repayments and their related interest charges are the two elements of debt servicing. They will affect net cashflows, but will not influence net cash benefits in the same manner. Here the crucial distinction arises: Net cashflows comprise all of the project-related cashflows, including those for debt servicing, while net cash benefits are affected by debt servicing cashflows only to the extent that income tax effects are involved. Another way of presenting this view is to say that the net cash benefits of a project are independent of its mode of financing. They are affected only to the extent that a particular financing method affects the income taxes payable. Net cash benefits accrue as a result of the project's operational performance and not because of the choice of financing. Net cash benefit can be regarded as directly accruing to the project, while it is not as easy to associate net cashflow directly with the project. To be more specific, if the project is aborted, the flow of cash benefits will be stemmed; however, its debt servicing cashflows will still have to be maintained, except in case of bankruptcy.

With this distinction firmly established, one can present a more succinct formula for the calculation of net cash benefits, regardless of the financing option selected for the initial investment:

> Revenues – Operating expenses – Fixed charges (which exclude depreciation and interest charges) – Income taxes + Marginal tax rate × (depreciation + interest).

In this formula debt servicing cash outflows and depreciation are completely omitted from the determination of net cash benefits. Attention is focused on the cash revenues and/or savings (taxes or otherwise) accruing to the project and the cash expenses it incurs due to its existence. Only the germane elements are dealt with.

Example

A hotel wishes to purchase two buses to be used for transporting guests to and from the airport. At present, it uses the service of an independent tour company which charges a flat fee of $22,500 annually. The hotel can purchase the two buses for $40,000. It has two options for raising the required funds: it can reduce its current account which has enough available cash, or it can borrow the money on a 5-year chattel 12 per cent mortgage. The mortgage is to be repaid yearly in equal instalments which comprise principal repayment and interest charges. Depreciation will be calculated on a straight-line basis over the vehicles' estimated 5-year life. It is assumed that salvage at the end of the vehicles' 5-year life will be $4,000. Operating cost is expected to be $12,000 annually. Assume a capital cost of 9 per cent.

Figures 1 and 2 present two solutions to the problem. In Fig. 1, financing is through 100 per cent debt, and in Fig. 2 the investment requirement is obtained completely by equity. Each analysis returns different net cash benefits, net cashflows and IRRs. Their similarities are based on the use of the general formula outlined above to compute the project's IRR:

1. Both exclude depreciation, interest, and principal repayments from the computation of net cash benefits.
2. Both include applicable tax-savings in the determination of net cash benefits.
3. In the computation of IRR, both disregard net annual cashflows.

The analysis has brought out two other important points. The first is that when debt financing, rather than equity financing, is used for a project, there is a tendency for the project to produce a higher IRR, as is evident from Figs 1 and 2. Normally, debt financing, because of its tax-savings, produces a lower capital cost than equity financing.

The other important consideration is this: if the net cashflow does not matter in the computation of the IRR, why then is it necessary to calculate it? The two examples illustrated have been sensitized to produce an answer to this question. Using IRR as the sole criterion for evaluation, Fig. 1 indicates that the project is expected to be profitable, while Fig. 2 shows that it is

Data section

Initial investment (cost of two vehicles):	$40,000
Estimated life	5 years
Salvage value.................................	$4,000
Annual operating expenses................	$12,000
Annual tour company's charge	$22,500
Chattel mortgage............................	$40,000
Mortgage interest	12 %
Mortgage term................................	5 years
Cost of capital	9 %
Income tax rate	35 %
Annual depreciation	$7,200

Answer section

5-year mortgage repayment schedule

Year	Total repayment ($)	Principal ($)	Interest ($)	Balance ($)
0				40,000
1	11,096	6,296	4,800	33,704
2	11,096	7,052	4,044	26,652
3	11,096	7,898	3,198	18,753
4	11,096	8,846	2,250	9,907
5	11,096	9,907	1,189	0

	Year					
	1	2	3	4	5	Total
Annual cost savings ($)	22,500	22,500	22,500	22,500	22,500	112,500
Less: annual operating costs ($)	12,000	12,000	12,000	12,000	12,000	60,000
Annual savings before tax-effects ($)	10,500	10,500	10,500	10,500	10,500	52,500
Less income taxes ($)	(3,675)	(3,675)	(3,675)	(3,675)	(3,675)	(18,375)
Add: tax-savings on interest ($)	1,680	1,416	1,119	788	416	5,419
Add: tax-savings on depreciation ($)	2,520	2,520	2,520	2,520	2,520	12,600
Add: salvage value ($)					4,000	4,000
Net cash benefits ($)	11,025	10,761	10,464	10,133	13,761	56,144
Less: annual debt service ($)	11,096	11,096	11,096	11,096	11,096	55,482
Net annual cash flow ($)	(71)	(336)	(632)	(964)	(2,665)	(662)
Internal rate of return	12.00%					

Figure 1 IRR computation (full debt financing).

Data section

Initial investment (cost of two vehicles):	$40,000
Estimated life.................................	5 years
Salvage value	$4,000
Annual operating expenses	$12,000
Annual tour company's charge...........	$22,500
Cost of capital	9%
Income tax rate	35%
Annual depreciation	$7,200

Answer section

	Year					
	1	2	3	4	5	Total
Annual cost savings ($)	22,500	22,500	22,500	22,500	22,500	112,500
Less: annual operating costs ($)	12,000	12,000	12,000	12,000	12,000	60,000
Annual savings before tax-effects ($)	10,500	10,500	10,500	10,500	10,500	52,500
Less income taxes ($)	(3,675)	(3,675)	(3,675)	(3,675)	(3,675)	(18,375)
Add: tax-savings on depreciation ($)	2,520	2,520	2,520	2,520	2,520	12,600
Add: salvage value ($)					4,000	4,000
Net cash benefits ($)	9,345	9,345	9,345	9,345	13,345	50,725
Net annual cash flow ($)	9,345	9,345	9,345	9,345	13,345	50,725
Internal rate of return	8.00 %					

Figure 2 IRR computation (full equity financing).

not expected to be financially viable. Both these decisions were obtained by comparing the IRR with the company's 9 per cent cost of capital. However, an investment proposal is evaluated not only on the basis of its profitability, but also on its debt servicing capacity. If both these yardsticks were applied to arrive at an accept/reject decision, both projects might be rejected. Under the debt-financing option (Fig. 1) the project appears profitable, but its capacity to generate adequate debt-servicing cashflows is precarious. When full equity financing is used, the situation is reversed – unprofitability is combined with good net cashflow generating potential. The results will show similar patterns if any combination of debt/equity financing arrangement is used.

Conclusion

Discounted cashflow methods, which include IRR, are the only theoretically sound techniques currently available for evaluating capital budgeting projects. With the advent of spreadsheet computer programs and pocket calculators with built-in financial functions, a significant amount of tedious work has been eliminated from the task of calculating a project's estimated IRR. Nevertheless, computers and calculators will process only what has been put into them. The dependability of the output and the reasonableness of the decision depend on the accuracy and validity of the input. These, in turn, depend on the analyst's ability to understand and apply relevant concepts correctly. This chapter has argued that one such problematic concept is the distinction between a project's net cash benefits and its net cashflows in discounted cashflow analyses, particularly IRR. It has made this critical distinction showing, conceptually, that interest on debt, depreciation, and principal repayments are irrelevant to the analysis, except for their income-tax effect. Consequently, it has argued that these items should be excluded from discounted cashflow models and replaced by the tax-savings on interest and depreciation. By using this general formula, it has been illustrated how the computation of IRR could be simplified regardless of the financing option selected.

Futher reading

Brigham, E. and Weston, F. J., *Essentials of Managerial Finance* (Dryden Press, 7th edition, 1985), pp. 352–5.

Coffman, D. C., *Marketing for a Full House, A Complete Guide to Profitable Hotel/Motel Operational Planning* (Cayuga Press of Ithaca, 8th edition, 1983), pp. 89–100.

Coltman, M., *Financial Management for the Hospitality Industry* (Van Nostrand Reinhold, 1979), pp. 176–87.

Hodgson, J. N., 'The feasibility study – determining the investment potential of a new hotel', *Cornell HRA Quarterly*, vol. 14, no. 3 (November 1973), pp. 9–30.

Lumby, S., *Investment Appraisal and Related Decisions* (Van Nostrand Reinhold (UK), 2nd edition, 1981), pp. 41–62.

RON BRATHWAITE and
AINSLEY O'REILLY

Recent developments in tourism research and education at the university level

Research applied to tourism started about 50 years ago. The pioneering work of Professor Glücksmann, Berlin was continued by two important publications: *Allgemeine Fremdenverkehrslehre* (*General theory of tourism*) by Professors Walter Hunziker and Kurt Krapf (St Gall and Berne); *Grundlagenlehre des Fremdenverkehrs* (*Basic theory of tourism*), by Professor Paul Bernecker (Vienna). As leading thinkers and strategists of the theoretical body of knowledge on 'Tourism', these three researchers subsequently induced a large number of colleagues from other disciplines such as sociology, psychology, geography and medicine, as well as established and junior exponents of tourism economics, to investigate and elucidate the tourism phenomenon. Furthermore, the International Association of Scientific Experts in Tourism (AIEST) has assumed the important role of a catalyst and initiator of numerous studies and therefore contributed substantially to the present state of research in tourism.

Out of the initial 10 years (1950–1960) of scientific efforts in the community of the AIEST tourism experts, it became clear that an extension of the research horizon, in the sense of interdisciplinary endeavors, was imperative. Questions such as space allocation and planning, carrying capacity of natural resources and strain caused by tourism ('ecology of tourism') and the complex aspects of human motivation and behavior related to tourism could be tackled due to the cooperation of geographers and social scientists. Researchers emphasized empirical and pragmatic approaches when studying these subjects. For the first time, the tenth congress of AIEST, which took place in Auvergne, France, in 1959, was not dedicated to a purely economic topic, but to space allocation in tourism in the context of regional development. Similarly, later congresses not only allowed for theoretical discussion, but fostered an application-centered dialog on a scientific level, underpinned by practical examples. Applied research was also the core interest of tourism research institutes, because tourism developed vigorously and practioners increasingly called for science-based assistance.

Owing to the strong practical emphasis of research in tourism and the fact that support for applied research often seems more forthcoming, fundamental research cannot always be realized to a desirable extent. Very often, the results of basic disciplines have to be examined in the light of their applicability to the tourist sector. Examples are the application of marketing to tourist businesses and the effects of planning and action, in the

tourist sector, with an ecological orientation. In some cases timelags have occurred between results of basic research and application to tourism.

The translation of methods from natural sciences to tourism has led to only very limited insights. An example is the carrying capacity of recreational space. Researchers tried for a long time to synthesize ecological and physical concepts with sociopsychological concepts (e.g. Bezzola, 1975 and Krippendorf, 1977). The efforts to elaborate a reasonable framework of quantified criteria for strain foundered, mainly due to the differences in possible operationalizations of constructs: in the domain of physical and ecological variables a relatively high level of operationalization and precision was attainable, in contrast to the sociopsychological domain, where subjective values, needs and behaviors prevail. There was imminent danger of apparent, yet meaningless or even wrong concepts being put into practice and the efforts were finally abandoned.

Nevertheless, the extensive work done in 'Man and Biosphere (MAB)', an integral and interdisciplinary research program by UNESCO, has generated interesting results concerning socioeconomic developments and ecological perspectives for mountain regions (see Brugger *et al.*, 1984). A comprehensive effort was made to model the interrelationships between cultural and socioeconomic systems and their natural environments and to study their long-term dynamic interaction. The results were presented in different scenarios for future tourist development, whereby ecological variables turned out to be crucial restrictions (cf. Krippendorf *et al.*, 1987). The MAB project is based on the systems perspective, which has the following advantages:

1. Integral thinking.
2. Process orientation.
3. A combination of analysis and synthesis.
4. Inclusion of feedback and iterations.
5. Interdisciplinary work.

One of the conclusions, which seems particularly interesting, was made by the MAB researchers, in the context of their study made in Grindelwald, a Swiss tourist resort: 'We have abandoned the claim for a closed, dynamic system, which would include the regulation of the anthropological and the ecological systems at the same time. The Grindelwald model is essentially an economic simulation model. Its endogenous dynamics are driven by investment behavior and its overall dynamics mainly determined by the exogenous tourist demand' (Apel, 1983).

Similar problems of quantification arose when cost–benefit analysis was applied to tourism. That method opens the door to subjectivity, for example when opportunity costs have to be quantified. At this point, the eminent relevance of socio-empirical research must be emphasized. An outstanding example for the German speaking countries is the Study Circle for Tourism (Studienkreis für Tourismus) in Starnberg, West Germany.

In an important contribution, Professor Mazanec, the director of the Viennese Institute of Tourism Research, pleaded for a reinforcement of empirical research in the domains of consumer behavior, conceptions of life, elements of personality, leisure and recreation (Mazanec, 1981). In his paper, Mazanec shows that preferences, lifestyles and patterns of behavior are potential constraints to the growth of leisure tourism. Consequently, the Viennese Institute is particularly dedicated to empirical research, which is a useful and important complement to the interests of the other Institutes. The authors is in full accordance with the claim of his colleagues (Ender *et al.*, 1983): openness toward neighbor disciplines of the social sciences is not grounded in esoteric curiosity or even desertion, but in the quest for an improved potential to solve real-world problems. Research in consumer behavior in the context of tourism research can, for example, be very relevant for the design of marketing strategies. As in other domains of knowledge, however, interdisciplinarity in tourism research is a difficult issue, although systems theory and system-oriented methodology facilitate multidisciplinary approaches to problem-solving (see, for example, Checkland, 1981).

A theoretical image of reality can basically be gained in three ways: by reductionist, holistic or systemic approaches (Kühne, 1982). Reductionism dissects a whole into single objects, as substantially closed, isolated units. The focus is on elements, not on interrelationships, and, if so, on few only. In economics, reductionist approaches are still the dominant mode of research. Holism in its radical form, represents the contrary: it regards wholes as nonseparable and therefore, nonanalyzable.

As Kühne (1982) formulated it, these limitations are sufficient to abandon both approaches and to search for a perspective, which enables one to grasp the peculiarities of the whole and the specific properties of the parts at the same time: 'A system is an open whole with relations between parts and with organization'. This definition includes five components: openness, whole, parts, relations and organization.

In the theoretical work of Kaspar (1986), he elaborated on a systems view of tourism. This perspective enables, and even cogently demands, the abandonment of one-dimensional thinking and the adoption of a multi-dimensional approach to tourism problems. As the tourism system is embedded into superordinate systems – economic, social, technological, political and ecological environments – a multidisciplinary perspective is imperative. The marked dynamics in the evolution of tourism, reflected in the emergence of new terms (for example 'soft tourism'), can adequately be grasped by the idea of an 'open system'. 'Open' means 'subject to environmental influences' and, at the same time, 'affecting the environment'.

Tourism subject and tourism object are component parts of the 'tourism system' as a whole. Interrelationships inside and outside the system fulfil a function of integration. Endogenous and exogenous factors disturbing the economic equilibrium have led to a tourism policy, which is increasingly shaped by governmental activities. In the market economies, the states have conceived their engagement as 'help for self-help' and hitherto left enough space for private initiative. Management and its improvement by means of scientific efforts continue to be important. For example, planning must be improved, not to become a rigid maxim, but to become an instrument of management to further the intelligence of organizations (Gaelweiler, 1987 and the chapter on *Strategic Management in Tourism*, p. 425).

The challenge for tourism research is to avoid simplistic models on the one hand and imbalances between the whole and its parts, on the other. As mentioned above, systems thinking implies the inclusion of multiple disciplines. The simple fact, that the academic Institutes of Tourism Research in German-speaking countries are mainly oriented toward economic research, demonstrates that interdisciplinarity is an ideal, difficult to achieve (see, for example, Krippendorf, 1988).

Contemporary research in tourism must be endowed with openness, both in the substantive, as well as in the methodological sense. To cope with the complexity inherent in the object of tourism research, closer cooperation and a continuous dialog across the borders of established disciplines will be imperative. At the same time, Ex-Minister Rudolf Eberhard's reminder, that practical problems must be the cardinal point of scientific research, which no researcher may neglect, should not be overlooked. 'Neither side should impose its viewpoint on the other; the one and only issue is complement each other' (Eberhard, 1969). An emphasis on complementarity has always been made in the work at the Tourism Research Institutes in German-speaking countries – Vienna, Munich, Berne, St Gall, Innsbruck. Furthermore, complementarity of theory and practice is vital. Practice-oriented research has been strengthened in the last few years.

In reviewing tourism research over 25 years, Kaspar stated with satisfaction that a development from a one-sided, economic approach toward a multidisciplinary one had taken place (Kaspar, 1975). At the same time, he remarked that one branch of research in tourism lagged behind the mainstream: management applied to tourist businesses. This is unfortunate, because such research is eminently important for the prosperity of the firms which constitute the tourist sector.

The dazzling increase of tourism – a manifestation of growing numbers of citizens who travel year by year – demands an appropriate structure to cope with these temporary mass-migrations. The emergence of tourism-oriented organizations, such as hotels, travel agencies and tourist offices, many of which have surpassed local, regional and even national and continental boundaries, presented new challenges for management.

The issues of management are numerous: human resources, finance, planning, organization and marketing are only some of the key areas of interest. The Institute of Tourism at the University of St Gall has made intensive and consistent efforts to cope with these challenges. Several publications on management issues have appeared (see particularly Kaspar and Kunz, 1982 and other volumes of the series 'St. Galler Beiträge zum Fremdenverkehr und zur Verkehrswirtschaft', 1982–1988). Fortunately, practice and theory have also become closer in the management domain of tourism research. Newer publications have applied valuable concepts in order to improve strategic management in tourism. A symposium recently held at the University of St Gall dealt with the issue 'Strategic potential for success: basis for effective management in tourism'. The conference closed with the conclusion, that further exploration of the approach of strategic potential for success presupposes further research as well as practice-oriented seminars (IFV, 1984).

The research activities outlined in this chapter are closely connected with education at the university level. Based on the European principle of the unity of teaching and research, members of the teaching faculty are at the same time directors of research institutes. This is the typical European model, but numerous American examples confirm the appropriateness of the connection.

Studies in tourism are highly practice-oriented. Involvement of faculty in dealing with the manifold problems in the real world of tourism enriches the educational process. The infrastructure of a research institute is a necessary prerequisite for the provision of advanced modes of learning, for example through case-studies, empirical research and bibliographical inquiries. Study programs in tourism, integrated into a comprehensive scientific education, are provided by the following European Universities: Surrey, Strathclyde, Swansea and Bradford (UK), Aix-en-Provence and Grenoble (France), Vienna and Innsbruck (Austria), Milan and Naples (Italy), Berne and St Gall (Switzerland).

Further reading

Apel, H., *Das dynamische Simulationsmodell Grindelwald*, MAB Information, no. 19 (University of Berne, 1983).

Bezzola, A., *Probleme der Eignung und Aufnahmekapazität touristischer Bergregionen in der Schweiz* (Haupt, 1975).

Brugger, E. A., Furrer, G., Messerli, B. *et al.*, eds, *The Transformation of Swiss Mountain Regions. Problems of Development between Self-Reliance and Dependency in an Economic and Ecological Perspective* (Haupt, 1984).

Checkland, P., *Systems Thinking, Systems Practice* (John Wiley, 1981).

Eberhard, R., *Aktuelle Fragen des deutschen Fremdenverkehrs* (Duncker & Humblot, 1969).

Ender, W., Fuhri, R., Mazanec, J. *et al.*, 'Von der Hotelbetriebslehre zur Management-Science des Tourismus? Zeitgemässe Aufgaben einer Betriebswirtschaftslehre des Fremdenverkehrs', *Der Markt*, no. 1 (1983), p. 41.

Gäelweiler, A., *Strategische Unternehmensführung* (Campus, 1987).

Institut für Fremdenverkehr und Verkehrswirtschaft an der Hochschule St Gallen, 'Strategische Erfolgspositionen – Grundlage wirkungsvoller Unternehmungsführung in Verkehr and Fremdenverkehr', *Instituts-Mitteilungen*, no. 36 (1984), p. 41.

Kaspar, C., *Le bilan des derniers 25 ans de la Recherche Touristique*, AIEST, eds (Gurtenverlag, 1975), pp. 1–4.

Kaspar, C., *Die Fremdenverkehrslehre im Grundriss* (Haupt, 3rd edition, 1986).

Kaspar, C. and Kunz, B., *Unternehmungsführung im Fremdenverkehr* (Haupt, 1982).

Krippendorf, J., 'Kritische Beurteilung bisheriger methodischer Ansätze zur Bestimmung der Belastbarkeit von Erholungslandschaften – Praktisches Beispiel für die Berücksichtigung von Belastungskriterien in der touristischen Planung, *The Tourist Review*, no. 1 (1977), p. 2.

Krippendorf, J. and Müller, H. R., *La-Haut sur la Montagne. Pour un Développement du Tourisme en Harmonie avec l'Homme et la Nature* (Kümmerly und Frey, 1987).

Krippendorf, J., *The Holiday Makers* (Heinemann, 1988).

Kühne, K., *Evolutionsökonomie* (Fischer Verlag, 1982).

Mazanec, J., 'The tourism/leisure ratio. Anticipating the limits to growth', *The Tourist Review*, no. 4, (1981), p. 2.

CLAUDE KASPAR

Resort development

Introduction

With the combination of leisure facilities, accommodation and business facilities, tourist resorts are blossoming in developed as well as developing countries. Resorts are set up within virgin sites or in established villages or cities. Their size varies from a few hundreds to tens of thousands of beds, in the form of, for example, hotels, hotel-apartments, second homes, villas and campgrounds. Funding can be public, private or a combination of both.

A resort's birth may result from the initiative of a conveyor: for example, the Canadian Pacific Railway created 'chalets' in the Rockies around 1900, and later developed them into luxurious 500 – room hotels which still flourish today (e.g. Banff and Lake Louise). The creation of a resort may also result from local initiatives, or correspond to a side-effect of large projects (development of a marina on a dam lake, as in Page, Arizona, on the banks of Lake Powell). It is usually assumed that the tourist should be busy with some activity, therefore another condition of establishing a resort is to fashion it around an activity. In the nineteenth century, the wealthy might have enjoyed thermal springs; since 1930 they may have taken skiing holidays.

Behavioral and social attitudes may change over the years, making formerly thriving resorts less popular. Owing to a change in the attitude toward water and also to a reduction of the relative price of transport, European tourists abandoned, in favor of sunnier coasts, a number of seaside resorts on the English Channel or the North Sea. One of the most difficult problems which developers may encounter today is the resuscitation of these charming old places. At present, the most attractive features generating a need for lodging on the spot are, in order of decreasing importance:

1. Aquatic and nautical activities (mostly in warm waters under sunny skies).
2. Mountain skiing.
3. Thermal springs or spas.

One of the key problems in establishing a resort remains the accessibility to it. It is so important that it is sometimes suggested that resorts should not be developed where the natural conditions are best, but where the clients are, which could lead to consideration of artificial reproduction of natural elements.

The exceptional quality of a site may, nevertheless, counter persistent access difficulties, as in the case of Val d'Isère, a top class ski resort located in the French Alps. There, there are 1.5 million skier-days over a 5-month season. When the snowfields were 'discovered' around 1930, by the fringe of Paris high society, the village (situated at an altitude of 1850 m) housed no more than 250 inhabitants, completely lacking public utilities. In 1987, the community had grown to 1,600 residents, roughly 100 retail businesses and 21,000 beds. The resort employs 1,500 salaried personnel, of which one third are employed all the year round. The lodging capacity is increasing at the rate of 8 per cent per year and the condominiums sell for US$2,500– 3,200 per inhabitable square meter. Managing three cable cars, three gondolas and fifty chair- and ski-lifts, the 'Société des Téléphériques de Val d'Isère' makes a good profit, with a net income to revenue ratio of 12 per cent. It has been able to finance 80 per cent of the 'snow-funicular', a US$10 million investment which was set in operation at the end of 1987. In addition to new improvements in accessibility (to the resort itself and to the snowfields) which are under way today, Val d'Isère plans to give its center an urban quality, and to increase the summer activity through the development of entertainment and specific products. Another subject of concern, without remedy until now, is the relative reduction in importance of hotels, which now represent only 11 per cent of the lodging capacity.

The Val d'Isère case clearly shows the benefits of a tourist development: multiplication of jobs and revenues, improvement of the roads and public services, demographic boost, revaluation of the residents' properties. Yet, at what price are the benefits gained? Huge investments must be taken on a long-term basis: it is assumed in France that the creation of one job related to mountain skiing corresponds to an investment worth US$150,000–200,000 in lodgings and equipment. On the other hand, developments based on secondary housing have increased the lodging volume five- to tenfold, thus overcrowding the landscape and increasing the probability of damage to the environment. In Vail, Colorado, individual firecamps had to be banned on weekends to prevent air pollution. If one adds to this picture that, due to a lack of professional training, the host population often occupies only seasonal jobs which are poorly paid and have no prospect of promotion, it is easy to understand that some communities, seeing their culture and their land degraded, may end up with an attitude of hostility against tourism and tourists, particularly in developing countries.

Once clearly aware that the resort constitutes a major enterprise for the community, there is a necessity to control all the resulting changes over the natural and human host environment. An honest process, analyzing thoroughly the costs and benefits for the host community, will therefore give evidence of a will to preserve nature's splendor and a prime concern to increase the community's welfare and wealth, rather than a desire only to maximize tourist spending. This implies an emphasis on synergism with the surroundings, in order to increase the benefits for the community given by income and employment multipliers.

Marketing and management

A resort's development takes place over a certain time. A thorough knowledge of the site's resources, and a careful study of the generating markets (present situation and long-term tendencies) are required in order to determine a range of varied products, compatible with one another and, if possible, complementary. Even if the main focus is on tourist stays, the market studies should not neglect the subsidiary demands which may contribute to stretching the periods of use (weekends, daytrips, training sessions etc.). The market shares liable to be captured depend on the one hand on the attractions available (quality, capacity) and, on the other hand, on the situation compared to rival resorts (accessibility, pricing levels).

The conceptual planning phase is intended to build on the experiences of this first study by identifying the following:

1. The project's aims and objectives.
2. The strengths or resources to be developed.
3. The equipment to be created.
4. The social and environmental implications.
5. The means to remedy the wrong effects.
6. The main lines of economic costs and returns.
7. Possibly, the aid (financial or other) to be granted by governments.

The achievement of a broad agreement over the global planning is a preliminary to the launching of expensive feasibility studies intended to specify and validate all of the quantitative data. These studies, necessary for the release of exterior financial support, are a first draft of the execution programs.

The government's role in the process may be extremely reduced and limited to the delivery of building authorizations. Thus, for example in North America and New Zealand, ski resorts or marinas are entirely financed (service roads included) through groups which own the property and manage the resorts. The intervention of public funds depends on the following:

1. The existence of a general political policy of aid for development.
2. The capacity for initiative of the regions or localities.
3. The fact that specialized investors create competition between the potential host communities.

Whatever the financing conditions, the developers must consider a certain number of thresholds determined by: the natural context (capacity of beaches, climatic conditions etc.), the state of equipment, and the economic conditions ruling the various businesses. In most cases, these thresholds may be overrun through an increase in expenditures, for example, a beach may be enlarged (as in Palma de Majorca), a delicate natural landscape may host a larger tourist population if it is properly protected and maintained. The most serious constraints result from climatic conditions which decide the season of a product. Keeping the facility open out of season sets a difficult problem of adjustment, because the number of the services needed to attract clients may risk economic losses due to low demand.

The existence of differentiated return thresholds for the different activities included in the resort's life emphasizes a specific characteristic of resort management. It is thus necessary to motivate, toward a unique objective, a set of professionnals whose mentalities, capacities and perspectives are essentially heterogeneous. The requirement of a positive attitude toward both the client and cost control requires a constructive association of individual and responsible partners. In particular, the daily success of human resources management generates the most delicate and most significant product on which a resort depends: its atmosphere.

Drawing on the image which acts as a means of commercial communication, the atmosphere must adjust to a market segment with a touch of originality. Too general an image, such as 'skiing in the sun', is ineffective because this situation is found in lots of places. It is far more efficient to offer, as Val d'Isère does. 'J.-C. Killy's resort': it implies a strong sports oriented inclination, as well as the possibility to actually meet there the star of a generation.

The reduction to an oversimplified image, which mass communication tends to impose, is not without danger for management or client. It is interesting to note that complex parties such as families, where tastes and aptitudes are diverse, when not opposed, feel inclined at the same time toward sports, cultural life, shopping and gastronomy. The urban diversification which this implies, requires a richer image. Another problem is that a strong image and an excellent reputation gained during a given season do not constitute a capital sufficient to guarantee success during another period of the year. For example, when the tourist office and several hotel managers of Saint-Tropez, the well known resort of southern France, decided to open during winter and launched a radio campaign in 1981–1982, they received approximately 40 information calls which were not followed up.

The management and promotion of a resort's image is the role of the tourist office. In order to avoid any mixing of roles, it is better to limit the tourist office's activity to the field of information. This is, by itself, a demanding brief, since it includes: the collection of all data relevant to the resort's life, the advertising and direct information to clients, and a permanent survey of the clients' opinions. The information must be precise and correct. The reliability of the received information is, for the client, a major pointer of the service quality. Conversely, a striking picture of the clients' reactions is a valuable incentive to professionnals.

Benefits

The economic benefits are direct, indirect or induced. The first type corresponds to tourists' purchases in the area, the second to purchases by tourism-related enterprises, and the latter to purchases by employees or local governments (if their incomes derive from tourism).

Another approach is to consider tourist spending as generating two sorts of revenue, according to the benefit to residents or nonresidents. The first step toward resort development may be to encourage direct benefits, but the key problem is to ensure the long-term maximization of indirect and induced benefits to the local community. As benefits are both economic and non-economic equal attention should be devoted to nonmonetary effects concerning public utilities, education, culture, and so on.

Implementation

Identification of tourist resources

There are two processes in identifying the sort of tourist development suitable for a site: the conclusion drawn from the existing practices, and the analogy with similar sites. Even if a group interested in a particular type of tourism is paying for the studies, it is essential to conduct open research covering the main markets of contemporary tourism. In the case of government-paid studies, political considerations should not impede an objective assessment of the value of available or potential attractions.

A survey of a site's resources mainly concerns the following:

1. Tourist attractions.
2. Climatic conditions.
3. Infrastructure and facilities.
4. Land reserves.
5. Labor availability.

The survey is completed with consideration of various qualitative elements: urban or rural quality, characteristics of architecture and landscape, cultural traditions, social and economic situations, attitude toward tourism (from host population and leaders) etc.

Development planning

The facilities chosen for the resort may address the main markets (such as beach and sun), or secondary ones (such as cross-country skiing). The values to preserve are collected in a program of concrete long- and short-term measures. This program concerns the natural and built heritage, the cultural values and the dignity of the host population.

The development program applies to the following:

1. The basic access equipment.
2. The public utilities.
3. The guest facilities (type, style, quantity).
4. Housing for employees and residents.

5. Sports, shopping and cultural facilities.
6. Informing and training the host population.
7. Marketing (advertisement, sales network etc.)

All the preliminary actions take place in space (land use planning), and in time (execution planning). While limiting the unproductive fixed assets, good planning aims at the delivery of coherent sets in a definitive state, in order to avoid repeated works liable to prejudice the resort's image.

Financing

The financing of major equipment, with returns stretching over a long period of time, is dominated by two problems: the role of imported capital, and the role of public funds. The need for imported capital applies in environments with limited or not very mobile capital. The risk of generating a tourist ghetto, isolated from the surrounding population, is toned down in the case of a joint-venture controlled by the host community.

The appearance of capital issued from local governments inevitably raises the question 'who pays, who benefits?', and requires that the taxpayers benefit as much as possible from the project. When communities enter risky operations such as the construction of chair- and ski-lifts, or the setting up of building operations, the public funding agencies tend to want benefits to be reinvested into public facilities, accompanying, reinforcing or serving a major business, or further development programs.

Image and awareness

The promotion of the resort's image is set through a continuous and strong effort of public relations, including actions as varied as the organization of cost-price stays for journalists and tourism professionals, or the organization or big events in order to get a large editorial coverage in the media. Another means of marketing relies upon word of mouth generated by satisfied clients and the local residents and employees. Lively internal communication within the community should mobilize all the residents to welcome tourists; public services, in particular, such as the post office and the police corps, should be correctly geared up.

The clients – the *guests* – must be continuously monitored without disturbing them or contracting excessive expenses. The processing, every season, of questionnaires left for anyone to complete is a good choice but the sample thus collected may be biased and it is important to periodically confirm the results (for example every 5 years) by a professional survey of 1,000–2,000 clients.

Details

Ultimately, it is the potential client who holds the key to the success of a development; he/she is sensitive to details. In a very competitive market, every detail counts, and any neglected item may give rise to a series of dangerous effects. As the project is settled, the chosen managers must be aware of all aspects of the operation. Are they able to give a coherent push, while still being responsive to remarks from clients, employees or . . . competitors?

Assessment

A project of some importance generally joins several partners and usually generates a public debate at some time during the planning process. During discussions with their partners or through meeting with opponents, the developers will face extremely varied questions.

The first type of question tends to put the project into its context. Who finances the studies? Who are the participants in the project and what are their respective roles? What objectives are set? According to the project's type, what are the key points of the process?

The complex quality of the development justifies questions corresponding to the multiple interests involved. What are the resources needed? What are the values to preserve? Considering potential demand, what products are valuable for the studied site? How are projected lodging types and capacities justified? What are the needs for basic service equipment, for guest facilities and for labor? Who pays what? What are the expected returns, particularly concerning the host community?

Have the project's potential sequential results been well analyzed? What steps will be taken to avoid or remedy any detrimental effects to the environment and the quality of life of residents? What means will be available for that task? Do all the projected services form a coherent and attractive grouping? How is the resort to be individualized to make it a more desirable destination than its competitors? How is its image to be promoted? How can results be improved in the low season?

Conclusion

A development project refers to political, social, environmental and economic factors which should not be limited to merely quantitative elements. The generation of marketable tourist products, in a given location, generally depends on several decision centers both local and external. Careful planning is necessary in fields ranging from construction to tourist communication. Items such as demand tendencies and partners' behavior, however, are liable to alter over a long period of time, requiring an evolutionary strategy, and flexible planning, allowing the possibility of reorientation after assessment of the results issued from the various phases of the action.

Focus on small business

A certain number of resorts are bound to remain small because of the characteristics of the site and product, or even because the main activity of the locality is of another type. Far from eliminating the usual problems (image, service quality etc.), a small size tends to increase risks of underemployment and overcrowding if initiatives are diffuse and poorly organized. The prosperity of family-type resorts relies on an internal and regional effort of coordination, led by the prospective studies, investments, training and marketing.

The small enterprise is not, however, a privilege of a small resort. In resorts created by large groups, the place reserved for small businesses represents the domain open to local initiatives. This approach properly managed, leads to more varied services for clients (particularly in catering and arts and crafts), while avoiding overcrowding which could destroy this aspect of the resort.

Further reading

Croizé, J.-C., 'Diversification et animation dans les stations de montagnes', *Revue de Tourisme* (January/March 1986), pp. 16–20. An approach to the actual evolution of the product and financing problems in alpine resorts.

Goeldner, C. R. and Dycke, K., *Economic Analysis of North American Ski Areas* (Colorado University, 1986). This report offers an evaluation of all the ratios to which the management of ski-resorts may refer.

Heskett. J. L., *Managing in the Service Economy* (Harvard Business School Press, 1986). In this basic volume Chapter 7 is particularly relevant: the author insists on the necessity for managers and employees to accede to 'service culture' in order to achieve good economic results.

Hutton, G., *Introduction to Resort Management* (Nelson Hall, 1982). Refering to numerous examples, the author emphasizes the role of positive public relations (Chapter 5) and the priority of the natural environment, and quality of equipment and service (Chapters 7–11 and 17).

Kaiser, C., Jr. and Helber, L. E., *Tourism Planning and Management* (CBI Publishing Co., 1978). This work, achieved by experienced professionnals, describes the objectives and content of planning. It contains a large number of checklists (Chapters 3, 5 and 13).

Krippendorf, J. and Muller, H., *Là-haut sur la Montagne* (Kümmerly and Frey, 1987). After an analysis of costs and benefits of tourism in a mountain locality (Chapters 1–3), the authors end with a report on the principles for a harmonious development between man and nature (Chapters 6 and 7).

Labenne, C., 'Diversification thermale et stratégie de gestion', *Espaces*, no. 70 (October 1984), pp. 7–11. Based on a survey of 62 establishments, this article summarizes the situation and strategy of thermal resorts in France.

Maybury, B., *Une Région et son Avenir: les Problèmes et les Chances du Tourisme en Bretagne* (SEATL, 1986) A brilliant case study raising the problems of adjusting old tourist regions to respond to changes in demand.

Pearce, D. G., *Tourist Development* (Longman, 1981). A geographical approach, analyzing a fair number of European seaside and mountain resorts.

Ritchie, J. R. B. and Goeldner, C. R. (eds), *Travel, Tourism and Hospitality Research* (John Wiley, 1987). This work presents the results and tendencies of research; Chapters 27–32 are particularly concerned with the problem of resort development. The authors present an analysis of all the operational techniques available in fields such as: cost–benefit analysis, human resources evaluation, social impacts and physical carrying capacity.

Smart, E. *et al.*, *Recreational Development Handbook* (The Urban Land Institute, 1981). The second part of this volume (pp. 25–151) is devoted to the principles of resort development planning. Many case studies enliven the text.

JEAN-CLAUDE CROIZÉ

Role of national tourist organizations in the United Kingdom

Introduction

Some of the principal problems raised by tourism are of an administrative nature. At a national level, state tourism authorities have been established to give an impetus to market growth and to help secure the integration of a fragmented and diverse industry. In the United Kingdom there exists a structure of four statutory national tourist boards. This chapter traces their origins, reviews their legislative basis, and discusses their subsequent evolution to the present day.

Origins

National government interest and involvement in tourism is a feature of the twentieth century. A group of commercial tourism interests formed a promotional agency in 1926 – the 'Come to Britain' movement – in order to stimulate the flow of foreign visitors to the United Kingdom. The value of its centralized promotional campaign was acknowledged by the Department of Overseas Trade in 1929. An Exchequer grant of £5,000 was voted to the movement which subsequently renamed itself the Travel Association of Great Britain. A final change of name saw the body become the British Travel Association. The annual Exchequer subvention remained for 40 years, and throughout the 1929–1969 period this nongovernmental organization acted as national government's 'chosen instrument for the purposes of promoting travel to and within the United Kingdom' (British Travel Association, 1969). By 1969 it had become heavily dependent on government subsidy, to the tune of over 90 per cent of its annual £3.2 million spend. Although it was chief paymaster to the Association, national government avoided guidance over policy and intervention in day-to-day management. It was a role later summed up by the *Economist* magazine as one of 'masterly inactivity' (*Economist*, 1971). By comparison the voluntary Scottish and Wales Tourist Boards, formed respectively in 1930 and 1948, were underresourced and lacking in official status. For the financial year 1965–1966, for instance, the Wales Board had an annual income of just £44,000 and the Board Chairman was obliged to stand as guarantor to a bank overdraft of £15,000!

The Development of Tourism Act 1969

This statute forms a watershed in the approach of national government to tourism in the United Kingdom. The late Lord Mancroft said of this measure:

> ...I am afraid that it is a muddled and messy little Bill. This is due, of course, to its devious political history, about which the less said the better. (House of Lords, 1969)

Its overriding political purpose was to boost the foreign exchange earnings associated with international travel to the United Kingdom (Heeley, 1975), hence the creation of a statutory overseas promotional agency – the British Tourist Authority (BTA) – and the Hotel Development Incentives (HDI) scheme. The BTA was in effect a revamped British Travel Association, while the HDI scheme was a 3-year cash injection of grant and loan and designed to improve and expand the country's hotel stock so as to meet the growing and increasingly sophisticated demands of tourists from overseas. Reflecting on the thinking behind the Act, a senior civil servant was later to remark:

> It seemed evident that we ought to be able to attract more tourists to this country... and I think the government believed that if they could give this process a bit of a push and enable it to happen rather faster than it might otherwise have happened, then this would be something that was worthwhile doing (Trade and Industry Subcommittee, 1972).

To the government of the day, then, the 1969 tourism legislation appeared as a modest and fairly painless way of winning more foreign exchange, thus capitalizing on the competitive advantages engendered by the devaluation of the Pound Sterling in 1967.

A subsidiary purpose of the 1969 Development of Tourism Bill was further to exploit the tourism potential of Scotland and Wales. The means to this end lay in statutory agencies: the Scottish Tourist Board (STB) and the Wales Tourist Board (WTB). These bodies were to promote domestically and to seek the improvement of facilities and services used by both overseas and home travelers. It is noteworthy that the original bill made no provisions for a comparable English agency. This led to fears among seaside tourism interests in England that their needs would not be well served by the BTA who in the bill had been given an 'add on' oversight of English tourism matters. In the event, a successful backbench amendment tabled by Sir Keith Joseph MP led to a separate agency for England being written into the Bill.

Interestingly, Joseph's amendment gained a wide basis of cross-party support amongst English, Scottish and Welsh MPs. As Ednyfed Hudson Davies, the Labour Member of Parliament for Caerphilly, was to recall some years later:

> ...the Conservative Opposition put down an amendment that there should be an English Tourist Board...there were some...who really felt quite strongly that there should be an English Tourist Board. I think they were representative of resorts.... But also...I think there was a flippant element, a fairly light air about the whole thing, that since the Scots and Welsh were having their own tourist boards, wouldn't it be nice if the English had their own tourist board as well. But what no one had really foreseen or calculated was that the Scottish and the Welsh members of the Committee – and I was among them – did have quite severe misgivings about the original structure. We felt that if there was to be too close a link between the promotion of England within Britain and the promotion of Britain abroad, that England might do too well on the overseas promotion, and that the voices of Scotland and Wales would not be fully heard...the result was that several of us voted with the Conservative amendment...to the astonishment of the Minister who had his bill collapse in his hands. (Davies, 1979)

The relevant junior minister, William Rodgers MP, was persuaded by this pressure, and the Bill was hastily redrafted to contain a provision for the establishment of an English Tourist Board (ETB).

Though billed as a new charter for tourism, the 1969 Act was as vague as to what policy the four statutory tourist bodies should implement, as it was woolly about roles and responsibilities. Only gradually were policy and administrative relationships to be clarified.

The first decade, 1970–1979

The first review of tourism legislation was in 1970 by a newly elected Conservative administration. Its conclusion was that the government's previous concentration on foreign exchange objectives in tourism had tended to obscure regional policy dimensions. In particular, tourism was seen as a way of 'evening up the balance between the major industrial areas and the rest of the country'. A minister with responsibility for tourism, the late Sir John Eden MP, suggested that:

> In failing over past years to realise the importance of tourism to our regional policies the full value of the domestic tourism market has been overlooked. The home holiday-makers are the backbone of the holiday industry in this country. (Eden, 1971)

The emphasis given to regional policy and to home as well as overseas markets signalled an affirmation of the need for the three country tourist boards (ETB, STB and WTB). It led the government to introduce a Tourist Projects Scheme (TPS) for which £1 million was allocated for the financial year 1971/72. The TPS scheme was to be administered by the country tourist boards, and it provided for grants to be made available to support capital expenditure on tourist facilities in those parts of the United Kingdom officially designated as development areas (in 1979 the intermediate areas were added). Investments located outside the development areas were ineligible for assistance.

TPS (or section 4) assistance could be offered to all categories of tourism facility (accommodation, catering, attraction, infrastructure etc.) and the decision to grant or refuse aid was at the discretion of the relevant country's tourist board. However, having introduced a TPS scheme, explicitly linked to the regional policy context, the government rejected suggestions that they should channel this assistance into specially designated tourism areas located within the development areas. As will be shown later, this decision was to be overturned some seven years later.

Following the election of a Labour Government early in 1974, the Department of Trade began a review of tourism which culminated in November 1974 in the announcement of the first ever set of ministerial guidelines for tourism. These confirmed that balance of payments and regional policy considerations were the prime factors justifying government aid for tourism, but intimated that Exchequer funding of the Tourist Boards would be unlikely to increase in real terms into the foreseeable future. The statutory national tourist agencies were also asked to reduce the existing 'heavy expenditure on generalized promotion both at home and overseas' (Department of Trade, 1974) and to seek wherever possible to put their activities on a self-financing basis, either by charging for services or by joint schemes which attracted financial partners (e.g. carriers, hotel groups, local authorities etc.). But the main thrust of the 1974 guidelines was the commitment to 'develop untapped potential for tourism in those areas that can readily absorb and benefit from more visitors, particularly in certain parts of the development areas'. The intention of the Secretary of State for Trade, Mr Peter Shore MP, was a radical one: a shift in the pattern of marketing and development expenditures away from the established and increasingly congested tourist centers (notably London) and towards less well known, economically 'fragile' ones located within the development areas.

The guidelines were to some extent contradictory: with a strong commitment to 'fragile' areas it was difficult to maximize either the balance of payments contribution made by tourism or industry sponsorship of tourist board activities. Moreover, the Boards and the tourist trade were largely united in the opinion that generalized promotion was essential if the United Kingdom was to have an effective presence in the market place, even if this perforce had to place a heavy stress on the symbols and attractions associated with the London gateway. For these and other reasons, it is arguable that the fundamental shift in programs and expenditure implied in the Shore guidelines never fully materialized. Nevertheless, heavy promotion of London and the North–South imbalance in tourism flows had been put on to the political agenda. A new emphasis was afforded to places off the tourist beaten track, the most notable expression of which was the so-called Tourism Growth Points (TGP) experiments. Three TGPs (Scarborough district, the High Pennines, and Bude/Wadebridge) were announced in 1977. Similar initiatives found expression in Wales and Scotland: notably at Blaenau Festiniog and in the South Wales valleys, and at Ballachulish in the Scottish Highlands. In each TGP an integrated series of proposals aimed at the provision of new plant and its subsequent marketing were drawn up by local working parties and implemented over a three-year period. Government, in conjunction with the tourist boards, played a lead role in selecting, coordinating and monitoring these development schemes into which section 4 assistance was heavily (though not exclusively) channeled. Nothing so 'dirigiste' had ever been attempted before, and the experience gained prompted a senior tourist board official to remark:

> Perhaps the principal lesson which has been learnt . . . is that local authorities, the other relevant Government agencies and representatives of private sector interests can be brought together in a constructive way to cooperate in planning for tourism and in setting up development packages which can draw finance from a wide variety of sources. (Mills, 1978)

The desire for a more planned, strategic approach to product development was reflected in two strategy documents published in the mid-1970s by the Scottish and Wales Tourist Boards.

By 1979 the official tourist board structure appeared to have a fairly secure future. That year saw the publication of a report by a government sponsored, interdepartmental committee which had looked into the cost-effectiveness of tourist board operations. Its main conclusion was that the four agencies were fulfilling a valuable role. The project support role of the country tourist boards via disbursement of section 4 grants was seen as an efficient instrument of regional policy: nearly all of the £18 million disbursed since 1971 had gone to small businesses and the vast bulk (99.5 per cent) of the projects assisted had turned out to be viable. Assistance had been concentrated in the accommodation sector, and a grand total of 5,000 jobs (FTEs) had been created. While the review recognized that the effectiveness of state sponsored marketing campaigns was more problematic – in the sense of comprehensive cost–benefit appraisal being impossible – it opined that in all probability such activities did yield an appreciable and positive return.

The tourist boards for their part could point to a UK tourist industry which in volume and value terms had been growing during the 1970s. While the number of domestic trips had remained roughly static over the period 1970–1978, inward visits by relatively high spending international tourists had risen by 88 per cent. The Boards inevitably highlighted the employment and balance of payments spin-offs: the British tourist industries were estimated to employ more than a million people, and net overseas earnings from tourism (the so-called travel balance) had jumped from £31 million in 1973 to £954 million in 1978.

These sorts of arguments had been used to rebuff a document highly critical of the government sponsored tourist board structure (Sherman, 1976). This had been published in 1976, and the following year was circulating in Conservative quarters. It was the work of Sir Alfred Sherman, a Tory Councillor in Kensington and Chelsea, and Director of the Center for Policy Studies which came under the aegis of Sir Keith Joseph (somewhat paradoxically a creator of the English Tourist Board!). Sherman described the tourist boards as a 'bizarre jungle of bureaucratic empire-building more reminiscent of the ancient regime in France than of a modern market economy'. Although the bulk of Sherman's arguments were biased and contained many weaknesses, the reference to a jungle bureaucracy was not entirely misplaced. The issues here were complex, but can be seen as having three main dimensions:

1. Areas of overlap, conflict and rivalry characterized relationships between the Tourist Boards. This was notwithstanding the fact that the four bodies made serious efforts to demarcate their functions and to cooperate in their common tasks. As early as 1970 a formal document had been drawn up demarcating responsibilities between the BTA and the individual tourist boards.
2. Links between the tourist boards, on the one hand, and agencies responsible for leisure, recreation and heritage on the other, proved difficult to articulate. The core problem here was that tourism as a policy field was a trade and industry matter and was therefore separated (organizationally and as a line of ministerial responsibility) from these related areas. In England, for instance, the Countryside Commission, the Sports Council, the British Waterways Board, the Water Space Amenity Commission, the Historic Buildings Council and the Ancient Monuments Board were responsible to the Department of Environment, which also bore a responsibility for environmental matters generally and for local authority planning. In addition, the Forestry Commission was responsible to the Ministry of Agriculture, Fisheries and Food. The need to forge agreed policies across the whole range of these organizations (and others) was recognized by government and the tourist boards, and had been made the subject of a special interdepartmental tourism study during 1973. But pinpointing these problems proved easier than reforming the Whitehall and Scottish and Welsh Office bureaucracies so as to emphasize linkages as opposed to 'separatism' across the tourism, recreation, heritage and planning spheres.
3. Areas of conflict were apparent between the country tourist boards and the area tourist structures they had helped to establish during the early 1970s.

These three sets of organizational problems and issues were to continue to occupy the attention of government into and during the 1980s.

1980 to the present day; Lamont's review and its aftermath

The importance of tourism as a job creator assumed increasing importance in this decade of rising unemployment. The development area limitation on section 4 assistance was reviewed by the Conservative government in 1980 (Roberts, 1980), and 2 years later it was decided that from 1 August 1982 projects throughout England, Scotland and Wales would now be eligible for assistance. By this time a fullscale review of the 1969 Development of Tourism Act was underway, the outcome of which was announced in the House of Commons in November 1983 by Norman Lamont MP, Minister of State for Industry (Department of Trade and Industry, 1983).

The Lamont review and guidelines asserted that the bias of previous government policies in favor of the less well known tourist areas had led to 'underselling London overseas' and 'were wrong'. Little in the way of detailed strategy is to be found in the Lamont guidelines, there is simply a list of measures for improving the United Kingdom's tourist products (e.g. improvements to historic railway stations, hotel services, extra signposting etc.) and a commitment to using tourism as a tool for urban regeneration and to revitalizing Britain's traditional seaside resorts. Their real significance lay in measures designed to end wasteful overlap between the British Tourist Authority and English Tourist Board. The ground for this was well laid, management consultants having been appointed in October 1982 with a brief to review critically the operations of both agencies so as to reduce spending and staff. Detailed plans were drawn up to eliminate duplication in publications and other programs, to merge common activities, and to devolve certain tasks to the English Regional Tourist Boards. To expedite the rationalization of BTA and ETB's activities, Lamont's statement announced the appointment of one person to be chairman of both boards, Mr Duncan Bluck, chairman of Cathay Pacific Airways. He took up office in April 1984. Most of the staff of BTA and ETB were eventually to vacate six separate offices and move into the same premises in Hammersmith, approximately 60 per cent of them within so-called common service departments covering publishing and information, corporate public relations, research, finance, training, administration and personnel. The two organizations were therefore partially amalgamated as a result of the Lamont review.

Occurring more or less side-by-side with the Lamont guidelines were announcements that the Scottish Tourist Board would be given limited powers of independent overseas tourism promotion and that improvements would also be made to the way Wales was marketed overseas. The latter fell short of giving WTB a direct presence abroad: instead a WTB Overseas Marketing Director was appointed to work in conjunction with a liaison executive at BTA.

Both STB and WTB had undergone major management reorganizations during the late 1970s and early 1980s respectively. Satisfying the national imperative to be doing a 'proper' Scottish and Welsh job was (and is) always going to be difficult for these two agencies. The tourism industries of both countries have become structurally weak during the 1970s and 1980s: the staple domestic market has not been growing in overall terms, and there is a predominance of remote and seasonal rural tourism which makes the achievement of commercial viability difficult. The Scottish and Welsh Boards have to endure the imbalance of size which exists between themselves on the one hand, and BTA/ETB on the other. Inevitably it is a potential source of tension that the bulk of the product sold abroad by

BTA is in England. And in both Scotland and Wales official sponsorship of the tourist sector is shared with other development bodies (Planning Exchange, 1986): in Scotland there is the Highlands and Islands Development Board (HIDB) and the Scottish Development Agency (SDA); in Wales the comparable organizations are Mid Wales Development, and the Welsh Development Agency.

Although in Scotland demarcation documents exist to delineate the respective tourism roles of STB, HIDB and SDA, interagency relationships remain problematic. A report issued by the Scottish Affairs Committee (Scottish Affairs Committee, 1985) called for a realignment of official responsibilities whereby STB would take over the tourism marketing activity of the Highland Board. Although this proposal was subsequently rejected by the Scottish Office, STB's chairman Alan Devereux had opined before the Committee that existing arrangements resulted in duplication and were 'nonsensical' (Heeley, 1985).

For the United Kingdom as a whole, 1985 proved to be a highly significant year for the tourism administration established by the 1969 Act. Commencing in January, a Parliamentary Select Committee undertook a major investigation into UK tourism, focusing on the conduct of tourism affairs at government level. A comparable all-Wales enquiry followed. In July an interdepartmental review of tourism chaired by the then Minister without Portfolio, Lord Young, produced a highly positive ministerial statement about tourism (Cabinet Office Enterprise Unit, 1985). In this, the emphasis was placed on minimizing obstacles to growth in tourism from within the public sector (e.g. Wages Council regulations, licensing laws, town and country planning controls etc.) and on improved training, rather than on increasing subsidy for promotion and development via the tourist board structure. September saw government cabinet changes shift the responsibility for tourism to the Department of Employment and away from the trade and industry sector. Lord Young assumed the mantle of Secretary of State for Employment, and established a tourism and small firms division to oversee BTA and ETB and to spearhead a tourism-led drive to create jobs and wealth. Arguably, he was the first minister in the United Kingdom to give a dynamic push to tourism and to grasp the importance of coordinated action by government departments.

The Parliamentary enquiry into UK tourism referred to above announced their conclusions in January 1986. The Trade and Industry Committee's report (Trade and Industry Committee, 1985) advocated the following:

1. That the Secretary of State for Employment should take over the ministerial responsibilities for tourism currently exercised in Scotland and Wales by the respective Secretaries of State.
2. That the four statutory national tourist agencies should be abolished and their functions reallocated.
3. That a newly-formed British Tourist Board (BTB) should exercise responsibility for all overseas tourism marketing.
4. The BTB should have a general oversight of domestic tourism affairs in England, Wales and Scotland but (wherever possible) it should devolve executive tasks (for advertising, promotion, project support, research etc.) to the appropriate

area tourist organization: in England the 12 regional tourist boards, in Scotland the 32 area tourist boards, and in Wales the three regional tourism councils.

All four recommendations were subsequently rejected by the government.

In March 1987 the Select Committee on Welsh Affairs produced its report (Welsh Affairs Committee, 1987). Among its central recommendations were that a requirement to conserve Welsh culture and the country's natural beauty be made an explicit objective of WTB, and that the Board be afforded a power of independent overseas promotion similar to the one enjoyed by STB. At the time of writing the government's response is awaited.

Assessment and conclusion

The interdepartmental committee which drew up the Development of Tourism legislation held its first meeting in 1967, the year designated as International Tourist Year. Looking back over the 20 years which have passed since then, four observations appear valid.

First, government influence on the tourist boards has essentially been a housekeeping one. Ministers and their civil servants have acted to eliminate waste and duplication and to prod the Boards in the direction of revenue generation. Approximately 24 per cent of tourist board income now derives from non-Exchequer sources – the comparable figure for 1976/77 was 16%, see Table 1. Policy influences have been slight. The existing Lamont guidelines are 'little more than a statement of good faith in the balance of payments contribution and the wealth/job creation of tourism, and in the desirability of achieving certain specified but largely uncontentious improvements to the country's tourist product' (Heeley and McVey, 1985). The sense in which Britain's national government does not nowadays even attempt to impose policies on the tourist boards is captured in the following statement by Norman Lamont:

> Perhaps I can draw a distinction here, I see my role and that of the DTI as being to set down the broad parameters of policy, our role is to emphasise that tourism is an extremely important industry, that it has enormous potential for employment growth, and it is my function to see other parts of government, other departments in Whitehall, do not obstruct the natural growth of tourism. When it comes to a tourism policy, if by 'policy' you mean should the emphasis be placed on seaside resorts, this part of the country, covered swimming pools, historic buildings, I think there is a lot of the responsibility is devolved to the boards. They are the people who are in the field, at the sharp end. (Trade and Industry Committee, 1985)

To be sure, BTA activities are governed by a detailed annual marketing plan and the country tourist boards are moving in the direction of a strategic, policy-based approach. ETB has a comprehensive five-year marketing and development strategy (English Tourist Board, 1987), the basis of the latter being in-

Table 1 Expenditure of UK statutory national tourist organizations (from annual reports of the various tourist boards).

	1971/72	1976/77	1981/82	1986/87
BTA				
Total income	4.5	10.7	23.1	33.3
Grant-in-aid	3.6	8.1	16.2	20.7
Revenue	0.9	2.6	6.9	12.6
ETB				
Total income	1.2	6.0	14.9	23.8
Grant-in-aid	1.0	4.1	8.7	10.8
Revenue	0.1	0.4	2.2	3.5
Section 4	0.1	1.5	4.0	9.5
STB				
Total income	0.6	2.5	7.0	10.9
Grant-in-aid	0.4	1.6	4.1	6.2
Revenue	0.1	0.2	0.9	1.6
Section 4	0.1	0.7	2.0	3.1
WTB				
Total income	0.5	2.0	5.4	9.2
Grant-in-aid	0.3	1.0	3.2	5.3
Revenue	*	0.2	0.5	1.4
Section 4	0.2	0.8	1.7	2.5
Combined Tourist Board incomes	6.8	21.2	50.4	77.2
Combined Tourist Board grant-in-aid	5.3	14.8	32.2	43.0
Combined Tourist Board section 4	0.4	3.0	7.7	15.1
Combined Tourist Board revenue	1.1	3.4	10.5	19.1

* Less than £50,000

novation and small business funds linked to a national network of local tourism development action plans (TDAPs). The Wales Tourist Board publishes a concise annual marketing statement (Wales Tourist Board, 1987), and in July 1986 embarked upon the preparation of a Framework Development Strategy. The Scottish Tourist Board's Business Plan issued in 1987 is a broad statement of marketing and development intent (Scottish Tourist Board, 1987). Whether those strategies are sufficient to give the industry the sort of policy lead it requires is the subject of debate.

Secondly, successive reviews and enquiries have broadly endorsed the value of the principal operational aspects of tourist board activity. Section 4 assistance has been judged as highly cost-effective. A recent report has suggested that this is especially the case when the grant awarding body operates proactively either 'by favouring particular types of project and/or concentrating assistance in selected geographical areas' (Cambridge Economic Consultants, 1986). However, from a national perspective the real wealth-creating significance of section 4 is arguably much lessened when account is taken of displacement effects – currently the subject of considerable study. On the marketing front, there is widespread assent that BTA sells the United Kingdom abroad in a professional and commercially oriented manner, and that overseas promotion is an important aid to capturing lucrative international markets. The rationale for domestic marketing by the county tourist boards has to be related to the reality of a highly fragmented industry in which the typical unit is the small business. Faced with intense competition from the powerful forces inducing Britons to take holiday abroad, some sort of collective state mechanism to market British products domestically appears necessary. Just how effective is that mechanism is a separate and much debated question.

Thirdly, for Scotland and Wales, the Development of Tourism Act represents at best a halfway house. The system is doubtless an improvement on the pre-1969 days when non-governmental agencies eked out a precarious existence on miniscule budgets. But the manner in which the STB and WTB are restricted in terms of their budgets, functions and influence means that they are continually perceived to fall short of meeting the legitimate national aspirations of the Scots and Welsh. Ways need to be found to upgrade significantly the status and resourcing of the two agencies.

A fourth and related issue is the question of the overlap between tourism and other policy fields, especially those of leisure, recreation, heritage and the environment generally. The late Sir Mark Henig in his time as first chairman of the ETB referred to this matter by issuing this clarion call:

> Somebody...will have to face the problem of co-ordination in a jungle of peripheral and often imperialistic bodies with overlapping interests...These people have all to work together, and there is no machinery, except good will, for talking. There is no machinery for telling each other what's happening. (Times, 8 August 1973)

The need for some high-level forum to articulate and coordinate policies across tourism and its related policy fields is as strong today as when Sir Mark made the above plea.

Further reading

British Travel Association, *Forty-First Annual Report for the Year Ending March 1969* (BTA, 1969), p. 11.

Cabinet Office Enterprise Unit, *Pleasure, Leisure – and Jobs: The Business of Tourism* (HMSO, 1985).

Cambridge Economic Consultants Ltd, *A Study of Section 4 Assistance to Tourism*, Final Report (CECL, February 1986), p. 119.

Davies, E. H., 'Tourism in British politics', A paper presented to a Tourism Society discussion meeting series on British Tourism at the Crossroads, held at the London Graduate School of Business Studies, 12 March 1979 (Tourism Society, 1979), p. 6.

Department of Trade and Industry Press Notice, *Tourism Review: Statement by Norman Lamont* (22 November 1983).

Department of Trade Press Notice, *New Guidelines for Tourism: Mr Shore's Announcement* (21 November 1974).

Economist (25 September 1971), see Special Article on Tourism in Britain, p. 13.

Eden, J., Speech to the English Tourist Board's conference at Coventry (17 May 1971).

English Tourist Board, *A Vision for England* (ETB, 1987). A separate document exists for the development and marketing strategies respectively.

Heeley, J., *A Study of Organisations Concerned with Tourism in the UK*, MSc Thesis (University of Strathclyde, 1975), Vol. 1, Chapter 4.

Heeley, J., 'Tourism: a highland stramash', *Quarterly Economic Commentary, the Fraser of Allander Institute*, vol. 10, no. 4 (1985), pp. 57–9.

Heeley, J. and McVey, M., *Tourism and Government Policy in Great Britain*, unpublished evidence to the Trade and Industry Select Committee enquiry, *Tourism in the UK* (4 February 1985).

House of Lords, *Parliamentary Debates*, vol. 303, col. 702 (1969).

Mills, S., 'A strategy for stimulating development by the private sector', unpublished paper (9 October 1978).

Planning Exchange Occasional Paper No. 22, *Strategy and Opportunities for Tourism Development* (the Planning Exchange, 1986).

Roberts, W., Speech by Parliamentary Under-Secretary of State at the Welsh Office delivered at the third National Conference on Local Government and Tourism held in Llandundo (24 October 1980).

Scottish Affairs Committee, Second Report, *Highlands and Islands Development Board* (HMSO, 1985).

Scottish Tourist Board, *Business Plan* (STB, 1987).

Sherman, A., *Tourist Study* (Centre for Policy Studies, August 1976).

The Times (8 August 1973), p. 19.

Trade and Industry Committee, *Tourism in the UK* (HMSO, 1985).

Trade and Industry Committee, Select Committee Enquiry, *Tourism in the UK*, Minutes of Evidence (12 June 1985), HC 172-x, pp. 286–7.

Trade and Industry Sub-Committee of the Expenditure Committee, *Public Money in the Private Sector*, Minutes of Evidence and Appendices (HMSO, 1972), p. 28.

Wales Tourist Board, *Marketing Plan 1987/88* (WTB, 1987).

Welsh Affairs Committee, *Tourism in Wales* (HMSO, 1987).

JOHN HEELEY

Sales promotion in tourism

Introduction

Successful sales promotion is sales enhancement, and may be defined as the collection of company sales activities contributing to the growth of sales. More fully, promotion may be defined as '...transmitting information, creating an awareness and an interest, finally resulting in a desire to buy' (Hague, 1985, p. 115), or, '...all the ways and means that a tourist development group or recreation enterprise can instigate or contrive to attract attention or enhance visitors to come to his enterprise' (Epperson, 1977, p. 271). There are essentially three kinds of promotion: advertising or media promotions, nonmedia promotions, and publicity. Advertising is where media, such as newspapers, magazines and television, are used to reach potential customers. Nonmedia promotions include direct mailing of potential customers, brochures and competitions. Publicity is gained by supplying the media with stories or other information, in order to induce free coverage by them, for example, as articles or programs.

It is really nonsense to talk colloquially of 'advertising *and* sales promotion' as the former is subsumed by the latter. Advertising is properly part of the *promotional campaign* of a company, and not a separate activity; likewise, the selection of appropriate media, or *media planning* as it is known, is also properly part of such a campaign. A promotional campaign should recognize the interplay of its various components, and should be used to co-ordinate all promotions by the company. As such, promotion is one of the four Ps of a company's *marketing mix*, namely its products, places of supply, prices and promotions. As such, promotion is only one part of a company's attempts to influence the buyer's response. When recognized as part of a company's marketing mix, it is clear that promotion should not be regarded as a luxury, but instead as vital for building up links with customers. Market research can be used to enhance the effectiveness of promotional spending by showing which messages have an impact and which promotions should be selected. Ideally, market segmentation analyses should precede promotions, to target potential customers. The effectiveness, or ineffectiveness, of promotions should also be monitored, and the mix of the promotional campaign reappraised. Other necessary promotional research includes studies of customers' images and motivations, and of sales techniques. Clearly, because of the range of tourism products and services, some promotions will be more effective in different sectors of the industry than in others. No blueprint can be offered; instead, this section will outline some principles of promotional implementation and evaluation.

Examples

Examples of promotions are so common as to need little introduction. Handbills, leaflets, brochures, newspaper and magazine advertisements, and television commercials are particularly common means of promotion in the tourism industry. Travel agents, national and regional tourist boards, district local authorities and tourist associations are well known promotional agencies in the United Kingdom. What is less well known is the comparative effectiveness of these promotional types and agencies.

Evaluation of promotions is less commonly undertaken by small businesses, which may frequently distribute their brochures by tourist associations or tourist information centers and assume that these are distributed as effectively as possible. In contrast, for example, is the Scottish Tourist Board, who in 1987 undertook their tenth successive travel trade monitoring survey. These surveys have been undertaken annually, in three waves (January, March and May) to monitor brochure stocks and exposure by travel agents, and to ascertain the agents' views of the brochures. This monitoring is undertaken as part of the Travel and Tourism Research Travel Agents' Omnibus Survey, and is only part of the STB's promotions evaluation strategy. The STB also undertakes marketing follow-up studies, to measure the comparative effect of their promotional campaigns, particularly assessments of their press advertising as a basis for brochure distributions, and of their television commercials. In 1986 the STB also participated in the surveying of visitors to tourist information centers to assess how these centers were meeting the needs of tourists. This survey was repeated in 1987.

Benefits

The benefit of a successful sales promotion campaign is the enhancement of sales; that is, the increase in business volume for the company, or for the companies which an agency is seeking to assist. These benefits may be achieved either by diverting tourists to the intended destination and away from another, or by generating tourist trips which would not have otherwise been made. In these terms, promotion is a pressure which a supplier can bring to bear on a person's decision to buy. It is important not to overstate what promotion can achieve. The most general benefit of promotion is the communication of information and, in particular, the highlighting of specific features. The latter is known in marketing jargon as the 'unique selling proposition', in which a unique feature of a product is promoted, the feature having been selected on the basis of an assessment of the buyer's needs. For example, some tourist boards have sought to define the mental images of their areas held by potential tourists in order 1. to promote those images which are both favorable and distinctive; 2. to 'correct' images; and 3. to indicate possible product developments.

In the 1970s the Scottish and Wales Tourist Boards sought to define the mental images which UK residents held of Scotland, Wales, the South West of England and the English Lake District. Clearly, built into this research design was a desire to compare the images held of Scotland and Wales with the images held of major competing destinations. Scotland's distinctive image was that it was seen never to be crowded, although this image was not particularly strongly held. Scotland's major disadvantage was that it was considered unknown as a destination by most persons surveyed, and that its facilities were perceived as poorer than in the South West of England. Mountains, the Highlands and the Islands were thought of most commonly as the best parts of Scotland for a holiday (Social and Community Planning Research, 1974). Findings of this kind imply a several fold promotional response. Firstly, the need to promote the destination, in this case Scotland, generally as a holiday destination. Secondly, the particular landscape qualities identified by the potential tourists, in this case the Highland scenery, may be exploited in advertising. Thirdly, either facilities need to be developed or those already existing need to be promoted. The importance of a promotional campaign, rather than disparate promotions, is evident in such planning.

Promotion may be used alternatively to build up an overall 'brand image', and contrasts with the concept of promoting a unique feature as the whole product is promoted as a range of common features. 'Brand images' are common in tourism, especially in the promotions of hotel chains and package holiday companies, but may also be found in the imagery used to promote Ireland, Scotland and Wales by the respective national tourist boards. The different characteristics of the brand are brought together for each product in a creative whole, and their salience is varied to meet the needs of specific groups. In essence, the buyer should be able to recognize the brand irrespective of the attributes of the particular product. Promotion may also be beneficial in influencing the activities of intermediaries, such as travel agents or tour organizers, and in reinforcing customer behavior. In particular, attitudes to areas may be dependent on past experience of trip making.

The short-term aims of promotion may be defined as follows:

1. Building an awareness of a destination or company.
2. Building a certain image.
3. Informing and educating.
4. Building loyalty to a destination or company.
5. Stimulating enquiries.
6. Stimulating bookings or visits.

These aims assume in turn a general model of holiday selection by tourists, as follows:

1. An original unawareness of the destination or company.
2. An awareness.
3. Comprehension or liking.
4. Conviction in favor of the destination or company.
5. Action or purchase.

The customer is therefore assumed to move through five stages of decision making and different types of promotion may be targeted to these stages.

Implementation

Promotion in tourism is directed both to potential customers and to intermediaries or agencies which in turn promote sales. The different kinds of promotion have their strengths and weaknesses. Media advertising in the general press or on television is particularly suitable for image building or where large and diverse audiences need to be reached. The major disadvantage of such advertising, particularly television commercials, is that it is ephemeral. Targeting is facilitated, however, by the ready availability of *media profiles*; these are delimitations of readers' or viewers' characteristics. The National Readership Surveys provide information on the social breakdown of newspaper readers, and these breakdowns are now usefully summarized along with other leisure data in *Social Trends*. The Scottish Tourist Board have also undertaken extensive readership surveys in its *National Survey of Tourism in Scotland* of 1985. The assumption behind the STB's analyses is that their market may differ in terms of accessibility via media. Magazines provide opportunities to target specific groups by their leisure or occupational interest. Magazines of this kind have the advantages also of being comparatively well read by their purchasers and of often being retained for subsequent inspection. Magazines may be used both to create a general awareness and to stimulate a response amongst specialist groups.

Direct mailing provides a further type of promotion. If based on past customers, such promotions may be of limited value for specific destinations as holidaymakers often seek different destinations. Such lists are however useful to companies or hotel chains promoting a range of destinations. Direct mailing may also be based on the socioeconomic selection of areas (see chapter on *Market Targeting* p. 247) or on bought-in mailing lists. For the travel trade, exhibitions are a further form of promotion. Supporting manuals and directories are important backups to exhibitions, and for general distribution to the trade. Publicity can provide a general educative or image-building role, but may have an ephemeral impact dependent upon the kind of media employed. Special 'events', such as a

Victorian week, are a further form of promotion commonly used in attracting tourists. Some events have a wide publicity value, such as the Manx TT Races.

Leaflets, handbills, brochures and other sales literature are further forms of promotion commonly used by the tourism industry. For example, the promoters of attractions frequently distribute handbills to other tourist sites in an attempt to stimulate visits to their own attractions by holidaymakers. Sales literature is suitable for educating and converting tourists, and commonly range in size from a handbill advertising a single attraction to area brochures advertising many attractions and types of accommodation. Literature of this kind may have a long term use as the material may be retained by the tourist. In promoting attractions such literature should include information on location, attributes of the attraction, special events, opening dates and times, how to get to the attraction, sources of additional information and services available.

The main intermediaries offer different services. Tourist information centers (TICs) variously offer local and national information services in the United Kingdom, and show markedly different rates of use. The spatial range of the areas they promote is surprisingly varied, as some centers have evolved as holiday information centers for nonlocal UK holidays. Policies of the centers vary considerably in how information is gained to promote destinations. UK travel agents frequently promote package holidays, which are frequently overseas holidays. 'Go as you please' holidaymakers have frequently to make their own arrangements or rely on successive tourist information centers (TICs) to 'book a bed ahead'. Tourism associations are in contrast associations of tourism industry producers, explicitly promoting their members' products. Epperson (1977) defines over 30 roles for such associations, but principally these center around the collective promotion of members' products, especially leadership, joint promotion and backup services. To these three major types of non-media promotional agencies may be added advertising agencies, which translate the advertiser's message into an appropriate form, select media and place the advertisements.

As well as these major media and nonmedia agencies, the entrepreneur should consider distributing local promotional material via hotels, restaurants, public houses, petrol stations, shops, local authority offices and other neighboring attractions. Joint promotional facilities at neighboring attractions can be mutually beneficial, helping the tourist to choose where next to visit and enhancing their overall experience of the destination. Local authorities have also traditionally promoted their districts, often in association with tourism associations, by producing accommodation brochures and other literature. The variation in UK local authority initiatives in this regard is very wide, and is dependent on the authority's own perception of the importance of tourism to its district's economy. With deindustrialization many local authorities are now appointing tourism officers and are actively promoting their districts as tourist destinations; effectively, this is broadening the promotions of local authorities from traditional seaside resorts to 'heritage areas'. South Wales provides a good example of the latter change, with many of the Valley authorities now actively promoting tourism in areas of redundant coalmining infrastructure.

Assessment

The evaluation of the effectiveness of promotion is at the same time critical but difficult. It is dangerous to assume that a promotion is having a significant effect in causing tourists to choose one destination rather than another. For example, advertisements on a regional television channel, promoting the attractions of an area to its residents, are unlikely to achieve much effect if the visitors to the attractions which are being promoted are not residents of the area, but largely tourists who are unlikely to have seen the television advertisements. The preliminary of a visitor survey and a follow up visitor survey inquiring about the visitors' sources of information about the attractions, would be invaluable in this instance to reveal the effectiveness of this particular campaign. More fully, the evaluation of promotional campaigns may have four objectives:

1. To test by recall how the promotion has informed the potential tourist.
2. To test the overall awareness of the potential tourist of the destination or company.
3. To test by additional research how past behavior has been reinforced.
4. To test by sales research how the campaign has affected bookings or visitor numbers.

Before evaluating any promotional campaign it is necessary to decide which of the above four objectives are being evaluated.

Basic to any evaluation is the concept of a 'control' group; namely, an area or group which has not been subject to the promotion. It is necessary to ask if these individuals behave any differently to those who received the promotion, or whether their images or recall is any different. If the groups are no different in these respects the promotion may well have been ineffective. Alternatively, before and after studies of potential tourists may be made, to assess how far, if at all, a promotion has affected their images, attitudes or behavior. Clearly, many promotions are untestable in terms of the public's overall images as, individually, products are often insignificant. In these cases, sales research may be the only sensible analysis.

Some promotions, in part, effectively test themselves. Competitions for holidays or coupons cut out from advertisements in newspapers and magazines are examples of this. However, the extent to which, by themselves, completed coupons or competition entries can reveal the characteristics of the customers is limited, and usually little more than the volume of reply by area of residence is measured. In contrast, major advertising campaigns should be fully monitored to assess the recall of potential customers, the translation of this recall into actions such as brochure requests, and, eventually, holiday taking. Examples of this kind of monitoring can be found across the range of media advertising, including the evaluation of campaigns using brochures, newspapers, television, and tube cards on the London Underground (Travel and Tourism Research, 1980; Research Bureau, 1983; Harris Research Centre, 1984; Feedback, 1986). As a preliminary to a campaign, experimental evaluation may be useful in order to identify the potentially most effective promotional material. Advertisements can be tested experimentally to show their impact, clarity and durability. Brochures also can be evaluated experimentally and examples of such studies include Travel and Tourism Research (1980) and Hoffman Research (1984 and 1986). Questions may include the extent to which a brochure succeeds in providing reassurance to those seeking it on the main negative aspects of the destination; reactions to specific aspects of brochure style and context; and the extent to which requirements for information are met.

Just because an agency has received promotional material does not mean that it will be prominently displayed. Monitoring of how many agents have brochures in stock, how many have spares, and how many have the brochures on display has been a recurrent Scottish Tourist Board exercise (e.g. Travel and Tourism Research, 1986; 1987). Likewise, depositing brochures in a TIC does not mean that most potential tourist customers will be reached even if the brochures are prominantly displayed, as most UK tourists do not visit these centers. During the 1970s, however, the use of TICs by holidaymakers did increase significantly, but from a very low base (Paveley, 1981).

Ultimately, evaluation concerns cost-effectiveness, that is, the effectiveness of a promotional type per pound spent. It is unwise to generalize across sectors of such a diverse industry as tourism; however, an example is illustrative. The Scottish Tourist Board has compared both the cost per brochure recipient deciding to holiday in Scotland *after* receiving a STB brochure and of *all* recipients holidaying in Scotland, for distribution via the travel trade and via mailing in response to media advertisements. Travel agents were found to be particularly cost-effective, especially for the target group – brochure recipients deciding to holiday in Scotland after receiving the brochure (Travel and Tourism Research, 1980). Travel agencies were doubly cost-effective: not only were they unpaid distributors of brochures, they had a higher 'conversion' rate in convincing the undecided to holiday in Scotland. Considerations of past cost-effectiveness should be an integral part of any promotional campaign, and, in the case of the example, the STB's continued purpose in monitoring the travel trade is clear from this analysis of costs.

Conclusion

Sales promotion involves a range of well-known techniques. Promotions should be both integrated into a promotional campaign and recognized as integral to building up links with customers. However, the mechanics of promotion are insufficient demonstration of its worth. The effectiveness of promotions should be investigated, and their effectiveness should not be assumed. Just because promotions are so common does not mean that any one promotion could not achieve more.

Focus on small business

The small business person is frequently best advised to measure the success of his or her promotions in terms of bookings or visits, and to question his guests or visitors on how they found

out about the accommodation or attraction. Simple market research techniques can formalize this questioning. Promotions via a local authority brochure or tourism association should be questioned for their effect. The entrepreneur should ask critically, 'How does the authority or association promote my attraction?' and 'Can the authority or association better promote my attraction?' The small business may also benefit from casual trade: in such cases, signposting, handbill displays in pubs and like places, and posters in shopping areas are critical. Short cuts in leaflet and handbill design may be gained by inspecting the literature produced by other attractions, and copying a clear, uncluttered, eyecatching and informative format. But, ultimately, competent market research is needed, particularly as the range and number of attractions, and thus competition, increases into the 1990s. Other than surveying one's own visitors, market research is properly a local authority or tourism association role, and the small business person should seek to convince these agencies of this need. The entrepreneur may be surprised to find just how few local authorities have a detailed understanding of the tourists visiting their districts, and of relevant market segmentations of these tourists.

Further reading

Baker, M. J., *Marketing. An Introductory Test* (Macmillan, 4th edition, 1985). This general marketing text includes discussions of advertising and campaign planning.

Cannon, T., *Basic Marketing. Principles and Practice* (Holt, Rinehart and Winston, 2nd edition, 1986). This is a general textbook covering the full range of marketing requirements and skills, including sales promotion and marketing mixes.

Central Statistical Office, *Social Trends* (HMSO). This annual statistical review includes a chapter on how people spend their leisure time, including media profiles.

Edginton, C. R. and Williams, J. G., *Productive Management Of Leisure Service Organizations* (John Wiley, 1978). This text includes a chapter on marketing, and in particular discusses the development of a marketing strategy and promotion.

Epperson, A. F., *Private and Commercial Recreation* (John Wiley, 1977). This book contains chapters on psychological motivations of tourists and on marketing. In particular, the book considers market analysis, marketing cycles, plans and programs. Attention is given to the strengths and weaknesses of the various promotional techniques.

Evans, J. R. and Berman, B., *Marketing* (Collier Macmillan, 3rd edition, 1987). This general marketing text includes chapters on the planning of promotions, and in particular on advertising and publicity.

Feedback, *Scottish Tourist Board and Frequent Tube Users*, Report to London Transport Advertising (Feedback, 1986). This report is available in the Scottish Tourist Board Library and assesses tube travelers' awareness of Scottish advertising, perceptions of Scotland as a holiday destination and holiday taking in Scotland.

Frain, J., *Principles and Practice of Marketing* (Pitman, 1986). This text reviews consumer behavior generally and the planning of marketing communications. Topics considered include the selection and use of communications media and campaign planning.

Hague, P. N., *The Industrial Market Research Handbook* (Kogan Page, 1985). This handbook is directed towards industries in which another producer consumes the products, rather than where the products are finally consumed. However, the book has a comprehensive review both of information that can be made available by market research and on the uses of market research. Of particular interest to the small business person is the extensive review of market research techniques and data presentation.

Harris Research Centre, *The Effectiveness of Area Tourist Board Promotions Research Project*, Report to the Scottish Tourist Board (Harris Research Centre, 1984). This report is available in the Scottish Tourist Board Library and reviews profiles of brochure applicants by media, the impact of media, holiday taking by brochure applicants and conversion rates.

Hoffman Research Company, *Research on Brochure Design for Area Tourist Boards in Scotland*, Report to the Scottish Tourist Board (HRC, 1984). This report is available in the Scottish Tourist Board Library and uses group discussions and 'Hall Tests' to measure reactions to brochures, amendments to styles and brochure usage.

Hoffman Research Company, *Research on Accommodation Brochures*, Report to the Scottish Tourist Board (HRC, 1986). This report is available in the Scottish Tourist Board Library and considers the advantages and disadvantages of brochure layout styles and opinions on reducing the number of accommodation brochures covering Scotland.

Hospitality Industries Research Centre, *Tourist Information Centres. Visitor Survey 1986* (3 volumes), Reports to the Scottish Tourist Board (HIRC, 1986). These reports are available in the Scottish Tourist Board Library and review sources of information on TICs, ease of finding TICs, views on staff and on information received, and visitor characteristics including travel plans.

Paveley, T., *Report of The Working Party to Review Tourist Information Centre Services and Support Policies* (English Tourist Board, 1981). This report is available in the English Tourist Board Library and reviews the roles of TICs, as a background for their development in the 1980s.

Research Bureau Ltd, *Scottish Tourist Board Marketing and Follow Up Study 1983, Final Report*, Report prepared for the Scottish Tourist Board (RBL, 1983). This report is available in the Scottish Tourist Board Library and reviews advertising recall and holiday intentions.

Social and Community Planning Research, *Attitudes to Holidays in Scotland and Wales* (Scottish and Wales Tourist Boards, 1974). This report is available both in the Scottish and Wales Tourist Boards' Libraries, and reviews holiday intentions, requirements and attitudes towards areas.

Travel and Tourism Research (Peter Hodgson and Associates) *Marketing Follow-up Study 1980*, Report to the Scottish Tourist Board (TTR, 1980). This report is available in the Scottish Tourist Board Library and reviews consumer and trade opinions of the STB's brochure, the effectiveness of its media campaign, the cost-effectiveness of the campaign and the promotion of holidays in Scotland by the retail travel trade.

Travel and Tourism Research (Peter Hodgson and Associates), *Scottish Tourist Board Holiday Brochures. Travel Trade Monitoring* (3 Volumes), Reports to the Scottish Tourist Board (TTR, 1986). These reports are available in the Scottish Tourist Board Library and review brochure display and distribution and travel agents' opinions.

Travel and Tourism Research (Peter Hodgson and Associates), *Scottish Tourist Board Holiday Brochures. Travel Trade Monitoring, January 1987*) (TTR, 1987). This report is available in the Scottish Tourist Board Library and reviews the display and distribution of Scottish skiing brochures, agents' opinions on the brochures and of the STB's central reservation service, and booking levels.

RICHARD PRENTICE

Science and technology
in tourism

Introduction

As the demand for tourism has increased, consumer behavior has not necessarily conformed to classic economic and marketing theory, because of rapid and sometimes unexpected advances in science and technology (S&T) (Massey, 1979; Naisbitt, 1987). The conventional ways of looking at consumer behavior (especially in tourism) are becoming outdated very quickly. For example, it is no longer possible to predict the purchasing habits of consumers of almost any product or service simply by labeling a group as 'upscale'. A world of paradoxes in tourism and leisure behavior is emerging where existing opposites operate simultaneously (Naisbitt and Aburdene, 1985). Greater sameness and greater diversity, plus greater security-seeking and greater risk-taking occur side by side. For example, there are skydiving accountants all over the place; campers who drive air-conditioned vans to 'rough it' in the woods; and, recreationists who drive air-conditioned cars to air-conditioned gyms where they sweat as much as they can. The same individuals may: shop at both down- and up-market shops; own a sizeable investment portfolio and trade it with a discount broker; fill a BMW with inexpensive self-serve gas; and, go to McDonalds at lunch and a four-star restaurant for dinner. Leisure lifestyle mosaics are often elusive, inconsistent, and contradictory (Massey, 1979; Perry, 1987; Plawin and Blum, 1987; Smith, 1985; Fensom, 1984).

Because of the tremendous amount of market segmentation that is occurring throughout the leisure and tourism industry, leading forecasters emphasize that the multiple-profile consumer is here to stay (McIntosh and Goeldner, 1984; Naisbitt, 1982). If any service industry provides anything without knowing how consumer tastes and preferences are rapidly changing because of new S&T, that industry is in for an expensive shock (Iacocca, 1984). As a result, the conventional ways of looking at tourism behavior are not only outdated but dangerous, and new approaches for analyzing the market need to consider the effects of oncoming S&T on future demand and supply (Naisbitt, 1987; Miller, 1986; Sivy, 1985; Kaufmann, 1983). Furthermore, in the tourism strategic planning game, many times it is the S&T *outside* the normal sphere of tourism research that can affect most dramatically tourism demand and supply patterns. Breakthroughs in these areas of S&T are the wild cards in the planning process. They often seem to appear on the scene unexpectedly

and create entirely new markets or significantly segment current ones.

This chapter describes some of the oncoming S&T that may have profound influences on tourism planning and development in the coming decades. Over 100 popular and scientific articles were explored in order to provide visions of how S&T will create new challenges and solutions in future tourism programming and planning.

Video

The video S&T of the twentieth and twenty first centuries will revolutionize traditional patterns of supply and demand for tourism. Breakthroughs in video S&T over the next 10–20 years will have counterveiling effects on tourism demand and the need to supply natural environments for tourism activities. The following expected scientific advances will probably create a *decrease* in demand and supply by taking various attributes of natural environments to the tourist, rather than generating a need for the tourist to travel to the actual environments.

1. Videocycles (a combination of a stationary exercise bike and a TV/VCR) will be used extensively by bikers at home to tour scenic routes in forested and urban environments, complete with exciting background music (Country Technology, 1987–88).
2. Image libraries will be available for home-viewing that will contain all the world's best art. Inexpensive flat panel-display devices will be available, throughout the house, with a resolution so good that viewing a projection will be like looking at the original oil painting (Long, 1987; Booth, 1986).
3. People will be able to create their own images and scenes on their television screens; the viewer will be able to simulate just about anything. For example, if a person wanted to enjoy a raft trip down the Grand Canyon of the Colorado river it will be possible to call up the image on a wall-size TV and with a raft at home the viewer will experience the sensation of the trip (Hartley, 1987; Rochester, 1986).
4. TV images will rival 35 mm film quality and be wall-

projection units. Digital TV will allow the viewer to become a participant in the actual production. For example, if a person puts a wager on the wrong football team, he can take a picture of the quarterback, superimpose him scoring the winning play, and at least get the thrill of having the play turn out the way he wanted it to (Long, 1987).

5. Sensavision TV will allow the viewer to feel temperature, humidity, smell, and to walk around in the scene because the whole room will be part of the TV set. With sensavision, viewers will be able to feel the thrill of victory or the agony of defeat in whatever activity they care to be in (Long, 1987).

6. As simulators become more realistic, people will be able to enjoy the breathtaking thrills of high-risk tourism experiences such as skydiving, mountain climbing, or underwater explorations with scuba gear without leaving home (Anon., 1987).

Meanwhile, a few examples of video S&T that will help to *increase* demand and create a greater need to supply on-site facilities include the following:

1. Video tapes will be used on location in specific recreational environments to train tourists to become more skilled at whatever they are doing – skiing, scuba diving or sailing, for example – so participants can almost instantly apply what they have seen on videotape to their activity (Sybervision, 1987).

2. In-room checkout to menu-driven displays on guest room televisions will be commonplace in resorts and hotels (McCoy, 1987; Cetron and Rocha, 1987).

3. Rather than read about a tourist destination in a travel guide, the average consumer will view travel video tapes of several potential destinations prior to making a decision about which trip to take (Kennedy, 1987; International Video Network, undated).

4. Existing flight simulators generally place a person behind the controls of comparatively tame private planes. In the future, computer programs will not only teach basic flying skills, but also provide instructions on advanced maneuvers and stunts. The characteristics of many different kinds of planes will be simulated – from World War I classics to rocket planes and experimental aircraft. Viewers will be able to put them all through their paces in the privacy of their own home (Electronic Arts, 1987).

Transportation

The overall effects of advances in S&T in transportation will be an *increase* in demand and supply for tourism activities. Future transportation will be faster, easier, and more comfortable.

1. Cars will contain many of the sights, sounds, and comforts of home: video map displays of the car's position, car phones, facsimile machines, lap-top computers that can send and receive data, answering machines, and sound systems for hightech compact disc players (Cook, 1987; Wiener, 1987).

2. Magnetic trains – trains that literally fly between cities on cushions of electromagnetism – will be making short trips (for example, Los Angeles to Las Vegas) faster than airlines can manage today (Black, 1984; Lemonick, 1987).

3. A new X-ray scanner will be used in airports to detect plastic weapons used by terrorists (Tracy, 1986).

4. The average price of a new car in the year 2020 will be $70,000 with a gas mileage of 100 miles per gallon (Naisbitt, 1986).

5. An aerospace plane, about the size of a Boeing 727 and able to take off and land at regular airports will fly coast to coast in about 12 minutes (Kristof, 1987; Siwolop, 1985).

6. Scheduled commercial flights from New York to Tokyo will take about two hours (Yeager, 1986).

7. A 25-passenger tilt-rotor aircraft will be used to provide short trips between major cities in Europe that are 600 miles or less apart. It will take off from downtown heliports and when aloft change to a conventional cruise flight; plus, it will cost half as much to operate but fly twice as fast as most helicopters (Siwolop, 1987).

8. Future commercial airplanes will be safer, cheaper to operate, more flexible in seating, and more comfortable (Schefter, 1987).

9. Multiple transportation cars that convert to an airplane will be fuel-efficient and economically accessible to the tourist (Kocivar, 1987; Hoyt, 1986).

10. Vertical take-off and landing vehicles – that cruise 225 mph above daily traffic – will be used for everyday personal and commercial use (Moshier Technologies, 1987).

Medicine

Major medical advances will enable people to live longer, healthier lives as science discovers new treatments for major disorders and even pushes back the frontiers of ageing itself. Consequently, the tourist population will probably be comprised of a greater proportion of more mature, physically active, healthier individuals who will seek a greater level of adventure and physical challenge than ever before. Some of those medical advances will include the following.

1. Many of the diseases that plague humans today – cancer, arteriosclerosis, arthritis, diabetes, and many infectious diseases – will fade from the scene in the next 20 years because effective ways to prevent or treat them will be found (Kluger, 1987; Bezold, 1985; Carey, 1985; Garr, 1987).

2. Genetic manipulation will help dispose of congenital defects (Cetron and O'Toole, 1982).

3. Research in combating AIDS will allow science to deal more effectively with problems of the immune system, and out of this will come, among other things, a dramatic increase in the success and number of transplant operations (Kluger, 1987; Carey, 1986).

4. In the next 20 years, there will be all kinds of transplants, including heart, lung, and brain-cell (Long, 1987).

5. There will be artificial livers, spleens, and pancreases (Cetron and O'Toole, 1982).
6. One great advance will be the discovery of some mechanism by which nerve tissue can be regenerated so that legions of paraplegics and quadriplegics can be rehabilitated (Long, 1987).
7. A portable, all purpose weapon against bites from snakes, scorpions, fire ants, bees, and wasps will be in the form of a stun gun that short circuits the consequences of the bite (Franklin and Davis, 1987).
8. Nonaddictive pain killers, more powerful than morphine, will be commonplace (Pelt, 1982).
9. There will be medicines that improve and restore memory, stave off senility, cure Parkinson's and Alzheimer's disease, and heal spinal cords (Kluger, 1987; Bezold, 1985; Cusumano, 1985).
10. Pills will be available that cure fear of flying and fear of heights (Cetron and O'Toole, 1982).
11. Medicines will be available that cure addictions to drug and alcohol (Bloom, 1985).
12. There will be hormones for controlling weight, memory and growth (Cetron and O'Toole, 1982).
13. Artificial hands, arms and limbs will be available (Walker, 1985; Kashi, 1987).
14. There will be artificial blood that can be given to a person with any blood type and that carries none of the risks of human blood (Pelt, 1982).

Recreation equipment

Here, as in the case with video, S&T advances in recreation equipment will cause both increases and decreases in tourism demand and supply; but probably, the overall effect will be more people spending more time, day and night, in outdoor environments at all times of the year.

1. Outdoor recreation clothing, although extremely lightweight and breathable, will be resistant to cold, rain, heat, and tearing, allowing the user to wear just one outfit for all climates and conditions (Scherer, 1987; Beercheck, 1986; Doran, 1986).
2. Night-vision glasses will allow individuals to participate in outdoor recreation activities in the dark; off-road vehicles will be driven at night without headlights (Shaker and Finkelstein, 1987).
3. Electronic and other devices will be worn by outdoor enthusiasts to improve hearing, touch, sense of smell, strength, and coordination (Shaker and Finkelstein, 1987).
4. Skycycles (one person light aircraft with wingspans of a DC-9 jet) – will be used to fly 25-plus miles or more at 15 miles per hour via pedal power (Ashley, 1987).
5. Ultralight two-person aircraft will be popular for touring and soaring in the 1990s (Campbell, 1986).
6. Inflatable boats that can be stored in a closet, carried to the water in the smallest car, and used in places that are not accessible by conventional boat will be used extensively in the future (Bignami, 1987).

7. Lazer tag, complete with space suit uniforms and starelyte guns that fire harmless beams of invisible infrared light at opponents day or night, will increase in home and outdoor recreation environments (*The Sharper Image*, 1986).
8. Because more people can be expected to participate in tourism and outdoor recreation activities if they can quickly learn and enjoy the skills required, sports equipment manufacturers will invent new equipment that enhances participant success (Wendland, 1986).
9. Audio communication transceivers, that will fit in a shirt pocket, will be used by vacationers to report emergencies, communicate with their workplace or home, remotely turn on and off appliances at home, and participate in certain types of work (Lundberg, 1985).
10. Technology for extracting oxygen from seawater will be used to fuel underwater recreational vehicles for exploring shipwrecks and underwater environments (Hoban, 1987).
11. Solar-powered bubbles (sunpods) will permit bathers to relax outdoors at home for an all-over tan even in below-freezing temperatures (Brody, 1984).
12. Innovations in equipment will allow off-road vehicles to be converted for wheelchair riders (Nachtivey, 1986).
13. Supersubs will be developed as a kind of undersea tour bus with oversized windows and an interior like a passenger plane (Sitwell and Sedgwick, 1984).

The natural sciences

The overall impact of new S&T in the natural sciences will be to increase both demand and supply for tourism. Emerging technology will immensely improve the quality of natural environments; probably more so in the next several decades than in previous centuries. The resultant increase in environmental quality will stimulate demand and supply for leisure activities in natural environments.

1. A chemical process will exist to embalm plants and young trees so they permanently can retain their life-like appearance in home environments (Bronson, 1987).
2. Rainbow trout weighing as much as 100 pounds and maturing five times faster than normal will be developed through genetic research. Similar achievements will be realized for salmon, tuna, and other commercial fish (Anon., 1985).
3. Techniques will be devised to communicate with one or more animal species that could eventually lead to the development of a universal translator device (Nobbe, 1987a).
4. Science will develop a grass that is self-weeding, can be grown in almost any climate or soil, needs no watering or fertilizer, and only needs to be mowed two or three times a year (Anon., 1987; Rayl, 1987).
5. Biotechnology will develop waste-eating bacteria to reduce or eliminate water pollution and toxic waste (Wallace, 1987).
6. Hunters in the United States will be able to hunt exotic wildlife from other parts of the world within a few hours drive of their residence (Hass, 1983).
7. Marine biology research will provide a means to understand,

predict, and perhaps even control the behavior of more useful or commercially valuable species; not just for human use but also for the species' own good (Nobbe, 1987b).

8. Extended weather forecasts of 2 or more weeks will be possible (Kiester, 1986; Heckman, 1987).

9. Science will develop a practical way to make drinking water from the ocean (Bowker, 1987; Glenn and O'Leary, 1985).

The built environment

Science and Technology in the built environment will cause both increases and decreases in the tourism demand–supply phenomena. Some of the items that will create increases include the following.

1. Massive, multi-storied, floating hotels will be moored off-shore and contain restaurants, shopping arcades, gymnasiums, and glass-enclosed elevators that carry tourists directly to the seafloor (Lawren, 1985).

2. Underwater hotels will attract the more adventurous leisure travelers who can peer at the undersea life through their bedroom windows (Barol and Belleville, 1987).

3. One-molecule thick glass that bends like Saran Wrap (Cling Film) and molded into many shapes will be used to create tourism structures that blend esthetically in outdoor environments and have interiors with summer temperatures throughout the year (Stewart, 1986).

4. Geotextiles, a filament produced from a variety of sources to form a nonbiodegradable fabric, will be used to stabilize erosion of scenic forest roads and trails (Schmidt, 1985).

5. Energy efficient earth shelters – those that use soil and sod for insulation – will be used in outdoor recreation facilities in hostile climates (Maranto, 1987).

6. Geothermal generators that use different water temperatures found layered through the ocean's depths will be used to power underwater villages (Lawren, 1987).

7. Electrolytic accretion (a process that uses dissolved matter in seawater) will be used to build artificial reefs and grow startling, reef-like submarine cities (Lawren, 1985; Phoebe, 1984).

On the other hand, certain other kinds of S&T related to the built environment will cause tourism demand to decrease.

1. Many homes of the future will become self-contained islands in terms of leisure lifestyle and entertainment potential. Developers will build homes that cater to the individual recreational appetites of the buyer (Sternlieb and Hughes, 1985; Lurz, 1985; Smay, 1985).

2. The theme parks of the future will be individual-experience centers where technology will let people role play...almost anything. For example, a Victorian-style high-tech house is presently being constructed than transports visitors back into a romantic version of the previous century. The house includes: a three-dimensional film theater that employs vibrating chairs to simulate motion, a scent-projection device that is coordinated with images on the screen, and a state-of-the-art sound system (Simmons, 1987).

3. Restaurants will use spatial image projections in which holograms in the shapes of mystical figures will magically appear beside customers' tables to take their orders (Simmons, 1987).

Computers, robotics, space

The coming revolution in computers, robotics, and space will cause major changes in demand–supply conditions that stretch imagination to the limit.

1. Fifty years from now, more of the world's surface may be used for farms, parkland, and wilderness because considerable quantities of industry will be moved into space (Asimov, 1983).

2. Robots will be built in the form of buildings that provide most of the services of modern hotels and that are run by an administrative computer (Barrett, 1985).

3. Robots will eventually figure greatly in planning many tourism related facilities and services, such as restaurants, landscaping, park design, and entertainment (Barrett, 1985; Reeve, 1987).

4. Robots will be used to perform hazardous tasks such as rescue operations in remote environments (Kashi, 1987; Anon., 1987).

5. Artificial intelligence in human form will be used in educational courses designed to enhance human negotiation, management, and leadership skills. These machines will instruct, counsel, and evaluate the student's participation (Knasel, 1986; Frand, 1987; Rogers, 1987).

6. Natural language software will be popular for mainframe and personal computers due to the higher fraction of novice users (Knasel, 1986).

7. Computer programs that can draw conclusions will be used by tourism managers to help formulate the best program mix for clientele and to manage vast natural resources for a multiplicity of uses (Chait, 1985; Kelly, 1985).

8. Computers will make it possible to read a journal or magazine aimed at the particular interests of an individual – a mass medium tailored to the individual (Dolnick, 1987).

9. A pocket-sized, voice-activated computer will be available that translates English into two or three languages (Stone, 1986).

10. Conflict-negotiation computer games will be used by resource managers to define and choose alternative courses of action regarding tourism development versus nondevelopment in wildland areas (Zweig, 1986).

11. Vandal-proofed computers will be installed at trail-heads and along the trail to explain better the value of the environment and interpret what is being observed (McCann, 1984).

12. Computers eventually will possess artificial intelligence and mimic human senses and attitudes (Rogers, 1987; Waterbury, 1987; Hoban, 1987).

13. A passenger module will be developed for the space shuttle that will carry passengers to an orbiting space hotel or act as a hotel module itself (Alcestis, 1983; Eskow, 1986;

Davies, 1985; Wolkomir, 1986).

14. Today's commercial airliner will be modified to become a space transport to deliver payloads to a low orbit for 90 per cent less than the cost of a NASA shuttle flight (Lawren, 1986).

15. Eventually, it will be possible to create robotic immortality – a deathless universe, in which life would go on forever by creating computer copies of our minds and transferring, or downloading this program into robotic bodies. Once one copy of the brain's contents had been made, it would be possible to make multiple backup copies. This would allow anyone to embark on any sort of adventure without having to worry about ageing or death. As decades passed into centuries, one could travel the globe and then the solar system and beyond (Fjermedal, 1986; Maranto, 1987; Dewitt, 1987).

Conclusion

Essentially, the whole process of tourism strategic planning boils down to planning on uncertainty. Uncertainty is the complement of knowledge – the gap between what is known and what needs to be known to make correct decisions. Dealing sensibly with uncertainty is not a byway on the road to responsible tourism management decisions, it is central to it. To cope with future tourism planning, management, and research, professionals need to be renaissance thinking women and men. The need to imagine, perceive, and gauge the future are paramount professional attributes of tourism professionals of tomorrow. The future tourism phenomena will be managed by today's professionals who look to the future and shape it into a strategic vision. The information presented in this chapter has been aimed at helping create that vision.

Further reading

Alcestis, O., 'NASA's space hotel,' *Science Digest* (April 1983), p. 58.

Anon., 'Superfish: genetics seeks 100-pound trout', *The Futurist* (February 1985), p. 3.

Anon., 'Now, artificial reality', *Newsweek* (9 February 1987), p. 56.

Ashley, S., '88-pound pedal plane', *Popular Science* (1987), pp. 70–3; 118–20.

Asimov, I., 'The 21st century: squinting into the crystal ball', *US News and World Report* (9 May 1983), p. A41.

Barol, B. and Belleville, B., 'Sleep tight, underwater', *Newsweek* (April 1987), p. 56.

Barrett, F., 'The robot revolution', *The Futurist* (October 1985), pp. 37–40.

Beercheck, R., 'Engineering: the winning edge', *Machine Design* (June 1986), pp. 26–32.

Bezold, C., 'Drugs and health in the year 2000', *The Futurist* (June 1985), pp. 36–40.

Bignami, L., 'Blow-up boating', *Boat Pennsylvania* (Summer 1987), pp. 4–7.

Black, R., 'Magnetic trains take off,' *Science Digest* (August 1984), p. 26.

Bloom, F., 'Brain drugs', *Science* (November 1985), p. 58.

Booth, S., 'Future vision', *Popular Mechanics* (July 1986), pp. 67–9.

Bowker, M., 'Fresh water from the ocean', *Popular Science* (April 1987), p. 57–8.

Brody, R., 'Sun bubble', *Omni* (June 1984), p. 52.

Bronson, G., 'Vegetable taxidermy', *Forbes* (May 1987), p. 145.

Campbell, J., 'Flying wing built for two', *Popular Mechanics* (October 1986), p. 60.

Carey, J., 'The brain yields its secrets to research', *US News and World Report* (3 June 1985), pp. 64–5.

Carey, J., 'Genetics and heart disease', *US News and World Report* (28 July 1986), p. 58.

Creton, M. J. and O'Toole, T., *Encounters with the Future: A Forecast of Life into the 21st Century* (McGraw Hill, 1982).

Cetron, M. J. and Rocha, W., 'Travel tomorrow', *The Futurist* (July/August 1987), pp. 29–34.

Chait, L., *Direct Marketing* (Hoke Communication, 1985).

Cook, W., 'Cars of the 90s', *US News and World Report* (August 1987), pp. 38–44.

Country Technology, 'Vital signs' (Country Technology, 1987/88).

Cusumano, J., 'Designer catalysts,' *Science* (November 1985), p. 12.

Davies, O., 'Space tourists', *Omni* (November 1985), pp. 30–2.

Dewitt, P., 'Dreaming the impossible at MIT', *Time* (31 August 1987), pp. 52–3.

Dolnick, E., 'Inventing the future', *The New York Times Magazine* (23 August 1987), pp. 30–3; 41; 59.

Doran, P., 'Winter world – getting technical', *Runner's World*, vol. 21, no. 11 (1986), pp. 43–8.

Electronic Arts, 'Chuck Yeager's advanced flight simulator'. (Video).

Eskow, D., 'Space city', *Popular Mechanics* (June 1986), pp. 27–30.

Fensom, R., 'Self enrichment travel', *USA Today* (September 1984), pp. 40–2.

Fjermedal, G., 'Surrogate brains', *Omni* (October 1986), p. 38.

Frand, E., 'Some terrific new product ideas', *Research and Development* (July 1987), p. 19.

Franklin, D. and Davis, L., 'Shocking snakebites', *Hippocrates* (May/June 1987), pp. 8–9.

Garr, D., 'Conic painkiller', *Omni* (May 1987), p. 128.

Glenn, E. and O'Leary, J., 'Productivity and irrigation requirements of halophytes grown with seawater in the Sonoran Desert', *Journal of Arid Environments* (July 1985), pp. 1–11.

Hass, R., 'Global reforestation', *Resources for the Future* (1983), p. 21.

Hartley, C., 'Video dreamland', *Audio-Visual Communications* (June 1987), p. 41.

Heckman, J., 'Tomorrow's weather', *The Futurist* (March/April 1987), pp. 27–9.

Hoban, P., 'Artificial intelligence', *Omni* (February 1987), pp. 24; 111.

Hoyt, W., 'Driving the future', *Popular Mechanics* (October 1986), pp. 77–9; 115.

Iacocca, L., *Iacocca, An Autobiography* (Bantam Books, 1984).

International Video Network (Video Travel library, undated).

Kashi, E., 'Part of life', *Hippocrates* (May/June 1987), pp. 46–53.

Kaufmann, W., 'Tourism in the twenty-first century, *Science Digest* (April 1983), pp. 53–60.

Kelly, *Computer in Landscape Architecture*, Landscape Architecture Technical Information, Series 8 (American Society of Landscape Architects, Washington DC, 1985).

Kennedy, H., 'Travel videos', *US News and World Report*, vol. 3 (August 1987), p. 65.

Kiester, E., 'Rain or shine', *Science Digest*, vol. 94, no. 9 (1986), pp. 48–53; 83.

Kluger, J., 'Body doubles', *Omni* (August 1987), pp. 48–9; 106.

Knasel, T., 'Artificial intelligence in manufacturing: forecasts for the use of artificial intelligence in the USA', *Robotics* (Elsevier Science

Publishers, 1986), pp. 357–62.

Kocivar, B., 'Flying porsche', *Popular Science* (May 1987), p. 39.

Kristof, N., '12-minute trip to coast is plane's goal', *The New York Times* (2 December 1987), Business Day: D-1.

Lawren, B., 'Floating hotel', *Omni* (February 1985), pp. 27–8.

Lawren, B., 'Private affordable space planes', *Omni* (December 1986), p. 157.

Lawren, B., 'The cities of Neptune', *Omni* (July 1987), pp. 37–40; 88.

Lemonick, M., 'Superconductors!' *Time* (May 1987), pp. 62–72.

Long, M., 'The 1987 seer's catalog', *Omni* (January 1987), pp. 37–40; 94–100.

Lundberg, O., 'Proposed mobile-satellite systems will offer users a wide range of services,' *Communications News* (June 1985), p. 51.

Lurz, W., 'Introducing NEST '85 – an exciting housing concept' *Professional Builder* (February 1985), pp. 1–10.

Maranto, G., 'Earth's first visitors to Mars', *Discover* (May 1987), pp. 28–43.

Massey, M., *The People Puzzle: Understanding Yourself and Others* (Reston Publishing Co., 1979).

McCann, R., "Communications is the goal in the computer world', *Parks and Recreation* (November 1984), pp. 33–5.

McCoy, M., 'Technology update', *Lodging Hospitality* (May 1987), pp. 72–3.

McIntosh, R. W. and Goeldner, C. R., *Tourism: Principles, Practices, Philosophies* (John Wiley, 5th edition, 1984).

Miller, W. F., 'Emerging technologies and their implications for America', *USA Today* (November 1986), pp. 60–4.

Moshier Technologies, 'The dawn of a new era in transportation may be closer than you think', *Discover* (May 1987), p. 15.

Nachtivey, R., 'In high gear', *Sports and Spokes* (January/February 1986), p. 17.

Naisbitt, J., *Megatrends* (Warner Books, 1982).

Naisbitt, J., 'A nation on wheels', *Popular Mechanics* (July 1986), pp. 173–90.

Naisbitt, J., *Trend Letter* (1987).

Naisbitt, J. and Aburdene, P., *Re-inventing the Corporation* (Warner Books, 1985).

Nobbe, G., 'Flippernauts', *Omni* (May 1987a), p. 37.

Nobbe, G., 'Fish talk', *Omni* (March 1987b), p. 28.

Pelt, D., 'Next best thing to whole blood?, *Insight* (12 October 1982), p. 51.

Perry, N., 'The economy of the 1990s – what the sober spenders will buy', *Fortune* (2 February, 1987), pp. 35–8.

Phoebe, H., 'Sponge power', *Omni* (September 1984), p. 2.

Plawin, P. and Blum, A., 'Great family vacations', *Changing Times* (July 1987), pp. 35–9.

Rayl, A., 'Dreamgrass', *Omni* (May 1987), p. 36.

Reeve, R., 'Where are the robots?', *Chemtech* (February 1987), pp. 72–5.

Rochester, P., 'The unreal thing', *Omni* (December 1986), p. 3.

Rogers, M., 'The next computers', *Newsweek* (April 1987), pp. 60–2.

Schefter, J., 'Engineering tomorrow's airlines', *Popular Science* (April 1987), pp. 49–52; 98.

Scherer, M., 'New wrinkles in old clothing', *Sierra* (January/February 1987), pp. 121–4.

Schmidt, D., 'Building better blacktops', *American City and County Administration, Engineering and Operations* (Communication Channels, June 1985), pp. 1–3.

Shaker, S. and Finkelstein, R., 'The bionic soldier', *National Defense* (April 1987), pp. 3–7.

Simmons, J. C., 'Christopher and Goddard: variations on a theme', *American Way* (15 July 1987), pp. 21–5.

Sitwell, N. and Sedgwick, J., 'Super sub of the future', *The Futurist* (June 1984), pp. 60–65.

Sivy, M., 'What we don't know', *Money* (November 1985), pp. 209–12.

Siwolop, S., 'Unsteady as she flows', *Discover*, vol. 6, no. 4 (1985), pp. 67–9.

Siwolop, S., 'It's a chopper – it's a plane – it's Europe's new air shuttle', *Business Week* (19 January 1987), p. 75.

Smay, V., 'Bolt and glue arched panels cut costs', *Popular Science* (August 1985), p. 13.

Smith, J. O., 'Mysterious weekends', *County* (January 1985), pp. 28–9.

Sternlieb, G. and Hughes, J., *The Good News about Housing* (Dow Jones and Co., August 1985), pp. 1–5.

Stewart, D., 'Fiber fabric structures', *Science Digest* (March 1986), pp. 58–62.

Stone, C., 'Computer translator', *Omni* (December 1986), p. 157.

Sybervision (Sybervision, 6066 Civic Terrace Ave., Newark, CA).

The Sharper Image (October 1986), pp. 1–2.

Tracy, E., 'A new X-ray scanner to hinder hijackers', *Fortune* (28 April 1986), p. 12.

Walker, P., 'Joints to spare', *Science* (November 1985), p. 57.

Wallace, J., 'Pollution solutions', *USAIR* (January 1987), pp. 58–62.

Waterbury, R., 'Computer/human interface 2000', *Assembly Engineering* (June 1987), pp. 70–3.

Wendland, M., 'New wave gear', *American Health* (July/August 1986), pp. 50–3.

Wiener, L., 'All the sights, sounds and comforts of home', *US News and World Report* (August 1987), p. 45.

Wolkomir, R., 'Beyond the challenger era', *Omni* (February 1986), pp. 27–30.

Yeager, C., 'America's orient express', *Popular Mechanics* (August 1986), pp. 73–5.

Zweig, C., 'Mayan vacation', *Omni* (December 1986), p. 157.

ELWOOD L. SHAFER and
GEORGE MOELLER

Seasonality

Introduction

The seasonality of tourism is simultaneously one of its most widely recognized features and one of its least well researched. Perhaps these two aspects are tied together, in that the acceptance of acute seasonal fluctuations in trade as being normal and even necessary on the part of its practitioners, has been a principal factor inhibiting research into the phenomenon. Indeed, Boyer (1972, p. 112) has suggested that not only was tourism 'born seasonal', but also that in this inheritance lies its 'original sin'. In relation to seasonality the innovatory work of BarOn (1976) stood as virtually the only significant contribution until about 1980. Nevertheless, enough material has now been gathered to indicate that patterns of seasonal fluctuation in the tourist trade have nothing inevitable about them, and that the emergence of seasonal patterns, the degree of their intensity, and their historic durability are all variables which can both merit and repay research.

Defining 'seasons' and 'seasonality'

By 'seasonality' in general we mean the tendency of tourist flows to become concentrated into relatively short periods of the year. Following the pioneering work of BarOn, it has become customary to distinguish between 'natural' and 'institutional' seasonality. The first of these refers to the impact of natural (especially climatic) features on the demand for or supply of tourism. In this respect, it is clear that the arrival of a monsoon, or rainy reason, will have a profound effect on the pattern of modern 'sunlust' tourism, and the development of ski resorts is unlikely in the absence of dependable falls of snow. There has been a tendency on the part of tourism specialists and practitioners alike, at least until recent years, to assume that natural features of this kind are the ultimate determining factor in shaping the pattern of sectoral activity. As Hartmann puts it: 'Tourism has been developed under seasonal auspices' (Hartmann, 1986, p. 25). It is important both from a theoretical and a practical point of view, however, to realize that seasonality in this 'natural' sense is not a simple matter.

Stynes and Pigozzi remind us (1983, p. 19) there is a tendency to assume that fluctuations are dictated directly by the features of the climate of the receiving area, whereas:

seasonality may...appear where climate is constant relative to other locations. For example, Hawaii may exhibit 'seasonality' because of the weather in Michigan and other northern states rather than any fluctuation in its own climate.

In fact, the relationship between tourist flows and such natural factors may be a highly complex and mediated one, and should never be taken for granted: it is overlaid everywhere by cultural (or 'institutional') factors.

At the most basic and general level (as Hartmann has emphasized) the conceptualization of time in seasonal terms is itself, a cultural and not a natural fact. It is quite wrong to make the ethnocentric assumption that one can invariably organize time into 'spring, 'summer', 'autumn' and 'winter'. The traditional Hindu calendar identifies six seasons: many African peoples recognize only two. These compartmentalizations of time, however, while they no doubt correspond in some measure to climatic changes, create definite divisions within processes which are more or less continuous. 'Seasons' are therefore, to some extent, socially significant periods of time, rather than naturally-occurring events. Time is evaluated with respect to some set of human purposes and cycles of activities.

The relevance of this abstract point to the more concrete problems of tourism is twofold. Firstly, the history of tourism shows that there have been important shifts over time in the seasonal preferences of tourists. Secondly, by no means all of those activities for which people engage in touristic travel are bound to specific climatic seasons of the year, even though they may exhibit 'seasonal' variation in their distribution.

Historical shifts in seasonal patterns

During the nineteenth century in Europe, when tourism was still largely an aristocratic phenomenon, prevailing ideologies of health were capitalized upon by spa towns. To the extent that the utilization of these resorts was seasonal, the medicinal use of their waters was dictated less by natural factors than by the complementarity of other social activities – the cycle of events at court, or the social life of the capital city, for example (Young, 1973, p. 13).

The early resorts of the Mediterranean coast, such as Nice and Opatija, also founded initially on a belief in the salutary value of sea bathing, offered the wealthy the comfort of a refuge from the rigors of the winter in Northern and Central Europe (Blazevic, 1976; Nash, 1979; Rudney, 1980). This pattern even shaped the early development of some southern UK seaside towns (Roberts, 1983). The shift to a dominant summer season only came after the First World War, and the interpenetration of 'natural' and 'institutional' factors in the shaping of seasonality is underlined by this shift.

The change from a winter to a summer season was associated with the extension of leisure time among the rising middle classes, and later among manual workers also. The summer holiday period for manual workers initially was dictated by the need for extra labor at the harvest. This pattern has persisted through inertia, and has been perpetuated by the fact that the principal school holidays of the year typically continue to coincide with the traditional harvest-time, even though the initial reason for this coincidence has disappeared. Certain types of leisure activity may, therefore, quite clearly be connected to natural (climatic) phenomena: but whether this becomes a 'holiday season' or not depends upon social factors which determine who is available to participate in these activities.

Other 'institutional' factors shaping seasonality

Other types of tourist activity relate little, if at all, to natural seasons. The peaks of tourist activity surrounding pilgrimages to the Christian holy places in Palestine, at Christmas and Easter, are dictated by the traditional calendar of the Churches, and the celebration of major events in the life of Christ. For the faithful, the Islamic pilgrimage to Mecca should be made in the month of *Dhu'l-Hijja*, which, since the Islamic calendar is lunar advances by about 10 days each year. Religious pilgrimages remain very important reasons for travel in many parts of the world, and may feature among the principal reasons for the pattern of seasonality in many tourist destinations. It is rather surprising, therefore, that they have received such passing attention in the literature on tourism.

Another type of tourism which has not attracted the attention in the literature which it possibly merits is 'congress tourism' – the holding of meetings of a business, academic, political or other character. Fighiera (1985) has documented a noticeable tendency to seasonality in the distribution of such events. A simple speculative explanation for these patterns might resort to the indirect impact of 'natural' factors – principally, to the availability of accommodation at relatively cheap rates in holiday resorts at times of the year which lie outside their normal peak season, although this latter may be dictated largely by climatic factors. It is plain from Fighiera's data, however, that the matter is more complex than this, in that climatically similar regions (the Netherlands and the United Kingdom, for example) do not report the same cycles in the distribution of meetings. Moreover, national and international events follow quite distinguishable cycles. Quite clearly, once again, any explanation will have to concentrate principally on configurations of institutional factors (timetables for the academic or parliamentary year, for example) which will interact with more conventionally seasonal factors.

Seasonality as a problem

Authors who have addressed themselves to the study of seasonal variability have typically seen it as a problem to be tackled, making much of the disadvantages which acutely skewed patterns of trade will entail. Manning and Powers (1984, p. 25) present us with a typical catalog of difficulties:

> Uneven distribution of use over time...is one of the most pervasive problems in outdoor recreation and tourism, causing inefficient resource use, loss of profit potential, strain on social and ecological carrying capacities, and administrative scheduling difficulties.

A very similar appraisal is given by Burkart and Medlik (1974, p. 67). To this catalog of disincentives, Mathieson and Wall (1982, pp. 38 and 49) add that, because of its seasonal character, tourism is an unstable export, which tends to have low customer loyalty, and one in which private investment in developing countries is reluctant to take an active interest – a point which is echoed by Archer (1973), in his study of Anglesey.

The specific concern of less-developed countries for the effects of seasonality is stressed by Yacoumis (1980, p. 84), who argues that unlike their more-developed sisters, they are typically unable to derive supplementary support from domestic demand. Whether the absence of domestic demand is a blessing or a blight in this respect remains to be argued, however, as the experience of countries such as Spain and Yugoslavia (in which there is a strong domestic demand for tourism services) suggests that the temporal coincidence of domestic and foreign demand actually may tend to exaggerate any problems of excessive seasonal concentration, rather than relieve them.

Archer also recognizes the positive role which tourism plays in the generation of employment, but draws our attention to the potentially destabilizing effects on other sectors of the local economy. In this he is supported by D'Amore (1976, p. 33) who sees tourism as attracting workers away from fulltime employment, thus discouraging other industries or types of economic activity from locating in the area. Tourism has also been criticized for its seasonal peaks coinciding with, rather than complementing, those of other equally seasonal economic sectors (principally agriculture), with which it therefore competes for the factors of production (Mathieson and Wall, 1982, p. 129). It is interesting, however, that these views have been challenged more recently by the work of Mourdoukoutas (1985), on the seasonal effects of employment in the Greek economy.

In a sociological study of the development of tourism in Yugoslavia, Allcock has argued that the seasonal character of the trade can be seen as one factor contributing to the institutionally weak position of the worker in self-managing institutions within the tourism sector (Allcock, 1986; 1987).

Jafari (1974) links seasonal fluctuations to the hostility which is sometimes generated within local communities towards tourism. More specifically, several studies have noted the association between tourism and crime (reviewed in Mathieson and Wall, 1982, pp. 150–2). There does seem to be a logical confusion which attends much of this argument, however, in that the authors are not always clear as to whether crime waves in tourist-receiving areas are simply to be explained by the fact that there is a time of the year when the population is greater (and more crimes are committed numerically, though not necessarily more in proportion to the greater population density) or whether the seasonality of tourism specifically generates higher crime rates.

BarOn has coined the term 'seasonal loss' to refer to the costs which may be attributed to the negative effects of seasonality (BarOn, 1976, p. 45).

In general, then, the discussion of seasonality in the literature seems to mirror much of the wider debate in the cost–benefit, or 'effects' tradition; although it is curious in this regard that there has been so little attention paid to the possible benefits to be attributed to seasonality. Only Hartmann (1986, pp. 31–2) unambiguously voices this interest:

> I would maintain that dead seasons are the only chance for a social and ecological environment to recover fully. A dormant period for the host environment is simply a necessity in order to preserve its identity.

This side of the case should certainly attract greater consideration in future research.

Measures to counteract seasonality

Given the prevailing tone of adversity with which the phenomenon of seasonality is discussed, it is not surprising to find that a good deal of the literature has been devoted to the search for measures which planners or managers within the industry might adopt in order to counteract seasonality. Four principal strategies have been canvassed in this respect: variation of the product-mix, diversification of the market, differential pricing strategies and state encouragement or facilitation of the 'staggering' of holidays.

Probably the most commonly-advocated strategy for the achievement of a more balanced flow of trade is variation of the product-mix (BarOn, 1976, pp. 44–51; International Hotel Association, 1985; Manning and Powers, 1984; Yacoumis, 1980). This involves the creation and marketing of attractions additional to those which provided the focus for the original development. Thus a beach resort might attempt to extend its season by mounting some special event, such as a golf festival; a winter sports resort might begin to advertise its potential as a center for climbing and mountain walking in the summer; a spa town might seek to even out its seasonal flow by appealing to the conference trade. A famous example of this strategy is the provision by the Lancashire seaside resort of Blackpool of 'illuminations' during the month of October, which would otherwise fall out of season. A curious failure to take advantage of this strategy is found in the Yugoslav city of Dubrovnik, which continues to mount its summer festival of the arts in August many years after its popularity has grown to the point that there is excessive demand for accommodation there in that month.

A subvariant of this approach to countering seasonality developed by several tour companies has been the 'two-center holiday'. This attracts the customer to a well-established resort with an accepted reputation, which may be suffering from excessive demand, but links a part of the holiday spent there to an extended visit to a less well-used resort, or one with different types of attraction. A typical two-center holiday will combine, for example, a week by the sea with a week in the country's capital city, or an ancient cultural center. From a national point of view this strategy does nothing to reduce the overall seasonal skew in the demand for its product; but it might serve to provide a better spatial distribution of the demand for its resources. The development of 'circuits' of attractions of this kind is a common device, which although it cannot be said to counter seasonality, at least may help to make its effects more manageable.

This approach to the management of seasonality may be particularly attractive to those areas whose attractions do appear to be prone to exceptionally steep 'peaking' of their seasonal pattern, but for whom the strategy of diversifying their product is inherently difficult, if not impossible – particularly National Parks (see Clawson and Knetsch, 1966).

The strategy of varying the product-mix (changing the product on offer) may, in practice, be closely tied to the strategy of diversification of the market (the attempt to present the product to new potential purchasers). Yacoumis commends this approach as one of the options available to tourism in Sri Lanka (Yacoumis, 1980, p. 97). Maynard has remarked upon the success of the Bahamas in diversifying its market, by moving beyond an established reliance on the United States to reach new custom in Canada and Europe (especially the United Kingdom and West Germany) (Maynard, 1979, p. 166).

Calantone and Johar (1984), in a complex analysis of the attitudes of visitors to parks in the State of Massachusetts, explore the applicability of an approach in terms of 'benefit segmentation'. They provide us with a typology of visitors to their region, differentiated by lifestyle and motivational structure. Their conclusion is not only that different kinds of people seek different kinds of benefits, but that the relationship between groups and the benefits they pursue is shaped by highly variable factors of their situation, such that:

> The types of people that seek a combination of benefits in one season may not be the same types of people that seek the same benefit during another season. (p. 23)

The implications of their study relate to both strategies directed at the product mix, and those which seek to diversify the market, and suggest that, while these might usefully be treated in relation to each other, their effective combination should clearly be based on more than hunches and rule-of-thumb. In any case, there is good reason to believe that this route may be a hard one, demanding very considerable effort and expenditure applied to both research and promotion, without assured gain.

The use of price differentials as stimuli to the market in periods outside the main season might be thought to be an obvious corrective to excessive seasonal concentration, in view of the widely-noted price-elasticity of demand for tourism. Surprisingly, however, pricing appears to have been viewed largely within the context of the overall competition between destinations.

Pricing policies may work in two directions in relation to seasonal congestion. Manning and Powers (1984, p. 25 ff.) for example, see the potential value of price reductions for attracting visitors during the low season. BarOn, by way of contrast (1976, pp. 44–5), reflects on the effectiveness of higher prices as a means of discouraging trade during the peak season. There appears to be little systematic study of the effects in practice of pricing in relation to seasonal flows. Burkart and Medlik (1974, p. 179), however, do point to the positive impact of the policy of the British Air Transport Licensing Board on the volume of winter travel in the early 1970s. Pricing incentives have probably been linked most effectively to strategies of market differentiation in the case of the several schemes (such as Saga Holidays) which have been developed specifically for the retired, who are free to take advantage of out-of-season offers.

Finally, considerable effort has been applied, especially in the European countries of the Organization of Economic Cooperation and Development (OECD), to influencing the pattern of seasonal concentration through various state-initiated measures directed at its institutional roots. The OECD has provided a useful, though highly condensed, review of these (OECD, 1986, pp. 50–1; see also Dubourg, 1985). Attention in the francophone countries has been systematically applied to the possibility of staggering the main school and industrial holidays over a longer period. Switzerland has made the most progress in this respect, but negotiations continue in France between the Ministry of Education, the SNCF (the national railway system) and other interested bodies. Already it is reported that there has been a fall in the number of enterprises closing completely during the traditional peak month of August, from 54 per cent in 1982 to 41 per cent in 1985.

A variety of other devices have been employed by governments to the same end. The French have instituted a series of awards to resorts for success in the *aménagement du temps*. The Greek government has made loans available for the construction of heated swimming pools. Yugoslavia has relied on tax concessions on the price of fuel oil for tourist establishments operating off-season. Such evidence as there is, however, suggests that it is very difficult to make an appreciable difference to distributions by these means.

Measuring seasonality: some conceptual issues

Because of the perceived importance of seasonality for the trade, and the potential value of policy measures or managerial practices which might affect the degree of seasonality, a good deal of attention has been devoted to the task of producing accurate measures of the phenomenon. In part, of course, one's capacity to assess with any degree of accuracy the seasonality of tourist flows is dependent upon the quality of the basic data from which calculations are made. The variable quality of material in this respect is well-known; but statistical issues of this kind will not be our concern here. Also, the methodological problems of measuring seasonality are not, in principle, different from those relating to the management of time-series data more generally. These wider technical issues of measurement will be set aside in this context. Our intention here is to focus upon a number of key conceptual points.

Talk of 'seasonality' probably typically calls to mind a relatively simple visual image: yet as BarOn has reminded us, in fact the temporal distribution patterns of tourist flows can be represented by a great variety of curves (BarOn, 1976, Diag. 9). In any one case, this curve will not reflect the impact of a single factor: it may, indeed, compound the results of a complex series of events. He himself stresses the importance of separating both conceptually and practically 'seasonality' from two other influences. The 'trend cycle' (possibly a tendency to overall long-term growth) needs to be separated from properly 'seasonal' fluctuations. Also, various 'irregular' factors (he cites here both regular institutional events such as religious festivals, and highly unusual events which may have an impact on the tourist trade, such as wars or acts of terrorism) need to be abstracted from the measurement of seasonality.

This general stance towards data is generally accepted within the field: but his typology of factors has been considerably refined by later work. Yacoumis (1980, pp. 88–9) in his study of Sri Lanka, stresses the need to further analyze 'seasonality' into sectoral and regional components, particularly when treating aggregate national data. Husbands (1986), in his examination of data relating to Mexico, distinguishes between two components of BarOn's 'trend-cycle' – trends in a general sense, and the specific effects of the business cycle. A further refinement is proposed by Sutcliffe and Sinclair (1980, p. 432), in their distinction between 'pure seasonality' and 'pattern changes'. They argue that the overall degree of seasonality in the demand for tourism to a particular destination may vary independently of the stability of the pattern (or general shape of the curve), illustrating their argument by reference to the development of Spanish tourism.

Considerable practical importance may attach to the measurement of seasonality, on the part of business, state or other public interests; and the nature of the policy or managerial alternatives which are open to them (or the extent to which one is to be preferred over another) may depend directly upon the measurements which are available to them and the predictions which result from these. There is consequently great interest in the work of Sutcliffe and Sinclair (1980) which takes a comparative look at a variety of measures which have been developed over the years. In particular, they subject data from Spain for the years 1952–1975 to analysis by three methods: Lorenz curves linked to Gini coefficients (see also Wanhill, 1980, for this method), the analysis of standard deviations, and an alternative measure derived from information theory. (Stynes and Pigozzi, 1983, and Fritz and Xander, 1982, present us with additional choices.)

Using the first of these, they calculate that the seasonality of Spanish tourism increased during the period in question by 45 per cent. Their information theory measure, on the other hand, indicated an increase of 120 per cent over the same interval. Although the correlation between the two measures was very high, and the measures produce similar rankings of years, they differ significantly in their estimation of the proportionate increase in seasonality. Although the authors do not spell out the business or policy implications of their findings, their work clearly stands as a warning of the hazards involved to those who venture into the quantification of seasonal phenomena.

Conclusion

Although the tendency of the tourist trade to develop strongly marked seasonal patterns of demand tends to be accepted as a fact of life in both academic and business circles, it is widely recognized that these pose many problems for both the tourist industry itself and for the wider host communities. In spite of its taken-for-granted character, however, seasonality is in principle subject to moderation, both as the result of spontaneous social and cultural change, and in response to policy. The difficulties of making headway against deeply entrenched institutional, cultural and economic patterns should not be underestimated: but the literature does indicate a wide range of possible measures which are worth exploring.

The possible practical responses to seasonality are linked to the problem of its measurement, as the appropriateness of, or even the need for, particular policies will depend upon our ability to say just which aspects of the distribution of demand are 'seasonal'. The whole area remains under-researched, however; and there is a clear need for both more intensive investigation of the phenomenon, and more adventurous state and business practice in response to it.

Further reading

Allcock, J. B., 'Yugoslavia's tourist trade: pot of gold or pig in a poke?', *Annals of Tourism Research*, vol. 13, no. 4 (1986), pp. 565–88. The author argues that the high degree of seasonality in employment is one of several factors which makes for the alienation of the worker in the Yugoslav hotel industry.

Allcock, J. B., 'Tourism and industrialisation: patterns of work and civic culture in conflict – some reflections on the Yugoslav case', *Problems of Tourism*, vol. X, no. 3 (1987), pp. 38–48. The article examines the conflict between the situation of seasonal workers in the Yugoslav hotel industry and the normative images of the worker in Yugoslav civic culture.

Archer, B. H., *The Impact of Domestic Tourism*, Bangor Occasional Papers in Economics, no. 2 (University of Wales, 1973). Archer suggests, in his study of Anglesey, that seasonality may act as a disincentive to investment in tourism.

BarOn, R. R. V., *Seasonality in Tourism: A Guide to the Analysis of Seasonality and Trends for Policy Making*, Technical Series no. 2 (Economist Intelligence Unit, 1976). This is one of the most important conceptual and methodological discussions of problems relating to seasonality yet produced. It remains a central reference work more than a decade after its publication.

Blaževic, I., 'Opatija – razvoj turizma i njegov utjecaj na transformaciju naselja', *Radovi Instituta Geografije Sveučilišta u Zagrebu*, vol. 13 (1976), pp. 267–98. This historical study of a Yugoslav resort documents the shift in seasonal pattern from a winter to a summer peak.

Boyer, M., *Le Tourisme* (Editions du Seuil, 1972). This is one of the few general discussions of tourism which gives adequate recognition to the importance of seasonality for the understanding of tourism.

Burkart, A. J. and Medlik, S., *Tourism: Past, Present and Future* (Heinemann, 1974). This major text in the economics of tourism illustrates the general tendency to take for granted the seasonality of tourism, while making several references to its effects.

Calantone, R. J. and Johar, J. S., 'Seasonal segmentation of the tourism market using a benefit segmentation framework', *Journal of Travel Research*, vol. XXIII, no. 2 (1984), pp. 14–24. The results of a complex questionnaire survey are analyzed to relate patterns of perceived benefits from national parks use to seasonal demand.

Clawson, M. and Knetsch, J. L., *Economics of Outdoor Recreation* (Johns Hopkins University Press, 1966). The authors draw attention to the fact that not all types of recreational facilities are prone to the same patterns and intensity of seasonal use.

D'Amore, L. J., 'The significance of tourism in Canada', *Business Quarterly*, vol. 41, no. 3 (1976), pp. 27–35. Within a general review of the economic value of tourism for Canada, the author considers the possibility that seasonality may discourage the mobility of labor.

Dubourg, J., 'Etalement des vacances: cent fois sur le métier', *Repertoire des Vacances*, no. 390 (1985), pp. 17–21. This article reviews attempts to diminish the skewed distribution of the tourist trade by means of the staggering of holiday periods.

Fighiera, G. C., 'Le caractère saisonnier des réunions', *Revue de Tourisme*, vol. 40, no. 3 (1985), pp. 14–19. The article presents the results of a world survey of the patterns of seasonal distribution in 'conference tourism'.

Fritz, R. G. and Xander, J., 'Estimating seasonality in time-series forecasting models', *Review of Regional Studies*, vol. 12, no. 3 (1982), pp. 1–10. The authors have provided a critical technical review of a wide series of methods of time-series analysis, in relation to their utility in estimating seasonality.

Hartmann, R, 'Tourism, seasonality and social change', *Leisure Studies*, vol. 5, no. 1 (1986), pp. 25–33. The article provides a useful conceptual discussion of seasonality, and considers its importance from a sociological standpoint. Particularly interesting is his suggestion that more attention should be given to the positive value of the seasonal pattern of trade in tourism.

Husbands, W. C., 'The cyclic behaviour of tourist flows: tourist arrivals in Mexico', *Revue de tourisme*, vol. 41, no. 2 (1986), pp. 19–22. Husbands' article offers one mathematical model for the analysis of seasonality. He is interested in particular in the disengagement of the effects of business cycles from seasonality.

International Hotel Association, 'South Asia to combat tourism seasonality', *Tourism Management*, vol. 6, no. 2 (1985), pp. 155–6. This is a report of a meeting of the IHA, illustrating the awareness within the business community of the importance of seasonality.

Jafari, J., 'The socio-economic costs of tourism to developing countries', *Annals of Tourism Research*, vol. 1 (1974), pp. 227–59. Among the several social effects of the development of tourism which the author considers in this general survey, he draws attention to the way in which seasonal fluctuations may encourage local hostility to the industry.

Manning, R. E. and Powers, L. A., 'Peak and off-peak use: redistributing the outdoor recreation/tourism load', *Journal of Travel Research*, vol. XXIII, no. 2 (1984), pp. 25–31. The authors report the results of a questionnaire study of visitors to eight Vermont campsites, in order to determine the possibilities for developing measures to encourage off-peak use. They favour the use of differential pricing mechanisms.

Mathieson, A. and Wall, G., *Tourism: Economic, Physical and Social Impacts* (Longman, 1982). This general text reviewing the literature in the 'impact' tradition of tourism studies, provides a succinct summary of the problems caused by seasonality generally cited in the literature.

Maynard, C. T., 'Tourism marketing for the Bahamas', *Caribbean Tourism: Policies and Impacts*, J. S. Holder, ed. (Caribbean Tourism Research and Development Centre, 1979), pp. 162–7. This paper presents an example of a successful attempt to moderate the excessive peaking of the tourist trade by the diversification of the market.

Mourdoukatis, P. G., *Seasonal Employment and Tourist Development: The Case of the Greek islands*, Ph.D. dissertation (State University of New York, Stony Brook, 1985). This thorough study of seasonal employment in tourism in the Greek islands suggests that the adverse effects of tourism on the wider structure of employment have typically been exaggerated in the literature.

Nash, D., 'The rise and fall of an aristocratic tourist culture, Nice: 1763–1936', *Annals of Tourism Research*, vol. 6 (1979), pp. 61–75. This valuable contribution to the history of tourism underlines the importance of the shift in seasonal patterns over time.

Organization for Economic Cooperation and Development, *Tourism Policy and International Tourism in OECD Member Countries* (OECD, 1986). There is a brief review of the several attempts made by OECD member countries to reduce the seasonal skew in their tourist trade by a variety of devices.

Roberts, R., 'The corporation as impressario: the municipal provision of entertainment in Victorian and Edwardian Bournemouth', *Leisure in Britain, 1780–1939*, J. K. Walton and J. Walvin, eds (The University of Manchester Press, 1983). This study illustrates the way in which even British resorts in the nineteenth century to some extent followed the Mediterranean pattern of seasonal use.

Rudney, R., 'The development of tourism on the Côte d'Azur: an historical perspective', *Tourism Planning and Development Issues*, D. Hawkins, E. Schafer and J. Rovelstad, eds (George Washington University, 1980), pp. 213–24. A further useful contribution to the study of the historical evolution of seasonal patterns in tourism.

Stynes, B. W. and Pigozzi, B. W., 'A tool for investigating tourism-related seasonal employment', *Journal of Travel Research*, vol. XXI, no. 3 (1983), pp. 19–24. The authors employ the method of harmonic analysis to data relating to northern Michigan in order to examine the influence of tourism on the wider pattern of seasonality in employment.

Sutcliffe, C. M. S. and Sinclair, M. T., 'The measurement of seasonality within the tourist industry: an application to tourist arrivals in Spain', *Applied Economics*, vol. 12, no. 4 (1980), pp. 429–41. The article makes a valuable contribution to the methodology of measurement in this area. In an analysis of data relating to Spain, several measures of seasonality are compared. Different measures yield quite startling differences in the estimation of seasonality. The authors also suggest that while the seasonality of the Spanish tourist trade has grown in the post-war years, the shift of pattern changes has been reduced.

Wanhill, S. R. C., 'Tackling seasonality: a technical note', *International Journal of Tourism Management*, vol. 1, no. 4 (1980), pp. 243–5. Taking off from a technical critique of the work of Yacoumis (1980), Wanhill advocates the use of Lorenz curves and Gini coefficients to measure seasonality.

Yacoumis, J., 'Tackling seasonality: the case of Sri Lanka', *International Journal of Tourism Management*, vol. 1, no. 2 (1980), pp. 84–98. The author draws attention to the need to distinguish national, regional and sectoral patterns of seasonality. He suggests also that the adverse effects of the seasonal character of tourism are likely to be more marked in less-developed countries. Several measures to encourage diversification are considered.

Young, G., *Tourism: Blessing or Blight?* (Penguin Books, 1973). Although this influential general discussion of the costs and benefits of tourism has little to say about seasonality, the author does acknowledge the importance of the historical shift in seasonal patterns of tourism.

JOHN B. ALLCOCK

Senior travel market

The importance of the elderly as a distinct segment of the travel market, results from their position (among the developed countries which generate most travel) as one of the largest age groups, fast becoming *the* largest. The main reasons for this are well-known. On the one hand, the post-World War II 'baby bulge' is now passing through middle-age, and starting to approach the retirement phase. On the other hand, people are tending to live longer. People aged over 100 in Europe now number several thousand. Indeed it has been suggested that by the year 2000 it will be usual for people to expect to live to 100.

A related feature of the elderly is that they are tending to retire earlier from fulltime employment. To some extent this is because of employers reducing their usual retirement ages, but also unemployment is becoming increasingly concentrated among people in their fifties. In addition, an increasing number of people in their fifties and early sixties are opting for part-time employment.

In the 1970s the travel industry concentrated its marketing efforts on attracting customers over the age of retirement (65 for men and 60 for women). Gradually, however, the travel industry has realized that retirement age is a confusing criterion. Instead, a rather broader view of the market situation is starting to emerge, the criterion of retirement age being replaced by the notion of the 'third age'. This involves a view of the human life span being divided into three distinct 'ages', the first being devoted to learning, the second to intense employment, and the third to progressive withdrawal from employment. For convenience, the 'first age' is becoming equated with those under 25, the 'second age' with those over 25 but under 50, and the 'third age' with those over 50.

Because of this changing market perception of the elderly it has until recently been difficult to develop a terminology which fits the market. Understandably the terms 'pensioners', 'old age pensioners (OAPs)' or 'retirees' are rapidly falling out of use in the travel industry. For a while a variety of other terms came into use; the most bizarre, 'grey panthers', was adopted by American Express. Gradually, however, use has focused on the phrase 'senior citizens' or its shorter form 'seniors'. This last term has several advantages from a market viewpoint. It has none of the negative connotations which are linked with terms such as elderly or aged. It provides a nice match with the term 'junior' which has already become widely accepted as a term which conveniently describes those in the 'first age'. It is readily understood and used in many languages, not just English. And as a single word it is readily convenient for use in marketing operations.

Thus defined, the senior travel market has several important characteristics. Most obvious is its growth and size. Taking all Europe excluding the USSR, by the year 2000 the number of people over 50 will (for the first time ever) exceed the number of people under 25. From now until the end of the century the number of juniors (unlike seniors) will fall continuously and rapidly. After the year 2000 an even more dramatic effect will take place, for in or around that year the number of people in the 'second age' will peak. This means that in little more than a decade the numbers of people both in the 'first age' and in the 'second age' will be starting to decline. With the continued accelerating growth of the 'third age' this means that people over 50 will, in around 20 years time, be the largest population group in Europe.

Within Europe there is a significant geographical split between the north and the south. As a general rule, the further north the higher is the market share represented by the 'third age', this being most pronounced in Sweden and Norway. Another example of this northern bias among developed countries is provided by Japan which will probably have the distinction of being the first country in the world where the elderly will out-number the middle-aged.

Another striking characteristic of the senior market is that it is an extremely wealthy group. It seems that in North America and Western Europe, and indeed in developed countries generally, people in the 'third age' already account for some three-quarters of all accumulated personal wealth and around one-half of all discretionary expenditure. These general facts do not conceal the existence of many poor and indigent people among the elderly. Indeed, among the elderly as a whole there are relatively more poor people than there are in any other age group. Nevertheless, it is important to remember that this group also includes a relatively large number of affluent high spenders.

Yet another striking characteristic of the senior market is its freedom to choose travel time. People in the 'first age' are largely governed by the rigid conditions of school/college term times and thus generally enjoy very little freedom of choice over when to travel. People in the 'second age' are highly constrained, not only by the leave arrangements at their place of work but also by the holiday arrangements at their childrens' place of education. In contrast, as people enter the 'third age' they tend to become increasingly flexible. Even those still in full-time employment tend to enjoy more flexibility over leave arrangements than in their middle-age. This flexibility does not only apply to the chosen season or month of travel; it also extends to the day of the chosen week, or even to the hour of the chosen day.

This flexibility in the market place is of fundamental importance to the travel industry which is everywhere geared up to serve an uneven flow of business, thus being inevitably condemned to some measure of unused off-peak capacity. Until the emergence of the senior market this unused off-peak capacity was considered to be virtually unsellable, its cost having to be recovered from sales at busier times. But increasingly in the 1980s suppliers in the travel industry have recognized that not only is the senior traveler an important market in his/her own right, but in addition he/she is the solution to the industry's widespread off-peak problem.

There is a further important, though hardly surprising, characteristic of the senior travel market: its members show a high inclination to travel for leisure and for other personal reasons. Throughout middle-age most people are prevented or inhibited from traveling as much as they would like. They look forward to their later years as a period when they will have more opportunity to travel, not only on short day trips and on short holiday breaks, but also on extended holidays and tours, perhaps even for several months.

Given the scale, growth, affluence, flexibility and inclination of the senior market, it might be thought that this was already a prime segment for the tourism industry. In fact this is not so. From comprehensive research in Europe and the United States it is clear that it is still a potential rather than an actual prime market.

The most convincing proof of this is from the massive survey into holidaymaking habits of people in the European Community (EC) carried out by consultants on behalf of the Commission during the spring of 1986. This survey covered almost 12,000 interviews spread evenly among the 12 countries of the EC. It showed, for instance, that the over 55 age group was the only group in Europe where more than half the respondents had failed to take one or more holiday (of four or more nights away from home) during the previous year. Even more striking was the fact that, among respondents over 55, as many as one in three claimed that they seldom or never went on holiday. It appears from the survey that the proportion of middle-aged people never or seldom taking a holiday is around one in six while the equivalent among young people is around one in ten.

Unfortunately there are no reliable statistics yet available within Europe for day trips and short breaks involving elderly people. As a matter of general observation it is widely believed that these two categories of travel (both of which are primarily domestic rather than international) are in fact dominated by seniors. There is also abundant evidence that most of this short-duration travel by seniors involves the use of heavily rebated off-peak transport by coach and rail and that most of this short-duration travel does not involve the use of commercial accommodation, the main form of accommodation being the homes of friends and relatives.

The picture which thus emerges is that the travel industry has yet to successfully exploit the senior travel market, particularly in the case of longer holidays.

In recent years travel industry leaders have become increasingly aware of this failure to exploit the senior travel market. Within Europe this led in 1985 to the convening of a major seminar in Cannes by the European Travel Commission and the International Hotel Association. By the end of the seminar two very disturbing facts were starting to emerge: the travel industry was failing to adapt its various products to suit the needs of the senior traveler. In general, senior travelers were faced with products which had been designed for the young or middle-aged. Indeed, the travel industry was failing even to communicate effectively with the senior travel market. For instance, a major European airline, Swissair, gave details of an experimental scheme it had operated (unsuccessfully) on behalf of the Association of European Airlines. Although it offered an attractive product in the form of heavily rebated off-peak fares to selected Mediterranean destinations the acceptance had been poor, mainly it seems because the airline failed either to inform potential travelers or to persuade them to accept their special offer.

It had been hoped that the European Travel Commission (ETC), working through the national tourism offices which together make up the ETC's membership, would make a concerted effort to tackle these twin defects in the European tourism system. Unfortunately, because of internal changes in the management and direction of ETC, this has failed yet to materialize. However, thanks mainly to liaison within the European Travel Action Group (ETAG), which periodically brings together senior representatives of all the international organizations concerned directly and indirectly with tourism in Western Europe, the word is spreading among those providing transport and accommodation facilities that more consideration must be given to the special needs of the elderly.

On a national level, several countries have acted to improve the marketing operation. The British Travel Association (BTA), for instance, in the winter of 1986/87 issued in the United States over 12,000 copies of a guide to off-peak Britain entitled 'Britain for the Very Good Years'. From this the BTA has subsequently built up a mailing list of potential senior travelers known to be interested in visiting the United Kingdom which it sells at a nominal charge to interested suppliers.

The main marketing development, however, has come not from the travel industry but from those bodies in Europe concerned with the welfare of the 'aged'. Since the early 1970s many European countries have taken seriously the need to improve the life quality of the elderly. In some countries this has taken the form of organizing subsidized holidays for the elderly. In other countries it has taken the form of offering a range of rebated facilities to the elderly. The country where this policy has been most successfully implemented is the Netherlands, where an elaborate system has gradually evolved. The basic tool here is a form of identity card known as Pass 65 which is issued to senior citizens through local municipal offices. This entitles the holder to a wide range of concessions, including transport and entrance to tourist attractions. The card is only a small part of an elaborate system, the main part of which is a well organized dual communications operation. On the one hand, working closely with the national and local tourism organizations in the Netherlands, there is continuing cooperation with the many parties responsible for supplying travel products. On the other hand, working closely with organizations concerned with the elderly, there is also continuing effort to ensure that up-to-date and accurate information on travel opportunities is passed through to potential travelers. The central feature of this dual approach to communication is a range of publications which are designed to inform both the travel industry and the senior traveler what travel opportunities are available using Pass 65.

Several years ago the Dutch authorities, responding to the expressed demand of senior travelers, started to develop the range of facilities to include countries outside the Netherlands. More recently, the Dutch have taken the initiative in persuading the main European political organizations – the Council of Europe and the European Commission – to support the idea of a pan-European version of Pass 65. Known provisionally as the Senior Euro Pass, support is gradually spreading for this project, and the present aim is to introduce an experimental scheme in 1990 with the object of having a fully developed system working throughout Europe by the year 1992 when the unrestricted internal market is due to come into effect within Europe.

An as yet unsolved element in the marketing operation is to involve the retailers and wholesalers who together make up the so-called 'travel trade'. A recent sign of the problem of involving travel agents in promoting senior travel was the decision by the world's largest wholesaler of packaged travel for senior citizens, Britain's Saga Travel, to no longer sell through travel agents but instead to concentrate on direct-sell. The irony here is that countless travel surveys show that senior travelers display a high interest both in using the services of travel agents and to buy packaged holidays, and yet in practice the use of travel agents and the purchase of package holidays by the elderly is unusually low. The reason for this seems to be that the travel trade have yet to start adapting to the needs of the senior traveler. They are still, usually unwittingly, offering a service which is designed to suit the young or middle-aged client. Until this is changed, the senior travel market will continue to fail to realize its full potential.

JOHN SEEKINGS

Service economy

Introduction

There has been considerable debate over the role which services play within the economy. Despite the fact that the service sector is the largest in the United Kingdom in terms of output and employment, it is the manufacturing sector which is usually regarded as being the key to economic growth. Furthermore, it is widely believed that services, particularly those which operate within the public sector, are 'unproductive' and even parasitic in relation to other activities. The evidence which is available does not support these views, neither does it justify the bias towards manufacturing industry. The service sector does create wealth and many of the services within it are complementary to manufacturing whilst others are substitutes.

Several problems are encountered in the analysis of the service sector, the most immediate being those of definition and measurement. The services do not conform to the standard assumptions of economic theory and the data available is poor, again reflecting the general neglect of this sector.

A service industry may be defined as any industry which produces an intangible product. The service economy comprises all such industries within the private and the public sectors of the economy. In the United Kingdom, the CSO (Central Statistical Office) groups services into the following categories:

1. Transport – bus, rail, air, sea (excluding private motoring).
2. Communication – post, telephone.
3. Distributive trades – wholesale, retail.
4. Insurance, banking, finance and business services.
5. Professional and scientific services – including health and education.
6. Miscellaneous services – cinema, sports, hotels and restaurants.
7. Public administration and defence – military and civil service.

The service economy in the United Kingdom accounts for over 55 per cent of total output, 67 per cent of total employment (see Fig. 1) and 40 per cent for consumer expenditure. It also makes a substantial contribution to the level of investment and to the balance of payments. In 1986, distribution, hotel and catering accounted for 8.8 per cent of gross domestic fixed capital formation, transport and communication 8 per cent and financial and business services 16.7 per cent. The United Kingdom is a net exporter of services, the majority of foreign exchange earnings being attributable to tourism, travel, financial services and other services such as consultancy and telecommunications.

Analysis of the service industries

The service industries have been neglected in the economic literature relative to agriculture and production industries. Several arguments have been advanced to explain this lack of emphasis, the most persuasive being that there is a lack of suitable definitions and measurements of output. Other explanatory factors are the predominance of relatively small firms, the significant number of nonprofit organizations in the service economy, the nature of employment (see below) and the 'sale without transfer of ownership' problem.

The difficulties associated with the measurement of output may be divided into two distinct types of problem: the definition problem and the measurement problem. In manufacturing industries, the definition of output, e.g. number of cars produced, also may be taken as the unit of measurement. In the service industries, however, the definition of output tends to be distinct from the means of measuring it. For example, if the output of a museum is defined as the display of historical artifacts, this does not suggest a unit of measurement. There are many services, such as education, for which the output may not be adequately defined and yet others, such as transport, where the simultaneity of supply and demand pose severe definition problems. For example, if the output of a bus service is defined to be the transportation of passengers from one location to another, it is implied that if no passengers use the service provided then there is no output.

There are many service industries in which the output may be defined, often precisely, but which still present the measurement problem. The most common approach to this problem is to use inputs as a proxy for output. This approach has been used extensively in the analysis of education and health services. An alternative approach, used in the analysis of multiproduct services such as banking, has been to choose a measurement of output which reflects the objectives of the research.

It is apparent that a search for suitable proxies for output in

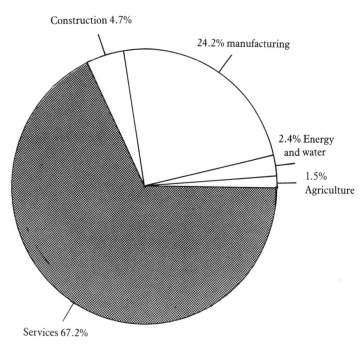

Construction 4.7%

24.2% manufacturing

2.4% Energy
and water

1.5%
Agriculture

Services 67.2%

Figure 1 Share of employment, December 1986 (*Source: Employment Gazette*, HMSO).

Closer examination of the pattern of employment within the service economy (see Fig. 3) reveals that female employees are in a majority in the distribution, hotel and catering and other services sectors and that part-time employment is dominant in the hotel and catering industry.

A striking characteristic of the service economy is the importance of intermediate demand for its output. When the growth of the services sector is analyzed, the myth of a boom in services fueled by consumer demand is quickly dispelled. The share of marketed services in consumer expenditure has not risen in recent years (see Fig. 5, below) and the demand for certain services, such as transport, has been displaced by manufactured durable goods such as cars. The impetus for growth stems from increasing demand for nonmarketed services such as health and education and also from intermediate demand for services such as banking, insurance, computing, design and consultancy. It has been estimated that about half of the employment in the service economy is related to tangible final products and less than one-quarter to direct provision of services to consumers.

In the United Kingdom the geographical distribution of service industries differs from that of manufacturing, with a marked concentration in the South East, particularly London, and in the provincial conurbations. This pattern reflects the fact that many services, such as banking, insurance and finance, professional services and public administration tend to be centra-

service industries does not solve the central problem which is that these industries are not amenable to most types of micro- and macro-economic analysis. If output cannot be adequately measured then neither can productivity, growth or economies of scale and the best allocation of resources cannot be determined.

Characteristics of the service economy

The service economy has several characteristics which distinguish it from the manufacturing and agricultural sectors. It has been noted that the share of services in the economy as a whole increases with the level of economic development, but that the size and growth rate of this sector varies between countries. This increase in the relative importance of the service economy may be attributed largely to increased government activity, especially in relation to the provision of education and health services, to the growth of financial and business services as business becomes more sophisticated and to rising demand for distributive and leisure services which is stimulated by higher income levels.

In terms of employment, the service economy is characterized by a high proportion of female employees and part-time working. In the United Kingdom in 1986, 54.2 per cent of employees in the service sector were female whereas the agricultural and production sectors employed a smaller proportion of females (see Fig. 2). It should be noted, however, that almost half of female employment in services was on a part-time basis but that the corresponding figure for males was around 11 per cent.

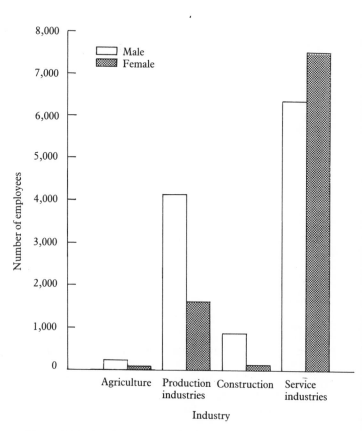

Figure 2 Employment by sex, March 1986 (thousands) (*Source: Employment Gazette*, HMSO).

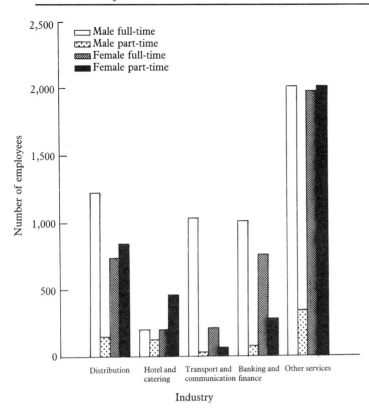

Figure 3 Employment in services, March 1986 (thousands) (*Source: Employment Gazette*, HMSO).

Table 1 Index numbers of output at constant factor cost for selected service industries (1980 = 100) (*Source:* Economic Trends, HMSO).

Year	GDP	Distribution; hotel and catering; repairs	Transport and communications	Other services	Total services
1980	100	100	100	100	100
1981	98.4	98.1	100.2	101.1	100.3
1982	100	99.9	99.3	102.8	101.7
1983	103.1	103.4	102.3	105.7	104.7
1984	106.5	108.2	106.3	109.6	108.9
1985	110.4	112	112.3	113.1	112.7
1986	113.6	117	116.7	117	117

finance and hotel and catering industries. Employment in other private sector services was either relatively stable (in the case of wholesale distribution), or declined slightly (in the case of retail and transport and communications). Employment in public sector services, notably public administration and health, rose over the period.

It can be seen from Fig. 5 that consumer expenditure on services, excluding rent, rates and water, rose slightly, from 25.75 per cent to 27.55 per cent of total expenditure at current

lized and that retail activities tend to be centered in urban areas.

Studies which have been conducted in the United Kingdom suggest that output per employee in services is higher than in manufacturing, but that productivity (as measured by the change in output per worker) grows more slowly. It is also suggested that services have weaker links, and therefore smaller multiplier effects, although interservice links are likely to be strong. A further assertion is that economies of scale are not likely to be present in the service industries, despite the fact that there is evidence that they exist in transport and communications and banking and finance. These findings should be regarded with caution in view of the problems of analysis outlined above.

Recent trends

Over the period 1980 to 1986, the service sector in the United Kingdom was rather more buoyant than the manufacturing sector, performing well in terms of output, employment and trade. Output in the service industries (measured at constant factor cost) rose faster than that of the economy as a whole (Table 1) thereby increasing their share of total GDP.

Between 1980 and 1986, total employment declined by almost 1.4 million whereas employment in the service sector increased by 0.74 million. However, as shown in Fig. 4, a large part of this increase may be attributed to the banking and

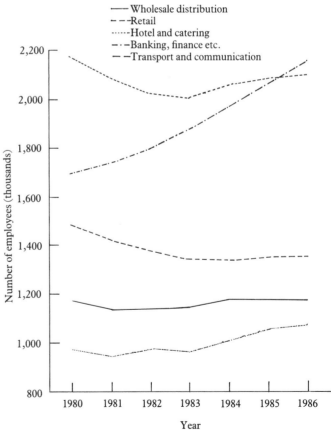

Figure 4 Employment in service industries, 1980–1986 (*Source: Employment Gazette*, HMSO).

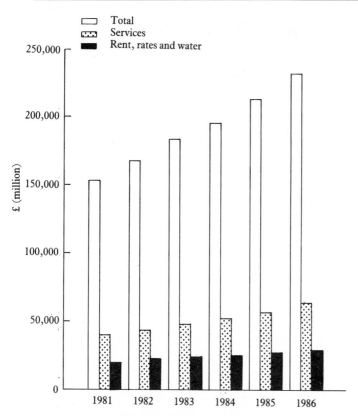

Figure 5 Consumer expenditure at current prices (*Source: Monthly Digest of Statistics*, HMSO).

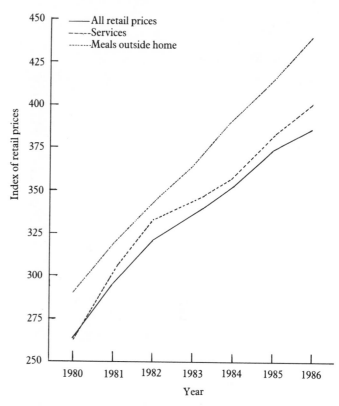

Figure 6 Movement in retail prices, 1980–1986 (*Source: Monthly Digest of Statistics*, HMSO).

prices. It should be noted, however, that service sector prices, particularly for meals purchased and consumed outside the home, rose faster than the general retail price index (see Fig. 6). In real terms, therefore, the proportion of total consumer expenditure which is devoted to purchasing services has remained relatively constant.

Conclusion: tourism in the service economy

Tourism is an important source of final demand within the service economy and therefore acts as a stimulus to output and employment creation. Tourism demand is spread over a variety of service industries, the most important being hotels, restaurants and bars, travel and passenger transport, tourism and sports facilities and the retail sector. Intermediate demand is generated as these industries purchase goods and services from other sectors such as agriculture, manufacturing, public utilities, wholesale distribution and business services.

Difficulties arise when attempting to identify the proportions of output and employment which are attributable to tourism precisely because the demand is for a diversity of products. Furthermore, the tourism related service sectors above cater for local demand in addition to domestic and international tourism. For example, it has been estimated that the share of employ-

ment supported directly by tourism is around 38 per cent for hotels and catering, 22 per cent for travel and passenger transport and 10 per cent for tourism and related leisure services.

In the United Kingdom, tourism makes a vital contribution to output, employment and invisible exports. Employment in hotels and catering and in tourism and related leisure services has grown steadily during the period 1980–1986 and forecasts of employment in these sectors indicate that they are likely to be an important source of job creation in the future.

Further reading

Central Statistical Office, *Monthly Digest of Statistics* (HMSO).

Daniels, P., *Service Industries: Growth and Location* (Cambridge University Press, 1982). An introduction to the character, growth and location of service industries in a variety of countries.

Department of Employment, *Employment Gazette* (HMSO).

Fletcher, J. and Snee, H, 'The need for output measurements in the service industries: a comment', *Service Industries Journal*, vol. 5., no. 1 (March 1985). A discussion which focuses on both definition and measurement problems with illustrations from various service sectors.

Fuchs, V., *Production and Productivity in the Service Industries* (Columbia University Press, 1969). A collection of papers on the topics of output measurement and productivity measures including studies of specific industries.

Gemmel, N., *Structural Change and Economic Development* (Macmillan, 1986). An examination of the process of structural change which pays patricular attention to the role of services in this process.

Parsons, D., 'Tourism and leisure jobs: a statistical review', *Service Industries Journal*, vol 7, no. 3 (July 1987). A review of the statistical data concerning employment patterns in tourism and tourism-related activities.

Whiteman, J., *The Services Sector – A Poor Relation*, Discussion Paper 8 (National Economic Development Office, 1981). A review of the role, performance and future prospects of the service sector in the United Kingdom.

JOHN FLETCHER and
HELENA SNEE

Site selection in tourism

Introduction

The managing director of a large theme park near London once said that there are three factors that determine the success of a leisure enterprise; these being: location, location and location. Some managers, therefore, would consider the process of site selection as the paramount factor in setting up a leisure enterprise. Location in turn can be approached in two ways. Firstly there is the suitability of the site for activity or range of activities that are to be carried out and secondly there is the accessibility of the site to the market.

This chapter will start by considering the purpose for which the site is to be used in relation to these two facets before proceeding to look at some of the methods of site selection that can be employed. It assumes that sufficient market research has been done to establish a viable level of demand although this may in fact be conditional on the site. Demand for a golf course may have been identified but if a site can only accommodate a short 9-hole course will the demand materialize and will it be able at a later stage to withstand the competition from a full 18-hole championship course? This might well depend on the level of demand and the locational circumstances in the area. This chapter will deal primarily with site selection and not with activity selection. In the case of the latter the location of the site has already been determined and the objective is to locate suitably viable activities on it.

Examples

The starting point is that the manager is looking for a 'home' for a certain activity be it a caravan site, a leisure park or an ice cream kiosk. The particular technical requirements of the activity need to be considered. These will include characteristics such as: area of land and/or water required, climate, building requirements, services and utilities, staffing, land for expansion, special activity and legal requirements and costs. Consider each of technical requirements, principally for a proposed marina:

1. Area of land or water; the size and form of a site is the basic starting point and these depend on the requirements of the activity in question. Need it be flat? Can it be long? What acreage is needed? In the case of a marina the number of boats that need to be accommodated will determine the area required, often using some form of standards/capacity approach – it is assumed that 80 yachts per hectare is a norm. Ideally it should be sheltered and in addition to the water area a similar land area is required for such items as car parking, where one space per berth is the normal standard but may increase to 1.5 or 2.

2. Climate; climatic conditions may be vital to the enjoyment of a range of outdoor pursuits. For marinas the strength and direction of prevailing winds together with the frequency and wave heights of storms are the determinants.

3. Building requirements; some activities such as indoor sports, conference facilities and museums will have very specific building requirements and might even require the utilization of a particular type and period of building. With regard to marinas the buildings are used to house the ancillary activities although as a minimum these are seen as being a marina office, showers and toilet facilities.

4. Services; most activities will require the basic services of water, electricity, sewerage, refuse disposal and telephone. The question normally to be considered is the cost of bringing them onto the site, the time that will take and the quantities in which they are required. In the case of a marina no extraordinary demands are made in this respect but on inland waterway sites boats are not allowed to discharge waste into the waterway and need to have a holding tank that will need to be emptied.

5. Staffing; the availability of suitable staff and their accommodation is an often overlooked item. For a marina shipwrights are required. In skiing areas the availability of instructors is important. In some locations it will be necessary to provide transport for staff if there is a lack of public transport or on site accommodation, both items adding to the cost of the venture. For some activities the accessibility of a hospital may be an important consideration, for instance various forms of motor racing.

6. Expansion; in addition to the site accommodating the principal activity the scope for ancillary activities that may or may not be under the control of the developer but which would add to the status of the site need to be considered. These might be important to the potential visitors' assess-

ment of the site. In marinas they include boatyard, sales, chandlery, clubhouse and restaurant facilities. In some cases the provision of residential accommodation may also be an item of importance.

7. Special technical and legal requirements; for some activities such things as safety zones or noise restrictions could be considered under this heading. If the site is not immediately suitable then the cost of installing them needs to be considered.

8. Costs; the capital development costs and subsequent running costs are also important items that will be influenced by the site. The need to instal lock gates can add to the capital costs just as dredging will add to revenue costs.

Having considered the various technical and other requirements of the activity or in some cases the range of activities themselves, it is necessary to proceed and look at the likely visitor demands of a site. These can be considered under the following headings:

1. Accessibility; this is often the single most important factor and can be subdivided into a two by two matrix. First of all there is accessibility in terms of real and perceived, and secondly there is accessibility to the site and to the activity on the site. On large and dispersed sites distances can be overcome by using features such as land trains or monorails and other transport gimmicks. A marina in South Wales might be perceived as being a considerable distance from say the Midlands despite the presence of motorways. Once in a marina, the distance to the sailing areas is important. If the site is highly accessible by land, but it can then take 2 hours sailing time (which in return is restricted by tidal access) to reach the main sailing areas, then another location should possibly be sought. Similarly, with skiing, how accessible are the ski slopes from the ski centers and villages?

2. Attractiveness; this quality is sometimes considered to be virtually impossible to measure. But visitors will often consider the general ambience of one site to be more attractive than another. When evaluating different sites this needs to considered but the importance of it will vary from user to user and activity to activity. For the sailor who sees a marina as somewhere to keep a boat the quality of the actual sailing area will be more important, but to the boat-owner who rarely ventures out, the setting of the marina is more important.

3. Safety and security; some sites, due to their design, layout and management, can either achieve or be perceived as achieving a higher level of personal safety than other sites. In the case of marinas it is not simply the provision of lifebelts that counts, but in, say, the club house would children be able to wander off and fall in? Often these are matters of design detail that can only be broadly considered at the site selection stage. More important in a marina is the aspect of security in terms of theft from boats, so while a city center site as part of a redevelopment scheme for a dock may seem attractive, allowing large numbers of people to wander at will might detract from the boat-owners' point of view.

4. Quality; the visitor will perceive quality as the standards set by the leaders in the field. Obviously quality has its price, therefore if to develop a site to minimum standards will

require charges equivalent to the highest level then it will be perceived as being bad value for money. In other cases, users will be prepared to pay more for a higher quality facility. In a marina, access for the boats to the sea at all states of the tide is a facility for which many are prepared to pay higher berthing charges to cover the necessary dredging and locking costs.

5. Range of facilities; this has already been mentioned under the technical criteria demanded by the activity itself. But visitors will often look at and consider the range of activities available particularly to nonparticipants. In other words, what are the opportunities to go shopping, sightseeing or to partake in a completely different activity?

Implementation

Site selection

Bearing all the preceeding information in mind the manager then has two tasks to undertake: site selection and site evaluation. Site selection, which involves identifying a number of alternative sites that can then be evaluated may take place on a macro or a micro scale. Invariably the larger the area of search then the more that is left to the manager's ability and intuition rather than any form of methodology. But the principal criteria even in broad terms will remain suitability of the area to accommodate the activity and accessibility to the market. If the activity has particular resource requirements such as skiing then the search will be dominated by looking at suitable resource areas. If, however, it has minimal resource requirements then market accessibility will dominate.

Most of the specific techniques involved take place at the regional or subregional scale:

1. Computerized mapping. This type of approach has been used more extensively in the United States, particularly in California and the west coast, than in the United Kingdom. Where there is a clear resource requirement, however, then the criteria can easily be set up using the activity requirements identified earlier in the process. Again, skiing is a good example, as the topography together with a climatic map can give areas that could provide suitable lengths of run gradient and snow cover. Setting up the necessary database is expensive and should possibly be done by an agency on a national basis.

2. Potential surface analysis. In many ways the forerunner of computer mapping, this technique, developed at Edinburgh University for the Scottish Tourist Board, has been used in the Lothian Region in Scotland, Sherwood Forest in England and in South Wales. As it is based on a 1 km grid, however, with each square scoring according to a predetermined criteria (this being summed to show the potential of each square) often as much information can be obtained by studying a map.

3. Aerial surveys. By using aerial surveys, which if not currently available from commercial sources can be specifically undertaken, desk-top map searches can be significantly en-

hanced as the actual ground cover, condition and boundaries can been easily seen.

In practice most site searches are likely to be desk-top searches in the first instance, using a combination of maps, local knowledge and consultations with local authorities, regional tourist boards and other agencies and consultants. Some of these might compile registers of sites that are considered suitable for tourist development, either in the ownership of the public or private sectors.

Site evaluation

Having established a number of alternative sites, some method of evaluation needs to be undertaken. Two methods that might be adopted are now considered.

Carrying capacity

This can be defined as the maximum number of people who can use a site without an unacceptable alteration to the quality of the physical environment and without an unacceptable decline in the quality of the experience gained by the visitors. Much has already been written on the subject of carrying capacity. Briefly one considers a site in relation to its physical, ecological, perceptual, economic and social capacities. The first two apply to the characteristics of the site itself. Obviously to set up a hide to watch rare birds would be counterproductive if the numbers to the site subsequently drove away the very attraction. Perceptual capacity is essentially reached at the point when visitors resent each other; this can depend on the particular market segment that is sought – some people like crowded beaches, others seek empty ones. Economic capacity is the number of people required on a site to achieve break-even point financially for a given level of investment. Social capacity is reached when the local community become resentful and antagonistic towards the visitor.

Obviously it is unlikely that these individual capacities will coincide. The manager has to determine which are more important and how, when a particular capacity is exceeded, the effects can be alleviated, managed and controlled. If the number of people visiting the hide to make it viable would drive away the birds then the manager has to decide either to reduce his costs or find another site. Allied closely to this approach are 'impact studies' that in many countries are required in the assessment of a development by government.

Scoring

A more commonly used approach is to consider each site against the criteria required by the activity and users of the activity as given earlier. This may be done on a formal basis as shown below where each site is scored against the activity requirements on a scale of 1–10, or informally. Similarly the actual scores and weightings might be done on the subjective basis of knowledge and experience or by using surveys of potential users. The weightings may have been obtained from earlier research. For instance, if people are asked to rank in order of importance features of a golf course – club house, surroundings, quality of greens etc. and are given the oppor-

Table 1 Selecting a marina site.

Criteria	Site A	Site B	Site C
Tidal access	8	5	5
Sail access	8	6	8
Road access	7	9	6
Surroundings	7	7	6
Incremental development	7	5	4
Services	9	9	9
Capital costs	4	6	5
Maintenance Costs	6	4	4
TOTAL	56	51	47

tunity to win a golfing holiday then this data can be used because it expresses the public's preferences.

Table 1 looks at the criteria considered in relation to selecting a marina site in a given area. Not all the selection criteria previously outlined have been used. The totals given in this instance are unweighted. If, for example, it was felt that road access was dominant then it could have been given sufficient weighting to give site B the highest score, but in that case the decision making is being dominated by one factor and the others can be disregarded, which may be the case for certain activities. Similarly the sites all score the same for the provision of services, so this could have been omitted.

Three other factors will also need to be assessed in relation to each site:

1. The availability of financial assistance in the form of grants or tax incentives could well influence the location or scale of development. In Britain these are principally available from the Tourist Boards and the EC. Such inducements are usually only available for the capital costs.
2. Having identified and even selected a site the problem of ownership remains. Initial site selection often only proceeds on the basis of sites that are likely to be available.
3. There are a range of sociopolitical constraints, the most dominant often being Planning Permission. While Green Belts, National Parks and Heritage Coasts are often perceived as areas where the pursuit of leisure and tourism activities are meant to take place, obtaining planning consent in them can often be a long affair. Also in some locations there is the likelihood of a small but vociferous and articulate group of residents and other interested parties who can influence the planning process, often leading to a public enquiry.

Conclusion

While location remains the dominant factor in site selection, a number of criteria, ranging from the technical resource base to market accessibility affect that location. At the end of the day the site selected must also be able to withstand competition over its projected lifespan. To do this it must have a perceived advantage in terms of the quality of the experience, its accessibility or its prices.

Further reading

Coppock, J. T. and Duffield J. S., *Recreation in the Countryside* (Macmillan, 1975). Explains potential surface analysis with reference to the Lothian Region in Scotand.

Gold S. M., *Recreation Planning and Design* (McGraw-Hill, 1980). Explains a number of site identification techniques.

Lawson, F. and Baud Bovey, M., *Tourist and Recreation Development* (Architectural Press, 1977). Gives a number of standards and activity requirements.

Leisure and Recreation: Market Appraisal and Marina Study, Unpublished report for the Welsh Development Agency on Marina sites in Milford Haven (1983).

Mathieson, A. and Wall, G., *Tourism: Economic, Physical and Social Impacts* (Longman, 1982). Looks at impacts and capacity.

Miles, C. N. W. and Seabrooke, W., *Recreational Land Management* (Spon, 1977). Explains the concept of carrying capacity and site evaluation techniques.

Oliver, D. M., 'Theme parks in UK', Paper presented to the Royal Institute of Chartered Surveyors, One day conference, Development of Theme Parks (January 1986).

Pigram, J., *Outdoor Recreation and Resource Management* (Croom Helm/St Martins, 1983). General background reading on site selection.

JAMIE ELWIN

Sociology of tourism

Introduction

Although the sociology of tourism has potentially a great deal to offer by way of both a theoretical and a practical understanding of the phenomenon, it has remained until recently a seriously underdeveloped area of the discipline. The reasons for this remain largely mysterious. In their introduction to a stimulating volume of essays concerned with the relation between gender divisions and the 'public/private' division in social life, Gamarnikow and Purvis (Gamarnikow *et al.*, 1983) advance what may be an explanation. They argue that, in general, sociology has in the past tended to concentrate its attention on the 'public' sphere (in which men tend to play a dominant role) relegating to the fringes of the discipline the study of the entire 'private' dimension of society (in which women's influence is far more prominent). Whereas this may not provide us with the whole picture, as we shall see below, it is probably one important reason why the study of tourism – along with the much wider sociological examination of leisure in general – has remained relatively underdeveloped.

It is worth noting one other significant weakness affecting the area, namely, its relative detachment from theoretical discussion. Specific studies typically have been content to rest at a descriptive level: and where theoretical ideas have been introduced, they have often remained implicit or been taken for granted. In spite of several forays into this field in Germany in the early post-war years (reviewed in Elaković, 1983) a disparate collection of findings failed to emerge as a rounded appreciation of the phenomenon, and the lack of any adequate theoretical articulation has made it easier to leave tourism on the margins of the discipline. It became commonplace at one time to bewail this situation in the literature (Ballossier, 1967; Forster, 1964; Greenwood, 1972). Indeed, Cohen remarked that 'strictly speaking, there exists no sociology of tourism' (Cohen, 1979, p. 31). Without dissenting entirely from these judgments, however, enough work has been done during the past decade to enable us to lay out several areas in which sociologists have been able to make worthwhile contributions to the understanding of tourism.

The review which follows concentrates on a number of general frames of reference which have either demonstrated their utility in the understanding of tourism as a social phenomenon, or which are deemed to be potentially very valuable in

this way. A large number of particular contributions made by sociologists to tourism studies are therefore not included here, they will find an appropriate place in other contributions to this Handbook, where they illuminate specific problems or issues dealt with by other authors.

'Impact' studies

An important stimulus to sociological discussion of tourism was the work of economists who, in the absence of a solid sociological literature, made amateur excursions into sociology in the course of their own work (see for example, Burkart and Medlik, 1974, Chapters 5 and 6; Young, 1973, Chapters 2 and 3). The dominant paradigm which shaped their work at this time was that of cost–benefit analysis. It is therefore unsurprising that much early sociological work should pick up the hints which they threw out, and concern itself with the extension and sophistication of the range of costs and benefits which might be attributed to tourism. Sociologists thus entered the study of tourism in the attempt to make 'tangible' the economist's 'intangibles'.

Probably the most influential study in this tradition was Turner and Ash, *The Golden Hordes* (1975). Their book, which conducted a brisk attack on tourism as the enemy of authenticity, the solvent of cultural identity and the bearer of class antagonism, set the sociology of tourism into a particular mould for a decade. Economics on balance provided a list of the economic benefits which were believed to flow from tourism: to this, sociology counterposed a roster of social and cultural costs. In relation to tourism research at least, sociology took over from economics its traditional role as 'the dismal science'.

The variety of 'impacts' listed by researchers is now enormous. (The literature in this genre is effectively reviewed in Mathieson and Wall (1982).) (See also de Kadt, 1979, especially the editorial introduction.) The following rather selective listing gives some indication of the breadth of the issues covered. Rivers (1973), Jafari (1974) and English (1986) have all highlighted the 'demonstration effect' of tourism, in holding out to members of the host community unattainable economic aspirations, with disruptive consequences. Cognat (1973), Greenwood (1976) and Smith (1978) have all made a feature of the 'impact' of tourism on local class and status structures. Wood (1984) in relation to South-east Asia, and Elaković and Brangjolica (1985) in relation to Yugoslavia, have studied aspects of the transformation of political structures under the impetus of tourism development. Poulsen (1977), Allcock (1983a) and de Weerdt (1987) concern themselves with aspects of migration or the reorganization of spatial relationships.

Several observers have dealt in one way or another with the consequences of tourist development for family structures, and in particular its impact on the position of women in society. While it is agreed widely that traditional family structures are weakened in this process, there are strongly contrasting evaluations of it. Reynoso Y Valle and de Regt, and Wilson (both in De Kadt, 1979) both present women as among the beneficiaries of tourism, gaining greater economic independence and status in the community (see also Lever, 1987). On the other hand Truong (1983) and Graburn (1983) draw our attention to the growth of prostitution and sex tourism, particularly in the Far East.

English (1986, pp. 50–3) and Mathieson and Wall (1982, pp. 150–2) both provide us with reviews of material in which the growth of tourism is said to be linked to the spread of a variety of other moral problems in the host society (see Cressey-Lind and Lind, 1986, for a valuable bibliography on the relationship between tourism and crime). This concern has been expressed in the form of the involvement of the World Council of Churches in the debate about the effects of tourism (O'Grady, 1981).

Greenwood (1976) in his Spanish research identifies several ways in which the cohesion of local communities can be said to have been weakened by the advent of a tourist-based economy. Aisner, on the other hand (1987), sees a connection between tourism and the strengthening of a sense of national identity in the region around Cuzco in Peru.

The list of effects attributed to the impact of tourism is compendious – no attempt has been made here to ensure that this review is exhaustive. Whereas this literature is enormously valuable in sensitizing us to the potential social importance of tourism, three principal dangers are worthy of comment.

In the first instance, because so few of these studies adopt a disciplined comparative approach to data, there is an acute danger of the overgeneralization of their results. Indeed, taken at face value, some of them may seem to present us with contradictory expectations about tourism and its social effects.

> Tourism is supposed to both stimulate local agriculture, by offering enhanced markets for local produce, and to result in the displacement and beggary of the farmer. The arts and handicrafts are expected to be corrupted, standardized and reduced to the lowest common denominator of taste, but they are also expected to be revived and reinvigorated, with tourism being perhaps the only force which rescues dying skills. Women are in danger particularly through the lowering of moral standards engendered by tourism – or possibly they stand to gain in freedom and dignity through a more equal participation in the labour market. Can they all be true? Are any of them true? How can we decide? (Allcock, 1983b, p. 348)

The second danger which attends 'impact' studies of tourism,

taken in isolation, is that they tend to promote a view of the host society which is 'normatively static' (Wood, 1980). In other words, they appear to imply a view of these societies as no more than the passive recipients of influences which are imposed on them from without. Whereas such an image of passivity may be appropriate in the case of some small and politically weak countries of the Third World, it is thoroughly misleading to assume that this model describes all (or even typical) situations in which tourism develops. Many of the socioeconomic changes which are documented in these studies would probably have happened to a greater or lesser extent anyway, in the process of industrialization (see below). Furthermore, these changes often come as a consequence of the pursuit of a 'modernity' which is actively sought by the population concerned. Tourism may indeed produce 'effects': but it would be folly to attribute to it all those consequences which attend the development of commodity relations, the market, or the modern state (see de Kadt, 1979, p. 12).

Finally, there is a problem of the theoretical isolation of individual findings about 'effects'. The sociology of tourism will grow more steadily where its material can be shown to be directly related to wider concerns within the discipline, enabling it to escape from the situation of intellectual overspecialization, almost amounting to ghettoization, in which it currently finds itself. (For some very perceptive comment on the general significance of this problem within sociology, see Elias, 1978, 'Introduction'.)

Escape from the limitations of the 'impact' or 'effects' mode of studying tourism is also of vital importance for its practitioners: for a discipline which confines itself to the question *'Cui bono?'* ('Who benefits?') has little practical application or interest.

Tourism and the sociology of leisure

One of the more obvious candidates for the task of providing a theoretical framework for the study of tourism is the sociology of leisure. Although there are several very promising points of anchorage here, students of leisure more generally have had little to say specifically about tourism – and students of tourism have generally failed to take advantage of the possibilities offered by a wider sociological appreciation of the nature of leisure. In his standard introduction to the subject, Dumazedier (1967, Chapter 6) affirms the importance of tourism to the study of leisure, but takes us little further. The situation seems to have progressed little if at all by the time of the publication of Roberts' text (1981); and Veal (1987) writing a quarter of a century after the first French edition of Dumazedier's work shows a general indifference to the topic. Although a recent special edition of the *Annals of Tourism Research* was devoted to the exploration of the 'interrelationships of leisure, recreation and tourism', little was achieved beyond the affirmation that the three ought to have something in common (Fedler, 1987). The plea by Krippendorf (1986) for the reintegration of the study of leisure, recreation and tourism is no more then programmatic.

In spite of this initially unpromising situation, it is within the sociology of leisure that one finds some of the most interesting ideas and materials in relation to which tourism might be interpreted. Although the social-scientific investigation of tourism is a relative novelty, the phenomenon itself is not. Historians of leisure have given us a number of invaluable studies which provide source materials for the student of tourism (Cunningham, 1980, which contains a particularly useful bibliography; Clarke and Chritcher, 1985; Hern, 1967; Walton and Walvin, 1983, for example). Three useful sociological points have emerged in particular from their work.

The first of these is a vigorous awareness of the class-differentiation of patterns of leisure, which can suggest a useful corrective to the tendency to generalize about tourists as an aggregate. If, in an age of mass tourism, to be a tourist is no longer the privilege of a particular stratum of society, then a number of questions are potentially illuminated by evidence about the composition of tourist flows. Generalizations about tourist behavior, or the possible 'demonstration effect' of tourism, are cases in point.

The second point is that historical study underlines the fact that patterns of leisure change over time. Tourism, as a cultural pattern, has emerged at a very specific historical juncture; the content of the tourist experience has not been constant; the bearers of tourism are not always the same groups. The one-time fashionable leisure pursuit of the European gentry, taking the waters in a spa, has now declined to the status of a minor eccentricity. There is, by the same token, no inevitability about the continuing vigor of tourism.

The third valuable legacy of historical studies of leisure is the way in which they point us firmly in the direction of treating tourism within the context of wider social and cultural processes. In following sections we will assess the significance of several of these.

The process of industrialization

One set of questions which the 'effects' approach to tourism tends to screen out is those which relate to its organization as a branch of economic activity. As we have already suggested, one of the best models available for the study of the development of tourism is that of the industrialization process. (A rather different view of the relationship between tourism and industrialization is presented by Krippendorf, 1986.)

Raymond Aron has given us a checklist of the characteristics of industrialization which, while it may be contested in detail by some sociologists, is certainly broadly acceptable (Aron, 1967, pp. 73–5).

First, the enterprise is completely separated from the family...

Secondly, an industrial firm introduces new forms of the division of labor...

Thirdly, an industrial enterprise implies an accumulation of capital...

Fourthly,...the idea of rational calculation is introduced...

The fifth feature of the industrial enterprise is the concentration of labor in the workplace.

The reader will immediately appreciate the appropriateness of these points as a generalized description of the 'tourist industry'. Examining the list, we can also see that many of the features of socioeconomic and cultural change itemized by the 'effects' school by no stretch of the imagination can be counted as unique effects of tourism. This observation has two significant consequences. In the first place, the field of tourism is no longer a mysterious and unexplored land, but one which in large measure is already familiar to us. In the second place, the challenge is issued to those critics of tourism who seem to assume that its adverse consequences could be avoided very simply. There is, in fact, no variant of the industrialization process which does not disrupt the traditional order of society, or induce a measure of 'culture shock' (Farnham, 1984).

This point is particularly relevant to discussion of the role of tourism in the economies of the least developed countries. The general argument within economics about tourism's relation to development and dependency has also emerged in a sociological form. Working the same seam of argument as Turner and Ash (1975), several writers of the same period have taken tourism to task for its role in the 'development of underdevelopment' (for example, Hiller, 1979; Perez, 1973; Shivji, 1973, and more recently, Erisman, 1983, and English, 1986). It remains entirely unclear, however, as to whether tourism does bring with it these contradictions and conflicts in an especially sharp form, and thus should attract the special attention of sociologists.

Rivers, for example (1973), has summarized the view of several writers, that international tourism is responsible for generating and reinforcing patterns of deference on the part of host populations. This view has been challenged by Allcock (1985), however, who makes a plea for more rigorous comparative evaluation of the results of individual studies in this respect.

Whereas economists have itemized some of the specifically economic characteristics of tourism, the task of identifying the sociological features of this sector which might lead us to believe that it has unusually disturbing consequences for the social fabric, has yet to be systematically undertaken.

Work and leisure

A central debate in the sociology of leisure has taken as its focus the distinction between 'work' and 'leisure'. The story is an old one, and there is no need to recapitulate it in full here. It will be useful, nevertheless, to draw attention to an important point which is now a commonplace of the literature. In everyday language we tend to counterpose 'leisure' and 'work', and consequently to equate 'leisure' with 'free time'. (The issues are reviewed, *inter alia*, in Lanfant, 1972; Rojek, 1985.) Clearly from a sociological standpoint, however, these distinctions are far from adequate as the bases for analysis. A single illustration will suffice in this context to make the point. The traditional housewife does not 'work' in the sense of being employed, or paid for her labor: but to suggest that she has copious 'free time', and spends her time in 'leisure' is an obvious nonsense.

Students of leisure have thus become accustomed to the fact that leisure is not simply 'free time', in either the sense of its being freely disposable time, or its having an unstructured quality. People often have regular and strong commitments to leisure activities, and the time which they spend at leisure may be highly structured. 'Leisure' is not the residue left over after socially significant time is disposed of; it participates in that structure of significances. The task of the sociology of leisure has come to be the exploration of that process of structuration, and its relation to wider social processes, which will include work.

The sociology of tourism is in danger of recapitulating that commonsense error about the nature of leisure, by assuming that the tourist experience is little more than 'time out' from the serious business of real life. It is seen as unstructured time, or at least, as time structured by the personal needs for recuperation of the individual tourist. Tourism is simply, in this view, negatively defined in relation to the everyday. Indeed, these assumptions are made quite explicitly in Jafari's discussion of 'the tourist system', where the tourist experience is described in terms of 'sacredness' (Jafari, 1987; but see also MacCannell, 1976, Chapter 1 and 2; Graburn, in Smith, 1978, pp. 17–31; Fine and Speer, 1985; Krippendorf, 1986).

One would not wish to deny the genuine interest of these contributions to the field. It is important to point out, however, that writing as they clearly do in the Durkheimian tradition, these authors ought to recall that 'sacredness' can only be defined in explicit relation to the 'profane'. The exceptional achieves significance only in counter-distinction to the everyday. Just as the sociology of leisure has been compelled, therefore, to rework the concept of leisure by examining the way in which it is wound into the total fabric of experience, so too the sociology of tourism must place its subject matter back into the wider cultural setting from which we have sought to lift it. It is appropriate to review here briefly three approaches which actually or (more typically) potentially address this task.

The quest for excitement

One of the most exciting developments in sociological theory in recent years has been the spreading interest in the 'figurational sociology' of Norbert Elias. Central to Elias' analysis of the long-term historical development of Western society and culture has been the concept of the 'civilizing process' (Elias, 1978; an excellent brief introduction to these ideas is given in the Preface and Introduction to Elias and Dunning, 1986). He argues that social development can be measured in terms of the advance of the 'triad of basic controls'. These are as follows (pp. 13–14):

1. The extent of society's control chances over extra-human nexuses of events, that is, over what we sometimes refer to rather loosely as 'natural events'.
2. The extent of its control chances over inter-human connections, or 'social nexuses'.

3. The extent to which each of its individual members has learned, from childhood onwards, to exercise self-control.

It is to the last of these that Elias refers as 'the civilizing process'. To the extent that the direct expression of violent action and emotion in society generally is progressively contained, regulated and stylized, one type of leisure activity takes on the character of a 'quest for excitement'.

> As a precise sociological term for this class is lacking, we have called it the 'mimetic class'. Most, though not all, leisure activities belong to it . . . . Here, as elsewhere, the quest for excitement, for the Aristotelian 'enthusiasm', in our leisure activities is complementary to the control and restraint of overt emotionality in our ordinary life. One cannot understand the one without the other. (Elias and Dunning, 1986, p. 66)

Although spare time and leisure activities can be compared along a variety of dimensions – the extent to which they are routinized, their place on the public/private continuum, and so on – 'one can say that all leisure activities embody a controlled decontrolling of restraints on emotions'. (p. 96).

Elias and Dunning have devoted their greatest efforts to the analysis of sport (and especially soccer) within this frame of reference, and tourism does not feature at all explicitly in their work. Nevertheless, the concept of a 'controlled decontrolling of restraints' offers a potentially highly fruitful starting point for the study of tourist motivations and the structure of tourist experiences. It indicates a way in which we might begin to give specific content to the hitherto rather generalized discussions of tourism in terms of 'sacredness'.

The quest for authenticity

Dean MacCannell's book *The Tourist: A New Theory of the Leisure Class* (1976), is very ambitious in its aims, in that he sees the tourist as not just another role-type to be placed alongside others, but as a standpoint from which the structure of modernity can be systematically surveyed.

> 'The tourist' is one of the best models available for modern-man-in-general . . . . Our first apprehension of modern civilization, it seems to me, emerges in the mind of the tourist. (p. 1)

The structure which displays the unity of modern culture is 'the attraction', which is 'precisely analogous to the religious symbolism of primitive peoples', it provides a means of approaching the 'total design of society'. Tourism emerges, for Mac-Cannell, as a secular substitute for organized religion, with 'public places' functioning as religious texts, containing representations of good and evil. He goes on to elaborate the process of 'sight sacralization', and to analyze sightseeing as ritual. The two elements which emerge as central to the structure of 'the attraction', turn out to be the establishment of the relationship of superiority of the tourist over the 'sight', and the demonstration of the 'authenticity' of the sight or attraction.

In some respects MacCannell's work suffers from the general defects of the structuralist tradition in which it stands, in that it elaborates the formal characteristics of a vehicle for analysis at the expense of the study of its content. We are left wondering whether *any* object is equally capable of sacralization as a 'sight', and may become the focus of ritual. It seems interesting to observe that they do work in this way: but just how do they work? We have a syntax, but in spite of his gestures in this direction, we really lack a 'semantics' of the 'attraction'. The potential interest of his vision of the tourist as engaged in a guest for 'authenticity' is shown, however, by the work of another author whose writing makes no acknowledgement of MacCannell, the Australian political scientist Donald Horne. Horne's empirical focus is much narrower than that of Mac-Cannell (he is only interested in 'the great museum') but nevertheless, for him the museum is the supreme exemplar of the tourist sight (Horne, 1984).

According to Horne, the structure of the tourist attraction is supported on the twin pillars of asymmetrical power relations and the affirmation of authenticity. Museums are 'about power': they all display the particular charisma of their patrons. The means by which their claims to power are made effective is the demonstration of 'authenticity'. ' "Authenticity" is the special magic of museums' (p. 16). What Horne is telling us is that instead of having a rather diffuse character, as presented by MacCannell, tourist attractions are engaged precisely in processes of legitimation. Tourist experiences are framed by the host to a particular end.

Horne's study may be rather one-sided, even within the specific context of the museum: but it does have great interest. MacCannell's work has become important as the stimulus to the examination of tourist performances (see, for example, much of the work collected in Cohen, 1985; also Brunner and Kirshenblatt-Gimblett, 1987). *The Great Museum* helps to build on, and give specificity to, this approach to tourism, while at the same time attaching tourism studies to the wider enterprise of the sociology of ideology.

The process of privatization

The concept of 'privatization' has not been fully domesticated in the vocabulary of English-speaking sociologists, originating as it does in the work of a group of German theorists. Jürgen Habermas is the writer who has probably done most to develop this idea. As with the two preceding sections, discussion of it is included here, not because of any large amount of sociological work already completed, in which it is applied to the study of tourism, but because – like the 'civilizing process' – it offers a very suggestive point of anchorage for a scatter of diverse observations about tourism which otherwise await organization in some coherent manner.

This process Habermas has identified as a very important moment in the development of a motivational crisis which affects advanced capitalist societies (Habermas, 1976, Part Two; see also Rojek, 1985). There is a crisis of motivation, he argues, in that such societies have hitherto been dependent upon tradi-

tional, precapitalist culture for important aspects of their motivational structures. In our present age, these elements of traditionalism are being undermined, without being replaced by something new. Areas of activity in society which formerly had some public, institutional status are thus being allowed to collapse into the realm of the private.

'Privatization' has to be understood in counter-distinction to the rather better-known sociological concept of 'structural differentiation'. Here the advancing division of labor generates new roles and complexes of roles, whose distinctiveness and interdependence with other aspects of social structure are recognized and institutionalized. During the process of privatization, however, the reverse is the case, in that the activities and structures within which they are collectively conducted are 'disestablished', so that their continuation, and the satisfaction of the needs which they serve, becomes the prerogative of private individuals, or at best of the family unit.

The interest of applying the notion of 'privatization' to tourism is twofold. In the first instance it suggests a framework for interpreting a number of tourist activities, especially those of a highly individualistic and hedonistic sort, such as sunbathing. For many tourists these play a far more important part in their holiday than do the kind of highly public events and attractions which provide the focus of MacCannell and Horne's work. Yet it is important that we realize that these are not just unstructured 'free time' – a nonsocial residue of time without significant connection with a wider context.

Secondly, an awareness of the privatized character of tourism also draws our attention to the composition of the flow of tourists. The transport and accommodation of tourists, and the marketing of tourism are in considerable measure in the hands of material available now dealing with 'tourist motivation', and attempts have been made to systematize knowledge of the role of the tourist. (Material on both of these areas is well reviewed in Pearce, 1982.) The first of these anticipates the tourist exself is consumed predominantly by small groups (especially the family) and individuals. To research into tourist performances we need to add the investigation of the process of tourist consumption – how the tourist 'reads', interprets, or acquires gratification from that which is offered. There is a good deal of material available now dealing with 'tourist motivation', and attempts have been made to systematize knowledge of the role of the tourist. (Material on both of these areas is well reviewed in Pearce, 1982). The first of these anticipates the tourist experience itself; and the second provides only a formal shell – a vehicle which potentially 'contains' this experience. The work on privatization implies that we should go beyond both of these sets of questions, to explore the ways in which the privatized individual does choose, order and assimilate such material.

Conclusions

All of the theoretical ideas reviewed here have a practical significance for our understanding of tourism, although that connection may at first seem indirect. The relevance of impact studies is the most straightforward, in that these expand in a variety of important ways our awareness of the range of consequences which are likely to attend upon the development of tourism within a host community. These consequences, as we now know in great detail, will extend well beyond the more obvious costs and benefits studied by economists, such as problems of opportunity cost or the provision of employment.

Sociological studies in the past have probably gone too far in their allocation to tourism of the blame for the adverse effects of economic change (although in this respect they have clearly been responding critically to the excessive optimism of economists). Nevertheless, it is vital that both business and state agencies involved in the promotion and management of the tourist trade are made aware of the likely significance of the decisions and policies for which they are responsible. The limiting of attention to costs and benefits solely in narrowly economic terms may well only defer to the future a growing number of serious problems which could undermine the original economic aspirations of developers. Sociological sensitivity in this area is probably economic good sense, rather than a luxury.

The direct applicability of other general frames of reference – the sociology of leisure and the 'quest for excitement', or the problem of 'privatization' – is less immediately clear, but nevertheless important. The intention of reviewing this succession of sociological frames of reference for the reader has not been simply to set out a kind of intellectual supermarket, in which one chooses theoretical ideas on the basis of their personal fit. The intention is also certainly not to leave the impression that sociologists cannot make up their mind about the character of tourism. General though these ideas are, they do have a very direct application to the understanding of tourism.

There is an acute danger on the part of those engaged in the discussion of tourism, whether they be principally interested in it from a business, a governmental or an academic point of view, to loosely overgeneralize its characteristics. There has been too much willingness to sound off confidently about 'tourism', *tout court*. Sociologists have an important contribution to make by drawing attention to the subtlety, complexity and diversity of the phenomenon.

In taking up the several sociological approaches reviewed here, we do not need to choose between 'rival' models of tourism, although there are obvious superficial contradictions between some of them. It is likely to be the case that those activities which we group together rather crudely as 'tourism' are actually quite diverse as social phenomena. They have different social and personal springs of motivation, and are located quite differently with respect to other social and economic processes. Policy or business decisions (as well as academic analyses) which fail to grasp these differences, are likely to fall seriously wide of their mark.

Futher reading

Aisner, P., 'Tourisme international au Cusco (Perou). Des impacts economiques aux répercussions socio-politiques', *Problems of Tourism*, vol. X, no. 3 (37) (1987), pp. 49–60. A relatively unusual attempt within the 'impact' tradition of tourism studies to confront the political aspects of change.

Allcock, J. B.,'Tourism and social change in Dalmatia', *Journal of Development Studies*, vol. 20, no. 1 (1983a), pp. 34–55. The article illustrates the interaction between spatial and social factors in the development of tourism, confirming independently the conclusions of Poulsen (1977).

Allcock, J. B., 'The development of tourism in Yugoslavia: some conceptual and empirical lessons', *Emerging Development Patterns: European Contributions*, I. Dobozi and P. Mandi, eds (EADI/Institute for World Economy of the Hungarian Academy of Sciences 1983b). Using data drawn from Yugoslavia to illustrate the argument, the author challenges the tendency to overgeneralize about tourism from very limited models.

Allcock, J. B., 'Waiting for Gojko: two one-act plays after Goffman', *The Sociological Review*, vol. 33, no. 3 (1985), pp. 532–43. The paper explores critically the thesis that tourism necessarily inculcates deferential attitudes on the part of host communities in developing countries.

Aron, R., *Eighteen Lectures on Industrial Society* (Weidenfeld and Nicholson, 1967). Aron provides a widely-accepted summary of the characteristics of the industrialization process, against which it is useful to compare tourist development.

Ballossier, R., 'Approche sociologique de quelques problèmes touristiques, *Cahiers du Tourisme*, serie C, vol. 3 (1967). An interesting early attempt by an engineer to draw attention to the need for tourism studies within a sociological framework.

Brunner, E. M. and Kirschenblatt-Gimblett, B., 'East Africa: tourist performances and representations', *Problems of Tourism*, vol. X, no. 3 (37) (1987), pp. 25–9. The authors examine the ways in which performances, both human and animal, are produced for tourists in East Africa.

Burkart, A. J. and Medlik, S., *Tourism: Past, Present and Future* (Heinemann, 1974). This highly influential standard work in the economics of tourism contains in Chapters 5 and 6 an attempt to extend its basic framework of cost-benefit analysis into the social domain.

Clarke, J. and Chritcher, C., *The Devil Makes Work: Leisure in Capitalist Britain* (Macmillan, 1985). A good example of the large body of work dealing with the social history of leisure.

Cognat, B., *La Montagne Colonisée* (Les Éditions du Cerf, 1973). This work is generally regarded as an early classic in the empirical sociology of tourism, providing a study of the transformation of class structure in an Alpine community.

Cohen, E., 'Rethinking the sociology of tourism', *Annals of Tourism Research*, vol. VI, no. 1 (1979), pp. 18–35. One of the principal figures in the development of the sociology of tourism draws together some central themes in the literature.

Cohen, E. (ed.), *Annals of Tourism Research*, vol. 12, no. 1 (1985). Special edition of the journal devoted to the study of tourist guides. The volume contains several pieces which add to our knowledge of tourism in terms of role models, and the study of tourist performances.

Cressey-Lind, M. and Lind, I. Y., 'Visitors as victims: crime against tourists in Hawaii', *Annals of Tourism Research*, vol. 13, no. 2 (1986), pp. 167–91. The authors provide not only a good contribution to the empirical study of the relationship between tourism and crime, but also an excellent bibliography.

Cunningham, H., *Leisure in the Industrial Revolution* (Croom Helm, 1980). Cunningham provides a good general overview of this aspect of British social history.

De Kadt, E. (ed.), *Tourism: Passport to Development?* (Oxford University Press, for the World Bank and UNESCO, 1979). In addition to his own excellent editorial introduction, De Kadt gathers thirteen original essays in this volume, which has now achieved the status of a standard reference work in the study of the social and cultural effects of tourism in developing countries.

De Weerdt, J., 'Espace rural et tourisme en France: orientations de la recherche', *Problems of Tourism*, vol. X, no. 2 (1987), pp. 83–93. This paper help to alert us to the importance of spatial dimensions to the changes associated with tourist development.

Dumazedier, J., *Toward a Society of Leisure* (Free Press, 1967). Dumazedier's text has become one of the major points of departure for work on the sociology of leisure in the formalist tradition.

Elaković, S., 'Turizam u funkciji moći ili emancipacije', *Kultura*, vols. 60–61 (1983), pp. 130–8. The author has provided a very concise review of the early tradition of the sociology of tourism among German scholars. Although written in Serbo-Croat, it may be more widely useful as a source of bibliographical reference.

Elaković, S. and Brangjolica, V., *Efekti i posljedice ekonomskih, socijalnih i drugih promijena pod utjecajem turizma na jadranskom području* (Fakultet za Turizam i Vanjsku Trgovinu, 1985). This is a very thorough and detailed piece of survey research, dealing with the social transformation of Dalmatia. It is particularly useful for its discussion of the effects of tourism on patterns of socioeconomic inequality and power.

Elias, N., *What is Sociology?* (Hutchinson, 1978). This more general introduction to sociological thought also contains a valuable brief summary of the author's seminal ideas about the importance of the 'civilizing process' in Western culture.

Elias, N. and Dunning, E., *The Quest for Excitement: Sport and Leisure in the Civilizing Process* (Basil Blackwell, 1986). The book collects ten essays by the authors, in which Elias' novel perspective on the general transformation of European culture is worked out with more specific reference to the study of leisure.

English, E. P., *The Great Escape? An Examination of North–South Tourism* (The North–South Institute, 1986). English has given us a first-rate brief survey of the issues in the debate about the role of tourism in the relationship between developed and underdeveloped countries. It includes a consideration of social and cultural as well as economic factors.

Erisman, H. M., 'Tourism and cultural dependency', *Annals of Tourism Research*, vol. 10, no. 3 (1983), pp. 337–61. The article examines the link between cultural, and politico-economic dependency in relation to tourism, within the specific context of the West Indies.

Farnham, A., 'Tourism and culture shock', *Annals of Tourism Research*, vol. 11, no. 1 (1984), pp. 41–57. This piece extends our range of interest in the 'impact' tradition.

Fedler, A. J. (ed.), *The Interrelationships of Leisure, Recreation and Tourism*, special edition of the *Annals of Tourism Research*, vol. 14, no. 3 (1987). An ambitious attempt to awaken interest in the importance of the links between three hitherto disparate areas of sociology. More important as a program than for its achievements.

Fine, E. C. and Speer, J. H., 'Tour guide performances as sight sacralization', *Annals of Tourism Research*, vol. 12, no. 1 (1985), pp. 73–95. There have not been many attempts to take up MacCannell's interesting insights into the quasireligious aspects of tourist experiences: but this is one.

Forster, J., 'The sociological consequences of tourism', *International Journal of Comparative Sociology*, vol. 2 (1964), pp. 217–27. Forster makes an early plea for the importance of a sociology of tourism, and draws attention to its importance for the structure of the labor force, work habits and stratification.

Gamarnikow, E., Morgan, D., Purvis, J. *et al* (eds.), *The Public and the Private* (Gower, 1983) The introductory essay suggests a reason for the systematic neglect of tourism studies in sociology.

Graburn, N. H., 'Tourism and prostitution', *Annals of Tourism Research*, vol. 10, no. 3 (1983), pp. 437–43. This is a review article which examines two important empirical studies in this area.

Greenwood, D. J., 'Tourism as an agent of change: a Spanish Basque case', *Ethnology*, vol. 11 (1972), pp. 80–91. Greenwood's research in Fuenterrabia in northern Spain has yielded a classic case-study of the social impact of tourist development which is particularly interesting for its comment on changing class structures. See also the following reference.

Greenwood, D. J., 'Tourism as an agent of change', *Annals of Tourism Research*, vol. 3 (1976), pp. 128–42. See also the previous reference.

Habermas, J., *Legitimation Crisis* (Heinemann, 1976). In this work this major contemporary German social theorist sets out his ideas on the cultural crisis within modern society, which has provided a point of departure for the sociological discussion of the process of privatization.

Hern, A., *The Seaside Holiday* (Cresset Press, 1967). A useful contribution to the social history of leisure.

Hiller, H. L., 'Tourism: development or dependence?', *The Restless Caribbean: Changing Patterns of International Relations*, R. Millett and W. M. Will, eds. (Praeger, 1979). This piece gives us a sociological challenge to the cost–benefit tradition in tourism studies, by placing tourism within a framework of 'dependency'.

Horne, D., *The Great Museum: The Representation of History* (Pluto Press, 1984). Horne has written an important contribution to the study of the tourist 'attraction', in which he examines museums as mediators of ideology.

Jafari, J., 'The socio-economic costs of tourism to developing countries', *Annals of Tourism Research*, vol. 1 (1974), pp. 227–59. A valuable attempt to extend the 'cost–benefit' framework beyond purely economic calculation, to the assessment of the social and cultural balance sheet of tourism.

Jafari, J., 'The tourist system: sociocultural models for theoretical and practical application', *Problems of Tourism*, vol. X, no. 3(37) (1987), pp. 3–17. Jafari provides a general schematic model of tourism which serves as a useful mnemonic, guiding the examination of the relationship of tourism to its cultural and social context.

Krippendorf, J., 'Tourism in the system of industrial society', *Annals of Tourism Research*, vol. 13, no. 4 (1986), pp. 517–32. The author argues that both recreation and tourism belong as integral components of the system of industrial societies.

Lanfant, M.-F., *Les Théories du Loisir* (Presses Universitaires de France, 1972). A systematic review is presented of the development of sociological theories of leisure.

Lever, A., 'Spanish tourism migrants: the case of Lloret de Mar', *Annals of Tourism Research*, vol. 14, no. 4 (1987), pp. 449–70. With respect to a Spanish resort, the writer considers changes in the class position of seasonal, migrant workers in tourism. Of particular note are her remarks about the gender composition of the labor force.

MacCannell, D., *The Tourist* (Schocken Books, 1976). MacCannell has provided us with an important attempt to produce a theory of the tourist, which focuses principally on the nature of 'the attraction' and its 'authenticity'. He makes ambitious claims for the general significance of tourism as a model for the wider understanding of modern societies.

Mathieson, A. and Wall, G., *Tourism: Economic, Physical and Social Impacts* (Longman, 1982). An excellent, compact and yet wide-ranging survey of the literature in the 'effects' tradition is provided by the authors, in a form accessible to the general reader.

O'Grady, R., *Third World Stopover* (World Council of Churches, 1981). This little volume had a dramatic effect on the stimulation of the debate about the impact of tourism on developing countries. In particular, it draws the reader's attention to the doubtful moral desirability of tourist-based development.

Pearce, P. L., *The Social Psychology of Tourist Behaviour* (Pergamon Press, 1982). This offers an unusual contribution to the literature, in that it is a student text in tourism which is principally addressed to the sociocultural and not the economic dimensions of tourism. It covers the literature widely, and deals with the social role of the tourist, tourist motivation, the contact between hosts and guests, and tourist perceptions of their environment.

Perez, L. A., 'Aspects of underdevelopment: tourism in the West Indies', *Science and Society*, vol. 37 (1973), pp. 473–80. Perez makes a stimulating contribution to the debate about tourism and its role in the 'development of underdevelopment', within a Marxist analytical framework.

Poulsen, T. M., 'Migration on the Adriatic coast: some processes associated with the development of tourism', *Population and Migration Trends in Eastern Europe*, H. L. Kostanick, ed. (Westview Special Studies on the Soviet Union and Eastern Europe, Boulder, Colorado, 1977), pp. 197–215. Poulson examines the way in which the growth of tourism on the Adriatic coasts of Yugoslavia has resulted in the slowing of population decline in the islands, and its concentration in urban areas.

Rivers, P., 'Tourist troubles', *New Society*, vol. 23, no. 539 (1973), p. 250. The essay outlines for a general readership the claims which have been made in the literature regarding the deleterious social effects of tourism.

Roberts, K., *Leisure* (Longman, 2nd edition, 1981). This book is a standard text in the sociology of leisure, providing a very clear review of the principal issues in the field.

Rojek, C., *Capitalism and Leisure Theory* (Tavistock, 1985). Rojek has provided a vigorous attempt to break out of the narrower conceptualization of the sociology of leisure, and to reintegrate it with some important general currents in contemporary sociological theory.

Shivji, I. G., *Tourism and Socialist Development* (Tanzania Publishing House, 1973). Drawing specifically on the experience of Tanzania, the author presents a forceful critique of the claims that tourism makes for economic benefit.

Smith, V. L. (ed.), *Hosts and Guests: the Anthropology of Tourism* (Basil Blackwell, 1978). Smith's anthology of 15 essays has been very influential in broadening the debate about the important of tourism be-

yond the economic considerations which dominated early discussion.

Truong, T.-D., 'The dynamics of sex tourism: the case of South-East Asia', *Development and Change*, vol. 14 (1983), pp. 533–53. This important piece of empirical investigation draws our attention to the the systematically structured exploitation of sex as a component of the tourist industry in South-East Asia.

Turner, L. and Ash, J., *The Golden Hordes: International Tourism and the Pleasure Periphery* (Constable, 1975). This book, vigorously written in a polemical style, constituted a landmark in the growth of awareness of and investigation into the social dimensions of the effects of tourism. Although it does suffer from the tendency to overgeneralize its conclusions, it is still well worth reading as a means of familiarizing oneself with the problems of the area.

Veal, A. J., *Leisure and the Future*, Leisure and Recreation Studies, 4 (George Allen & Unwin, 1987), Veal examines the likely future changes in leisure in industrial societies in relation to the expected changes in the nature and pattern of work.

Walton, J. K. and Walvin, J., *Leisure in Britain, 1780–1939* (Manchester University Press, 1983). The editors have brought together 11 original studies in the history of leisure in Britain, several of which are directly relevant to the study of tourism.

Wood, R. E., 'International tourism and cultural change in Southeast Asia', *Economic Development and Cultural Change*, vol. 28, no. 3 (1980), pp. 561–81. The author develops a clear and forceful critique of the tendency within tourism studies to treat host societies as 'normatively static – the passive recipients of change wrought by tourism'.

Wood, R. E., 'Ethnic tourism, the state, and cultural change in Southeast Asia', *Annals of Tourism Research*, vol. 11 (1984), pp. 353–74. The article explores the way in which international tourism increasingly involves the restructuring of the relationship between the state and local cultures.

Young, G., *Tourism: Blessing or Blight?* (Penguin, 1973). Chapters 2 and 3 are good examples of the attempt by economists writing in the cost–benefit tradition to extend the range of consideration given to noneconomic factors in assessing the impact of tourism.

JOHN B. ALLCOCK

State tourism policy

Introduction

Before World War II, government intervention was, generally speaking, limited to areas which concerned tourism only indirectly. The war climate, however, gave rise to a series of police, customs, monetary and sanitary requlations that largely restricted tourist movements. During the second half of the 1940s and most of the 1950s, governments worked towards facilitating tourism once again.

Having recognized tourism as an effective and efficient foreign exchange earner (and suffering from a continuous lack of hard currency for their reconstruction efforts), the European governments started busily promoting their country as a tourist destination to their neighbors and the Americans. The Eisenhower administration, on the other hand, had rejected the proposal that the federal government become involved in tourism promotion.

The extraordinary growth in tourism demand led the governments to make use of this industry in attaining national objectives. Furthermore, public opinion was ready to accept that the State take over certain industries (such as the national airline or rail system) considered to be important for the country as a whole, even though the liberal philosophy would have them come under the private sector.

Although policies relating to tourism development went through similar changes in most industrialized countries, it is evident that history, socioeconomic conditions, the political philosophy of the respective government and the extent to which tourism supply was developed, have all had a large influence.

Justification

The complexity of the tourism phenomenon demands a certain control by government and a tourism policy which orients, but does not restrict, private initiative. Any comprehensive policy is confronted, however, by the ambiguity of the tourism sector: the State expects this industry to serve the national economy (foreign exchange, job creation etc.), but also to respond to the leisure needs of the population. And since any economic development represents a charge for the environment, government is confronted with another paradox: a well-preserved environment is one of the main tourist attractions, but with tourism comes its inevitable degradation. The objectives government sets itself, and which are directly dependent on the principles that justify its intervention, will determine the tourism policy it later implements.

Social aspects

The often excessive industrialization and urbanization as well as the stressful pace of daily life in the modern world must periodically be counterbalanced by a rest for the body and mind in the interest of humanity: for the individual's well-being of course, but also because a relaxed person is more likely to accept other people's right to be different.

Tourism can, in fact, be a precious tool for international understanding, for as the guest learns about the culture of his host, the same is to some extent true the other way around. But this industry can also help revive local economies threatened by emigration for lack of economic activity or improve living conditions in regions where the local population alone could not finance certain heavy investments such as airports or sewer systems. In very underdeveloped nations, however, tourism often costs more in social and economic terms than it contributes.

Economic aspects

The economic consequences for the (material) well-being of a society are easier quantified than those of a social or environmental nature. It is thus these economic and financial considerations that are normally put forward to justify any government intervention in the field of tourism. But a tendency to underestimate the subtle links between different branches of industry, and to consider only some of its principal aspects, has often led governments to be unaware of the costs involved or the advantages induced by the tourism demand.

A major concern for all governments is the earning of foreign currency in order to maintain their capacity to import or to pursue their development efforts. This supply of hard currency is particularly important for lesser developed, non oil-exporting nations whose economic structure is rarely very diversified, and for the socialist countries whose currencies are not internationally accepted. In these cases, tourism can be an effective and efficient foreign currency earner. On the other hand, some countries, such as West Germany and Japan, encourage their nationals to go abroad. Their commercial balance being excessively positive, 'exporting' their tourism demand helps reduce international criticism.

Although the vast majority of holidaymakers stay within their own country, few governments have actually attached any great importance to domestic tourism. Except for certain traditional tourism-receiving countries (Spain, Italy, Greece etc.), its economic and fiscal importance far outweighs that of international tourism in the industrialized world. For example, in the United States, only 4 out every 100 tourists are foreign. Studies are currently underway at a national and international level better to measure the contribution made by domestic tourism.

The tourism industry's potential for creating and maintaining employment has always been used to justify any tourism development. A study undertaken by the British Department of Employment showed, for instance, that 1 million jobs were directly supported by tourism spending in the United Kingdom in 1983, to which another 500,000 had to be added in supplying industries. This is nearly 8 per cent of the working population. However, some 30 per cent of these jobs are part-time or seasonal, and the low job qualifications lead to a high turnover rate within the industry. These are the considerations that tourism development detractors usually highlight.

The rural regions are most attractive to those tourists looking for a change of scenery. Thus tourism not only brings a new economic activity and job possibilities to lesser developed areas, but also contributes to a redistribution of revenues, which have a tendency to be concentrated in a few highly developed parts of a country. But a mono-activity is always dangerous for a region's economic and cultural survival, and tourism should therefore never be more than a motor for development.

Environmental aspects

Contrary to other industrial branches, which consider the environment to be of value if it produces material wealth (which degrades it...), tourism accords the natural, preserved areas the highest value since its own quality depends directly on that of the environment. But who has not seen the results of overuse? The protection and improvement of the natural surroundings, monuments etc. are therefore essential for tourism development (to protect their inherent amenity value), on the one hand, and for the local population, increasingly aware of environmental problems, on the other.

It is vital to determine the tourist carrying capacity of an ecosystem in constant evolution. The reciprocal interactions between the 'living space' and the 'living being' continually modify, in fact, the states of equilibrium. The importance of a comprehensive land-use policy, taking into account the various degrees of compatibility between activities, is of utmost importance since space or land has a finite quality. The competition between various uses for the same parcel of land is the reason for the often unrelenting price spiral in prime tourist regions.

Objectives

The overall objective that any tourism policy must set itself, and which must itself contribute to attaining even more general objectives outlined by government, is to guarantee the following:

1. The optimal satisfaction of the individual's tourism needs, including the low income groups and the disadvantaged, while taking into account the interests of the local population.
2. The rational use of resources so as to facilitate holidaymaking and to assure the efficiency, if not the profitability, of the tourism installations.
3. The quality of the environment while respecting the carrying capacity of the different ecosystems.

Time/society objective

If tourism is fully to play its role within a social policy, it must (*ipso facto*) be an activity available to the largest number of people. This requires actions concerning the rhythm of work (and school) on a daily, weekly and yearly basis. More flexible working hours and calendars would relieve the pressure on prime holiday periods: weekends, public holidays, summer months, etc. The concentration of school and industrial holidays in a short period of the year particularly reduces the efficiency of the tourist industry, and the effectiveness of regional development. It entails increased high-season prices and a degree of congestion which is uncomfortable for both the tourist and the local population.

Reducing the working hours should contribute not only to shorten the hours worked per week, but especially to lengthen the annual holiday period. Medicine has proven that a period of at least 4 weeks is needed annually to restore the human organism to full capacity. But as important as these aspects are, a lack of information and knowledge on how to organize one's vacation time is a major handicap for many people. Staying at home is not an effective alternative to a change of scenery from a physiological and psychological point of view.

Getting away temporarily from social constraints can also help a person reach self-fulfilment. However, the tourist must dispose of his full liberty of movement. It has been one of the major objectives of the industrialized countries to slowly break down all obstacles to international tourism, but as the ongoing work of the Organization for Economic Cooperation and Development (OECD) and the European Community (EC) shows, this is a very long process. The tourist must furthermore have sufficient knowledge so that 1. his personality can fully express itself, 2. he will not be in conflict with the local population due to lack of comprehension, and 3. he will not suffer from the greed that is often the result of tourism as a dominant activity. To protect him further, many governments have adopted a consumer protection policy, to safeguard the tourist's interests against any shortcomings in the services offered by tour operators and travel agents as well as against misleading advertisements.

It seems only just that the local population, literally invaded once or twice a year by the tourists, should profit from this phenomenon not only economically but also socially. Tourism can contribute to a better comprehension between people, but it can give rise to conflict in customs and moral standards. In any case, if the ratio tourist/inhabitant becomes too high, friction is almost inevitable, and this must be taken into account by any regional development program. The local population should also be allowed to profit from the advantages tourism development can procure, such as access to the attractions and facilities created to satisfy the tourists' needs. Especially in the lesser developed and socialist countries, this is quite often not the case. For instance, casinos, certain hotel bars and restaurants or resorts (Club Méditerranée...) are 'off limits' to the locals.

Revenue/economy objective

The efficiency of the main elements of the tourism industry – lodging, restaurant and recreational facilities, transportation, tour businesses – depend directly on the personnel's competence. Of course, the supply must present a good quality/price ratio, be diversified and permit as far as possible an all-weather use, since improving the rate of occupancy/utilization will improve its profitability.

Employment in the tourism industry generally speaking lacks prestige: working hours are usually longer than the norm, holiday periods demand even more work, work is often only seasonal and the pay does not always compensate for all these drawbacks. But in order to optimize the productivity of this sector, it is necessary to employ not only a qualified but also a motivated work force, both factors that depend on the quality of the working conditions.

The democratization of the demand on one hand, and the influence of fashion and advertising on the other, have given rise to a very heterogenous demand. The supply must therefore be diversified to comply with the wishes of both domestic and foreign tourists. But this new race of tourists is also more aware of its rights as consumers and, influenced by the media, more demanding when it comes to the quality of the services rendered. Thus it is often necessary to modernize the current supply and to improve the comfort of the facilities. The financial cost involved demands the extension of the tourist season, which will not only improve the rate of occupancy/utilization, but will also better justify the environmental charge of the tourism development.

A balanced tourism development requires a close watch on the environmental constraints and the carrying capacity, which implies that demand will be directed away from certain poles that have reached saturation towards lesser developed regions. But at the same time, the government must be aware that too great a dependence on a seasonal activity such as tourism can very quickly destabilize a whole region and should therefore encourage a multi-activity economy even in areas whose future seems to lie with tourism.

Effective marketing can also help improve the profitability and spread of any tourism development. A close collaboration between public and private tourism organizations is necessary to determine the target markets on which the diversifed supply is based. Any marketing campaign should be intensive, systematic and, above all, coordinated.

The State also has a large role to play on the demand side: a sufficient discretionary income is necessary to make a vacation affordable. The government has a wide range of options at its disposal. The basic income can be fixed through minimum-wage legislation; family and rent allowances, child benefits etc. can increase the basic income for many households; vacation funds or holiday vouchers, reduced cost of transportation or lodging, holiday villages subsidized by public funds, etc. are some of many possibilities to help people overcome the revenue barrier to vacations. The economic policy with respect to buying power, interest rates, revenue redistribution and inflation control can also play a key role in encouraging or dissuading tourism demand.

Space/environment objective

A poorly controlled tourism development will inevitably bring with it its own destruction because of the excessive charge it will put on the environment. A balance must be found between the different types of zones:

1. With minimum access and maximum protection.
2. Protected but with access by tourists.
3. Essentially agricultural but for recreational use.
4. For intensive use by tourism and recreation.

A judicial land development also implies the integration of the facilities into the surrounding environment, as well as the conservation and rehabilitation of those buildings that constitute the cultural and historical heritage of a country. A vacation or leisure architecture makes provision for the architectural style of the region. The construction style must furthermore respect the human scale, alternate built-up surfaces and green areas and keep access to natural sites open. The dispersion of constructions can be as damaging to the environment as the creation of tourist ghettos (sometimes the size of a town), and which remain unoccupied three-quarters of the year.

A functional agriculture can help maintain the landscape not only from an esthetical point of view, but also from an ecological one: mountain pastures and meadows that are closely cropped fulfil a protective function for the mountains, as do dunes and plantations along the coastline. Landscaping can improve the attractiveness of any site, be it urban, natural, cultural or historic.

Conclusion

While the three major objectives all contribute to achieving the general goal, there are numerous conflicts among the secondary objectives. It follows that priorities must be established beforehand, which must also concord with the finalities set by government. The degree of importance accorded to any one objective as well as the means chosen to implement it, are, however, a direct function of the overall economic climate and the ideology of the political party in power.

The choices made at any given moment will determine the direction taken by the tourism policy. But the objectives serve essentially as principles, and must be translated into reality. It is the strategies that serve as a link between the objectives and the practical measures. Contrary to the determination of objectives and strategies, the actual carrying out of strategies is the responsibility of the authorities directly concerned as well as of business and private individuals.

Further reading

Airey, D., 'Tourism administration in the USA', *Tourism Management*, vol. 5, no. 4 (December 1984), pp. 269–79. Although the signature of the National Tourism Policy Act 1981 seemed to be a very positive step towards federal support for tourism, the Administration has not followed through on the promise in subsequent years. This is a very interesting analysis on the power play behind the Act, its objectives and shortcomings.

Commission consultative fédérale pour le tourisme, *Conception Suisse du Tourisme*, Bases de la politique du tourisme, Rapport final, Berne (1979). An excellent attempt to establish a framework for a comprehensive tourism policy.

Commission of European Communities, *A Community Policy on Tourism Initial Guidelines*, Bulletin of European Communities (supplement 4/1982). The communication by the Commission illustrates the large number of Community policies, which directly or indirectly, have a bearing on tourism and which must therefore be given a 'tourist dimension'. Topics cover freedom of movement and protection of tourists, working conditions for those engaged in tourism, transport, regional development, and safeguarding the European heritage.

Edgell, D. L., 'United States international tourism policy', *Annals of Tourism Research*, vol. 10, no. 3 (1983), pp. 427–34. This article describes the key mechanisms in the United States for tourism policy making.

Krapf, K., 'L'intervention de l'Etat en matière de tourisme', *Revue de Tourisme*, no. 2, (1951), pp. 111–15. Although very old, this article has not lost any of its basic value as a concise analysis of the different economic regimes and how they intervene in the field of tourism.

Médecin, J., *Une Politique du Tourisme pour la France* (Secrétariat d'Etat au Tourisme, 1978). This policy paper, put out by the French government, was the first attempt to state in clear terms what the tourism policy should be and where it should lead.

Organization for Economic Cooperation and Development, *Decision–Recommendation of the Council on International Tourism Policy* (OECD, November 1985). The Decision–Recommendation is part of a vast, intersectorial work program on the liberalization of trade-in-services undertaken by the OECD since 1981. It contains three parts: global objectives, obligations to be met by each member country, and directives as to how to reach the objectives.

Organization for Economic Cooperation and Development, *Tourism Policy and International Tourism in OECD Member Countries* (OECD, yearly). This publication contains policy developments and tourism information for individual member countries.

Organization of American States, *Hemispheric Policy on Tourism Development and Strategy for Implementation*, Occasional Papers (OAS, 1979). A very short paper outlining the main tourism objectives.

Richter, L. K., 'Fragmented politics of US tourism', *Tourism Management* (September 1985), pp. 162–73. The article examines the evolution and structure of tourism in the USA, leading to the conclusion that the impact of tourism politics is little understood or appreciated by the national administration.

Richter, L. K, 'Political implications of Chinese tourism policy', *Annals of Tourism Research*, vol. 10, no. 3, (1983), pp. 395–413. A study of the abrupt change in the Chinese tourism policy and its repercussions from a political, social and economic point of view.

Ronkainen, I. A., 'The conference on security and cooperation in Europe, its impact on tourism', *Annals of Tourism Research*, vol. 10, no. 3 (1983), pp. 415–26. A very good study of the inner workings of international conferences and the impact they may have on individual countries' policies.

MARION JOPPE

Statistical measurement in tourism

Introduction*

Tourism statistics had long lagged behind most industry statistics until the early 1980s. Then, services began to be recognized as an important issue for which efforts to improve the quantitative and qualitative assessment of this emerging sector of the post-industrial era had to be made. Attempts have since been made to ensure that tourism gets its appropriate share in this reorganization and that revisions of international systems and classifications are made, which could allow a better assessment of the significance of tourism as an economic sector. At the business level, secondary sources of tourism data provide valuable information for desk research conducted within the overall framework of market research, an essential element of marketing strategy. In exploiting this information, users have to be aware of data deficiencies in order to make the best use of this low-cost and readily available material.

History

When using tourism statistics, one is confronted with the lack of reliable and meaningful data and the absence of a universal tourism statistical system. The principal reasons for this are threefold. Firstly, tourism is difficult to identify because it is not a single industry in the conventional sense, but an amalgam of several parts of many industries supplying goods and services to visitors and nonvisitors alike. Secondly, like most service industries, tourism has been neglected in the past on the grounds that, compared to traditional industries such as manufacturing or agriculture, it had not proved to be important in domestic production or international trade. Above all, however, this situation mainly reflects the low priority accorded to service statistics in general, and tourism statistics in particular, by governments and international organizations responsible for developing statistical systems likely to produce adequate data for decision making.

The first step towards an international recognition of the importance of measuring the tourism phenomenon came from the UN Conference on International Travel and Tourism held in Rome in 1963 which recommended a 'Definition of "visitor"

and "tourist" for the purpose of international statistics'. This was followed by the publication during the 1970s by the World Tourism Organization (WTO) of a series of guidelines on definitions and classifications for national as well as for international tourism statistics. The Organization for Economic Cooperation and Development (OECD) Tourism Committee associated itself with the main concepts underlying the guidelines by recommending its member countries to use the two criteria for defining 'visitors', i.e. the main purpose of trip and the country of residence of the traveler. These efforts, intended to provide more insight into the movements of people, were insufficient to provide the appropriate tools to appraise the significance of tourism as an economic sector because they were not integrated into the already existing and internationally-recognized statistical systems.

This opportunity arose in the mid-1980s with the introduction of services in the Uruguay Round, and the international political weight they thus gained prompted governments to support efforts aimed at improving trade-in-service statistics. In this context, the decision taken by the UN Statistical Commission in 1976 to work towards harmonization of international economic classifications was timely, as are the ongoing revisions of the System of National Accounts (SNA) (the last version dates back to 1968) and the International Standard Industrial Classification (ISIC) (the last version was drawn up in 1968) and also the set up of a Central Product Classification (CPC) applicable to goods and services. Furthermore, the International Monetary Fund (IMF) has initiated the revision (5th edition) of its Balance of Payments (BOP) Manual (4th edition was issued in 1977).

These actions are expected to bear fruit at the beginning of the 1990s with the publication of new or revised international guidelines. A large number of international organizations have been invited to participate in the preparatory work, ensuring that services are fairly represented in the final proposals; the WTO, the OECD and Eurostat have been particularly active. In the case of certain service industries which cut across a number of other industries or sectors, e.g. information, energy and tourism, their integration into ISIC or CPC has proved to be difficult, if not impossible; it has therefore been suggested that tourism be treated on an *ad hoc* basis in an annex to the final versions of the proposed classifications. It is also expected that the revised BOP Manual will take into account certain realities of the tourism industry by breaking down its transport and travel accounts in such a way that, for example, passenger trans-

---

* The views expressed are those of the author and do not necessarily represent the views of the OECD.

port, pleasure and professional travel can be separately assessed.

All this work at the international level may look promising for the future of service industries in general, but it will never satisfy all the specific needs of individual industries at the desired level of detail. In fact, what businessmen, policy makers or researchers need in tourism is readily available quantitative material containing as much comprehensive data as possible on demand and supply, to be used in setting up marketing information systems, input/output analyses, or satellite accounts.

Terminology

The proposed improved WTO terminology takes into consideration the necessity to adapt the concepts used in other systems, such as the definition of 'resident agent' used in national accounting and in the balance of payments. The main elements of this terminology are now briefly summarized to the extent that they constitute the background to most of the guidelines presently available to the providers of official tourism statistics. As such, they represent the 'ideal' situation and not necessarily the one which the user might encounter when exploiting them (for further explanations, see the section on 'Data sources and deficiences' below).

There is general consensus that, for statistical purposes, a 'visitor' is a person traveling for less than a specific period of time (or more than a specific distance) to a place other than of his usual environment and whose main purpose of visit is other than to exercise an activity remunerated by an entity within the place visited. WTO proposes that three types of tourism be defined:

1. International tourism – inbound (external) plus outbound tourism.
2. Domestic tourism – tourism within (internal) plus inbound (external) tourism.
3. National tourism – tourism within (internal) plus outbound tourism.

Figure 1 sets out the international classification of travelers. On this basis, the international visitor combines the following:

1. The international tourist, i.e. an international visitor staying at least one night (but not more than one year) in the country visited and whose main purpose of visit can be classified under pleasure, professional or other tourism purposes.
2. The international excursionist, i.e. an international visitor who does not stay overnight in the country visited.

On the other hand, the domestic visitor is made up of the following:

1. The domestic tourist, i.e. a domestic visitor staying at least one night in a place other than that corresponding to his usual environment and whose main purpose of visit can be classified under pleasure, professional or other tourism purposes.
2. The domestic excursionist, i.e. a domestic visitor who does not stay overnight in the place visited.

In general, tourism statistics obtainable from secondary sources (those which assemble data produced by primary sources) should be able to provide information on both tourism demand and tourism supply. Total tourism demand is the consumption generated by economic agents performing internal, external and outbound tourism. These 'tourism agents' include persons, households and enterprises as well as government and private institutions. For each type of demand, statistics available usually provide the following data on individuals performing tourism:

1. The number of visitors during the reference period.
2. The duration of their visit.
3. Their place of origin (countries or areas).
4. Their destination (countries or regions within the country).
5. The periods during which they arrive.
6. Their means of transport.
7. The type of accommodation they choose.
8. Their demographic and socioeconomic characteristics.
9. The purpose of their visit.
10. Their reasons for taking the trip.
11. The means by which they organized the trip.
12. The amount of money they spent by type.
13. Their image of the country or area visited as a place for tourism.
14. Their degree of satisfaction after the trip.
15. Their opinion on prices, quality of service, tourism facilities, infrastructure, etc.

Tourism supply is composed of all goods and services necessary for tourism to take place, e.g. resources, infrastructure, and industries producing such goods and services either as characteristic tourism industries or tourism-related industries. It is customary that the following information on production units concerned with direct tourism consumption is available:

1. The tourism product provided by the production unit.
2. Its current tourism reception capacity.
3. The degree to which current tourism supply is utilized and the relationship between supply and demand.
4. The unit's economic performance.
5. The employment generated by the tourism production activity.
6. The prices for tourism goods and services.
7. The potential for growth in supply over the short, medium and long term.

An important feature of tourism supply is the coverage of the various types of accommodation into two broad categories: hotels and similar establishments, and supplementary means of accommodation. The first category originally aimed at covering four basic types of establishment, hotels, motels, boarding houses and inns; this list has been modified to take account of the various options present worldwide and it now includes roadside inns, beach hotels, residence clubs and similar establishments providing hotel services, tourist residences and similar accommodation arranged in rooms and providing limited hotel services. The second category, which originally provided

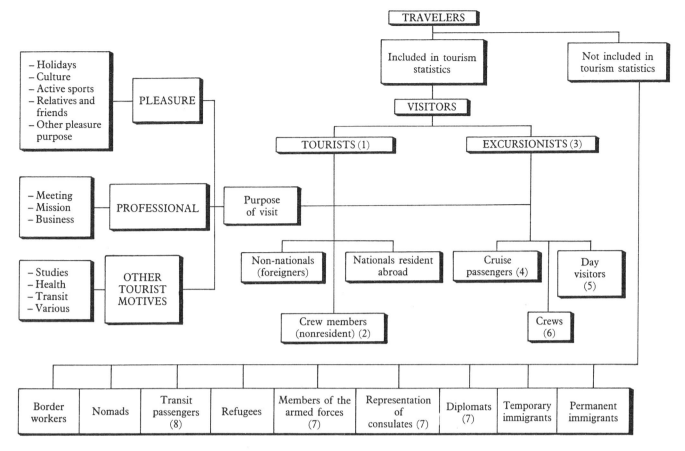

1. Visitors who spend at least one night in the country visited.
2. Foreign air or ship crews docked or in lay over and who use the accommodation establishments of the country visited.
3. Visitors who do not spend the night in the country visited although they may visit the country during one day or more and return to their ship or train to sleep.
4. Normally included in excursionists. Separate classification of these visitors is nevertheless recommended.
5. Visitors who come and leave the same day.
6. Crews who are not residents of the country visited and who stay in the country for the day.
7. When they travel from their country of origin to the duty station and vice-versa (including household servants and dependants accompanying or joining them.)
8. Who do not leave the transit area of the airport or the port. In certain countries, transit may involve a stay of one day or more. In this case, they should be included in the visitors statistics.

Figure 1 Classification of travelers. (*Source:* World Tourism Organization).

information on all the other accommodation facilities, has now been broken down into supplementary and special establishments, and private or special tourist accommodation.

Applications to business

Market research is essential for the development of the right marketing strategy involving the analysis of market opportunities through market segmentation. As part of the marketing program, this takes the form of selection of target markets for a fixed given supply or the modification of the quality and/or quantity of supply to meet the specific needs of actual or potential target markets. To do so, businesses have two basic techniques at their disposal, desk and field research. Desk research is performed by gathering as much information as available from secondary sources and by arranging it in a fashion which shows the gaps in the required data and thus the areas to be covered by field research work. Field research generally includes the search for more detailed and refined qualitative information based on questionnaires, interviews or sample surveys conducted by a specialized inhouse service or by an outside consultant.

Enterprises or agencies directly or indirectly concerned with the provision of goods and services to visitors all need to perform market research. This is typically the case for national departments responsible for tourism, tourist boards (national or regional), tour operators, airlines, hotels, and recreational attractions.

Data sources and deficiencies

For desk research covering information on demand and supply in more than one country, it is advisable to start off with basic data easily obtainable from secondary sources, e.g. from international organizations such as the OECD or the WTO. While they can provide valuable and comprehensive time series data with regard to demand, this is not always the case for supply or investment, for which the information is often sparse, if it exists at all. Furthermore, the larger the organization, the less likely it is to be able to provide very recent data covering most of its membership.

On the other hand, more recent disaggregated information on any given country is available directly from governmental agencies (such as departments responsible for tourism, national statistical offices, central banks), or from quasi- or nongovernmental bodies (national airlines, railway or coach companies, national hotel associations, national travel agency associations, or any association of suppliers of tourism services [restaurants, tour guides etc.]).

Although the majority of countries accept the guidelines on statistical measurement of tourism demand and supply in principle, practice has shown that these guidelines often came too late to be implemented, involved high costs which could not be met, or implied considerable technical and legal changes which could not be undertaken. The main deficiencies in these types of data come therefore from the lack of international comparability due to differences in definitions and coverages, and from changes in methodology which can render any statistical series inconsistent over time. Examples of this can be found in the lack of certain data across-the-board, incomplete coverage of certain types of demand, or nonexistent information on important features of supply. However, if one can assume that these errors and omissions are consistent through time, it may therefore be advisable to consider the elements under review by determining their trends rather than their overall volumes.

One way for the producers of statistics to fill in the gap between what is covered by the statistics published in an international context and what should be covered according to agreed principles and concepts is to enrich the tables with appropriate methodological footnotes. At the national level, attention should also be given to the provision of copies of the questionnaires or forms used to gather the material. These last two suggestions would be of great help to potential users.

Existing tourism statistics provide most of the quantitative elements for determining the trends of international and internal demand, and for the characteristics of visitors and of trips; in general, they answer the basic questions: who? when? where? what? and how? However, these statistics are very poor at measuring aggregated demand or at determining its qualities, particularly in providing replies to 'why' found in opinions and attitudes of visitors. On supply, data readily available include material on capacity, occupancy, employment and prices, but data on investment is scarce and far from being representative of the state of the industry.

International inbound tourism demand is usually measured by the receiving country on an annual basis using one or more of three methods. Frontier counts can only provide limited information beyond volumes, modes of transport or ports of entry (examples of the use of this method can be found in Japan, New Zealand and Spain). Sample surveys enable a large quantity of data to be gathered, quantitative as well as qualitative, ranging from total volume of visitors to choice of accommodation (including second homes or houses of friends and relatives), degree of satisfaction, and expenditure by type (e.g. in Canada, Portugal and the United Kingdom). Registration at means of accommodation allows more limited, but more precise data, to be assembled on origin, duration of stay and on certain characteristics of the tourist (e.g. Finland, Italy and Switzerland); however, by definition these ignore the excursionist and the types of accommodation not registered for fiscal or other reasons, such as stays with friends and relatives or in other private accommodation, including facilities rented from individuals.

International outbound tourism is normally measured at regular intervals by generating countries using sample surveys applied to returning residents; the elements to be covered can be as numerous as time, money, and availability of volunteers permit (as in Canada and in the United Kingdom). This is often associated with the quest for information on national internal tourism; in this case, the same survey is conducted on the national territory with the aim of measuring total national tourism demand. Household surveys or micro-censuses furnish this type of data at regular intervals of 1 to 4 years; they contain as many detailed questions as the law permits, but are often limited to trips of at least four overnight stays. Within the OECD area, 12 countries conduct such enquiries yearly while seven other countries do it on a regular basis but with a longer time-span, generally every 3 or 4 years. In certain cases, data gathered by this means cover national outbound tourism, which might be used to fill in the gaps in the existing tourism measurement system of the destination/receiving country.

An area which has received particular attention, although it still deserves more work, is data on international tourist receipts and expenditure, i.e. the credit and debit sides of the travel account of the balance of payments which every country of the world publishes. For the most part, this data is assembled by central banks, using the 'bank reporting method'. There are only a few exceptions; in the OECD area, these exceptions concern Canada, Ireland, Switzerland, the United Kingdom and the United States, which use an 'estimation method', and Australia and Italy which use a 'mixed method'.

The 'bank reporting method' is essentially based on the registration by authorized banks or agencies of transactions taking place when a traveler buys or sells currencies prior to or following a trip abroad. To identify those travelers as 'visitors' and to distinguish these tourism transactions from any other transactions, such as the export of capital, this implies first that the purpose of the transaction can be identified. Secondly, it also assumes that all relevant transactions are recorded. In practice, however, this is difficult or impossible to achieve, due to transactions being settled outside the banking system, misclassification of banking transactions, or nonreporting by the banks. In many cases, it also includes parts of other accounts which cannot be separated from the travel account, e.g. workers' earnings or transportation. Most notably, users have to be aware of two major pitfalls. Firstly these figures are not necessarily gross data because of some nettings taking place in the process, e.g. through clearing arrangements between travel agents in different countries or through the export of domestic banknotes by travelers and the import of some portion of it through foreign travelers for its use in the country of origin; this leads to the question of whether or not a time series of travel account data reflects the size of international demand. Secondly, the geographical breakdown, if available at all, is provided according to the denominations of the currencies and not to the origin / destination of the visitors; this means that most of this data is not reliable for measuring demand in expenditure terms by generating markets.

On the other hand, the 'estimation method', based on sample surveys, has so far provided the best and most reliable information on travel expenditure. These surveys are generally conducted at points of entry/departure of nonresidents or re-entry of residents. With time and experience, countries using these methods have refined their methodologies and improved the accuracy of the material so assembled, the main sources of errors remaining the ones inherent to sample surveys, i.e. sampling errors and response biases (e.g. recall difficulty). Besides providing aggregate figures, this method has the advantage of making available detailed statistics on expenditure by purpose of trip, destination, and type of expenditure. (A practical way to find out what may be available is to get a copy of the questionnaire used by the authority concerned.)

The 'mixed method' has been developed by governmental authorities concerned with the gaps and deficiencies of the bank reporting method. It is a process which enables the transactions statistics to be weighted in accordance with the magnitude of travel expenditure and visitor flows to/from the country concerned through the use of information available from other sources, e.g. visitor surveys or data provided by foreign receiving countries. Though this method is not widespread at present (only two OECD countries have reported using it – Australia and Italy), it has raised interest among a number of countries using the bank reporting method, which are considering improving their methods and hence the reliability of the data they produce.

Conclusion

In carrying out work in any service sector, including tourism, one becomes rapidly aware of the inadequacies of the statistics available: there are major gaps in the coverage, inappropriate classification systems, and problems related to accuracy and timeliness. Some solutions are being sought at the international level, but these will not bear fruit in the immediate future. Meanwhile, businessmen, policy makers and researchers will have to continue to use existing tourism statistics, especially the ones available at low cost from secondary sources and which provide a large quantity of information useful for market and desk research. However, because of their deficiencies, these data have to be used with care, taking advantage of their usefulness in showing general tendencies but bearing in mind the

gaps that exist between the quantitative material available and the phenomenon to be measured. Once these are recognized, they can be filled in by field research directed to the particular need conducted by an inhouse service or an outside consultant.

Further reading

BarOn, R., *Tourism and Travel Data – A Comprehensive Handbook on World Travel* (Euromonitor Publications, 1988). This handbook presents a comprehensive review of the different methods of measuring and analyzing travel data used throughout the world and provides a complete and practical guide to international sources of travel trade statistics.

Chadwick, R. A., 'Concepts, definitions and measures used in travel and tourism research', *Travel, Tourism, and Hospitality Research: A Handbook for Managers and Researchers* (John Wiley, 1987). This article discusses different approaches for the harmonization of the terminology, definitions and classifications used in travel and tourism.

Horwath & Horwath International, *Worldwide Hotel Industry* (Horwath & Horwath International, annual since 1950). This booklet summarizes the main trends in hotel operations of more than 1,000 hotels in the world divided into five regions: Africa and the Middle East, Asia and Australia, North America, Europe, and Latin America.

O'Hagan, J. and Waldron, P., 'Estimating the magnitude of tourism in the European Community: data deficiencies and some results', *Journal of the Statistical and Social Inquiry Society of Ireland* (1989). This article presents the first comprehensive approach to measuring the importance of tourism of the 12 countries of the European Community in macroeconomic terms, quantifying total tourism employment and total receipts generated by domestic and international tourism as well as payments to carriers.

Organization for Economic Cooperation and Development, Report by the Tourism Committee, *International Comparability of Tourism Statistics Published by OECD Countries – Receipts and Expenditure* (OECD, 1986). This handbook provides the basic information for the user of OECD tourism statistics on receipts and expenditure and emphasizes the methods used and the main problems encountered by countries using either the bank reporting or the estimation method.

Organization for Economic Cooperation and Development, Report by the Tourism Committee, *International and National Tourism Demand in Member Countries, 1970 to 1985*, special issue (OECD, 1988). Data also available on tapes or diskettes.

Organization for Economic Cooperation and Development, Report by the Tourism Committee, *Tourism Policy and International Tourism in OECD Member Countries* (OECD, annual since 1961). See in particular the statistical annex published annually and Chapter V of the 1987 edition dedicated to an OECD pilot project on the integration of tourism to the national accounting system.

Pannel, Kerr, Forster, *Trends in the Hotel Industry, International Edition*, (annual). This booklet presents the main trends of the development of hotel operations in different parts of the world, in particular Canada, South America, Europe, Middle East, Pacific, South East Asia, South Asia, and Oceania.

Pisarski, A. and Hawkins, D. E., *US Travel Statistics and Information Sources: An Inventory and Assessment* (Hawkins & Associates, 1988). This study, conducted for the European Travel Commission, provides the prospective users of data related to the American traveler with a guide to potential primary and secondary sources of information likely to assist them in their cost effective use of the material available. This is one of the first studies of its kind published on any given country.

United Nations, *Provisional Guidelines on Statistics of International Tourism*, statistical papers, series M, no. 62 (UN, 1978).

Withyman, M., 'The ins and outs of international travel and tourism data', *International Tourism Quarterly*, no. 4 (Economist Publications, 1985). This article presents a criticism of data published by secondary as well as primary sources pointing out their main pitfalls. It deals with inward and outward visitor statistics, with special attention devoted to tourism statistics published by the OECD, the WTO and the United Kingdom.

World Tourism Organization, *Guidelines for the Collection and Presentation of International Tourism Statistics* (WTO, 1981).

World Tourism Organization, *Determination of the Importance of Tourism as an Economic Activity within the Framework of the National Accounting System* (WTO, 1983).

World Tourism Organization, *Draft Revised Definitions of Visitor, Tourist, Excursionist for Domestic and International Tourism*; *Draft International Standard Classification for Tourism Statistics by Countries and Regions, Purpose of Visit, and Age Group*; and *Draft Classification of Economic Characteristics of Visitors by Type of Activity, Occupation, Professional Situation, and Socio-Economic Categories* (1984 and 1986), to be published in *Guidelines for tourism statistics* (WTO, forthcoming).

World Tourism Organization, *Methodological Elements for Developing a Tourism Balance of Payments* (WTO, 1987).

World Tourism Organization, *Methodological Supplement to World Travel, and Tourism Statistics* (WTO, 1985).

World Tourism Organization, *Yearbook of Tourism Statistics* (WTO, annual since 1975) (prior to 1975, published by the former International Union of Official Travel Organizations).

LOUISE ALLARD

Strategic management in tourism

Introduction

This chapter applies the latest theory of business strategy to the specific requirements of the tourist sector. The article analyzes the principal purpose of strategic management – the development and the enhancement of sustained earnings potentials, as the prerequisite of long-term business success. Further, it identifies the determinants of earnings potentials, namely market position, experience, customer problem, problem solutions and other factors which determine competitiveness. The key parameters of strategic business management and their interrelationships are addressed. We will show that some concepts, already well established in industrial strategy, are also relevant to tourism. Of course, not all factors relating to tourism can be fully covered here; however, the theoretical explanations will be supplemented by numerous practical examples from the tourism and leisure sectors.

In the 1970s great progress was made in the theory and practice of strategic management. A reliable knowledge of the nature of long-term patterns in business processes, and their underlying causal structures, has emerged (see especially Gaelweiler, 1987; Porter, 1980; 1985). The concept of 'strategy' is misused frequently nowadays, and the extension of its meaning has led to misunderstandings and errors. Strategy is not the same as procedure, although this is often believed to be the case: normal procedures in an organization are not strategies.

The old Greek origin of the concept of strategy leads us towards an understanding of this term. The word is derived from 'stratos', something comprehensive and superior, of higher importance. The word strategy is also derived from the Greek 'agein' which means to act or guide. Strategy means thinking, decision making and actions towards superior long-term goals, without being deflected by short-term advantages, disadvantages or variations.

Orientation parameters

Increasingly, over the last few years strategic and operational management have been separated. This differentiation is not just theoretical. As the complexity and uncertainty faced by organizations have increased, an understanding of this differ-

ence has become essential to maintain the effectiveness of top management.

Traditional management science more or less equated profit with 'the ultimate purpose of business'. As a result, even now the error is made of using short-term data to produce wrong long-term conclusions. It is often forgotten that last year's profit has little bearing on the future prospects of a business; less, for example, than sales growth has on profits.

Meanwhile, we have learnt that profit is not the main goal of an organization, but forms only part of the hierarchy of target and control parameters relevant for management of a business (Fig. 1). The shortest-term objective of management is solvency, which is determined by operating income and expenditure. Anybody who understands even a little about accountancy knows that solvency and profit are different things. This difference is due to the timespan between the occurrence of costs and revenue on the one hand, and of income and expenditure on the other. It follows that expenditure and profit will not necessarily have an immediate effect on solvency.

The longer profit is lacking in an organization, the more difficult it becomes to maintain solvency. Profit exerts a causal effect on liquid assests, and thus plays the role of an advance warning with regard to the solvency of an organization. This has been known ever since double-entry bookkeeping was invented by Luca Pacioli in about 1500. But only in relatively recent times have we gained a more precise understanding of the fact that solvency and profit alone cannot be the ultimate business objectives.

The customer, the competitive situation in the tourist industry, and general economic conditions, have become much more difficult. The timespans available for adapting to changes in external circumstances have become much shorter. On the other hand, timescales required for implementing long-term effective projects cannot be arbitrarily reduced, for example the development of new products and services, the creation of extra capacity, organizational changes and improvement of human skills. It becomes problematical to control an organization exclusively for profit, because the indications derived from profit accounting change more quickly than adaptive procedures can be taken. The controlling mode in profit-oriented management is based on desired-from-actual deviations. It has to be complemented by a controlling mode, which focuses on the long-term causes of profit and loss.

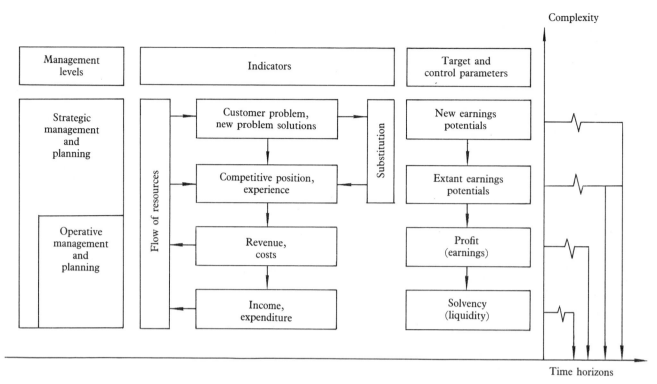

Figure 1 Hierarchy of target and control parameters in management (Gaelweiler, 1980a).

Solvency and profit are operative control parameters, but they are overshadowed by other control parameters on the strategic level: earnings potentials, in other words the capability of producing earnings (profit) at a future date and over long periods. The core task of strategic management is to build and maintain sustained earnings potential; this corresponds to systematic creation of the prerequisites of future earnings and liquidity. This task includes the consideration of long-term liquidity effects derived from a strategy. Again, control of earnings potential is not an object in its own right, but only supports the primary objective of any business: to ensure its continued viability and development in terms of enduring prosperity and vitality.

Parameter relationships

The relationship between control parameters on the strategic plane on the one hand and the operational plane on the other has to be elucidated further (Gaelweiler, 1987, Chapter VII):

1. As shown in Fig. 1, control of the earnings potential involves in much longer-term view than control aimed at earnings or profit requirements.
2. Large positive earnings are always a better basis for the control of solvency than low or negative earnings. Similarly, a large and secure earnings potential is a better basis for later profits than a small, uncertain earnings potential. However, neither is profit in itself a guarantee of adequate solvency at a later stage, nor can earnings potentials produce assur-

ance of later profits. Earnings potentials create favorable conditions and good chances of future profit, but they cannot guarantee such profit in the future.

3. Positive or negative earnings in the sense of profit accounting will occur in every organization, irrespective of the actual use of such accounting. This thought also applies to earnings potentials. The existence or nonexistence of earnings potentials and of their actual effects with regard to a specific firm will arise quite independently of whether or not management understands the importance of such parameters.
4. Under the same circumstances, different control parameters can change in opposite directions, e.g. solvency could be negative in spite of good earnings. Further examples are found in organizations or business divisions having great profit potential which, however, can only be realized if several years' negative returns are accepted. Just as profit and solvency must be separately managed at all times, control of earnings potential requires individual and independent attention.
5. The objective of the creation and maintenance of earnings potential is usually incompatible with the maximization of present profit. In view of the hierarchy of objectives stated above, achievement of profit is not an objective in itself, but rather a derived objective.
6. In simple words, operative effectiveness is based on 'doing things right', while strategic effectiveness results from 'doing the right things'. The choice of markets, creation of competitive advantage, development of products, resources and skills are issues of strategic business management. Opera-

tive management is concerned with the efficient use of these prerequisites.

7. Strategies can be described in terms of operative criteria (profit, solvency), but not decided on the same criteria as operative measures. Profit is a standard of operative management, competitiveness of strategic management. A similar pattern applies to the relationship between the strategic level and normative levels of management, which cannot be illustrated in detail here (see Schwaninger, forthcoming). On the normative (or 'corporate policy') level, viability and development are the comprehensive criteria of effectiveness. The perspective of normative management, which involves values, ethical and esthetical considerations, will often shed a different light on a decision than criteria of the 'lower levels' do. A project, for example to adapt a new product, can perfectly make sense from the profit and earnings potential perspective and yet, the broader outlook may qualify it as inappropriate. The product may be unacceptable from a corporate policy perspective, because it is incompatible with ethical standards or the social responsibilities of management. Managers are increasingly aware not only of the fact that they can't do all they want (strategic perspective) but also that they should not do all they could (normative perspective).

Coming back to the strategic level, we should further elaborate on strategically relevant indicators. The present state of knowledge in the field of strategic management allows us to identify the crucial factors affecting the earnings potential and long-term solvency by a method which is similarly systematic, just as double-entry bookkeeping allows us to calculate business profit. In recent years, the control parameter 'earnings potential' has differentiated between extant and new earnings potentials.

Extant earnings potentials

Extant earnings potentials are determined by the market position and the business specific experience of the organization. Experienced managers understand the importance of a strong market position (competitive position) as a requirement for long-term profit. 'Strong market position' is not just a term important for large companies. For example, in a holiday resort it is not only the Grand Hotel which can be a market leader (i.e. in the luxury class), even a small business can be the leader in its market sector or segment, or can at least achieve a strong position. We all know of small hotels having the reputation of 'the friendliest medium-price family hotel in the region'.

The good relationships between such firms and their customers allow them to survive through crises and hard times. Other examples are found among the relatively small travel businesses which have become leading specialists for certain customer groups (e.g. senior citizens, youngsters) or products (e.g. theater journeys, hiking tours, travel to particular destinations). One can gain a strong market position by achieving one or more specific competitive advantages, which can be defined partly in quantitative and partly qualitative terms.

Quantitative indicators

Quantitative indicators for many types of tourist businesses (e.g. travel agencies, mountain railways and restaurants) are determined by market share. Having obtained a large proportion of the market, the organization is likely to have gained specialized experience in the particular field; this leads to potential cost advantages and makes it less vulnerable (exceptions to this rule occur in those cases where large market shares are attained entirely by financial investment – 'buying of market share'). The greater the experience, the better are the chances (not always utilized) for producing cost-effective products and for efficient organization of the various functions. Market share and experience are approximate indicators of the product- and -market-specific know-how gradually accumulated in a particular business area. The absolute levels of these indicators do not say anything accurate about the strategic situation of the business, but they become more significant when compared with the corresponding levels of the relevant competitors. Hence, two factors to assess our own competitive position are as follows:

1. $\text{Relative market share} = \dfrac{\text{Own market share}}{\text{Marketing share of strongest competitor}}$
2. Cost advantages and disadvantages.

Cost advantages and disadvantages which can be derived from the relative market share can be quantified approximately on the basis of the experience curve, derived from the 'learning curve'. The experience curve is defined as follows: each time the cumulative experience (i.e. the cumulative volume of output) is doubled, a cost reduction potential of the order of 20–30 per cent per unit (i.e. of the per item cost) is created, at least for those cost components which constitute their own value-added*, and based on constant money value (Fig. 2). This feature applies as well to an industry as a whole as to individual businesses.

The experience curve has been studied empirically (Henderson, 1972) and is substantiated by the PIMS (profit impact of market strategy) studies by the SPI Institute which also show a strong positive correlation between relative market share and long-term profitability. This means that there is a potential for higher profitability as the organization's own market share and, in particular, the relative market share, grow. Schwaninger has shown in an empirical study that the learning curve model can be translated to tourist businesses. This does not preclude the possibility that its application to specific cases may be problematical (Schwaninger, 1984a; cf. Hart *et al.*, 1984).

Qualitative indicators

There are further important indicators for assessing the existing earnings potentials, apart from the relative market share and the experience curve (see also Buzzell, 1987). These are mainly qualitative factors which determine the competitive position but it is to some extent possible to quantify them. Parameters

---

* Value-added in this connection is taken in a simplified form as the difference between total costs and purchased material costs.

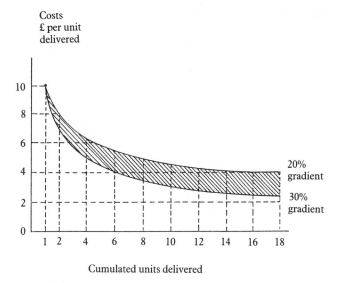

Figure 2 The experience curve plotted on linear axes (Gaelweiler, 1986).

which are likely to affect market share and therefore the propensity to make profits, will include factors such as: the attractiveness of the product offered to the customer, the quality of the product, utility of the product to the consumer, the price/performance ratio, technological and informational skills, service level and the marketing effectiveness, always in relation to relevant competitors.

In many tourism businesses, profit achievement is not necessarily linked to high market share and learning curve levels. Here the key factor which determines the competitiveness of an organization is the attractiveness of the service offered, which itself depends on items such as locality, quality of natural and sociocultural factors, tourist infrastructure etc.

The above qualitative factors, just like market share, must not only be assessed in an absolute sense but also compared to relevant competitors. All assessments should be based on customers' views rather than on an inward looking perspective.

Application of indicators

Applications of market position and learning curve as indicators for strategic management and planning, require an understanding of the following further connections:

1. The experience curve does not occur necessarily like a law of nature. Instead, it is the result of taking full advantage of cost-reduction possibilities. This, of course, is a major task of effective management. It follows again that the learning curve is not necessarily discernible in every individual business. Empirical results have shown, however, that there are competitors in each industry which succeed in realizing their available cost-reduction potentials, thus creating an earnings potential, at least in the long run.

2. A firm having the best cost ratios should also, other things being equal, have the best profit potential. It is well known that prices vary in the form of step functions and can practically change overnight. However, cost reductions take much longer to achieve, because there are always remnant costs which cannot be so quickly controlled. A competitor who succeeds in gradually reducing his unit costs in accordance with the experience curve, achieves a better starting position and gains pricing leeway which facilitates maintenance, or even an increase, in market share.

3. Relative market share contains significant information value. It is a figure which expresses, in a highly condensed way, the relative strengths of competitors, as well as possible cost levels, and therefore gives pointers relating to the prospects of surviving in a particular market or in a particular market segment. The experience curve indicates, as a logical consequence, that organizations having only a small market share are particularly vulnerable in the long term. On the other hand, a high relative market share represents a good starting position for generating earnings.

4. The concept of the learning curve does not necessarily demand growth in a business, although this is often mistakenly assumed. Market share and the experience curve are indicators specific to individual markets and product groups. Therefore, accurate definition of the relevant market/product units is imperative. It should be noted that the competitive game is played less on the level of the company as a whole than on the level of individual business systems. These can be defined as specific configurations of customer-problems, customer-groups, products/services, technologies and distribution channels, within the context of certain competitors and, eventually, under consideration of regional aspects (Schwaninger, 1987). Quite often, a segmental subgrouping (for example in customer groups, or price classes) can be helpful in differentiating diagnosis and in determining strategy.

5. Since the experience curve only applies to homogeneous market/product units, it furnishes a rational foundation for the principles of concentration and variety reduction in business. The principle of concentration of effort states that one's efforts should not be split across too many customer groups and products. Since fixed costs generally rise exponentially with increased product range, it is important to control both product range breadth and depth. In short, we have to avoid dealing with too many products. The method of trying to compensate decreases in turnover by enlarged product range (for example by increasing the number of items on the menu) is usually dangerous because it is likely to have a severe negative impact on profit.

6. It is often mistakenly believed that the experience curve only applies to lower price-group businesses. The favorable long-term profitability achieved by some market leaders in upper end class segments of travel, as well as the higher price levels of some leading hotels, were not only obtained through above-average quality and value offered to customers. These profits are also a result of unit costs maintained and controlled carefully along the experience curve. The corresponding per item cost reductions can result from cutting cost elements (rationalization), from productivity increases

and also from an improved ability to match capacity to demand or from better capacity utilization. The last aspect is particularly important for the capital-intensive hotel businesses. The two possibilities of cost reduction do not refer to separate 'laws' but to partial aspects of the experience curve. Successful long-term reduction of per item costs, whether by capacity matching or by better utilization of extant resources, are results of long-term learning processes.

7. Accurate calculation of the experience curve is not always feasible. Nevertheless, the fundamental rules defined by this curve are valid in principle and can form useful guidelines for strategic planning at the business level.

Wrong conclusions to be avoided

It would be wrong to conclude from these remarks on market position and experience curve that all good strategy must aim at increasing market share, or that it should always be possible to achieve profit increases by increased market share. For one thing, market-share increases cannot be achieved economically in many start-up situations (e.g. in stagnating markets, or when faced with powerful competitors or the inability to install innovations). Secondly, increases in market share do not usually have an immediate effect but only produce increased profits after some time, especially if they are based on true competitive advantage, and not purely on price wars. Thirdly, the strength of market position is not entirely defined by market share but, as shown above, by other factors. In some cases, an increase in market share can even reduce the attractiveness of the services offered which, in turn, could dampen demand in the long term. (This applies, for example, to holiday resorts where ecological and sociopsychological resources are subject to excessive strain.) The fourth consideration is that profit can be increased not only as a result of current, but also as a result of earlier market growth if cost-reduction potentials are implemented retrospectively where this potential is available from the past. Finally there is an upper limit beyond which increases in market share will have an unfavorable effect on a business because they generate increased resistance of governmental institutions and the public at large (cf. the debates and regulations with regard to fusions of major US and UK airlines).

New earnings potentials

A strong market position and a high level of experience in a particular business area still cannot predict whether an organization will be able to remain in the market and be competitive in the future. Market share can be rapidly lost as a result of new and better products/services. Timely awareness of such events requires indicators which reach further than correct market position and learning curve.

Customer problem

The widest ranging strategic indicators are customer requirements or customer problems, provided they are defined independently of particular solutions (Levitt, 1975). It is known that the way a certain customer problem is solved, can vary substantially, both in form and in timescale.

Thinking in these terms is still rare in the tourist industry. Frequently, the customer problem is defined on the basis of what the vendor of a particular solution offers. Management may not be aware that different solutions are available, or at least possible. For example, the requirement for 'active holidays' can be met by the following solutions: holidays at home; local holiday tourism; and activity holiday trips. Within each of these a number of suitable leisure activities can meet the stated requirements. For activity holiday trips, club holidays, or holiday packages in a hotel with a wide program of leisure activities may be employed. Another option might be hiking tours, where the activity itself consists of moving from one holiday accommodation to the next.

Experts in tourist marketing have analyzed this aspect, and have coined the phrase 'substitution competition'. Studies up to now have been more concerned with substitution from a static perspective, taking account only of already available, and competing, solutions. The solution-invariant definition of the customer problems enlarges functional and temporal horizons, so that the following types of solutions can be matched to specific customer requirements (Gaelweiler, 1987):

1. Solutions available at the moment, whether they are offered by one of the tourism sectors or not. An example would be a new leisure center at the edge of a large city which can meet the need for a change of atmosphere and for recreation. The same requirements can be met by several nearby tourism resorts. As these various solutions for the same customer problem are in different phases of the life cycle, this perspective shows the dynamics of substitution competition.

2. More recent solutions, still under development in one's own business but also in competing businesses and in other sectors. Examples could be the new forms of restaurants still under study to meet growing customer requirements for integral and organic food products.

3. Potential problem solutions which are still at the research stage. These are fundamentally new but rather uncertain in their probability of achieving success, and are still a long way from commercial realization. Until a few years ago, teleconferences and the home shopping of tourist services were included in this category.

Substitution processes

The role of new, and potentially new, solutions to problems is to completely or partially replace old solutions. This phenomenon is termed a substitution process. The tourist industry has not paid enough attention to the replacement of old by new services, processes and technologies. We should remember that lifestyle and change of values during the past several decades have led to substitution processes which are clearly discernible and, in some cases, still going on:

1. Appreciable sections of the hotel industry have been substituted by other kinds of accommodation. In Switzerland, for example, the proportion of nights spent in hotels and

similar establishments fell from 58 to 48 per cent of total accommodation nights between 1970 and 1984.

2. During the last 30 years, 'parahotels' have gained in importance. In addition, new forms of accommodation similar to hotels, such as holiday clubs and those offering extensive leisure and sports facilities, as well as active support from social contacts among the guests, have increased their market shares.

3. Products have also been developed where the innovation is based on new financing and utilization models (for example apartment hotels and new forms of apartment timesharing).

4. A change, which will have enormous effects on the hotel and catering sector, is taking place in the restaurant industry. System catering is taking further market share from traditional gastronomy and will engender new 'species' of restaurants. ('System catering' refers not only to fast food chains such as MacDonalds and Burger King but also to networks of more sophisticated operations such as the Swiss Moevenpick group.)

It is a characteristic of substitution processes that a new problem solution never achieves 100 per cent penetration of the total market, but manages only a partial market penetration. As an example, package tours which have reached a substantial share of the total travel market (34.5 per cent in West Germany in 1986 [StfT, 1987]), will probably never arrive at an overall market penetration even close to 100 per cent, although the substitution process is still going on.

In product substitution, only that part of the market is replaced for which the new problem solution is more suitable to requirements than the traditional solutions. Therefore, innovations tend to split the market, since some of the customer problems continue being better met by traditional solutions (Gaelweiler, 1987).

Experience shows that totally or partly new customer problems arise in the course of time, which require the development of new solutions. For example, newer kinds of restaurant have not only replaced part of the traditional restaurant market, but also largely satisfy customer requirements which were previously only latent or just beginning to appear.

The structuring of customer problems

In service industries, the definition of customer problems, and therefore of the appropriate solutions, is considerably more difficult than in many industrial sectors. The intangible, emotional and value-associated aspects of marketing in the service industries are particularly significant and wide ranging. The method of structuring customer problems, which differentiates between original and derived customer problems, is substantially due to experience in industry (Gaelweiler, 1980b). Schwaninger has applied this rationale to several service industries and it can also be applied to the tourism and leisure industries.

Original customer problems tend to be long lasting. As far as can be judged with our present knowledge, it is very unlikely that they will disappear. Derived customer problems, however, are liable to change. The existence of these derived problems was only caused by the characteristics of specific problem solu-

tions. Therefore these 'derived' problems themselves are liable to change as new problem solutions emerge. 'You run the risk that you will innovate away, integrate away or rationalize away, the very customer problems you wish to satisfy' (Gaelweiler, 1987).

Fig. 3 shows an example of the structure of a customer-problem in the tourist industry. This indicates clearly that different solutions can be threatened by integration to a higher level, or by fundamental changes of the problem solutions on their corresponding levels.

Innovation and long-range perspective

If there were such a thing as an Archimedian point for strategic management, then this would be the customer problem. This is the reference basis with the largest material and timescale horizons. It provides impulses for innovations. It yields the most meaningful reference points for development and for marketing of new problem solutions including the necessary quantitative assessments of market potential. One should not equate 'new problem solutions' with 'new products'. New problem solutions with increased innovative effects are generally not limited only to a new product. On the contrary, they involve changes to several, or all, components of a business system (services marketed, technology, distribution channel, target groups and customer problems) and to their interplay (Buaron, 1981; Schwaninger, 1984b).

A long preparation time must be allowed for the creation of new earnings potentials; they create immediate key requirements for personnel, intellectual, financial and material resources which are not matched, at this time, by appropriate inflow of cash and which will not provide profits initially. Consider for example the time required to design completely new hotel or restaurant formulae and to develop these commercially. Other examples are the long lead times required before a resort can establish a reputation as a golfing center, or the effort to be made before a town creates a name for its theater festival.

On the other hand, it can be shown that wrong strategic decisions can have long-term and even irreversible consequences:

1. High capital intensity is a fundamental characteristic of the hotel industry. Therefore, if a hotel has been badly planned, then it is extremely difficult to change strategy at a later stage.

2. In a holiday resort the original (natural) facilities are of prime importance as a long-term prerequisite for profit. Environmental spoiling or damage of local culture does not lead to an immediate fall in turnover or profit, but in the long run they can have enormous effects on the regional ecology and on the socioeconomic vitality of a resort. Thus short-term maximization of profit can lead to long-term failure. Krippendorf's fear that tourism will itself be destroyed by tourism has become well known and has, in fact, been substantiated in several cases (Krippendorf, 1981). Referring to ecology, the changes are long term; for example, we know that a forest, once destroyed, may need decades to grow again or even be lost for ever.

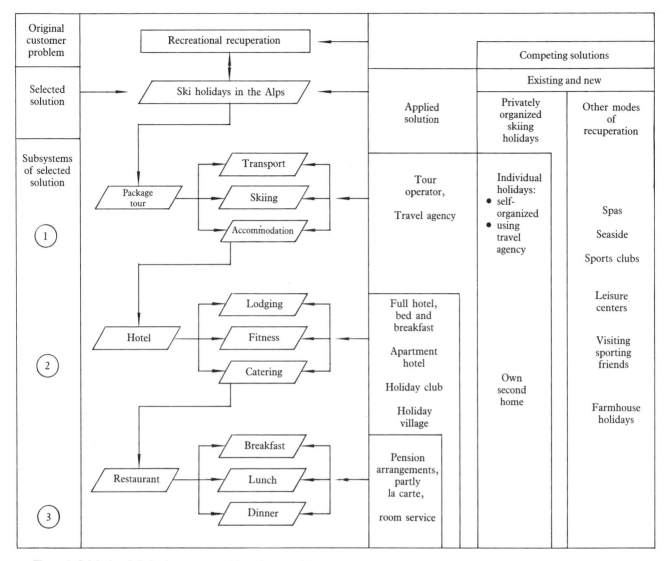

Figure 3 Original and derived customer problems in part of the tourist industry.

Conclusion

The purpose of this chapter has been to apply the basic concepts of business strategy to the tourist industry. It concentrates on strategy at the business level. In large, diversified companies, the integration of business strategies to overall corporate strategies involves further reflection on portfolio-management, synergy, economies of scope and sharing activities etc. (Hax and Majluf, 1984; Porter, 1987; Rowe *et al.*, 1985).

The earlier the management of individual tourism companies, or of holiday resorts or regions start to deal with the long-term issues discussed in this article, the better they can address strategic challenges. The examples of several innovators show that it is not always necessary to be a large and powerful company to be able to cope with change.

Long-term market developments and substitution processes

can, in most cases, be identified long before they result in reduction of business for the organization involved. The earlier the corresponding warning signals are analyzed and understood, the more latitude may still be available for adaptive action. The essence of strategic thinking is to recognize early how to act from the start, in order to ensure long-term and enduring profitability.

The considerations put forward show that the data from operative accounting (balance sheets, profit and loss accounts) tell us relatively little about the long-term opportunities for an organization. Profit is the wrong indicator by which to assess or justify future strategies. Wrong strategies usually cannot be corrected by economically justifiable means once their negative effects show up in the current profit and loss statements.

The management of holiday resorts must learn to take a long-term view, especially in respect of the natural environment and its sensible development, as well as of the visual amenities of villages and of the countryside. In view of the diminishing natural resources, there is a growing awareness in the tourist industry that nature and the countryside are integral components of the solution of customer problems, which deserve a high degree of care. Tourism, more than any other business, depends on the quality of natural resources. The conservation, protection and upgrading of the ecological and sociocultural resources must be first priority issues of strategy, because these are critical factors of success.

The interactions on the strategic plane are often hard to recognize because of the long time intervals between cause and effect. To understand these requires not only a deep, business-specific knowledge, but also a high capability of abstract thinking.

The associated mental discipline is absolutely essential for effective strategic management. Without this discipline, those responsible will find it difficult to take decisions involving the sacrifices necessary at present to ensure future earnings. For example, an environmentally responsible attitude to the countryside, the critical resource in a holiday resort, will only be accepted if the people involved understand the priority of strategic objectives (e.g. avoidance of further random building development) and are not diverted by the glance of short-term advantages (for example, profits from change of zoning, or sale of land).

Strategic thinking also requires that 'weak signals' announcing future events should not be ignored just simply because those appear to be still far away. We must not forget that long-term causal interactions occur whether or not we are aware of them.

Further reading

Buaron, R., 'New game strategies', *McKinsey Quarterly* (Spring 1981), pp. 24–40.

Buzzell, R. D., *The Pims Principles: Linking Strategy to Performance* (Free Press/Collier, 1987).

Gaelweiler, A., 'Zum Stand der Unternehmungsplanung heute' (Present status of business planning), *Rationalisierung*, vol. 31 (1980a), p.32.

Gaelweiler, A., 'Die wachsende Bedeutung des Ingenieurs im Markt' (The growing importance of the engineer in marketing), *VDI Reports*, no. 282 (1980b), pp. 11–20.

Gaelweiler, A., *Unternehmungsplaning* (Corporate Planning) (Campus, 2nd edition, 1986).

Gaelweiler, A., *Strategische Unternehmungsführung* (Strategic Management) (Campus, 1987).

Hart, W., Spizizen, G. and Wycoff, D. D., 'Scale economies and experience curve: is bigger better for restaurant companies?', *Cornell HRA Quarterly*, vol. 25, no. 1 (May 1984), pp. 91–103. This article, which is otherwise wideranging, unfortunately may give the false impression that the learning curve defines the need for growth of a business. See also the discussion in the section on 'qualitative planning parameters'.

Hax, A. C., and Majluf, N. S., *Strategic Management* (Prentice Hall, 1984).

Henderson, B., *Perspectives on Experience* (Boston Consulting Group, 4th edition, 1972).

Krippendorf, J., *Die Landschaftsfresser* (The Environment Destroyers) (Forschungsinstitut für Fremdenverkehr, 3rd edition, 1981), p. 45.

Levitt, T., 'Marketing myopia', *Harvard Business Review* (September/October 1975), pp. 26–44; 173–81.

Porter, M., *Competitive Strategy* (Free Press, 1980).

Porter, M., *Competitive Advantage* (Free Press, 1985).

Porter, M., 'From competitive advantage to corporate strategy', *Harvard Business Review* (May/June 1987), pp. 43–59.

Rowe, A. J., Mason, R. O. and Dickel, H., *Strategic Management and Business Policy* (Addison-Wesley, 2nd edition, 1985).

Schwaninger, M., *Spielt die Erfahrungskurve in Fremdenverkehrsunternehmungen?* (Has the learning curve a place in tourist businesses?) (St Gall Management Centre, 1984a).

Schwaninger, M., 'Zur Marktstrategie einer Nummer 2' (On the marketing strategy for a number 2 business), *Management Zeitschrift IO*, vol. 53, no. 3 (1984b), pp. 136–40.

Schwaninger, M., *Integrale Unternehmungsplanung* (Integral Planning) (Campus, forthcoming)

Schwaninger, M., 'A practical approach to strategy development', *Long Range Planning*, vol. 20, no. 5 (1987), pp. 74–85.

Studienkreis für Tourismus, *Urlaubsreisen 1986* (Holiday Travel 1986) (StfT, 1987).

MARKUS SCHWANINGER

Strategic planning for tourism: governmental view

Introduction

Corporate planning is a difficult task in all industries because it is concerned with the uncertainties of the future. It is especially difficult in the tourism industry for two reasons. The first relates to the inescapable involvement of national governments in defining the objectives of tourism policy. The second relates to the diversity of the activities which collectively constitute the tourism industry.

All corporate planning must start from a precise definition of the purpose of the business or the 'mission role' as it is often called. In a normal business organization this is something on which the board of directors and the owners can and must agree. The basic purpose of the tourism industry is, however, something which only governments can agree. And, if they do not, the tourism industry is likely to be left with some impossibly difficult decisions about its future course of development.

Strategic objectives and policies

There is a very wide choice of strategic objectives for tourism open to governments and, quite often, governments choose objectives which are mutually contradictory. Even more often there is a confusion between the definition of the purposes of policy and the more specific objectives, or action measures, which are needed to achieve the central purposes of policy.

In a report 'Tourism Policy and International Tourism in OECD Member Countries' (OECD, 1987) each of the 24 countries has something to say about the policies which they are pursuing. Many of the policy statements give prime place to the following three strategic objectives:

1. The stimulation of national economic growth.
2. The maximization of foreign exchange earnings.
3. The creation of jobs.

Amongst other strategic objectives the following six are frequently cited:

1. The promotion of a favorable national image.
2. The protection of the natural environment.
3. The protection of cultural heritage.

4. The improvement of the quality of life.
5. The protection of consumer interests.
6. The promotion of balanced economic development in different regions of the country.

Conflicts can obviously arise between these objectives. For example, the maximum stimulation of economic growth can be in conflict with the protection of the natural environment and/or the preservation of the social structure of the country. Many developing countries have experienced severe social and political strains because of the contrasts between the lifestyles of foreign visitors and those of the local population. And, in some of the richer countries, foreign tourists are sometimes regarded as inimical to the way of life of those who do not directly benefit from their expenditures.

The Japanese government, recognizing that international tourism in the past has made only a small contribution to the national economy, has recently defined the principal objectives of tourism policy as:

1. To contribute towards the furtherance of international friendship.
2. The development of the national economy.
3. The enhancement of the life of the Japanese people.

To achieve these strategic objectives the following policies are now being pursued:

1. To stimulate the inflow of foreign tourists and improve the reception services for them.
2. To establish tourist resorts and routes for foreigners on a comprehensive and integrated basis.
3. To ensure the safety of tourists while traveling and make it more convenient for them.
4. To relieve excessive concentration of tourists at specific resorts.
5. To facilitate family travel and other travel by the general public.
6. To develop tourism in underdeveloped regions.
7. To protect, cultivate and develop tourist resources.
8. To maintain the beauty of tourist resorts.

This kind of precise definition of purpose and objectives will vary greatly from country to country depending upon differences in economic, social and political circumstances. Moreover, for each particular country, the definition of purpose and objectives must be updated over time to reflect changes in those circumstances. In the United Kingdom, for example, less importance is currently attached to the objective of foreign exchange earnings than was the case a decade ago. Balance of payments considerations have been replaced by job creating developments as the top priority of national tourism policy.

This change of emphasis was well illustrated in the statement of aims and objectives in the English Tourist Board's statement of its strategy for tourism development in England (ETB, 1987). The ETB gives pride of place to the following objective:

> to maximise tourism's contribution to the economy through the creation of wealth and jobs – we aim to create a further 250,000 jobs over the next five years.

The importance of tourism in the creation of employment is also a central theme in the report which Medlik (1985) produced for the Confederation of British Industry. The twenty recommendations of this report are mainly addressed to the government and they underline the point made earlier that government objectives for tourism should be clearly enunciated and that there should be an unequivocal commitment to the pursuit of those objectives.

Planning requirements

The most crucial aspect of strategic planning is that there should be a unifying purpose agreed by government to ensure that the diverse elements of the tourism industry move forward in the same direction. This is the second factor which presents special planning problems in this industry. Doubts are sometimes expressed whether it is, in fact, legitimate to speak of the tourism 'industry'. What is indisputable is that tourism involves sectors of many industries like accommodation, catering, transport, travel agencies, entertainment, exhibition centers, shopping and sightseeing. The tourism business has been well described by Leonard Lickorish, former Director General of the British Tourist Authority, as a 'grand confederacy' of economic activities. Two things follow from this. First is the need for an organizational framework to coordinate the activities and future plans of these disparate segments of the industry. The World Bank (1972) put this point very plainly when it said: 'The tourism sector can develop adequately only when given an appropriate government and semi-government institutional framework.' This is a basic requirement for successful strategic planning in such a diverse economic activity. But the second point, of equal importance, is that the diversity of the industry leads to the requirement for a system of indicative planning. This has been well recognized by the British Tourist Authority (1984) in these words:

> The BTA cannot 'order' the future development of British tourism. Many external factors will influence the future scale and pattern of demand. Even if these could be forecast accurately, many independent authorities and commercial organisations will make the decisions which determine whether the supply of facilities is properly matched to demand.

Strategic planning in such circumstances is, therefore, a matter of providing a set of guidelines which, on the one hand, offer plausible and soundly based forecasts of future demand potential and, on the other, give practical advice to encourage co-ordinated decisions to be taken by all sectors of the industry.

This statement highlights the key requirements of successful strategic planning for tourism. All future planning is based on forecasts of future potential demand, even though it is generally recognized that most forecasts turn out to be wrong. We have to base many current decisions on the view we take of the future and market forecasts are, therefore, an inescapable aspect of decision making in the tourism industry, as in all other industries. What has come to be called 'single line' forecasting has been replaced in many organizations by so-called 'scenario' forecasting in which a range of future positions are evaluated. But, no matter how the future is studied, and no matter how sophisticated the sensitivity evaluations of alternative scenarios, investment and other decisions do have to be made on the basis of the most likely view of the future. Forecasting techniques are therefore an extremely important aspect of strategic planning.

A joint approach to forecasting future tourism traffic has been adopted in Europe, through the cooperation of the 21 national organizations which are members of the European Travel Commission. One of the outcomes of this cooperation was a report *European Tourism in 1990* (ETC, 1983). The ETC has also set up the European Travel Action Group (ETAG) which continues to monitor and report on trends in European tourist traffic and to propose the actions which members should take to ensure the most effective exploitation of market opportunites. These ETAG initiatives are a collective approach to the requirements identified in the quotation from the BTA report which refers to the need to give practical advice to encourage coordinated decisions by all sectors of the industry.

The strategic planning process has two essential stages. The first, which has been discussed at some length, is the identification and agreement of the purposes of policies. The second is the definition of more specific objectives and, from them, the formulation of the action programs which should be followed to achieve the strategic purposes of policy.

An input/output approach is often very helpful in this second stage of the planning process. This involves asking the questions: 'What inputs are needed to ensure that the strategic ob-

Table 1 Input/output analysis of tourism policies.

Essential inputs	Necessary outputs	Resulting policies
Money	Adequate profits	Financial objectives
Men	Good conditions of employment	Employment policies
Markets	Products giving value for money	Marketing policies
Public acceptance	Meeting public concerns	Social and environmental policies

jective are achieved?' and then: 'What outputs are necessary to earn the essential inputs?' The elements of this approach are illustrated in Table 1. In tourism, as in all other industries, the three most vital inputs are the three Ms: Money, Men (and women!) and Markets. These essential inputs can only be won if the industry is producing the necessary outputs for the following:

1. To attract the capital it needs it must earn adequate profits.
2. To attract skilled managers and employees it must offer attractive conditions of employment.
3. To win customers it must design and price products which are effectively marketed and give good value for money.

In addition to the three Ms, there is another vital input for the tourism industry: public acceptance of what the industry is doing and producing. If a majority of the public decides that certain aspects of tourism development are unacceptable, then the best laid plans will founder. This is why environmental considerations and social policy implications are so vital in the formulation of tourism action programs.

Strategic planning must face up to some very difficult questions in this area and, particularly in developing countries, there are often serious conflicts of interests to be resolved. The late and highly respected Indian expert, Som Chib, discussed in a lecture the social and environmental implications of tourism policy for his own country. He accepted that tourism must make a maximum contribution to earning foreign exchange and he recognized that this could most easily be achieved by concentrating tourism marketing on high spending foreign visitors. But he was deeply concerned about the social implications of such a policy and said:

I do not subscribe to the view that we should mainly concentrate on upscale high-spending visitors. We would in fact be promoting a type of tourism which would open ourselves to the charge sometimes made by sociologists that modern tourism is a form of neo-colonialism.

He concluded that the development of tourism must have a larger human purpose and that domestic tourism should also be developed to ensure that the industry produced benefits which would help to unify the country and would guard against resentment of foreign visitors.

Considerations of this kind must be an integral part of a strategic plan for tourism in any country. Such considerations are just as important as the economic and marketing aspects of the plan because, if they are neglected, and in consequence the development of tourism does not have general public support, the overall plan will fail just as surely as it would if it did not have adequate financial support or adequate human skills to provide its services.

Further reading

Aviation and Tourism International, *European Tourism in 1990* (European Travel Commission, 1983).

British Tourist Authority, *Strategy for Growth – 1984 to 1988. Guidelines for Tourism Planning and Marketing* (BTA, September 1984).

Chib, S., *Perspectives on Tourism in India* (Sardar Patel Memorial Lectures, New Delhi, October 1981).

English Tourist Board, *Tourism Strategy – A Vision for England* (ETB, 1987).

Medlik, S., *Paying Guests* (Confederation of British Industry, July 1985).

Organization for Economic Cooperation and Development, *Tourism Policy and International Tourism in OECD Member Countries* (OECD, September 1987).

The World Bank, *Tourism – A Sector Working Paper* (World Bank, June 1972). This is a seminal paper on tourism policy.

STEPHEN WHEATCROFT

Structure of tourism

Introduction

Attempts to define tourism, whether as an industry, as a phenomenon, or both, have concerned researchers for decades. Such definitional explorations and articulations have indeed contributed to the understanding of tourism as a field of inquiry, but often at the expense of isolating tourism from the structures which support and conditions which espouse it. The purpose of this chapter is to promote a holistic treatment of tourism by proposing alternative models to view, structure, and explain it, both for theoretical explorations and practical applications. However, because of space limitations, only the models, not their use, are discussed.

Two earlier articles are used in preparing this chapter. One views tourism as a sociocultural phenomenon (Jafari, 1987) and the other as an industry (Jafari, 1982). The former concludes that 'Tourism is the study of man away from his usual habitat, of the touristic apparatus and networks, and of the ordinary and nonordinary worlds and their dialectic relationship' (Jafari, 1987, p. 158). This definition is adopted to guide the discussion in this chapter. It is first dissected to reveal some of the deeper structures and functions and then reassembled to present a holistic view on tourism.

Tourism is a study of man away from his usual habitat, . . .

Man's desire to be away from home is directly related to his/her home context, the study of which would illuminate the structures and conditions which give birth to touristic motives and expected benefits. Without having understood the tourist (the central person in tourism), touristhood (the state of mind), and the touristic network (which responds to his needs), the student of tourism has only a superficial frame of reference.

To begin, for a visual metaphor, one may imagine a springboard of resilient material which enables the tourist to leap temporarily into the nonordinary tourism world and then fall back into the ordinary life. This metaphor, to suggest the form and flow of a *tourist* model, includes the base board itself, the player, the leap and return motions, and the animated airborne spirit (Fig. 1). In action, the player sinks into the board, only to emerge to the surface, to rise above it, to suspend in the air, to

maneuver, and to return to the base – only ending one cycle before beginning another.

In the pattern of this springboard metaphor, six components and processes involved in the construction of the model can be proposed: the corporated body of the ordinary life which breeds the need or desire to leave the springboard behind (Fig. 1, WA); the process of emancipation which includes the act of departure and the sense of freedom from the basal confinement (AB); the touristic animation which is fueled when the tourist is placed in that distinctly nonordinary outer time and space (BC); the process of repatriation which is the inevitable return from the 'temporary' tourist position to the 'constant' reality of the base (CD); the homeward touristic flow which incorporates into the ordinary mainstream (DX); and the interim ordinary life which continues despite the tourist's absence from home (AD).

Corporation: a body of entangled forms and forces

Graphically, an individual is positioned on the springboard of ordinary (daily) life which constitutes the 'corporation' component of the tourist model (Fig. 1, WA, or the same component in Fig. 2). The corporate body is composed of substances and conditions which incubate the motivation for travel to an outer zone, away from the daily springboard. This ordinary platform may be viewed from different angles, with function and structure as its two main vistas.

The first vista frames the functional explanations or factors which are commonly attributed to the need to get away from it all. It provides for notions and motions induced at physical, personal, cultural, and professional levels which lead to the desire or search for escape, recreation, restoration, rejuvenation, visiting friends and relatives, networking, sightseeing, lifeseeing, and much more. These motivations, mostly nurtured in the course of ordinary life, include a *melange* of causes and effects that can perhaps be distinguished by the tourist himself or by the researcher who labels and categorizes them.

The second vista brings into focus a structural series of long ordinary and short nonordinary sequences in one's life. The ordinary comprises the mundane, profane, daily life whose procession loses strength due to its own ordained, rhythmic course; while the nonordinary is the heightened state of mind resulting from the departure from the ordinary ranks. This structural arrangement allows differentiation between the two

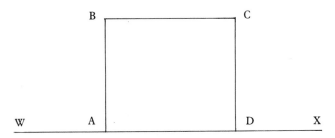

Figure 1 The springboard metaphor.

planes and thus distinguishes tourism, somewhat similar to religion and pilgrimage, from the ordinary orders. Therefore, the structural vista captures more than the corporation base by juxtaposing the ordinary and nonordinary states in one frame.

Regardless of how the ordinary forms and forces are viewed and explained, the touristically directed flow begins to surface and collect momentum during the 'emission' stage located at the end of this first component of the model. The person begins first mentally and then physically to prepare for touristhood.

Emancipation: distancing from the ordinary world

This second component of the model (Fig. 1, AB, or the same component in Fig. 2) is actually a process, indeed an important one. Here the individual is emancipated from the ordinary bounds into the unbounded realm of the nonordinary: he is metamorphosed into a tourist. This transformation process may be divided into two phases of 'separation' and 'declaration'.

The first is merely a *spatial notion*. Beyond the corporation component, separation includes the act of taking off from the ordinary platform, passing through the 'gates' of departure, and/or traveling toward the magnet. For some, the separation process may even include passing through the 'gates' of arrival, reaching the magnet, and even settling down in tourism sanctuaries. These, as spatial 'markers,' all emphasize the increasing distance between home and the magnet. But touristhood is more than traveling away from the usual habitat (the basis on which tourism statistics are formed) – it is also a state of mind.

Declaration as the second phase of emancipation acknowledges that, in addition to spatial travel, the individual may also need to cross beyond his home's sociocultural thresholds. This important process is aided by several touristic items, many symbolic in nature. Suitcase, camera, tourist shirt, oversize hat,

and traveler's checks, though metaphoric, ease the transition into the realm of touristhood or the nonordinary. Even the earlier spatial markers contribute to the declaration process.

But that is not all. Most significantly, while away from home, the real identity of the traveler is disguised. His own face becomes an anonymous 'mask' behind which he hides. This mask and the above tourist symbols together induce an emancipative magic. They provide him with touristic cues, moods, and tones to which he responds and contributes playfully. The declaration process – when internalized by the tourist and externalized for those around him – 'legalizes' his new status, 'legitimizes' his action, and even 'sacralizes' his pursuit. The new lifestyle is welcomed by himself and 'understood' by others, and thus he can proceed with little or no interference from the ordinary bounds into the nonordinary world. In other words, through the new identity and role, the individual is transformed into a tourist, familiar 'clothing' and anxieties are shed for a new state of mind. The new soul begins to take a firmer hold of the body and mind in which it assumes residency during the sojourn. The tourist, 'adequately' masked, attired, equipped, and transformed, has now entered the state of touristhood.

As may be clear, the two emancipative phases work together to transform one into a tourist – separation signifies the *growing* distance between him and the ordinary, while declaration denotes the *shrinking* distance between him and the nonordinary. Combined into one, the emancipation whole disconnects the cords of the ordinary womb and suddenly the tourist is born into the nonordinary world.

Animation: a life of nonordinary flotation

As the transformation into touristhood proceeds, the ordinary community of the tourist assumes the 'back-home' position, its impounding culture is relegated to the *residual* culture for a backdrop position, and the *tourist* culture of the new world pervades (Jafari, 1983). In other words, the ordinary temporal, spatial, and cultural dimensions are 'distanced' into a past, and the nonordinary of here and now becomes the new reality. The *tourist* culture, as the *modus operandi et vivendi* of 'tourisdom,' begins to define and redefine roles, rules, notions, motions, forms, forces, expectations, processes; and the notion of animation (i.e. filled with a new spirit, courage, or resolution – a dictionary definition) captures this lubricant or illusive state of flotation, detachment, disengagement, disconnectedness, or spontaneousness transcending ordinary bounds, away from it all (Fig. 2, animation component).

Antistructural utterances, as opposed to the culturally shaped and sanctioned life at home, if now expressed are within the new norm. While ordinary needs may also be met, it is the ludic forces and leisure desires which are especially awakened when the foreground and backdrop cultures assume their respective positions. The new touristic mode actually invites antistructural manifestations and tourism assumes the qualities of play. Articulation of these points will further clarify the notion of animation and its accommodating frame.

As immersion into touristhood deepens (not at a uniform degree for all), the tourist continues to peel away the homebound cultural layers (what remains is the *residual* culture) until

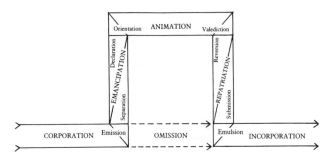

Figure 2 A tourist model.

he is detached enough to let go of himself. The tourist begins to internalize the idea that he is no longer imprisoned by his former self but is transformed into a new person with a new identity (the tourist), that he is playing on a new stage (the magnet), and that he is living up to the rhythm of a new culture (the *tourist* culture). The animated mode is hence augmented in that out-of-time and-place, now a world apart from the realities of back home. The tourist becomes the character and the *tourist* culture the script; and when the emancipated spirit or soul is lifted to the new height, immersion into the *tourist* culture has taken place, the tourism trance is in progress, and everything can be only a dream away. The tourist may now ignore not only the cultural norms of home but also those of the magnet. Breaking the rules becomes actually one of the principles of touristhood, and the tourist quickly excuses himself or is excused: 'he is only a tourist, he does not know any better'. Even the police tolerate a greater range of disorderly behavior by the tourist than the resident. The tourist assumes or knows that in this nonordinary playground his animated behavior can be acceptable. If not, he can always resort to his status: he simply throws his weight around and others oblige.

An important notion which illustrates a not-so-unusual practice in tourism is inversion (the search for and emulation of a life different from or opposed to what the tourist has in his ordinary world). 'King for a Day' and 'Peasant for a Day' are among a vast range of inversions possible in the world of nonordinary. The new king wants to experience in one week what seems missing the rest of the year. True, many of the touristic expenditure are beyond one's usual budget; but in this nonordinary world, the rules of ordinary consumerism do not apply. Hence flashing credit cards is the norm, while paying the bills is not. The matter of payment is in a world apart from the tourist – a problem located in another time and place.

Fantasy, illusion, or dream has further deepening effects. It is the sort of freedom or animation that the player on the springboard senses once suspended in the air or the sense of flotation once the surfer is on the top of a rolling wave. The expressive thrust of touristic fantasy, which both fuels and is fueled by the *tourist* culture, further nurtures and lubricates touristic manifestations. Fantasy becomes the ink with which tourism's script is written and its magnet sketched, especially so under the powerful influence of travel advertisement. Tourism, this powerful illusive opiate, can cause many closed doors of the ordinary to open in the land of the nonordinary. It can even extend the already long list of touristic S's (snow, sun, sand, sea, surf, sex) to include even *sin*.

In short, the animation component includes much of the spatial (magnet), temporal (sojourn), cultural (*tourist* culture), and other touristic dimensions. It is where the nonordinary is mostly located and where the animated characters are played (without implying that the magnet and the animation occupy the same space or position for all tourists, or that tourism is always illusive). While the nonordinary spirit could take control as early as the departure from the mundane platform, for analytical purposes the early stage of the animation component may be designated as the 'orientation' period – the tourist settles in touristic sanctuaries (e.g. hotel), takes care of the essentials, and is oriented to the surroundings. Beyond this point, all sorts

of touristic animations, flotations, and rituals become the main thrust of the sojourn. The final stage, 'valediction', sees the curtains coming down, indicating the end of the performance (Fig. 2, animation component). The apprehension that the nonordinary occasion is over turns into reality as the preparation for the return begins.

Repatriation: return to the ordinary platform

What goes up must come down: the tourist returns to the springboard. The repatriation component represents the transformation process from the nonordinary back to the ordinary state and, similar to the emancipation, is made up of two integrated phases (Fig. 2, repatriation component).

First, the process of 'reversion' from the nonordinary world begins as the departure time approaches. The tourist must leave the spatial, temporal, and cultural zones of tourism behind. The psychological retransformation dawns on the tourist first and culminates in the physical departure from that animated world. The actual descent to the ordinary, whether by land, air, or sea, for example, provides opportunities for other ritualistic goodbyes to touristhood.

Second, the process of 'submission' includes the resurrection of the former self and the reaffirmation of and yielding to the ordinary world. Here the cultural backdrop and foreground begin to switch positions. In other words, the whole of the *residual* culture which had assumed the backdrop position during the sojourn, and whose vacated post had made room for the *tourist* culture, now claims its former full position. With this process in progress, the nonordinary gradually submits to the ordinary controls.

As the psychological and physical 'distance' between the magnet and the tourist increases, the effect of the submission is deepened. By the time of 'touchdown' on the ordinary platform, the foreground *tourist* culture should have transformed into no more than a backdrop, now located in the past, and the tourist returns into his ordinary self.

Incorporation: tourism subsumed in the ordinary mainstream

The tourist finally arrives home. But, the touristic flow from the nonordinary world has not run an isolated course. It merges with the mainstream or is 'incorporated' into its ordinary body which, in the first place, showed the way to the detour option.

In terms of the springboard metaphor, upon touchdown, the individual finds himself in the depressed or the 'emulsion' space (Fig. 2, incorporation component). The depression may represent not only the pressure of landing (physical 'exhaustion') but also the state of mind (which has been on a 'trip') and the 'shock' of reentry. Beyond the emulsion stage lies the rest of the mainstream.

Since the incorporated component of the tourist model represents a conditioned and conditioning slice of life, it brings into focus both the contribution of tourism to the ordinary and the process which leads to another departure in the next cycle. This retrospective and prospective view of tourism reveals the significance of functional–structural relationships that tourism articulates between the two worlds of ordinary and nonordinary, with the latter more than complementing (balancing, patterning, or influencing) the former.

Omission: the underpass of tourism

By focusing on the touristic flow as such, one may lose sight of the ordinary current which flows in spite of the tourist's absence from home. This relinquished current constitutes the 'omission' component of the tourist model (Fig. 2, omission component). Despite its position, it is not extraneous to tourism, but is actually an essential constituent in the construction of the model. Significantly, it brings to light the uninterrupted flow of the mainstream, the foundation on which the nonordinary arch of the model rests, and the underpass onto which the tourist may fall back.

In duration, the omission is the same as the nonordinary flow; it is the span between the emission and emulsion points of departure and arrival. As the omitted body lengthens, the reentry culture shock is more probable and thus, for example, more real for the returning expatriate who may feel more disconnected than the tourist. Therefore, in this respect, the difference between the reentry 'shock' of the tourist and expatriate is a matter of degree, not kind.

The above six components approximate the touristic forms and flows. With each component in its place, the whole tourist model is assembled (Fig. 2), presenting a comprehensive view of the tourist and the touristic transformation not evident before. *Not that every tourist and his every act exactly copy or explain the model in its entirety, but that the model accounts for and subsumes various touristic patterns.* To study the tourist, it is necessary to understand him with respect to these ordinary–nonordinary transformative processes and dimensions.

. . . of the touristic apparatus and networks, . . .

The second part of the earlier tourism definition calls for models focusing on touristic apparatus and networks. To many, tourism is not the ordinary–nonordinary transformation, but a giant *industry* whose huge private and public resources actually respond to various touristic needs of travelers away from home. This 'hardware' dimension of tourism is often mistakenly taken to represent tourism as a whole. The industry is but one dimension of tourism, and it too needs to be studied and understood.

To place the myriad tourism goods and services in a 'tangible' context, tourism may be likened to a market basket of goods and services, for a *basket* model. In selecting his destination, the tourist chooses a particular market basket which is composed of both the attractions he seeks and the goods and services which accompany them. Figuratively speaking, throughout his trip, the tourist purchases experiences (related to the attractions and the goods and services) and places them in the basket. For analytical clarification, the contents should be distinguished from the basket itself.

The contents

The great variety of goods and services consumed by the tourist while away from home comprise the contents of the bas-

ket. These products may be divided into two groups: the Tourism Oriented Products (TOPs), and the Resident Oriented Products (ROPs).

The TOPs encompass all those goods and services which are directly related to the tourism industry. They are often produced especially for the tourist, for direct economic return. The producers of these goods and services may be categorized as accommodations, restaurants, transportation, travel agencies and tour operators, recreation and entertainment, and other tourism-related services. Some of these 'typical' tourism products/businesses have already grown to enormous magnitudes or industries in themselves.

The ROPs, in contrast to TOPs, are produced primarily for consumption and use by the resident of the host community, yet they may be consumed by the tourist as well. They include almost all other goods and services, whether produced by private or public interest groups. Examples of ROPs include infrastructure, police force, hospitals, bookstores, and barber shops, to name a few. While some ROPs may be of only incidental use or value to the tourist, the industry cannot function with the TOPs alone. Therefore, the ROPs are also essential, though to various degrees. In fact, inferior quality of ROPs can reduce the appeal of a destination, as may be the case for some developing countries.

By distinguishing the TOPs from ROPs, it is not intended to draw a solid line between them. Actually, the two groups of goods and services are often interwoven and they may be consumed by the host and guest alike. Moreover, what may be considered TOPs in one destination, could be considered ROPs in another. Nevertheless, the distinction is useful not only to demonstrate the vast variety in the products and their varying production orientation, but also to encourage visualization of the *content* of the basket in a discriminating fashion – a distinction which may prove useful to private and public tourism planners and developers.

The basket itself

Carrying on with the metaphor of the tourism market basket of goods and services, the tourist puts his chosen TOPs and ROPs in the basket. The basket or container is composed of and 'shaped' by the tourism attractions or Background Tourism Elements (BTEs) which may be divided into three groups.

First is the *natural* BTEs. They represent all the nature-oriented resources lumped together: water resources, weather conditions, forests, mountains, scenic resources, and more. Second is the *sociocultural* BTEs. They include all sociocultural conditions, atmospheres, or activities such as history, religion, tradition, politics, artwork, ceremonies and festivals unique to the host community. Third is the *manmade* BTEs. They represent physical creations of man which include historical buildings, monumental symbols, religious shrines, and traditional or even modern architectural structures.

It is important to point out that the BTEs do not necessarily conform to the above three categories. In reality, they are intermixed. But while one can name many destinations with appealing mixtures of BTEs, there are also those which more clearly fall into one category (e.g. Niagara Falls). As an added note of explanation, the BTEs are not necessarily beautiful or esthetically pleasing. Many attractions do not necessarily induce pleasing experience or are not socially sanctioned, such as ruins of World War II, earthquake disasters, ghettos, gambling, and prostitution. Yet these BTEs can serve as major tourism attractions for many destinations.

Individually or collectively, the BTEs give 'character', 'flavor', or 'personality' to the TOPs and ROPs. They uniquely dress up a community and create a 'tourismagnetic' atmosphere. Thus, the BTEs are the hidden substances or *background* resources of the tourism industry which shape the image a country or region portrays. Together, they form the basket or container for the TOPs and ROPs. Without the container, the contents cannot take any shape of their own. The BTEs are the *raison d'être* of the tourism industry. Assembled, the TOPs, ROPs, and BTEs represent the touristic apparatus and networks (mostly products of private and public involvements) which contribute to creating and (re)presenting the nonordinary stage on which the animated tourist performs.

...and of the ordinary and nonordinary worlds and their dialectic relationship

Beyond the transformative ordinary–nonordinary–ordinary tourist model and the touristic apparatus and networks of the basket model of the tourism definition lies still a much larger context or construct. As may be clear from the above discussion, tourism is not an independent event but a part of and a means to other ends. It exists when the tourist-generating (ordinary) and the tourist-receiving (nonordinary) systems are connected. But, for analytical pursuit, it is necessary to treat each of these two systems separately and then together in order to combine the earlier tourist and basket models to propose an all-inclusive tourism model.

The generating system

As the tourist model indicates, the tourist is emanated because his ordinary system nurtures or incubates the need to escape; the touristic flow is outward because the system 'promotes' extraneous mobilization; the flow runs an antistructural course because the system's ordinary bounds prohibit the unwinding of many endogenous disorders; the flow carries home the nonordinary treatment because the system 'benefits' from this exogenous process. Viewed from this angle, the tourist generator or market appears in the central position, with the receiving systems or destinations positioned in its 're-creative' orbits.

To illustrate, the generating system can be a country, a state, or a metropolitan city, depending on how the analytic boundaries are drawn. While the system is to serve its people (workers), it has now risen above them all – they work for the system. As it operates, it drains its workers physically and mentally. But they, when 'tired out', do not function effectively. Therefore, the system must annex re-creative subsytems (subs or satellites) for the treatment of 'exhaustion' and 'voids' which accumulate in the course of its ordinary mainstream. The nonordinary treatment for some of its people includes re-creation

of exhausted physique – to relax and restore toward a new optimum. For others, the treatment may be for anomie – to temporarily become kings or queens, somebody or nobody, for an elevated sense of fulfilment. For all, the satellites can provide a vast variety of opportunites to restore the depleted or rusted parts, to 'expand' mind and body, to get 'refills' and/or 'uplifts', to have been away from it all. When the processing is complete, these re-created workers are 'readied' to resume their positions in the main system.

Therefore, the annexation of the nonordinary satellites, positioned in the outreaching orbits, is in the interest of the generating system. Without this externalization process, the system then has to provide for suitable internal substitutions, or it may 'burn out'. In this view, tourism appears as a functional and structural detour from the mainstream (an internally generated outpour, an externally processed treatment, and an internally subsumed inpour) in order to enhance a harmony native to the generating system.

The receiving system

It is also necessary to place the receiving (host) system, where the touristic apparatus and networks of the basket model are mostly located, in the center of several tourist generating hubs. From this angle, the host is seen accommodating within its own ordinary bounds the nonordinary touristic outpours from different tourist generators. Foreign to the host, each inflow contains external substances (residual culture) native to that tourist generator. Thus, the receiver is dealing with several such substances, each representing a different hub, with little or no accord among them. In addition, there is the tourist culture which represents the common pattern or rhythm evident among all tourists. There is still the local culture of the host, or its own ordinary structure. This local culture is now seen side-by-side with the heterogeneous residual cultures and the rather homogeneous tourist culture, both foreign to it. The private and public makers and shapers of the tourism market basket of the host system, quite influential in many instances, represent still another involuted set of internal and external forces. These cultural and operational conditions constitute a 'culture mix' unique to each receiving system (Jafari, 1983).

This all brings into light a significant perspective. The new synthesized 'ordinary' (particularly assimilation of the *local*, *tourist*, and *residual* cultures) can gradually replace the original ordinary mode of the host, which still will have to meet not just the nonordinary needs of all different tourists, but also the ordinary requirements of its own people.

Moreover, as implied earlier, the ordinary and nonordinary are contradictory propositions (e.g. one reinforces the structure, the other promotes antistructure; or one upholds work, the other promotes play). They are often two incompatible systems. Nevertheless, the host, as the re-creative satellite of several generating systems, may pay insufficient attention to its own compounded ordinary requirements, potentially leading to a 'borrowed burn out' not totally of its own making. The receiving system is forced to deal with much more than what it has bargained for, a proposition that the recent literature on host–guest relationships (see, for instance, recent issues of *Annals of Tourism Research*) has addressed.

Interdependence of the systems

Observations from either position reveal that the give-and-take processes between the generating and receiving partners structurally combine them into one integrated whole. From this perspective, it becomes evident that, contrary to previous assumptions and practices, the generating system also needs to be concerned with the well-being and affairs of the receiving system. This point may require further elaboration.

It is in the interest of the tourist-generating system not only to respond properly to the touristic demand of its people, but also to contribute to the development of its re-creative satellites and to 'absorb' and 'pay for' some of the impacts of the vacations taken in someone else's backyard. After all, it is the generating system which stands to benefit most, not necessarily the receiving one which is commonly believed to bank the cash. Thus argued, for example, it is the city of Chicago which 'owes' much to Wisconsin and Michigan, or it is the European Community which owes much to Tunisia and Senegal as their re-creative satellites. This is not a unilateral but a mutual prescription. It takes efforts to coordinate the touristic flows in order to minimize frictions and maximize prospects. This calls for a systems-level cooperation and financial involvement beyond the direct expenditure by tourists from the generating market and the investment or commitment by operators in the receiving magnet.

The tourism model

By juxtaposing the tourist and basket models, a new model emerges. For this purpose, the flow of the tourist model (Fig. 2), moving from left to right, is converted to a circuitous motion (Fig. 3). Here the two worlds of ordinary (generating system) and nonordinary (receiving system) appear as an integrated whole. They together form a megasystem, an interconnected structure, or the context for a tourism model.

As an all-inclusive construct, the new model denotes that tourism is more than the ordinary–nonordinary transformative processes; that it is more than the generating markets, the receiving destinations, and their touristic apparatus and networks; that it is more than development, marketing, promotion, foreign exchange, multiplier effect, and employment; that it is more than acculturation, demonstration effect, and cultural enrichment or commoditization; that it is more than documentation and evaluation of its costs and benefits; and hence it is larger and more significant than the sum of its parts and dimensions. As such, the current tourism industry view on tourism which is concerned mostly with attracting and catering to the tourist fails to recognize the place of tourism beyond its business dimensions. Tourism certainly represents much more.

Beyond the specific lies the megasystem in which tourism flows in and out and connects practically all generating ordinary markets and receiving magnets worldwide. It clearly indicates that *tourism is not simply the act of going away, tourism is also coming home*. This proposition signals the important assimilation role that tourism plays in today's global community.

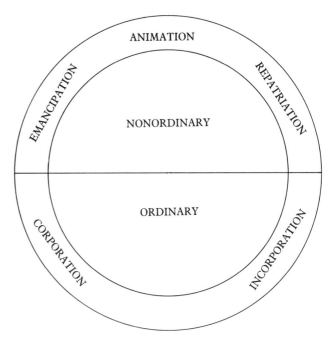

Figure 3 A tourism model.

The analytic isolation of the touristic paradigm from the megasystem represents the tourism system to which the above three models (tourist, basket and tourism) belong. This abstracted whole constitutes the disciplinary domain in which touristic forms and forces should be contextually studied in order to understand and accommodate the structured and structuring, the influenced and influencing dimensions of the phenomenon or industry known as tourism.

Futher reading

Jafari, J., 'Tourism market basket of goods and services: components and nature of tourism', *Studies in Tourism Wildlife Park Conservation*, T. V. Singh, J. Kapur and D. P. Singh (eds) (Metropolitan Book Company, 1982), pp. 1–12.

Jafari, J., 'Understanding the structure of tourism', *Tourism and Culture: A Comparative Perspective*, E. C. Nabel, ed. (The University of New Orleans School of Hotel, Restaurant and Tourism Administration, 1983), pp. 65–84.

Jafari, J., 'Tourism models: the sociocultural aspects', *Tourism Management*, vol. 8, no. 2 (1987), pp. 151–9.

Acknowledgements

This paper has benefited from the work of several authors acknowledged in an earlier publication (Jafari, 1987).

JAFAR JAFARI

Systems approach in tourism: the Saint Gall Management Model

Introduction

From the scientific point of view, the Saint Gall Management Model represents an attempt to extend logically the 'system oriented science of business and industrial management' to the management problems of all kinds of companies and other similar social systems (Ulrich and Krieg, 1973, p.5).

Contrary to the trend of earlier theories on management towards a closed system concept, Ulrich and the Saint Gall school start from an open system concept. An open system is characterized by its exchange relations with its environment. The systems approach in general and particularly the concept of open, dynamic systems have the big advantge that they take a broader view rather than single-sided and isolated considerations. The concept represents an ordering concept that makes it possible to analyze, describe and synthesize different viewpoints from an overall perspective.

The advantages of systems thinking stem from the fact that systems thinking involves the following (Ulrich and Krieg, 1973, p.12):

1. Integral thinking.
2. Process-oriented thinking.
3. Interdisciplinary thinking.
4. Analytic and synthetic thinking.
5. Pragmatic thinking.

System oriented management consists generally of the principle that concepts, representations, knowledge and methods from system theory and cybernetics are taken up, interpreted and applied to management problems. The enterprise is considered as an open system, that is purposeful and capable of action, and fulfils productive functions in a changing environment. The management which incorporates the design, control and development functions, appears in a cybernetic framework as an information processing subsystem. In constant interaction with a transforming environment, the management sets objectives, fixes conditions, shapes the enterprise as a real system in a way corresponding to its purpose, and sets up and controls the necessary goal-oriented processes.

System oriented management means moreover that individual managers orientate themselves within the framework of a management system, that is designed according to the cybernetic concept that has been indicated. Therefore, 'system oriented' must not be simply equalized with 'systematic', because it implies the application of new organization and management principles. It must be added that the systems approach, thanks to its integrating and interdisciplinary character, is particularly adequate to lead to a management science based on various experience and knowledge fields, with a multidimensional ordering system to understand and represent the necessary concepts. (Ulrich and Krieg, 1973, p. 14)

To summarize, the Saint Gall Management Model is of outstanding usefulness to grasp real-life issues, the more so, as social systems are understood as open systems, so that the manifold influences and situations can be permanently and globally processed as information and taken account of in management decisions.

Management in the tourism industry

The Saint Gall Management Model comprises four components: company; management; organization; manager's tasks (Ulrich and Krieg, p. 16). Kaspar and Kunz have applied the principle of the Saint Gall Management Model to the tourist industry (Kaspar and Kunz, 1982). It was particularly important to take into account the specific features of the tourist trade. As all the fields of management do not have the same importance in all the types of tourism firms, all the types of enterprises/businesses have not been covered in each chapter. More emphasis in the applications is given to hotels, tour operators and travel agencies, and tourist resorts as travel destinations. Other enterprises such as tourism transport firms, sports facilities, tourist offices, health resorts, and spas have been taken into account according to the significance of their management tasks.

Our assessments have shown that modern management concepts and methods have only been applied to tourism in a very limited way. This neglect is difficult to understand because the science of management is essential for the success and survival of tourist enterprises, which have a significant impact on the national economies. Exceptions are the international hotel chains and the large travel organizations which, in recent years, have put into practice more and more management theory.

Obviously, the small company structure of most tourism enterprises has delayed the acceptance of modern management methods, particularly because the flexibility of staff organization, and customer appeal (repeat business), helped them to overcome any difficulties. Management blunders and faulty investments have been compensated over many years by the accelerating growth of the tourist markets. Nevertheless it has become more and more acceptable to try to solve the resulting problems through cooperative approaches, such as voluntary hotel chains, interest partnerships, common purchasing, advertising and sales organizations.

The significance of the environment to tourism enterprises

The system thinking that forms the basis of the Saint Gall Management Model underlines the significance of the influences of the environment on the enterprises (Kaspar, 1986). Neglecting any of the environmental factors leads to a wrong evaluation of the chances of success, and hence to wrong behavior and faulty investments. The environmental factors to be taken into account are shown in Fig. 1.

The 'spheres' cannot be influenced by the enterprise but are important factors influencing it. Their significance for the individual tourism business depends strongly on international, national, regional and local conditions, which underlines the necessity of understanding and processing their concrete relevance for the firm concerned.

Management as a steering system for information processing

The importance of diagnosing the environment surrounding the tourism firm becomes fully clear with the characterization of management as an information processing steering or control system (Ulrich and Krieg, 1973). To develop the processes

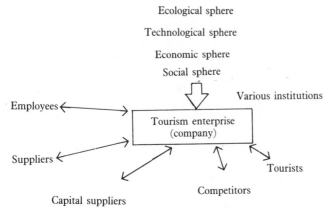

Figure 1 The environment of the tourism enterprise.

that must be carried out, the management must determine the following:

1. The objectives.
2. The means or potential capabilities necessary to attain these objectives.
3. The processes suitable for the use of available means.

The *determination of the objectives* within the framework of general management concerns fixing the main objectives, i.e. the general aims of the enterprise. At the same time, coordination measures must be taken to attune the partial objectives to the main objectives, and these partial aims to each other. The 'main' objectives of the enterprise concern, among others, the definition of the services that must be supplied to the market in order to satisfy the needs of potential customers. They also include goals related to the social behavior of the firm, the intended earnings and their use etc. For example, a hotel will specialize in a specific type of guest (e.g. those that like sport) and, because of this objective, neglect other segments of the market (e.g. aged guests). A travel organization must, for example, decide whether, on top of supplying packaged products, it will also be in the retail business, and if it will specialize in a certain type of trip, such as hiking tours.

The *determination of the means*, within this framework, comprises fixing the necessary *resource potential* to attain the general objectives, i.e. the capability, in the broadest sense of type and scope, and the overall organization structure of the company. For many tourist enterprises, fixed assets represent the major component of resource potential. For example, for a transport firm, specializing in ski resort tourism, these include generally one (or more) main road(s) from the resort to the skiing area (primary installations) and additional transport installations in the ski area (secondary installations). The fixed assets of a hotel consist essentially of the building, machines, equipment, and furniture. Managing and executive collaborators just as information, energy and raw materials of various types also belong to the resource potential ('input'). The determination of these elements of the resource potential is the task of the general management within the scope of the determination of means.

The *determination of the processes* is a task of general management inasmuch as the steering processes cannot be localized only in part of the company. Examples of issues relating to processes are: in hotel or restaurant kitchens, conventional cooking versus fast food production; for a ski-resort transport installation, building a cable railway or a skilift; in the sale of tours, extension of the choice through ancillary services (insurance, sales of voyage equipment and documentation).

The following points are important in characterizing the decisions to be taken by the general management of the enterprise:

1. As the decisions are original, and are not derived from elsewhere, the motivations and value representations of the people belonging to the decision center play an important role.
2. The freedom of decision of these people is limited by the requirements and influences of the environment, as well as by the characteristics and development potential of the business.

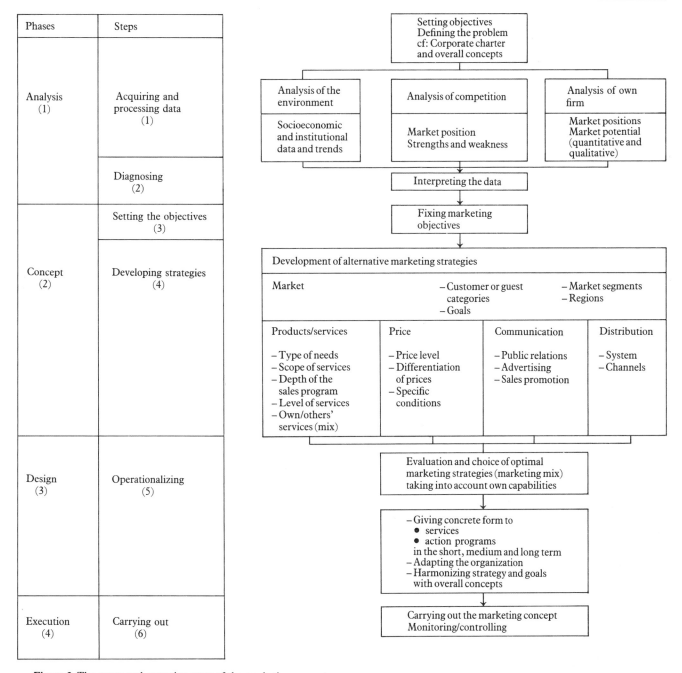

Phases	Steps
Analysis (1)	Acquiring and processing data (1)
	Diagnosing (2)
Concept (2)	Setting the objectives (3)
	Developing strategies (4)
Design (3)	Operationalizing (5)
Execution (4)	Carrying out (6)

Figure 2 The stages and operating steps of the marketing concept.

3. The decisions concerning the general management that have important and mostly long-term effects, often involve substantial risks or uncertainty.

Structure of the management of tourist enterprises

The management of tourist enterprises can be divided into the following elements:

1. *Corporate policy:* determination of objectives and principles to guide the firm, in a corporate charter (guiding principles), a corporate concept (content-oriented) and a management concept (management-oriented).
2. *Planning:* as a quantified and scheduled specification of corporate policy.
3. *Marketing:* policy and strategy according to the market, including the design of services, prices, advertising, sales promotion, distribution.

4. *Finance:* obtaining, using and administrating financial resources.
5. *Organization:* a local-oriented management of the behavior of the enterprise by defining structure, and distributing tasks and responsibilities.
6. *Physical organization of the enterprise:* this aspect is important for tourist enterprises because of their high intensity of fixed assets.
7. *Management of the collaborators:* particularly important in touristic activities where services and management personnel operate in the presence of the clients.
8. *Information system:* it should provide the most important decision support for management. Information has become a strategically crucial resource, also on the operations level.
9. *Monitoring and rationalization:* the objective is to increase the efficiency of the organization.

It is not possible within the scope of this introductory chapter to go into the details of each element; they have been extensively described by Kaspar and Kunz (1982). We will however illustrate the advantages of the process-oriented and systematic procedures according to the Saint Gall Management Model, using the example of tourism marketing, which has led to the largest successes in the practice of tourism management. Great help was provided for this by the truly practice-oriented work of publications on marketing in the tourist trade for example Zolles *et al.* (1981).

The application of the systems analysis principle in marketing

Marketing in tourism is particularly suited for the application of the system analysis process, which includes the topical search for variants of solutions for a given objective (optimal marketing of touristic services) within certain constraints (environment, competition and own relative strengths/weaknesses). This process, in other words, consists of an operational (i.e. implementable) concept that is systematically worked out. The contents and procedure (phases, working steps) of the marketing concept are clearly illustrated in Fig. 2 (Droege *et al.*, 1981).

Conclusion

The arguments set for the significance of a market-oriented business policy in the tourist trade (tourism marketing) (Kaspar and Kunz, 1982, p. 127) can just as well be used as an indication in favor of a general improvement of management in the tourist trade:

1. Tourism firms offer services that depend on the presence of guests, so accurate correspondence of services offered with customer needs is imperative.
2. Tourism services have a truly complementary character, as tourists ask for a service package including transport, accommodation, catering activities.
3. A fixed offer is confronted with an elastic demand which leads to a particularly high sales risk.
4. The tourism trade is relatively capital intensive (means of transportation, accommodation, catering, equipment for sports and leisure facilities).
5. A relatively large number of substitutes exist both in terms of capital goods and especially from other touristic offers.
6. The tourism market has changed from a seller's to a buyer's market, which requires particular care in assessing demand for any decision concerning the firm.

The worldwide increase of competition in the tourist trade, reduced profit margins, increasing cost of personnel and capital are important factors that call for a systematic application of the solutions offered by modern management theory, which could become decisive for the future of the tourist trade.

Further reading

Droege, W., Bufe, R., Sturm, F., 'Röntgenbild eines Heilbades', *Der Fremdenverkehr und das Reisebüro*, part 3/81 (Darmstadt, 1981), p. 71.

Kaspar, C., 'Die Fremdenverkehrslehre im Grundriss', *St. Galler Beiträge zum Fremdenverkehr und zur Verkehrswirtschaft*, vol. 1 (Haupt, 3rd edition, 1986). System thinking applied to the tourist trade.

Kaspar, C. and Kunz, B., *St. Galler Beiträge zum Fremdenverkehr und zur Verkehrswirtschaft*, vol. 13 (Haupt, 1982).

Ulrich, H. and Krieg, W., *Das St. Galler Management-Modell* (Haupt, 2nd edition, 1973).

Zolles, H., Müller, R. and Ferner, F. K., *Marketing Praxis für den Fremdenverkehr* (Orac, 1981).

CLAUDE KASPAR

Tangibility of the intangible travel product

Introduction

A consumer spends money on buying some physical object, such as a car, or to take part in an activity, such as travel, or a combination of both, such as food cooked and served. It is possible to measure, if only crudely, what the consumer has bought, and to compare purchases by different consumers (for instance, different types of holiday). This is essentially what is meant by the 'tangibility' of a product. With any purchase, however, what matters is the resulting experiences that the consumer either undergoes of expects to undergo. It is difficult to measure these experiences with precision or compare the experiences of one consumer with those of another in an objective manner. This lack of measurability is indicated by the term 'intangibility'.

The experiences of each traveler differ from those of every other traveler in some way. These differences are part of the intangible benefits, the sensations of well-being, acquired by each traveler. They are difficult to identify except as broad aggregates of feelings or sensations. The extent of the benefits and their value can be even harder to measure, since they vary with the personality and disposition of the recipients.

However, the travel operator needs to measure the extent to which it satisfies the various expectations of the consumer in relation to the cost of resources used in providing the services. Benefits and costs have to be compared at some stage of the process on the same basis. The intangible benefits have to be put in some tangible form. For instance, comfortable accommodation has to be expressed in terms of the physical attributes of the room and its furnishings, in such a way that degrees of perceived comfort can be identified.

Examples

Hotels and other service providers are generally concerned to present a caring and efficient image. Such concepts of caring and efficiency can be identified with certain attributes of the service provided, such as timeliness in restaurant service and making the customer feel welcome. These attributes are, however, subjective. To determine how good the service is, the management needs some measuring device. For instance, one measure of timeliness could be that guests have their order taken within three minutes of being seated in the restaurant. A measure of welcome could be that the customer is addressed by name at least once during the course of the meal.

The firm has three tasks: to decide on the particular measures to be used (such as time between sitting down and order being taken); to decide how numerical values for the variables are to be interpreted (e.g. one minute scores ten points, two minutes five points); and to decide on the relative importance of the different measures (e.g. a timeliness point may be worth two personal concern points).

In this way, the firm can assess whether improvements in the service provided are really happening. It must ensure that the measure used will reflect (though not necessarily be the same as) consumer perceptions of quality.

Benefits

Converting intangible benefits into some tangible form may seem difficult, but decisions about markets, products and resource usage are either based on this kind of explicit process or else they imply certain assumptions about consumer perceptions and supply costs. Explicit analysis reduces inconsistencies and encourages the firm to be outward-looking and receptive to nuances of consumer behavior rather than attempting to fit consumers into a predetermined mould. Above all, it is an essential contribution to the ongoing process of quality assurance.

As indicated above, concepts are turned into attributes which are then turned into measures. Thus the first stage is to identify significant factors influencing consumer travel and tourist behavior, which will help identify the particular service attributes required by different types of customers. Various writers have indicated the following influences on tourist behavior.

Travel to and use of a location tends to follow a certain pattern. A relatively unexplored area is discovered, perhaps by accident, by individuals using local guides on an *ad hoc* basis. The travelers require a considerable amount of highly individualized information and activity organization. As the tourist site develops there is increasing improvement in amenities and formalization of information and tourist activity. Private or public agencies (travel operators and so on) provide cheap, mass-produced, standardized information and activity. At the upper end of the market, individual exploration continues, but the traveler must buy the special and relatively expensive information and organization required, or produce it himself. Other travelers will be able to use the formalized knowledge that is readily and cheaply available to provide for their own self-guided exploration. The type of knowledge that they want to buy will become increasingly sophisticated.

Modern travel, especially longer distance travel has been associated with economic growth. This has not been accidental. Households have changed their consumption patterns to spend their extra income on new activities or more expensive forms of existing activities, such as holidays abroad instead of at home. Consumers have also cut down on time spent on relatively unattractive activities by buying market substitutes. Changes in household size and structure have tended to reduce the importance of family centered consumption and increased individualistic consumption in the market. This is particularly so in smaller households, especially those without dependent children, where the relative cost of market consumption is low. For instance, a meal for a family in a restaurant becomes more expensive the larger the family unit, even when the price per person stays the same.

The falling relative cost of consumer durables, such as cars, has encouraged households to provide more of their own simple travel and tourism services. The consumer has tended to upgrade the general level of travel services bought in the market, in terms of quality and complexity. Even today the consumer has only a limited amount of time to enjoy his extra consumption. Indeed, increased leisure is only part of the answer, since it becomes increasingly expensive in terms of lost income, so the consumer will want to make more effective use of the time available. Thus, the speed and efficiency of service will become more important as consumers try to cut the time cost of travel. Consumers will also want to reduce uncertainty in travel and tourist purchases to reduce the cost of searching for suitable products. Along with specific demand for products, travelers have become more specific about acceptable standards basing their demand on known, commercially available products.

Implementation

The desires of consumers and the requirements of efficient production have to be reconciled. So the travel operator has to proceed from the intangible perceptions of the consumer through to the tangible resources used, and back again through physical improvements to the product to improve the consumer's experiences. This should be regarded as an iterative, ongoing process.

The firm must identify those experiences sought by the consumer and the basic economic conditions determining the methods of production that will be practicable in the long run.

The operator can then make a structural analysis of the travel process. This will pinpoint those activities or situations where customer satisfaction can be directly translated into the tangible use of resources. The analysis may be divided into a number of major parts. For instance, a holiday may be split into the components: travel to destination – stay at destination – return travel home. Each part will be subdivided in turn into smaller parts, including once-only events (such as arrival at hotel) and repetitive events (meal service). This continues until all the significant stages are delineated. Here, of course, major problems may arise.

Managers have to identify critical points of the process, where control can be effectively exercised over the resources used. With limited managerial resources, not everything can be dealt with down to the last detail. Some things have to be left to the operatives or personnel actually concerned with delivery of the services. Indeed, given the need to develop service awareness in many fields, such delegation is to be encouraged.

There are, however, three perspectives on the consumption process: the management's; the operatives'; and the customers'. It is not difficult to see that there can be considerable divergence between the different perspectives on both what is desired by the consumer and how in terms of actual activities these desires are to be met. To overcome this, effective channels of communication have to be established that deal with these points specifically. Although consumers may have unrealistic expectations that can be modified by direct or indirect service interaction, many of the problems of divergence will have been caused through the production-centeredness of managers and the workforce, with managers seeking routine, stability and control status, and the workforce seeking craft or skill development and status.

The process of analysis can be split into four basic stages.

Stage 1

This is largely qualitative and it has three aims:

1. To identify general types of market.
2. To identify those experiences that the consumer values.
3. To identify those activities and products that ensure those experiences.

These may be pursued at the same time rather than sequentially.

Purchase decisions depend on household or business goals and production activities. The market for consumer travel can be split into various segments according to type of vacation desired, which can be related to the type of consumer and their socioeconomic status and values.

A consumer's travel program comprises a mixture of activities and products, produced by the consumer or bought from firms or a combination of both. The program continues for a period of time and may be important in itself, the traveler being concerned almost entirely with the experiences gained during travel, for instance, on a sea-going cruise. Alternatively, travel may be a means of getting from A to B. Consumer satisfaction depends on the efficiency and effectiveness with which he is delivered to his destination. These in turn depend on the extent to which the travel process has improved his capabilities for further consumption activity (or production activity in the case of the business traveler). In practice, there is usually a mixture of both.

A travel operator may offer a range of services. The firm may simply arrange delivery of the traveler or provide a package deal once there. In the former case the operator provides a standardized service to a large number of buyers (for instance, through scheduled air or rail services); in the latter the operator takes the initiative in organizing the tour, providing, among other things, information.

A travel program provides the consumer with a bundle of characteristics providing varying degrees of satisfaction. Two different sets can be identified: *general* and *personal* service characteristics. The general characteristics represent the elements of the commodity that are generally available to all consumers and are often physical, tangible elements. Their value to the consumer reflects:

1. Adaptability to customer requirements. For instance, a traveler uses a scheduled air service together with his own time and other resources to complete a particular activity. The plane ride is the same as the one bought by the next consumer, the use to which it is put is similar, but the end product for the two individuals is different.
2. Reliability in performance. Every product carries a risk that it will not conform to specification. This risk is a cost to the consumer that varies with the chances of failure and the costs of failure. A reputation for reliability reduces the perceived risk to the consumer.

The Personal Service Characteristics are the personal elements of the product. They are essentially subjective and depend for their value on being consistent with the individual's own special requirements. Two important service characteristics are timing and location (for instance, of train services).

Stage 2

The qualitative analysis must become quantifiable and geared towards the producer:

1. Measure the contribution of each subactivity to overall value.
2. Identify the resources used in that activity.
3. Measure the contribution of these resources to the value of that activity, as perceived by the consumer.

This obviously requires a good understanding not only of the production and delivery systems available but also an appreciation of the relative costs of different resources.

Where potential markets are large, the firm can improve its position by concentrating on increasing standardization where possible, with off-the peg provision, either from the firm's travel unit or from a central supply unit (for instance, accommodation facilities bought from a hotel). The firm will be better able to cope with fluctuations in demand from different types of customers, since it will be able to switch resources from one market to another more easily. Even for smaller markets, the firm can reduce costs by standardizing the type of service offered, effectively cutting the costs of switching personnel and other resources from one market to another. The provision of a particular service is reduced to a few components that are provided by rather similar processes.

Alternatively, where markets are small and varied or are for composite products requiring two sets of tourist activities, the various requirements of such a group can be met through inter-unit cooperation. Where this is not practicable, the firm will concentrate on providing highly individualized services rendering high value. Thus the efficient firm considers two important features of the product: standardization and personalization. It will have a small number of standard product ranges; but each product will be cheaply differentiable, with easy to make variations valued by consumers (for instance, optional day trips on package tours).

The travel operator has to bear in mind the inherent risks in providing for a market that is continually changing and developing. Where a firm successfully positions a new product in the market, the rewards can be high. These will, however, lead eventually to adjacent market positioning by rivals and a decline in the profitability of the particular product. The improvement and refinement of provision will continue but further cost reductions will diminish through time. At the same time, economic change alters the pattern of consumption. Certain characteristics may retain their value for consumers, but the relative efficiency of existing commodities in supplying those characteristics will decline and so will their value to the consumer.

Stage 3

The analysis centers on provision by the firm:

1. Measure the cost of the resources relative to the value generated.
2. Change the mix of services to reduce waste of resources and to identify new avenues of development.

Stage 4

Decisions are implemented.

Devise a procedure for implementation. This will vary with the size of the problem and type of organization. Staff have to understand the need for change and must perceive tangible benefits for them from the improvement in performance.

Assessment

The process of implementation requires constant evaluation. Managers should themselves experience, where possible, consumer reaction and ensure receptivity among staff. This means looking at the attitudes that one is trying to instil into staff during training, getting both management and staff wholeheartedly committed to perceptible and measurable standards of quality, and not just to a woolly-minded concept of service.

Conclusion

It is a common fault in the provision of services that suppliers hide behind the smokescreen of 'service' or even 'personal service' as if this allows them to escape the need to evaluate honestly just what the consumer wants. Too often personal service degenerates from 'service to a person' to 'service by persons': the consumer is then neglected in favor of convenience for the producer.

Yet, the increasing sophistication of the consumer and the diffusion of technological possibilities requires a closer analysis of the consumer's needs. Converting intangible concepts into tangible components is a difficult process, but becomes increasingly necessary.

Focus on small business

The process of analysis and evaluation can be carried out as effectively in the small firm as in the large, since generally the actual unit of service (a particular travel package) is small. The small business manager may have more difficulty in standing back from everyday activities to give sufficient importance to these matters. On the other hand, given the commitment it may be easier to get the feel of the market and develop empathy with

Further reading

Butler, R. W., 'The concept of a tourist area cycle of evolution: implications for management of resources', *Canadian Geographer*, vol. 24 (1980), pp. 5–12. This article develops the application of the life cycle concept to a tourist area. Its depiction of the various stages should be of use to tour operators in assessing the potential of various localities.

Cohen, E., 'The tourist guide, the origins, structure and dynamics of a role', *Annals of Tourism Research*, vol. 12, no. 1 (1985), pp. 5–29. This article looks at the changing role of the guide as tourism develops and can be related to the changing information needs of the traveler.

Fine, E. C. and Speer, J. H., 'Tour guide performance as sight sacralisation', *Annals of Tourism Research*, vol. 12, no. 1 (1985), pp. 73–95. An interesting article putting a sociological perspective on what travelers are looking for from tourist spots.

Lancaster, K. J., 'A new approach to consumer theory', *Journal of Political Economy*, vol. 74, no. 2 (1966). The author of this article sets out his goods' characteristics approach to consumer behavior.

Levitt, T., 'Marketing intangible products and product tangibles', *Cornell HRA Quarterly* (August 1981). An interesting and significant article on marketing.

Lewis, R. C., 'Isolating differences in hotel attributes', *Cornell HRA Quarterly*, vol. 25, no. 3 (November 1984), pp. 64–77. This article illustrates the use of some simple multivariate techniques to quantify differences in consumers' perceptions between hotels.

Martin, W. B., 'Defining what quality service is for you', *Cornell HRA Quarterly*, vol. 26, no. 4 (February 1986), pp. 32–8. This article looks at aspects of service quality and how intangible indicators can be expressed in tangible ways.

Martin, W. B., 'Measuring and improving your service quality', *Cornell HRA Quarterly*, vol. 27, no. 1 (May 1986), pp. 80–7. This article looks at the ways service quality can be measured and suggests strategies for implementing improvements.

Oppedijk van Veen, W. M. and Verhallen, T. W. M., 'Vacation market segmentation: a domain-specific approach', *Annals of Tourism Research*, vol. 13, no. 1 (1986), pp. 37–58. This article considers the variables determining the set of attractive choice alternatives, those that are important in the choice of vacation, and establishes a value hierarchy. It is also useful in that it relates type of holiday desired to socioeconomic factors, including family type.

Winston, G. C., *The Timing of Economic Activities* (Cambridge University Press, 1982). The book provides a theoretical analysis of the timing of production and consumption activities and the implications of economic growth.

Sheldon, P., 'The tour operator industry: an analysis', *Annals of Tourism Research*, vol. 13, no. 3 (1986), pp. 349–65. This article, among other things, shows that similarity of characteristics between package tourists is greater than that between nonpackage tourists.

PETER CULLEN

Taxing international tourism

Introduction

Tourism has been one of the phenomenal growth stories of the second half of the twentieth century. Figures from the World Tourism Organization, shown below, indicate the speed of this growth:

1966	$ 13.3 billion
1976	$ 44.4 billion
1986	$115.0 billion

Many commentators now confidently forecast that tourism will be the biggest single international 'export' by the year 2000. Even if this is not the case, it will represent an enormous sum and, almost without exception, form an important sector in the economy of every country in the world.

There is no official estimate of the breakdown of spending on tourism between international and domestic. The figure for international tourism is shown above, but many countries cannot estimate the value of their domestic tourism. The generally accepted view is that domestic tourism is bigger than international tourism – probably about 60 per cent domestic to 40 per cent international. This would give a figure approaching $300 billion for 1986 for total worldwide spending on tourism.

As traveling throughout the world becomes easier, and if the price does not increase in real terms, it is inevitable that the amount spent on domestic tourism will fall as a share of total tourism spend. This is not to suggest that domestic tourism will fall dramatically, but its growth will not be as fast as that of international tourism.

The case for taxing international tourism

In the very nature of things, governments are continually looking for ways of raising more taxation as their expenditure continues to grow each year. In its infancy, tourism was spared from taxes because the yield would have been insignificant. However, an increasing number of governments are now levying taxes on goods and services bought by tourists. The reason is simple. Once consumer spending on a sector of the economy reaches a certain level, it pays governments to consider levying taxes. If administrative costs are too high, it will not pay govern-ments to levy a tax. This means that one must, regrettably, now assume that the taxing of tourist services is here to stay. It will certainly be the case while spending on tourism continues to grow. Government treasuries are only too well aware that the best taxes are those that come from a sector of the economy that is growing. One has only to look at the yield from tobacco tax in the United Kingdom over the years, to appreciate that there is a limit to the level of tax which can be levied on a commodity whose sale is declining. Even so, a steep increase in the tax can still yield additional revenue if the demand is relatively inelastic.

There is a need, though, for governments to appreciate the difference between domestic and international tourism. International tourism is an invisible export and many people argue that it is unfair for a government to tax such an invisible export, as a visible export is not taxed. However, a major difficulty arises since it is almost impossible to differentiate between someone who is booking a hotel room as to whether they are a domestic or a foreign visitor. If it is a foreign visitor, one can be certain if the booking has been made by a tour operator from overseas. However, if it is a foreign visitor who had traveled independently, it would be unjust to make him pay the tax if block bookings from abroad were exempt from taxation.

Examples

By far the most important tax levied on tourists in major European countries is Value Added Tax. The yield from this in the United Kingdom from tourists runs to hundreds of millions of pounds.

The British Tourist Authority has for many years urged the British Government to tax the foreign visitor at a lower rate of value added tax than the standard rate. The British Govern-ment has decided, so far, not to introduce any preferential rate for VAT on services. However it is interesting to note that the European Commission in Brussels is proposing that a standard rate of between 14 and 18 per cent and a preferential rate be-tween 4 and 8 per cent be introduced when harmonization of VAT is due to take place in 1992. This demonstrates the accept-ance by EC officials that there is a valid argument for taxing certain services at a lower rate if a proportion of the sales are bought within that country by a nonresident – in other words, it is an invisible export.

In the case of shopping, a system has been devised in the United Kingdom as well as in other countries, whereby visitors can reclaim the amount they have paid in value added tax (VAT) by carrying the goods as hand luggage when they leave the country and displaying them to the Customs Officer. He can identify that they are being exported from the country and the departing visitor can reclaim the tax from the shop where the goods were bought on returning to his country of residence. This system, although somewhat cumbersome, has proved popular with tourists not only in the United Kingdom but in other countries as well.

Value added tax is not the only indirect tax which is levied on tourists. They also pay UK tax when they buy such items such as alcohol, tobacco, petrol etc. It is estimated that the yield to the British Exchequer in 1987, including VAT, is likely to be of the order of £750 million. It is therefore not surprising that governments increasingly rely on tourism to help provide a small but useful sum of revenue for their Exchequer.

The equivalent of VAT in the United Stated are 'sales taxes'. These are fixed at a lower level than VAT rates (of the order of 6 per cent) and are levied not by the Federal Government but by the individual states. These taxes cover a wider spectrum than VAT. Where goods have been bought there is no system whereby the tourist can recoup the tax on leaving the country. If the taxes were levied at a higher rate (as with taxes in European countries) it might well pay states to introduce some form of Personal Export Scheme to enable the tourist to reclaim the tax but whilst it is at a relatively low level, the cost of administering such a scheme would outweigh the amount of the tax charged.

The increasing spread of taxes on tourists

In recent years there has been an ominous development in the introduction of tourist taxes on residents traveling abroad from certain countries, particularly from Scandinavia. This is the Departure Tax, which is levied on every passenger departing on a charter flight. For some years representations have been made at the meetings of the Organization for Economic Cooperation and Development (OECD) Tourism Committee that these taxes, which have an adverse effect on traffic flows, should be removed. Scandinavian Governments have argued that the tax is considered purely as a revenue raiser for the Exchequer and in no way is meant to deter citizens from traveling outside of their own country. It has to be admitted that tourist statistics support this argument – to take one example, the tax in Sweden has been progressively increased from 100 Kroner to 300 Kroner (from about £10 to about £30) – and yet spending by Swedes traveling abroad, particularly to sunshine destinations where most of the charter flights go, has continued to increase.

Such a tax distorts travel in two ways. It is not imposed on coach tour operators, motorists taking the ferry out of Sweden, or scheduled air passengers. So, its effect is to disadvantage one sector of the travel market out of Sweden from the rest. It seems most unlikely that the Swedish Government is actually trying to do this but the effect of the tax is to do just that.

Another way in which the tax distorts the market is in dis-

couraging weekened charters, because it is not an *ad valorem* tax but a fixed tax. It therefore does not bear so heavily on 2-week charters to the Mediterranean as it does on a weekend charter to the United Kingdom. Such charters have great potential for bringing tourists either for shopping or for such events as football matches. A fixed tax, however, increases the total cost of the package by a far higher percentage than with the cost of a 2-week charter. There is, therefore, a good case to be made for changing a fixed rate into an *ad valorem* rate to avoid distorting the charter market. It should also appeal to governments in that the yield could grow appreciably!

Departure tax

In 1983, Portugal introduced a departure tax of £5 for each overseas visitor leaving the country. Again, it was meant to be a simple revenue raiser but there was severe criticism from the travel trade because it meant they had to collect the tax before visitors traveled to Portugal. If the tax had been collected at the point of departure, many tourists would have been unable to pay the £5 as they may well have run out of money.

There was so much criticism at the imposition of this tax that the Portuguese Government withdrew it at the end of 1983. So far, no other country has followed the example of Portugal with a blanket charge for foreign visitors leaving a country. It is to be hoped that the travel trade's criticism will have discouraged other countries from imposing such a tax.

Security tax

In view of the regrettable increase in terrorist activities, particularly over the last 10 years, it is inevitable that the majority of governments now levy some form of security tax at airports to help defray the cost of providing security guards. There seems little hope of persuading governments, or airports, to absorb this tax into their general running expenses and one has to accept that these taxes are here to stay. Admittedly, as taxes go, they are relatively insignificant.

Another tax recently introduced into the United States has been levied to help pay for the cost of customs officials and immigration officials at US airports. This tax is normally added to the price of an airline ticket.

Road tax

A new and more ominous tax has recently been introduced in Switzerland where foreign motorists are required to pay a toll for using Swiss motorways when driving through the country. It is understandable that the Swiss Federal Government should want to defray part of the cost of building these motorways by charging motorists who use them such a fee, particularly if they are driving straight through Switzerland *en route* for another country and spending little, if anything, in Switzerland. Belgium has recently started to consider whether they also should initiate such a tax. Like Switzerland, a lot of traffic passes straight through Belgium from countries such as Holland and West Germany to France and other destinations. Whilst the tax is regrettable, one has to accept that governments can justifiably argue that if a motorist is using a road paid for by taxes by the Swiss tax payer, he should at least help to pay towards that cost.

What is worrying about this road tax is the fact that it can spread so quickly to other countries. Almost as soon as Belgium had announced that they were considering a road tax, the Dutch and West German Governments protested vigorously and said that if Belgium was to introduce such a tax they would give serious thought to it themselves.

The only reason for doing this is to try and persuade the Belgian Government to drop such a tax. This is, in a sense, a form of blackmail by saying that if you introduce this tax, we will do the same. This is the most worrying thing about the spread of tourist taxes. Governments think up new ideas and if the newly levied tax proves a useful revenue earner, other governments leap on to the same bandwagon.

Visa charge

In spite of improvements in facilitation for tourist movement throughout the world, many countries still require visas before a tourist can enter that country. The United States, for example, requires visas from all countries except Canada and Mexico, although, recently, there has been a proposal in Congress to abolish visas from eight countries as an experiment. (US Embassies do not charge for issuing visas so that although they are an irritant, they are unlikely to deter prospective travelers.)

In 1986, following a spate of bomb outrages in Paris, the French Government introduced visa requirements for all countries in the world with the exception of other EC countries and Switzerland. At the same time, a charge was levied of approximately £6 for issuing the visa. This new law has resulted in much criticism, particularly from Scandinavian countries who feel that they are being unjustly discriminated against. Evidence suggests that it has deterred many Scandinavians from visiting France, so this form of taxation on the tourist is resulting in lost business.

The same appears to be the case with travelers from the United States to France. The indications are that in 1987 traffic growth is not as large as to other European countries such as the United Kingdom.

Assessment

No doubt governments will try to think of schemes in the years ahead for taxing the tourist even more. If there should be a severe recession in world tourism in the years ahead, one could justifiably argue that such taxes should at least be reduced, if not abolished. However, whilst tourism continues to flourish and grow governments are able to argue that they are not in any way inhibiting its growth by levying additional taxes.

Nonetheless, it is important that a close watch is kept on the spread of international tourist taxes. There are two inter-governmental tourist organizations well placed for doing this. One is the World Tourism Organization (WTO) which has its headquarters in Madrid. The majority of world countries are members of this Organization and there are therefore opportunities at its meetings for the subject to be discussed and a view taken as to whether such taxes should be discouraged.

The other organization is the OECD whose Tourism Committee meets twice a year. That Committee has, for some time, been discussing the impact of tourist taxes and has often spoken out strongly against them, but any decision or recommendation by the Committee cannot in any way be binding upon governments. It can only point out the dangers inherent in taxing international tourism.

Conclusion

There seems to be little doubt that tourist taxes will continue to spread with the growth in tourist spending. International bodies can and, one hopes will, object but government treasuries will always continue to look for additional ways of raising revenue.

Whether the spread of such taxes will become so onerous that it discourages tourist flows remains to be seen. Even more importantly, if it does, will governments be prepared to reduce such taxes to discourage a further decline in traffic? It would be a very useful academic exercise if someone could estimate at what point additional tourist taxes are likely to lead to a slow-down, if not a downturn, in tourist spending.

The most likely downturn in tourist spending in the years ahead will almost certainly occur from extraneous factors such as terrorism or a sharp increase in the price of oil. The worrying thing is then that governments will find that the yield from tourist taxes fall significantly as overall spending falls. No government likes to find itself running short of revenue. It is hoped that in such a situation, governments would not fall back on raising the rate of the tourist tax to make up the lost yield. If they were to do so then it could lead to a serious downturn if tourists vote with their feet and stop traveling. The chances of this are admittedly remote, but it is a possibility that should never be overlooked.

CHARLES D. BARNARD

Technological change and competitive marketing strategies

Introduction

Technology is one of the key influences on the competitive process in the travel industry. Technological change directly affects price competition through achieving cost savings; for example, the communications costs between, on the one hand, principals and, on the other, travel agencies. At the same time, information technology enables an increased volume of transactions to be handled rapidly and effectively. Forms of nonprice competition are also affected by the adoption of new technologies. Travel offerings can be differentiated from one another in terms of their presentation, such as, the use of videos to advertise holidays and in terms of their distribution and, here, the development of electronic direct sell is one variant. Indeed, the introduction of information technologies by travel organizations is having dramatic impacts on the structure of the industry. This process is changing the way business is conducted; one example is the use of public access ticket machines for airflight bookings (Bruce 1983; 1987). Currently, there is a race to introduce new technology and to develop value-added applications, such as, direct debit facilities for travel agencies. The 'shapers' of technological change are keen to reap the benefits of such activities before others follow. As the industry is characterized by intense rivalries, an expanding market but low profit margins, it is clear that companies operating in the travel industry cannot strategically afford to neglect the opportunities and threats posed by new technologies. This is particularly true for those companies aiming to not only establish but to retain a competitive advantage.

The theme of this chapter is to reflect on the introduction of information technology by travel organizations and in so doing to examine how technical change relates to the competitive nature of the industry. This will allow an exploration of some of the links between technology and the development of competitive marketing strategies within the travel industry.

Technology and the competitive process

The competitive process in any industry is obviously complex and determined by many contingent factors. Michael Porter (1980) has outlined some of these, including the power of buyers and the potential threat of new entrants. In the travel industry, the threat of new entrants may occur as new technologically created opportunities appear. It may be that developments in communications technologies affect the movement of poeple as poeple chose to use the new media rather than moving themselves to communicate over long distances. Consequently, the volume of travelers may fall and instead business people could begin to hold teleconferences and potential holiday travelers may take 'instant trips' with audiovisual media. If travel companies fail to exploit such potentially novel market opportunities, then other companies presently located outside the industry may well do so. This situation would alter the relationships defining the competitive nature of those currently providing travel offerings.

Some commentators perceive of competitiveness as a 'race' with 'winners and losers' (Georghiou *et al.*, 1986). Moreover, they regard technological change as a major ingredient determining the 'rules of the competitive game'. Georghiou *et al.* claim that: 'industrial competitiveness depends on a process in which new products and processes are continually introduced, improved and replaced'.

From this perspective, competitive strategies have to take account of technological changes and the market opportunities they may present in the shorter and in the longer term. In other words, a competitive marketing strategy has to have the capacity to identify 'leading' technologies, spot value added applications and be flexible to implement and respond to technological changes. In other words, strategy making may not be the rational process it is so often portrayed and it may not be so climactic either (that is, a big, one-off decision). Rather it is incremental, more of an ongoing and open-ended process. The question arises: what marketing strategies are feasible for companies operating in a constantly changing technological environment?

Examples

Generic marketing strategies

Porter (1980) outlines three main types of 'generic marketing strategies' which, he argues, can lead to a sustainable competitive position. These are 'price' or 'cost leadership', 'focus' and 'differentiation'. For Porter, a competitive strategy based on cost leadership indicates that the supplier is driven by the need to reduce costs and to compete on the basis of low cost. This strategy of price-cutting and low costs is almost a precondition for all companies in the travel business.

A focus strategy, on the other hand, refers to the identification of an exclusive market niche wherein the customer base demands specialist goods, for example, longer-stay holidays for the elderly. The suppliers' offerings are directed to the provision of attributes which satisfy the exclusive tastes and requirements of the customers in the specialist market niche. For differentiation, effort is given to producing offerings with attributes which separate out one supplier's offerings from those of its competitors, for example, adding value to a communications network by introducing new facilities like direct debiting to agencies.

Porter maintains that the three strategies of cost leadership, focus and differentiation are mutually exclusive. A company can base its strategy on one or the other of these approaches but if it combines them, then it is in danger of becoming 'stuck in the middle' and ultimately it will fail to compete effectively. However, there have been criticisms of Porter's notion that the three competitive strategies of cost leadership, focus and differentiation are mutually exclusive. Notably, Hall (1980) found in his survey of 64 US companies that a combination of strategies was crucial to success, for example, cost leadership plus focused branding or cost leadership with differentiated offerings. This is apparently often the case in the travel industry where the market leaders in the tours operators' segment clearly blend .together different approaches, such as cost leadership with focus and/or differentiation.

How do such concepts of competitive marketing strategy apply, if at all, to the shaping of the competitive process in the travel industry, with the advent of technological change? Some of the changes occurring with the adoption of interactive videotex are revealing from this point of view.

Facing technological change

Perhaps the most recent and widespread adoption of information technology in the travel industry has been that of interactive videotex. This technology has enabled the computerization of the communications between principals and agencies and has radically affected the distribution process of travel offerings. The rate of take-up of this technology is quite phenomenal. Within 5 years of its introduction to the industry, late in 1979, about 90 per cent of British agents used videotex systems for, at least, checking latest availability, up-to-date prices and to obtain general travel information, such as exchange rates. Over 85 per cent of all package bookings are now made through videotex. Videotex technology has become an integral facet of the distribution infrastructure of the travel industry and there are various videotex networks in operation. As well as British Telecom's Prestel travel services private systems have been designed and are managed by principals and carriers. The 'TOPS' system of Thomson Holidays is famous.

Benefits

Why was interactive videotex so quickly implemented by all sectors of the travel trade? Before interactive videotex was adopted, the main communications between the principals and agencies about the range of travel offerings, their availability and price was via telephone, mail and telex. Booking and confirmation procedures were time consuming with possible loss of custom and travel companies were unable to realize the full value of their products and services; for example, airseats were not filled and so flights went with empty seats. The technology offered great benefits for upgrading the communications between those providing travel offerings (the principals) and those distributing (the agencies) these to the end-user, the customer. Computerization allowed the immediate distribution of information about availability in airline seats and hotel accommodation and for the electronic confirmation of reservations. It became easier to make car-hire bookings and so on.

The early adoptors of interactive videotex, both principals and agents, were able to gain a competitive advantage by cheapening the cost of communications between principals and agents by improving the speed of turnover of their transactions which added substantial value to the business. Cost reductions were possible through the decrease in mail and of written communication, via shedding of labor in the reservations and enquiry departments of the principals (Bruce, 1983). The effects on customer service were important in that agencies with trained staff using videotex databases could give up-to-date information about availability and prices of travel offerings to customers which resulted in increased custom and revenue for those agencies possessing electronic information systems.

The principals introducing interactive videotex had various levels of commitment to the technology. One approach to technological/competitive strategy was taken by Thomson Holidays now regarded as a technological leader in the industry. From the start, this company was keen to exploit the potential of videotex technology and designed and developed its own network, TOPS. The competitive advantage conferred by this approach was that access to TOPS was restricted only to those agencies trained to use the system. This ensured that Thomson's travel information was easily selected by the agencies' staff selling its travel offerings. The system was designed to provide security about the offerings so that competitors could not obtain commercially sensitive data about, for example, the firm's load factors. In December 1986, the company took the step of making reservations for its package holiday possible by videotex only. During 1987, the company doubled its business, increased its market share by 10 per cent and kept its average prices at the 1986 level. The Deputy Marketing Manager, Colin Palmer, attributes much of this business success and ability to gain and retain on competitive advantage to effective implementation of technological change. He writes:

> This has allowed us to shake up the market with dramatic pricing moves in the sure knowledge that we had the systems in place to soak up the extra demand! The ability to handle bookings on a massive scale and to cope with the huge surges in demand that are a feature of the package holiday business has been an important factor in keeping Thomson in front of every other UK tour operator year after year.

The success of this tour operator in exploiting the potential offered by technology has not been shared by others. One of its main competitors introduced a videotex system about the same time as Thomson Holidays but because of its inability to connect the technology's potential with its business objectives, the company lost support from agencies who preferred to use TOPS to alternative systems. This tour operator has, in the last two years, redesigned and implemented its own version of a videotex network which is similar in many respects to that of TOPS. The company would not be able to compete in terms of price without having undergone this technological change. However, the facilities offered by the principals to the agents differentiate the system from that of its competitors. The main differentiating features focus on 'human factors' features so that agency staff can quickly locate the tours requested by the customer and also find alternatives if the first choice is unavailable.

For the agencies, the adoption of videotex meant quite fundamental changes to the working practices and layout of their offices. Some of these as they affect employee attitudes to job motivation are described in the chapter on *Effects of New Technology on the Job Motivation and Job Design of Travel Agent Employees*, p. 123. In terms of the competitive performance of agencies, the technology has had an effect on cost-effectiveness, particularly because a larger volume of transactions can be handled without additional cost and the technology simplified and reduced the time taken for booking, confirmation and the checking of availability and latest prices.

The business advantages offered by interactive videotex encouraged its rapid and widespread adoption. It has now become one of the travel trade's main standards and it is not possible to compete without some sort of videotex system. This technological change has opened up the doors for further automation. The direction of technological change to secure a competitive position is twofold: first, a continuation of the process of identifying and implementing value-added applications to the existing network, for example, debit facilities for agencies so that agents will become locked into or use the system of one tour operator rather than another and, second, a continual survey and review of new technologies to pursue marketing opportunities arising from these.

Value-added applications

Value-added applications can be made by introducing improvements to existing systems, particularly to enhance the ease and comfort and speed of operation. Indeed, there are problems with the existing technology installed in agencies. These can be rectified and in so doing may lead to an improved customer service. Various problems are mentioned below. It can take agency staff a day to enter or 'log-on' to the databases of the principals and carriers in order to check availability and to make bookings. This can lead to the build up of bottlenecks, loss of custom and empty seats. This can be extremely time-consuming and frustrating for both agency staff and customers. Automatic dial-up procedures to search the computerized reservation systems of the principals and carriers is required for agents. The installation of ticketing for retailers would help process late bookings. The provision of print-outs for customers to take away with them can alleviate any misunderstand-

ings and provide reassurance for the customer. Having two terminals on agency desks so that the customer can see the screen at the same time as the clerk is making the booking would help. Not all problems are created by technology. A 'technicist' focus can mean that human problems are not dealt with which are crucial in affecting consumer purchase behavior. Creating an atmosphere which makes the purchase of travel offerings pleasurable is one facet of this – a relaxed ambience in the agencies where the client can survey printed material and videos about travel offerings and where the entire needs of the holidaymaker are provided, such as selling of suntan lotion and sunglasses. Further, new technology could help agencies' marketing ventures. Microcomputers and word processors could be used to adminster surveys to establish customer demands and to advertise particular travel products.

The next steps

The drive to gain and sustain a competitive advantage affects the behavior of the major players in the travel industry as they realize the contribution that technological change can make to competitiveness. Consequently, the major players are on the alert to identify and experiment with new technologies. What are some of the future trends likely to impinge the travel world? Cable and satellite communications will become increasingly prevalent. Principals and agents could exploit these technologies to directly book hotel rooms with hoteliers located in Spain, Greece or wherever.

Public-access ticketing will become more commonplace for air and train bookings and will extend to eventually encompass other travel offerings. As with retailers in other service areas this trend to 'self-service' will grow, although the travel consumer has to be confident the information is comprehensive, accurate and reliable and that liability is guaranteed if something goes wrong.

Another trend is the use of videotex/videodiscs in agencies. The customer will be able to watch videos of holiday destinations and simultaneously acquire information about availability and price.

A significant advancement is that denoted by 'fifth generation' software, for example, expert systems (Feigenbaum and McCorduck, 1984). This type of software is intended for decision-support functions and potentially has various uses for the travel industry, although these are for the longer term. The customer may be able to specify certain parameters defining travel requirements, such as, date of travel, length of stay, price etc., and the system would generate a range of alternatives for the customer to select. The applications currently are much more mundane and are for fairly structured areas of decision-support like route planning, scheduling and data processing than in the areas of decision making and replacement of experts.

Assessment and conclusion

Technology is an essential component in the competitive performance of companies and serves to change the 'rules of the competitive game' of industries. It affects the balance of power of the relationships governing the structure of an industry. In this chapter, various types of competitive strategies have been delineated, following Porter, and discussed in relation to the travel industry. The example of the adoption of interactive videotext was drawn upon to show how effective exploitation of technology, along with a clearly defined set of objectives, determined the sustainable advantage of those creating technological opportunities and also altered the types of competition structuring the travel industry, for example, price competition. Technological change also enabled other forms of competitive advantage like differentiation, to be combined effectively with price competition.

The rate of adoption of technological change in the travel trade is related to the competitive strategies of the travel companies. Companies that have successfully taken up and used technology in the past will be more likely to continue to do so and to make the introduction of new technology an integral part of their corporate strategy. Such 'shapers' of technological change often set up procedures (for example, think-tanks consisting of people from different departments in their own company and with representatives from equipment suppliers and so on) to search for developments in technology, assess these and relate them to their own position in the travel industry. The harnessing of technology can affect the competitive 'rules of the game', as interactive videotex has done, for the travel industry with some companies gaining a sustainable competitive advantage over time through their ability to exploit the technology.

It is likely that the quantity of information technology employed in the industry will increase and the main industrial players are on the alert to identify the 'leading-edge' contenders. The main cost savings are in the communications link between principals and agencies for the distribution of products and services. Here, principals can differentiate themselves in terms of the value-added applications they provide for agents on their videotex networks, such as direct debiting. Eventually the adoption of fifth generation technologies could well improve the quality and speed of customer's purchasing behavior and decision making. This is a whole new area for possible automation. In the meantime, such technology will be adopted to improve the scheduling and route planning activities of principals. Focusing on technological change can mean a neglect of a 'customer orientation'. A balance has to be made between the improvements technology can bring and other changes, such as a greater investment in marketing. Effort at the retail end of the industry to make the selling experience more professional and

pleasurable, the introduction of marketing ideas, such as market segmentation and catering for the entire needs of the travel consumer, would provide commercial benefits.

Already trends are discernible in this direction with the revamping of high-street retail outlets. Maybe there will be a move towards a greater specialization within the industry with some companies focusing on particular market segments and providing products for these. A new type of agency may emerge which moves away from the high-street booking shop to more of a travel consultancy providing individualized travel packages made up of a 'mix and match' of available travel offerings. Sophisticated information systems could be used to achieve the optimum travel package.

Technological change is not 'out of control' but is closely integrated to business goals and objectives. Addressing technological futures and developing plans in accordance with competitive marketing strategies is the way forward for those operating in the tourism industry.

Software/databases

Talisman, Travel Agency Computer System from Data Management Group, London (01-888-6779).

Travelpack, Management and Accounting System for Travel Agents from Independent Computer Co. Ltd, Altrincham, UK; (061-941-6065).

Further reading

Bruce, M., 'Information technology: changes in the travel trade', *Tourism Management* (December 1983), pp. 290-5.

Bruce, M., 'New technology and the future of tourism', *Tourism Management* (June 1987), pp. 115-20.

Feigenbaum, E. and McCorduck, P., *The Fifth Generation: Artificial Intelligence and Japan's Challenge to the World* (Pan Books, 1984).

Georgiou, L., Metcalfe, J. S., Gibbons, M., *et al*, *Post Innovation Performance: Technological Development and Competition* (MacMillan, 1986).

Hall, W., 'Survival strategies in a hostile environment', *Harvard Business Review* (September–October 1980), pp. 75–85.

Porter, M., *Competitive Strategy* (Free Press, 1980).

MARGARET BRUCE

Theme and leisure parks

Introduction

The concept of the recreation park is fairly old. In Europe, the birth of this concept was seen during the eighteenth century, when large royal parks (Versailles, near Paris or the Prater, in Vienna) started to be equipped with either short-lived or permanent attractions. Other roots include the popular fair, whose modern aspect, the fun fair, is directly in competition with the theme parks.

During the nineteenth century, the United Kingdom saw its seaside resorts being gradually equipped with attractions on the piers. It was in the United States, however, that the first series of parks with popular attractions developed in urban outskirts. Prototypes located around New York were Coney Island (1887) or Steeplechase Park (1897, still in operation), and the number of parks was approximately 1,500 in 1920, including the famous Luna-Park (1904), which was the first theme park. The lack of renewal of the product – classical merry-go-rounds – during the 1930s economic crisis was the cause of the decline of most of these centers.

A new breath came with Disneyland in Los Angeles in 1955. The 17 attractions, endowed with the emblems of Walt Disney's characters, created an immediate and durable success, with returns two to three times over the most optimistic estimates. Thirty years later, Disneyland has 57 attractions and around 10 million visitors annually. The park initiated the establishment of nearly 400 restaurants and 12,000 rooms in 130 hotels. Here is the first main application of the theme park principle: to motivate visitors (especially families) during one day or more. To do this it is necessary to make them dream ('I want the public to feel they're in another world' *Walt Disney*). The subconscious and the imagination of people is caught through the variation of one theme in a series of subthemes and the multiplicity of sideshows whose scenic arrangement is organized in minute detail.

Today, there are almost 2,000 leisure parks in the United States, of which two are mega-parks (Disneyland and Disney World in Florida) and 38 are large regional parks (e.g. the Six Flags programs, Cedar Point, and Seaworld). In Europe there are at least 20 large parks already in existence or still being developed: Phantasialand, near Köln (West Germany), De Efteling (Netherlands), Walibi, near Brussels (Belgium), the Jardin d'Acclimatation, Mirapolis and Disney in Paris (France)

etc. The recreations park format is not exclusive – animal parks, sports/leisure parks, aquatic parks, floral parks and open-air museums also can be included as leisure parks. A general definition of the leisure parks could be: a site, uniting in a single enclosure, a series of attractions and activities and completed with a number of important side services such as cafeterias, restaurants, shops and lodgings.

Such attractions contribute to tourism development. The leisure parks are able to increase tourist spending locally by generating specific flows or by extending the length of the visitors' stay. It is very important, however, to ensure a basis of local customers in considering the location of a park. It must benefit the urban region or the existing tourist destination.

The scale of influence determines the portion of activity devoted to the local community and to domestic or international tourism. Most of the parks share the following characteristics:

1. The presence of huge parking lots (0.5 to 1.0 hectare of parking space for 1.0 hectare of attraction) in relation to the proportion of bus travelers and families.
2. Areas between 20 and 50 hectares devoted to the attractions alone.

If we consider the investments and the attendance, however, the similarities end:

1. Exceptionnal programs with an international influence, like the Disney mega-parks have an annual attendance which may be over 10 million (23 million in 1983 for Disneyworld-Epcot, Florida, with a turnover of more than US$600 million); these programs need 10,000–20,000 permanent salaried personnel and now require initial investments more than the $1.5 billion which the complex of Disney World–Epcot cost.
2. Programs of regional interest (in the United States) or national interest (in Europe) correspond to an annual attendance of 1–4 million; 100 to 300 permanent salaried personnel are needed, to which are added 300 to 700 temporary personnel at certain periods; these programs require an initial investment of $50 to 100 million, for a turnover worth $15 to $50 million.
3. Programs of local interest (or regional in Europe), correspond to an annual frequenting of approximately 100,000–500,000 people; they employ 50 to 100 salaried personnel

and require an initial investment of $5 to $15 million, for a turnover worth $2 to $5 million.

Marketing and management

In the case of the construction of a large park, the governments are concerned about the following:

1. The entertainment for and image of the city or the region.
2. The economic returns and job creation.
3. The need for new or reinforced public infrastructure.
4. The impact on the landscape.

It is now easy to understand that in certain countries or for certain programs there is a question of choice to be made between a public utility service management, and a profit-oriented company management, or an intermediary system.

Considering a public utility service management, the decision to minimize the costs in order to deliver a defined social benefit is possible only if a clear definition of the objectives is set. The traditional inclination of the public service management to create a free or semi-free access is not without danger in a business whose costs are far from being insignificant. They include: the investments for renewal of the attractions; the maintenance costs; the costs of reception and monitoring in order to avoid disorder and pillaging. Therefore, even an entirely publicly-funded enterprise will need to set up, a certain number of private businesses which pay a rental fee or a fraction of the maintenance costs, and contribute through their effective presence to the activity, the reception and the security.

The path is then set toward a management working on two levels:

1. Overall management, which may be public or private, responsible for the basic equipment and the common shared spaces, the park's marketing, the general pricing, the general activity and surveillance etc.
2. Distributed management, in which each activity or service is run by legally independent entities, usually small private companies.

A thorough study of the potential clientele and of its conditions of mobilization is necessary to the success of a leisure park. Added to a precise definition of the side services, the study must define three major factors:

1. The open season, which should be as long as possible to justify a heavy investment.
2. The maximum possible attendance during the peak vacation season, so that space and activities can be organized accordingly.
3. Pricing thresholds.

Marketing techniques vary from product to product and according to the segments of clientele:

1. The approach to the tourist clientele, especially from abroad relates to the general scheme of tourism marketing; in this field, the marketing is set through tour-operators and packages including lodging.
2. The regional clientele requires a different approach, relying

upon the density and the characteristics of a population living in a given area; one must specify that approximately 80 per cent of the clientele visiting a regional park live within a 2-hour car drive of the site; here the marketing is based on the direct motivation of families, the contact with bus tourists and the mobilization of groups such as schools, companies' welfare activities, youth organizations etc.
3. The parks specializing in sports are aimed mostly at local clientele but require specific precautions such as:
   (a) an analysis of the demand for the various types of activities;
   (b) an adequate definition of the standard of the activities offered;
   (c) a correct account of the role played by sports' associations in the enrolement of the participants and in the operation of the equipment.

A park's popularization also relies upon the organization of large entertainments in order to get a large editorial impact in the media (sports parks), as well as strong and repeated advertising campaigns which may absorb as much as 10 per cent of the returns of a theme park.

For reasons of equity and management efficiency, the pricing is almost always divided into entrance fees and additional charges for certain services, attractions or activities. In a theme park, the entrance ticket usually opens a right to all of the attractions, but the shops, the drinks and restaurants, which represent 30 to 40 per cent of the total returns, are managed separately. It is interesting to set up systems which encourage attendance during the less popular periods or days, such as groups pricings or, for sports parks, season tickets. The overall pricing strategy must tend to ensure a profitability rate in the short and long term of the capital invested in a private profit-oriented perspective, but the strategy might also limit itself to ensuring all or merely a portion of the maintenance costs, in the case of public investments.

Implementation

Programming

The key problem of programming lies in assembling around a few leading elements, a mix varied enough to be attractive, and coherent enough to promote a strong image of the park.

The supporting services will include, at least, cafes and bars, and restaurants and shops adapted to the volume and characteristics of the clientele. Integrated lodgings (also adapted) may be required in several cases, e.g. for international attendance, top level sportspersons, residential workshops etc.

Costs

The very essence of the parks (ground surface and the need for a quality image) implies that two items require specific attention. They are, on the one hand, the basic equipment (parking, roads, watering systems...) and on the other hand, the landscape architecture (land movements, plantings, ornamental lakes...). Grouped together, these two items make for approximately 20 to 30 per cent of the initial investment.

Another crucial item is related to the attractions and involves a series of techniques emanating from film and television studios: staging, animated scenarios, electronic regulations and commands etc.

Financing

The basic equipment pays off over a very long period, but the attractions are perishable products, characterized by a very rapid ageing. The need to hold the public's attention through new attractions requires the provision of an annual renewal investment, worth between 5 and 10 per cent of the initial investment.

A constant problem lies in the division of the investment between public and private. As a minimum, the public investment should concern the services – access roads and drainage, for example. Yet, in a number of cases (local parks, sports' facilities etc.), one may assume that a large part of the initial financing came from public funds.

Architectural and landscape design

The general space design must consider two important points:

1. The waiting time at the entrance gate, at the various attractions and at the restaurants. Measured for a standard day during the high season, these waiting times must stay within bearable limits while emphasizing the crowd effect, because the entertainment comes from the park *and* the crowd.
2. The need for land reserves, within or next to the park, which will provide for new and enriched attractions, in the medium and long term.

Concerning the architectural and landscape design, the dominance of amusement and playing themes tends to exclude anything resembling suburban architecture. Two methods exist which classically help solve the difficulty: dream architecture with exuberant artefacts, particularly for theme parks; a sober design which is in keeping with the regional traditions, which recalls a fashionable countryside and tries to endow large equipment with a warm and attractive appearance.

Assessment

A park development raises, from the first sketches, a certain number of specific questions which continue to be pertinent to further management. Which type(s) of attractions or activities, what scale of influence is planned? How does the park fit into regional development? What should be the proportion of regional and tourist clientele? What are the characteristics of various segments of the potential clientele, in terms of leisure? Considering the tendencies of the concurrence, what share of the market is to be expected?

Once the product and the clientele targets are determined, the park must be built and operated. Are the attractions, the activities and the services mutually reinforcing to form a coherent mix? Are the physical programming and the cost estimates precise and reliable? How much flexibility of the product has

been maintained in the medium and long term? Are the private and public responsibilities clearly defined, and have the various financing sources been combined in an optimal way? Considering the park operation, how are the various managements articulated? Is the park's management able to ensure both the technical maintenance and the answers to the evolution of the demand? Are the number and quality of the personnel adapted to the objectives? What is done to develop flexibility, initiative and the sense of hospitality? In terms of its principles and value thresholds, does the pricing correspond to marketing objectives and expected recovery rates? How and through what means will the park's image be marketed? What are the future plans to develop the activity beside the natural peaks of the demand?

Conclusion

The best parks aren't necessarily those whose access is expensive, nor those free or practically free. The successful programs are those which satisfy the following criteria:

1. Add to the quality of life in an area.
2. Increase the prestige and attractiveness of a tourist destination.
3. Use, largely or totally, self-funding for investment.
4. Create revenue and jobs.

Such programs reveal a know-how which may be valued in different ways (e.g. consultation by others or creation of a chain of parks).

At the cross-point of dreams in practices and techniques, the theme and leisure parks probably make up a product of the future. Following a period of intensive construction, it is now time to imagine that a period of selection through competition will occur. It is often assumed that a part of the initial investment could be paid by public funds, for example through a partial or total payment of the land acquisition costs; however, the reliance on the taxpayer should not become a management principle. In the absence of private funds, there is a risk of having to manage a distribution of scarcity, the consequences of which would rapidly become apparent in the quality of the product. The management should therefore sponsor a flexible and objective study of the market in order to define and establish products ensuring good return rates.

An arrangement associating an organization (public or not), owner of the basic equipment, and one or more operators, leaseholders, may prove to be pertinent. A setting of this type allows for diversification of the initiatives, while still maintaining control over the whole program.

Finally, another major condition of success is the assembly of competent and motivated operating and managing personnel.

Focus on small business

Large leisure parks contribute to the creation or development of a quantity of small businesses, 1. by requiring all sorts of tradesmen for operation and maintenance, and 2. by creating the opportunity of setting, within the park or nearby, a series of small service businesses in the field of tourism and leisure.

Moreover, it must be emphasized that due to a limited surface area, to the nature of the activities (e.g. aqualands), or to the scarcity of attractions, a great number of parks are small businesses themselves, in terms of their turnover and the number of employees. These businesses may focus on a local clientele or complete the range of attractions of a tourist resort. Their relatively modest size is not a reason to dispense with the need for strict management and marketing adapted to the situation.

Further reading

Bovaird, A. G., Tricker, M. J. and Stoakes, R., *Recreation, Management and Pricing* (Gower, 1984). The authors address the wide variety of countryside recreation facilities (leisure parks only indirectly, giving relevant observations about pricing techniques (Chapters 1 and 8)).

Coltier, T., 'Les parcs à thème', *Espaces*, no. 73 (April 1985), pp. 18–21; no. 74 (June 1985), pp. 24–7; no. 76 (October 1985), pp. 11–13. Extracts from a doctorate thesis, the three articles present a history of theme parks, an analysis of their content and an approach to the management problems.

Coronio, G. and Muret, J. P., *Loisirs, Guide Pratique des Equipements* (Centre de Recherche d'Urbanisme, 1978). With a great number of concrete examples concerning costs, attendances and usual management principles, this book is still the best introduction, in French, to the knowledge and conception of leisure equipment.

Farrel, P. and Lundegren, H. M., *The Process of Recreation Programming: Theory and Technique* (John Wiley, 1978). After an analysis of the groupings of activities, the authors focus the conclusion on a range of areas to be evaluated, such as leadership, program philosophy and goals and physical planning processes.

Heskett, J. L., *Managing in the Service Economy* (Harvard Business School Press, 1986). Even though the author never directly discusses parks, the management principles and concepts discussed in Chapters 1, 2, 3 and 4, must be considered as perfectly relevant (targeting the market segment, clearly defining the product etc.).

Kraus, R. G. and Curtis, J. E., *Creative Administration in Recreation and Parks* (Mosby Co., 1973). The book deals with the physical, sociological, methodological and administrative conditions for developing programs.

Patin, V. and Bauer, F., *Les Parcs Recréatifs en France* (DATAR, 1986). Through a series of variables such as the initial investment, pricing and attendances, the study conducts a comparative analysis of the major parks, not only in France but also in Europe and North America. Also present is an analysis of the demand for types of product.

Rougerie, J., Ruob, J. M., Van Yan, T. *et al.*, 'A thème ou Aquatiques', *Paysage Actualité*, no. 91 (October 1986), pp. 32–65. A series of case studies concerning parks, still as projects or under construction, in France.

Zehnder, L. E., 'The costs and benefits of tourism – an analysis of Florida's Disney World', Congrès de l'AIEST 1982 (*Publications de L'AIEST*, 1982), pp. 81–95. A case study of the most visited park in the world: initial investment and the first 10 years of operation.

JEAN-CLAUDE CORZÉ

Tour management

Introduction

Although tour operation and tour management may appear to the lay person to be similar, they describe two very different activities. A tour operator is an organization (or individual) which identifies and develops inclusive tours, which are then offered for sale. A tour manager, by contrast, is someone who plans for and accompanies a group of tourists on a tour (or a part of a tour), checking arrangements and handling any problems which arise. Some tour operators will include the services of a tour manager in their inclusive tour, but many do not. Occasionally, a tour manager may plan and sell his own tours, and accompany the group on tour. These are likely to be specialist tours, covering an aspect of history, architecture or sport. However, most tour managers are *not* involved in this aspect. Accordingly, this chapter will examine the role of tour managers in accompanying tours.

In the early days of overseas travel, rich people employed couriers and guides to help them with their journeys, dealing with customs, exchange rates, language problems and even prejudice which was targeted at them. The environment for tourists in Europe was very different in the nineteenth century from current times, and there were even more serious barriers to travelers than there are today. Thomas Cook's tours aimed to provide the services of these couriers to a wider market. He had identified a clear market need – people who wanted to travel, and who did not want to be responsible for all their arrangements. In doing so, he laid the foundation for the modern tour manager's role. Even now, when overseas travel is much more widely enjoyed, many people still want this service.

In recent years, many companies have been changing focus to listening to customers' needs and ensuring that employees treat customers with respect and courtesy. The growing importance of marketing orientation and of customer care programs have both had an impact on tour operators' desires to provide tour managers and develop their role. While skilled tour managers have often been considered essential for luxury and/or touring holidays, they are now being used in a wide range of tour programs.

The tour manager acts as a representative of the tour operator, confirming all reservations and arrangements on the trip, and communicating with head office on these matters. He/she may be involved in establishing the schedule for a tour, or this may be set by the tour operator. The tour manager has to deal with unforeseen problems with facilities or reservations, emergencies arising from illness or accidents to tourists and, more generally, to help the tour group get the most from their trip.

Tour managers may be based in one area or country, or may travel across countries or continents. Some specialize in short trips; others prefer longer tour programs. Tour managers can be employees of a tour operator or freelance (self-employed) tour managers. Some tour managers may hold a fulltime job outside the travel industry, only accompanying tours on an irregular basis. Teachers, the clergy, artists and people with relevant specialist interests or abilities fall into this category.

Tour managers differ from resort representatives. They will only work with one group at a time, and their role is to establish a rapport with this group. Resort representatives are normally responsible for several groups and are less likely to build this personal relationship with an entire group. Tour managers are available to their tour members at all times throughout the tour; resort representatives are likely to have specific and limited consultation times. Some tour managers may also act as guides. Others will offer only general advice and may liaise with official guides in particular towns or areas.

Many of the tasks involved in tour management seem straightforward and uncomplicated. The reality is far different. Passenger lists issued by the tour operator will often vary from those who turn up as part of the tour, and this will mean that all reservations throughout the tour need adjustment. Most tours will have their share of accidents, illness, people mislaying property and/or crime. Some group members may even become separated from the tour. Occasionally, someone may leave or join the group in the middle of the tour. All these factors, and more, will mean constant work for the tour manager.

The abilities and personality of the tour manager may be a critical factor in the success of a tour. Tours which have been beset by problems, whether through illness, transport breakdowns, weather or lack of planning by the tour operator, may be viewed as successful by the group, if their tour manager has been effective and caring.

Examples

An educational tour operator offers study programs for American high school students, including multicenter (or roving) programs. Teachers in the United States recruit and supervise groups of students (normally about ten students per teacher), and there are normally about 50 people (including teachers) in each tour party. This is a very competitive market, and teachers select between the operators on their reputation for quality and reliability.

These tours are relatively low cost, and are fully inclusive of tuition, accommodation, meals, sightseeing and all transport (mainly rail or coach). The tours last for up to 6 weeks, and have full schedules. Each arrangement (for food, accommodation etc.) needs confirmation to ensure that the reservation has been received and is correct, as the consequences of a problem could be substantial. For example, it can be almost impossible in the peak season to find accommodation for about 50 people at short notice. In addition, teachers *must* be in contact with their students, as they are responsible for them, so it is not possible to split the party into different hotels etc. If a coach fails to arrive for a tour, there is no time to reschedule the visit because of the tight program. Further, although the teachers who bring groups are interested in the countries they visit, most do not speak a foreign language. Accordingly, they would not always be capable of solving problems on their own.

These tour managers are chosen for their abilities to cope with problems which might arise, and not as guides. Many of the tour managers are graduates and can assist in the educational aspects of the tour. In addition to dealing with reservations, the tour managers are encouraged to build relationships with the party members, and to be seen as a general adviser to the group. This tour operator prefers young tour managers (up to age 25) because it believes that they can relate better to the students, and that their knowledge and enthusiasm could add to the students' enjoyment of the program.

The cost of using a tour manager on this type of program is justified in the increased reliability of bookings for meals, tours etc., and in the confidence it gives the teachers who recruit the members of the party. Thus even a budget tour operator can benefit from tour management.

Benefits

One of the advantages in buying an inclusive tour is that the tour operator is responsible for making and confirming all arrangements. This product is ideal for the visitor who wants a break from responsibility. However, often the arrangements are not always as reliable as either the tour operator or the tourist would like. This may not be a major problem for a resort based package tour, where flight, accommodation and transfers are the only elements of the inclusive tour. However, for tours which include more elements, confirmation of arrangements is a vital element in the success of the tour. As mentioned earlier, the fact that a tour manager is used can 'add value' to the tour operator's package and position it as a superior tour. This positioning shows the customer that to the company the efficiency and quality of its tour matters. This positioning feature is a fundamental benefit of using tour managers.

Another benefit of using tour managers is that the tour operator can get feedback on the quality of restaurants, hotels, coaches, etc, which are used. If they fail to meet an agreed standard, then alternatives or compensation (for the passengers) may be sought. The tour operator may authorize the tour manager to buy drinks for group members or to plan an evening's entertainment at the company's expense to compensate for poor meals or unfortunate incidents. In this way, the tour manager can turn disgruntled passengers into satisfied ones.

The tour manager can also add to the quality of holiday experience, by offering assistance with many of the tourist's problems. He can explain different currencies and exchange rates and can recommend restaurants, shops, foods, wines, local products, independent excursions etc. A tourist who enjoys any of the experiences recommended by the tour manager will have increased satisfaction with the tour, the tour manager and the tour operator. A knowledgeable tour manager can thus act as a good salesman for the operator, resulting in increasing brand preference and possibly recommending the operator to others. It is often said that the tour manager should be a salesman. However, it is important that he/she should sell the tour operator, and not him/herself. Many tour managers sell themselves in an attempt to get high tips; by selling the company, they should get repeat business, and the tour manager should get continued employment.

In addition to gathering information on satisfactory facilities, the tour manager can gather valuable information on the features of the tour which the holidaymakers find most or least enjoyable. This can help the tour operator in designing and promoting future tours. More astute tour managers can gather a considerable amount of qualitative data about the holidaymaking habits of the group members, their holiday selection process and their brand loyalty to particular operators. In addition, tour managers can obtain the market's reaction to new destinations. Many operators fail to recognize the value of this information.

A further benefit of using tour managers is that the tourists can be advised on the local culture, and its customs and taboos. For example, a tour manager may advise his party on dress, drinking and eating habits which are appropriate to each area. Not only does this advice benefit the tourist, but also it means that the host community are treated respectfully by the party.

Implementation

The decision to use tour managers can reduced the demands on head office staff once the tour is underway, but it must be set up carefully. The tour manager is often the only representative of the company who is likely to be in direct contact with the group, so he/she must be completely reliable and capable of presenting the operator in a good light. Accordingly, it is important for the tour operator to consider the selection and training of tour managers.

Recruitment of tour managers with the appropriate skills and experience is an important step. Tour operators need to determine the required knowledge, experience and skills for their tours. These may include language skills, knowledge of the areas visited on the tour, problem solving skills, social skills and knowledge of first aid. The importance of each of these attributes will vary depending on the type of tour. Some operators place a high priority on previous experience in tour management; others will take on fresh recruits who show sufficient aptitude and enthusiasm. Generally, there will be many applicants for any position in tour management, because it is viewed as a glamorous job. The reality is often far from this, with long hours and little free time during a tour. It is important to check that applicants appreciate the nature of the work which is involved.

Tour managers' salaries vary in quantity and form between companies. Some operators offer tourist managers a salary throughout the year; others pay a salary throughout the season only. Alternatively, an operator may pay a basic salary, expecting the tour manager to boost this through commission from shops, attractions etc., or selling additional tours. This can often result in problems for the tour operator, as the tour manager's need to boost his/her earnings may damage his/her relationship with the group.

All tour managers should be trained in the operator's procedures in itinerary listing, voucher checking and processing etc. Some role playing experience of handling problems, using real case details where possible, can help even the most experienced tour managers develop their skills. Training sessions can also cover new destinations, check-in procedures, customs and visa requirements.

The tour manager has a considerable amount of preparation prior to a tour. The tour itinerary is the starting point for this preparation. A copy of this will be given to all group members, so it is important that it is finalized at least 3 weeks in advance of the trip, to enable them to know contact dates and addresses. Only a few tour managers are responsible for this aspect. In most cases, tour managers are given these itineraries, although their level of detail will vary. The tour manager should examine these itineraries to determine which meals, accommodation and transport arrangements have been made, and with whom. He/she can then undertake the first check on each of these reservations, confirming current group numbers. The tour manager should examine the journey plan, identifying journey routes and lengths (to plan rest, photo and shopping stops), establishing which borders will be crossed and what form the passport and custom controls take at each, and listing the key towns which will be visited or passed *en route*.

Before meeting his group, the tour manager should collect the book of vouchers (to be used in payment of services), obtain any necessary customs forms or visas, and gather a supply of luggage labels, insurance forms, identifying stickers for coachers, posters and badges bearing the tour operator's name and logo. The final thing which should be collected is the current passenger list, detailing names and accommodation and meal requirements of the tour group. This will change until the last minute (and even then might not be accurate), but it is a tour manager's basic tool. Tour managers may arrange a pre-tour meeting for some specialist tours where advance preparation is required.

Once the tour is underway, the tour manager becomes involved with managing the administrative duties (booking, checking and processing vouchers) and managing people (tour members, drivers, guides, hotel and restaurant managers etc). The people management issues will vary, but they may be fundamental to the success of the tour (the author helped avert a local coach driver's strike while working as a tour manager!) or superficially trivial, but central to a tour member's enjoyment (such as obtaining marmalade rather than jam for his breakfast). The longer tours will inevitably result in social pressures between some members of the party. Ensuring that all members are treated equally becomes a very important aspect of the tour manager's role. If one party has an inferior room in one location, then the tour manager should ensure that his room is equal to other group members (or better) in the next location. Some tour managers have complex patterns to move group members one row back or forward on coach trips to ensure such equality!

Tour managers personal skills will often determine their success while on tour. They need to be able to build relationships with group members in a short period of time, to listen to their problems and objectives, yet be able to control the conflicts, anger and stress which will occur during the tour. In addition, it is important that the tour manager can be assertive; like airline cabin staff, he/she must take full responsibility for looking after the safety of group members if any major problem arises. Towards the end of a tour, when the tour manager will be tired because of the long hours involved in the role, this can become more difficult.

Some tours have gaps in the program which allow group members some free time. Tour managers may offer optional programs at these times, which can be organized in one of three ways. First, the tour manager may recommend a tour provided by a local coach operator (or equivalent) which has been approved by head office. He receives no money for booking tourists on this type of trip. Secondly, where the head office has no policy on these trips, he can offer the same types of tours, but claim commission on each participating group member. Thirdly, he can establish his own tours and take the risk (and rewards) associated with their success. There can often be conflict where the tour manager has the potential to earn extra income. His/her desire to earn more money may result in a 'pushy' sales approach, which can upset some group members. Accordingly, some companies forbid these money-earning schemes on particular tours.

Tour managers can also earn commission from shops and tourist attractions. By registering with them, and asking group members to mention his/her name when making payment, he/she can earn a proportion of what the tourists spend. The exact percentage will vary between establishments, but can be quite substantial. Tour managers should be responsible about this type of payment, and not encourage group members to buy goods which are of a poor quality or which they do not want just to obtain commission. Some tour operators will list shops, discotheques, restaurants etc. which they find acceptable, and even encourage their tour mangers to promote these.

The final task of the tour manager is the management of the tour affairs and reporting of these to the operator. Most tour operators will give tour managers a 'float' of travelers' checks to cover all expenses incurred in the normal routine of the tour, and to cover sudden problems (such as requiring taxis if a coach fails to appear, and there is a chance that a train or air connection may be missed). All expenses must be detailed precisely and reports prepared on a daily basis. In addition, the tour manager should note the quality and reliability of the coaches, accommodation, restaurants etc. which are used and report this back on a regular basis. The operator can then ask the provider to improve these services or move his business to an alternative supplier, ensuring that future tours following a similar route should not be faced with the same problems. The tour manager must be conscientious about this reporting, as it is the fundamental form of quality control for the tour operator.

Assessment

There are many different aspects which should be considered when evaluating the use of tour managers. First, you should evaluate the cost of providing tour managers against the benefits which they bring. Secondly, you should assess whether they are enhancing the quality of the tour for its participants. Finally, you need to determine the quality of the tour manager's individual performance.

Evaluating whether the use of tour managers justifies the costs of employing them is clearly a complex task. Any one problem in a tour could result in the tour operator incurring several times the value of a tour manager's salary and expenses. However, some operators have chosen to reduce the likelihood of problems through vertical integration policies, acquiring coach operators and hotels. By establishing their own quality standards in these operations, there should be fewer problems with arrangements. Other operators have combined many of the duties of a tour manager into the coach driver's role. Some operators view this as a cost saving; others view it as a potentially dangerous practice, because of the long hours involved in undertaking a tour manager's responsibilities fully. In practice, it is not practicable for a driver to undertake all the duties of a tour manager. This inevitably has an effect on the group's perception of his performance.

The tour manager's role in enhancing a tour is a vital one. Indeed, it is claimed that the difference between a resort representative or transfer courier and a tour manager lies in their ability to increase the enjoyment or pleasure experienced by their group. Building a relationship with the customers can help the tour manager to identify their interests. This means that any tour can be customized around the needs, and that often two tours on the same route will not be entirely identical. Questionnaires at the end of the trip to assess satisfaction is one way of measuring the quality of the relationship with a group. Questions should be worded to identify whether the tour manager has added to their enjoyment of the tour.

The quality of the tour manager's performance is one area which should be specifically addressed in this end-of-tour questionnaire. The tour manager is the operator's representative, and if he is considered lacking, then the company's tour will also be considered lacking. Usually, there is little direct supervision of the tour manager on the tour, so it is important to obtain honest opinions about whether he/she has fulfilled his/her role effectively. Questions should address personality, availability, whether he/she showed interest in the tour and its party, knowledge of the areas visited or favoritism of any group members. The tour manager can encourage party members to complete the questionnaire and return it to him before departure. Some companies pay a bonus to tour managers which is based on the percentage of questionnaires returned and the percentage with good ratings. These questionnaires should be sealed by the party members to conceal any personal comments. Some tour managers will try to read comments and destroy questionnaires which report unfavorably on them. Accordingly some companies will send out reminder questionnaires if the original response rate is particularly low.

The questionnaire at the end of a tour does not measure the ability of a tour manager to reduce or solve problems. A good tour manager should only tell his group of any problems when it requires a change in plans or when they are kept waiting because of an obvious problem or delay. Company reports should be designed to identify the situations when the tour manager has averted a problem. In addition to providing an evaluation of the tour manager's abilities, it highlights problems which other tour managers may face or which should be considered when developing future programs. The tour operator should also check the honesty and completeness of the tour manager's expenses reports.

Conclusion

Some inclusive tours are accompanied by a tour manager, whose role is to assist tour members in obtaining the maximum benefit and enjoyment from their trip and also act as the representative of the tour operator with the tour group. Achieving these aims involves a wide variety of duties and usually means very long hours of work. In addition to handling administrative aspects of the tour, the tour manager is also involved in managing relationships with tour members and suppliers, and also between group members. Accordingly, a skilled tour manager will not only be well-organized, but also have good social skills.

Use of tour managers is not restricted to specialist or up-market operators. Other companies, such as those specializing in the 'over-sixties' or youth markets, may also use them, because of the specific needs of these markets. The costs of using a tour manager need not be high. They can result in cost savings in administrative time at head office, as well as increasing brand loyalty (and through this, reducing future promotional costs).

The tour manager is often the only member of the tour operator's staff who will meet tourists directly. It is important that the tour operator is aware of this and selects and trains tour managers with care, and monitors their performance on tours. Tour managers should also report on the quality aspects of the tour, and on market characteristics and behavior. This information can be useful in planning future programs.

Focus on small business

Tour management is appropriate to any size of business, but small businesses may particularly value personal service, and thus place a high priority on the use of tour managers. The information which tour managers can collect as part of their duties is especially important for a small business, as it is unlikely that they can justify the staff costs involved in establishing quality control checks on their suppliers, nor on gathering qualitative information from their market.

Some tour managers build their own tours, and develop their own businesses around them. These are normally specialist tours which are based in the regions in which the tour operator has most experience or around a topic of special interest. Examples of these include tours to the French wine-making regions, and fishing or golfing tours to Ireland and Scotland. Tour managers are involved in general management duties on tour for their operators, so administratively, the transition to building tours is not difficult. Those tour managers who have listened to their market while on tour will be able to develop tours which meet real market needs.

Further reading

Argyle, M., *The Psychology of Interpersonal Behaviour* (Pelican, 4th edition, 1983). A classic text by one of the most prolific writers on interpersonal skills, this book covers the theory and its application. Chapter 11, on applications of these skills, and Chapter 12, on training in social skills, are especially relevant.

Beaver, A., *Mind Your Own Travel Business* (Beaver Travel, 1980). This comprehensive two volume publication is a manual for travel agency personnel; Chapter 11 describes tour operation activities.

Bishop, J., *Travel Marketing* (Bailey Bros and Swinfen, 1981). Chapter 10 of this well-known and practical text examines 'Tour building', but reflecting the needs of its market, focuses on functional and administrative aspects suggesting use of local agents at the departure airport and the destination, rather than tour managers.

Peters, T. J. and Austin, N. K., *A Passion for Excellence* (Collins, 1985). Part 2 of this book focuses on customers, and addresses many of the issues which underlie the principle of using tour managers, such as adding value to the product, but also stresses the importance of all employees being made to realize the value of customers to the company – an important lesson for tour managers.

Peters, T. J. and Waterman, R. H., *In Search of Excellence* (Harper and Row, 1982). Chapter 6 introduces the concept of getting close to the customer, and aspects of quality management.

Reilly, R. T., *Handbook of Professional Tour Management* (Merton House, 1982). A very practical guide about the various activities involved in tour management, and the qualities required of tour managers.

Swinglehurst, E., *Cook's Tours* (Blandford Press, 1982). A history of the development of Thomas Cook's tours, identifying when and why tour managers were used with groups.

Young, Sir G., *Tourism: Blessing or Blight?* (Penguin Books, 1973). Chapter 1 outlines the historical development of tourism, including the role of the courier in the development of the package tour.

LYNN PARKINSON

Tour wholesaling

Introduction

Tourism is an unusual product because it consists of many component parts. A trip usually includes accommodation, air and/or ground transportation, food, entertainment and sightseeing. This creates an opportunity for middlemen to combine appropriate and complementary components of a trip before selling them to the traveler as a single product at a single price. Tour wholesalers (or tour operators) exist solely to provide this service, however sometimes travel agents perform this function on a small scale. Tour wholesalers, then, act as intermediaries between suppliers in the travel industry and consumers – they negotiate with suppliers and sell to consumers. Tours can be sold either directly to the consumer or through a travel agent.

Tour wholesaling first became a significant part of the travel industry in the 1950s when air transportation made it possible to transport large numbers of people quickly over long distances relatively inexpensively. Also for the first time the general public had enough disposable income to spend on travel. Since volume is critical to successful tour wholesaling (to be discussed later), these two factors were important in providing the volume needed to boost the industry. Tour wholesaling has continued to develop since the 1950s, assisted by the advances in information and communication technologies in the last few decades.

In the United States there are currently over 1,000 tour wholesalers, varying considerably in size and stability. Only 32 belong to the United States Tour Operators Association (a professional association which requires financial and ethical standards of its members). It has been estimated that 65 per cent of all travel agent sales of tours are with these 32 companies. In fact, in 1975 a study by Touche Ross found that 3 per cent of all tour wholesalers earned 30 per cent of the total revenue and handled 37 per cent of the passengers. In Europe, the tour wholesaling industry has similar characteristics to those in the United States – there are a few large, stable firms that dominate the market and many smaller firms which are often less stable.

Tour wholesalers create many different kinds of tours. Some are very basic and consist only of, say, transportation to the destination and accommodation, and allow travelers flexible departure dates. Fly – drive packages are further examples of these basic tours. At the other extreme are multidestination tours which include all food, entertainment, sightseeing, escorts and gratuities in addition to accommodation and transportation. There has recently been an increase in the number of firms offering special interest tours. Examples of such tours are outdoor and adventure tours, historic and archeological tours, art-lovers' tours, honeymoon packages and gourmet tours. Some tour wholesalers (such as Four Winds Travel) are now designing shorter tours and allowing travelers to put them together in various combinations.

Examples

Thomas Cook could be considered the first tour wholesaler when he arranged the first tour in England in 1846. His firm has subsequently become one of the largest tour wholesalers in the world, and has its own retail travel agencies. These retail outlets provide marketing arms for Thomas Cook tours, thereby eliminating commission payments to travel agencies. American Express is another successful tour wholesaler offering tours worldwide. In addition to offering escorted group tours, American Express has recently designed independent packages, sometimes called 'freelance itineraries'. These allow travelers to pick and choose from a selection of components listed in a brochure to make their own customized vacation. As travelers become more knowledgeable about destinations and more adventurous these types of tours are expected to increase. American Express also has retail travel agencies, and of course its huge credit card operation. The success of these two wholesaling giants is partly because they have diversified their operations to include functions other than tour provision.

Diversification by purchasing other firms in the travel industry is common among tour wholesalers. Many own their own hotels, airlines or ground transportation. Thomson Travel, the largest tour wholesaler in the United Kingdom, has its own retail travel agencies, its own air charter firm (Britannia Airways) as well as its own direct selling operation (Portland Holidays). Britannia Airways is Europe's biggest independent charter airline and carried 5.5 million passengers in 1986. In Hawaii, the largest volume tour wholesaler, Pleasant Hawaiian Holidays, owns its own hotels and tour buses. Diversification such as this provides a lower-cost structure, higher volume and more competitive pricing, and seems to be almost essential for firms to gain a competitive edge.

In some cases the diversification goes the opposite way. There are numerous examples of airlines and hotels starting their own tour wholesaling operations. In West Germany, LTV started life as a charter airline in 1955 and is now a holding company for a number of tour wholesalers. Many international airlines also create and sell their own tours – TWA, British Airways, United and American Airlines are a few examples. Tours are also being offered by motorcoach companies and railways.

Benefits

Tour wholesaling provides substantial benefits to the suppliers of travel-related products to the consumer, and to the travel agents. Tour wholesaling *may* also benefit a tourist destination. Each one of these benefit areas will now be discussed separately.

Suppliers

Suppliers of travel-related products benefit from tour wholesaling because it assists them in marketing their product. It is easier for a hotel to fill its rooms if a tour wholesaler blocks most of them for its tour groups. Not only does tour wholesaling increase occupancy or usage rates, but it also reduces promotional costs for the supplier. Instead of having to target individual consumers, they are able to focus their marketing efforts on tour wholesalers who book large blocks of rooms, airline seats etc. When tour wholesalers block book in this way, it not only reduces the marketing costs for the supplier, but also transfers some of the risk of doing business from the suppliers' shoulders to those of the tour wholesaler.

A supplier and a tour wholesaler may engage in one of two different types of contract – a block purchase or a block reservation. A block purchase is where the tour wholesaler actually buys units from the supplier by fronting the money before the tours are sold. In this case the tour wholesaler shoulders all of the risk. If tour wholesalers are unable to sell all the tours, they absorb the loss. This type of contract is less common than the block reservation, where the tour wholesaler only pays for the units that are occupied, and so is less at risk. This type of contract is most common in the travel industry, but the discount given to wholesalers is less because less risk is transferred.

Consumers

Consumers benefit from tour wholesaling in a number of ways. First of all, costs of locating information on the destination are reduced. The consumer simply looks through brochures and chooses the tour that is most attractive. The tour wholesaler researches the destination and its facilities, and given that the consumer trusts the tastes of the tour wholesaler, no further research of attractions, accommodation, restaurants etc. is needed. With the introduction of independent packages, a little more decision making must be done by the consumer. Second, transaction costs and the hassle of making reservations are also re-

duced since communications and bookings with many different suppliers (e.g. hotel, airline, rent-a-car) are reduced to one with the tour wholesaler.

A third major benefit that tour wholesalers provide for consumers is lower-priced vacations. This is especially true for high volume destinations such as Hawaii and Spain. When tour wholesalers negotiate with suppliers, they receive a discount that reflects the volume of business that is being supplied. It has been estimated that these discounts can vary between 10 per cent (minimum travel agent discount) to over 50 per cent. If the discounts are high and the market for tours is competitive enough, the tour operator may pass some of these discounts on to the consumer. It then becomes cheaper for the consumer to purchase a tour from a wholesaler than to purchase the individual components of the vacation separately from each of the suppliers. Indeed, there are instances where the cost of an inclusive vacation from a tour wholesaler is cheaper than the cost of the round trip air fare. Sheldon (1986) has shown that for basic tours to the Hawaiian Islands (containing only transportation and accommodation) the discount to the consumer is about 15 per cent whereas for inclusive escorted tours the discount is less, and often there is a premium.

Consumers also enjoy benefits while they are on the tour. Less time needs to be spent on organizing and planning. Local arrangements, language problems and other hassles are taken care of by the guide or by the company's representative. This is especially valuable for older travelers who may not be able to cope alone. For some, the companionship from traveling on a tour is valued, as is the feeling of security and safety – especially when traveling in strange places. These benefits, of course, will be valued differently by different people. Those who like freedom and independent travel would see these as disbenefits.

Travel agents

The travel agent is given approximately the same commission percentage for selling a tour as for selling the individual components. But in order to earn that amount, only one transaction with the wholesaler is required instead of many with the individual suppliers, and so the efficiency of the agent is improved. Tour brochures give complete information on the vacation and its components and so the agent needs to spend less time researching the destination and its facilities than if the components were being sold individually. Instead, the travel agent needs to be knowledgeable about the different tour wholesaling companies so that advice can be given to the consumer about which companies are reputable and reliable.

Tourist destinations

The destination to which tours are being wholesaled may benefit but it also may suffer. Tour wholesalers often have an interest in keeping a destination attractive to its clients. It is common, therefore, for tour wholesalers to invest in the destination by providing attractions or other facilities to improve the desirability of the destination. On the other hand, a destination may experience negative impacts from the large numbers of tourists that wholesalers deliver at its doorstep. Examples of negative impacts are overcrowding, pollution, environmental deterioration or social unease on the part of the resident population. The type of tourists that the tour wholesaler provides may not be in keeping with the destination's image. It is therefore important for the destination to play an active role in deciding which tour wholesalers should bring tours to the destination and how many tourists the destination can handle.

Implementation

Setting up in business as a tour wholesaler is relatively easy and little capital outlay is required compared to many other industries. Knowledge of the destination to be served, a means of communication, marketing skills and the ability to negotiate with suppliers are the major requirements. Because entry into and exit from the industry is relatively easy, there has been, and continues to be, a considerable amount of instability in the industry. In 1978 there were 588 firms in the US industry; by 1985 that number had grown to 1,001, although only 34 per cent of those in business in 1978 were still in business in 1985. The situation is similar in European countries and seems to be characteristic of the industry.

Once set up in business, the tour wholesaler must be able to generate volume to stay in business. Volume is critical for the wholesaler to obtain discounts with suppliers. When the tour wholesaler negotiates with suppliers, the sizes of the discounts are dependent not only on volume, but also on past performance, and to some degree the financial standing of the company. Volume is critical to getting good rates, which in turn allows the wholesaler to price the tours competitively. When the prices are attractive to the consumer this generates more volume. Once a firm is established and can generate high sales through advertising, operating efficiency, or specialized knowledge of the destination, economies of scale are generated, in both direct and indirect costs.

For those firms unable to generate enough volume to compete with the giants in the industry, it is possible to be successful by capitalizing on some specialized knowledge, and by carving out a niche in the market. Examples of how this can be done are:

1. To specialize in tours to a particular destination where the wholesaler has some special knowledge of the facilities.
2. To create special interest tours for a particular market segment such as historic, adventure or archeological tours. Special interest tours and customized tours are becoming increasingly popular, and so this area is fruitful for smaller firms.

Most tour wholesalers work with a long lead time. They usually plan tours 1 to 2 years in advance, so that they can make the necessary arrangements and have the brochures in travel agencies 6–12 months before the tour dates. Tour wholesalers may also list their tours in the airline reservation computer systems such as American Airlines' SABRE and United Airlines' APOLLO. When working with block reservations, tour wholesalers usually require payment from clients 35 days in advance with elaborate cancellation policies. Thirty days in advance the tour operator must notify the supplier of the number of units required. The supplier is then free to sell any unused units. Since deposits and payments come in before the tour date and payments to suppliers are not due until after the tour date, the tour wholesaler may have a large cash float and is able to earn interest on the balance. In times of low demand, however, the tour operator may experience cashflow problems and become insolvent.

Even though it is difficult to obtain figures on profitability in the industry and undoubtedly they vary from company to company, it appears as though on both sides of the Atlantic, currently profit margins are slim at about 3 per cent (after deduction of overheads, payments to suppliers and indirect expenses), and the industry is very competitive.

Assessment

Tour wholesaling is a very significant part of the travel industry and is likely to continue to be so. Areas of concern that need to be addressed are as follows:
1. What can be done to protect the consumer against the instabilities and bankruptcies of the less established firms?
2. How can the consumer be protected against misleading or incorrect information contained in brochures?
3. Should international standards be created for tour wholesalers and their products to notify the consumer more directly about the quality of the products?
4. Should more attention be given to researching the types of tour packages the consumer wants?
5. Do consumers want escorted group tours? If so, are they appropriate for all destinations? Or instead, do consumers want to take advantage of the tour wholesalers' volume discounts only and be independent once they arrive at the destination? Market research of all kinds will be helpful to determine consumer trends in vacation choice.
6. Should the increasing trend towards consolidation and diversification within travel industry firms continue? Is it fair on the smaller companies? Or is that an irrelevant question that only the market place should decide?

Conclusion

Tour wholesalers are important middlemen in the travel distribution system. By negotiating with suppliers they create a product that the consumer values for its convenience and for its competitive pricing. The risk that many tour wholesalers assume has led to many short-lived firms in the industry. Tour wholesalers that are diversified and own airlines, hotels and travel agencies seem to be the most successful. The nature of tour packages that are sold is changing as more and more special interest tours and independent packages are being created.

Focus on small business

Although volume appears to be the key to successful tour wholesaling, the analysis above has shown that there are opportunities for small businesses in tour wholesaling. They are, however, fewer than in other industries and should be embarked on with care. Small companies are most successful if they are able to carve out a special niche for themselves by providing either special interest tours to a well-researched and understood market segment, or by specializing in a particular destination about which the wholesaler has indepth knowledge. As the traveling public's tastes are changing to prefer more customized vacations with special interest and educational value, opportunities for smaller companies do exist. Small businesses often find it more difficult to justify the necessary costs of marketing the tours once they are designed. If the company has a 'ready made' clientele then success is more likely.

Software/databases

Airline Reservation Systems (*Apollo, Datas II, PARS, Sabre, System One*) all provide online access to tour wholesalers' listings by destination.

Further reading

Abbey, J., 'Package tour design: A comparative study of demographic and life style information', *Tourism Recreation Research* (June 1982), pp. 11–17. This paper reports the results of a controlled experiment which attempted to determine the relative effectiveness of lifestyle information compared to demographic data in designing package travel tours.

Askari, H., 'Demand for package tours', *Journal of Transport Economics and Policy* (January 1971), pp. 40–51. This paper first analyzes the role of travel agents, tour operators and airlines in setting up a package tour, then estimates the demand for the product.

Bredemeier, J., 'US tour operator industry', *Travel and Tourism Analyst* (May 1986), pp. 29–36. The article presents a survey of growing competition and costs in the US tour operator industry.

Curran, P. J. T., *Principles and Procedures of Tour Management* (CBI Publishing Co., 1978). The book emphasizes the concept and basic procedures of tour management. It also outlines the profession and its problems.

Drexl, C., 'Tour operators in West Germany', *Travel and Tourism Analyst* (May 1987), pp. 29–43. This article presents a survey of the package tour market in West Germany: who the operators are and methods they use to sell their product.

Fitch, A., 'Tour operators in the UK', *Travel and Tourism Analyst* (March 1987), pp. 29–43. The author provides a survey of the industry in the United Kingdom, its markets and product diversification.

Godwin, N., Berkely Agency of Mineola, NY, 'Operators' memo spells out legal liability for tour operators', *Travel Weekly* (2 April, 1987), pp. 18–19. This article provides legal advice to tour operators.

Hall, P., 'Travel marketing: the role of the tour operators', *Travel and Tourism Analyst*, pp. 3; 6 (January 1987). The article emphasizes the tour operators' role and function in travel marketing – assembly, compositioning, quality control. The paper also defines the classes of tour operators.

McLellan, R. W. and Noe, F. P., 'Sources of information and types of messages – useful to international tour operators', *Tourism Recreation Research*, pp. 27–30. This paper explores two facets of travel industry communication – knowledge of where tour operators get information (sources) and what information they seek (types of messages).

Nordren, L. F., Insight, Inc., *Opportunities Unlimited – A Guide to Group Travel* (American Society of Travel Agents, 1975). This booklet gives an overview of concepts, basic skills and knowledge of group tour business. It is some assistance to those owners and managers who accept the constancy of change and adapt to the pursuit of increased group business.

Phillips, R. G. and Webster, S., *Group Travel – Operating Procedures* (Van Nostrand Reinhold, 1983). This book explains how any travel agency may work with group travel. Each chapter gives instruction, information, and samples of forms to be used in working with a typical group.

Reilly, R. T., *Handbook of Professional Tour Management* (Merton House Publishing Company, 1982). This handbook provides an understanding of the tools one needs to succeed in tour management. It formally introduces the prospective manager to the field, and explains the skills necessary to succeed as a professional tour manager.

Sarbey de Souto, M., *Group Travel Operations Manual* (Merton House Tourism Publishers, 1985). The book presents knowledge and skills of group tour operations.

Schuchat, M., 'Comforts of group tours', *Annals of Tourism Research*, vol. 10 (1983), pp. 465–77. The paper evaluates the potential of the tour group and is an ethnographic account of the roles of the group in the travel experience.

Sheldon, P. J., 'The tour operator industry: an analysis', *Annals of Tourism Research*, vol. 13 (1986), pp. 349–65. This paper analyzes the function and structure of the domestic tour operator industry. An industry analysis is also performed. The second part of the paper analyzes different types of package tours to the Hawaiian Islands. Suggestions are made as to how industry may become more stable in the future.

Sheldon, P. J. and Mak, J., 'The demand for package tours: a mode choice model', *Journal of Travel Research*, vol. 25, no. 3 (Winter 1987), pp. 13–17. The article presents a model that explains a traveler's choice of vacation mode. The model is tested using logit analysis and survey data on travel to the Hawaiian Islands.

Stachnik, J., 'Costing is a science, pricing is an art', *NTA Courier* (March 1986), pp. 87–91. This article summarizes presentations by John Stachnik which suggest a new way of thinking about costing and pricing of a package tour.

Touche Ross and Company, *Tour Wholesaler Industry Study* (Touche Ross, 1975). This is a comprehensive survey of the US tour operator industry and includes results of a survey of travelers as to how they view tour packages.

United States Tour Operator Association, *Ethics in U. S. Tour Operations – Standards for Integrity* (USTOA, 1978). This booklet presents the ethics and standards in US tour operations, emphasizing the tour operators' rights and obligations. Chapter 1 gives an excellent overview of the tour operators' function, history and responsibilities.

PAULINE J. SHELDON

Tourism balance analysis

Introduction

International tourism has a major impact on the balance of payments for many countries. Overall, the 1986 level of international tourism receipts was US $115 billion, which represents approximately 6 per cent of the total value of international trade. However, the balance of expenditures by tourists traveling abroad and receipts from incoming tourists varies considerably from country to country and region to region.

International tourism receipts are defined as the receipts of a country resulting from payments for goods and services made by international visitors during their stay in the country visited. In general, they exclude all forms of remuneration resulting from employment, as well as international fare receipts. International tourism expenditures are defined as payments for goods and services made by residents of a country visiting abroad, and again in general exclude all forms of remuneration resulting from employment, as well as international fare payments.

In practice, it is not always possible to distinguish between the currency and country of origin of a visitor. Visitors from various countries may use US dollars or other strong currencies during their stay, and when data on tourism receipts are derived from reports by commercial banks, the breakdown by country is according to the type of currency and not the country of origin of the visitor. In particular, therefore, the data on receipts from the United States may be overestimated in certain cases (see World Tourism Organization, 1986). International fare receipts and expenditures should, in principle, cover all modes of international transport. However, in many cases the data merely refer to air transport, and in others to air and sea or air and rail.

Overall, caution should be exercised in interpreting the following tables. The definitions and methods of compiling the statistics vary across countries so the data are often not strictly comparable. In spite of the various deficiencies associated with international tourism receipts/payments and international fare receipts/payments figures, however, the tables provide useful information regarding the sign and approximate size of the tourism balance.

Examples

The tourism balance is shown for the major regions of the world in Table 1. It can be seen that the region with the most favorable tourism balance is Europe, but there are sharp differences within this total. In fact, apart from Southern Europe which has a massively positive tourism balance (reflecting the importance of sun/sea/sand tourism), the only area within Europe where receipts exceed expenditure is Eastern Europe. The combined deficits on the tourism account for Northern and Western Europe are of a similar order of magnitude to the deficit of North America, the continent with the worst tourism balance. By contrast, Central and South America, and in particular the Caribbean, show healthy surpluses on their tourism accounts. Tourism receipts slightly exceed expenditure for Africa as a whole; this is brought about by a large positive tourism balance in Northern Africa (where some countries bordering the Mediterranean attract considerable numbers of European tourists) and a smaller positive tourism balance in Eastern Africa, which are offset by negative tourism balances in the other regions of Africa. In East Asia and the Pacific and South Asia tourism receipts are considerably higher than tourism expenditure, whereas the high income oil exporters of the Middle East bring about a large negative tourism balance in this region.

International fare payments are considered in Table 2, where the fare balance is shown for major regions. The actual figures relate to different years as the availability of recent data varies from region to region. However, large negative fare balances arise for the Americas and East Asia and the Pacific, whereas Europe achieves a high positive fare balance. Within Europe, however, Northern Europe shows a substantial negative balance, which is more than compensated for by the large positive balances in Southern and Western Europe. Similarly, within the Americas fare receipts exceed fare expenditures by a considerable margin in both Central and South America and the Caribbean, but this is more than offset by the large negative balance in North America.

Both international tourism receipts and international tourism expenditures are greater for Europe than any other major region, and Table 3 shows the breakdown for individual European

Table 1 Major regions of the world: tourism balance 1985 (US $ million) (*Source*: WTO, 1986).

	Receipts	Expenditure	Balance
Africa	2,854	2,764	90
Eastern Africa	409	299	110
Middle Africa	133	281	−148
Northern Africa	1,352	753	599
Southern Africa	610	631	−21
Western Africa	350	800	−450
Americas	26,625	29,039	−2,414
North America	14,719	21,168	−6,449
Central and South America	7,132	6,603	529
The Caribbean	4,774	1,268	3,506
East Asia and the Pacific	11,308	10,312	996
Europe	62,779	49,195	13,584
Eastern Europe	1,433	717	716
Northern Europe	11,565	13,132	−1,567
Southern Europe	22,481	4,392	18,089
Western Europe	26,191	30,423	−4,232
Middle East	4,477	6,779	−2,302
South Asia	1,523	537	986

Table 3 Individual European countries: tourism balance 1986* (US$ million) (*Source*: OECD, 1987).

	Receipts	Expenditure	Balance
Austria[†]	6,928	4,207	2,721
Belgium	2,269	2,887	−618
Denmark	1,759	2,113	−354
Finland	597	1,070	−473
France	9,580	6,383	3,197
Greece	1,835	498	1,337
Iceland[‡]	42	77	−35
Ireland[§]	659	683	−24
Italy	9,853	2,758	7,095
Netherlands	1,906	4,430	−2,524
Norway	992	2,429	−1,437
Portugal	1,583	333	1,250
Spain	11,945	1,503	10,442
Sweden	1,543	2,811	−1,268
Switzerland	4,240	3,378	862
Turkey	1,228	312	916
United Kingdom[‖]	7,921	8,686	−765
West Germany	7,826	20,664	−12,838

* The amounts, other than for Ireland, Italy, Switzerland and the United Kingdom, refer to receipts and expenditure registered in foreign currency grouped regionally according to the denomination of the currency.
[†] Including international fare payments.
[‡] 1985 figures.
[§] Excluding receipts from and expenditure in Northern Ireland. Receipts exclude all passenger fares, but expenditure excludes passenger fares to Irish carriers only.
[‖] Including estimates for the Channel Islands receipts and expenditure, and cruise expenditure.

countries in 1986. The most favorable tourism balance is achieved by Spain (US $10.4 billion), followed by Italy (7.1), France (3.2), Austria (2.7), Greece (1.3) and Portugal (1.3). Countries with positive tourism balances of less than US$ one billion are Turkey and Switzerland (0.9 billion). The least favorable tourism balance is achieved by West Germany (−US$ 12.8 billion). Although tourism receipts for West Germany exceed those of countries such as Austria and Switzerland (which have positive balances), the massive tourism expenditure of US$ 20.1 billion gives West Germany by far the worst tourism balance in Europe (the second least favorable balance is − US$ 2.5 billion, which is achieved by the Netherlands). Other countries with negative tourism balances of more than US$ 500 million are Norway (−1.4), Sweden (−1.3), the United Kingdom (−0.8) and Belgium (−0.6).

The international fare balance for individual European countries is depicted in Table 4, but as with Table 2 the data refer to different years. Greece, in contrast to other Southern European countries such as Italy, Spain and Turkey, has a negative fare balance, whereas Finland, in contrast to other Northern European countries such as Norway and the United Kingdom, has a positive fare balance. Although Sweden shows a positive balance, air transport is excluded, and its inclusion would be likely to cause a negative balance.

Table 5 examines the tourism balance for selected non-European countries. The major destination in Eastern Africa for international tourists is Kenya, and here receipts from international tourism exceed expenditure by US$ 80 million. This is, however, dwarfed by the positive tourism balances achieved by the Northern African countries of Morocco (US$ 370 million) and Tunisia (US$ 508 million). By contrast, Nigeria shows a large deficit on its tourism account (−US$ 352 million).

Table 2 Major regions of the world: international fare balance (US$ million) (*Source*: WTO, 1986).

	Year	Fare receipts	Fare expenditure	Fare balance
Americas	1982	4,091	5,986	−1,895
North America	1982	3,262	5,656	−2,394
Central and South America	1982	959	330	629
The Caribbean	1981	71	25	46
East Asia and the Pacific	1982	1,333	2,579	−1,246
Europe	1982	15,876	12,078	3,798
Eastern Europe	1981	333	283	50
Northern Europe	1984	1,378	2,169	−791
Southern Europe	1984	1,135	517	618
Western Europe	1984	5,579	4,751	828

Table 4 Individual European countries: international fare balance – rail, air, sea and road transport (US$ million) (*Sources*: WTO, 1986; OECD, 1987).

	Year	Fare receipts	Fare expenditure	Fare balance
Austria*	1986	348	105	243
Belgium	1984	2,632	2,363	269
Finland	1985	225	161	64
France	1982	6,306	6,079	227
Greece	1986	12	97	−85
Ireland	1986	210	139	71
Italy†	1985	979	340	639
Norway	1984	591	1,474	−883
Spain	1986	707	221	486
Sweden‡	1986	518	336	182
Switzerland	1986	1,162	790	372
Turkey§	1986	214	2	212
UK‖	1982	1,537	1,897	−360
West Germany¶	1986	2,255	2,427	−172

* Rail, air, inland waterways and road transport.
† Air and sea transport.
‡ Sea and rail transport.
§ Air, sea and rail transport for receipts; rail transport only for expenditure.
‖ Air and sea transport.
¶ Air, sea and rail transport.

In North America both Canada and the United States achieve a negative tourism balance. International tourism expenditures by the USA are US$ 3 billion below the level for West Germany, but international tourism receipts are 5 billion higher. Thus the US tourism balance of −US$ 4.7 billion is nowhere near as unfavorable as that for West Germany (−12.8). In Central and South America, Brazil and Mexico achieve substantial positive tourism balances, whereas in Argentina and Venezuela international tourism expenditures exceed international tourism receipts. The Caribbean countries of the Bahamas, Jamaica and Barbados all show positive tourism balances – 0.7, 0.4 and 0.2 billion US dollars respectively. These compare very favorably with the balances achieved in Kenya and the Seychelles, for example, where the joint figure is US$ 0.1 billion.

In East Asia and the Pacific, Singapore and Thailand achieve substantial positive tourism balances, whereas Australia, Japan, Malaysia and New Zealand achieve negative tourism balances. The level of international tourism expenditure greatly exceeds the level of international tourism receipts in Japan, giving rise to a tourism balance of −US$ 5.7 billion, a less favorable tourism balance than that for the United States.

The Middle Eastern country with the highest level of net international tourism receipts is Egypt (US$ 0.7 billion). On the other hand, the high income oil exporting countries of Kuwait and Saudi Arabia show deficits on the tourism account of −1.9 and −1.1 billion US dollars, respectively, even though Saudi Arabia attracts a high level of tourism receipts as a result of pilgrim expenditures.

In South Asia the country with the highest level of international tourism receipts and most favorable tourism balance (US$ one billion) is India.

Table 5 Selected nonEuropean countries: tourism balance (US$ million) (*Sources*: WTO, 1986; OECD, 1987).

	Year	Receipts	Expenditure	Balance
Eastern Africa				
Kenya	1984	96	16	80
Seychelles	1985	51	9	42
Northern Africa				
Morocco	1984	440	70	370
Tunisia	1983	573	65	508
Southern Africa				
South Africa	1984	610	651	−41
Western Africa				
Nigeria	1983	102	454	−352
North America				
Canada	1986	3,853	4,295	−442
United States	1986	12,913	17,627	−4,714
Central and South America				
Argentina	1984	602	681	−79
Brazil	1985	1,739	1,146	593
Mexico	1985	2,900	2,262	638
Venezuela	1984	358	955	−597
The Caribbean				
Bahamas	1984	802	106	696
Barbados	1983	252	26	226
Jamaica	1984	407	20	387
East Asia and the Pacific				
Australia	1986	1,366	1,925	−559
Japan	1986	1,443	7,138	−5,695
Malaysia	1984	535	1,119	−584
New Zealand	1985	277	416	−139
Singapore	1985	1,754	615	1,139
Thailand	1985	1,171	280	891
Middle East				
Egypt	1984	860	146	714
Jordan	1985	555	452	103
Kuwait	1985	103	1,988	−1,885
Saudi Arabia	1983	2,073*	3,152	−1,079
South Asia				
India	1983	1,203	227	976
Pakistan	1985	186	207	−21

* Pilgrim expenditures.

Benefits

Tourism can benefit a host country in various ways including the generation of income and employment, but often the major benefit is seen as the generation of foreign exchange. Gibbons and Fish (1986, p. 17) note that 'Many countries face balance of payments difficulties because of a deficit in the trade account or capital account or in both', and international tourism can help to alleviate balance of payments problems.

Assessment

Tourism balance analysis examines the net contribution of the tourism industry to foreign exchange earnings, but the analysis of international tourism receipts and expenditures has several limitations; for example, the definitions used vary from country to country, there are limitations associated with sample surveys used to collect expenditure data, and where bank foreign exchange records are used for data purposes various inadequacies are present. (For a discussion of the problems associated with data on tourist expenditures and receipts see the chapter on *Statistical Measurement in Tourism*, p. 419 and White and Walker, 1982.)

A further point is that international tourism generates balance of payments effects which are far more complex than the initial net tourism balance. In particular, the extent to which inward tourism expenditures generate import demand in the host country will have a major impact on the foreign exchange generating ability of tourism. (This point is further developed in the chapter on *Impact of Tourism* p. 215.)

Conclusion

In spite of the limitations associated with tourism balance analysis, the examples considered give an indication of the impact of international tourism on the balance of payments for various countries and regions of the world. Future trends in tourism balances will be largely determined by future flows of international tourists, and a discussion of the factors influencing these flows is presented in the chapter on *Forecasting International Tourism Demand: The Econometric Approach.*

Further reading

Gibbons, J. D. and Fish, M., 'Dynamics of the U.S. international tourism market, 1970–84', *Journal of Travel Research*, vol. XXIV, no. 4 (Spring 1986), pp. 17–24. Analysis of US inward and outward tourist flows and tourism expenditures split by five major regions. Examination of US balance of expenditures.

Organization for Economic Cooperation and Development, *Tourism Policy and International Tourism* (OECD, annual). Detailed statistics on tourism expenditures and receipts for OECD countries, plus tourism balance sheet for major regions. International fare payments are also given.

White, K. J. and Walker, M. B., 'Trouble in the travel account', *Annals of Tourism Research*, vol. 9, no. 1 (1982), pp. 37–56. Discussion of limitations associated with data on tourism expenditures and receipts.

World Tourism Organization, *Yearbook of Tourism Statistics* (WTO, annual). Most comprehensive worldwide collection of statistics on tourism expenditures and receipts. International fare payments are also given.

STEPHEN F. WITT

Tourism demand elasticities

Introduction

Several elasticities are used in demand analysis. These measure the responsiveness of demand to small changes in the determining factors. For example, the (own) price elasticity of demand is defined as the percentage change in quantity demanded divided by the percentage change in price that brought it about, and in general is negative. When the percentage change in quantity is less than the percentage change in price (absolute value of the elasticity is less than unity) demand is inelastic, and when the percentage change in quantity is greater than the percentage change in price (absolute value of the elasticity is greater than unity) demand is elastic. If demand is inelastic, then a price reduction reduces total expenditure on the good and a price rise increases expenditure, whereas if demand is elastic a price reduction increases expenditure and a price rise reduces expenditure. Clearly, therefore, the impact of a price change on total expenditure on the good (which is equal to the gross revenue of the sellers) depends critically on the magnitude of the elasticity. Estimated elasticities of the demand for tourism are therefore of considerable value to the tourism industry.

The income elasticity of demand is defined as the percentage change in quantity demanded divided by the percentage change in income that brought it about, and is usually positive, but negative elasticities are not uncommon. Goods with positive income elasticities are termed normal (or superior) goods, whilst those with negative income elasticities are termed inferior goods. Normal goods can be further subdivided; if the income elasticity is less than unity the good is a necessity, whereas if it is greater than unity the good is a luxury. We would normally expect the income elasticity of demand for international tourism to be positive, and indeed that foreign holidays would commonly be regarded as luxuries.

The responsiveness of the demand for one commodity to changes in the price of another commodity is measured by the cross-elasticity of demand, which is defined as the percentage change in the quantity demanded of good X divided by the percentage change in the price of good Y that brought it about. Complementary goods are those for which cross-elasticity is negative and substitutes those for which cross-elasticity is positive. In tourism demand the role played by substitute (or competing) offerings may be marked.

There are many studies in which econometric models of in-

ternational tourism demand are estimated. Demand functions are specified in various forms of explain either the number of tourist visits or tourist receipts/expenditure, and empirical results are presented. The general structure of such models and the justification for the inclusion of the various explanatory variables are discussed at length in the chapter on *Forecasting International Tourism Demand: The Econometric Approach* p. 163.

The most commonly specified mathematical form for international tourism demand functions is log-linear. Here a multiplicative relationship is postulated:

$$Y = aX_1^{b_1} X_2^{b_2} \ldots X_k^{b_k} e^u \qquad (1)$$

where

Y is the demand for international tourism
$X_1, \ldots, X_k$ are the influencing variables
u is a random error term
$a, b_1, \ldots, b_k$ are parameters
$e \simeq 2.178$ is the base of natural logarithms.

In order to render equation (1) amenable to estimation using the usual technique of ordinary least squares, it is necessary to take logarithms of the variables (to the base e), which yields an equation which is linear in the natural logs (ln) of the variables:

$$\ln Y = \ln a + b_1 \ln X_1 + b_2 \ln X_2 \\ + \ldots + b_k \ln X_k + u \qquad (2)$$

An ordinary least squares regression of $\ln Y$ on $\ln X_1, \ldots, \ln X_k$ yields estimates of the parameters $b_1, b_2, \ldots, b_k$ in equations (2) *and* (1).

The log-linear transformation is often employed because the multiplicative model (1) corresponds to the assumption of constant elasticity. The derivative of Y with respect to X_1 in equation (1) yields:

$$\partial Y/\partial X_1 = ab_1 X_1^{b_1-1} X_2^{b_2} \ldots X_k^{b_k} e^u \\ = bY/X_1 \qquad (3)$$

But the elasticity of Y with respect to X_1 is defined as:

$$q_{YX_1} = \partial Y/\partial X_1 \cdot X_1/Y \qquad (4)$$

Substitution of equation (3) into equation (4) gives

$$q_{YX_1} = b_1 \qquad (5)$$

Hence b_1 is the constant elasticity of Y with respect to X_1, and in general b_j is the constant elasticity of Y with respect to X_j, $j = 1, 2, \ldots, k$.

Consider the following demand function:

$$Y = aX_1^{b_1} X_2^{b_2} X_3^{b_3} e^u \tag{6}$$

where

Y is the demand for foreign holidays from a given origin to a given destination
X_1 is origin country consumers' disposable income
X_2 is the price of a foreign holiday to the destination
X_3 is the price of a foreign holiday to a substitute destination.

In equation (6) the parameters b_1, b_2 and b_3 may be interpreted as elasticities; hence b_1 is the income elasticity of demand, b_2 is the own-price elasticity of demand and b_3 is a cross-price elasticity of demand.

Examples

In this chapter the results of a study by the authors are presented in which a comparison is made of outward tourism from four major generating countries to their important destinations. The estimated coefficients of the variables explaining international tourist flows from the four origins to six destinations each are examined, these flows being: France to Italy, Morocco, Portugal, Spain, Switzerland and the United Kingdom; West Germany to Austria, France, Italy, Spain, Switzerland and Yugoslavia; the United Kingdom to Austria, France, West Germany, Greece, Italy and Spain; and the United States to Canada, France, West Germany, Italy, Mexico and the United Kingdom. In each case the data used in estimation were annual and covered the period 1965 to 1980. Data on tourism flows for UK outward tourism were disaggregated according to air or surface travel, and hence separate models were estimated for the two transport modes. For the other origins, France, West Germany and the United States, only aggregate models were estimated, and to provide greater comparability aggregate models were additionally estimated for the United Kingdom.

The basic model is specified as follows:

$$\ln \frac{V_{ijt}}{P_{it}} = \alpha_1 + \alpha_2 \ln \frac{Y_{it}}{P_{it}} + \alpha_3 \ln C_{jt} + \alpha_4 \ln CS_{it}$$
$$+ \alpha_5 \ln EX_{ijt} + \alpha_6 \ln TA_{ijt} + \alpha_7 \ln TAS_{it}$$
$$+ \alpha_8 \ln TS_{ijt} + \alpha_9 \ln TSS_{it} + \alpha_{10} DV1_t$$
$$+ \alpha_{11} DV2_t + \alpha_{12} DV3_{it} + U_{ijt} \tag{7}$$
$$t = 1, 2, \ldots, 16 \ (1 = 1965, \ldots, 16 = 1980)$$

where

V_{ijt} is the number of tourist visits from origin i to destination j in year t
P_{it} is the origin i population in year t
Y_{it} is personal disposable income in origin i in year t (1980 prices)
C_{jt} is the cost of living for tourists in destination j in year t (1980 prices)

CS_{it} is a weighted average of the cost of tourism in substitute destinations for residents of origin i in year t (1980 prices)
EX_{ijt} is the rate of exchange between the currencies of origin i and destination j in year t
TA_{ijt} is the cost of travel by air from origin i to destination j in year t (1980 prices)
TAS_{it} is a weighted average of the cost of travel by air to substitute destinations from origin i in year t (1980 prices)
TS_{ijt} is the cost of travel by surface from origin i to destination j in year t (1980 prices)
TSS_{it} is a weighted average of the cost of travel by surface to substitute destinations from origin i in year t
$DV1$ is a dummy variable which picks up the effects of the 1973 oil crisis
$DV1_t = 1$ if $t = 10$ (1974) or 11 (1975)
$= 0$ otherwise
$DV2$ is a dummy variable which picks up the effects of the 1979 oil crisis
$DV2_t = 1$ if $t = 15$ (1979)
$= 0$ otherwise
$DV3$ is a dummy variable which picks up the effects of the 1967–69 UK currency restrictions (applies to UK origin models only)
$DV3_{it} = 1$ if i refers to the UK and $t = 3$ (1967), 4 (1968) or 5 (1969)
$= 0$ otherwise
U_{ijt} is a random disturbance term
and $\alpha_1, \alpha_2, \ldots, \alpha_{12}$ are unknown parameters.

In addition, a trend term $\alpha_{13}t$ and/or lagged dependent variable term $\alpha_{14} \ln (V_{ij(t-1)}/P_{i(t-1)})$ is incorporated in the model for those origin–destination pairs where the preliminary empirical results indicated that this may be necessary.

As is usual in demand analysis, income and the prices of substitutes are included as explanatory variables in the model in addition to own price. (A full discussion of the forms of the various price variables are given in Martin and Witt, 1988.) Exchange rate is included as an additional explanatory variable on the grounds that some consumers may be more aware of exchange rates than destination costs of living for tourists and hence may be driven to use exchange rate as a proxy variable. (For a full discussion of the role of exchange rates in international tourism demand models see Martin and Witt, 1987.) The oil crisis dummy variables represent the psychological impacts of the crisis on foreign tourism demand. In addition, the 1974–1975 dummy variable allows for the detrimental effect of the 1974 Turkish invasion of Cyprus on foreign tourism to Greece (applies to the United Kingdom to Greece tourism flows only). The UK Government applied a £50 foreign currency limit to holidays abroad from late 1966 to late 1969 (fares excluded) in an effort to stem the outflow of foreign currency; hence the currency restriction dummy variable is included to capture the resulting distortion in international tourism demand. The trend variable mainly reflects a steady change in the popularity of the holiday over the period as a result of changing tastes, and may take on either a positive or negative coefficient.

The lagged dependent variable allows for habit persistence; once people have visited a country and liked it, there is a tendency to reduce risk by returning. (A full justification for the inclusion of a lagged dependent variable in models of international tourism demand is given in Witt, 1980.)

Equation (7) is estimated for each origin–destination pair over the period 1965–1980, together with various subsets of this equation. A 'best' model is then selected for each origin–destination pair on the basis of several criteria such as a statistically significant F statistic, 'correct' estimated coefficient signs, the absence of autocorrelation, a relatively high R^2 value, a relatively high number of statistically significant coefficients, and relative forecasting performance over the period 1981–1982. The latter criterion – the ability of an econometric model to forecast accurately outside the sample estimation period – is widely regarded as a strict test of model validity. (A full explanation of the selection procedure is given in Martin and Witt, 1988.)

The estimated coefficients for the best model for each origin–destination pair are presented in Tables 1–6.

Assessment

The empirical results presented in Tables 1–6 are now interpreted and assessed. In Table 1, for example, for travel from France to Switzerland the estimated income elasticity implies that a 1 per cent increase in real per capita income results in a 2.819 per cent increase in the per capita demand for tourism, *ceteris paribus*, and the estimated tourists' cost of living elasticity implies that a 1 per cent increase in costs in real terms results in a 1.242 per cent decrease in per capita demand, *ceteris paribus*.

In the models where an exchange rate variable appears, the interpretation is not quite so straightforward. When interpreting one variable the remaining variables are assumed to remain unchanged, i.e. a 1 per cent rise in an explanatory variable leads to a corresponding increase/decrease in demand, *ceteris paribus*. However if exchange rates change and the origin country's currency becomes stronger, it is unlikely that all other variables will remain unchanged. Travel costs are calculated in the currency of the origin and are therefore not directly affected by changes in exchange rate, but other cost variables have been derived taking exchange rates into account. For example, the cost of living in a destination variable is adjusted by exchange rates before being put into real terms. A change in exchange rates will therefore almost certainly affect other variables in the model, unless price changes exactly offset the effect of the change in exchange rate. If this latter is the case, price levels as stated in the currency of the origin country do not change, i.e. price increases in the destination will be exactly offset by the destination currency becoming weaker.

Table 1 Best models for France outward tourism.

Explanatory variable	Destination					
	Italy	Morocco	Portugal	Spain	Switzerland	United Kingdom
$\ln \frac{Y}{P}$	2.573 (3.28)★	2.213 (16.46)★	0.772 (2.56)★	3.289 (2.26)	2.819 (2.46)★	2.756 (7.16)★
$\ln C$	−0.634 (−2.14)		−0.993 (−5.39)★		−1.242 (−3.26)★	
$\ln CS$	3.637 (5.89)★		0.810 (2.90)★		1.053 (1.30)	
$\ln EX$						
$\ln TA$						
$\ln TAS$				0.109 (0.14)		
$\ln TS$	−0.472 (−1.68)			−0.557 (−1.00)		−0.708 (−2.14)
$\ln TSS$						0.600 (2.01)
$DV1$	−0.138 (−2.79)★		−0.008 (−0.025)	−0.080 (−0.78)	−0.022 (−0.43)	−0.204 (−2.74)★
$DV2$				−0.103 (−0.26)	−0.034 (−0.50)	
$DV3$						
TREND	−0.217 (−4.71)★			−0.095 (−0.52)	−0.150 (−2.57)★	
R^2	0.745	0.951	0.964	0.711	0.969	0.953

The figures in brackets are *t* values
★ Indicates significant at 5% level.

Table 2 Best models for West German outward tourism.

Explanatory variable	Destination					
	Austria	France	Italy	Spain	Switzerland	Yugoslavia
$\ln \dfrac{Y}{P}$	1.292 (31.04)★	1.750 (4.32)★	1.233 (11.67)★	3.505 (17.24)★	4.923 (3.78)★	3.369 (16.58)★
$\ln C$	−0.755 (−4.17)★	−1.984 (−2.63)★		−0.063 (−0.11)	−1.250 (−1.72)	
$\ln CS$						
$\ln EX$						
$\ln TA$		−0.903 (−3.68)★			−0.932 (−2.18)	−1.071 (−2.28)★
$\ln TAS$		3.260 (4.79)★		1.047 (2.23)★	2.803 (3.09)★	
$\ln TS$	−0.037 (−0.46)		−0.011 (−0.04)	−0.771 (−1.59)		
$\ln TSS$			0.271 (1.38)			1.346 (3.04)★
$DV1$					−0.040 (−0.30)	
$DV2$	−0.109 (−3.91)★					
$DV3$						
TREND					−0.122 (−2.09)	
R^2	0.987	0.968	0.954	0.973	0.896	0.979

The figures in brackets are t values
★ Indicates significant at 5% level.

Table 3 Best models for US outward tourism.

Explanatory variable	Destination					
	Canada	France	Italy	Mexico	United Kingdom	West Germany
$\ln \dfrac{Y}{P}$	0.372 (0.18)	4.683 (2.21)	0.421 (0.71)	3.523 (7.97)★	2.431 (6.38)★	4.058 (6.07)★
$\ln C$	−0.364 (−0.39)	−1.299 (−2.58)★			−0.428 (−1.98)	−1.345 (−5.10)★
$\ln CS$		4.898 (1.76)				
$\ln EX$						
$\ln TA$		−0.078 (−0.32)			−0.198 (−2.44)	
$\ln TAS$	0.156 (0.58)					
$\ln TS$	−0.355 (−0.64)					
$\ln TSS$						
$DV1$		−0.173 (−1.66)	−0.154 (−2.14)			
$DV2$	−0.042 (−0.38)					
$DV3$						
TREND	−0.018 (−0.36)	−0.182 (−1.56)				
R^2	0.776	0.581	0.571	0.941	0.897	0.747

The figures in brackets are t values
★ Indicates significant at 5% level.

Table 4 Best models for UK total outward tourism.

Explanatory variable	Destination					
	Austria	France	Greece	Italy	Spain	West Germany
$\ln \dfrac{Y}{P}$	4.550 (24.00)*	1.952 (4.26)*	0.387 (0.31)	4.394 (10.63)*	1.775 (1.97)	2.387 (6.16)*
$\ln C$	−0.235 (−1.60)	−0.946 (−5.50)*	−5.605 (−8.59)*	−1.608 (−7.64)*		−0.361 (−1.75)
$\ln CS$	0.130 (0.23)	1.410 (5.54)*				
$\ln EX$	1.859 (6.62)*				0.637 (1.18)	
$\ln TA$						
$\ln TAS$			0.492 (1.07)			0.540 (3.03)*
$\ln TS$			−0.394 (−0.41)	−0.081 (−0.83)	−0.155 (−0.26)	−1.765 (−3.73)*
$\ln TSS$			5.069 (5.21)*		0.921 (1.10)	
$DV1$	−0.258 (−10.64)*		−0.420 (−3.12)*	−0.179 (−4.43)*	−0.022 (−0.26)	−0.265 (−4.27)*
$DV2$	−0.619 (−10.23)*					
$DV3$	−0.061 (−2.82)*	−0.264 (−4.93)*				−0.052 (−1.60)
TREND				−0.111 (−11.42)*		0.056 (2.82)*
R^2	0.991	0.977	0.976	0.913	0.911	0.895

The figures in brackets are *t* values
* Indicates significant at 5% level.

Table 5 Best models for UK outward tourism by air.

Explanatory variable	Destination					
	Austria	France	Greece	Italy	Spain	West Germany
$\ln \dfrac{Y}{P}$	1.331 (1.99)	3.197 (5.30)*	5.029 (4.00)*	5.377 (10.34)*	2.733 (3.77)*	5.144 (8.73)*
$\ln C$	−1.403 (−4.50)*	−0.617 (−3.82)*	−2.569 (−3.66)*	−1.443 (−5.46)*		
$\ln CS$						
$\ln EX$	2.258 (14.94)*					1.060 (7.24)*
$\ln TA$	−1.122 (−5.21)*	−0.295 (−2.57)*				
$\ln TAS$						
$\ln TS$						
$\ln TSS$	6.305 (8.44)*					
$DV1$			−0.235 (−1.49)	−0.219 (−4.29)*		−0.475 (−6.35)*
$DV2$	−0.604 (−5.60)*	−0.108 (−0.99)				−0.197 (−1.40)
$DV3$		−0.408 (−9.82)*				
TREND		−0.065 (−4.00)*		−0.115 (−9.67)*		
R^2	0.972	0.916	0.952	0.910	0.926	0.782

The figures in brackets are *t* values
* Indicates significant at 5% level.

Table 6 Best models for UK outward tourism by sea/land.

Explanatory variable	Destination					
	Austria	France	Greece	Italy	Spain	West Germany
$\ln \dfrac{Y}{P}$	1.743 (2.01)	2.295 (2.83)★	1.821 (2.71)★	1.852 (2.56)★	2.508 (4.79)★	0.995 (3.00)★
$\ln C$	−0.679 (−1.38)	−0.531 (−1.88)	−1.104 (−1.28)	−1.880 (−5.24)★	−2.253 (−5.07)★	−1.321 (−3.64)★
$\ln CS$	3.308 (2.64)★	2.653 (2.92)★			1.837 (3.13)★	1.174 (3.33)★
$\ln EX$	1.827 (2.93)★	1.062 (1.54)				
$\ln TA$					1.491 (5.94)★	0.372 (2.39)★
$\ln TAS$						
$\ln TS$	−4.337 (−5.54)★			−0.239 (−1.29)	−1.697 (−3.54)★	−3.174 (−3.97)★
$\ln TSS$	2.266 (2.58)★					2.258 (1.99)
$DV1$	−0.374 (−5.78)★		−0.314 (−1.48)			
$DV2$	−0.367 (−3.44)★		−0.451 (−1.59)			
$DV3$						−0.105 (−2.99)★
TREND				−0.096 (−5.46)★		0.050 (3.33)★
R^2	0.978	0.970	0.492	0.867	0.888	0.909

The figures in brackets are *t* values
★ Indicates significant at 5% level.

The opposite extreme position is if prices in the destination do not change at all when exchange rates change. If one interprets the exchange rate variable as usual, i.e. *ceteris paribus*, one is implicitly assuming that the first extreme position holds, i.e. price changes in the destination exactly offset the exchange rate changes. However, if one believes that this is not the case it is still possible to calculate the effect of the change in exchange rate by working through the whole model. This entails calculating what effect a 1 per cent increase in the relative position of the exchange rate will have on the price variables. For example, taking the United Kingdom as the origin country and France as the destination, if the price of accommodation for 2 weeks in France is 4400 FF and the exchange rate is 10 FF to the £, the cost in the origin currency is £440. If the exchange rate improves by 1 per cent to 10.1 FF to the £, the price falls to £435.64 (a fall of 0.99 per cent). Thus one calculates the net effect on per capita demand by adding the effect of a 1 per cent upwards movement of the relative exchange rate to the effect of a 0.99 per cent fall in price, etc.

Similarly, if one is looking at what the effect of a 1 per cent increase in a price variable will be, *ceteris paribus*, one is assuming that the price rise is caused solely by a rise in the price level. This must be so or the *ceteris paribus* statement is not valid, because if the price rise is caused by movements of exchange rates, other price variables will clearly not remain unchanged. Therefore, if an exchange rate variable does appear in a model, one has to be clear what assumptions are being made when one is interpreting the model.

The coefficients of the dummy variables are interpreted somewhat differently; for travel from France to Switzerland the estimated coefficient of the dummy variable relating to the 1979 oil crisis implies that this event resulted in a 3 per cent reduction in the demand for tourism ($e^{-0.034} = 0.97$), which implies a decline of 3 per cent from the level of demand which would otherwise have been achieved. This may be shown by focusing solely on the two relevant variables. In 1979

$$\ln V_t/P_t = \ldots -0.034 + \ldots \tag{8}$$

In 1978, i.e. the year before the oil crisis

$$\ln V_{t-1}/P_{t-1} = \ldots + 0 + \ldots \tag{9}$$

as the dummy variable takes the value 1 in 1979 and 0 otherwise.

Subtracting equation (9) from equation (8) yields

$$\ln \left. \frac{V_t}{P_t} \right| \frac{V_{t-1}}{P_{t-1}} = -0.034$$

Taking antilogs

$$\frac{V_t}{P_t} \left| \frac{V_{t-1}}{P_{t-1}} \right. = 0.97$$

i.e. 1979 demand would have been 97 per cent of the demand in 1978; thus a reduction of 3 per cent is indicated.

The trend variable may be interpreted as follows using periods 11 and 12 as an example:

$$\ln V_t/P_t = \ldots \; -0.150 \times 12 + \ldots$$
$$\ln V_{t-1}/P_{t-1} = \ldots \; -0.150 \times 11 + \ldots$$

Therefore for any two sequential periods

$$\ln \frac{V_t}{P_t} \left| \frac{V_{t-1}}{P_{t-1}} \right. = -0.15$$

and thus

$$\frac{V_t}{P_t} \left| \frac{V_{t-1}}{P_{t-1}} \right. = 0.86$$

indicating that demand from France to Switzerland is falling at a rate of 14 per cent per annum.

A few general points should be noted in the following analyses. Where multicollinearity exists, the size and significance of the variable coefficients in the models may be distorted. Where high values of R^2 are obtained, this implies that the models fit the data well and there can be considerable confidence in the empirical results. By contrast, where the R^2 values are not particularly high, caution should be exercised in drawing conclusions. Similarly, statistically significant coefficients allow for greater confidence. Finally, coefficient estimates obtained from simplistic models containing only one or two explanatory variables should be treated with caution.

France outward tourism

Four out of the six models have high R^2 values; only the models for Italy and Spain have low values. Given the sizes of the estimated income coefficients, which, with the exception of holidays to Portugal, are greater than 2, it appears that the French regard a foreign holiday very much as a luxury. This result may have been distorted by the presence of multicollinearity between income and other variables, but the only income coefficient not statistically significant is that for Spain. In the three models where C appears, CS is also present, implying that when the French consider costs, they do not look at the cost in the destination alone, but also at costs in substitute destinations. Neither the exchange rate nor the cost of travel by air variables appear in any model. This suggests that the French tend not to take notice of exchange rates *per se* when taking holidays abroad and air fares are not an important factor in international travel demand from France to the destinations considered. With respect to the latter variable, this may be because air travel is a small proportion of total demand or because the travelers by air are not price sensitive. The cost of travel by surface seems more important, appearing in three models, and in

two cases is accompanied by a substitute travel cost variable. However, none of the variable coefficients are significant.

Additional support for the hypothesis that the French are very aware of surface travel cost is the rate of occurrence of the oil crisis dummy variables, which appear in all models for which surface travel is a clear option (NB a surface cost variable for Morocco was not trend in the estimation process). In the two models where the 1974–1975 dummy variable is significant, the implied effects are quite large: a fall of 13 per cent for Italy and 18 per cent for the United Kingdom. There appear to be clear downward trends for Italy, Spain and Switzerland from France, with falls of 20 per cent, 9 per cent and 14 per cent respectively.

The implications generally with respect to French outward tourism are as follows:

1. Increases in income will lead to substantial increases in demand.
2. The absolute and relative costs of the holiday are fairly important, particularly in the case of Switzerland and Italy (where relative cost seems very important).
3. The psychological impacts of the oil crises, which affect perceptions regarding the cost of surface travel, are very marked.
4. The underlying trends for Italy, Spain and Switzerland are downwards.

West German outward tourism

All the models have reasonable R^2 values, with only the Swiss model having a value less than 0.9. The income elasticities are all significant but the destinations do appear to be regarded in different ways. The nearest destinations have income coefficients lying between 1 and 2 with the exception of Switzerland. The three remaining countries have very high income coefficients, and are thus seemingly regarded very much as luxury goods. This split makes sense – in general, bordering countries are easier to reach. Comparing Austria with Switzerland, as countries with similar attractions, e.g. winter skiing, Switzerland is clearly more up-market and this possibly accounts for its higher income coefficient.

Absolute cost seems quite important to the West Germans with the destination tourists' cost of living variable entering four models. The exchange rate variable does not appear in any model. This may be because the West Germans are aware of the fact that exchange rates are not good indicators of cost or because of the presence of multicollinearity between, in most cases, income and exchange rates and in some cases exchange rate and C. Travel cost variables, both absolute and substitute, appear much more frequently in the West German models than they do in the French models, with every model including an absolute cost variable and the only model which does not include a substitute cost variable being that to Austria. The oil dummy variables only appear in two models, the 1974–1975 variable indicating a 4 per cent fall in the model for Switzerland and the 1979 variable indicating a fall of 10 per cent for travel to Austria. The only West German model with a trend variable is that to Switzerland, indicating a fall of 11 per cent per annum.

Thus, for West Germany, the implications regarding international tourism are as follows:

1. Increases in income will lead to increases in tourism demand, but the effects will vary between countries, with Spain, Switzerland and Yugoslavia benefiting most.
2. Switzerland, France, Austria and Spain will all lose demand if prices rise, but the first two destinations are particularly price sensitive with elasticities greater than 1 in absolute value.
3. West Germans are very aware of travel costs. They are not only interested in absolute costs, but regard other destinations, using the same mode of travel, as substitutes and are also prepared to switch to alternative modes of transport.
4. The only country suffering from an underlying downward trend is Switzerland.

United States outward tourism

Building models from the United States proved difficult, which may be due to the very low propensity to travel abroad from that country. This difficulty is reflected in the R^2 values, with only the models for Mexico and the United Kingdom having values of 0.9 or above, and the former model is rather simplistic containing only one explanatory variable. It is, therefore, not possible to draw many conclusions from these models.

The main factors affecting demand appear to be income and absolute costs. Most overseas holidays seem to be regarded as luxuries with high income coefficients. The exception is Italy. This may be because:

1. Old family ties are felt particularly strongly by Italians and much of the travel is visits to friends and relatives.
2. There is a very strong pull to Italy for the Roman Catholics in the United States, who would tend to regard such a trip as a necessity.

United Kingdom outward tourism

The three sets of UK models will be considered together as the effect that disaggregation has on the variable coefficients is of interest. The majority of the 18 models have R^2 values of at least 0.8. The model for the United Kingdom to Greece by surface is poor with an R^2 value of only 0.492. In all cases multicollinearity between many of the variables is a problem, which makes interpretation difficult and perhaps is the reason why the sizes of some of the variable coefficients seem either surprisingly high or low. For example, when looking at the coefficients of the income variables in the United Kingdom to Austria models, an elasticity of 4.550 is indicated in the total model whilst estimates of 1.331 and 1.743 are found in the air and sea models, respectively.

One pattern which does seem to emerge is that the income variable coefficients are higher in models explaining air travel than surface/land travel. This seems sensible as air travel is usually regarded as more of a luxury than surface travel. It also appears that the British generally regard international holidays as a luxury with the income coefficient lying between 1.331 and 5.377 in all but two cases. Absolute cost seems to be important.

In only one model does no price variable appear – the United Kingdom to Spain by air. This model is suspect as it is very simplistic with only one explanatory variable. In all other models either a cost of living or exchange rate variable is present. Multicollinearity between the C and EX variables is a problem in the Italian models, and to a lesser extent in the Greece and Spain models. However, the remaining three destinations are not affected and thus bear scrutiny.

Holidays by air seem more price sensitive than by surface for Austria and France, although the surface models incorporate substitute cost variables as well. The British do seem to take exchange rates into account and appear to be very responsive to any movements, especially in the case of Austria. When looking at travel costs, multicollinearity is again a problem in all cases. However, what does seem apparent is that holidays by surface travel are sensitive to actual and substitute prices.

The oil crises do seem to have had a marked effect on total demand, although this is not as strongly indicated in the disaggregated models. The coefficient of the oil crisis dummy for 1974–1975 for Greece in the total model is higher than for the other destinations, as expected, given the threat of war between Greece and Turkey in 1974. However, this is not reflected quite so clearly in the air and surface models. The currency restriction dummy variable appears in just under a third of the models and, in each of these, the effect indicated is negative. All of these are countries regarded as relatively expensive destinations. The indicated effects range from falls of 5 per cent to 34 per cent in per capita demand. In the total models an upward trend of 6 per cent per annum is estimated for travel to West Germany and a downward trend of 11 per cent to Italy. Downward trends are also identified for travel by air to France (6 per cent) and to Italy (11 per cent). Outward tourism by sea/land to West Germany is estimated to be going up by 5 per cent per annum whilst to Italy a downward trend of 9 per cent per annum is indicated.

As with the United States, overall conclusions are made difficult by the presence of multicollinearity, however the following points probably hold:

1. The British regard holidays whether by air or sea/land as luxuries.
2. Demand is price sensitive.
3. Exchange rates are considered in the decision making process.
4. Substitute destinations and modes of transport are factors influencing tourism demand.
5. The psychological impact of the early oil crisis was marked.
6. Currency restrictions did have an effect on the number of holidays taken in higher cost destinations.
7. France and Italy are suffering from downward trends, whilst West Germany is experiencing an upward trend.

Conclusion

The set of explanatory variables which appears to influence the demand for international tourism varies considerably from one origin–destination pair to another, and according to transport mode where the data are disaggregated. Where a variable does not appear in an equation, this implies that the variable coefficient is zero. For example, in many cases a substitute price variable is not present, which suggests that the cross-elasticity of demand is zero. Furthermore, the estimated coefficient sizes show considerable variation across the various tourism flows, both with regard to origin and destination.

Estimated demand elasticities permit an evaluation of the likely impact of changes in the demand determinants. For example, if income in a particular generating country is expected to grow by 5 per cent, the differing impact on tourism flows to the various destinations can be assessed. Similarly, the effects of changes in air fares, surface transport costs, exchange rates, tourists' living costs etc. can be evaluated.

Further reading

Archer, B. H., *Demand Forecasting in Tourism*, Bangor Occasional Papers in Economics No. 9 (University of Wales Press, 1976). Discusses the concept of tourism demand elasticity in Chapter 1.
Lipsey, R. G., *An Introduction to Positive Economics* (Weidenfeld and

Nicolson, 6th edition, 1983). For a discussion of demand elasticities see Chapter 9.
Martin, C. A. and Witt, S. F., 'Tourism demand forecasting models: choice of appropriate variable to represent tourists' cost of living', *Tourism Management*, vol. 8, no. 3 (September 1987), pp. 233–46. An empirical comparison of the use of a specific tourists' cost of living variable with a general consumer price index in the context of tourism demand forecasting models.
Martin, C. A. and Witt, S. F., 'Substitute prices in models of tourism demand', *Annals of Tourism Research*, vol. 15 (1988). An empirical analysis of the impact of prices of competing holidays on international tourism demand.
Witt, S. F., 'An abstract mode-abstract (destination) node model of foreign holiday demand', *Applied Economics*, vol. 12, no. 2 (June 1980), pp. 163–80. Construction and estimation of econometric model to explain UK outward holiday visits by destination, transport mode and independent/inclusive tour using pooled cross-section and time series data.

In addition to the references listed, many econometric studies of international tourism demand in which estimated elasticities are presented are given in the *Further Reading* section of the chapter on *Forecasting International Tourism Demand: The Econometric Approach* p. 163.

CHRISTINE A. MARTIN and
STEPHEN F. WITT

Tourism destination area development (from theory into practice)

Introduction

The last decade has seen the evolution and application of the concept of tourist destination zones (TDZ), or tourism destination areas (TDA) in many countries. The more sophisticated developments and applications have taken place in the United States, Canada and the United Kingdom.

This chapter is intended to look at this field of development, to see how and why it has evolved and been applied. It addresses a number of questions:

1. What sort of theoretical base and assumptions underpin this approach?
2. What practical use and value does it have in the fields of tourism development, management and marketing?
3. How do tourism products relate to destination zones, and are they demand-led or supply-based?
4. In a time of moves towards tourism planning processes, and integrated tourism planning, does this type of 'TDA' approach conflict with or complement these trends?
5. Where a tourism destination area approach has been used, what practical and functional advantages have resulted?
6. With action programs and flexible strategies now to the fore, in the tourism world, can they be linked to, or even integrated with, the tourist destination area approach to tourism planning?

Concepts which underpin a new phase of tourism development

The explosion in the scale of international tourism movements in the last 15 years has led to a refining in our concepts of tourism, and of the *tourist system*, and the *tourism environments*, which are especial concerns to the functioning tourist industry – as providers, servicers, planners, developers, managers and marketeers of tourism. What then, first of all, is the tourist system?

The *tourist system* (as shown in Fig. 1) suggests that tourism sits within physical, technological, social, cultural, economic and political environments. It involves two types of region: those which are tourist-generating regions, and those which are tourist-receiving or tourist destination regions. Part of the tourist industry functions in the generating regions: the ticketing services, the tour operators and travel agents, plus the marketing and promotional activities of the competing destination regions. The channels of transport and communication form the linking part of the tourist industry – where air, land and water transport may carry the tourists to and from the third part of the tourist industry: the functioning tourist industry in the destination region. Here the essential accommodation sector functions (with its manifold forms of provision), including the catering and drinks industry. The entertainment industry, tourist attractions and events, plus shopping outlets are here to cater for tourists (and to varying degrees the resident population too). The full range of tourist services is supplied in the destination region.

In handling the *tourist destination regions*, it can be seen that these will vary in scale, size and target markets they serve, but will need some coherent structures for their planning, development, management and marketing. This is where the idea of *tourist destination zone* or *tourism destination area* planning comes in.

First, however, it is useful to examine that of the '*tourism environment*' (Fig. 2), which needs to be understood and accepted, prior to applying the *TDZ* or *TDA* approach. The tourism environment is a model of a system which has both dynamic and static components. Based on the images, perceptions, information available, financial means and attitudes of one group of people (the tourist population), potential tourists will choose the single or multiple destinations that will form part of their tourism experience. Their socioeconomic characteristics, interests, demands, culturally determined and financially influenced will link to the seasons/times they will take their tourist journeys. Transportation and communications will then take the tourist to the destination regions, and from airports, seaports, frontier road crossing, railway stations etc. to their destination accommodation, and from that to attractions, to shopping and information services, and so on.

The attractions at the destinations are the things for tourists to see and to do, they may provide the incentives to travel (sun, sand, sea, sex, through to many specialist interest aims). This,

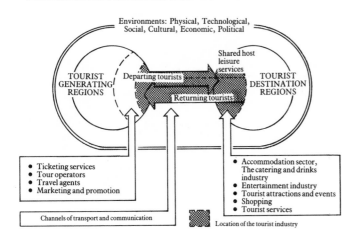

Figure 1 The tourist system (after Leiper, substantially amended by the author)

in turn, all requires the underpinning services and facilities – accommodation, catering and shopping at the destinations. Finally a key second population is involved – the host population and culture at the destination area, linked to the sets of resources at that place: the archaeological, architectural and man-built heritage, the natural heritage resources, and the host culture/cultural resources and subcultures with which the visitors may, or may not wish to interact.

Our definitions of the tourist industry, and its five component key sectors have greatly improved in the last decade, and in the same period a theory-base for tourism has developed. That theory base earlier grew out of economics, with the concepts of costs, benefits, the tourism multiplier, and has led on to developments in applied sociology, anthropology, and psychology. From writers like Dean MacCannell in the USA, Valene Smith, Erik Cohen, Stanley Plog, and others, we can start to structure concepts of stages of tourism developments, types of tourist motivation and preferred products and experiences. In conceptual terms, we have reached a stage where we can distinguish mass and minority markets, general and special interest tourisms, and know at which stage and in which sorts of place these may be combined, separated, distinguished.

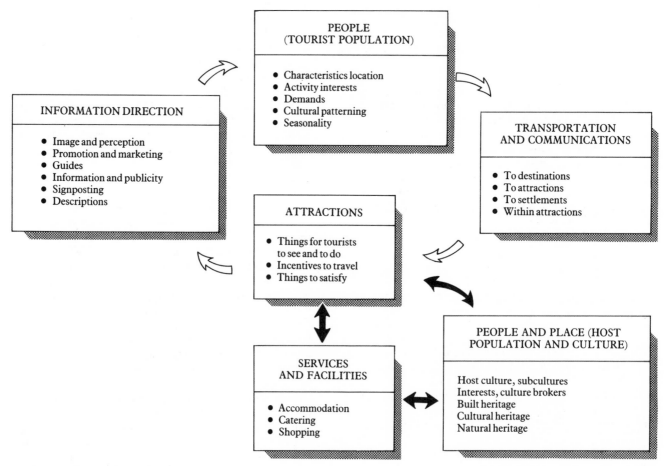

Figure 2 The tourism environment

Tourism product development and the development of tourist destinations

Because tourism – as a worldwide phenomenon, and complex set of provider industries – has expanded to a vast extent in a mere 20 years, understanding of the phenomenon, of the many types of tourism, understanding of the planning development, management and marketing needs have been uneven, and is generally at a grossly underdeveloped stage throughout the world. Even the simple concepts explained in Figs 1 and 2 are not understood in many countries which today host tourism. Consequently, the travel-trade idea of having 'tourism products', like the products of other industries, has been imperfectly understood. Other industries produce physical products, whereas tourism is seen to have much more brittle or fragile products – the experience the tourist has of his travel, of being at his destination, at the attractions, the human interactions, the resource-based nature of experiences and so on. It is not just therefore the assembling of product components, like transport, hotels, attractions, services and so on, but the fit of real experience to advance expectation of the tourist. It has to do with 'product integrity', i.e. how far is what is supplied the same as what is marketed, and therefore expected? Tourists invest high expectations in the 'magic' of their tourism experiences which they may want as a climax of their year – a social, spiritual or other type of annual refueling of the individual.

This means that tourism products involve quality factors of experience, and product assembly and integrity, as much as, if not more than quantitative aspects. A gregarious or big fun resort experience requires a scale and variety and vitality of provision at a tourist destination. At the opposite polarity, there is the isolative tourist who seeks wilderness untrammelled by the presence of other visitors.

In consequence, the 1970–1990 period has seen the evolution of a new type of tourist product categorization incorporating variegated types of tourist destination, scale and character: big seaside resorts, to city tourism, island tourism, industrial area tourism, to ski resort areas, to spas, to river basins, forest zones, desert and grassland safari zones, arctic and antarctic zones, conserved nature resource regions and so on. Tourism planning processes have increasingly been shared in the planning of these different types of region or destination area, but the products have often lacked adequate differentiation and increased identity. In a time of expansion of the number of tourist products, competition grows, and diminished identity of some destinations diminishes their chances of success.

Central and local government often act as key providers of infrastructure, on to which the commercial sector (in some countries) or the public sector (in other countries) may place the tourism superstructure. Government and public administration are often obsessed with functional provisions within administrative boundaries. Thus tourism plans for districts or regions often conflict with the functional boundaries of a destination area, to serve all the needs of one or more distinct sets of tourists. Thus a mechanism is needed which satisfies effective demands and needs of the tourists, regardless of governmental boundaries, and functional jurisdictions; this, it is suggested, is a key reason for the evolution of a concept like the *TDA theory.*

Tourist destination zones and destination areas: evolution of a concept, and its application

In the period from 1972–1982 on the North American Continent, the concept of the tourist destination zone evolved, partly through the work of Professor Clare Gunn, and interactions between him and a number of other thinkers. The fullest development of this field – in its American applications – was to be found in Canadian work at the end of the period. Gunn's work on 'Vacationscape' at the start of a period of expansion in leisure and tourism provisions, in North America, the Carribean and the mid-Pacific areas, gave a first range of concepts of demand and supply, interpreted in conceptual destination area terms. One can see the evolution from a stage where Gunn classified Destination Zones on a spatial basis (see Fig. 3) via the stage of differentiating the spatial structure and functional types of destination (the *Community Attraction Complex* of Gunn, shown in Fig. 4) on to State-wide or Province-wide Tourism Strategies, with highly differentiated tourism development zones, as indicated in the work of Balmer, Crapo & Associates (1977) in Ontario (see Fig. 5).

What is very important about the work done in the Province of Ontario, and work done for the Canadian Government is that the TDZ/TDA concept has evolved into a flexible tool for subregional product development, and for marketing thematically; this tool can be used for a small area, high population destination point (like a big city) or for an extensive, natural-resource zone, with a very small population, used for low-capacity, active, outdoor holidays. The methodology too (as indicated in Fig. 6) provides an approach which can be easily integrated with process-planning, and such techniques as the PASOLP (products analysis sequence for outdoor leisure planning) approach to Integrated Tourism Planning. It is for this sort of reason that planning done on tourism strategies in the United Kingdom in the 1970–1980 period, which had been more based on the Rockefeller Commission's resource development approach, has been able to be integrated with the US/Canadian Destination Area methodology during the 1980s.

What are tourist destination areas or zones now?

There are now several definitions for such areas, and these take into account factors including administrative (e.g. for organizations), marketing (e.g. for themes), site development (e.g. resort *not* area/region), or existing development (i.e. an area may already have many attractions, but no clue as to its future market potential except as indicated by the past). The terms are therefore used here to mean: *A coherent area of potential for tourism destination development based upon significant tourism factors – past, present, and possible future.*

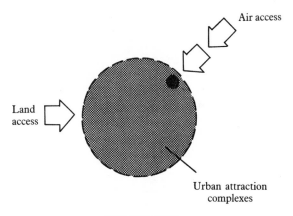

URBAN ZONE

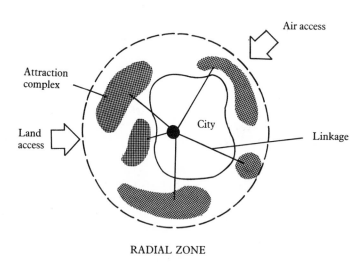

RADIAL ZONE

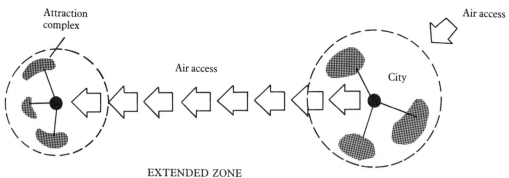

EXTENDED ZONE

Figure 3 Destination zones classified on a spatial basis (*source:* Gunn, 1972).

The basic premises of the definition are as follows:

1. The concept of destination *is* the tourism product, i.e. the product is the resource plus the development of that resource.
2. Development can be by government, or private, or non-profit/charity sector.

3. The principal component of the tourism product is attractions, supported by ancillary services and facilities. Thus the components of the tourist system in the light of the detailed tourism environments provide the guidelines.

The terms or definitions should not be misinterpreted. They are not intended as terms to be used autocratically by someone

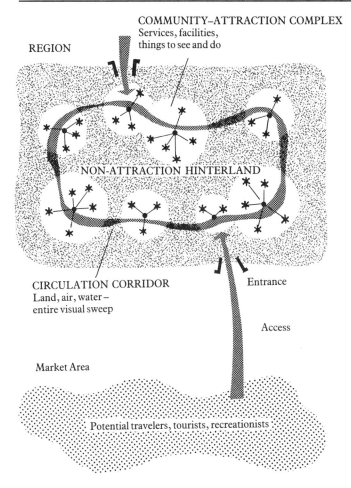

REGION

COMMUNITY–ATTRACTION COMPLEX
Services, facilities,
things to see and do

NON-ATTRACTION HINTERLAND

CIRCULATION CORRIDOR
Land, air, water –
entire visual sweep

Entrance

Access

Market Area

Potential travelers, tourists, recreationists

Figure 4 The community attraction complex (*source:* Gunn, 1972).

remote from the local scene or inflexibly when identified in a government document.

'Tourist Destination Zone or Area' does not imply rigidity or permanence of function. It *must be dynamic* – able to accept the changes in markets, and the changes in provision of supply, a market responsive in tourist destination supply over time.

The term excludes the touring side of tourism, but zones should include both 'touring circuit' and 'focused' types of tourism development. Thus touring routes or corridors may link destination areas, or be within them, and part of them. Touring circuits may include, for example, the visiting of natural resources, historic tours, scenic tours, and major event participation.

Criteria for the selection of tourism destination development areas

Balmer and Crapo in their Ontario work used the following criteria in the identification of areas, in order of importance (see Fig. 7):

1. Natural resource base:

(a) except in areas which are urban dominated, zones should incorporate areas having high capabilities for intensive recreation, especially all the year round activities and opportunities;
(b) areas should contain natural landscapes which provide esthetically appealing settings for tourism activities.
2. Population:
(a) areas should be close to major markets (i.e. a large population with the desire and ability to participate) or be easily accessible via transport channels to such markets;
(b) areas should be accessible to the labor market necessary to service the tourism industry.
3. Transport:
(a) areas should have access from major road routes;
(b) areas should also have *access* by a variety of modes (train and bus as well as car) to draw on as wide a market as possible;
(c) areas should contain an efficient *internal* circulation network which brings in the following considerations:
(i) the existence of routes between attractions and service centers that are attractive and efficient;
(ii) the availability of and potential for developing a variety of modes by which tourists can travel within the areas;
(iii) the existence of and potential for developing tours which can use unique methods of transport that relate to an area's development theme or image.
4. Attractions/events:
(a) areas should contain attractions and events of the scale likely to be attractive to at least regional markets, and preferably to draw on national (and sometimes international) markets;
(b) areas should contain clusters of attractions and events which together:
(i) show a diversity of appeal;
(ii) can be packaged to attract year-round visits;
(iii) do not need the degree or scale of ancillary development which would be required by a series of dispersed single attractions;
(c) areas should, wherever possible, include historic or cultural landscpes which are capable of encouraging tourist visits by forming the basis for the development of historical and cultural attractions and events.
5. Image and cohesiveness:
(a) areas should have common features on which to develop a regional identity (historical/cultural/physical/manmade etc.) which can be readily identified and associated with the geographic area;
(b) although administrative boundaries need to be recognized, they should not be paramount when clarifying a cohesive image for marketing development.
6. Services and facilities:
(a) areas should contain service centers that are able to, or have the potential to, provide good service to tourists and tourist facilities in the area;
(b) areas should contain service centers that can themselves provide potential attractions.

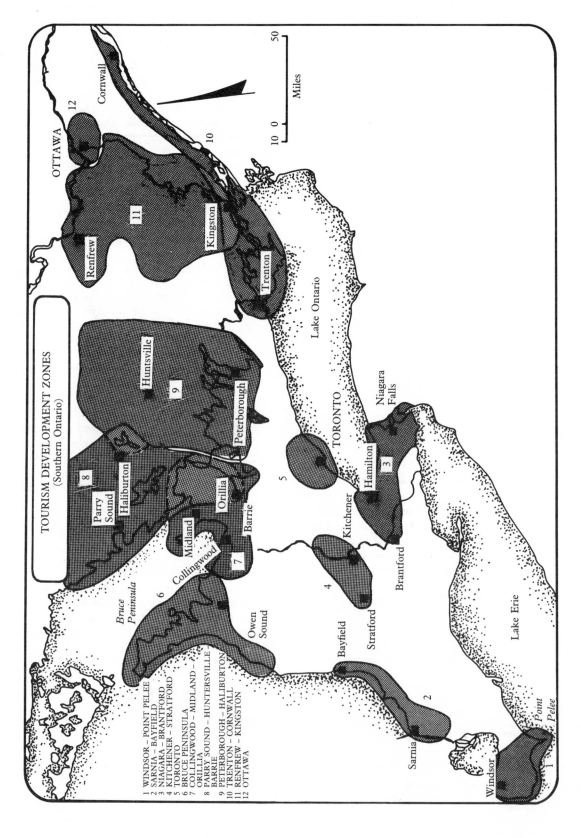

Figure 5 Tourism strategies: tourism development in Ontario – a framework for opportunity (*Source:* Balmer, Crapo & Associates, 1980).

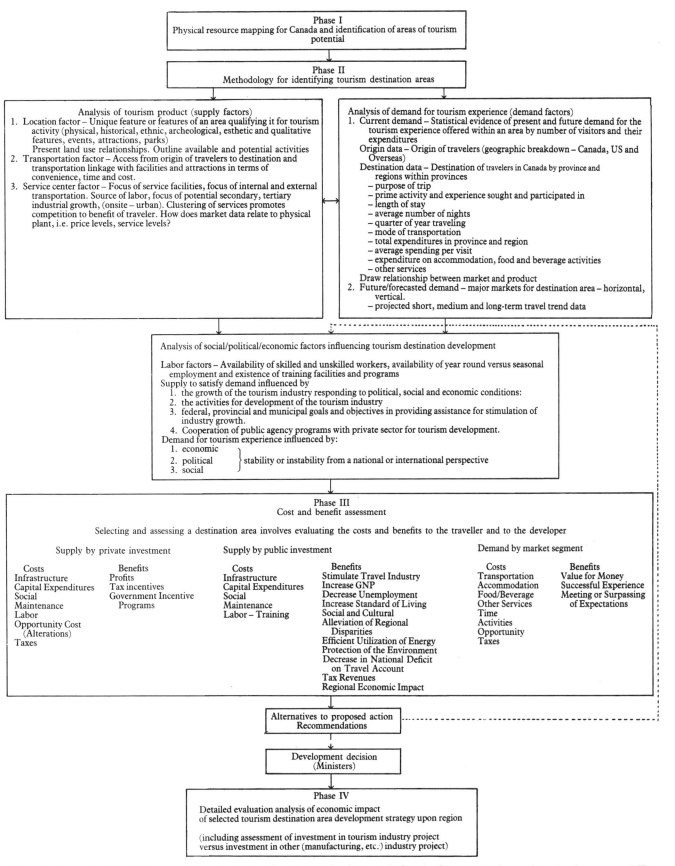

Figure 6 Process for identification, analysis and selection of tourism destination areas in Canada (Gunn, 1982) (*Source:* Canadian Government Office of Tourism).

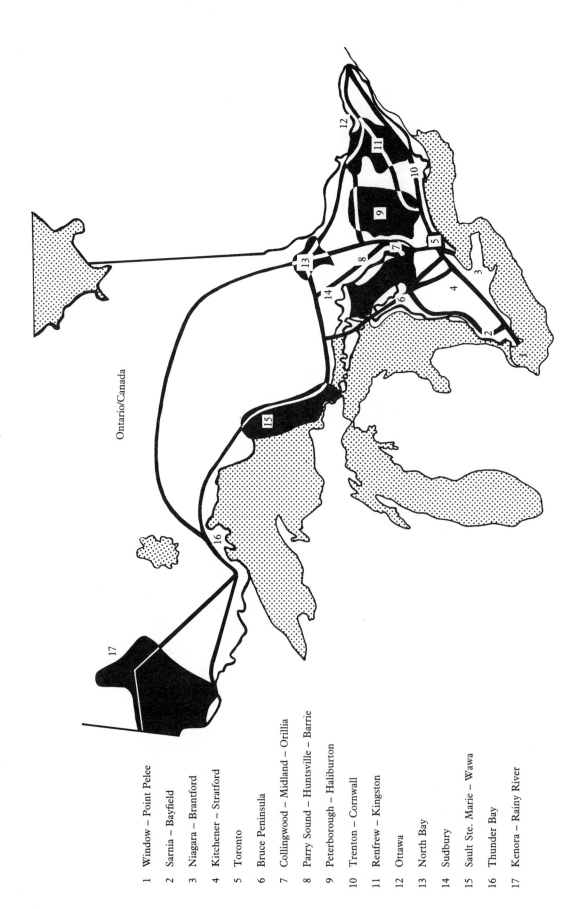

1   Window – Point Pelee
2   Sarnia – Bayfield
3   Niagara – Brantford
4   Kitchener – Stratford
5   Toronto
6   Bruce Peninsula
7   Collingwood – Midland – Orillia
8   Parry Sound – Huntsville – Barrie
9   Peterborough – Haliburton
10   Trenton – Cornwall
11   Renfrew – Kingston
12   Ottawa
13   North Bay
14   Sudbury
15   Sault Ste. Marie – Wawa
16   Thunder Bay
17   Kenora – Rainy River

Ontario/Canada

Figure 7   Ontario strategy for tourism development (*Source:* Government of Ontario).

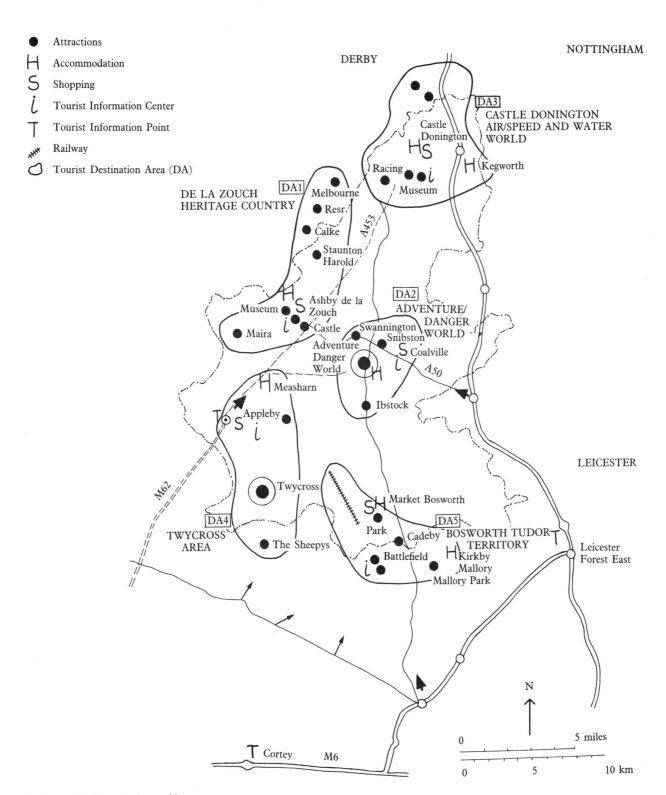

Figure 8 North-west Leicestershire strategy.

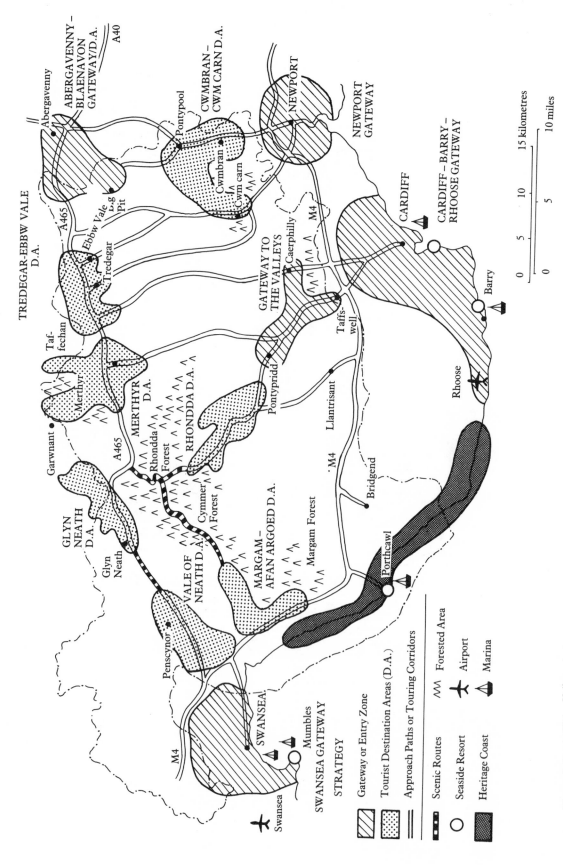

Figure 9 South Wales Valleys strategy.

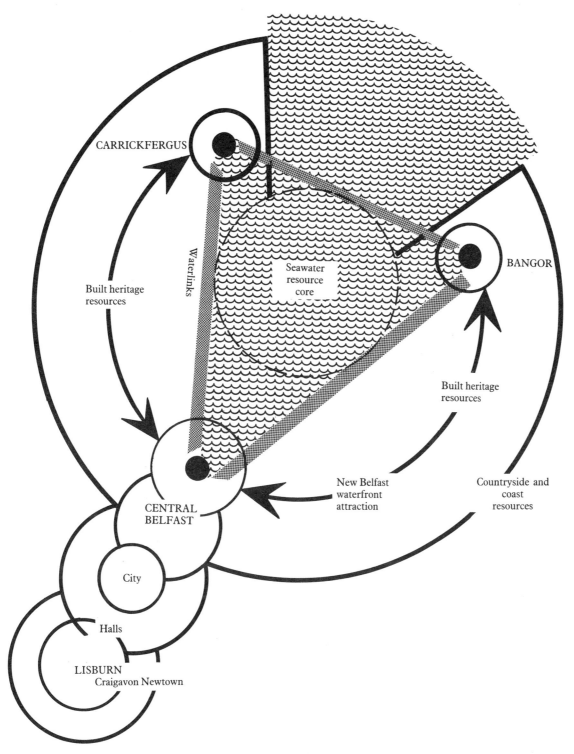

Figure 10 Greater Belfast tourist strategy.

The process of assessment of the potential for tourism development is a three-phase one, including research of physical and resource factors (twinned with segmented demand analysis), research of program factors and action programs related to time parameters, with conclusions and delivery system recommendations for realization of destination potential within timespans. Six sets of studies of international market trends, plus five types of national market trends (as well as development trends) are built into this process. Tourist destination areas have been well built into the model Canadian studies.

Recent European experience in the field

During the 1980s at least four UK studies have applied the TDA concept to several development zones:

1. Realizing the tourism potential of the South Wales valleys – done for the Wales Tourist Board by CURS (Centre for Urban and Regional Studies), University of Birmingham (Travis & Associates, 1983/84).
2. The North-west Leicestershire tourism potential study (Travis & Associates, 1984).
3. The Greater Belfast Tourism Study – by PIEDA (1987).
4. The West Cumbria Tourism Strategy – by PIEDA (1988).

Tourist products and strategic development have thus been integrated into these mixed sector, tourism strategies. To quote the North-west Leicestershire study:

> Rather than tourist changes being handled piecemeal in north-west Leicestershire, it would be advantageous to develop the tourist offering in an integrated way, so that accommodation, shopping and tourist services, are related to the location of attractions. If these are all integrated in a development-zone, or zones, then identity, image, as well as general convenience, and advantages in tourist packaging and marketing can be achieved.

The idea of 'tourist destination areas', used by the authors in their South Wales study, is appropriate for economic regeneration strategies, because each such destination-area can give a *distinctive and different set of offerings*, enabling thematic marketing, and special appeal.

Tourist destination areas are areas of very limited physical extent, in this instance not less than 3 and not more than 7 miles across, which can have a perceptual identity to a tourist market, and include most of the following three sets of characteristics:

(a) *One or more attractions*, treated thematically for marketing, so as to give one or more 'products' with appeal to specific sectoral markets
(b) A set of *services and facilities*, including accommodation, catering, toilets, shopping, information and publicity – for residents and visitors.
(c) *Transport and communications*, high accessibility, spare capacity, and possible treatment in relation to tourism, e.g. via landscaping, signposting, stopping and service points (for tourist information, toilets, catering etc.) as well as for interpretation.

Key diagrams from the Leicestershire, South Wales and Greater Belfast Studies are illustrated here (Figs 8, 9 and 10).

The South Wales and Belfast Studies further developed concepts of gateway, approach paths, touring corridors and scenic routes, as well as highly differentiated development pockets, with thematic, and contrasting but complementary features.

Conclusion

The TDA approach enables adaptive, and action-oriented strategies, which can achieve new tourism products in limited timespans, fitted to viable market demands, and encouraging viable products of integrity. Dutch work (Broos and Ziegler, 1984) on regional tourism strategies (or TROPs) has lacked an adequate economic dimension, and has not clearly differentiated a range of new tourism products fitted to target markets. Current Tourist Action Programs in the United Kingdom lack many dimensions of the earlier Canadian and US work. The four British case studies referred to attempts to *integrate* action-planning or programs, with development zone strategies.

In this field the theoretical base has underpinned a pattern of practice, which is proving to be useful in planning, development and management, and is now being tested in marketing. Market research has been part of the strategic planning process employed. The technique – rooted in Gunn's ideas, developed and adapted by Travis in British work – fits tourism product supply to viable market demand, and has been found to be functionally of direct practical value. Tourism planning of the PASOLP type (evolved by Lawson and Baud-Bovy, 1977) can and is being easily integrated with this approach to give an extended and matured form of integrated planning for tourist destination areas.

Further reading

Balmer and Crapo Inc., *Tourism Development in Ontario: A Framework for Opportunity* (Balmer and Crapo, 1980).

Balmer, Crapo & Associates, *A Review of Existing Tourism Zones and Suggested Primary Tourism Destination Zones* (Balmer and Crapo, 1977).

Broos and Ziegler, *Integrated Tourism and Recreation Planning for the '80's – Experience in the Netherlands* (Heidemij Consultancy, 1984).

Gunn C. A., *Vacationscape: Designing Tourist Regions* (BOBR, University of Texas, 1972).

Gunn C. A., *Tourism Development: Assessment of Potential in Texas* (1979a).

Gunn C. A., *Tourism Planning* (Crane Russak, 1979b).

Gunn C. A., *A Proposed Methodology for Identifying Areas of Tourism Development Potential in Canada* (Canadian Government Office of Tourism, 1982).

Lawson, F. and Baud-Bovy, M., *Tourism and Recreation Development: A Handbook of Physical Planning* (Architectural Press, 1977).

PIEDA, *The Greater Belfast Tourism Development Study* (Northern Ireland Tourist Board, 1987).

PIEDA, West Cumbria Tourism Strategy (Cumbria County Council, 1988).

Ruest G., *The Tourism Destination Zone Concept* (1979).

Travis, A. S. & Associates, *Recreation Planning for the Clyde* (Scottish Tourist Board, 1970).

Travis, A. S. & Associates, *Realising the Tourism Potential of the South Wales Valleys* (Wales Tourist Board, 1983/84).

Travis, A. S. & Associates, *The North-west Leicestershire Tourism Potential Study* (Leicestershire County Council, 1984).

ANTHONY S. TRAVIS

Tourism in difficult areas

Introduction

'Difficult areas', in tourism terms, may be defined as satisfying three conditions:

1. They have a small tourism base in terms of receipts and/or visitor numbers.
2. They may be regarded as unsuitable for tourist development because of a poor 'image', unfavorable social or economic factors such as a declining industrial base or poor environmental conditions.
3. They are in need of infrastructural improvement.

Difficult areas will tend to have a combination of these problems, although research has shown that there are significant and interesting variations between them.

Tourism can play an important role in regenerating inner cities and derelict areas. The transition from a predominantly manufacturing-based economy to a predominantly service economy often based in different locations has resulted in many declining or depressed areas throughout the industrialized world. Labor market adjustment has left pools of unemployed workers, often concentrated in inner cities or outer city housing estates. Tourism is labor-intensive and generates many unskilled or semiskilled jobs – precisely the kind needed in older centers of populations. In addition, tourism development can play a major role in improving the quality of life not only for tourists but also for local residents. Such an improvement in facilities and culture can have an important effect on self confidence and self esteem of residents of depressed areas, leading to self-sustaining projects and growth.

Many of the more successful examples of tourism development in difficult areas are brought about by a sustained partnership between the public and the private sectors. The role of local authorities, or local government bodies, is crucial. Such local authorities can become catalysts for private sector initiatives. The development of dynamic partnerships of this kind has implications which go beyond tourist development to a growth philosophy which may yield important benefits in much wider areas of economic and social activity.

The relatively low cost per job created and the possibility of rapid realization of job development potential are further elements which commend tourism as a job generator. However, it is too weak a reed to carry the whole of an area's job creation hopes. It must be part of an integrated strategy. Here too, care is necessary as tourist development may conflict with other job-creating policies.

Examples

A considerable amount of case study work has been done on tourism in difficult areas. Much of this work has been conducted in the United Kingdom and North America. Examples of towns and cities which have significantly improved facilities, economic activity, image and employment by tourist-related development include Boston, Baltimore and Lowell, Massachusetts in the USA and Bradford, Glasgow, Manchester and Calderdale in the United Kingdom. At a more micro level, individual areas of dereliction in towns have been transformed by tourism and leisure developments: examples here are dockland areas in London, Bristol, Liverpool and Gloucester and canal developments, e.g. the Rochdale Canal in Lancashire, UK and Camden Dock, North London. The use of neglected, disused or change of use buildings as tourist attractions, often as a tourist center in their own right is also well documented, e.g. Piece Hall, Halifax, Yorkshire; Covent Garden Central Market Building, London; and Temple Meads Railway Station, Bristol. The linking of wider areas in a single integrated strategy of access and/or promotion is also evident in the Welsh Valleys, 'Destination Humberside' and 'Great English City Breaks'.

Urban tourism

Several studies of urban tourism have been completed, generally examining visitor characteristics and purpose of visit. It is difficult to generalize from a small number of studies and limited amount of data but there appears to be a growth in short-break holidays from which urban centers can profit by shrewd marketing policies. Figures for large towns in the United Kingdom (1982) gave the following picture of bednights: short holidays 14 per cent, long holidays (at least four nights) 40 per cent, visiting friends and relatives 24 per cent, business/conference 20 per cent, other 3 per cent. The sector which has been attacked with most vigor is the short-break holiday segment.

Implementation

In the promotion of difficult areas, it is essential that as many key participants as possible cooperate in an integrated strategy. It is essential for the public and private sectors to comply to an agreed strategy. Local and central government funding of infrastructural improvement can be the key to unleashing private sector activity.

Further, it is important that such a strategy should be focused: a scattergun attack on many markets and segments of markets is unlikely to reap benefits. Difficult areas need to define their strengths and opportunities and to recognize and attempt to reduce their weaknesses as tourist destinations. Local cultural and historic attractions must be identified and made accessible and inviting to visitors. Any famous associations, for example with film and television locations, must be exploited, and museums well marketed. Special interest holidays can be developed to export unique or unusual aspects of the locality. Generally, research has shown the most important market segment to be the short-break holiday – often at weekends and often the second (or more frequent) holiday. Weekend packages are not necessarily the only successful market segment for difficult areas. The attraction of foreign visitors, the conference trade, business tourism and specialist holidays also can be important contributors.

There is often a case for an integrated strategy across a wider region ('Destination Humberside') in order to achieve viability as a discrete destination, or similar areas coming together in joint marketing efforts ('Great English City Breaks'). Such cooperative efforts need careful management, but have great potential.

The implementation of such strategies requires good organization. The evidence so far is for the commitment of too few resources to the organization of tourism in local (and central) government. Tourism must compete with other activities from a limited budget. However, to maximize the effectiveness of resource use, greater numbers of specialized tourism managers are required in local government.

Conclusion

Difficult areas, with a combination of a small tourism base, unfavorable image and poor infrastructure, can, with the right public and private action, develop as tourist centers in their own right. Research (mainly in the United States and United Kingdom) has shown that short-break holidays are the most promising market focus for tourist development. Careful marketing is required with attention paid to the particular attractions of the local area. Cooperative strategies, linking difficult areas with stronger attractions may also be an appropriate approach.

Tourism has an important role to play in the regeneration of difficult areas. It can provide jobs at relatively low cost and can raise an area's prestige and self-esteem. The jobs created are usually relatively unskilled – precisely those jobs for which there is most need in difficult areas. Management of the process is crucial and a well-organized, targeted approach with specific market segments as foci is necessary.

Further reading

Blank, U. and Petkovich, M. D., 'Research on urban tourism destinations', *Travel, Tourism and Hospitality Research*, Part 4, J. R. B. Ritchie and C. R. Goeldner, eds (John Wiley, 1987), Chapter 9. This chapter examines the techniques of conducting urban area tourism research, in particular impact studies.

Buckley, P. J. and Witt, S. F., 'Tourism in difficult areas: case studies of Bradford, Bristol, Glasgow and Hamm', *Tourism Management*, vol. 6, no. 3 (September 1985), pp. 205–13. A pioneering study of the context of tourist development in difficult areas with an investigation of the potential and appropriate strategies for each area. Points out the importance of a properly focused, targeted marketing approach.

Buckley, P. J. and Witt, S. F., 'Tourism in difficult areas II. Four north of England case studies: Calderdale, Leeds, Manchester and Scunthorpe', *Tourism Management*, vol. 10, no. 2 (June 1989). This article compares and contrasts four areas with similar backgrounds and locations and attempts to delineate viability as a discrete tourism destination. Provides pointers to opportunities for difficult areas.

English Tourist Board, *Tourism and the Inner City*, Planning Advisory. Note: 3 (ETB, 1980). A guide for local authorities on tourism planning and management in inner city areas. Includes sections on the impact of tourism developing strategies and interesting case studies. Appendices cover short notes on related projects not covered as full cases and sources of finance.

English Tourist Board, Incubon, *A Study of Tourism in The East Midlands* (ETB, 1975) Interesting, though now dated, study of a region including information on visitor characteristics.

Falk, N., 'Baltimore and Lowell: two American approaches', *Built Environment*, vol. 12, no. 3 (1986), pp. 145–52. Part of an issue on the theme of 'Revitalizing inner-city neighborhoods: six case studies'. In examining Baltimore's inner harbor and Lowell's historic textile mills it shows the importance of public-private cooperation and the emergence of a 'new type' of entrepreneur-planner. These key individuals require a range of skills from insight and resourcefulness to organizational ability.

Hall, P., 'Urban development and the future of tourism', *Tourism Management*, vol. 8, no. 2 (June 1987), pp. 129–30. Short article by an influential Professor of Geography highlighting the role which tourism can play in economic development strategies for older cities, in particular its job creating role for the unskilled. Uses examples mainly from the United States.

Hughes, H. L., 'A note on local authorities and tourism', *The Service Industries Journal*, vol. 3, no. 1 (March 1983), pp. 87–92. Local authorities are key participants in many instances of developments in difficult areas. This article examines their potential for successful ventures.

Jansen-Verbeke, M., 'Inner city tourism: resources, tourists and promoters', *Annals of Tourism Research*, vol. 13, no. 1 (1986), pp. 79–100. This long article is part of a special issue on 'Consumer Research in Tourism'. An empirical investigation based on historic Dutch cities and centered on interviews with day visitors. Presents a model of inner city tourism relating the product (inner city environment) to the tourist and the 'promoters' (image building and product improvement). Gives a profile of inner city visitors – activity patterns, importance of product characteristics, the role of promotion.

Travis, A. S., 'The tourism potential of outworn industrial areas',

Problemy Turystyki (Problems of Tourism), vol. 1 (1985), pp. 7–14. This article, published by the Instytut Turystyki, Warsaw, briefly surveys developments in tourism in specially adapted industrial areas and presents the major findings of the Wales Tourist Board study on realizing the tourism potential of the South Wales Valleys (see the following reference), emphasizing particularly the problems of access. Linking the remoter valleys to the major centers of population and changing the attitudes of the residents in the destinations emerge as crucial problems.

Travis, A. S., *Realizing the Tourism Potential of the South Wales Valleys* (Wales Tourist Board, 1984). This report identifies the major problems in developing tourism in the valleys, notably communications, attitudes of local residents and interest groups, lack of accommodation of the required quality, inadequate catering and public provision. A comprehensive resource appraisal is carried out on built resources, industrial archaeology, cultural and natural resources. The strategy requires building an integrated destination with a commitment to tourism.

Vandermey, A., 'Assessing the importance of urban tourism', *Tourism Management*, vol. 5, no. 2 (June 1984), pp. 123–35. Develops a model of urban tourism systems, and ways in which potential needs may be identified based on Calgary, Canada, Examines the limitations on conducting urban tourism research, notably data deficiencies and presents a conceptual model of the urban tourism system. The article examines the accommodation profile of Calgary and methods of assessing visitor expenditure to assess the impact of urban tourism.

PETER J. BUCKLEY

Tourism information systems

Introduction

In this era of the computer, databases, and the information explosion, the subject of tourism information systems inevitably must be explored. Even before the advent of computers, individuals developed procedures designed to collect and catalog tourism information and disseminate it to users. Although not computerized, these early efforts effectively provided tourism information to decision makers. Today, computer technology has been embraced making it possible to access and retrieve information easily and in one place.

Examples

General collections

Several organizations have developed special collections of travel and tourism related information which are now available to tourism executives, government officials, academicians, and students. Use of these general tourism information data banks can save a great deal of time and result in a comprehensive literature search on a desired topic.

One of the oldest, most comprehensive systems is the TOURISM REFERENCE AND DATA CENTRE (TRDC), 3rd Floor West, 235 Queen Street, Ottawa, Ontario K1A OH6, Canada, (613) 995–2754. This center maintains the most complete computerized collection of tourism-related information in Canada. The holdings of more than 5,000 books and documents include research papers, statistics, surveys, analyses, journals, conference proceedings, speeches, proposals, feasibility studies, legislation, guide books, bibliographies, and more. Information on this material is held in a data bank which can be accessed by TRDC staff or by the users of remote terminals in other parts of the country.

The computer system at TRDC is a bilingual, bibliographic information storage and retrieval system which allows users to search the holdings using 1,500 key words or 'descriptors'. Information is classified into eight major sectors: transportation, accommodation, conventions, hospitality services, events and attractions, recreational activities and facilities, education and tourist-related enterprises. The descriptors can be used singly or in combination to produce the information required.

Searches can be undertaken, for instance, by subject, author, sponsor, date, document type, geography, or various combinations of these. Although the information has been compiled to assist the industry and officers of Tourism Canada, it is also available to the general public.

A second general collection is the TRAVEL REFERENCE CENTER, Business Research Division, Campus Box 420, University of Colorado, Boulder, Colorado 80309, (303) 492–5056. Established in 1970, this reference center exists both to assist the travel industry in finding information sources and to house a comprehensive collection of travel studies. The center, which was established as a joint venture of the Travel and Tourism Research Association (TTRA) and the Business Research Division of the University of Colorado, Boulder, comprises the largest collection of travel, tourism, and recreation research studies available at any one place in the United States.

Cataloged according to the Library of Congress system, the present collection numbers over 8,000 documents and is growing daily. The collection was computerized in 1985 and literature searches can be done using 973 descriptors. Major documents have been abstracted and each document is classified under a number of descriptors. Users can request a literature search of the database by one or more of the descriptors and receive an annotated bibliography of the relevant materials.

A comprehensive collection of the world literature on tourism is maintained at the CENTRE DES ETUDES TOURISTIQUES, Fondation Vasarely, 1 Av. Marcel-Pagnol 13090, Aix-en-Provence, France, (42)270507. Headed by Rene Baretje, the center publishes *Etudes et Mémoires*, a reference book of studies in tourism. The 25 volumes issued to date have recorded over 36,500 documents. The center also publishes *Touristic Analysis Review* every quarter. The center has recently computerized its collection, and users may now search this database of over 30,000 books and papers. Users who need to know the international literature on tourism and leisure will find this to be an excellent data bank.

A final major general collection is LEISURE, RECREATION AND TOURISM ABSTRACTS, Commonwealth Agricultural Bureau, Farnham Royal, Slough SL2 3BN, United Kingdom, (02814) 2281. This quarterly journal is sponsored jointly by the Commonwealth Agricultural Bureau and the World Leisure and Recreation Association. Prepared by the Commonwealth Bureau of Agricultural Economics and published by the Commonwealth Agricultural Bureau, the journal offers a database which can be searched online. Relevant literature on leisure, recreation, and tourism can be found quickly and printouts of information can be obtained in minutes, thus saving hours of manual effort. The LRTA database is available as a subfile of CAB ABSTRACTS – subfile R3 on DIALOG; subfile 3R on ESA QUEST and DIMDI. Searches should be confined to the subfile. LRTA is an internationally accessible online database dedicated solely to the international literature on tourism, leisure, and related subjects. For further information, contact Margaret Leighfield, LRTA, CBAE, Dartington House, Little Clarendon Street, Oxford OX1 2HH, United Kingdom.

Statistical and other databases

Numerous North American and European organizations have developed data banks to provide assistance for travel decision makers and travel researchers. The types of services, specific holdings, and method of acquiring information vary from bank to bank, and interested users should contact the organization that maintains the type of data they are interested in. Some examples follow.

IATA Statistical Information System (ISIS) (PO Box 160, 1216 Cointrin-Geneva, Switzerland, 022–983366) offers a computerized information service on airline traffic, capacity, revenue and costs which is available to member airlines and affiliated interests. It provides timely, easily accessible statistics on commercial air transport. ISIS consists of a centralized database and a number of easy-to-use programs which allow retrieval, processing, analysis, and display of information compiled by IATA.

INS – US INTERNATIONAL AIR TRAVEL STATISTICS (US Department of Transportation, 400 Seventh Street, SW, Washington, DC 20590) maintains monthly time series showing the number of passengers flying between the United States and other ports. Data are broken down according to passenger citizenship, flight type, and the nationality of the carrier.

TRAVEL INDUSTRY INDICATORS DATA SERVICE (James V. Cammisa, Jr., Inc., PO Box 6627, Miami, FL 33154, (305) 868-3818) maintains industry facts on consumer data and trade statistics from the *Travel Industry Indicators* research library in its data bank. Information available covers all sectors of the travel industry and is drawn from newsletter research files. Sources are documented.

DIALOG (Information Services, Inc., 3460 Hillview Avenue, Palo Alto, CA 94304, (415) 858-2700), includes the CAB Abstracts, a comprehensive file of the 26 journals published by the Commonwealth Agricultural Bureau in England. CAB Abstracts contain a subfile entitled *Leisure, Recreation and Tourism Abstracts*. Subject areas covered in LRTA are leisure, recreation, and tourism; natural resources; tourism; recreation activities and facilities; culture and entertainment; and home and neighborhood activities.

The future

The above examples illustrate a few of the tourist information systems available to the public. Because these systems are so

useful, they have attracted the attention of the World Tourism Organization, which has conducted a survey on documentation resources and systems available for the travel and tourism sector and which plans, among other activities, the establishment of the *World Tourism Information Exchange Centre (WTIEC)*. The establishment will occur in two stages: a preparatory phase (1988–1989) and a pilot program (1990–1993) for setting the center in operation.

Creation of WTIEC is an important major development in tourism information processing. The data and documentation gathered by the WTO's survey should serve as key elements for drawing up a world inventory of the documentation systems existing nationally and internationally for the tourism sector and also for preparing, during 1988–1989, a feasibility study for the WTIEC project as well as the preliminary version of a multilingual thesaurus for information processing in the field of tourism.

For further information contact Mr Patrice Tedjini, Chief, Documentation Section, World Tourism Organization, Capitan Haya, 42, 28020 Madrid, Spain 5710628.

Benefits and implementation

For years, computers have been used for payroll, accounts payable, accounts receivable, reports and numerical analysis. Today, however, automation and data processing have moved out of the accounting department, and organizations can use databases, research, and other information to develop a total tourism information system to aid in decision making, in marketing, in customer services, or to accomplish a special purpose.

The importance of these developments must not be underestimated. Information technologies are reaching a critical mass, and organizations and their employees now think about doing their jobs with the computer in mind. The personal computer has increased the potential to develop and use a tourism information system because, through the personal computer, many users overcame their unfamiliarity with and fear of computers. In addition, the PC restored control over information to the manager. Because managers can now manipulate data themselves on personal computers, they are eager users and are hungry for more and better information. Managers are now receptive to what a tourism information system can do for them.

A tourism information system, or TIS, has four major components: the hardware, the database, the software and analytical package, and the communications link. The system puts together the pieces and makes the TIS a tool for management. The hardware provides the vehicle to become operational. The data bank provides the ability to store and retrieve information, which ranges from internal company records to demographic statistics. The software and analytical package allow the manager to retrieve, combine, and compare data. Graphs can be created, means figured, standard deviations computed, cross tabulations made, and multiple regressions calculated. The final component is the communication link between the user and the system. The system can be structured so the tourism manager can obtain information from the system in a number of ways. He or she can receive periodic reports, query the database for special reports, or use simulation models to develop various scenarios. Systems can be designed to provide information and communication with customers as well as managers.

Companies and tourism promotion organizations have been developing tourism information systems of varying degrees of sophistication for some time. Some examples of these efforts follow.

Minnesota travel information system (Limback, 1987)

The State of Minnesota has developed a travel information system as an aid in carrying out the state's marketing responsibilities. The Minnesota travel information system is made up of four sets of data:

1. The inquiry and order taking information (name, brochures, media sourcing information).
2. The seasonal calendar of events and attractions.
3. The follow-up survey that evaluates the travel behavior of people who have called the information center, including information on whether they vacation in Minnesota, how much money they spent, some demographics, and activity preference data.
4. The accommodations database.

The purpose of the system is to provide vacationers with the information that meets their unique needs by narrowing the entire population of vacation possibilities to the subset that they define as desirable.

The accommodations database module of the information system is somewhat unusual for a state tourism office. When vacationers who call the office express preferences for accommodations and certain amenities, the travel counselors answering their inquiries use the menu-driven computer system to access the accommodations database and assist the caller. There are five menus, and the first two, geographic area and accommodation type, are used in all searches. On the accommodation amenity menu, the travel counselors can choose up to seven criteria. The software then sorts through the data to find the accommodations that meet the requirements. These properties either are given to the traveler over the phone or are mailed, as a printout, along with other pertinent information.

For marketing reasons, Minnesota's travel counselors provide a personal link between the traveler and the information system. However, the system has the capability to be used by the traveler directly.

The Minnesota system is a marketing tool for the sales force and an information tool for management. It provides data to researchers so they can better understand the market and it provides tourism planners with a powerful data set.

Maine's tourism information system (Richard, 1987)

Maine's tourism information system lists all the state's tourist-related activities, services, and facilities by town, county, and tourism region. It provides introductory general narratives and specific narratives for each activity and associated businesses.

The Maine system was developed by the Maine Division of Tourism and the Maine Occupational Information Coordinating Committee. Data in the system came from a questionnaire that was sent to 498 communities, and the system has been designed to serve a number of functions, a tool which can be used by information centers and by travel agents to plan packages or to respond to specific inquiries. It is also a tool which can be used to measure supply in the context of feasibility and market studies. Finally, the system can generate a quantified 'quality of life' matrix which has been useful in addressing social issues as well as tourism concerns.

Currently the system is being used by the public and private sector, with the public sector dominating. The following illustrate some uses to which it has been put:

1. Conducting feasibility and market studies on behalf of firms such as Pannell, Kerr, Forster.
2. Determining room counts and attractions services in conjunction with a contemplated resort or hotel.
3. Helping develop Maine's case against location of a nuclear waste repository.
4. Planning conventions and conferences.
5. Conducting studies of local infrastructure needs, e.g., services and utilities.

An additional use would come from tourist information centers and travel agents within the state, who could supply more detailed information to tourists once they are in-state.

Maine has enhanced this first system by building a new system called the Maine Hospitality Data Base, which is an inventory of all lodging accommodations. Maine thus has a rapid response file to answer questions regarding meetings, convention, and group travel markets. Using this system, the meetings planner could assemble a configuration of hotel rooms, meeting rooms, restaurants, activities and attractions, and eliminate the need to plow through a mountain of literature. The data source for this system is a by-product of the TRAITS (Travel Analysis and Information System) inventory developed for Maine.

Conclusion

While numerous other examples could be given, this brief chapter has illustrated the types of tourism information systems that exist and indicated the potential for the future. Although some barriers to adoption exist, such as fear of and resistance to new technologies, high cost, perceived lack of need, and lack of appreciation by uninformed personnel, such systems are the way of the future. As widespread adoption occurs, innovative and strategically minded organizations will develop even more sophisticated information systems and move on into integrating expert systems.

Further reading

Gamble, P. R., 'Some implications of computers for hospitality managers', *International Journal of Hospitality Management*, vol. 1, no. 1, pp. 3–10.

Hill, M., 'Tapping online data banks', *Cornell HRA Quarterly*, vol. 24, no. 3 (November 1983), pp. 18–25.

Kasavana, M. L. and Cahill, J. J., *Managing Computers in the Hospitality Industry* (The Educational Institute of the American Hotel & Motel Association, 1987).

Kaupp, R., 'Avoid frustration and use a good information system', *Marketing News* (14 March 1986).

Lavon, Z. B., *Information Systems in the Food and Lodging Industry, Theory and Practice,* Cornell University, School of Hotel Administration, May 1975).

Limback, L., 'The computer medium and your travel marketing message', *Technology and Tourism* (Travel and Tourism Research Association, 1987).

Mayros, V. and Werner, D. M., *Marketing Information Systems* (Chilton Book Company, 1982).

Report of the Committee on Transportation Research Information Systems (National Technical Information Service, November 1972).

Richard, W. E., 'Maine's tourism information system: a tool to measure supply', *Technology and Tourism* (Travel and Tourism Research Association, 1987).

Strang, W. A., *Evaluating the Potential for a Small Business Information System in Wisconsin* (College of Business, University of Wisconsin-Madison, July 1979).

Technology and Tourism: A Growing Partnership (Travel and Tourism Research Association, Bureau of Economic and Business Research, University of Utah, 1986).

Teicher, J. S., 'Telecommunications revolution', *Cornell HRA Quarterly*, vol. 23, no. 1 (May 1982), pp. 53–6.

CHARLES R. GOELDNER

Tourism legislation

Introduction

Once objectives have been fixed and strategies determined, government must give them a legal framework to direct economic development. The degree of freedom left to the other economic agents depends on its own ideology. In spite of this legal 'framework', it is not, however, possible to speak of a tourism law as a coherent body of texts, since it is formed by calling on all branches of law (constitutional, administrative, civil, commercial etc.).

Two characteristics of the tourism sector – the constant dependence of the tourist on those rendering the services and the currency foreign tourists bring in – have led governments to become very rapidly involved in this field, involvement which has above all produced special regulations assuring a close control of its activities. The government can limit itself to strictly technical or administrative intervention or, on the contrary, enlarge it to include all aspects of the economy. The modes of enforcement of its laws can take the form of encouragement, coercion, punishment, dissuasion etc. Among this 'display' of legal, financial, economic means at its disposal, the public authorities must choose those that they consider most apt to help them realize their tourism policy.

The implementation of social and temporal objectives

The judicious use of work and leisure time not only facilitates access to holidays, and therefore to a more open personality, but also eases the intolerable overcrowding in certain tourist regions. Thus, contacts between tourists and hosts can be more personal and less prejudicial. On a daily and weekly level, most countries fix the maximum length of work time, with special measures for minors and women (no night work, for example). Sometimes these texts also impose the official weekly closure. But collective agreements play a very important role, especially in the tourism branch, in adapting the working conditions to the needs of the sector (the hospitality industry, for instance, is particularly busy when others are inactive such as holidays and weekends). As far as the paid annual holiday is concerned, most countries have instituted a more or less lengthy period, whether through law, salary negotiations or collective agreements.

These measures are usually accompanied by details concerning the time of year, the splitting up of the vacation time etc., which can have a direct influence on the staggering of holidays. But the rigidities of the school calendar are often invoked to justify those of the industrial sector. West Germany is usually cited as an example of how to desynchronize school breaks: the departure and return dates are pre-determined for each region for a period of 7 years, so that each year the starting date moves forward by a week.

The right to vacation time and the freedom to travel are closely linked. Thus the right to come and go freely is considered to be not only one of the fundamental rights of mankind (see, for instance, the Helsinki Agreement, 1975), but also the basis for the expression of tourism demand. To protect this precious liberty, a proliferation of agreements on international, multinational and bilateral cooperation has taken place, aiming at the suppression of visas, easing customs and immigration formalities and limiting health requirements.

All these facilitations in favor of tourists imply their protection, since far from home they are even more vulnerable, particularly so when in a foreign country where they do not even speak the language. Governments can either rely on professional codes of ethics, legislate or adopt administrative measures in order to protect the tourist, control the activities of transport companies and those of tour operators and travel agencies. The most widespread government action concerns the publicity and other promotional activities of the travel industry, but many countries have gone as far as legislating on the obligations and responsibilities of travel 'merchants'. In 1970, the International Convention on the Travel Contract was adopted in Brussels in order to harmonize the different legal provisions and assure the tourist of obtaining a maximum of information and protection in his relations with travel agents and tour operators. Unfortunately very few countries ratified this convention, with the result that each country's approach to handling this problem differs. Few also are the countries that have adopted measures to indemnify tourists who are victims of an insolvent agency. The United States, Japan and France, for instance, require a surety bond, while Canada, Denmark, Sweden and the United Kingdom, among others, have opted for the setting up of a reserve fund. There are many more countries that collect complaints from tourists at a national level and arbitrate on the disputes, either through mutual agreement (e.g. Austria and the Scandinavian countries) or through a constraining order (e.g. the Netherlands). In many cases, however, arbitration is left to the travel agents' associations.

The orientation of the tourism market

The efficiency of the measures relating to time will have direct repercussions on the use of tourism and leisure facilities. A demand spread over a longer period of time will render these facilities more profitable, which can also increase their competitiveness. Many installations, however, cannot receive clients outside the period for which they have been constructed (summer/winter) or cannot adapt to a more diversified clientele since their conception was unifunctional. A more discriminating clientele and their changing vacation habits thus force modernization, adaptation and diversification on the tourism supply agency. Partly because of the heavy investments this requires and partly to encourage businessmen to increase their efforts, all countries who consider themselves to have a vocation in the field of tourism have, at one time or another, set up a variety of measures to assist them directly (financial aid), indirectly (fiscal aid) or in kind (land transfer, technical and administrative assistance etc.). The granting of aid is usually discretionary, theoretically in order to permit the differentiated development of tourism facilities, but more often for strictly political reasons: grants limited to certain geographical regions, certain categories of accommodation etc.

According to the priority objective sought (economic development, foreign exchange earnings, increased tax income etc.) one measure will be preferred over the others. The granting of subsidies or grant aid at 'sunk cost' are not a common form of finanical assistance in tourism, with the exception of state-owned transport companies, and are usually limited to the following objectives:

1. The protection and stimulation of an emerging or modest sector.
2. The development of an economically weak region.
3. The improvement of the comfort offered by the lodgings, in some cases in order to bring in more currency.
4. The support of social tourism and spa cures.

Almost all countries do, however, grant loans for a more or less lengthy period to the tourism sector (from 20–25 years for construction, 8–12 years for the modernization and extension of facilities), since the tourism businesses encounter many problems when trying to secure a loan on the commercial market, because of their small size and a return on investment that is deferred in time. While interest-free loans are rare, interest relief subsidies are a much more common practice. In fact, this type of subsidy allows governments to assist more projects with a given amount of money than a preferential loan scheme. Their efficiency, however, depends entirely on the accompanying clauses. Thus, for instance, Belgium grants a subsidy to the credit institution concerned so that the interest rate is reduced by 3 to 4 per cent for a period of 3 years, which is a good way of supporting projects during their start-up period. On the other

hand, the United Kingdom had opted for a subsidy that reduced the interest rate by 3 per cent on half of the loan (1.5 per cent for the total) for a period 4 years, a much less effective measure, especially for those projects requiring a heavy investment outlay. Government or some designated institution will also sometimes guarantee the loan granted by a commercial bank, who might otherwise hesitate to grant a loan for a project requiring a large capital expenditure and which has a rate of return on investment that might be lower than in other branches of industry.

The total or partial exoneration from direct taxes is a practice that is particularly common in the lesser developed countries since it does not call on the often scarce government funds. Since fiscal advantages do not usually intervene during the planning and construction process, when capital outlay is heaviest, but rather once the business is running or after profits are already being earned, taxation incentives only have a limited impact in encouraging the development of the tourism sector. Since the lesser developed countries must often seek foreign investment funds for tourism, Governments offer guarantees relating to the repatriation of capital and profits, rather than requiring that revenues be reinvested within the country as they usually tend to do to protect the national economy.

The transfer of land, for a token rent or of a choice location, can also act as an investment incentive, as can work permits for foreign workers: the lack of qualified workers can be a handicap in lesser developed countries, while the highly developed ones lack menial help. But government can also finance studies, provide technical assistance and the logistics required by major tourism projects, as well as financially aiding professional training programs.

Government actions in favor of tourism supply are sometimes accompanied by efforts in favor of demand. The work legislation is, of course, at the base of these efforts for the majority of the population, but insufficient revenues are a real barrier to holiday making for many people. A few governments have therefore studied a variety of consumer subsidies, ranging from special holiday funds and saving accounts to subsidized holiday schemes in order to circumvent this one major handicap. But usually their aid is more discrete, like reducing the cost of public transport, or left to public and private social, welfare or religious organizations. These institutions sometimes receive government grant aid, either as general operating subsidies or as investment grants, which allows them to reduce the cost of services offered. In this respect, the free enterprise philosophy, which suggests that 'distortion' of choice by way of low prices is to be avoided, contrasts sharply with the philosophy extolled in the socialist countries and where holidays are heavily subsidized and encouraged.

The preservation of the tourism patrimony

The legal texts concerned with planning and development can be divided into two categories: either they deal with preserving the natural environment, or they try to improve it. Especially in the highly developed and industrialized nations, the awakening of an ecological conscience has led to such a proliferation of texts and measures, that it has become a most difficult field.

The texts dealing with conservation aim at one of two objectives: 1. direct or indirect land control, and 2. the constitution of green areas. Land control measures can be further subdivided into those aiming at preventing speculation and those tending to preserve the monuments and sites that have historical cultural, esthetic or natural values. However, the mode of enforcement can be very different as the cases of France and the United Kingdom illustrate. While France has created 'deferred development zones' (ZAD) where the State or its representatives exercise a preemptive right in order to protect the reference price, the United Kingdom has preferred to install a system whereby all land suitable for development will eventually pass into the hands of the municipalities. In the meantime, a development land tax is applied to the increase in value resulting from a construction permit. When it comes to the preservation of sites and monuments, France and the United Kingdom (as well as many lesser developed countries) have opted for the procedure of inventory and classification, which gives the authorities a right to impose (and enforce) a number of constraints, such as the restriction to modify the physical aspects of a building. But the law can also provide for the purchase of these sites and monuments: for example, by the Administration in Canada, by private interests and particularly public utility associations (National Trust in the United Kingdom, National Trust for Historic Preservation in the United States). Another very effective measure is the constitution of green belts around agglomerations, which preserve the city's character and provide recreational facilities for the population.

National parks exist the world over, although their definition varies from country to country. Although the supreme objective of these parks is always the protection of nature, visitors are treated differently: Canada represents one extreme, where all construction within the park boundaries is forbidden. France is less strict and allows the construction of accommodation and welcome facilities in the peripheral zones. The United States, on the other hand, does not consider conservation to be a self-sufficient goal, but rather something that procures pleasure for the visitor. England goes even further in this sense by stipulating that the designation of 'national park' permits the improvement of the facilities and access, since the land generally speaking remains in private hands.

All these countries have installed a 'hierarchy' of green areas. At the top are the few national parks, where conservation remains the priority. Underneath come in far larger numbers the natural regional parks in France, the country parks in England, the provincial parks in Canada, the outdoor recreation parks in the United States etc. Although protection is important in these parks, the priority is given to the relaxation, the rest and the education of visitors. At the base of the pyramid is the very large number of open spaces, many situated within city limits, of forests or even of paths and bridleways that can be found in all countries and whose main function is recreational.

Of major interest for tourism are also the measures that protect, and allow access to riverbanks, lakeshores and seashores. Beside legislation declaring these areas state property and/or controlling their use, a multitude of governmental and private organizations have as their main objective the acquisition of land along the sea and rivers. The law has often given them immense powers to accomplish this task, including the right to expropriate the land and the inalienability of their property.

All these measures of safeguard are rarely isolated, but are more and more often integrated into vast land improvement schemes through development plans. Even the most liberal countries resort to planning when it comes to land management, in order to define the governmental options in such matters as urbanization, industrialization, infrastructures and transportation. These plans should ideally take recreational and tourist facilities into account on the same basis as other land uses, but unfortunately, that is often not the case. France and the United Kingdom can be cited as exceptions: respectively, the 'land occupation plans (POS)' and the 'structure and local plans' define possible land uses, the nature and importance of constructions allowed and are the base for any building permit.

In the United States, where plans as a legal tool are not yet a normal practice, it is interesting to notice that one of the very few sectors that has been the object of just such legislation is that of outdoor recreation: in 1963, the Outdoor Recreation Resources Commission (ORRC) was created by law, and one of its tasks is to formulate, and keep up-to-date, a national outdoor recreation plan which takes into account all federal plans.

The difference between these two legal approaches becomes even greater when it comes to the application of the plans: while in the first two cases this is the responsiblility of public bodies, in the United States it is often left to private interests. These will receive technical and financial incentives to encourage them to undertake what in other countries would be considered to be a public service and thus a government responsibility. But France and the United Kingdom also differ in the way legislation has dealt with the implications of these plans. In the latter case, a public enquiry is obligatory in order to familiarize the public with the project(s) and take its recommendations into account. The French legislation, on the other hand, is far more authoritarian, and public consulation is discretionary.

Last but not least, in the urbanized and highly industrialized nations, an increasing importance is attached to maintaining a functional agricultural industry, the only effective way to assure the upkeep of the existing landscape. Measures in favor of the rural population are varied and multiple:

1. Statutory: zoning laws and dispositions concerning fallow land and the scattering of plots due to the construction of second homes.
2. Technical: agricultural counselling services to help with the modernization and diversification of farming concerns, or how to earn a complementary income through the rental of rooms.
3. Financial: subsidies to grow (or not to grow) certain products, loans and grants to encourage the construction of certain tourism facilities that help revive rural and mountainous areas.
4. Fiscal: employment creation within the framework of a regional economic expansion often benefits from a reduction of the tax burden, while the revenue earned from room

rentals can be exempt from commercial taxes.

5. Training: in order to prepare the rural population for economic, and especially tourist, development, they must be trained for the jobs created, and courses (usually subsidized) are set up by the Chambers of Commerce or other organizations.

Assessment

Any analysis of government's direct and indirect intervention shows that the authorities do not understand (or ignore) the interdependence between the various economic factors contibuting to the tourism system. It is even possible to affirm that their intervention has never been systematic nor, very often, has it been guided by an easily perceptible objective. And since tourism policy is always subject to the more global policies of the moment, each change in the policy leaves the initiated measures more or less hanging in the air while the authorities are interested in some other aspect of tourism. The majority of the legislative texts adopted during each period are not modified to comply with the change in direction.

It is only when a problem arises that government tries to compensate by taking another sectoral and partial measure, while rarely revising or withdrawing the old texts. The consequence, true in all countries, is a multiplication of texts since no one ever takes stock of the situation, that is to say repeals the legislation no longer applied, raises the incoherencies and the incompatibilities, points out the conflicting interpretations between existing texts and fills in the gaps left by the successive provisions.

Conclusion

The options at governments' disposal to implement an agricultural policy, for instance, clearly demonstrate the interpenetration of the social, economic and environmental aspects of legal measures. But in spite of the line of action set out by the policy objectives and the legal framework of their statutory existence, the interpretation and application of the laws is usually left to the more inferior hierarchical levels. Since each administrative level has its own powers, and often its own policy, it is not surprising to find great differences in the application (or the non-application) of many texts. In certain cases, a bylaw can be overridden by a ministerial order; the mayor, prefect or even a minister can authorize a nonconformity to the law; or the provisions are simply – voluntarily or involuntarily – ignored.

Further reading

Anolik, A., 'The role of the lawyer in tourism', *Tourism Management* (March 1986), pp. 50–2. The author looks at the law of tourism as a new and emerging field. The analysis is limited to the judicial and statutory definitions of the duties owed to travelers and to each other, by travel agents, tour operators, and common carriers (including airlines).

Arrago, R., *Les problèmes fonciers et leurs solutions* (Berger-Levrault, 1969). Although dated, this book deals with all the problems relating to land and its development. The author also deals with the various approaches adopted by different countries, their strengths and weaknesses.

Ascher, B., 'Obstacles to international travel and tourism', *Journal of Travel Research*, vol. XXII, no. 3 (Winter 1984), pp. 2–17. Following the work undertaken by the OECD and WTO, this article identifies and examines restrictions on the international tourist trade. Particular attention is given to government actions and regulations, classifying them in a very logical and comprehensive manner.

Bodlender, J. A. and Davies, E. J. G., *A Profile of Government Financial and Grant Aid to Tourism* (World Tourism Organization/ Horwath & Horwath International, 1984). Prepared for the Working Party on Investment in Tourism of the WTO, the paper sets out the principal methods by which governments can provide financial and fiscal aid for tourism projects. Case studies in selected countries have been employed to illustrate the current or past use of the various forms of aid and their effectiveness.

British Tourist Authority, *Legislation Affecting Tourism in the UK* (BTA, 1982). A fairly extensive list of texts that directly and indirectly affect the tourism industry.

Economic Commission for Europe, *Planning and Management of Leisure Zones, Including The Improvement of The Natural Environment*, vol. 7 (United Nations, 1975). The authors look at how to create leisure zones, while protecting the environment. The report is partially based on Clare Gunn's ideas on creating pre-parks.

Howard, D. and Crompton, J., *Financing, Managing and Marketing Recreation and Park Resources* (Wm.C. Brown Company, 1980). Chapter 9 deals with the legal aspects of managing recreation and park law, as well as personnel law, liability, risk management and public relations law. It also provides a brief review of legal research methods and reference materials.

Leslie, D., 'Tourism and conservation in national parks', *Tourism Management* (March 1986), pp. 52–5. The author looks at how tourism may support, and be supportive of, conservation, citing the Lake District as an example. After analyzing the various sources of conflict of interest, due to the fact that the National Parks in the United Kingdom are not owned by the people, the author calls for a clearly defined government policy, supported by effective legislation.

Mosse, E. and Lesage, J. L. *et al.*, *Etude RCB sur l'aménagement du temps* (Ministères de la Culture et de l'Environnement, de l'Economie et des Finances, de l'Industrie, du Commerce et de l'Artisanat, 1978). A detailed look at how 'time' is regulated in the OECD countries: workday and week, annual holidays, retirement. An exhaustive list of statutory measures and collective agreements in force is given for each country.

Organization for Economic Cooperation and Development, *Consumer Protection in the Field of Air Travel* (Consumer Policy Committee, 1980). An attempt to analyze and classify the various approaches to consumer protection, limited to ABC flights, within the member countries of the OECD.

Servoin, F., *Institutions Touristiques et Droit au Tourisme* (Masson, 1981). An indepth analysis of the various branches that make up the tourism industry and the laws that regulate them. France is the only country taken into consideration.

MARION JOPPE

Tourism marketing management

Introduction

Marketing management is the 'analysis, planning, implement-ation and control of programs designed to create, build and maintain beneficial exchanges and relationships with target markets for the purpose of achieving organizational objectives'. This definition by Kotler is deliberately broad since he is an advocate of the view that basic marketing principles have general application to many areas such as products, services, places, people and social causes. Certainly he would consider marketing to be applicable to tourism and therefore the general management process defined above to be an appropriate starting point to this article.

Whilst accepting the definition, it is clear that some of these topics will have received attention elsewhere in this book. Therefore an overview of the marketing management process will be considered sufficient in this offering, with particular attention to the specific problems which will be met in applying it to tourism and how they affect the managerial task. Finally there will be a brief consideration of organizational aspects to assist in management.

The marketing management process

All firms, and functions within them, of no matter what size or industry must go through the following broad process:

1. They will analyze their current situation to see where they are going.
2. They will state where they would like to be by defining their objectives and assess the discrepancy/gap between these two.
3. Some broad strategies will be devised to help ensure that the firm will end up where it wishes to be rather than where it is headed at the moment. The bigger the gap which emerges from steps 1 and 2 the more dramatic/risky are the strategies likely to be.
4. Finally some detailed planning will be necessary to imple-ment these strategies and a control mechanism devised to monitor these plans.

Let us expand on this process somewhat.

The analysis will be by means of an internal and external audit. Here management considers strengths and weaknesses (internal factors) and opportunities and threats (external factors). This is commonly called a SWOT analysis. It sounds a somewhat elementary stage, but in fact is critical. It is conducted in the context of competitive and market forces and indicates the differential advantage an organization may have. Members of the firm must seek to prioritize items within the audit and achieve a consensus so that action may be proposed, or further information sought through more formal research.

Some objectives will probably be given the marketing mana-ger from board level although he may have been consulted in their establishment. Ideally these objectives must be realistic, quantitative and hierarchical. The company will seek a certain return on investment. To achieve these the company will require marketing to achieve a certain market share or turnover. To achieve these targets a tour operator may require a certain oc-cupancy rate from his flights and accommodation. Quantifying objectives in this way throughout the firm allows for the use of management by objectives, increasing motivation and the like-lihood of achieving targets.

Strategies must now be established to achieve objectives. These are important long-term decisions determining the general direction to be taken by the firm (stategies aim at doing the right thing, i.e. effectiveness; tactics are concerned with doing things right, i.e. efficiency). Strategies will vary depen-ding on objectives but here a growth objective will be assumed, which is reasonable in the tourism industry at present.

At the very senior level a marketing manager/director may be concerned with merger/takeover decisions, either to diversify and spread risk or to integrate and seek greater control. In a high risk industry such as tourism, integration is the more common; hence Horizon Travel's ownership of Orion Travel, holding in Bass Horizon Hotels Ltd and recent acquisition of Wings/OSL. In such a growth market firms are cash hungry and are less likely to have the funds to diversify into nonrelated areas.

Marketing managers normally will be much more directly involved with the less dramatic intensive growth strategies. Can objectives be achieved by penetrating existing markets with existing offerings, or must products and/or target markets be adjusted? Penetration would be when a tourist attraction, 80 per cent of whose customers come from its own region nevertheless decides that more mileage exists, adapts its promotion mix appropriately and continues to target its own area. An illustration of product/market extension would be tour operators' development of packages for the growth market (e.g. Intasun's 18–30 club).

All the options above would use established marketing concepts. For example, the marketing manager from his earlier analysis would consider what differential advantage he may have over competition, which market segments will be the most advantageous and how to position his offering within that segment.

To this point strategic considerations have been paramount, but now more detailed technical factors emerge and the manager considers his marketing mix. What ancillary factors can be added to the offering to increase its attractiveness (e.g. free insurance on a package, free and plentiful parking at an attraction)? Are price discounts feasible? Can customers pay by instalments? How should the advertising budget be allocated between different media? What copy would be most effective? What incentives can be offered to operators/agents?

As these considerations emerge into the marketing plan considerable detail is involved, especially in a large firm. How this might be handled is considered later. Also as the positioning of the product is determined and the outline plan established the objectives given by the firm can be translated into goals for component parts of the marketing plan. For example, advertising objectives/goals cannot be established until the media are determined and these will depend on the positioning and segment selected and so on. Of course once this final hierarchy of objectives is agreed, then control of the plan becomes much easier as it is seen whether or not targets are being met.

Key difficulties in tourism marketing

The above process has universal value to all levels and functions in the firm. The marketing principles mentioned are also of general use but their application naturally varies by and within industries. Below are key areas where tourism differs from most other operations and these will require specific management consideration when drawing up plans.

People and Quality Control

For services generally it is argued that the marketing mix (i.e. Promotion, Product, Price and Place) should contain a fifth 'P', People, since they will invariably be involved at the point of purchase and simultaneous use of the product. Therefore the staff performance will be critical to customer satisfaction. It is more difficult to control the quality of an employee's performance than that of a machine and this applies particularly to international operations such as large hotel chains or airlines. Therefore the standard of the offering in tourism cannot be guaranteed to the same extent. However one of the key functions of marketing is to create a consistent image and differential advantage for a product so that customers are loyal to it and perhaps willing to pay more for it. If this is difficult then

competitors are forced back onto price competition. There is clearly a danger that this is happening between tour operators. A key task of marketing management in tourism must be to attempt to avoid such price wars. Moreover, if the performance of selected employees is to be such that they are seen as a key element of the marketing mix then clearly the marketing manager in tourism must be involved in the recruitment and training of such staff, to a greater extent than in other industries.

In 1982 British Airways (BA) reported a loss of £108 million and had debts of over £1,000 million. BA stood for 'bloody awful' to most people. With the appointment of Lord King as Chairman and Colin Marshall as Chief Executive the company has been turned around and since 1984 consistently makes profits of around £200 million per annum. This has been due to major staff pruning and cost cutting but Marshall also masterminded an image-building campaign, a reorganization into profit centers (using both product groupings and markets/routes as centers) and also a 'Putting People First' program which stressed not only the importance of the staff/customer interface, but also the importance of the 19,000 staff in direct contact with the customers 'looking after themselves' to ensure their good performance, and the duty of the remaining 20,000 to service the direct contact staff. The aim is that BA staff become its key diffential advantage in the eyes of the all important customer.

A corollary of the above is that if people are critical to the delivery of the product then the marketing manager must involve himself in the operating end of the business. Marketing managers for hotel chains must be interested and have some say in the performance of staff within hotels, just as airline chief executives must accept responsibility for the training of cabin staff.

Fluctuating demand/rigid supply

In many ways it could be argued that this is the classic marketing problem in all firms. Manufacturers make large investments with long lead times for an uncomfortably unpredictable demand. Yet it can be argued that these problems are exaggerated in tourism, particularly on the demand side.

Supply can require high capital investment for accommodation or airports but also there is the inability to store the offering, traditional in services. This becomes a real problem when faced with a lumpy tourism demand (due to seasonal factors) which is unpredictable due to the many forms that leisure might take and the hitherto discretionary nature of spending upon it. Add to this the fluctuation in the exchange rate and incidence of terrorism which bedevil international tourism and the difficulties facing the marketing manager are clear.

The traditional precaution would be to undertake market research. Yet some of the variables mentioned above are hardly predictable by clairvoyancy let alone standard research procedure. The marketing manager must be prepared to adjust plans so that fixed capacity is taken up. Whatever has been said earlier about avoiding price wars, the price cut which still contributes to fixed costs is a natural response. As this becomes a feature of the late holiday season however the informed customer delays choice to benefit from the offers. Should the manager cut back on supply? Not so long as the late buyer is making some contribution to overheads perhaps. Yet price wars do little for image and create dissatisfaction among customers paying the correct price.

Whatever late offers are made circumstances prevent targets being achieved on some occasions. This is an almost inevitable feature of the industry. For large firms diversification into other industries to spread risk may seem appropriate. If firms themselves do not have funds and in growth situations this is difficult, mergers on appropriate terms with firms in more stable industries might well be attractive.

Firms in the travel industry in the United Kingdom frequently have backing from large parent companies (Table 1). In addition, Hogg-Robinson (Travel) has recently been the subject of a takeover bid from the Trustee Savings Bank.

Horizon Travel and the International Leisure Group are exceptions. They are themselves parent companies and whilst expanding by merger they are tending to stay at present in the broad travel/tourism business.

Impact on society

The inseparability of the purchase and use of tourism products has further implications for the marketing manager. Marketing's role is generally seen as the satisfaction of the wants of the target market. The relatively new concept of societal marketing suggests that it should also consider enhancing the consumer and society's long-term well-being. Firms appear sympathetic to this concept but unless legislation or public pressure is brought to bear, they are able to ignore it. Certainly the marketing manager successfully selling chemicals in Europe is unlikely to worry if his firm is polluting a river in England. Not so in tourism however, where thoughtless development can ruin an environment and therefore product offering. Thus, particularly in the public sector the marketing managers must be heavily involved in planning/environmental aspects. Even if the environment is not destroyed there may be a change in the product's character necessitating approaches to new segments of the market. Indeed the marketing of tourism may be much more about managing and redeploying demand rather then increasing it (i.e. the controlled reduction of demand). Demarketing (reducing demand) is a concept which may have real value for some aspects of tourism.

Nonbusiness organizations

Tourism organizations range from those in the private sector where income is derived directly from customers, to those in

Table 1 Ownership of travel firms.

Travel firm	Parent company
Thomas Cook	Midland Bank
AT Mays	Bank of Scotland
Pickfords Travel	National Freight Consortium
Thomson Holidays	International Thomson
Lunn Poly	Organization

Table 2 Officers responsible for tourism in Northumbria/Cumbria.

Base department for tourism		Title of respondent	
Chief executive	7	Tourism (officer)	7
Planning	6	Leisure/recreation	6
Leisure	4	Press/public relations	4
Recreation	3	Administration	3
Public relations	2	Economic development	1
Libraries	1	Librarian	1

the public sector, which are partly or wholly subsidized. This confuses the marketing task in the public sector since not only must an organization appeal to its customers but also to its various providers of funds. These sources may well have varied objectives/motivation; for example, in sponsoring a theater. Arts Councils may be satisfied with high attendance and bringing culture to wider audiences, but the local authority may seek to increase employment. This implies attracting additional spending to the region and therefore promoting to customers outside it.

That local authorities themselves have differing perceptions of objectives for tourism can be seen from the reporting relationships discovered in research among officers responsible for tourism in Northumbria/Cumbria and indeed in the different offical titles given to these officers. Table 2 is a breakdown from 24 respondents (from a total of 33 authorities in the region).

Coordination of planning

The coherence of plans within a firm is absolutely critical; the strategies of functional areas in a firm will support the corporate strategy, will be compatible with each other and all will seek to achieve set objectives by satisfying customers. However in tourism this is more difficult as there are many elements involved in the satisfaction of customer demand. Tour operators thrive on this, offering the standard package providing both accommodation and transportation; there are many other elements involved in the provision of a holiday such as myriad private operators as well as the public authorities within the area. These should cooperate to provide a balanced overall offering or one focused towards a particular target market if that is appropriate, yet smaller firms in the infrastructure may compete rather than cooperate and local authorities may pursue independent policies which could conflict with the strategies put forward by the National and Regional Tourist Boards. In addition to this many tourist attractions are themselves dependent on a range of bodies each with an interest in their planning and marketing. This presents particular problems for the marketing manager who must control his own operations but also attempt to understand/influence a vast range of other organizations.

During the 1970s the plan was conceived to build a reservoir in a remote valley in North Northumberland (Kielder) for industrial purposes. By the time it was completed in 1982 however, industries, and therefore their need for water, had declined. There was now a need to promote the reservoir as a tourist attraction. How was this to be achieved? A Tourist

Development Action Program (TDAP) was established to assist in this. The key parties included the Forestry Commission, Northumbrian Water, National Trust, Northumberland County Council, Tynedale District Council and the Northumbria Tourist Board. The reservoir was the responsibility of Northumbrian Water; the surrounding land belonged to the Forestry Commission. To develop the accommodation fully, private finance was required; to obtain this improved roads were required and planning permission necessary from the local authorities. This is typical of the ramifications of such a public sector development. Who has responsibility for the marketing of the reservoir? To the extent that the Regional Tourist Board was, how could the marketing manager satisfy the needs of all parties? TDAPs are formed specifically to encourage cooperation between parties, but they are not universally successful.

Managing tourism marketing

The manager's job is not only to draw up plans, but also to make them work. There is no right way to do this since there is such a variety of firms in the industry. All recent management theory stresses the need to consider situational factors before determining the organization and management of an organization. This is too large a topic for this chapter but at the risk of oversimplification it is fair to say that a firm which is large and international, carrying out routine and urgent tasks, and operating in a stable environment, tends to be run in a formal manner with a hierarchical organization structure. Yet in reality such criteria may provide conflicting guidelines. Many firms in tourism are large, international with routine tasks, but invariably operate within a turbulent environment. This problem is resolved by accepting that organizational structure/cultures need not apply to the entire firm, but departments within it. Thus even within marketing the research departments and the sales force will be organized in different ways because of their different tasks/environments.

Having established a flavor for the marketing department, there is the question of handling staff. It is generally felt that participative management leads to greater motivation. Yet delegation/participation can only occur if the staff have skill and experience. This is a matter for managerial judgment but again points to the importance of correct recruitment and training of staff.

What tasks is the marketing manager expected to fulfil? The assumption seems to be that he will manage the process outlined earlier. But this is not necessarily the case; it will vary greatly by size of firm and we must consider this in some detail. In a small firm, and there are many within tourism, the manager will look after the whole firm; marketing management will take a portion of his time, and will have to compete with several other demands. In the large firm on the other hand a marketing manager will concentrate on marketing full time and deal with only part of the management process. For example the marketing director will take a long-term view of the market and

probably participate in the setting of overall objectives for the firm and the allocation of resources and effort between different products. The marketing manager will consider in more detail the targeting of resources using an appropriate differential advantage and setting subobjectives for component parts of the plan. Junior management will then coordinate, monitor and control the elements of the marketing mix to achieve the various goals. This latter task is clearly a complex one in very large organizations and specialized roles have developed; firms use either a product manager or a market manager.

The product (or brand) manager was developed initially in fast-moving, consumer goods industries where the company offered a variety of products to a single, relatively stable market. Hence, given this market stability, the product manager can devote attention to his product becoming the acknowledged expert on it within the company. The alternative approach is the market manager. This is where the company provides a single or similar products to multiple complex markets. This manager develops a thorough understanding of customer behavior and of the market for which he is responsible. Both the product and the market manager provide expertise and detailed attention to elements of the plan which would otherwise be impossible in large organizations. A weakness is that they lack the authority to match the responsibilities they carry, yet they are increasingly found in some form in many marketing departments.

These product/market alternatives are not mutually exclusive. Under its marketing director Jim Harris, British Airways employs both modes with eight market/route centers and three business types centers (i.e. cargo, tours and charters). However generally firms tend to one or the other. Thomsons the major UK operator has product managers in charge of its many brochures/programs. Detailed attention can then be given to the individual planning for each brochure. Inghams (the UK subsidiary of Hotelplan) runs a relatively up-market and less complex operation and therefore organizes six junior managers into its three major markets, Austria, Switzerland and Italy, ensuring that little extra quality for customers at their holiday destination. Tourist Boards in England also organize themselves and therefore their marketing by region, acknowledging the differences between each, and the need for a thorough knowledge of each area.

Conclusion

This chapter has considered the marketing management process, the aspects of it which will require particular attention in tourism, and some concepts which might help the manager to implement his plan satisfactorily. It concludes with the point that in a large firm a manager, depending on his position in the hierarchy, may be responsible only for a part of the plan.

The discussion should also have alerted us to another point however. The marketing manager to be successful in tourism must not confine himself to purely marketing matters. Certainly there are particular problems specific to marketing with which he must concern himself; the fluctuating demand and the lack of brand loyalty for example.

In the private sector, however, the problem of product quality must be met to achieve brand loyalty. This implies an involvement with staff not only in his own department but in operating departments far removed from head office. In the public sector he must satisfy many publics and seek coordination from authorities which have their own frequently conflicting interests to consider. Additionally cooperation with planning is essential to safeguard the very attractions which customers are visiting.

All of this implies an acceptance that the role of all personnel in tourism organizations is the satisfaction of the tourists/customers and the protection of their long-term interest. The marketing manager has a role to play in gaining acceptance of this view. Of course this does not suggest a preeminence for marketing. In tourist traps such as Oxford or York planning will play a vital role. In relatively undiscovered regions, such as Northumbria, marketing and promotion are vital. Firms must, however, focus on tourist satisfaction if the correct balance is to be established and overall planning to be successful.

Focus on small business

As already hinted the arguments put forward in this chapter certainly have widespread application. The planning process outlined initially is universally applicable. However whereas in a large firm the marketing manager will only be responsible personally for part of it, in the small firm the owner needs to apply it across the whole firm, not just the marketing tasks. The danger here is that all his time is spent on urgent but routine operations; there is no time for the strategic thinking mentioned earlier – no time to maintain the records which allows them to monitor their plans. To overcome a natural lack of time and funds, small firms must concentrate their limited resources on a particular niche in the market. As the owner will have knowledge of this well-defined market anyway the need for expensive research is reduced as are promotion costs.

Small firms frequently group themselves regionally into Tourism Associations. They then coordinate their strategy for promotion and become a pressure group to influence local government planning for tourism. In this way the problems of lack of coordination mentioned earlier can be offset. However this voluntary association must be professionally organized and members willing to commit resources if it is to work.

Small firms have a distinct advantage in the training of personnel and the quality control of delivery. The owner's influence on service levels will be strong; he will lead by personal example.

Small businesses are common in tourism and running them is never easy. Because of their size, they are more at the mercy of uncontrollable variables. However they must use basic planning procedures, and set aside time for monitoring and controlling plans from internal records. Then sensible adaptation to their situation will help them succeed.

Further reading

Bagozzi, R. P., 'Marketing as exchange', *Journal of Marketing* (October 1975), pp. 32–9. Fits marketing principles generally within the framework of an exchange process. Therefore marketing in the public sector is more complex, there will be several 'publics' or markets, but it is still marketing.

Cowell, D., *The Marketing of Services* (Heinemann, 1984). On services generally a very useful book, with Chapters 3 and 4 of particular relevance here.

Fisk, G., 'Criteria for a theory of responsible consumption', *Journal of Marketing* (April 1973), pp. 24–31. An early introduction to the concepts important in societal marketing.

Fitch, A., 'Tours operators in the UK', *Travel & Tourism Analyst* (March 1987). A very good review of this sector of the industry reviewing the competitive position of the major operators and their marketing strategies.

Foster, D., *Travel and Tourism Management* (Heinemann, 1985). A good review of the overall subject with Chapter 7 expanding several points mentioned in this chapter.

Galbraith, J. R., *Strategy Implementation – Structure, System and Process*, (West Publishing Co., 2nd edition, 1936). Particularly useful in considering the structures in complex organizations, the need for decentralization and, given that, the means of achieving integration and control.

Hanton, J., *Training Needs for Tourism in Northumbria and Cumbria*, unpublished Research report sponsored by PICKUP, conducted at Newcastle Polytechic (1986). This research deals with several sections of tourism, such as tourist attractions and recreation centers, in addition to local authorities.

Hersey, K. and Blanchard, K. H., *Managing of Organisational Behaviour: Utilising of Human Resources* (Prentice Hall, 3rd edition, 1977). Includes the Life Cycle Theory of leadership. Different situations require different styles of leadership. The level of maturity of staff is a key determinant. (Blanchard, K. H. *Leadership and the One Minute Manager* (Fontana/Collins, 1986) – a popular version.)

Kotler, P., *Marketing Management: Analysis, Planning and Control* (Prentice Hall, 5th edition, 1984). For many the definitive textbook on marketing. Chapters 1 and 2 give a particularly good review of the subject and there is some specific discussion of service marketing in Chapter 15. Treatment in this specific field of tourism is not a strength of the book as Kotler is arguing for the general applicability of marketing principles.

Kotler, P. and Levy, S. J., 'Broadening the concept of marketing', *Journal of Marketing* (January 1969), pp. 10–15. The general applicability of marketing principles is supported, whether in the private sector, profit or nonprofit making organizations.

Kotler, P. and Levy, S. J., 'De-marketing, yes demarketing', *Harvard Business Review* (November/December 1971), pp. 74–80. Argues that marketing is not always about achieving growth. The planned reduction of demand can also be a legitimate objective.

Luck, D. J., 'Broadening the concept of marketing – too far', *Journal of Marketing* (July 1969), pp. 53–5. A rejoinder to Kotler and Levy (1969).

MacDonald, M. B. H., *Marketing Plans; How to Prepare Them. How to Use Them* (Heinemann, 1984). The title says it all; a valuable review of the marketing planning procedure.

McEwan, J., 'UK travel agencies – future marketing strategies' *Tourism Management* (June 1987). A most interesting review of potential strategy options for travel agents in the future. This particular edition of Tourism Management contains several interesting articles on future marketing in the industry.

Porter, M. E., *Competitive Strategy: Techniques for Analysing Industries and Competitors* (Free Press, 1980). An interesting book on strategic management, particularly in providing alternative strategies which might be appropriate in different market conditions (Chapters 10–12).

Schmoll, G. A., *Tourism Promotion* (Tourism International Press, 1977). Takes a very broad view of promotion and therefore there are many insights for marketing.

MALCOLM MARTIN

Tourism marketing mix

Introduction

Understanding the marketing mix is essential for marketers to have a true marketing orientation, rather than a selling or product orientation. Marketers with a selling orientation rely on promotion to try to create a demand for their product. But these marketers do not necessarily have a product that meets the consumers' need; and the price and place may not be right. Marketers with a product orientation feel a good product sells itself. But a good product may be overpriced, impossible to access, or be unheard of by the consumer. Both the selling and product orientations ignore the variety of factors which affect consumer demand – this is the marketing mix.

The marketing mix is the combination of the 4 Ps of marketing: product, promotion, price and place, which the tourism marketer manages in order to reach his goal of making demand equal supply. The marketing mix has been called a 'recipe for success'. All ingredients of the marketing mix must complement each other and be emphasized in a balanced manner. Probably the most common error is to emphasize promotion at the expense of the other elements of the marketing mix.

Examples

The Hyatt Hotel in Hawaii has developed a marketing mix to appeal to one of its major markets, the Japanese tourist. Their service has been adapted to appeal to this market: menus and service directories are in Japanese and there is a two-person staff to assist Japanese guests. A 'push' promotional strategy is used; a fulltime sales manager keeps good relations with Japanese tour wholesalers and travel agents. Pricing can be high because Japanese consumers are willing to pay for quality. Distribution, or 'place', complements the marketing mix in two ways. Special efforts are made to develop and keep good relations with the trade (described above). Also, physical distribution is easy because Hawaii is the closest US destination to Japan. In fact, it is this element of the marketing mix which is the impetus for the other three elements.

Club Med's basic product – escape from civilization – remains, but Club Med has repositioned itself from a hedonistic holiday place to a family and business destination. They offer programs for families with children and plan to create programs for couples with infants. As a business destination, Club Med has locations with conference rooms and even computers. Promotion is being changed to reflect a more wholesome atmosphere. Club Med's pricing strategy reflects their 'escape from civilization' positioning – all fees, including those for transportation, are included. No cash is used in Club Med locations: Club Med resorts are located in beautiful areas which are not to hard to access, since the Club Med visitor wants to slip easily from 'civilization' to vacation.

Benefits

Proper management of the marketing mix is essential for success of tourism marketing. The marketer must attend to all elements of the marketing mix: product, promotion, price and place. The element of the marketing mix which tends to be overemphasized is promotion. Promotion which promises something which the tourist does not actually experience may work once for some tourists. But if tourist expectations are not met, the tourist will never return, and bad word-of-mouth recommendations will prevent other tourists from traveling to that destination even once. Product, price and place must also be integrated into the total marketing mix, in a consistent manner. When all elements of the marketing mix complement each other, the benefits are twofold: 1. the combination of elements interact synergistically, creating a much more effective marketing strategy; and 2. the consumer is not perplexed, and dissatisfied, by conflicting signals, e.g. a high price tour with poor accommodation.

Implementation

Product

Tourism marketing organizations such as hoteliers and individual attractions can create, plan and control their product relatively easily. These tourism marketers face the problems of other service marketers, e.g. lack of standardization of the product/service due to the human element involved and the fact that the product is consumed as it is created. However, they can decide the basic product design and then implement strategies to produce that design.

Ski resorts have repositioned their product from the 'dare-devil' market to older skiers and families. Easier ski slopes and lifts have been developed to appeal to these groups. Completely new products can be developed by tourism marketing organizations, for example The Royal Scotsman, a lavish train ride through Scotland.

Tourism organizations operating on a macro level, e.g. regional tourist boards, often claim they have no control over the product. However, they can to some extent influence the product offered. Tourism boards of regions known for scenic beauty must work to ensure that the scenery remains clean and natural. Singapore's Tourism Task Force has been faced with the task of preserving Singapore's exotic flavor in the face of urban renewal.

The Jamaican Tourist Board's brand management has taken the form of making Jamaica a friendly place for visitors. They ran a campaign in Jamaica to inform their population of the benefits of tourism and to encourage Jamaicans to make visitors feel welcome.

Having a product which meets the needs of customers is the most basic concept of marketing. Tourism marketers, as service marketers, do not have complete control over each tourist's experience of their services; regional tourist boards have less control over their product. However, as the above examples show, brand management is possible.

Promotion

As a component of the marketing mix, overall promotion strategy must be considered. The tourism marketer's message to the target market, through promotion, must be consistent with the actual product offered. Consider the examples described under 'product'. Ski resorts can promise older skiers and families that this sport is fun and relaxing, because the easier ski trails *are* fun and relaxing. The Royal Scotsman can offer a 'travel extravaganza' because the accommodations *are* lavish. Regional tourist boards should only promise benefits which they can actually offer: beautiful scenery, or, in the case of Singapore, a bit of old Asia. Jamaica can advertise itself as a friendly place only if Jamaicans treat tourists in a friendly manner.

Price

Price must reflect the type of tourist product being promised through promotion and, ultimately, the product itself. Higher prices can be charged for extra services which the consumer perceives as desirable enough to be worth the cost. The Royal Scotsman train experience costs £300 per day, because it offers adventure and great luxury. A more extreme product/price combination is a weekend at Oakbrook Hills Hotel outside Chicago for two for $20,000. Services include airfare from anywhere in the world, playing polo with the Oak Brook Polo team, and dinner for up to 12 people at the Waterford Restaurant.

Marketers hoping to price high should heed the advice of one ski resort marketer: 'You can't nickel and dime tourists who are spending big money on a ski vacation' (Rademan, 1987).

Sometimes, when managing the marketing mix, pricing becomes one of the foremost problems. For example, New York State found, through research, that young, less affluent families were the main customers for upstate New York wilderness areas. Tourist organizations should not try to upgrade and price very high, unless they are making a conscious effort to change their target market to one which is known to be willing and able to frequent such attractions.

The marketing mix should be managed to make demand equal to supply. However, tourism marketers should be wary of using pricing as a demarketing strategy when demand is greater than supply. During Philadelphia's US bicentennial celebration, hoteliers increased rates exorbitantly. This created bad relations both with tourists and tour operators.

Pricing can be used as a promotion tool. For example, Taiwan has offered a 'Three Frees' promotion to attract new tourists. First time visitors staying more than 3 days get one free night in a hotel, a free city tour and hotel transfer, and a free hamburger, in case they are tired of oriental food. Canada has promoted the low value of the Canadian dollar to Americans. However, this has only occurred on certain radio advertisements, to prevent a perception of cheapness of the product.

Control of pricing in the marketing mix is complicated when foreign tourists comprise a major portion of a marketing organization's target market. When the tourism marketers' currency is highly valued, foreign visitors find that destination more expensive. In order not to price themselves out of the market, tourism marketers may have to consider lowering their prices (and therefore profits).

Place

The 'place' element in the marketing mix includes both channels of distribution and physical distribution. Channels include tour wholesalers, e.g. tour operators, and retailers, e.g. travel agents. Tourism marketers should choose channels which are consonant with the other three elements in the marketing mix. A luxury hotel or tourist attraction should choose tour operators and emphasize promotion to travel agencies with upscale images.

Similarly, tourist attractions aiming towards families should choose tour operators which specialize in this market and travel agencies located in residential neighborhoods. The other aspect of 'place', physical distribution, takes on unique meaning to tourism marketers. Rather than getting the product/service to the market, the consumer must be able to travel to the tourist destination. Usually, this means travel should be easily available and convenient. Although most tourism marketing organizations do not have direct control over transportation, they can try to convince appropriate personnel (usually in government) to make necessary changes. Airports must be large enough to handle demand, be efficient, and be safe. The same is true for other modes of transportation – bus, train, ships and highways. Reasonably direct transport should be available from major markets to the tourist destination. In fact, major markets should be defined in part by availability of transportation. For example, Jamaica only advertises in US markets with good air connections to Jamaica.

Again, all elements of the marketing mix truly complement each other.

Assessment

Ultimately, effectiveness of the marketing mix is measured in sales. If sales are down, the tourism marketer should first examine the overall marketing mix – are all the elements consistent with each other? If they appear to be consistent, each element of the marketing mix must be evaluated. Marketing research should be used to measure consumers' perceptions of the different elements of the marketing mix. Basic questions to be answered are: Does the tourism product meet the needs of the target market? If not, what can be done to change the product/service? If the product is acceptable to the target market, the marketer should see if the problem lies in promotion, i.e. is the target market adequately informed about the product? If not, more emphasis in the marketing mix should be placed on promotion. Is the price the level that the tourist is willing and able to pay? Tourism marketers should make sure they have not priced themselves out of the market. Does the tourism organization have good relations with tour wholesalers and travel agents? Finally, is the tourist destination easy to get to? If not, local government must be convinced of the need to improve access to the area.

Conclusion

The marketer must determine the marketing mix that appeals to his tarket market. Having done this, he must determine whether any elements of his marketing mix should be changed. For example, Mexico repositioned itself from an area rich in culture to a resort area, due to the demands of its target market. The tourism marketer must consider all elements of the marketing mix when planning his marketing strategies. Product, promotion, price and place must be consonant with each other. When all ingredients have been carefully evaluated and planned, the marketing mix recipe will be successful.

Focus on small business

Small businesses must manage the promotion mix. They must decide their own product offering, determine the appropriate price, and promote those benefits which their tourism product offers the consumer. Even on limited budgets, promotion can be accomplished through cooperative advertisements. The physical distribution component of 'place' is not under the control of the small business. However, small businesses should work together to approach appropriate government officials regarding the improvement of access to their areas.

Small businesses should also work together and with their re-gional tourist boards to ensure that their region is appealing to tourists. Unpolluted resort areas, planned and controlled urban development, and safety are just a few of the issues that all tourism organizations, whatever their size, are concerned about.

Further reading

Carnba, A., 'Welcoming the Japanese tourist', *Advertising Age*, vol. 52, no. 23 (15 June 1981), p. S29. Discusses Hawaii's marketing strategies aimed towards Japanese tourists, a major market segment.

Boydell, M., 'Tourism sparks more plans for new attractions', *Asian Business*, vol. 23, no. 2 (February 1987), pp. 42–4. Gives Taiwan's marketing strategy, including positioning, brand management, and the 'Three Frees' promotion.

Fitch, E., 'Signing celebration sparks showtime', *Advertising Age*, vol. 58, no. 17 (20 April 1987), pp. 5–6. Describes Philadelphia's 'We the People 200' marketing campaign to celebrate the 1787 Constitutional Convention.

Gerrie, A., 'Mixing business with pleasure', *Marketing*, vol. 28, no. 3 (17 July 1986), pp. 27–31. Describes how the United Kingdom is taking advantage of nostalgia for national heritage. Includes new attractions being built by Tussaud's and the Royal Scotsman train tour.

Greenley, G. E. and Matcham, A. S., 'Problems in marketing services: the case of incoming tourism', *European Journal of Marketing*, vol. 17, no. 6 (1983), pp. 57–64. Excellent description of the problems of marketing an intangible service such as tourism. However, the authors take the view that the product cannot be modified. As described above, this is not completely true, although modification may not be as easy as for a manufactured product.

Haas, A., '$20,000 for a two-night stay – with amenities', *Philadelphia Inquirer* (26 July 1987), p. 4-H. Describes a luxurious weekend at the Oakbrook Hills Hotel.

Higgins, J. and Rose, S., 'Luring the travel trade: the grand illusion', *Marketing Communications*, vol. 9, no. 7 (July 1984), pp. 11–14; 61. Gives differentiation strategies by different marketers, e.g. hotels and cruise marketers, aimed towards different market segments.

Rademan, M. C., 'Ski town prediction: obstacles ahead', *Planning*, vol. 53, no. 2 (February 1987), pp. 17–21. Discusses repositioning of skiing to a safer, easier family sport. Excellent discussion of product changes and pricing suggestions.

'Resort promotion', *Marketing and Media Decisions*, vol. 15, no. 8 (August 1980), pp. 129–39. Describes promotional strategies from several areas, including Bahamas, New York, Bermuda and Canada.

Sullivan, K., 'Planners try to balance old and new in Singapore', *Asian Business*, vol. 21, no. 8 (August 1985), pp. 38–40. Describes Singapore's Tourism Task Force effort to save historical buildings which makes Singapore attractive to tourists and to rejuvenate Chinatown, also a major attraction.

Zacharia, C., 'Brand management: Jamaica makes it – again', *Madison Avenue*, vol. 26, no. 10 (October 1984), pp. 30; 32. Description of several aspects of Jamaica's marketing strategy. Excellent marketing orientation.

JUDY COHEN

Tourism marketing research

Introduction

Marketing research in tourism is the systematic gathering, recording, and analyzing of data about problems related to the marketing of tourism services. The five most common types of tourism marketing research activities are as follows:

1. Determination of market characteristics.
2. Measurement of market potentials.
3. Market share analysis.
4. Sales analysis.
5. Studies of tourism business trends.

The marketing research process is a systematic procedure linking together the marketing researcher, the marketing decision maker and the sources of relevant information concerning a particular problem. The key to the process is planning. The marketing research process has its roots in scientific research and the scientific method. In practice, however, marketing research studies in tourism range from the 'quick and simplistic' to carefully planned, systematic empirical investigations of hypotheses. Marketing research usually is conducted on request to provide information relevant to the solution of specific problems as they occur. Its two basic functions are to gather information and test hypotheses which are useful for marketing decision making.

Examples

A number of research studies have assessed the intensity of attitudes towards travel in general and have found them strong. Given an imaginary windfall of £1,000 and directed to spend it on something, a majority of people in one study stated that they would spend it either on household improvements or on travel. Few people stated that they would spend the unexpected money on a new automobile, home entertainment, new clothes, hobbies, or local recreation. A recent survey of single adults between the ages of 18 and 40 disclosed that 82 per cent of those people rated travel as either a moderately or highly important part of their lives.

Tourists have shown a growing interest in exploring nontraditional destinations in search of new experiences. This is one reason why Finland has been discovered by tourists, but, perhaps the most important factor has been the intensive information and marketing activity of the Finnish Bureau of Tourism, which has made tourism the third largest industry in Finland. Who are the tourists? Of the 2,300,000 foreign tourists, about half come from the other Scandinavian countries and the other half are nonScandinavian. Of the nonScandinavians, about 40 per cent come from West Germany and the remainder are from the United States, the United Kingdom, Belgium, France, Switzerland, Italy, and so forth.

It would perhaps be assumed that the Finnish people would feel pleased with the country's success in attracting foreign tourists. On the contrary, the people have very mixed feelings. The rapid growth of tourism has been accompanied by several problems. Firstly, the tourist influx is highly seasonal. Nearly 50 per cent of the tourists come in the 3 months of June, July and August. Secondly, most of the tourists come from lower- or middle-income classes with small travel budgets; they live in tents or trailers; they bring their own food; in a word, they spend very little money in Finland. Furthermore, they crowd the Finnish vacation spots at a time when the Finnish people are also on vacation and seeking rest and relaxation. This has led to many complaints. Thirdly, Finnish environmental groups have complained that their scenic land, particularly the lake area and Lapland, is being threatened with ruin. The Lapps have complained about the litter and about tentfuls of tourists who camp next to their previously peaceful summer cottages. The Finnish Bureau of Tourism recognizes that it has a new problem to solve. The earlier problem was to attract people to Finland. They succeeded but now are forced to adopt new objectives.

Benefits

The marketing research process is a tool that helps tourism managers wisely or adequately resolve marketing problems. Many tourism companies are geographically separated from the bulk of their markets. Collecting information about these distant markets is essential so that management can make intelligent decisions about what is needed in far away places. Also, important information is seldom obvious. Accurate answers to important behavioral questions may be essential in deciding effective strategies, yet the answers may be difficult for management to answer without conducting research. Executive isolation is another reason for collecting market information. Relying on collected market information enables them to make effective decisions relating to all target markets. Finally, accurate and carefully researched information is needed because of the high cost of making a mistake. Tourism management cannot afford to risk making a wrong decision on the basis of mere hunches or guesses. Too little information results in needless risk, but attempting to collect too much information involves excessive costs. Therefore, it is prudent for management to make a trade off between the cost of collecting and analyzing additional information, and the expected cost of making a wrong decision if the information is not collected. Neither marketing research nor marketing information systems can, however, eliminate all uncertainty and risk.

Implementation

At the initial stage of the marketing research process, a particular problem confronts the company or organization; usually this problem should be specifically and correctly defined. To help identify the true problem(s), a company should conduct a situation analysis, which is an investigation of the factors internal and external to the firm or organization that potentially relate to the problem area. In a situation analysis, the marketing manager or researcher relies on secondary data, which is data that has already been collected or published. For purposes other than the one immediately at hand, the secondary data could come from internal or external sources. Secondary data should be used whenever possible because they are readily available and are relatively low cost compared with primary data.

After having defined the specific research objectives and consulted the secondary data available, the market researcher can lay out the research design and then proceed to collect the necessary primary data. A research design is a blueprint or map for obtaining and collecting the primary data needed to solve a particular research problem.

Qualitative or motivational research can be very useful for exploratory purposes. It is designed to find the 'emotional hot buttons' of the tourist in relation to a particular subject, by bringing hidden stimuli up to the level of conscious awareness. Qualitative research involves many techniques ranging from indepth interviews to group discussions. Focus groups are of value in measuring the influence of group interactions on behavior, which is somewhat analogous to a reference group talking over a tourist product's merits. In the give and take of focus group discussions, tourists often reveal attitudes and perceptions that they would not make evident through other data collection modes. Furthermore, motivational research contributes to the process of questionnaire design. The most appropriate type of survey depends upon the nature of the information sought, the required sample size, and the location of subjects.

A variety of methods can be used to collect primary data, and each method has certain situations for which it is most ap-

propriate. The three principal methods for collecting primary data are as follows:

1. The observation method where data are obtained by watching human behavior.
2. The survey method where people are questioned directly by telephone, mail or personal interviews, and
3. The experimental method in which the researcher assesses how changes in manipulated variables affect other variables; the factor to be assessed is called the dependent variable, and the factors that affect it are called the independent variables.

All methods for collecting data require some type of data collection form. When designing a questionnaire, it is not easy to develop effective questions. There are, however, six criteria to consider for an effective question; it must be relevant, clear, brief, inoffensive, unbiased, and specific. Several basic types of questions can be used; open-ended, structured, indirect rating scales, semantic differential, control, semi-open, graphic rating scales, verbal scales, filter, likert scales, and thurstone scales, among others. Since even the experienced marketing researcher can make mistakes, many companies insist on questionnaire pre-testing, which consists of administering the questionnaire to a small group before using it to gather information from the entire survey group.

Almost all marketing research projects require a sample of the population because it is too costly in terms of time and money to contact all the people in the study population. A representative sample can be obtained using a good sampling plan. There are two basic types of sampling plans; a probability sampling plan and a nonprobability sampling plan. In a probability sample, each individual in the population has a known probability of being selected. Because there is a known probability for each individual, the researcher can estimate what is known as sampling error. Sampling error is a measure of the extent to which the sample can be expected to mirror the population on the characteristics or phenomena being studied. On the other hand, in a nonprobability sample, the probability of a person being included in the sample is unknown; thus the sampling error cannot be assessed. The major types of sampling plans are shown in Fig. 1.

With simple random sampling, every element in the population has an equal chance of being selected as part of the sample. In stratified sampling, the population is broken down into more homogeneous segments (strata) according to a common characteristic and a random sample of each of these segments (a stratum) is conducted. With cluster sampling, the total population can be broken down into a number of mutually exclusive groups (usually geographic area) where each element in the population belongs to one and only one group. A random sample of these groups is then selected and, if necessary, a random sample of elements in the selected clusters could be chosen.

Within the nonprobability sampling methods, the judgment sample utilizes judgment and experience to select the sample elements that will best contribute to the study. With convenience sampling, data are collected from people who are most conveniently available. Finally, quota sampling can be applied when the sample elements are collected at the convenience of

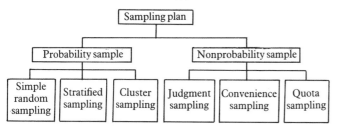

Figure 1 Major types of sampling plan.

the interviewers but the characteristics of the sample are matched against certain quota. The advantage of nonprobability sampling over probability sampling is that it is less expensive; its drawback is that the individuals chosen in nonprobability sampling may not be representative of the relevant population.

Once the data have been collected, the marketing researcher must be able to analyze them. There are many techniques for analyzing data, and it is fair to say that there is no single best technique for all situations. Most marketing research projects, however, involve explanatory studies where analysts examine two or more variables. This is called multivariate analysis. After the analysis, it is the reponsibility of the research team to interpret the data for management.

A research project should not be forgotten upon completion; in the final stage the analysts should specify follow-up procedures. Proper follow-up procedures anticipate changing conditions or incorrect conclusions that may have been drawn because of erroneous assumptions or other reasons. By performing follow-up studies, possible trouble spots may be uncovered before it is too late to take corrective action.

Assessment

Tourism managers need to pinpoint the exact types of information needed. In doing so, they should answer the following questions:

1. What type of decisions do you regularly make and what information do you need for them?
2. What types of special studies do you need?
3. What types of information would you like to get that is currently unavailable?
4. How should the information be reported, in terms of both form and frequency?
5. What improvements in information would you like to see?

By itself, though, simply spending money on research is no guarantee of useful results. Some studies merely verify the obvious; others are performed haphazardly. Whether the research is done internally or contracted from outside sources, it is management's responsibility to be in a position to assess a research project's usefulness and to judge whether or not it represents a quality piece of work. This is accomplished by understanding the nature of objectivity and the scientific method.

Conclusion

Management's need for information is ongoing and ever-increasing. Marketing research should be undertaken with a predetermined strategy in mind; it consists of planning for, obtaining, analyzing and interpreting all the facts necessary to make an intelligent decision concerning a particular problem. It involves systematically obtaining and analyzing information about a market, such as what tourists want, need, think, and feel. The need for solid marketing information is ongoing for routine and daily marketing operations in tourism. Objective, and therefore very useful, information is best obtained by following the marketing research process, which involves following seven steps: becoming familiar with the area and specific definition of the research problem, developing testable hypotheses, determining the specific information that is needed to test the hypotheses, developing the data collection instrument, acquiring the data, analyzing the data, and establishing follow-up procedures.

Focus on small business

While the involvement in the marketing research function varies from one tourism company to another, practically all firms, of any size, do some marketing research. There is a direct correlation between size of a tourism company and the size of its marketing research department. Size of the company, however, is not the only determinant. The overriding factor is the anticipated benefit associated with the cost of the department; the more extensive and frequent the marketing research analyses required, the larger the personnel and operating budgets. The size of the department also increases as its tasks become more complex. Nevertheless, small companies in tourism should use simple methods of collecting market information, such as marketing intelligence systems, internal reports, customer databank, and survey research.

Software/databases

The Survey System, Creative Research Systems, 1649 Del Oro, Petaluma, CA 94952, USA. This system now offers a CRT interviewing option because interviewing and tabulating in one microform printer package is the most efficient way to handle questionnaire data. The system also produces blank questionnaire forms. It has the ability to code and report the actual text of reponses to open-ended questions.

Microtab, Microtab Incorporated, PO Box 472, Newton, NJ 07860, USA. This is a microcomputer-based table production software. Excellent tabulation capabilities: 10,000 questionnaire capacity and recoding. Uses logical progressive menus.

P-Stat, P-Stat Incorporated, PO Box AH, Princeton, NJ 08542, USA. Permits: unlimited number of respondents, weighting and ranking, factor analysis, descriptive statistics and other statistical procedures.

Statpac Gold, Walonick Associates Incorporated, 6500 Nicollet Avenue South, Minneapolis, MN 55423, USA. You get a complete data manager, basic and advanced statistics, tables, windows, graphics, and utility program library.

Further reading

Aaker, D. A. and Day, G. S., *Marketing Research* (John Wiley, 1986). This essential book has a comprehensive coverage of all the important steps in marketing research.

Boyd, H. W. Jr., Westfall, R. and Stasch, S. F., *Marketing Research: Text and Cases* (Irwin,1981). Good coverage of important topics and excellent case studies.

Buell, V. P., *Marketing Management – A Strategic Planning Approach* (McGraw-Hill, 1985). This book includes a well-balanced chapter (6) on marketing research and marketing information systems.

Churchill, G. A. Jr., *Marketing Research: Methodological Foundations* (Dryden Press, 1981). This book has strong emphasis on the issue of methodology of analysis.

Churchill, G. A. Jr., 'A paradigm for developing better measures of marketing constructs', *Journal of Marketing Research* (February 1979), pp. 64–73. This article discusses the importance of developing good measures in marketing.

Deshpande, R., 'The organisational context of market research use', *Journal of Marketing*, vol. 46, no. 4 (Fall 1982), pp. 91–101. Good discussion of the role of market research within the organizational context.

Gross, C. W. amd Peterson, R. T., *Marketing – Concepts and Decision Making* (West Publishing Co., 1987). This book has an excellent chapter (7) on marketing research and information systems, which includes useful examples and illustrations.

Kress, G. J., *Marketing Research* (Prentice Hall, 3rd edition, 1988). The book emphasizes a 'how-to' approach to research procedures.

Labaw, P., *Advanced Questionnaire Design* (ABT Books, 1981). This is an excellent book on the problem of questionnaire design.

Lusch, R. and Lusch, V. N., *Principles of Marketing* (Kent Publishing Co., 1987). This book contains a comprehensive chapter (4) on the marketing research process and the marketing information system, including many illustrations, examples and action problems.

Mayo, E. J. Jr. and Jarvis, L. P., *The Psychology of Leisure Travel* (CBI Publishing Co., 1981). An excellent book which provides useful insights into motivational research.

Parasuraman, A., *Marketing Research* (Addison-Wesley, 1986). A good overview of contemporary issues in the marketing research process.

Peterson, R. A., *Marketing Research* (Business Publications, 1982), pp. 234–43. Excellent coverage of all the most relevant issues in the field of marketing research.

Tull, D. S. and Hawkins, D. I., *Marketing Research: Measurement and Method* (MacMillan, 3rd edition, 1984). This is a classic book in the marketing research literature.

LUIZ MOUTINHO

Tourism marketing strategies

Introduction

The literal meaning of the word strategy is 'the art of the General', deriving from the ancient Greek word for General, 'strategos'. To the tourism manager the term strategy has come to mean the type of decision made by the tourism company president or, at regional/country levels, on the relationships between the organization/tourism activity and the environment. In other words, tourism marketing strategy attempts to describe certain critical decisions that define the framework and direction of overall tourism marketing management and provide answers to the following kinds of questions: In what specific activity should the country/organization be in terms of mix of tourist products/services and customers? What course of action should the organization pursue (emphasis, timing, priorities)? How should tourism marketing resources be acquired and deployed? What major market opportunities are most compatible with the management definition of tourism marketing goals, objectives or missions? Tourism marketing strategy could take place at both 'micro' organizational level and/or 'macro' regional or country levels.

Examples

Development of a national (or state) tourism strategy has taken place, for example, in Michigan, USA. Designated an 'all-American City' in 1984, Traverse City (Michigan) was a growth area for tourism, attracting an average of about 10,000 visitors per day during the summer season and a fair amount at other times of the year. One problem of the area though has been over-optimism of its tourist 'pull' by residents, and this has been dealt with by the creation of a Traverse City Area Convention and Visitors' Bureau, which had the job of strategically promoting the area to all types of potential visitors, and developing local facilities.

Other work has been done in developing tourism marketing strategies in Massachusetts, USA, by examining the out-of-state 'auto tourists' to this state between autumn 1984 and autumn 1985. The results, gained from questionnaires handed out at turnpike locations and information booths randomly accessible to visitors, of which 40 per cent were returned, seemed to produce informative and reliable data on which future marketing strategies for the state could be formulated.

Development of a marketing strategy at 'micro' organizational level, has been successfully demonstrated by Sunmed Ltd, for example. This firm, having identified the natural geographical progression of popular holiday destinations across the Mediterranean towards Greece and noticing the abundance of cheap accommodation in the region, began operating a 'quality' package holiday to Greece that carried 374 people in 1973 and experienced growth from then on. Their initial marketing strategy included using the following:

1. An unusual, truthful brochure.
2. Consumer advertisements in national newspapers.
3. Many direct sales to clients answering the newspaper advertisements.
4. A small percentage of sales through traditional travel agents.

This proved very successful, increasing their customers to 5–6,000 people by the late 1970s. A still more specific strategy was developed, though, that included: firstly 'improving distribution through the travel agent', which Sunmed achieved not by increasing the agents' commission (which was the method that many companies employed) but by offering agents extensive 'displays', in windows and events; employing road representatives to distribute this material; and educating the 'counter staff' that they believed sold their holiday with trips to Greece, videos, a staff newsletter, training courses, etc. Sunmed also increased consumer awareness with advertisements in Sunday papers and color magazines, as well as television advertising in the peak Christmas/New Year period. Furthermore, a substantial drive was launched to 'find new resorts' in Greece as a method of expanding.

Sunmed also adopted a policy of offering UK regional departure airports, a highly risky policy at that time, which paid off after 2 years, with the consumers appreciating the added convenience. All this was achieved by maintaining middle-of-the-road pricing levels, which seemed to project an image of quality and reliability in a turbulent market. Indeed, so successful was this particular marketing strategy that Summed was able to 'ride the storm' of the early 1980s price war between the major tour operators, whereas other smaller firms fell; their strategy of continued growth and adaptation to certain market conditions was probably the key to success.

Sunmed Holidays provides an excellent example of *marketing inclusive tours*. This sector of the business is one which has been expanding in recent years, although Sunmed's situation differs slightly from the other operators in the industry in that it was not formed as a subsidiary of a larger organization operating in another area of the travel business, and so was not able to benefit from the marketing advice, gleaned from experiences, that they could impart. Sunmed, though, did follow the pattern of recognizing the demand for a certain type of holiday in a very price-elastic market, equally noting that the need was for a comfortable hotel, sun and an amenable view and not for any particular brands or names of these facilities, and thus met this demand by providing a standardized tourist product in the 'package tour'.

The format of a tour operator's strategy, according to these observations, is to develop a range of tours that will each cater for different, though similar, markets, and list these in one glossy brochure with one booking form. From there the priority will be to distribute these 'packages' through travel agents (from which 90 per cent of bookings will be expected to originate) and advertise their existence through mass media techniques. Consequently the experience of the tour operators in Western Europe in recent years in terms of marketing strategy has been either one of *diversification* – developing new services to offer to new markets or customers, like Sunmed; or *acquisition* – the buying of another organization that may or may not operate in the same service or market area.

Benefits

The basic objectives of tourism strategy are: to match the tourism firm's strengths with market opportunities; to avoid threats posed by competition and environmental changes; and to remedy weaknesses in the firm's organization and operations. It is not enough to generate tourist arrivals or achieve a certain market share but, rather, it is necessary to produce profitable tourist product sales and profitable market penetration.

There are four major stages in the formulation of a marketing strategy (see Figure 1), as follows:

1. Segmenting the marketing, i.e. identification of potential tourists' destinations and needs.
2. Defining constraints, particularly environmental and competitive factors.
3. Formulation of tourism marketing objectives.
4. Allocation of marketing resources (chiefly through the tourism marketing mix).

The benefits of a tourism marketing strategy identification include: the efficient allocation of marketing resources; the ability to develop marketing planning; identification of target market segments; and satisfaction of tourists' needs and wants.

Implementation

The first step in planning a tourism marketing strategy is likely to be one of confirming corporate/organizational objectives and developing these into marketing ones; and often the most relevant aims of tourism are growth and profitability. Growth is usually incurred through adjustments to the *product mix* – developing new products and ceasing provision of, or modifying, existing products – or by increasing the number of markets served, or both. Whilst profitability is often deemed by marketing staff to entail either: increasing sales by expanding the market size; increasing sales by increasing the market share; or by improving productivity through decreasing costs or adjusting the *sales mix*. These two aims, therefore, with the different methods of attaining them, are the major long-term objectives of mainstream tourism marketing, and therefore must be taken into consideration in developing a strategy. In practice however the formulation of marketing objective(s) is a function of the SWOT analysis, i.e. examination of environmental threats and opportunities as well as strengths and weaknesses in the organization (see Figure 1).

Tourism marketing strategies can be broadly categorized into two groups: *growth strategies*, comprising marketing strategies whose overall predominant character is related to a certain pattern of objective of market growth; *competitive (or market share) strategies*, comprising strategies that focus on tourism's market

Figure 1 SWOT analysis.

Stages in tourism marketing strategy			Examples/elaboration
1. Segmenting the market			Business travelers Conference market Demographic segmentation: youth, family, divorcees etc. Social class segmentation Family tours market Pilgrims
2. Defining constraints (particularly competitive and environmental factors)			Economic, political, social and cultural conditions Governmental, legal and technological forces Competitive situation and rivalry
3. Formulating marketing objectives			Satisfy tourists' needs Increase market share Increase tourists' loyalty to a destination Bedroom/bed occupancy rate Occupancy stability Improve tourist destination image
4. Allocation of marketing resources (via tourism marketing mix)	(a) product		Attractions Atmosphere Facilities Package variety
	(b) place		Location Accessibility Direct channels of distribution Indirect channels of distribution
	(c) promotion		Advertising in appropriate media Promotional literature Destinations images Brochures Sales representative
	(d) price		Price reduction packages Discrimination pricing Seasonal variations Group discounts

share competitive position. Whichever strategy a tourism firm decides to apply, it is determined largely by the marketing objectives and the target market.

For example, it is important to attempt to reduce the problem of tourism seasonality and improve capacity utilization by promoting an all-year tourism zone, creating new off-peak demand and by attracting other activities to hotel capacity. A 'pipeline' strategy (a continuous charter flights program) could be used in the low season, carrying specific 'interest target groups'. To maximize tourist satisfaction and to utilize best the facilities year-round, some action must be taken to minimize the level of variation of demand from the peak to the off-season.

Two specific strategies for dealing with this situation are the multiple use (involving supplementing peak season attractions) and price differentials. Basically there are three major strategies for tourism as follows:

Market penetration strategy

This usually focuses on gaining market share at the expense of competitors. This may be achieved through creating a differential advantage via any of the elements of the marketing mix. This is undoubtedly the most popular strategy prevalent amongst tourist firms. A well-planned penetration strategy would also win new tourists through its better understanding of their needs.

Market extension strategy

This is designed to reach new types of tourists by modifying the firm's present tourist products. By planning in advance of the actual launching of a new tourist product, its life could be extended or stretched out through predetermined actions designed to sustain its growth and profitability.

Market development strategy

This means that the tourist firm will seek new classes of tourists for its products or will add salient product characteristics to the existing line. This strategy seeks to widen its appeal to attract tourists from segments of the market which the firm in the past has not concentrated on. Such a strategy may either attempt to receive the new types of tourists in addition to its traditional ones, or may resolve to replace its past market segment appeal. Of the marketing mix variables, the most important factors that should be considered when this strategy is adopted are quite obviously promotion and product development. The market development strategies are of three types:

1. *The tourist product differentiation strategy:* This is designed to differentiate each tourist subproduct in real or psychological terms. A differentiated marketing strategy should be applied with different marketing mixes designed to satisfy several market segments. Promotional expenditures may increase as unique promotional mixes are developed for each market segment.
2. *The reformulation strategy:* This includes specific tourist programs which are designed to ameliorate some attributes of the tourist products, in order to satisfy the needs of the present tourist market. A product reformulation strategy means that the tourist firm sets out to build upon its present

market through developing new products. The application of this strategy may help to define the particular range of tourist products which would match with the specific motivations of the target tourist market.
3. *The innovatory strategy:* This focuses on expanding the tourism target markets either by segmenting the broader market or converting nontourists. An innovation strategy means that the tourist organization will seek to satisfy new tourists with new tourist products and services. A real innovation strategy searches for significant tourism innovations, not just 'new and improved' products.

Assessment

More recent studies on tourism marketing strategies indicate that strategy selection in this industry should be based on four factors: the size of the segment or submarket; tourists' sensitivity to the differences between tourist hotels, airlines, travel agencies etc.; the distinctiveness of these tourist establishments and companies; competitors' marketing strategies. In general, however, a tourism marketing strategy should have the following characteristics:

1. It should have a long-term time horizon, i.e. a strategy should relate to expected and/or possible developments in the market place, technological developments, trends and competitors' policies.
2. It should be decided at the top echelons of organizational decision makers and should involve *all* the functional areas and activities, not just marketing management.
3. The expected level of *risk* of any selected strategy should be considered.
4. It should fully attempt to exploit national and international opportunities.
5. It should be compatible with existent resources, strengths and opportunities.
6. It should be translated into plans, i.e. a strategic tourism plan in writing has to be developed as a result of a strategy, if it is to be implemented.

Conclusion

Operating in an environment of competition and inflation, the tourism industry must place greater emphasis on more efficient and objective-oriented marketing management. The world spending on tourism today exceeds $600 billion per annum, greater than the total world spending for health care or for military purposes. The employment of a marketing approach and relevant marketing methods will enhance the tourist firms with improved profitability and a larger market share. This could be achieved, in practice, via tourism marketing that is basically a three-stage process: analysis of the tourist's needs; designing a product/package to meet these needs; and communicating the availability of the tourist product via advertising, sales promotions and public relations. Unfortunately, too many tourist firms omit the first two stages and concentrate mainly on the third, leaving out marketing planning and policy. As every tourist organization must consider how it can build and protect a strong competitive and growth position, the critical question is the selection of an appropriate marketing strategy for tourism that might be suitable to different tourist market/product/competition situations.

Focus on small business

Most small tourist organizations have the following characteristics:

1. They have a limited number of products and services, and/or a relatively narrow/specific group of customers or geographical areas. Opportunities to spread the risk through large portfolios of products and markets seldom exist.
2. Limited resources and capabilities, in finance, management and personnel.
3. They are more flexible, dynamic and could react more rapidly to changes in the environment.

Taking into consideration these characteristics the two most suitable marketing strategies for small firms are as follows:

1. Concentration on a regional tourism expansion/growth, rather than national development. This will require development of tourism products and services that require less investment, yet offer high quality to selected market segments.

2. Niche strategy i.e. to select and defend a specific strong position in a particular segment of the market. Certain small tour operators, hotels, airlines, regional tourist offices etc., have specialized and concentrated on a particular niche in which they have found a profitable and lucrative market.

Further reading

Allen, T., 'Marketing by a small tour operator in a market dominated by big operators', *European Journal of Marketing*, vol. 19, no. 5 (1985).

Buttle, F., *Hotel and Food Service Marketing – A Managerial Approach* (Elm Publications, 1986).

Dan, R. E. T., 'Strategy is different in service businesses', *Harvard Business Review* (July/August 1978), pp. 48–64.

Greenley, G. E. and Matcham, A., 'Marketing orientation in the service of incoming tourism', *European Journal of Marketing*, vol. 20, no. 7 (1986).

Harris, K., Forster and Co., 'Developing a marketing strategy', *Cornell HRA Quarterly*, vol. 15, no. 3 (November 1974), pp. 34–48.

Holloway, J. C., *The Business of Tourism* (Holt, Rinehart and Winston, 1983).

Medlik, S., *The Business of Hotels* (Heinemann, 1980).

Meidan, A. and Lee, B., 'Marketing strategies for hotels', *International Journal of Hospitality Management*, vol. 1, no. 3 (1982).

Reilly, R. T., *Travel and Tourism Marketing Techniques* (Merton House Publishing, 1980).

ARTHUR MEIDAN

Tourism multiplier effects

Introduction

Wherever tourism activity takes places it will generate a variety of economic impacts. These impacts may be studied at the national level, or by examining the effects of tourism on some specific destination. Tourist visitors make expenditures on transportation, accommodation, food and beverage and other tourist-related services. Part of the monies spent by tourists, in each of the above categories, will leak out of the circular flow of income in the form of imports and savings, but the remaining portion will be respent in the economy on factors of production. Thus, the initial, or first round of tourist expenditure will generate a second round of expenditure (of a lesser magnitude than the first round) which will in turn generate a third round effect and so on. This process of repercussionary transactions will continue until the amount of expenditure circulating within the economy (as a result of the initial level of tourist expenditure) becomes negligible. The relationship between the initial amount of tourist expenditure and the resultant effect upon the economy, is the essence of the multiplier concept.

Tourism multipliers can refer to the economic impact of tourism expenditure upon the level of output, income, employment and foreign exchange of the national or regional economy.

Concept of the multiplier

The concept of the multiplier was first noted during the latter half of the nineteenth century, when it was recognized that changes in the level of activity in one industry could bring about changes in the level of activity in other industries and, therefore, create a *multiple* effect throughout the economy. The size of this multiple effect will largely be determined by the strength and extensiveness of intersectoral linkages, which will, in turn, generally be determined by the overall size and development of the economy. If it is found that a change in the level of demand for the output of one industry creates a ripple effect throughout the economy, it is important that the policy makers know the magnitude of this effect in order to implement rational economic planning.

The tourism multiplier refers to changes in the level of income, employment, output and inflow of foreign exchange generated by a change in the level of tourism expenditure. For instance, if tourism expenditure increased by, say 10 per cent, then some of this additional expenditure may be spent on accommodation in hotels. The additional revenue to hotels will then be re-spent on food and beverage, furniture and fittings, wages, salaries and distributed profits, government taxes and fees etc. Also, some of this extra revenue may 'leak out' of the economy in the form of imports which also includes profits, dividends, interest etc., paid to persons or companies not resident within the boundaries of the economy in question. Those persons who receive the additional money spent by the hotel sector will respend part of it within the economy on goods, services and factors of production and part of the additional money will be respent on goods, services and factors of production outside the economy. Furthermore, some of the additional money may be saved. Money saved and money spent abroad are both leakages and, in this way, the money in circulation decreases with each successive round of expenditure.

The various levels of impact created by the change in tourist expenditure, as it circulates throughout the economy, can be subdivided into three distinct categories:

1. The *direct effect:* the amount of income (employment, output etc.) created in the tourist sectors as a direct result of the change in tourist expenditure, e.g. wages, salaries and distributed profits in hotels, restaurants and tour companies.
2. The *indirect effect:* the amount of income etc., created by the increased expenditure of the tourist sectors on goods and services from their suppliers in the domestic economy (which may, or may not, be directly related to the tourist sectors). The indirect effect also includes the effect of the increased demand created by the suppliers to the tourist sector to their suppliers, and so on, throughout the economy.
3. The *induced effect:* as income levels increase throughout the economy, as a result of the direct and indirect effects of a change in tourist expenditure, some of this additional income will be respent on goods and services within the domestic economy. This repercussionary effect on the demand for domestically produced goods and services will increase income, output and employment etc., yet again. This is known as the induced effect.

The multiplier is expressed in terms of a ratio, generally the ratio of direct, indirect and induced changes in an economy, to the direct (initial) change which occasioned it. Great care must be exercised when comparing multiplier values of different economies, however. Misleading conclusions may be derived because of the differences in the way in which the multiplier is calculated and because of the different multipliers which may be computed. There are six tourism multipliers which may be calculated for any economy.

1. The output multiplier. This demonstrates the ratio of direct, indirect and induced changes in output, to the initial change in the level of tourism expenditure.
2. The sales or transactions multiplier. This is very similar to the output multiplier described above, but it does not include additions to inventories or stocks which may be occasioned by the initial change in tourist expenditure.
3. The income multiplier. This demonstrates the direct, indirect and induced additions to the domestic income generated by the additional tourist expenditure.
4. The employment multiplier. This is similar to the above multipliers, but shows how many fulltime equivalent job opportunities are supported, throughout the economy, as a result of the increased tourist expenditure.
5. The government revenue multiplier. This multiplier demonstrates how much government revenue is created by each additional unit of tourist expenditure. It generally includes all forms of government revenue – taxes, licences, fees and charges, less subsidies and grants paid out by the government to those sectors directly and indirectly involved in the provision of tourist-related goods and services.
6. The import multiplier. When tourists make expenditures in the hosting nation, part of the monies spent will go on domestically produced goods/services and part will be spent on imported goods and services. The same is true when those sectors involved directly with the provision of tourist goods/services make purchases from other sectors within the economy. Similarly, the suppliers to the tourist-related sectors will purchase some of their factors of production from within the economy and import the rest. Thus, it is useful to know how much of the total tourist expenditure stays within the economy and how much 'leaks out' in the form of imports. Thus, the import multiplier demonstrates the value of imported goods and services associated with each additional unit of tourist expenditure.

Multipliers 1, 2 and 3 are used fairly frequently during economic studies of tourism impact. Multipliers 4, 5 and 6 are becoming more common. The employment multiplier is the least reliable of all the multiplier concepts because of two factors. First, if it is derived from an input–output multiplier model, or an *ad hoc* multiplier model, it is generally linked to either income or output in a linear fashion. Thus, it assumes a proportional relationship between employment and these other variables, whereas employment is theoretically assumed to be linked to output (income) in a nonproportional manner because of the existence of economies of large scale production and the use of technology etc. Secondly, it assumes that all existing employees are fully utilized so that an increase in tourist activity will inevitably lead to an increase in the level of employment. This is clearly not always the case and additional demand may be met

by either greater utilization of the existing labor force, or by production reorganization. Nevertheless, the employment multiplier provides a useful tool for examining the number of fulltime equivalent job opportunities which are supported by tourist activity and for making sectoral comparisons (with caution).

Ad hoc multipliers

The basic framework which underlines the *ad hoc* multiplier can be traced back to the notable work of Kahn and, subsequently, Keynes, who expressed the multiplier as

$$k = \frac{1}{1 - c + m}$$

where

k = the multiplier
c = the marginal propensity to consume (i.e. the proportion of income which is spent on goods and services)
m = the marginal propensity to import.

The multiplier value is determined by the propensities to consume and import. The larger the propensity to consume, the greater the size of the multiplier. The larger the propensity to import, the smaller the multiplier value.

Although it is inadvisable to generalize about the multiplier values, it may be said that, in general, the smaller the economy, the smaller the multiplier. This is largely because 1. a small economy tends not to have the sectoral interdependencies which circulate the monies spent during the first round of expenditure and 2. there is likely to be a high marginal propensity to import associated with small economies.

Input–output multipliers

These are multipliers derived from input–output models and are described elsewhere in this book p. 223.

Conflict between different income multipliers

There are conflicting views about tourist income multipliers:

1. Type I income multipliers. This is the ratio of the direct plus indirect income generated by tourist expenditure to the direct income generated.
2. Type II income multipliers. This is the ratio of the direct plus indirect plus induced income generated by tourist expenditure to the direct income generated.
3. Type III income multipliers. This type of multiplier takes into account the fact that the pattern of consumption may change as incomes increase (as a result of the increased tourist expenditure). However, this type of multiplier does not present any conflicts which are not present between the type I and II multipliers.

The multipliers defined above do not provide the policymakers with information which is useful for planning purposes.

What is needed is a multiplier which demonstrates how much income (output, employment etc) is generated directly, indirectly and induced by one extra unit of tourist expenditure. It is now common practice, therefore, to express the tourism income, employment and government revenue multipliers as a ratio of tourist expenditure to total income, employment and government revenue generated. In this way the policy makers are able to see just how much income etc. is generated by each additional unit of tourist expenditure. The multipliers can also be constructed in such a way as to distinguish between different categories of tourists. This type of information is invaluable when attempting to determine which tourist groups are most beneficial to the economy.

Multiplier analysis is not without its weaknesses. There are three areas where the usefulness of multiplier analysis may be called into question. First, it is necessary to make some assumptions about the linearity and constancy of production functions and consumer behavior which contradict marginalist theory. Although multiplier analysis may be criticized from this viewpoint, it is possible to circumvent many of the problems associated with the assumptions by the careful construction of detailed and complex models. The assumptions of the basic model also ignore the source of the change in autonomous expenditure, differences in methods of production between establishments within the same industrial sector and the possibility of supply constraints occurring within the economy. Finally, the basic, static model does not take into account the time period necessary for the various rounds of impact to take effect. The data requirements of model construction increase dramatically as the researcher attempts to circumvent each of these problems.

Secondly, the availability of data is rarely adequate to undertake multiplier analysis. This means that the researcher will often need to undertake extensive data collection by survey. This makes multiplier analysis an expensive and time consuming method of analysis.

Thirdly, there have been many recorded instances of multiplier analysis being incorrectly applied. This is not so much a criticism of multiplier analysis as of ill-equipped researchers who undertake such analysis.

Examples

Table 1 contains tourism income multipliers for national economies, regions, and towns and cities which were calculated using similar methods of analysis. The results were taken from published and unpublished reports. It can be seen from Table 1 that the multiplier values tend to decrease as the analysis moves from large national economies down to individual cities.

Further reading

Archer, B. H., *Tourism in the Bahamas and Bermuda: Two Case Studies*, Bangor Occasional Papers, no. 10 (University of Wales Press, 1977). An analysis of tourism and its economic impact in the Bahamas and Bermuda.

Archer, B. H., *Multipliers: The State of the Art*, Bangor Occasional Papers, no. 11 (University of Wales Press, 1977). This is a comprehensive piece of work covering the development of multiplier theory, multiplier construction and their practical applicability.

Boserup, M., 'A note on the prehistory of the Kahn multiplier', *Economic journal*, vol. 79 (1969), pp. 667–9.

Bryden, J. M., *Tourism and Development: A Case Study in the Commonwealth Caribbean* (Cambridge University Press, 1973). This is essentially a very thorough piece of work using cost–benefit analysis to determine the economic impact of tourism, but it does include an analysis of the tourism multiplier in the Caribbean.

Bryden, J. M. and Faber, M., 'Multiplying the tourist multiplier', *Social and Economic Studies*, vol. 20, no. 1 (1971), pp. 61–82. An excellent work which shows just how wrong multiplier analysis can be if applied incorrectly and then goes on to compare the East Caribbean multipliers with their own, correctly applied analysis.

Keynes, J. M., 'The multiplier', *The New Statesman and Nation* (1 April 1933), pp. 405–7.

Pollard, H. J., 'Antigua, West Indies: an example of the operation of the multiplier process arising from tourism', *Revue de Tourisme*, no. 3 (1976), pp. 30–4. A description of the results of a study undertaken to analyze the contribution made by tourism to the economy of Antigua in 1967.

Sadler, P. G., Archer, B. H. and Owen, C. B., *Regional Income Multipliers: the Anglesey Study*, Bangor Occasional Papers, no. 1 (University of Wales Press, 1973). This work demonstrates the difficulties involved in constructing multipliers at the subnational level.

JOHN FLETCHER and
HELENA SNEE

Table 1 Tourism income multipliers.

Geographical area	Income multiplier value
Turkey	1.98
United Kingdom	1.73
Irish Republic	1.72
Jamaica	1.27
Egypt	1.23
Dominica	1.20
Cyprus	1.14
Bermuda	1.09
Hong Kong	1.02
Mauritius	0.96
Antigua	0.88
Bahamas	0.79
Fiji	0.72
Cayman Islands	0.65
Iceland	0.64
British Virgin Islands	0.58
Gibraltar	0.57
Door County, USA	0.55
Sullivan County, USA	0.44
Gwynedd, North Wales, UK	0.37
East Anglia, UK	0.34
Kendal, Cumbria, UK	0.30
Edinburgh, Lothian, UK	0.28
Brighton and Hove, UK	0.22
Winchester, Hampshire, UK	0.19
Bournemouth, Dorset, UK	0.18

Tourism policies in the public sector

Introduction

A *policy* may be defined as a course of action calculated to achieve specific objectives. Objectives are general directions for the planning and management of tourism, and are based on identified needs within market and resource constraints. Policies are the specific guidelines for the day to day management of tourism, covering the many aspects of the industry's operation. In simple terms, policies attempt to maximize the benefits and minimize the adverse effects of tourism, and as such are part of the planned development in a region which is necessary to create, develop, conserve and protect tourism resources. The future success of the tourism industry will depend heavily on the policies formulated for managing its development, growth and maturity (Edgell, 1987, p. 23).

Policies are relevant to both the public and private tourism sectors. Policies in the private sector are designed to give corporate direction for a profit motive, and as such are opportunist. Policies in the public sector are more concerned with the benefits of tourism for the community and have to play a more strategic/coordinating/leadership role in the development of tourism. Airey (1983, p. 10) identified a measure of agreement as to the issues underlying government involvement in six European countries: improved balance of payments, employment creation, the reduction of seasonality and encouragement of environmental protection. However, it is the local authorities who are largely responsible for presenting tourism to the visitor (House of Commons, 1985, p. xxxvii). This chapter will concentrate on the policies for tourism in the public sector in the United Kingdom, although the role of private investment in tourism will be shown to be an essential part of the public sector's strategy.

The importance of the public sector in tourism policies is reflected in the evolution of tourism policies which can be envisaged in three phases based on those suggested by Gravel (1979). The first phase, pre-1960s, was characterized by the public sector taking a *laissez faire* attitude towards tourism. Any policies at this time focused on specific markets or sites with little attempt to consider the wider implications of proposals or projects. This nonintegrated approach is known as 'hard' tourism. During the second phase, from the 1960s, the social implications for host communities and the impact upon the environment was recognized in policies. This integrated approach is known as 'soft' tourism. This change can be attributed to the growing role of the consumer's value judgment as against that of the producer, the increasing assertiveness of the native population in the tourist region and more restrictive attitudes towards tourism (Krippendorf, 1982, p. 144). Such control is enforced by public intervention in the industry's operation. A third phase is now possibly evident in the United Kingdom, with the public sector actively encouraging private investment in tourism within their own development control constraints. This would seem to represent a combination of 'hard' and 'soft' tourism in policy formulation.

The development of policies for tourism in the United Kingdom reflects the changing relationship between the public and private sectors. The growth of resort towns in the late nineteenth century was largely motivated by the commercial self-interest of individual entrepreneurs, although some local public authorities (in the form of Corporations or Municipal Authorities) began to assume responsibility for infrastructure, attractions and promotion after the reform of local government between 1884 and 1894 (Heeley, 1981, p. 63). Central government showed no interest in tourism. For example, between 1926 and 1969, travel to and within the United Kingdom was promoted by a group of private tourism interests, and the voluntary Scottish and Welsh Tourist Boards (created 1930 and 1938) did not receive recognition from central government (Kendell and McVey, 1986, p. 17). Grants and incentives for tourism projects were excluded from Regional Development Policy between 1934 and 1965 (Heeley, 1981, p. 65). Tourism was not a political issue and suffered from a lightweight image in comparison to manufacturing industry (Cooper, 1987, p. 249).

Central Government involvement in tourism began with the Development of Tourism Act, 1969. This Act was introduced to increase foreign exchange earnings from overseas visitors through the British Tourist Authority, and to encourage domestic tourism, through the national tourist boards. The principal factors for government assistance to tourism at this time were balance of payment and regional policy considerations. Consequently, section 4 grants (of the 1969 Act) only made finance available for tourism projects located in Development Areas/Intermediate Areas. The Conservative government's review of tourism in 1983 laid emphasis on improving the country's tourist products, the revitalization of the traditional seaside resorts and the role of tourism in urban regeneration) Kendell and McVey, 1986, p. 18). In September, 1985, government responsibility for tourism was transferred from the Department of Trade and Industry to the Department of Employment emphasizing the importance attached to the role of tourism in reducing unemployment through re-training and employment schemes such as 'Action for Jobs'. The heightened political interest in tourism allowed the English Tourist Board to introduce Tourism Development Action Programs (TDAPs) for areas with significant tourism potential. These areas would be looked on favorably for the designation of Section 4 grants. This change meant that assistance was switched to regions with the best tourism potential, rather than for regional policy considerations. The identification of a clear and consistent tourism policy in the United Kingdom is difficult (Heeley, 1981, p. 75; Kendell and McVey, 1986, p. 20; Cooper, 1987, p. 253) because of the changes outlined above and the complexity of the institutional framework for tourism.

The operation of tourism policies in the public sector in the United Kingdom at present occurs at three distinct levels (national, regional and local), with a large number of public agencies at each level (see Fig. 1). There are a great number of agencies with responsibilities for tourism mainly because the industry extends into so many sectors of the economy. Inter-

national directives (e.g. from the World Tourism Organization or the European Community) could be added to the diagram, since they represent significant influences, particularly in terms of sources of funding for tourism projects. For example, the Sandcastle Indoor Resort Complex in Blackpool, which opened in June 1986, received about a quarter of its £16 million cost from the European Regional Development Fund. There is scope for duplication and conflict amongst the agencies involved because of the lack of policy direction (Middleton, 1974, p. 35).

Nevertheless, the emphasis of policies for tourism is clearly different at each of the levels. White (1976, p. 153) distinguishes between tourism policies at the national scale, which provide a means of affecting the balance of payments, while policies at the regional or local scale use the tourism sector as a means of influencing regional development. Policies at the national level are broad directives, e.g. the English Tourist Board's encouragement of new innovative large scale projects, such as indoor leisure complexes, all-year holiday villages and marina/harbor developments to encourage the growth of tourism (ETB, 1987, pp. 16–17). It is the function of policies at the regional/local level to translate and implement these directives into specific developments. Public agencies at the local level are in a difficult position, having to recognize local resources and

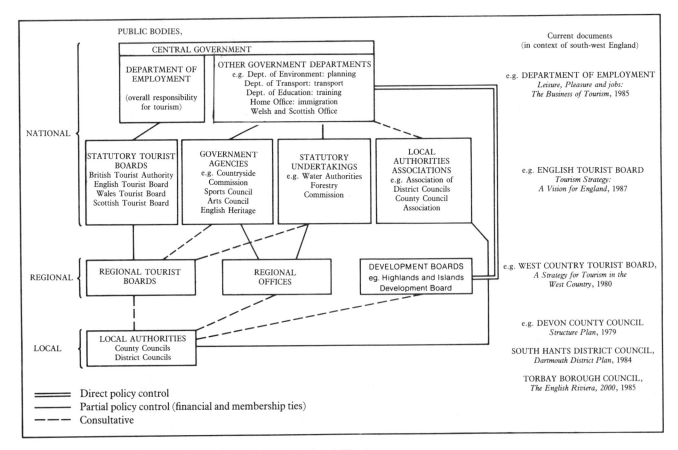

Figure 1 Institutional framework for tourism policies in the United Kingdom.

needs, yet having to respond constantly to the changing opportunities emanating from contemporary government philosophy.

The traditional involvement of local authorities in tourism in the United Kingdom has been directed towards their responsibilities for the provision of local tourism infrastructure (e.g. car parks, town trails, visitor centers, customer services and litter collection), and in maintaining an attractive environment for tourism through their development control responsibilities. These roles have led to the formulation of supportive and restrictive/regulatory policies respectively. However, as both traditional resorts and new areas attempt to benefit from the 'tourism boom' of the 1980s and take advantage of government incentives for tourism, many local authorities have become increasingly involved in tourism promotion and in encouraging the efforts of the private sector. This new role has led to the formulation of more innovative policies for tourism, which involve a strong marketing element. Such policies are evident in the work of many local authorities in recent years (refer to Williamson and Dowling, 1980; ADC, 1981; Clarke, 1986). This chapter will consider the action taken in Portsmouth and Bournemouth, UK, to illustrate this approach.

Examples

Following the Government Defence Review in 1981, Portsmouth was faced with the loss of 3,500 jobs in the naval dockyard. A lack of vacant land reduced the scope for manufacturing or office expansion and, not being a development area, it was unlikely that grant aid for economic development would be forthcoming from the Central Government. A policy decision by the city council encouraged the development of tourism in an attempt to create new employment opportunites. Portsmouth's seaside location and existing infrastructure provided a base for further development, although the tourism product was changed from 'sunny Southsea' based on its resort area to that of 'Flagship of Maritime England' based on the presence of historic ships and 500 years of naval history. A marketing strategy to exploit the area's maritime heritage involved capital investment from the city council which, in turn, stimulated major development by the private sector. It has been estimated that by 1986, tourism-related investment totalling £200 million had created 3,000 new jobs at a cost of £5,053 per job, of which £1,834 per job was public money. Tourism's annual contribution of £150 million in 1986 to the local economy represented nearly 10 per cent of local income.

Recent policy initiatives in Bournemouth, an established tourist resort at a later stage in its product life cycle, have addressed the problem of seasonality and that of attracting new markets. By adopting policies aimed at attracting new visitors during the shoulder season, the Tourism Department has helped to improve occupancy rates and lengthen the period of tourist income for all sectors of the industry. This should enhance the prospects for future growth because three-quarters of all tourists to the town are repeat visitors. To this end a series of festivals have been established, the benefits of which will now be described.

Benefits

Bournemouth's Power Boat festival held in September benefits from sponsorship which not only covers much of the running costs of the events, but also enables the town to host traditionally high-spending representatives of the commercial sponsors. The festival receives considerable media coverage giving travel writers something new to report about a resort which can only gain from free publicity of this kind. It can produce impulse purchase by readers or television viewers at a particularly opportune time, increasing bookings for the September/October shoulder period.

The media attention helps to project an image of Bournemouth which assists in attracting specific target markets. The Power Boat festival appeals to a wide range of spectators, but the events are more oriented toward the young and especially participants of the sport. Information and promotional material aimed at the latter can be easily directed through the relevant specialist magazines. This promotional tool is equally appropriate to other kinds of events (e.g. bowling weekends and ballroom dancing weekends).

Another festival in Bournemouth, the Health Week held during June, requires the participation of local residents. Voluntary groups and sports clubs exhibit displays and stage events in connection with the identified theme. The host population provide and become a tourist attraction in themselves. The value in resource terms to the Tourism Department is clearly evident, but a further consequence is the sense of identity, with Bournemouth and its tourism industry, felt by the participating residents. A similar improvement in the sense of place and a feeling of local pride has been experienced by residents in Portsmouth, where a quantifiable result has been an increase in attendances at sporting, entertainment and other public events.

Tourism's role in boosting community confidence and in revitalizing areas has been noted in other, less tangible, ways. In the wider economy businesses of all kinds are able to attract new investment and both recruit and retain good quality personnel. The tourism activity helps to foster a perceptual picture of the area; that of being a location which is progressive and where 'things happen'.

A confidence of this kind can be equally important, if not more so, in rural areas. Increased social and economic activity resulting from tourism can help support marginal services; provide additional resources which, although designed for visitor use, can also be consumed by locals; and promote conservation, for example through the re-use of redundant buildings. The number of new jobs created in rural areas might not be dramatic but population levels could be maintained due to an improvement in the diversity and balance of the employment structure.

Implementation

The following description represents a sequential model of policy implementation for tourism development. It demonstrates the rationale for each stage and the relationship between them and is based on a schema which has been applied successfully in Portsmouth. This framework allows social, economic, political and environmental factors, as they affect any particular location or organization, to be taken into account.

Stage 1 – Local political support
Portsmouth City Council first made a policy decision to adopt tourism development as a means of achieving politically desirable objectives. It was recognized that resources, both human and financial, would need to be allocated. Commitment from council leaders to support policies designed to achieve the overall objectives is critical throughout the process of implementation.

Stage 2 – Organizational structure
The establishment of a suitable structure within the local authority system is not only an indication of political commitment, but also provides the necessary framework for successful managerial practice. Fig. 2 illustrates the middle and senior level positions within the Portsmouth structure, which exhibits a marketing orientation. This orientation is expressed by the Chief Officer making both a philosophical and operational input across the functions of the city council. The Chief Officer also has direct access to the Chief Executive. Private investment

can be thwarted by bureaucratic procedures so access to decision makers creates the opportunity to gain an, often necessary, quick response.

Tourism officers working in the public sector are increasingly recognizing their strategic role. They must establish a position whereby they are consulted about all issues which affect an area's ability to host tourism. Planning applications for major developments, which will change an area's character or physical appearance, or for changes of use by hotels, which will reduce the stock of accommodation, are obvious examples.

Stage 3 – Product enhancement
A strategic evaluation of local resources is the prerequisite for further development. Initial investment might need to be publicly funded to act as a catalyst for future private sector involvement. The investment must however be directed towards identified infrastructural needs or weaknesses in the product range or quality. This analysis must be related to the needs of prospective markets.

It is also important to cultivate the support of local residents. This can be fostered through a good working relationship with the local press. Positive publicity helps to develop a constituency which is favorably disposed towards tourism and this can only further the prospects for the commitment of public funds by local politicians.

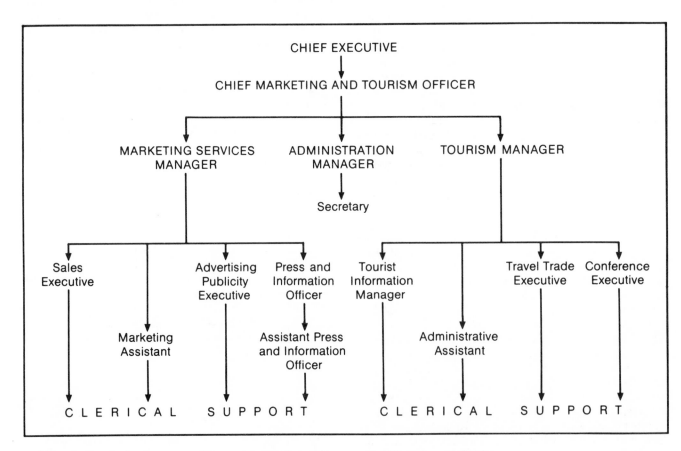

Figure 2 Organizational structure of Portsmouth City Council Department of Marketing and Tourism.

A common characteristic of the first three stages is that they are basically introspective, establishing an appropriate political, organizational and product environment locally. The following stage focuses on the wider environment.

Stage 4 – Promotional and development strategy
The main areas of activity at this stage include the following:

1. Adopting promotional techniques to attract identified markets.
2. Seeking private investment.
3. Encouraging political support from Central Government.

The promotional campaign must be realistic, based on the local industry's ability to attract and accommodate target markets. It should also consider distribution issues, such as making booking arrangements through the city's brochure, as straightforward as possible. Cooperation with both regional and national tourist boards is likely to be of value at this stage. Recognition of Portsmouth as a TDAP by the ETB not only enhanced opportunities for grant aid, but also improved the viability of local tourism initiatives. It is important to take advantage of credibility achieved through policies implemented during the first three stages. Potential investors and government ministers have been invited to the area to convince them of its potential for further tourism growth. The final stage involves the process of monitoring and is discussed in the following section.

Assessment

Information providing feedback about the consequences of policy implementation is critical for the successful management of tourism in the area. To this end Portsmouth tourism department addresses the following questions:

1. Is it operating in a way which enables it to ensure quality control within, and provide the necessary service for, the local tourism industry?
2. Is it gathering market information which enables it to monitor changing trends in demand and levels of visitor satisfaction?
3. Is it monitoring the economic impact and scale of investment in tourism?
4. Is it maintaining support from the local residents and promoting a favorable attitude towards tourism?

In summary, are the policies achieving the objective initially established for the tourism strategy?

Conclusion

Policies are essential for the proper creation, development and maintenance of a successful tourism industry. This is achieved through innovative, supportive and restrictive/regulatory policies which form part of the marketing strategy of local authorities. Policies for tourism have become increasingly influenced by central government involvement since 1969, although adaptation to suit local circumstances remains critical. Successful implementation of policies at the local level requires support both from the local authority and from a number of different groups, involving the visitors, the local tourism industry, the local resident population, government agencies and the travel trade.

Focus on small business

People managing small businesses in the tourism industry may presume that their day to day activities are unaffected by public sector policies. An active local authority tourism department, like Portsmouth, maintains a close working relationship with all sectors of its tourism industry which is composed of a high proportion of small enterprises. The local business is able to benefit from market information collected by the city department and the tourist boards. It is also represented in promotional activities organized by these agencies and participates in their package programs. It is very much a case of knowing how to exploit opportunities resulting from policies emanating from all levels of the public domain. The availability of grant aid from tourist boards is an obvious example, but forms of assistance, from local authority tourism departments and from government bodies, to train and recruit employees are becoming increasingly valuable.

Further reading

Adley, R. and Gregory, C., *A Policy for Tourism?* (Conservative Political Centre, 1977). A recognition of the importance of tourism to the UK economy.

Airey, D., 'European Approaches to Tourism', *PTRC, Developing Tourism* (PTRC (Planning and Transport Research and Computation), 1983), pp. 1–14. Identifies main themes of tourism policy in six European countries.

Ashworth, G. J., 'The selling of Norwich: marketing the historic city', Paper presented at Urban Geography Study Group, IBG, Annual Conference, Portsmouth Polytechnic (1987).

Ashworth, G. J. and Bergsma, J. R., 'New policies for tourism; opportunities or problems', *Tijdschrift voor Economische En Sociale Geografie*, vol. 78, no. 2 (1987), pp. 151–9. Investigates tourism in the Netherlands, 1960–1987.

Association of District Councils, *Tourism: A Handbook for District Councils* (ADC,1981). Suggested best practice for district councils in promotion of tourism in own area.

Banks, R., *New Jobs from Pleasure* (The Bookshop, 1984). Presents a strategy for creating new jobs in the UK tourist industry.

Bosman, M. A., *A National Tourism Policy for Great Britain: Proposals for Action* (EMI Hotels and Restaurants Ltd, 1975). Stresses the urgent need for a positive policy for tourism in the United Kingdom.

Cabinet Office (Enterprise Unit), *Pleasure, Leisure and Jobs* (HMSO, 1985). This is the UK Government's most recent statement of attitudes towards opportunities in tourism.

Clarke, A., 'Local authority planners or frustrated tourism marketeers?',

The Planner, vol. 72, no. 3 (1986), pp. 23–6. Outlines the marketing approach to planning and details application by Gwent County Council in the 1980s.

Commission of the European Communities, *A Community Policy on Tourism: Initial Guidelines*, Bulletin of the EC, Supplement 4/82, (EC, 1982). Highlights the main issues to be considered when formulating the 'tourist dimension' of community policies.

Cooper, C., 'The changing administration of tourism in Britain', *Area*, vol. 19, no. 3 (1987), pp. 249–53. Outlines administrative developments for tourism by the Conservative government, 1979–1987.

Countryside Commission, *Annual Report*. Annual publication detailing policies and action in the countryside.

Countryside Commission, 'Recreation 2000', *Countryside Commission News*, no. 18 (1985), p. 1. Proposals for formulating new recreation policies to the year 2000.

Crouch, S., 'Marketing can improve your economic health: the Portsmouth Experience', *Local Government Policy Making* (June 1986), pp. 75–9. Explains how marketing can be introduced into local government and the contribution it can be expected to make in improving the economic health of an area.

Department of Employment (Enterprise Unit), *Pleasure, Leisure and Jobs: The Business of Tourism* (HMSO, 1985).

Department of Employment, *Action for Jobs in Tourism* (Central Office of Information, HMSO, 1986). Promotional document from government department responsible for tourism, setting out rationale for job creation in tourism sector.

Devon County Council, *County Structure Plan* (DCC, 1979). Chapter 10, pp. 107–13.

Edgell, D. L., 'Recent US tourism policy trends', *Tourism Management* vol. 3, no. 2 (1982), pp. 121–3. Outlines the US National Tourism Policy Act, 1981.

Edgell, D. L., 'The formulation of tourism policy: a managerial framework', *Travel, Tourism and Hospitality Research*, J. R. B. Ritchie and C. R. Goeldner, eds (John Wiley, 1987), pp. 23–33. Introductory explanation of the formulation of tourism policy as an aid in the planning and management of tourism.

English Tourist Board, *Planning for Tourism in England* (ETB, 1981). Presents a review of the planning system in relation to tourism development.

English Tourist Board, *Tourism Enterprise by Local Authorities* (ETB, 1982). An assessment of new tourist developments by local authorities.

English Tourist Board, *Tourism and Leisure: The New Horion* (ETB, 1983). Reviews market and development trends and identifies the main areas for growth in the future.

English Tourist Board, *Tourism and Leisure: Investing in the Future* (ETB, 1983). Identifies the types of investment considered by the ETB to be essential to the success of tourism and leisure in the 1980s.

English Tourist Board, *Tourism Strategy: A Vision for England* (ETB, 1987). Presents clearly defined aims and objectives for tourism development and marketing in England. This presents the Board's current policy strategy.

Gravel, J. P., 'Tourism and recreational planning', *Urban and Regional Planning in a Federal State: The Canadian Experience*, W. T. Perks and I. M. Robinson, eds (Dowden, Hutchinson and Ross, 1979), pp. 122–34.

Heeley, J., 'Planning for tourism in Britain: an historical perspective', *Town Planning Review*, vol. 52, no. 1 (1981), pp. 61–79. Traces the historical development of regional and local planning for tourism in the United Kingdom from origins in the period up to 1914 through the planning response to tourism during the inter- and post-war eras.

House of Commons, *Tourism in the UK*, Report and Proceedings of the Trade and Industry Committee, Session 1985–86 (HMSO, 1985).

Hughes, H. L., 'Government support for tourism in the UK', *Tourism Management*, vol. 5, no. 1 (1984), pp. 13–19. The nature of government support for tourism in the United Kingdom is examined.

Jenkins, C. L., 'Tourism policies in developing countries: a critique', *Tourism Management*, vol. 1, no. 1 (1980), pp. 22–9. Illustrate the critical importance of policies for tourism in developing countries.

Kendell, P. and McVey, M., 'Tourism and politics: the British experience', *Leisure Management*, vol. 6, no. 8 (1986), pp. 17–20. Provides a review of successive government intervention in tourism in the United Kingdom.

Krippendorf, J., 'Towards new tourism policies', *Tourism Management*, vol. 3, no. 3 (1982), pp. 135–48. Stresses the importance of environmental and sociocultural factors in tourism policy and calls for a fundamental political transformation in the conception of tourism and recreation.

McIntosh, R. W. and Goeldner, C. R., *Tourism: Principles, Practices, Philosophies* (John Wiley, 1972), pp. 304–11. Outlines the necessity of planning for tourism.

Middleton, V. T. C., *Tourism Policy in Britain: the case for a radical reappraisal* (Economist Intelligence Unit, 1974). Describes the lack of policy guidance from government to the national tourist boards.

Mill, R. C. and Morrison, A. M., *The Tourism System: An Introductory Text* (Prentice Hall, 1985). Chapters 9, 10 and 11 present a review of strategies, formulation and regulation in tourism policy.

Morrissey, J., 'Tourism and the public sector', *The Planner*, vol. 72, no. 6 (1986), pp. 17–18.

National Conference on Local Government and Tourism, Conference Papers LNCLGT, UK, (undated) Collection of papers on role of local authorities in the development of tourism.

Sessa, A., 'The tourism policy', *Annals of Tourism Research*, vol. 3, no. 5 (1976), pp. 234–47. Defines and explores the need for tourism policy.

Smyth, R., 'Public policy for tourism in Northern Ireland', *Tourism Management*, vol. 7, no. 2 (1986), pp. 120–6. Explains the lack of coordination of activities or effective forums for tourism interests in Northern Ireland.

South East England Tourist Board, *Regional Tourism Strategy for South East England* (SEETB, 1987). Presents a regional tourism strategy to foster economic and social benefits while having regard to the exceptional environmental qualities of the region.

South Hants District Council, *Dartmouth District Plan* (SHDC, 1984), pp. 30–2; 36–43.

Southern Tourist Board, *A Strategy for the Southern Tourist Board Region Towards 1990* (STB, 1987). Identifies the areas of awareness, cooperation and investment as the key to the success of the plan.

Torbay Borough Council, *The English Riviera 2000: An Integrated Tourism Strategy for Torquay, Paignton and Brixham* (TBC, 1985). This publication was submitted to the English Tourist Board for the Resort 2000 competition held in 1986.

West Country Tourist Board, *A Strategy for Tourism in the West Country* (WCTB, 1980).

Williamson, R. and Dowling, M., 'Resort planning', *The Planner*, vol. 66, no. 6 (1980), pp. 151–3. Investigates policies adopted in the resorts of Scarborough, Great Yarmouth, South Shields and Llandudno.

White, P. E., 'Tourism and economic development in the rural environment', *Economy and Society in the EEC: Spatial Perspectives*, R. Lee and P. E. Ogden, eds (Saxon House, 1976), pp. 150–9.

Further reference material can be obtained from two government agencies whose responsibilities are directly or indirectly related to tourism. The libraries of the English Tourist Board, London and the Countryside Commission, Cheltenham are sources of relevant information. The

English Tourist Board holds a wide range of data, including the results of its annual monitoring of investment in tourism. Documents at the Countryside Commission refer to tourism activities in rural areas. The policies for tourism within each county and district council in the UK are outlined in the respective Structure Plan or Local Plan. An annual review of international policies for tourism is available from: Organization for Economic Cooperation and Development, *Tourism Policy and International Tourism in OECD Member Countries* (OECD, Paris).

Acknowledgments: The authors wish to thank Mr K. Male, Director of Tourism, Bournemouth Borough Council, and Mrs S. Crouch, Chief Marketing and Tourism Officer, Portsmouth City Council, for their advice and assistance with this paper. Thanks are also due to Miss J. Wyatt for drawing the illustrations.

GRAHAM P. BROWN and
STEPHEN J. ESSEX

Tourism positioning strategies

Introduction

A tourist product's positioning is the place a product occupies in a given market, as perceived by the relevant group of tourists; that group of tourists is known as the target market segment. The concept of product positioning is linked with market segmentation and market targeting. Product positioning is the act of formulating a competitive position for the tourist product and a subsequent detailed marketing mix. In other words, it affects directly all other marketing decisions.

A tourist product's position is established by focusing marketing strategy efforts towards a particular international target market having specific product preferences. A tourist product's position is then assessed by consumers' perceptions of how the tourist product compares to other products in the market on relevant tourist product attributes. Product position is the place the tourist product occupies in the consumer's mind with respect to a small number of key attributes, which can be tangible or intangible.

Product positioning helps a tourist company to achieve a sustainable competitive advantage. Tourist product positioning involves the placement of the product in relation to local competitive offerings in a given market segment. Once a target market has been chosen, the tourist organization may develop a new product for this market or reposition an existing product through product modification or change in promotional policy. A tourist product's position is affected not only by actions it initiates but also by the activities of its competitors.

The potential value of international product differentiation is then based on the introduction of 'differential advantages' to the tourist product, in terms of product attributes, features, services, level of quality, style and image, price range, and other key elements that will shape in a positive manner the perception of the consumer. The company should then make adjustments, through tourist product modification, or changes in promotion, channels, or pricing strategies to bring the product in line with the desired product position.

Examples

Ramada Inns is the third largest lodging chain in the world, yet it is saddled with many rundown units and an increasingly downscale image. Management is now attempting to buy back many franchise units and either renovate or sell the inns. The sale of some locations will provide capital for renovation of others. Ramada ultimately will be repositioned as a finer, more exclusive lodging environment.

Both Marriott Corporation and Hyatt Corporation promote their hotels to upper-income businessmen and professionals. Marriott tends to emphasize luxury, while Hyatt dwells on the fact that it offers herbal teas and other natural foods in its restaurants. Marriott is appealing to the 'achiever' (according to the SRI-VALS classification), while Hyatt is appealing to a more inner-directed customer. Hyatt may fare better in the end, because in SRI's (Standford Research Institute) view, given the growing importance of the 'experiential' and 'societally conscious' segments among business travelers, this can be seen as a very smart positioning.

New York Air positions itself against the Eastern Shuttle as a competitive comparison position, in terms of the most relevant product attributes, such as in-flight service, scheduling, fares, comfort etc. This comparative positioning is only applied in relation to the concentrated New York Air's market.

Australia, New Zealand, and the South Pacific Islands have been positioning themselves as a single tourism destination in terms of their promotional strategy designed to attract US holiday visitors.

Benefits

The notion of positioning recognizes that tourists or consumers of tourist services evaluate and buy products based on perceptions and images that are unique to each tourist product or brand. Any tourist company can create a position through market segmentation and product differentiation. A tourist product can be differentiated, bringing out its unique benefits to the intended target market, in order to create a desired position in the tourist's mind. Tourist product positions are established by selecting a target market that values specific attributes, and designing tourist products that capitalize on those attributes. In the case of repositioning, new marketing strategies must be designed to shift a tourist product's place in the market to the desired position.

New tourist products are designed to achieve a particular

position in a market. An old or existing tourist product might be repositioned in the market by altering specific tourist product attributes to fill a new position. In either case, positioning and repositioning strategies force marketing managers to assess carefully the local competition, tourist perceptions of each tourist brand in the market, and to determine the tourist product attributes in designing new products and marketing existing ones.

Perceptual mapping tracks tourist perceptions of a tourist product or brand over time. If a tourist product's position shifts over time as a result of changes in tourist perceptions, needs and preferences, or with the introduction of new tourist brands into the market, repositioning strategies are required to re-establish the desired position. Perceptual maps can also be used to identify tourist market segments. As a strategic marketing tool, perceptual maps can identify target markets formed by clusters of tourist product attribute preferences. A perceptual map can provide a more detailed picture of how tourists perceive different tourist products or brands and their attributes.

Perceptual maps can also be used to identify new tourist product opportunities in international markets. New products can be positioned in gaps that appear in those markets. However, a new product will not succeed just because it is unique. Gaps in the perceptual space are meaningless unless potential consumers are to be found in them.

Implementation

Effective product positioning helps to serve a specific market segment by creating an appropriate concept in the minds of tourists/customers in that international market segment:

1. *Perceived positioning.* A product's positioning is not in the product or even in the advertising. It is in the mind of the tourist. Two identical tourist products may be perceived as different; on the other hand, two quite dissimilar products may be perceived as being similar. A desired positioning is one that clearly distinguishes a tourist product from its competition on attributes considered important by the relevant market segment.
2. *Positioning and the competitive set.* A tourist product's competition includes a primary set of other tourist products and a secondary set of other products that are not similar but may be used as substitutes. The definition of competitive sets is, once again, in the tourist's mind.

When tourism marketers introduce a product, they attempt to position it so that it seems to possess the characteristics most desired by the relevant target market. This projected image is crucial. Each tourist has a location in the market structure that corresponds to the characteristics of that of the buyer's ideal product. Although a given tourist product possesses many characteristics only a few will be important in the consumer's decision-making process. These critical attributes are used to differentiate among the competitive offerings. In some cases, tourism companies can exploit regional differences in perceptual maps for several product categories in order to reposition brands through selective advertising changes.

Positioning has no value in itself, only in its effect on the target market segment. There are seven ways to position a tourist product:

1. Based on specific product attributes or features. This is a very common approach.
2. Based on the benefits of the tourist product to tourists or customers. This is strongly related to positioning on product features; generally it is more effective.
3. By specific usage. This is related to benefit positioning.
4. By user category.
5. Against another tourist product. This strategy ranges from implicit to explicit comparison of products and benefits. Explicit comparison can take two major forms. First, one can use a comparison with a direct competitor aimed at attracting tourists from the compared tourist product, which is usually the tourist product category leader. Alternatively, there is no attempt to attract the consumers of the compared product, but rather to use the comparison as a reference point.
6. Tourist product class dissociation. This type of positioning is somewhat less common; it is particularly effective when used to introduce a new product that differs from the typical products in an established tourist product category.
7. A hybrid positioning strategy combines two or more of these approaches. The hybrid positioning strategy typically requires multiple branding strategies.

A new tourist product can also be positioned with respect to an attribute that competitors have ignored. Sometimes, a tourist product can be positioned in terms of two or more attributes simultaneously. Another positioning strategy is to associate the tourist product with usage. Tourist products can, of course, have multiple positioning strategies, although increasing the number involves difficulties and risks. Often a positioning by usage strategy represents a second or third position designed to expand the market. Another positioning approach is to associate a tourist product with a user or a class or users. For example, special interest tours have been positioned by associating them with specific consumer lifestyle profiles. Some other critical positioning decisions involve tourist product–class associations.

In most positioning strategies, an explicit or implicit frame of reference is the competition. Often the major purpose of this type of positioning is to persuade tourists that a brand is better than the market leader (or other well-accepted tourist brand) on important attributes. Positioning with respect to a competitor is commonly done in advertisements in which a competitor is named and compared. An example of this has been seen in the amusement park market: Six Flags' Magic Mountain has run advertising campaigns in which it compares itself with Disneyland. A company can position a product or service to compete head-on with another brand or to avoid competition. Head-to-head positioning may be appropriate even when the price is higher and if the product's performance characteristics are superior. Conversely, positioning to avoid competition may be best when the product's performance characteristics are not significantly different from competing brands.

The general approach to determining a product's position includes the following steps:

1. Construct a 'map' of the product's perceptual space by comparing its salient features and benefits with tourists' evaluations of how existing brands relate to the ideal point. This process is called perceptual mapping.
2. Plot the positions of existing brands.
3. Isolate or identify company brands for which there are no preference points and preference points for which there are no company brands. These indicate possible untapped tourist product opportunities.
4. If product opportunities exist, use marketing research, research and development, advertising, and other marketing mix variables to develop new tourist products and brands or to reposition existing ones.

Old products, new positions

There are four basic strategies for change. First, the tourist product may be repositioned to appeal to a new segment. This may involve changing the product, or perhaps just changing the way it is marketed. Second, the marketer may attempt to add a new target segment, while trying to hold on to the old segment. This is normally done by introducing a new product to appeal to the new segment, while keeping the old product targeted to the old segment. Sometimes, however, it is possible for one tourist product to appeal to several market segments. Third, the size of the existing target segment may be increased. This is a difficult task because tourists must change their minds: people in other segments must adopt beliefs that will move them to the target segment. Fourth, the structure of the market itself may be changed. If a new product is really new, the universe of potential tourists for the product category may change, and possibly grow. The perceived relationships among tourist

products in the market will change, new attributes will become important, and the relevant characteristics defining target segments will also change.

There is actually a fifth strategy, which is no change. Often this is the best course. After all, a tourist product may be repositioned away from its existing target segment and then never reach its proposed new target segment. Or a new tourist product may simply take over an existing product's segment, without enlarging the market. The tourist organization has then spent a lot of money to stand still. Clearly, positioning can be crucial to a tourist company's survival in a market. A tourist product's relevant vital signs (such as growth rate, market share, sales, and profits) should be broken down by positioning and segment. Then, the existing tourist product portfolio should be analyzed for its projected performance under alternative marketing strategies and environmental scenarios.

Multidimensional scaling techniques provide a set of computer algorithms that allow a tourist company to develop perceptual maps. These perceptual maps are visual configurations based on attributes of each tourist product or brand in the market as perceived by tourists or customers. The multidimensional scaling technique allows product positions to be mapped, providing a visual representation of each tourist product or brand competing in the same market. However, assessing tourist product positions using multidimensional scaling has some major drawbacks. The attributes that tourists or customers use in evaluating tourist products and brands must be identified. These attributes must then be used as input variables to a variety of multidimensional scaling computer programs, such as MDSCAL V and PC-MDS.

Assessment

When used with market segmentation and market targeting, product positioning/repositioning sets the guidelines for designing an effective marketing strategy. Marketing mix policies have to be consistent with each tourist product's positioning statement. Many tourist companies are continually deciding which markets to serve and which tourists, customers, or clients in each market offer the most growth and profit potential. Market data (e.g. demographics, psychographics, benefits sought, usage rate, user status, response functions, etc.) can be collected in order to find the specific tourist market's evaluative criteria. The product attribute and feature criteria are chosen to compare tourist target markets. The most relevant tourist product attributes and 'differential advantages' are then matched to visitor/tourist profiles – market segments that might be attracted to these tourist product qualities. Furthermore, the demand patterns of a feasible combination of tourist profiles should then be analyzed. The tourist product portfolio should be evaluated on each STP (segment, target, and positioning dimensions) vector as well as taking into account the specific competitive sets. Tourism marketing strategies can then be developed on the basis of repositioning decisions.

Based on the analysis of competitive positions, a tourism company might pursue several marketing positioning strategies, such as low cost strategies, product differentiation strategies,

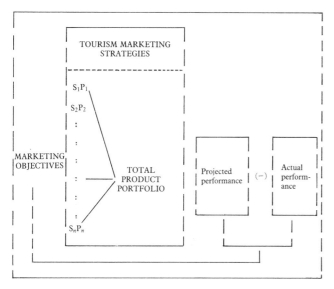

Figure 1 Strategic path in international positioning. S = segment; P = positioning.

and market niche strategies. Ideally, the positioning strategy should be sustainable and not easily matched by competitors. A tourism marketer should not consider the overall market positioning of a tourist product, but rather attempt to assess the positioning of the product as perceived by various market segments. One area in which new research is emerging is the relationship of positioning and segmentation strategy to the tourist product portfolio decision.

Conclusion

Tourist product positioning/repositioning strategies are useful only within a sound marketing approach. Product positioning is established only after a thorough analysis of each tourist product or brand in the competitive market, each tourist product or brand's unique attributes, and how they are perceived by tourists or consumers.

Product positioning is a key element for effective marketing. Once positioning is accomplished and the tourism company establishes 'share of mind', it will be translated into 'share of market'. Therefore, product positioning really means sales and return on investment.

Positioning is more encompassing than advertising. It provides a reason for people to be receptive to advertising and sales messages, while holding advertising, public relations, sales promotion, and sales together. Positioning provides a pre-existing reason for people to be receptive to a tourism firm's promotional messages. Once developed, it should be consistently carried out in all of the firm's communications activities.

The interactive process between tourist product positioning and market selection system provides a winning combination for the design of international marketing strategies and the subsequent achievement of results' maximization.

Focus on small business

Any small hotelier, travel agent, or anyone else operating a small tourist business can apply the positioning concept and its techniques. The best way to do so is to track the sales patterns and tourist/customer profiles for their products which might be used by various audiences.

Few small businesses in the industry recognize how important their companies are to the expanding business of tourism. The application of positioning strategies for the development of small tourist businesses can be effective and profitable. New market opportunities can be defined and pursued; crucial segmentation and concentration strategies can be implemented; new tourist products can be developed; low-budget promotional campaigns can be defined and launched; after-sales service policies can be pursued in order to capture more repeat business; an overall marketing plan can be devised as well as marketing strategies designed to attain realistic goals and objectives; and tourist/customer segment analysis can also be utilized.

Small businesses in tourism can develop perceptual maps based on available published data, small samples of customers, and their own experience. These perceptual mapping procedures will enable them to better define positioning strategies designed to help the growth of their businesses.

Further reading

Aaker, D., *Multivariate Analysis in Marketing* (Scientific Press, 1981). Clear and concise explanation and examples of multidimensional scaling and its application.

Bagozzi, R., *Principles of Marketing Management* (Science Research Associates, 1986), pp. 244–51; 693–6. An excellent marketing management text that gives detailed examples of various positioning strategies.

Bryant, B. E. and Morrison, A. J., 'Travel market segmentation and the implementation of market strategies', *Journal of Travel Research*, vol. XVIII, no. 3 (Winter 1980), pp. 2–6. This article indicates how the segmentation approach should be used to implement marketing strategies.

Crask, M. R., 'Segmenting the vacationer market: identifying the vacation preferences, demographics, and magazine readership of each group', *Journal of Travel Research*, vol. XX, no. 2 (Fall 1981), pp. 29–33. This article deals with the application of segmentation techniques as related to media planning.

Domzal, T. J., 'Product positioning and repositioning', *Beacham's Marketing Reference*, W. Beacham, R. T. Hise and H. N. Tongren, eds, vol. II (Research Publishing, September 1986), pp. 709–12. Brief and clear overview of the concept of product positioning and repositioning. It includes a good range of examples.

Etzel, M. J. and Woodside, A. G., 'Segmentary vacation markets', *Journal of Travel Research* (Spring 1982). This article presents perspectives about segmentation issues as related to the vacation market.

Lewis, R. C., 'Positioning analysis for hospitality firms', *International Journal of Hospitality Management*, vol. 1, no. 2 (1982), pp. 115–18. This article explains the mechanisms of positioning analysis that might be used by hospitality firms.

Lewis, R. C., 'The positioning statement for hotels', *Cornell HRA Quarterly*, vol. 22, no. 1 (May 1981), pp. 51–61. This is a good article dealing with positioning issues applied to the hotel industry.

Mill, R. C. and Morrison, A. M., *The Tourism System: An Introductory Text* (Prentice Hall, 1985). This is an innovative book which contains many parts directly related to the issue of developing tourism positioning strategies. Special attention should be given to chapters 2, 4, 5, 8, 12, 14 and 15.

Nykiel, R. A., *Marketing in the Hospitality Industry* (CBI Publishing Co., 1983), pp. 25–33. This book includes a good and pragmatic chapter (3) on positioning in line with consumer preferences.

Wind, Y., 'Going to market: new twists for some old tricks', *The Wharton Magazine*, vol. 4, no. 3 (1980). This is an excellent article on the positioning concept. It relates positioning strategies to portfolio models, giving many examples of the concept application. The article also describes the most important ways to position a product.

Wind, Y., *Product Policy* (Addison-Wesley, 1980). Offers a comprehensive coverage of the product policy area, including a detailed chapter on product positioning.

LUIZ MOUTINHO

Tourism promotion mix

Introduction

The tourism promotion mix consists of four elements: advertising, personal selling, publicity and sales promotion. Advertising includes paid communication through mass media (television, radio, cinema, print), and more direct forms of communication such as direct mail. Personal selling refers to one-to-one communication, such as travel agent suggesting tour destinations to a customer.

Publicity consists of promotion which has not been paid for, e.g. articles in travel sections of newpapers or magazines. Sales promotion is generally defined as promotional activity not fitting into the other categories. It includes activities designed to generate an immediate response from the audience, such as special price discounts, and 'not elsewhere classified' promotions, for example contests and 'special items' such as T-shirts. These are designed to generate interest in and excitement about a tourist attraction or destination.

The promotion mix, like the marketing mix, is a blend of the four types of promotion. Each element of the promotion mix must complement each other, i.e. must communicate similar or at least nonconflicting messages to each target market. The target market can be divided into two general segments: channels of distribution (e.g. tour operators, travel agents) and the ultimate consumer.

The tourism marketer's goal in managing the promotion mix is to maximize successful communication to chosen target markets. Of course, the promotion mix must be managed within the budget constraint of the tourism marketer.

Examples

The premier example of successful promotion has been the I Love New York (ILNY) campaign. New York State was the first US state to diversify from using just brochures and start using television advertisements. New York's campaign has received much free publicity, no doubt in part due to the exciting stars such as Elizabeth Taylor who appeared in the television advertisements. Another clever strategy which New York used was *not* to copyright their ILNY logo. The marketers were hoping (correctly) that commercial manufacturers would use the logo on a variety of paraphenalia from T-shirts to matchbooks to spoonrests. Thus New York got both free publicity and sales promotions. New York has also used innovative promotion strategies to reach the travel trade in Europe. Broadway casts are flown to European cities such as Paris to give short Broadway performances.

In the early 1980s, Hawaii creatively stretched a small budget to counter a negative image of crime. A variety of organizations – hotels, banks, tours, and airlines, paid for space in advertising inserts in major magazines, including *Time* and *Newsweek*. *Newsweek*, in turn, used the Hawaiian travel theme for display boards in airports. *Time* used the theme in advertisements in travel trade publications. More publicity came through Bloomingdales, the famous New York department store, which featured a special Hawaiian theme, including displays in store windows and in the store itself. Bloomingdales also advertised their Hawaiian theme and further promoted it with a press party. Sales promotions for the Hawaiian promotion campaign included an 'Island recipe' contest in Reader's Digest. This contest was supported by advertising from Macadamia nut, ham and rum companies. As a result, Reader's Digest ran a sweepstake for a Hawaiian trip.

Both New York and Hawaii have used a variety of means to promote themselves and let others help promote them, while communicating consistent messages. They have both been very successful by creatively manipulating the promotion mix.

Benefits

By understanding promotion to be multifaceted, the tourist organization marketer can maximize his communication potential. The elements of promotion work synergistically. A budget devoted exclusively to brochures, or even television advertising, will not be as effectively used as a budget which has brochures, mass media advertising, good relations with the mass media for publicity purposes and with the trade, and special promotions to generate excitement.

Implementation

Advertising

The basic advertising message can communicate something in general about the tourist attraction/destination, or specific events or characteristics. For example, in the United States, after the success of the ILNY campaign, many states have started their own general slogans, 'Indiana has it all', 'You've got a friend in Pa', 'Escape to Wisconsin'. When competition all sounds alike, however, the tourism marketer needs to differentiate his product/service. Illinois, for example, has promoted special events through radio and magazine advertisements. Differentiating one's product/service from competition is especially important when the potential tourist is not familiar with the destination, e.g. does not differentiate between Taipei and Tokyo.

Marketing research should be used to determine what image, if any, your tourist product/service has in the eyes of your target market. The tourism marketer can then determine the most positive perceived image to promote. For example, Mexico has repositioned itself from a cultural attraction to a resort area. To reach tour operators and travel agents, advertisements can be placed in trade magazines.

Mass media advertising *is* feasible under tight budgets; advertising dollars can be stretched using cooperative advertisements from several tourist organizations, e.g. tourist sites, hotels, and airlines.

Although less common, direct mail advertising can be used to reach the final consumer. Montana has been very successful using their 'Invite a friend' campaign. State residents were asked to send names and addresses of friends and relatives from out-of-state. The Governor then wrote letters to them, inviting them to visit Montana.

Personal selling

Personal selling to the final consumer usually is done by travel agents. Personal selling has the advantage of immediate feedback from the customer. Tour agents should determine the customer's needs: do they seek relaxation, culture, the exotic? How long a vacation do they have? What price range is acceptable? Do they have special needs, such as traveling with children? The travel agent can then suggest appropriate destinations, but they are more likely to suggest a particular destination if the tourism organization providing it has in turn promoted itself well to travel agents. To some extent the tourist organization can promote to the travel agent through personal selling. In an unusual promotion, Canada's Minister of Tourism toured five US cities. One of his tasks was to meet with travel agents and tour operators.

Publicity

Publicity is not paid for, and not under the direct control of the tourism organization. However, the tourism marketer can take steps to try to obtain favorable publicity. The most common way to manage publicity is to send news releases to the media to inform them of special events or news. The tourism marketer must remember, however, that news releases must include newsworthy subject matter. It must be timely and be of special interest to the audience.

A more effective means of getting publicity is to offer free trips to travel writers. To increase the probability that the travel writers are favorably impressed with the tourist destination, staff should be available to help the travel writer. If the travel writers are foreign, multilingual staff should be available. The results of a successful trip by a travel writer will be commendatory stories in magazines, newspapers etc. Since publicity has more source credibility than advertising, the importance of good relations with travel writers cannot be overstated. The ultimate publicity through travel writers is to host a national or international travel writer convention. To win approval as a convention site, however, takes a promotion campaign in itself to the appropriate decision makers at the travel writers' association.

Publicity can also be obtained for a tourist destination through media fiction, e.g. movies. By having a movie with a pleasant setting take place in the tourism marketer's region, positive publicity is obtained for that region. For example, the city of Chicago has an office whose goal is to promote Chicago as a location for movie making. Although the primary motivation is economic development from the movie making activities, a different secondary benefit has been promotion of Chicago as a tourist destination. These movies have helped show Chicago to be a beautiful city, rather than one run by gangsters.

Sales promotions

Sales promotions to consumers include special activities such as contests, sweepstakes, sales (price promotions), and special merchandise. Sale promotions generally play a secondary role in the promotion mix – they can help support other activities, but should not be the focus of the tourism marketer's promotion mix.

Contests and sweepstakes which include trips to the tourist destination help gain awareness of the destination and can add a perception of excitement about the destination.

Price promotions can include discounts from one or more attractions in a region. For example, as part of its celebration of the centennial of the Statue of Liberty, New York State offered 'Liberty Passports', which included discount coupons for New York State hotels, restaurants, and attractions. Thus, upstate New York was promoted along with New York City festivities. Price promotions should be used with caution, however. The tourism marketer does not want the potential traveler to associate the destination with cheapness or to consider the tourist site as a possible destination only during special price promotions.

A common form of tourism sales promotions is special merchandise. T-shirts, key chains etc. can generate 'word-of-mouth' about the tourist destination.

Sale promotions to the trade can include all of the above, but are also likely to include 'familiarization tours', or 'fam tours'. These are free trips for travel agents and travel wholesalers to let them experience firsthand the tourist destination. Successful fam trips are necessary to facilitate a 'push' strategy, in which the channels of distribution promote the tourist destination to the next channel member, and ultimately the consumer.

Assessment

Several questions must be considered when evaluating the promotion mix. The most basic question is, 'Is one clear message being communicated?' For example, advertisements should not emphasize luxury if price promotions are communicating a message of economy. If travel writers are emphasizing the resort atmosphere of a tourist destination, then the tourism marketer should think twice before emphasizing cultural attractions.

The second question to consider is, 'Is the right amount of emphasis being given to each element in the mix?' Here, the two limiting factors are budget constraints and creativity. Even within severe budget constraints, tourism marketers have been able to take advantage of the synergistic quality of the promotion mix. As a rule of thumb, advertising and publicity are generally most important; personal selling is important to the trade; and sales promotions add extra reinforcement to the overall promotion theme.

Conclusions

Of the four types of promotion, the tourism marketer has greatest control over advertising and sales promotion. Both advertising and sales promotion are created, implemented, and paid for by the marketer. On the other hand, personal selling is generally done indirectly through travel agents; publicity is generated through the media. It is therefore important for the tourism marketer to maintain good relations with both the travel trade and with media. This can be accomplished through a well-directed marketing campaign aimed towards these targets. Ultimately, the tourism marketer can increase his overall promotional impact by managing all four elements of the promotion mix: advertising, personal selling, publicity and sales promotion.

Focus on small business

Managing the promotion mix is just as important to small businesses as to large tourism organizations. Small businesses should work cooperatively to advertise. Personal relationships with the trade should be cultivated. This can be accomplished simply through pleasant interactions when the tourism marketer comes into contact with travel operators or travel agents. Publicity can be managed through news releases. Although free trips for travel writers are generally out of the small business's budget, small businesses should work with regional tourist boards to be kept informed, if possible, of travel writers who happen to be in the region. The small business can then invite the writer to visit his attraction/service. In sales promotions, the most common type of merchandise has been the simple matchbox with the name of the attraction on the cover; other low-cost items are also in the small business budget.

Software/databases

Microvations Inc., 455 Beaver Ruin Road, Suite 114, Lilburn, GA 30247, USA. Microvations operates over 100 computer-based Touch and Go databases for tourists. They are located in public access places in the United States. The advertiser can input up to 18 lines of information to communicate to the potential customer.

World Viewdata Services Ltd, 33–35 Crouch End Hill, London N8 8DH, UK. Major tourism advertisers can, for an annual fee, input information on their services. The database is available to 6,000 travel agents plus some businesses with travel departments.

Further reading

Auchmutey, J., 'New image has Australian tourism hopping', *Advertising Age*, vol. 56, no. 65 (1985), pp. 24; 31. Describes the repositioning of Australia from the cute koala to sophisticated humor.

Brock, J. L., Larson, J. D., Muhs, W. F. *et al.*, 'Drawing the out-of-state tourist to Montana', *Montana Business Quarterly*, vol. 23, no. 3 (Autumn 1985), pp. 2–7. Describes marketing research done on American's image of Montana and the state's 'Invite a friend' campaign.

'Canadian marketing blitz lures U. S. tourists back after decline', *Marketing News*, vol. 18, no. 18 (1984), pp. 1; 6. Describes Canada's Minister of Tourism tour of the United States. Good examples of unusual strategies.

Candler, J., 'Travel writers put Michigan on front page', *Advertising Age*, vol. 57, no. 39 (1986), p. S5. Describes promotion strategies to encourage the Society of American Travel Writers to hold their annual conference in Michigan, and the benefits of the convention.

Clark, E., 'Big Apple bites back', *Marketing*, vol. 21, no. 12 (1985), pp. 21–4. Describes the 8-year-old ILNY campaign.

Cohen, J., 'Promotion of overseas tourism through media fiction', *Proceedings: Special Conference on Tourism Services Marketing* (The Academy of Marketing Sciences and the Marketing Dept. Cleveland State University, 1986), pp. 229–37. Describes how to use placement in movies to promote tourist destinations.

Dreyback, M., 'Cooperative advertising, Hawaiian style', *Marketing and Media Decisions*, vol. 17, no. 1 (1982), pp. 68–70. Describes a very creative plan used by Hawaii to stretch a small budget and overcome negative images.

Howe. R., 'Luring 'em with brass and class', *Marketing and Media Decisions*, vol. 17, no. 6 (Spring 1982), pp. 189–200. Discusses beginnings of ILNY campaign.

McGeehan, P., 'Illinois peddles events from around the State', *Advertising Age*, vol. 57, no. 39 (1986), pp. S17–S18. Describes Illinois' campaign which focuses on specific events, rather than using a general campaign for the whole state.

Nardelli, R., 'In search of the good ad', *Advertising Age*, vol. 52, no. 25 (1981), p. S18. Cites two problems in tourism advertisements: advertising agencies do not give them to the appropriate creative team, and the advertisements do not differentiate the tourist attraction from competition.

Norwood, M.L., 'Promotion speaks language of foreign tourists', *Advertising Age*, vol. 53, no. 49 (1982), pp. M11; M14. Gives a multiplicity of strategies used by Florida to increase tourism from abroad.

Phillips, L., 'Main attraction not only show in New York State', *Advertising Age*, vol. 57, no. 51 (29 September 1986), p. S2. Shows how nearby attractions can try to 'piggyback' on special events, in this case the Statue of Liberty centennial celebration.

JUDY COHEN

Tourism quality

Introduction

Provision of a high quality tourism experience is a major challenge for all those involved in this dynamic industry. This difficulty is primarily due to the complex nature of both the tourism industry and the concept of service quality. The travel and tourism industry is comprised of a diversity of hospitality services provided by the public and private sectors. Additionally, the tourism experience encompasses varying degrees of interaction with the host community; including residents, businesses, and government. Such a highly labor-intensive industry has enormous potential for variable quality. The delivery and improvement of quality tourism services is crucial to maintaining or increasing tourism activity.

Traditionally, the concept of service quality has not been easy to define or measure. Its subjective nature makes it difficult to determine what factors contribute to service quality. As a result, perceptions of service quality by those who provide tourism services and those who consume them may differ. In such cases management employs service performance standards which may not be consistent with consumers' perceptions and expectations. An agency may not always be attuned to what constitutes high quality to its customers, so managers make decisions based on their own perceptions and preferences. For example, LaPage (1983), working in the area of camping, suggests that there is increasing evidence of substantial differences between managerial and camper perceptions of ideal locations, designs, facilities, supervision, and maintenance of parks.

Although service quality has been characterized by a variety of management-oriented definitions, there is support in the marketing literature for the argument that the customer assesses service quality by his or her perception of the way in which the service is performed. This viewpoint promotes service quality as the outcome of a comparison between a consumer's expectations of a service and what is perceived as delivered. The gap between these determines the level of quality from the tourist's perspective.

Examples

One company within the travel and tourism industry which has a formalized quality control program utilizing customer input is American Airlines. This company boasts a commitment to service excellence. This began prior to deregulation of air transportation in the United States, during a time when airlines could differentiate themselves more often on quality of service than on price. The commitment still persists in the form of a service quality program which includes a corporate culture fostering employee dedication and excellence; operations standards which are regularly monitored; and inflight traveler surveys. All facets of the program are directed at pleasing customers by meeting or exceeding their expectations for service. This approach is successful because management embraced the service quality goal and effectively communicated it to both customers and employees.

An international hotel chain offers another example of a formal service quality program. Recently the hotel chain embarked on a campaign where all employees promise to do their best to encourage guests to return. In the front of hotel lobbies a display of this promise with employees signatures was prominently featured. Employees are exposed to national educational programs either directly or indirectly by management. This serves to instil a 'work for the guest' attitude. Franchised hotels use the national standard operating procedures. Compliance to these is monitored by local management and periodically by an inspector.

To further ensure service quality, this hotel chain offers guests the opportunity to rate the hotel on a report card and a restaurant comment card. The report card is sent directly by the guest to the national office. Hotels which receive the best 'grades' are presented awards at the annual company conference. This acts as a valuable incentive to encourage high quality performance.

The mass experience of a national chain reduces or eliminates the need for individual experimentation on service quality evaluation. Individual inns enjoy national reputation, advertising, and training programs. National scale hotels and other hospitality services employ formal service quality strategies out of necessity to control a decentralized operation. Franchising has proven to be one successful approach to controlling quality in hotel and other tourism services.

Benefits

High quality of service by a tourist destination suggests increased demand for that area. That is one reason why quality of tourism services is receiving more attention from both academic and managerial perspectives. The prevalent concern is with addressing service quality from the tourist's perspective. Managers need to know the components of a quality tourism experience in order to provide for it effectively.

Many destinations have traditionally sought to attract as many tourists as possible. This can be an expensive strategy for sustaining or increasing market share of tourist travel. One alternative is to concentrate on generating repeat tourist business. By providing high quality services, tourism producers are more likely to entice first-time and repeat visitors. Tourists who have a quality experience are likely to communicate favorable reports to friends and relatives. This creates both repeat business and potential new business. Unfortunately, the reverse is also possible. If a quality tourism experience is not attained, then tourist business is lost. Not only will the unhappy tourists not return to the destination, but they will tell others about their disappointment. Word of mouth communication has strong credibility among family, friends, and reference groups, all of whom the potential tourist may hold in regard. This further strengthens its impact.

Tourism businesses may also be able to reduce expenditures by concentrating on what tourists expect for quality service and allocating resources accordingly. Information gained through service quality investigation can be utilized to focus marketing strategy. For example, promotional efforts and service delivery consistent with tourist expectations of a quality experience, may reduce the likelihood of disappointed tourists. Presentation of an accurate image is essential.

Implementation

The subjective nature of service quality has led management to define, describe, and delimit it in quantifiable, objective, but often arbitrary standards. Service quality has been explained in physical, situational, and behavioral terms; that is, what is delivered, the circumstances of the delivery, and how it is delivered. Service quality standards are commonly determined by providers' past experiences, and they often reflect the physical and technical aspects of a service because these are the most easily measurable. This outcome-oriented definition has been termed technical quality.

An alternative approach to assessing service quality has been to measure functional quality, which is the manner in which a service is delivered. This aspect has been proposed as being a more important criterion of quality to consumers. Even if the facility (restaurant) is clean and the service delivery meets high operational standards (timeliness of food arrival), a negative impression can be generated through poor employee–customer interaction (e.g. by an unpleasant waiter). This negative impression can override well-executed technical quality aspects.

Recent research using a multi-attribute approach has integrated the technical and functional components. Five main dimensions of service quality were identified: tangibles, reliability, responsiveness, assurance, and empathy.

Tangibles represent the physical facilities, equipment, and appearance of personnel. These can be assessed by reviewing such elements as cleanliness, design of facilities, the working order of equipment, and the way employees are dressed. Tangibles can create atmosphere. The tangible dimension of a service is one of the few things that a potential customer can know and evaluate in advance of purchase and/or participation.

Reliability refers to the ability to perform the promised service dependably and accurately. The key is the promised service. Promises made through a destination's promotional efforts can contribute to tourists' expectations. Consistency of performance with projected image is important to reliability, and subsequent perceived service quality. Tourists are most often disappointed in quality when services are not delivered as promised.

Responsiveness is the willingness to assist and provide prompt attention to tourists. Tourists expect their requests to be handled quickly and accurately so their vacation plans proceed smoothly. Responsiveness may be described as an attitude.

Assurance indicates courteous and knowledgeable service providers who convey trust and confidence. Assurance encompasses elements of credibility, competence, and security. Credibility is another of the few items regarding a service that can be evaluated in advance. For example, the reputation of an airline can be checked before traveling with that carrier. Assurance is a reflection of the knowledge and competency of service providers. This can assist in the reduction of perceived risk of travel, for either physical or financial security reasons.

The empathy dimension includes caring, individualized attention to tourists. Empathy expresses an understanding of tourists' needs, which can be transformed into services to meet those needs.

Assessment

The difficulty in evaluating quality in tourism services stems from three distinctive features which are unique to service industries, such as tourism. These features of intangibility, heterogeneity, and inseparability of production and consumption are present to varying degrees in every service and have been widely discussed in the marketing literature.

Services are performed and experienced, and although the performance of many services is aided by tangibles (such as airplanes in the provision of transportation), what is actually purchased or obtained is the experience. Intangibility is, in essence, what differentiates a service from a product, which is purchased and literally taken in hand. This makes it difficult for the providers of tourism services to understand how tourists evaluate their services. Intangibility can also make it hard for service providers to exercise the necessary control for offering uniform quality of service delivery.

Heterogeneity refers to the potential for variability in service delivery. This is especially prominent in tourism services because a substantial labor component is involved. The quality of tourism services is largely dependent upon the actions of people such as tour guides, restaurant and hotel personnel, tourist bureaux staff, park and campground employees, and residents of the host community. For example, the nature and quality of interactions between hotel personnel and guests are likely to vary among staff members and from day to day. This can create a gap between what the hotel management plans to deliver and what the guest actually encounters.

The third characteristic, which is inseparability of production and consumption, describes how tourism services are often rendered and experienced simultaneously. This usually requires the presence of both the provider and the consumer during the delivery process. Evaluations on quality of performance are made at this stage. Because the tourist often participates in delivery of a service, the performance and its subsequent quality can be impacted by the tourist's actions, mood, and cooperativeness.

In addition to these unique characteristics of services, there are three types of properties which are integral to consumer evaluation processes in services. These are search experience, and credence properties. Search properties apply to those attributes which a consumer evaluates before engaging in the service. These are primarily tangibles which are physical representations of the service, such as facilities, equipment, appearance of personnel, and sometimes other recipients of the service. Such properties are the easiest for the tourist to evaluate.

Experience properties refer to attributes which can only be specified during or after consumption of the service. They are usually present in highly people-based services, such as those comprising the tourism industry. The experiential nature of tourism services makes them more difficult to evaluate because they lack durability which is a feature often linked with quality in products.

Credence properties are those elements which are beyond the capability of the consumer to evaluate, even after consumption. For example, at a symphony concert, the audience is unlikely to possess the training to formally evaluate the talents of the musicians. Credence properties predominate in services delivered by specialists or professionals because of the high level of expertise usually required to perform such services.

The majority of tourism services, due to their intangibility, are low in search properties and high in experience properties. The heterogeneity characteristic of services heightens the relative importance of experience properties because of the inevitable variability in service delivery from one occasion to another.

Examination of search, experience, and credence properties reveals that evaluation of tourism service quality is both process and output oriented. Tourism services are experiential in nature.

This fosters evaluation of service quality both during and after service delivery. The tourist, as participant, is an integral part of the service enabling him or her to make an assessment while the service is being performed, as well as after it has been performed.

Conclusion

The challenge of providing high quality tourism experiences becomes less difficult when tourism producers know what tourists expect from their services, and what they feel is important to quality. This can most effectively be accomplished through careful assessment, first of tourists' expectations for a quality experience, and second, of tourists' perceptions of the quality of service received. A comparison of tourist expectations with their perceptions of service provides an evaluation of service quality and indicates which areas of service quality are satisfactory and which need improvement. Through such ongoing evaluation and modification, quality in tourism services can be achieved and improved.

Focus on small business

The tourist's overall experience is comprised of numerous smaller encounters with a variety of tourism service providers. Area tourist associations could benefit from a coordinated effort to assess tourists' perceptions of service quality in their region, and integrate the results into the area's overall marketing plan. For example, an area perceived as providing a safe environment for vacationers could highlight this attribute in order to reduce perceived risk of traveling to that destination.

Evaluation of service quality is often undertaken as a means of risk reduction. The types of risk may include time, financial, social, and psychological. Risk reduction strategies employed by marketers commonly include attempts to increase certainty that the service will be performed well. Previous studies have reported that reliability is both a highly expected and highly important dimension of service quality. Promotion of quality aspects may elevate a destination's image and increase tourist traffic to that area, benefiting local businesses.

Further reading

Assael, H., *Consumer Behavior and Marketing Action* (Kent Publishing Co., 1984). Chapter 6 deals with consumer perceptions and marketing strategies for risk reduction.

Berry, L. L., 'Services marketing is different', *Services Marketing*, C. H. Lovelock, ed. (Prentice Hall, 1980). This article describes special challenges and opportunities in services marketing.

Berry, L. L., Zeithaml, V. and Parasuraman, A., 'Quality counts in services too', *Business Horizons* (May/June 1985), pp. 48–52. The article discusses what causes problems in service quality and ways to improve quality.

Cosby, W. E., 'American Airlines a commitment to excellence', *Emerging Perspectives on Services Marketing*, L. Berry, L. Shostack and G. Upah, eds (American Marketing Association, 1983). An address by the Vice President of Passenger Services for American Airlines on the company's focus on service excellence and quality.

Crompton, J. L. and Lamb, C. W., *Marketing Government and Social Services* (Prentice Hall, 1986). The book discusses how marketing concepts can be utilized in the delivery of government and social services. Special attention should be given to Chapters 2–4 and 11 which deal with differences in public and private sector marketing plans, evaluation procedures, and communication networking.

Klaus, P. G., 'Quality epiphenomenon: the conceptual understanding of quality in face to face service encounters', *The Service Encounter*, J. Czepiel, M. Solomon and C. Surprenant, eds (Lexington Books, 1985).

LaPage, W. F., 'Recreation resource management for visitor satisfaction', *Journal of Parks and Recreation Administration*, vol. 1 (1983), pp. 37–44. The article discusses differences between camper and management perceptions of quality.

MacKay, K. J., 'An investigation of service quality in a municipal recreation setting'. Unpublished thesis, Department of Recreation and Parks, Texas A&M University (1987). Research results on relative importance of service quality dimensions to service consumers are presented.

McIntosh, R. W. and Goeldner C. R., *Tourism: Principles, Practices, Philosophies* (John Wiley, 4th edition, 1984). Chapters 6, 7, 9 and 14 deal with tourism demand/supply, marketing, and the tourist's perspective on quality.

Parasuraman, A., Zeithaml, V. and Berry, L. L., 'SERVQUAL: a multiple item scale for measuring consumer perceptions of service quality', Working Paper (Marketing Science Institute, 1986). An approach to assessing service quality using five dimensions of service quality resulting from earlier research.

Parasuraman, A., Zeithaml, V. and Berry, L. L., 'A conceptual model of service quality and its implications for future research', *Journal of Marketing*, vol. 49 (1985), pp. 41–50. The article presents a model of service quality based on the results of service quality research.

Shostack, G. L., 'Breaking free from product marketing', *Journal of Marketing* (April 1977), pp. 73–80. New concepts and strategies for services marketing are explored.

Solomon, M., Surprenant, C., Czepiel, J. *et al*, 'A role theory perspective on dyadic interactions: the service encounter', *Journal of Marketing*, vol. 49 (1985), pp. 99–111.

Upah, G., Berry, L. L. and Shostack, L., 'Emerging themes and directions for services marketing', *Emerging Perspectives on Services Marketing*, L. L. Berry, L. Shostack and G. Upah, eds (American Marketing Association, 1983). This article discusses functional and technical aspects of service quality.

Zeithaml, V., 'How consumer evaluation processes differ between goods and services', *Services Marketing*, C. Lovelock, ed. (Prentice Hall, 1981). This article presents differences between consumer evaluation processes for goods and services, and proposes strategic marketing implications.

Zeithaml, V., Parasuraman, A. and Berry, L. L. 'Problems and strategies in service marketing', *Journal of Marketing*, vol. 49 (1985), pp. 33–46. This article presents of overview of services marketing literature. The article also reports research findings of service firms' problems and strategies.

KELLY J. MACKAY

Tourism retailing

Introduction

Tourism, regardless of the country in which it occurs, is an industry served by a myriad of businesses at the retail level, the majority of which are small businesses. Tourism retailing is predicated upon business practices and market concepts which exist in all retail envirnoments, however, there are additional market conditions within tourist destinations which present unique challenges to the operation of a successful tourism retailing operation.

Perhaps the most difficult market phenomenon with which tourism retailers must deal is the seasonality of their business cycle. While all retailers operate in a dynamic market environment, the tourism retailer's demand pattern is skewed significantly. Skewed demand patterns result in inefficiencies stemming from undercapacity use during some time periods and overcapacity use at others. This phenomenon translates into exaggerated management, personnel and ecological problems.

An underlying difference between retailing in general and tourism retailing is that many publics (political leaders, residents and business people) play a role in directing and controlling tourism development within an area. Aside from the resulting promotional problems which will be discussed later, strategic management problems at several levels surface. In general, residents usually support controlled business development in their community, knowing that businesses will contribute to the expansion of the tax base and employment opportunities, in addition to improving the overall quality of life. Frequently, this is not the case in a community destined for tourism development, however. The tourism retailer is frequently viewed as a conduit to the demise of the community, thus making it difficult to secure political, financial or community support to operate its business. It is impossible for tourism retailers, singularly or collectively, to be successful in a milieu of community discontent.

Due to the nonlocal nature of tourists, it is not uncommon to have a mutual lack of knowledge between retailers and tourists. This results in a unique market environment where tourists are generally unaware of retail offerings in the tourist areas and retailers have a limited understanding of tourist market segments. This situation presents pecuniary problems to the tourism retailer in matching consumer needs with appropriate merchandise assortments, reaching and promoting the store to tourists, evaluating promotional efforts, developing and sustaining a retail image, and encouraging store patronage and loyalty.

This chapter will focus on market components and business practices which represent the divergence of tourism retailing from retailing in general. Business management concepts will be discussed from a practical standpoint to assist academics and tourism retailers in developing systematic planning techniques.

Examples

The importance of shopping as a tourist activity should not be understated. Whether a traveler is on a business or pleasure trip, shopping is the first and last thing done upon arriving and departing from a tourist location. One Arizona study revealed that shopping was the main objective for 61 per cent of the Mexicans visiting that state. Another study of nonbusiness visitors to Atlanta indicated that 56 per cent had shopped at a mall while in Atlanta.

In many of the major US convention and tourist areas retailers are developing elaborate marketing plans to lure conventioneers and tourists into their stores. Fashion shows, wardrobe consultations, makeovers, day trips for shopping and luncheons are only a few of the campaigns which are being promoted to tourists by companies such as Bloomingdales, Neiman Marcus and Rich's. The interest of retailers in being included in the itinerary of tour bus packages has added another dimension to their promotional plans. Because of the unique vehicles through which these campaigns are promoted, there may be greater opportunities for target marketing strategies.

Benefits

It is not an overstatement to say that tourism development within most tourism dependent areas can best be described as uncoordinated and spontaneous, resulting in a market environment which is fragmented and inefficient. Coupled with these micro problems is the macro problem of the highly competitive nature of tourist destinations within a world tourism market. In order to address these problems the notion of strategic planning for the 'total tourist destination' becomes critical and central. Strategic planning and the overall 'image' development of a tourist location becomes the responsibility of political leaders, residents of the community, and business people. Aside from the planning difficulties this presents, there may be political pressures at the local, regional or state level to position the image of the tourist location different from that of the residents or business persons. What this translates into is a centralized strategic planning process which circumscribes business development to present a unified image of the entire tourist location which can be packaged and promoted.

While the centralized planning agenda of a tourist destination is predicated on the notion that the overall quality of a tourist destination is enhanced by each individual tourism operator, a question arises as to the individual retailers' sovereignty to engage in business planning. The net result is that a retailer wishing to open a business within a tourist location must realize that the output from the centralized tourism planning process may be more pervasive than anything he/she does within the business planning process. A second caveat is that the tourism retailer must clearly understand the centralized mission of the tourist destination in order to creatively position a store so that it reflects and complements the image of the tourist destination.

Implementation

Location

First-time tourists know little about any aspect of the tourist location, especially the retail offerings. Frequently, the first-time visitor spends considerable time in orienting himself to the amenities of the tourist area and during this orientation period may be unconcerned with particular retail availabilities. Therefore, location is often the most critical factor in increasing store patronage. Convenience may be the major attribute used in the decision to patronize a store, especially for tourists not having cars.

A planned clustering of stores in a tourism destination, as in any retail environment, can be of benefit from a retail patronage standpoint. The location, compatibility and mutual attraction of the retailers can be a prime strategy to generate traffic while assisting tourists to gain economies of shopping effort. However, this retail clustering approach must be further supported by uniform store hours, easy accessibility, available and free parking, and proximity to lodging facilities.

Product mix

Because tourism retailers conduct little, if any, market segmentation, relatively little is known about their customers, the tourists. The lack of key target market consumer profiles makes the development of appropriate merchandise assortments very difficult. Frequently, this results in tourism retailers offering similar merchandise assortments due to a lack of target marketing. While most tourism locations are comprised of many different types of retailers, due to a lack of creativity in store development all too often it is the 'gift shop' or 'tourist trap' image which is pervasive. After all, does one tourist destination need 25 fudge shops with an almost identical product assortment?

In an attempt to develop a unique, differentiated and targeted product assortment, retailers should be mindful that tourists frequently desire to purchase products which reflect the culture, mores or traditions of the destination. It is incumbent upon the tourism retailer to offer high quality products from local artists, craftspersons and producers. A creative approach to merchandise mix assemblage should offer an ample assortment of unusual gifts and personal items with a local flavor, keeping in mind that authenticity of the locally produced product is key. Information about the local artist or craftsperson provided by the tourism retailer will add to the charm of the product, increasing the opportunity for a sale.

Retailers should keep in mind that the size or configuration of a product may preclude a tourist from purchasing it. As air travel continues to be an important travel mode for tourists, baggage size restrictions, fragility and manageability need to be considered when developing a product mix. Additionally, the tourism retailer may need to provide packaging and airport delivery service to entice the tourist to buy.

Pricing

A tourist area is usually characterized by a high degree of retail concentration and saturation which is located in close proximity to the tourist attracting feature(s). This artificial clustering of retail establishments promotes a highly competitive market structure. This means that retailers with homogeneous merchandise mixes will experience a great deal of price competition and therefore should differentiate through unique product offerings.

One way in which department and specialty stores, in general, have thwarted competition from discounters and off-price retailers is by developing a merchandise mix heavily reliant upon brand name and private label merchandise. While little research has been conducted to analyze merchandise mix issues for tourism retailers, it has been indicated that brand loyalty is not an important attribute in store patronage for American tourists when in a US tourist destination. Some research does suggest, however, that brand names, especially luxury brand name products, are important in increasing store patronage among international visitors within US tourist destinations.

Little research has been conducted to analyze tourist gift buying. It is felt that expenditures for gifts represent an important part of tourists' retail expenditures. Research supports the notion that tourists do not arbitrarily buy gifts; they have a specific person(s) and corresponding price point(s) in mind when they purchase. Knowledge of the intended recipient of the gift will help the retailer to make appropriate gift suggestions. This knowledge base will also assist him in future merchandise price lining decisions.

Promotion mix

In recent years the tourism industry has become more sophisticated in its promotional efforts. The importance of market segmentation strategies and development of the promotional mix are being recognized today. To this end, a multitiered promotional effort has evolved which is significantly different from the general retailing promotional process. While the level of specificity of the promotion message changes, tourism destinations are promoted at the national, regional (multi-state), state, regional (within a state) and local levels by a multitude of publics: government, Chambers of Commerce, travel writers, trade organizations, private tourism retailers, among others. In this highly promotional environment it is crucial that promotional messages are coordinated, consistent and accurate. Individual tourism retailers must, then, creatively channel their promotional campaigns to reflect the overall image of the tourist location yet focus messages which emphasize their individual competitive advantages. Because so many special interest groups are involved in tourism promotion it may make it more difficult for a retailer to get over a clear promotional message which differentiates his store from other similar stores.

Another useful strategy for retailers located in tourist locations attracting many international visitors would be to hire multilingual sales personnel. The practice of having sales personnel who speak several languages could be promoted and provide a strategic advantage in developing store loyalty or at least increased store patronage.

Distribution

Retail demand in a tourist destination could be described as an 'outshopping' phenomenon. Outshopping is the practice of shoppers who live in one area and travel to another to shop. While outshopping is a practice with which all retailers have to deal, outshopping typically represents the major portion of revenues for tourism retailers. Due to the outshopping nature of tourism retailing, retailers know relatively little about the characteristics of their consumers. Therefore, the target market in a tourist area is perceived to be 'the tourist' which tourism retailers view as one homogeneous group and little, if any, market segmentation and target marketing is conducted.

Assessment

One could argue that due to the unique business environment of tourism, strategic planning is critical. But do tourism retailers have a complete understanding of strategic planning or its benefits? The word 'strategy' has been so overused that many business operators believe that if they have formulated a 'strategy' to accomplish a task that they, in fact, are engaged in strategic planning. Further, few tourism retailers make a clear distinction between operational and strategic management. While both are necessary, they have significantly different purposes and components. Another common misconception in business planning is the emphasis on the monolithic goal of short-term profit maximization to ensure business success. The use of last year's profit loss or gain as a forecast for the level of business success for the next year is a commonly used financial tool.

Combining the aforementioned planning difficulties of tourism retailing with the fact that there is no industry operating information for comparison, compounds the problem when attempting to evaluate business performance. Development of planning strategies in the light of industry operating ratios are critical to the development and sustenance of a viable tourism business.

The real resistance of tourism retailers to strategic planning stems from the perception that it requires two resources that many do not have a great deal of – either capital or sophisticated expertise in planning techniques. Coupling these two objections with the fact that strategic planning pay-offs are usually of a long-term nature, tourism retailers become disenchanted with the lack of immediate results, abandoning future attempts at systematic planning.

Conclusion

Tourism retailing is big business and is forecasted to become even bigger. Projections indicate that tourism will become the world's leading industry by the year 2000. Due to these trends, the tourism industry has enjoyed growth in many areas with little systematic planning for development.

While the potential for economic development and employment expansion through tourism retailing is present in virtually every state, systematic planning and a marketing approach is critical to realizing this potential. The small-scale entrepreneurial nature of tourism retailing should not be an excuse for *ad hoc* planning and business management. With systematic decision making and sound business administration skills coupled with creativity, tourism entrepreneurs can maintain economically viable businesses and contribute to the employment base and economic stability of their communities.

Focus on small business

Over 95 per cent of the businesses that serve the tourism industry are small businesses and many of them are undercapitalized. Because of these two characteristics, their ability to survive long periods of adverse economic conditions is often limited. While no statistics are available to profile business failures among tourism retailers, there is reason to believe that their failures are as high, if not higher, than those of businesses as a whole. Facing statistics which suggest that nine out of ten new businesses fail in the first 2 years should provide impetus for 'building a better mouse trap'.

Research projects

Holecek, D. F., 'Travel, tourism and recreation resource center', Michigan State University, East Lansing. This research project is currently in progress. Upon completion, the results will identify: 1. computer and communications technologies which can provide quick and simple access to tourism data, 2. voids in tourism investment information, and 3. alternatives for the dissemination of secondary databases for small businesses.

Pulver, G. C. and Aronson, N. R., 'Measuring community trade area capture', University of Wisconsin, Madison. The objective of this research project was to identify the effects of varying factors on a community's capture of consumer expenditures. Retail trade performance was examined using the Census of Retail Trade and Service Industries data.

Klar, L. R. and Warnick, R. B., 'Tourism impacts and development alternatives from the local government perspective', University of Massachusetts, Amherst. This project is currently in progress. Its objective is to correlate variations in tourist expenditures and tourist industry revenues with selected governmental expenditures and socio-economic variables associated with the quality of life in tourist communities. A microcomputer model will be used to analyze the data.

Sternquist, B., Pysarchik, D., Davis, B. *et al*, 'Toward achieving Michigan's rural employment potential – the role of resort area retailing', Michigan State University, East Lansing. Database of tourim retailers focused on the analysis of business planning techniques and market segmentation.

Further reading

Burdenski, H., 'Tourism: America's hottest industry', *Tourism Services Marketing: Advances in Theory and Practice*, vol. 2 (Academy of Marketing Science, 1986), pp. 3–12. This article analyzed current trends in tourism with an emphasis on target marketing and an analysis of the marketing mix.

Carusone, P. S. and Moscove, B. J., 'Special marketing problems of smaller city retailers', *Journal of Academy of Marketing Science*, vol. 13 (Summer 1985), pp. 198–211.

Davis, B., Pysarchik, D. T., Sternquist, B. *et al*, *A Profile of Tourism-dependent and Nontourism-dependent Retailers*, Research Report, no. 484, Michigan State University Agriculture Experiment Station, East Lansing (6 November 1986).

de Gennaro, N. and Ritchey, R. J. 'Mexican visitors to Arizona identified as valued market', *Arizona Review*, vol. 27, nos. 8–9 (August/September 1978), pp. 1–9.

Gee, C. Y., Choy D. J. L. and Makens, J. C., *The Travel Industry* (AVI Publishing Co., 1984). This book is a comprehensive presentation of concepts and practices of the travel industry.

Jafari, J., 'Anatomy of the travel industry', *Cornell HRA Quarterly* (May 1983), pp. 71–7. Explores the various components of the travel industry and then analyzes this industry from a holistic viewpoint.

LaFarge, R. W., Reese, R. M. and Stanton, W. W., 'Identifying and attracting consumer outshoppers', *Journal of Small Business Management*, vol. 22 (January 1984), pp. 22–9.

Lime, D. W., *Large Groups in the Boundary Waters Canoe-area – Their Numbers, Characteristics, and Impact*, Note NC-142 (USDA Forest Service Research, 1972).

Maddox, R. N., 'Factors contributing to satisfaction with tourism: the residents' view', *Tourism Services Marketing: Advances in Theory and Practice*, vol. 2 (Academy of Marketing Science, 1986), pp. 76–84. Explores public acceptance of tourism by residents of a community.

Manning, R. E. and Powers, L. A., 'Peak and off-peak use: redistributing the outdoor recreation/tourism load', *Journal of Travel Research*, vol. XXIII (Fall 1984), pp. 25–31.

McIntosh, R. W., *Tourism: Principles, Practices, Philosophies* (Grid Inc., 1977). Indepth coverage of the component parts and practices of the tourism industry.

Meidan, A., 'Marketing strategies for tourism', *Tourism Services Marketing: Advances in Theory and Practice*, vol. 2 (Academy of Marketing Science, 1986), pp. 294–310. This paper discusses the formulation and implementation of marketing strategies for tourism.

Omura, G. S. and Cooper, M. B., 'Three strategic planning techniques for retailers', *Business*, vol. 33, no. 1 (January/February/March 1983), pp. 2–8. This article applies three popular strategic planning techniques to retailing.

Schwaninger, M., 'Strategic business management in tourism', *Tourism Management* (June 1986), pp. 74–85.

Sternquist, B., Davis, B., Pysarchik, D. T. *et al*, *Profiles of Marquette and Mackinac Island Tourists: Results of A Summer 1985 Survey*, Research Report, no. 481, Michigan State University Agriculture Experiment Station, East Lansing (January 1987).

'Tour stops', *Chain Store Age, General Merchandise Trends* (April 1986), pp. 11–15. The article discusses strategies undertaken by retailers to increase revenues from tourists.

US Travel Data Center, *The 1984–85 Economic Review of Travel in America* (USTDC, 1985).

US Travel Data Center, 'Travel takes third place in US employment scene', *Travel Weekly* (USTDC, 1985) p. 3.

DAWN THORNDIKE PYSARCHIK

Tourist destination image

Introduction

Product image is an integral part of that product, much like its other attributes, such as, quality, function, price, design or value. Traditional marketing research, as well as studies in psychology and sociology, have established that perceptions of a product or a service play an important role in an individual's choice of that particular product or service. In other words, the purchase decision is determined not only by the product's performance characteristics, but also by the consumer's perception of its personality or image. Therefore, the study of product images is an essential component of the marketing research process, in which the perception of a product is evaluated and then strategies are devised which aim at strengthening, altering or even creating an image.

A tourism destination can be viewed as one of the products of the tourism industry. It is a uniquely complex product – composed of, among other factors, an area's climate, infra- and suprastructure, services, and its natural and cultural attributes – but, nevertheless, a product. It is reasonable to assume, then, that a tourism destination also possesses an image. In fact, some pioneering research in image as a factor in tourism development, as well as a wave of recent works on the subject do confirm this assumption (e.g. Britton, 1979; Crompton, 1979; Goodrich, 1978a, 1978b; Hunt, 1971, 1975; Mayo, 1973, 1975; Pearce, 1980; Sternquist-Witter, 1985). Hunt (1975) maintained 'all places have images – good, bad and indifferent – that must be identified and either changed or exploited' (p. 7). Thus, travelers and potential travelers hold images of destinations, and, moreover, the choice of a destination is influenced by the individual's perception of alternative possibilities, whether these perceptions happen to be true or not.

Although the topic of this chapter necessarily limits the scope of the discussion to destination images, it must at least be pointed out that this is not the only subject of study in the broader field of image in travel and tourism. Mayo (1976), for example, studied the perceived images of airlines. LaPage and Cormier (1977) investigated images of recreation activities. They also noted that individuals employed in the tourism industry are capable of projecting positive or negative images. Finally, it has to be pointed out that images of leisure have also been studied and it has been shown that they have been changing over time (Neulinger and Breit, 1971).

Having determined that people perceive images of various aspects of the tourism industry, it is appropriate to ask what exactly is image? Some authors (Hunt, 1975; Mayo, 1973) consider image an impression, or even a simplified impression. Others place image into a broader context, equating it with knowledge. But, 'an image is not necessarily objective knowledge. Rather, it is subjective knowledge. Knowledge carries the implication of validity and truth. Image connotes what I believe to be true, or what you as an individual person believe to be true' (Markin, 1974, p. 121). In this sense image may be defined as 'our own personalized, internalized and conceptualized understanding of what we know' (p. 121).

Examples

Building on the knowledge of image as a factor in destination development and promotion, images of a wide variety and types of locations have been examined. This impressively long list of destination image studies includes works on, for example, the images of Ireland (Ehemann, 1977), Florida, California, Mexico, Hawaii, the Bahamas, Jamaica, Puerto Rico, the Virgin Islands (Goodrich 1978a, 1978b), the Third World (Britton, 1979), United States (McLellan and Dodd Foushee, 1983), Yugoslavia, Greece and Romania (Telisman-Kosuta, 1987) etc.

Responding to the results of image studies of the Netherlands, this country was able to create innovative and successful promotional campaigns (Fisher, 1984). Studies had shown that Holland had a positive image in the US market, but that this was a nostalgic vision of old Amsterdam, tulips, Gouda and Edam cheese and the always dominant and ubiquitous windmill. In order to stimulate visitors to travel throughout the country, instead of making only a brief stopover in Amsterdam, the Netherlands Board of Tourism offered special bonuses as an incentive to visit the countryside with points given for each province visited. Efforts were also made to promote the cultural variety of the country. A new promotional vehicle, the Holland Culture Card (a cultural credit card), was implemented, which in conjunction with the 'museum pass', 'meet the Dutch' welcome parties and an effort to promote lowlands high cuisine resulted in increased exposure of cultural riches.

A 1971 study by Hunt, in which state images of Colorado,

Montana, Utah and Wyoming were analyzed, is another example of an image study which proved to be the basis of future promotional activities. More precisely, Hunt identified many areas where, specifically, Utah's image could be improved. In accordance with those recommendations various promotional messages were initiated to reposition the state's product. From 1971 to 1983 nonresident travel to Utah fluctuated, but evidence indicated it was steadily on the increase. There were no new studies, however, addressing a possible change in the state's image. Therefore, in 1983 (Gartner and Hunt, 1987) the 1971 study was replicated, testing the hypothesis of a positive correlation between image change and visitation level. Results indicated that for every activity and attraction analyzed, in no case was image change negative and in many cases it was positive. It was, thus, concluded that, among other factors, successfully changing state image will result in that state becoming a more desirable destination.

Benefits

The importance of studying images lies in the relationship between perception and behavior. In other words, the central question is whether one's ideas and beliefs about a destination, i.e. one's image, influence one's travel behavior.

The pertinent travel and tourism literature indicates there is a relationship between travel behavior and our cognitions and beliefs about a destination. Hunt (1971) stressed that 'what . . . potential customers think about the natural environment, climate and people of a region may shape perceptions or images which detract from or contribute to successful development' (p.1). Similarly, Goodrich's (1978b) research demonstrated 'a strong and direct association between respondents' preferences for a vacation destination and their perception of that destination. That is, the more favorable the perception of a given vacation destination, the more preferred that destination will tend to be' (p. 11). Chung's (1985) and Telisman-Kosuta's (1987) work echoed much the same findings. LaPage and Cormier (1977) furthermore noted that 'in many cases, it is probably the image more than the factual information that produces a tourist's decision on where to travel' (p. 21).

Knowing that there is a positive correlation between destination image and visitation allows us to maintain that when an individual has made the decision to travel the choice of destination is influenced by the individual's perception of alternative possibilities. What this implies in practical terms is that image studies can result in direct guidelines at to actions which need to be undertaken in order to create a more successful destination. It must be pointed out, however, that while image is a significant variable weighing upon the success of a destination, its relative magnitude as compared to other factors such as access, population concentrations, physical facilities and so forth still remains a question.

Since destination images are one of the determinants of travel behavior, it is essential to understand how they are formed. The most obvious answer to this question is, why may be called, the mechanism of direct experience. Having had contact with a destination or a group of people enables one to form a set of ideas and beliefs about that destination or group from first-hand experience. More commonly, however, images seem to be developed in complete absence of contact with the object. Our images of the world around us are, most often, the product of the culture and the subculture in which they are developed. Beginning at home, a large part of our cognitive map regarding our own and other cultures is transmitted from parents to children through generations. There are also many sources of information and images outside the family, especially in complex societies with extremely diversified communication systems. These include the mass media, school teachers, textbooks, fiction, political parties, religious teachings, as well as other people, and particularly travelers who recount their experiences. Each is a powerful fountainhead of an individual's knowledge. In addition to these 'organic images' resulting from lifelong socialization processes, destinations may also have 'induced images' (Gunn, 1972). The latter are brought about by a conscious effort of development, promotion, advertising and publicity on the part of the tourism industry.

Implementation

Once the image a destination projects to potential visitors has been determined, it is possible to assess whether that image is realistic, whether it needs to be moved closer to reality, and whether it is easily differentiated from perceptions of others locations with similar attributes. Depending on the outcome, a proper marketing strategy has to be developed. The basic goal of such a marketing communication program would be to reinforce the positive images, or to bring information to potential customers about characteristics they are not aware of or of which they have a distorted view, or even to attempt to build a desired destination image.

It must be pointed out, though, that there are several factors which make the process of image change and particularly of image building a difficult task. In the first place, by the nature of the product, destinations are not in a position where they can greatly alter their physical characteristics. Working within given limitations, destinations have to strive to build their images around unique attributes which give them a competitive advantage and which can be marketed successfully. The second hurdle arises from the fact that a destination is able to create an image only to the extent that it can control the information reaching potential visitors. Tourists are, however, likely to be exposed to numerous informational stimuli about a location, many of which may contradict the information provided by the destination's marketing efforts. In this sense, images are also difficult to build.

Nevertheless, there are numerous marketing tools which can be implemented in creating a desired image. The most obvious one, and certainly the most prevalent one is advertising. Specific advertising messages in combination with specific visual effects, delivered through a specific medium can be used to paint a desired picture. Furthermore, placing stories in the mass media is a cost-effective way of reaching a large audience.

There is also a wide variety (with plenty of room for new, imaginative alternatives) of special promotional and information-disseminating techniques, including, for example, programs built around a certain theme, familiarization trips offered to travel writers, travel agents and tour operators, special incentives, seminars and so on.

It has been noted, however, that promotional messages produced by the tourism industry more often strive to create false and partial images of destinations and their people, than they attempt to communicate factual and truly worthwhile information. Nettekoven (1976) noted countries are usually depicted in terms of the 'beach, sun, palms, untoched landscape, . . . friendly population, amusement potential, quality of hotel beds, number of courses of meals, and measurements of the hotel swimming pool' (p. 53).

Both the tourists and the host populations stand to lose from false and shallow images. Image building which creates a 'false reality' is, at best, selling and perpetuating a harmless lie, but nevertheless a lie. At worst, this can become a path to robbing a culture of its authenticity. False destination images have a negative effect on the tourist as well. 'For the [tourist], the contrast between image and reality often produces disappointment or anger on arrival, and bogus images constrain the learning potential of travel, one of its most durable and valued rationales. If places are perceived either as composed of nothing more than beaches, sun, and obsequious, smiling locals, or, at the other extreme, as some mystical paradise, visitors are much less likely to learn anything about the real place. The experience is reduced to validation of clichés and stereotypes' (Britton, 1979, p. 323). In addition, a tourist who 'has been had' once is unlikely to return again. Therefore, in the short run, creating a fictional paradise in the minds of potential visitors may be a profitable idea, but in the long run it is not a wise policy to follow.

Assessment

Diagnosing a destination's perceived strengths and weaknesses on relevant tourism attributes is a valuable guide in making specific modifications or additions, in the tourism facilities themselves and also in the destination's marketing support. Moreover, it is important to realize that a given destination image has to be periodically re-evaluated. Images are not static and they change over time (Gartner and Hunt, 1986; Mayo and Jarvis, 1981; Pearce, 1982). Although at first we tend to reject messages which conflict with our existing images, research has shown that such resistance is not usually infinite. Messages which are often repeated or which come with unusual force will be able to alter the image (Boulding, 1956). In some cases images can change in a very short period of time, while in others that transformation can be a very slow process. Whatever the case may be, this implies that the key concept in the study of destination images is not merely 'image evaluation', but 'periodic image evaluation'.

Another point to be kept in mind when addressing the issue of destination image evaluation is the regional variation of image. Research has confirmed a positive correlation between physical distance from a destination and the image of it. Increased distance covaries with increased reality distortion. Conversely, increased proximity covaries with increasingly more detailed and clearer pictures (Crompton, 1979; Gould and White, 1974; Hunt, 1971). Thus, marketers must evaluate the regional variations in the image of destinations, so that appropriate messages can be directed at the different regions.

A remaining question related to the evaluation of destination images deals with the manner in which they are measured. In fact, measurement is the basic problem in the study of images. They are difficult to express, highly subjective and sometimes even subconscious. As such they are not easily quantifiable. Therefore, unlike gauging temperature, for example, it is impossible to measure the direction, or the intensity, or the salience of an image in any direct way. Researchers have, however, developed a number of methodological techniques which enable them to infer images from responses to measuring instrument stimuli and which allow them to quantify highly subjective data.

One of the simplest methods of image measurement is the rank order technique. For instance, vacation destinations are typically ranked in order of preference. Furthermore, various types of scales are frequently used to measure images. Although they differ in type and in the way they are constructed (e.g. Likert scales, semantic-differential scales, descriptive scales, evaluative scales etc.) the objective of all scales is to assign to the subject's image a numerical score along a continuum ranging from *highly favorable* at one end to *highly unfavorable* at the other (Crompton, 1979; Goodrich, 1978a; 1978b; Hunt, 1971; Mindak, 1965). Image can also be measured using open-ended questions and through indepth interviews. Finally, a series of projective techniques is a very interesting, but a seldom used method of data collection in image studies. The projective tests include word-association, sentence-completion, picture interpretation questions or the balloon test (Kassarjian and Robertson, 1973.).

Conclusion

Travelers and potential travelers hold images of alternative tourism destinations. Thus, destination image is a crucial component of a destination's tourism product. Furthermore, it has been found, tourists' choice of a vacation destination is greatly influenced by his or her perceptions of it. All of this makes a continuous assessment of a destination's image, as it exists in the minds of potential customers, a prerequisite to meaningful marketing strategy and a destination's general capability of maintaining a competitive position in the marketplace. More precisely, image studies aim to result in pointers as to the type of specific promotional and other activities needed to, for example, improve a negative image or one ridden with misconceptions, to maintain a positive one or to even create an image altogether.

Focus on small business

By the nature of the subject matter, it seems logical destination image studies should be of particular interest to national, regional or local tourism organizations, such as the National Tourism Offices and their State and local counterparts. These are the 'supra' organizations responsible for marketing a destination as a whole.

A tourism destination is obviously composed of numerous smaller components, however. From our knowledge of image, it is reasonable to assume each one of them – a hotel, a club, a restaurant, a transportation company, an information service, a museum or other attraction – projects certain images as well, thus contributing to overall destination image. In this sense, evaluation of these 'sub-images' is important to the overall success of the destination as a whole.

Apart from linking images of specific components within the destination's tourism industry to a broader destination image, each business involved in tourism has to be aware of the significance of image as an integral component of any product and of its capability to influence significantly, or even determine, buyer behavior. Consequently, how consumers perceive a specific business or a particular organization is extremely relevant to the success of their marketing efforts.

Further reading

Boulding, K. E., *The Image – Knowledge in Life and Society* (The University of Michigan Press, 1956). This work advances an interesting theory of image as the basis of buyer behavior.

Britton, R. A., 'The image of the Third World in tourism marketing', *Annals of Tourism Research*, vol. 6 (1979), pp. 318–29. This article deals with the disparity between the advertised image and reality, especially in relation to Third World countries.

Chung, M. H., *Images of Four East Asian Countries*, unpublished master's thesis, George Washington University, Washington, DC (1985). This study describes images of Japan, South Korea, Hong Kong and the Philippines as perceived by American travel writers. It also deals with the relationships between image and physical, distance, and image and visitation.

Crompton, J. L., 'An assessment of the image of Mexico as a vacation destination and the influence of geographical location upon that image', *Journal of Travel Research*, vol. 17, no. 4 (1979), pp. 18–23. Descriptive and importance dimensions of Mexico's image are measured. The article further explores the relationship between favorability of image and distance.

Ehemann, J., 'What kind of place is Ireland: an image perceived through the American media', *Journal of Travel Research*, vol. 16, no. 2 (1977), pp. 28–30. This article reports on the images of Ireland as determined by content analysis of American printed media.

Fisher, H., 'Travel research: the catalyst for worldwide tourism marketing (catalysts in Europe and Down Under)', *Proceedings of the Travel and Tourism Research Association Fifteenth Annual Conference* (1984), pp. 95–7. This report describes the promotional problems and solutions encountered by the Netherlands Board of Tourism.

Gartner, W. C. and Hunt, J. D., 'An analysis of state image change over a twelve year period (1971–1983)', *Journal of Travel Research*, vol. 26, no. 2 (1987), pp. 15–19. This report analyzes changes in the state of Utah's image. The study tests a hypothesis dealing with the correlation between image and nonresident visitation.

Goodrich, J. N., 'A new approach to image analysis through multidimensional scaling', *Journal of Travel Research*, vol. 16, no. 3 (1978a), pp. 3–7. Images of nine tourist attracting regions are presented. This article also describes an approach to portraying images of tourist regions through the use of multidimensional scaling.

Goodrich, J. N., 'The relationship between preference for and perception of vacation destinations: application of a choice model', *Journal of Travel Research*, vol. 17, no. 2 (1978b), pp. 8–13. This article demonstrates that preferences for tourist destinations are largely dependent on the favorableness of perception of those destinations.

Gould, P. and White, R., *Mental Maps* (Penguin Books, 1974). A geographer's perspective on perception.

Gunn, C. A., *Vacationscape – Designing Tourist Regions* (Bureau of Business Research, The University of Texas, 1972). A comprehensive text on tourism development.

Hunt, J. D., *Image – A Factor in Tourism*, unpublished doctoral dissertation, Colorado State University, Fort Collins (1971). A pioneering work in image as a factor in destination development. Images of Wyoming, Montana, Utah and Colorado are studied.

Hunt, J. D., 'Image as a factor in tourism development', *Journal of Travel Research*, vol. 13, no. 3 (1975), pp. 1–7. This article discusses images of four Rocky Mountain states. It reports on a broader work exploring the role of image in tourism development.

Kassarjian, H. H. and Robertson, T. S., *Perspectives in Consumer Behavior* (Scott, Foresman and Company, 1973). In the introductory remarks the authors deal with methodological considerations in consumer behavior studies.

LaPage, W. F. and Cormier, P. L., 'Images of camping – barriers to participation', *Journal of Travel Research*, vol. 15, no. 4 (1977), pp. 21–5. Images of camping's attractions and environment are studied, as a means of identifying new market prospects and marketing strategies for overcoming the perceptual barriers of many prospective campers.

Markin, J. R., Jr., *Consumer Behavior – A Cognitive Orientation* (Macmillan, 1974). A cognitivist view of the role of image in buyer behavior.

Mayo, E. J., 'Regional images and regional travel behavior', *Proceedings of the Fourth Annual Travel Research Association Conference* (1973), pp. 211–17. In an effort to contribute to our understanding of destination choice, this study discusses the role of impulse decision making in the vacation setting, reports on attractiveness ratings of eight 'Discover America' regions, and on the process of constructing a multidimensional attitudinal map of these areas.

Mayo, E. J., 'Tourism and the national parks: a psychographic and attitudinal study', *Journal of Travel Research*, vol. 14, no. 1 (1975), pp. 14–17. This article reports on two techniques – multidimensional scaling and psychographics, as a means of discovering attitudes of tourists toward National Parks as vacation destinations.

Mayo, E. J., 'Airline choice: the role of perceived images', *Proceedings of the Seventh Annual Travel Research Association Conference* (1976), p. 257. This article discusses a study in which, using multidimensional scaling, differences in airline images are analyzed.

Mayo, E. J. and Jarvis, L. P., *The Psychology of Leisure Travel* (CBI Publishing Co., 1981). This book presents consumer behavior concepts as related to tourism.

McLellan, R. W. and Dodd Foushee, K., 'Negative images of the United States as expressed by tour operators from other countries', *Journal of Travel Research*, vol. 21, no. 2 (1983), pp. 2–5. Images of the United States among potential travelers and how these affect their travel behavior are discussed.

Mindak, W. A., 'Fitting the semantic differential to the marketing problem', *Dimensions of Consumer Behavior*, J. U. McNeal, ed. (Appleton Century Crofts, 1965), pp. 257–65. The problems of measurement in consumer behavior studies are discussed.

Nettekoven, L., 'Mechanisms of intercultural interaction', *Tourism – Passport to Development?*, E. de Kadt, ed. (Oxford University Press, 1976). This chapter deals with intercultural relations between indigenous populations and foreign tourists.

Neulinger, J. and Breit, M., 'Attitude dimensions of leisure: a replication study', *Journal of Leisure Research*, vol. 3, no. 2 (1971), pp. 108–15. This paper reports on the identification of five relatively independent dimensions in the leisure domain which allow the measurement of leisure attitudes.

Pearce, P. L., *The Social Psychology of Tourist Behaviour* (Pergamon Press, 1982). In Chapter 5 on 'Tourists and the environment' pre-and post-travel evaluations of destinations are discussed.

Sternquist-Witter, B., 'Attitudes about a resort area: a comparison of tourists and local retailers', *Journal of Travel Research*, vol. 24, no. 1 (1985), pp. 14–19. This article compares images of a resort area as held by two groups.

Telisman-Kosuta, N., *Images of Yugoslavia, Greece and Romania*. Unpublished master's thesis, George Washington University, Washington, DC (1987). This study reports on both the descriptive and the evaluative aspects of Yugoslavia's, Greece's and Romania's image. The study also attempts to determine the relationship between image and distance, between favorability of image and visitation, and between image and likelihood to recommend a destination.

NEDA TELISMAN-KOSUTA

Tourist market segmentation

Introduction

Market segmentation is an important element of a marketing strategy. Kotler, one of the leading marketing specialists, defines market segmentation as '...the subdividing of a market into homogeneous subsets of customers, where any subset may conceivably be selected as a market target to be reached with a distinct marketing mix' (Kotler, 1972, p. 166). In his definition Marty makes a distinction between a statistical technique and a marketing policy: 'Segmentation is both a statistical technique, which makes it possible to divide a population into homogeneous groups, and a marketing policy, which consists of dividing a market into homogeneous segments each having its own distribution channels, different motivations etc.' (Marty, 1971, p. 98).

Segmentation is very close to what the French call 'typologie'. Whereas segmentation is a 'descendant process' (we split up the population into groups), typology is an 'ascendant process'. In the latter case we start with individuals and bring them together into larger and larger families or groups, the individuals who form those families being very similar and the differences between the families the greatest possible. In reality the distinction between segmentation and typology is rather a question of method, as we shall see below (see Clustering).

Tourist market segmentation is not an academic notion but, as we stress, a strategy to achieve the most efficient use of marketing resources (Schwarz, 1984). This is quite well underlined in the description of marketing by Burkart and Medlik: 'A tourist market may be identified corresponding to each tourist product. In this sense, the term market is used to describe the collective of buyers and potential buyers of each tourist product. The identification of this corresponding market, a segment of the total market, is of the greatest importance. If the marketing effort is to be cost-effective, it must be at a minimum level to avoid waste by reaching only that fraction of the total market which is likely to be attracted, and at the same time on a sufficiently large scale to reach some threshold level below which the marketing effort would be ineffective' (Burkart and Medlik, 1974, p. 194). We must never forget that there is not only a great variety of tourist products (each country, region, resort or operator is seeking to offer more and more specific products) and different tourist consumers, but that the cost of a promotion action is very high. This forces a tourist agency, which promotes a tourist product, to define a clear group of customers who are useful in the framework of a market. It is a systematic approach that permits the marketing planner to select the strategically most important segments and then to design brands, products, packages, communications and marketing strategies around them. It infinitely simplifies the setting of objectives (Yankelovich, 1964). In other words, segmentation is not only related to promotion or distribution; it can also be very useful for adapting the tourist products (e.g. quality of hotel, manmade infrastructure) to the chosen segments.

Several factors have made segmentation more and more a necessity: first, the possible economies of scale due to standardization (e.g. sun destinations); second, the higher welfare level of the population and the differentiation of the needs; third, the increased competition between tourist destinations, and fourth, marketing research has been stimulated by a scientific approach (e.g. SPSS computer program) (Verhage and Cunningham, 1981, Chapter 7).

Segmentation requirements

In order to achieve an efficient use of marketing resources segmentation should respect a number of conditions. Kotler (1972, p. 168) gives three requirements:

1. Measurability, or the degree to which quantified information exists or is obtainable on a particular buyer characteristic. Not all characteristics are susceptible to easy measurement. This can be particularly the case with some psychographic variables or benefits sought.
2. Accessibility, or the degree to which the firm can focus its marketing efforts on chosen segments. There should be a link between the segmentation and the instruments of the marketing-mix (product formulation, promotion, distribution).
3. Substantiality, or the degree to which the segments are large enough to be worth considering for separate marketing.

Major segmentation variables

A hotelkeeper, a travel agency, a regional tourist board, at whatever level they may operate, are confronted with two basic factors. First, the tourist product is not very flexible. The basic attraction of the product (e.g. climate, sun, mountains, history) is to a great extent given. Second, the resources are limited. This implies that undifferentiated marketing or differentiated marketing with a product and/or a marketing program for all segments is not efficient or at least very difficult to apply. Therefore we must opt for concentrated marketing. The latter is a question of choice of a limited number of segments.

What are the possible variables which can be used to segment the market? In the literature and also in practice, very often a distinction is made between five groups of variables: geographic, demographic, socioeconomic, psychographic and buyer behavior. This classification does not mean that a combination of factors of two or more groups is excluded; on the contrary, in practice a combination is the rule.

Geographic segmentation is very popular and efficient in the tourism sector. There are several geographic variables. The two most important ones are the regional breakdown and the city size or the degree of urbanization of a population. It is highly recommended to concentrate all efforts in a few geographical markets rather than to spread the resources into many countries and/or regions for which we do not have the necessary instruments. We also need to keep in mind that in the tourism sector word-of-mouth publicity is very significant (e.g. in the case of a hotel or a resort). The more the efforts are concentrated in depth (i.e. on a limited number of regions), the more benefits we reap from word-of-mouth publicity. Urbanization is a second important geographic variable. *Ceteris paribus*, holiday participation is much higher in large conurbations than in small towns or rural areas.

Demographic segmentation speaks for itself. The marketer distinguishes different groups on the basis of such variables as age, sex, family size and life cycle. To this group we can add other variables, such as race and religion. For tourist market segmentation, age and life cycle – which are to a certain extent mutually related – are very important variables.

Socioeconomic segmentation is mainly based on income, education, occupation and social class. For any tourist product questions should be raised such as 'Who can afford it?' and 'Who might be interested?' The Socioeconomic classification is well-known. Table 1 shows a UK National Readership Survey

classification (Jicnars, 1984). In fact such a classification covers several of the above mentioned socioeconomic variables.

Here, one important remark should be made. There are many destinations that appeal to tourists of certain classes more than others, not only because of income or education but also due to the basic needs of the tourists. In the last decade marketers (also in the tourism sector) have given more and more prominence to lifestyle or personality traits. This brings us to the psychographic variables as the fourth category of segmentation.

Very different types of holidaymakers can be distinguished within this group of variables. Each of these types has a preference for one or more tourist products. They have their own characteristics with respect to readership of newspapers and periodicals, leisure activities etc. In other words several of these psychographic groups are measurable and accessible. However, there is still a lack of available personality variables.

The fifth segmentation group is based on buyer behavior variables. For the tourism sector three factors are very important. The first is what we call benefit segmentation based on holiday or travel benefits (de la Beaumelle, 1977; Burkart and Medlik, 1974, p. 196; Calantone and Johar, 1984, p. 14; Kaynak and Yavas, 1981; Taylor, 1986); the other two tourist-buyer behavior variables are: resort or regional loyalty and marketing factor sensitivity (e.g. price elasticity, quality, publicity, sales promotion).

It is hard to say what the most important variables in tourism marketing are. Much depends on who is involved in the marketing: an accommodation unit, a resort, a region. On the whole, the main variables are place of residence, degree of urbanization, age, family life cycle, income, social status, and the tourist benefits sought. The practical applications are a combination of several variables (e.g. the population of North and South Holland in the Netherlands, aged 50 and over, class C1 and C2, seeking calmness and beautiful nature). This is an illustration of the so-called market-matrix approach. It is further possible for a tourist destination to distinguish within a geographical unit of residence (e.g. a region) several market segments (e.g. age groups), to which we may use special communications.

Segmentation methods and examples

Above we explained that an essential characteristic of segmentation is the subdividing of the market into homogeneous subsets. The application of one or more of the variables leads to a homogeneity with respect to one or more chosen factors (e.g. geographical segmentation and age). But within that so-called homogeneous market segment there is still a very great heterogeneity as far as tourist benefits sought or psychographic behavior are concerned. In particular the benefits that are sought constitute a very important element in tourist market segmentation. When an agency promoting the Belgian coast is selecting one or two age groups in a number of regions in West Germany (based on market research), one does not know what share of that market may be interested in the tourist product offered, in other words how many can find, at the Belgian coast,

Table 1 Socioeconomic segmentation in the United Kingdom.

Group	Social status	Percentage of adults
A	Upper middle class	3.1
B	Middle class	13.9
C1	Lower middle class	22.1
C2	Skilled working class	28.4
D	Working class	18.0
E	Those at the lowest level of subsistence	14.5

the benefits sought. Therefore, more sophisticated research is necessary. Three methods may be applied. For each of these methods a short description is given below with the essence of the techniques. For more details we refer to a number of publications. For all three techniques a practical example follows.

Cluster analysis

Cluster analysis is a technique very often used in tourist market segmentation. It leads to a typology of tourists to which we referred in our comment on the definition of segmentation. The objective of cluster analysis is to find groups of objects which are similar with respect to some criteria. The resulting object clusters should be as homogeneous as possible within clusters and as heterogeneous as possible between clusters.

Basically, we are dealing with the similarity of the objects that can be seen as the resemblance of their profile over a set of variables. Many methods are available for combining objects into clusters. In general, these methods fall into three groups: linkage methods, variance methods and centroid methods. All are based on a matrix of distances between pairs of objects. They differ in how they estimate distances between clusters at successive steps (Green and Tull, 1970, Chapter 13; Aaker, 1971; Mazanec, 1984, pp. 18–19).

A practical case study is the application of cluster analysis to the Belgian holiday market. The starting point is the significance given by the Belgian potential tourists to 29 holiday aspects and/or benefits (attributes) of a holiday (e.g. looking for rest, cultural enrichment, beautiful landscape, scenery, cosy atmosphere in typical resorts, to practice one's hobbies, good food etc.; Westvlaams Ekonomisch Studiebureau, 1986). These attributes must not be confused with holiday motivation.

In a second step the potential holidaymakers were combined into clusters based on the weight they gave to the above mentioned 29 possible holiday aspects or benefits. The algorithm used for determining cluster membership is based on nearest centroid sorting, that is, a case (i.e. a potential tourist) is assigned to the cluster for which the distance between the case and the center of the cluster (centroid) is the smallest.

The outcome of this analysis suggests that the Belgian holiday market can be segmented into seven groups, each of them interested in different holiday benefits (Fig. 1).

1. The active sea-lovers (5 per cent of the potential holiday-makers). The respondents of this group stress sea and beach, to practice active sport and to enjoy entertainment.
2. Contact-oriented holidaymakers (10 per cent). Important holiday aspects are hospitality, to make time for each other, to make contact with other people, to be in a pleasant group.
3. The nature lovers (12 per cent). The respondents of this cluster underlined the importance of beautiful landscapes and scenery. This group has a rather passive attitude towards different holiday aspects.
4. The rest seekers (26 per cent). In this large group one element dominates: seeking rest.
5. The discoverers (10 per cent). These holidaymakers attach significance to elements such as contact with other people, cultural enrichment, to experience a lot.

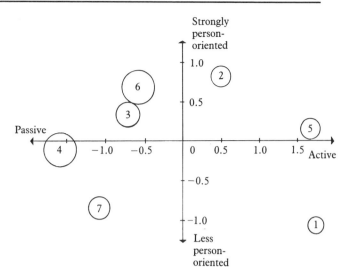

Figure 1 Situation of the seven clusters within the market of the potential holidaymakers.

6. Family-oriented sun- and sea-lovers (27 per cent). Several elements seem to be of great importance such as beautiful landscape, scenery, to make time for each other, hospitable reception, good food, holiday attractions for children, sea and beach and Southern Europe.
7. The traditionals (10 per cent). The respondents who belong to this group underline safety and no surprises, familiar surroundings, looking for rest and good food.

Of course these clusters can and should be related with, for instance, the respondents' demographic and socioeconomic characteristics, as well as with their actual holiday and media behavior. Considering the attractions and characteristics a tourist region can offer, an efficient segmentation can be implemented.

Multidimensional scaling

Multidimensional scaling techniques (MDS; Green and Tull, 1970, Chapter 7; Aaker, 1971) are used for analyzing respondent data on perceptions and preferences. The basic purpose of these techniques is: given a set of distances between objects or a rank order of distances between objects, try to find a geometrical configuration of points representing these objects, in such a way that the interpoint distances or the rank order of interpoint distances closely match the original input values. MDS transforms the input data in a geometrical way so that objects which are similar are close to each other in space. We can compare the relative similarities of pairs of objects in terms of their interpoint distances.

We applied MDS on the above mentioned outcome of the cluster analysis. The matrix of pairwise distances between the clusters served as input. The clusters were described by their centroid, that is the average value of the objects contained in the cluster on each of the variables making up the object's profile. A configuration in a two-dimensional space was derived, whose interpoint distances represented the input data in the best possible way. Taking into account the position of the clusters on the graph and the kind of benefits sought by these clusters, it is possible to find out the significance of the axes. The horizontal axis clearly deals with the degree to which one is active during the holidays. The vertical axis can be interpreted as the (non)person oriented nature of a holiday. These seem to be the basic dimensions by which one can describe and segment the Belgian holiday market (Fig. 1).

The diameters of the circles in Fig. 1 are directly proportional to the market size of the clusters. The distance between the clusters should be interpreted as a standard of the disparity between the different clusters. From Fig. 1 it can be deduced that clusters 4 and 5 are very different.

The practical significance of the results of this method can be illustrated as follows. A destination which is offering a very active holiday should pay attention to clusters 1 and 5, which together only represent 15 per cent of potential holiday-makers.

AID-analysis

AID stands for Automatic Interaction Detector. Its purpose is to group respondents with similar characteristics. Similarity among respondents is determined by the value of a particular continuous dependent variable for those respondents (Morgan and Sonquist, 1963, pp. 415–34).

AID successively splits up a sample of respondents in such a way that the variance of the dependent variable is explained at a maximum. It does so by selecting the appropriate categories of the independent variables. It differs from cluster analysis in two respects. First, AID makes a distinction between one continuous dependent variable and one or more nominal independent variables. All variables used in a cluster analysis are interval-scaled independent variables. Second, the grouping in AID is based on the value of a selected single dependent variable. In cluster analysis all variables are simultaneously considered.

We found an application of this method in the WES-study 'Tourist behaviour and attitudes of the Belgian population' (Westvlaams Ekonomisch Studiebureau, 1983). The dependent variable in this study is gross holiday participation. In this AID-analysis four independent variables were applied: geographical area, degree of urbanization, age and income. Twenty five groups were distinguished. The highest holiday participation was found with respondents with a monthly income of 50,000 Belgian Francs and more, living in one of the five Belgian conurbations (Fig. 2). From this analysis we can derive that income and, in secondary order, degree of urbanization contribute the most to the differences in gross holiday participation. This is, of course, an important conclusion with respect to the segmentation of the Belgian tourist market.

Conclusion

Market segmentation is an important element of a marketing strategy in tourism. We have to define target markets as homogeneous groups. The main arguments in favor of segmentation are as follows:

1. The scarcity of resources.
2. The efficient use of resources.
3. The adaptation of tourist products.
4. The optimum means of communication with the market.
5. The formulation of the best marketing plan.

Segmentation should, however, not be an academic exercise and each segment should be measurable, accessible and substantial.

The major segmentation variables can be classified in five groups: geographic, demographic, socioeconomic, psychographic and buyer behavior (especially benefit segmentation). In certain cases a more sophisticated approach may be required. Therefore, a number of methods can be applied such as cluster analysis, multidimensional scaling and AID-analysis.

Focus on small business

Segmentation is an essential element of market strategy at all levels: for individual firms or groups of firms, resorts, regions or countries. For any business, segmentation can give an indicator in what direction the product should be adapted. It is furthermore necessary to get the best financial results with the limited available marketing resources. However, an individual business cannot ignore the market segmentation arrived at and used for marketing at a higher level, in which it operates, such as a resort, a tourist region or even a whole country.

Further reading

Aaker, D. A. (ed.), *Multivariate Analysis in Marketing: Theory and Application* (Wadsworth Publishing, 1971). Part 2, Chapter C deals with cluster analysis.

Aaker, D. A. and Day, G. S., *Marketing Research* (John Wiley, 1986). Part IV, Chapter 17 deals with multidimensional scaling and cluster analysis.

Burkart, A. J. and Medlik, S., *Tourism. Past, Present and Future* (Heinemann, 1974). Part VII deals with marketing in tourism.

Brandt, S. A., 'Dissecting the segmentation syndrome', *Journal of Marketing* (October, 1966). The author deals with the problems of selecting segmentation variables.

Calantone, R. J. and Johar, J. S., 'Seasonal segmentation of the tourism market usng a benefit segmentation framework', *Journal of Travel Research* (Fall 1984). An attempt to segment the travel market by showing how different factors influence choice in different seasons.

Crask, M. R., 'Segmenting the vacationer market: identifying the vacation preferences, demographics, and magazine readership of each group', *Journal of Travel Research* (Fall 1981). The author identifies five vacation segments having distinct vacation preferences.

Denner, A., *Principes et Pratique du Marketing* (J. Delmes, 1971).

de La Beaumelle, S., 'A contribution to market-segmentation in tourism research', *Seminar on Travel and Tourism* (1977). This is an illustration of benefit segmentation based on travel benefits.

Dhalla, N. K. and Mahatoo, W. H., 'Expanding the scope of segmen-

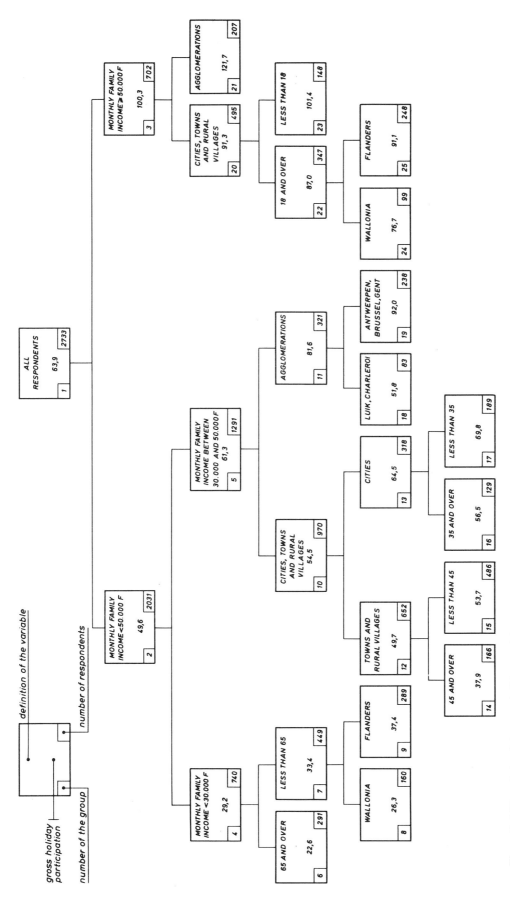

Figure 2 AID-analysis of the gross holiday participation of the Belgian population, 1982.

tation research', *Journal of Marketing* (April 1976). This article also concerns the problems of selecting segmentation variables.

Etzel, M. J. and Woodside, A. G., 'Segmenting vacation markets: the case of the distant and near-home travelers', *Journal of Travel Research* (Spring 1982). This article presents an approach to the study of near-home and distant travelers as target segments for travel marketing.

Green, P. E. and Tull, D. S., *Research for Marketing Decisions* (Prentice Hall, 1970). A synthesis of traditional and new research methods used in marketing decision making – explores the current developments in marketing research (multidimensional scaling, see Chapter 7; cluster analysis, see Chapter 13).

Haley, R. I., 'Benefit segmentation: a decision-oriented research tool', *Journal of Marketing* (April 1976).

Hirsch, R. D. and Peters, N. P., 'Selecting the superior segmentation correlate', *Journal of Marketing* (July 1974). This is another article dealing with the problems of selecting segmentation variables.

Jicnars, *National Readership Survey* (1984). An application of socio-economic classification in the United Kingdom.

Kaynak, E. and Yavas, U., 'Segmenting the tourism market by purpose of trip', *Tourism Management* (June 1981). An application of segmentation in general and benefit segmentation in particular.

Kotler, P. H., *'Marketing Management–Analysis, Planning, Control'* (Prentice Hall, 1972). This is a general handbook on marketing. Chapter 6 deals with market segmentation.

Marty, A. G., *Gestion Commerciale. Connaître et Satisfaire le Client* (J. Delmes, 1971). This publication is a general handbook on marketing.

Mazanec, J. A., 'How to detect travel market segments: a clustering approach', *Journal of Travel Research* (Summer 1984), pp. 18–19. A cluster-analytic approach to benefit segmentation is described using an illustrative example drawn from the Austrian domestic travel market.

Morgan, J. and Sonquist, J., 'Problems in the analysis of survey data and a proposal', *Journal of the American Statistical Association* (September 1963).

Schwarz, J. J., *Pour une Approche Marketing de la Promotion Touristique* (Office du Tourism du Canton de Vaud, 1984). This can be considered as a handbook on tourism marketing.

Smith, W. R., 'Product differentiation and market segmentation as alternative marketing strategies', *Journal of Marketing* (July 1956). This article concerns a classical contribution of marketing.

Taylor, G. D., 'Multi-dimensional segmentation of the Canadian pleasure travel market', *Tourism Management* (September 1986). This is a case study of selecting appropriate segments and the use of multidimensional segments.

Verhage, B. and Cunningham, W. H., *Marketing: A Managerial Approach* (South Western Publishing, 1981). This is a handbook of marketing. Chapter 7 deals with segmentation.

Westvlaams Ekonomisch Studiebureau, *Toeristische Gedragingen en Attitudes van de Belgische Bevolking in 1982* (1983). This report deals with the holidays of the Belgian population in 1982. It contains an AID-analysis of gross holiday participation.

Westvlaams Ekonomisch Studiebureau, *Les Belges en Vacances. Comportements et Attitudes en 1985*, vol. 5: *Typologie du Style de Vacances et de Vie des Belges* (1986).

Yankelovich, D., 'New criteria for market segmentation', *Harvard Business Review*, vol. 42. (1964). The author underlines the role of segmentation with respect to the timing of promotion and advertising.

NORBERT VANHOVE

Tourist needs and motivations

Introduction

The needs of tourists can basically be classified into two categories. The first includes those needs that differ from those of nontourists only through the place where they must be satisfied, and maybe also by their intensity. These are the basic requirements for food and lodging and such needs for items and services such as clothing, newspapers, books, films, cigarettes, hair cuts, telephone, banking etc.

The second category includes those needs that do not, or rarely exist at the place of residence. First come the transport requirements of the tourist, but buying souvenirs, visiting places of interest, going in for specific sports, or using special tourist transport means are other important examples.

Historical development

Pleasure travel is evidently not one of the fundamental needs of mankind. Historic sources nevertheless show that at all times people traveled, although journeys often meant difficulties and deprivation.

> It was always want, for biological or economic reasons, that induced men to travel. The caravans of the nomads had geographical and climatic causes. Never was the idea to move for war expeditions, of ancient people, due to pleasure. The first people that freely decided to travel far were traders. With a few exceptions, from ancient times to the 18th century all travel was limited to very small minorities, and for specific and definite aims. Soldiers and couriers, heads of state and scholars, students and beggars, pilgrims and criminals were seen on the roads; but mostly and always traders and merchants (Enzensberger, 1962).

The Old Testament includes many indications of commercial contacts between the peoples of the Middle East. To travel of one's own free will for adventure and pleasure, rest or recreation, culture or other reasons was quite rare and generally reserved for emperors and kings (for example in old China and Egypt). A well known tourist of antiquity is the Greek historian Herodotus (around 500–424 BC).

The first expansion of this form of free tourism happened at the time of the late Roman Empire. This is the exception mentioned by Enzensberger (1962):

> From the beaches of Tuscany to the Gulf of Salerno, the West Coast of Italy was a playground for tourists. Marble villas and luxurious hotels received the guests. Rhodes, Asia Minor and Egypt were preferred destinations for pleasure trips. There were scheduled boat crossings, travel agencies, change offices and festivals; even the interest in museums, a characteristic of modern tourism, already existed.

Wagner (1970) writes, correctly, that the organization and administration of this empire could only be maintained through an 'extensive system of facilities for travellers' their perfection, after the demise of Rome, was only available again in Europe at the end of the eighteenth century. One should also note in this context the remarkable road network of the Romans, with couriers and post systems, and chains of hostels.

The surviving descriptions of the touristic activities of the upper classes of the time show obvious similarities with today's situation, mainly concerning travel motivations, but also specific touristic equipment and ancillary activities. There existed already at that time clear 'flight from the city' tourism to the more pleasant climate of the mountains of Albania, 'health tourism' in the form of sea voyages or health resort treatments prescribed by doctor, 'recreation tourism' in luxurious environments as well as culture tourism to historical and religious sites in Greece and Egypt, and so on. 'For the recreation and luxury tourism of the Romans, baths has an essential role. Bajä in the bay of Naples was the best known destination, it was called in Antiquity "the hostel of the world". The season lasted the whole year. The guests that came from as far as the Near East provinces of the Empire, from Egypt or Phoenicia found elegant new hotels, as well as temples to worship their gods' (Wagner, 1970). There were also indications of gourmet restaurants, guides, souvenir shops, inscriptions made by tourists on tombs and so on. And the wise Seneca already stigmatized the depravity and shamelessness of the tourists in Bajä.

After this very modern sounding description one would be tempted to say 'nothing new under the sun'.

In the Middle Ages these opportunities of the earlier tourist trade disappeared and the Roman roads and other travel installations gradually became derelict. As a new variation on tourism, the pilgrims and pilgrimages came to the fore, making their mark in militarily-organized crusades that influenced the history of culture and religion for centuries. That things didn't remain respectful of God, pious and gentle, is testified by numerous historic sources.

Although the quoted number of participants is impressive (under Louis XII 100,000 Frenchmen are said to have left for Palestine, which can be compared with today's mass tourism phenomenon), nevertheless the Middle Ages generally showed a very low travel intensity; people were definitely sedentary. The servility of the peasants and the rules of the corporations in the cities gave little opportunity for mobility.

> The scholar was unhampered and free to move, he visited important schools and enjoyed his travels as a way of life. The traders, as always before, traveled. Marco Polo is the best known example (1254–1323). He discovered unknown kingdoms the existence of which was not believed on his return. His name is still today a symbol for touristic enterprises that lead to little known places. (Wagner, 1970)

New impulses to travel came during the years of discoveries, although the motives of the famous sea captains and conquistadores had little to do with tourism.

In the seventeenth century came the knight-errant who traveled foreign courts, which was thought of as part of the education of young nobles. But this form of tourism disappeared with the demise of the feudal system. In the eighteenth century the better classes started anew to go to spas; this led to the development of health resorts such as Baden-Baden, Aix-les-Bains and many others.

The breakdown of the feudal system of the Middle Ages, and the new spiritual mobility due to the age of enlightenment and the French Revolution, found its welcome counterpart in travel methods. There were more comfortable travel coaches, the network of roads was becoming denser and the lodgings better. All this led to a trend to undertake voyages freely – for culture, leisure, pleasure or other reasons.

There are deep roots of modern tourism in English, French and German Romanticism. The main trends: discovering nature, virgin landscapes and past history, are still, today, driving forces of tourist migrations. Romantic attractions for faraway places and the ideals of classical education were the main motivations for these art and pleasure trips, which were described by authors such as Goethe and Hölderlin, Balzac and Chateaubriand, Lord Byron, Keats, Shelley and others. Enzensberger (1962) interprets the romanticism as a reaction against the start of industrialization and political restoration, as a supposed escape route from the selfmade reality. This escapism is illusory because the civilization-breaking progress that the citizen wanted to flee was followed by mass tourism.

> Just as the tortoise in the fable waits ironically for the panting hare at the winning-post of the race, the tourist always meets his refutation already there. This dialectic is the motor of its development; because far from any thought of renouncing the running match for the price of freedom, after each defeat he tries harder. (Enzensberger, 1962)

Pure forms of the romantic ideology of tourism include mountaineering and discovery travels, with the character of an expedition. Both can be understood by the fascination of the 'elementary', the 'untouched or virgin', the 'adventure'. Again Enzensberger (1962) draws attention to the dialectic of the process and to the similarity with performance sports. 'As the untouched can only be appraised by contact, it is essential to be the first there. So travel becomes a competition for the first climb, to attain records'. Introduced in 1787 by de Saussure's first climb of Mont-Blanc, mountaineering had its first boom in the second half of the nineteenth century. The English took up the lead and they, as is known, founded the reputation of Switzerland as a country for tourism.

It is not by chance that it was the British who pioneered the new forms of tourism (the discovery by Thomas Cook of organized all-inclusive tours is another example). The fact is explained by the close correlation between the expansion of industrial civilization and the development of tourism. Against this background one should also mention the development of railway networks, that in its time gave a decisive developmental push to tourism.

Until World War I, the 'new rights of people to free themselves from their own civilization by going far away' (Enzensberger, 1962), remained an exclusive right of the privileged classes that could afford the free time: mainly the nobility and the independent bourgeoisie. The breakthrough to today's mass tourism of broad population strata happened only with the gradual acceptance of the idea of legally guaranteed holidays for all workers, with full salaries. It is essentially this social conquest which made the quantitative and qualitative aspects of modern tourism basically different from all the tourism forms of earlier times. General mobility received decisive impulses, and in particular mass tourism, through the increasing numbers, after World War II, of the motor car, and later the progress in air transport.

Prerequisites and motivations of today's mass tourism

Seen on a world scale, mass tourism must be interpreted today as a phenomenon of the industrial nations. Only in those countries are the following prerequisites *simultaneously* available to broad social strata:

1. A need to travel and nostalgia.
2. Adequate free time to satisfy this need to travel.
3. Adequate financial means to satisfy these travel wishes.
4. Adequate transport and a touristically relevant infra- and suprastructure.
5. The general political acceptance or even encouragement of mobility, freedom of movement, and tourism as natural society activities, i.e. the lack of basic political, administrative or other limitations.

These five basic prerequisites for tourism are linked and reinforce each other, at least partly. The need to travel as such is stimulated by the availability of the prerequisites given above, and can thus not be interpreted as a temporary escape from civilization. That would be an inadmissible simplification. The touristic heyday described during the Roman Empire can also be explained by the fact that the five prerequisites for tourism were at the time simultaneously available, even if limited to the social levels privileged by birth or situation.

When analyzing the travel motivation of today's tourists, one finds not only a broad pallet of tourism needs, but also large differences concerning origin and social stratum, for tourism needs. Thus, tourist travel requirements have neither general nor permanent validity. They are, rather, inserted in the historical, geographical, political, economic and technological environment of the time and can only be understood by taking these into account.

Our own research shows, additionally, that hardly any single trip can satisfy all the touristic needs of a person. Each type of trip can only cover part of the needs. It follows that motivation research in the field of tourism remains incomplete if it is limited to a single voyage (for example the last main vacation trip); one should tend towards an observation style that considers the travel behavior of the same individual over a longer period of time (at least a whole year). This will be demonstrated by the travel motivation of a sample of Swiss people.

Examples

Answering the question of the type of travel they had made during the 1973–1982 decade, at least once, we received from adult Swiss people the answers displayed in Table 1 (Reisemarkt Schweiz, 1983).

This shows that each adult Swiss who, during the last decade, has taken part in travel (90.1 per cent of all adults) has tried, on

Table 1 Tourist behavioral patterns of the Swiss people.

Type of travel made at least once between 1973 and 1982	Percentage of adult Swiss ($n = 4,331$)
Holidays at the seaside	57.4
(Summer) holidays in the mountains	39.4
Circular tours/discovery trips	39.4
Winter sports holidays	35.7
Visiting family/friends (as main travel objective)	32.8
Travel to visit cities	22.9
Holidays by a lake	20.4
Holidays in the countryside	12.7
Culture or study travel	9.7
School or firm excursion	8.7
Visiting for definite occasions/events	7.8
Taking part in a congress/conference	5.7
Cruise	5.5
Health or fitness holidays of own free will	4.9
Cures ordered by the doctor	4.3
Language courses or similar in a foreign language region	3.5
Various other types of travel	1.5
	312.3
Has not traveled, no data	9.9
	322.2

Table 2 Tourist motivations of the Swiss people.

Travel motives	Percentage of all trips made in 1982 ($n = 9,789$)
1. To meet family, acquaintances, friends	23.0
2. For active sports	14.0
3. To be outdoors	14.0
4. Sun and warmth	14.0
5. To get to know new places, for new impressions, to see something different	17.7
6. To remain healthy or recover health; to regain one's strength	10.4
7. To enjoy the beauty and excitement of a specific landscape	9.2
8. To have time for each other (family, partner, friend)	8.9
9. To discover other countries; to see the world; to get to know the locals	8.6
10. To relax and switch off	8.5
11. To get away from everyday routine, to change environment	7.6
12. The attraction of mountains	6.7
13. To stay in a more agreeable climate	6.0
14. To let oneself be spoilt, to enjoy life	5.7
15. The appeal of water	5.6
16. To be with pleasant people, to enjoy companionship	5.4
17. Hiking	5.4
18. To escape the time and performance stress, to have time for everything	5.4

average, 3.5 different types of tours, illustrating how varied tourists' needs are.

Further insight is provided by the detailed analysis of travel during the year 1982. For each private trip of four or more nights duration, undertaken in that year, we asked for the most important motivation, out of a list of 30 different items. Compared to the total of all tours, Table 2 classifies the most often named travel motives (with at least 5.0 per cent of answers) (Reisemarkt Schweiz, 1983).

The list shows that participating in tourism fulfils a whole series of important sociological functions that otherwise can only be poorly satisfied, or not at all; this explains, at least in part, the high propensity of the Swiss for travel. These sociological functions are as follows:

1. To compensate for the many deficits that everyday life in a working performance society inevitably brings:
   (a) social deficits or deficits in human contacts and friendliness;
   (b) climatic deficits (the urge for sun and warmth);
   (c) deficits in movement and activity, deficits in sports activities;
   (d) deficits in the closeness to nature; in the enjoyment of scenery; in outdoor recreation;
   (e) deficits in experiences and change, repression of the discovery and action urges;
   (f) deficit in enjoyment, luxury and prestige;
   (g) lack of freedom.
2. Physical and psychological recovery from stress, the pres-

sure of performance and the monotony of everyday life, finding again or keeping physical and mental well-being.
3. Widening horizons, satisfying curiosity, self-realization, increase of the feeling of one's own value.
4. Self-reward; self-indulgence.

Conclusion

In view of the numerous needs that holiday travel must satisfy, consciously or unconsciously, one can understand sayings such as 'voyager c'est vivre' or 'the vacation weeks are the best weeks of the year'. One understands also why tourist demand everywhere has been astonishingly recession-proof and that holiday trips today are practically considered to be among the 'essen-

tials' of life. Tourism has become an integral part of our modern way of life; if it did not yet exist, it would be immediately invented in the interests of mankind.

Further reading

Enzensberger, H. M., 'Eine Theorie des Tourismus', *Einzelheiten I – Bewusstseins-Industrie*, Enzensberger (ed.) (*Suhrkamp Verlag*, 1962), p. 179 ff.
Reisemarkt Schweiz 1982/83, results of the Swiss Holiday-Survey of the Institute for Tourism at the University of St.Gallen (1983).
Wagner, F. A., *Die Urlaubswelt von Morgen – Erfahrungen und Progonsen* (Eugen Diederichs Verlag, 1970) p. 15ff.

HANSPETER SCHMIDHAUSER

Tourist product

Introduction

The concept of the tourist product is central to understanding the meaning and practice of management in all sectors of the travel and tourism industry. It has important implications for the marketing of commercial organizations and national and regional tourist offices; it is also highly relevant for planning and development, both in its community aspects and as a focus of feasibility studies for commercial organizations.

From a marketing standpoint, products are defined by the leading American marketing author, Kotler, as 'anything that can be offered to a market for attention, acquisition, use, or consumption that might satisfy a want or need. It includes physical objects, services, persons, places, organizations, and ideas' (Kotler, 1984, p. 463). As such, product decisions in any industry, not only tourism, are the focal point of all marketing activity, around which the other aspects of the marketing mix (pricing, promotion and distribution) are organized. In the short run, marketing tactics for tourism products are concerned with managing demand around available product capacity; in the long run, marketing strategy is concerned with product positioning, development and enhancement around the identified needs of target segments.

In the travel and tourism industry, tourist products can be understood on two levels:

1. The total tourist product, which comprises a combination of all the service elements which a tourist consumes from the time he/she leaves home, to the time of return. This product is an idea, an expectation, or a mental construct in the customer's mind, at the point of sale.
2. The specific, mainly commercial products, which are components of the total tourist product, such as the product offers of accommodation, transport, attractions, and other facilities for tourists, such as car rental and ski hire.

This article is concerned only with the first level, defined as the total tourist product, as it is perceived on the demand side by tourists (for leisure, business, or any other purpose), and as it is conceived on the supply side by National Tourist Offices (NTOs), and Regional and Local Tourist Offices (RTOs and LTOs), responsible for one or more tourist destinations. On the supply side, the total tourist product view is also that adopted by tour operators who, acting on behalf of customers, put together or 'package' the individual components of travel, and market them as entities.

From this introduction, the total tourist product can be defined as 'a bundle or package of tangible and intangible components, based on activity at a destination. The package is perceived by the tourist as an experience, available at a price' (Middleton, 1988).

Components of the total tourist product

The components view of the total tourist product defined above fits precisely with the overall concepts of products developed by other authors dealing with services, such as Sasser *et al.* (1978) and Shostack (1982). There are five main components in the total product, which are discussed separately below:

Destination attractions

These are the elements within the destination's environment which, individually and combined, serve as the primary motivation for tourist visits. They comprise *natural attractions*, such as landscape, seascape, beaches, and climate; *built attractions*, such as historic townscape (e.g. Paris, London and Rome), or new townscape as in newly built resorts (e.g. Orlando, Florida, or Languedoc Roussillon resorts in France), and the wide range of purpose-built, managed visitor attractions such as industrial heritage sites in the United Kingdom, theme parks (particularly in the United States) or the Darling Harbor project in Sydney, Australia. They also comprise *cultural attractions*, such as theater, museums, and presentations of history and folklore, many of which are organized as festivals and pageants; and *social attractions*, defined as opportunities to meet with, or 'encounter' the residents of destinations, and experience their way of life, to some extent.

For business and other nonleisure tourists, such as visitors to friends and relatives, the primary motivation is provided by their connections or associations with the destination, although the leisure attractions may still be an influence and used by such visitors, and the components analysis of the total product remains valid in every other respect.

Destination facilities

Destination facilities (sometimes referred to as 'amenities') are defined as the elements within the destination, or linked to it, which make it possible for tourists to stay at destinations and to enjoy and participate in the attractions. They include accommodation of all types, restaurants, cafes and bars, transport at the destination including car rental and taxis, and other services such as retailing, hairdressing, and visitor information. There is inevitably some overlap between attractions and facilities, for example where a famous hotel becomes an attraction in its own right and the primary motivation for a visit. Even so, its principal business function is to provide facilities and it should be classified as such.

Accessibility

This is defined in terms of the relative ease or difficulty with which customers can reach the destinations of their choice. Access is a matter of transport infrastructure, such as airports, harbors, motorways and rail networks. It is also a matter of transport technology which alters the costs of travel and the time it takes to reach destinations. For example, the development and rapid expansion of tourism in the Pacific/Asia area in the 1970s was made possible primarily by the technology of wide-bodied, longhaul, 'Jumbo Jets', which radically improved the timing and reduced the cost of transPacific travel.

Images

Images, meaning the ideas and beliefs which people hold about all forms of products they purchase or contemplate, are a property of all forms of tourist product. Destination images are not necessarily based on experience or fact but they are usually very powerful motivators in leisure travel and tourism decisions. For example, of the millions of Americans and Europeans who have never visited Las Vegas in Nevada, USA, there can be very few who do not carry in their minds some image of the experiences such a destination offers. It is always an essential objective of destination marketing in tourism to sustain, alter, or develop images, in order to influence prospective buyers' expectations. Images are the logical focus for much of destination promotion.

Price

This is the sum of what it costs for travel, accommodation, and participation in a range of selected services at the destination. The price of tourist products varies by choice of accommodation, such as de luxe or economy, season of the year, the types of activity chosen, and the distance traveled to a destination.

Examples

The practical relevance of the components view of the total tourist product concept can most easily be recognized in the context of planning a new destination, such as a ski resort. The attraction is based on the scenic appeal of potential sites, the range and quality of the ski slopes available, and the architectural appeal of the built environment of the resort's structures.

Facilities are purpose-built around the needs and wants of the prospective visitors in quantities identified by market feasibility studies. Other facilities include ski-lifts, restaurants, bars, ski-hire, and so on, designed to meet the needs of target segments. Access is a matter of roads to the resort, provision of car parking and bus parking, and access to the nearest airport. A new resort will have to have an image for the purpose of promotion, and a style which projects its attractions and individuality. Such an image, for a new resort, will typically reflect the intrinsic qualities of the destination region and the design, quality and style of its attractions and its built and social environment. Price will be a function of the attractions and facilities provided, with a range of prices according to the needs of target visitor segments.

A second example can be seen in the internationally famous 'I Love New York' campaign organized by the State in the late 1970s following an extensive program of market research among prospective visitors. For the City of New York (the full campaign covered the whole State) at the start of the marketing campaign, the theaters, entertainments and shopping in Manhattan existed, the hotels, restaurants, bars, and night clubs were there, the transport to and within New York City existed; in fact all the basic components of attractions, facilities, access and price were already in place. During the 1970s, however, these components were mainly pursuing their own individual narrow focus of business interests and they did not add up to a very appealing entity to many out-of-town visitors, unless they already knew the city and how to get the best out of it. The marketing skill was first and foremost to bring together and package the product elements in ways designed to appeal to customers and facilitate their purchases, especially focusing on the entertainment, cultural, and accommodation opportunities provided by the city – in other words, organizing the total tourist product delivery. With the product delivery organized, the campaign image was developed to encapsulate the benefits offered, and all the five components of the total tourist product were brilliantly and successfully brought together in the famous logo and strap line now familiar around the world.

Practical marketing implications

Five main practical implications can be drawn from this tourist product concept.

First, is the implication for market research. There are few 'facts' and 'truths' in the marketing of tourist products. Products are ideas in the minds of tourists, and can only be understood through a process of consumer research referred to above in the case of New York City and State. Market research is necessary initially to define perceptions and attitudes to the tourist products sought, and subsequently to measure the extent to which their delivery creates satisfaction. Research is the basis for effective tourism promotion as well as for product development.

Secondly, unless it is secured by management decisions as in the packaging arrangements made by tour operators, there is no automatic matching or harmony between the components of the total product, such as accommodation, transport and attractions, which are seldom under the same ownership. Even within the same sector there will usually be many different organizations, each with different and often conflicting objectives and interests. It is the dispersion or fragmentation of control and ownership within the tourist industry and the relative freedom of individual organizations to act according to their own perceived self-interests, which makes it difficult for NTOs, RTOs and other bodies to exert much coordinating influence either in marketing or planning. Most destinations deal with a large number of total products for a wide range of segments, but the long-term future success of a destination must involve coordination and recognition of mutual interests between all the components of the total tourist product.

Thirdly, reflecting their interdependence within the total product, there is considerable potential for collaboration in marketing by the component producers in different sectors. This potential for cooperation was termed 'complementarity' by Krippendorf (1971). How it works in a product development context can be understood from the ski resort example noted earlier. Collaboration is also highly relevant to the promotion of products such as those described for New York. In the United Kingdom, at national and regional level, there has for years been participation in joint advertising, print and public relations initiatives sponsored by tourist organizations, in which the participants seek synergy in the spending of budgets too small individually to have a significant impact on prospective consumers.

Fourthly, the fact that many changes in tourist destinations are not planned but happen naturally through the effects of structural changes in market demand, adds to the need to understand the total products for development and promotional purposes. The loss of popularity of Northern Europe's seaside resorts over the last decade is a case in point. The approach to solutions to their problems lies in reappraising customers' overall destination needs and wants in the light of modern competition, followed by systematic planning for the tourist future of such destinations on a holistic basis.

Fifthly, understanding the total tourist product through the eyes of consumers provides a natural focus for the images of destinations, as illustrated in the New York example earlier. In England, the successful promotion of short holiday breaks in Autumn and Spring was developed throughout the 1970s and 1980s by the English Tourist Board, using a campaign entitled 'Let's Go', which was used consistently for advertising, for the name of the brochure of product offers, and for sales promotion and merchandising. The same promotion has been very useful in stimulating the accommodation industry to develop the supply of its own commercial products within the overall, integrating theme.

Conclusion

'Since all tourists arrive somewhere to do something, the destinations concerned are the most important bases of the product "package" which the consumer buys' (Medlik and Middleton,

1973, p. 32). The concept of the tourist product, defined as a total experience, provides a practical integrating framework for analyzing and managing tourism movements at the destination, relevant both for marketing, and for planning and development purposes. The concept is relevant both to destination interests, such as NTOs and RTOs, and to the suppliers of individual component services, such as accommodation and attractions. 'In terms of demand for products, product formulation involves analyzing and assessing consumer requirements (existing and potential) and identifying homogeneous groups of potential purchasers [segments]. . . . In terms of supply, product formulation involves analyzing and assessing the product elements, and identifying [total tourist products] from the range of possibilities available at any destination. . .' (Medlik and Middleton, 1973, p. 35).

Focus on small business

Small businesses, like large ones, are part of the total products offered by destinations. Because their budgets are too small to make a major impact on customer perceptions, they have an even greater interest in collaboration and cooperative marketing than their larger competitors. For several decades, small businesses at destinations, such as hotels, guest houses, caravan parks and attractions, have joined in collaborative marketing by paying for entries in resort guides. Over the years, many of these guides have become locked into traditional formats and images that have little relevance to modern market needs. The long-term interests of smaller businesses lie in finding more imaginative, customer-relevant extensions to these existing, somewhat primitive forms of collaboration.

Also relevant to smaller businesses is marketing cooperation between different sectors (especially accommodation and attractions) in which each can act as a promotional and distribution point for the other. Such cooperation may lead to the possibility of cooperative product formulation, advertising and promotion campaigns, joint representation at workshops, and so on.

Further reading

Reflecting their foundation in the principles of marketing, as well as their relevance to the management of tourism and structure of the travel and tourism industry, the essential concepts relating to products will be found in varying forms in British and American texts dealing with marketing and with tourism. Useful references are noted below:

Baker, M. J., *Marketing: An Introductory Text* (MacMillan, 4th edition, 1985). In Chapter 3, discussing aspects of demand and supply, Baker puts a leading British view of the marketing principles underlying the provision of consumer products of all kinds.

Burkart, A. J. and Medlik, S., *Tourism: Past, Present and Future* (Heinemann, 2nd edition, 1981). In their first edition (1974) and second edition, the authors outlined the core product concept as comprising three main elements of 'attractions, accessibility, and amenities' (or facilities) in their Chapter 4, defining the meaning and nature of tourism.

Go, F. M., 'Development of new service products for the leisure travel market – a systems view', *The Tourist Review*, no. 2 (1981), pp. 9–19. The concept of the total tourist product is, by definition, a systems view because of the interrelationship between the components. Go brings out and illustrates this point, highlighting product planning implications.

Holloway, J. C., *The Business of Tourism* (Macdonald and Evans, 2nd edition, 1985). In his introduction to tourism (Chapter 1), Holloway adopts the three core product characteristics of attractions, amenities (facilities), and accessibility in defining what is offered at tourist destinations.

Jeffries, D., 'Defining the tourist product and its significance in tourism marketing', *The Tourist Review*, vol. XVII, no. 1 (1971), pp. 7–13. In this early article, Jeffries sets out the fundamental view that all tourists buy packages, whether or not they use the services of tour operators and travel agents.

Kotler, P., *Marketing Management: Analysis, Planning and Control* (Prentice Hall, 5th Edition, 1984). In Chapters 1 and 15, Kotler explains in full detail the essential concepts of consumer needs, wants, and the search for utilities or benefits which underlie customers' views of all products.

Krippendorf, J., *Marketing et Tourisme* (Herbert Lang, 1971).

McIntosh, R. W. and Goeldner, C. R., *Tourism: Principles, Practices, Philosophies* (Grid, 4th Edition, 1984). Although the authors of this well known US tourism text do not analyze the tourist product as outlined in this article, the same principles will be found in their analysis of the five main elements in 'tourism supply'. These are, using their terms, 'natural resources, infrastructure, superstructure, transportation, and hospitality resources'.

Medlik, S. and Middleton, V.T.C., 'The tourist product and its marketing implications', *International Tourism Quarterly*, no. 3 (September 1973) pp. 28–35. This article, which has also been published elsewhere, sets out the essential components view of the total tourism product, comprising attractions, facilities and access. The components of Image and Price were added subsequently by Middleton in 1979.

Middleton, V. T. C., 'Tourism marketing – product implications', *International Tourism Quarterly*, no. 3 (1979), pp. 36–46. In this article, Middleton reviews the earlier contribution of 1973, and discusses the meaning of marketing component sector products, within the context of the total product.

Middleton, V. T. C., 'Product marketing – goods and services compared', *The Quarterly Review of Marketing*, vol. 8, no. 4 (July 1983), pp. 1–9. This article challenges the commonly held view (at that time) that manufactured goods are products and services are not. He offers a spectrum of buyer behavior characteristics relevant to both goods and services, and coins the phrase 'FMCS' for fast moving consumer services.

Middleton, V. T. C., 'Profitability through product formulation strategies', *The Practice of Hospitality Management II* (AVI Publishing Co., 1986), pp. 377–89. This summary of a conference paper sets the formulation of product strategies for hotels in the context of the overall tourist product.

Middleton, V. T. C., *Marketing in Travel and Tourism* (Heinemann, 1988). In this book the concept of the tourist product is referred to in several places. Chapter 8 deals specifically with product concepts, and in Chapters 20 to 24 the author explains them with illustrations in each of the main sectors of the industry: Tourist Attractions, Transport Operations, Accommodation, Inclusive Tours and Packages, and Destination Marketing.

Murphy, P. E., *Tourism: A Community Approach* (Methuen, 1985). Reference is made to the tourist product throughout this interesting book which tackles the issues in planning and developing what is called a 'Community's Tourism Product' (p. 37). The author develops a resource based components view of the total product from a community planning standpoint.

Sasser, W. E., Olsen, P. R. and Wyckoff, D. D., *Management of Service Operations* (Alleyn and Bacon, 1978). In Chapter 2 of this relatively early contribution on the nature of marketing service products, the authors set out their view of most service products as 'bundles' of both goods and services.

Shostack, G. L., 'How to design a service', *European Journal of Marketing*, vol. 16, no. 1 (1982), pp. 49–63. The author of several important articles on the nature of service products, Shostack adopts what he calls a 'molecular' view of products, intended to demonstrate the structural relationships which exist within service products of the individual elements of which each is comprised.

Schmoll, G. A., *Tourism Promotion* (Tourism International Press, 1977). In Chapter 2, Schmoll discusses the nature of the tourism product and the meaning of what Krippendorf defined as 'complementarity' within the context of the structure of the tourist industry.

Wahab, S., Crampon, L. J. and Rothfield, L. M., *Tourism Marketing* (Tourism International Press, 1976). The authors include a discussion of the tourist product in Chaper 2 of this book, in which they stress their view that tourist products are best defined through travel motivations. This is a behavioral view of products reflecting the fact that such products are ideas in the minds of customers at the point of sale.

VICTOR MIDDLETON

Tourist product life cycle

The product life cycle (PLC) describes the evolution of a product as it passes through the stages of introduction, growth, maturity and decline with the growth of product sales following an S-shaped pattern (which has its basis in biological studies). The PLC has evoked both acclaim and disparagement in marketing: on the one hand it is a simple concept describing the evolution of adoption of a new product by consumers. It hypothesizes that products have a limited life, profits rise and fall at different stages of the PLC and products require different marketing strategies at each stage. On the other hand, despite its logical and intuitive appeal, it is difficult to operationalize and use the PLC for say, forecasting or decision taking.

Each stage of the PLC is characterized by certain marketing considerations (Table 1). At 'introduction' sales grow slowly because of the need to create awareness of product benefits and overcome buyer inertia. Most purchases are trial and marketing tries to stimulate word-of-mouth promotion, commence advertising, obtain publicity and establish distribution. Often a financial loss is sustained because of product development and marketing costs. By the 'growth' stage customer recognition and acceptance leads to a broadening of the market with rapid growth of sales and some repeat purchases. At this stage profits are realized because marketing expenditure is reduced. Competitors may also enter the scene, particularly from companies which 'follow' in order to reduce commercial risk and avoid the expense of introducing a new product. Once penetration of the potential market has reached saturation, growth subsides and levels off and profits stabilize or decline. Sales are mainly repeat purchases and growth is dependent on the potential buyer group and the level of competition. By this stage distribution channels are all filled. Eventually consumers lose interest in the product as new ones emerge or tastes change, and sales decline as fewer and fewer people repurchase.

Not all PLC curves follow the standard S-shape and a number of variants exist. For example, the fad PLC is characterized by rapid growth and an equally rapid collapse of sales. Some leisure products follow this pattern – skateboards, hula hoops and discotheques. Fads enjoy tremendous media coverage, are often accompanied by much pre-launch publicity and rapid adoptions attract a specific market and are nonnecessities which are visibly consumed. Of course, fads are a problem for marketing decision takers as buyer behavior is so volatile.

The extended PLC has an extended maturity stage with high repeat purchases providing a stable volume of sales (and little loss of sales to other competitors). In the tourism field products which exhibit this pattern include luxury hotels, holidays and food service outlets.

Other PLC forms include the cycle/recycle pattern with a second cycle caused by a promotional push in the decline stage. The scalloped pattern consists of a succession of cycles based on the discovery of new product characteristics, uses or users.

Examples

Although it could be argued that the tourism product is the sum of travel experiences from anticipation to recall, the destination is a key element of the product. Destinations go through a cycle of evolution similar to the product life cycle. Simply, numbers of visitors replace sales of a product. Some writers suggest three stages to this tourism area cycle of evolution – discovery, local response and initiative, and 'institutionalization' – but a more detailed framework is now generally accepted. This begins with 'exploration' by small numbers of visitors who are adventurous by nature and tend to shun institutionalized travel. They are attracted by the natural beauty or culture at the destination but numbers are restricted by lack of access and facilities. At this stage the attraction of the destination is that it is as yet unchanged by tourism and contact with local people will be high. Parts of Latin America and the Canadian Arctic are examples here.

In the 'involvement' stage, local initiatives to provide for visitors and later advertise the destination result in increased and regular numbers of visitors. A tourist season and market area emerges and pressure may be placed on the public sector to provide infrastructure. The smaller, less-developed Pacific and Caribbean islands are examples of this stage.

The 'development' stage sees large numbers of visitors arriving, at peak periods perhaps equalling or exceeding the numbers of local inhabitants. The organization of tourism begins to change as control is passed out of local hands and external companies emerge to provide up-to-date facilities, which may alter the appearance of the destination. In this very success lies the roots of failure, however. With increasing numbers and popularity the destination may suffer problems of

Table 1 Implications of the product life cycle (*Source*: Doyle, 1976).

	Introduction	Growth	Maturity	Decline
Characteristics				
SALES	Low	Fast growth	Slow growth	Decline
PROFITS	Negligible	Peak levels	Declining	Low or zero
CASHFLOW	Negative	Moderate	High	Low
CUSTOMERS	Innovative	Mass market	Mass market	Laggards
COMPETITORS	Few	Growing	Many rivals	Declining number
Responses				
STRATEGIC FOCUS	Expand market	Market penetration	Defend share	Productivity
MARKETING EXPENDITURES	High	High (declining %)	Falling	Low
MARKETING EMPHASIS	Product awareness	Brand preference	Brand loyalty	Selective
DISTRIBUTION	Patchy	Intensive	Intensive	Selective
PRICE	High	Lower	Lowest	Rising
PRODUCT	Basic	Improved	Differentiated	Rationalized

overuse and deterioration of facilities. Regional and national planning and control will have become necessary in part to ameliorate problems but also to market to the international tourist-generating areas as visitors become more dependent upon travel arrangements booked through the trade. Parts of Mexico and the north and west African coasts exemplify this stage.

In the 'consolidation' stage the rate of increase of visitors has declined although total numbers are still increasing and exceed permanent residents. The destination is now a fully fledged part of the tourism industry with all the major franchises and chains represented and there is an identifiable recreational business district. Many Caribbean and northern Mediterranean destinations are examples here.

At 'stagnation' peak numbers have been reached and the destination is no longer fashionable. It relies on repeat visits and business use of its extensive facilities and major efforts are needed to maintain the number of visits. The destination may by now have environmental, social and economic problems. The Costa Brava typifies this stage.

In 'decline', visitors are lost to newer resorts and the destination becomes dependent on a smaller geographical catchment for day trips and weekend visits. Property turnover is high and tourist facilities such as accommodation are converted into other uses. Alternatively, the authorities may recognize this stage and decide to 'rejuvenate' by changing the attractions. Introduction of a casino (as at Schveningen (Netherlands) and Atlantic City (USA), is a common response. Similarly some destinations capitalize on previously unused natural resources, such as winter sports, to extend the season and attract a new market. These facility developments often reflect joint public/private sector ventures to seek new markets and invest in the destination in order to reach a cycle/recycle pattern.

As with the PLC the shape of the curve will vary but in this case is dependent upon the rate of development, access, government policy, and competing destinations – each of which can delay or accelerate progress through the various stages. Indeed development can be arrested at any stage in the cycle. Only tourist developments promising considerable financial returns will mature to experience all stages of the cycle. In turn the

length of each stage, and of the cycle itself, is variable. At one extreme instant resorts such as Cancun (Mexico) or timeshare developments move almost immediately to growth; at the other extreme well-established resorts such as Scarborough (England) have taken 350 years to move from exploration to rejuvenation.

Benefits

The true test of the PLC or tourist area life cycle is whether they can be operationalized as a tool for planning and managing products or tourist areas. Both are useful as descriptive tools to provide a versatile organizing framework for product planning and strategy. The main determinant of strategy is expected market growth, and other factors include distribution of market shares, degree of competition and profitability. Each of these vary at different stages of the PLC and a different marketing mix is appropriate. They can also be used as forecasting tools, although here they are less successful because of the differing lengths of the stages and the difficulty of obtaining standardized sales histories or long runs of visitor arrivals data.

One particular benefit of the tourist area life cycle is as a framework for understanding how destinations and their markets evolve. Tourist destinations are dynamic, with changing provision of facilities and access matched by an evolving market in both quantitative and qualitative terms. Different types of tourists seek different experiences. Plog (1974) suggests that tourists can be characterized as allocentric (adventurous, ever seeking new destinations), or psychocentric (seeking familiar destinations and the security of the travel trade). Midcentrics have some of both of these characteristics and represent the bulk of the market. Plog envisages a destination appealing to allocentrics in the early stages of evolution, to midcentrics in the later stages of 'development' and 'consolidation' and to psychocentrics in 'stagnation' and 'decline'. In other words successive waves of different numbers and types of tourists with distinctive preferences, motivations and desires populate the resort at each stage of the life cycle.

Implementation

There are two basic, though interrelated, uses of the life cycle: as a guide for strategic decision taking and as a forecasting tool. The life cycle approach can be used to characterize the main marketing challenges at each stage (Table 1). At introduction, concern is with building up a strong market position and developing experience and economies of scale before competitors enter. In the growth stage emphasis changes to building market share through increased use of the product and preempting competitors' customers. As maturity approaches defence of share against competitors becomes important, as does maintaining margins and cashflow by cost control and avoiding price wars. However, once sales or visitor numbers stabilize management should not await decline as inevitable but should seek to revitalize sales or visits. The danger here is that the marketing effort involved in such activities may be better placed elsewhere in the portfolio of products (i.e. resources should be allocated to where they generate the greatest contribution). By decline the task switches to preventing a cash drain in products with no future.

The overall lesson here is for companies to have a portfolio of products at different stages of the PLC so that, for example, mature products generate the cash needed for investment in new products.

Some argue that it is erroneous to assume that the determinant of marketing strategy is stage in the life cycle and the task is to utilize the stages of the life cycle to develop and evaluate marketing strategy. This can be done in two basic ways:

1. Life extension is a planned series of actions to ensure that sales or numbers of visitors and profitability are sustained for as long as possible.
2. Incorporation of other inputs such as data on market share, the competitive environment and profitability.

For tourist destinations these decisions are less straightforward as other factors have to be taken into account. Destinations represent an investment in a community as well as the built fabric and the implications of the 'decline' stage are more severe than for a manufactured product. Seasonal unemployment, a depressed business community and falling property prices are symptomatic of this stage. There is therefore a need for longer-term planning at tourist destinations and a recognition of the implications of the tourist area life cycle. In other words, visitors may not increase continually with time, and if they do, this in itself has implications if the original attractions and competitiveness of the destination are to be safeguarded. This may be achieved by constraining growth of resorts to within manageable capacity levels and developing in sympathy with the community.

Use of the life cycle approach as a forecasting tool depends upon the ability to isolate and predict the forces driving it. Most forecasts assume a constraint on long-run growth, an S-shaped diffusion curve, homogeneity of customers and give no explicit consideration of marketing decisions or the competition. Forecasts can be successful if these limiting assumptions are acceptable and sales data are available to give stable parameter estimates.

Frustratingly for forecasters, retrospective studies have shown that much sales data fit the PLC. This empirical evidence can be summarized as: sales of most products follow the PLC pattern; profits peak during rapid growth and problems of competition increase as the cycle progresses; the average length of the PLC is decreasing; there is no regularity in the length of the stages of the PLC; and the PLC can be temporarily bent by heavy promotional expenditure. Work is also beginning to evaluate the tourist area life cycle using empirical data but the scarcity of long runs of historic information on visitor numbers is a problem here.

Assessment

The life cycle approach has many critics, in part drawn by its very simplicity. Some argue that far from being an independent guide for decisions the PLC is determined by the strategic decisions of management and heavily dependent on external factors such as the competition, development of substitute products, swings in consumer taste and government legislation. Other more detailed criticisms include:

1. The danger of reacting to warning signs which may have been misinterpreted. The PLC is often criticized as a prescriptive tool because there is poor empirical validation for shape or length. Clearly the life cycle approach is product- or destination-specific, each stage is variable in length, and the shapes and patterns differ. The life cycle, it is argued, does not therefore provide sufficient insight into the development of policy or planning for tourist areas or products. It may also be imprecise as a guide for strategy because it ignores competitive settings and profit considerations.
2. Its main uses for decision taking and forecasting are in doubt. In particular the wisdom of pursuing a standardized marketing strategy at each stage has been questioned and it is also imprecise as a forecasting tool and difficult to calibrate because of the lack of long runs of data on visitor numbers or sales.
3. The difficulties of identifying stages and turning points. Identification of turning points is important in the later stages of the cycle given the increased cost of reacting as the need for change becomes more obvious. Turning points can be identified by use of leading indicators such as growth rate of sales or visits, level of ownership or visits compared to market potential, percentage of first-time buyers or visitors, number of competitors, levels of prices and profits, advertising, promotional and price elasticity, and emergence of new products meeting customer needs more effectively. The variety of possible shapes of the curve and acceleration or delay due to external factors make it difficult to identify the stage reached by a destination or product. This can be done by plotting rate of change of sales or visitors. For destinations, other measures may be visitor expenditure, type of tourist, market share or profitability.

4. The level of aggregation is unclear. Different shapes of the PLC emerge for product categories and forms (where external influences are important) compared to brands (where company decisions are dominant). Geographical scale is important for the tourist area life cycle as each country is a mosaic of resorts and tourist areas (which in turn contain hotels, theme parks etc.) and depending on the scale taken each may be at a different stage in the cycle (compare for example resorts in northern and southern France) The unit of analysis is therefore crucial and should be determined by the intended use of the information.

5. The life cycle assumes a homogeneous market but the market can be divided into many segments and a perfectly logical stance would be for, say, a destination to introduce segments sequentially. Equally, geographical segmentation would produce differing curves for, say, domestic and international visitors etc.

6. For the tourist area life cycle, decline is rooted in visitor numbers exceeding capacity levels at the destination. But capacity is a notoriously difficult concept to operationalize. Also, no single capacity threshold exists for a destination – physical, environmental and psychological capacity may each be different. Of course, neither does this take account of spatial nor temporal variations, such as seasonality with the attraction of crowd-tolerant visitors in the peak season and others in the quieter off-peak.

Conclusion

The main utility of the PLC is as an aid to understanding the evolution of tourist products and destinations and it thus provides guidance for strategic decision taking. This suggests that tourism businesses and destinations should adopt a long-term planning horizon in order to utilize the PLC as an organizing framework for marketing and development decisions. However, for destinations the implications of these decisions are severe, particularly in the decline stage, as tourism is closely enmeshed within the economy and community. The PLC is much less successful in providing detailed prescriptions for marketing actions. This is because the life cycle is product- or destination-specific and there is little empirical validation of its shape or length to allow generalizations to be made. The PLC is therefore useful as an aid to strategic thinking but is difficult to operationalize for day-to-day marketing actions.

Focus on small business

The life cycle approach is difficult to operationalize for small businesses. Its main lessons are:

1. The importance of being aware of the stages of the life cycle and the various strategic options at each stage.
2. The importance of adopting a long-term planning horizon.
3. The importance of keeping accurate records of sales or visitor numbers to help identify turning points.

4. The importance of monitoring actions of competitors and demand changes in the marketplace.
5. The desirability of maintaining a portfolio of products at different stages of the cycle.

Software/databases

Databases relating to the PLC are primarily those of company sales histories which largely remain confidential. Historic records of visitor arrivals at destinations are more readily available, but at the resort scale, where most work on applying the tourist area life cycle has concentrated, historic runs of data are rare. The richest source of this type of data is for small island destinations which normally have historic visitor arrivals figures.

Cooke and Edmondson's LIFER (life cycle forecaster) is an attempt to produce computerized forecasts based on the PLC. It is outlined in Cooke, E. and Edmondson, B., 'Computer aided product life cycle forecasts for new product investment decisions', *Increasing Marketing Productivity and Conceptual and Methodological Foundations of Marketing*, T. Green, ed. (American Marketing Association, 1973), pp. 373–7.

Further reading

Brownlie, D., 'Strategic marketing concepts and models', *Journal of Marketing Management*, vol. 1 (1985), pp. 157–94. Pages 161–71 in particular give a balanced and informed account of research into the effectiveness of the PLC as a strategic planning tool.

Butler, R. W., 'The concept of the tourist area cycle of evolution: implications for management of resources', *Canadian Geographer*, vol. 24 (1980), pp. 5–12. The most explicit account of the tourist area life cycle and the catalyst for subsequent research.

Buttle, F., *Hotel and Food Service Marketing. A Managerial Approach* (Holt, Rinehart and Winston, 1986). Useful overall summary of marketing in this sector but particularly pertinent is Section 1 on the product.

Day, G. S., 'The product life cycle: analysis and applications, issues', *Journal of Marketing*, vol. 45 (1981), pp. 60–7. Useful summary of the issues to introduce a special issue of the journal devoted to the PLC.

Dhalla, N. K. and Yuspeh, S., 'Forget the product life cycle concept', *Harvard Business Review*, vol. 54 (1976), pp. 102–10. A lively critique of the PLC.

Doyle, P., 'The realities of the product life cycle', *Quarterly Review of Marketing* (Summer 1976), pp. 1–6. A general overview of PLC theory.

Haywood, K. M., 'Can the tourist area life cycle be made operational?', *Tourism Management*, vol. 7 (1986), pp. 154–67. Effective summary of the life cycle approach in tourism and a realistic assessment of the problems of operationalizing the concept.

Hofer, C. W., 'Toward a contingency theory of business strategy', *Academy of Management Journal*, vol. 18 (1975), pp. 784–809. A detailed account of strategic marketing action based on the PLC.

Hovinen, G. R., 'A tourist cycle in Lancaster County, Pennsylvania', *Canadian Geographer*, vol. 25 (1981), pp. 283–6. A practical examination of the life cycle approach, basically supportive but outlining specific differences from the idealized model.

Kotler, P., *Principles of Marketing* (Prentice Hall, 3rd edition, 1980).

Special attention should be paid to the PLC outlined in pages 350–7.

Levitt, T., 'Exploit the product life cycle', *Harvard Business Review*, vol. 43 (1965), pp. 81–94. Detailed guidance on putting the PLC to use.

Meyer-Arendt, M. J. 'The Grand Isle, Louisiana, resort cycle', *Annals of Tourism Research*, vol. 12 (1985), pp. 449–65. An application of the life cycle concept to a specific case on the same lines as Hovinen (1981).

Middleton, V. T. C., *Marketing in Travel and Tourism* (Heinemann, 1988). Thorough overview of marketing in tourism but see, in particular, the section on products in tourism.

Plog, S. C., 'Why destination areas rise and fall in popularity', *Cornell HRA Quarterly*, vol. 14, no. 4 (1974), pp. 55–8.

van de Weg, H., 'Revitalization of traditional resorts', *Tourism Management*, vol. 3 (1982), pp. 303–7. A case study of the practical problems of rejuvenating an ailing resort.

Wall, G. and Marsh, J., *Recreational Land Use: Perspectives on its Evolution in Canada* (Carleton University Press, 1982). A collection of papers with many case studies of the tourist area life cycle.

CHRIS COOPER

Travel choice behaviors

Introduction

For travelers the choice of a vacation spot is an important decision: vacationers carefully evaluate the options that are available to them in the travel market. The goals of vacationers are to have a good time and to involve leisurely activities when they are vacationing. In this sense, they look for perceived need satisfaction and a unique set of utility parameters to determine their final destination.

For instance, hot weather and summer sports may be the predetermined needs of summer travelers who prefer to go to the southern seaside resorts. On the other hand, winter travelers may be influenced by winter sports such as downhill or cross-country skiing, and so prefer to travel to the northern states where winter sports are popular. They rate the quality of winter resorts according to snow conditions, skiing space, turnaround speed, prestige, time on the slope, ski classes offered, various peripheral services, lift capacity, and cost. Most of the summer and winter travelers' activity packages include the following:

1. Sightseeing (museums, national parks, and cities).
2. Commercial recreation (tennis, gambling, skiing, and nightclubs).
3. Water-oriented activities (swimming and sunbathing).
4. Such outdoor activities as camping and picnicing.

Examples

Vacation spots provide consumer services and intangible goods that are consumed at the point of purchase. Satisfied or dissatisfied behaviors should thus be stated at the end of vacation time. Studies of travel behaviors indicated that in-state travelers are more likely to revisit the same vacation sites and to use cars to reach their destinations. Also, they tend to be younger and watch more television than out-of-state travelers. Travelers often follow friends' recommendations in the selection of vacation spots and both color and black and white newspaper advertisements on vacation spots were found to be very influential. Also, evidence demonstrated that marketing strategies for vacation spots should emphasize low cost vacation packages and vacations taking less than six days to attract more in-state and out-of-state tourists.

In selecting a vacation spot, on the other hand, travelers evaluate the overall travel time and the excess travel time, and compare them with the cost of travel. In doing so, they investigate the perceived risk in terms of cost, comfort, convenience, and safety, and choose their mode of travel. For example, there is evidence that income and education have significant positive effects on travel behaviors, while the presence of children younger than 6 and older than 18 have greater negative effects.

Research methodology

To investigate the behavioral characteristics of summer travelers versus those of winter travelers, a study was conducted in several cities in the New England (USA) area. A questionnaire originally developed by Etzel and Woodside and successfully used in their study was revised and adapted for this research. Questionnaires were hand-distributed to a convenience sample of 100 respondents in Vermont, which is famous for its winter resorts, and an additional 100 respondents in Massachusetts, which is famous for its summer resorts. Distribution and collection of questionnaires took two weeks, and at the end of the second week, 160 usable questionnaires were returned.

Data were analyzed in the SPSS^X computer program by using a stepwise discriminant analysis technique. The stepwise discriminant analysis is a multivariate data analysis method and involves deriving the linear combination of the two or more independent variables that will discriminate best between defined groups.

In discriminant analysis, the dependent variable is called the discriminant score; researchers usually look at the discriminant scores of each group, and test their statistical significance. The discriminant coefficients determine the contribution of each independent variable to the discriminating score. Independent variables with large coefficients have larger discriminatory power than independent variable with small coefficients. The signs of coefficients indicate positive contribution or negative contribution to the discriminating score.

Findings

The responses of summer travelers demonstrated that the purpose of their travel was most often rest (42 per cent), and that these travelers were away from home for 1–3 nights. The mode of travel most often selected by summer travelers was car (52 per cent). Eighty-eight per cent felt that their trip was neither inexpensive nor expensive. Summer travelers tended to be 30 years old or younger (66 per cent), single (61 per cent), college educated (78 per cent), and earning over $12,000 a year (87 per cent). Twenty-seven respondents (64 per cent) were male and fifteen (36 per cent) were female.

Behavioral characteristics of summer travelers indicated that they watched 1–15 hours of television a week and read *Time* Magazine (71 per cent), *Playboy* (50 per cent), *Sports Illustrated* (43 per cent), *Business Week* (33 per cent), and *Fortune* (29 per cent). The majority did not use a travel agent (70 per cent), and carried gasoline company cards (43 per cent), Master Card (43 per cent), American Express (36 per cent), and Visa (36 per cent). On average, they listened to 3–15 hours of radio a week and indicated that their chances of returning to the same vacation site was 50 per cent or better.

The responses of winter travelers, on the other hand, differed from those of summer travelers. Although, like summer travelers, their principal purpose of travel was rest (58 per cent), winter travelers stayed 3–9 days away from home (73 per cent). The most popular mode of travel among winter travelers was plane (71 per cent). Fifty per cent of the respondents spent over $1,100 per trip and felt that their trip was neither expensive nor inexpensive. Their average age was 40; 61 per cent had no children. Thirteen respondents (34 per cent) were female, and 25 (66 per cent) were male. Forty seven per cent were single and 53 per cent married. Fifty-eight per cent had college degrees. The majority of winter travelers earned less than $30,000 annually and watched television 3–15 hours a week (68 per cent). Sixty-eight per cent listened to radio 6–25 hours a week.

The behavioral characteristics of winter travelers showed some similarities to those of summer travelers. For example, the majority of them read *Time* Magazine (58 per cent), followed by *Playboy* (48 per cent), *Sports Illustrated* (42 per cent), *Business Week* (34 per cent), and *Fortune* (32 per cent). Their average stay out-of-home was nine nights (74 per cent). They either occasionally (45 per cent) or never (42 per cent) used travel agents, and carried Visa (55 per cent), Master Card (55 per cent), Gasoline Company (58 per cent), and American Express (37 per cent) cards. Over 50 per cent indicated between a 30 and 50 per cent chance of revisiting the same vacation site.

Lifestyle of summer and winter travelers

In the questionnaire, there were 40 questions related to the response categories of lifestyle, personality, and need/values of the respondents. Likert-type questions were used in this

section, and each question had five categories ranging from strongly disagree to strongly agree. Mean responses of summer and winter travelers to each response category are shown in Figs 1, 2 and 3.

Summer travelers disagreed with winter travelers on several personality, lifestyle, and need/values criteria. For example, summer travelers tended not to read during their trips as much as winter travelers. Also, they tended to give a relatively low importance to visiting historical places, being close to nature, taking a vacation once in a lifetime, and asking for advice regarding destination. Summer travelers, in addition, were not so interested as winter travelers in applying vacations to the intellectual development of their children. On the other hand, they agreed with winter travelers that travel helps them to forget daily problems, to break monotony, and to find excitement. Summer travelers were more active than winter travelers and tended to change the pace of their lives during their trips. Like winter travelers, summer travelers found their trips enjoyable and worth taking again.

When the responses of winter travelers were analyzed in terms of personality, lifestyle, and need/value criteria, they felt that winter travel was emotionally refreshing, helped them to forget daily problems, and was an enjoyable experience; therefore, winter travelers indicated a strong tendency to take the same trip again. Also, they tended to believe that winter travel helped them to break the monotony of life, was fun, changed the pace of life, and encouraged them to engage in sports and to meet new people. However, winter travelers tended not to visit historical places, not to feel that they owed their families a vacation, not to ask advice, not to look to vacations as important toward building self-confidence, and not to value vacations as important toward the intellectual development of their children.

The results of the discriminant analysis, on the other hand,

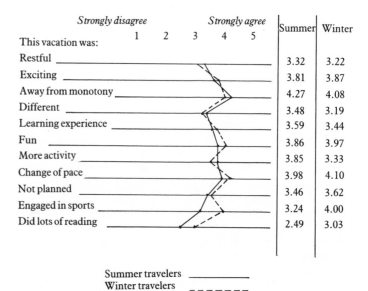

Figure 1 Lifestyle characteristics of summer and winter travelers.

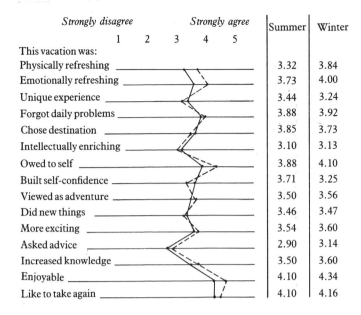

Strongly disagree Strongly agree 1 2 3 4 5	Summer	Winter
This vacation was:		
Physically refreshing	3.32	3.84
Emotionally refreshing	3.73	4.00
Unique experience	3.44	3.24
Forgot daily problems	3.88	3.92
Chose destination	3.85	3.73
Intellectually enriching	3.10	3.13
Owed to self	3.88	4.10
Built self-confidence	3.71	3.25
Viewed as adventure	3.50	3.56
Did new things	3.46	3.47
More exciting	3.54	3.60
Asked advice	2.90	3.14
Increased knowledge	3.50	3.60
Enjoyable	4.10	4.34
Like to take again	4.10	4.16

Summer travelers ————————
Winter travelers – – – – – – – –

Figure 2 Personality characteristics of summer and winter travelers.

Strongly disagree Strongly agree 1 2 3 4 5	Summer	Winter
This vacation was:		
Close to nature	2.78	2.89
Fulfilled responsibility	3.56	2.78
Owed to family	3.00	2.31
Cultural value	3.41	2.86
Took once	2.39	2.47
Valuable for children	2.80	2.53
Different activities	3.40	3.17
My friend took also	3.61	3.81
Recommend	3.15	3.44
Site not important	3.54	3.58
Met new people	3.83	4.00
Visit historical places	2.54	2.63
My friend impressed	3.50	3.55

Summer travelers ————————
Winter travelers – – – – – – –

Figure 3 Needs/values of summer and winter travelers.

demonstrated that age, education, number of children, and total number of travelers were significant demographic factors, and that cost of travel, dollar evaluation of travel, Visa Card, Diner's Club, and travel agents were significant economic factors. Self-confidence, family responsibilities, obligations to family, physical refreshment, participation in sports, and enjoyment were significant lifestyle, personality and need/value (behavioral) factors. Table 1 shows the breakdown of significant demographic, economic and behavioral factors between summer and winter travelers.

Discriminant coefficients of demographic factors indicated that age, total number of times traveled, number of children, and level of education, made relatively large contributions to the discriminant function of summer travelers. Since summer travelers tended to be younger than 30 and college graduates, and tended to have at least one child, their distinctive demographic characteristics may be used as a base for market segmentation.

Economic factors were more significant to the winter travelers than to the summer travelers. Cost-of-travel and evaluation of travel expenses had the largest contribution to the discriminant function of winter travelers who tended to feel that their travel was neither expensive nor inexpensive. The average cost of a trip to a winter traveler was between $500 and $700, and a Visa Card was used during the travel. Winter travelers tended to use travel agents. Diner's Club Cards had a negative contribution to their discriminant function.

Lifestyle, personality, and need/value factors such as family responsibilities, self-confidence, vacation site, and travel owed to family had the largest negative contribution to the discriminant function of summer travelers. This result indicates that increased family responsibilities and self-confidence may cause the reduction of summer travel. However, winter travelers enjoyed their trips and engaged in sports.

Table 1 Discriminant functions coefficients of demographic, economic and behavioral factors.

Predictor variables	Summer travelers	Winter travelers
Demographic factors		
Age	5.410	1.752
Number of children	6.240	2.941
Number of trips	12.323	9.372
Education	38.385	28.912
Economic factors		
Cost of travel	1.406	2.145
Dollar evaluation of travel	17.820	23.289
Visa card	5.644	13.259
Diner's Club	− 8.249	− 4.365
Travel agent	32.319	36.321
Behavioral factors		
Fulfilled family responsibility	− 4.229	− 4.046
Vacation site recommended	− 0.969	− 0.085
Owed to family	− 4.367	− 3.463
Physically refreshed	2.551	3.020
Helped to build self-confidence	− 9.642	− 6.168
Enjoyed	1.069	7.208
Owed to self	− 0.900	0.828
Engaged in sports	0.619	4.120

Implementation

Tourism is a service industry and its products have to be consumed at the place where the product is offered to prospective vacationers. Dissatisfaction causes the refusal of utilizing tourism facilities and this decision results in great financial loss for tourist places. Therefore, implementation of the findings of this study suggests that the promotion strategy for summer and winter resort areas should be designed to influence the young and well-educated parents of small families. Also, the attractions and activities already available in resort areas should satisfy the needs of this segment. However, for winter tourists, the average cost of each trip should be kept competitive. If this is accomplished, winter travelers are likely to enjoy their trips and return to vacation sites for year-round attractions and sports. Winter and summer resort areas are competing with each other at the same time to attract the same group of traveler for different purposes. To be successful the resorts should provide excellent service for the money and keep the standards and quality above the expectations of vacationers.

Assessment

Travel choice behaviors in general indicate that travelers show distinctly different socioeconomic, demographic, psychographic, behavioralistic, and travel-related characteristics. The research efforts, therefore, should be channeled to investigate the major factors effecting these differences, and to make necessary suggestions for application of different marketing and promotion strategies. The following are some of the questions which need to be answered:

1. What are the environmental differences between summer and winter resort areas?
2. What are the marketing objectives of summer and winter resorts?
3. Are there differences in marketing objectives implied to each group?
4. What are the distinct characteristics of winter and summer travelers?
5. What are the market segments of each group?
6. What are the possible marketing strategies which will help to reach them?
7. Would different promotional strategies be required to influence their decision?
8. Should different pricing strategies be applied?
9. Should channel strategy be different for summer and winter travelers?

Understanding behavioral differences will help tourist organizations to develop and apply more effective plans, organization and control models. It is certain that the summer/winter vacation spots will gain a great deal from this effort.

Conclusion

Since the behaviors of tourists and their expectations from vacation spots are determining factors in choosing one mode of vacation or another, this study of summer and winter travel behaviors provides evidence that cost of travel, family size, age, education, sporting activities, family responsibilities, and self-confidence in travel distinguish the behavior of summer travelers from winter travelers. Summer travelers tend to be young and college-educated and have one child. Their family responsibilities and confidence have a negative effect on their travel interests. Although winter travelers indicated concern with cost of travel, they used Visa Cards, engaged in sports, and enjoyed their trips.

Further reading

Barff, R., Mackay, D. and Olshavsky, R. W., 'A selective review of travel-mode choice models', *Journal of Consumer Research*, vol. 8, no. 4 (March 1982), pp. 370–80. This article deals with major advances in travel-mode choice modeling. The mode-choice studies are assessed, and possible directions for future development are suggested.

Etzel, M. J. and Woodside, A. G. 'Segmenting vacation markets: the case of the distant and near home travelers', *Journal of Travel Research*, vol. 20, no. 4 (Spring 1982), pp. 10–14. This article presents evidence about characteristics of near-home and distant travelers as target segments for travel marketing.

Graham, J. E. L. and Wall, G., 'American visitors to Canada: a study in market segmentation', *Journal of Travel Research*, no. 3 (Winter 1978), pp. 21–4. This article describes the socioeconomic status of United States visitors to Canada. Using factor analysis, four market segments are developed: sightseeing, commercial recreation, water-oriented activities, and outdoor living.

Greig, P. J., 'Recreation evaluation using a characteristics theory of consumer behavior', *American Journal of Agricultural Economics*, vol. 65, no. 1 (February 1983), pp. 90–7. This article attempts to build an outdoor recreation management problem and analytical model which retains all the attributes of Lancaster's theory.

Hair, J. H., Jr., Anderson, R. E. and Tatham, R. L., *Multivariate Data Analysis: With Readings* (Macmillan, 2nd edition, 1987). The book emphasizes the theory, concepts and application of multivariate analysis as a research tool. Special attention should be given to Chapter 3.

Hagemann, R. P., 'The determinants of household vacation travel: some empirical evidence', *Applied Economics*, vol. 13, no. 6 (June 1981), pp. 225–34. The article attempts to estimate the determinants of household vacation travel. It deals with the relationship between probability of household travel and the level of expenditures given that the household does travel.

Heggie, I. G., 'Putting behavior into behavioral models of travel choice', *Journal of Operations Research Society*, vol. 29, no. 6 (1978), pp. 541–50. This paper focuses upon household travel behaviors and modeling. It suggests that models of behavior may have to become more human and less mathematical.

Kaynak, E., 'Developing marketing strategy for a resource-based industry', *Tourism Management* (September 1985), pp. 184–94. This article examines the implications of defining a new market segment for generating foreign currency. It suggests the offering of activity packages which facilitate more tourism resources, with advertising aimed at a well-defined market segment.

Kaynak, E. and Yavas, U., 'Segmenting the tourism market by purpose of trip: a profile analysis of visitors to Halifax, Canada', *International Journal of Tourism Management*, vol. 8, no. 6 (June 1981), pp. 105–11. This paper investigates the usefulness of segmentation by purpose of trip through a case study of tourism and travel to Halifax. Canada. It suggests that purpose-oriented segmentation can be used with other segmentation correlates.

Woodside, A. G. and Ronkainen, I. A., 'Travel advertising: newspaper versus magazines', *Journal of Advertising Research*, vol. 22, no. 3 (June/July 1982), pp. 39–43. The article examines the effects of black and white newspaper advertisements versus color magazine advertisements for national tourism promotion programs. Results suggest that newspaper advertisements out-perform those in magazines for both the black and white and color campaigns.

Woodside, A. G. and Etzel, M., 'Vacation travel behavior and perceived benefits of home state residents', *Business and Economic Review*, vol. 26, no. 2 (April 1980), pp. 28–35. This paper provides information about travel-related behaviors of home state residents and benefits received in relation to behavior modification.

UGUR YUCELT

Travel industry information systems

Introduction

Information is the life blood of the travel industry. Travelers, travel agencies, and travel industry suppliers all need information. Travelers need information about destinations and their facilities, prices and schedules, and about dates of attractions, exhibitions and events. Travel agents need easy access to travel product information, rates and regulations, visa and health regulations, and reservation procedures. Travel industry suppliers need information on the status of their business for control and planning purposes, and on their clients, potential clients and the competition for marketing purposes. Firms with access to information have a natural competitive advantage over those that do not, and so travel industry information systems are critical to business success.

Information systems in the travel industry have special characteristics. Travel industry information constantly changes – schedules, fares and rates change, festivities and attractions vary from month to month, visa and health regulations change, new promotional programs are introduced periodically, and tour packages are redesigned each season. Another special characteristic is that information on components in the travel industry must also be accessible by other components because of the complementary nature of tourism products. Also the information must be easily accessible from many places around the world. The intangibility of the tourism product places extra emphasis on the need for information.

For the purposes of this chapter, travel industry information systems will be discussed in three different categories:

1. Those which travel planners (travel agents, travelers and corporations) use to access information on and make reservations for all travel products. These cover all sectors of the travel industry.
2. Reservation systems used by an individual company with many different locations, e.g. a hotel chain.
3. Those used by a single company for processing and storing internal accounting, inventory, planning and marketing information.

Computer technology has dramatically enhanced the ability to handle travel industry information flows, and travel industry computer systems exist in each of the three categories. This chapter will focus on computer supported information systems, although nonautomated ones do exist. Examples of nonautomated information systems are the services offered by destination tourist bureaux and travel centers which provide brochures and literature on the destination.

Examples

The first category of information systems are exemplified by computer reservation systems (CRS) developed by airlines. These were originally designed to facilitate the operations of the particular airline, but they have developed to become much broader in scope and are now the main arteries of travel industry information. They provide access to complete trip planning and reservation information for all sectors of the industry (accommodation, cruises, transportation, tours, currency exchange, attractions, destination information etc.) There are currently five major CRS systems in the United States. They are: Sabre (developed by American Airlines), Apollo (developed by United Airlines), SystemOne (developed by Eastern Airlines which has subsequently been bought by Texas Airlines), PARS (developed by TWA and now part owned by Northwest), and Datas II (which is owned and developed by Delta Airlines). CRS systems are extremely profitable for the five vendor airlines and so separate companies have been created to operate the automation division. Terminals to access these databases were first put into travel agencies in the mid 1970s and today they are in over 90 per cent of all US travel agencies and an increasing number of those in Europe and Asia. The databases can also be accessed by travel departments of corporations and by individual travelers who have their own personal computer.

In Europe videotext technology has been used to create equivalent travel industry information systems. The videotext system in the United Kingdom, which is operated by British Telecom, is called Prestel and can be found in 90 per cent of travel agents' offices. Prestel can also be easily accessed by consumers from their home television sets – a major advantage of videotext technology. Prestel contains thousands of pages of information on many different topics with about one-quarter of those pages on the travel industry. For example, tour operators list their tours, prices, and booking rules and British Airways lists flight information. European airlines are now negotiating with United and American airlines to develop CRS systems similar to those in the United States, but it is unlikely that they will replace videotext.

Some destinations are using a modified version of videotext technology to create information systems on their facilities and attractions. These systems enable travelers to access pages of information on restaurants, shops and attractions from small stand-alone terminals located in airports, hotel lobbies and other public places.

Examples of the second category of travel information systems are hotel reservation systems and car reservation systems. Unlike the CRS systems discussed above, these systems handle information that is company-specific only and are not directly accessible by travel agents or consumers for trip-planning purposes. Holiday Inn Hotels, for example, has an information system called Holidex that links together all its properties and enables reservations to be made in any Holiday Inn from any other Holiday Inn or from one of the regional reservation offices. The system is also used for marketing and planning purposes. Sheraton Hotels has a similar reservation system (called Reservatron) as do most of the large hotel chains and car rental companies.

Examples of the third category are companies in the travel industry which simply need systems to handle the information and accounting flows within their own business. For example, travel agencies need to keep track of their clients and their accounts; individual hotels need information systems for room management, forecasting, food and beverage control and payroll; tour operators need information systems to handle their inventory and cost analysis. The types of systems that have developed for this category are of two types. First, there are systems specifically developed for that section of the travel industry. For example, there are specially designed travel agency back office systems, restaurant management systems and hotel property management systems. They are developed by professionals who understand the specific requirements of that sector of the industry. The second option is to use generic business applications such as spreadsheets, accounting packages, payroll packages or forecasting packages.

Benefits

The first category of travel industry information systems facilitates the trip planning process significantly. Travel agents no longer have to refer to large volumes such as the *Official Airline Guide* which quickly become out-of-date. Instead they are able to access on-line, up-to-date information on most facilities in the industry from a single terminal. Also, because individual travelers and corporations have some access to these systems, they can research trips for themselves and not be dependent on travel agents. These systems can also enrich the vacation experience because travelers know ahead of time the kinds of attractions and events that are likely to be going on in the destination. This is preferable to relying on serendipity to locate an event of interest when on vacation. The systems also provide an excellent channel through which suppliers can promote their products effectively.

The second category of information systems provide better control of inventory and therefore higher usage or occupancy rates for hotels, airlines and other travel industry companies. The database permits management to immediately access figures showing the status of the company such as load factors, occupancy rates, no-shows, and revenues. Another major benefit of these information systems is that they offer companies extra marketing power by allowing airlines, hotels and car rental companies to store customer profile information. Databases usually contain demographic and behavioral information on clients that can be used effectively for marketing purposes and to personalize future stays (or journeys) of the repeat client. In the hotel industry, for example, an online database allows the front desk clerk to know immediately that the guest checking in prefers a nonsmoking room, likes a wake-up call at 7 a.m. and has a birthday during the stay. An airline or travel agency can keep files on seat preference, frequent flyer accounts and other items that will help to achieve brand loyalty from consumers. Airlines also use their computer systems for many other purposes such as crew scheduling, and message switching.

Implementation

To implement the first category of travel information systems, millions of dollars and a commitment to research and development are needed. There must be a single location for the central computer and the storage of data. The central computer is usually a large mainframe, or there may be four or five mainframes attached together to handle the huge message and storage volume. This central computer is then connected via telecommunication links to thousands of terminals around the world. It is also connected to other travel industry computers so that interline itineraries and entire vacations that include accommodation and ground transportation can be planned.

There are three ways that these computers can be linked together – by using the ARINC network, the SITA network or by direct access links. The ARINC network is managed by Aeronautical Radio Incorporated to facilitate communications between airlines. It is located in Annapolis, Maryland and has switching centers in Los Angeles, Chicago, and Dallas. This network connects travel industry computers in the United States. If international telecommunication links are required the SITA network must be used (Société Internationale Telecommunication Aeronautique). This network uses different technologies in different parts of the world (some faster than others) but is able to connect travel industry companies worldwide. More recently, some travel industry companies have installed their own telecommunication links to allow faster communications with other travel industry computers than ARINC and SITA can offer. These are called direct access links.

For a travel agency wishing to implement such a facility it is relatively straightforward, but costly. Travel agencies can lease or purchase terminals to access these CRS systems. They need a modern and dedicated electrical and telephone circuit. Maintenance and support are provided by the vendor airline.

Implementation of the second category of information systems is also a major undertaking. Travel companies wishing to create and implement their own reservation systems would be wise to consider purchasing systems that have already been developed rather than reinventing the wheel. Refinements may be necessary but programming a system from scratch is not always the most efficient approach. If the company has some unique characteristics, in-house development may be preferable.

In the third category, a business wishing to implement a computer system to handle internal information flows should first of all analyze its needs and create a Request For Proposal (RFP). Research into possible vendors should also be done by talking to other users, by reading trade publications, and by attending trade shows where products are demonstrated. Often it is also possible to obtain demonstration disks for programs that run on personal computers. This is not a feasible option for larger systems. The RFP will generate proposals and sometimes site visits from possible vendors. Turnkey systems (which include the hardware, software, installation and training) are available for most sectors of the travel industry. After a system is chosen and installed, a monthly maintenance contract is usually purchased.

Another available option is to use general business information systems and tailor them to fit a travel company. Although this can be a cheaper option, it may be less desirable than software that has been specifically designed for the travel industry.

Assessment

Well-designed information systems can make the travel industry operate more efficiently. Reservation systems are especially important and it is logically appealing that there be one single travel industry reservation system for all travel planners to use. The CRS developed by the airlines have filled this void, but not perfectly. Information displayed by the CRS has been and is still, allegedly, biased so that the vendor airline is favored over competitors. Bias has been the subject of much debate and legislation in the United States. Should the airlines that have put so much time and money into developing these information systems be allowed to reap additional profits through bias and restrictive contracts with travel agents? Or should they be forced to remove the bias and be less restrictive on the contracts? The consensus in the industry and in the courts is that the bias should be removed.

Questions arise as to whether a single neutral (i.e. nonbiased) industry reservation system should ever be developed? If so, who should develop it, finance it and operate it? There have been a number of attempts to create such a system – indeed it was even given a name for a while: Neutral Industry Booking System (NIBS), but all attempts have so far failed. Instead, the five airline CRS are becoming established as the industry information and reservation systems. This seems logical as the infrastructure and the hardware are all in place and the software is developed. Whether one system will eventually incorporate all others and become the single travel industry information system is yet to be seen.

Will videotext technology continue to play an important role

in providing users with travel industry information? It is valuable as an inexpensive way of providing the population at large (through their television sets) with information. A limitation is that it does not easily lend itself to interactive transactions as the reservation systems do. Society will soon reach the point where every home has a personal computer and a modem and will be able to access any information system in the world. As individuals are given more access to the airline reservation systems, an important question arises – 'What will be the future role of travel agents?'

Conclusion

The travel industry needs efficient information systems in many different forms. Information systems that travel planners can use to assist in the research and reservation process are very important. Airline reservation systems have become the main sources for such information. There is however room for other nonbiased destination information systems that the prospective traveler can use to locate information on attractions and facilities. Company-specific information systems to handle accounting, marketing, reservation and operational information are becoming increasingly popular in travel industry companies. Many sectors of the travel industry have hesitated to use information technology, arguing that computers do not fit well into a service industry. Experience is showing that computer information systems instead improve service levels by reducing mundane tasks and freeing personnel for more attentive customer service.

Focus on small business

Only a few years ago, small companies in the travel industry found it difficult to justify the cost of creating an information system using computer technology. This is no longer the case. As computers become smaller, quicker and cheaper, even the smallest companies can afford systems. For example, computer systems for hotels used to be only justifiable for those with more than 400 rooms. Now there are microcomputer based systems that are feasible for hotels with less than 100 rooms. Previously, another limitation for small businesses was that it was infeasible to hire skilled computer programmers to operate the system. Today this is not the case. Information systems are user-friendly and so skilled computer programmers are not needed. Instead, a few hours with a manual or a trainer is adequate. Small businesses such as tour operators and attractions may also find that the industry-wide computer reservation systems provide efficient and cost-effective ways to market their products.

Software/databases

AZTEC Hotel Information System, NY. AZTEC provides a daily
bulletin of hotel industry news, information on supplies, goods and

services, new hotels, renovations and an industry library containing marketing statistics and other information sources.
The five US CRS: Apollo, Datas II, Sabre, SystemOne, PARS; Prestel and Travicom in the United Kingdom.

Further reading

Anon., 'Information technology applications in travel and tourism', Special Report no. 47 *International Tourism Quarterly*, no. 3 (1983), pp. 37–43. This report highlights some of the applications of information technology in the travel and tourism sector, concentrating on aspects of better information, and improved transactions.

Booth, R., 'Automation in the travel industry', *Tourism Management*, vol. 4, no. 4 (December 1983), pp. 296–8. This article discusses the impact of automation on the travel agency. Videotext and the British multi-access reservation switch called Travicom are explained.

Bruce, M., 'Information technology: changes in the travel trade', *Tourism Management*, vol. 4, no. 4 (December 1983), pp. 290–5. This article discusses different information technologies, with special emphasis on videotext, and analyzes their use and impact on the travel industry.

Geller, N. A., 'How to improve your information system', *Cornell HRA Quarterly* (August 1985), pp. 19–27. This article outlines a systematic plan for creating a hotel executive's information system. The author attempts to assist the reader to identify company needs and thereby identify the information that is of most urgent interest to the company.

Godwin, N., *Complete Guide to Travel Agency Automation* (Delmar, 2nd edition, 1987). This book provides a guide to the kinds of automation available to travel agents. It offers assistance in how to shop for automated information systems.

Green, D., 'Videotext and UK package tour companies', *Tourism Management*, vol. 4, no. 4 (December 1983), pp. 289–301. This article reports on how videotext technology has been used by UK tour operators to facilitate their operations. Thomson Holidays is used as an example.

Kasavana, M. L., *Hotel Information Systems* (CBI/Van Nostrand Reinhold, 1978). This book provides insight into manual methods of handling hotel information flows and introduces advancements in computer technology and their impact on hotel reservation systems.

Martin, J., *Viewdata and the Information Society* (Prentice Hall, 1982). This book analyzes viewdata (videotext) technology and discusses its impact, problems, applications and future. It specifically addresses the travel industry in Chapter 17 and gives examples of Prestel's travel applications.

Noguchi, Y., 'Japan's information oriented society and the travel industry of the future', *International Travel Journal* (January 1986), Parts I and II. This is a report based on a presentation given by the Director of Kinki Nippon Tourist Co. at the 5th Japan Congress of International Travel. It is a good, broad-based discussion of the role that information plays in the travel industry.

Sheldon, P. J., 'The impact of technology on the hotel industry', *Tourism Management*, vol. 4, no. 4 (1983), pp. 269–78. This paper describes the different areas of hotel operations that can be improved with information technology. It also suggests trends for future developments.

Sheldon, P. J., 'Computers – tourism applications', *Tourism Management* (September 1987). This article reports on a survey of 56 State Tourism Offices in the United States and Canada on the degree to which they are using information technology to process information on visitors.

Var, T., Sheldon, P. J., Liu, J. C. *et al*, 'Tourism and computers: quo vadis?', *Annals of Tourism Research*, vol. 13 (1986), pp. 109–28. This paper outlines computer applications in the travel industry by referring to three critical areas: the role of computers in tourism planning and research, the industrial applications of new technology, and the role of education in this 'high tech/high touch' society.

Wardell, D., 'Hotel technology and reservation systems', *Travel and Tourism Analyst* (January 1987), pp. 45–56. This article gives a good background to airline reservation systems and the role they play as the travel industry's major information systems.

Wardell, D., 'Hotel technology and reservation systems', *Travel and Tourism Analyst* (June 1987), pp. 33–47. This article is a survey of the developments in and challenges facing the most underautomated sector of the travel industry.

Welburn, H., 'Travel selling and distribution: new technology and trends in Europe', *Travel and Tourism Analyst* (July 1987), pp. 3–15. This report looks at the impact of new information technology on the selling and distribution of travel.

PAULINE J. SHELDON

Trends in international tourism

The growth of world tourism

By any criteria tourism is a major world industry. Throughout the 1970s international travel accounted annually for over 5 per cent of world exports and it has maintained this share during the 1980s.

Despite the world fuel crisis of the early 1970s, tourist arrivals increased from 160 million in 1970 to 274 million in 1979, see Table 1. The world recession in the first half of the 1980s and in particular the rise in fuel prices at the beginning of the decade merely slowed down the rate of increase. The desire to travel proved stronger than many researchers had forecast and previous measurements of price and income elasticities were no longer applicable in the 1980s. In 1980 world tourist arrivals increased by 4 per cent, followed by a further 1.4 per cent in 1981. 1982, however, was a poor year internationally. As the recession bit deeper into the economies of the main generating countries tourist arrivals fell for the first time since comprehensive central records have been kept. Tourism, however, is a resilient industry and by 1983 recovery had started with a rise of 2.4 per cent in international arrivals followed by over 7 per cent in 1984, a further 6 per cent in 1985 and 2 per cent in 1986 when the total reached an estimated 340 million.

In money terms tourism has more than maintained its position during the recent recession. International tourism receipts rose from $17.9 billion in 1970 to $83.3 billion in 1979. Receipts continued to rise in the 1980s. Even in 1982 when receipts fell by over 5 per cent, world exports declined by over 6 per cent. By 1984 receipts were starting to recover and by 1985 had reached $110 billion (5.68 per cent of world exports; see Table 1).

One of the most interesting aspects of international tourism over the last two decades has been the different reactions of tourists to the recessions of the early 1970s and early 1980s. The first recession caused only a slowing down in the rate of increase in international travel, whereas the effects of the second recession were felt for about three years and not all countries have fully recovered to their previous levels. The economies of the western world reacted more speedily in the 1970s to the rise in fuel costs, substantial though they were, and the upward trend in travel continued. In the early 1980s, however, the rise in fuel costs was only one among several factors which triggered off a recession which had longer-term effects on disposable incomes and the costs of travel. In both decades, however, the desire to travel proved stronger than many researchers had forecast – the populations of the main generating countries now regard holidays as a near essential part of consumer expenditure and individuals protect their holidays even at the expense of many other forms of consumption.

The composition of world tourism

Despite the magnitude of international tourism, the 330 million international tourist arrivals in 1985 represented only about 150 million people (or some 3 per cent of the world population). Moreover, about 30 per cent of these visits were for business purposes (including attending conferences and trade fairs), or for family, short study or health reasons. In other words, only about 230 million visits were for 'holiday' purposes. As disposable incomes and leisure time increase the residual tourist market for the future is enormous.

Most international travel is still shorthaul to nearby countries. Of the 330 million international tourist arrivals in 1985, about 180 million took place *within* Europe and 22 million *within* North America. Although these continents have experienced an *absolute* growth in international tourism during the last two decades (Tables 2 and 3) their relative share of the market has declined. North America's share has fallen from over 17 per cent of arrivals and almost 20 per cent of receipts in 1970 to 10 per cent of arrivals and 14 per cent of receipts in 1986, whereas Europe's share has remained more stable at over 70 per cent of arrivals and 63 per cent of receipts in 1970 to 67 per cent of arrivals and 58 per cent of receipts in 1986. Although many areas of the world increased their relative shares of the market during the 1970s, only the East Asia and Pacific Region continued to gain relative to other areas during the 1980s. The factors influencing the continual growth in this region were the opening up of new air routes, the provision of cheaper travel and accommodation packages, increased marketing and promotional activities and the increased disposable income in countries such as Japan which created growth in intraregional travel.

Over three-quarters of all international tourism expenditure is accounted for by countries in Europe or North America.

Table 1 International tourist arrivals and international tourist receipts, 1950–1986 (adapted from WTO, 1986, vol. 1).

Year	Arrivals (millions)	Receipts (US$ millions)
1950	25.3	2.1
1960	69.3	6.9
1970	159.7	17.9
1971	172.2	20.9
1972	181.9	24.6
1973	190.6	31.1
1974	197.1	33.8
1975	214.4	40.7
1976	220.7	44.4
1977	239.1	55.6
1978	257.4	68.9
1979	274.0	83.3
1980	284.8	102.4
1981	288.8	104.3
1982	287.0	98.6
1983	293.9	98.3
1984	315.4	102.5
1985	333.0	109.6
1986	340.0 (est)	115.0 (est)

Even with allowances made for intraregional tourist flows *within* the continents of Europe and North America, about 43 per cent of the remaining international tourist movements to other countries are generated from Europe and North America. Japan is the only substantial tourist origin country outside these continents with 2 per cent of the world total, although in terms of expenditure Saudi Arabia now ranks within the top ten generating countries (Table 4). Indeed the importance of these countries (Europe and North America) to world tourism can be gauged by the fact that throughout the present decade their tourist expenditure has consistently accounted for between 47 and 49 per cent of the world total (Table 5). Over this period West Germany's contribution has declined from $20.6 billion in

1980 to $14.6 billion in 1985 whilst the United States has increased from $10.4 billion to $17 billion. These data, however, give no indication of the balance between longhaul and short-haul traffic. On a world scale almost 80 per cent of foreign travel and about 37 per cent of tourist expenditure including fares takes place between neighboring countries. Although West Germany, for example, provides more international visitors than any other country (over 48 million in 1985), almost half of its traffic is to countries with a common frontier and less than 5 per cent is longhaul. The principal longhaul travelers are residents of the United States and Japan with the United Kingdom third (Table 6).

Four of the five principal tourist-generating countries are also among the leading destination countries. Indeed, the United States is (1985 figures) both the main generator and receiver of tourist expenditure. In 1985 the seven principal destination countries received over 45 per cent of all international tourists and almost 53 per cent of international tourist expenditure (Table 7). France, Spain and Italy together received over 89 million tourists (over a quarter of the world total). The Mediterranean area as a whole received over 120 million international visitors compared with 7.8 million in the Caribbean, 9 million in Africa and 46.6 million in the whole of Asia and Australasia.

More important, however, for the world economy is the distribution of international tourism flows and receipts between the rich and poor areas of the world. Tables 8 and 9 show the situation in 1981 and 1985. Whereas the low and lower–middle income economies have gained slightly over the period in both absolute and relative terms, the vast majority of world tourism is still received by industrial market economies. Not all lower income countries have been able to convert increases in tourist arrivals into increased receipts from tourism. Kenya, for example, experienced an increase of 45 per cent in tourist arrivals from 1981 to 1985 but its receipts from tourism fell by 26 per cent, whereas, on the other hand, Barbados with a less than 2 per cent increase in visitor arrivals, gained a 17 per cent increase in receipts.

Table 2 International tourist arrivals by region, 1950–1986 (adapted from WTO, 1985; 1986, vol. 1).

Year	Tourist arrivals (thousands)							
	Africa	North America	Latin America	East Asia and Pacific	Europe	Middle East	South Asia	World
1950	524	6,180	1,305	190	16,839	197	47	25,282
1960	780	14,000	2,705	680	50,351	630	180	69,296
1970	2,407	27,400	9,248	4,859	113,000	1,864	912	159,690
1980	6,413	35,376	18,270	19,981	195,966	5,821	2,280	284,107
1981	8,046	35,891	17,573	23,446	195,289	6,160	2,443	288,848
1982	7,646	34,099	16,797	24,521	194,490	6,983	2,422	286,958
1983	7,854	32,932	18,344	26,839	199,433	6,053	2,489	293,944
1984	8,618	32,326	19,729	31,302	214,405	6,513	2,466	315,359
1985	9,070	32,487	20,307	36,985	224,488	7,115	2,539	332,991
1986 P	8,800	34,000	21,650	39,500	227,500	6,000	2,550	340,000

Data for Taiwan are excluded; the figures for some countries still include excursionist arrivals; methods of estimating visitor arrivals vary from country to country and readers are referred to the explanatory notes in the WTO references.
P: Figures for 1986 are provisional.

Table 3 International tourism receipts by region, 1950–1986 (adapted from WTO, 1985; 1986, vol. 1).

Year	Tourism receipts (US$ millions)							
	Africa	North America	Latin America	East Asia and Pacific	Europe	Middle East	South Asia	World
1950	88	668	392	30	890	26	6	2,100
1960	178	1,388	1,064	195	3,918	89	35	6,867
1970	400	3,519	1,281	1,100	11,200	300	100	17,900
1980	1,992	12,342	13,180	7,465	61,654	3,228	1,549	101,410
1981	2,878	14,715	14,563	8,899	57,240	4,130	1,871	104,296
1982	2,767	13,740	11,628	9,334	55,577	3,886	1,666	98,598
1983	2,612	14,006	10,529	9,800	55,824	3,920	1,647	98,338
1984	2,517	14,247	11,485	10,432	58,054	4,130	1,617	102,482
1985	2,854	14,719	11,906	11,308	62,779	4,477	1,523	109,566
1986 P	2,900	15,650	12,250	12,500	66,500	3,700	1,500	115,000

Methods of estimating tourism receipts vary from country to country and readers are referred to explanatory notes in the WTO references.
P: Figures for 1986 are provisional.

Table 4 Principal tourist-generating countries, 1985 (calculated from WTO, 1986, vol. 2).

Rank	Country	Expenditure		Departures	
		US$ billions	% of world total	millions	% of world total
1	United States	17.0	17.2	38.1	10.8
2	West Germany	14.6	14.8	48.4	13.8
3	United Kingdom	6.3	6.4	24.9	7.1
4	Japan	4.8	4.9	7.4	2.1
5	France	4.6	4.7	28.3	8.1
	Top five countries	47.3	48.0	147.1	41.9
	Rest of world	51.3	52.0	204.2	58.1
	World total	98.6	100.0	351.3	100.0

The world expenditure total differs from those in Tables 1 and 3 because of incomplete reporting on a country by country basis.

Table 5 Principal tourist-generating countries, 1980–1985 (calculated from WTO, 1985, 1986, vol. 1).

Country	Expenditure (US$ billion)					
	1980	1981	1982	1983	1984	1985
United States	10.4	11.5	12.4	14.0	16.0	17.0
West Germany	20.6	17.5	16.2	15.1	14.1	14.6
United Kingdom	6.9	6.5	6.2	6.0	6.2	6.3
Japan	4.6	4.6	4.1	4.4	4.6	4.8
France	6.0	5.8	5.2	4.3	4.3	4.6
Top five countries	48.5	45.9	44.1	43.8	45.2	47.3
Rest of world	50.6	52.3	49.1	49.1	47.5	51.3
World total	99.1	98.2	93.2	92.9	92.7	98.6

The world totals are shown lower than those in Tables 1 and 3 because of incomplete reporting on a country by country basis.

Table 6 Principal shorthaul and longhaul tourist-generating countries, 1985 (calculated from WTO, 1986, vol. 2).

Country	Departures			
	Shorthaul (millions)	Longhaul (millions)	Total (millions)	Longhaul as a % of total
United States	17.1	21.0	38.1	55.1
West Germany	46.3	2.1	48.4	4.3
United Kingdom	21.3	3.6	24.9	14.5
Japan	2.5	4.9	7.4	66.2
France	26.4	1.9	28.3	6.7

Shorthaul refers to destinations within the same tourism region (as defined by the WTO); longhaul refers to destinations outside the same region.

Table 7 Principal tourist destination countries, 1985 (calculated from WTO, 1986, vol. 1).

Rank	Country	Receipts		Arrivals	
		US$ billions	% of world total	millions	% of world total
1	United States	14.1	12.9	19.3	5.8
2	Italy	8.8	8.0	25.0	7.5
3	Spain	8.1	7.4	27.5	8.3
4	France	7.9	7.2	36.7	11.0
5	United Kingdom	7.0	6.4	14.5	4.4
6	Austria	6.0	5.5	15.1	4.5
7	West Germany	5.9	5.4	12.7	3.8
	Top seven countries	57.8	52.7	150.8	45.3
	Rest of world	51.8	47.3	182.2	54.7
	World total	109.6	100.0	333.0	100.0

Arrivals data are less meaningful expressed in percentages of the world total because some tourists visit more than one destination on the same journey.

Table 8 International tourist arrivals by nature of destination economy, 1981 and 1985 (adapted from WTO, 1986, vol. 1).

Nature of destination economy	Number of visitors (thousands)		Share of world total (%)	
	1981	1985	1981	1985
Low income economies	10,814	21,077	3.74	6.33
Lower middle income economies	17,169	20,696	5.94	6.22
Upper middle income economies	34,786	43,746	12.04	13.14
High income oil exporters	254	223	0.09	0.07
Industrial market economies	178,039	197,202	61.64	59.22
East European nonmarket economies	37,342	38,665	12.93	11.61

The classifications used are based on those adopted by UNCTAD.
The sums of these columns do not agree with the data in Tables 1 and 3 because of incomplete reporting.

Table 9 International tourism receipts by nature of destination economy, 1981 and 1985 (adapted from WTO, 1986, vol. 1).

Nature of destination economy	Receipts (US$ millions)		Share of world total (%)	
	1981	1985	1981	1985
Low income economies	2,820	3,052	2.70	2.79
Lower middle income economies	6,514	8,846	6.25	8.07
Upper middle income economies	19,570	16,306	18.76	14.88
High income oil exporters	2,036	2,493	1.95	2.28
Industrial market economies	66,488	71,807	63.75	65.54
East European nonmarket economies	1,392	1,433	1.33	1.31

The classifications used are based on those adopted by UNCTAD.
The sums of these columns do not agree with Tables 1 and 3 because of incomplete reporting.

Factors affecting future trends

Of the factors likely to affect the demand for international tourism during the next 10 years, some are largely or partly outside the control of the destination countries, others can be influenced by the manner in which tourism is managed and developed in the host country.

The principal long-term factors affecting demand are demographic changes, the amount of leisure and holiday time, changes in consumer preferences and economic growth in the main generating countries. Among the short-term factors at work are the costs of travel, relative prices and exchange rates, marketing and promotion, as well as extraneous factors including legal and political difficulties and wars.

Many of these factors are the subject of other papers in this Handbook, but it is pertinent to examine in this context the findings of a recent forecasting study by the Economist Intelligence Unit (1985). The principal factors considered in the study were as follows:

1. Projected changes in real household disposable incomes.
2. Projected changes in the costs of travel abroad relative to domestic prices.
3. Other time-related growth trends.
4. Constraints imposing a 'ceiling' on travel abroad during the period under consideration (up to 1995). The 'ceiling' was determined in terms of the amount of time available for foreign travel by the employed population of the main origin countries.

The Economist Intelligence Unit forecast that, after an expansion during 1973–1983 of under 6 per cent per annum in real tourist expenditure (including fares), growth would rise to 7 per cent per annum up to 1990 and then to 8 per cent per annum during 1990–1995. The consequences would be at least a doubling of real tourism expenditure by 1995. The researchers also forecast that by 1995 Japan would become the second largest tourist expenditure-generating country after West Germany, with the United States and United Kingdom in third and fourth places, and with Saudi Arabia moving into fifth place to overtake both France and Canada. In terms of nights spent abroad however, the present five main origin countries would maintain their positions in the league (Table 4), largely because of their substantial shorthaul origin travel. Longhaul travel's share of the market from the twenty principal origin countries was forecast to increase significantly over the period 1983–1995 – in terms of number of visitors from 6.1 per cent to 8.5 per cent; visitor nights from 27.3 to 32.9 per cent and visitor expenditure from 37 to 44.9 per cent. Among the main generating countries, higher than average rises in longhaul traffic were forecast for France and the United Kingdom.

Conclusion

On a world scale fewer than 4 per cent of the world's population take international holidays and 80 per cent of international demand is generated by less than 20 countries. Although the *rate* of growth in world travel has fallen each decade since the 1960s, the absolute growth has been very substantial. Income increases have been more than sufficient to offset the effects of price rises. Tourism has proved remarkably resilient in the long run to the effects of wars and other extraneous influences. The available research suggests that growth will continue well into the next century and that the rate of increase is unlikely to fall and may even rise over the next 10 years.

Further reading

Cleverdon, R., *International Business Travel: A New Megamarket* (Economist Intelligence Unit, 1985).

Edwards, A., *International Tourism Forecasts to 1995*, Economist Intelligence Unit Special Report no. 188 (April 1985).

Leisure Consultants, *Leisure Forecasts 1987–1991* (Leisure Consultants, 1986). Analysis and forecasts of several leisure sectors including UK inward and outward international tourism. Annual forecasts of trip numbers and consumer spending on holiday accommodation (with no origin/destination country breakdown).

Tourism Management (vol. 8, no. 2, June 1987) contains the proceedings of the international conference on *Tourism in the 1990s* held in London in November 1986. Papers of particular relevance are:

Chew, J., 'Transport and tourism in the year 2,000', pp. 83–5.

Davies, E., 'Shaping tourism trends – the commercial perspective', pp. 102–4.

Frechtling, D. C., 'Key issues in tourism futures', pp. 106–11.

Lickorish, L., 'Trends in industrialized countries', pp. 92–5.

Martin, W. H. and Mason, S., 'Social trends and tourism futures', pp. 112–14.

Rodrigues, C. J., 'European travel – the way ahead', pp. 134–6.

Shackleford, P., 'Global tourism trends', pp. 98–101.

World Tourism Organization, *Regional Breakdown of World Travel and Tourism Statistics 1980–1984* (WTO, 1985).

World Tourism Organization, *Yearbook of Tourism Statistics*, vols. 1 & 2 (WTO, 1986).

World Travel Overview 1986/87 (American Express Publishing Corporation, 1986). Econometric analysis and forecasts of US outward international travel. Annual forecasts of visitor numbers and expenditure for main destination countries up to 1990. Visitor numbers also split by purpose (business, holiday, visits to friends and relatives).

BRIAN H. ARCHER

Trends in leisure and tourism for 2000–2010: scenario with consequences for planners

Introduction

It is usually predicted that the economic and social climate over the next 20 years will produce a strong increase in tourism. Although there are clearly discernible limits to the growth of tourist demand in the industrialized countries, new markets will emerge, due to changing economic conditions, modified consumer behavior and new technologies. Increasing leisure time will be allocated to other uses besides travel. The composition of the tourist population will alter, with increasing proportions of, for example, senior citizens. There will be greater emphasis on individual/self-determined holidays, and on educational and active recreational pursuits. Increasing environmental awareness will affect planning policies and tourist demand, but natural environments, the critical resource of tourism, will become scarcer. An ecological, long-term approach to tourism planning is postulated.

This scenario deals with the probable trends in leisure time and tourism until the years 2000–2010. Reference is made particularly to the situation in the industrialized countries of Western Europe. The aim is not to present a definitive picture of developments over this period. It is far more important for this scenario to help the planners concerned with leisure time and tourism to come to terms with future changes than merely to describe future conditions. Thus we must examine any distinguishable and important trends with a view to answering the question: 'What decisions have to be taken now or in the coming years to make adjustment to these trends possible, in good time?'

Although the subject of this scenario is defined by the terms 'leisure time' and 'tourism', certain statements are made which deliberately transcend rigid boundaries between disciplines so that more general lines of thought are not discounted from the start. This chapter deals with a base scenario which portrays the most likely trends on the strength of a critical study of the most important sources. The various interactive factors considered are shown in Fig. 1. Low probability and high impact events, such as the effects of major military conflict or collapse of the economic system, are not considered, as these would require the preparation of crisis or catastrophe scenarios.

Economic aspects

According to most futurologists, the economic future will be characterized by greater amounts of freely disposable income, an increasing proportion of city dwellers and a further fall in working hours for employees. Even if it is assumed that the rate of these changes will slow down, experts a few years ago anticipated considerable rates of growth for tourism between 1980 and 2000:

1. The World Tourism Organization (WTO) anticipated an annual growth rate of arrivals in cross-border tourism to be between 4.5 and 5.5 per cent (Krippendorf, 1979, p. 6).
2. Half the experts in the Swiss Delphi poll anticipated growth rates in the region of 3 to 3.5 per cent, in other words, approximately a doubling of the number of tourist arrivals within 20 years (Krippendorf, 1979, p. 6; Kibedi, 1981).
3. Herman Kahn forecast that in the year 2000 tourism will be the largest industry and the most important export sector in the world. He calculated that by then expenditure on tourism may well have risen fivefold, corresponding to an annual growth rate of about 8 per cent (Kahn, 1979).

More recent estimates from the United Kingdom go even beyond these growth rates (Lickorish, 1987): the Economist Intelligence Unit (EIU) forecasts world tourist spending (including fares and in constant 1983 US dollars) will almost quadruple within only 10 years, from 100×10^9 (US billion) in 1985 to 367×10^9 in 1995. For countries in the Organization for Economic Cooperation and Development (OECD), the Honorary Vice-Chairman of the European Travel Commission (ETC) reckons on travel expansion that could even be superior to the massive expansion of the past. (The average per annum growth rate of international arrivals was 9.7 per cent between 1964 and 1985, in the sample of the 12 countries comparable over that period [OECD, 1965; 1986].)

Yet in the traditional industrial countries the economic perspective is generally one of greatly decelerated growth and stagnating disposable per capita incomes. Even today, the desire to travel in these countries seems to get close to saturation levels, and sensitivity to prices is increasing (Mazanec, 1982).

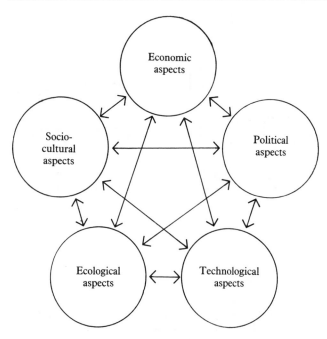

Figure 1 The interaction of relevant dimensions contributing to the scenario of future trends in leisure and tourism.

The limits to tourist expansion are already detectable. The forecasts mentioned above for growth in tourism, particularly that by Herman Kahn, are likely to be over-optimistic to some extent, at least as far as the traditional industrialized nations are concerned (note also that the WTO has revised its forecast downwards to 1990 [Chew, 1987]). In countries like Switzerland, Sweden and Norway the net travel intensities (percentage of travelers in the overall population), which are over 75 per cent, are not likely to increase significantly anymore. In several large countries, however, where the variance of travel intensities between urban and rural areas is larger, e.g. France, West Germany, United Kingdom (net travel intensities between 57 and 60 per cent), there is still some growth potential (Edwards and Cleverdon, 1982).

Energy costs

It is remarkable how rarely the energy problem is addressed in connection with future trends in tourism. The conclusion to be drawn from three large-scale energy studies (by the World Energy Conference, International Institute of Applied Systems Analysis [IIASA] and Exxon) is that, globally speaking in the long term, we must expect bottlenecks in the supply of energy (Fells, 1982). This contrasts with the possibility, which according to Vester exists in principle, of reducing total energy demand by 40 per cent without a consequent loss of output (Vester, 1984). On balance, there is reason to suppose that, notwithstanding temporary slumps of oil prices, the period of cheap energy is over – at least for some decades to come. If, as predicted, fuel costs rise appreciably, we can expect the following:

1. There will be an accelerated shift from private to public means of transport.
2. Potential longhaul tourist flights will be replaced by shorter ones.
3. Business trips will be replaced by communication via satellite to a greater extent than would otherwise have been the case.
4. Unprofitable domestic air traffic routes will be superseded and highspeed trains will come to the fore.

It is to be assumed that such phenomena will occur in the 1990s, and for the following reason: if the price per unit of fossil energy increases in real terms by 6 to 8 per cent per year, in other words if it doubles within about 10 years, it will only be possible to offset part of this extra cost by appropriate rationalization★ and better occupancy rates. This could, in the long term, result in increases in transport tariffs which would have a dampening effect on the growth of travel and the economy in general (Guldimann, 1983). That may turn out to be an important constraint on longhaul tourism in general. Yet, even if European longhaul flights expand less than forecast (Rodrigues, 1987), the trend which promises to make the Asia-Pacific region 'the boom area for tourism by the year 2000' (Chew, 1987) will not be jeopardized, due to the enormous 'internal' potential of that area.

The informal economy

Although there are discrepancies between the forecasts, and differences in opinion (particularly with regard to the prospective growth in expenditure for tourist consumption) it should be indisputable that there will be a further long-term increase in leisure time, although probably at a lower rate than in the past (Owen, 1979). The question arises as to whether the extra free time available outside the professional sphere will be used by individuals for consumer purposes or for productive purposes and in each case to what extent.

We can see today that the 'informal' sector of the economy is on the increase. By this we mean the productive activities which are not recorded in the national accounts, such as housework, DIY, social work in self-help groups, social networks and so on. This informal sector will probably continue to increase in importance (Toffler, 1981).

Demand and supply

Even though the volume of travel in the industrialized countries has grown considerably, the tourist market worldwide has changed from a seller's market to a buyer's market. On a global scale, competition from new developing destinations and facilities will increase further. Significant structural changes in progress give a rough idea of how the situation might appear in 15 to 20 years time.

On the supply side, there has been a disproportionate increase in the types of lodging provided by the 'parahotel' business in

----

★ This assumption seems plausible in the light of a fuel scenario conceived by Dr Zumstein and the author at St Gall Management Centre.

relation to the traditional hotel business. In addition, a major proportion of traditional hotels have had to develop new product strategies to match the growing demand for more active holidays. Holiday clubs, parks and villages, and hotels offering active leisure pursuits, are experiencing higher than average increases in demand. It is likely that the market share of the traditional hotel types will continue to shrink.

If increasing leisure time leads to an increase in the time spent on holiday trips*, it is likely that tourist demand will demonstrate a reduction in the nightly average expenditure budget. There will be a resultant increase in the willingness to spend holidays in cheaper accommodation, with a lower volume of services consumed, and to reduce the distances traveled as well. Opinion polls have shown that if the need arose to make cutbacks, people in West Germany and Austria said holidays and journeys would be the first items that they would cut back on (Emnid Institute, 1982; Austrian Chamber of Commerce, 1982), while people in Switzerland placed them in fourth place behind jewellery, confectionery, radio/television equipment and furnishings (Scope Institute, 1982). Those questioned did not explicitly state that they would shorten the length of their holidays.

A price-elastic tourist demand need not necessarily imply an end to all travel – after all, travel as such has become close to being a 'basic need' – but is more likely to result in demand for cheaper holidays. Thus, the market share of low-price accommodation will probably rise. If, as expected, the price elasticity of tourist demand increases, we can look forward to further significant shifts in market shares among the various countries (Shackleford, 1979). Swiss experts, however, do not believe that the market share enjoyed by Switzerland will change radically by the year 2010 (Krippendorf, 1979, p. 18).

Seasonal variation

Efforts to reduce the seasonal fluctuations in tourist flows will make further progress. In line with the growth rates for supply and demand, this will have an impact on occupancy, profitability and the ability of tourist facilities to adapt to changing needs. Better and more varied products will probably be available for off-season periods.

Sociodemographic change

The following segments of the tourist market are likely to gain in relative importance and therefore grow at above average rates (AIEST, 1985): senior citizens and active middle-aged persons between 50 and 65 (also called 'young' senior citizens), singles (particularly those under 35), 'YUPs' (Young Urban Professionals), guest workers, youngsters (the number of young people traveling is increasing rapidly but supply is not yet well geared to them), young families, double income families (particularly 'Dinks': double income, no kids). Psychographic and lifestyle segmentations will identify more specific clusters of travelers.

---

* Such an increase will not be proportional. A decreasing marginal propensity to travel with further growth of free time available is probable (see comments on alternative pastimes, below).

Sociocultural aspects

Research carried out in several countries, in particular a large-scale study by the Stanford Research Institute, indicates that there is a clearly defined trend away from an 'outward-directed' lifestyle towards 'inward-directed' and 'integrated' values (cf. Mitchell, 1981). Several recent studies (Krippendorf, 1987) indicate that 'post-materialistic values' (growing nonmaterialistic needs, environmental care, diminishing concerns about career, prestige and status etc.) will gain in importance. Materialistic lifestyles will not vanish, but a polarization between exponents of material and nonmaterial values is likely to take place.

A strong trend is leading away from standardization towards an ever greater diversity in lifestyles and incites new approaches to life and recreation. The limits of mass tourism are recognizable not only from the quantitative, but also from the qualitative point of view. The following trends are apparent and probably of a long-term nature (Schwaninger, 1984):

1. Further increasing differentiation and pluralization of demand.
2. Emergence of new specialized markets and market segments.
3. A decrease of physically and culturally passive forms of vacation in favor of more active pastimes.
4. A shift towards maximizing individual liberty in recombining elements for custom-made holiday packages (modular product design).

The growing need for nonstandardized services and individualized tourist behavior is directly linked to the following:

1. The quest for self-determination (emancipation) and 'do-it-yourself'.
2. The advanced level of travel experience in the population, which goes hand in hand with more selective, critical and quality-oriented approaches to individual holiday planning as well as growing sophistication of demand and rationality of choice.
3. An increasing desire to relate to nature, to gain first-hand experience and to engage in active pastimes (e.g. 'hobby holidays', trekking holidays, farm tourism);
4. Higher levels of environmental consciousness and sensitivity to the quality of life in general.
5. The increasing effort to learn, which often manifests itself in serious attempts to get to know foreign cultures.

The suppliers of tourist services will increasingly offer service packages which directly address specific customer problems and provide travelers with more opportunity to shape their holidays as they wish. 'Activities, experiences, participation and learning will all be key elements in the future' (Martin and Mason, 1987). Adventure holidays, sports and health trips, sabbaticals and learning holidays will all become more popular. The demand for 'soft' forms of transport and tourism, including 'back-to-nature' activities will show a marked increase. Overall, an increasing share of tourists will procure a 'holistic' type of recreation, trying to avoid one-sidedness and in search of an 'overall balance' of body, soul and mind. More and more travelers will define their concept of a 'rich holiday' rather in terms of the depth than in terms of the diversity of their travel experiences.

Not only will the worldwide travel market itself be characterized by an ever greater range of possible types of travel and destinations, but competition from substitutes will also continue to increase. The range of alternative uses to which free time can be put is constantly expanding, a trend which is likely to continue over the next 20 years. Apart from travel, these options can be characterized as follows:

Leisure within the home (or in the vicinity)

Leisure-oriented design of living space, children's playgrounds near to dwellings, public leisure facilities in residential areas, centers or leisure parks, green-belt areas around cities will all be central to current leisure policies.

Education and further training

To a certain and ever increasing extent, life is becoming a permanent learning process owing to the rapid rate of change in professional structures and technologies. The spectrum of educational facilities and opportunities is being continually enriched, even though the educational and professional routes are further being formalized, under the direction of public institutions. Nevertheless, there is a clear trend towards the pluralization and liberalization of education and training in general, thanks to private initiatives: companies set up their own training centers and training courses, groups of individuals form their own educational establishments based on progressive and 'alternative' pedagogic concepts, and so on. This applies to all levels, from primary school to university, but especially to training in specific technologies, skills or professional profiles.

Schools of the future will not be institutions for imparting knowledge so much as integrated centers for education, culture and leisure.

Use of leisure time for productive purposes

The following variants are relevant:

1. Paid work to increase disposable income.
2. Home-based production, which means not only a greater degree of self-service on the basis of tasks 'delegated' by industry to the consumer (such as collecting, assembling, repairing and maintaining products) but also increased production of an agricultural or handicraft type. This type of production is often carried out on a community basis.
3. Sociocultural: this category includes all types of social, political and cultural involvement. The social cooperation networks which even today are expanding rapidly and which in 20 years are likely to supply a significant proportion of social services, are a prominent example.

In view of the expansion of the 'informal' economy and a certain shift, for technological reasons, of professional activities to the traditional domicile, the boundaries between leisure time, work and living are becoming increasingly hazy. Also the individual will have more opportunities to arrange his working hours and leisure time as he pleases. Flexitime, job-splitting, job-sharing, individual arrangements regarding holidays and pensions etc. will become commonplace.

Ecological aspects

Concern for the environment will be in future far more widespread among the population than it is today. The growing appreciation that man and nature share a common fate will have promoted a conservationist approach at many levels. Even today, we can see an increasing environmental awareness in public opinion. This manifests itself in a growing tendency to reject those foreign tourist spots which have already exceeded their tolerance levels, not only in the opinion of the experts but also from the point of view of the consumers (Krippendorf, 1979, p. 92).

The inhabitants of tourist areas, some of whom have exchanged their initial euphoria at the influx of tourists for blatant resistance, will increasingly adopt realistic strategies to retain their independence and protect their environment. For example, the dilemma facing mountain regions concerning the balance between destruction of the landscape by tourist monoculture, and desolation on account of depopulation, will be handled better than it is today, by means of multi-faceted development – revalorization of mountain farming, including unconventional methods such as game farming, vegetable cultures, and blending with other branches of the economy.

The planning authorities and political institutions, thanks largely to the pressure of public opinion, will contribute to a development in the interests of man and the environment, by defining appropriate planning guidelines and ensuring that they are followed.

In many areas, however, this effort will come too late in view of the high level of destruction that has already taken place. Destruction of natural resources vital to tourism will not be stopped immediately. As a consequence, decline of some traditional destination areas (due to gradual spoilage or, in some cases, due to environmental catastrophes) and rise of 'substitutes' in unspoiled surroundings will probably continue (unfortunately) to a certain extent. Furthermore, artificial leisure environments will be created as a partial (and weak) compensation for the degraded natural milieu; these are increasingly evident in many destination areas. Such developments will continue until society implements tourism strategies which reconcile man and nature (Swiss MAB, 1983–1987; Krippendorf, 1987).

On the other hand, growing environmental sensitivity is likely to stimulate substantial efforts to protect, conserve and upgrade the natural as well as the sociocultural milieu. In response to a question raised by a WTO exponent (Shackleford, 1987), we maintain that the demand for 'soft forms of tourism' will be a volume market by 2010, or even 2000. On the supply side, it is to be hoped that there will be a change towards a long-term planning mentality, which should substitute for narrow-mindedness and shortsighted profit-maximization.

Even the best hotels and restaurants in tourist resorts can only thrive if they are embedded in an intact environment. An ecologically viable strategy is the prime prerequisite for success.

As far as the provision of accommodation facilities is concerned, already a dramatic rearrangement of priorities, due to growing environmental awareness, has begun. If in the past the accent was on the erection of new buildings, the future should see a comprehensive program of renovation: according to a Delphi poll, by 2010 40 per cent of all Swiss hotels will have to be completely renovated (Krippendorf, 1979, p. 55). The transformation of historic buildings or other old buildings into training and leisure establishments, and the shaping of the environment to accommodate leisure activities, both in the home and its close vicinity, will gain considerably in importance.

Technological aspects

Technological developments will have serious effects, particularly in those areas where originally isolated technologies can be combined. In the leisure sector, this applies primarily to the converging technologies of telecommunications, data processing and office machines.

An increasing proportion of professional work will not be site-dependent. This leads not only to new forms of social organization and interaction but also to a certain shift of professional activity to the home of the working individual. Thus, the boundaries between work, living and leisure time become less rigidly defined.

The new technologies give rise to new sales and distribution systems. New economic groupings engaged in the battle for the holiday visitor (banks, clothing and sports shops, supermarkets, restaurants, lottery kiosks and petrol stations) are at present complicating the established network of sales channels. In the years to come, however, electronic distribution, for example, will lead to drastic structural change, including substitution of existing sales channels. The Imholz travel agency, which a few years ago almost completely replaced the traditional booking of holidays in branch offices by telephone bookings, is a precursor of this development and gives some idea of the possibilities. Another example is the airlines business, where computerization will stimulate innovation, dictate structural changes among airlines and travel agents. The quest for more efficient distribution will also lead to new alliances within and between firms of these sectors.

Yet, computerized services will also breed new opportunities for those travel agents who will succeed in counselling their customers better. The new technologies will further specialization. New types of travel agencies will emerge, which will have the character of consulting rather than of booking agencies, using information systems to design individualized travel packages out of available offers (Bruce, 1987).

According to a report to the Club of Rome, microelectronics will lead to a stagnation or fall in employment in certain service industries, at least for some time (trade, banks, insurance companies, public administration, offices, information, rail and sea

transport). In the branches which form the subject of this chapter (air transport, education, hotels, restaurants) and a few others (research and development, social services in the widest sense, including health, welfare, counselling, rehabilitation, road transport) however, there should be a positive effect on employment, spurred on by developments in the field of microelectronics and optronics (Friedrichs and Schaff, 1982).

Political aspects

The influence of public institutions on the leisure sector will continue to grow. Sociopolitical motives, as part of the effort to humanize working conditions, are aimed at reducing the statutory number of working hours and to promote the involvement of companies and public authorities in the field of leisure policies. Economic motives are aimed at sharing out an evidently shrinking volume of human work so that full employment is guaranteed.

Particularly in tourism, there is a trend towards increasing amounts of planning and also protectionist intervention at national and international levels. Positive efforts to curtail the ecologically damaging effects of human leisure activities are being taken more and more seriously, and are meeting with some success.

Political and planning decisions in our society take longer the less they are based purely on the representation principle. For some years now, there have been increasing demands for participation by the people concerned, for example inhabitants of tourist regions. In future, these demands will be better met than has so far been the case. Not only is the view gaining ground that incorporation of those concerned in the planning processes leads to better results, but there are better and better means available which contribute to the efficient handling of such complex decision processes (cf. Schwaninger, 1987).

Prospects for planners

It was stated at the start of this chapter that this scenario represented the 'most likely' trends. These trends are based on the realistic premise that not only individuals, but also our institutional and social systems, retain a capacity to learn.

In the past, plans often covered too short a period and were too one-sided – two characteristics which commonly go hand in hand. This had undesirable ecological, social and also economic consequences which were often of a long-term nature and, in some cases, irreversible.

The most important challenges faced by those responsible for planning in the leisure and tourist sector, and those affected by it, can be summarized as follows.

Integral planning
It is necessary to replace the old dominating and unidimensional planning concepts with integral, systematic planning which would be more adequate to cope with the complexity of

real systems. From the field of cybernetics we know that one-sided planning jeopardizes self-regulation and thus the viability of a system: if a leisure facility or a holiday location is planned from the basis of a single viewpoint (be it exclusively economic, technological, ecological, social or esthetic) the outcome can only be unsatisfactory. Integral planning calls for the incorporation of all these aspects and components of knowledge in the process of analysis and design. Thus it is not only interdisciplinary but also transdisciplinary in character. Namely, to realize socially and ecologically viable strategies (which will be high priority issues in many destinations) such planning should not be limited to consulting reports. All constituents ('stakeholders') that embody relevant knowledge (and 'stakes') should contribute to the planning process (for applications, see Ackoff, 1981). In a tourist resort, not only representatives of tourist institutions and hotels should be included, but also exponents of sectors such as trade, agriculture and forestry and, ultimately, all citizens.

Long-term thinking

The attractiveness of advantages expected in the short term is often in conflict with the need to obtain long-term facilities, in other words to care for and build up the resources which will form the basis for the future. The knowledge gained over the past few years on the long-term nature of fundamental cause-and-effect relationships inherent in tourism business systems requires us today, more than ever, to think strategically. Thinking in terms of large-scale, long-term relationships gives us the opportunity to concentrate on overall targets, such as the maintenance of a healthy natural environment, without being led astray by short-term fluctuations. In many destinations, the design of ecological policies and strategies will be of primary importance to maintain long-term viability. These postulates are substantiated in the chapter on *Strategic Management in Tourism* p. 425.

Consistent action

With regard to leisure and tourism a number of plans and concepts have been elaborated, which contain a considerable amount of integral planning and long-term thinking (see, for example, Advisory Committee on Tourism of the Swiss Government, 1979). 'Strategic plans' or 'policies' are essential foundations for coherent action in the future. Putting them into practice requires commitment of decision makers at all levels. A legal framework of tourist policy will be helpful, but the understanding of those concerned is the essential prerequisite for commitment. This holds particularly when short-term sacrifices are necessary in order to maintain long-term viability, for instance, when ecological strategies are at stake. Also in this respect, the basis for effective implementation of strategy is set by involving the constituents of the system in its design.

Further reading

Ackoff, R. L., *Creating the Corporate Future* (John Wiley, 1981), p. 65 *et seq*; 163 *et seq*.

Advisory Committee on Tourism of the Swiss Government, *Schweizerisches Tourismuskonzept* (The Swiss Tourism Concept), (Swiss Transport and Energy Department, 1979).

Association Internationale des Experts Scientifiques du Tourisme, *Trends of Tourist Demand* (AIEST, 1985).

Austrian Chamber of Commerce Poll, *Tiroler Tageszeitung* (23 December 1982), p. 9.

Bruce, M., 'New technology and the future of tourism', *Tourism Management*, vol. 8, no. 2 (June 1987), p. 119.

Chew, J., 'Transport and tourism in the year 2000', *Tourism Management*, vol. 8, no. 2 (June 1987), p. 83.

Edwards, A. and Cleverdon, R., *International Tourism to 1990* (Abt Books, 1982), pp. 29–37.

Emnid Institute Poll, *Die Welt* (August 1982).

Fells, I., 'Energieperspektiven für das 21. Jahrhundert' (Energy prospects for the 21st century), *Neue Zürcher Zeitung* (21 April 1982), p. 63.

Friedrichs, G. and Schaff, A., eds, *Microelectronics and Society: For Better or Worse: A Report to the Club of Rome* (Pergamon Press, 1982).

Guldimann, W., 'Luftverkehr an der Jahrtausendwende' (Air transport at the turn of the century), *Neue Zürcher Zeitung* (8–9 January 1983), p. 31.

Kahn, H., *Die Zukunft der Welt 1980–2000* (The Future of the World 1980–2000), (Molden, 1979), p. 297.

Kibedi, G., 'Future trends in international tourism', *Tourist Review*, vol. 36, no. 1 (1981), p. 3. Results of a Delphi Poll commissioned by the International Tourism Symposium in Washington DC, which made a virtually identical forecast to that of Krippendorf.

Krippendorf, J., *Tourismus in Jahre 2010 – eine Delphi-Umfrage über die zukünftige Entwicklung des Tourismus in der Schweiz – Interpre-tionen und Schlussfolgerungen* (Tourism in the year 2010 – a Delphi Poll on Future Trends in Tourism in Switzerland – Interpretations and Conclusions), (Forschungsinstitut für Fremdenverkehr, 2nd edition, 1979).

Krippendorf, J., 'Ecological approach to tourism marketing', *Tourism Management*, vol. 8. no. 2 (June 1987a), p. 176. Cites a Delphi study on travel needs by the year 2000 by the Swiss Corso Group in 1984 and the Romeiss-Stracke study on tourism and new lifestyles, 1985.

Krippendorf, J., *Là-haut sur la Montagne. Pour un Développement du Tourisme en Harmonie avec l'Homme et la Nature* (Kummerly and Frey, 1987b).

Lickorish, L., 'Trends in industrialized countries', *Tourism Management*, vol. 8, no. 2 (June 1987), p. 93.

Martin, W. H. and Mason, S., 'Social trends and tourism future', *Tourism Management*, vol. 8, no. 2 (June 1987), p. 112.

Mazanec, J., 'The tourism leisure ratio, anticipating limits to growth', *Tourist Review*, vol. 36, no. 4 (1981), pp. 2–12; *Hotel Review*, vol. 17 (1982), p. 5.

Mitchell, A. and MacNulty, C., 'Changing values and life styles', *Long Range Planning*, vol. 4 (1981), pp. 37–41.

Organization for Economic Cooperation and Development, *Tourisme International et Politique du Tourisme dans les Pays de l'OCDE* (1965 and 1986).

Owen, J. D., *Working Hours – An Economic Analysis* (Lexington Books, 1979), pp. 12 ff.

Rodrigues, C. J., 'European travel – the way ahead', *Tourism Management*, vol. 8, no. 2 (June 1987), p. 134.

Schwaninger, M., 'Forecasting leisure and tourism', *Tourism Management* (December 1984), pp. 250–7. Compare with: 'Proceedings of the international conference on tourism in the 1990s, November 1986', *Tourism Management*, vol. 8, no. 2 (June 1987).

Schwaninger, M., 'A practical approach to strategy development', *Long Range Planning*, vol. 20, no. 5 (1987), pp. 74–85.

Scope Institute, *Schweizer Handelszeitung* (1 April 1982).

Shackleford, P., 'Planning for tourism', *Futures*, vol. 11, no. 1 (February 1979), pp. 32–43.

Shackleford, P., 'Global tourism trends', *Tourism Management*, vol. 8. no. 2 (June 1987), p. 101.

Swiss MAB (Man and Biosphere) Program, *Final Reports* (1983–1987).

Toffler, A., *The Third Wave* (Bantam Books, 1981).

Vester, F., *Neuland des Denkens* (New Modes of Thought), (DTV, 1984).

MARKUS SCHWANINGER

Appendix I
General information
sources and databases

The chapter on *Tourism Information Systems* contains detailed information regarding several major information sources and databases. A more general selection of information sources and databases is briefly reviewed in this section.

American Express Publishing Corporation, *World Travel Overview*, New York, annual. Contains statistical information on travel patterns, with the emphasis on US tourism.

Anbar Management Publications, *Marketing and Distribution Abstracts (Personnel and Training, Marketing and Distribution, Top Management)*, Wembley, UK. Published eight times yearly (in association with the Institute of Marketing) to provide information on research/currently published articles in these areas, including those concerned with tourism.

Baretje, R., *Etudes et Mémoires*, Centre des Etudes Touristiques, Aix-en-Provence, France. Contains a comprehensive inventory of the world literature on tourism. Over 25 volumes have been issued to date and have recorded over 36,500 documents (which are housed in the Centre) classified according to subjects, countries and authors. Computerized.

British Tourist Authority and English Tourist Board, *Research Publications Available from the British Tourist Authority and English Tourist Board*, London. Reports and publications of the two tourist authorities. A useful guide to sources of statistical material.

CAB (Commonwealth Agricultural Bureau) International, *Leisure, Recreation and Tourism Abstracts*, Bureau of Agricultural Economics, Oxford, UK, quarterly. All abstracts are available worldwide as a subfile in the CAB ABSTRACTS-Database (on DIALOG). The single internationally accessible online database concerned only with the literature on tourism and related subjects.

CACI INC, *Market America*, Fairfax, Virginia. Online database providing retrieval of demographics (census and updates), sales potential, and market segmentation information for any US area.

Data Courier, *ABI/INFORM*, Louisville. This computerized database contains periodical citations on articles that deal with all aspects of business management and administration, including those concerned with tourism. Available on DIALOG.

Finsbury Data Services, *Textline*, London. Online database covering over 1,000 newspapers and trade journals. Particularly relevant are specialist databases D: Marketing and Media, and K: Travel.

Horwath and Horwath International, *Worldwide Hotel Industry*, New York, annual. Contains statistical results of a survey of hotels around the world.

Hotel, Catering and Institutional Management Association, *Bibliography of Hotel and Catering Management*, London, quarterly. Covers articles in over 60 related periodicals.

International Air Transport Association, *ISIS (IATA Statistical Information System)*, Geneva. A computerized database relating to commercial air transport.

International Air Transport Association, *World Air Transport Statistics*, Geneva, annual. The authoritative source of worldwide airline statistics.

Marketing Institute International Corp., *Business Referral Network*, Washington DC. Online database which helps cultivate and target organizations, individuals, and other business people for business development and helps establish a network of key companies and individuals that either refer business to your firm or to which business is referred.

Nettleton Travel Research Center, *Nettleton Travel Research Reports*, Virginia. Statistical analysis of monthly international airline traffic departing from and arriving in the United States.

Organization for Economic Cooperation and Development, *Tourism Policy and International Tourism in OECD Member Countries*, Paris, annual. Contains statistical information on tourism in 24 OECD member countries. Also economic analysis of tourism trends and recent government policy actions.

Pacific Asia Travel Association, *Annual Statistical Report*, San Francisco, annual. Contains statistical information on tourism in 30 Pacific/Asia nations.

Pannell, Kerr, Foster Worldwide, *Trends in the Hotel Industry, International Edition*, Huston, annual. Contains the statistical results of a survey of hotels around the world.

Tourism Canada, *Tourism Reference and Data Centre (TRDC)*, Ottawa. The Centre maintains the most comprehensive online collection of tourism-related information in Canada, and covers over 5,000 documents.

Tourism Society, *Tourism Society Annual*, London. Contains statistical information covering all sectors of the UK tourism industry.

University of Colorado in conjunction with the Travel and Tourism Research Association, *Travel Reference Center*, Business Research Division, University of Colorado, Boulder. Contains over 8,000 travel, recreation and tourism documents to date, the largest collection of tourism-related research studies available in the United States. Cataloged by C. R. Goeldner and K. Dicke in the nine-volume *Bibliography of Tourism and Travel Research Studies, Reports and Articles*. Computerized.

University of Surrey, Oxford Polytechnic and Dorset Institute of Higher Education Libraries, *Articles in Hospitality and Tourism*, UK. A monthly cross-indexed listing of articles appearing in 60 periodicals and journals.

US Department of Transportation and Transportation Research Board, *TRIS (Transportation Research Information Service)*, Washington, DC. An online database giving information on modes of transport. Provides abstracts of documents, data holdings, and research reports.

US Travel Data Center, *Economic Review of Travel in America*, Washington DC., annual. The authoritative source of data on travel and tourism in the United States.

US Travel Data Center, *US Travel Data Bank*, Washington, DC. Online access to information including spending, Travel Price Index, travel flow analyses, and traveler demographic data.

Waters R., *Travel Industry World Yearbook*, *The Big Picture*, Child and Waters Inc., New York, annual. Compendium of global tourism statistics.

World Tourism Organization, *Yearbook of Tourism Statistics*, Madrid, annual. The most comprehensive collection of official government tourism statistics available, covering 140 countries and territories.

Appendix 2
Computer software

APM (**Adaptive Perceptual Mapping**), Sawtooth Software, Ketchum, ID, USA. The APM System's interview learns which products are familiar to the respondent and which attributes are important (up to 30 products and 50 attributes), then asks only relevant questions. Besides producing traditional maps, APM has a simulator that lets you alter respondents' perceptions of products or insert new products, then estimate the likely effects of marketing those changes.

Close, Close Corp., 125 Cambridge Park Dr., Cambridge, MA 02140, USA. Closed-loop sales and marketing productivity system consisting of a central marketing database. It integrates five stand alone, module systems – direct mail, inquiry response and tracking, filed sales support, and management analysis and planning; used on IBM mainframes.

Conquest Consumer Information System, Donnelley Marketing Information Services, Stamford, CT, USA. Identifies emerging markets, selects new services for existing markets, evaluates retail sites, develops target marketing programs, and creates advertising strategies.

Encore, Ferox microsystems Inc., Suite 1205, 1701 N. Fort Myer Dr., Arlington, VA 22209, USA. Sales analysis, new product analysis, and pricing analysis. Usable on IBM-compatible micros, MS-DOS.

Forecast Plus, Walonick Associates, 6500 Nicollet Ave. S., Minneapolis, MN 55423, USA. A forecasting package containing various forecasting routines; also permits model-building using regression analysis. Usable on microcomputers.

John Deighton, Hanover, New Hampshire, USA. Mapping of cross-tabulation tables. Finds the best spatial representation of a table's row and column elements, and plots the two-dimensional solution; it can be used to create product positioning maps.

Lotus 123, Lotus Development Corporation, Consort House, Victoria Street, Windsor, Berkshire, UK. Versatile spreadsheet package capable of performing many useful financial calculations.

MAPPS, Maritz Market Research Inc., St Louis, MO, USA. This is a sophisticated product planning and positioning system. MAPPS gives a thorough market profile. It is possible to discover what is important to customers, their reasons for buying and current satisfaction levels, how your product measures up (or can be improved), your sales potential, etc. Perceptual mapping procedures let you visually compare the results.

Market/EIS (Market and Economic Information Systems), Marketing Systems GmbH, FRG. Effect of marketing mix as well as other situations can be studied through this system.

Marksman, Control Data Corp., Business Information Services, 500 W. Putnam Avenue, Greenwich, CT 06836, USA. Integrates product, customer, prospect, sales, and marketing data for analysis; monitors sales activity, buying patterns, product margins, and price discounts for more profitable sales and marketing programs; advertising support, delivers maximum return on advertising dollars spent through improved planning, implementation, and tracking of media campaigns; sales management; identifies and measures marketing program needs and success relative to investment made.

MKTSIM (Marketing Simulation Model), Spring Systems, Chicago, Illinois, USA. Organizes information about a brand, product, and its competition, fits a model to this information, and then simulates the effects of various marketing strategies.

Multiplan, Microsoft Ltd., Excel House, 49 De Montfort Road, Reading, Berkshire, RG1 8LP, UK. Versatile spreadsheet package capable of performing many useful financial calculations.

Orion, Comshare Inc., 3001 S. State St., Ann Arbor, MI 48108, USA. A forecasting package containing various forecasting routines; also permits model building using regression analysis. Usable on mainframes.

Pulse/Qseg, Pulse Analysis Inc., Ridgewood, New Jersey, USA. Performs market segmentation and profile analysis. Includes generation of ASCII file with segments ready for post analyses; completely labeled and sorted output.

RATS (Regression Analysis of Time Series), VAR Econometrics Inc., PO Box 19334, Minneapolis, MN 55419-0334, USA. An econometric package useful for model building and calibration in tourism, and also forecasting.

Statgraphics, Statistical Graphics Corporation, 2 Wall St., Princeton, NJ 08540, USA. A forecasting package containing various forecasting routines; also permits model building using regression analysis. Usable on microcomputers.

System W, Comshare Inc., 3001 S. State St., Ann Arbor, MI 48108, USA. Can be used as decision support software for marketing and strategic planning. Usable on mainframes.

There are many well-known statistical/econometric packages which can be used for model construction and calibration in the tourism field, such as SPSSX, SAS and TSP. Many of such mainframe packages have now been developed and modified to run on microcomputers.

Index of contributors

Index